Routledge Handbook of Sports Development

Sports development has become a prominent concern within both the academic study of sport and within the organisation and administration of sport. The *Routledge Handbook of Sports Development* is the first book to comprehensively map the wide-ranging territory of sports development as an activity and as a policy field, and to offer a definitive survey of current academic knowledge and professional practice.

Spanning the whole spectrum of activity in sports development, from youth sport and mass participation to the development of elite athletes, the book identifies and defines the core functions of sports development, exploring the interface between sports development and cognate fields such as education, coaching, community welfare and policy. The book presents important new studies of sports development around the world, illustrating the breadth of practice within and between countries, and examines the most important issues facing practitioners within sports development today, from child protection to partnership working.

With unparalleled depth and breadth of coverage, the *Routledge Handbook of Sports Development* is the definitive guide to policy, practice and research in sports development. It is essential reading for all students, researchers and professionals with an interest in this important and rapidly evolving field.

Barrie Houlihan is Professor of Sport Policy in the School of Sport, Exercise and Health Sciences, Loughborough University, UK.

Mick Green was a Senior Lecturer in Sport Policy and Management in the School of Sport, Exercise and Health Sciences, Loughborough University, UK.

Routledge Handbook of Sports Development

Edited by
Barrie Houlihan and Mick Green

Routledge
Taylor & Francis Group

LONDON AND NEW YORK

First published 2011
by Routledge
2 Park Square, Milton Park, Abingdon, Oxon, OX14 4RN

Simultaneously published in the USA and Canada
by Routledge
270 Madison Avenue, New York, NY 10016

Routledge is an imprint of the Taylor & Francis Group, an informa business

© 2011 Barrie Houlihan and Mick Green

The right of the editor to be identified as the author of the editorial material, and of the authors for their individual chapters, has been asserted in accordance with sections 77 and 78 of the Copyright, Designs and Patents Act 1988.

Typeset in Bembo by Taylor & Francis Books
Printed and bound in Great Britain by
TJ International, Padstow, Cornwall

British Library Cataloguing in Publication Data
A catalogue record for this book is available from the British Library

Library of Congress Cataloging in Publication Data
A catalog record for this book has been requested

ISBN13: 978-0-415-47996-7 hbk
ISBN13: 978-0-415-47995-0 pbk
ISBN13: 978-0-203-88558-1 ebook

To Mick Green

Contents

Contents

Contents

Illustrations

Figures

Tables

Boxes

Preface

When Simon Whitmore, Routledge's commissioning editor for sports books, approached me in 2008 with the idea for a handbook of sports development, my first reaction was that a book that attempted to define the boundaries and content of this aspect of sports policy and practice was badly needed, but that the editing of such a text would also be a daunting challenge. As I was having this initial discussion with Simon I was already thinking about whom I could bring on board as a co-editor. The obvious choice was the person in the next office to me, Mick Green, with whom I had already worked on a number of books and articles and who, I knew from experience, possessed the necessary knowledge, organisational skills and enthusiasm for such a project.

Over the following couple of months Mick and I had many discussions about the scope and structure of the handbook and whom we might approach as contributors. Mick was as much the architect of the handbook as I was and was equally excited as the early chapters began to arrive and we could begin to see the book take shape. Sadly, Mick fell ill towards the end of 2008 and died early the following year. Among the many sorrows occasioned by the death of a colleague, the fact that Mick died before he could see the fruits of his labour is a minor one in comparison to the loss felt by his partner, relatives and friends, but it does serve to remind us once again of the contribution he made to the social scientific study of sports policy. We can only speculate as to the contribution he might have made had his academic career run its full term. This book is dedicated to his memory.

Introduction

Barrie Houlihan

Definition of a policy area or of a set of government activities is nearly always problematic: what starts as an apparently straightforward process of positivist-oriented empirical description soon becomes mired in ambiguity as attempts to define 'sports development' confirm. Rejecting the positivist approach to policy analysis, Fischer (2003: 51) argues that 'To accurately explain social phenomena, the investigator must first of all attempt to understand the meaning of the social phenomenon from the actor's perspective ... the actor's own motives and values.' Furthermore, the meaning of policy is not static as will be made clear below in relation to sports development. While the investigation of policy will generate empirical data of great value to the policy analyst, the data are unlikely to produce social categories sufficiently robust to satisfy the positivist researcher. One of the reasons for the need to treat empirical observations with care is that they are often related to a specific time and place. Thus concepts such as 'regular participation', 'sport', 'physical education', 'physical activity' and 'moderate exercise' have all been redefined over the last forty years. A second reason why positivist methods are insufficient to define a policy area is that, despite regular expressions of commitment to evidence-based policy, policy-makers are just as likely to be influenced by the mythology that develops around policy and which takes on the status of 'truths' even though the evidence base is weak. According to Coalter (2007: 9), 'such myths contain elements of truth, but elements which become reified and distorted and "represent" rather than reflect reality, standing for supposed, but largely unexamined, impacts and processes.' Coalter's argument has much in common with Hajer's (1995) concept of policy 'storylines' which, according to Fischer (2003: 88), 'function to condense large amounts of factual information inter-mixed with the normative assumptions and value orientations that assign meaning to them ... [Storylines] stress some aspects of an event and conceal or downplay others.' Sports development is replete with such myths and storylines, which generate and preserve (generally positive) perceptions of sports development on the basis of weak evidence. While it is important to acknowledge that sports development is far from unique in having a weak evidence base (criminal justice, defence, education and even medicine all have their share of storylines and myths), Coalter's injunction to 'think more clearly, analytically and less emotionally about "sport" and its potential' (2007: 7) is important to bear in mind. In other words any attempt to define sports development and assess its impact needs to be accompanied by a healthy dose of scepticism.

With our scepticism primed, there are a number of possible starting points for definition. One might take the statements of policy-makers as a logical starting point for specifying the objectives and activities that constitute the core aspects of sports development given that in many countries 'sports development', however we might eventually define it, is usually publicly funded. Yet experience would indicate that policy-makers are prone to play rather fast and loose with meaning, perhaps not to an Orwellian extent, but with sufficient elasticity to give us pause in accepting their definition as a natural point of departure for analysis. Politicians have a tendency to routinely 'vaguely over-aspire.' However, even when policy-makers establish a clear set of goals for a policy, they are often diluted, adapted and subverted as they move through the process of implementation. The lack of resources at the local level might require a dilution of goals, the peculiarities of the local context may necessitate policy adaption and political opposition may result in a policy being subverted from its original goals (Pressman and Wildavsky 1973; Hill and Hupe 2009).

An alternative starting point is to examine the activities of those who self-define their work as 'sports development'. Many of these practitioners are employed by public sector organisations or by national sports organisations, although a significant number are employed by non-sport organisations that use sport to attract young people so that personal or community development objectives can be addressed. Taking practitioners as the starting point soon highlights the difficulties of this approach as a series of boundary problems rapidly emerge. There are many examples of practitioners who seek to achieve non-sports objectives through attracting people, young people in particular, into sport: the youth worker who uses sport to engage young people so that she can undertake personal development activity; the member of a religious body who uses sport as the basis for missionary work; and the political activist who uses sport as a way of attracting and retaining members. It is certainly a moot point whether these practitioners should be considered to be engaged in sports development when it is clear that they would not define sports development as their primary concern. However, it is undeniable that much 'high quality' (another contested concept) sports development takes place outside the expected organisational contexts of schools, municipalities and sports clubs.

In some policy areas, medicine being the classic example, the boundary maintenance function is undertaken by a professional body. In the UK, for example, the British Medical Association is highly influential not only in deciding how doctors are trained and when they are fit to practise, but also in determining what is considered legitimate medical treatment. This scope and depth of influence is clearly lacking in the area of sports development. In almost all countries entry to the occupations associated with sports development, such as sports development officer and coach, is very open. Where licensing does exist it tends to be organised and enforced by the state rather than by a professional body. However, while there are relatively few examples of the state controlling access to the practice of sports development and coaching, the state, in most countries, plays a crucial role in defining what sports can be developed (at least at public expense). Most states that provide a public subsidy to sport define the scope of the subsidy and may prioritise funding and thus development activity in relation to Olympic sports, the more martial sports or traditional sports, depending upon political priorities such as the pattern of diplomatic relations or the imperatives of nation-building.

An analysis of the role of the state serves to draw attention to the importance of the concept of power and the fact that any definition of sports development will reflect the associated set of power relations. Definitions of substantive policy areas such as sports development are the outcome of a set of prior decisions not only about who is to be targeted, for what purpose, in what way and by whom, but also about how the need for action is identified, who has the power to define need and who determines that sufficient change/development has taken place. The long-standing debate within the global economic development literature about the nature of the development process and to whose advantage it operates, albeit with many more significant consequences for people's lives than sports development, is a valuable point of comparison. The power of international organisations often located in rich countries to define 'good development' and the conditions to be met by the countries being developed certainly has parallels in many of the countries covered in this Handbook. The balance of emphasis (and resources) between elite and mass sport, between competitive sport and non-competitive physical activities and between age groups and genders is almost always the outcome of the operation of policy networks of varying degrees of exclusivity.

The exercise of power is a thread that runs through much of this Handbook. Part 1 provides ample evidence of the role of privileged social groups and organised interests in defining the structures within which the contemporary experience of sport takes place and also in imbuing the activity of sport with its supposed moral aura and its mystique of character-building. Part 2 illustrates the extent to which states dominate the contemporary context for sports development and also the degree to which they have accepted uncritically the late nineteenth-century mythologising. The next four Parts contain chapters that demonstrate not only the extent of instrumentalising of sports development, but also the way interest coalitions have emerged around fields of sports development, with elite sports development being supported, in many countries, by a particularly effective coalition of interests. Throughout the study of sports development the voice of one group is conspicuous by its absence – that of those being developed. It is undeniable that there are many examples of sports development activities that create welcome opportunities to participate in sport and where the developers take steps to identify the preferences of those targeted for development. However, there are still many examples, perhaps the majority, where sports development is something that is done *to* the particular target group (whether they are women, young people, the impoverished, or even elite athletes), sometimes something that is done *for* them, but it is rarely something done *by* them. Power over resources rarely moves from the funder or provider to the consumer or object of development.

In summary, attempts at defining the scope, objectives and impact of sports development need to take account not only of the underlying power relations between policy actors, but also of the limited evidence base and the influence of storylines on policy. With these strictures in mind it is appropriate to review existing attempts to define sports development. One, perhaps wishfully simple, view of sports development is that it is about 'getting more people to play more sport'. However, this definition over-emphasises the role of sport in 'sports development' and underplays the instrumental attitude of most governments to sport (i.e. the non-sport objectives that sport is thought to be able to achieve). Collins (1995: 21) expands on this definition and suggests that sports development is 'a process whereby effective opportunities, processes, systems and structures are set up to enable and encourage people in all or particular groups and areas to take part in sport and recreation or to improve their performance to whatever level they desire.' Collins' definition, given in 1995, reflects an aspirational viewpoint and was the product of a time when sports development was associated more closely with increasing participation, and when participation was organised around a traditional range of sports delivered through a framework of public provision and voluntary clubs. Collins' definition is also interesting because it emphasises the creation of opportunities (which people are free to take advantage of or not) rather than emphasising behavioural change where indifference to sport is perceived as the core problem. Another definition from the 1990s reflects this alternative and more interventionist approach. In addition to referring to the creation of opportunities for participation and improvement, the definition also notes that 'Sports development is a process by which interest and desire to take part may be *created* in those currently indifferent to the message of sport' (Sports Council North West 1991: 3, emphasis added). While Collins' definition stresses the role of sports development activity in the creation of outputs, that is, opportunities for sports development to take place, the latter definition stresses outcomes (increased participation or improved performance).

Since the 1990s a new dimension to the definition of sports development has emerged and it is normative and moralistic – it is less 'sport for sport's sake' and more 'sport for good'. Hylton and Bramham (2008: 2) argue that 'sport development is more accurately a term used to describe policies, processes and practices that form an integral feature of the work involved in providing sporting opportunities and *positive* sporting experiences' (emphasis added). This is a view of sports development reinforced in 2006 by the then Minister for Sport, Richard Caborn, who argued that 'if we are to prove that the [sport] sector can address government's agendas across the UK, and ... what it can do for others, be it tackling the obesity crisis in health, greater social inclusion in our communities and of course producing world class talent for our 2012 athletes and beyond – then it needs to be fit for purpose' (ISPAL 2006, quoted in Hylton and Bramham 2008: 3). This utilitarian and instrumental notion of sports development is a long way from the creation of opportunities envisaged by Collins in the mid 1990s.

It will become clear from the chapters in this Handbook that sports development is highly contested in terms of objectives (which range from talent identification and development, through enhanced health to moral improvement), practices (ranging from the development of sport-specific technical skills to recreational 'fun days') and practitioners (ranging from career sports development officers and coaches to youth workers and religious missionaries). Moreover, there is, in many countries, an actual or emerging tension between three orientations to sports development. The first identifies the promotion of participation in sport as the central concern much along the lines of the *sport for all* policy of the Council of Europe; the second prioritises talent identification and development; and the third treats sport as an instrument to achieve a variety of non-sport objectives related to health, community development and education, for example. The ambiguity, uncertainty and tensions surrounding sports development policy and practice are, in part, a consequence of the adaptability of sport and its capacity to attract young people, but also a consequence of its attraction to government as a relatively low-cost, high-visibility and malleable response to a wide range of social policy issues. There is little indication that these characteristics of sports development will alter in the near future. What the chapters in this Handbook capture is not only the scope and diversity of sports development, but also its highly politicised character and its dynamism.

References

Coalter, F. (2007) *A wider social role for sport: Who's keeping the score*, London: Routledge.
Collins, M. (1995) *Sport development locally and regionally*, Reading: Institute of Leisure and Amenity Management.
Fischer, F. (2003) *Reframing public policy: Discursive politics and deliberative practices*, Oxford: Oxford University Press.
Hajer, M. (1995) *The politics of environmental discourse*, Oxford: Oxford University Press.
Hill, M. and Hupe, P. (2009) *Implementing public policy: Introduction to the study of operational governance*, London: Sage.
Hylton, K. and Bramham, P. (eds.) (2008) *Sports development: Policy, process and practice*, London: Routledge.
Pressman, J. and Wildavsky, A. (1973) *Implementation*, Berkeley, CA: University of California Press.
Sports Council North West (1991) *Sportsnews factfile: Sports development*, Manchester: Sports Council.

Part 1
The influences on sports development
Introduction: The constraints of history

Barrie Houlihan

'One would expect people to remember the past and to imagine the future. But in fact … they imagine the past and remember the future.'

Lewis Namier (1942)

Even with relatively recent areas of governmental interest such as sport it is not possible to ignore the significance of history. All policy development is, by equal measure, facilitated, mediated and constrained by the historical context within which it takes place. At one level this self-evident proposition is a simple reminder that in order to understand the type of sports development that emerges in a country one needs to look beyond the contemporary context of factors such as wealth, political party control of government and international relations. At a more significant level the admonition to 'take account of history' requires the policy analyst to address a series of complex questions regarding the study of history. Perhaps of greatest importance is the question 'What or whose history?' The four chapters in this Part examine the influence of some of the main institutions to shape the emergence of sports development not only in the United Kingdom and former British colonies, but also in many other developed and developing countries – the private education system, the military, religions and nationalism. Each of these institutions is an organisational representation of a set of values about what constitutes acceptable sport and also the purposes for which it should be supported and promoted. Furthermore, while these institutions shaped and, to varying degrees, continue to shape contemporary British sport policy, there are other influences that could also be profitably explored particularly in relation to other European and North American countries, including labour organisations/trade unions, political parties and commercial organisations such as sports equipment manufacturers and bars/public houses.

Yet the acknowledgement of the significance of the historical context of sports development is of only limited analytical value unless there is some method for determining which elements of history are significant. Assessing the significance of historical events and patterns requires the

5

application of social science, especially sociological and political science analysis. As has been argued by Bergsgard *et al.* (2007: 39), who refer to the work of Benson (1982), Sabatier (1998) and Jenkins–Smith and Sabatier (1994) suggest that a framework for the analysis of the significance of historical institutional patterns and arrangements is through the use of the metaphor of levels of cultural embeddedness. Of particular importance is the identification of policy dispositions that are located in the deep structure of a society and would include attitudes towards private property, the role of the state, the relationship between the state and the individual, and the relationship between generations and genders and which are slow to change and continue to shape all aspects of public policy including sports development. Assertions of the transformative impact on public policy of post-modernity (or even modernity) can be greatly exaggerated due to a lack of appreciation of the power and resilience of deep structural values. Deep structural values or policy predispositions often manifest themselves as 'storylines' (Fischer 2003) where historical 'facts' become embroidered, as Lewis Namier, quoted at the beginning of this introduction, acknowledged, and take on an ideological (or mythological) status that engenders a strong commitment to particular policies irrespective of the strength of the evidence available.

An acknowledgement of the importance of historical context can lead researchers to a consideration of the relevance of the concept of path dependency when analysing sports development. Path dependency suggests that initial policy decisions can determine future policy choices: that 'the trajectory of change up to a certain point constrains the trajectory after that point' (Kay 2005: 553). As noted elsewhere (Houlihan and Green 2008: 17):

> Path dependency is also connected to the broader policy analysis literature on the importance of institutions which, for Thelen and Steinmo, are seen as significant constraints and mediating factors in politics, which 'leave their own imprint' (1992: 8). Whether the emphasis is on institutions as organisations or as sets of values and beliefs (culture) there is a strong historical dimension which emphasises the 'relative autonomy of political institutions from the society in which they exist; … and the unique patterns of historical development and the constraints they impose on future choices' (Howlett and Ramesh 1995: 27).

In his analysis of welfare regimes in Europe Esping-Andersen (1990, 1999) provides strong support for a soft version of path dependency, arguing that in many countries distinctive types of welfare regime (liberal, conservative and social democratic) have emerged over time and generated a set of values and practices that not only influence the identification of issues as public problems, but also set the parameters of the policy response. Thus it may be argued that the extent to which current participation levels in sport are perceived as a problem for government will be influenced by the nature of the welfare regime, as will the response to the problem in terms of the extent of state involvement, the promotion of market solutions, the extent of public subsidy, etc. Cultural history, reflected in the attitudes of institutions such as religions, the military and the education system towards sport, creates policy predispositions that are likely to be reinforced and compounded by the slow accumulation of policy decisions. The processes and organisational structures through which organised sport emerged in a country's history need to be seen as institutions in relation to current policy choices, with path dependency capturing the insight that 'policy decisions accumulate over time; a process of accretion can occur in a policy area that restricts options for future policy-makers' (Kay 2005: 558).

Acknowledging that 'history matters' is fairly uncontroversial; what is much more problematic is determining the extent to which history matters and what history matters. In relation to the countries included in this collection it is possible to point to deeply rooted values systems that have withstood wars, authoritarianism, economic collapse and invasion. Confucianism in China, Taiwan and Japan, Protestantism in Denmark and Sweden, and Islam in the Arab world are deeply entwined in the fabric of daily life of countries and have been for many hundreds of years and forcefully influence, even if mainly indirectly, perceptions of the importance of sport and the practice of sport. However, much more recent historical events have also left their mark on the context for sports development policy. The experience of Nazi occupation in Denmark and the Nazi domination of sport in Germany have led both countries to safeguard the autonomy of the sports system and made governments reluctant to become too directly involved in community-level sport. One consequence of an acknowledgement that the history of a country, both distant and recent, provides a significant constraint on policy innovation is that the opportunities for policy transfer between countries are more limited than might at first be assumed. For example, a country that aspires, as the United Kingdom currently does, to emulate the participation levels of Finland is assuming that policy can be transferred from a social democratic culture to one that has stronger roots in neo-liberalism.

The opening chapters in this Handbook are not intended to provide a comprehensive review of the history of the roots of sports development nor a thorough discussion of the significance of history for the emergence of sports development. Rather they have been selected to draw attention to the importance of taking account of the historical context within which policy is formulated, to examine four areas deemed to be of especial relevance to the shaping of sports development in many developed and developing countries and to act as a reminder that good social science analysis relies heavily on good historical research.

References

Benson, J.K. (1982) 'Networks and policy sectors: A framework for extending inter-organisational analysis', in: Rogers, D. and Whitton, D. (eds) *Inter-organisational co-ordination*, Iowa: Iowa State University.

Bergsgard, N.A., Houlihan, B., Mangset, H., Nødland, S.I. and Rommetvedt, H. (2007) *Sport policy: A comparative analysis of stability and change*, Oxford: Butterworth-Heinemann.

Esping-Andersen, G. (1990) *The three worlds of welfare capitalism*, Cambridge: Polity Press.

——(1999) *Social foundations of postindustrial economies*, Oxford: Oxford University Press.

Fischer, F. (2003) *Reframing public policy: Discursive politics and deliberative practices*, New York: Oxford University Press.

Houlihan, B. and Green, M. (2008) (eds) *Comparative elite sport development: Systems, structures and public policy*, Oxford: Butterworth-Heinemann.

Howlett, R. and Ramesh, M. (1995) *Studying public policy: Policy cycles and policy sub-systems*, New York: Oxford University Press.

Jenkins-Smith, H. and Sabatier, P. (1994). 'Evaluating the advocacy coalition framework', *Journal of Public Policy*, 14, 3, 175–203.

Kay, A. (2005) 'A critique of the use of path dependency in policy studies', *Public Administration*, 83, 3, 553–71.

Namier, L. (1942) 'Symmetry and repetition', in: Namier, L. (ed.) *Conflicts: Studies in contemporary history*, Basingstoke: Macmillan.

Sabatier, P. (1998) 'The advocacy coalition framework: revisions and relevance to Europe', *Journal of European Public Policy*, 5, 1, 98–130.

Thelen, K. and Steinmo, S. (1992). 'Historical institutionalism in comparative politics', in: Thelen, K., Steinmo, S. and Longstreth, F. (eds) *Structuring politics: Historical institutionalism in comparative analysis*, Cambridge: Cambridge University Press.

1

Sports development in the nineteenth-century British public schools

Martin Polley

Sports development is a key component of contemporary British sport. The sports development system, based around central government policy and local authorities' application of it, influences every aspect of sport, from the hosting of the Olympic Games through to the provision of exercise classes for the elderly. The system is a channel through which governments target social, economic, and cultural problems. Sport has many features that make it attractive to the state for such ends. For example, it can help to promote social cohesion, particularly in multicultural communities. It can provide a place for the dispersal of excess energy, particularly amongst young males, that might otherwise be directed into anti-social or criminal activity. It can promote good health and thus help to reduce the costs that sickness causes to the economy. Sport can also help to generate economic activity, through hosting events, building infrastructure, and sports tourism. These and other classic functionalist readings of sport give it an appeal to governments, and sports development is central to governments' attempts to reach these objectives. (See Jarvie 2006: 17–41 for an overview of key social theories.) Anyone with a professional or academic interest in contemporary British sport needs to look at sports development critically, and to appreciate its political and ideological nature (Hylton *et al.* 2001; Houlihan and White 2002; Green and Houlihan 2005).

The chapters in this book explore contemporary sports development in great detail and from a variety of positions. To help set the scene for these present-centred discussions, this chapter's purpose is to promote debate about the historical roots of sports development. Contemporary sports development has its most obvious origins in the 1960s, when, as part of the work of a maturing welfare state, Conservative and Labour governments began to take an active interest in how sport was run. Since then, governments have managed sport to promote wider social policy objectives relating to health, education, social inclusion, multiculturalism, crime, and many other areas. We can trace the evolution of sports development through the history of the Sports Council and it successor bodies, and through the emergence of a funding and policy network involving central government, local government, quangos, sports' governing bodies, and clubs (Coghlan with Webb 1990; Polley 1998: 12–34). An understanding of this recent history is essential if we wish to have a perspective on why contemporary sports development is like it is, what the main agencies are, and how they inter-relate. Exploring this contemporary history can take us into causation and context, into the ways in which political, social, and economic needs inspire policy, and into the ways in which people have used sport to respond to the problems of their times. Such historical enquiry can also help us to understand how different ideologies can influence sports development, as it can show up the links between political parties' intellectual and philosophical bases and how they have acted towards sport.

However, historians of sports development are not simply interested in narratives of how the present system came about. Essential as this is, it is also instructive for us to cast our gaze beyond recent political history, and to go further back than the influential Wolfenden Report of 1960 (Wolfenden Committee on Sport 1960). By looking for longer-term precedents and influences, we can root contemporary sports development deeper in history. Moreover, by looking in a comparative way at earlier systems that appear to share some common features with contemporary sports development, we can ask historical questions to illuminate both past and present: questions about the links between ideology and action; about the inter-relationships between providers and participants; and about the ways in which sport has been promoted through both financial support and cultural approval. With this remit, the sporting culture of British public schools in the nineteenth century emerges as an obvious contender for consideration.

There was something both systematic and developmental about what happened in the schools during this period. What Honey said of the schools as a whole can also be applied to their sports: 'the public schools ... emerged or adapted themselves during the [nineteenth] century in such a way as to constitute a *system*, an articulated and coherent set of schools serving a common set of social functions' (Honey 1977: xi, emphasis in original). It was a time in which schoolboy games changed rapidly from being relatively unstructured pastimes into being central to elite educational life. Sports attracted funding and facilities, the kind of features we associate with modern sports development. Moreover, these public school sports were closely tied to political objectives. Sports became associated with schoolmasters' desire to control pupils' spare time and to channel their excess physicality into acceptable activities, and with boys' sense of political allegiance with their schools as communities. Sport also became underpinned by an ideology, with orthodox values relating to class, gender, religion, national and racial identity, and imperial duty all tied up with how boys played football, rugby, and cricket. These sports were later exported around the world by former public school boys working for British military, imperial, religious, and trading interests, helping to create a global culture of team games based in part on the value systems of the British public schools. It was in the public schools that games first became linked to the notion that sport could act as a panacea for any and every problem facing the individual and the community, a notion that remains embedded in contemporary sports development, despite its fallacy. With these challenging points of comparison, it is fitting to explore the sports culture of these schools as one of the ancestors of modern sports development.

There is a rich and diverse literature on this subject. Indeed, one of the pioneering works of academic sports history, Mangan's *Athleticism in the Victorian and Edwardian Public School* of 1981, was devoted to the subject, which has helped it to become a central theme in the historiography of British sport. Mangan combined archival work in selected schools with a contextual analysis of the meanings that sports took on (Mangan 1981). Mangan also wrote the key text on the links between these school sports and the development of sport throughout the British Empire (Mangan 1985). Dunning and Sheard concentrated on football codes in the schools, especially Rugby's version, in their historical sociology, *Barbarians, Gentlemen and Players* (Dunning and Sheard 1979). Other sports historians have taken up these books' themes and have explored various aspects of the public school sports, including Dewey on Eton (Dewey

1995a, 1995b) and Collins on Rugby (Collins 2009), while some criticism of the apparent primacy of the public schools in developing team games has come from Harvey (Harvey 2005). Fletcher shifted attention to girls' experiences in *Women First* (Fletcher 1984). The intense debates that ensued between Harvey and Dunning around the importance of the schools (Harvey 2001; Dunning 2001), and the fact that Mangan's and Dunning and Sheard's key texts have gone into second editions (Mangan 2000; Dunning and Sheard 2005), illustrate the continued centrality of this subject to sports historiography. The role of sport has also been explored by historians of the public school system as a whole, such as Mack (1939, 1971), Honey (1977), and Chandos (1984). These works place the development of games in the wider context of the changes that schools as a whole went through in the nineteenth and early twentieth centuries. In addition to this academic work, which typically combines detailed analysis of the primary evidence with a critical awareness of contexts, a number of schools have their own accounts that narrate their sporting history. These tend to lack contextual awareness, particularly on such crucial issues as class and gender politics, but they provide us with details, chronicles, statistics, and anecdotes (see Polley 2007 for guidance on different types of sports history writing). Money's *Manly and Muscular Diversions* is a synthesis of this literature (Money 1997). Both academic and institutional histories draw on varied primary sources, including school records, logbooks, prospectuses, government enquiries, and curricula, as well as the literature that the pupils created in their magazines and poems. Taken together, this literature shows that there was a shift in school sports in the nineteenth century during which games became organised, codified, and regulated, and imbued with certain ideological values.

The picture that emerges from this literature suggests that there was a system in place by the start of the twentieth century. What is particularly interesting for our current concerns is that this system delivered – apparently without too much conflict – the two objectives that Houlihan and White (2002) have seen as a tension in modern sports development. There was both 'development of sport', through the creation of rules, the establishment of competitions, and the expansion of facilities; and 'development through sport', with games promoted as a way to improve the physical, mental, social, and moral well-being of the boys. It is around these themes of 'development of sport' and 'development through sport' that we will now consider the place of the nineteenth-century public schools in the history of sports development.

The changing schools and their sports

It is beyond the remit of this chapter to provide a list of what the public schools were, or a full account of how and why they changed during the nineteenth century. Mack, Honey, and Chandos work well as guides to the schools themselves and their shifting role, while Mangan (2000) provides a good overview of the changing role of sport within the context of these wider changes. However, some context is necessary. First, the schools that are considered in this debate are those that were outside state control, and were funded by various means, including endowments, charity, and fees. Mangan gives the most accessible list of the different types of schools, and of the main schools themselves (2000: 2–3), such as the 'Great Public Schools' explored by the Clarendon Commission in 1861 (Charterhouse, Eton, Harrow, Merchant Taylors, Rugby, St Paul's, Shrewsbury, Westminster, and Winchester), various denominational schools (such as the Roman Catholic Ampleforth and the Quaker Bootham), 'Proprietary Schools' set up as businesses with shareholders (such as Malvern), 'Elevated Grammar Schools' (such as Sherborne and Uppingham), Anglican schools established by Nathaniel Woodward (such as Lancing), and 'Private Venture Schools' owned by individuals as businesses (such as Loretto and Radley). There were many differences between these schools, both in terms of the quality of education they delivered and the prestige they afforded to pupils and their parents, and we can learn much about the growth of the industrial and commercial middle classes through the boom in schools and the nuanced differences between them. Broadly, more people were willing and able to pay for their sons (and later daughters) to be educated than in previous periods, and so schools adapted to meet this rising demand. This included the foundation of new schools, and the expansion of existing ones.

Schools also adapted their curricula and cultures in order to cope with the rising demand and the new populations that industrial wealth brought. Wiener's *English Culture and the Decline of the Industrial Spirit 1850–1980* (Wiener 1981) remains a provocative introduction to the debate surrounding these changes, with his emphasis on how businessmen and tradesmen saw public schools as a way of gaining social mobility for their sons. As Ready put it in his scathing attack on 'Public School Products' in 1896, 'the upper middle classes ... wish to do the best by their boys; and they have been made to believe that this is the best' (Ready 1896: 424). Wiener's concern was with the effect that this emphasis on tradition and the classics had on British entrepreneurship (Wiener 1981; see also Rubinstein 1993: 102–39). For our purposes, the changing demographics of the schools formed a context of change within the schools. There were changes in curricula and teaching quality, for example, as parents became more obviously customers than they had been before. New money brought new buildings and specialised spaces. One of the biggest of these changes came in relation to sport. Rising numbers of boys, the attendant social order problems that came with this rise, and sport's emergence as a cultural phenomenon that can act as a focus for group identity, form the context for the burst of development that went on in the schools.

Such changes require human agency as well as contextual change, and this came from various sources. Thomas Arnold, headmaster at Rugby from 1828 until 1842 is popularly associated with the development of school sports. Mangan and others have shown that, while Arnold's role in educational reform was significant, his interest in sport was minimal (Mangan 2000: 14–18). Other masters and headmasters, such as Cotton at Marlborough, Vaughan at Harrow, and Almond at Loretto were more instrumental, each of them promoting sport both within the curriculum and beyond it. In addition, initiatives came from pupils at some schools, such as the Harrow Philathletic Club (Mangan 2000: 28–31).

The results of these initiatives varied from school to school. On the whole, by the end of the nineteenth century, sports took up a large amount of the time of most public schoolboys, and team games had become synonymous in the public eye with many schools' identities. Events such as the Eton v Harrow cricket match at Lord's made this visible to the wider public. Sport became an important part of what we would now call many schools' brands, and the 'cult of athletics' to which the new sports had given rise within the schools became well known enough to be praised by the military and parodied by the satirical magazine *Punch*. In addition to changes within the educational establishment, schools' development of sport had a bearing on games across society. The codification and organisation of various football codes, athletics, and other sports all owed debts to what had happened in the public schools. While the debate over the relative role of the schools continues, there was clearly enough of an influence for us to agree with Mangan: that the development and adoption of school sports, and the ideal types of behaviour and attitude that went with them, 'had extensive educational and social repercussions' (Mangan 2000: 1). With this context in place, we can now consider the public school system as a form of sports development, and as a precedent for our current systems. We will do this by taking Houlihan and White's two forms of sports development. In what way did the schools provide for the development of sport? And in what ways did they attempt to develop people through sport?

Development of sport

Before the mid-nineteenth century, boys at public schools played a variety of games. Typically, these games made use of available spaces, either within each of the school's buildings, or on open ground nearby. There is plenty of literary and administrative evidence of such activities as swimming, wrestling, running, archery, football, cricket, hunting and tennis in many of the schools from the late medieval period onwards (Money 1997: 29–64). These games were essentially distractions, spare time activities that had limited amounts of official school patronage, and they were not seen as a formal part of the pupils' development. Sports varied from school to school with variations in geography and architecture, so that the kind of football played at Winchester, for example, was defined by the relatively limited space at the top of St Catherine's Hill where games took place, while the fives at Eton was defined by the buttresses outside the chapel. Typically, sports were localised, regulated by oral traditions, limited by available space, and perceived to be of little educational value. Although new attitudes towards physical health came into educational circles in the renaissance (Brailsford 1969: 67–121), their impact on curricula was limited.

With the contextual shifts outlined above, and the new interest taken in sport by key individuals amongst both staff and pupils at various schools, there was a great deal of development in the nineteenth century that changed these limitations. The development of sport under this agenda took various overlapping forms, but we can tease out some trends here: the codification of sports; the construction of facilities for sport; and the creation of regular events and competitions. Through these themes, we can see the instrumental development of sport through which schools provided the opportunities for more regular play.

The possession of rules and regulations is one of the characteristics that differentiate a sport from physical activity. Rules and regulations give an activity order, allowing all who play it to know what kind of conduct is allowed and what is not, and they create agreed objectives, predictable outcomes that allow all involved to agree on what results mean. This is obvious to anyone involved in modern sport, but it is worth stepping back from that common sense position, and to remember the evolutionary and developmental nature of rules.

As Holt and others have shown, many sports had forms of rules long before the nineteenth century, so it would be simplistic to claim that the public schools invented the notion of playing to regulation (Holt 1989: 12–73). However, we do see many of the schools regulating their different games in this period, and those regulations influencing sports outside the schools, particularly as old boys took their games with them into their working lives. Football at Harrow, for example, gradually became codified during the course of the nineteenth century, with pitch sizes, permitted and prohibited moves, and team sizes stable by the 1900s. Similarly, Winchester College football adopted set rules and pitch sizes from the 1820s onwards. The most famous rule making is perhaps that of Rugby's football, which has become shrouded by the William Webb Ellis myth (Dunning and Sheard 2005: 52–53; Collins 2009: 11). The myth apart, it is true that by the mid-1840s the distinct elements of handling, scrummaging, and tackling were structured into the game. We see similar rules across the sector, with each school having codes for its own version of football, including Westminster in the 1850s, Repton in 1862, and Shrewsbury in 1866. Beside the various football codes, Winchester, Eton, and Harrow all codified their versions of fives in the second half of the nineteenth century. These rules involved the specific layout of each school's playing area and thus were specifically local, but they allowed for certainty of outcomes and agreed objectives.

Alongside the creation of rules, there was also a wave of facility building. All of the schools that survive from this period still have significant sports grounds: a mapping analysis of the environs of Eton, for example, shows football, tennis, cricket, rowing, archery, shooting and other sports all having their own defined spaces and buildings, while the southern section of modern Winchester is still dominated by College's playing fields. This designation of space for school sport, what Mangan called 'the solid superstructure of facilities' (Mangan 2000: 70), was perhaps the feature of the school sports that has most resonance with contemporary sports development.

Once the schools were committed to sport, they raised money in various ways to fund the facilities. The development was in part linked to growing school populations, but it was more firmly linked to the schools' belief in sport's value. Some of Mangan's figures show the scale of this investment, with Harrow's land devoted to sport increasing from eight acres in 1845 to 146 acres in 1900, with Marlborough's sport spaces rising from two to 68 acres in the same period, and Loretto's going from no space to 22 acres (Mangan 2000: 71). For outdoor games such as the various football codes, this expansion created more and better pitches, and allowed multiple pitches of increasingly defined size to be placed near each other for simultaneous matches. The increase also allowed for new buildings devoted to sport. Some schools had devoted spaces from much earlier, like Winchester's fives court from 1688 (Money 1997: 72), but the expansion in the nineteenth century was vast.

A few examples will have to suffice to indicate the trends. In 1840, Eton gained a purpose-built block of four fives courts, which relieved pressure on the original chapel site and allowed for more frequent usage. By 1894, Eton had 50 courts. Rugby had its own Racquet Court built in the 1870s with indoor courts for fives and squash (Money 1997: 77, 170–1). Eton, Harrow, and Westminster all built boathouses on the Thames, as did Shrewsbury on the Severn and Winchester on the Itchen. Gymnasiums were built at many of the schools, for indoor exercises and boxing, while some also invested in swimming. Pavilions for changing and refreshments also sprung up for the cricketers and footballers. Although many architectural and plant developments in public school sports took place in the twentieth century, the template was in place by 1900, by which time many schools were becoming as well known for their pitches and pavilions as they were for their chapels, cloisters, and classrooms.

As well as rules and facilities, we see the emergence of regulated teams and regular competition in all sports, another type of development. The older schools had traditional distinctions, particularly between boarders and day boys, which sports had long helped to maintain, as in the College v Commoners football games at Winchester from early in the nineteenth century, and the Collegers v Oppidans in the Eton Wall Game. These identities formed the basis for teams in ways that we would recognise them today. The house system also became central to internal school sports. In most of the schools under consideration, houses fielded teams for all sports, and there was fierce competition between them for school honours. Competitions were variously based on both league and knockout models, both of which were influential when sports like football and rugby spread nationally later in the century. In rowing, cricket, and athletics, similar competitions based on the houses also took off. And with competitions came awards and trophies, with cups, medals, and colour systems all commonplace by the end of the century. Rewards were thus about prestige and honour rather than money. The survival of the school identity into adulthood for some boys, as manifested in the old boys' clubs, suggests how well this system worked.

There was also, by this time, a flourishing culture of inter-school matches in a range of sports. The most famous was the Eton v Harrow cricket match at Lord's, which became an annual highlight in the calendars of the two schools and their pupils' families, and in the London social calendar. Headline events such as this were underpinned by a huge growth in what contemporary parlance called 'foreign' fixtures – that is, matches against other schools. Money gives a good account of the cricket fixtures that had been established by the 1850s, including West-minster v Charterhouse and Cheltenham v Marlborough. Football was trickier at first because of the diversity of rules, but as the 1846 Cambridge rules, the 1863 Football Association rules, and the 1871 Rugby Football Union laws filtered back to the schools to define the different codes, regular foreign matches took place alongside each school's own peculiar version. Westminster and Harrow began to play each other in the late 1850s, with Eton, Charterhouse, Lancing, Marlborough, Clifton, Rugby and other schools also becoming involved in such fixtures.

We should not claim that the public schools invented these features of sport: as with anything else in sport, all modern features have many causes and precedents. Certainly a glance at the history of folk football gives us many examples, all predating the public school innovations, of teams being based on geographical location or economic status, of rules and regulations being known and respected, of regular fixtures – albeit annually rather than weekly – and of material and symbolic rewards being given (Hornby 2008). What makes the public school experiment different is the rapidity with which a system emerged that contained all of these features: 'the whole system', as Ford wrote in the 1890s 'is entirely modern, most of it a development of the last forty years' (Ford 1898: 289). Here then was wholesale development of sport through investment in space and buildings, through the creation of teams and competitions, and through the codification of rules. When we reflect on how what went on in the schools became a template for many later competitions, we can see an influence going way beyond the schools. Moreover, when we note how old boys from a number of schools – particularly Shrewsbury, Harrow, Charterhouse, Westminster, and Eton for football, and Rugby for rugby – took lead-ing roles in creating nationally agreed rules for their games between the 1840s and 1900, then we can appreciate that this was, in the long run, about far more than the simple development of sport for elite schoolboys.

All of this development did not happen by accident, but nor was it a conspiracy by masters to keep their adolescent charges occupied. Investment of time, money, land, and cultural capital into sport happened because the power holders in the schools believed it to be worthwhile for pedagogical, financial, and marketing reasons. The developments were hegemonic in a Gram-scian sense, with the interests of the masters, the governors, parents, and pupils coming together to inspire developments (for Gramscian theory as it applies to sport, see Hargreaves 1986; Jarvie 2006: 28–29). This is shown well in Mangan's analysis, where he stresses the role of pupil-based clubs in setting up events as well as the role of masters in changing the curriculum and investors and benefactors in paying for it all. It is through this angle – the recognition that many stake-holders felt that all this sport was in their interests – that we can approach the second of Houlihan and White's tensions in sports development. How did the public school system develop people through sport?

Development through sport

As well as being about creating opportunities, contemporary sports development aims to develop people through sport. At its simplest, the assumption underpinning this is that sports improve people. This improvement may be about physical health, seen most obviously in relation to current obesity debates, or it might be about social behaviour, seen where sports activities are promoted in areas of high juvenile crime as approved alternatives to car theft and substance abuse. While there are clearly many success stories here, it is important for us to approach this model cautiously: sport can never be a panacea for all of society's and the individual's ills. For our current purposes, it is clear that the way in which the public schools promoted sport in the nineteenth century has become an influential model for the notion that sport can develop people. As such, we need to look at what masters and pupils believed sport did for them, and how these beliefs were informed by an evolving ideology of athleticism. As Mangan has shown, this ideology has to be seen in its nineteenth century context as an amalgam of Christianity, Darwinism, and imperialism. It emphasised the Christian's duty to be physically strong and morally pure, the Briton's duty to be ready and able to serve the Empire, and the basic tenets of evolution with their emphasis on natural selection and the survival of the fittest.

It is impossible to unpack the relationship between actions and ideas at this distance in time, and to claim with certainty that games were developed as a way of teaching an ideology and modelling good behaviour. Such a claim would assume a conspiracy on the part of masters, and the hegemonic ways in which sport was taken up suggests that many boys saw sport as being in their interests. Instead, it is safer to see a value system and an ideology gradually developing in line with the regulatory and infrastructure developments. By the end of the century, the ideology was central to the public school experience. So how was it supposed to develop people?

Physical improvement was one feature. The boys who made up these schools' populations did not come from the industrial slums that were causing havoc to the health and life chances of generations of working people. However, there was a growing belief in the innate goodness of physical health during the nineteenth century, as well as a recognition that the fittest boys were likely to make the hardest workers and the best soldiers once they left school. Almond, head-master of Loretto, probably the leading ideologist of athleticism, was blunt in his emphasis on the benefits of games: 'they supply active *exercise*, which is quite as important a factor of vig-orous health as ... drainage, pure water, or pure air' (Almond 1881: 287). The emphasis on outdoor exercise linked to a growing knowledge of the benefits of fresh air. Rowing and ath-letics were seen as good developers of strength, stamina, and wind, while contact sports devel-oped muscle and endurance. Sport's role as a way of developing health, rather than for any extrinsic rewards, was a solid part of the public school approach. Almond, in his reply to Ready's criticisms of public school life noted above, was forthright on this point, when he criticised masters who did not encourage their pupils to play sport:

> They are robbing the blood of its red corpuscles, they are narrowing the chest and increasing the liability to phthisis, they are impairing the energy and high spirits which ... come to the front in life, they are doing something towards wearing out the race.
>
> *(Almond 1897: 90)*

Sports were also held to develop the boys' social skills. The type of socialisation that team games, in particular, offered, provided boys with the chance to learn about leadership, team-work, loyalty, commitment, and how to place the side above the self. Welldon described the skills that sport taught boys as being 'promptitude, resource, honour, co-operation and unself-ishness' (Welldon 1906: 406), and he saw sport rather than academic lessons as being able to supply these qualities, which were the basic ingredients of 'the character of a gentleman'. These were all qualities that were greatly valued within school, and the house system gave a clear focus for it. Sporting boys became seen as role models and as promising material for contributing to society outside school. 'Give me a boy who is a cricketer,' wrote Ridding, Headmaster of Winchester (1866–84). 'I can make something of him' (quoted in Money 1997: 67). Part of the thrust of this aspect of sports development came from the high levels of delinquency, crime, and disorder that had characterised many of the schools earlier in the nineteenth century. Riots at Winchester, stone throwing at Harrow, hunting and torturing animals everywhere (Holt 1989: 78–81): sport then became 'an antidote to vandalism, trespassing and indiscipline' (Mangan

2000: 33), a means of social control that had the triple benefit of supervising the boys' time, tiring them out, and teaching them better ways of behaving. This also linked in to what the system's defenders saw as sport's ability to develop people morally, as vigorous team games were also seen as an antidote to the inevitable homosexuality and masturbation of these all-male adolescent environments. Many of the defenders of the system wrote scathingly of the type of boys who tried to get out of sports, and they were invariably characterised as effeminate and thus other. Collins, in his analysis of Thomas Hughes' *Tom Brown's Schooldays* of 1857, shows how such 'miserable little pretty white-handed curly-headed boys' were legitimate targets for bullying from the orthodox football-playing boys (Collins 2009: 92). In short, sports were believed to develop boys into healthy, vigorous, heterosexual men who could bring their skills, their talents, their healthy bodies and morally pure minds to the service of the nation and the empire. To quote Almond again: 'the most robust nation is the happiest and the greatest' (Almond 1897: 92).

The rhetoric surrounding this aspect of sport in the public schools was powerful. Those who did not fit in were stigmatised as degenerate, spoiled, molly-coddled, and ultimately unBritish. Those who did fit in were praised for their bodies and characters and excused for any intellectual short-comings, as shown in schoolboy poetry and fiction, school magazines, and cartoons in *Punch* with their hearty stereotypes. From these aspects of the Victorian schools' sporting cultures, we could argue that rather than develop the boys in rounded ways, it was narrowing in its effect. It created heroes out of those who disparaged 'book-learning', and legitimised bullying and abuse when they were targeted at anyone who did not fit in with the orthodox, hearty, masculine stereotype.

Conclusion

The innovations in sport that the reformed and new schools undertook during the nineteenth century have had a great impact, both within the schools and outside them. All of the schools under consideration, and new ones that have been founded since the period, still place a great emphasis on sport. From their marketing materials to their old boys' and girls' teams, and from the investment in plant to the employment of ex-professionals as coaches, sports still figure massively in the life of the schools. The ideological emphasis has changed, and the aim may be to create the developed global citizen rather than the unquestioning imperial servant or soldier, but there is still a clear belief that if the schools develop sport, and then encourage their pupils to develop through sport, then the benefits will be obvious. The innovations also had an impact on girls' schools in the late nineteenth and twentieth centuries, with hockey, netball, and lacrosse at Cheltenham Ladies' College (founded in 1853) and Roedean (founded in 1885) taking on similar roles to football and rugby at the boys' schools, as places where girls could learn social skills while improving their health. Grammar schools and aspirational state and faith schools have also been influenced by the public school sports model, with house teams, colours, and the lessons of good sport being important parts of their cultures. This centrality of such ideas in school-based literature has taught them to successive generations of children, with team games and their attendant honours and moral lessons being key parts of the action at every fictional boarding school from Richards' Greyfriars to Enid Blyton's Mallory Towers, and from Willans and Searle's St Custard's to Rowling's Hogwarts.

The public school system has also had a huge impact on the wider development of sport. Many aspects of international sport can trace some of their origins to the developments that took place in British public schools in the nineteenth century. Pierre de Coubertin believed that school sports were central to Britain's late Victorian imperial power, and he based his

Olympic Games in part on their rules and cultures (MacAloon 1981: 43–82). The international profiles of cricket and rugby union are still strongly based on the old British Empire, reminders of the role of ex-public schoolboys in taking their games with them overseas. Ex-public school boys played leading roles in the codification of football, rugby, swimming, and athletics. The long-running emphasis on amateurism (particularly in rugby union and athletics), on playing the game in the right spirit, on playing for honour and health rather than for material rewards, on competing being more important than winning: all of these platitudes come direct from the public schools. Similarly, the anti-intellectualism of many involved in sport today – in schools, in universities, and in professional and voluntary sports clubs – continues to echo the criticisms that sport's enthusiasts in the schools made of their book- and art-loving contemporaries. In this way, we can see that some of the legacies of the Victorian schools' innovations have been negative.

The public school system provides an interesting precedent for our contemporary sports development system. It has many features that we can recognise as being similar to sports development, such as its systematic nature, its emphasis on investment in amenities and projects, and its possession of an underlying assumption that sport can improve people and society. It involved the development of sport and the development of people through sport, and it had knock-on effects into other areas of life in the communities in which it happened. It used sport to tackle crime, poor health, and social problems. In this way, the model fits. However, there are also some disparities between the two systems, so much so that it could be anachronistic to attempt such a comparison. The two systems come from such vastly different contexts, and were created for different purposes. School sports were created to help the training – physical, social, and moral – of a tiny minority of people, the sons of the richest families in nineteenth-century Britain. Modern sports development is based in the principles of the welfare state, and even though it can be accused of elitism when it concentrates on high-level sport over grass-roots projects, this is an elitism based on skill rather than wealth, on merit rather than social class. Any notions of inclusion, multiculturalism, sport for all except the wealthiest, and dis-ability sport would simply have made no sense to the masters and the boys of the nineteenth-century schools. However, sports history is in part about finding the roots of phenomena in modern sport: and it is clear that on these grounds we can see the sports and games of the Victorian and Edwardian public schools as a significant ancestor of contemporary sports development.

References

Almond, H. H. (1881), 'Athletics and Education', *Macmillans Magazine*, XLIII, pp. 283–94.
——(1897), 'The Public School Product (A Rejoinder)', *New Review*, XVI, pp. 84–98.
Brailsford, D. (1969), *Sport and Society: Elizabeth to Anne*, London: Routledge and Kegan Paul.
Chandos, J. (1984), *Boys Together: English public schools, 1800–1864*, New Haven: Yale University Press.
Coghlan, J. with Webb, I. (1990), *Sport and British Politics Since 1960*, Basingstoke: Falmer.
Collins, T. (2009), *A Social History of English Rugby Union: sport and the making of the middle classes*, London: Routledge.
Dewey, C. (1995a), '"Socratic Teachers": Part 1 – the opposition to the cult of athletics at Eton, 1870–1914', *International Journal of the History of Sport*, vol. 12, no. 1, pp. 51–80.
——(1995b), '"Socratic Teachers": the opposition to the cult of athletics at Eton, 1870–1914. Part II – the counter-attack', *International Journal of the History of Sport*, vol. 12, no. 3, pp. 18–47.
Dunning, E. (2001), 'Something of a Curate's Egg: comments on Adrian Harvey's "An Epoch in the Annals of National Sport"', *International Journal of the History of Sport*, vol. 18, no. 4, pp. 88–94.
Dunning, E. and Sheard, K. (1979), *Barbarians, Gentlemen and Players: a sociological study of the development of Rugby football*, Oxford: Martin Robertson.

——(2005), *Barbarians, Gentlemen and Players: a sociological study of the development of Rugby football*, 2nd edn, London: Routledge.

Fletcher, S. (1984), *Women First: the female tradition in English physical education, 1880–1980*, London: Athlone.

Ford, L. (1898), 'Public School Athletics', in Cookson, Christopher (ed.), *Essays on Secondary Education*, Oxford: Clarendon Press.

Green, M. and Houlihan, B. (2005), *Elite Sports Development: policy learning and political priorities*, London: Routledge.

Hargreaves, J. (1986), *Sport, Power and Culture: a social and historical analysis of popular sports in Britain*, Cambridge: Polity.

Harvey, A. (2001), 'An Epoch in the Annals of National Sport: football in Sheffield and the creation of modern soccer and rugby', *International Journal of the History of Sport*, vol. 18, no. 4, pp. 53–87.

——(2005), *Football: The First Hundred Years: the untold story*, London: Routledge.

Holt, R. (1989), *Sport and the British: a modern history*, Oxford: Oxford University Press.

Honey, J. R. de Symons (1977), *Tom Brown's Universe: the development of the Victorian public school*, London: Millington.

Hornby, H. (2008), *Uppies and Downies; the Extraordinary Football Games of Britain*, London: English Heritage.

Houlihan, B. and White, A. (2002), *The Politics of Sport Development: development of sport or development through sport?*, London: Routledge.

Hylton, K., Bramham, P., Jackson, D. and Nesti, M. (eds) (2001), *Sports Development: policy, process and practice*, London: Routledge.

Jarvie, G. (2006), *Sport, Culture and Society: an introduction*, London: Routledge.

MacAloon, J. J. (1981), *This Great Symbol: Pierre de Coubertin and the origins of the modern Olympic Games*, Chicago: University of Chicago Press.

Mack, E. (1939), *Public Schools and British Opinion, 1780–1860: the relationship between contemporary ideas and the evolution of an English institution*, New York: Columbia University Press.

——(revised edition, 1971), *Public Schools and British Opinion since 1860: the relationship between contemporary ideas and the evolution of an English institution*, New York: Greenwood Press.

Mangan, J. A. (1981), *Athleticism in the Victorian and Edwardian Public School: the emergence and consolidation of an educational ideology*, Cambridge: Cambridge University Press.

——(1985), *The Games Ethic and Imperialism: aspects of the diffusion of an ideal*, London: Viking.

——(2000), *Athleticism in the Victorian and Edwardian Public School: the emergence and consolidation of an educational ideology*, 2nd edn, London: Routledge.

Money, T. (1997), *Manly and Muscular Diversions: public schools and the nineteenth-century sporting revival*, London: Duckworth.

Polley, M. (1998), *Moving the Goalposts: a history of sport and society since 1945*, London: Routledge.

——(2007), *Sports History: a practical guide*, Basingstoke: Palgrave.

Ready, A. W. (1896), 'Public School Products', *New Review*, vol. 15, no. 22, pp. 422–29.

Rubinstein, W. D. (1993), *Capitalism, Culture and Decline in Britain, 1750–1990*, London: Routledge.

Welldon, J. E. C. (1906), 'The Training of an English Gentleman in the Public Schools', *Nineteenth Century*, 60, pp. 396–413.

Wiener, M. (1981), *English Culture and the Decline of the Industrial Spirit 1850–1980*, Cambridge: Cambridge University Press.

Wolfenden Committee on Sport (1960), *Sport and the Community*, London: Central Council for Physical Recreation.

2

Jewish and Christian movements and sport

Andrew R. Meyer

In the second half of the nineteenth century, the marriage of Christian religious ideals and the philosophy of physical culture established a cultural ideology stressing the importance of sports participation and physical prowess that remains in Western sport today. Contemporary theorists interested in sport have detailed the pivotal role the muscular Christian movement has had in shaping Western perceptions of sport and physical exercise (Ladd and Mathison 1999; Putney 2001; MacAloon 2006). The blending of religion and sports philosophy created clear and justified connections between the norms and values of Christian theology and physical activity. Religious sports movements are evidence of shifts in how Western societies conceive of the body, physical activity, and the fundamental way human beings perceive themselves in the world.[1] Though Europe maintained a predominantly Christian population, there were non-Christians[2] whose theological epistemologies were not as open to the physical exercise movements of the time; in this light, this essay focuses on Jewish tradition and the physical movements that arose from it in the nineteenth and twentieth centuries.

Within fifty years of muscular Christianity's establishment, muscular Judaism, a related "physical" movement, emerged. In 1897 Jewish physician and Zionist Max Nordau called for the physical education of the Jewish people, with the aim of rescuing Eastern and Central European Jews[3] from their disadvantaged social circumstances. Yet muscular Judaism, as an established movement, did not last or become the overwhelming physical view of European Jews because of two limiting conditions. First, European Jews had historically been barred from participating in athletic programs because of the social stigmas associated with being Jewish and therefore non-athletic. Second, within the Jewish community there was a negative perception of athleticism contributing to the cultural disconnect between Jews and nineteenth-century European physical culture. The overall social perception of Jews as weak and passive was thus preserved, especially when compared to the physically active, combatant, and muscular Christian standard.

This chapter explores the traditional Jewish anti-athletic gender ideology and discusses the emergence of muscular Judaism,[4] its predecessors and lasting effects. Readers should understand that muscular Judaism's overall goal was for social improvement within communities, while muscular Christianity aimed for spiritual purity. Also explored is the modern turn toward using sport for social and spiritual improvement. Ultimately this study is about sport and religion, a historical and cultural exploration of the normativity of physical activity and the role of sport within religious communities.

Traditional Jewish views on gender and sport

Recent world events, such as the December 2008 Israeli invasion of the Gaza Strip, bombs, tanks, and able-bodied Israeli soldiers demonstrated the military strength of a nation seemingly under constant attack. This flexing of Israeli national "muscle" contradicts the historical perception of a weak, feeble, non-combative Jew. Jews were depicted by media outlets as reactionary, strong, and aggressive—which are quite contradictory to traditional cultural perceptions.

In describing a traditional Jewish male, or a *mentsh*, Daniel Boyarin (1997) characterized him as a gentle, genderless and passive individual, whose main responsibility was to the "ethics of the household, of the extended family, and a sphere of the domestic." He kept himself from the "purview of the masculinist ideals of the alien cultures in which ... Jews lived," and continued the traditions of "rabbinic opposition to European romantic 'masculinism'" (Boyarin 1997: 37). The Zionist movement in the late nineteenth century sought to change these historical descriptions and establish a strong Jewish nation state (Goldscheider and Zuckerman 1984; Presner 2007). One may argue that Israeli military conflicts, such as the 2008 Gaza reactionary measure, demonstrate that the historical stereotype of passive and effeminate Jewish masculinity has become less prominent, and that Jewish Zionism ultimately achieved its goals.

By the end of the eighteenth century, Romantic Era and Jewish definitions of masculinity were under revision because of changes in the fundamental organization of society (i.e. industrialization and the nation state). Muscular Christianity was a result of these changes in gender ideology, incorporating traits of the new social perceptions of manliness. While a clear and distinct shift was made within Christian theology to include sports and physical exercise, muscular Judaism struggled with its theological values; there existed a distinct gap between Jews who accepted their physical prowess and sought to develop it and those who remained loyal to traditional (non-athletic) ideals. For example, most eastern European Jews had a general dislike for athletics. This more orthodox vein of Judaism saw sport as exemplifying European fascination with vulgarity and violence and was thus labeled "un-Jewish." These activities distracted young Jews from their studies and work, and were fundamentally at odds with their orthodox upbringing (Riess 1998: 15).

An overall shift in gender identity was needed to bring muscular Judaism to full light. One early attempt to include emerging concepts of the Jewish male athlete resulted from the late nineteenth-century Zionist movement, expressed in the written works of and speeches made by Max Nordau. Described by Ernest Gellner (1983) as "diaspora nationalism," the proponents of Zionism regard it as a national liberation movement, with the explicit goal of Jewish self-determination within their European countries and ultimately the creation of a Jewish state. As a shift in Jewish gender ideology occurred in less orthodox communities of Europe (Germany, England and Austria), Jews became involved in the westernization process of Europe, one in which the "Muscle-Jew" became a figure almost identical to his Aryan confreres and especially the "Muscular Christian" (Boyarin 1997: 37). Nordau stated that Zionism "after all, was explicitly designed to produce a Jewish version of the *Mannerbund*, a culture of Muscle-Jews" (Nordau 1892: 336).

Nordau attempted to use Zionist ideology to change European social perceptions of the physical inferiority of Jewish men. Much of his major literary work *Degeneration* (1892) addresses the mental and cultural changes European Jews were called to make in order to overcome their social circumstances. Out of this written work, Nordau addressed the Second Zionist Congress in 1898, which called for the physical action of Jews throughout Europe. The totality of Nordau's work expresses his desire for a stronger, proactive, muscular Jew. Inciting members of the Jewish community to be more active and rise above their lowly social condition, he was asking for a shift in gender ideology and Jewish approach toward physicality. He states, "the degenerate who shuns action, and is without will-power, has no suspicion that his incapacity for action is a consequence of his inherited deficiency of brain," (Nordau 1892: 20) echoing the muscular Christian ontological connection between mental purity and physical prowess. He implored Jews to physically rise out of the ghettos and challenge the age-old label of low-class, weak citizens of the world, and to take pride in their Jewish heritage, and affirm their cultural right to nationhood.

Physical ability within a national identity was the fundamental premise Nordau used in his attempt to shift traditional gender ideology. As Nordau described, Jews had two options: to join the physical movements and be counted as equals within their nations, or continue to hold onto traditional values and perpetuate the ostracism they had endured for centuries. Nordau and Zionism had early success in Europe by establishing programs that offered Jewish citizens the opportunity to develop their bodies and challenge the anti-Semitic label.

Non-Jewish Europeans had stereotyped Jewish men as weak, non-confrontational, and studious. The traditional male label was not much different within Jewish communities. The Jew who sought the qualities of the new man was vilified by many within his community (Gilman 1986). Nordau's 1898 Zionist Congress address on creating "muscle Jews" challenged the traditional Jewish discourse at the time, which equated these muscle-seeking Jews with low forms of civilization. Critics used terms like "Goyim naches"—a contemptuous term for those who exhibited characteristics of non-Jewish masculinity: physical strength, martial activity, aggressiveness, and contempt for and fear of the female body (Boyarin 1997: 78). Nineteenth-century European Jews were well aware of the Romantic version of "manliness," but many perceived Christian "masculine humanity" as "very low, crude, primitive, violent, and cruel" (Boyarin 1997: 79). From the start, Nordau's attempt to change traditional Jewish gender norms and increase physical activity challenged perceptions of both Jews and non-Jews alike.

The theories of Max Nordau certainly lay the foundation for what was to become the movement of muscular Judaism. Nordau describes the Jews as a people who had been subjected to discrimination for so long that they internalized the discrimination as an unfortunate result of birth. Despite the air of overall resistance, Nordau did reach some members of the Jewish community and sparked the formation of Zionist athletic organizations as well as a Jewish gymnastics journal (Die Jüdische Turnzeitung). Nordau used the ideas of nationalism to convince Jews opposed to his ideas that being physically active was important for the community at large. One of the aims of the Zionist movement was to be included in national movements (Goldscheider and Zuckerman 1984), and with nationalism sweeping the continent strong physical bodies were necessary for strong national bodies.

Muscular Christianity and muscular Judaism

Arguably, what came to be the foundation of western sport ideology was the muscular Christian movement, premised on emerging cultural values like duty, honor, and industriousness. Mid-nineteenth-century educators, politicians, and writers infused these ideals in their work, and physical education followed suit. While historical views within Christian theology clearly describe the sinful nature of the physical body, a challenging view of traditional Christian corporeality was published when Charles Kingsley first popularized notions of a "healthful and manly Christianity," in his 1855 novel, *Westward Ho!* (Bundgaard 2005: 25–6). Using the term muscular Christianity, new connections between notions of manliness and godliness were infused into both spiritual and physical health, in which a healthy physical body became equated with a healthy spirit, encapsulated in the phrase *mens sana in corpore sano* (a healthy mind in a healthy body) (Young 2004: 90).

The connection between muscular Christianity and the progressive social movements of the times is also well documented; "muscular Christians, energized by a postmillennial view of progress, a sense of duty, and a concern for health, used the dynamic environment fostered by the technical revolution to engage the gears of the sports machine in culture" (Ladd and Mathison 1999: 27). Using muscular Christianity as a guide, scholars have illustrated the connections between industrial society, its perceptions of the body, and the role religious communities have in determining sports ideology.

Apparent at the foundation of muscular Christianity is a spiritual concern, enhanced through physical activities. One founding author of the movement, Thomas Hughes, illustrates the muscular Christian attitude toward physical activity in *Tom Brown at Oxford*:

> The least of the muscular Christians has hold of the old chivalrous and Christian belief, that a man's body is given to him to be trained and brought into subjection, and then used for the protection of the weak, the advancement of all righteous causes, and the subduing of the earth which God has given to the children of men.
>
> *(1861: 83)*

Charles Kingsley also endorses physicality as a main muscular Christian focus for spiritual enhancement, writing in *Health and Education* (1874) that:

> games conduce not merely to physical but to moral health; that in the playing fields boys acquire virtues which no books can give them; not merely daring and endurance, but, better still, temper, self restraint, fairness, honour, unenvious approbation of another's success, and all that 'give and take' of life which stands a man in such good stead when he goes forth into the world, and without which, indeed, his success is always maimed and partial.
>
> *(cited in Ladd and Mathison 1999: 15)*

Scholars point to Kingsley and Hughes as benchmark authors of muscular Christian physical ideology (Watson, Weir and Friend 2005).

Three themes can be extracted from this above passage about muscular Christians and the role they play in the world. First, muscular Christians were heralded as physically fit and manly. Second, they were to produce moral goodness with the bodies they trained. And lastly, muscular Christianity dedicated itself to keeping Christian ideals and God involved in any physical activity. The founders of muscular Christianity held as their "core ideology" manliness, morality, and health, "focused on the transformation of society, assuming that participation in games and sports by adolescent males had inherent value immediately and in later life" (Ladd and Mathison 1999: 16).

In a recent article on gender in education, Rob Boddice (2009) explores the influence parents and students had on muscular Christian ideology in their schooling. Historically, muscular Christianity has been described as a physical movement beginning at British schools such as Rugby and Eton. Boddice provides evidence that, much like the Jewish Viadrina (discussed below), the sports ideology at these schools began with the desires of parents to have their sons learning Romantic masculine values. It is also well documented that the boys themselves pushed to keep games as an integral part of their schooling experience. Boddice argues, "Hughes was really disseminating the parental vision of what public schools ought to be encouraging ... It was parents, not masters, who subscribed to 'the ethical value of games as the source of good sense, noble traits, manly feelings, generous disposition, gentlemanly deportment [and] comradely loyalty'" (Boddice 2009: 161). Looking at this impetus for muscular Christian ideals in British educational rubric reveals the important role secular pressures can have on religious ideology.

There is one differing premise separating the muscular Christian and muscular Judaism writings; their sense of purpose. Muscular Christianity was a movement premised on religious and spiritual betterment. Muscular Judaism was defined as an exercise to raise the Jews from their lowly social conditions through physical competition. It is important to state that sport can have multiple justifications within religious communities. In looking at the cases of muscular Judaism and muscular Christianity, what can be demonstrated is that sport has been used for social and spiritual purposes by religious organizations. Through this comparison one can understand that spiritual enhancement can only become the focus of a muscular movement once social conditions allow.

Early Jewish sports movements

Prior to Max Nordau, and the muscular Judaism movement, Jewish students at German universities had become caught up in their own physical movements. One of the earliest Jewish physical movements, the Viadrina, involved twelve students who established a dueling society at the University of Breslau in 1886 (Boas 1981: 1001). The goal of the Viadrina was to create a space for Jewish physical activity that German universities had either failed to create or offered with unacceptable conditions. In the organization's founding statement there is an appeal to the personal pride and self-respect of fraternity men and gymnasts who tried mightily to socially "pass" at the expense of their Jewish identity. In one founding document it is stated that:

> We are either completely excluded from these communities or offered membership in a form and under conditions unacceptable to most of us. A strict exclusion of Jewish fellow-students is to be found particularly in the sports clubs, which are of such eminent importance above all for students ... Our association is to be, first of all, a place for physical training of every kind: gymnastics, fencing, rowing, swimming. We have to fight with all our energy against the odium of cowardice and weakness which is cast on us. We want to show that every member of our association is equal to every Christian fellow-student in any physical exercise and chivalry ... We hope to acquire a firm foundation for this self-respect and self-confidence by studying Jewish history, the deeds and suffering of our ancestors.
>
> *(Goldscheider and Zuckerman 1984: 88)*[5]

The Viadrina offered Jewish students an opportunity to prove, on the athletic field that they were as manly as their fellow Germans. We see in these founding statements evidence that this organization was for the social improvement and equality of young Jewish men.

Arguably, the Viadrina would not have evolved had it not been for the "Turner movement," an early nineteenth-century politically nationalistic/gymnastic movement initiated by Friedrich Ludwig Jahn (1778–1852). Jahn's Turner movement pervaded German society in the early part of the nineteenth century with the intention of building German national pride through gymnastics (Mechikoff and Estes 2006: 172). Though often cited as anti-Semitic, Jahn tolerated

Jewish students joining in with his gymnastics classes, challenging the general German academic practice of Semitic exclusion. He included Jews because the Turner movement was premised on the nation and not religious affiliation (Gurock 2005: 35). As a result of their exposure to Jahn's nationalistic physical movement, German Jews developed an understanding of nationalistic pride and the importance of equating physical prowess with national identity.

Jewish sport programs always needed to be respectful of the deeply held tradition of religious study. It seems that the late nineteenth-century Jewish student body at German universities justified their physical interests by doing what muscular Christianity had done: combine religious traditions with newly defined sport ideals. These Jewish students claimed—reiterated in Nordau's speeches—that "physical strength and agility will increase self-confidence and self-respect, and in the future no one will be ashamed of being a Jew" (Goldscheider and Zuckerman 1984: 88). The combination of physical competition and Jewish study allowed Jews to establish a more comfortable position within German society and maintain a balance between modern physical expression and traditional Jewish values. But at this point there exists no evidence that these students were using sport for spiritual improvement.

After two decades of fighting, sometimes in street fights when anti-Semitic remarks were leveled at Viadrina members, the groups had become an unpopular option among German Jewish students. By the time Max Nordau addressed the Second Zionist Congress in 1898, the Jewish sport fraternities had all but disappeared.

Muscular Judaism's emergence and lasting effects

The totality of his written work and addresses at Zionist Congresses establishes Max Nordau as the central figure of the muscular Judaism movement. Focused on what he believed was "a missing corporeal upbringing" (Presner 2003: 282), Nordau's aim was twofold in developing Jewish sporting organizations: first, to provide a space for sport, developed for Jews who had been barred from other athletic spaces. The second goal for Nordau's sports programs was to demonstrate that the Jewish male could have athletic prowess. These goals were similar to those of the Viadrina, and again we see muscular Judaism's overall trend toward social enhancement, not spiritual.

As a result of Max Nordau's address to the Zionist movement, the *Juedische Turnerschaft* and the *Bar Kochba*, Jewish sporting organizations were created. These organizations were to provide settings suitable for Jewish student athletes struggling to combine European physical culture with traditional Jewish culture in an attempt to demonstrate that sports were a worthy Jewish activity. They called upon members of the German Jewish community to "fight with us for our Judaism by cultivating [the study of] Jewish history and literature [and] by steeling [our] bodies." Remaining faithful to Nordau and his vision, these organizations existed for "physical fitness, combined with education in Jewish heritage and the belief in the Jewish nation" (Gurock 2005: 33).

We know that it was "in accordance with an emancipatory ideology that accepted and internalized anti-Semitic figurations of an emasculated Jewish Otherness," that the sports organizations Nordau called for were intended "to demonstrate that Jews could develop the same physical potential and abilities as non-Jews" (Bunzl 2000: 240). One successful example of Nordau's efforts was the SC Hakoah Wien, an Austrian Jewish football club established in 1909 (Hughes 1996: 62). Their presence and progress culminated in the 1924–25 season when the club emerged victor of the Austrian league championships. But the rise of Nazi anti-Semitism stifled further developments in Austria and the Jew was once again relegated to an impoverished physical and social position. It was not until the 1990s that Jewish soccer teams would re-emerge in

Austria (Bunzl 2000: 233). Even before the rise of the Nazis and the eventual Holocaust, Jewish communities faced harsh discrimination, where old views of who and what Jews were supposed to be held firm throughout Europe (Brunstein 2003: 4). The anti-Semitic social environment of Europe at the time, as well as continued Jewish opposition to physical culture, were likely the root causes of muscular Judaism's inability to remain a prominent physical movement.

However, elements of muscular Judaism ideology are evident in various activities outside of the anti-Semitic environment of nineteenth-century Continental Europe. Other examples in Europe demonstrate that physical movements were successful in bettering the social perception of the overall Jewish population. Within these communities again we see the inclusion of Jewish athletics for social improvement and not based on theological arguments like the muscular Christians.

As early as the seventeenth and eighteenth centuries, a significant number of British pugilistic Jews "fought professionally and were the pride of some of their people" (Gurock 2005: 28). Anglican Jews were exposed to the sweeping British sporting culture of the mid-nineteenth century. A more democratic sentiment toward the Jewish populations existed in Britain, where even special academic accommodations were made if exams coincided with holy or Sabbath days. By political mandate in 1856, British Jews gained admission to Oxford and Cambridge. At these universities, "athletics became an extracurricular option," with Britain's, "own select group of Anglicized Jew" (Gurock 2005: 34). Jewish athletics also appeared in British state schools as well. Early in their education, British Jewish children demonstrated their athletic skills along with their Gentile classmates, as well as participated at Jewish youth clubs and Zionist Maccabi programs. In such settings they could "overcome their so-called 'Jewish Tardiness … in maturing a capacity for team-effort'" (Gurock 2005: 35). The inclusion of Jewish citizens coincides with muscular Christian ideals, which were becoming popular and spreading in British physical education programs by the early 1860s.[6] Much like the experience during the Turner movement in Germany, British Jews became involved in their national muscular movement.

In the late nineteenth century, in view of the ban on Turner gymnastics in Prussia and a vibrant muscular Christian movement in Britain, America appeared to be a ripe environment to expand.[7] As British and German Jews set sail for America at the dawn of the twentieth century, they entered a social and sporting culture unlike any the world had ever known.

Cities along the east coast of the United States with significant German populations, including Jewish immigrants in the late nineteenth and early twentieth centuries, witnessed Turner gymnasiums spring up. Inherent in their founding ideology and compatible with the democratic ideals of the United States, religious affiliation for the Turners was rumored to be of little importance. The inclusion of Jewish immigrants into these clubs offered a chance to feel socially accepted and to feel one with the emerging American national image. In fact, to work and survive in their new neighborhoods, Jews needed to be physically strong. One Cincinnati social club newsletter stated that "man is the main thing, and that Jew, or Mohammedan, is a matter of minor importance … Manliness, the improvement of the body, the development of a robust physique stood as the core value of the American Turner creed" (Gurock 2005: 35). Within the new American Turner organizations the Jewish body could be developed without the long-standing social discrimination that existed in Europe.

Of course there were some remnants of anti-athletic perceptions by eastern European immigrants. These populations came to America with an understanding that participation in sporting activities was still not a worthwhile life option. "First generation Jewish parents were as strongly opposed to athletics, if not more so, than any other immigrants. Not only were they unfamiliar with sports in the Old World but in America they regarded athletics as a waste of time that served no useful function … sport was a dangerous force that taught inappropriate social values, drew children away from traditional beliefs and behavior, and led to overexertion and accidents" (Riess 1998: 64). To demonstrate the negative sentiments of Eastern Jews toward sport, one of the worst insults a parent or grandparent could level at children was "you baseball player, you" (Riess 1998: 15). Yet, as these early Eastern Jewish immigrants settled in, first- or second-generation German Jews took it upon themselves to introduce their Slavic brothers and sisters to American culture, particularly though sport. As with all attempts at cultural change, first-generation Eastern European Jewish children were unavoidably and overwhelmingly influenced by the American athletic culture. As these young generations grew older, many used sport as a way to acclimate to American society.

Using sport as a means of social integration and social mobility worried some Jewish religious leaders. Elderly religious members of American Jews feared that young Jews would become engaged "in the worst aspects of sporting pursuits, participating not as athletes but as spectators at the track, gambling with racing forms in their hands" (Gurock 2005: 37). It is at this time we see a moral concern entering the Jewish sporting dialogue. This is a notable shift in how sport is used within religions, and not just in a Jewish context. Jewish religious leaders had begun to accept sport as a worthy activity and now began to fear for the spiritual well-being of their followers, not just their social mobility. Moral, ethical, and spiritual concerns became the focus of American Jewish sporting organizations because, in a sense, American Jews were no longer struggling against an entrenched social anti-Semitic culture. In this new environment, Jewish leaders realized the need for the creation of religiously based sport organizations where they could have a positive influence on the athletic education of their members. The liquor-free and almost smokeless environment of the Young Men's Hebrew Association (YMHA) became the place for young Jews to fulfill their athletic desires. In the last quarter of the nineteenth century, new YMHAs were built in various cities across the United States. These social clubs incorporated older, traditional libraries and sitting rooms, to go along with a new athletic element. The inclusion of sport-specific space in YMHAs mirrors its predecessor, the YMCA. "By 1890, as many as twenty cities had such Jewish-run facilities, complete with trained instructors who were graduates from the 'Turner' colleges of the period" (Gurock 2005: 37), demonstrating the lasting influence of the Turner movement on Jewish athletic culture.

Athleticism became an entrenched program for the YMHA. Similar to the Christian purpose for having athletic space, the social and moral aims of the YMHA certainly demonstrate a pronounced change in the Jewish approach to sport and physical culture. Organizers of early American YMHAs were impressed with the success of the YMCA (Kaufman 1999: 54) in their creation of an organization that combined faith, culture, education, and physical recreation activities.[8] Other Jewish leaders built new temples with sport-specific areas. Rabbi Henry Berkowitz of Kansas City developed a plan in his own Temple B'nai Jehudah which would include athletic areas, libraries, music rooms, and social halls to be included in his synagogue. His hope was to "lure those who came to play to stay and pray" (Gurock 2005: 39).

Even rabbis who did not believe in establishing gymnasia in their own temples saw the benefits of establishing Jewish-run athletic organizations, acknowledging that Jews were caught up in the sports movements of early twentieth-century America. If there were no Jewish organizations to offer physical recreation, young Jews would seek it elsewhere. Detroit's Rabbi David Franklin was clearly against having a gym in his temple or anywhere near his holy sanctuary. Begrudgingly, he had to approve of such activities and arenas, stating that, as a "self-defense measure," these opportunities must be established for Jewish youth, "since the gymnasium of the YMCA," was the only one available to his Jewish boys, and because "at the YMCA young Jewish children were being taken away 'on the Sabbath morning', and were being 'inculcated with the gymnastic instruction and elements of Christianity'" (Gurock 2005: 41).

The physical culture in America pervaded all aspects of society, and Jewish immigrants decided they wanted to keep their children in Jewish programs, gymnasia, swimming pools, and recreational organizations. The shift in Jewish sentiment toward a more sympathetic view of sport and athleticism began with the social concerns of the community, and later came to include Jewish immigrants' spiritual needs. While the efforts of Zionist Max Nordau and his muscular Judaism movement are not regarded as lasting because of the anti-Semitism and continued traditional Jewish sentiments toward masculinity and physical culture that pervaded European culture, they were certainly influential elsewhere. Envisioned to be a movement of social improvement and equality, muscular Judaism moved beyond this to include similar spiritual concerns in the United States. Here, the cultural environment allowed for more social mobility and communal cohesion. It was the physical culture of America (a result of the muscular Christian movement, Turner gymnastic education, and American idealism) that changed Jewish attitudes toward sport and physical activity.

Conclusion

The blend of sport and religion has become a part of Western sport ideology. Beginning with the muscular Christian movement and evidenced in muscular Judaism, sport has been used in religious communities for spiritual betterment as well as social progression. These two related movements reflect some of the fundamental beliefs of sport in its contemporary social role. Muscular Judaism had at its core the push to prove Jewish men could be just as manly and physical as their Gentile neighbors. Through athletic competition, they could show both Jews and non-Jews alike that they were able bodied, which would in turn prove that Jews were not second-class citizens, and make others see that they were a physical force worthy of respect.

Muscular Christians had at their core the moral improvement of the individual. An athletic Christian could better his morality through physical exercise by expelling pent-up energy that he might use in other sinful ways. Athletes could prove they matched up with the Romantic ideals of what it meant to be a man: physical strength, marriage, aggressiveness, and oppositional attitudes toward feminine traits, as well as prove their spiritual purity.

While each religion's physical movement was initiated with different aims, there is a mutual theme that unites the two, an essential trait to any physical-based religious movement: the betterment of their religious community. Both wished for self-sacrifice, self-restraint, duty, and responsibility—essential Judeo-Christian character traits that are also found in almost every formal religion around the globe. Also, both religions changed because of these physical movements. The "muscular movement" challenged the traditional Jewish introspective ontology to a more outward-looking Romantic view of masculinity and sport. Muscular Christianity altered the fundamental Christian belief that the body was something to be denied, punished and inherently evil. Each changed their metaphysical positions using sport, for the purpose of moving their communities in progressive ways.

In recent decades, many scholars have discussed the strong connections that exist between sport and religion (Guttmann 1978; Giamatti 1989; Hoffman 1992, 2010; Ladd and Mathison 1999; Preece and Hess 2009). The evidence provided in this essay supports a claim that sport can be a useful tool for both social and spiritual progress. The Zionist movement and Nordau's work presented European Jews with a new approach to improve their social status using physical means. Christians became aware of a new approach to better their health and spirit through physical activity and sport, changing a long-standing view about the inherent sinfulness of the body. In changing their metaphysical views of sport and physicality each religious community benefited in profound ways.

The effect of muscular Christianity can be seen in the way sports are played in the modern world. Muscular Judaism's impact is felt on a much smaller scale, evident in YMHAs, Jewish Community Centers (JCCs) and the World Maccabi Union (the international Jewish sports organization). It is argued that muscular Judaism's existence was short-lived and of lesser notoriety because the use of sport and physicality was such a challenge to both external and internal cultural hegemony. It is interesting to consider an alternate course of world history if muscular Judaism had originally been a movement for the spiritual betterment of its followers and not a social movement where individuals had to prove their basic human worth. In both instances however, muscular Judaism and muscular Christianity used sport as a progressive and beneficial tool, demonstrating the intimate tie that sport and religion share within human communities.

Notes

1 Other "muscular religious movements" during the second half of the nineteenth century have been topics of research. For example, Joseph Alter (2004) has explored the relationship between muscular Christianity and Hindu masculinity; Richard Kimball's (2008) work on muscular Mormonism demonstrates the lasting effects of sports policy within their religious framework; and Mark Freeman (2009) has conducted research on muscular Quakerism. These movements in general demonstrate the importance of sport within religious social frameworks.

2 According to *The Jewish Encyclopedia* (Singer and Adler 1901–1906), the total number of Jews living in Europe during the first years of the twentieth century was just under nine million (80 percent of the world Jewish population). At the time Europe had a total population of 408 million, making Jews 2.2 percent of the European population (United Nations 2004: 6).

3 Nordau writes of the necessity of creating a new type of Jew—corporeally strong, sexually potent, and morally fit—as the precondition for realizing the national goals of Zionism. After providing an overview of the steadily deteriorating situation of Jews in Russia, Romania, and Galicia—what he terms "the classic countries of Jewish suffering"—he argues that the Jews themselves must change their desperate historical situation and that it is "Zionism [that will] awaken Judaism to new life" (Presner 2003: 269).

4 The term "muscular Judaism" was first used by Max Nordau in his opening speech to the Second Zionist Congress, August 28, 1898. This term was meant to realize the nationalistic goals of Zionism by inspiring the European Jewish community to appreciate the benefits of physical strength for moral fortitude.

5 Cited in Asch, A. and Philippson, J. (1958). 'Self-Defence in the Second Half of the 19th Century: the emergence of the K.C.,' *Leo Baeck Institute Yearbook*, Vol. III, New York: Oxford Journals, pp. 123–5. (K.C. was the Kartell Covenant, a national association of German Jewish students.)

6 See, for instance, the discussion of the Clarendon Commission on Public Schools discussions of sports, parental roles, and "muscular Christianity" in Boddice, R. In 'loco parentis? Public-school authority, cricket and manly character, 1855–62,' *Gender and Education*, 21(2), 2009, pp. 159–72.

7 Charles Follen, Charles Beck and Francis Lieber, all members of Jahn's Turner movement, moved to the United States as immigrants in the mid- to late 1820s. All three men brought with them Jahn's physical philosophies to gymnastic programs at Harvard University, the Boston Gymnasium, and the Round Hill School in Northampton, Massachusetts (Mechikoff and Estes 2006: 175–6).

8 For a detailed analysis of the connections between the YMCA and the YMHA see David Kaufman's *Shul with a Pool* (1999), pages 52–56.

References

Asch, A. and Philippson, J. (1958). 'Self-Defence in the Second Half of the 19th Century: the emergence of the K.C.,' Leo Beck Institute Yearbook, Vol. III, New York: Oxford Journals, pp. 122–39.

Alter, J. (2004). 'Indian Clubs and Colonialism: Hindu masculinity and muscular Christianity,' *Comparative Studies in Society and History*, 46(3): 497–534.

Boas, J. (1981). 'German Jewry's Search for Renewal in the Hitler Era as Reflected in the Major Jewish Newspapers (1933–38),' *The Journal of Modern History*, On Demand Supplement, 53(1): D1001–24.

Boddice, R. (2009). 'In loco parentis? Public-school authority, cricket and manly character, 1855–62,' *Gender and Education*, 21(2): 159–72.

Boyarin, D. (1997). *Unheroic Conduct: the rise of heterosexuality and the invention of the Jewish man*, Los Angeles, CA: University of California Press.

Brustein, W. (2003). *Roots of Hate: anti-Semitism in Europe before the Holocaust*, Cambridge: Cambridge University Press.

Bundgaard, A. (2005). *Muscle and Manliness: the rise of sport in American boarding schools*, Syracuse, NY: Syracuse University Press.

Bunzl, M. (2000). 'Resistive Play: sports and the emergence of Jewish visibility in contemporary Vienna,' *Journal of Sport and Social Issues*, 24(3): 232–50.

Freeman, M. (2009). 'Fellowship, Service and the "Spirit of Adventure": the Religious Society of Friends and the outdoors movement in Britain c. 1900-1950,' *Quaker Studies*, 14: 72–92.

Gellner, E. (1983). *Nations and Nationalism: new perspectives on the past*, Ithaca, NY: Cornell University Press.

Giamatti, A.B. (1989). *Take Time for Paradise: Americans and their games*, New York: Summit Books.

Gilman, S. (1986). *Jewish Self-Hatred: anti-Semitism and the hidden language of the Jews*, Baltimore, MD: Johns Hopkins University Press.

Goldscheider, C., Zuckerman, A. (1984). 'The Formation of Jewish Political Movements in Europe,' *Modern Judaism*, 4(1): 83–104.

Gurock, J. (2005). *Judaism's Encounter with American Sport*, Bloomington, IN: Indiana University Press.

Guttmann, A. (1978). *From Ritual to Record: the nature of modern sport*, New York: Columbia University Press.

Hoffman, S. (ed.) (1992). 'Recovering a Sense of the Sacred in Sport,' *Sport and Religion*, Champaign, IL: Human Kinetics Books, 153–9.

Hoffman, S. (2010). *Good Game: Christianity and the Culture of Sports*, Waco, TX: Baylor University Press.

Hughes, A. (1996). 'Muscular Judaism and the Jewish Rugby League Competition in Sydney, 1924 to 1927,' *Sporting Traditions, the Journal of the Australian Society for Sport History*, 13(1): 61–80.

Hughes, T. (1861). *Tom Brown at Oxford*, London: Macmillan.

Kaufman, D. (1999). *Shul with a Pool: The 'Synagogue-center' in American Jewish History*, Hanover, NH: Brandeis University Press/University Press of New England.

Kimball, R. (2008). 'Muscular Mormonism,' *International Journal of the History of Sport*, 25(5): 549–78.

Ladd, T., Mathison, J. (1999). *Muscular Christianity: Evangelical protestants and the development of American sport*, Grand Rapids, MI: Baker Books.

MacAloon, J. (2006). 'Introduction: muscular Christianity after 150 years,' *The International Journal of the History of Sport*, 23(5): 687–700.

Mechikoff, R., Estes, S. (2006). *A History of Sport and Physical Education: from ancient civilizations to the modern world*, 4th edn, Boston, MA: McGraw Hill.

Nordau, M. (1892). *Degeneration*, 4th edn, New York: D. Appleton and Company.

Preece, G., Hess, R. (2009). *Sport and Spirituality: an exercise in everyday theology*, Adelaide: ATF Press.

Presner, T. (2003). 'Clear heads, solid stomachs, and hard muscles: Max Nordau and the aesthetics of Jewish regeneration,' *Modernism/modernity*, 10(2): 269–96.

Presner, T. (2007). *Muscular Judaism: the Jewish body and the politics of regeneration*, London: Routledge.

Putney, C. (2001). *Muscular Christianity: manhood and sports in Protestant America, 1880–1920*, Cambridge, MA: Harvard University Press.

Riess, S. (1998). *Sport and the American Jew*, Syracuse, NY: Syracuse University Press.

Singer, I., Adler, C. (eds) (1901–6). *The Jewish Encyclopedia*, New York: Funk and Wagnalls.

United Nations Populations Divisions (2004). The world at six billion, www.un.org/esa/population/publications/sixbillion/sixbillion.htm, accessed 29th August 2010.

Watson, N., Weir, S., Friend, S. (2005). 'The Development of Muscular Christianity in Victorian Britain and Beyond,' *Journal of Religion and Society*, vol.7.

Young, D. (2004). *A Brief History of the Olympic Games*, Oxford: Blackwell Publishing.

3

Sports development, nations and nationalism

Alan Bairner

Nation states and stateless nations alike contribute to the development of sport for many and varied reasons, amongst them domestic solidarity, international prestige, and the physical and psychological well-being of their people. With specific reference to nationalism as a political ideology, the most common motivations have been imperialist expansion and anti-imperialist resistance. The purpose of this chapter is to examine ways in which nationalism has made a vital contribution to sports development. The chapter begins with a brief discussion of the relationship between sport and nationalism, with special attention being paid to the British (or, to be more precise, the English) experience and to the diffusion of sport as an imperialist project. The main focus of the chapter, however, is on two particular case studies – Ireland and Taiwan – with the aim of demonstrating the complex relationship between sport, nationalism and post-colonialism in relation to sports development. The chapter ends with a commentary on the threat posed by globalisation to the traditional linkage of nationalism and sports development.

Sport and nationalism

At the most basic level of analysis, it is easy to see the extent to which sport, arguably more than any other form of social activity in the modern world, facilitates flag waving and the playing of national anthems, both formally, at moments such as medal ceremonies, and, informally, through the activities of fans (Hoberman 1984; MacClancy 1996; Cronin and Mayall 1998; Bairner 2001; Smith and Porter 2004). Indeed, there are political nationalists who fear that by acting as such a visible medium for overt displays of national sentiment, sport can actually blunt the edge of serious political debate (Jarvie and Walker 1994). No matter how one views the grotesque caricatures of pseudonational modes of behaviour and dress that so often provide the colourful backdrop to major sporting events, one cannot escape the fact that sport and nationalism, no matter how that concept is understood, are closely linked. It is important to appreciate, however, that the precise nature of their relationship varies dramatically from one political setting to another and that, as a consequence, it is vital that we are constantly alert to a range of different conceptual issues (Bairner 2008, 2009).

For example, like the United Nations, sport's global governing bodies, such as the International Olympic Committee or the Fédération Internationale de Football Association (FIFA), consist almost exclusively of representatives not of nations but rather of sovereign nation states. It is also worth noting that pioneering figures in the organisation of international sport, such as Baron Pierre de Coubertin, the founder of the modern Olympics movement, embodied a commitment both to internationalism and to the interests of their own nation states. Thus, whilst de Coubertin could write enthusiastically about a sporting event that would bring together young (male) athletes from across the globe, he was also specifically concerned with the physical well-being of young French men in the wake of a demoralising defeat in the Franco-German War. As Hill (1992: 6) observes, 'it was not primarily because he was an internationalist that Coubertin pursued the Olympic ideal; rather, he saw this as the best way of promoting sport of the finest type, his efforts to balance intellectual and physical education in French schools having failed'.

As for the Olympics themselves, it is worth noting that although the Cold War is normally understood as a contest between the rival ideological visions of capitalism and communism, nationalism also played its part not only in terms of international competition between the United States and the Soviet Union but also within the Soviet bloc. Hungary and Czechoslovakia's rivalry with the Soviet Union in water polo and ice hockey, respectively, although provoked by ideological differences and their consequences, were also rooted in national pride. Indeed, simply by becoming an *international* competition in 1908 as opposed to one that sought only to bring together competitors representing no one but themselves, the Olympic Games have had a major subsequent impact on ensuring that sports development and the nation are inextricably linked.

It should also be recognised that sport has contributed hugely to gendering the nation. Whereas the relationship between gender and national identity in general has been relatively underexplored, the role of sport in the context of that relationship has been almost totally ignored, even by sports scholars. Yet, Jennifer Ring (2009) draws our attention to the anomalous description of baseball as 'the national pastime' of the United States in relation to gender. Noting that, on 21 June 1952, Commissioner Ford Frick banned women from playing minor or major league baseball, Ring (2009: 20) comments, 'If baseball is the national pastime, the implication is that women are not part of the nation.' Similarly, in England, the Football Association instituted a ban on women's football on 5 December 1921, which was not lifted until 29 November 1971 (Williams 2003). Thus, another national sport was formally reserved for male members of the nation. Traditionally women have either been excluded from sport or encouraged to play for their own sakes – principally for the sake of their health. There has been little sense that female athletes carry with them the hopes and ambitions of the nation. Like war, sport has customarily been regarded as men's work. There have been some notable exceptions to this general rule, primarily emanating from state socialist societies such as the German Democratic Republic, Rumania and the Soviet Union itself. Indeed, the most interesting contemporary example is provided by the female boxers (Lee 2009) and footballers of North Korea, and with the failure of that closed society's men's football team at the 2010 World Cup Finals (Lee and Bairner 2009), the propagandist value of women athletes may well remain high, at least in the short term.

Whilst in most cases the nation states that constitute the membership of international sporting bodies such as the International Olympic Committee are coterminous with nations, the fact remains that numerous nations throughout the world, as well as other forms of collective belonging, are stateless and thus denied representation in international sporting competition just as they are in the corridors of global political power. Here too the Olympic movement has ensured that sports development and nationalism are interwoven. For example, despite the fact that the right to host the Games is granted to individual cities, those cities themselves are generally also seen as representative of their respective nation states. In the case of host cities such as Montréal and Barcelona, however, the opportunity arose to promote the sporting, and concomitantly the political, aspirations of what are seen by many as the submerged nations of Québec and Catalonia, respectively (Kidd 1992; Hargreaves 2000).

As the examples of Montréal and Barcelona reveal, when considering the relationship between sports and nationalism, it is important to think in terms both of nation states and of nations. This also provides the means whereby sport's connection with nationality and also with national identity can be separately explored. It is also useful to bear in mind that sport often acts as a window through which we are able to examine a whole range of social developments and to test a variety of theoretical concepts and perspectives. With specific reference to the relationship between sports and nationalism, observing the world of sport offers insights into the relevance and reliability of such concepts as ethnic and civic nationalism and the validity of explanatory approaches to the rise of nations and nationalism such as primordialism and modernism. Sport can also provide important insights into varieties of imperialism, the cultural politics of anti-imperialist struggle and postcolonial legacies (Bairner 2008). However, despite a growing literature on the relationship between sport and nationalism, the precise impact of nationalism on sports development has received little attention. One way of trying to understand this impact is to look at the ways in which sport has developed (or has been developed) in societies in which the struggle for national identity has been a major political concern over extended periods of time.

There are two extreme ways in which nationalism can impact on the development of sport. First, national ambition can be instrumental in sport's diffusion. In the case of the United Kingdom, for example, diffusion took place in two directions – from England to the other constituent parts of the nation state, from members of the upper classes to subordinate groups in British and Irish society and, finally, from Britain to the various corners of its Empire. Educational institutions played a vital role in the emergence and rapid growth of modern sport in England, as did organised religion. Indeed the two often worked hand in hand inspired by Christian headmasters in the public school system – hence the origins of the term, 'muscular Christianity'. As Dunning (1990: 91) points out, 'whatever the degree of adequacy of this hypothesis, it is certainly the case that public schools were the central loci of the development of embryonic forms of soccer and the rival rugby code.' Subsequently the diffusion of British games, at least in the formal British Empire, owed much to Christian missionaries as well as to official functionaries of the Empire.

The alternative manner in which nationalism can influence sports development is through the ring fencing of certain sports in the interests of national purity. Although cricket is still closely associated with Englishness, neither the English nor the British more generally used this particular strategy, such were their expansionist aims. More recently, at one level the United States has witnessed the construction of a relatively insular sporting culture. But that too has been influenced by expansionist ambitions, both political and sporting, not least in relation to the spread of baseball, traditionally described as America's 'national pastime' but now played with skill and enthusiasm in such disparate societies as Cuba, the Dominican Republic, Japan and South Korea. Rather it was with the formation of the Gaelic Athletic Association (GAA) in 1884, in direct response to the diffusion of British games in Ireland, that there emerged what was to become one of the most successful of all attempts to harness sport to a nationalist cause and, in so doing, to develop sport in interesting and successful ways.

Gaelic games and the origins of sports development in Ireland

By the 1880s, a number of British sports were already well established in Ireland – scarcely surprising given the island's close proximity to Britain and the close family and other personal

33

ties between the British and the Irish, particularly within the Anglo-Irish Establishment. As with the development of modern sport in England, the role of educational institutions was vital. Upper-class Irish boys attended boarding schools in England and subsequently Oxford and Cambridge universities where they were exposed to the feverish process of sports development that had begun in nineteenth-century England. They returned to Ireland eager to pursue their interests particularly in cricket, rowing and rugby. Meanwhile, the British army's presence in Ireland created a growing interest in the so-called 'garrison games' of association football and hockey, whilst in the north-eastern corner of Ireland, Protestant working-class men in Belfast, influenced by developments in the west of Scotland, also embraced football (Bairner 1996). However, it would be wrong to assume that British games were only taken up by the Protestant Irish upper classes, functionaries of the British state and the unionist workers of what in due course was to become Northern Ireland. For example, there is growing evidence of cricket being played by lower middle-class Catholics (Bracken 2004; Hunt 2007), whilst the leading Catholic schools were as likely to encourage British games as were their Church of Ireland counterparts, and urban Catholics also began to take up football (Cronin 1999). Indeed, the founder of the GAA, Michael Cusack, was himself an enthusiastic cricketer and rugby player, as were numerous other major figures in the history of Irish nationalism, and had taught his pupils these sports before deciding on a new course of action (Rouse 2009). It was against, and in response to, the backdrop of the growing popularity of British games in Ireland that the GAA emerged.

Again, it is important to recognise the influential role played by schools and teachers, like Cusack himself, and also by religion, although unlike in England, where the Catholic Church had tended to follow the example of Protestant denominations in relation to sport, in Ireland it was the Catholic Church, despite intermittent concerns about some of the more politically radical figures in the Association, that would assume the leading, and increasingly exclusive, role as far as Gaelic sport was concerned.

Gaelic games, according to Cronin (1999: 116), 'have played a central role in definitions of Irish nationalism.' Indeed the GAA's contribution in this regard has been twofold – first, to provide cultural ballast to the efforts of a constitutionally submerged nation to achieve statehood and, second, since partition in 1921 to help to consolidate and promote the Irish Free State (and, subsequently, the Republic of Ireland) whilst simultaneously providing an important vehicle for the continuing expression of a distinctive Irish national identity within the nationalist community of Northern Ireland. These aspects of the GAA's history are instructive for a wider debate concerning the relationship between sport and the construction and reproduction of national identities in other parts of the world. As David Daiches (1952: 9) wrote, in a different context, 'there are two ways in which a baffled and frustrated nation can attempt to satisfy its injured pride.'

> It can attempt to rediscover its own national traditions, and by reviving and developing them find a satisfaction that will compensate for its political impotence; or, accepting the dominance of the culture of the country which has achieved political ascendancy over it, it can endeavour to beat that country at its own game and achieve distinction by any standard the dominant culture may evolve.
>
> *(Daiches 1952: 9)*

In challenging the emerging hegemony of British games, the GAA clearly eschewed the latter course of action. But it went even further than the former by its insistence that political independence rather than compensation was one of its key objectives. To that end, not only were most of its activities to be distinctively Irish, its approach to sport would also differ from the British model, not least through an emphasis on the symbiotic relationship between sport and community.

The GAA, community and sports development

The leaders of the GAA, fearful that their activities might be unable to compete with more established sports, adopted a policy of banning from the Association members who had been found guilty of playing or watching foreign games. This particular rule was not removed from the GAA's statutes until the 1960s, by which time it was apparent to all that Gaelic games had firmly established themselves in the nation's sporting culture. Indeed, in the years that have followed, the GAA has become a modern, self-confident governing body, capable of transforming Dublin's Croke Park into one of Europe's most impressive stadia and of showing magnanimity – for the sake of the nation – by modifying another of its rules in order to allow rugby union and soccer international matches to be played at Croke Park during the reconstruction of Lansdowne Road. Anomalies remain, however, and are explicable only by exploring what arguably represents the GAA's unique contribution to sports development.

Within the overall context of sports development and specifically in relation to high-performance sport, it is remarkable that it is theoretically possible for the best Gaelic footballer in Ireland to be playing for one of the weakest club sides and for a county with no real expectations of winning a major trophy – 'no hopers', if you like. Only when the relationship between the player, his community and parish, and his Gaelic club is explained does this make any sense. Also unfamiliar to a non-Irish audience is the extent to which Gaelic clubs are more than places where sports are played. Birthday parties are held in them, concerts, engagement parties and so on. Indeed in Belfast, and other towns in the north of Ireland during the so-called 'troubles', Gaelic clubs were widely regarded (erroneously, in some cases, as tragic events were to prove) in nationalist communities as safer and more easily accessed leisure spaces than downtown bars and clubs.

The relationship between sport and community is, of course, by no means confined to the GAA. In England, for example, many professional football clubs were formed by churches, eager to strengthen the bond between religion and the people who lived in a particular town or city district. As Brown *et al.* (2009: 2) note, 'many of today's most successful clubs and particularly the longest established clubs have their origins in "community organisations" such as churches, social clubs or work's teams.' Even more illuminating in terms of the overall context of this book is the manner in which grass-roots sport and elite sport have long enjoyed a symbiotic and mutually supportive relationship in the social democratic societies of northern Europe (Meinander and Mangan 1998). There are echoes of this phenomenon in the organisation of Gaelic games. Certainly, unlike modern professional soccer clubs in England, the GAA has never had to act self-consciously in relation to local communities. Gaelic clubs have been and remain integral parts of their respective communities and, as such, have provided an example that clubs in other sports, in Ireland and elsewhere, have seldom, if ever, been able to emulate.

Links with the Catholic Church although greatly diminished in importance still remain, with most Gaelic clubs inextricably associated with the parish and with the schools that serve it. Thus, in Ulster, Gaelic football's MacCrory Cup is a prized goal for the Catholic grammar schools that annually contest it. In addition, the all-Ireland Sigerson Cup, competed for by institutions of higher education, confers on its winners a status that far exceeds that which is associated with awards in British university sport. Thus, teachers have over time replaced the clergy as dominant figures in developing Gaelic games, whilst the GAA and its member clubs have themselves introduced more modern coaching structures so that the continued development of the sports for which it has responsibility can be assured. As noted above, given the popularity in Ireland of football and, to an only slightly lesser extent, rugby union, it has never been possible for the GAA to become complacent. Its early attempts to ban those who were found to have played or watched foreign games were irrefutable indications of a protectionist, perhaps even a paranoid, perspective. Today, however, although other sports have also evolved in relation to coaching and development, there is a greater sense within the GAA that the nation can be served by a variety of sports, albeit maintaining that Gaelic games remain the purest expression of sporting Irishness – a concept that in itself is constantly evolving as the GAA seeks to develop its games within the immigrant communities made up of the so-called 'new Irish'.

Colonialism and the origins of sports development in Taiwan

In terms of the study of national identity and more specifically the relationships between sport and national identity, Taiwan (or the Republic of China – ROC) provides a fascinating case study. According to Roy (2003: 1), 'Taiwan's present circumstances are peculiar and intriguing' – scarcely surprising given the island's complex history. Equally, it should come as no surprise that a country with such a unique past has also experienced a complex history in terms of both sports development and the construction of national identity and the relationship between the two. The country has been influenced by a long and remarkably varied experience of colonialism. The link between this experience and sport was first established with the arrival of European and American Christian missionaries and educators who sought to make sport and games integral to the education process in imitation of their own western experience.

For example, in 1882, Dr George Leslie MacKay founded the Oxford Study Hall (the predecessor of today's Taiwan Theology College), and later launched the Tamsui Girls High School (the predecessor of today's Tamsui High School). In 1885 the English Presbyterian Church established the Presbyterian Church High School (the predecessor of today's Chang Rong High School). All of these schools, like many schools in Ireland, were subsequently to enjoy an outstanding reputation for sporting excellence. The question of whether there had been a conscious effort on the part of schools to promote modern exercise and physical education prior to the Japanese occupation remains unanswered.

What is undeniable, however, is that, when the Japanese began their occupation of Taiwan in 1895, the sports curriculum in schools began to play an important role in promoting a Japanese identity. This approach was further advanced during the era of Japanese colonialism, most notably with the introduction of baseball, itself ironically having been introduced to Japan as a consequence of American expansionism. The sport's popularity grew rapidly in Taiwan. However, this was no simple exercise in sports development. As in numerous other colonial contexts, sport was used to create dutiful citizens, willing to accept the colonists' authority and values. This was particularly apparent in the treatment of the island's aboriginal population. It can legitimately be argued that, to a significant extent through baseball, not only was armed resistance crushed but cultural indoctrination through systematic (re)education was also imposed on aborigines to the extent that their own identities were much eroded. After being co-opted by the state, aborigines transferred their legendary courage onto the diamond and played an important role in the development of Taiwanese baseball. In addition, baseball helped to enhance mutual understanding through games between opponents from different ethnic backgrounds. For example, the Jianong (Kano) was a tri-ethnic competition involving Han Chinese,

Japanese and indigenous peoples, with Ami aborigines accounting for a high percentage of the players. Furthermore, as we shall now see, attempts to use sport to promote the assimilation of aboriginal people did not end with Japanese rule (Yu 2004).

Defeated by the Communists in mainland China, the Kuomintang (KMT) under the leadership of the Chiang Kai-shek government decamped to Taiwan and thus began the contestation between the governments of the People's Republic of China (PRC) and of the ROC, which persists to the present day. One of the main objectives of the KMT leadership has been to ensure that the Taiwanese people identify themselves as Chinese and, just as the Japanese colonial rulers sought to use baseball to maintain obedience to their rule without quite making the population Japanese, so, in subsequent years, baseball has been used to underline Taiwan's Chinese identity (Yu and Bairner 2008). It is particularly instructive to note the ROC's use of Little League Baseball (LLB) competitions in the United States as part of its nation-building process. It is clear that the KMT, the governing party throughout this period, used LLB as a cultural resource to achieve its political objectives. Young players were hailed as role models for the 'Chinese Nation', with which Taiwanese people were proudly identified, and through which the ethnically divided society was integrated. In addition, LLB triumphs were used to indicate to overseas Chinese, and also to the outside world as a whole, that the ROC represented a more genuine Chinese nation than did the PRC.

With the emergence of a major opposition party in the form of the Democratic Progressive Party (DPP), which is more interested in raising a distinctive Taiwanese consciousness, there has been yet another development. Just as the island's aboriginal people are valued ideologically as a factor in the case for independence, their disproportionate contribution to Taiwanese baseball has not gone unnoticed (Yu and Bairner 2010).

Enlisting Taiwanese aboriginals for the sporting nation

The Japanese wanted to transform 'savages' into civilized beings. The KMT, in turn, used baseball to enhance international visibility and construct an overarching notion of a 'Chinese Nation' so as to win the support of overseas Chinese, consolidate its rule in Taiwan, and Sinicize the aborigines (Yu 2007; Yu and Bairner 2008). More recently, the pro-independence DPP administration, which took office for the first time in 2000, like the KMT before it, albeit with very different objectives, has also recognised the potential role of baseball. International success for Taiwanese teams combined with the personal achievements of Taiwanese players in Major League Baseball in North America become valuable factors in the construction of a distinctively Taiwanese identity. Regardless of the political party in power, all of this has implications for the development of baseball and, in particular, for the education of young aboriginal players.

Recognising the sporting potential of aborigines, not least in terms of promoting national pride and unity of purpose, the KMT government established two Physical Education (PE) Experimental High Schools, in Taidong and Hualian, in the late 1990s to allow pupils to focus their attention on sport. Both of these are full of tribal athletes. Some teachers have warned of the dangers of condemning student-athletes as young as thirteen to be little more than sport machines with no additional skills. It seems that, on one hand, the government conveniently extracts the cheap labour of aborigines to achieve its goal of international visibility. On the other hand, aborigines become more and more convinced that sport is the most likely, perhaps the only, way for them to obtain fame and earn money. It is a familiar story. Comparisons can certainly be made with the experience of young African American athletes (Hoberman 1997). Moreover, unlike in the United States (Hoberman 1997) and Australia (Tatz 1995), where racism also exists but where sport is valorised by many, in Chinese society all occupations relating to physical labour tend to be despised. Yet, acculturation supported by racial stereo-typing has shaped aboriginal thinking into accepting that Han Chinese are academically superior while they themselves are better athletes (Yu 2004).

While many local tribal people applauded the move to set up PE schools, it is important to examine the trajectory of their alumni. In 1996, Taidong PE Experimental High School accepted its first 28 junior high players, only two of whom were Han Chinese. Only seven still play baseball and not all of them are likely to progress to the professional game. The rest are now at the bottom of the social scale, working as street vendors selling sautéed periwinkle, truck drivers, or bricklayers (Yu and Bairner 2010). This drop out rate is very high. However, there is a widespread tendency to focus on the success stories and to ignore the plight of those who have dropped out of baseball. Indeed, officials use the successful examples to uphold the PE school policy. Since sports performance can mean promotion for education officials, it is not surprising that baseball teams are encouraged to win championships both domestically and internationally.

There is considerable evidence, therefore, of the close relationship that has existed in Taiwan over an extended period of time between sports development and the construction and repro-duction of various national and quasinational identities. Whilst the central concern of genera-tions of politicians has undeniably been with the identity issue per se, it cannot be denied that partially as a consequence of their various ambitions, sport, and in particular baseball, has been substantially developed. To return to the political issue, however, although sports development has certainly been conceived as part of a national project, questions remain as to which nation is at stake, to whom that nation belongs and who pays the highest price.

Conclusion

It would be an oversimplification to argue, not least on the basis of only two case studies, that nationalism has been a major driving force in sports development. At the same time, it is clear even from the examples offered in this chapter that nationalism has undeniably been deeply implicated in the processes whereby sport has been accepted and then further developed in particular societies. Whether the nation will continue to loom as large in the future is another matter.

Despite the resilience of traditional pastimes such as *pelota* in the Basque country and sumo in Japan as well as organisations such as the GAA, many would argue that there are strong grounds for believing that the link between nationalism and sports is becoming weaker and that the very existence of international competition is threatened by the twin forces of globalisation and consumer capitalism (Miller *et al.* 2001; Giulianotti and Robertson 2009). Athletes migrate from one nation state to another in rapidly increasing numbers and not only to play for different clubs (Maguire 1999; Lanfranchi and Taylor 2001). In many cases, the move also involves the adoption of a new sporting nationality. This process has been notably exemplified in the global movement of Kenyan and Ethiopian runners – representing their 'real' nation at one major event and oil-rich countries such as Qatar and Bahrain or even the United States at the next. Furthermore, it is increasingly believed that, whilst most professional athletes in team sports continue to represent the nation states of their birth, their true feelings of loyalty are for their clubs and even for their corporate sponsors. This leads to concerns that in soccer the European Champions' League has now virtually surpassed the World Cup in terms of its significance for players and that, in most sports, major competitions will in the long run involve representatives of Nike, Adidas and a host of other corporations, with nations and even long-established sports clubs having greatly reduced importance. At present, the Ryder Cup in golf pits golfers from various European nation states against their counterparts from the United States, providing a relatively rare opportunity for the expression of American sporting nationalism prompted by international, or more accurately intercontinental, competition. But how realistic are fears that competition between nations is in the process of being superseded by a transnational, global sports culture?

First, we should always be cautious when we talk about the transformation of modern society into globalised post-modernity. Throughout the history of modern sport, which is itself not much older than that of most of the world's nation states, players have moved from one country to another. Furthermore, 'national' teams have always reflected the movement of peoples and the creation of diasporic populations. Indeed, the fact that some nation states now select representatives on the basis of the place of birth of one or more of their grandparents is little more than a reversal of that particular trend. If the host state's national selectors show little interest in a particular athlete, then it becomes increasingly likely that another set of selectors will. All of this suggests that, whilst there may indeed be more anomalies than ever before with respect to who represents the nation, the actual phenomenon of representing a nation that is not fully one's own (whatever that actually means in relation to the idea of authenticity) is in no way new. Between the 1940s and 1960s, it was possible for one of the greatest soccer players of his time, Alfredo Di Stefano, who was born in Argentina into a family of Italian immigrants, to play for three different national teams – Argentina (7 caps), Colombia (4 caps) and Spain (31 caps). The life of this one sportsman alone is indicative of the extent to which modern sport has always thrown up issues surrounding the concepts of nationality and national identity.

The question of whether or not to cast the net wide in order to improve national representation in various sports is an interesting one not least in relation to sports development. In rugby union, for example, the recruitment of players born in New Zealand, Australia and South Africa to northern hemisphere national teams and of Pacific islanders to New Zealand's All Blacks can be seen as part of an attempt to maintain high standards, which subsequently helps to create 'national' role models and increased interest in the sport from young people. In this sense, the strategy can be presented as an aid to sports development. Alternatively, this practice might also be seen as one whereby young native-born people note what is happening and infer that it is increasingly unlikely that they and their like will ever represent the nation in the face of competition from outside. Hence, they are lost to the sport, the indigenous, grass-roots development of which inevitably suffers. It is a difficult balancing act and one that will continue to be addressed by governing bodies so long as national performance in international competition continues to be an important measure of sporting success. It should be added, however, that for the most part, throughout this period, the overwhelming majority of people who have represented their countries at sport have had remarkably strong ties with the nation state in question. In most instances, that is where they (or at least their parents) were born or else they have come to live there at some stage in their lives and have acquired citizenship and with it a legally recognised nationality. In addition, as suggested earlier, an even greater majority of fans have always been irrevocably tied to their respective national teams and representatives.

This is not to deny that it is easier than ever before for sports fans to watch, to support and to wear the colours of nations other than their own. Yet most choose not to do so. One can understand the decision of a Kenyan athlete who opts to represent Qatar. Sports fans who are motivated to any degree by the relationship between sport and nationalism are largely stuck with the nation or the nation state to which through national identity and/or nationality they can be said to belong. It should be added though that this type of fan is also most likely to be attracted to team sports or to major events, such as the Olympic Games, at which athletes compete as representatives of their nation states. As far as more individualistic high-level competition is concerned – in tennis, for example, or golf – it becomes easier for a fan to celebrate the achievements of a chosen player regardless of his or her place of origin. Once again though it is fair to say that this has always been the case; it is not the consequence of increasingly influential forces of globalisation or of the chaos that is believed by some to characterise the post-modern condition.

There is no denying that sport is constantly affected by social change. Sports that were once played only in certain places – national sports according to one set of criteria – are now played throughout the world. American influence, whilst insufficient to allow sports such as baseball and American football to supersede soccer in most parts of the world, has clearly impacted on the ways in which a sport such as soccer is now played, packaged, mediated and observed. The fact remains, however, that sport is still far more likely to contribute to the perpetuation of strongly held, local regional and national identities than to the construction and consolidation of a homogeneous global culture (Bairner 2001). This is scarcely surprising since sport is central to the construction and reproduction of particularistic identities that are very different from the idea of a global culture that is so often heralded but which evokes so little emotion. For the time being, the relationship between sports and nations remains strong, although it is equally apparent that this relationship manifests itself in a wide variety of ways. Sport can help to promote the image of a nation state but it may also bring shame and financial ruin. Sport can unite a nation state; but it may not. Sport can often be the most important symbol of the continued existence of a submerged nation. Sport can allow nations and nation states alike, as well as regions and other localities, to resist cultural homogenisation. Yet it can also serve the purposes of global capitalism. Like nationalism itself, sport is Janus-faced (Nairn 1997). Perhaps for that reason alone their continued relationship is secure.

Sports development has clearly been aided by the links between sport and nationalist ambitions, whether expansionist or resistant. Nationalism has not been the only political ideology to contribute to sports development in this way. But arguably it has been one of the most persistent and, despite the pressures of globalisation, it remains the most robust.

References

Bairner, A. (1996) 'Ireland, Sport and Empire' in K. Jeffery (ed.), *An Irish Empire? Aspects of Ireland and the British Empire*. Manchester: Manchester University Press: 57–76.
——(2001) *Sport, Nationalism, and Globalization: European and North American Perspectives*. Albany, NY: State University of New York Press.
——(2008) 'Sports and Nationalism' in G. H. Herb and D. H. Kaplan (eds), *Nations and Nationalism. A Global Historical Overview. Volume 3 1945–1989*. Santa Barbara, CA: ABC-CLIO: 991–1004.
——(2009) 'National Sports and National Landscapes: In Defence of Primordialism', *National Identities*, 11 (3): 223–39.
Bracken, P. (2004) *Foreign and Fantastic Field Sports – Cricket in County Tipperary*. Thurles, Co. Tipperary: Liskeeveen Books.
Brown, A., Crabbe, T. and Mellor, G. (2009) 'Introduction: Football and Community – Practical and Theoretical Considerations' in A. Brown, T. Crabbe and G. Mellor (eds), *Football and Community in the Global Context. Studies in Theory and Practice*. London: Routledge: 1–10.
Cronin, M. (1999) *Sport and Nationalism in Ireland: Gaelic Games, Soccer and Irish Identity since 1884*. Dublin: Four Courts Press.
Cronin, M. and Mayall, D. (eds) (1998) *Sporting Nationalisms. Identity, Ethnicity, Immigration and Assimilation*. London: Frank Cass.
Daiches, D. (1952) *Robert Burns*. London: Bell.
Dunning, E. (1990) *Sport Matters. Sociological Studies of Sport, Violence and Civilization*. London: Routledge.
Giulianotti, R. and Robertson, R. (2009) *Globalization and Football*. London: Sage.

Hargreaves, J. (2000) *Freedom for Catalonia? Catalan Nationalisms, Spanish Identity and the Barcelona Olympic Games*. Cambridge: Cambridge University Press.

Hill, C. R. (1992) *Olympic Politics*. Manchester: Manchester University Press.

Hoberman, J. (1984) *Sport and Political Ideology*. London: Heinemann.

——(1997) *Darwin's Athletes. How Sport has Damaged Black America and Preserved the Myth of Race*. Boston, MA: Houghton Mifflin.

Hunt, T. (2007) *Sport and Society in Victorian Ireland: The Case of Westmeath*. Cork: Cork University Press.

Jarvie, G. and Walker, G. (1994) 'Ninety-Minute Patriots? Scottish Sport in the Making of the Nation' in G. Jarvie and G. Walker (eds), *Scottish Sport in the Making of the Nation. Ninety-Minute Patriots?* Leicester: Leicester University Press: 1–8.

Kidd, B. (1992) 'The Culture Wars of the Montreal Olympics', *International Review for the Sociology of Sport*, 27 (2): 151–64.

Lanfranchi, P. and Taylor, M. (2001) *Moving with the Ball: The Migration of Professional Footballers*. Oxford: Berg.

Lee, J. W. (2009) 'Red Feminism and Propaganda in Communist Media: Portrayals of Female Boxers in the North Korean Media', *International Review for the Sociology of Sport*, 44 (2/3): 193–211.

Lee, J. W. and Bairner, A. (2009) 'The Difficult Dialogue: Communism, Nationalism and Political Propaganda in North Korean Sport', *Journal of Sport and Social Issues*, 33 (4): 390–410.

MacClancy, J. (ed.) (1996) *Sport, Identity, and Ethnicity*. Oxford: Berg.

Maguire, J. (1999) *Global Sport. Identities, Societies, Civilizations*. Cambridge: Polity Press.

Meinander, H. and Mangan, J. A. (1998) *The Nordic World. Sport in Society*. London: Frank Cass.

Miller, T., Lawrence, G., McKay, J. and Rowe, D. (2001) *Globalization and Sport. Playing the World*. London: Sage.

Nairn, T. (1997) *Faces of Nationalism: Janus Revisited*. London: Verso.

Ring, J. (2009) *Stolen Bases. Why American Girls don't Play Basketball*. Urbana, IL: University of Illinois Press.

Rouse, P. (2009) 'Michael Cusack: Sportsman and Journalist' in M. Cronin, W. Murphy and P. Rouse (eds), *The Gaelic Athletic Association 1884–2009*. Dublin: Irish Academic Press: 47–59.

Roy, D. (2003) *Taiwan. A Political History*. Ithaca and London: Cornell University Press.

Smith, A. and Porter, D. (eds) (2004) *Sport and National Identity in the Post-war World*. London: Routledge.

Tatz, C. (1995) *Obstacle Race: Aborigines in Sport*. Sydney: University of New South Wales Press.

Williams, J. (2003). *A Game for Rough Girls? A History of Women's Football in Britain*. London: Routledge.

Yu, J. W. (2004) *Baseball in Taiwan: Politics, Participation, and Culture* (unpublished PhD thesis). Coventry: University of Warwick.

——(2007) *Playing in Isolation: A History of Baseball in Taiwan*. Lincoln, NE: University of Nebraska Press.

Yu, J. W. and Bairner, A. (2008) 'Proud to be Chinese: Little League Baseball and National Identities in Taiwan during the 1970s', *Identities: Global Studies in Culture and Power*, 15 (2): 216–39.

——(2010) 'Schooling Taiwan's Aboriginal Baseball Players for the Nation', *Sport, Education and Society*, 15 (1): 63–82.

4

The military, sport and physical training

Tony Mason

The first match played by the famous Wanderers football team took place in September 1864. Their opponents were a team of army officers from Aldershot. The game lasted two and a half hours and the Wanderers won by a single goal to nil. In the second half of the nineteenth century, the officers' team of the Royal Engineers at Chatham was one of the pioneers in the development of the passing game in Association Football. They paraded their skills during a Christmas visit to Nottingham and Sheffield in 1873 and won the FA (Football Association) Cup in 1875. Sport was one of the few ways in which soldiers and sailors might mix more or less freely with their civilian neighbours. Commanding Officers (COs) increasingly encouraged it. The COs of the Guards Depot at Caterham, Surrey organised an athletics meeting, not only for the benefit of the troops in the camp but also for the 'edification' of the residents in the neighbourhood. It was held on Easter Monday and by 1890 was attracting 5,000 spectators with some of the events open to civilians.

In many respects it might be argued that a relationship between the two sporting worlds was an obvious one. One of sports' more endearing characteristics is its ability to bring people from different spheres together, in what is a social as well as a competitive environment. But it is important to remember that in the later nineteenth century and beyond, the British public tended to be ambivalent about their sailors and soldiers. Although enjoying the public displays provided by military bands on ceremonial occasions and excited by the imperial exploits of an age of small wars, they had a low opinion of the rank and file in both arms. Usually recruited from the pool of unskilled labour, the ordinary seamen and soldiers were often thought to be no better than they ought to be. Prone to drunkenness and frequenters of prostitutes, they were often believed to be responsible for hooliganism in public places and were frequently refused entry to pubs, music halls and other places of entertainment. Both the British Army and the Royal Navy had the reputation of being poor employers. No respectable working man would join either service save as a last resort. Sport became one of those areas of social life where these judgements might be challenged.

This was, perhaps, the most important of a number of ways in which organised sport could be seen to be of benefit to the armed services. It is not too difficult to compile a list of the others, such as improving the physical fitness of all ranks, and boosting unit morale and *esprit de corps*. It was also often argued that it helped to cement inter-rank relations without threatening the essential hierarchal structure and that sporting prowess when exhibited by an individual or a team brought not only publicity but also prestige and enhanced reputation. It might even aid recruitment (see Mason and Riedi 2010). What follows is an exploration of the growing relationship between civilian and military sport during the late nineteenth and twentieth centuries, with emphasis being placed not so much on what civilian sport did for the military but rather more on how far sport in the armed services contributed to the wider world of civilian sport.

It is worth reminding ourselves that the growth of sport in Britain in the 50 years or so after the Great Exhibition of 1851 was considered by many who saw it as one of the wonders of the age. Not only did the number of individual sports expand: the numbers of mainly men who played and watched increased dramatically especially after 1870. Moreover, the social composition of participants and sport's geographical range both widened (see Tranter 1998). Sport became an important part of the curriculum not only in the public and grammar schools but also in the elementary schools to which most children went. It was increasingly organised on a national scale as clubs banded together in associations, and there was also an expansion in the employment of a small group of professionals at the elite level of several sports. The timing of sporting activity was radically altered by the spread of the five-and-a-half-day working week. Saturday afternoon became not only the main time to play sport: it also became the most popular time to watch it. The football codes of Association, Rugby League and Rugby Union were the biggest crowd pullers. By 1909 over a million people were watching football matches in the English and Scottish leagues. Athletics, boxing, horseracing and cricket also had many supporters. Moreover, many sports were developing an international dimension. British sportsmen frequently competed abroad and welcomed overseas rivals to these shores. It could be argued that the first Modern Olympic Games was the one staged in London in 1908, at which the rivalry between the British and Americans had a very modern ring to it. Nevertheless, sport and its associated idea of fair play had become very much a part of the social and ideological make-up of the British. It was increasingly one of the characteristics attributed by foreigners to the rulers of the largest Empire the world had ever seen. Moreover an awareness of all this was available to most parts of it, given the coverage of sport in books, specialist magazines, boys' comics and both the daily and weekly press. In 1913 Lloyds' Weekly News, which sold a million copies every Sunday, published a series of articles, 57 all told, on famous sporting regiments, which underlined how far this remarkable expansion of sport had also infected the British Army (see Lloyd's Weekly News, 30th March 1913–3rd May 1914). In fact, military sport was increasingly represented to the civilian world in a series of publications ranging from specialist papers, such as the Navy and Army Illustrated, to those largely aimed at male youth, like the Boys' Own Paper and the Boys' Realm, whose leading story for its Christmas edition of 1910 was about a young soldier who was 'Every Inch a Footballer' (The Boys' Realm 443, Vol. X, 26 November 1910).

The emergence of military sport

By the beginning of the twentieth century sport was already an important part of military life but largely as a result of an unofficial and grass-roots movement. The main impetus for its development came neither from the Admiralty nor the War Office, but from a younger generation of officers who had played sport at their public schools and officer training establishments, such as Dartmouth, Sandhurst and Woolwich. When the Royal Flying Corps was formed in 1912, it immediately set up an officers' sports fund financed by compulsory subscription for the

> promotion of all forms of sport and recreation ... [on the grounds that sports] are of such paramount importance in the creation and maintenance of the esprit de corps and good fellowship, essential for officers in the fighting forces.
>
> (RAF Officers' Sports Fund n.d. (1918) Air 2/71 F8465, TNA)

However, it would be quite wrong to ignore the contribution made to the organisation and administration of sport in the armed services by the other ranks and especially the non-commissioned officers (NCOs), and it was army footballers who not only led the way in establishing a service-wide competition but also joined the civilian Football Association, eventually to be followed by the football associations set up by the Navy and the RAF.

There were many benefits to be had on both sides. Civilian Sports organisations were keen to control all activity within their sporting and geographical areas, and military men had the time and energy to help with the burdens of administration and management. Major Francis Marindin, of the Royal Engineers, was actually President of the Football Association from 1874 to 1890, although he was not in the Army for all of that time. The National Sporting Club, which was one of the organisers of professional boxing for over 20 years after 1891, had many military officers as members, and pan-sport organisations, such as the British Olympic Association, founded in 1905, were never without a quota of serving or retired officers eventually from all three services. The National Playing Fields Association, established in 1925, was pretty much the idea of a retired Brigadier General, Basil Kentish, who had been very active in the promotion of sport in the Army, since before the First World War.

An interesting example of a more direct military influence on the sporting development of one particular town can be found by briefly examining the coming of professional football to Portsmouth. Of course Portsmouth was a town with some dependence on the military, being both an important naval base and home to several army units. Influential local figures had tried and failed, in the early 1890s, to establish a team which would be representative of the town. It was left to the Royal Garrison Artillery (RGA) to produce one which quickly attracted the attention of the local press and spectators alike. The team won the Army Cup, twice, but established its wider credentials by reaching the final of the FA Amateur Cup, in that competition's second season in 1895–96. It also became the first Portsmouth team to win the Hampshire Senior League. Increasingly they were the team to beat, watch and talk about. Success promotes ambition and the Gunners applied for and were admitted to a place in the newly formed second division of the Southern League, the championship of which they won at their first attempt in 1897–98, a season in which the team played a total of 47 matches. This proved to be the best of times. The First Division was a much tougher proposition, containing formidable professional combinations such as Bristol City, Southampton and Tottenham Hotspur. Portsmouth (RGA) finished bottom of the league and were later suspended by the Football Association for infringing the regulations on the expenses of amateurs. But during the winter of 1898–99, a series of discussions between local business and sporting interests led to the formation of the professional Portsmouth Football Club, and one of the two NCOs who had been responsible for running the artillery team joined the new club's Board of Directors. The Portsmouth Evening News underlined the crucial legacy of this 'unique Army team, a collection of brilliant players which made the Association game in Portsmouth' (quoted in Smith 1999).

The influence of the military

The remainder of this chapter will be devoted to examining how the military continued to exert powerful influences over civilian sport in both peace and war until well into the twentieth century. It will do this by exploring a particular branch of sports, the equestrian, a specific ideology, that of amateurism, and particular periods in which the military had an especially important role in civilian life, during the two World Wars and the almost two decades of peace-time conscription after 1945.

The importance of the horse in the British armed services between the First World War and the Second World War cannot be underestimated. This was particularly true of the Army in India but also of the service at home. The influence of the cavalry on British equestrian sport could almost be described as a monopoly. Even after 1918, the Army seems to have had an obsession with horses. Students at the Army Cavalry School at Weedon hunted three or four times a week every year between 1918 and 1939. When Mike Ansell, later President of the British Show Jumping Association, was an officer in the 5th Royal Inniskilling Dragoon Guards he toured the United States and Canada with the British showjumping team in 1931, all four members of which were cavalrymen. Polo was almost *de rigeur* among the officers. Ansell again visited the United States to play polo for the Hurlingham Club in 1935 and had no sooner returned than he left for India to play some more. In that epitome of modernity, the Royal Air Force, its Sport Control Board approved the formation of an RAF Polo Association in 1935.

Olympic Equestrian events were linked to male military officers until well into the twentieth century. All 44 competitors for the showjumping and the three-day event teams at the 1948 Olympics had military backgrounds. The British Team included a Brigadier, two Lieutenant-Colonels and three Majors. The Spanish team was led by a General. No wonder there was a serious discussion about whether military uniforms should be worn. Midway through the team dressage an official noticed that one of the Swedish team was wearing a Sergeant's cap. It did not prevent them from winning the gold medal but several months later he was 'disqualified for not being of commissioned rank'. Most of the equestrian events had been held at Aldershot and the horses had been bought from the British Army. The British three-day event team that won gold at the Olympics of 1968 and 1972 included two army officers, Richard Meade, from the 11th Hussars and Captain Mark Phillips, from the 1st Queen's Dragoon Guards.

Equestrian sports were a way of life even if part of their appeal, especially to the military, was the element of danger attached to them. The Modern Pentathlon, of course, was an event designed with the military in mind and as late as 1976 the leading member of the British Olympic team, Jim Fox, was a Sergeant in the Royal Electrical and Mechanical Engineers. It was no longer a sport reserved for officers and Jim Fox, who had been placed fourth in the individual event at the 1972 Olympics in Munich, was in the team of three that won the gold medal. Winter Sports were also attractive to the officer class. The British bobsleigh team in 1948 was made up of four RAF officers who had eight Distinguished Service medals between them (see Ansell 1973; Hampton 2008).

If the influence of the military on equestrian sport was of long standing, how much more important was its role during the periods of World War and conscription between 1914–18 and 1939–62? In 1931 General Sir Charles Harington had expressed his confidence that it had been 'leather' that had played one of the greatest parts in the victory of the Allies in the First World War:

> Few have realised what we owe to the boxing glove and the football, the two greatest factors in restoring and upholding moral[e].
>
> *(see Army Sports Control Board 1931 and subsequent editions)*

Behind the lines on all the fronts, in Italy, in the Middle East, as well as on the Western Front, and at many naval bases such as Scapa Flow, sport certainly seems to have played an important part in the lives of many sailors, soldiers and airmen. It helped to boost morale by providing amusement, distraction and a link with home and civilian life in what was a military largely made up of civilians in uniform. It drew on a sporting tradition in the services which, as we have noted, was already well established by 1914, itself one of the notable features of British modernity. The purpose of service sport had never been wholly recreational, but it was during the war of 1914–18 that it became more integrated into the military system.

After the Somme battles in 1916, infantry units were reorganised into smaller groups of fighting men. These sections and platoons were to be the location for the creation of what was often called the true soldierly spirit, and sport was to be one of the means of promoting it. The point was clearly made by the 1918 version of the instructions of the General Staff on the training of platoons:

> too much attention cannot be paid to the part played by games in fostering the fighting spirit.

If the platoon commander

> produces the best football team in the Battalion, he will have done a great deal to make it the best platoon.
>
> *(General Staff 1918)*

The days of the troops were to be divided between training in the mornings and games in the afternoons. Rest days were also to include sports, which were to play a part in cementing good relations between units. This further emphasised a growing belief among the military authorities in the general importance of physical training when out of the line. It was also seen to have a part to play in the rehabilitation of injured men. Nor should we underestimate the way in which service sport could provide opportunities to play that were not always available to the less well off in 'civvy street'.

By the later years of the war, therefore, sport had become part of military routine. It was not a surprise that when the end of the war was followed by a potentially difficult period of demobilisation, military hierarchies turned to sport, along with an expansion of service education to keep men occupied and reasonably content. It could be argued that the military also played a significant role in re-establishing post-war sport by organising the Inter-Theatre of War sporting championships in 1919. Qualifying events in boxing, cross-country running, football and rugby were held both at home and abroad, with the finals taking place in the United Kingdom during late April and May 1919. The rugby tournament was almost the only organised rugby taking place in Britain in the spring of 1919 and it had been put on by the Army Rugby Union. A New Zealand fifteen won the final against an England side playing under the title of the 'Mother Country'.

Sport may not have won the war but it had played a real part in the experiences of many men in all three arms. It is worth repeating this, because it provided a rare arena in which military and civilian preoccupations overlapped; it was a link with home and one of the activities that helped to make war bearable. Although it clearly contributed to the shaping of military ends, it also reinforced the civilian tradition of sport. It helped to keep sport going at home when the vocal opposition of a minority of patriotic militants had threatened its continuance in the early months of the conflict. Perhaps the Chief Medical Officer of Health at the Board of Education, Sir George Newman, exaggerated when he said that the way sport had been used by the military pointed towards a future in which Britain would become a nation of players, rather than spectators, ushering in a new age of mass participation in civilian sport (Bourke 1996: 183–4). But in the context of its role in the war his exaggeration was pardonable.

Furthermore, the War Office Committee on Shell Shock, reporting in 1922, acknowledged the usefulness of sport in preventing neurosis among front-line troops. Organised recreation behind the lines was placed ninth out of 14 factors believed to have helped mitigate the effects of war. Ninth was a position well below morale, discipline and good officers, but above home leave and the controlled use of rum. Sport promoted fitness, the spirit of competition and variety for both mind and body. Well before the outbreak of the Second World War the value of sport's role in boosting morale and esprit de corps in the armed services had been widely accepted. Sport had grown as essentially a voluntary activity almost from the military grass roots but by 1919 it had become too important to evade control from the centre. At the end of the war all three arms were provided with Sport Control Boards to oversee the sporting life of the services and to improve its funding. And one of their main aims was to form connections with sporting organisations outside the services in all matters that might affect service, sport and games.

World War Two was in some ways different to the War of 1914–18. Between the evacuation of Dunkirk in May 1940 and D-Day in June 1944, most British servicemen were stationed at home. Over half the Army, about 1.5 million men, spent most of the war in Britain, as did many members of the other two services. Moreover, more mechanised forces and a growth in the size of the military service sector required to keep the front-line troops supplied meant that a higher proportion of airmen and soldiers were non-combatants. Many young officers who had been impressed by the value of sport during 1914–18 were in more senior positions and therefore better able to influence events. The fact that there was inevitably a good deal of waiting around for the action to start meant a lot of time to fill and boredom to alleviate. Sport was one of the activities that helped to ease the strain.

War was not quite the surprise in 1939 that it had been in 1914. During the 1930s several national sporting organisations, including the Rugby Football Union and the Football Association were urging their players to join the Territorial Army. As the possibility of war became a probability the players of several clubs such as Bolton Wanderers, Norwich City and Liverpool joined up. The FA and the Army co-operated in a scheme to recruit professional footballers as physical training instructors.

There was a general agreement that civilian morale was as important as that of the military and a much stronger feeling among the authorities that the participatory and spectacular parts of sport were of equal value. Football in particular staged a whole series of internationals, with teams selected almost entirely from conscripted players. Crowds were large, producing significant monies for benevolent funds and wartime charities.

There was occasional criticism that leading sportsmen were given favourable treatment and some suggestions that the commitment to playing the game may have undermined military efficiency. The fall of Singapore in 1942 was a particularly serious moment in the war and for a while sport was confined to weekends. But as circumstances improved the restrictions were lifted. There was little talk about war being another form of sport and a much clearer sense that war was a game that had to be played to win. Clearly it would be wrong to exaggerate the role played by sport in the war. But it would also be a mistake to ignore not only the part it played, but also how it served to emphasise that civilian and military sports were not really separate spheres.

The military and post-war sport

The continuation of conscription in the post-war world serves to emphasise the point. It had been reintroduced in 1947 with all males between 18 and 26 required to serve for 12 months. This was extended to 18 months in November 1948 and to two years in September 1950. It was ended in 1960 and the last man was released in 1963. It provided fresh opportunities for military sports organisations to co-operate with civilian ones. In 1955 the Amateur Athletic

Association, for example, drew up a scheme that enabled member clubs to inform their military representatives when athletic club members were coming up for National Service. Articles appeared in the athletics press stressing that the military welcomed young athletes and there was civil–military collusion in placing many prominent sportsmen. In the years of post-war austerity military sports facilities were often better than civilian ones – even the Army Sport Control Board admitted as much to the Wolfenden Committee (Central Council of Physical Recreation 1960). Many different sports were available at a wide range of units: 13 different ones at RAF Walton, for example, in 1960.

Many leading sportsmen benefitted. Derek Ibbostson claimed he had never been so fit than when in the RAF, and Gordon Pirie thought seriously about becoming a regular, which would enable him to train without bothering about those little problems thrown up by life, such as work, food, clothes or shelter. Brian Hewson did sign on for three years and never regretted it. Only the professional footballers, and their managers, complained, the former that playing for their units on Saturdays meant they were unable to earn money from their clubs, the latter that their players got into bad habits on the field. For those who ran service teams, life had never been so sweet. Indeed Lt Colonel Gerry Mitchell even sat on the FA Committee that selected the full international side during the 1950s. National Service clearly strengthened the links between civilian and military sport that had been boosted by the war and generally provided good copy for the media in their representations of service life.

Perhaps the most important influence that military sport exerted over its civilian counterpart was its long-term support of the ideas embedded in the notion of amateurism. Before the First World War there appears to have been some ambivalence on the part of the military authorities as they tried to shape a sporting tradition that had never been distinguished by an absence of money. Both sailors and soldiers, for example, had been allowed to compete for money prizes in athletics and boxing. The aim was to encourage those sports that appeared to have particular military value. Boxing was also often bracketed with rugby as being an activity likely to promote a tough masculinity. Sometimes this had led to conflict with civilian sports and a sense of injustice to particular individuals. The Amateur Athletic Association for example, felt strongly that money prizes amounted to professionalism. Private Dunne of the Royal Irish Fusiliers was not allowed to compete in the 1908 Olympic Games in the long and triple jumps because he had been a recipient of money prizes at army sports.

Yet a more conciliatory attitude was adopted in the case of football. Here, the Army Football Association took the side of the national governing body in its dispute with the breakaway Amateur Football Association. By the early 1900s football had clearly established itself as the favoured sport among the other ranks. Before 1914 both the Army and Navy had hundreds of football clubs, but only a handful playing rugby, which was largely an officers' sport. Most other ranks had never played it. In fact, in order to encourage rugby's growth in the armed services, the Rugby Football Union actually gave a cup for a regimental knock-out tournament, a form of competition they did not really favour for the civilian game. The Army Rugby Union, meantime, tried to stimulate the participation of the ordinary soldier by imposing a limit of eight officers in each regimental team. It is not clear whether this stratagem had the desired effect; but it is interesting to note that officers in the military provided a greater number of England rugby internationals than any other occupational category between 1871 and 1939 (Collins 2009: 216–18). The Army FA meantime had supported the Football Association in major part because it did not want its teams being banned from playing against civilian teams in membership with the FA, the vast majority. Moreover, when some professional football clubs began to see the services as a new and relatively inexpensive pool of potential players, the FA passed new rules that largely allowed the practice. Buying a man out of the service could not be stopped entirely, however, and Bombardier Billy Wells, later British heavy weight champion, was probably the most famous sportsman to benefit.

Both World Wars led to some modification of amateur principles in the services, most notably in rugby where Union and professional League players would play both with and against each other, which was impossible in civilian sport. But after 1914–18 there was also a strengthening of the opposite tendency. We have already noted how service sport was reorganised from above with the setting up of the Sport Control Boards. One of the reasons for this and a result of it was a short-lived attempt by some in the military to purify civilian sport, to raise the tone of it to what it was alleged to have been in the wartime Army. It was the pursuit of a chimera. But it did have some impact in ridding the military of the professional boxer. In 1924–25 the Army Boxing Association held parallel championships for what were termed amateurs and service professionals. It was a drive for a purer form of amateurism, which only the Navy resisted. But from 1926 the Imperial Services Boxing Association championships were entirely amateur.

After 1945 post-war conscription brought many young professional sportsmen into the forces especially boxers, cricketers and footballers. One result was to make it difficult for men on regular engagements to represent their units and especially to play for their service as a whole. In fact it could be argued that the support of amateurism by the military actually helped to undermine it by showing what could be done when sportsmen and women were allowed to spend more time on practice and training for their event. Many examples could be given, but two must suffice. Bill Nankeville, the middle distance runner who had been called up in 1944, decided to sign on for a further year because he believed service life would be more conducive to his preparations for the 1948 Olympics. In the meantime, at RAF Benson in Oxfordshire, a group of rowers were collected together and followed a regime of practice and fitness training and a focus on the sport that might have been found in an American college or a Soviet sports school. Finally, it needs to be said that the hierarchical structure of military life did not always go down well in civilian sporting circles. It was expected that the hurdler, Group Captain Donald Finlay, would captain the British team at the 1950 Empire and Commonwealth Games in Melbourne, but protests from members of the team led to a civilian appointment.

It is tempting to see the 1948 Olympics as one of the high points of military influence in civilian sport. Not only were many of the competitors still in uniform or very recently demobilised, but, in a Britain exhausted by six years of war, military camps were used for housing the competitors, fencing took place in the army gymnasium at Aldershot, equestrian competitors stayed at Sandhurst, and RAF Uxbridge was probably the nearest thing to an Olympic village. Even the telephone exchange at Wembley Stadium was staffed by military personnel, and the captain of the British team was the aforementioned then Wing-Commander Donald Finlay. It is hard not to agree that the period from 1939 to 1960 as a whole was one in which the military's relationship with civilian sport was closer than at any time since 1918. After the First World War the reduced size of the services meant that between the wars the forces became as marginal to the national sporting life as they were to national life as a whole. With the end of conscription at the beginning of the 1960s the process of downsizing the military was repeated and its sporting influence correspondingly again reduced. It could still play a part in producing athletic champions: Chris Akabusi and Kelly Holmes spring immediately to mind. But, in the latter case, it is notable that she had been a successful athlete at school and had almost abandoned her running in the Army and was persuaded to take it up with a new seriousness by civilian coaches. Moreover, a successful athlete no longer relies on almost automatic promotion in the military and therefore could not be expected to devote themselves full time to sports training. Finally, much more money can now be made in the world of civilian sport where the former ideological and social prescriptions of amateurism no longer apply (see Holmes with Blake 2005).

Tony Mason

References

Ansell, M. (1973) *Soldier on*, London: Peter Davies.
Army Sports Control Board (1931) *Games and Sports in the Army*, London: War Office.
Bourke, J. (1996) *Dismembering the Male: Men's Bodies, Britain and the Great War*, London: Reaktion Press.
Central Council of Physical Recreation (1960) *Sport and the Community: The Report of the Wolfenden Committee on Sport*, London: CCPR.
Collins, T. (2009) *A Social History of English Rugby Union*, London: Routledge.
General Staff (1918) S.S. 143, *Instruction for the Training and Employment of Platoons*, London: War Office.
Hampton, J. (2008) *The Austerity Olympics: When the Games Came to London in 1948*, London: Aurum Press.
Holmes, K. with Blake, F. (2005) *Black, White and Gold*, London: Virgin Books.
Mason, T. and Riedi, E. (2010) *Sport and the Military: The British Armed Forces 1889–1960*, Cambridge: Cambridge University Press.
Smith, K. (1999) *Glory Gunners: The History of Royal Artillery (Portsmouth) FC*, Bognor Regis: K.S. Publications.
Tranter, N. (1998) *Sport, Economy and Society in Britain 1750–1914*, Cambridge: Cambridge University Press.

Part 2

The contemporary context of sports development

Introduction: Government and civil society involvement in sports development

Barrie Houlihan

In much of western and northern Europe, North America and former British colonies the infrastructure for sports development activity was established by voluntary organisations firmly located in the fabric of civil society, with religious organisations, political organisations and private educational institutions being of especial importance. Over the last 60 years or so the state in most of these countries – the United States being an important exception – has steadily expanded its investment of resources and its influence over the form that sports development has taken and the objectives that have been adopted. As a result it is essential to acknowledge the increasingly important role of government in shaping contemporary sports development, but it is equally essential not to lose sight of the substantial contribution – in terms of capital assets and voluntary labour – that still comes from civil society.

Dealing first with the role of government and the motives for government involvement in sport in general, and sports development in particular, it is common to highlight the degree of instrumentalism involved and the relative lack of a recognition or acknowledgement of an intrinsic justification for investment of public money in sport. Governments are portrayed as acting, with varying degrees of cynicism, to exploit the properties of sport and of civil society sports organisations for non-sporting objectives such as diplomatic advantage, nation-building, health improvement, economic regeneration, the development of social capital or the tackling of complex social welfare issues. Governments, it is argued, are willing to acknowledge that a minimum level of literacy and good health, for example, do not need an instrumental justification for the investment of public money and are seen as being 'good in themselves'. Sport, by contrast, is rarely accorded such a privileged status and is treated in a much more casual way, being routinely incorporated to serve broader domestic or diplomatic objectives or simply to enhance political party advantage.

Such arguments, which I have made on a number of occasions myself, prompt wider reflections on the role and nature of the state and the relationship between the state and civil society. The first consideration is whether sports policy is actually treated in a more instrumental fashion than other policy areas such as education, transport and health. For both the neo-pluralist and neo-Marxist there is a broad agreement that business interests have a substantial, if not a determining, influence over public policy and, accepting this basic analysis, that welfare policy is an instrument designed to support the interests of business. However, the relationship between the interests of business and public policy is often mediated by other powerful interests such as the professions (for example, teachers, doctors and engineers) and also by the need for governments in democracies to seek legitimacy from the electorate. Consequently, it might be argued that the stronger instrumental utilisation of sport than other policy areas is due in part at least to the absence, in many countries, of powerful mediating interests such as a professional organisation or a strong sports confederation. However, it might also be argued that, unlike health, transport and education, which are all services that benefit from more or less universal demand, sports participation, particularly in competitive sport, is a sectional interest. One consequence of the sectional nature of the demand for competitive sport (as opposed to physical activities such as keep fit classes or jogging) is that competitive sport interests and advocates need to find ways to attempt to universalise the benefits of public investment in sport. Thus the huge investment in many countries in supporting the interests of a tiny minority of elite athletes is universalised through appeals to the capacity of medal success to generate national unity or a national 'feel-good' factor or to demonstrate national superiority. Similarly, investment in youth and school sport is universalised by claims that sports participation will contribute to improved academic attainment, improved behaviour and a reduction in truancy. Consequently, what might at first appear to be the exploitation by governments of sport for non-sporting purposes might be a necessary condition for leveraging public funds into what is a set of minority (albeit a substantial minority) interests.

The contemporary context of sports development may be characterised in many countries as one where the volume and profile of sports development is the outcome of, on the one hand, the recognition by governments not only of the malleability of sport as a response to some complex social problems, but also of the high visibility and relatively low cost of sport interventions and, on the other, the necessity to broaden the coalition of interests supporting public investment in sport by claiming a universality of beneficial outcomes of sports participation and/ or sporting success. The chapters in Part 2 illustrate the range of governmental motives for public funding of sport and also the way in which governmental involvement shapes the activities of sports organisations and clubs.

The opening chapter in Part 2 by Donnelly and Harvey is an important reminder that, while government in many countries is of increasing significance in influencing sports development activities it still remains heavily dependent on close cooperation with the not-for-profit or voluntary sector. Donnelly and Harvey's chapter highlights the strains emerging in relation to volunteering in sport. At one level the strong volunteer base in many sports enables them to maintain their roots firmly in civil society and retain some distance from the expectations of government. At another level volunteers enable the survival of sports clubs and activities that are seen as less useful to government. However, one consequence of the weakening of the volunteer base is to steadily increase the dependence of sports organisations on professional staff and indirectly on government. What is clear from the analysis provided by Donnelly and Harvey is both the crucial contribution of volunteers to the scale and scope of sports provision in a community and the fragility of that contribution.

Andrew Adams' chapter on sport and social capital illustrates, *inter alia*, the extent to which government has sought to utilise the voluntary sports infrastructure to achieve broader social goals associated with social inclusion and the generation of social capital. Equally important is the demonstration that the chapter provides that governmental ambitions for sport are built on a fragile evidence base and are characterised by a high degree of 'moral inflationism'. Moreover, the chapter amply illustrates the conceptual incoherence of the favoured Putnamian strand of social capital that had so effectively captured the imagination of many western governments. The chapter by Smith and Haycock examines a specific area of sports development – disability sport – and one where voluntary activity is also central to contemporary provision. Two features of disability sport are evident from the study; first, the relative neglect of sports provision for people with disabilities in the UK, but also the scope for innovation at the regional or home country level. While policy vacuums may indicate neglect of a set of needs they might also reflect uncertainty on the part of policy-makers and can often provide important opportunities for policy entrepreneurs to shape the nature of sports development provision. However, it is hard to avoid the conclusion that the rhetoric of greater social inclusion through sport has a hollow ring when the impact on disability sport is considered.

Kevin Hylton's discussion of social integration through sport echoes a number of the themes raised in the previous two chapters. Of particular significance is the tendency for sport's capacity to achieve social integration to be overstated and for discrimination to be conceptualised primarily as a problem of inter-personal relations rather than as an organisational (or institutional) or a societal (structural) issue. Hylton's conclusion that there is evidence of sport's capacity to 'contribute something to the social integration agenda however, that *something* requires clearer exposition' is an urgent invitation for more investigation of the role of sports development in this area of social life. The final contribution, by Mahfoud Amara, is a reminder of the significance of culture and the extent to which culture mediates our experience and perceptions of sport. In addition, the chapter also illustrates the capacity of states to be highly selective in terms of their engagement with international sport. While many of the Arab states have developed an acute interest in elite level sport, both as participants and as hosts of events, few have demonstrated an equal willingness to invest in the promotion of mass sport.

Volunteering and sport

Peter Donnelly and Jean Harvey

[S]port cannot operate in this country [Canada] without the total substructure of volunteers. The money isn't there ... the organization isn't there ... the volunteer is the lifeblood of sport.

(cited by Safai 2005:174)[1]

Volunteering is unpaid work. It involves time, energy, skills and/or abilities given freely in a context outside an individual's home. The 2007 Canadian Survey of Giving, Volunteering and Participating (CSGVP 2009: 10) defined volunteering as 'doing activities without pay on behalf of a group or organization'.[2] A similar definition was used by Sport England in its national survey of sports volunteers: 'individual volunteers helping others in sport and receiving either no remuneration or only expenses' (Taylor *et al.* 2003: 6). Explicit in these definitions, and in all of the research relating to sports development, is the restriction to volunteering in groups, clubs, or organizations. National surveys show that large numbers of people report informal voluntary work, helping another individual or a small group of individuals,[3] but little is known from an academic perspective about this type of volunteering, and there are no studies of informal volunteering in sport and recreation.

Neo-liberalism and the growth of volunteering

Volunteering in organizations has its roots in the nineteenth and early twentieth centuries, and has two sources. The first involves the growth of voluntary associations such as the Boy Scouts, the Red Cross and, for the purposes of this chapter, various local, national and international sports associations. In the case of sport, volunteerism is embedded in the values of amateurism, and sports were run by participants, ex-participants and other interested persons who volunteered their services. The second is related to the emergence of liberal reformers establishing charitable social welfare organizations to counter the excesses of unrestrained capitalism. Since that time, the state in high-income countries took over many aspects of social welfare, replacing volunteers with professionals.

This latter aspect of volunteerism reveals the double-edged nature of the activity in modern times. On the one hand, low tax and reduced government (neo-liberal) regimes since the 1980s have ideologically created a situation in which necessary services, once paid for and provided collectively (through taxes), have been cut, and often had to be replaced by volunteer work (e.g. fund raising for and volunteering in state schools following cuts to education budgets). The continued contraction of the state in the provision of social services, growing recognition of the limits and inequities of the market, and even the scale and impact of national and international disasters on global and local social life, have stimulated academics and policy-makers to investigate in greater depth the ways in which volunteerism often serves as a less effective replacement for state services. On the other hand, there is evidence that volunteerism may contribute to social cohesion, citizenship and civil identity (CVI 2001), and a growing acceptance that volunteering should be fostered and promoted in all areas of social life: 'voluntary activity contributes to the reinforcement of relations of confidence/trust and of reciprocity. At the same time it creates and reinforces social cohesion, with all of the connected advantages that this implies for individual and collective well-being/health' (ISUMA 2001: 8).[4] In recognition of its importance, 2001 was marked as the International Year of Volunteers (IYV).

What surveys tell us about volunteering

Surveys provide rich and informative data about a variety of matters, but there are some inherent limitations that must be taken into account. First, they extrapolate findings from samples, and while there are well-established methods for generating representative samples, data loss is inevitable. For example, in the surveys discussed below, a sample of more than 23,000 people is used to provide data about volunteerism among a population of 33 million Canadians; and a sample of 13,000 non-profit and voluntary organizations is used to provide data about volunteerism in an estimated 161,000 registered and incorporated organizations (thus, grass roots organizations and citizens' groups that are not registered or incorporated are not even sampled). Second, surveys are sometimes conducted only once, so it is difficult to know if the data are representative, and impossible to know if there is change over time; or, in a series of surveys, the methods and questions may be changed, thus making comparisons over time quite unreliable.

The latter is the case for the major surveys of volunteerism in Canada. The National Survey of Giving, Volunteering and Participating (NSGVP) was carried out in 1997 and 2000, providing comparative data for those two years. The methods, questions and name were changed in 2004, and the Canadian Survey of Giving, Volunteering and Participating (CSGVP) provides comparative data for 2004 and 2007. The National Survey of Nonprofit and Voluntary Organizations (NSNVO) was carried out in 2003, and because its intent, sample, and methods were different from the CSGVPs, it provides somewhat different information about volunteers – but provides an interesting point of comparison for sports volunteering.

As a baseline for interpreting the subsequent discussion of sports volunteering, in the most recent CSGVP (2009), 12.5 million Canadians reported volunteering in the previous year – some 46 per cent of the population aged 15 and over. This increased from 45 per cent in 2004, but actual numbers increased by 5.7 per cent (due, in part, to increases in the population aged 15 and over). By comparison, the NSNVO (2005) found that 19 million volunteer positions were reported by organizations – an indication that some volunteers work for more than one organization or carry out more than one task in an organization. However, both surveys report that volunteers contribute over 2 billion hours in a year – the equivalent of more than 1 million full-time jobs. Although the total number of hours devoted to volunteering has increased by over 4 per cent since 2004, the average hours contributed remains at approximately 167 per year. However, this average is misleading, since a small number of volunteers tend to do the most work – the top 25 per cent account for more than 78 per cent of the total hours, and the top 10 per cent average more than 421 hours per year and account for 52 per cent of the total hours.

This chapter examines volunteerism in sport, and its relationship to sports development, by first considering the scope and significance of sports volunteerism, difficulties involved in measuring sports volunteerism, the origins of and changes to volunteering in sport, and the forms of sports volunteerism. This is followed by an examination of who volunteers in sport and why; the time devoted to and tasks involved in sports volunteerism; the challenges and obstacles to volunteerism in sport; the training, support and recognition of sports volunteers; and sports volunteerism and social capital.

Volunteerism in sport

The scope and significance of sports volunteerism

It is widely reported (and supported by data) that sport (and recreation) volunteerism, at least in Canada, Norway and the UK, is among the largest single categories of volunteerism – in other words, no other form of volunteer service, not even religion, involves more volunteers than sport (and recreation).

Volunteers have been and continue to be a vital component of national and local sports systems, contributing extensively to sports development through the organization, governance and administration, and delivery of sport (see for example, in Canada: Doherty 2005; Macintosh and Whitson 1990; Macintosh et al. 1987; Rhyne 1995; Slack and Hinings 1987; Smale and Arai 2002, 2003; NSNVO 2005). As Taylor et al. (2003: 140) acknowledge in the case of British sport, the benefits of volunteering can be felt in a number of different ways: 'For volunteers [themselves], it provides friendship, enjoyment and satisfaction; for clubs, it enables them to exist; and for communities, it sustains sports participation, from which a number of social benefits can be derived' (see also Eley and Kirk 2003).

In a number of countries volunteer administrators, coaches, judges and referees represent the first stage of sports development – they are integral to the socialization of young children into sport as they learn about and participate in community recreational leagues. Highly skilled officials, medical clinicians and sports scientists are also crucial volunteers who ensure the delivery of high-performance sport and the success of high-performance athletes; for example, volunteer clinicians conduct the delivery of medical services for elite sport in many countries. Between these extremes, volunteers carry out numerous tasks in sport. Much of that work goes unrecognized and is under-researched.

As noted in the opening quote, 'sport cannot operate … without the total substructure of volunteers.' This implication is reinforced by numerous statements in various research studies and reports about sports volunteers. As Andreff et al. (2009) note, the pyramid structure of European sport is 'based on mass sport operating thanks to significant voluntary work.' They go on to note that volunteerism represents a supply of free labour, without which European sport could not function and develop (Andreff 2009). Several attempts have been made to place a monetary value on the work of volunteers, although the variety of work carried out by sports volunteers makes it difficult to assign costs as if it was necessary to hire someone to carry out the work (the 'replacement cost').[5] Thus, volunteer work is often valued as equivalent to the average wage. Taylor et al. (2003) estimated that the 1.2 billion hours worked each year by volunteers in sport were equivalent to 720,000 full-time jobs (FTEs), valued at £14 billion. However, Andreff et al. (2009) point out that, regardless of the monetary evaluation, the value of the contribution that volunteerism makes to sport is invariably greater than the total of public funds devoted to sport. They estimate [using an extremely conservative calculation of the value (replacement cost) of volunteerism as equivalent to half the average wage] that the value of volunteer work is more than four times larger than public funding for sport in Germany, three times larger in Denmark, twice the total amount in Austria, Finland and France, six times larger in the Czech Republic, and nine times larger in the Netherlands.

Difficulties in measuring sports volunteering

The limitations of survey data, and the problems of finding comparative data were noted previously. The Taylor *et al.* (2003) estimate of 5.8 million sports volunteers (15 per cent of the population of England) providing 1.2 billion hours each year (approximately 720,000 FTEs), was largely based on data provided by surveying a sample of 8,500 adults. In Canada, if we compare data provided by organizations (NSNVO 2005) with population survey data (CSGVP 2009), the data from organizations indicate that there are 5.3 million volunteer 'positions' in sport and recreation, some 28 per cent of all volunteer positions, while population survey data suggest that there are 1.38 million volunteers in sport and recreation, some 11 per cent of all volunteers.[6] Strikingly, the two surveys report a similar number of total volunteer hours per year (over 2 billion), but the CSGVP reports that sport and recreation volunteers work 17 per cent of the total hours, while the NSNVO reports that they work 23 per cent of the total hours.

The problem with these data becomes even more apparent when attempts are made to compare them with European data. For example, in Andreff's (2009) recent survey of 14 European countries, the time spent by volunteers in sports clubs and associations in each country was re-calculated on the basis of FTEs (40 hours per week). The FTE totals for some Western European countries were as follows: Denmark – 42,000; Germany – 210,000; Finland – 30,590; France – 271,000; Italy – 125,000; Netherlands – 118,575. The 720,000 FTEs reported by Taylor *et al.* for England seem astonishing by comparison. A similar calculation using Canadian data suggests that there are approximately 178,500 FTEs (using the CSGVP) or 241,500 FTEs (using NSNVO data on volunteer positions). Similarly, LeRoux *et al.* (2000) calculated the number of sports volunteers per 1,000 population for various European countries: Finland – 60; Sweden and Denmark – less than 50; Germany – less than 40; France and UK – 26. More recently, Andreff *et al.* (2009) reported a range from less than 15 to 102 sports volunteers per 1,000 population in their sample of European countries. By this same calculation, Taylor *et al.*'s (2003) English data suggest that there are 150 sports volunteers per 1,000 population, and Canada's figures for sport and recreation volunteers would be 42 (CSGVP) or less than 150 (NSNVO, using volunteer positions). The point here is to suggest that data on sports volunteers may not be reliable, are extremely difficult to compare, and need to be interpreted with caution.

Origins of and changes to volunteering in sport

As noted above, volunteerism in sport is grounded in the original amateur ideals of sport.[7] Volunteer support for the development of sport was assumed in the days of strict amateurism, even at the highest levels of sport. The officials (referees, umpires and judges) for amateur sports were also amateurs. This was, in many ways, a manifestation of the higher social class origins of amateur sport and of the status of sport for wealthy and educated individuals, characterized by Bourdieu (1978) as disinterested practice – to show too much concern about the outcome was considered to be an aspect of professionalism, gentlemen were honourable, and no gentleman would ever question the decision of a fellow gentleman who was officiating.

As 'amateur' international sport achieved political significance during the Cold War (between the 1950s and the 1980s), concern was expressed in countries still imbued with the amateur tradition about the professionalization of athletes, coaches and the entire sports systems in 'Communist' countries and the United States (via the athletic scholarship system). The 'amateur' countries realized that they also had to change if they were to be internationally competitive, and state funding began to be channelled to 'amateur' sports. This was followed by concern that international sport and national teams could not be run effectively by, what were termed in Canada, 'kitchen table' amateurs.[8] Government funding in many high-income countries led to the appointment of paid staff and national team coaches in national sports organizations (NSOs), but the struggles over power and decision-making between the university educated (in new sports sciences disciplines) professional administrators and the volunteer committees went on for some time (see Slack 1985; Slack and Hinings 1992).

In Canada, there is a substantial body of research on the ways in which volunteer sports administrators and executives contribute to the administration and delivery of organized sport (e.g. Auld and Godbey 1998; Beamish 1985; Doherty and Carron 2003; Inglis 1994; Slack and Hinings 1987; Yoshioka and Ashcroft 2002, 2003). One of the key themes emerging from this body of literature concerns the ways in which the structure of the Canadian sports system, and its transformation over time, facilitates and challenges what volunteers are able to accomplish.

A number of researchers have specifically examined the relationships between volunteer and professional sports administrators in Canada's high-performance sports system (e.g. Auld and Godbey 1998; Beamish 1985; Inglis 1997; Kikulis et al. 1995; Macintosh and Whitson 1990; Slack 1985). Some argue that, as the Canadian high-performance sports system became more professionalized, rationalized and bureaucratized (although, as Slack and Hinings (1987) point out, not in a uniform or linear fashion), volunteers perceived themselves to be in an ambivalent position. On the one hand, they understand that volunteers are integral to the delivery of sport in Canada given the size, scope and range of Canada's physical, political and social landscape; on the other hand, they feel subservient to the goals, motivations and the decision-making power of professional sports administrators (Auld and Godbey 1998; Macintosh and Whitson 1990; Macintosh et al. 1987; Safai 2005; Slack and Hinings 1992). Other researchers found that professional sports administrators perceive their roles in an ambivalent way in relation to the goals, motivations, and decision-making power of volunteer-dominated boards and executive committees – in other words, a complete shift in control from volunteers to professionals has not been accomplished (Frisby 1986; Kikulis et al. 1995; Thibault et al. 1993; Thibault 1996). Auld and Godbey (1998) emphasize that the relationships between professional and volunteer sports administrators is complex, multi-faceted and contingent on the type of sports organization under study; and there is a need for more research on the relationship between these stakeholders, particularly with regard to their (perceived and actual) power, or lack of power, in organizational decision-making, policy development and implementation. Professional administrators have established a powerful position within 'amateur' sport, but still must negotiate some decisions with volunteer boards, and the organizations as a whole survive on the work of volunteers.

The professionalization and bureaucratization of NSOs and international sports federations (IFs) has been reinforced since the 1980s by the commercialization of international sport. New funding in the form of sponsorship and media rights contracts has helped to create a class of very wealthy and unregulated IFs, now mainly located in tax shelter countries. At the highest levels of international and Olympic sports, notions of amateurism have all but disappeared, and professionalized coaching has become the norm. However, the salaried bureaucracies, professional coaches, and sources of funding are highly concentrated at the highest levels of sport, and sports systems still depend primarily on voluntary labour at the grass-roots and developmental levels of sport.

Forms of volunteering in sport

It is possible to identify three main types of volunteering in sport (see Note 3 for two other types): major event volunteering; volunteering for grass-roots and community sport; and volunteering for high-performance sport. Research on volunteering in sport tends to combine the latter two and, for several reasons, major event volunteering is beyond the scope of this chapter. Volunteering at major sports events such as the Olympics and the Commonwealth Games is a significant aspect of volunteering, but it is short term (lasting only for the period of the event), and while the same benefits as other forms of sports volunteering are often attributed to major event volunteering (civic engagement, networking and learning transferable skills), this form of volunteering is not usually associated with sports development. However, Downward and Ralston (2006 p. 333) did question, in the case of the Manchester Commonwealth Games, whether volunteering at major sports events affects sports development in terms of 'interest, participation and subsequent volunteering in sport'. They found some limited evidence to that effect, but also found that various other factors needed to be in place that would encourage volunteers to shift their participation from a single event to ongoing voluntarism in sport. Thus, volunteering at major sports events may only have an indirect effect on sports development, and while there is a growing body of research that considers the characteristics of such volunteers, and the ways in which they and the event benefit from their participation, that research was not considered to be immediately relevant for this volume.

The most frequent form of volunteering in sport is directly connected to sports development – it is found at the youth/community/grass-roots levels of sport, where volunteers engage in all of the tasks necessary for the organizations to function – coaching, fundraising, administration, event planning, officiating (refereeing, judging, timekeeping, etc.) and so on. The NSNVO in Canada found that almost three-quarters (73 per cent) of sport and recreation organizations had no paid staff – they were entirely staffed by volunteers.

Related, and sometimes directly linked to the grass-roots level, is the more traditional form of sports volunteering – club/league/organization/federation administration at the higher levels of sport (including voluntary administrative and committee work in NSOs and IFs). At the regional and national levels this form of volunteering was formerly criticized as the 'kitchen table' form of sports administration; however, such volunteers now often work with paid staff in the organizations. These volunteers are also sometimes referred to by the derogatory terms, 'badgers' or 'blazers' – referring to the jackets with organizational emblems on the pockets that are often worn by officials and administrators volunteering at major events (e.g. track and field or swimming competitions).

Volunteering at the high-performance sport level may also involve individuals with specific skills – for example, the medical staff (physicians, physiotherapists, massage therapists, and so on) who accompany national teams to major games; or individuals who officiate at major events ranging from regional competitions to national and international levels. This level of volunteering would also include the volunteer board members of international and national agencies (e.g. the World Anti-Doping Agency; Canadian Centre for Ethics in Sport), committees (e.g. the International Olympic Committee; Commonwealth Games Canada), commissions (e.g. the IOC Medical Commission) and so on. The two types of volunteering are linked at the intersections of grass-roots and high-performance sport, and volunteers may progress through the ranks from a local club to a regional, national or international level of sport. The research literature rarely makes a distinction between these two levels of volunteering.

Who volunteers and why?

The profile of Canadians who volunteer in sport is somewhat similar to the overall profile of Canadian volunteers. According to the CSGVP (2009), the highest rates of volunteering in general are found among young Canadians with higher formal education and higher household incomes; they have school-aged children living at home, and they are religiously active. Doherty's (2005) data for volunteers in sport was extrapolated from the 2000 NSGVP. She found that the typical sports volunteer was male (64 per cent vs 36 per cent female; for volunteering in general there is a slightly higher proportion of females – 47 per cent vs 45 per cent male), 35–44 years of age, a college or university graduate, married with dependents at home, in full-time employment, and with a household income of C$60,000–99,000. Taylor et al.'s (2003) study of sports volunteerism shows a similar profile. Sports volunteers in England are predominately men (67 per cent), the majority of male and female volunteers are between the ages of 35–59 years (40 per cent), and are employed full time (56 per cent).

Canadians cite various reasons for volunteering. According to the CSGVP (2009): 93 per cent wish to make a contribution to their community; 77 per cent want an opportunity to use their skills and experiences; 59 per cent have been personally affected (or know someone who has been affected) by the cause the organization supports; 50 per cent want to explore their own strengths; 48 per cent use volunteering as an opportunity to network or meet other people; and 47 per cent volunteer because friends or family members volunteer. Again, the reasons given by sports volunteers are similar, but not identical. Doherty (2005) found that a similar proportion of sports volunteers wanted to support a cause in which they believed (an amalgam of several motives noted above) and to explore their own strengths. However, a higher proportion of sports volunteers cited 'using their skills to help,' and 'because they know someone who is affected by the organization.' Younger sports volunteers gave more emphasis to volunteering 'because friends were involved.' Using a somewhat different set of indicators, Taylor et al. (2003) found that English sports volunteers gave both intrinsic (a desire for social benefits, and wanting to put something back into the club) and extrinsic (wanting to help as a parent) reasons for volunteering. Young volunteers also gave 'future work' as an extrinsic motive.

With regard to how people become involved, Canadian volunteers in general were almost evenly divided between being asked by someone to volunteer (48 per cent) and those who approached an organization having learned about it from advertising or news media (45 per cent). However, Doherty (2005) found that becoming involved in volunteering because one's children were involved was a significant reason, and one relatively unique to sports volunteering. This is also captured in the motive of 'knowing someone who is affected by the organization' and is also, as noted, the main extrinsic reason for sports volunteering in England. Harvey et al. (2005) also found that there were aspects of 'mandatory volunteering' in Canadian sport where, for example, parents were required to volunteer one day a month in some capacity (e.g. fundraising) in their child's swimming club as a condition of their child's enrolment in the club, or where a reduced registration fee for their children was offered to parents who volunteered with a club.

The 2000 NSGVP did reveal that, in general, the perception that volunteering can help secure paid employment is growing and solidifying with almost a quarter of survey respondents – particularly younger volunteers (55 per cent of volunteers aged 15–24 years) – citing future career improvement and advancement as their reason for volunteering. The 2007 CSGVP (2009) still indicates that 23 per cent of all volunteers give 'improving job opportunities' as a motive. As Brock (2001: 58) notes:

> If community service is justified as a means of improving employment prospects … it encourages a more self-interested, if not cynical, approach to volunteering rather than one based on altruism and a sense of social responsibility. While the two may not be exclusive, it might not be desirable to connect them too tightly in the minds of young people.

In terms of sport and recreation, this motive only appears in the Taylor *et al.* (2003) data noted above. However, there may be an indirect connection in North America where youth volunteering is often an expectation on applications for university scholarships, and on applications to better universities. Sport is an area in which many young people participate as volunteers and often assume leadership roles (cf. Eley and Kirk 2003), and many academics in the fields of physical education, kinesiology/sports sciences recognize that their students often have a great deal of volunteer experience. There is a clear need for more research on this relatively materialist aspect of volunteering.

In addition to future job and education possibilities, many other benefits of volunteering are cited. Doherty (2005: 9) points out that volunteering is a leisure activity, and it must have the characteristics of a leisure activity; it is also 'an exchange between the organization and the volunteer … [t]he needs of both must be met in order for the relationship to be satisfying and effective, and maintained.' The organization's needs are straightforward – free labour; the benefits to the volunteer are more diverse. The CSGVP (2009) indicates that self-improvement is by far the most important benefit reported by volunteers – the development of interpersonal skills (66 per cent), communication skills (45 per cent), organizational or managerial skills (39 per cent), and increasing knowledge (34 per cent). Doherty (2005) found that sports volunteers reported the same type of benefits: using their skills and experience; obtaining new skills and experience; making a difference in a successful organization; and developing social relationships. In addition, coaches of youth sports reported the satisfaction of seeing skills improve.

Time devoted to, and tasks involved in sports volunteerism

As noted in a previous section, in countries such as Canada and England sport and recreation represents the single largest volunteer sector in society. However, the data are inconsistent for Canada: the NSNVO (2005) estimate of 5.3 million sport and recreation volunteer positions working a total of 483 million hours per year gives an average of 91 hours per year for each volunteer position; while the CSGVP (2009) estimate of 1.38 million volunteers working 357 million hours per year gives an average of 259 hours per year for each volunteer. The national average given by the CSGVP for volunteering in general is 167 hours per year; however, a higher average for sport and recreation is consistent – although sport and recreation volunteers represent 11 per cent of the total volunteer population, they contribute some 17 per cent of the total volunteer hours. Using different survey methods, Taylor *et al.* (2003) estimated that there were 5.8 million sports volunteers contributing 1.2 billion hours per year, giving an average of some 208 hours per year for each volunteer. In both Canada and England the surveys acknowledge that the averages are misleading, because a small proportion of the volunteers contribute a high proportion of the hours.

The number of FTEs represented by these volunteers has been noted previously, and it is clear that the 'replacement cost' for volunteer work in sport and recreation would be substantial. However, for some scholars, such as Godbout (2002; see also Robichaud 1996), volunteerism is a gift of time, energy and civil spirit between individuals; thus, to quantify volunteerism is reductionist, symptomatic of neo-liberal ideology, and creates the risk of the commodification of volunteer work. Godbout (2002; see also Lesemann 2002) advocates the adoption of alternative models of understanding. Rather than employing market-based categories such as hours of contribution, replacement cost value, and so on, such models would characterize volunteerism in relational terms in order to better recognize and understand volunteerism as a relationship between individuals. It is appropriate to keep these alternatives in mind when considering the problems of volunteering and how to resolve them.

The type of tasks carried out by volunteers in sport was briefly noted previously. In specific terms, the research suggests that volunteers carry out all of the tasks necessary for organized sports to exist. Rhyne (1995) notes that volunteers contribute their skills and time mainly in coaching/training (69 per cent) and organizing/supervising events and activities (69 per cent); followed by fundraising (55 per cent); providing information (52 per cent); and teaching (49 per cent). Volunteers were also involved in driving (44 per cent), refereeing/judging (43 per cent), recruiting volunteers (41 per cent), being a committee member (38 per cent), being a board member (37 per cent), performing office work (36 per cent), collecting/preparing and/or distributing food or other items (36 per cent), and making and/or selling items (26 per cent). Doherty (2005) confirms these main activities, pointing out that substantially more sports volunteers are involved in organizing and supervising activities and events, and teaching and coaching than is the case with volunteers in general in Canada.

As the figures above indicate, most volunteers in sport carry out multiple tasks. In England, Taylor *et al.* (2003: 42) found that: 'Volunteers recall on average between four and five roles fulfilled in their sports volunteering in [2002].' Doherty (2005) notes that older volunteers are more likely to be involved in multiple activities. Rhyne (1995), Doherty (2005) and Taylor (2003) also documented marked sex differences for some types of volunteer activities. For example, Doherty (2005) points out that men are more involved in organizing activities and coaching, and to a lesser extent in board/committee work; women are more involved in organizing activities, fundraising and committee/board work, and to a lesser extent in coaching (see also, Chafetz and Kotarba 1995). Rhyne (1995) found that men were more likely than women to be involved in coaching/training (80 per cent vs 57 per cent) and judging/refereeing (49 per cent vs 35 per cent); while more women than men were involved in recruiting volunteers (43 per cent vs 38 per cent), organizing events and activities (74 per cent vs 6 per cent), office work (44 per cent vs 29 per cent), collecting/preparing food and other items (44 per cent vs 29 per cent), and in making and selling items (32 per cent vs 21 per cent). The extent to which volunteering in sport replicates and helps to reproduce traditional sex roles is worthy of further research.

Recruitment and retention: Challenges and obstacles to volunteering in sport

Recruiting and retaining volunteers is a crucial issue for many organizations. For example, in Canada the NSNVO reported that just over half of the organizations reported having problems recruiting the type of volunteers needed, and finding board members; just under half of the organizations reported having problems retaining volunteers. These problems are exacerbated in sports organizations, where the NSNVO (2005) reported that sport and recreation ranked third (after 'law, advocacy and politics' and 'health') as organizations reporting these problems. Some 65 per cent of sport and recreation organizations reported difficulties in recruiting the type of volunteers needed to meet organizational needs; 64 per cent reported problems in obtaining volunteer board members; while 58 per cent reported difficulties in retaining volunteers. In Europe, Andreff *et al.* (2009) point out that: 'Voluntary work is hardly renewed at the same pace as before although it is a first order human resource for mass sport functioning and a foundation of what makes the European model of sport so specific.' This trend was also noted by Taylor *et al.* (2003) who calculated that there was one 'lapsed' sports volunteer for every two current volunteers.

One possible limitation in the recruitment and retention of volunteers in sport was noted by Beamish (1985), who documented the socioeconomic and demographic characteristics of sports executives in voluntary sports associations. He found that the organizations were often domi-nated by highly educated women and men (predominantly men) from upper socio-economic status groups. Beamish points out the ways in which such individuals, by virtue of their heightened social, cultural and economic capital, relate more easily to the government, and retain greater decision-making power over the ways in which sport should be delivered and transformed (see also Macintosh and Whitson 1990). He also notes the social reproduction of volunteer cohorts in that individuals may implicitly and explicitly select future generations of volunteer sports administrators based on their (often expertise-specific) network of contacts (e.g. promotion, marketing and accounting, etc.).[9]

Sharpe (2003) documents similar trends with regard to recruitment and retention in the delivery of sport and recreation at the grass-roots or community level. Volunteer administrators expressed their frustrations about the officials they had to deal with in the external environment (e.g. school boards, city councils and parks and recreation departments), not just in terms of the complex administrative rules and procedures that had to be followed, but also in terms of the loss of special treatment regarding facility reservations, fees or priority that was a result of budget cutbacks under emerging neo-liberal policies. With regard to the former, participants readily acknowledged the difficulty facing volunteer executive committees because of their lack of specialized knowledge in areas such as marketing, management, law or accounting. This added to the workload of existing sports volunteers, and deterred a number of the participants from continuing their involvement with the organization and/or from additional volunteer contributions.

Nichols *et al.* (2003) identified similar concerns among volunteer sports administrators in the UK. Their research reveals the increasing levels of perceived and actual government pressure on sports volunteers associated with the increasing complexity of administrative tasks and increased demand for professional practices. Much like NSOs in the Canadian sports system (see Slack and Hinings 1992), UK sports governing bodies depend on central government for funding and must therefore comply with government initiatives. Sports organizations do not exist in a socio-political and economic vacuum and they feel the consequences of widespread government fiscal restraint and budget cutbacks alongside increasingly complex administrative work (see also Thibault 1996). This results in additional administrative work for sports organizations and their volunteers, regardless of their size.

Volunteer sports administrators do not necessarily disagree with government initiatives (e.g. those around sexual harassment, child protection, applications and accountability for funding, and so on). However, the need to comply with these initiatives means more work downloaded to existing volunteers who increasingly need skills in sports management and administration. The implications are greater for smaller sports organizations with a smaller volunteer base; Sport England attempted to address these concerns through such initiatives as the Volunteer Invest-ment Programme (VIP). The increasing demands on sports volunteers contributes to volunteer stress and attrition, and discourages others from becoming involved; it becomes more proble-matic when the reasons that volunteers want to become involved do not resonate with the goals and vision of the organization. Taylor *et al.* (2003) conclude that whenever any extra work is downloaded to volunteers, the organization must first convince volunteers that it is to their advantage rather than just an additional burden. Rhyne's (1995) study of sports volunteerism in Canada identified many of these same issues.

In general the reasons for not volunteering, or for dropping out of volunteer work, are the same for sports volunteers as for volunteers in general. Lack of time (67 per cent) is by far the most frequent reason given by the Canadian population (CSGVP 2009), and that is also given as the main reason in surveys of sports volunteers (Doherty 2005; Taylor *et al.* 2003). Related reasons, such as the conflicting demands of family and paid work, were also given, and more women than men reported a lack of time. Many individuals felt that they were unable to make a long-term or year-round commitment to volunteering in sport, or stated that they had already contributed enough (e.g. in money, or former volunteer work). A significant number of individuals surveyed stated that they did not know how to become involved, or that no one had asked them to become involved. More sport-specific reasons included increasing age (feeling that the energy demands and activities of sport were more relevant for younger persons) and people feeling that they lacked the (sports) skills needed to volunteer in sport. Doherty (2005) suggests a model that incorporates personal barriers (e.g. time, work, family and lack of skills) and organizational barriers (e.g. increasing demands on volunteers and poorly run organizations).

Rhyne (1995: 19) acknowledges a number of challenges to volunteering in sport, including factors related to training, support and recognition:

> Difficulties may arise either from the volunteer's personal circumstances or from problems encountered in the course of the volunteer work. Financial costs to the individual, responsibilities to family, work or other commitments, difficulties arranging childcare and transportation as well as not having necessary skills fall in the personal circumstances category. Disliking the way an organization is run, not enjoying working with paid staff or other volunteers and lack of recognition for what they do can make it difficult for volunteers during the course of their involvement.

This is quite significant for volunteerism in general, and for sports volunteerism in particular, given that a smaller number of volunteers are being required to assume greater workloads and to acquire (or take on volunteer positions with) specialized skills (Rhyne 1995; Sharpe 2003; Taylor *et al.* 2003).

Training, support and recognition

Training, screening, orientation, appropriate supervision, support and recognition are all increasingly being seen as important factors by organizations that employ volunteers. However, these factors are among the more difficult to implement, especially in sports organizations, and there is very little research on these issues. In Canada, one-third of non-profit and voluntary organizations reported difficulties in providing training for their volunteers, and for volunteer board members (NSNVO 2005). There are reasons (below) to expect that this percentage is significantly higher in sports organizations. In addition to recruitment and retention problems Taylor *et al.* (2003) found high levels of burnout resulting from significant amounts of work being carried out by a few volunteers, and pointed out the need for initiatives that raise the profile and recognition of sports volunteers, provide support and training for volunteer work, offer management plans to support sports organizations with volunteers, and promote good volunteer management practice in the form of basic training (Taylor *et al.* 2003).

Many non-profit organizations have now developed detailed outlines of good practices in the employment of volunteers. For example, even small organizations such as the Camrose and District Volunteer Centre (Camrose, Alberta, Canada) have developed *A Template for Non-Profit Organizations on Developing an Orientation Manual for Volunteers* (2008). Their orientation is grounded in the Canadian Code for Volunteer Involvement, developed by Volunteer Canada for the International Year of the Volunteer (2001) and updated in 2004 in partnership with the Canadian Administrators of Volunteer Resources. The *General Principles* outline the mutuality of the relationship between volunteers and organization:

> Volunteers have rights. Voluntary organizations recognize that volunteers are a vital resource and will commit to the appropriate infrastructure to support volunteers.
>
> - The organization's practices ensure effective volunteer involvement.
> - The organization commits to providing a safe and supportive environment for volunteers.
>
> Volunteers make a commitment and are accountable to the organization.
>
> - Volunteers will act with respect for beneficiaries and the community.
> - Volunteers will act responsibly and with integrity.

> *Volunteer Centre of Camrose [Alberta] and District [www.whyvolunteer.ca]. www.whyvolunteer.ca/*
> *FCKeditor2FC1/UserFiles/File/Volunteer%20Orientation%20Manual%202008%20Feb%*
> *2011.pdf (accessed October 2009)*

Such codes are developed with the underlying understanding that volunteers will be screened, trained, supervised, and supported in their work by paid staff.

In the case of sport, the NSNVO (2005) found that almost three-quarters (73 per cent – a much higher proportion than for non-profit and voluntary organizations in other sectors) of the organizations had *no* paid staff – they were run entirely by volunteers. This obviously has consequences for the aspects of good practice outlined above – screening, orientation, training, support and recognition. In order to develop effective practices in organizations with no paid staff, already over-stretched volunteers must take on additional tasks; and because there is often more demand than supply for volunteers in sports organizations, such effective practices may not always be implemented, and there may be no individuals who are responsible for, or skilled in implementing them. In Canada, the only mandatory aspect of training is for coaches, who are expected to obtain a basic level of coaching certification. With regard to screening, following some sexual abuse cases in sport in the 1990s, there is now a requirement for volunteer coaches to undergo a police check. Researchers have also pointed out how multi-tasking is a frequent characteristic of volunteerism in sports organizations, and this also creates difficulties for recruitment and training. For example, Taylor *et al.* (2003: 42) note that: 'any initiatives to increase formalisation and specialisation of key roles within voluntary sports organizations need to be flexible enough to preserve the "mucking in" culture that pervades many of these organizations'.

Taylor *et al.* (2003) acknowledge that sports organizations that have been successful in retaining and fostering their volunteer support actively train, support and recognize their volunteers in a number of informal and formal ways. They cite a number of best practices derived from three case studies. For example, in one sports organization's written volunteer recruitment/management strategy:

> Members are identified as being potential committee volunteers. They are approached if trusted and a good relationship exists with them. If they agree [to volunteer], they are

mentored by the outgoing incumbent for a period of time. No one person is expected to do a task without support. Committee members therefore gain knowledge of a range of tasks and essentially form a support group. Also non-committee volunteers are not expected to complete tasks without support. This helps volunteers to feel welcomed and supported and not isolated and resentful. Each volunteer is supported with training where necessary ... paid for by the club.

(p. 99)

While recognition for volunteer contribution is not a significant source of motivation for individuals to volunteer, it does have an effect on volunteer satisfaction, retention and even recruitment (e.g. Farrell *et al.* 1998; Inglis 1994; Johnston *et al.* 1999, 2000). The CVI (2001: 5) recommends the development and implementation of 'a multi-year campaign of promotion, recognition and outreach ... to help Canadians better understand and appreciate volunteer activity and encourage them to volunteer.'

Sports volunteerism and social capital

Although it is broadly accepted that volunteerism is a strong contributor to social capital, how sports volunteerism contributes to social capital, what forms of social capital are generated by sport, or whether sport really does contribute to social capital are still under question (Maguire *et al.* 2002). The idea of social capital has been interpreted in various ways, but all refer to 'various social and moral relations that bind communities together' (Coalter 2010: 1215). The concept achieved popularity, and has generated a great deal of research, since it became linked to 'third way' politics during the 1990s. Putnam's (1993: 167) claim that social capital consists of ' ... features of social organization, such as trust, norms, and networks, that can improve the efficiency of society by facilitating coordinated action,' was cited widely. Research suggested that communities with higher levels of social capital (or communities comprised of individuals with higher levels of social capital) were characterized by various positive social indicators such as better physical and mental health, and lower rates of crime.

Despite widespread research and policy interest in social capital in the last 15 years, and the fact that a key text in the field references a competitive recreational activity (Putnam's (2000) *Bowling Alone*), there is limited research on social capital in sport, especially as it relates to sports volunteerism. Harvey *et al.* (2008), in a pilot study, found a strong relationship between volunteerism in sport and social capital; the results were even stronger when controlling for gender and age. However, the results do not permit any assumptions about the direction of the relationship – do individuals with higher social capital become involved as volunteers in sport, or does volunteering in sport produce higher levels of social capital? Despite limited research evidence, the latter is widely assumed by individuals in the sport and policy communities. In the only other study of sports volunteerism and social capital, Tonts (2005) provides various examples to demonstrate that sports volunteers provide key resources to their communities, including time, expertise, and material resources. He argues that individuals may gain social capital through their volunteer work.

The various theoretical approaches to social capital are evident in the stated motivations of volunteers – learning new skills, and perhaps transferable skills, is a characteristic of Coleman's (1988) 'pragmatic' approach; Lin's (2001) network approach and Bourdieu's (1986) 'investment' approach are evident in Tonts' (2005) suggestion that the social capital gained from sports volunteering may benefit individuals when they need access to resources they do not possess; and Putnam's (2000) popular 'civic engagement' approach is evident in the idea of 'wanting to give something back to the [sports] community.' However, Coalter (2007) and Tonts (2005), considering Putnam's (2000) categories of *bonding, bridging*, and *linking* social capital, warn that the sense of identity and belonging generated in, for example, a sports club may actually facilitate the exclusion of certain individuals along race, gender and social class lines. Coalter (2010: 1215) argues that, '[t]o be most effective [in terms of promoting social inclusion], sports clubs need to seek to promote bridging and linking social capital.'

Conclusions

Volunteers are a vital structural component of sport, and volunteerism is one of the main determinants of sports development in particular, and sports sector capacity in general. Without the 'mucking in' culture of sports volunteerism in the UK, the 'Can-do' attitude of sports volunteers in Canada, or the dedication and multi-tasking work of sports volunteers everywhere in the world, sports as we know them would not exist. Volunteers affect every level of almost every sport, from the first steps in learning sports skills among children to the treatment of injuries among high-performance athletes.

This situation has emerged partly as a result of the amateur traditions of sport, and partly because, although many state and local governments (at least in high-income countries) consider sport to be important, it is not always seen as vital. This is especially the case when taxes and public spending are being cut, physical education is given less significance in school curricula, and municipal recreation programmes and facilities are reduced and subject to user fees. Sports volunteers, individuals who do consider sport to be vital to the life of their community, or who just want to ensure that their own children have an opportunity to participate, take up the slack and make sports programmes work. Their willingness and enthusiasm have helped to create both opportunities and positive experiences for many millions of sports participants.

And yet, evidence from Canada, England and other countries suggests that the system is under strain. A small proportion of volunteers carry out the vast majority of the volunteer work; recruitment and retention are major issues; and, despite limited public funding, the regulatory environment in which sports exist is becoming increasingly complex in terms of liability and safety issues, equity requirements, the need to ensure disability access, and the need to screen, train and support volunteers in their work. Sharpe (2003: 446) notes that:

> It is the need to successfully negotiate the increasingly complex regulations, procedures, and policies from institutions in the external environment that leads many informal groups toward professionalization. Indeed, the main reason why leisure groups employ paid staff is that they need a professional answer to the formal environment. However, there are other consequences that accompany a move toward professionalization. One is that it may reduce the diversity of grassroots volunteers so that professional training becomes a prerequisite for involvement.

The issue of recruitment was a major concern of the Canadian Voluntary Initiative (CVI), which noted: 'one conclusion is that the vast majority of Canadians might be open to volunteering if their concerns were addressed (e.g. lack of time) or they were made more aware of, and welcomed to, volunteering opportunities' (CVI 2001: 27). Therefore, 'addressing the issue of real and/or perceived lack of time availability will constitute the single most significant challenge in arresting and offsetting the current decline in volunteering rates' (CVI 2001: 27).

The need for volunteer labour in most sports organizations, especially those with no paid staff, is often so pressing that it is almost impossible for them to pay attention to the support and needs of the volunteers. Individuals may be pressed into volunteer situations where they are on their own with the clients (players), feel under-trained or inadequate to the tasks, or feel over-whelmed by the workload requirements. It is a tribute to the 'mucking in / Can-do' traditions of sports volunteerism that so much is accomplished under such circumstances, but the needs of both volunteers and the organizations must be considered in order to plan appropriately. Doherty (2005) makes two important observations:

- Volunteering is considered a leisure activity and so, by definition, it must be relaxing, refreshing, and/or rejuvenating, meet one's social and/or intellectual needs, provide an opportunity to exercise, and/or provide an opportunity to learn or display competence and mastery.
- Volunteerism is an exchange between the organization and the volunteer. The needs of both must be met for the relationship to be satisfying and effective, and maintained.

Notes

1 Throughout the chapter, Canada is used as an exemplar. This limitation is imposed for two reasons. First, many high-income countries conduct national surveys of volunteerism, and it is not possible in the space limitations of this chapter to provide meaningful national comparisons. Second, volunteerism in sport is an area of study characterized by limited research, and a substantial part of that research has been carried out in Canada, although other data are cited where relevant. Our intent is to provide data that will encourage readers to find comparative examples in their own countries; or readers may use the sport examples provided here to generate comparative data.

2 Interestingly, the definition now includes 'mandatory community service', the oxymoronic 'compul-sory volunteering' that is now required as a part of the sentencing of some offenders, or as part of school completion requirements in some jurisdictions.

3 For example, some 84 per cent of Canadians reported this type of informal volunteering in the most recent survey (CSGVP 2009). Informally helping others is likely to be widespread in sport, but is not included in this chapter primarily because there is no available research. Similarly, volunteering in international development through sports projects and initiatives is a growing field of sports volunteerism, but there is very little research on this aspect of volunteering (e.g. Darnell 2007). Volunteer work in international development through sport may or may not include aspects of sports development – it is not included in this chapter.

4 Original in French: *l'activité bénévole contribue à renforcer les liens de confiance et de réciprocité. Elle crée et renforce tout à la fois la cohésion sociale, avec tous les avantages connexes que cela implique pour le bien-être individuel et collectif.*

5 There is a pressing need for research in this area. In a rare instance, *Sport: The Way Ahead* (Task Force Report 1992: 87) acknowledged that the 'estimated value of service of voluntary Canadian medical staff attached to the Canadian team attending the [1991] Pan American Games in Cuba was C$118,000'; however, this figure does not take into account the costs the volunteers accrued in their personal professional practices (e.g. replacement clinicians, clinic overhead costs, and so on).

6 An additional difficulty resulting from Canadian data is that both recent surveys (CSGVP and NSNVO) combine 'sports and recreation' as a single category. Thus, the calculations based on Canadian data would be reduced significantly by removing volunteers in recreation, but it is impossible to determine by how much. However, the general point about comparative data stands, and the situation in Canada is much improved over the former population surveys (NSGVPs) where sports and recreation were in a category combined with arts and culture.

7 There is very little volunteerism associated with professional sport, apart from charitable work by professional players (often a contract obligation) and crowd control work by members of supporters' clubs.

8 Amateur sport organizations were run by volunteers on shoestring budgets; meetings of club and organizational administrators were often held at a member's home to save expenses. This volunteer form of administration began to be characterized in a rather derogatory way by an emerging group of professional sports administrators, as 'kitchen table' administration.

9 Another form of social reproduction is evident in sports volunteerism. Since such volunteering tends to involve middle-class individuals, and is often motivated by children's involvement in sports, access to

the support provided by sports volunteers tends to be more readily available in high- and middle-income communities than low-income communities. Children in low-income and minority communities who do not grow up experiencing a tradition of volunteering are then less likely to become volunteers themselves.

References

Andreff, W. (2009). 'Sport financing in times of global recession'. Paper presented at the Play the Game International Conference, Coventry, UK, 8–12 June.

Andreff, W., Dutoya, J. & J. Montel (2009). 'Sport financing: European model facing a risky future?' *Play the Game News*, 30 March. www.playthegame.org

Auld, C.J. & Godbey, G. (1998). 'Influence in Canadian National Sport Organizations: Perceptions of professionals and volunteers'. *Journal of Sport Management*, 12(1), 20–38.

Beamish, R. (1985). 'Sport executives and voluntary associations: A review of the literature and introduction to some theoretical issues'. *Sociology of Sport Journal*, 2(3), 218–32.

Bourdieu, P. (1978). 'Sport and social class'. *Social Science Information*, 7(6), 819–40.

——(1986). *Distinction: A Social Critique of the Judgment of Taste*. London: Routledge & Kegan Paul.

Brock, K.L. (2001). 'Promoting voluntary action and civil society through the state'. *ISUMA: Canadian Journal of Policy Research*, 2(2), 53–61.

Chafetz, J.S. & J.A. Kotarba (1995). 'Son worshippers: The role of Little League mothers in recreating gender'. *Studies in Symbolic Interaction*, 18, 217–41.

Coalter, F. (2007). *A Wider Social Role for Sport: Who's Keeping the Score?* London: Routledge.

——(2010). 'Social capital'. In R. Bartlett, C. Gratton & C. Rolf (eds), *Encyclopedia of International Sports Studies*. London: Routledge, p. 1215.

Coleman, J. (1988). 'Social capital in the creation of human capital'. *American Journal of Sociology*, 94, S95–120.

CSGVP (2009). *Caring Canadians, Involved Canadians: Highlights from the 2007 Canada Survey of Giving, Volunteering and Participating*. Ottawa: Statistics Canada.

CVI (2001). *Canadian Volunteerism Initiative: The Report of the National Volunteerism Initiative Joint Table*. Ottawa. ON. *www.vsi-isbc.ca/eng/cvireport*

Darnell, S. (2007). 'Playing with race: Right to play and the production of whiteness in "development through sport"'. *Sport in Society*, 10, 560–79.

Doherty, A. (2005). *A Profile of Community Sport Volunteers / Volunteer Management in Community Sport Clubs*. Toronto: Parks and Recreation Ontario / Sport Alliance of Ontario.

Doherty, A. & A. Carron (2003). 'Cohesion in volunteer sport executive committees'. *Journal of Sport Management*, 17(2), 116–41.

Downward, P. & R. Ralston (2006). 'The sport development potential of sports event volunteering: Insights from the XVII Manchester Commonwealth Games'. *European Sport Management Quarterly*, 6(4), 333–51.

Eley, D. & D. Kirk (2003). 'Developing citizenship through sport: The role of sport in promoting volunteerism and community service'. *Journal of Sport and Sciences*, 21(4), 288–300.

Farrell, J.M., Johnston, M.E. & G.D. Twynam (1998). 'Volunteer motivation, satisfaction, and management at an elite sporting competition'. *Journal of Sport Management*, 12(4), 288–300.

Frisby, W. (1986). 'The organizational structure and effectiveness of voluntary organizations: The case of Canadian national sport governing bodies'. *Journal of Park and Recreation Administration*, 4(3), 61–74.

Godbout, J. (2002). 'Le bénévolat n'est pas un produit'. *Nouvelles Pratiques Sociales*, 15(2), 42–52.

Harvey, J., Donnelly, P. & M. Lévesque (2005). *Volunteerism: Researching the Capacity of Canadian Sport – Research Report*. Ottawa: Sport Canada.

Harvey, J., Lévesque, M. & P. Donnelly (2008). 'Sport volunteerism and social capital'. *Sociology of Sport Journal*, 24(2), 206–23.

Inglis, S. (1994). 'Exploring volunteer board member and executive director needs: Importance and fulfillment'. *Journal of Applied Recreation Research*, 19(3), 171–89.

Inglis, S. (1997). 'Shared leadership in the governance of amateur sport: Perceptions of executive directors and volunteer board members'. *Avante*, 3(1), 14–33.

ISUMA (2001). 'Le bénévolat'. *ISUMA: Canadian Journal of Policy Research*, 2(2), 8–9.

Johnston, M.E., Twynam, G.D. & J.M. Farrell (1999/2000). 'Motivation and satisfaction of event volunteers for a major youth organization'. *Loisir et Société/Society and Leisure*, 24(1/2), 161–77.

Kikulis, L., Slack, T. & B. Hinings (1995). 'Does decision making make a difference?: Patterns of change within Canadian National Sport Organizations'. *Journal of Sport Management*, 9(3), 273–99.

LeRoux, N., Camy, J., Chantelat, P., Froberg, K. & A. Madella (2000). *Sports Employment in Europe*. Lyon: European Observatoire of Sports Employment.

Lesemann, F. (2002). 'Le bénévolat: De la production "domestique" de services à la production de "citoyenneté"'. *Nouvelles Pratiques Sociales*, 15(2), 25–41.

Lin, N. (2001). *Social Capital: A Theory of Social Structure and Action*. Cambridge: Cambridge University Press.

Macintosh, D., Bedecki, T. & Franks, C. (1987). *Sport and Politics in Canada: Federal Government Involvement Since 1961*. Montréal & Kingston: McGill-Queen's University Press.

Macintosh, D. & D. Whitson (1990). *The Game Planners: Transforming Canada's Sport System*. Montréal & Kingston: McGill-Queen's University Press.

Maguire, J., Jarvie, G., Mansfield, L. & J. Bradley (2002). *Sport Worlds: A Sociological Perspective*. Champaign, IL: Human Kinetics.

Nichols, G., Taylor, P. James, M., King, L., Holmes, K. & R. Garrett (2003). 'Pressures on sports volunteers arising from partnerships with the central government'. *Loisir et Société/Society and Leisure*, 26(2), 419–30.

NSNVO (2005). *Cornerstones of Community: Highlights of the National Survey of Nonprofit and Voluntary Organizations, 2003*. Ottawa: Statistics Canada.

Putnam, R. (1993). *Making Democracy Work: Civic Traditions in Modern Italy*. Princeton: Princeton University Press.

Putnam, R. (2000). *Bowling Alone: The Collapse and Revival of American Community*. New York: Simon & Schuster.

Rhyne, D. (1995). *Volunteerism in Sport, Fitness and Recreation in Ontario*. Toronto: Recreation Policy Branch, Ontario Ministry of Culture, Tourism and Recreation.

Robichaud, S. (1996). 'Du réseau à l'institution: Le bénévolat en mouvement'. *Swiss Journal of Sociology*, 22(2), 329–46.

Safai, P. (2005). *A Critical Analysis of the Origins, Development and Institutionalization of Sport Medicine in Canada*. Unpublished doctoral thesis. University of Toronto, Toronto.

Sharpe, E.K. (2003). '"It's not fun any more": A case study of organizing a contemporary grassroots recreation association'. *Loisir et Société/Society and Leisure*, 26(2), 431–52.

Slack, T. (1985). 'The bureaucratization of a voluntary sport organization'. *International Review for the Sociology of Sport*, 20(2), 145–66.

Slack, T. & B. Hinings (1987). *The Organization and Administration of Sport*. London, ON: Sports Dynamics.

Slack, T. & B. Hinings (1992). 'Understanding change in National Sport Organizations: An integration of theoretical perspectives'. *Journal of Sport Management*, 6(2), 114–32.

Smale, B. & S. Arai (2002/2003). 'Recontextualizing the experiences of the volunteer'. *Leisure/Loisir*, 27(3/4), 153–9.

Task Force Report (1992). *Sport: The Way Ahead [Report of the Minister's Task Force on Federal Sport Policy]*. Ottawa: Supply and Services Canada.

Taylor, P., Nichols, G., Holmes, K., James, M., Gratton, C., Garrett, R., Kokolakakis, T., Mulder, C. & L. King (2003). *Sports Volunteering in England: A Report for Sport England*. Sheffield: Leisure Industries Research Centre.

Thibault, L. (1996). 'Employee turnover in non-profit sport and leisure organizations'. *Loisir et Société/Society and Leisure*, 19(1), 265–80.

Thibault, L., Slack, T. & B. Hinings (1993). 'A framework for the analysis of strategy in nonprofit sport organizations'. *Journal of Sport Management*, 7(1), 25–43.

Tonts, M. (2005). 'Competitive sport and social capital in rural Australia', *Journal of Rural Studies*, 21, 137–49.

Yoshioka, C.F. & R.F. Ashcroft (2002/2003). 'Leadership traits of selected volunteer administrators in Canada'. *Leisure/Loisir*, 27(3/4), 265–82.

6

Sports development and social capital

Andrew Adams

The observation that social capital represents a 'sack of analytical potatoes' (Fine 2001) may well be applied to sports development, where it seems that everyone is an expert, has an opinion or has experiential insights that confer expertise. As Long has argued, disagreement in sport is often based on 'belief rather than evidence' (2008: 236), reinforcing what Coalter has referred to as the 'mythopoeic' (2007a: 9) status of sport where sport is viewed as 'self-evidently a good thing' (Rowe 2005). This over generalising of sport has impacted upon both the 'emergence of sports development as a political issue' and more importantly its 'systemic embeddedness' (Houlihan and White 2002: 230–31) into national and regional policy frameworks in the UK. Sports development's emergence as a field of both policy and practice is as an adjunct to broader trends in social and economic policy making.

Social capital has been used in various contexts for over a century, having been first coined by Marx and used later by Hanifan and Dewey (Farr 2004). Like sport, social capital has been discussed, dissected and elaborated on by many social scientists, politicians and policy makers and yet like sport it remains a stubbornly contested term with competing theoretical perspectives each indicating its value as both object and subject of policy. Possibly the simplest definition of social capital has come from the Organisation for Economic Cooperation and Development (OECD) which has stated that it includes 'the networks, norms, values and understandings that facilitate cooperation within or among groups' (OECD 2001: 4). Within government in the UK, the Strategy Unit identified social capital as consisting of the 'networks, norms, relationships, values and informal sanctions that shape the quantity and cooperative quality of a society's social interactions' (Strategy Unit 2002: 5). In essence, what both of these definitions capture is, in the sense of John Stuart Mill's 'conjoint action' or Adam Smith's 'a sense of duty', a potentially powerful social mechanism for overcoming the problematic notion of collective action.

While social capital can be thought of as a 'diffuse' concept (Coalter 2007b), it is clear that it is more than just a useful analytical tool, for, as much of the literature concerning social capital and sport attests to it, or a particularised version of it, it has become embedded within the social policy infrastructure of the UK (see Coalter 2007a, 2007b; Adams 2008; Bradbury and Kay 2008). Indeed internationally where voluntary associationalism is part and parcel of specific sports development infrastructures, social capital has often been identified as a key driver of sports policy. In Canada, for example, research at one level has specifically sought to inform and guide public policy (see for example Canadian Policy Research Initiative 2005), whilst at another level it has sought to interpret and understand grass-roots sport experiences in light of policy applications of social capital (Donnelly and Kidd 2003; Sharpe 2006; Perks 2007). Internationally it would seem that the intersection between sports development and social capital has crystallised around the pursuit of a number of common and persistent social policy agendas and discourses, of which active citizenship and social inclusion have been prominent. In respect of the UK, Coalter (2007b) has outlined the potential role that sport and sports clubs can have in enabling forms of social capital to be formed and the impact this can have on the possible outcome of policies implemented. Bradbury and Kay (2008) meanwhile, highlight the social capital policy context of the promotion of volunteering to young people, noting that their data indicated that young people were positively inclined towards active citizenship and civic participation and felt more socially connected through volunteering in sport.

It is this aspect of social capital that is fundamental in locating sports development as a conduit, through which aspects of social and community development can be incorporated into a particular political project. The coming to power of New Labour in 1997 and its adoption of pragmatic Third Way politics, modernisation, an ethic of accountability and an emphasis on governance rather than government has been eloquently dealt with elsewhere (e.g. Levitas 2000; Houlihan and White 2002; Lister 2004; Coalter 2007a, 2007b; Adams 2008; Bradbury and Kay 2008; Houlihan and Green 2009). It is sufficient at this juncture to note that in the UK, New Labour's social investment strategies have been based on a particular version of civic communitarianism which, in valorising the active citizen, has employed social capital within the notion of 'rights and responsibilities' (Giddens 1998; Blair, 1999). The promotion of volunteering (see for example Halfpenny and Reid 2002) has provided an opportunity structure for the successful promotion of social capital via the active citizen and through volunteering to establish 'bonds of trust and commitment … and encouraging people to work together for common purposes' (Blair 1996: 116–17). It is in this regard that the promotion of volunteering in sport, often referred to as 'capacity building' in policy documentation became part of the mantra of sports development and those seeking to promote the role of sport in forming social capital (DCMS/Strategy Unit 2002; see also Adams 2008). The upshot is that the twin policy outcomes of promoting sports participation and forming social capital have become unwitting bedfellows in what Green has referred to as an 'unprecedented' embracing of policies for sport and physical activity by the British government (Green 2007).

The use of social capital within policy-making circles, particularly when considered in relation to sports development, has all too often suffered from a conceptual vagueness that largely stems, as Field notes, from its journey from 'metaphor to concept' (Field 2003). In part this is attributable to the enduring disagreement concerning what social capital is and what it does, which for Fine has resulted in a 'web of eclecticism in which the notion of social capital floats freely from one meaning to another with little attention to conceptual depth and rigour' (Fine 1999: 9). Certainly many have considered the concept to resemble the reconstruction of old thinking in new packaging (e.g. Edwards and Foley 1997; Portes 1998; Tarrow 1998; Fine 2001), while others have focused attention onto the 'conceptual stretching' that is apparent in the many different uses and applications of this particular concept (Portes 1998; Johnston and Percy-Smith 2003). Indeed many writers, commentators and policy makers have identified social capital with the contemporary socio-political zeitgeist, and have seized upon and viewed the concept as a new therapeutic remedy for the ills of society (e.g. Weitzman and Kawachi 2000, also see Halpern 2005). As a consequence it is understandable why Johnston and Percy-Smith (2003: 332) have referred to social capital as 'the contemporary equivalent of the philosopher's stone'. If anything, the explosion of interest in the UK has arguably reached the second stage of Portes' cautionary warning that social capital has evolved (like other promising social science concepts) 'from intellectual insight appropriated by policy pundits, to journalistic cliché, to eventual oblivion' (Portes 1998: 1).

This chapter has three objectives: first, to outline the three principal theories of social capital (henceforth referred to as strains), re-focusing the vagueness with a particular concern to embed each strain within its particular conceptual framework. Second, the chapter addresses how social capital and sports development can be viewed within a policy framework that promotes a strategic orientation to social capital outcomes. The discussion and analysis is informed by a range of public documents produced by government, together with a series of 31 interviews conducted with a range of senior officials across one single county council area in England (Adams 2009). The chapter concludes by summarising how research into sports development and social capital refutes rather than fulfils Portes' melancholic prophesy.

Defining social capital and attendant conceptual frameworks

The modern usage of social capital stems primarily from political science, economics (rational choice theory) and sociology, and is essentially based on the writings of three academics who each provide the basis for a distinct school of thought or strain of social capital (Lewandowski 2006; Maloney *et al.* 2000; Grix 2002). Robert Putnam, who is widely considered to have popularised the concept, is the driving force behind the democratic strain, which according to some (e.g. Grix 2002) is the most dominant strain. James Coleman, taking a lead from Becker and writing in the 1980s, provides the basis for the rational strain, and Pierre Bourdieu, from his structuralist beginnings writing mainly in the 1970s, infuses the critical strain.

The democratic strain

It is Putnam's work that provides the back-story to the democratic strain of social capital. Putnam originally used the concept to examine different levels of civic engagement in Italy (1993) before going on to analyse the decline of civic engagement in the USA (2000). In *Making Democracy Work* (1993: 167) Putnam defined social capital as 'features of social organisations, such as trust, norms, and networks' that can improve the efficiency of society by facilitating coordinated actions. For Putnam it was the volume of horizontal networks, norms of reciprocity and trust in the north compared to the south of Italy that accounted for the differing levels of civic engagement. Putnam terms these networks, norms and trust 'social capital'. This social capital was what laid the key foundation for civic activity. It is noteworthy that in *Making Democracy Work* social capital is very much a *post hoc* concept, appearing only in the last chapter to account for the phenomena examined within the book.

The publication of *Bowling Alone* (2000) sought to develop this thesis concerning politics and democracy and extend it to explain the apparent decline of social capital in the USA (Putnam 1995, 1996). In this seminal book Putnam indicates that social capital refers to 'connections among individuals – social networks and the norms of reciprocity and trustworthiness that arise from them' (Putnam 2000: 19). This definition shifts the emphasis towards networks as the wellspring of social capital. However, there is little conceptual depth afforded to this notion of social capital in *Bowling Alone* and this vagueness prefigures much of the debate concerning the apparent confusion between process and outcome (see for example Newton 1999; Maloney *et al.* 2000; Foley and Edwards 1996, 1998, 1999). The democratic strain, with its emphasis on trust, reciprocity and the context within which they are fostered, thus proposes a neo-Tocquevillean 'civic-culture' (Almond and Verba 1963) approach to social capital which has had enormous academic, political and policy-making appeal. The basis of the civic-culture approach rests with the employment of a macro-level approach (using large-scale quantitative data sets) to explain how generic problems of collective action might be overcome. In so doing the democratic strain frames social capital in the context of the public goods (Almond and Verba 1963; Coalter 2007b) that it might provide for overcoming generic problems of collective action. This apparent indication of causal flows allied with the production of social benefits highlights this strain's policy-making appeal and helps to explain Putnam's audiences with two former US presidents and one former British Prime Minister (Lemann 1996).

The main assertion of the democratic strain is that normative social networks are fundamentally intertwined with and within the abundance of associational life that exists outside both the state and private sectors. Furthermore, a predisposition to engage in voluntary associationalism is assumed to be an indicator of the strength of the civic core of any given society. Both implicitly and explicitly voluntary associational activity is implicated as the prime means of community development and connectedness necessary to provide the trust, reciprocity, norms and values that enable communities to be more effective in meeting their collective ends (Coalter 2007b).

The democratic strain is notable for its attempt to pinpoint causes of civic activity and focuses on the establishment of networks, norms and trust as social capital. Furthermore, the desire to establish causality for the rise and decline in social capital in the USA led Putnam to conclude in *Bowling Alone* (2000) that this decline is mainly due to the passing of a 'long civic generation'. This generation was not only very civically engaged, but also socialised more and had higher levels of trust. Putnam, in following De Tocqueville's 'art of association' (2003), placed voluntary associationalism as the primary means for establishing sociability, norms and trust as social capital. In this respect Putnam's use of the metaphor of the lone bowler was intended to signify the decline in organised associationalism and the rise of individualism and the impact that this had for societal democratic structures, given that, as associationalism decreased, so did civic engagement, sociability and trust. Thus, the democratic strain invites a clear association between the output of civil society organisations (CSOs) and the pursuance of democratic values and structures with the desire to 'build solidarity in a secular society exposed to the full rigours of a global market and committed to the principle of individual choice' (Leadbeater 1997: 35).

There seems to be some agreement among writers that the democratic strain of social capital is limited by its conceptual hinterland or apparent lack of one. Coalter (2007b) refers to a set of 'apparent correlations' in Putnam's work that substantiate the logic of the democratic strain, while others such as Portes (1998) and Johnston and Percy-Smith (2003) refer to the inherent tautology of the concept in this strain. A clear example is in the strain's reliance and confusion on the issue of trust. In positing trust as a definitional component and key contributor to the creation of social capital, the democratic strain becomes problematic because of the circularity and tautology inherent to explanations based on such logic (Arrow 1999; Misztal 2000; Woolcock 2001). The tautology is created because trust is positioned as both: a) a creative variable and b) the product of that creation. In this guise trust implicitly tends to incorporate a retroactive analysis, which in excluding a number of other factors produces explanations that are both simplistic and misleading. Thus to say that a group formed through voluntary association is more trusting than individuals outside the associative network is a tautology, because the premise of collective action based on trust is a consequence of trusting individuals coming together in the first place (Portes 1998).

This conceptual underdevelopment is also apparent in the use of the bonding and bridging distinction employed in particular by Putnam in *Bowling Alone*. In essence bridging social capital, forming links with people unlike me, is inclusive, as it involves 'weak ties' (Granovetter 1973), facilitating relationships with individuals on the basis of acquaintance. Bonding social capital, forming links with people like me, is exclusive, reinforcing established relationships particularly within the family and also within a particular social group of which one may be a member. For Putnam, bridging social capital is a 'kind of sociological WD40' whilst the bonding variety is a 'kind of sociological superglue' (Putnam 2000: 13). Whilst the rational and critical strains of social capital tend to overlook this distinction (focusing on strongly bonded networks – homophilous interaction), the democratic strain maintains its importance especially in relation to bridging capital. A key problem with bridging social capital is in its measurement, which by Putnam's own admission is difficult to distinguish from the bonding type. Notwithstanding these limitations the bonding/bridging social capital distinction is vital in order to differentiate between contrasting types of social interaction that can yield very different benefits.

Many of the apparent conceptual problems of the democratic strain stem from Putnam himself who has shown little interest in going beyond a conceptual pragmatism to discuss and analyse how other factors such as the political and economic might impinge on the processes described. A clear inference from Putnam's work is that the democratic strain of social capital can only ever provide a partial explanation of civic engagement. In particular, Putnam omits a serious consideration of structural factors (Grix 2001) as well as focusing on civil society to the exclusion of 'the exercise of power, and the divisions and conflicts that are endemic to capitalist society' (Fine 2001: 191). It is in this respect that social policy and sports development have become conflated in a potent mixture that appeals to those who wish to infer that sport can contribute to the provision of public goods whilst increasing social trust and tolerance.

The rational strain

The democratic strain of social capital is acknowledged by Putnam to be clearly influenced by James Coleman in his formulation of the rational strain of social capital. Coleman mainly considered social capital in relation to the creation of human capital and primarily used the concept to look at education and the related issue of youth in supporting the community. For the rational strain, in following Coleman, 'Social capital is defined by its function. It is not a single entity but a variety of different entities, with two elements in common: they all consist of some aspect of social structures, and they facilitate certain actions of actors' (Coleman 1988: 98).

The rational strain thus views social capital as a functional multi-entity that is defined via the actions of actors in terms of what it does productively. This interpretation has been criticised for its tautological logic which, in failing to separate 'what it is from what it does' (Edwards and Foley 1997), leads to a situation where causes and consequences become confused (Portes 1998). The rational strain, however, is fundamentally concerned with the role of social capital as a concept to facilitate action and, although the definition undoubtedly facilitated the proliferation of processes being labelled social capital (via Putnam), it is not fair to blame Coleman for this. Coleman, unlike Putnam and those of the democratic strain, only used the concept to examine one aspect of social relations, and separating it from the role it plays in his broader work is a misuse of his version of the concept.

The rational strain is situated first and foremost within Coleman's broad theoretical project to balance economic and social theories with his concern for action. In this respect the rational strain encompasses social capital within a broader conceptual framework as part of a theory that attempts to combine the economic and social streams in much of Coleman's work (1987, 1988, 1994). Whilst for Ostrom (1999), also operating within the rational strain, social capital is used as part of a second-generation collective action theory. The rational strain encompasses a problematising of the sociological stream: an absence of an 'engine of action' resulted in an over-socialised view; and of the economic stream: the overstating of the role of the individual 'flies in the face of empirical reality' (Coleman 1988: 96). Generally the sociological stream emphasises structure and the economic stream highlights agency, and Coleman sought to synthesise the two streams and use the notion of social capital to assist in this process. In this regard his aim was to 'import the economists' principle of rational action for use in the analysis of social systems proper, including but not limited to economic systems, and to do so without discarding social organisation in the process. The concept of social capital is a tool to aid in this' (Coleman 1988: 97). For Coleman social capital plays a vital role in what is in essence a modified theory of rational choice that takes into account the wider social environment of the individual.

The rational strain of social capital is therefore relational and inheres in the relationships and the interactions of individuals and infers that individuals approach their connectedness with the view to 'maximising their utility' (Coleman 1988). Social capital is also considered to be context dependent, in that what constitutes social capital in one situation may not in another, and this follows both spatially and temporally, which Coleman refers to as its 'limited fungibility' (1988). In this regard social and public 'goods' are created by individuals pursuing their own rational desires (their self-interest) in a socially relational context. Importantly within the rational strain there is a recognition that individuals may have differential access to 'resources', which tends to operate at a subconscious level and hence social capital does not tend to be distributed evenly either.

Coleman identifies six ways that types of social relations can 'constitute useful [social] capital resources for individuals' (1994: 306). These are obligations and expectations, information potential, norms and effective sanctions, authority relations, approachable social organisation and intentional organisation. All of these relational types represent the possibility of action within a framework within which trust and trustworthiness are created (Coleman 1988). To this extent the rational strain relies on context: to establish reciprocity that elicits obligations or 'credit slips' (Coleman 1988: 102), to ensure reliability of information and to maintain norms and effective sanctions that exist to facilitate a generalised environment of trust and help to prevent what could be a Hobbesian free-for-all (Coleman 1987). A further key element to the rational strain is 'network closure' (Coleman 1988, 1994), which refers to the reinforcing of social norms via the social structure. Closure operates from dyads and triads upwards to large, complex societies and acts as a way of sanctioning behaviour via normative processes, thereby reducing potential expenditure costs in the operation of a network. Closure tends to occur where members of a network know, or are known to, each other and are therefore able to influence the behaviour of other members via strong normative effects. In situations such as this the relations between different individuals and institutions become mutually reinforcing and ensure reciprocity (repayment of obligations) and the imposition of sanctions.

With such a strong emphasis on the economic principle of maximising utility guiding individual choice, the essential question facing the rational strain concerns the collective activity that is at the heart of sporting participation. It is overly simplistic to argue that individuals coming together for the sake of sport do so first and foremost because of a desire to express their self-interest. Indeed the rational strain imposes a strong social structural understanding to the context of any social capital so that theoretically any social capital is embedded in relations and therefore the social structural context of those relations is important. In this respect Coleman's argument that social capital has limited fungibility is played out in particular circumstances that highlight how social capital that might facilitate actions in one particular context may be useless or harmful in another (Coleman 1990).

Although Coleman is not fully convinced of the potential for voluntary associations to offer the same possibility for social capital as 'primordial' institutions such as the family (1994), he does acknowledge that associations may be social capital for those who can invest in them. In other words the rational strain implicitly accepts that sports participation may be exclusionary as much as it is inclusive, given that for those who have access to particular incidents of sports participation, then what they experience there is social capital.

The critical strain

In similar fashion to Coleman, Bourdieu's conceptualisation of social capital grew out of his concern for education and educational achievement, although for Bourdieu other forms of capital, notably cultural, economic and symbolic, are fundamental to understanding how social capital operates. Furthermore in dismissing methodological individualism Bourdieu affirms 'the primacy of relations' (1977), imbuing his work with a highly social and historical contextual slant. Bourdieu and Wacquant (1992: 119) define social capital as 'the sum of the resources, actual or virtual, that accrue to an individual or a group by virtue of possessing a durable network of more or less institutionalised relationships of mutual acquaintance and recognition'. Thus for Bourdieu social capital is used to benefit either an individual or a group and as such does not provide for the public benefit per se, but rather is linked to how particular agents use social capital to exploit the other forms of capital in their possession. In essence, social capital in this context creates the milieu within which one is able to operate successfully, in terms of activating and realising one's economic and cultural capital.

Bourdieu (1977) saw capital as the key structural determinant in any given society at any given time, with agents operating in 'fields', utilising 'strategies' within wider 'practices' that relate to a specific 'habitus'. Indeed the concepts of habitus and field are important elements in Bourdieu's work. Habitus essentially refers to a process of socialisation that moulds an individual's world-view and forms a subconscious group identity. Bourdieu wrote thus: 'The structures constitutive of a particular type of environment (e.g. the material conditions of existence characteristic of a class condition) produce *habitus*, systems of durable, transposable *dispositions*, structured structures predisposed to function as structuring structures' [original emphasis] (Bourdieu 1977: 72).

Structures can therefore help transmit the disposition of the group to individuals, with factors such as taste and general perception being rooted in an individual's cultural background. According to Bourdieu individuals can also identify those with similar dispositions such that habitus 'is both the generative principle of objectively classifiable judgements and the system of classification ... of these practices' (Bourdieu 1984: 170). Thus habitus presents itself as 'a life-condition' that has a particular structural position within a system that Bourdieu referred to as a 'field'. For Bourdieu, a field is

> a network, or configuration, of objective relations between positions objectively defined, in their existence and in the determinations they impose upon their occupants, agents or institutions, by their present and potential situation ... in the structure of the distribution of power (or capital) whose possession commands access to the specific profits that are at stake in the field, as well as by their objective relation to other positions.
>
> *(Quoted in Jenkins 2002: 85)*

These networks are vital for social capital transmission and aid group identity, particularly as membership of a group, according to Bourdieu, allows an individual to accrue social capital resources. For voluntary sports clubs (VSCs) these concepts have some important ramifications, which will be explored in more detail later, suffice to say that fields are the networks that foster collective assets, and the occupants of those fields share habitus, which reinforces the group's identity. These concepts are relevant to understanding Bourdieu's approach to capital insofar as 'the structure of the distribution of the different types and subtypes of capital at a given moment in time represents the immanent structure of the world' (Bourdieu 1997: 46). Moreover one's relationship to, and possession of, forms of economic, cultural and social capital determines one's social world and one's relationship with other social worlds. For Bourdieu, while all capital stems from, but is not reducible to, the economic, it is the disguised aspect of cultural capital that makes its benefits all the more undetectable and less penalised. In this respect Bourdieu refers to the transmission of cultural capital as 'the best hidden form of hereditary transmission of capital' (Bourdieu 1997: 246).

Thus implicit in Bourdieu's use of social capital is his rejection of economism and acknowledgement that social capital is a disguised and transformed form of economic capital that is 'never entirely reducible to that definition' (the more transparent a form of capital, the easier its conversion to economic capital in the ultimate equation) (Bourdieu 1997: 246). Furthermore 'Acknowledging that capital can take a variety of forms is indispensable to explaining the structure and dynamics of differentiated societies' (Bourdieu and Wacquant 1992: 119). In this sense, capital, for Bourdieu, is a social construct mainly identified through its meanings to the parties involved and also through its effects and those that are privy to them. It is therefore not individual utility maximisation that constructs the social and economic worlds inhabited by individuals; rather, it is their differential access to capital that is the key driving and determining force (Foley and Edwards 1999). According to Bourdieu therefore, power is inescapably linked to the notion of having and using social capital, a quite different approach to the more benign approaches to social capital discussed thus far. Power is exercised by individuals operating to reproduce their social position, and social capital functions in a transmutative fashion to reinforce one's symbolic and hence cultural capital. This corresponds with Bourdieu's concern for the reflective status that cultural capital confers on those who possess and are knowledgeable about this form of capital.

Sports development and the intentional creation of social capital

In considering the level of articulation between policy frameworks and aspects of social policy implementation this chapter now goes on to explore the extent to which governments (focusing on the UK in particular) hold, or have held, expectations (i.e. strategic policy applications) concerning the capacity of sport to contribute to the formation of social capital. It is clear that the propensity for sport to be organised, and participated in, within VSCs, tends to be viewed as an aspect of civil society. The apparent social fact that it occupies a large portion of volunteer activity has provided the key context for the sports development/social capital nexus (Taylor *et al.* 2003; Adams and Deane 2009). Indeed the context for the New Labour government (1997–2010) position was set out by Tony Blair when he argued that 'social capital matters too [as well as human capital] the capacity to get things done, to cooperate, the magic ingredient that makes all the difference. Too often in the past government programmes damaged social capital ... In the future we need to invest in social capital as surely as we invest in skills and buildings' (Blair 1999). For policy makers this stance signified an appreciation not only that 'relationships matter' but that government can and should have a place in facilitating social capital through appropriate investment. This became cemented within government circles with the publication of a Strategy Unit discussion paper that identified 'economic efficiency, equity and civic or political arguments for government intervention to promote the accumulation of beneficial kinds of social capital' (Aldridge *et al.* 2002: 7). For Blair and New Labour, and within an overarching communitarian orientated Third Way, these arguments for social capital creation had a distinct resonance within the policy articulated for sports development (DCMS 2000; DCMS 2002; Sport England 2008). In the main this was due to the heavy emphasis on volunteering in providing sporting activity and opportunities for participation. Thus the promotion of sports participation, predicated on the reinvigoration of the voluntary and community sector (VCS), is fundamentally tied to re-establishing the active citizen as a precursor to the active community (Marinetto 2003). In this sense the aim of government is to expand the capacity of the sports VCS to provide services to and for their citizenry, where volunteering and volunteerism become central to the development of the necessary social capital.

Whilst not the focus of this chapter, the context for sports development provided by modernisation is fundamental in making sense of how social capital has become interwoven within sports policy aimed at such basic outcomes as increased participation. Suffice at this juncture to note that modernisation may be both a process and an outcome, necessitating the constant examination and alteration of social practices in light of incoming information about those practices. Thus social practice and activity is constantly reviewed, which politically has ensured that New Labour's Third Way principles (rights and responsibilities – Fairclough 2006) established a "" … team" a "community" of some sort to be the body that both experiences and undertakes modernisation' (Finlayson 2003: 96). As a context for social capital formation modernisation of the sports sector reflects the 'high political salience of sport and physical activity programmes' as well as having the dual purpose of 'a grand project of national renewal' and the effective delivery of objectives associated with grass-roots sports programmes (Houlihan and Green 2009).

Interpreting social capital and sports development at local government level

Much of the translation of social regeneration, modernisation and the formation of social capital at the local level which has focused on encouraging VSCs to become part of what Sport England has referred to as the sport delivery system (Sport England 2007). In this respect an acceptance of managerialist tendencies inherent in central government corporatism required an adaptation to new strategic and structural realities which for one Chief Leisure Officer meant (Interview 7, 21st November 2006) that 'those clubs that are progressive and are going to embrace change and do things in a way that the Government, Sport England and the local authorities want them to do, they are going to be the clubs that are going to thrive'. In essence the trajectory follows the dominant social capital policy structure of the democratic strain in ensuring network and relationship expansion on the assumption that social level benefits would inevitably follow. Indeed the language of the majority of interviewees (Adams 2009) indicated that notions of 'forward thinking' and 'being proactive', 'development minded' and 'enlightened' were vital to the sports development process enabling VSCs to be both open to, and working with a variety of agencies and organisations, in partnership arrangements to develop the activities of a particular club. Partnership working is an explicit realisation of the multiagency ethos. A key mechanism to 'mixed economies of welfare' (Giddens 1998, 2000) and subsequently a given for the realisation of sports policy infused by the democratic strain of social capital. This has at least two consequences important for a consideration of a strategic social capital position: first, VSCs were encouraged to look to external agencies as partnership working becomes critical in the 'mixed economy', so that, as a senior Sport Development Officer stated, 'It will encourage a club to make links with its local authority, sports development unit and all the sports clubs partnerships ... [and] will start to encourage a club to look outwards rather than just being totally internally focused' (Interview 2, 3rd June 2006). Second, support for VSCs becomes a structural necessity in establishing an appropriate 'institutionally thick arena' (Imrie and Raco 2003) within which 'service level agreements' at the national governing body (NGB)/county sport partnership (CSP) level tie VSCs in further to both NGB and CSP strategic aims and objectives. In essence, as an NGB Regional Manager observed, 'The challenge is trying to get clubs to think outside their own structure' (Interview 16, 11th September 2006).

The importance for sports development lies with the apparent entrenching of the enabling role of central and local government within an outsourcing culture that embraces the practices of the corporate world, and which resonates with social capital theory in terms of developing and reinforcing the importance of 'weak ties' (Granovetter 1973) and/or 'bridging capital' (Putnam 2000) as desirable outcomes. This returns us to the problematic notion of the democratic strain's conceptual coherence for, as VSCs are absorbed into policy-delivery frameworks, then tensions arise concerning the perceived positive societal level social capital outcomes as derived from a particular solution to collective action problems. For a Senior Education Officer this misappropriation of VSCs is potentially challenging because 'they [VSCs] don't *serve* necessarily, because the very nature of the voluntary club is a group of people who got together to do tiddlywinks, because they wanted to do tiddlywinks, not because they suddenly woke up one morning and had a road to Damascus experience and thought: We must provide tiddlywinks for this community' (Interview 1, 18th May 2006). From this evidence the rational promotion of those sports development practices at grass-roots level (which may include the aims and objectives of organisations outside the VSC) does not necessarily take into account the mutual-aid nature of VSCs. The upshot for the potential to develop the democratic strain of social capital that acts as the social 'WD40' facilitating democratic 'mores' (Putnam 2000) and structures becomes circumscribed by the very nature of those individuals who come together within a VSC.

A politically useable resource?

The apparent abandonment of the arms-length principle by New Labour (Oakley and Green 2001) in the practice of sports development has ensured that social capital outcomes have been interwoven into countywide structures both at a formal and informal level. Indeed the notion of quality of life can be seen to be a further 'politically useable resource' (Allison 1986) which, in addition to health, social order and local and national prestige, is both indicative of governmental welfaristic leanings and a rationale for greater state interest and involvement in sport provision and the outcomes of sports participation. Although quality of life may be considered a somewhat vague and imprecise interpretation or measure of a variety of policy outcomes it has a resonance with both social capital and what has been referred to as 'atomised citizenship' (see for example Pattie *et al.* 2004). Atomised citizenship essentially results from an over-individualised and de-socialised approach to social policy outcomes, essentially where individuals anticipate the benefits of policy without active participation or acceptance of the implications or outcomes of particular policies. In this respect quality of life is as much about counteracting such atomised citizenship as it is a key tactic implicit in the development of norms and values that cohere within and amongst communities. The democratic strain of social capital predicated on voluntary activity is a key factor in establishing such normative connectivity, which the Leader of the County Council identified in commenting that 'our social policy is that the County Council take the view that by supporting voluntary sports clubs or voluntary activity anyway is good for the quality of life for the County, across all disciplines' (Interview 26, 15th May 2007).

Clearly the role of sport in developing one's perceived quality of life is not a new phenomenon; 'sport for all' in the 1970s was not only an attempt to ameliorate the problems in people's lives but moreover a continuation of the dominant welfarism and Keynesian approach to social policy through sport (Houlihan and White 2002). Similar echoes can be heard in the clear articulation, found within *Game Plan*, where the ability of sports organisations to access government funding depended on their willingness to address broad social 'problems' such as obesity levels, crime reduction and social cohesion. *Game Plan* addressed these issues in more managerial and neo-liberal terminology and drew attention to the potential for inefficiency within VSCs, stating that 'voluntary provision might be inadequate in some way', requiring government intervention to increase 'social welfare' as a strategic outcome (DCMS/Strategy Unit 2002: 76). Indeed, as Green (2004) has argued, the relationship between sport and social outcomes is both 'symbiotic and overtly instrumental', and has precipitated a form of 'new localism' (Stoker 2006) in sports development structures, not least in the reinvigoration of South East regional offices, but also Regional Sports Boards, County Sports Partnerships, and more recently Community Sports Networks

The embeddedness of this symbiosis is apparent in the expectation that local authorities will develop a range of strategies, from the local sport and recreation to the cultural, that are clearly driven by modernising reforms (Cabinet Office 1999) and more particularly by the target-orientated structure within which effective sports development is increasingly judged. Within one English county council's Cultural Strategy, culture is identified as being 'instrumental in achieving or contributing to the achievement of the wider objectives of a local authority' (County Council 2003: 3), with sport being cited as being of value for health and community safety. Fundamental here is the acceptance of social-facing or democratic social capital as an outcome of essentially individually driven activity. Moreover, the capacity of sport to contribute to the development of this particular strand of social capital is evident by the common association of the value of sport with achieving social objectives. For the County Council Leader this meant meeting particular social policy outcomes 'we are charged by government with the wellbeing of the people of [the County] and by wellbeing is meant moving towards prevention rather than the cure ... and in all of this sports as part of our culture, sports play a *very very* important role' (Interview 26, 15th May 2007).

It is not surprising that sports development is viewed primarily in social policy terms, reflecting the 'core policy paradigms' of New Labour: namely pragmatism, community and 'third way' politics (Houlihan and White 2002). Furthermore, these core policy paradigms in defining New Labour also tailor particular policy strands which, in invigorating particular policy networks, have also incorporated the moral inflationism that is at the centre of the democratic strain of social capital's moral and normative outlook. The outcome is that core issues such as modernisation, the mixed economy of welfare and social inclusion have become wrapped up in the promulgation of social capital through a reinvigorated civil society and in particular an attempt to reconnect citizens to each other and to their particular communities primarily via the voluntary associationalism of sports clubs. According to one senior Regional Sports Board member 'as a club ... you have got a role to play in your community ... what are you doing about improving children's' health, getting kids off the streets and not committing crimes ... getting kids involved in sport doing something positive with their lives ... ' (Interview 5, 5th July 2006). This comment was typical of the moral inflationism surrounding sport, which casts VSCs in a particularly virtuous light. The increasing acceptance of VSCs into the architecture of delivering sports development objectives is thus apparently legitimated on the basis of accepting the arguments of the democratic strain that they are engines of forming social capital and that VSCs are not just vital for the members of those clubs, but also vital to the quality of life of any particular community.

Conclusion

This chapter has reviewed the three key strains of social capital theory and examined the intersection between sports development and the policy context that has provided the impetus for policy makers to identify social capital formation as a key rationale for the promotion of sports participation at grass-roots level. The policy debate regarding sports development has been dominated by the democratic strain of social capital, although this review has argued that the democratic strain of social capital is conceptually weak and methodologically flawed. The empirical evidence that has been presented suggests that stakeholders have a clear strategic orientation to social capital outcomes, which at the policy level has tended to be manifested in notions of quality of life. Indeed, the linking of VSCs with this metaphor indicates that the democratic strain is not only accepted but undergoes a form of local level translation (Skille 2008), which has implications for the utilitarian value of VSCs as the major providers of sporting opportunities within a modernised delivery framework.

The evidence also lends a counterpoint to the suggestion that policy-led interventions aimed at creating social capital will tend to fail (Coalter 2007b) given that the emphasis placed upon VSCs by stakeholders is not in the sport-specific development 'of' sport mould, but is more to do with fostering the associated norms and values that are presumed to come with VSC participation. In other words senior stakeholders tended to view the associational value of the VSC in line with policy expectations in terms of recreating Tocquevillean 'mores'. In this respect the mere fact of promoting participation within and through VSCs facilitates the policy recognition of the VSC as more than just a sports organisation. Rather, the VSC is positioned as a communal source of generalised trust and social norms that potentially give rise to mutual obligations and cooperative action. The point here is that the perception of the VSC is relocated, in policy-orientated terms, from autonomous to 'manufactured' civil society (Hodgson 2004) enabling the by-products of associational engagement to be deliberately sought. In this respect the formation of social capital may be deliberately or knowingly sought as a deferred or sequential policy output.

It is clear from this review that the democratic strain of social capital, notwithstanding allusions to a number of conceptual approaches, which include collective action theories, new institutionalism and human capital, does not exhibit the conceptual depth of either the rational or the critical strain. It is also clear that, whilst not explicit in most areas of policy generation and implementation, social capital has become absorbed within policy discourses and subsequently has had an implicit, almost covert effect in the construction and implementation of sports development policy. Furthermore, because the democratic strain of social capital is really the only one to go down the route of externalising the outcomes of individual networks to the societal level, the importance of parsimony and conceptual coherence is paramount. Without wishing to labour this argument, the lack of conceptual coherence within the democratic strain gives rise to some obvious tautologies that have important ramifications for much sports development that is predicated on the existence of VSCs.

References

Adams, A. (2008). Building organisational/management capacity for the delivery of sports development. In V. Girginov (Ed.), *Management of Sports Development*, Oxford: Butterworth-Heinemann.

——(2009). *Social Capital and Voluntary Sports Clubs: Investigating political contexts and policy frameworks*. Unpublished PhD thesis, Loughborough.

Adams, A. and Deane, J. (2009). Exploring formal and informal dimensions of sports volunteering in England. *European Sport Management Quarterly*, 9 (2): 119–40.

Aldridge, S., Halpern, D. and Fitzpatrick, S. (2002). *Social Capital: A Discussion Paper*. London: Performance and Innovation Unit.

Allison, L. (1986). *The Politics of Sport*. Manchester: Manchester University Press.

Almond, G. and Verba, S. (1963). *The Civic Culture*. Princeton: Princeton University Press.

Arrow, K. (1999). Observations on Social Capital. In P. Dasgupta and I. Serageldin (Eds), *Social Capital: A multifaceted perspective*. Washington DC: The World Bank.

Blair, T. (1996). *New Britain: My vision of a young country*. London: Fourth Estate.

——(1998). *The Third Way: New politics for the new century*. London: Fabian Society.

——(1999). *Keynote Speech to NCVO Annual Conference*. London: NCVO.

Bourdieu, P. (1977). *Outline of a Theory of Practice (Trans Richard Nice)*. Cambridge: Cambridge University Press.

——(1984). *Distinction: A social critique of the judgement of taste*. London: Routledge.

——(1997). The forms of capital. In A. Halsey, H. Lauder, P. Brown and A. Stuart-Wells (Eds), *Education: Culture, economy and society*. Oxford: OUP.

Bourdieu, P. and Wacquant, L. (1992). *An Invitation to Reflexive Sociology*. Chicago: University of Chicago Press.

Bradbury, S. and Kay, T. (2008). Stepping into community? The impact of youth sport volunteering on young people's social capital. In M. Nicholson and R. Hoye, *Sport and Social Capital*. Oxford: Butterworth-Heinemann.

Cabinet Office (1999). *'Modernising government', Cm. 4310*. London: The Stationery Office.

Canadian Policy Research Initiative (2005). Social capital as a public policy tool, available at http://policyresearch.gc.ca/doclib/PR_SC_SocialPolicy_200509_e.pdf

Coalter, F. (2007a). *A Wider Social Role for Sport: Who's keeping the score*. London: Routledge.

——(2007b). Sports clubs, social capital and social regeneration: 'ill-defined interventions with hard to follow outcomes'? *Sport in Society*, 10 (4): 537–59.

Coleman, J. S. (1987). Norms as social capital. In G. A. Radnitzky and P. Bernholz (Eds), *Economic Imperialism: The economic method applied outside the field of economics*. New York: Paragon House.

——(1988). Social capital in the creation of human capital. *American Journal of Sociology*, 94 (Supplement): S95–120.

Coleman, J. (1990). *Equality and Achievement in Education*. Boulder, CO: Westview Press.

——(1994). *Foundations of Social Theory*. Cambridge, MA: Belknap Press.

De Tocqueville, A. (2003). *Democracy in America and Two Essays on America (Trans: Gerald, E, Bevan)*. London: Penguin.

Department for Culture Media and Sport (2000). *A Sporting Future for All*. London: DCMS.

Department for Culture Media and Sport/Strategy Unit (2002). *Game Plan: A strategy for delivering the government's sport and physical activity objectives*. London: DCMS.

Donnelly, P. and Kidd, B. (2003). 'Realising the Expectations: Youth, character, and community in Canadian sport'. *The sport we want: Essays on current issues in community sport*. Ottawa: Canadian centre for ethics in sport.

Edwards, B. and Foley, M. (1997). Social capital and the political economy of our discontent. *American Behavioural Scientist*, 40 (5): 669–78.

Fairclough, N. (2006). Tony Blair and the language of politics. *Open Democracy* downloaded 2.5.2007, available at www.opendemocracy.net/articles/ViewPopUpArticle.jsp?id=3& articleId=4205

Farr, J. (2004). Social capital: A conceptual history. *Political Theory*, 32 (1): 6–33.

Field, J. (2003). *Social Capital*. London: Routledge.

Fine, B. (1999). The developmental state is dead – long live social capital. *Development and Change*, 36: 1–19.

——(2001). *Social Capital versus Social Theory*. London: Routledge.

Finlayson, A. (2003). *Making Sense of New Labour*. London: Lawrence and Wishart.

Foley, M. and Edwards, B. (1996). The paradox of civil society. *Journal of Democracy*, 7 (3).

——(1998). 'Beyond Tocqueville: Civil society and social capital in comparative perspective'. *The American Behavioural Scientist*, 42 (1): 5–20.

——(1999). 'Is it time to disinvest in social capital?' *Journal of Public Policy*, 19 (2): 141–73.

Giddens, A. (1998). *The Third Way: The renewal of social democracy*. Cambridge: Polity Press.

——(2000). *The Third Way and its Critics*. Cambridge: Polity Press.

Granovetter, M. S. (1973). The strength of weak ties. *American Journal of Sociology*, 78 (6): 1360–80.

Green, M. (2004). Changing policy priorities for sport in England: The emergence of elite sport development as a key policy concern. *Leisure Studies*, 23 (4): 365–85.

——(2007). Governing under advanced liberalism: Sport policy and the social investment state. *Policy Sciences*, 40 (1): 55–71.

Grix, J. (2001). Social capital as a concept in the social sciences: The state of the debate. *Democratisation*, 8 (3): 189–210.

——(2002). Introducing students to the generic terminology of social research. *Politics*, 22 (3): 175–86.

Halfpenny, P. and Reid, M. (2002). Research on the voluntary sector: An overview. *Policy and Politics*, 30 (4): 533–50.

Halpern, D. (2005). *Social Capital*. Cambridge: Polity Press.

Hampshire County Council. (2003). *Enjoying Hampshire: Hampshire's Cultural Strategy*. Winchester: Hampshire County Council.

Hodgson, L. (2004). Manufactured civil society: Counting the cost. *Critical Social Policy*, 24 (2): 139–64.

Houlihan, B. and Green, M. (2009). Modernization and sport: The reform of Sport England and UK Sport. *Public Administration*, 87 (3): 678–98.

Houlihan, B. and White, A. (2002). *The Politics of Sport Development: Development of sport or development through sport*. London: Routledge.

Imrie, R. and Raco, M. (2003). Community and the changing nature of urban policy. In R. Imrie and M. Raco (Eds), *Urban Renaissance? New Labour, community and urban policy*. Bristol: Policy Press.

Jenkins, R. (2002) (2nd edn). *Pierre Bourdieu*. London: Routledge.

Johnston, G. and Percy-Smith, J. (2003). In search of social capital. *Policy and Politics*, 31 (3): 321–34.

Leadbeater, C. (1997). *The Rise of the Social Entrepreneur*. London: Demos.

Lemann, N. (1996). Kicking in groups. *The Atlantic Monthly*, 277 (4): 22–26.

Levitas, R. (2000). Community, utopia and New Labour. *Local Economy*, 15 (3): 188–97.

Lewandowski, J. D. (2006). Capitalizing sociability: Rethinking the theory of social capital. In R. Edwards, J. Franklin and J. Holland (Eds), *Assessing Social Capital: Concepts, policy and practice*. Newcastle: Cambridge Scholars Publishing.

Lister, R. (2004). The Third Way's social investment state. In J. Lewis and R. Surrender (Eds), *Oxford Welfare State Change: Towards a third way?* Oxford: Oxford University Press.

Long, J. (2008). Researching and evaluating sport development. In K. Hylton and P. Bramham, (Eds), *Sports Development: Policy, process and practice* (second edition). London: Routledge.

Maloney, W., Smith, G. and Stoker, G. (2000). Social capital and associational life. In S. Baron, J. Field and T. Schuller (Eds), *Social Capital: Critical perspectives*. Oxford: OUP.

Marinetto, M. (2003). Who wants to be an active citizen? The politics and practice of community involvement. *Sociology*, 37 (1): 103–20.

Misztal, B. (2000). *Informality: Social theory and contemporary practice*. London: Routledge.

Newton, K. (1999). Social capital and democracy in modern Europe. In J. W. Van Deth, M. Maraffis, K. Newton, and P. F. Whiteley (Eds), *Social Capital and European Democracy*. London: Routledge.

Oakley, B. and Green, M. (2001). Still playing the game at arms length? The selective re-investment in British Sport 1995-2000. *Managing Leisure*, 6: 74–94.

Organisation for Economic Cooperation and Development (2001). *The Well Being of Nations: The role of human and social capital*. Paris: OECD.

Ostrom, E. (1999). Social capital: A fad or a fundamental concept? In P. Dasgupta and I. Serageldin (Eds), *Social Capital: A multifaceted perspective*. Washington DC: The World Bank.

Pattie, C., Seyd, P. and Whiteley, P. (2004). *Citizenship in Britain: Values, participation and democracy*. Cambridge: Cambridge University Press.

Perks, T. (2007). Does sport foster social capital? The contribution of sport to a lifestyle of community participation. *Sociology of Sport Journal*, 24: 378–401.

Portes, A. (1998). Social capital: its origins and applications in modern sociology. *Annual Review of Sociology*, 24: 1–24.

Putnam, R. (1993). *Making Democracy Work: Civic traditions in modern Italy*. Princeton: Princeton University Press.

——(1995). Tuning in, tuning out: The strange disappearance of social capital in America. Political Science and Politics. The 1995 Ithiel de Sola Pool Lecture: 664–83.

——(1996). The strange disappearance of civic America. *The American Prospect*.

——(2000). *Bowling Alone: The collapse and revival of American community*. New York: Simon & Schuster.

Rowe, N. (2005). Keynote paper. *How many people participate in sport? The politics, practice and realities of measurement – the English experience*. International Association for Sports Information, Beijing Sport University.

Sharpe, E. (2006). Resources at the grassroots of recreation: Organisational capacity and quality of experience in a community sport organisation. *Leisure Sciences*, 28: 385–401.

Skille, E. A. (2008) Understanding sport clubs and sport policy implementers: A theoretical framework for the analysis of the implementation of central sport policy through local and voluntary sport organizations. *International Review for the Sociology of Sport*, 43 (2): 181–200.

Sport England (2007). *Sport England Policy Statement: The delivery system for sport in England*. London: Sport England.

——(2008). *Sport England Strategy 2008–2011*. London: Sport England.

Stoker, G. (2006). *Why Politics Matters: Making democracy work*. Basingstoke: Palgrave.

Strategy Unit (2002). *Social Capital: A discussion paper*. London: Cabinet Office.

Tarrow, S. (1998). *Power in Movement: Social movements and contentious politics* (Second Edition). Cambridge: Cambridge University Press.

Taylor, P., Nichols, G., Holmes, K., James, M., Gratton, C., Garret, R., Kokolakadikis, T., Mulder, C. and King, L. (2003). *Sports Volunteering in England 2002*. London: Sport England.

Weitzman, E. R. and Kawachi, I. (2000). Giving means receiving: The protective effect of social capital on binge drinking on college campuses. *American Journal of Public Health*, 90 (12): 1936–9.

Woolcock, M. (2001). The place of social capital in understanding social and economic outcomes. *Isuma: Canadian Journal of Policy Research*, 2 (1): 1–17.

7

Sports development and disability

Andy Smith and David Haycock

Over the last 30 years or so the promotion and development of sport, together with the increasing use of sport and physical activities as vehicles of social policy designed to achieve a range of other non-sport objectives, have become common features of government sports policy and sports development-related activity in many countries. This tendency has been strongly associated with the parallel tendency for government and other state agencies to become increasingly interventionist in setting the sports policy agenda and, hence, the sports development work that emerges from it. Although the steady increase in government and state involvement in sport has, to an extent at least, been accompanied by a comparable growth in analyses of that involvement and the changing nature of sports development activity more generally, little attempt has been made to examine the provision, development and co-ordination of sporting opportunities for one key target group of sports development professionals: disabled people. The objective of this chapter, therefore, is to begin to address this deficiency by examining some of the key issues associated with disability sports development. In particular, we shall consider how disability and the experience of impairment have been defined and explained before reflecting upon how this has come to inform the emergence and development of disability sport in Britain. Having considered the trend towards the mainstreaming of disability sport in the period since the 1990s, the chapter briefly examines the practice of disability sports development in local authorities in England and Wales. The chapter concludes with a review of the issues that are raised by our analysis and reflects upon the extent to which disability sport may be integrated into wider sports policy and development activity in the future.

Models and explanations of disability

As Thomas and Smith (2009) have noted, in order to understand something about the complex relationships that exist between modern sport, disability and society it is useful to have some appreciation of various theoretical explanations of disability. In the context of sports development, this is important because the ways in which disabled people have been treated historically by other members of the wider society, as well as how disability and the closely related concept of impairment have been conceptualized, are vital prerequisites for understanding how disability sports development has emerged and currently exists in practice (Thomas 2008; Thomas and Smith 2009).

It is generally accepted that definitions of disability can be grouped into two broad categories: medical or social. The medical model or personal tragedy theory presents disability as the consequence of an impairment that is owned by an individual and that results in a loss or limitation of function or some other 'defect' (Barnes and Mercer 2003; Oliver 1990). This individualized view of disability came increasingly to inform much social and welfare policy, particularly during the post-1945 period, and was strongly associated with the growing power of the medical profession and other practitioners (e.g. educational psychologists) to define disability as a medical problem believed to be located within the individual that can only be 'cured' through medical intervention and rehabilitative therapy.

The traditional view of disability began to be widely criticized from the late 1960s by several political campaigns led by the disabled people's movement across Europe and North America who argued that the medical definition of disability focuses exclusively on the personal limitations of disabled people and presents impairment as the sole cause of disability. It was also argued that these medicalized views ignored how perceptions and experiences of disability (and other sources of social division such as gender and social class) are socially constructed and vary over time, and from one society to another (Barnes and Mercer 2003; Barnes *et al.* 1999; Shakespeare and Watson 1997). In this regard, it was argued that a social model or explanation of disability was needed to redirect attention to the need to change the attitudes and actions of people in the wider society towards those considered disabled and specifically to address:

> the impact of social and environmental barriers, such as inaccessible buildings and transport, discriminatory attitudes and negative cultural stereotypes, in 'disabling' people with impairments.
>
> *(Barnes and Mercer 2003: 1)*

Although the social model of disability has been criticized for failing to acknowledge the centrality of impairment and experience of disability to disabled people's lives (Hughes and Paterson 1997; Shakespeare and Watson 1997), the emphasis it places on the socially constructed nature of disability is thought to have helped improve and enabled disabled people to take greater control over their own lives than they did previously (Barnes and Mercer 2003; Oliver and Barnes 2008). The shift from medical, individualized definitions to more socially constructed explanations of disability that pay greater attention to the social constraints that are believed to 'disable' people is also thought to have helped bring about significant government policy change (Thomas and Smith 2009). Perhaps the most significant policy change in Britain was the Disability Discrimination Act (DDA) that came into force in July 1996 to tackle the discrimination faced by disabled people in society (Barnes and Mercer 2003; Oliver and Barnes 2008). The DDA defined discrimination as:

> treating someone less favourably than someone else, for a reason related to the disabled person's disability – than it treats (or would treat) others to whom that reason does not (or would not) apply; and cannot show that the treatment is justified.
>
> *(HMSO 1995: s,20(1),2.5)*

The DDA focused on employment, the provision of goods, facilities and services and the management of land and property, and identified someone as disabled if they 'have a physical or mental impairment which has a substantial and long term adverse effect upon their ability to carry out normal day to day duties' (HMSO 1995 organizations, 19(1),(a)5). The Act also stated that it was unlawful for a service provider (including sports development providers) to discriminate against a disabled person (with sensory, physical and learning impairments, but not mental illness) 'by refusing to provide (or deliberately not providing) any service which it provides (or is prepared to provide) to its members of the public' (HMSO 1995 organizations, 19 (1),(a)5). Following a series of other amendments since the original Act in 1995, an extended DDA was passed in 2005. The revised DDA, which made it unlawful for private clubs (such as sports clubs with 25 or more members), for example, to exclude disabled people because they have a disability, placed greater emphasis on the responsibility of public bodies (such as Sport England and local authorities) to promote equality of opportunity for disabled people. The revised DDA 2005 also extended the definition of disability to include those who are identified as having a range of mental health problems, are HIV positive, have multiple sclerosis, and cancers of various kinds. It is important to note, however, that, with the exception of those impairments and conditions referred to above, the Act does not stipulate that someone is 'disabled' if they have a specific impairment. Rather someone who is disabled is defined as such when there is a longlasting (meaning lasting, or likely to last longer than 12 months) impact on normal day-to-day activities (which include eating, washing, walking and going shopping), and when these affect one of the various personal 'capacities' cited in the Act (e.g. mobility, manual dexterity, speech, hearing, sight and memory).

While within a sporting context every person who is identified as 'disabled' under the DDA can, in theory, be included within sport, this is by no means guaranteed because there may be few opportunities or pathways for those with specific impairments or conditions to participate in sport whether at the mass participation or higher levels of the sports development continuum. Indeed, for reasons we shall explain later, the provision and co-ordination of mass sporting opportunities for anyone who identifies themselves as being disabled according to the DDA is largely the responsibility of the Home Nations Disability Sport Organizations (English Federation of Disability Sport [EFDS], Federation of Disability Sport Wales [FDSW], Scottish Disability Sport [SDS], and Disability Sport Northern Ireland [DSNI]). Provision, especially towards elite levels of sports participation, is constrained by the existence of impairment-specific, segregated, sports development pathways that are provided by the International Disability Sport Organization (IDSO) or the International Paralympic Committee (IPC). The Deaflympics, for example, are organized separately for those who are deaf or hard of hearing, the Paralympics are provided for elite athletes who are blind/visually impaired, or have a physical impairment (e.g. amputee, cerebral palsy, wheelchair user), and elite sport opportunities are provided for those with learning disabilities by the International Sports Federation for Persons with an Intellectual Disability (INAS-FID). Thus, whilst disabled people may be defined as disabled under the conditions of the DDA and may be able to participate in sport at recreational levels, they may not be able to participate at higher levels of disability sport within a particular sport because a sporting pathway does not exist (e.g. a person with a mental health problem may play boccia recreationally in a club environment, but there is no performance pathway for that individual at international level).

The emergence and development of disability sport

Sports clubs for deaf people are widely acknowledged to be the first formally known contexts in which disabled people engaged in a variety of sports with, alongside or separate from non-disabled people (DePauw 2009; Thomas and Smith 2009). The emergence and development of other modern forms of disability sport can, however, be traced back to Britain, specifically England, during the 1940s when the British Government requested that Sir Ludwig Guttmann (a neurosurgeon) should open the National Spinal Injuries Centre (NSIC) at the Stoke Mandeville Hospital in Aylesbury, England (DePauw 2009; DePauw and Gavron 2005; Thomas and Smith 2009). The NSIC was originally established to provide therapeutic activities that would enhance the physical and psychological well-being of large numbers of soldiers and civilians who had acquired a range of impairments, particularly spinal cord injuries (SCIs), during the Second World War (Guttmann 1976). Despite this initial rationale, physically disabled people were subsequently encouraged to engage in sport to promote their rehabilitation back into civilian life. It was on the basis of these supposed benefits of sport that Guttmann and his fellow hospital workers developed opportunities for disabled people to participate in more organized and competitive sports at the recreational and elite levels. Perhaps the most significant contribution made by Guttmann, and the International Stoke Mandeville Games Federation (ISMGF) that he formed, was the inauguration of the Stoke Mandeville Games. The Games were first held in 1948 and were one of the first international sports competitions for wheelchair athletes in England. Sports clubs and hospitals were invited to attend Stoke Mandeville that year, to coincide with the opening of the Olympic Games being held in London (Thomas 2008; Thomas and Smith 2009).

Following the perceived success of the Games, the British Paraplegic Sports Society (BPSS) – which later became the British Wheelchair Sports Foundation – was established in 1948 to provide regular training and competitive opportunities initially for those with SCI, and later for wheelchair users, to participate in sport. Since the scope of the activities of the BPSS was rather limited, the British Sports Association for the Disabled (BSAD) was inaugurated by Guttmann and colleagues in 1961. The BSAD became the recognized national body with responsibility for providing, developing and co-ordinating sport and recreation opportunities for those disabled people with impairments (but especially those with SCI) not catered for by the BPSS. During its early years the BSAD developed a network of clubs and regional associations with full-time staff to support a regional and national events programme, together with a wide range of training and development initiatives to support local authorities, national governing bodies and schools (Thomas 2008; Thomas and Smith 2009).

By the mid-1980s the BSAD came to be recognized as playing a crucial role in the emergence and development of disability sport in England and elsewhere. With support from the Sports Council (a national government agency for sport), the BSAD acted as a governing body on behalf of disability sports organizations (DSOs) and was seen as a successful provider and co-ordinator of a regional club network and comprehensive national events programme catering for athletes with a range of physical and sensory impairment (Minister for Sport Review Group 1989). The dual role of the BSAD was not without criticism, however, for by the late 1980s BSAD was seen as failing to provide either an 'effective unified voice for disability sport or an efficient organisational infrastructure for competition' (Thomas 2008: 214). This perceived failure became more pronounced as a plethora of DSOs (e.g. Cerebral Palsy Sport) were established with a specific remit to improve the range and quality of sporting opportunities for disabled people by acting as providers for, and lobbyists on behalf of, those with particular physical, sensory and learning impairments.

The proliferation of DSOs did not go unnoticed by the Sports Council, which was also becoming increasingly involved in the development of sport policy for disabled people. From the 1970s the Sports Council placed particular emphasis on facility building that was significant in increasing levels of participation among the general population. It was recognized, however, that these reported increases had done little to improve the involvement of under-participating groups such as disabled people. Consequently, during the early 1980s, 'there were clear signs of a shift away from facility provision … to a strategy of concentrating resources on particular sports or sections of the community' (Houlihan and White 2002: 33), which to some extent included disabled people. The Sports Council began delivering a series of projects that epitomized the 'Sport For All' principle that placed local authorities, alongside the emerging DSOs, at the heart of local sports provision for disabled people. More specifically, the Sports Council operationalized its commitment to 'Sport For All' and enhancing participation among low participant groups in the early 1980s with three major initiatives: first, through the *Action Sport* programmes that were developed in 1982; second, in its publication *Sport in the Community: The Next Ten Years* (Sports Council 1982); and third, in some of the National Demonstration Projects (NDPs) launched in 1984 (Sports Council Research Unit 1991). Although the promotion of sports development for disabled people was acknowledged in each of these innovations, it was of marginal interest to the Sports Council, and disability sports development did not form part of its national strategy for the promotion of 'Sport For All', even though it was recognized that failing 'to tackle the needs of [disabled people] would put the Council in breach of its Royal Charter' (Sports Council 1982: 7). Indeed, when policy was developed for disability sport 'this rarely amounted to more than funding other organisations that were pursuing a more innovative and inclusionary vision of "Sport For All"' (Thomas 2008: 214).

The lack of policy focus on the sports participation of disabled people within local authorities in favour of other under-participating groups continued in the Sports Council's (1988) follow-up strategy, *Sport in the Community: Into the 90s*. With the exception of some local authorities such as Northamptonshire, and governing bodies such as the Amateur Rowing Association, who were cited as 'using innovative schemes to promote mass participation opportunities for disabled people' (Thomas 2008: 214), very little attention was paid to the sports development needs of disabled people in government policy. In fact, during the 1980s the promotion of sport for disabled people in local authorities was only really explicitly recognized and promoted in the Minister for Sport's Review Group's report, *Building on Ability*, which summarized the findings of a large and wide-ranging review of the organization and provision of sport for disabled people in Britain (Minister for Sport's Review Group 1989). The Review Group identified that there was considerable variation in the ways in which disability sport was delivered and prioritized within the sports development services offered between local authorities, with some authorities seen as pursuing 'their obligations with diligence, imagination and generosity' while others were doing 'little more than pay lip-service to the needs of disabled people' (Minister for Sport's Review Group 1989: 23). Despite this differential practice, the Review Group emphasized that 'at a local level, the main providers of sporting opportunities are the local authorities, sports clubs, and disability sports clubs such as those affiliated to BSAD' (Minister for Sport's Review Group 1989: 10). Within this context, the Review Group recommended that local authorities and home country sports councils 'should assume responsibility for ensuring the provision and co-ordination of sport for people with disabilities at a local level' (Minister for Sport's Review Group 1989: 10) and that consequently the Sports Council should embed local authority disability sports provision in its future policies and strategies. In the period between the 1960s and 1980s, therefore, local authorities made a significant contribution to the organization and administration of disability sports development, even though this was curtailed somewhat by the introduction of Compulsory Competitive Tendering, the need to control local government spending (Coalter 2007; Houlihan and White 2002), and 'a marked lack of sustained political interest and direction in sport' (Houlihan and White 2002: 52) that continued into the early 1990s.

Mainstreaming disability sports development

As Thomas (2008: 216) has noted, following the publication of *Building on Ability* 'there occurred during the 1990s a gradual policy shift by the Sports Council towards the mainstreaming of disability sport' to which both local authorities and governing bodies of sport were expected to make a contribution. This was reinforced in the various 'Frameworks for Action' published by the Sports Council in which it placed considerably more emphasis on the ways in which the principles of equity should be embedded across all levels of the sports development continuum. In relation to disability sports development, it was recommended that the Sports Council should work with governing bodies and DSOs at a local level to promote participation and equity for disabled people. Although the position statement the Sports Council developed in relation to disabled people did not generate much impact, in its policy statement, *People with Disabilities and Sport*, the Sports Council suggested that sport for disabled people was at a stage where 'having developed its own structures, it [the provision of disability sport] move from a target approach to the mainstream' (Sports Council 1993: 5). In this regard, in keeping with the proposals made in *Building on Ability*, the Sports Council recommended that there should be a gradual shift of responsibility for the organization and provision of disability sports development away from the national DSOs (NDSOs) towards mainstream, sport-specific governing bodies and, at the local level, local authorities. In the process, the Sports Council identified those groups (e.g. NDSOs, facility managers and teachers) whom it considered were, and should be, involved in the policy network of disability sport. Even though it failed to define clearly the roles and responsibilities of those groups, the emphasis that the Sports Council placed on mainstreaming and the expectation that mainstream bodies would take on more responsibility for delivering disability sport provided clear evidence of the ways in which central government was becoming increasingly interventionist in setting the disability sports policy agenda (Thomas and Smith 2009).

In light of the continued concern surrounding the co-ordination and activities of the various agencies involved in disability sports development, together with wider political concern about integration and inclusion, in 1996 the Sports Council convened a National Disability Sport Conference to review the organization and structure of disability sport in England. One outcome of the conference was the establishment of a Task Force to facilitate 'the mainstreaming of disability sport in England by the year 2000' (Sports Council Disability Task Force 1997: 2). The Task Force prepared a series of proposals to meet this objective that were subsequently presented in June 1997 when the Conference was reconvened to receive these recommendations and the results of the consultation exercise. Collins (1997: 3) reported that while there were voices of discontent, the Conference 'marked the first occasion on which a representative national consensus on the future structure and role of disability sport can be seen to have been achieved'. The majority of the participants at the meeting agreed that a new umbrella organization with responsibility for disability sport in England was required to help provide a more secure basis on which to develop more strategic and effective disability sports policy and practice (Thomas and Smith 2009). This organization became known as the English Federation of Disability Sport (EFDS), which was established in 1998 and became the organization recognized by Sport England as the 'umbrella body responsible for coordinating the development of sport and recreation' opportunities provided for disabled people by DSOs and NDSOs (EFDS 2000: 8). In 2005 responsibility for co-ordinating disability sports events in partnership with mainstream governing bodies of sport passed to Disability Sport Events, as the EFDS focused more explicitly on raising awareness of the sporting needs of disabled people among mainstream sports partner organizations such as governing bodies and County Sport Partnerships (Thomas and Smith 2009).

As Thomas and Smith (2009: 43) have noted, the encouragement that Sport England gave to the creation of the EFDS as a separate organization with responsibility for disability sport in England 'was interpreted by some as further evidence of the lip-service it paid – and continues to pay – to disability sport as a central policy concern'. They also point out how, since its formation, the relationship between the EFDS and some NDSOs has been characterized more by conflict than consensus, which has limited the extent to which the EFDS has been able to achieve its formally stated objectives (Thomas and Smith 2009). Notwithstanding the significant contribution that it makes to the provision of disability sport, it also seems that the continued failure of the EFDS and other organizations to provide a clear policy direction for disability sport 'represents something of a missed opportunity to improve the organizational structure of sport for disabled people' (Thomas and Smith 2009: 46). More particularly, although the inauguration of the EFDS marked a significant moment in the maturity of disability sports development, 'it appears to have increased, rather than helped improve, the fragmented, complex and cumbersome nature of the organization of disability sport that has emerged during the course of the last half a century or so' (Thomas and Smith 2009: 46). In light of the organizational complexity that characterizes disability sports development, in the rest of this chapter we shall examine the ways and extent to which local authorities in England and Wales are important contexts for providing, developing and co-ordinating sporting opportunities for disabled people.

Disability sports development in England: the role of local authorities

During the mid-1990s the sports development needs of disabled people in local authorities in Britain was, at best, pushed to the margins of sports development policy – if not in the practices of local authorities – as state involvement in setting the national sports policy agenda began to increase quite substantially (Thomas and Smith 2009). Although the political salience of sports policy and development grew following the replacement of Margaret Thatcher by John Major as leader of the Conservative Party in 1990, and the subsequent election of his Conservative government two years later (Houlihan and White 2002), much sports policy (e.g. *Sport: Raising the Game* [DNH], 1995) under the Conservative Party marginalized considerably the role of local government and made little reference to mass participation ('Sport For All') or to local authorities who are the key vehicles of its promotion (Houlihan and White 2002). The explicit emphasis was not on mass participation or providing sporting opportunities for specific groups such as disabled people, but on the dual policy objectives of enhancing school sport and elite performance, with a more efficient and streamlined structure for the organization of sport also cited as a key priority (DNH 1995; Houlihan and White 2002). The contribution made by local authorities to the provision of sport for disabled people was not surprising given the Conservative government's long-standing antipathy towards local authorities (Houlihan and White 2002). However, as Thomas and Smith (2009: 56) have noted the 'failure to integrate this provision into the wider sport development policy priorities of government may … have come to threaten the extent to which those within disability sport were able to maintain and enhance levels of participation and the quality of disabled people's experiences of sport at local authority level.'

Following the election of the Labour government in 1997, the retained policy emphasis on school and elite sport was accompanied by a renewed commitment to the promotion of 'Sport For All' and to the role of local authorities, who were once again seen as important partners in the delivery of government policy goals in relation to mass participation (DCMS 2000). As part of the 'Third Way' approach to much Labour government policy, and the prevailing tendency for sports policy priorities to shift away from the development of sport and achievement of sport-related goals towards the use of sport to achieve other desired social objectives, local authorities were also seen as being important to the delivery of broader social and welfare policy goals. This is particularly the case in relation to the achievement of greater social inclusion and meeting the needs of those considered vulnerable to social exclusion (such as disabled people) in local communities (DCMS 2000; DCMS/Strategy Unit 2002; Sport England 2008a). In *A Sporting Future for All*, published by the Labour government in 2000, for example, it was claimed that:

> Sport can make a unique contribution to tackling social exclusion in our society ... We fully recognise that this is not something that sport can tackle alone but by working with other agencies we believe it can make a significant contribution.
>
> *(DCMS 2000: 39)*

Social inclusion was a central policy theme that also ran through aspects of *Game Plan*, in which it was also suggested that if sports participation was to increase in the future, especially amongst under-represented groups such as disabled people, then particular attention needed to be placed on enhancing the provision, development and co-ordination of opportunities at the local rather than national levels (DCMS/Strategy Unit 2002). Despite the funds that are available for those working in local authority sports development and the continued emphasis that was placed on the role of local authorities in the provision of sport for disabled people, it was made clear in *Game Plan* that:

> Sport and physical activity are not always seen as a priority at a local level ... As a result, sport and leisure expenditure is often the first to suffer if resources are reduced. A significant proportion of budgets is spent on the management and maintenance of facilities (rather than the strategic development of sport and recreation).
>
> *(DCMS/Strategy Unit 2002: 183)*

While criticism was directed towards the provision of sporting opportunities that are available to all groups, particular criticism was made of the role played by local authorities in enhancing participation amongst under-represented groups such as disabled people (DCMS/Strategy Unit 2002). It was also suggested that, in view of the widespread variation in the level of investment in sport between different local authorities, clearer sporting priorities and objectives that focused on the needs of local communities needed to be established; better strategic planning for sport was required; and practical steps to improve services and bring about a 'joined up' approach to the delivery of sport and physical activity to local residents needed to be undertaken (DCMS/Strategy Unit 2002). More recently, Sport England (2008a: 3) have pointed to the importance that sporting organizations and especially governing bodies should place on working with 'local authorities in order to ensure that sport benefits from being included in [a range of local strategic service plans such as] Local Area Agreements (LAAs), Sustainable Community Strategies, Comprehensive Area Assessments and the Living Places Partnership programme'. In addition, they claim that, together with the benefits of promoting sport for sport's sake among groups such as disabled people, sport 'can make a contribution to many of the shared priorities with local government, local strategic partnerships, and the other local and regional partnership structures' (Sport England 2008a: 3) that have been developed to meet a myriad of political priorities related to the social inclusion agenda.

It is within this emerging policy context that much disability sports development currently operates in local authorities in England. As Thomas and Smith (2009) have noted, however, our understanding of the nature and extent of local authority disability sports provision has been severely hampered by the lack of systematically collected and published data that currently exist in both the academic and professional press. In light of the dearth of available data, Thomas and Smith (2009) conducted case studies of disability sports provision in three local authorities in England. On the basis of their research, they suggested that, despite some similarities, 'there exists differential policy and practice between individual local authorities and that, as a consequence, the sporting experiences and opportunities available to disabled people may vary considerably – perhaps very considerably – from one local authority to another' (Thomas and Smith 2009: 71). As in other areas of sports development work, there was, for example, considerable variety in the range and number of sports clubs and competitions available to disabled people in each authority. In addition, as part of the alleged need to become more 'socially inclusive', some local authorities have established disability sports development plans and policies and established a comprehensive range of programmes designed to co-ordinate and promote opportunities for disabled people to engage in a variety of sports and activities at recreational and more competitive levels. In other local communities, the sports opportunities available for disabled people and the commitment and/or ability of those working in local authorities to organize and promote disability sport have been considerably less developed by comparison (Thomas and Smith 2009).

Having examined the activities and role played by local authorities in the delivery of sporting opportunities for disabled people in England, in the next section we shall examine disability sports provision that currently exists in Wales.

Disability sports development in Wales: the role of local authorities

In September 1997, after the success of the Labour government in the General Election, the Welsh electorate voted via a referendum to create a devolved Welsh Assembly with the power to identify (initially) non-primary legislation and make decisions at local level regarding health, education and local government. Following the referendum, the Welsh Assembly Government (WAG) was formed through the Government of Wales Act 1998 and many of the powers that had previously been held by the Welsh Office and the Secretary of State for Wales were transferred to the more democratically accountable Assembly Members (AMs). Two years earlier, the Sports Council for Wales (SCW), whose role it is to advise the WAG on all sporting matters, published *Willing and Able: The Provision of Sports Opportunities for Children with Disabilities* (SCW 1995). In it the SCW claimed that not only do sports development officers and departments have an important role to play in facilitating formal and informal sports opportunities for disabled children, there were 'huge variations between localities in terms of service delivery' (SCW 1995: 18) and that provision was more dependent on where disabled children lived rather than what they actually needed or wanted in terms of their sports development. Indeed, notwithstanding the inauguration of the Federation of Sports Association for the Disabled (Cymru) (FSAD) in 1990, sports development programmes were still regarded as being reactive to the sporting needs of young people. In *Willing and Able* the SCW also noted that, although the provision of taster days for young disabled people interested in sport were seen as successful, few follow-up activities were available within their local communities and there was a notable lack of continuity and opportunities for them to engage in disability sport outside school (SCW 1995).

In 1998 the SCW framework document, *Young People First*, which was the first strategic plan under the newly devolved government, encouraged organizations to develop their provision of sport and physical activity to young disabled people. The need for the introduction of Disability

Sport Development Officers (DSWDOs) to be funded jointly by Lottery monies and local authorities was also identified and the SCW said that it would:

> review the co-ordination of sporting provision for people with disabilities at local level and fund ... local authority development officers with a focus on the development of sport specific disability clubs.
>
> *(SCW 1998: 9)*

Consequently, a programme intended to develop grass-roots sport for disabled people was established in 1999 as part of a National Lottery-funded partnership between the FSAD, the SCW, and local authority sports development departments. It is claimed that the pro-gramme helped increase the number of sport-based opportunities that were available to disabled people across Wales from 1,200 in 2002 to 320,000 in 2008/9 (House of Commons 2009). In 2004, the FSAD was rebranded and restructured to become the FDSW. The community scheme, now also rebranded as Disability Sport Wales (DSW), currently receives just in excess of £0.5 million National Lottery monies that support the part-time employment of a DSWDO, managed jointly by the FDSW National Development Manager and at local level by the Sports Development Manager/Principle Leisure Officer, within each of the 22 local authorities across Wales.

Since the late 1990s, DSW and DSWDOs have endeavoured to achieve greater consistency in disability sports provision across Wales. FDSW also established a unified National Delivery Plan within which differential variations in sports participation and the sporting needs of dis-abled people in rural and urban Wales are to be addressed by the programmes delivered by DSWDOs. The aim of the DSW programmes is to 'increase the number of people taking part in sport and physical activity by developing quality led community based opportunities throughout Wales' (FDSW 2008: 1). During the first cycle of employment (2000–4), commu-nity officers focused on recruitment, induction and training and were expected to develop *Moving Forward*, the first holistic disability sport strategy for Wales (FSAD 2003). During the second cycle (2005–8) the DSW scheme became more strategic in its objectives and began to be aligned more closely with the key objectives of *Climbing Higher/Dringo'n Uwch* (WAG 2003) in which the WAG outlined its vision for 'an active, healthy and *inclusive* Wales, where sport, physical activity and active recreation provides a common platform for participation, fun and achievement' (WAG 2003: 6 emphasis added). In addition, the DSW scheme continues to provide programmes intended to extend opportunities for disabled people to participate in sport alongside non-disabled people and has since begun to underpin the performer pathway that feeds into national elite sports performance programmes, particularly the pan-disability Academy launched in October 2006. In this regard, the increasingly strategic development of sport-specific activity within the DSWDOs work programmes are intended to make a contribution to the growing – albeit partial and inconsistent – trend towards mainstreaming sports development opportunities for disabled people among sports governing bodies (FDSW 2008).

It is notable, however, that despite the growing professionalization of sports development in Wales and the introduction of DSWDOs with a specific remit of developing, facilitating and co-ordinating sporting opportunities for disabled people in local communities, the role of DSWDOs has remained largely marginalized within some Sports Development Units (FDSW 2008). In some authorities the DSWDO has been identified as the 'expert' in disability sport and is, therefore, responsible for the organization and sometimes delivery of disability sport opportunities, rather than being a facilitator who encourages colleagues to provide inclusive sports events and activities, thus integrating disability sport objectives into wider sports development plans. In this regard, the DSWDO (some of whom are disabled) has been identified as the sole person responsible for the planning, delivering and monitoring of disability sports development activity. The tendency to identify the DSWDO as an 'expert practitioner' in relation to disability sport would appear to legitimize the willingness of sport-specific development officers to delegate responsibility for the co-ordination and delivery of disability sports activity to the DSWDO.

Notwithstanding the differential engagement of DSWDOs in the provision of sport for disabled people in local authorities following the organizational changes that have occurred since the late 1990s, disability sports development in Wales has typically been based on a 'bottom up' model of sports development. This approach and the appointment of 22 DSWDOs based in local authorities appears to have had a degree of success in extending and co-ordinating sporting opportunities and provision for disabled people across all local authorities in Wales. It may also help provide a framework through which national sports policy objectives for disability sport can be met and sustained (FDSW 2008; House of Commons 2009).

Disability sports development: reflections and future directions

Since the 1960s the number, range and kinds of organizations (including local authorities and governing bodies) with a responsibility for delivering disability sports development has increased substantially in a rather complex and ad hoc way. Indeed, although there now exists a wider range of sports that are provided more regularly in a wider variety of contexts for disabled people with a range of impairments, the roles and responsibilities of those involved in the provision of sporting opportunities for disabled people have tended to overlap with those of other organizations (Thomas and Smith 2009). It is also the case that, in some respects, the practice of disability sports development has emerged relatively independently from other innovations in the sports policy and development fields, for disability sport has rarely been the focus of any sustained or clearly defined political and policy commitment in Britain (Thomas 2008; Thomas and Smith 2009). This is certainly the case in some of the more recently released sports policies; for example, only passing reference is being made to the role that governing bodies are expected to play in the promotion of disability sport in *Playing to Win* (DCMS 2008), which was published by the DCMS in 2008, and in Sport England's latest strategy document for community sport (Sport England 2008b). In Wales, however, disability sports development has been integrated more clearly into the new Local Authority Partnership Agreements (LAPAs) that are intended to distribute future funding via the SCW to local authorities to provide them with greater autonomy to deliver disability sport within their communities with the intention of bringing about 'cultural change in local authorities through developing a cross authority action plan which … commits to new ways of working and demonstrates a commitment to increasing sport and physical recreation resulting in sustainability of participation' (SCW 2009: 7). In light of the growing emphasis that is coming to be placed on LAPAs, it may be that in the future responsibility for disability sports development will be that of a range of appropriate local authority staff who will be expected to utilize the knowledge and expertise of, rather than expect delivery from, the DSWDO to co-ordinate and facilitate the provision of sporting opportunities for disabled people in local communities.

In relation to local authority provision in England especially, it is also clear that, despite the policy commitment to 'Sport For All' and social inclusion, 'there does not appear at present any coherent policy – or, indeed, anything approaching it – designed to enhance either the mainstream or segregated sports development provision for disabled people between local authority areas' (Thomas and Smith 2009: 71). This is likely to remain the case given the tendency for the

British government to adopt a largely hands-off approach to the delivery of its disability sports policy goals by encouraging organizations such as the EFDS and NDSOs to assume responsibility for doing so. Even though this has continued in the period since the 1990s when the process of mainstreaming disability sport and the rhetoric of social inclusion have become increasingly salient politically, sport and physical activity for disabled people continues to be offered in largely segregated settings away from non-disabled people and is dependent on the particular priorities of individual local authorities and governing bodies. In light of the current political and policy climate where broader social and welfare policy goals are prioritized alongside sport-specific objectives, and if the best guide to predicting the future of local authority disability sports development is an understanding of previous and existing provision, then it is probable that disability sport will remain nothing other than loosely integrated into the sports development activities of some local authorities and, for that matter, governing bodies (Thomas 2008; Thomas and Smith 2009). Finally, as Thomas and Smith (2009: 156) have noted, despite the growing emphasis that has come to be placed on inclusion, the process of mainstreaming disability sport and 'the increasing political interest in, and support of, disability sports development at all levels, it is likely that this level of interest and support will remain, by degrees, limited; policy commitment is likely to remain marginal; and responsibility for the organization and delivery of disability sport will be kept at arms length from direct government involvement'.

Acknowledgements

We would like to thank Fiona Reid from the Federation of Disability Sport Wales, Cardiff, for her contribution to the sections on disability sports development in Wales.

References

Barnes, C. and Mercer, G. (2003) *Disability*, London: Polity Press.
Barnes, C., Mercer, G. and Shakespeare, T. (1999) *Exploring Disability. A Sociological Introduction*, Cambridge: Policy Press.
Coalter, F. (2007) *A Wider Social Role for Sport*, London: Routledge.
Collins, D. (1997) *Conference Report: National Disability Sport Conference. Report from conference held on 22/06/97 at Kings Fund Centre, London*, London: Sports Council.
Department for Culture, Media and Sport (DCMS) (2000) *A Sporting Future for All*, London: DCMS.
——(2008) *Playing to Win: A New Era for Sport*, London: DCMS.
Department for Culture, Media and Sport (DCMS)/Strategy Unit (2002) *Game Plan: A Strategy for Delivering Government's Sport and Physical Activity Objectives*, London: DCMS/Strategy Unit.
Department of National Heritage (DNH) (1995) *Sport: Raising the Game*, London: DNH.
DePauw, K. (2009) 'Disability sport: historical context', in H. Fitzgerald (ed.) *Disability and Youth Sport*, London: Routledge.
DePauw, K. and Gavron, S. (2005) *Disability Sport*, 2nd edn, Champaign, IL: Human Kinetics.
——(2004) *EFDS Development Framework Count Me In: 2004–2008*, Crewe: EFDS.
Federation of Disability Sport Wales (FDSW) (2008) *Proposal to Extend the Disability Sport Wales Community Programme 2008–2012*, Cardiff: FDSW.
Federation of Sport Associations for the Disabled (FSAD) (2003) *Moving Forward*, Cardiff: FSAD.
Guttmann, L. (1976) *Textbook of Sport for the Disabled*, Oxford: HM & M Publishers.
HMSO (1995) *Disability Discrimination Act*, London: HMSO.
Houlihan, B. and White, A. (2002) *The Politics of Sports Development: Development of Sport or Development Through Sport?*, London: Routledge.
House of Commons (HoC) (Welsh Affairs Committee) (2009) *Potential Benefits of the 2012 Olympics and Paralympics for Wales: Eighth Report of Session 2008–2009*, London: Stationery Office.
Hughes, B. and Paterson, K. (1997) 'The social explanation of disability and the disappearing body: Towards a sociology of impairment', *Disability and Society*, 12: 325–40.

Minister for Sport's Review Group (1989) *Building on Ability*, Leeds, Department of Education: The Minister's Review Group.

Oliver, M. (1990) *The Politics of Disablement*, Basingstoke: Macmillan.

Oliver, M. and Barnes, C. (2008) '"Talking about us without us?" A response to Neil Crowther', *Disability and Society*, 23: 397–9.

Shakespeare, T. and Watson, N. (1997) 'Defending the social model', *Disability and Society*, 12: 293–300.

Sport England (2008a) *Shaping Places through Sport: Building Communities. Developing Strong, Sustainable and Cohesive Communities through Sport*, London: Sport England.

——(2008b) *Sport England Strategy 2008–2011*, London: Sport England.

Sports Council (1982) *Sport in the Community: The Next Ten Years*, London: Sports Council.

——(1988) *Sport in the Community: Into the 90s. A Strategy for Sport 1988–1993*, London: Sports Council.

——(1993) *People with Disabilities and Sport: Policy and Current/Planned Action*, London: Sports Council.

Sports Council Disability Task Force (1997) *Recommendations of the Future Structure and Integration of Disability Sport in England*, London: Sports Council.

Sports Council Research Unit (1991) *National Demonstration Projects: Major Lessons and Issues for Sports Development*, London: Sports Council.

Sports Council for Wales (1995) *Willing and Able: The Provision of Sports Opportunities for Children with Disabilities*, Cardiff: SCW.

——(1998) *Young People First*, Cardiff: SCW.

——(2009) *Newsletter: Clubs, Coaching and Competition* (February), Cardiff: SCW.

Thomas, N. (2008) 'Sport and disability', in B. Houlihan (ed.) *Sport and Society: A Student Introduction*, 2nd edn, London: Sage.

Thomas, N. and Smith, A. (2009) *Disability, Sport and Society: An Introduction*, London: Routledge.

Welsh Assembly Government (WAG) (2003) *Climbing Higher/Dringo'n Uwch*, Cardiff: Sport Policy Unit.

8

Sport and social integration

Kevin Hylton

This chapter is circumspect in its approach to the exploration of social integration through sport. Social integration is a transnational agenda and as such its significance for sports development is traced through policy endorsements from the United Nations, through the European Union, the UK Government and its national sport agencies. While social integration is considered in relation to its possible advancement using sport as a tool, the interconnection between sport and social integration is also considered in relation to fundamental cultural and structural inequalities in society. The concept of social integration is used to refer to a number of related policy discourses and, 10 years after the 1999 Macpherson Report (Macpherson 1999), its potential for success is framed using a critical 'race' lens as a proxy for many other intersecting social factors requiring consideration in sports development.

In 1994 at the level of the United Nations the UK Government signed up to a set of proposals, later ratified as the Copenhagen Declaration, which involved a focus on social integration as one of the three key objectives of development (UN 1994; UN 2007: 19). For most policy-makers the two objectives relating to reductions in poverty and unemployment were less elusory than the objective of social integration, which remained in need of further elaboration. The UN, which emphasised a process of participatory dialogue to support the complex policy focus on social integration that underpinned most of the UK Government's social policies through the mid-1990s and 2000s, took on this challenge. Participatory dialogue is presented as one piece of a complex jigsaw that includes equality policies, systems of justice and educational interventions that contribute to social integration. Since the mid-1990s sport has been consistently and visibly part of policy implementation strategies for active citizenship, active communities, social inclusion, social cohesion, neighbourhood renewal and regeneration. Social integration is used here as an umbrella term to draw together these policy discourses.

Tony McNulty MP (speaking when Parliamentary Under Secretary in the Office of the Deputy Prime Minister) encapsulated a common view of sport's place on the social agenda as a vehicle to mend a dysfunctional society or community. He stated (Smith Institute 2003: 11) that,

> Having nowhere to go and nothing constructive to do is as much a part of living in a distressed community as poor housing or high crime levels. Sports and active recreation

provide a good part of the answer to rebuilding a decent quality of life. Getting involved can be good for health, it can lead to people learning new skills, making new friends and to a strengthened community spirit.

McNulty and other politicians are part of a transnational infrastructure that accepts the role of sport as a necessary aspect of social policy. The European Union constitutes part of this influential policy network that concurs that sport has a definite place in strategy development if progress to a socially integrated nation and a socially integrated Europe is to be realised.

> Sport makes an important contribution to economic and social cohesion and more integrated societies … The specific needs and situation of under-represented groups therefore need to be addressed … The Commission believes that better use can be made of the potential of sport as an instrument for social inclusion in the policies, actions and programmes of the European Union and of Member States.
>
> *(European Union 2009: 2.5)*

A socially integrated society is an ideal vision that few would (or even, could) disagree with. Integration is a concept used in the vernacular to reflect the 'melting pot' culture of a society undifferentiated by 'race', class, gender, disability, faith, or sexual orientation. Social integration is used to depict a process that is dynamic and ongoing, a goal to aim for and a state that has been achieved. In addition, it has been argued by the UN that social integration can be viewed in three distinct, if at times conflicting, ways: a) an inclusionary goal; b) an imposition; or c) in a descriptive idealistic sense. Social integration is rarely viewed as anything less than positive; however, where sport or particular forms of physical activity and recreation opportunities are imposed, then the recipients are likely to think otherwise. Social integration has also been referred to as a panacea or a crucial foundation stone for a fully functioning and mature society. Designing initiatives to achieve inclusionary goals involves a focus on social justice, equality and empowerment, hence offering a sense of why there is a very clear overlap or even conflation of social integration and the policy discourses above. The UN reinforces this conflation of discourses, as does the UK Government, through their regular interchange of prominent policy rhetoric of inclusion and participation as components of the process of social integration. For example, the UN refers to 'overcoming exclusion, promoting inclusive institutions and promoting participation … these are among the key elements of social integration processes' (UN 2007: xv).

In most cases integration is used in relation to those outside or excluded from mainstream facilities, services or decision-making. As in the Policy Action Team 9 report (PAT 9) (Home Office 1999), community self-help is considered central to renewing the social fabric and empowering and sustaining active citizenship in local neighbourhoods. This PAT was one of 18 established to determine the contribution of various government departments and public services to neighbourhood renewal and social inclusion. The place of sport in the UK Government's social inclusion strategy was outlined in the UK National Action Plan on Social Inclusion 2003–5 (DWP 2003). The progress report from the PAT 10 report, which focused on sport and the arts (DCMS 1999), recommended:

- [That] at national, regional and local levels all relevant agencies that contribute to delivering social inclusion and community development are advised on … the significant contribution that sport can make to the successful achievement of their objectives

- [making] social inclusion a key part of the work of all sports funding bodies
- [taking] positive action to redress the imbalance that exists in positions of leadership
- [listening] to the views of local people and partnerships
- [that] local authorities link the value of sport to the wider benefits of health, inclusion, regeneration, education and crime prevention
- [placing] sport at the heart of local objectives.

(DCMS 2001: 11)

These recommendations resonated powerfully with the sports policy of the time, *A Sporting Future for All* (DCMS 2000), which coherently wove many of these recommendations into its plans for sport in the community. The PAT's recommendations were also closely related to good practice in community development where it was common to see these approaches promoted (Hylton and Totten 2007a). These discourses of inclusion and integration are most often used in the context of communities, whether they are framed by politics, interests, experience, or geography. Ethnic communities are regularly the focus of these policies and practices intended to encourage their integration into wider local, regional, national and even European communities/societies. Ethnicity, 'race', nation, cultural heritage, faith and community are key characteristics of an integra-tionist debate. These characteristics intersperse with class, gender and other intersecting and complex social factors outlined in the PATs' deliberations which distinguish the 'integrated', 'included' and 'cohesive' communities from the 'segregated', 'excluded', and 'fragmented' outsider communities.

Social integration in practice

Figure 8.1 is adapted from the stages of social relations model developed by the UN (UN 2007: 6). The Figure is meant as a developmental rather than prescriptive tool to understand the dynamics of social relations and their stages in the social integration process. At first glance half the stages can be viewed as positive (coexistence, collaboration, cohesion) and the other half negative (fragmentation, exclusion and polarisation). However, the 'negative' stages should be viewed as opportunities or formative stages leading to the more cohesive relations aspired to in a process leading to social integration.

The model can be used to frame prominent sports and social development policies and contexts in the UK if it is understood that the model is heuristic and interpretive in nature. The assumption is that there is not necessarily a mechanical shift in any society from a state of critical fragmentation, exclusion or polarisation to a more strengthened environment of coexistence, collaboration, terminating at a point of social integration. The model is useful in contemplating critical moments in sports development that have been the catalyst for policy developments or a change in vocational practice and as such can be used strategically in an educational sense to identify the rationales for past and present scenarios in the sports and social agenda. For example, there is evidence, from the Chair of the Commission for Racial Equality, of comm-unities in the UK becoming more stratified and segregated on racial and ethnic lines (Phillips 2005). This was partially informed by events in the north of England explored and reported by Ted Cantle and John Denham (Denham 2001; Cantle 2002). In attempting to identify good practice in the provision of public services, the Community Cohesion Review Team (chaired by Cantle) and an inter-departmental Ministerial Group on Public Order and Com-munity Cohesion (chaired by Denham) identified a number of factors as contributing to the breakdown in community cohesion and an increase in racial tension over recent years that have clear implications for the relationship between 'race', sport and social integration. Some of the main points have a direct relevance to sport and its organisations and they include a lack of

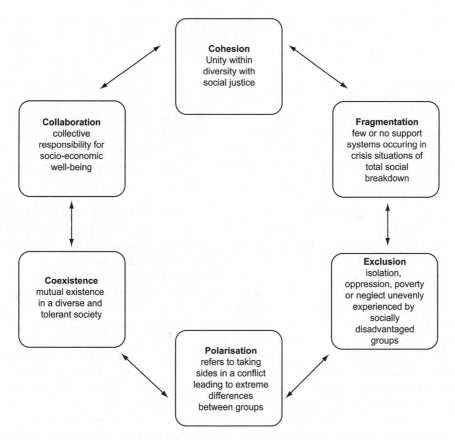

Figure 8.1 Stages of Social Relations Model (adapted from the United Nations model) (2007: 6)

adequate social, recreational, leisure, sporting, and cultural activities. The UN model is useful then in simply conceptualising the process of polarisation and the potential for sport to reduce the differences between (and within) groups. However, an understanding of the complex social factors that explain how and why the polarisation developed would be needed to inform any intervention (Cantle 2002). Such interventions could include cross-cutting responses that aim to incorporate stakeholders in education, and involve the community and voluntary sector, employment, faith organisations, and social and cultural networks that would include sport as a partner.

However, some issues are less amenable to analysis than others and require a great deal of insight and awareness of complex social processes. In an information-gathering exercise with local football clubs across Leicestershire to inform policies designed to increase sporting partici-pation amongst black and minority ethnic communities, Bradbury *et al.* (2006) found that most of the black and minority ethnic players were concentrated at a few clubs. Significant numbers from the majority-black and minority ethnic clubs viewed their organisations as symbolic meeting points for diverse ethnic groups. Long *et al.* (2009) advise those in sports development that they should recognise the cultural relevance of these sporting formations. Where sports developers can recognise the safety, racial and religious purpose of particular sport/community-led organisations then, through mutual existence there can be movement from purely cultural toleration to collaboration and active citizenship. Long *et al.* (2009: 41) suggest that,

In the current climate, such clubs in Asian communities may be viewed with suspicion as sites of potential radicalisation. Alternatively, they may represent the starting point to strengthen ethnic identities – sites for ethnic integration or sites of resistance to racism.

Observations of community fragmentation and exclusion resulting in parallel existences raise complex questions which need a more sophisticated response than *purely providing sport*. Yet without focusing the minds of sports policy-makers and practitioners on the potential value of innovative, appropriate initiatives for social integration there is the risk of further polarisation. An understanding of complex social processes could lead policy-makers and practitioners to utilise sport in conjunction with other social opportunities to encourage communities to develop beyond the minimum levels of tolerance and mutual coexistence advocated by the UN.

The model in Figure 8.1 can be used in a prospective way to anticipate or predict change given the previous policy cycles in UK sport. Donnelly and Coakley (2002) make links between social inclusion and social closure in line with the more recent policy concerns with the multiple characteristics of deprivation that are associated with social exclusion. Social capital generation is a popular strategy to combat social exclusion as it is considered to result in increased social ties and thus community renewal. Increased social capital is reported to be an outcome of strengthened social relations and community cohesion. However, in his analysis of social capital, Field (2003) agrees that networks can actually promote inequality due to their restrictive access to the means of accruing social capital through association. Thus, where sport networks operate with a noticeable inability to include others, the likely long-term effect is to further reinforce social division. By ignoring these social relations in sport and by making naïve assumptions about the integrative capacity of sport we are reinforcing the marginalisation and power differentials that black and minority ethnic people face in other social arenas. Some connections are clearly more useful than others in terms of their ability to build bridges and open up opportunities. This has been particularly emphasised by the emerging literature on racial exclusion, racism and sport (Carrington and Mcdonald 2001; Long and Hylton 2002; Hylton 2009; Long *et al.* 2009).

Polsby, in his study of local community policy-making in the United States (1963: 4) asked three questions: 1) who participates in decision-making?; 2) who gains and who loses from alternative possible outcomes?; and 3) who prevails in decision-making? The literature concerning 'race' and sports administration indicates clearly that generally black and minority ethnic communities or networks neither decide nor gain from the outcomes of the sports policy process. Consequently, ROTA (Race on the Agenda 2001) argues that due to the levels of inequality and racism in many areas in England it is necessary to recognise and fund community-led organisations as they are well placed to provide culturally sensitive services. Although community groups are generally established to concentrate on the interests of their users and members, there are many examples where community groups have been set up as a result of social injustice (Solomos and Back 1995; Home Office 2001). Examples are provided by McLeod *et al.* (2001) who argue that the earliest documented forms of black self-help in England came as a result of black people recognising that mainstream services were unable to provide adequately for their needs including those related to housing, health, education, community and advocacy services. With reference to the UN stages of the Social Relations Model and considering Marsh's (1998) conclusion that policy networks reflect the structured inequalities in society whilst reflecting their members' interests, raises interesting questions about exclusion and inclusion in sports policy networks.

How can sport work to build the capacity of socially excluded groups to a level of either mutual coexistence or a point of collaboration and independent sustained development? Social ties and their development can be viewed as capital that is unequally distributed in sport as well as a process that reinforces racialised inequality and yet, just as we can identify these negative consequences, there could also be opportunities to proactively challenge the structure of sport to enhance self-determination opportunities and to challenge these apparent negative power relations (Field 2003). Further, Hylton (2008: 6) critiques how sport networks can promote inequality due to their restrictive access to the means of accruing social capital through association. The bonding and bridging processes that help develop social capital in sport networks are clearly affected by the social characteristics of individuals and groups in society (Long *et al.* 2000; Carrington and Mcdonald 2001; Donnelly and Coakley 2002; Hylton 2009). The distribution of social capital in sport reflects the incomplete project of social integration as practice, process and end state (Nicholson and Hoye 2008).

The politics and practice of social integration through sport

It can be argued that the use of sport as a tool for social integration brings with it a commitment to a particular form of politics of rights, justice, and empowerment which, Donnelly and Coakley (2002) argue, can be subverted by competing agendas in mainstream provision. One implication of Donnelly and Coakley's argument is that it is necessary to distinguish those interventions and initiatives with an inclusive community development approach and those with a paternalistic, 'top-down' or social control perspective. For some minority ethnic groups, a social integration strategy might be seen as a less than benevolent state trying to impose a sovereign culture that swamps their own. In relation to community sports development Hylton and Totten (2007a) describe this paternalistic approach as deploying community as a label without recognising that a particular set of practices and values is implied that have been identified by the UN as 'a set of guiding principles of unity within diversity with social justice' (2007: 4). The challenge for sport is how to lay down the necessary structures and opportunities that engage individuals and communities through a process of participatory dialogue that ensures an inclusive provision that recognises diverse social needs.

The UN Briefing Paper for the World Summit for Social Development (UN 1994) counsels against the uncritical assumptions that policy-makers and practitioners often hold in relation to social integration. This resonates with the relatively unproblematised assumptions that many policy-makers have around the benefits of sport and the capacity of sport to change individuals and communities for the better just by making it available and through increasing participation. Coalter's (2007: 7) use of the term *sporting evangelism* sums up those policy-makers and practitioners whose blind belief in the goodness of sport leads them away from the big questions concerning how we know that sport is being effective and, if it is to be effective, what kind of sport and under what circumstances. The need to consider these complex questions is daunting for many and it is only recently that stakeholders in sport have begun to ask such questions even if the answers and research are slow to follow. The UN's argument is to counsel influential policy-makers and practitioners away from expediency and treating sport as a panacea when considering sport's contribution to social agendas. The UN reported that,

> It is intellectually easy and often politically expedient to assume that grave problems of poverty and injustice can be alleviated through including people formerly excluded from certain activities or benefits. Yet, in many cases, the existing pattern of [sports] development itself may be unviable or unjust.
>
> *(UN 1994: 3)*

Kevin Hylton

For example, sport in the UK has been regularly criticised for being ineffectively structured to accommodate high numbers of low and non-participants who tend to be located in lower socio-economic groups, and among whom black and minority ethnic groups, older age categories, those with lower sports ability and women are over-represented (Collins and Kay 2003; Jarvie 2006; Whannel 2008; Hylton and Morpeth 2009). Further, in relation to the legacy promises made on behalf of London 2012 that revolve around cohesion and integration, as a result of the various benefits made available through the development and participation processes of the Olympics, Hylton and Morpeth (2009: 224) state that

> It can be demonstrated through research by the Government's sport development body, Sport England, that there are many unmet needs amongst minority ethnic groups in comparison to their white peers and from this it is hard to see how the legacy promise of increased participation is somehow going to affect these structural fractures as a result of London 2012.

On this basis, the promise of social integration is unlikely to occur *just by providing sport* where there are structures in place that themselves reinforce social exclusion and the pattern of social stratification in participation indicated in the Sports Equity Index (Sport England 2001) and do little to address the unmet needs of sport's governing bodies as outlined by Wheeler (2000).

Sport, 'race' and culture

It is clear that when social integration is mooted it is integration into society that is the goal. However, a side effect of these policy deliberations is that culture and/or ethnicity are homogenised and reified thus making the proposition of integration seem unproblematic (Archer 1996). The notions of cultural cohesion or ethnic fragmentation remain unproblematised leading to social integration being perceived 'as imposition' as signalled by the UN. In sport there have been few debates that question ideas of universalism (Jarvie 1991) or inter/intra-ethnic differences (Amara *et al.* 2005; Long *et al.* 2009). In their analysis of sport as a vehicle for urban regeneration and social inclusion, Coalter *et al.* (2000) were concerned by these issues as a number of the studies they reviewed were premised upon narrow views of ethnic groups. Long *et al.* (2009) go on to posit that this process of universalism is also reflected in common sporting stereotypes and reductionism that can lead to prejudice, discrimination, inequality and racism.

Sport's basic properties and structural capacity to meet the social integration agenda must be viewed more sceptically given the findings from the 2003 Home Office Citizenship Survey (Home Office 2004). In this survey sport's capacity for social integration came under particular scrutiny because people reported that they were more likely to meet regularly others from a different ethnic background at the shops (56%); in restaurants, pubs, cinemas and community centres (47%); in the neighbourhood (31%); than through sports and fitness activities (17%) (Home Office 2004: 160). These findings were reinforced in a 2008 study (DCLG 2008) in which 62% reported that they were more likely to mix socially with others from a different background at the shops; 45% in pubs, clubs, cafes or restaurants; and 30% in groups clubs or organisations (which may or may not include sport). Clearly sport has the potential to facilitate an inclusive, integrating process, but the important question is 'under what conditions'? The analysis by Amara *et al.* (2005) stands as one of the few studies that examines the ways in which sport has been used for the purposes of promoting social inclusion, in this case among asylum seekers and refugees. The case studies undertaken by Amara *et al.* explored how sport projects can be used to promote social justice and to work towards the elimination of discrimination with most having a clear emphasis on promoting social inclusion, social integration and community cohesion.

However, the temptation to 'transplant' these ideas from Amara *et al.*'s work needs to be balanced by an acknowledgement that sport- and community-focused projects are often place specific. In the Citizenship Survey there was a significant association between where people lived and the nature and regularity of their relationships with others from different ethnic backgrounds. For example, residents in ethnically mixed neighbourhoods were more likely to say that they have more regular contact with people from different ethnic backgrounds, and residents in the most densely ethnically mixed areas reported that they were significantly more likely to have regular contact. Perceptions of community cohesion also vary based upon ethnicity, as it was found that black and minority ethnic people were more likely than their white counterparts to report positively in relation to the extent of local community cohesion. This finding was the same across all areas, even in the most ethnically mixed areas, but did not take into account the existence of variation between and within ethnic groups, which provides an additional layer of complexity. These variations are further complicated by age and sex which were most effectively captured in research by Rowe and Champion on sports participation and ethnicity (2000).

Sport has regularly been viewed as a window to society and its customs and practices. Various sources have been critical of the covert and overt forms of prejudice, discrimination and racism manifest in sport, which is still clearly a problem in wider society. The increasing profile of far right politics and the high levels of perceptions of prejudice reported in the Citizenship Surveys reflect the gargantuan task to be tackled in sport and other public policy arenas. The variation in perceptions of racial prejudice by ethnic group should also be a consideration for those evaluating the success of social integration and sport's role in working towards it.

Sport, social integration and the state

Writers such as Parekh (2000) and Markus (2002) have been critical of those who argue that the state must remain neutral in conducting its duties in relation to the social integration agenda. In analysing what people mean by 'integration' Parekh (1998, 2000) explored five different ideologies that have affected state policy direction:

- the state as culturally neutral
- the state as a promoter of a single national culture that expects assimilation
- the state as a sponsor of a liberal view that unites around a single public political message that encourages, in the private sphere, tolerance for diversity with distinct communities being empowered to develop this message
- building on the third ideological variant, the fourth ideological position removes the barriers between the public and private spheres so that the private realm has more influence on the public. As in Figure 8.1, the state as a promoter of recognition rather than tolerance of cultural diversity, is a stronger message that comes through here, just as communities are encouraged to become more interdependent and cohesive
- the state as a sponsor of independent separated communities that work within its legal and civil framework.

In Hylton's (2003) analysis of local government policy and practice with regard to race equality and sport a significant number of policy-makers' and senior officers' views fell close to one of the less attractive categories, such as the notion of a neutral state, or a single national culture. It is hoped that, in recognising these differences, local government councillors and officers can see how each starting point on integration can affect the way they provide for their local communities.

There is a well-documented history of central government's attempts to manage issues of social integration, race-relations and equality that stem predominantly from the sponsored work programmes that encouraged workers to migrate to Britain from the New Commonwealth following the passage of the 1948 British Nationality Act (see Parekh 2000: 69). This policy of encouraging immigration must be juxtaposed with subsequent policies intended to control further black immigration such as the 1971 Immigration Act. The policies of encouraging and then controlling immigration were underpinned by assimilationist and integrationist ideologies and produced, in the 1950s and 1960s, ethnocentric education policies, which are still evident in the contemporary dominant racialised ideologies (Gillborn 2009). The policy of assimilation of black children was more focused on allaying the fears of a white society that felt threatened with 'losing their heritage' than respecting the cultural background of black and white people. As a consequence black children were forced to adjust to the cultural values of the white educational system rather than experiencing 'race'-centred policies that celebrated black identity (Flagg 1997). In rejecting this notion of assimilation due to its failure in achieving the goal implicit in the 'melting pot' ideology on which it is based, Brown (1970) argued that towns were sites of stratification due to the pathologising of immigrant groups and their subsequent problems of settling in which would impact clearly upon accessing public sport services.

Cultural diversity was singled out as one of the main causes of social stratification in 1960s Britain by Home Secretary Roy Jenkins and more recently managing cultural diversity became one of the core elements for achieving a socially integrated society identified by the United Nations in 2007 (UN 2007). Jenkins put particular emphasis on the integration of culturally diverse groups. To Jenkins racism was not a matter of racial oppression and exploitation of 'race' and class but of cultural differences and their acceptability. The public confusion on 'race' and racism was exaggerated through dominant racist discourses emphasised by senior politicians such as Enoch Powell in the 1960s and Margaret Thatcher in the 1980s. In fact, the year before Thatcher became Prime Minister in 1978 she claimed that Britain was being 'swamped' by immigrants from the New Commonwealth and Pakistan, thus symbolising the contradictions, racial prejudice and institutional inequality amongst public sector policy-makers.

It was not just the Conservative party that made capital out of the politics of 'race'. Between the 1960s and 1980s both the Conservative and Labour parties 'exploited the fears raised by the immigration of Blacks and Asians' (Gilroy 1987; Holmes 1991). During this period the messages sent to local government and their communities over racial acceptance and toleration lacked direction and coherence. By the late 1980s, when the Race Relations Act (1976) was almost 15 years old, cultural pluralism had developed into versions of multiculturalism and had become institutionalised in an ideology that asserted that the tackling of cultural diversity was a problem for black people in the country and it was not an issue of institutionalised racism, unlike the stark conclusions reached, in more recent times, by Macpherson (1999), Ouseley (2001) and Gillborn (2009).

The issues surrounding the public sector response to new communities, racism and social justice found their most potent expression in mainly Labour-controlled local authorities, often as a response to the policies of the Conservative government in the 1980s. However, it was in the 1980s when at least some degree of consensus was established between the major political parties and between central and local government that there needed to be a more focused approach to racial equality. One of the major catalysts for this was the civil disobedience in the early 1980s, often referred to as riots, that prompted a public sector response which, on one level, was designed to pacify dysfunctional (black) youths, and which on another level was recognition that this was a symptom of deeper, and potentially more socially destructive, problems. In hindsight, the inception of the Action Sport demonstration projects, while a politically opportunistic reaction to some of these issues, was also the first coherent response to what are recognised now to be complex social issues and objectives (Rigg 1986).

Although a discourse of political equality developed over this period at national government level, the discourse was often not translated into practice at local level. However, the problems of translating the emerging equality discourse into practical policy at local level were further compounded as state-sponsored welfarist sports projects gave way to liberal minimalist provision, as adopted by the Conservative New Right in the early 1990s, and reflected in the new-managerialism that gained popularity in the public sector. The same framework that promoted economy, efficiency and effectiveness was the one that ignored social objectives and therefore social integration (Clarke 1994; Hylton and Totten 2007a; Hylton and Totten 2007b). One of the major drawbacks of the contracting process introduced in the Local Government Act (1988) and an integral part of New Right liberalism was that the achievement of social objectives was not an integral condition of their implementation. Social objectives around this time were seen as non-commercial or anti-competitive and consequently few local authorities incorporated social objectives into the contracts to manage sports facilities that went to tender (Ellis 1994; Escott 1996). It is not unreasonable to suggest that progress on social objectives actually deteriorated under compulsory competitive tendering (Clarke 1994). However, the next phase of local government regulation, Best Value, introduced by Labour after its victory in the 1997 general election could be seen as, at best, unclear on social justice. One interpretation of the Local Government Act (1999), which covered all local government functions from early 2000, was that it gave added impetus to local authorities to reduce expenditure by becoming more strategic and innovative: an alternative interpretation is that it provided a menu from which a diet of excuses could be read about racial equality in sport (Thomas and Piccolo 2000). It is under this ever-changing landscape of national regulation and local implementation that local authorities have to tailor their social integration activities to meet the needs of their local communities.

In Hylton's (2003) analysis there were examples of processes at work in each of the case study local authorities of 'Eurocentric'[1] approaches, such as the prevalence of positions on equal opportunities that used an integrationist paradigm typical of those less tolerant ideas on diversity highlighted by the UN. Gilroy (1987), Alibhai-Brown (2001) and others have criticised the racialisation processes in British society that have constructed a discourse on 'race', identity, and nation that 'denies those who deviate from the norm which characterises the British collectivity' (Alibhai-Brown 2001: 103). This process of alienation and exclusion ultimately reinforces an imagined homogenous cultural identity that protects tradition against 'outsiders', and 'immigrants' who themselves have to make important cultural decisions about self, identity and community. A forced cultural integration through sport effectively becomes an assimilationist policy. These approaches negate the identity claims of black and minority ethnic people whilst at the same time alienating them and reaffirming a 'white cultural identity' (Parekh 1998, 2000).

In her assessment of the cultural neutrality of a liberal democratic state Markus (2002), in agreement with Parekh (1998, 2000), asserted that in pursuing the equality of all its citizens the state should be critical of itself where it aligns itself with a particular ethnic or racial group. The question for local authority integrationists is 'integration into what?' ideally into a healthy and happy society dependent upon a degree of cohesion, unity or sense of belonging. Provision that maintains an uncritical perpetuation of mainstream norms, traditions and values commonly associated in practice with the dominant white community, is likely to reinforce social inequalities. This relative impartiality of the state in terms of not developing proactive distributive or redistributive practices (that go some way to equalising outcomes and treating some people *unequally* as a result) creates a context in which the inequalities in provision can remain unchanged and social integration remains purely rhetorical. This further maintains the everyday white privilege that Delgado and Stefancic (1997) and Long and Hylton (2002) warn against and propose as a new frontier for critical 'race' theorists. As Markus (2002: 395) argues:

> All these considerations lead to the conclusion that the impartiality of the state and its desirability ought to be evaluated selectively, examining how far it contributes to the reduction of the privileged position of the majority where it is detrimental to the cultural heritage and cultural identities of other groups.

The importance of sport and other cultural activities as vital elements of inclusive and cohesive communities has also been brought into sharp relief over recent decades with civil disturbances and the public sector response to them. Similarly, mass migration to the UK recently from European countries and previous diasporic movements have led to a defensiveness towards sovereign cultures of Britishness or Englishness through calls for assimilation, integration and multiculturalism. In addition, combating social exclusion and promoting social cohesion, neighbourhood renewal and social integration arguably continue these discourses of inclusion into something that most sociologists would say is imagined, but in political and vernacular terms is an identifiable cultural phenomenon. This phenomenon is also revealed in discourses around citizenship, that have become more defined and overt since the war on terror, following the destruction of the World Trade Centre in New York on 11 September 2001, compounded by the civil unrest in Bradford, Oldham and Burnley that year, and the terrorist attacks in London on 7 July 2005.

The challenge for sport

The challenge for sport is that it cannot tackle social integration alone. One of the structural challenges to be faced in attempts to achieve social integration, and relevant to each equality Act, is that discrimination occurs at the personal (individual), organisational (institutional) and societal (structural) levels. Ironically, nearly a decade after Ouseley (1990) raised his concerns about the level of racism in British institutions, the 1999 Macpherson report endorsed his concern with a definition of institutional racism in relation to the Metropolitan police force. More recently the 10-year review of the Macpherson report revealed that the same problems persist within the Metropolitan police, a conclusion that has implications for policy and practice within other public arenas including sports development. For example, in relation to sports development Sport England's Equity Index (Rowe and Champion 2000; Sport England 2001) noted that the proportion in the Pakistani and 'Black Other' categories who wished to take up a sport in which they currently do not participate were 54% and 81%, respectively, above the norm for the population as a whole. Curiously the survey only touched upon experiences of racial discrimination even though in some categories one in five experienced racism (Sport England 2001). This silence on 'race' can be viewed as symptomatic of the institutional response and the values and assumptions underpinning public sector sport. Conversely, using guidance from the UN Stages of Social Relations model in Figure 8.1, it could be an opportunity to ensure a more concerted attempt at understanding social dynamics and sport's response to social integration.

An example of positive change occurred in 1999 when Sport England conducted research into its own activities and products only to find that minority ethnic communities in Derby, Leicester and Nottingham did not have equal access to them. To counter this problem it identified a need for greater coordination of sports opportunities, a need for community groups to work together, and a need for racial equality support for local governing bodies of sport/ sports clubs (Wheeler 2000). This recognition of the need for race-equality support in the experimental Active Communities projects is an indicator of emergent ideas on the need to focus jointly on community development and social integration through sport. At a more strategic policy level the DCMS, in fulfilling the social inclusion objectives of the Government, has developed a strategy that draws on the discourse of valuing diversity, active communities, and social inclusion. This strategy draws upon recommendations from the European Union that reinforce the DCMS recognition of national concerns by seeking guidance and support (some financial) internationally (DCMS 2009). On social inclusion and under-represented groups the DCMS stated that

> The Sport England Strategy 2008–11 includes specific undertakings to create opportunity for all. The strategy makes clear that developing the girls' and women's game, disability sport and reaching out to diverse communities must be a key priority for the sport's national governing bodies.
>
> *(DCMS 2009)*

Policy analysts and policy-makers need to move beyond rhetoric to consider the structural constraints and the power dynamics affecting participation in sport and society. A culturally sensitive approach to policy is worthy of further consideration as a 'colour-blind' or other intersecting 'issue-blind' approach only reinforces social exclusion in policy formulation. Marginalising social integration causes inconsistencies and fragmentation in service delivery. This has been underlined by the emphasis placed upon working with key stakeholders and community-led groups by the UN, EU, and various non-governmental organisation reports and declarations to promote social integration.

In summary, sport's capacity as a tool for social integration is challenging in what may seem to be a crowded conceptual terrain of policy discourses. As a tool with a set of properties sport has documented capacity to contribute something to the social integration agenda. However, that *something* requires clearer exposition in terms of its efficacy in specific conditions. Sports development is clearly vulnerable by itself and requires a closer melding of effort and resources with other public policy arenas and stakeholders if aspiration is to become reality and policy gaps are to disappear.

Historically, social integration policies have been affected by wider cultural and structural concerns, demographic and political shifts and public sector responses to them. The response by sport has been inconsistent and yet there is evidence at local, national and international levels of a will to change, as hopefully practice follows policies. Where this practice adopts the politics of social integration, defined as *unity within diversity with social justice*, it will remain a constant test of the willingness of the structures of sport to respond to the needs and wants of diverse communities.

Note

1 *Eurocentric* refers to processes that legitimate or defend the interests of those in power in Western society. In UK society the most prevalent in positions of power tend to be male, middle class and white. The insidiousness of Eurocentrism is such that dominant ideologies are based upon this paradigm, thus perpetuating the hegemony of Eurocentric knowledge and power effortlessly. This process is similar but different to *Anglocentrism*, where England or Britain is centralised.

Kevin Hylton

References

Alibhai-Brown, Y. (2001). *Who do We Think We Are: Imagining a New Britain*. London, Penguin.
Amara, M., D. Aquilina, *et al.* (2005). 'The Roles of Sport and Education in the Social Inclusion of Asylum Seekers and Refugees: An Evaluation of Policy and Practice in the UK, European Year of Education through Sport', Report to DG Education and Culture, European Commission. Loughborough, Institute of Sport and Leisure Policy, Loughborough University and Stirling University.
Archer, S. (1996). *Culture and Agency: The Place of Culture in Social Theory*. Cambridge, Cambridge University Press.
Bradbury, S., T. Kay, and Nevill, M. (2006). *Black and Minority Ethnic Inclusion in Leicestershire and Rutland Affiliated Football Clubs*. Loughborough, Institute of Youth Sport, Loughborough University.
Brown, J. (1970). *The Un-Melting Pot: An English Town and its Immigrants*. London: Macmillan.
Cantle, T. (2002). *Community Cohesion: A Report of the Independent Review Team*. London, Home Office.
Carrington, B. and I. Mcdonald (2001). *'Race' Sport and British Society*. London, Routledge.
Clarke, A. (1994). 'Leisure and the New Managerialism'. In J. Clarke and E. McLaughlin, eds, *Managing Social Policy*. London, Sage.
Coalter, F. (2007). *A Wider Social Role for Sport*. London, Routledge.
Coalter, F., M. Allison, and Taylor, J. (2000). *The Role of Sport in Regenerating Deprived Urban Areas*. Edinburgh, University of Edinburgh Centre for Leisure Research.
Collins, M. and T. Kay (2003). *Sport and Social Exclusion*. London, Routledge.
DCLG (2008). 'Citizenship Survey April-September, England'. *Cohesion Research Statistical release 6*, Department for Communities and Local Government.
DCMS (1999). 'PAT 10 Report'. London, DCMS.
——(2000). 'A Sporting Future for All'. London, Department for Culture Media and Sport.
——(2001). 'Building on PAT 10: Progress Report on Social Inclusion'. London, HMSO.
——(2009). 'International Sport Strategy'. London, Department for Cuture Media and Sport.
Delgado, R. and J. Stefancic (1997). *Critical White Studies*. Philadelphia, Temple University Press.
Denham, J. (2001). 'Building Cohesive Communities: A Report of the Ministerial Group on Public Order and Community Cohesion'. London, Home Office.
Donnelly, P. and J. Coakley (2002). *The Role of Recreation in Promoting Social Inclusion*. Toronto, Laidlaw Foundation.
DWP (2003). 'UK National Action Plan on Social Inclusion 2003–5'. London, Department for Work and Pensions.
Ellis, J. (1994). 'Developing Sport Through CCT'. *Recreation* 53(9): 31–3.
Escott, K. (1996). 'Equal Opportunities Strategy for CCT'. Birmingham, Centre for Public Services.
European Union. (2009). 'Using the Potential of Sport for Social Inclusion, Integration and Equal Opportunities'. Retrieved June 2009.
Field, J. (2003). *Social Capital*. London, Routledge.
Flagg, B. (1997). 'Anti-discrimination law and transparency: barriers to equality?' In R. Delgado and J. Stefancic, eds, *Critical White Studies*. Philadelphia, Temple University Press.
Gillborn, D. (2009). *Racism and Education: Coincidence or Conspiracy?* London, Routledge.
Gilroy, P. (1987). *There Ain't No Black in the Union Jack*. London, Routledge.
Holmes, C. (1991). *A Tolerant Country? Immigrants, Refugees and Minorities in Britain*. London, Faber and Faber.
Home Office (1999). *Policy Action Team 9 – Community Self-help*. London, Home Office.
——(2001). 'Strengthening the Black and Minority Ethnic Voluntary Sector Infrastructure', www.homeoffice.gov.uk/acu/strng2.html.
——(2004). *Citizenship Survey: People Families and Communities 2003*. London, Home Office.
Hylton, K. (2003). *Local Government, 'Race' and Sports Policy Implementation: Demystifying Equal Opportunities in Local Government*. Leeds, Leeds Metropolitan University: 1 v.
——(2008). 'Race Equality and Sport Networks: Social Capital Links'. In M. Nicholson and R. Hoye, eds, *Sport and Social Capital*. London, Butterworth-Heineman.
——(2009). *'Race' and Sport: Critical Race Theory*. London, Routledge.
Hylton, K. and N. Morpeth (2009). '"Race", Sport and East London'. In G. Poynter and I. MacRury, eds, *Olympic Cities: 2012 and the Remaking of London*. Farnham, Ashgate.
Hylton, K. and M. Totten (2007a). 'Community Sport Development'. In K. Hylton and P. Bramham, eds, *Sports Development: Policy, Process and Practice (2nd Edition)*. London, Routledge.

——(2007b). 'Developing Sport for All? Addressing inequality in sport'. In K. Hylton and P. Bramham, eds, *Sports Development: Policy, Process and Practice*. London, Routledge.

Jarvie, G. (1991). *Sport, Racism and Ethnicity*. London, Falmer.

——(2006). *Sport, Culture and Society: An Introduction*. London, Routledge Taylor and Francis.

Long, J. and K. Hylton (2002). 'Shades of White: An Examination of Whiteness in Sport'. *Leisure Studies* 21(1): 87–103.

Long, J., K. Hylton, Welch, M. and Dart, J. (2000). *An Examination of Racism in Grass Roots Football*. London, Kick it Out.

Long, J., Hylton, K., Ratna, A., Spracklen, K. and S. Bailey (2009). 'A Systematic Review of the Literature on Black and Minority Ethnic Communities in Sport and Physical Recreation; Conducted for Sporting Equals and the Sports Councils by the Carnegie Research Institute, Leeds Metropolitan University, Sporting Equals, Birmingham', www.sportingequals.org.uk/DynamicContent/Documents/BME% 20Final%20Full%20%20Report.pdf

Macpherson, Sir William, of Cluny (1999). *Report of the Stephen Lawrence Inquiry* (Cm4262-I). London, The Stationery Office.

Markus, M. (2002). *Cultural Pluralism and the Subversion of the 'Taken-for Granted' World*. Oxford, Blackwell.

Marsh, D. (1998). *Comparing Policy Networks*. Buckingham, Open University Press.

McLeod, M., D. Owen, and Khamis, C. (2001). *Black and Minority Ethnic Voluntary Organisations: Their role and future development*. York, Joseph Rowntree Foundation.

Nicholson, M. and R. Hoye (2008). *Sport and Social Capital*. Amsterdam; London, Elsevier/Butterworth-Heinemann.

Ouseley, H. (1990). 'Resisting Institutional Change'. In W. Ball and J. Solomos, eds, *Race and Local Politics*. London, Macmillan.

——(2001). 'Community Pride Not Prejudice: Making Diversity Work in Bradford'. *Presented to Bradford Vision by Sir Herman Ouseley*. Bradford, Bradford Vision.

Parekh, B. (1998). *Integrating Minorities*. London, Routledge.

——(2000). *The Future of Multi-ethnic Britain*. London, Runneymede Trust.

Phillips, T. (2005). 'After 7/7: Sleepwalking to Segregation', speech given by CRE chair Trevor Phillips at the Manchester Council for Community Relations. 22 September 2005, www.humanities.manchester.ac.uk/socialchange/research/social-change/summer-workshops/documents/sleepwalking.pdf

Polsby, N. (1963). *Community Power and Political Theory*. New Haven, Yale University.

Race on the Agenda (2001). Briefing No. 5; Supporting the Black Voluntary Sector, www.rota.org.uk/briefing/support.html

Rigg, M. (1986). *Action Sport – an Evaluation*. London, Sports Council.

Rowe, N. and R. Champion (2000). *Sports Participation and Ethnicity in England National Survey*. London, Sport England.

Smith Institute, T. (2003). *Sport, Active Recreation and Social Inclusion*. London, The Smith Institute.

Solomos, J. and L. Back (1995). *Race, Politics and Social Change*. London, Routledge.

Sport England (2001). *Sports Equity Index*. London, Sport England.

Thomas, H. and F. Piccolo (2000). 'Best Value, Planning and Racial Equality'. *Planning Practice and Research* 15(1/2): 79–95.

UN (1994). 'Social Integration: Approaches and Issues'. *UNRISD Briefing Paper No. 1, World Summit for Social Development*. New York, United Nations Research Institute for Social Development.

——(2007). 'Participatory Dialogue: Towards a Stable, Safe and Just Society for All'. New York, United Nations.

Whannel, G. (2008). *Culture, Politics and Sport: Blowing the whistle, revisited*. London, Routledge.

Wheeler, J. (2000). 'Leicester Racial Equality and Sport Project Preparation Report', Leicester, Leicester City Council.

9

The importance of culture

Sport and development in the Arab World – between tradition and modernity

Mahfoud Amara

Discourses on the development of contemporary sport as well as sports development practices are shaped by history, including the history of nation-state formation, and by culture (or ideology), including traditions and religious beliefs. 'Development' is in itself a historically contested concept. For some, development means a break with the past. Past here is usually associated with decadence, irrationality and metaphysical beliefs. For others, particularly in ex-colonised societies, development is conditioned by a reconciliation with the past. Past here is synonymous with authenticity.

In the Arab world, the concept of development in the sense of modernisation and progress or in the sense of reclaiming an authentic past is yet to be studied (deconstructed) in relation to sports phenomenon in general, and in relation to the field of sports policy (or politics) in particular. Therefore, this chapter discusses the model of the nation state, as a form of socio-historical development (Amin and El Kenz 2003), in the Arab world. It analyses the ways in which sport was mobilised in the assertion of populist nationalism and national unity beyond class/ethnic divides as well as around Pan Arab and Pan Islamic ideologies. Sport has been recently organised as a means for integrating the new world system characterised by the end of a bipolar system, replaced by the American hegemony, liberation of financial movement and multiplication of multinationals. As a consequence, the declining discourse on Pan Arab solidarity and secular state's development ideologies such as *Ba'athism* in Syria and Iraq or socialism in Algeria has been replaced by the dominant discourse of economic (neo)liberalism (*infitah*) and regional economic cooperation, excluding (or at least delaying) discussion of principals of democratisation, individual emancipation and citizenship rights.[1] This shift in discourse explains, according to El-Kenz (2009), the manipulation of 'history' and 'tradition' as sources of 'authenticity' in the legitimisation of one-party-states and monarchy-states rules (in fusion with religious institutions and business interests) in the region. Moreover, accepting the values of free movement of capital and products has not involved either the free movement of people between Arab borders or between the Arab region and other regions. In the same vein Beker and Aarts (1993: 93) contended that:

> the limits of liberalization are the result of the weak position not only of the state, but also of national non-state actors *vis-à-vis* their counterparts in the world market. This weakness

is in turn the corollary of underdevelopment. It was precisely the failure of statist economic policy (socialist or otherwise) to bring about development that led to its rejection.

El-Kenz goes as far as to claim that the Arab world today is witnessing an end of a historical cycle for its *étatique* (state-driven) development, which started with the Egyptian revolution led by 'the free officers' in 1952, and ended with the American occupation of Iraq:

> In the Arab region, countries which adopted a position of 'positive neutrality' [in the bipolar world system] such as Egypt, Syria, Algeria and Iraq, have ended up ruined, by internal conflicts (or occupation as in Iraq's case), or as a result of strong economic and political pressures on governments and 'civil societies', for the other countries. The fall of the Soviet Union and the war in Afghanistan marks the end of the first cycle of post-colonial Arab history and its developmentalist ideology. The new cycle opens on different perspectives. The peaceful Arab world can and should welcome neo-liberal experience of capitalism already underway in the Occident, in a number of Asian countries, as well in the Gulf countries and in Mexico.
>
> *(El Watan 31/03/09, p.5, translated from French by the author)*

In terms of structure the chapter first examines sport and nation-state formation and ideologies of development in the Arab world. The Pan Arab Games and Pan Islamic Games are illustrative examples of the Arab world's engagement with Islamic values and secular ideologies, including modern sport. The next section explores the increasing strategy of Arab countries of development through sport in bidding for/and staging of major sports events as a scheme for urban regeneration, strengthening internal and external political legitimacy and integration of the global sporting infrastructure as well as for the commercial value of sport.

Sport and nation-state formation in the Arab World

As a reaction to the Eurocentric and essentialist view of nationalism and also as a direct result of the history of colonialism, a new 'Third World' form of nationalism has emerged. The objective of this 'accepted' or 'necessary' nationalism, as described by Said (2002), was to bring to light those long-deferred and denied identities, and mobilise them around the nationalist cause for independence. As a result, 'black' and 'Arab' cultures previously viewed by colonialist intellectuals and politicians as features of a 'subordinate race', fit only for colonialised and subaltern status, became celebrated as the features of national and supra-national unity and resistance against imperialism (e.g. Third Worldism, Pan-Arabism and Pan-Africanism). This call for self-determination expressed in political and intellectual terms, took the form – due to the scale of the revolutionary and counter-revolutionary violence – of an attempted rupture with the colonial society (historically, geographically and ideologically). The revolutionary model of nation-state building in post-independent Algeria, at least until the late 1980s, is a case in point.

> After the liberation of Algeria in 1962 one of the principle tasks of the FLN was to re-establish the integrity, the centrality, and the sovereignty of the Muslim Algerian identity. With the creation of a new governmental structure of Algeria came an educational programme focused first on the teaching of Arabic and on Algerian history, formally either banned or subordinated to programmes stressing the superiority of French civilisation.
>
> *(Said 2002: 365)*

115

It should be noted, however, that the political determination for separatism from the coloniser did not go as far as to completely refute the epistemological foundations of nationalism, and particularly its homogeneous (most of the time imposed) notion of national unity. The Western philosophy of identity and its definition of nationalism, or nationhood and nation state (considered in the literature as an invention of modern and secular Europe), were completely assimilated by the newly independent states. The process of assimilation, which happened most of the time at the expense of regional and sub-national (ethnic, linguistic or religious) identities, was considered as the 'supreme' solution for the preservation of national sovereignty, interest, and security from external threats (such as neo-imperialism and Zionism).

In relation to state ideologies the Arab World was divided between socialist, communist, Baathist and Nassirist varieties. If we look at the example countries in North Africa, Algeria picked a militant and revolutionary type of socialism largely inspired by the soviet model, emerging within an ideological atmosphere of Third Worldism; Tunisia opted for a reformism based on two sequences: first, socialist and then liberal (at least in economic terms); Morocco adopted a non-contested, but tolerated (economic) liberalism by the presence of an important public sector (Santucci 1993). In the Arabian Peninsula, there are examples of customary discourses of state formation and national glory, such as Saudi Arabia's – or al Saud's family – battle for a unified Arab Peninsula, Oman's ancient history of maritime expansion in Africa, and Kuwait's recent history of liberation from Iraqi invasion. However, state building in the Gulf countries, which is depicted in Arab *Ba'athist* and *Nasserist* propaganda as pure colonial construction (i.e. former protectorates of Britain, with the exception of Saudi Arabia and Northern Yemen), has been faced with serious internal and external challenges. As an example of the many internal and external challenges, we can cite the past *Ba'athist* and *Nasserist* secular ideologies, Saudi (*Wahabi*) hegemony, Iranian political and religious doctrines, and, after the First and Second Gulf Wars, the so-called 'Islamist Salafi Jihadi' peril (Garesh and Vidal 2004). In terms of state-citizen relations everything happened in the Arabian Peninsula as if a social contract – a reciprocal agreement, socio-economic stability in exchange for political pluralism – was signed between the ruling families and the populations (nationals and non-nationals). This takes (in ideal terms) the following form:

> The ruler is ex officio the primary beneficiary of the oil revenues, which he re-allocates as benefits to nationals throughout the country. This redistribution of funds and key benefits thereby reinforces the traditional structure of the state and undermines oppositions ... The Gulf states are informally stratified, with nationals, who are safeguarded with significant financial entitlements, followed by workers and employees of various ethnicities ranked by job categories ... Nationals direct day-to-day distribution of the oil wealth, while the expatriate workers ensure its production ... The basic social contract is two tiered: mutually beneficial, informal entitlements for nationals and tax-free and relatively high salaries for skilled guest works.
>
> *(Fox* et al. *2006: 11–14)*

Despite the shared sense of belonging to the Islamic faith, Arab countries can be divided in relation to the practice of Islam as a source for their legislation into:

- Revolutionary–modernist: such as Tunisia, Algeria, Syria and Libya. Ranging from semi-secularist to secularist, they adopt a hybrid judicial system inspired by *Shari'a* law (particularly in relation to questions of civil law such as: inheritance, property and family) and are heavily influenced by the Western juridical system.

- Conservative or 'traditionalist': such as Sudan and Mauritania. They claim to adopt an 'Islamic system of governance' and the rule of the Islamic court inspired by *Shari'a* law (including criminal law).
- Monarchies: such as Oman, Kuwait, Qatar, UAE, Saudi Arabia, Bahrain, Morocco and Jordan. Their political systems are based on the traditional legitimacy of the ruling family, a form of legitimacy according to Karava (1998: 76) deeply rooted in the history and Arabo-Islamic cultural heritage of the country. This heritage takes a different (religious) dimension in Morocco, Jordan and Saudi Arabia, where dynastic rulers justify their positions on the grounds of being descendants of the Prophet (*Sharifs*), and for the Saudi family, the guardian of Islam and its two holiest cities (Mecca and Medina).

Today, particularly in the Arab World, the collapse of socialism and the absence of a convincing new secular ideology have played a role in the manifestation of other forms of nationalism. As a result, national identities based on religious as well as ethno-linguistic and regionalist solidarities (e.g. Kurd and Arab Sh'ia in Iraq)[2] are competing with 'secular' party-states/ monarchy-state nationalism (Arkoun and Goussault 1990). Religion, which used to be the sole domain of the state, is mobilised today as a political tool for protest often intended to discredit Arab states' policies for development, their capacity for ideological mobilisation and their claimed position as the sole agent of technological, economic, social and cultural transformation.

The Arab nations are hesitating between the options of becoming a political entity according to the Western model of the nation state; of forging a cultural identity shared with the rest of the Arab nations that constitute the Arab World; or assuming a larger identity, that is as part of the Islamic (*Umma*) community, as a strategy to halt the growing popularity of 'Islamists' movements (Hussein 1997). Individual national interests and regional economic blocs, such as the Gulf Council and the Maghreb Union, have taken the place of the idea of the 'common interests of all Arab nations' and considerations of unity. Formerly constructed around the secular values of political and cultural regeneration, moral and political origins, and more importantly on 'historical legitimacy', the notion of national unity is itself being questioned today. These tensions are also reflected in the sporting domain.

The process of the diffusion of Western sport into Arab countries has taken different means and routes. One of the major influences was the presence of colonialism in its different forms, namely direct colonialism, annexation or protectorates. Sport was part, though with different degrees of intensity, of the colonial strategies for integration into the colonial order. It was also used alternatively by nationalist movements as a tool for resistance against colonialism and as part of the struggle for independence. In the case of the Arabian Gulf States (members of the Gulf Council) the introduction of modern sport was mainly through multinational petroleum companies and labour migration. In the aftermath of independence, the appropriation of the dominant model of sport by newly independent countries was seen as inevitable, taking into account the multiple uses of sport as an element for political, social and cultural recognition. The adoption of this universal language (sport) was accomplished by the integration of newly independent countries, during the 1960s, into the homogeneous and pre-established sporting and administrative structure, rules and regulations of the international sports federations (particularly FIFA and the IOC), as illustrated in Table 9.1.

Sport came to be regarded as an effective arena for future international contact between North and South, East and West. As Wagg (1995) claims:

Table 9.1 Integration of the Arab World into the International Sports Community: The examples of the International Olympic Committee (IOC) and International Federation of Football Associations (FIFA)

	IOC	*FIFA*
Egypt	1910	1923
Lebanon	1948	1936
Syria	1948	1937
Iraq	1948	1950
Tunisia	1957	1960
Morocco	1959	1960
Sudan	1959	1948
Mauritania	1962	1970
Libya	1962	1964
Algeria	1963	1964
Jordan	1963	1956
Saudi Arabia	1965	1956
Kuwait	1966	1964
Somalia	1972	1962
Bahrain	1979	1968
UAE	1980	1974
Qatar	1980	1972
Yemen	1981	1980
Oman	1982	1980
Djibouti	1984	1994
Comoros	1993	2005
Palestine	1993	1998

> Soccer has always been considered to be one of the most important modernizing forces of the continent [Africa]. The degree of competence an African state has achieved is measured on the soccer pitch. ... The World Cup Tournament, the ability to compete at the highest level, has become the ultimate measure of progress.
>
> *(Wagg 1995: 37)*

Hence, sport played an important role in Arab states' policies in the formation of nation states, to become an important element in the Pan Arab ideology as a measure of cooperation, integration and unification between Arab populations.

However, one can nevertheless suggest that the commitment of formerly colonised nations to the international sporting community was not straightforward. The newly independent countries have also used international sporting events, and particularly the media coverage that such events attract, as a space to express their regional, political and ideological concerns (such as anti-imperialism and pan-Africanism), which has led sometimes to a real situation of crisis (for example; Black September at the Munich Olympics in 1972; and the boycott of the Olympic Games to denounce apartheid in South Africa in 1976). The use of sport to express the developing world's discontent reached its peak with the initiation of the Games of the New Emerging Forces (GANEFO).[3] The GANEFO were initiated by Indonesia (the most populated Muslim country) under the leadership of Sukarno, the father of the Indonesian revolution and one of the principal leaders of the Non-Aligned Movement. The Games were held for the first (and the last) time in Jakarta in 1963[4] (Luton and Hong 2007).

As for today, in the alleged era of globalisation, sport is an ingredient of the general strategy of transformation from socialism or controlled liberalism to the market economy and thus openness toward the 'liberal' world. This is clearly evident today in the Gulf region. Commercial sport, previously prohibited and equated with neo-imperialism and (colonial) exploitation (at least in ex-socialist countries), is being accepted as the norm in the transfer of Arab societies into the market economy, in the injection of local capital into the global market through the staging and sponsoring of major sports events and global sports clubs (e.g. Manchester City FC, Arsenal FC), or in the marketing of the Arab region, particularly the Gulf region, as a tourist destination where 'modernity' and 'authenticity' co-exist.[5]

Pan Arab and Pan Islamic Games

The Pan Arab Games were established by the League of Arab Nations in 1953 as a means of expressing cultural unity between Arab people across nation-state boundaries. It intended to provide an opportunity for Arab youth to increase their awareness about the development projects, traditions and cultural diversity in different Arab states. The other goals of the games were to provide a competitive environment for Arab youth to enhance their sporting skills, which would allow them to better represent their nations (and their Arab identity) in international sporting festivals like the World Cup and the Olympic Games.

The establishment of the Pan Arab Games could also be seen as a part of the globalisation process reflected in the creation of regional games (mini-Olympics) following the establishment of the Mediterranean, Pan American and Asian games. These games were all recognised by the International Olympic Committee (IOC) in the 1970s. However, although the Pan Arab Games apply international sports rules and regulations and follow the amateur sports code, they are not under IOC patronage. Interestingly, the IOC and the International Sport Federations (ISFs), which had effectively opposed all attempts at fragmentation of international sport space or organisation of any parallel (ideologically) competitive games, did not raise any objections to the foundation and development of the Pan Arab Games.

The Arab countries located around the Mediterranean have throughout the history of the games been dominant in terms of sporting performance. This is in part a reflection of early acceptance of sporting culture in their societies compared with other Arab states as a result of (imposed or negotiated) urbanisation and modernisation. Furthermore, the secularisation process favoured the participation of both genders; which consequently gives those countries a significant advantage in the final table of medals. Even though some countries in the Arabian Peninsula like Saudi Arabia hold a higher position in the Pan Arab Games Association and play an important role in financing the Games (for example, in the case of the Lebanon Games 1997),[6] these countries have yet to host the event. This, it could be argued, is due to ideological and cultural barriers, particularly in relation to female participation, which is limited to some events such as the chess and the shooting competitions (Henry et al. 2003).

As an example of games that favour Pan Islamic identity and in which most Arab states take part is the Women's Islamic Games, which offer an alternative (but not in total opposition to other International sporting events) venue for Muslim women to compete in sport. Created in 1993 and organised by the Islamic Federation of Women's Sport (IFWS), the Women's Islamic Games has increased Muslim women's participation in sports, but this comes only within the context of sports events closed to males and the media. The main objectives of the Women's Islamic Games are to organise different sports competitions for female athletes that pay attention to Islamic beliefs (e.g. dress code, modesty and women-only settings) while strengthening solidarity among Muslim women. The fourth edition of the games, which were held in September

2005 in Teheran, gathered 1,587 female Muslim (and for the first time non-Muslim) athletes (including athletes with disabilities) from 42 Muslim and non-Muslim countries (including the United States, the United Kingdom, Russia and Japan), who competed in 18 different disciplines such as taekwondo, karate, futsal (five-a-side soccer) and table tennis. Although for some women athletes the Women's Islamic Games are the only occasion to compete at the international level, the games nonetheless suffer from a lack of a public female audience, little media attention and low standards of competition (Pfister 2006).

The other recent attempt at organising sports competitions that promote Pan Islamic identity is the Islamic Solidarity Games. In 2005, Saudi Arabia hosted the first ever Islamic Solidarity Games. Said to be the largest sporting event after the Olympic Games in terms of number of participants and sports, the Solidarity Games attempt to rebuild a sense of Islamic unity and reinforce the universal values of Islam as the second largest religion in the world.[7] The games were organised under the patronage of the Organization of the Islamic Conference (OIC) and the Islamic Solidarity Sports Federation. The objectives of the Islamic Solidarity Sports Federation are: to strengthen Islamic solidarity among youths; promote Islamic identity in sports; inculcate the principles of non-discrimination according to the precepts of Islam; advance cooperation among member states on issues pertaining to sport; unify positions in international sporting events and cooperate with international sporting bodies; preserve sports principles; and promote the Olympic movement in the Muslim World. The first edition of the games, held in Saudi Arabia, witnessed the participation of 7,000 athletes (all male), including Christians, from 54 Islamic countries competing in 13 sports.[8] The next two tournaments had been scheduled for 2009 in Iran (postponed for April 2010[9]) and 2013 in Syria.

Development through sport: the bidding and the staging of mega-sports events

The policy for bidding for staging regional and international sports events, as highlighted in Table 9.2, has been a component of development strategies of Arab countries, particularly those in North Africa. Tunisia organised the first major international Games, the Mediterranean Games of 1967, only 11 years after its independence from France in 1956 (Errais 2004). Another significant example is Algeria, which in 1975, after only 13 years of independence, staged a major regional event – the Mediterranean Games. Articles published in El-Moudjahid newspaper, which appeared between 23 August and 10 September 1975, reinforce Finn and Giulianotti's (2000) argument on state legitimation and sport:

> The revolutionary regime in Algeria has always accorded major importance to the youth of this country. The proof is in the building of sports facilities in *wilayates* [departments]. This approach is symbolized by the Olympic complex of 19 June [the day of the military coup, called officially the day *du réajustement de la revolution*], where the Mediterranean Games of Algiers will take place … Those projects were promoted for a precise objective, the building of a large-scale infrastructure aimed at facilitating the promotion of sports participation for all young Algerians … All invited delegations, the majority of whom had come to Algeria for the first time, declared admiration for the achievement of our country. Emerging from the people, the revolutionary regime works for the people. It is within this vision that the Algerian Sport University and Olympic City of 19 June were constructed.
>
> *(El-Moudjahid newspaper, quoted in Amara and Henry 2004)*

Table 9.2 Selected major international sports events hosted in the Arab region

Example of major international games	Arab cities
African Games	1978 Algiers, Algeria; 1991 Cairo, Egypt; 2007 Algiers, Algeria
Mediterranean Games	1959 Beirut, Lebanon;
	1967 Tunis, Tunisia; 1975 Algiers, Algeria; 1983 Casablanca, Morocco; 1987 Latakia, Syria; 2001 Tunis, Tunisia
Pan Arab Games	1953 Alexandria, Egypt;
	1957 Beirut, Lebanon;
	1961 Casablanca, Morocco;
	1965 Cairo, Egypt;
	1976 Damascus, Syria;
	1985 Casablanca, Morocco;
	1992 Damascus, Syria;
	1997 Beirut, Lebanon;
	1999 Amman, Jordan;
	2004 Algiers, Algeria
Asian Games	1974 Tehran, Iran; 2006 Doha, Qatar
Jeux de la Francophonie	1989 Rabat, Morocco
Football African Cup of Nations	1957 Sudan; 1959 Egypt; 1965 Tunisia; 1970 Sudan; 1982 Libya; 1986 Egypt; 1988 Morocco; 1990 Algeria; 1992 Senegal; 1994 Tunisia; 2004 Tunisia; 2006 Egypt
Football Asian Cup of Nations	2000 Lebanon; 1996 UAE; 1988 Qatar; 1980 Kuwait

Despite winning a number of competitions to host major sports events, not all bids have been successful, especially when the bids have been to host major global competitions. A recent case is the (unsuccessful) bidding by Morocco and Egypt to stage the 2010 FIFA World Cup, despite the fact that Morocco recruited the American Allan Rothenberg, who was the chief of the FIFA inspection team for the 2006 World Cup, to advise on bid strategy (Ben El Caid 2004). This was the fourth bid from Morocco to stage the football World Cup, having previously bid in 1994, 1998 and 2006.

The strategy for staging international sports competitions has taken on a significant dimension lately in the Arabian Gulf region. In an effort to diversify state revenues by developing and promoting other industries such as hospitality and tourism, real estate, retail, technology, communication and finance,[10] huge investments have been made in the staging and sponsoring of international conferences, trade and art exhibitions.[11] The aim is to market the new 'open' and 'liberal' Arabian Peninsula as the must-go-to destination for tourists and businessmen and to build a new identity as an emerging model of (liberal) monarchies that have succeeded in finding the right balance between, on the one hand, Western 'efficiency' and, on the other, the 'authenticity' of Arab culture. The fruits of these intense marketing and public relations strategies are starting to become visible. This has reached an unprecedented level with Qatar staging the Asian Games (second biggest international sports event after the Olympic Games),[12] followed by its (unsuccessful) bidding to stage the 2016 Olympic Games.

In an interview with *Observer Sport*, Hassan Ali bin Ali, the chairman of the Doha 2016 Olympic bid gave a taste of Qatar's ambition and strategy of development through sport:

Our Sport infrastructure is among the best in the world and we are certain we can build on our previous sporting experience to host the greatest celebration of sport in the world …

121

In Doha we have a world class-sporting infrastructure. We hosted the 2006 Asian Games – the world's second largest multidiscipline event after the Olympics, putting on what has been called the best, biggest, most widely reported and highest standard Asian Games ever[13]

Qatar will host the Asian Football Cup 2011 and is already bidding to host the 2022 FIFA World Cup.

Other examples of mega sport events and projects taking place in the Arabian Gulf region include:

- The Bahrain International Circuit (US$150 million), the only desert track in the world to stage the Formula 1 Grand Prix. The circuit was named after the official sponsor, the Gulf Air Bahrain Grand Prix, and is held in partnership with Toyota in the automotive industry, Arcapita in banking, and Batelco in telecommunications. In 2009, Abu Dhabi will follow Bahrain's example by joining the F1 with a second Middle Eastern round of the FIA Formula One World Championship.
- The Dubai World Cup of horse racing, inaugurated in 1996, awards a huge purse of US$6 million to the winner – the largest offered in all racing. Chief supporting races for the 2008 meeting are the US$5 million Dubai Duty Free and the US$5 million Dubai Sheema Classic. Also on the card are the Dubai Golden Shaheen and UAE Derby, both worth US$2 million, and the US$1 million Godolphin Mile.[14]
- Dubai international power boat racing.
- Qatar Super Grand Prix athletics meeting.
- The International Cycling Tour of Qatar.

The other interesting phenomenon in the commercialisation of sport is the booming industry of media sports broadcasting. If we look at the Arab World, the number of Arab state-run, private free-to-air, and pay-per-view TV sports channels has significantly increased in the last 10 years thanks to satellite broadcasting technology. TV broadcasting offers diverse sports programmes; debates; documentaries; and national, regional, and international sports competitions, ranging from traditional sports such as camel and horse racing to extreme sports such as the Offshore Powerboat Championships. The dramatic rise in sports channels has also brought increased competition in the advertising market, valued in 2003 according to industry estimates at US$300 million. Private sports channels, previously dominated by Arab Radio and Television network (ART) and more recently *Al Jazeera* TV sports network, are challenging the old concept of locality, particularly state sovereignty, and demonstrating that the power over media and communications no longer lies solely within nation-state borders (Amara 2007).

Speaking about the future strategy of ART, the owner of ART group, Sheikh Saleh Kamel, had already declared in a press conference back in 2001 that:

'sport is the spinal cord of the whole operation … It is also the main point of contention in a region where millions religiously watch soccer games whenever they're on TV'. He further said that he hoped to 'obtain exclusive rights to every major tournament and sporting event in the region – maybe even local championships and club league games'.

(Atia 2001)

ART did not wait too long to put its strategy into practice. The media group paid £220 million to acquire the exclusive rights (for some a monopoly) to broadcast the FIFA World Cup for 2006, 2010 and 2014.[15]

Conclusion: challenges for sports development and development through sport

This chapter highlights examples of ways that sport has been integrated into ideologies of development in the Arab World, and more recently as a strategic component for development and the negotiation of the post-oil era in the Arabian Gulf region (i.e. in urban regeneration, city branding, the improvement of the tourism sector and investment in the global sports market). One could argue, however, that in opposition to revolutionary Arab states that have adopted a secular populist model of state building (which is generally in crisis today) and that in sport have taken a pro-active position in utilising sport for national mobilisation and international prestige (e.g. Egypt, Tunisia, Morocco and Algeria), the growing interest in the industry of sport in the Arabian Peninsula has not been followed by a successful policy of promoting mass sport at national level, and to a lesser extent participation in international sport competitions. With the exception of a few sports such as football, horse riding, shooting, athletics, table tennis and hand ball, countries in the Arabian Peninsula are still falling behind in terms of promoting participation and developing a national high-performance sports strategy. Although there have been some improvements recently, for instance in the building of Aspire Academy in Qatar, countries in the Arabian Peninsula are still depending on foreign coaches and players to run their domestic leagues, and on the naturalisation of athletes (usually from Africa and Eastern Europe) to perform at the highest level. That said, even in those Arab countries with an established history of participation in international competitions, their performances have been insignificant, particularly in the Olympics, when compared with other developing countries in Asia and Latin America. This is illustrated in the following table:

Table 9.3 Best Arab performances in recent summer Olympic Games

	Best performance		Medals		
Olympic Games	Country	Position	Gold	Silver	Bronze
2008	Bahrain	52	1	0	0
	Tunisia	52	1	0	0
	Algeria	62	0	1	1
2004	Morocco	36	2	1	0
	Egypt	46	1	1	3
2000	Algeria	40	1	1	3
	Morocco	58	0	1	4
1996	Algeria	34	2	0	1
	Syria	49	1	0	0
1992	Morocco	31	1	1	1
	Algeria	34	1	0	1

Whereas some Arab countries, in relation to the development of sport, have to overcome obvious political and socio-economic problems such as poverty, rapid population growth, insecurity, illiteracy, and even military occupation (in Iraq and Palestine), others have to face cultural challenges, such as:

- Traditions, which have a particular impact on girls' participation in sport and which require that the provision of sports programmes and the environment in which they are organised is suitable from a religious and cultural viewpoint.

- The dominant (and for some invasive) Western culture of modern sport.
- The marginalisation of sport as a subject of study and as a profession, with sport remaining predominantly considered as a non-serious domain of amusement and play.

Finally, we cannot have development in society, and in sport, without providing opportunities for Arab people, including athletes and sports spectators, to exercise their citizenship rights (including the right to practise sport). Furthermore, one could argue that sport at the level of popular culture (sport for all) and high performance has been 'captured' by nationalist/political interests and used to further particular political (partisan) or mercantile objectives rather than being supported and nurtured as a social pastime and an element in community life. The negative repercussions of this are being felt in a number of ways. For instance, in health terms, there is a high rate of obesity amongst youths in the prosperous Gulf countries. In the Arab World, health problems related to lifestyle (e.g. dietary habits, smoking) and lack of physical practice are amplifying.[16] In politico-social terms, the over-political manipulation of sport has turned sports arenas (particularly football stadia) into a space for youth to express their frustrations and their dissatisfaction (sometimes with violence) with Arab states' policies for development. The violence following the 2010 World Cup qualifier play-off between two north African and Arab nations, Algeria and Egypt, is symptomatic of the social unrest in the Arab World.

I finish with the following statement by Malek Bennabi, which perfectly summarises the crisis of civilisation and development (of ideas) in the Arab World, located according to him in the confusion of progress with the accumulation of material:

> instead of constructing a civilisation, we have sought to accumulate its products ... the outcome of Islamic renaissance has not, during the last fifty years, been a construction but rather an accumulation of materials.
>
> *(Bennabi 1970: translation by the author)*

Notes

1 The UNDP Arab Human Development Report 2002 summarises the deficit of development in the Arab World into the following points: the Arab World: scores above sub-Saharan Africa and South Asia in world human development rankings by region, but below East and South East Asia and Latin America; in GDP per capita it outscores South East Asia, indicating that the Arab World is more wealthy than it is 'developed'; in rankings of human rights, participation, and democracy, however, the Arab World scores last among all regions of the world; in rankings of women's role and status in society, it scores second to last, outdone only by sub-Saharan Africa; adult illiteracy in the Arab World is still above 50%, particularly among women, and rates of enrolment in formal education lag behind global averages – again, more so for women (Salem 2003).

2 The Kurdistan Regional Government (KRG) signed an international partnership with Wales and Iran. The aim as stated in the web page of the Regional Government Ministry of Youth Sport is to initiate and deliver independent sports in the Kurdistan Region, 'in a way that is integrated with Iraq at the national level, that builds on the strength of new and existing international partnerships, which will help the KRG to develop their aim to compete at the highest levels of international sport as a region', www.mosy-conference.info/

3 The games of the New Emerging Forces were founded by Indonesia to challenge the hegemony of the International Olympic Committee. The first and last Asian GANEFO games were held in December of 1966 in Phnom Penh, Cambodia in which 15 nations participated.

4 The People's Republic of China paid US$18 million for the transportation costs of all delegations. More than 2,200 athletes and officials from 48 regions including France, Italy, the Netherlands, Belgium, Finland and the Soviet Union attended the Games.

5 A recent rule adopted by FIFA has made the professionalisation of all elite football leagues compulsory by 2011.

6 Lebanon received US$28 million from Saudi Arabia and Kuwait to help in the construction of sports facilities destroyed during the civil war (Jordan Times, 8 April 1999).

7 It is interesting to make a parallel here with the Maccabi Games, which are the games of the Jewish communities around the world.

8 Reported in Middle East North Africa Financial Network, 22 June 2005, http://www.menafn.com

9 The official web page of the 2nd Islamic Solidarity Games, which were due to be held in Iran from 9 to 25 April 2010 is: www.isg2010.com/en

10 Major projects include Dubai International Exhibition Centre; DUBAILAND; Dubai Festival City; Saddiyat Island in Abu Dhabi; King Abdullah City in Saudi Arabia; Amwaj Island project and The Durrat resort in Bahrain; Bahrain World Trade Centre; the Bahrain Financial Harbour, The Wave project and Blue City Oman; The Pearl island in Qatar; the Buobyan Island and the new Subiya City in Kuwait.

11 In exchange for a sum said to be from US$800 million to US$1 billion, France will rent the name, art treasures and expertise of the Louvre to a new museum to be built in Abu Dhabi. It is one of five museums planned for a multibillion-dollar tourist development on Saadiyat Island off Abu Dhabi, www.iht.com/articles/2007/01/12/features/louvre.php. For more information about Saadiyat Island visit the following address (www.saadiyat.ae/).

12 With a budget of US$2.8 billion, it is the biggest event after the Olympics in terms of the number of countries represented (45), sporting events (39), volunteers (45,000), viewers (cumulative audience of 1.5 billion), and broadcasting (2,000 hours of television coverage).

13 Doha 2016 bid committee hired the services of Mike Lee, described by The Observer as the man who masterminded London's successful bid to host the Games before setting up his company Vero communication. They also hired the services of Andrew Graig, a Detroit-based British executive who also worked for London (MacKay 2008).

14 See the Dubai World Cup official web page (http://dubairacingclub.com/dubaiworldcup/).

15 In buying all sports broadcasting rights from ART sports network, Aljazeera Sport has strengthened its hegemony over the Arab market.

16 'Top regional nutrition experts warned that Gulf nationals are among the worst affected. If the trend continues, young people in the Gulf region will be more susceptible to chronic diseases such as heart problems, diabetes, cancer and high blood pressure, which account for 50 per cent of premature deaths, according to the 400 experts gathered for a three-day conference aimed at formulating an Arab strategy to combat obesity and promote physical activity. (The National Newspaper, UAE, 20 January 2010).

References

Amara, Mahfoud (2007) 'When the Arab World was mobilised around the FIFA 2006 World Cup', The Journal of North African Studies, 12:4, 417–38.

Amara, M., Henry, I. (2004) 'Between globalization and local "Modernity": The diffusion and modernization of football in Algeria', Soccer & Society, 5:1, 1–26.

Amin, S. and El-Kenz, A. (2003) 'Le Monde Arabe: Enjeux Sociaux', Perspectives Méditerranéennes (Paris: L'Harmattan).

Arkoun, M. and Goussault, Y. (1990) Religion, pouvoir et société dans le Tiers Monde; entretien avec Mohammed Arkoun (Paris: Presses Universitaires de France).

Atia, T. (2001) 'No More Free TV', Al-Ahram Weekly On-line 526, 22–28 March, http://weekly.ahram.org.eg/2001/526/li3.htm

Ben El Caid, S. (2004) 'La Coupe du Monde de Football au Secours du Maroc', Confluences Méditerranée – N°50 ETE, pp. 75–8.

Bennabi, M. (1970) Le probleme des idées dans le monde musulman (Cairo: Dar El Fikr).

Beker, M. and Aarts, P. (1993) 'Dilemmas of development and democratization in the Arab World', International Journal of Political Economy, Spring, pp. 87–107.

El-Kenz, A. (2009) 'Le Cycle Arabe II and III', El Watan Newspaper (March 31, page 5 and April 29, page 7).

Errais, B. (2004) 'Discours sportif à vocation méditerranéenne: L'exemple tunisien, 1956–85', Confluences Méditerranée – N°50 ETE 2004.

Finn, T. and Giulianotti, R. (2000) *Football Culture: Local Contests, Global Visions* (London and Portland, OR: Frank Cass).

Fox, W.J., Sabbah, N.M. and al-Mutawa, M. (2006) *Globalisation and the Gulf* (London: Routledge).

Garesh, A. and Vidal, D. (2004) *The New A-Z of the Middle East* (London: I.B.Tauris).

Henry, I., Amara, M. and Al-Tauqi, M. (2003) 'Sport, Arab Nationalism and the Pan-Arab Games', *International Review for the Sociology of Sport*, 38:3, 295–310.

Hussein, M. (1997) 'L'individu postcolonial', in Luc Barbulesco and Abdelouaheb Meddeb (eds), *Post-colonialisme: décentrement déplacement, dissémination*, 164–74 (Paris: Débale, Maisonneuve and Larose).

Karava, M. (1998) 'Non-democratic states and political liberalisation in the Middle East: A structural analysis', *Third World Quarterly*, 19:1, 63–85.

Luton, R. and Hong, F. (2007) 'The polarization of sport: GANEFO – a case study, in sport, nationalism, and orientalism', in F. Hong (ed.), *The Asian Games* (London: Routledge).

MacKay, D. (2008) 'Doha's Olympics: If we build it, they will come', *The Observer*, p. 22.

Mazen Mahdi (2010) 'Arab nations come together to tackle teenage obesity', *The National Newspaper*, UAE, 20 January, www.thenational.ae/apps/pbcs.dll/article?AID=/20100121/FOREIGN/701209815/1138

Pfister, G. (2006) 'Islam and women's sport, Focus: Islam in a changing world', *SangSaeng*, 15 (Summer).

Said, E. (2002) *Reflections on Exile and Other Essays* (Cambridge, MA: Harvard University Press).

Salem, P. (2003) 'A concept paper, the Lebanese Transparency Association', www.transparencylebanon.org/2006/Archives/Human%20Development-%20Corruption.PDF

Santucci J.-C. (1993) 'Etat, légitimité et identité au Maghreb: Les dilemmes de la modernité', Confluences, 06, Printemps.

Wagg, S. (1995) *Giving the Game Away. Football, Politics and Culture on Five Continents* (London and New York: Leicester University Press).

Part 3

Sports development and young people

Introduction: Socialisation through sport

Barrie Houlihan

Although sports development has, in most countries, a relatively short history of fifty or sixty years, there is a much longer history of the politics of young people's involvement in sport. Much of this long history has focused on the legitimacy of physical education within the school system and, if considered legitimate, then its content and objectives. As Polley made clear in his contribution to Part 1, the role of school sport in the socialisation of the young members of the social elite in the UK was well established by the last quarter of the nineteenth century. Sport in schools as a vehicle for instilling leadership qualities among socially privileged groups rapidly spread internationally and with relatively little debate; much more controversial was the role of sport in relation to the youth of a country who were not part of the social elite. In some countries, Ireland for example, the role of the state in providing physical education and sport was strongly contested. Following independence from Britain, the provision of physical education (mainly in primary schools) deteriorated rapidly. In the draft Irish constitution reference was made to the role of the state in ensuring minimum levels of education, including physical education. However, the reference to physical education was removed due to pressure from the Catholic Church, which declared that all matters physical were the proper responsibility of the family, not the state. The final version of the constitution confirmed the state's marginal role in physical education as reference was made to the responsibilities of the family for the 'religious and moral, intellectual, physical and social education of their children'. However, and somewhat ironically, it was the Church that eventually encouraged the state to re-engage with the issue of school physical education, when a 1951 report of the Commission on Youth Unemployment, chaired by Archbishop McQuaid, argued that physical education did have a positive role to play, but suggested that physical education could be linked to organised sport, the Gaelic Athletic Association, over which the Catholic Church had considerable influence. Similar, highly politicised, debates over physical education can be found in other countries. In Portugal, for example, the introduction of physical education was prompted by a concern for military training of the young and later by eugenicist concerns over physical and moral degeneration. Meanwhile, in many other European countries, the former East Germany and Soviet Union in particular, school physical education was considered the primary site for instilling nationalist and socialist values in the young.

The chapters in this Part of the Handbook provide five contrasting national approaches to sports development for young people, with differences evident in terms of motives, objectives and processes. Lesley Phillpots' examination of sports development for young people in England highlights the significant investment by government in recent years and the broad range of outcomes expected of the investment. Given the scale of public investment, it is not surprising that the strategy has had a substantial positive impact on participation levels among the young. However, as Phillpots points out, these achievements have also heightened some latent tensions in the policy area, including those between educational objectives and physical activity/sport skills objectives and between social policy objectives (behavioural change) and sports development. In their examination of youth sport in France, Lhéraud, Meurgey and Bouchet emphasise the fluid nature of sporting identify among the young and the shifting patterns of the cultural consumption of sport. In particular they draw attention to the under-researched nature of the interconnection between socio-economic characteristics and sports participation, sports spectating and the consumption of sports information. Implicit in much of their analysis is a questioning of the capacity of organised sport and publicly funded sport to keep pace with the changes in the behavioural patterns among youths.

Carlsson and Hedenborg's analysis of Swedish youth sport provides an important contrast to both France and the UK. Whereas the latter two countries have strong centralist direction of youth/school sport, Sweden has allowed its sports Confederation considerable discretion in sports development. Although the Swedish state provides substantial financial support for sport through the Confederation there is a high level of trust between the two organisations, which results in the Confederation possessing considerable autonomy. Despite the very different organisational systems for youth sport many of the issues that have shaped policy are common to all three countries. Of particular note is the recognition given to sport as a vehicle for the socialisation of young people into the values of good citizenship and social inclusion. However, where Sweden diverges from France, but most notably from the UK, is in the clearer concern to resist the over-commercialisation and professionalisation of young people's experience of sport. If commercialisation and professionalis-ation are central causes of concern in Sweden, they are taken for granted as aspects of youth sports development in the USA. Moreover, the centralised nature of the youth sports development policy-making process, whether through government agencies or autonomous confederations, is absent in the USA. Consequently, Bowers, Chalip and Green identify federalism and capitalism as the two 'systematic conditions guiding sport development'. Unlike most advanced industrial countries, youth sport in America has developed independently of the state, first through the activities of not-for-profit organisations such as the Young Men's/Women's Christian Associations, but more recently through a range of commercial organisations such as Little League Baseball. In addition to youth sport organisations motivated by religion and profit there is the extensive pattern of school sport which is divided between private and state schools, with the latter directly shaped by the policy of the local school boards at city or municipal levels. Overall, Bowers *et al.* paint a picture of a highly frag-mented structure of school/youth sport which not only makes any notion of a sports development strategy or system highly problematic, but which seems particularly ill-prepared to respond to the social and especially the health problems facing young people. The authors refer to the 'façade of coordination' which belies a system geared more to inter-sector competition.

Tien-Chin Tan and Chin-Fu Cheng outline a youth sports strategy and system in Taiwan which, in contrast to the European examples, has a clear focus on fitness and talent identification and development with evidence of a lesser concern with socialisation and citizenship. Nevertheless, the government's interest in investing in youth baseball is closely linked to nation-building and political symbolism. While talent identification and development is a clear priority, the recent concern with the decline in physical fitness among school children is rapidly becoming a pressing concern. With regard to the relationship between the investment for elite success and decline in the physical fitness of school students, Tan and Cheng are right to question whether the continued prioritisation of elite success is partly responsible for the neglect of school sport for the mass of students. The final chapter in Part 3 explores the role of international organisations in relation to youth sport. On the one hand it might seem paradoxical that what would appear to be a clearly domestic policy issue, sport provision for young people, has stimulated the interest of so many international organisations. Yet the level of interest and involvement of so many international organisations should come as no surprise given the highly politicised nature of youth sport, as outlined at the start of this introduction. The content, form of delivery and objectives of school and youth sport raise crucial global issues about citizenship, democratic values and health. As Naul and Holze outline, there has been a steady increase in the interest shown by international organisations in promoting and defending youth sports programmes. The number of policy actors active in the area is broad, ranging from education-focused bodies such as the European Physical Education Association, to international sports organisations such as FIFA and the International Olympic Committee, to international governmental organisations such as UNESCO and the European Union. The number of organisations with an interest in school/youth sport is indicative of the controversial nature of school/youth sport provision: yet the plethora of organisations is also indicative of the competition to define the purpose of sports development for young people. Of all the aspects of sports development covered in this Handbook, youth sport is by far the most politicised.

10

Sports development and young people in England

Lesley Phillpots

Over the last 30 years there has been an increased interest and focus on sports development across the UK, with responsibility for policy delivery devolved to the four home countries who, through Sport England, sportscotland, the Sports Council for Wales and Sport Northern Ireland fulfil separate roles within their individual nations. Since devolution it has become more difficult to refer to a 'UK-wide' sports policy because, whilst there are still major commonalities in policy in the four countries, since devolution these differences have increased, to the extent that each country needs to be considered as a separate policy domain. The reader should not therefore assume that the features identified in the case of England would be reflective of youth sport policy in Scotland, Wales and Northern Ireland.

Mapping the territory of youth sport development in England is extremely difficult as its delivery involves a disparate range of agencies and a plethora of sports initiatives that have become increasingly interconnected with policy areas such as health and education. Since the mid 1990s, sport's political salience in England has increased incrementally, and UK government investment has led to an abundance of sports opportunities for young people. The publication of the sports policy document *Sport: Raising the Game* (DNH 1995) was a watershed for youth sport in the UK and signalled a significant shift in sports development practice from mass participation, to a more targeted approach that prioritised sporting excellence and youth sport (Green 2006; Houlihan 2000; Kay 2000; Kirk 2005). From the mid 1990s onwards, there was unprecedented growth in government investment in sports initiatives that focused upon young people. A renewed political enthusiasm for sport in general and its potential to contribute to elite sport outcomes and broader social welfare agendas, led to a sustained period of government support for youth sport in England.

In seeking to outline sports development policy and practice in England, it is important to acknowledge the complex interface between overlapping policy areas such as education, health, coaching, community welfare, economic development and youth work (Kirk 1992; Lentell 1993; MacDonald 1995; Pickup 1996). The chapter begins with a brief account of the values and principles that have underpinned and shaped youth sports policy and practice in England and in particular, the role of schools, sports clubs and local government sports development teams. The intention is to provide the reader with an account of youth sports development that highlights the 'discursive storylines' that have punctuated policy and practice in England (Bergsgard *et al* 2007; Green and Houlihan 2004; Houlihan 2005).

Mass participation, facility building and 'Sport for All' (1960–70)

During the 1960s, the Council of Europe spearheaded a debate that focused on the role of sports development in addressing the right of all individuals to participate in sport (Allison 1998; Coalter *et al* 1986; Coghlan and Webb 1990; Evans 1994; Green 2006). Mirroring debates in Europe surrounding mass participation, the creation of a UK Advisory Sports Council in 1965 signalled a renewed political desire for a more planned and strategic approach to sport and recreation in the UK. The Sports Council's initial role was to increase public provision of recreational opportunities for everyone through local authority programmes, whilst also delivering elite sport objectives (Coalter 1988). The UK government's agenda for sport was largely driven by its desire to use sport as a tool to tackle broader societal issues such as urban disorder and by public demands for both an increase in recreational provision for the general public and greater support for Britain's sporting achievements on an international stage (Green and Houlihan 2005; Social Exclusion Unit 2000; Rowe and Champion 2000).

The 1970s was characterised by a shift from a voluntarist approach to sport, to one of growing central government intervention and control (Coalter 1988, 1990, 2002, 2007; Green 2004; Henry 2001). UK government policy priorities for both sport and recreation focused primarily on social welfare objectives and the provision and construction of public sport and leisure facilities (Coghlan and Webb 1990; Collins 2003; McIntosh and Charlton 1985). In June 1972, the Conservative Government announced its intention to enhance the status and widen the responsibilities of its Advisory Sports Council by rebranding it as the GB Sports Council. One of its first policy initiatives was the *Sport for All* campaign (1972) which sought to use the power of sport to transform individuals and to encourage all members of the community to participate in sport (Houlihan and White 2002; Hylton and Totten 2007).

Its rationale reflected similar sports policy developments in Europe and the social democratic principles of the Labour Government at that time (Houlihan 1991; Houlihan and White 2002). The underpinning social welfare objectives led to the funding of sports initiatives that focused upon disadvantaged inner city youth and were juxtaposed with increased investment in elite sport priorities as a response to growing public demand. These two distinct commitments illustrated the 'underlying tension between the community welfare view of sports development (development through sport) and the perception of sports development as a synonym for talent identification and elite development (development of sport)' (Houlihan and White 2002: 24).

Conflict and confusion (1970s and 1980s)

The policy context for sports development during the 1970s and 1980s was characterised by disharmony, fragmentation and a lack of clear leadership among the various sports bodies involved in the delivery of youth sports (Green 2006). Indeed its parlous state was reflected in Roche's description of sports development as 'one of the most divided, confused and conflictive policy communities in British politics' (1993: 78). The power and influence of the GB Sports Council was compromised by the fiercely independent nature of sports organisations such as the national governing bodies for sport (NGBs), the Central Council of Physical Recreation (CCPR) and the British Olympic Association (BOA), who were resistant to any attempts to interfere in their affairs. As a consequence, there was a lack of any strategic lead in sports development strategy during the 1970s and 1980s (Roche 1993). Although local authorities were the major facilitators in the provision of sports development opportunities within their local communities, they were often unclear about how their role in youth sport delivery overlapped with other agencies such as NGBs, sports clubs and schools (Cowell 1977; Green 2006).

Sports development and schools (1980s and 1990s)

The commonly held assumption of NGBs and sports clubs at the start of the 1980s was that schools would supply them with a steady flow of keen young people wishing to play their respective sports (Evans and Penney 1995; Penney and Evans 1997, 1999; Talbot 1995). However, a number of exogenous factors and changes to the political landscape during the 1980s and 1990s had a significant impact upon the relationships between schools, sport clubs and NGBs (Houlihan 1991). A decline in the national birth rate, an increase in leisure options available to young people and the introduction of a broader range of sports activities onto the PE curriculum meant that traditional sports such as cricket, rugby and athletics had to compete more intensively for talented young people (Talbot 1995). The years between 1986 and 1988 represented a particularly difficult period for PE teachers, who were held responsible by right-wing politicians, the government, and the media for the poor performances of national sports teams and the general decline in the country's moral standards (Evans 1990, 1992; Kirk 1992, 1999). Ensuing debates surrounding whether PE should be retained as a compulsory subject in state schools pushed youth sport onto the political agenda. The realisation that PE might no longer be taught in all state schools led to collective lobbying by the major team sports on behalf of PE (Mason 1985). Its eventual inclusion within the national curriculum for schools was a symbolic representation of the Conservative Government's priorities for PE and youth sport and focused predominantly upon the needs of elite sport (Penney and Chandler 2000). Significantly, the creation of a National Curriculum for Physical Education (NCPE) in 1989 raised the profile of school sport and contributed to renewed government and public interest in youth sport in England.

John Major and youth sport development in the UK

Henry (1993) and Houlihan (1997) suggest that the appointment of Prime Minister John Major in November 1990 contributed a significant change to the British government's approach to sport. The publication of *Sport: Raising the Game* (DNH 1995) was a key UK sports policy document in which John Major described sport as a binding force between generations and a defining characteristic of nationhood and local pride. The policy had a twin emphasis on sporting excellence and youth sport and, significantly, it focused on the development of opportunities for young people to engage in sport and to fulfil their sporting potential. Schools and teachers were 'identified as key agents for realising successful policy implementation' (Houlihan 2000: 174) and for shaping British success on an international stage. It heralded a marked shift away from previous sports development strategies that focused upon mass partici-pation and community recreation, towards more targeted support for elite sport initiatives and youth sport (Green and Houlihan 2005; Roberts 1995).

As a sports policy document, it laid the foundations for new partnership arrangements between sports organisations and the subsequent creation of innovative organisational, financial and administrative frameworks to shape the future direction of sports policy and its delivery for young people (Green 2004). A range of new youth sport initiatives were created and funded through a new National Lottery scheme (established in 1994) in which sport was identified as one of its 'good causes'. This new funding stream precipitated a growth of youth sport oppor-tunities in England during the 1990s. These included Sport England's *Active Schools* programmes (which provided award schemes for quality sport and physical education in schools) and the Youth Sport Trust's TOPS Programmes. The Youth Sport Trust was established in 1994 as a registered charity with funding from wealthy benefactor and businessman Sir John Beckwith, the National Lottery and British Telecom. Its mission was to build a brighter future for young people by creating opportunities to receive a high-quality introduction to sporting opportunities through activity-based programmes. This charitable organisation focused upon improving sporting opportunities for young people of all abilities both in school and within local communities through its TOPS sport programmes. Their success marked the beginning of the Youth Sport Trust's significant commitment to, and influence upon, youth sport policy and practice in England.

Schools and partnership approaches to the delivery of youth sport

Parallel with these developments, were changes in schools that also had a profound effect upon the organisation and delivery of youth sport. In 1994, the launch of the Specialist Schools Programme allowed state secondary schools to deliver innovative and effective teaching and learning in one area of subject expertise. Sport became the chosen focus for some secondary schools that, as a consequence of additional government funding, were required to work with local primary and secondary schools and community groups for the benefit of young people. The expectation was that specialist schools were outward looking and, through innovative, consultative and collaborative practices, would work to improve the quality of sports provision for young people in collaboration with local and national partners (DfES 2005; Evans *et al* 2002). Specialist Sports Colleges became a key partner at the hub of new sport partnership networks. As a condition of funding, these schools were required to engage with local businesses and community groups, sport governing bodies and sports development units in order to develop sustainable sporting opportunities that promoted youth participation (Evans *et al* 2002). Operating at the intersection of multiple policy agendas and interests and managed by the Youth Sport Trust, Specialist Sports Colleges were responsible for raising academic standards in schools, facilitating local community sports development initiatives and supporting NGBs in the delivery, identification and development of sporting talent (Houlihan 2000).

During the 1990s, this renewed interest in sport led to an exponential growth in youth sport initiatives. The Labour manifesto for the 1997 election outlined the government's belief that sport should enhance the nation's sense of community, identity and civic pride. *England, the Sporting Nation* (Sports Council 1997) was the starting point for New Labour's vision for sport in the new millennium. It demonstrated a commitment to the continuation of youth sport policy initiatives and reflected many of the values that had been a feature of *Sport: Raising the Game* (1995).

The Labour Government's desire to address social exclusion led to the re-establishment of sport as a tool for tackling these problems and encouraging active citizenship (Oakley and Green 2001). The government's modernising agenda inevitably impacted upon policy arrangements for youth sport. Sport England took the lead in directing and co-ordinating sports policy delivery by launching initiatives such as the *Active Schools, Active Sports* and *Active Communities* programmes. In June 1999, the Labour Government announced funding for a new multi-agency initiative to create six hundred Schools Sport Co-ordinators to arrange competitive fixtures and improve links between schools and sports clubs. The programme was a collaborative venture between Sport England, Department of Culture, Media and Sport (DCMS), Department for Education and Employment (DfEE), the New Opportunities Fund (NOF) and the Youth Sport Trust (YST). Schools became central hubs for youth sports policy objectives because of their potential to draw together the threads of all the policies for youth sport. It signalled an exponential growth of sports activities involving schools, sports coaches, sports development officers and NGBs in the provision of youth sport. As a consequence, this led to a blurring of the boundaries between the delivery of physical education in schools and community sport provision for young people (Flintoff 2003).

A clearer 'Game Plan' for Young People in the UK (2000 onwards)

A Sporting Future for All (DCMS/DfEE 2000) highlighted the Labour Government's intention that sport in the community and schools and world-class sport should contribute to the social and cultural well-being of the nation. Critically it also provided 'an organizational and administrative framework for the shape and direction of sport policy into the twenty-first century' (Green 2004: 373). It consolidated the dual emphasis upon youth sport and elite sport initiatives and the report's 'Implementation Plan' announced the government's intention to transform school sport through an 'entitlement to sport and physical education for all 5–16 year olds' (DCMS 2001: 13). Specialist Sports Colleges and School Sports Co-ordinators were highlighted as key structural components in a new dynamic infrastructure for youth sport (DfES/DCMS 2003). A five-point plan focused upon rebuilding school sports facilities, the creation of 110 Specialist Sports Colleges, the extension of sporting opportunities beyond the school day, the appointment of School Sport Co-ordinators linked to Specialist Sports Colleges and access for talented 14–18-year-olds to high-quality coaching. Most notably, it emphasised the obligation of education, sport and community partners to work together to deliver sports policy outcomes for young people.

The Physical Education, School Sport and Club Links (PESSCL) strategy

The launch of the national PESSCL strategy in 2002 represented a major commitment by the Labour Government to restructure the delivery of youth sport in the UK (Flintoff 2003). The overall objective of the strategy was a joint DfES and DCMS Public Service Agreement (PSA) target:

> to enhance the take up of sporting opportunities by 5–16 year olds. The aim is to increase the percentage of school children in England who spend a minimum of two hours each week on high quality PE and school sport within and beyond the curriculum to 75 per cent by 2006.
>
> *(DfES 2003:2)*

The strategy was administered through a board of representatives from professional PE associations, head teachers, the Office for Standards in Education (OFSTED), the Qualifications and Curriculum Authority (QCA), Sport England, DCMS, DfES and NGBs. The overarching strategy declared that 'all children, whatever their circumstances or abilities, should be able to participate in, and enjoy, physical education and sport' (DfES/DCMS 2002: 1).

Moran (2005) suggests that, during this period, policy was framed by the Labour Government's desire for administrative decentralisation and the introduction of quantifiable performance indicators through PSA targets. The PESSCL strategy adopted new delivery arrangements for youth sport in which key agencies worked in partnership to meet policy outcomes that were tightly managed and controlled by government. The national PESSCL strategy initially included nine interlinked work strands: Sports Colleges, School Sport Partnerships, School-Club Links, the Gifted and Talented programme, the QCA PE and School Sport Investigation, Step into Sport, Swimming, Sporting Playgrounds and Professional Development. The initiatives were an attempt to create a cohesive framework for youth sport that placed sports colleges and school sport partnerships as key structural components upon which a new sports infrastructure for young people was to be built.

School sport partnerships

School sport partnerships were established in 2000 as networks of primary and secondary schools linked to specialist sports colleges. They received additional government funding to enhance and increase sporting opportunities for all children in a partnership. They sought to improve standards of performance across a range of sports and to increase the number of qualified and active coaches, leaders and officials in schools and local sports clubs (IYS 2004: 1). Partnership Development Managers (PDMs) were created as full-time posts to manage local partners such as sports clubs, local authority sports development units and NGBs and to deliver youth sport policy objectives.

In order to strengthen the links between school sport partnerships and community sports clubs, the School-Club Links work strand focused upon increasing the proportion of young people directed from schools to high-quality club sport. The initiative was enhanced by a range of in-school coaching sessions and the establishment of after-school satellite and junior clubs, community clubs, festivals and competitions aimed at improving pathways from school to club sport. A Gifted and Talented work strand targeted the identification and development of potential young sporting talent through a multi-agency approach. Multi-Skills Academies were also created that were managed and supported by Sports Coach UK (scUK) and the Youth Sport Trust in order to support talented 9–12 years olds. Step into Sport was another multi-agency initiative that involved schools, local education authorities (LEAs), County Sports Partnerships,[1] NGBs and sports clubs in promoting volunteering and leadership opportunities among young people.

A new National Schools Competition Framework was announced in December 2004 as the final piece of the PESSCL jigsaw. The aim was to create a world-class competitive structure for school sport that focused upon improving levels of participation and the identification of talented young performers. Competition Managers were appointed to manage and co-ordinate the delivery of the new framework through a programme of inter-school competitions. The purpose of this new initiative was to rebuild and reintegrate high-quality competitive opportunities that ensured that talented young people had a seamless pathway from school competitions to the competitive structures of sport.

Young people, sports development and active citizenship

The publication of *Game Plan* (DCMS 2002) demonstrated the Labour Government's intention to increase levels of sport and physical activity amongst children and young people. *Game Plan* focused on physical activity, child-centred sport, lifelong opportunity and social inclusion and was indicative of New Labour's broader social investment policy priorities (cf Esping-Anderson *et al* 2002; Green 2006; Lister 2003). Sport England's *Framework for Sport in England* (2004) outlined its new vision and priorities that ensured that young people would be able to '*start, stay and succeed*' in sport and active recreation. As part of Sport England's modernisation delivery plan (Sport England 2004), the target was to increase by 3 per cent the number of young people participating in sports at least 12 times a year. Responsibility for its delivery was devolved by Sport England to Regional Sports Boards and County Sports Partnerships (CSPs). NGBs were required to engage in the delivery of the PESSCL strategy as a condition of their funding. The creation of new local community sports structures meant that NGBs, LEAs and local authorities were directly accountable to Sport England through a performance management system. CSPs supported the delivery of the PESSCL strategy and community sport provision and had an explicit remit to support youth sport by facilitating an increase in club membership through the Club Links element of the PESSCL strategy (Sport England 2005).

Local authorities and youth sport development

Local authorities traditionally played a key role in ensuring that young people had access to sports facilities and coaching in England. However, their power diminished as schools, regeneration partnerships, CSPs, NGBs and commercial sports clubs became increasingly influential in the delivery of youth sport at local level (Jeffery 2003). Research conducted by the Centre for Leisure and Sport Research suggested that whilst sports development teams should be core to the provision of local authority services, their work was often poorly defined and often solely based upon filling the gaps in local sporting provision left by other agencies (Coalter 2002). As a consequence, an assortment of organisations and charities assumed more prominent youth sport delivery roles, whilst local authority sports development teams increasingly existed at the periphery of youth sport acting as enablers rather than deliverers (Glover and Burton 1998; Henry 2001; Ravenscroft 2004).

Publication of the Sport England Report *Shaping Places through Sport* (2008b) highlighted how local authorities and their partners should use sport to build stronger, healthier, sustainable and more prosperous communities. The report outlined the contribution that sport could make to delivering PSA target 12 (to improve the health and well-being of young people) and PSA target 14 (to increase the number of children on the path to sporting success). Sports development teams were required to work in collaborative partnerships with Local Strategic Partnerships (LSPs) and Local Area Agreements (LAAs) to meet the interests and needs of children and young people. The *Local Government and Public Involvement in Health Act* (DoH 2007) provided a list of named partners such as Primary Care Trusts (PCTs), Youth Offending Teams, District Council Authorities and Sport England who had a 'duty to co-operate' with local authorities in the development of LAAs and targets.

Youth sport development and the London 2012 Olympic Games

The successful London 2012 Olympic bid had an undoubted effect on the range of sports opportunities available to young people in the UK. The publication of the DCMS 2012 Legacy Action Plan (LAP) Before, During and After: Making the most of the London 2012 Games (2008a) outlined the government's legacy ambitions for the London 2012 Olympic and Paralympic Games. The plan focused upon using the Games to increase participation in youth sport, to address young people's underachievement and disaffection, and to support young people in making healthy lifestyle choices. To inspire this element of the population, three government-funded London 2012 programmes were launched, which included: the UK School Games, the Young Ambassadors programme and an annual National Talent Orientation Camp to bring together the best 14–17-year-old young athletes.

With a burgeoning and increasingly complex infrastructure for youth sport in England, the launch of *Playing to Win: A new era for sport* (DCMS 2008b) was an attempt to restructure and rationalise sports provision. Three agencies were given responsibility for discrete areas of delivery. The Youth Sport Trust was accountable for PE and school sport; Sport England for the management and delivery of community sport, whilst UK Sport's remit was the development of elite sport. These new structural arrangements were regarded as the key pillars for a decade of sport and high-profile events in which England would fulfil its sporting potential (Andy Burnham, Minister for Sport, 14 May 2009). The Youth Sport Trust spearheaded the rebranding and expansion of the PESSCL strategy, which was renamed the *PE and Sport Strategy for Young People* (PESSYP). Launched in January 2008, it created an innovative world–class system for youth sport that was informed by the views of children and young people. The PESSYP strategy was the joint responsibility of the Department for Children, Schools and Families (DCSF) and the Department for Culture, Media and Sport (DCMS) working in partnership with the Department for Business, Innovation and Skills (BIS) and the Department of Health (DoH). The new strategy included 10 work strands, which are listed in Table 10.1.

Table 10.1 Summary of PESSYP work strands

Work strand	Partners	Delivery objectives
Club links	Sport England, Youth Sport Trust, National Governing Bodies and the Child Protection in Sport Unit	To create high-quality environments that encourage participation of children and young people. Talent development, incorporating the principles of the Long Term Athlete Development model. To recruit and develop coaches and volunteers to provide the best possible activity programmes. To create sports club opportunities for young people that are welcoming, safe, high quality and child friendly.
School sport coaching	School Sport Partnerships, Youth Sport Trust, Sport England and sports coach UK	A step-change in the quantity and quality of coaching offered to young people in sport. To drive up standards of coaching children. A positive contribution to the *Five Hour Offer.* TOP-UP coaching grants to all SSPs to build on local relationships and coaching programmes.
Competition	Consortium Management Group: Youth Sport Trust, Association for PE and sports coach UK	A national network of Competition Managers to work with School Sport Partnerships on inter-school sport. To increase the number of young people engaged in regular competitive opportunities. National School Sport Week.
Continuing professional development	Youth Sport Trust	To train and develop PE teachers and other sports professionals to deliver high-quality targets set by DCSF and PSA target.
Disability	Youth Sport Trust	Establishment of network of 450 Multi-Sport Disability Clubs across SSPs. A club sport experience for all young disabled pupils who are not able or do not wish to access inclusive provision.
Extending activities	County Sport Partnerships/Sport England	Providing activities in areas of deprivation. Sustainable opportunities in sporting activities for young people from the 'semi sporty population segment' to take part in during term time.
Gifted and talented	Youth Sport Trust	To support schools in identifying and supporting talented pupils in PE and sport, to help them to realise their full potential – both in sport and education, especially high achievers, pupils at risk of underachieving and those from disadvantaged areas.

Table 10.1 (continued)

Work strand	Partners	Delivery objectives
Infrastructure	School Sport Partnerships, Further Education Sport Co-ordinators, County Sports Partnerships and NGBs	School Sport Partnerships will remain the key driver for young people's high-quality sports opportunities within and beyond the curriculum. CSPs will play an enhanced role in the delivery of the *Five Hour Offer*. NGBs will continue to play a key role in supporting the delivery of many work strands including Club Links, Step into Sport, Competition Managers.
Leadership and volunteering (Step into Sport 08-11)	Youth Sport Trust and Sport England	A pathway of leadership and volunteering from KS3 to KS5 (aged 11–19). An introduction to Leadership roles through the PE Curriculum using Sport Education through to School-Based Volunteering and ultimately young people as Community Volunteers.
Swimming	DCSF and Amateur Swimming Association (ASA)	DCS Families and ASA commitment to improving School Swimming 2009 to 2011.

The Further Education Sports Co-ordinator (FESCO) programme

A further addition to the raft of sports initiatives for young people was the creation of a formal structure of sports activities for 16–19-year-olds. As part of the PESSYP strategy, the FESCO programme was added to the existing School Sport Partnership arrangements. It was supported by government funding directed through an SSP hub site, but ring-fenced for individual FE Colleges. The intention was to increase opportunities for young people in further education, to participate, perform, lead and volunteer in sport. This meant that students in FE colleges experienced a coherent transition from the secondary school sports system to the FE sports sector, and from FE colleges into community sport. Another objective of the FESCO initiative was to enforce a process of sports development planning that was linked to existing external sports networks. Whilst each FE Co-ordinator was recruited and appointed by individual FE colleges, their work was conducted in liaison with PDMs, CSPs and Community Sport Networks. It represented a final element of a more structured and systematic approach to youth sports development practice.

Conclusion

Youth sport in England is a complex policy area in which a range of organisations, interests and agendas exist. Over the past two decades there has been a concerted attempt, led by the UK government, to clarify the delivery systems for sport. Three organisations, namely the Youth Sport Trust, UK Sport and Sport England, have emerged as the key agencies responsible for the delivery of school sport, elite sport and community sport, respectively. These new structures and initiatives have developed as a consequence of significant government investment in sport and have had a marked impact upon the number of young people who engage in sport and physical activity in England. The DCSF School Sport survey (2007/08) reported that 90% of pupils in SSPs participated in at least two hours of high-quality PE and out of hours school sport in a typical week. This meant that the 2008 PSA target of 85% participation had been exceeded by five percentage points. A range of other surveys attested to how young people were playing a wider range of sports in their leisure time (IYS 2008) and the Active England Programme report (Sport England 2008a) outlined how its initiatives had increased participation in sport and physical activity amongst 636,000 young people in England.

Whilst there is much to be positive about regarding the future of youth sport in England, researchers have highlighted the inherent tensions that arise when partners from education (whose remit is to focus upon outcomes such as raising academic achievement, behaviour and attendance) compete with the demands of elite sport (Houlihan 2000, 2001; Penney 2004). The steady growth of youth sport initiatives in the last three decades is indicative of a trend towards drawing on sport as a vehicle for policy implementation and as a tool to address broader government agendas such as reducing knife crime, tackling obesity, producing future Olympic medallists and improving academic standards in schools (DCSF 2008; Green 2006). Such competing agendas inevitably arise in a policy area of diverse interest groups involved in partnership arrangements that are heavily dependent upon short-term government funding and support (Bailey 2009; Grix 2009; Penney and Jess 2004; Phillpots and Grix 2010). The range of competing discourses and organisations involved in youth sport in England ensures that policy making and delivery is a complex and challenging process (Houlihan 2000). Nevertheless, the restructuring and strengthening of youth sport structures in England has undoubtedly improved the sports opportunities available to young people and at the start of the twenty-first century they have an unsurpassed range of opportunities to engage with, and to develop through sport.

Note

1 There are 49 County Sports Partnerships across England. Each CSP comprises a small core staff group and a wider partnership of different agencies committed to providing a high-quality single system to help people to access and benefit from sport.

References

Allison, L (1998) Sport and Civil Society, *Political Studies*, 46, 4:709–26.

Bailey, R (2009) *Positive Youth Development Through Sport*, London: Routledge.

Bergsgard, N A; Houlihan, B; Mangset, P; Rommetvedt, H and Nodland, S I (2007) *Sport Policy: A Comparative Analysis of Stability and Change*, Oxford: Butterworth-Heinemann.

Burnham, A (2009) *Hosting the rugby World Cup would boost football's 2018 bid*, www.guardian.co.uk (accessed 14/5/09).

Coalter, F (1988) *Sport and Anti-social Behaviour. A Literature Review.* Research Report, Scottish Sports Council.

——(1990) The mixed economy of leisure in Henry, I P (ed.) *Management and Planning in the Leisure Industries* (pp 3–31), Basingstoke: MacMillan Press.

——(2002) Sport and Community Development: A Manual, Edinburgh: sportscotland.

——(2007) *A Wider Social Role for Sport: Who's Keeping the Score?* London: Routledge.

Coalter, F; Long, J and Duffield, B (eds) (1986) *Rationale for Public Service Investment in Leisure*, London: Sports Council and Economic and Social Research Council.

Coghlan, J and Webb, I M (1990) *Sport and British Politics Since 1960*, Brighton: Falmer.

Collins, M F (2003) *Sport and Social Exclusion*, London: Routledge.

Cowell, D W (1977) The Marketing of Local Authority Sports Centre Services, *European Journal of Marketing*, 11, 6: 445–56.

Department for Culture, Media and Sport (DCMS) (2000), *A Sporting Future for All*, London: HMSO.

DCMS (2001) *The Government's Plan for Sport*, London: HMSO.

——(2002) *Game Plan: A Strategy for Delivering Government's Sport and Physical Activity Objectives*, London: DCMS.

——(2008a) *2012 Legacy Action Plan* Before, During and After: Making the Most of the London 2012 Games, London: DCMS.

——(2008b) *Playing to Win: A New Era for Sport*, London: DCMS.

DCMS/DfEE (2001) *Sporting Future for All*, London: DCMS/DfEE.

DCSF (2008) *School Sport Survey*, London: DCSF.

DfES & DCMS (2002) *Learning Through PE and Sport*, Nottinghamshire: DfES Publications.

——(2003) *Learning Through PE and Sport. A Guide to the Physical Education, School Sport and Club Link Strategy*, London: DFES.

DfES (2003) *A New Specialist System: Transforming Secondary Education*, London: DfES.

——(2005) *An Evaluation of the School Sport Partnership Programme*, London: DCMS/DfES.

DNH (1995) *Sport: Raising the Game*, London, DNH.

DoH (2007) *The Local Government and Public Involvement in Health Act* (2007), www.opsi.gov.uk/acts/acts2007/ukpga_20070028_en_1 (accessed 20/02/09).

Esping-Anderson, G; Gallie, D; Hemerijck, A and Myles, A J (2002) *Why We Need a New Welfare State*, Oxford: Oxford University Press.

Evans, D; Whelan, J; Neal G (2002) *Best Practice in Sports Colleges*, Loughborough: Youth Sports Trust.

Evans H (1994) *Service to Sport: The Story of the CCPR 1935–1972*, London: Pelham.

Evans J (1990) Defining a Subject: The Rise and Rise of the New PE? *British Journal of Sociology of Education*, 11, 2: 155–69.

——(1992) Authority and Representation in Ethnographic Research Subjectivity, Ideology and Educational Reform: The Case of Physical Education *in* Sparkes, A (ed.) *Research in Physical Education and Sport: Exploring Alternative Visions* (pp 231–47), London: Falmer Press.

Evans J and Penney D (1995) Physical Education, Restoration and the Politics of Sport, *Pedagogy, Culture & Society*, 3, 2: 183–96.

Flintoff, A (2003) The School Sport Co-ordinator Programme: Changing the Role of the Physical Education Teacher? *Sport, Education and Society*, 8, 2: 231–50.

Glover, T D and Burton, T L (1998) A Model of Alternative Forms of Public Leisure Services Delivery *in* Collins M F and Cooper I S (eds) *Leisure Management: Issues and Applications*, Wallingford, Oxon: CAB International.

Green, M (2004) Changing Policy Priorities for Sport in England: The Emergence of Elite Sport Development as a Key Policy Concern, *Leisure Studies*, 23, 4: 365–85.

——(2006) From 'Sport for All' to not about 'Sport' at all? Interrogating Sport Policy Interventions in the United Kingdom, *European Sport Management Quarterly*, 6, 3: 217–38.

Green, M and Houlihan, B (2005) *Elite Sport Development: Policy Learning and Political Priorities*, London: Routledge.

Grix, J (2009) Assessing the Impact of UK Sport Policy: An In-depth Case Study of the Governance of Athletics in the UK, *International Journal of Sport Policy*, 1, 1: 31–49.

Henry, I P (1993) *The Politics of Leisure Policy*, Basingstoke: MacMillan.

——(2001) *Sport in the City: The Role of Sport in Economic and Social Regeneration*, London: Routledge.

Houlihan, B (1991) *The Government and Politics of Sport*, London: Routledge.

——(1997) *Sport, Policy and Politics: A Comparative Analysis*, London: Routledge.

——(2000) Sporting Excellence, Schools and Sports Development: The Politics of Crowded Policy Spaces, *European Physical Education Review*, 6: 171–93.

——(2001) Citizenship, Civil Society and the Sport and Recreation Professions, *Managing Leisure*, 6: 1–14.

——(2005) *Sport and Society: A Student Introduction*, London: Sage.

Houlihan, B and White, A (2002) *The Politics of Sports Development*, New York: Routledge.

Hylton, K and Totten, M (2007) in Hylton K and Bramham P (eds) *Sports Development: Policy, Process and Practice*, London: Routledge.

IYS (2004) *School Sport Partnerships: Annual Monitoring and Evaluation Project Report for 2004*, Loughborough: Loughborough Partnership.

——(2008) *The Impact of School Sport Partnerships on Pupil Attainment*, Loughborough: Loughborough Partnership.

Jeffery, C (2003) *Devolution: Challenging Local Government?* York: Joseph Rowntree Foundation.

Kay, T (2000) Sporting Excellence: A Family Affair? *European Physical Education Review*, 6: 151–62.

Kirk, D (1992) *Defining Physical Education: The Social Construction of a School Subject in Post War Britain*, London: Falmer Press.

——(1999) *Ways of Thinking about the Relationship between School Physical Education and Sport Performance*. Paper presented at the CRSS/EPER Conference of Physical Education and Sporting Excellence, University of Leicester, September 1999.

——(2005) Physical Education, Youth Sport and Lifelong Participation: The Importance of Early Learning Experiences, *European Physical Education Review*, 11: 3–239.

Labour Party (1997) *New Labour: Because Britain Deserves Better. General Election Manifesto*, London: Labour Party.

Lentell, B (1993) Sports Development: Goodbye to Community Recreation? *in* Brackenridge C (ed.) *Body Matters: Leisure Images and Lifestyle*, Eastbourne: Leisure Studies.

Lister, R (2003) Investing in the Citizen-workers of the Future: Transformations in Citizenship and the State under New Labour, *Social Policy and Administration*, 37, 5: 427–43.

MacDonald, I (1995) Sport for All – 'RIP'; a Political Critique of the Relationship between National Sport Policy and Local Authority Sports Development in London, *in* Fleming, S; Talbot, M and Tomlinson, A (eds) *Policy and Politics in Sport, PE and Leisure*, Brighton: Leisure Studies Association.

Mason, V (1985) *Young People and Sport – A National Survey*, London: OPCS.

McIntosh, P and Charlton, V (1985) *The Impact of Sport for All Policy 1966–1984*, London: Sports Council.

Moran, M (2005) *Politics and Governance in the UK*, Basingstoke: Palgrave.

Oakley, B and Green, M (2001) Still Playing the Game at Arm's Length? The Selective Re-investment in British Sport, 1995–2000, *Managing Leisure*, 6: 74–94.

Penney, D (2004) Policy Tensions being Played Out in Practice. The Specialist Schools Initiative in England, *Journal of Critical Education Policy Studies*, 2: 1.

Penney, D and Chandler, T (2000) Physical Education: What Future(s)? *Sport Education and Society*, 1, 1: 47–57.

Penney, D and Evans, J (1995) Changing Structures, Changing Rules: The Development of the 'Internal Market', *School Organisation*, 15, 1: 13–21.

——(1997) Naming the Game. Discourse and Domination in PE and Sport in England and Wales, *European PE Review*, 3, 1: 21–32.

——(1999) *Politics Policy and Practice in PE*, London: E & FN Spon.

Penney, D and Jess, M (2004) Physical Education and Physically Active Lives: A Lifelong Approach to Curriculum Development, *Sport, Education and Society*, 9, 2: 269–88.

Phillpots, L and Grix, J (2010) *The Increasing Politicisation of Youth Sport Policy Delivery in the UK: A Case Study of School-Club Links*, European Physical Education Review (forthcoming).

Pickup, D (1996) *Not Another Messiah: An Account of the Sports Council 1988–1993*, Bishop Auckland: Pentland Press.

Ravenscroft, N (2004) *Sport and Local Delivery*, Brighton: Chelsea School, University of Brighton.

Roberts, K (1995) Young People, Schools, Sport and Government Policies, *Sport Education and Society*, 1, 1: 47–57.

Roche, M (1993) Sport and Community: Rhetoric and Reality in the Development of British Sport Policy *in* Binfield, J and Stevenson, J (eds) *Sport, Culture and Politics* (pp 72–112), Sheffield: Sheffield Academic Press. Routledge.

Rowe, N and Champion, R (2000) *Young People and Sport National Survey 1999*, London: Sport England.

Social Exclusion Unit (SEU) (2000) *Report of Policy Action Team 16: Learning Lessons*, London: SEU.

Sport England (2004) *The Framework for Sport in England: Making England an Active and Successful Sporting Nation: A Vision for 2020*, London.

——(2005) *County Sports Partnerships Performance Management Framework*, www.sportengland.org/taes_for_csps_final.doc (accessed 12/04/07).

——(2008a) *Sport and Physical Activity: Active England Final Report*, London.

——(2008b) *Shaping Places Through Sport*, www.sportengland.org/executive_summary_web_version.pdf (accessed 9/09/08).

Sports Council (1997) *England The Sporting Nation*, London: The Sports Council.

Talbot, M (1995) Physical Education and the National Curriculum: Some Political Issues, *Leisure Studies Association Newsletter*, 41: 20–30.

11

The development of sport and youth in France

Jean-Luc Lhéraud, Bernard Meurgey and Patrick Bouchet

When researchers refer to individuals as 'chameleons' (Simmons 2008), 'paradoxical and fragmented' (Firat and Venkatesh 1993) or as guided by a quest for eclecticism and hedonism (Hetzel 2002), they all emphasize the fact that behaviour has become less predictable and stable than in the past. Whether this is *'consumer made'* (Cova 2008), or that is the consequence of consumerism, or the emergence of a 'plural man' (Lahire 2005), these writers observe transformations in the relations between society and individuals and the emergence of heterogeneous practices particularly in the field of leisure and sports. In this context, we can reflect upon the complex ways in which youth (from 3 to 24 years of age) articulate, adjust and regulate (or not) their behaviours in relation to sport and the contexts of its consumption. Hence, in France, one could investigate why the young are not active enough, especially girls. In other words, why they do not follow international guidelines that recommend the equivalent of one hour of physical activity every day. According to a summer 2009 study published by the Agence Française de Sécurité Sanitaire des Aliments (French food standards agency): 'exactly 43.2% of teenagers … reach a level of physical activity [that leads] to health benefits … more than six boys out of ten against fewer than one girl out of four [reach the recommended standard]'. But what does physical activity mean? The European Union working group 'Sport and Health' defines it as 'any corporal movement associated with muscular contraction which increases the consumption of energy compared to levels observed at rest'[1] and includes in that definition physical activities undertaken in an organized form (managed by a third party) or self-organized (done alone) at home, in public areas or specialist sports facilities and sites.

Previously, a period of 20 minutes per day was recommended, then new Anglo-Saxon studies recommended regular periods of activity of an average intensity. Health studies suggest that children are physically able to begin a sport at the age of six. Children under six need to move and expend their energy every day since this is necessary for the development of their motor abilities and coordination, but doing sports has been continually on the decrease over the past few decades. Today's teenagers are 40 per cent less active than they were 30 years ago. According to French data from the international Health Behaviour among School-Aged Children survey (2008), 'more than one out of two young people do not use an active form of transportation (by foot, bike or roller blade) to go to school'.[2] Furthermore, the development of transportation and the arrival of digital technology – with its all-powerful screen (computers, game consoles, cell phones, etc.) has increased sedentary habits which are accompanied by the development of obesity. On average, 3–17-year-old children spend roughly three hours a day in front of a screen, and this amount of time increases with age. Yet, according to The European Food Information Council: 'physical or sports activity is a major determinant of the mental and physical state of health of individuals and populations at all ages of life'.[3]

Faced with these observations, the French Institute of Biomedical and Epidemiological research on sports set an objective that 80 per cent of children from the ages of 3 to 18 should do at least one hour of physical and sports activity per day. This target was set despite the recognition that the number of hours devoted to physical activity and sport in school diminishes with age and that girls' reluctance to do sports increases with age. In order to overcome this low level of physical activity among youth, federal and non-federal associations currently aim to develop non-competitive leisure activities, open to all in keeping with this population's prioritization of socializing and having fun. The conventional wisdom is that an active youth has more of a chance of becoming an active adult if physical activity is pleasurable, which is an aspect of physical activity and sport that is not always appreciated by those responsible for delivery. As a result, numerous sports brands (video games, equipment, etc.) and free-lance workers (coaches, physical therapists, etc.) are attempting to offer products that are likely to make physical exertion and relaxation in 'private' areas (at home, in gyms, etc.) attractive to young people disappointed with the 'traditional' range of activities and sports on offer.

In order to analyze the development of sports among youth in France, we believe that it is necessary to understand not only the evolution of supply and demand which is concretized in ways of doing sports, but also the consumption of sporting goods common to other westernized countries and specific to France.

The range of sports opportunities for youth in France

The polysemy of sport enables an extremely varied discourse on its virtues and on the rationale for doing sport (education, citizenship, health, well-being, expression, etc.) particularly for youths between the ages of 3 and 24. In France, those who offer sports activities for the young are divided into four major categories: the national education system through its physical education classes and extracurricular activities associations; federal (and non-federal) associations that issue membership cards for competitors or young officials; public policies through national or local programmes; and specialist private organizations. These categories reflect the current offer and, of course, they are not mutually exclusive; young people can do sport simultaneously or consecutively with several providers.

The provision of sport in the education system

The scholastic provision of sport is of two types, one being compulsory: physical education classes (PE), and the other voluntary through membership of a school's sports association. Four educational levels exist in France: nursery, primary, secondary school and university.

- *In nursery school:* the national curriculum provides for a daily session of compulsory PE for 3–5-year-old children that involves sessions to discover and develop motor activities and, in theory, represents an annual total of 280 hours (2 hours times 4 days times 35 weeks). Nursery schools do not have extracurricular associations.
- *In primary school:* the national curriculum states that the students (aged 6–11 years) must have at least three hours a week of PE, with a minimum of two sessions a week. As a rule, the teachers give these classes, but some activities (swimming, outdoor sports, gymnastics, etc.)

can be taught by visiting specialists certified by the board of education. In theory, these classes represent an annual total of 210 hours of sport (2 times 3 hours times 35 weeks). In addition, students may choose to participate in extracurricular activities through school associations affiliated to the Elementary School Sports Club (Union Sportive de l'Enseignement du Premier degré: USEP). USEP has about 900,000 members in almost 12,000 associations directed by a hundred or so departmental (local government) committees.

- *In junior and senior high school:* PE is a scholastic discipline for young people between the ages of 12 and 18 according to the national curriculum, and each school is also obliged to create a scholastic sports association. In junior high school, the 6th graders (11 years) have 4 hours of PE per week and the 7th and 8th graders and freshmen (12–14 years) have 3 hours per week, while the sophomores, juniors and seniors (15–18 years) in high school have 2 hours. Therefore, students have 455 hours of sports in total in junior high school and 210 hours of sports in high school in their compulsory PE classes unless they receive a dispensation (see Table 11.1).

Parallel to the general plan for all students, the schools can create 'scholastic sports sections' which offer students the opportunity to do sport intensively within the education system. More than a million students participate in what is part of the National Scholastic Sports Club (Union Nationale des Sports Scolaires: UNSS) and can participate in more than 70 different disciplines during the championships. The national project of the UNSS revolves around three themes: the promotion of sports, competition and responsibility among students. Decentralized service providers (31 at regional and 100 at departmental level) are in charge of the coordination and the promotion of this programme in France. The UNSS is a member of the management committee of the Comité National Olympique et Sport Francais (CNOSF) and it is also affiliated with the International Sport School Federation (ISSF).

- *At university:* PE classes are no longer compulsory for young people over 18 and students are free to choose their physical activities. Therefore, activities are proposed and organized on each campus by two university institutions[4]: the French Federation of University Sports (Fédération Française de Sport Universitaire: FFSU), a parallel organization to the UNSS, and the University Service for Physical and Sports Activities (Service Universitaire des Activités Physiques et Sportives: SUAPS) which is a service department found in all universities. The

Table 11.1 Theoretical number of hours of PE calculated on the basis of 35 weeks of classes

Level	Hours of PE per week	Weeks of classes	Total hours of PE
6th	4	35	140
7th	3	35	105
8th	3	35	105
Freshmen	3	35	105
Total hours of PE in junior high school (11–14 years)			*455*
Sophomore	2	35	70
Junior	2	35	70
Senior	2	35	70
Total hours of PE in high school (15–18 years)			*210*
Total hours of compulsory PE at the secondary level			*665*

This is the theoretical number of hours of PE (official instructions) from which time spent in travelling and changing clothes must be deducted.

FFSU groups together all the university associations and its goal is the promotion and organization of competition for university students and students attending the Grandes Ecoles (competitive entrance higher education establishments). During the day, but outside teaching hours, the SUAPS offers various physical activities in response to student demand. The physical activities offered are generally non-competitive, not traditional and social such as climbing, diving, golf, skiing aerobics, dance and yoga.

The number of young members of scholastic and university associations was estimated at 2,410,000 in 2003 (see Table 11.2). Since the 1990s the development of school sports has been a subject of reflection focused on three themes: health (health education, nutrition and obesity), the struggle against social exclusion (immigration and social integration) and scholastic organization (search for better school planning).

Provision for participation in single sports, multi-sports and free sports

The sports federations in France are in charge of organizing and promoting participation in their fields. The Code of Sport (a government regulation) distinguishes between the federations which have government approval and those which have, in addition, received delegated powers. The management structure of each federation is pyramidal with the clubs, represented by a committee on the departmental level, at the base, with a league at the regional level and, finally, at the top, the federal authorities. The sports federations (about 100) include 14,000 single-sport, multi-sport and free sport clubs in France.

- *Single-sport federations* have general authority to manage all the sports activity in their field whether it be high-level sport, amateur sport, professional sport or recreational sport. In principle, the federation has the authority to issue membership cards, which provide the legal and institutional basis of the relationship between the athlete and the federation. The government through the sports minister closely supervises the federal sports federations. Close supervision

Table 11.2 Percentage of young people with a sports membership card by type of federation in 2003

Type of federation	Number of sports membership cards delivered (in thousands)	Percentage aged under 20 with membership cards	Origin of membership cards held by the young	Estimated number of young with membership cards (in thousands)
Single sport Olympics federation	6,983	60%	54%	4,300
Single sport non-Olympics federation	2,497	25%	8%	625
Multi-sports and free sports federation	2,189	25%	7%	552
Scholastic and university federation	2,535	95%	31%	2,410
TOTAL	14,204	56%	100%	7,887

Source: Census of qualified sports federations, 2003 (Ministry of Sports – Statistical Mission 2005)

is a specific characteristic of the French federal model producing a hybrid organizational model which combines freedom of association and government supervision. The organization of sport in France can consequently best be described as a public service with private management. Between 1943 and 2003, the different single-sport federations saw their membership increase significantly, but then stagnate over the following years.

- *Free sport or multi-sport federations* have general authority to organize and promote several sports disciplines. Thus, members of these federations could participate competitively in several disciplines with their unique multi-sport membership card. The origin of these large multi-sport or free sport federations in France is linked to workers', religious or secular movements, to the rural environment or to the sector providing support for people with disabilities. Between 1943 and 2003 the membership of multi-sport and free sport federations remained relatively stable compared to other federations. In 2003 they had 552,000 young members (see Table 11.2) in numerous federations or clubs, although 20 federations accounted for the vast majority of members.

- *The number of young people participating in sports associations* in France is high, representing 56 per cent of total association membership (15 per cent for those under 9 years, 25 per cent for those between 10 and 14, and 25 per cent for those between 15 and 19) (Stat Info no. 05–01, February 2005, p.1–2). The number of young non-scholastic members is estimated at 5,477,000 (see Table 11.2) with almost 4,300,000 single-sport members in Olympic disciplines. In many federations more than half the membership comprises those aged 19 years and under (see Table 11.3).

- *The crisis in the competitive sports model for youth.* Until the early 2000s the federal sports model had been an effective framework for youth participation, but the diversification of sports and of participants is shown by a drop in participation in competitive sports. The official figures from the Sport Ministry for 2001 speak for themselves: 26 million French people between the ages of 15 and 75 claim to do sports at least once a week, while the total number with sports association membership amounts to 10 million and the actual number of competitors is estimated to be roughly 5 million (the difference is due to the fact that an individual can have several memberships cards, for example, a club membership and a scholastic membership). The differential is then 21 million French people who do some sport, but outside the traditional system.

A change in federal sports provision towards a sports economy based on demand has been observed over the past 10 years partly in response to the high level of drop-out from sport during adolescence (Machard 2003) but also to the changing motivations of those young people who continue to participate, including a greater concern with a 'return to nature' and a more consumerist attitude. In the late 1990s it was acknowledged that the 'federal clubs' were not adapting to the changed expectations of the young. In fact, the real problem confronting these structures continues to be how to adapt to the demands of youth in our consumer society without the traditional sports associations 'losing their soul' and having to dilute their provision of traditional sport. Faced with these challenges, beginning in 2002, the Ministry of Health and Sports initiated a policy to develop the social and educational function of federal sports for all, but particularly for those with the most difficulty in accessing sport.

National and local public plans for youth sport participation

In 1998, with the aim of ensuring the greatest access possible to sport for young people, the Sports Ministry implemented an experimental plan called 'coupon sport'[5] intended to encourage participation, particularly by young people whose families are eligible for a school

147

Table 11.3 Federations (with more than 100,000 members) in 2003 with the highest proportion of young members

Federation	Note	9 years and under	10–14 years	15–19 years	Total of 19 years and under	Percentage of membership aged 19 years and under
French Soccer Federation	(ec)	349,134	459,769	318, 147	1,137,050	62.5%
French Tennis Federation		137, 350	254,212	149,776	541,338	50.4%
French Federation of Judo-Jujitsu, Kendo and related disciplines		227,576	156,048	51,030	434,654	79.9%
French Equestrian Federation		90,045	153,847	79,093	322,985	69.8%
French Basketball Federation		36,675	130,452	105,638	272,765	63.9%
French Handball Federation	(ec)	61,765	113,526	53,320	228,611	75.4%
French Gymnastics Federation		91,261	58,630	22,055	171,946	74.5%
French Swimming Federation		44,398	74,145	28,983	147,526	68.2%
French Karate and Martial Arts Federation		41,392	59,856	28,822	130,070	64.9%
French Athletic and Cultural Federation		64,016	44,566	19,266	127,848	58.7%
French Rugby Federation		20,302	46,937	45,660	112,899	50.7%
French Table Tennis Federation	(ec)	19,795	51,498	31,642	102,935	57.0%

Source: Census of qualified sports federations done in 2003 (Ministry of Sport – Statistical Mission) (Stat Info no. 05-01, February 2005, 4)
Notes:
(ec): categories calculated based on the categories communicated by the federations concerned
ec = data provided by the federation
Figures do not add to 100% due to rounding

allowance. Further plans were proposed (in collaboration with other Ministries) to avoid the drop-off in sports activities of teenagers. The principal aim was that the educational and sport activities of the young person would be the object of a common project shared by all policy actors and service providers. The objective was to harmonize teaching, peripheral and extracurricular hours throughout the country. This is the origin of national plans currently being implemented (see Annex 1) such as the Local Education Contracts (Contrats Educatifs Locaux: CEL) which affirm the intention to ensure genuine educational continuity for young people with all the partners concerned (families, government – particularly the teachers, sports associations and communities). The objectives of the CEL are clearly defined: to develop access to cultural and sports activities for all children and adolescents, particularly the most disadvantaged, to improve scholastic results, to establish an effective framework for this project with the participation and cooperation of the different actors in education, to involve young people in the actions undertaken, to organize the training of leaders and to verify their qualifications. The priority beneficiaries are children under 16 (2–5 years: 20.7 per cent, 6–11 years: 46.1 per cent, 12–16: 27.1 per cent, over 16 years: 6.1 per cent).[6] Physical and sports activities represent the sphere of activity favoured (they make up 95 per cent of the contracts). The CEL coexists with other plans in most cities (see Annex 1).

Moreover, the Vacation and Leisure Centres (Centres de Vacances et de Loisirs: CVL) and the Leisure Day Centres (Centres de Loisirs Sans Hébergement: CLSH) (about 33,000)

Table 11.4 The sports activities preferred by the young during their summer vacations (%)

Age	Equestrian activities	Canoe-kayak, rafting and water activities	Windsurfing	Tennis
Under 10 years	26	6	2	11
10–14 years	23	29	16	23
15–19 years	12	11	25	11
20–24 years	3	6	13	9
Over 25 years	36	48	44	44
Total	*100*	*100*	*100*	*100*

Source: INSEE, 2004 vacation survey in Ministry of Sport – Statistical Mission (2007)

are public services offering physical activities and other services in the form of sports vacations for schools (30,000 trips per year). In 2007, about 1,126,300 young people attended a CVL (source: Department of Youth and Popular Education, Department of Vacations and Leisure for Minors, April, 2008): 16,000 nursery school children (4–6 years), 447,100 for 6–12 years, 662,600 for 13–17 years; in addition, 232,300 teenagers (under 18) attended stationary and touring camps. The most sough-after sports among young people during their summer vacations are equestrian and water activities, windsurfing and tennis (see Table 11.4).

Alongside, and complementing these organizations, the communes (local administrative districts) created their 'Municipal School for Sports' (Ecole Municipale des Sports: EMS) over recent years. Far from wanting to compete with the sports clubs, which also offer an introduction to single disciplines, these schools answer the demand for multidisciplinarity made by young persons who are not yet specialized in a particular sport (the 'zapping generation'). These EMSs, organized and managed by the municipal service of sports, are arranged around the school calendar and offer five to six rather general activity sessions which more often serve as an introduction to traditional disciplines. The children can discover 'ball games', 'racket games', 'gymnastics activities', etc., which is a good springboard for future participation in sports (whether in a club or not). With the development of greater inter-communal cooperation, these EMSs are managed increasingly by groups of communes.

Finally, at the beginning of the 2007 school year, the Minister of Education wanted to use what had already been put in place by the communities to develop a plan for 'educational support' after school (mainly between 4 pm and 6 pm, four days per week, in three areas: aid with homework, participation in sports, and artistic and cultural activities). This educational support is supervised by voluntary teachers and municipal workers, as well as sports associations.

The private services specialized in physical activities for the young

Historically, few private organizations in France have specialized in sports activities for the young compared to the scholastic, associative and public provision. Vacation clubs, beach clubs and summer camps existed, of course, and offered physical activities to children during the school vacations. These seasonal services were never fully inventoried although they had to request certification (commercial, state or local) in order to operate in France. But over the past 20 years, especially in large French cities, the development of private provision of sports activities for youth has been observed, two examples of which seem to have met with a certain success: Sports Elite Jeunes and The Little Gym®.

Sports Elite Jeunes[7] (SEJ or Sports Training Camps) provide sports vacation programmes for children from 7 to 17 adapted to each individual's level. Numerous sports are offered as well as advanced language classes, remedial education courses, early learning activities and trips abroad. Everything is designed for these children's vacations: the environment, varied programmes, personalized follow-up and permanent supervision. Twenty-two camps are located throughout France and offer multi-sport and training programmes or specialized programmes such as ski-snowboard camps.

The concept of The Little Gym®[8] was developed by Robin Wes, a professor of physical education and psychomotricity, who opened his first centre in 1976. His revolutionary concept answered a dual need: a) to give sport an educational value by creating a non-competitive programme for stimulating the physical, emotional, social and intellectual development of children (from 3 to 12 years); and b) to offer a programme to develop motor capacities also accessible to children under the age of 3. With more than 300 franchises in over 19 countries, The Little Gym® is currently the world leader in programmes designed to develop children's motor capacities. Several centres exist in France where they have met with considerable success and further centres are planned.

The sport activities of French youth

Nearly 20 million individuals, or roughly 31.4 per cent of the working population in France were under 25 years of age in 2007 (see Table 11.5). Their sports activities show wide variations according to their age bracket and the socio-cultural characteristics of their activity.

Age and youth sport activity in France

The variations in sports participation according to age (Aubel *et al* 2007) show a very clear break between the school years (nursery and primary school, junior and senior high school, and after obtaining their diploma) and later years concerning the rate of participation, the range of activities selected and the mode of participation.

Young children: doing sports under supervision

The three most popular sports for very young children in France are dance, gymnastics and judo – all activities that offer the possibility of doing sports under supervision at a younger age

Table 11.5 Age distribution of those aged under 25 in 2007

Age group	Male	Female	Total
0–4 years	2,050,505	1,960,742	4,011,247
5–9	2,015,564	1,923,316	3,938,880
10–14	1,952,013	1,860,932	3,813,245
15–19	2,077,724	1,995,013	4,072,737
20–24	2,046,604	2,012,338	4,058,836
Total under 25	*10,142,604*	*9,752,341*	*19,894,945*
Young people under the age of 25 as a % of the working population	*16.0%*	*15.4%*	*31.4%*

Source: INSEE, civil status; population at 1 January 2007, in Ministry of Health (2007)

than that proposed by other sports. However, the parents' decision plays a major role during this period of a child's life and often reflects the preferences of parents rather than those of their children. Perhaps not surprisingly these sports also have the characteristic of being more frequently abandoned than other sports. This parental initiation into sport also helps structure the significance of gender in relation to adult participation. The traditional roles are already (or are being) established. Girls do dance and gymnastics: in 2002, the gymnastics federation issued 18 per cent of its membership cards in dance and gymnastics to children of 6 and under (which corresponds to 40,000 children, 79 per cent of them female). Boys do judo: in 2002, the Judo-Jujitsu federation issued 12 per cent of its membership cards in judo to children of 6 and under (60,000 children, 76 per cent of them male).

Children and teenagers: the age of eclecticism and the everyday athlete

A large proportion of children and adolescents do sports outside the school setting, but about one-third do no more than what is strictly compulsory in school. The fact that adolescents very often choose to do certain sports independently is linked to the multitude of activities in which they participate: the young report that they participate in an average of seven sports/physical activities. Teenagers, typically, seem to choose a sport that they will do in a club, but also play other sports outside the club structure. Nevertheless, the proportion of young people who take part in competitive sport in these clubs is only 19 per cent, although this proportion is higher than that of young adults (see Table 11.6) and the overall percentage of children and teenagers who do sports (64.1 per cent, see Table 11.7) is significantly higher than that of the French population as a whole.

There is a relatively high level of participation in sport during free time by youths aged between 10 and 14 (74 per cent). Participation by 4–9-year-olds is lower, possibly because they are too young to participate in a certain number of activities in an after-school association in spite of the efforts made by many sports in this direction (baby-gym, baby swimmers, etc.). In addition to the intrinsic attraction of sport, the reason for the high participation rate among 10–14-year-olds is probably more pragmatic. When children are not in school, the parents must find activities, especially sporting ones, for their offspring who are not sufficiently autonomous to be left at home without supervision.

If we observe the regularity of children's and teenagers' participation in sport (Table 11.8), 16.7 per cent of them generally do sports almost every day, and 54.3 per cent two or three times per week. If the total of those who do sports at least once a week is added, then 95 per cent

Table 11.6 Sports participation by age (15 years and older) and by type of participation

Age range, years	Percentage participating in sport	Percentage involved in sport in a club or association	Percentage involved in competitive sport
15–24	90	46	19
25–34	84	37	10
35–44	83	35	9
45–54	72	28	6
55–64	67	31	7
65 plus	37	20	3
Total	71	34	10

Source: INSEE, 'Cultural and sports participation' survey, 2003 in Ministry of Health (2007)

Table 11.7 Percentage of children and teenagers who do sports

Age range	Non-participants	Participants
4–9 years	39.3%	60.7%
10–14 years	26.0%	74.0%
15–19 years	43.7%	56.3%
Total	35.9%	64.1%

Source: Aubel *et al.* 2007

Table 11.8 The frequency of children's and teenagers' sports participation

Age range	Every day or almost	2 to 3 times per week	Once a week	Every 2 or 3 weeks	Once a month
4–9 years	8.7%	47.6%	41.9%	1.8%	0.0%
10–14 years	21.3%	59.2%	17.3%	2.2%	0.0%
15–19 years	22.5%	57.4%	18.4%	0.8%	0.9%
Total	16.7%	54.3%	27.0%	1.8%	0.2%

Source: Aubel *et al.* 2007

of the children and teenagers have a sports pastime. A direct link exists between the frequency of doing sports and club membership. Whatever the sport, teenagers do sport more regularly when they do it in a club than when they do it independently. On average, 94 per cent of those in a club do sports more than once a week against only 52 per cent who do sports independently. Therefore, it can be hypothesized that belonging to a club is linked to a high regularity of participation and results in a strong involvement with competition. But the very idea of competition is one of the factors that is shown to be a disincentive to participate for the majority of teenagers!

Moreover, an examination of the sports played shows an important eclecticism of the physical activities, as well as a noticeably different profile. Thirty-six point seven per cent of children and teenagers participate in at least six activities, and 61.1 per cent in at least four. Among the 25 most cited sports, the number of those in which the 'young' are over-represented is particularly important (19 out of 25) compared to 'all ages'. Although the ranking of the popularity of the 25 sports preferred by the young is not the same as that for 'all ages' (see Table 11.9) there are few different sports. Sports traditionally available in schools that feature on the list of 'sports for the young' include swimming (compulsory in 6th grade), table tennis, badminton, track and field, gymnastics, etc. In addition to these 'school classics', team sports hold a good place particularly because they relate to 'street' versions of sports such as soccer and basketball.

Choice of sport is also influenced by social status, for example, the highly elitist image of golf in France compared to Scotland or Ireland, and by income. The level of sports participation increases with the parents' income and level of education. The sports chosen for young children by parents will often be abandoned at adolescence, although this does not indicate the end of all physical activity. Quite the contrary, it is more of a sign of independence, a shift toward new orientations in other activities that are not necessarily sporting. Some activities, such as those related to sports which involve sliding, are an especially revealing example of a particular mode of the social construction of the self. Sometimes, contrary to generally accepted ideas, the young surfer in France (surf, snowboard, windsurf) is not a rebel. The commitment to this type of risky

Table 11.9 The 25 sports preferred by the young

Sports/activities	From 4 to 18 years (%)	All ages (%)
Swimming	48.5	37.5
Bike riding/hybrid biking	48.5	32.5
Soccer	40.5	16.2
Basketball	25.7	8.2
Gymnastics	22.6	11.2
Badminton	22.5	11.0
Table tennis	21.5	11.8
Roller blading/roller skating	20.5	8.6
Track and field	20.2	6.8
Mountain biking	17.4	13.9
Downhill skiing	15.5	12.1
Handball	15.4	4.2
Hiking/trekking	11.7	21.3
Fishing	10.8	10.5
Tennis	13.4	8.8
Martial arts (judo, karate, etc.)	13.4	5.1
Boule/pétanque/bowling	15.1	21.9
Jogging/running	14.1	16.0
Ballet, contemporary dance, etc.	14.0	7.4
Ice skating	12.2	5.6
Equestrianism	12.0	5.3
Outdoor cycling	10.0	9.0
Canoe/kayak/rowing	4.6	4.3
Body building	5.3	9.4
Fitness	2.4	7.9

Source: Aubel *et al.* 2007

sport, which often involves an apparatus, is less of a rebellion than a way to achieve social construction through physical activities. Knowing oneself, one's capabilities, limits and ability to master precise techniques appear to be necessary assets for doing disciplines with a 'strong social image' well.

Those over 18

Sports participation declines around the age of 20: this coincides with the low incomes of students and the low and often precarious income of young workers and the development of other interests; the most often mentioned at this age are cultural activities, girlfriends, etc. Nineteen–22-year-olds are often involved with final exams and the beginning of university studies (almost 75 per cent of an age group earns a high school diploma in France). Young adults do a little less sport, tend to drop out of clubs, have fewer membership cards, and young women do less competitive sport. The transition to work, with modest incomes and/ or living at home, also explains this loss of interest. However, this trend is reversed among young adults between 23 and 24 years of age. Those in this age group have a higher rate of club membership than those between 19 and 22 and also a higher rate of participation in competitive sport.

The socio-cultural characteristics of doing sports in the school setting and associations

Entering junior high school accentuates the relation that exists between sports participation and the process of social construction by young people. Strong disparities emerge at the end of this period: while 81 per cent of the boys from advantaged socio-economic environments do sports, the percentage for girls from modest socio-economic environments is only 40 per cent. Participation also differs with the educational track being followed. Participation is lower among those on the professional (vocational) track, in contrast to those following the academic or technical track in high school: 71 per cent in contrast to 81 per cent for boys and 40 per cent as opposed to 63 per cent for girls.

This difference reflects the elaboration of the social construction of sport that progressively leads French teenagers toward their identity according to one of two broad types. The first is constituted of those who go to high school, have a higher rate of doing sports than the average and who come from environments in which the parents' levels of education and income are high. The second type is constituted of those who choose to follow vocational tracks, whose rate of doing sports will diminish and who come from environments in which the parents' level of education and incomes are significantly lower.

The sports that teenagers choose, most often in the framework of an association, are those that call the most for learning rules and techniques (for example, martial arts, gymnastics, dance) and sports that are played in pairs or groups (combat sports, tennis, soccer, handball, etc.) because the club is also a place where one can meet partners and opponents. On the contrary, outdoor sports such as biking, climbing, circus activities or water sports that involve gliding, as well as those often done only during the vacations, such as skiing and ice-related sports, are done independently.

Family is an important influence on club participation and obtaining a membership card in France. In particular, the children whose father does a sport are enrolled in a sports club and have a membership card more often than others. In all, teenagers from advantaged environments and involved in social life will have a mode of doing physical activities that is part of a social model and facilitates their own integration with others.

Three determining factors play a role in young people's decision to drop out of organized sports: the constraints of training, the problem of mastering the technique and the feeling of not being 'good'. These three factors are strongly evoked by young people who do not or no longer do sports beyond the scholastic obligation. Doing sports outside the structure of the clubs appears less as a refusal of a supervised activity than a way to do sports in a less restrictive and less demanding context, and turned more toward individual or group pleasure, which is less expensive for some. In fact, it seems legitimate to think that the refusal to do highly structured sports is partly linked to a range of provision that is not adapted to what young people want. In order to answer this second need, for the past several years, numerous sports and scholastic associations have developed activities involving different sports that are played according to rules that are not necessarily those recognized by the corresponding federation, but which do encourage the young to participate. While this situation is not new in France, its current scale is. Thus, the young express the desire to do sports outside the federation 'model' of competition for reasons linked to pleasure, relaxation, health, social interaction, etc.

Beyond 'doing' sport: the construction of youth participation

The construction of young French athletes' interest in and perception of sport seems to be articulated around two main axes: a 'cultural' axis linked to the consumption of information and sporting events, and a 'consumerist' axis particularly linked to the use of sporting goods and sports video games.

Cultural consumption of information and sporting events

The cultural consumption of information and sporting events by the young French is marked by strong masculinity and a strong affinity for doing sports (Lefèvre 2001). While 69 per cent of male teenagers do extracurricular sports activities, almost 90 per cent of them watch sporting events on television, two out of three read sports newspapers, and one out of two attend sporting events. Hence, important differences appear in relation to the degree of involvement: for the most assiduous (participation in sport 'once a week and more'), television predominates (2 out of 3) followed by reading (1 out of 2), then followed by going to games (1 out of 5). The multiple consumption of sports newspapers and sporting events is high as it concerns four out of five teenagers. Watching sports on television seems to be the corollary of an interest in reading specialized newspapers and going to games.

A masculine predominance exists in the consumption of 'sports culture' related to the fact that more boys than girls do sports in the context of clubs and competitions. In all, the difference between girls and boys regarding the consumption of sporting events (respectively, a ratio of 1 to 2.8) is much higher than the difference regarding sports participation (1 to 1.3). The mode of consumption also reflects social divisions, with the young of modest socio-economic backgrounds more likely to be spectators at matches while the more affluent young are higher consumers of specialized sports newspapers.

The importance of the sports culture for the 12–17-year-olds is also shown by a consumption of information about sport that is more common than sports participation on the one hand and, on the other hand, a strong affinity between these two systems of sports consumption. Participation and the consumption of 'sports culture' are certainly linked; however, this relation is not reciprocal. Thus, the athletes who have membership cards and compete are more numerous among the amateurs of sports television, sports reading and matches. Moreover, the consumption of televised sports programmes is highly associated with competition.

Finally, it appears that the consumption of information and sporting events adds to the coherence of the totality of young people's recreational activities. The consumption of televised sports programmes is strongly correlated with the consumption of television in general; it is also linked to playing video games, using a computer and the amount of time spent with friends. Going to matches in a sports facility is linked to time spent with friends, playing video games and going to a discotheque. Reading specialized newspapers is associated with reading and using a computer. There is a high level of coherence in the pastimes adopted by youths, with sport ultimately a frequent cultural synonym for play, sociability … in short for curiosity and variety. The sports culture that is associated with physical activity has an important influence on the management of the free time of young people.

The consumption of sporting goods and sports video games

The consumption of sporting goods and sports video games seems to attest to a new quantitative and qualitative evolution, which transforms the conception of sports development among youth in France.

The uses of sporting goods brands by the young

Youth is a period in which toddlers and teenagers currently represent new consumer targets. They constitute an important target for sporting goods brands since those who are committed to them during this period of life have a good chance of continuing to be customers for many years, even if scholastic or professional changes are likely to break this commitment. Hence the attention given to this part of the market by many sporting goods brands, particularly those selling sportswear. Marketers consider that the young of the 'Y generation' (those born around the 1980s) are their prime targets because they are in the process of building their identity, which involves the consumption of products and brands that resonate with their chosen referent group(s). The choice of activities, friends and dress style during this pre-adult period is fundamental for being accepted or integrated in a given group (rappers, lolitas, skaters, etc.). The impact of sporting goods brands on young people in France has been continually increasing both qualitatively and quantitatively. In 2003, the 10 most preferred sportswear brands of young French boys were (in descending order): Adidas, Nike, Reebok, Décathlon, Levi's, Quiksilver, Fila, Complices, Champion USA and Lacoste. The preferred brands of the girls were: Pimkie, Jennifer, Nike, Adidas, Etam, Décathlon, Levi's, Reebok, Camaïeu and Naf Naf (Garnier and Guingois 2003).

Current publicity campaigns aim directly at this young clientele which is seen as easily captivated and largely uncritical when faced with the profusion of products available on the market. Some authors, such as Quart (2004), even think that children are hostages of the main brands and all kinds of media, since children are vulnerable to the marketing strategies directed at them. Moreover, the professional sports leagues have also learned this lesson. As institutional brands, their main targets for derivatives (team shirts, shorts, caps, scarves, etc.) are those under 18 years of age. These products are promoted through the systematic association of international sporting goods brands with professional clubs in order to commercialize derivatives or co-branded merchandise aimed at young club fans.

A more recent phenomenon, that of the 'babies', is a niche for the sporting goods brands that aim at developing ranges of activities and products adapted to this market segment. This is exemplified by The Little Gym® established west of Paris which aims to answer a dual need: a) to give sport its educational value by creating a non-competitive programme to stimulate the physical, emotional, social and intellectual development of children (from 3 to 12 years); and b) to offer a programme to develop motor capacities accessible to children under the age of 3. The sporting goods manufacturers launched products specifically designed for toddlers such as the Baby Gym Shoe (winner of the Reddot Design Award) by the trendy brand Domyos of Oxylane Group, geared for 1–4-year-old children who do gymnastics or those in a child care centre (these types of shoes are ergonomic and follow very closely the anatomy of the foot in this age bracket). This is not to mention the 300 ml Sport Bottle Sipper with a no-drip straw manufactured by the brand Nûby for babies from 12 months, which allows toddlers to run, jump and play as they like while holding a bottle!

Youth and the e-sport culture

Video games sell 3.7 times more than CDs: in 2008, the sales of video games increased by 18.8 per cent, while sales of CDs dropped by 14.3 per cent in France. Overall, in our opinion, the e-sport culture blends two categories of sports sub-cultures: that of the player consumers who confront each other in virtual sports competitions and that of the video game players who generate a real physical activity in relation to virtual people. In both cases, the e-sport culture is part of a deeper societal movement in which real, hyperreal and virtual worlds are more and more intertwined in sports consumption as well as in the purchase of sporting goods brands. One of the emblematic cases of success for all young generations concerns the sector of multiple players on the internet. This type of experience is found in the French Final of the PES League, the virtual French soccer championship sponsored by Thierry Henry (FC Barcelona) and Didier Drogba (Chelsea FC) which was held on 1 July 2007 in the Stade de France. Almost 22,000 players participated in the events in France with 60,000 applications to participate. Whatever the physical activity behind competitions, groups of friends, young people and adults confront each other through on-line video games throughout the day. Roughly 400,000 virtual groups are estimated to exist worldwide, involving 27 per cent of net surfers.

New technologies have also revolutionized the approach to sports at home for the young and, more surprisingly, for the 50 years and older population (which the designers of software and game consoles did not foresee!). With Nintendo's Wii Fit, Play Station 2 Kinetic and Nintendo DS' 'My Personal Coach', doing sport in front of one's television or on a console has nothing virtual about it. In 2008, Wii Sport became the best selling game in the history of video games, with 40.52 million copies sold since its launch. 'Nintendoland's' influence over the global games market is because this brand knew how to target two groups of consumers, the young and the over fifties, with user-friendly games to stimulate the brain and sports games with simplistic graphics. The latest brand success, the Wii Balance Board, allows reproducing body movements on television to lose weight, dance, play music, etc.

The development of this e-sport culture poses a public health problem: energy expenditure is less important than having fun with friends or the family, and the game rules for these virtual physical activities cannot be transferred to real sport. But Wii Fit's advance emulates the EA Active Sports of Electronic Arts, which is more orientated toward balance and physical resistance, with a jogging, boxing and tennis mode for burning calories. In any case, those who offer sports services (public and private associations) are confronted by an original competitor with considerable power that cannot be ignored. Moreover, some hope exists of a positive link between participating in sport and playing video games among French teenagers. According to Peter (2007), almost seven out of 10 teenagers who do sports at least once a week spend the same amount of time playing video games against only a little less than half of those who do not do sports. A positive relationship exists between doing sports and playing video games since the probability of an athletic teenager playing video games is multiplied by 1.2 compared to a non-athlete. How can this relation between physical action done in the real world and played in a virtual world be interpreted? Playing video games is based on the fact that the player finds his information on a screen; just as in doing sports with uncertainties such as roller blade, tennis or soccer, the teenager must find the necessary information in his visual environment. It is then possible to hypothesize that a relation exists between playing virtual physical video games and doing sports based on visual uncertainty. And this link remains positive independent of sex, age or even the social class, but does vary between sports. For example, a teenager who plays soccer regularly is about 2.5 times more likely to be an enthusiast of video games than a teenager who swims.

Conclusion: The diversity of French youth and sport

The structuration of our contemporary societies is considered more and more as a set of configurations that form a social context with multiple dimensions. The young are diverse and their engagement with sport depends on their particular circumstances: their choices and their participation in sports can be carried out in diverse complementary and even paradoxical ways in the scholastic, family, associative or consumerist frameworks. These new behaviours seem to be underlain by two matrices of the contemporary, juvenile sports experience: 'orientated toward oneself vs. orientated toward others' (Holbrook 1999) and 'goal vs. instrumental' (Holt

1995). This original situation in France must be taken into account by all of the political and social actors who still consider sport as a unique vector of integration and health!

Annex: The different national and local youth sport providers

- **Contrat de Ville (CV) (City Contract)**: 'it constitutes the framework in which the Government, the local communities and their partners in concert are committed to implementing territorial policies of social development and urban renewal, with the aim of combating the social decline of certain areas of our cities' (Ministère de l'Emploi de la Cohésion Sociale et du Logement; www.ville.gouv.fr/infos/ville/index.html).
- **Contrat Enfance (Childhood contract)**: this is a contract of the objectives and the co-financing made between the Family Allowance Office and a partner such as a territorial community, a group of communes, an enterprise or a Government department. Young people in the CVL and CLSH programmes can benefit from this financial aid.
- **Contrat local d'accompagnement à la solidarité (CLAS) (Local contract for scholastic support)**: this applies to children in primary, junior and senior high schools primarily in problem urban areas. Its mission is to promote scholastic success and to reinforce the involvement of parents in the education of their children.
- **Contrat Local de Sécurité (CLS) (Local security contract)**: this is a contract established by all the actors involved in the fields of prevention and security.
- **Contrat Temps Libre (CTL) (Free time contract)**: a contract signed by the territorial community and the CAF (Family Allowance Office) and other partners for children from 6 to 16 years of age.
- **Ecole ouverte (Open school)**: under this inter-ministerial plan launched in 1991, schools remain open for elementary, junior and high school students who do not go away on vacations. The open school primarily applies to children and teenagers who live in socially disadvantaged areas or in difficult economic and cultural contexts. The funds allocated by the Government in 2007 amounted to 15.8 million euros and made it possible to aid 137,748 students in 745 voluntary schools. A total of 737 schools planned on participating in the programme in 2009–10.
- **Ville Vie Vacances (VVV) (City Lifestyle Vacations)**: these programmes make it possible for children and teenagers at risk or in need of support to have access to leisure activities and educational support during school vacations.

Notes

1 Source: http://ec.europa.eu/sport/library/doc/b23/doc472_en.pdf (consultation: January 2008).
2 Source: www.euro.who.int/mediacentre/PR/2006/20060508_1 (consultation: January 2008).
3 Source: www.eufic.org/article/fr/sante-mode-de-vie/activite-physique/artid/condition-physique-adolescents-europeens (consultation: June 2009).
4 Moreover, historically, numerous associations were created to indicate a link with the university by integrating the letter U in their acronym: DUC, Dijon University Club; PUC, Paris University Club, etc.
5 This is an individual incentive to do the sport of one's choice in the form of a € 20 bill, valid for two calendar years after its date of issue. The Coupon Sport can be used to pay for joining fees, membership, classes or training sessions in a large number of associations or sports clubs that signed an agreement with the National Agency for Vacation Cheques. This coupon is available for youths between 9 and 18, youths between 16 and 25 who are monitored by welfare services; and those with disabilities.
6 Source: Direction de la Jeunesse et de l'Education Populaire, bureau des politiques éducatives territoriales (Stat-info n° 03–02 de février 2003, p. 3).
7 Source: www.sportselitejeunes.fr (consultation: June 2009).
8 Source: www.thelittlegym-eu.com (consultation: January 2008).

References

Aubel, O., Lefèvre, B. and Tribou, G. (2007), *Sport et sportifs en France*, Observatoire du sport FPS/IPSOS.

Comité National Olympique et Sport Francais (CNOSF) (2005) *Politiques sportives féderales et politique territoriales*, Rapport du CNOSF, Paris: CNOSF.

Cova, B. (2008), *Consumer Made*: quand le consommateur devient producteur, *Décisions Marketing*, 50, avril-juin, 19–27.

Firat, F. and Venkatesh, A. (1993), 'Postmodernity, the Age of Marketing', *International Journal of Research in Marketing*, vol. 10, n°3, 227–49.

Garnier, J. et Guingois, S. (2003), 13–20 ans: les champions du mixage culture, *LSA*, p. 48–52.

Hetzel, P. (2002), *Planète conso. Marketing expérientiel et nouveaux univers de consommation*, Paris, Editions d'Organisation.

Holbrook, M.B. [Ed.] (1999), *Consumer value: a framework for analysis and research*, London-New York, Routledge.

Holt, D.B. (1995), 'How consumers consume: a typology of consumption practices', *Journal of Consumer Research*, 22, 1–16.

Lahire, B. (2005), *L'homme pluriel*, Paris, Armand Colin.

Lefèvre, B. (2001), La consommation d'informations et de spectacles sportifs: un pilier de la culture sportive adolescente, in *Les adolescents et le sport* (2001), Rapport du MJSVA et INSEP, Paris, 129–36.

Les adolescents et le sport (2001), Rapport du MJSVA et INSEP, Paris.

Les pratiques sportives en France (2002), Rapport du MJSVA et INSEP, Paris.

Machard, L. (2003), *Sport, Adolescence et Famille*, rapport de propositions remis à Lamour J.F., Ministère de la Santé, de la Famille et des Personnes Handicapées – Ministère délégué à la Famille – Ministère des Sports.

Ministry of Health (2007) *Les chiffres-clés de la jeunesse, bulletin du ministère de la santé, de la jeunesse, des sports et de la vie associative*, Paris: Ministry de la santé, de la jeunesse, des sports et de la vie associative.

Peter, C. (2007), Goût pour les jeux vidéo, goût pour le sport, deux activités liées chez les adolescents, *Culture Prospective*, Agence Française pour le Jeu Vidéo, 16 mai 2007, p. 1–2.

Quart, A. (2004), *Nos enfants otages des grandes marques*, Paris: Village Mondial.

Simmons, G. (2008), 'Marketing to postmodern consumers: introducing the internet chameleon', *European Journal of Marketing*, vol. 42, 3–4, 299–310.

World Health Organization (2008), 'The health of students aged 11 to 15 years in France', *Health Behaviour in School-aged Chindren (HBSC)*, press release, September 2008, Ministry of Education.

12

The development of youth sport in Sweden

Bo Carlsson and Susanna Hedenborg

Today approximately two-thirds of all Swedish children participate in organized sports and most children encounter sports within the educational system, as physical education is part of the compulsory curriculum (Swedish Sport Confederation 2007). Outside school, children's organized sports activities are connected to the sports movement, which is organized within the Swedish Sport Confederation, that is, Riksidrottsförbundet (RF). RF has a strong position in Swedish society and is to a large extent self-governing in relation to the government (Norberg 2002; Ministry of Culture 2008). However, it is still heavily dependent on public subsidies for activities for youth and children.

In this chapter we will provide an overview of children's involvement in sports activities in Sweden, mainly from the mid-nineteenth century onwards. The aim is to explain and examine the way in which children and youth participate in sport, with a focus on physical education and the development of the sports movement. We will, in addition, outline the governance issues and policy related to Swedish youth sport. We will also identify and discuss several problems that have occurred in the running and administration of youth sports in Sweden. In this respect we will try to relate our discussion to gender, as sport has traditionally been connected to boys, men and masculinity. The chapter ends with a reflection on contemporary and future trends and possible directions in the development of youth sport in Sweden, in which we focus on the present amalgam of physical education and the sports movement.

Physical education

In the first section we will provide a historical account of the development of physical education. Notably, in Sweden as in other Western societies, in the early modern period sport was probably part of the socializing process of children and youth in several ways. Knowledge of how to dance and play was necessary for young people, at least from the upper classes, during the seventeenth and eighteenth centuries. Fencing, horse riding, modern languages, music and art were activities which were part of the education of young men in schools and universities, whereas women were taught dance in the private sphere. The ability to dance was seen as good for the body as well as for the soul (Ulvros 2004).

The manner in which sport was part of poor children's lives is more difficult to know. As was the case with the adults, it is likely that children and young people participated in popular games. When it comes to physical education for poor children the school regulation documents from 1649 include a part about physical exercises. Even so, it is difficult to know how much this affected children and youth in practice, as we do not know whether physical exercises were compulsory. In the school regulation documents from 1807 gymnastics was mentioned again (Blom and Lindroth 1995: 272–3), and judging by a discussion on teachers' wages in one of the schools for poor boys in Stockholm, physical education as a school subject had been introduced for boys as early as the eighteenth century. Whether this was the case for all schools is unclear. Furthermore, not until the late nineteenth century did most children attend school on a regular basis. Therefore it is impossible to say how many children were actually involved in physical education before this time.

It is clear that physical education was discussed during the nineteenth century and that the introduction of the school subject was slow – not least for financial reasons. Moreover, the introduction was slower in the elementary schools (which were compulsory from 1842) than in the secondary schools. Not until 1919 was 'gymnastics, play and sports' introduced as a subject in the elementary schools and in 1928 it became mandatory in secondary education (ibid: 270).

During the nineteenth century there was an ongoing discussion on physical education in relation to secondary education. In these schools physical education and sport were seen as an important part of the socializing process, in which boys and young men were made more masculine, not least as these young men were expected to be able and prepared to defend the country. The actual contents of physical education were discussed and altered over time. During the nineteenth century dance lost its status to Ling gymnastics and towards the second half of the nineteenth century dance even became associated with sin. This connection grew stronger over time and during the beginning of the twentieth century dance was attacked several times. The criticism was aimed at dance being physical and sexual – especially that which is performed with a partner (Ulvros 2004). Up until the 1920s military exercises were important for young men. However, Ling gymnastics was questioned in secondary education as well – sport, as practised in the British Public Schools, became increasingly more important. Sport was believed to promote a more individualistic and competitive mentality useful to those expected to rule others.

When schooling became available to a greater number of people towards the end of the nineteenth century (even though elementary schooling was compulsory from the mid-nineteenth century, not all children attended), physical education for the poorer classes, boys as well as girls, was developed (Lundquist-Wanneberg 2004). Ling gymnastics became important in the schools that admitted boys from the lower social classes of society. Ling gymnastics was seen as a means to socialize these boys into collective subordination. In contrast to young men from the upper class, these boys were to be brought up to be men who were willing to cooperate rather than rule. The importance of Ling gymnastics in elementary schools remained strong as far as the 1950s.

However, Ling gymnastics changed over time. The postures developed by Ling were criticized at the beginning of the twentieth century and, instead of the traditional idealistic posture, the Swedish gym teacher and inspector Ellen Falk emphasized new postures that were 'energy-saving'. The importance of an energy-saving posture was connected to the fatigue debate from the latter half of the nineteenth century.

Except for being dealt with according to social class, physical education was connected to gender and developed according to this. Gender-adjusted Ling gymnastics was created by Elli Björkstén. She developed a women's gymnastics which supposedly included more free movements than traditional Ling gymnastics. According to Björkstén, there were significant differences between boys and girls and therefore it was important to develop these differences within physical education as well. Up until puberty boys and girls could exercise together, but after the onset of puberty girls were supposed to engage in aesthetic exercises, which developed agility, flexibility and grace, whereas boys were to engage in sports that increased strength, determination and performance. Girls were seen as weak, due to their reproductive function: for girls all energy was supposedly directed towards sexual development. Girls were also considered to be non-aggressive and non-competitive, whereas boys needed sport to sublimate aggressiveness. Boys' development could go wrong and in order to direct it in the desired way, involvement in sport was necessary. It is obvious that physical education brought forward, or mirrored, two different types of socially constructed citizens: boys strong with stamina and girls supple and graceful (ibid).

As has already been mentioned, physical education changed during the 1950s, as the aim of the elementary schools was no longer collective subordination. At the time competitive sport was accepted for boys from the lower social classes too (ibid). In other words, from the 1950s onwards physical education was not regulated in relation to social class when it came to men. Boys and girls were, however, still separated and believed to need different kinds of physical exercise up until the reform of the school curriculum in the 1980s. From the 1980s physical differences between boys and girls were given less prominence in curriculum design. However, in 1994 gender differences were re-emphasized (Sandahl 2005).

The sports movement and the development of youth sport

Simultaneously, as physical education was being organized for an increasing number of children in schools towards the end of the nineteenth century the Swedish sports movement was becoming established. This section will shed light on this development, concluding with a presentation of the current organization of youth sport.

In order to understand the development of youth sport in Sweden, we have to start with a short clarification of the organization of the Swedish sports movement, and the regulation of sport in general. First, the organization and regulation of the sports movement can be conceptualized as having a huge degree of autonomy and self-regulation due to the fact that sport has historically been perceived as having a more frivolous character and, in relation to its formal organization, having been heavily connected with idealism and voluntarism, that is, activities that take place in the field of leisure far removed from the market.[1] Besides, the State has generally taken an inactive standpoint in relation to sports policy and sports governance, which have instead basically developed internally in the general associations of sports and sports clubs. However, perhaps more accurately, the State position towards sport in Sweden can be conceptualized as being 'actively neutral' (Norberg 2003). The State, for instance, has supported sport financially since the early nineteenth century and more formally since 1913, but has not, in a historical perspective, placed any particularly political pressure on the regulation of sport and the normative development of sport in general. The relation has relied on an 'implicit contract' (Ministry of Culture 2008: 126–33), in which the State supports the autonomy of the movement, and tacitly trusts that the sports movement's utilization of the financial support relates beneficially to 'societal values' (ibid).[2] Besides, there are no substantial political conflicts in history related to the State's position in sport.

In this light, the sports federations have been able to connect autonomy and public support (ibid), at least ideologically. In this respect, the Swedish sports model has been able to uphold *a normative autonomy* regarding values and morals (Carlsson and Lindfelt 2010). What is important to stress, however, is that the question of the autonomy of sport must, in a more general approach, be related to, for instance, the State's financial support of sport as governmental funding has been crucial, particularly for the development of youth sport.

In contemporary Sweden almost all organized sports are governed by the Swedish Sports Confederation. In this respect, the confederation is an umbrella organization with the task of supporting its member federations and representing the whole Swedish sports movement in contact with the state organizations, politicians, and so on. It is also the RF that defends the legitimacy of sport and reports on the current state of sport, arguing for its social value and illuminating its extent and importance as well as monitoring participation in sport. For many Swedes, involved with the RF, it was through membership in their local clubs that they for the first time came into contact with particular elected roles and the practice of the democratic process.

In the process of building the Swedish welfare state during the second half of the twentieth century there has been a strong interest in children and young people. However, the socializing of these groups was not necessarily associated with sports to begin with. Instead, strong criticism was directed towards competitive sports in general. The possibility that competitive sport could influence adversely the socializing process in relation to the development of 'good' citizenship was obviously considered as threatening – especially when connected to young people. As we have already mentioned in connection to physical education, it was not considered beneficial to educate the majority of young people to become competitive. However, from the 1950s onwards the attitudes towards sports changed. The shifting attitudes towards young people and sports can be connected to public discussions on youth problems and socializing issues. During the 1940s and 1950s young people's education, leisure, alcohol habits and criminality were debated.[3] Youth was considered to be a problem group and it was stated that young people – mostly young men, in relation to sport – ought to be integrated into the Swedish welfare state. The popular movements were deemed to play an essential role in the socializing process, and not least organized sports were seen as an important tool in order to mould the new citizens (Patriksson 1987; Toftegaard-Støckel et al. 2010).

The new function of sport was not only talked about but actually put into practice as well. In 1942 a youth committee was established by the Swedish Sports Confederation (Peterson 1993). The committee was supposed to work with young people above the age of 14. This age limit was set as the associations organizing sports in schools were supposed to concentrate on the children below that age (Wijk 2001: 95). At this time many young people finished school when they were 14–15 years old and for this group, especially for young men, sports were seen as a good leisure activity. Youngsters with too much free time were thought to be in danger of acquiring undesirable habits.

The Swedish Football Association was the first to establish a specific youth committee in 1948 in order to increase the number of boys playing football. At the time there were already young men playing football within the association. In 1943 8 per cent of the football clubs had youth sections which, by 1947, had increased to 20 per cent (Peterson 1993: 64–65). Apart from meeting the specific development needs of football, the committee was supposed to work against youth criminality and alcohol abuse (ibid: 65). Shortly after the establishment of the committee the Football Association had created activities like diploma-bearing courses connected to technique development, had increased cooperation between schools and authorities and organized leagues at local, regional and national levels for young people (ibid: 66). The Football Association even sent instructors to one of the largest summer camps for children (ibid).

When the youth committee in the Football Association was established there were no equivalents in the other sports associations. However, several other sports associations developed youth sections over time. Within the Equestrian Association, the issue of youth was discussed as early as the 1940s; however, youth were not viewed as more important than any other horse riding group (Minstry of Finance 1946). Even so, the establishment of a new equestrian association in 1948 made a difference to young people who wanted to ride, as the association gave sub-sidies for the building of indoor horse-riding schools and provided discount tickets to young people. In 1958 the importance of equestrian sports for young people was commented on within the association. Horse riding and participation in a horse-riding school were then seen as important socializing opportunities (Hedenborg 2009).

These actions clearly had an impact on the development of sports participation. In 2006 the most popular sports for 13–20-year-olds measured by the number of members in the associations were football (110,000) and floor bandy (52,000) for boys, and football (63,000) and horse riding (46,000) for girls. If the number of times that people take part in a sport are counted, football (almost 2,000,000 times in 2006) and horse riding (about 600,000 times in 2006) are the most popular sports. As football and horse riding seem to be important activities for young people today it is interesting to survey how the associations connected to these sports acted in order to promote and include young people in the takeoff phase of children's sports.

The Swedish sports model is entirely dependent on the voluntary support of local leaders as well as on public financing, especially from local government and the widely spread club system. It is estimated that 600,000 Swedes have one or more positions as leaders in the Swedish sports movement. Almost all of them fulfil their duties without any financial compensation. Sports leaders in Sweden are, thereby, motivated neither by financial rewards nor by personal ambition.

Besides, Swedish sport in general has traditionally been governed and formed by a relatively heavy emphasis on education, welfare and socialization, due to its implicit position in the pro-gress of the Welfare Society (Norberg 2003). In the policy of RF, as well as of the Swedish special sports associations, we can notice an emphasis on sport (football) as relevant to education, welfare, rule orientation, as well as public health, social integration, cultural and mutual understanding, etc. At the same time there has been an emphasis on elite sport, due to the ideology that elite sports nourish the horizontal sports organizations and that sports at the basic level are the foundation of elite sport and international success.

However, the idealistic virtue of sport as 'spiritual welfare' and 'physical education' should not be driven too far, not even in the Nordic countries, because this traditional conception of sport has for a long time operated face to face with an idea of sport as entertainment and even as sports industry. Football has played a crucial role in this transition (Carlsson 2009); a transition in which sport, particularly in football and hockey, has mapped out its modernity in the bor-derline between welfare and entertainment, idealism and commercialism (Norberg 2009).

Youth sport policy

In our time children's and adults' activities are largely kept apart. Ideally, adults are supposed to work, whereas children are supposed to play, attend childcare institutions and school. This is possibly a relatively new separation, as it is likely that children at least up until the nineteenth century participated with adults in sport and play, as well as partaking in working life. In paintings by the Dutch artist Pieter Brueghel from the sixteenth century, adults and children are pictured playing, dancing and practising sports. The use of art as a historical source is of course questionable; however, written sources demonstrate that children's and adults' lives were more closely linked through work before the early twentieth century than during our own times. That is not to say that everyone did or could do the same thing. Work and leisure were coded according to gender and social class as well as associated with different age groups – young boys did not perform the same chores as old women. Even though children's and adults' leisure activities are kept apart, an interesting paradox connected to children's sports activities today is that they have to a large extent been modelled on adult sports.

However, when it comes to policy, the Swedish Sports Confederation (RF) and the Swedish special sports associations produce different directions and guidelines for youth sport. Sport, to start with, is categorized according to age and the level of ambition. Children's sport is generally considered to extend to the age of twelve, and youth sport to the age of twenty. In children's sport the emphasis is on play and the possibility to engage children in different sports. A child's *general sporting development* is the norm for children's sport. Although competition is an aspect of the game, it must always be conducted on the children's own terms.

These demands on sport are even more crucial in light of its role in the social fostering of children and young people. In this respect, the sports movement, including its authority the RF, claims to be constantly seeking to develop and improve its activities, and to adapt them in accordance with the needs and wishes of athletes, leaders and parents. By the concept of 'good at sport and good sport' the RF means sporting activity 'that promotes democracy, welfare, equality, fair play, healthy finances, respect for others, voluntary commitment, and environmental awareness'.

We will even find statements in the RF collection of policies directed towards children and youth sport, protecting the *play element* in sport from the power of conquest and triumphs, as well as guarding the welfare of children and the individual development of children and youth. For most children, sports offer, together with family and school, primary socialization, and in this respect it must be guided by quality and rights, rights that are connected to free will, independence and empowerment.

Not surprisingly all statements of official policy and ideology are often very hard to realize in the practice of sport, considering its tradition – and phenomenology – of conquest and victory. Consequently, several conflicts and disputes have emerged, not only in relation to equality, fair play and respect for others, but also in relation to the question of health and fostering on various levels. In spite of an increasing public debate, the agenda has historically been set by the sports organizations and has been related to an emphasis on the long-established self-regulation in and of sport.

Due to the fact that RF operates rather autonomously as a self-regulated system, the development of values and the production of policy are prepared and implemented internally. Naturally, the character of policy outputs is in some degree inspired by or responding to external societal values (such as gender and ethnic discrimination, and social integration). In this internal production of youth policy we find first of all an emphasis on 'the play element'. The RF writes: 'In youth sport we are playing, and give the opportunity to experience different sports. The youths' multitalented development stands out as the norm for the training. However, competition is a part of the play, but has to be conducted according to the individual kid's situation' (Swedish Sport Confederation 2005: 5). Accordingly, in the vision of the RF, sport is brilliant for youth, if it is correctly implemented. Sport contributes to a flexible development, and all young people, the RF states, ought to have the opportunity to participate in sport, at school, in sports clubs or spontaneously in the local environment. Sport serves, in addition, as a beneficial socialization arena, and by the planned organized activity the RF 'will have affirmative positive impact on young people's attitudes and values' (ibid: 7). Furthermore, the RF considers that the intrinsic values in sport focus on honesty and fair play (ibid: 8). It is also argued that the work of the RF should have an impact on an individual's lifelong interest in sport and physical activity.

Clearly, ambitious claims regarding social and psychological development are highlighted in the RF's policy of youth sport. However, the standards and the preconditions for the realization of these claims are not discussed seriously in this policy formulation (cf. Ministry of Culture 2008), apart from the statements that youth sport should be 'correctly implemented' and 'healthy for the youths'. The youth policy is complemented with several recommendations, upholding for instance that: competition should be defused; alternative forms of competition should be developed and tested; competition should be individualized according to talent and individual status; and, if competition occurs, it should focus on the individual's progress.

Problems and trends attached to the traditional conception of youth sport

Despite the RF's majestic policy formulations as well as its strong development and huge impact on society in general, youth sport and the Swedish sports movement have faced several problems and challenges. Regardless of an overwhelmingly positive attitude toward (youth) sport in society in general there have been, in this perspective, some indications that not all youths have acquired positive experiences of and feelings towards sport and the sports movement, and the manners and culture of institutionalized sport (Carlsson and Fransson 2005). It is also obvious that there is a visible discrepancy between the vision of the sports movement of a good youth sport experience and social scientists' descriptions and analyses of youth sport in practice (Ministry of Culture 2008).

An inventory of problems and dilemmas provides us with the following short analysis. As in most countries, there has been a substantial discussion about various selection processes connected to youth sport, with an emphasis on inclusion and exclusion due to social capital, gender, family circumstances, geography and ethnicity as well as talent (Swedish Sport Federation/R& D 2004a; Ministry of Culture 2008: 25). In addition, the family's familiarity with particular sports and their inside knowledge of the sports movement appear to be important elements of cultural capital, excluding, for instance, immigrants and other groups not acquainted with the Swedish model (Trondman 2005). The problems related to transportation to sports facilities have also been observed, both in relation to exclusion and the dependency on adults (Carlsson and Fransson 2005).

Clearly, social and political ambitions – 'sports for all' – fade away to some degree in practice. There have, however, been several attempts to come to terms with various forms of selection, such as the avoidance of league competitions (Swedish Sport Federation/R& D 2002), adapted and modified forms of youth sport (Swedish Sport Federation/R& D 2006), as well as reduced fees for underprivileged groups (Swedish Sport Federation/R& D 2004b). In order to attract new groups to sport, we find 'Handslaget' [A Handshake with Sport], a State-supported project in schools, as well as the idea of miniature arenas for spontaneous sports activities in a local environment. However, 'Handslaget' suffers from the dilemma of assimilating sports competition (the logic of the sports movement) with physical education (Peterson 2008). Besides, the initiative of 'spontaneous sports arenas' has not, according to the early evidence, directed new – and physically inactive – groups to sport. On the contrary, the young – regularly boys – that are already involved in sports clubs seem to have received an extra sports ground.

In the effort to improve the quality of youth sport, different special sports associations make various attempts to modify the character of youth sport by introducing smaller grounds, shorter periods of play, adapted equipment, and alternative and more discretionary rules, etc. (Swedish Sport Federation/R& D 2006). These attempts at modifying youth sport are normally beneficial but have, at the same time, to face the problem of the 'image of "real" sport', and the conception of youths as 'adults in miniature' (Carlsson and Fransson 2005; cf. David 2005).

Furthermore, while the Swedish sports movement asserts its ability to support social integration and the development of good ethics and societal values, studies among young people present a picture of an experience characterized by varying degrees of elitism, authoritarianism, ranking and masculinity (Fundberg 2003).

A different problem is related to the position and marketing of the sports movement, as well as the organization for future development. It is obvious that, in this context, young people today are not so devoted and faithful to sport, or at least to particular sports or sports clubs, as earlier generations. They will change between different clubs as well as between sports and even refrain from sport for periods. Clearly, in light of current developments, the traditional club-based model has difficulty in coping with an individualized society and pluralistic lifestyles (Carlsson 2004).

This problem poses a crucial challenge for the Swedish sports movement, namely the dependency on idealism and voluntarism. Without doubt, in a historical and still valid perspective the number of volunteers participating as leaders has been crucial and important. The numbers are – surprisingly – still increasing, and in 2008 we found 600,000 adults working as non-paid leaders at leisure activity. But compared to former generations of volunteers, current leaders (parents) put less time and involvement into sports clubs. Today most parents participate only as leaders in their own children's club and only during their child's period of involvement. We did not find evidence of the longer periods of less self-interested engagement found among earlier sports enthusiasts.

In sum, we can observe that there are more parents engaged in sport, often related to the provision of transport and their role as 'helicopter parents', but in the main with less depth of commitment to sport. From another group of parents we observed the application of increasing pressure upon the young for instrumental sporting success, even at an early age (Swedish Sport Federation/R& D 2004c). Parallel to this process, the number of professionals in youth sport is increasing (Seippel 2010). As a result, there seems to be a growing mixture of professionals and volunteers (ibid).

The demands for success, and the willingness to pay for it, directs attention to a recent challenge for the sports movement; that is, the rising commercialization of youth sport, even in Sweden. We find nowadays several commercial projects focusing on exclusive training for talented young people as well as projects integrating entertainment, amusement and physical activity, for instance Sport Camp, branded by Stadium sportswear (Cardell 2008, 2009). Obviously, this business-oriented direction of youth sport is something different from the concept the RF embodied in the 'sports for all' policy.

Mixing physical education and the Swedish sports movement in schools

We have claimed that 'Handslaget' [A Handshake with Sport] is facing problems in practice, due to the assimilation of sports competition and physical education. This problem is examined more fully in this section.

Today there seems to be a narrowing of the activities organized by the Swedish sports associations and via physical education in school. The development is connected to, and probably explained by, some of the questions that are posed in the contemporary debate concerning the sports associations' problems, such as not reaching everybody, particularly girls, immigrants, children who have parents with low incomes; failing to address increasing obesity among children and youth; and decreasing hours of physical education in school. Furthermore, recent research has indicated that those who are active are doing more and more but that those who are physically inactive are increasing in number (Engström 2002). One solution to these problems has been the provision of financial subsidies by the government to the sports associations in order to enable them to address the issues.

In 2003 the financially subsidized 'Handslaget' campaign was started, with €950 million at its disposal over a four-year period. The campaign, which focused on the sports associations, had five goals which included increasing the recruitment base of children and young people within the sports associations; the support of sporting girls; keeping the fees down; working against drug use; and cooperating with schools. The campaign was to be run over a period of four years and has now been followed up with evaluations and a new campaign ('Idrottslyftet') with similar goals.

Almost 50,000 projects within the sports associations were initiated by the first campaign. More than 10,000 of them were concerned with the cooperation between sports associations and schools. The cooperation was carried out in several ways. In some schools children were given the opportunity to try different sports activities or were provided with information from the sports associations. In other schools sports coaches participated in or were responsible for some hours of physical education. Most of the representatives involved from the sports associations and about 50 per cent of the schools reported that they had appreciated the cooperation. Several of the associations had continued or planned to continue the activities within schools after the initial campaign was concluded. Evaluation of the projects also demonstrated that the cooperation met with some problems such as the difficulty of reaching inactive children and children with special needs. According to the evaluation, part of the explanation was the lack of education relevant to these issues among the sports coaches and the fact that sports and physical education are possibly organized according to different logics. The former explanation is connected to the logic of competition, and the latter to the logic of the development of motor skills (Engström 2008). Furthermore, the competence of physical education teachers appears to be undermined through the increasing involvement of unpaid and voluntary sports leaders as a complement to, or substitute for, paid school personnel (Peterson 2008: 85).

In this respect, what are the implications when voluntary sports clubs take over the responsibility for physical activities during school hours – 'for society, for the school, for the sports clubs and for the children involved' (ibid: 86)? Using Luhmann's concepts, they rely on different determined codes and rationalities, and in the view of Bourdieu, the crossing of fields often gives rise to a number of problems. As Peterson states: 'club sport is good at what sports club sport does', and 'what takes place during school time, shall take place during school time' (ibid: 92–93). Consequently, a more effective investment from the Government would be resources to strengthen the subject of physical education in the schools, increasing the hours of sport, supplemented with qualified teachers. However, the sports movement has established a strong image – 'brand' – in society in general in relation to youth sport and health.

New directions or ... ?

In the following section we intend to present two different, but rather novel and developing, approaches – and challenges – to the traditional concept of a self-regulated (and autonomous) sports movement. In this respect we will emphasize different processes or actions in civil society, as well as in the State, which will have consequences for the future development of the sports movement.

First of all, in Sweden there are several non-governmental organizations – such as, 'allFair', 'Friends' and 'Children's Right in Society' – that all are fighting different forms of malpractice in youth sport. There is, naturally, analogously with a rising commercialization, a demand for an increasing professionalization of sport in general, including youth sport. Traditional ideals of fair play have to be revitalized by putting the emphasis on professional ethics, which departs from social and moral education and a quality audit of the practice of sport. The spotlight on ethics puts a stress on organization, leadership and coaching in youth sport. An excellent illustration of these demands on youth sport is the rise of different NGOs dealing with negligence in sport. 'allFair', for instance, deals with the problematic relationship between adults, psychological pressure and competition in youth sport. The 'Friends' organization works to address bullying and hazing in sport. 'Children's Right in Society' is focused on exclusion as well as harassment in youth sport. All of them take as their reference point the UN Convention on the Rights of the Child (David 2005) and highlight sports practices that are according to the 'best interest of the child'. From a socio-legal perspective this step, the rise of interest groups, can be regarded as a prelude to potentially stronger political-legal interests which, in the longer term, might generate legal actions (Carlsson 1998; Hoff 2004). This possibility puts pressure on the sports movement's development of youth sport.

Secondly, in March 2007 the Ministry of Culture set up an external evaluation regarding the public financial support given to sport. The 'implicit contract' was subsequently illuminated and scrutinized. One aim of the evaluation was to investigate the, often asserted, positive influence of sport on society, and particularly on public health and youth development, an impact that had been – up to this date – more or less assured and indisputable. As a rule, the RF has previously conducted internal evaluations of the quality and impact of sport. In the evaluation the inves- tigators focused on several problems, but were especially interested in three subjects: children's right, the request for external evaluation, and the problem of financing sport by relying on pool (lottery) revenues (Ministry of Culture 2008). By focusing on comparing and weighing two different official aims in youth sport – the fostering of competition ['tävlingsfostran'] and the fostering of democratic values ['föreningsfostran'] – the report analyzes the dilemma of youth sport. The investigator states that competition, in the logic of the internal value/phenomenology of sport, has misled and deluded those who subscribe to the view that sports participation achieves political/societal aims related to democracy and socialization into positive social values (ibid: 271ff). Consequently, what the State essentially pays for, in the 'implicit contract', seems to be harder to implement due to the logic of sport. As a conclusion, the report upholds the importance of implementing the UN Convention on the Rights of the Child in the sports movement, thereby integrating 'the perspective of the child' in the analysis and in the imple- mentation of different actions. Furthermore, the evaluation of the sports movement has to be made by an external organization, in contrast to the earlier internal method. The govern- ment proposal, in February 2009, draws explicitly on the report. The proposal will support the development of youth sport in line with the UN Convention and require that the evaluation of youth sport be conducted by an external organization.[4] It is also proposed that the funding from the pool (lottery) disappear to be replaced by increased and more predictable governmental financial support (Governmental Proposal 2009).

Conclusions

From an international outlook, in Western countries such as the USA, Canada, New Zealand and England, physical activity and physical education belong broadly to the school realm. Youth sport in Sweden, as in Scandinavia in general, has a somewhat different relationship to physical education. It can be carried out in schools or in the sports movement. During 1940–68 in Sweden, as in Denmark and Norway, it was sport in the sports clubs that increased

(Toftegaard-Støckel *et al.* 2010). Since the late 1960s the State's interest in youth sport has expanded, especially in Norway and Sweden. Many municipalities in the Scandinavian countries built sports facilities in that period. Until recently, before for instance the 'Handshake with Sport' programme, there was little or no cooperation between school sport and club sport. Historically, 'they strongly disagreed on a number of issues regarding sport itself and the possible effects of sport participation' (ibid). But since 2000 there have been a number of projects, supported by the State, which aim to increase youth sport participation, in sports clubs or in the mixture of sports movement organizations and schools.

A lesson to be drawn from our analysis of the development of youth sport in Sweden is that the organization of sport has to face different challenges. First of all, there is a demand for the professionalization of the sports movement through, for instance, evaluations and audits of compliance with Conventions on children's rights. Secondly, we find novel, but rather immature, commercial interests becoming involved in youth sport in Sweden. In collaboration, the processes of professionalization and commercialization make demands on the ideology of voluntarism and idealism. This process of 'sport in transition', mixing voluntarism/idealism with commercialism as well as professionalism will be an interesting direction in Swedish (youth) sport. In light of the ideology of participation and inclusion, however, increasing commercialization of youth sport appears to be an uncertain matter. Nevertheless, it confronts the domination of the sports movement.

Furthermore, when crossing the fields of physical education and the sports movement we highlight the paradox inherent in sport in Sweden and in the phenomenology of sport in general, as being both an excluding and an including system, as being both elitist and democratic. By using the RF sport as the model for physical activity and physical education in school, the sports project presents its limitations. Our vision of the future development of youth sport in Sweden, related to this problem, is an emphasis on 'sport' in sports clubs, related to children's rights and the generation of social benefits, and improved physical activities and physical education in school, consistent with the logic of 'learning for life'.

Notes

1 Perhaps a fairer conceptualization of the Swedish sports model will be sport as a 'semi-autonomous system', because of governmental support through the tax systems. Despite the economic input, the State has, in a historical perspective, never put any kind of political pressure on sport, even though the State has regarded sport and its organisation as an important component in the Welfare Society (Norberg 2003).
2 This relation involves, however, an intrinsic tension between the autonomy of sport and the governance of the State. The right of association and associations' right to self-regulation are politically supported by the State. On the other hand, the State normally has to secure that its spending is effective and used in a legitimate way.
3 This moral discourse was, however, less intensive in Sweden compared to other countries.
4 The Centre for Sport Research [Centrum för idrottsforskning, CIF] will become responsible for conducting the evaluation of the Sport Movement.

References

Blom, K. A. and Lindroth, J. (1995) *Idrottens historia. Från antika arenor till modern massrörelse* [The History of Sport: From Ancient Amphitheatres to a Modern Popular Movement]. Farsta: SISU Idrottsböcker.
Cardell, D. (2008) 'Pop-Sportens fält' [The Field of PopSport], *Sociologisk forskning,* 2: 76–80.
——(2009) *Barndomens Oas* [The Oasis of Childhood]. Örebro: Örebro University.
Carlsson, B. (1998) *Social Steering and Communicative Action.* Lund: Lund Series in Sociology of Law, no. 4.
——(2004) 'The Image of Reality and Legality in Digital Sport', *Moving Bodies,* 4.

——(2009) 'Insolvency and the Domestic Juridification of Football in Sweden', *Soccer and Society*, 10 (3/4): 477–94.

Carlsson, B. and Fransson, K. (2005) 'Youth Sport in Light of the Swedish Sports Confederation and the Children's Right in Society, e.g.', *idrottsforum.org*. www.idrottsforum.org/articles/carlsson/carlsson_fransson/carlsson_fransson051130.html (published 30 November 2005; accessed 25 August 2010).

Carlsson, B. and Lindfelt, M. (2010) 'Legal and Moral Pluralism: Normative Tensions in a Nordic Sports Model in Transition', *Sport in Society*, 13 (4): 718–33.

David, P. (2005) *Human Rights in Youth Sport: A Critical Review of Children's Rights in Competitive Sports*. London: Routledge.

Engström, L.-M. (2002) 'Hur fysiskt aktiva är barn och ungdom?' [How Physically Active are Children?], *Svensk Idrottsforskning*, 3.

——(2008) *Forskning om Handslagets genomförande och resultat – en utvärderande sammanställning* [An Evaluation of Research on the Handshake with Sport]. Stockholm: Riksidrottsförbundet.

Fundberg, J. (2003) *Kom igen, gubbar! Om pojkfotboll och maskuliniteter* [Boys, Football and Masculinity]. Stockholm: Carlssons bokförlag.

Governmental Proposal (2009) *Statens stöd till idrotten* [The State's Support to Sport], 2008/09:126.

Hedenborg, S. (2009) *Till vad fostrar ridsporteu? En studie au ridsporteus utbildningar* (The rearing of children and young people within one of the Swedish horse riding organization) Educare 1, 61–78.

Hoff, D. (2004) *Varför etiska kommittéer?* [Why Ethic Committees?]. Lund: Lund Series in Sociology of Law, no. 20.

Luhmann, Niklas (1985) *The Sociology of Law*. Routledge.

—— (2004) *Law As A Social System*. Oxford University Press.

Lundquist-Wanneberg, P. (2004) *Kroppens medborgarfostran. Kropp, klass och genus i skolans fysiska fostran 1919–1962* [Body and Civic Education: Body, Class and Gender in Physical Education 1919–62]. Stockholm. PhD thesis.

Ministry of Culture (2008) *Föreningsfostran och tävlingsfostran – En utvärdering av statens stöd till idrotten* [Democratic and Competition Fostering: An Evaluation of the State's Support to Sport]. SOU 2008:59. Stockholm: Fritzes.

Minstry of Finance (1946) *Riktlinjer för den framtida jordbrukspolitiken* [Policy for Agriculture in the Future]. SOU 1946:46, Betänkande avgivet av 1942 års jordbrukskommitté del 2. Stockholm: Nordstedts.

Norberg, J.R. (2002) *Riksidrottsförbundets hegemoni* [The Hegemony of the Sport Confederation], in Lindroth, J. and Norberg, J. R. (eds) *Ett idrottssekel. Riksidrottsförbundet 1903–2003* [A Century of Sport: The Sport Confederation 1903–2003]. Södertälje: Fingraf.

——(2003) *Idrottens väg till folkhemmet* [Sport and its Way to the Welfare Society]. Malmö Studies in Sport Science, no. 1. Stockholm: SISU Idrottsböcker.

——(2009) 'Football, Football Pools and the Unexpected Arrival of Sports in Swedish Welfare Politics', *Soccer and Society*, 10 (3/4): 418–37.

Patriksson, G. (1987) *Idrottens barn: Idrottsvanor, stress och utslagning* [The Children of Sport: Habits, Tensions and Exclusions in Sport]. Stockholm: Friskvårdscentrum.

Peterson, P. (1993) *Den svengelska modellen: Svensk fotboll i omvandling under efterkrigstiden* [The Swenglish Model: The Transformation of Swedish Football After World War II]. Lund: Arkiv.

——(2008) 'When the field of sport crosses the field of Physical Education', *Educare*, 3: 83–98.

Sandahl, B. (2005) *Ett ämne för alla? Idrottsämnet i grundskolan 1962–2002* [A Subject for All: Physical Education in the Primary School 1962–2002]. Stockholm. PhD thesis.

Seippel, Ø. (2010) 'Professionals and Volunteers: On the Future of a Scandinavian Sport Model', *Sport in Society*, 13 (2): 199–211.

Swedish Sport Federation/R& D (2002) *Barn & innebandy. En kvalitativ undersökning om innebandyspelares attityder till system utan tabeller* [Youth and Floor Ball: A Qualitative Study of System without Gradings]. FoU 2002: 4. Stockholm: Riksidrottsförbundet.

——(2004a) *Varför lämnar ungdomen idrotten?* [Why Are the Young Leaving Sport?]. FoU 2004: 3. Stockholm: Riksidrottsförbundet.

——(2004b) *Kostnader för barns idrottande* [The Expenditures of Youth Sport]. FoU 2004: 2. Stockholm: Riksidrottsförbundet.

——(2004c) *Föräldraengagemang i barns idrottsföreningar* [Parent's Involvement in Youth Sport]. FoU 2004: 8. Stockholm: Riksidrottsförbundet.

——(2006) *Regler och tävlingssystem i barn-och tidig ungdomsidrott* [Rules and Competition in Youth Sports]. FoU 2006: 2. Stockholm: Riksidrottsförbundet.

Bo Carlsson and Susanna Hedenborg

Swedish Sport Confederation (2005) *Idrotten vill* [Sport Wants]. www.rf.se/ImageVault/Images/id_164/scope_128/ImageVaultHandler.aspx (accessed 27 June 2009).
——(2007) *Idrotten i siffror* [Sport Statistics], www.rf.se/ImageVault/Images/id_121/scope_128/ImageVaultHandler.aspx (accessed 27 June 2009).
Toftegaard-Støckel, J., Strandbu, Å., Solenes, O., Jørgensen, P. and Fransson, K. (2010) 'Sport for children and youth in the Scandinavian countries', *Sport in Society*, 13 (4): 625–42.
Trondman, M. (2005) *Unga och föreningsidrotten. En studie om föreningsidrottens plats, betydelser och konsekvenser i ungas liv* [Youth and the Sport Movement: The Impact and the Consequences of Sport in the Lives of the Young]. Stockholm: Ungdomsstyrelsen.
Ulvros, H. (2004) *Dansens och tidens virvlar. Om dans och lek i Sveriges historia* [The Whirl of Dance and Time]. Lund: Historiska Media.
Wijk, J. (2001) 'Idrott, ungdom och dansbaneelände. Om den svenska idrottsrörelsens begynnande engagemang som ungdomsfostrare på 1940-talet' [Sport, Youth and the Misery of Dance Pavilions: The Swedish Sport Movement's Involvement in the Fostering of Youths in the 40s], in *Idrott, historia och samhälle*, no 1.

13

Beyond the facade

Youth sport development in the United States and the illusion of synergy

Matthew T. Bowers, Laurence Chalip and B. Christine Green

As this Handbook attests, the recent emergence of scholarship seeking to understand cross-national differences in sports development systems has generated more thorough efforts to characterize the ontological and ideological distinctions between the policies and programmes designed to cultivate elite athletes and encourage mass participation (cf. Chalip *et al* 1996; Green and Oakley 2001). Scholars and practitioners interested in understanding sport in the United States may be surprised to learn that the systems undergirding youth sport development are remarkable as much for their lack of interconnectedness as for their production of successful elite athletes on the international stage (B. Green 2005). Despite the high-profile nature of the latter systemic output, it is the facade of coordination at the input stage that serves as the primary focus of this chapter.

The utility of sports development has been established as having two fundamental components: the cultivation of elite athletes for national teams and the encouragement of mass rates of sport participation (e.g. M. Green 2007; Palm 1991). Although these two goals of sports development represent conceptually distinct enterprises, they are inexorably tied to one another through the need of elite sport programmes to draw from a deep pool of athletes in their search for developable talent (Broom 1991; Stovkis 1989). In explicating the theoretical framework for the pyramid model of youth sport development in which the relatively few high-performing elite athletes are supported by a broad participation base, B. Green (2005: 248) notes that in the United States systems of development 'have emerged haphazardly'. Moreover, 'sport programmes occur at various levels and in many places but are often ambiguously linked. At times, they might even be in conflict' (B. Green 2005: 248). While such an assertion may seem counterintuitive given the country's undisputed success in elite competition, the genesis of this uncoordinated system is readily ascribable to a hegemonic sociopolitical agenda that has pervaded the modern sports policy landscape in the United States (Sparvero *et al.* 2008).

Prior to the 1972 Summer Olympic Games in Munich, the United States had no guiding legislation specifying sports development policies, which was consistent with the country's historical reticence to introduce federal control into traditionally private sectors (Chalip 1995). However, with the internationally televised administrative failures and underperformance by American athletes in Munich serving as a focusing event, an undercurrent of concern about preserving national prestige during the Cold War mobilized governmental efforts to form a central administrative body under the Amateur Sports Act. The problem, however, was that establishing federal control over sport was perceived by many as consummate to adopting the Soviet model of sports governance, an outcome precluded by the political climate of the period. The unwillingness of the government to make substantive changes to the levels of federal control permitted over sport in America ultimately led to an impotent legislative outcome designed to rationalize the preservation of the status quo. Ultimately, Chalip contends,

> This is significant because the focus on administrative rationalization eliminated consideration of alternative or supplementary policy options. For example, redress of socioeconomic inequities in sport access and development of grassroots sports programs were given scant attention. It was tacitly assumed that inequities would be redressed and new sports programs created if the upper levels of sport governance were rationalized. Neither equal access nor program development were pursued as distinct goals of policy action, despite the fact that earlier research, White House reports, and congressional hearings had identified both as necessary components of an effective sport policy.
>
> *(Chalip 1995: 9)*

With such a neutered sports governance policy (i.e. the 1978 Amateur Sports Act) still representing the only legislative framework for sports development in the United States, it becomes more apparent as to how the veneer of international success could be misperceived as system-level coordination. As a result of this lack of federal policy, at least in terms of Olympic sport development, United States youth sport development is comprised of a number of autonomous governing bodies whereby each operates independently and is accountable only to the international governing body responsible for a given sport. Further, the lack of top-down coordination is both reflective of and pursuant to the creation of the two primary systemic conditions guiding sports development in this country: federalism and capitalism.

Not unique to the United States, federalism is a type of governance structure in which regional and local governments are granted independent powers and responsibilities (M. Green 2005). In American sport, this approach often manifests itself in the presupposition that youth sports operate as a local matter until an athlete reaches a certain level of accomplishment, at which point regional and national organizations assume control over the development of the athlete (B. Green 1992). Naturally, this type of system has both benefits and drawbacks as a means for developing athletes. On the one hand, local control theoretically affords more efficient use of financial and human resources in designing and implementing sport programmes. On the other hand, inequalities with regard to the calibre and funding of programmes produce broader disparities in the cultivation of a national talent pool from which to draw elite athletes (or, for that matter, in the sustenance of maximal participation levels).

Having economic, political, and ideological roots in a capitalist system of market economy also contributes to the reliance on a multitude of relatively uncoordinated sports development channels. As was evident in the ideological discomfort that emerged from the policy discussions regarding the Amateur Sports Act, issues pertaining to sports development are often viewed as best resolved through free market principles in which the quality of sport programme will be sufficiently regulated through competition (cf. Sparvero *et al* 2008). The assumption, therefore, is that ineffective sports programmes will not meet the demands of the consumers and will thus be replaced by better-functioning programmes through market forces. B. Green (2005: 248) recognizes the fallaciousness of this assumption, however, in noting that 'there is something ideologically comfortable about a sport system that has many different (sometimes competing) organizations. It smacks of laissez faire, open markets, and democracy. Our system, however, is neither laissez faire nor democratic.' In reality, the end product of a federalist system of sports development (with little legislative guidance) that is also predicated on capitalist principles to ensure the success of its programmes, is a sports development model in which chaos reigns.

The remainder of the chapter explores the three primary youth sport development paths that have emerged from this apparently disjointed system, with a focus on interpreting the distinct roles of each in the development system. Through briefly deconstructing the structural and operational differences between youth sport development in the private sector, the school system, and the municipalities, a more thorough explanation of the unique challenges discouraging the linkage and coordination of these sports development channels becomes possible.

Youth sport in the private sector

Prior to the mid-1950s, the majority of organized youth sport experiences for children and early adolescents occurred within (not-for-profit) social agencies such as the Young Men's Christian Associations and Young Women's Christian Associations, Boys and Girls Clubs, and Boy Scouts and Girl Scouts (Seefeldt and Ewing 1997). Since the advent of Little League Baseball in 1954, however, youth sports have moved towards a model of adult-led organizational structures housed primarily within private, pay-for-play organizations like Little League and Pop Warner Football.

Over the last few decades, youth sport outside of the school system and the direct jurisdiction of municipal parks and recreation departments has emerged as the primary development stream for elite youth sport at all ages, no longer simply younger children. Given the capitalist ideological and economic framework of the United States, the notion that market forces would render a competitive environment in which the private sector is viewed as the most effective means of development may not be surprising. However, the recent marked consolidation of elite sport development into the private sector merits further discussion.

Traditionally, elite youth sport development in the United States began for children in the private organizations, primarily because the school systems have been resistant to organized interscholastic sports competitions in early childhood education for safety and financial reasons (Eitzen and Sage 2003). With the increasing competition for limited collegiate athletic scholarships and professional opportunities, an emphasis on early specialization for elite youth athletes has become commonplace (Baker 2003). However, whereas in previous eras development would begin within the quasi-privatized confines of Little League, before transitioning back to the interscholastic sector during the middle school and high school years, many youth sport athletes (or, perhaps more accurately, the parents of many youth sport athletes) are electing to remain in the private sector as either a supplement or a replacement to interscholastic sports participation.

For example, basketball is a sport that has recently been at the centre of the debate over private sports development channels versus interscholastic sports. In this particular sport, summer participation in Amateur Athletic Union (a private, pay-for-play club system) competition has overtaken high school basketball as the primary forum through which to gain the exposure and credibility requisite to earn a college scholarship (Whitaker 2006). Given the privatized nature of the programming, concerns have emerged about the high-profile commercialization of the sport through shoe company sponsorships and profiteering. Consequently, this youth sport environment has become emblematic of the constant struggle between preserving the espoused values of amateurism and childhood while promoting a youth sport development system that borders on professionalization (Hohler 2006).

The most extreme form of this cultural movement toward professionalization is evidenced through the success of organizations such as IMG Academies, which immerse child prodigies in a highly expensive boarding school-style sports training programme where athletes attend on-site classes in the morning and dedicate the rest of the day to training in their respective sport. In reference to the pressures and demands placed upon children at IMG and academies like it, Hyman (2009: xiii) notes how 'the bigger is better model of youth sports delights adults … only kids are losers here'. In some sports, such as volleyball, for-profit private enterprises (sometimes called a 'school' or a 'club') have emerged. These programmes are run as entrepreneurial ventures, although many do not make a profit. Examples of experiences in the high-pressure youth sport development approaches are pervasive in individual sports like gymnastics and figure skating (Ryan 2000). Each of these instances embodies the delicate balance between opportunity and abuse that exists in the often-unchecked elite youth sport development model in the private sector.

The delivery of youth sport through entrepreneurial and social service organizations has been complemented for over a century by sports programmes provided by religious organizations. These include the Catholic Youth Organization (CYO), the Jewish Community Centers (JCCs), and an array of individual protestant churches. In many instances, sports facilities are included on church grounds for purposes of training and competition. In other cases, such as the JCCs, the sports facilities and programmes are provided at a central location for young people from several different churches (or synagogues).

The significance of sport for church organizations has varied origins, but is typically linked to other services intended to inculcate religious values that are appropriate to whichever sect offers the sport. Consequently, in many instances, the relevance to religion takes precedence over sporting excellence. However, the overall social trend toward increasing emphasis on winning over mere participation, even for children, has caused the degree of pressure in many of these environments to increase. Indeed, among Protestants, 'muscular Christianity' has become sufficiently pervasive that organizations like the Fellowship of Christian Athletes have emerged as increasingly significant purveyors of the notion that achieving sporting excellence is also to witness for God.

The array of organizations offering sport for youth – some of which are strictly entrepreneurial, some of which are still grounded in social service missions, and some of which are religiously affiliated – combines with the lack of any system for coordination or any policies at national, state, county, or local levels to create a patchwork of youth sport opportunities through which there is no definitive pathway. Further, the quality of coaching and administration varies among these organizations, and is often inconsistent as volunteers or low-paid part-time workers make up the majority of staff. Despite several attempts to create systems to train coaches and administrators, none has been widely accepted and implemented. The nature of competitions can also vary, and a sport may operate in separate leagues under rules that bear little resemblance to those formulated by the national governing body (NGB) that runs the sport in the United States or by the sport's international federation (IF). For example, during the summer, many communities organize swimming clubs, which come together to compete under their own sets of rules. In short, the patchwork of private sports organizations remains an uncoordinated and unregulated mix of high- and low-quality organizations, each operating in its own way, and sometimes even competing in leagues of their own.

Youth sport in the school system

Traditionally, systems for elite youth sport development for popular American sports, particularly during adolescence, have been housed within the interscholastic sports sector as a result of its direct tie to intercollegiate sport, which is the post-secondary elite sport development outlet for many sports (particularly baseball, basketball, swimming, track-and-field, and American football). While the degree to which some youth sports still rely on interscholastic competition for youth sport development has receded in some sports (e.g. basketball), sports like high school football are as inextricably linked to the school systems for elite development as ever.

Guttmann (1988) emphasizes the uniqueness of such integration between the academic and athletic educational pursuits relative to models of youth sport development in other parts of the globe, where sports at the university level are maintained under the autonomy of the students themselves, not highly institutionalized athletic departments. He notes, 'The most remarkable aspect of this situation is that American academics, apart from a bemused or embittered minority, accept this curious state of affairs as if it were part of the unalterable order of nature' (Guttmann 1988: 103). Although there are many who question the integrity of such an emphasis on athletics within academic institutions at both the high school and college levels, the reality of the inter-scholastic sports sector as a primary youth sport development arm is undeniable (e.g. Fejgin 2001). The more important issue, therefore, becomes what impact this relationship has on the youth sport development system.

For one, the systemic link between high school interscholastic sports and intercollegiate sports has a trickle-down impact on the spectrum of sports alternatives offered at the high school level. On the one hand, high school sports like baseball or softball (with a direct intercollegiate counterpart) are often a priority in terms of funding and resources because of the existence of an established development outcome: college scholarships, and in turn, community notoriety. As is illustrated in works such as *Friday Night Lights*, prominent high school sports in America (like football) often serve as a symbolic representation of the communities in which they are played (Bissinger 1991). On the other hand, emerging sports and sports without established collegiate counterparts, such as rowing or lacrosse (in some parts of the country), often face immense challenges in carving a niche within established interscholastic sports development infra-structures, particularly given funding constraints endemic to public school systems.

Another repercussion of the direct tie between interscholastic sport and intercollegiate sport is the dearth of advancement opportunities for youth who either lack the skills or talent necessary to participate in high school or college sport, or do not attend college for academic or financial reasons. In the United States, the opportunities for adolescents and young adults who fall into these categories are severely limited, which in turn precludes many young people from pursuing organized sport after adolescence. While intramural sports are available as an alternative for those who attend college but are not varsity- or club-level athletes, the lack of programme options outside of the intercollegiate framework is a major hindrance to optimizing participant advancement and retention for sports development systems throughout the lifespan.

The American school sports system is often misunderstood by those who view it from the outside. There is not, in fact, a single school sports system. There are private schools, many of which maintain their own leagues and rules. The many public schools are governed at city or county level, so the systems and rules by which sport is delivered in the schools (and even which sports are included among those offered) vary substantially across the country. There has been effort in some states to coordinate competition systems among public schools, and various coaches' associations and associations of school administrators have sought to promote improvements in school sport. However, each school district remains autonomous, and can choose how to run the sports it offers. A school may be constrained by the requirements of the league to which it belongs, but leagues are fundamentally local, and schools run the leagues, so those requirements are the ever-changing product of aggregate local preferences, rather than any systematic policy.

Youth sport in the municipalities

Often missed during debates over whether the private or interscholastic sector is truly the most effective channel for elite development, the municipal parks and recreation departments are charged with two implicitly unenviable tasks. The first is to assume responsibility for sustaining the mass participation component of the American youth sport development system for those children who lack the skill to participate at either the interscholastic or private (club) level. The second task is to deliver youth sport programming to those who lack the financial resources to pay for the right to participate in the private sector (cf. Taylor *et al.* 2007). As a result of these responsibilities, municipal parks and recreation programmes become perceived as intrinsically inferior to the other sectors and are often relegated to the default development option for those who are less skilled or of a lower socioeconomic standing. Moreover, this relegation is indicative of the broader philosophical issue that, regardless of sector, mass participation is a secondary concern to elite development, and that mass participation is thought to function as merely a means to the end of developing elite athletes (B. Green 1992).

Irrespective of the implicitly diminished stature of the municipal sports development sector, parks and recreation departments are charged with providing the most diverse array of sports (and other leisure) programmes to the broadest range of individuals; in fact, in the United States, municipal parks and recreation departments are often one of the few outlets to provide organized sports participation opportunities to the adult population (Van der Smissem 2000). As government-run, government-funded enterprises, in many respects parks and recreation departments are asked to do the 'most with the least' within the American youth sport development system. In particular, the municipal sports development arm is charged with providing sports programmes to younger children coming from lower socioeconomic backgrounds whose families do not have the resources to afford the costs associated with pay-for-play, private sector sport programmes. In essence, then, given the aforementioned lack of opportunities for pre-adolescent children to participate in interscholastic sports programmes, parks and recreation become the de facto option for participation outside of the private sector. In spite of this commendable role in the youth sport development system, the rather nebulous connection between the three sectors and the fact that the parks and recreation segment provides comparatively lower-calibre sport training (often organized through parents and volunteer coaches) make transitioning and advancing athletes an unsystematized, ad hoc process.

Of course, there are as many variations to parks and recreation department programming as there are parks and recreation departments. Like the schools, parks and recreation are either the responsibility of the city or the county; whether city or county varies in different parts of the country. Cities and counties also vary in terms of facilities and finances so, consequently, the services that parks and recreation can provide also vary. There are also regional differences in the popularity of sports. For example, lacrosse is popular in the northeast, but not particularly popular in the southwest. Similarly, surfing is popular in California and Florida, but not feasible in the inland states. Consequently, the nature of programmes – which sports are offered, and with what quality – varies among communities. There is no governance or regulatory system to standardize or to provide quality control to publicly run sport.

Challenges of promoting youth sport development

Combining an understanding of the structural differences among the primary delivery systems for youth sport with knowledge of the sociopolitical underpinnings guiding youth sport development, it becomes easier to comprehend how a seemingly straightforward process can devolve into a complex amalgam of competing practices and ideologies. In spite of the fact that there are instances of both well-leveraged, coordinated linkage between sectors and successful ad hoc, ephemeral coordination, the endemic nature of the many impediments to linking the development sectors often makes efforts to sustain coordination intractable. For example, the previous sections have demonstrated the systemic inefficiencies of both vertical and horizontal athlete transitions; that is, different sectors afford different opportunities depending on the age and ability of the child. Given the insufficient coordination of these sectors, children can easily fall through the proverbial development cracks.

In fact, the systems can work against one another. Although in some communities sports facilities are shared by the schools and parks and recreation, in other communities school facilities (which may be the only ones in town) are unavailable. If insurance costs or agreements with unions whose workers maintain school facilities make it expensive for schools to make gymnasia, pools, or other facilities available outside school hours, then those facilities are closed to the public. In like manner, the presence of school sports has often precluded the development of community-based clubs for those same sports. Similarly, the prestige associated with school sports excellence has made it difficult for sports that are not offered by schools (which are the vast majority of sports) to establish themselves in the community, because the necessary social support is eroded by the focus on school sport. In some sectors of the country, school coaches have passed rules prohibiting training outside school, limiting the hours that can be trained, and preventing training on weekends. These are anti-excellence rules that reduce the demands on school coaches, but that also discourage potentially elite athletes.

In some cases, the systems are not in conflict; they simply operate in parallel. For example, many church leagues are independent of any other sporting organization. Similarly, many so-called 'recreational' leagues (e.g. summer swimming leagues) have rules to preclude athletes who have trained with elite sporting organizations. The upshot is that moving to another level of training or competition can be difficult for a child to do, particularly if there are social consequences for leaving a system in which relationships have been built.

Beyond the differences in funding, organizational structures, and cultures there are deeper social forces at work that also constrain the potential for youth sport to expand beyond traditional taxonomic conceptions. The professionalized sports model is so ingrained in the collective American psyche that it is difficult to develop and sustain sports programmes that do not conform to this image. Although one would expect youth sport organizations to incorporate more diverse participation alternatives and developmentally beneficial policies aimed at generating more positive sport experiences for a broader range of youth, this is rarely the case. Instead, the professionalized sports models of our entertainment-based sports system pervade our youth sport settings as well.

Parents play a major role in youth sport settings, often volunteering as coaches, officials, and administrators. Further, parents' attitudes and perceptions have been shown to directly and indirectly affect their children's evaluations of their skill, their satisfaction with their sports participation, and their psychological involvement with the sport (B. Green and Chalip 1997). In short, the role of the adult in shaping the youth sport experience appears to have a critical and measurable impact in the development process. Unfortunately, this impact often manifests itself in counterproductive forms of behaviour.

Not all youth sport programmes adhere to the professionalized model. Modifications to this model range from equal playing time requirements and the use of small-sides games (e.g. 5v5 soccer), to non-competitive, play-based programmes that use modified equipment and modified rules. Modifications are typically incorporated to better provide child-centred, developmentally appropriate activities. These programmes have also been shown to develop the basic skills necessary for more traditional youth sport participation. However, modified programmes struggle for acceptability (B. Green 1997). While both children and parents report satisfaction with the skill development and emotional outcomes of modified youth sport, some parents have expressed concern that the alternative programme merely serves as a distraction from 'real sport'. Because it does not conform to the ubiquitous professionalized model of sport, it does not represent a legitimate youth sport experience. The resulting pressure to conform to professionalized forms and values makes it difficult to maintain the modifications. Instead, programmes are often compelled to adopt elements of the traditional youth sport programmes (Chalip and Green 1998). Chalip and Scott (2005) encountered similar parental resistance to atypical, developmentally focused programming within a youth swimming league. The authors witnessed the detrimental impact of rivalrous factions of parents precipitating the near disbandment of the league, and recommended that proactive policies be implemented to prevent parental issues from detracting from the macro- and micro-level potential for youth sport development.

Conclusion/future

Evaluating the efficiency and effectiveness of the American model of youth sport development ostensibly hinges upon a fundamental debate over taxonomic classifications regarding both what constitutes sports development and how the ultimate goal of sports development is defined at the national level (i.e. mass participation or elite performance). As we have demonstrated, the international success of elite athletes and teams does not necessarily equate to an adequately coordinated development system that promotes and sustains sports participation throughout the lifespan for the non-elite athlete. Given the present obesity epidemic confronting the United States, the saliency of this disparity cannot be overstated. In fact, a 2008 report by the Centers for Disease Control and Prevention (CDC) found that in 2005–6, only one-third of adults in the United States participated in regular leisure-time physical activity, while an equal number were considered to be obese (US Department of Health and Human Services 2008: 24). For American youth, the trends are equally disturbing. According to the CDC's National Center for Health Statistics, in the period between the mid-1970s and the mid-2000s, the prevalence of childhood obesity increased dramatically across all age ranges: for children aged 2–5 years, the prevalence increased from 5.0 per cent to 12.4 per cent; for those aged 6–11 years, prevalence increased from 6.5 per cent to 17.0 per cent; and for those aged 12–19 years, prevalence increased from 5.0 per cent to 17.6 per cent (Centers for Disease Control and Prevention 2009). In either case, be it adults or children, these statistics are not reflective of a well-functioning, well-coordinated sports development system.

There are obvious advantages to using sport (broadly defined) as a means to encourage physical activity. The CDC recognizes physical activity as a key to fighting obesity, but it has not used sport as a tool. Rather, the CDC promotes exercise despite popular resistance to its painful and boring nature. Why exercise rather than physical play (i.e. sport)? The answer is grounded in the fundamentals of the American sporting system. The huge variety of sporting organizations and the variations among those even in the same taxonomic group (e.g. schools, parks and recreation) make it a difficult system with which to work; however, the more fundamental problem has to do with the emphasis on excellence, particularly within the schools. Children (especially adolescents) must compete to 'make the team,' and more are excluded than are included. Thus, the very values of the American sporting system are inconsistent with its use as a public health tool. As a result, an alliance that has the potential to add outreach for the CDC and resources for sport has so far been deemed unworkable.

In addition to confronting issues of obesity and non-participation (or drop-out), youth sport in the United States faces significant challenges related to those who *do* participate. Among the major issues with which youth sport must contend are the increasing social pressure for early specialization in a particular sport, a culture of 'professionalization' that detracts from the playful, participatory nature of youth sport, and the increasing imposition of adult values and parental/coach abuse and misconduct (Brower 1979; Fraser-Thomas *et al* 2005). In fact, some sociological researchers have even suggested that youth sports have become so untethered from their anthropological and biological roots in conceptions of play as to represent an 'impoverished' individual and social experience (Devereux 1976). A scant few authors concerned with youth sport have considered the consequences of a systemic shift away from more play-like sport experiences (e.g. informal, neighbourhood sports) to increasingly earlier formal sport experiences (cf. Ogden 2002). Attempting to understand sports development without engaging with issues such as these renders an inherently incomplete, if not myopic, assessment of the state of youth sport development in the United States.

Compounding these more sociocultural concerns are the policy issues identified in this chapter. The facade of coordination that permeates youth sport in America is a misleading representation of a system that is constrained by the absence of a central governing body to oversee and direct youth sport development. In addition, the political and economic foundations of federalism and capitalism commingle to promote inter-sector competition rather than coordination. Further confounding efforts to link the private, scholastic, and municipal development sectors are the self-perpetuating resource disparities and social stigmas that promote the private and scholastic sport sectors as legitimate options for athlete advancement, while relegating the municipal sector as the de facto route for those without. When opportunities emerge to expand and diversify programming, or to optimize cross-leveraging between sectors, parental preconceptions about the value and function of youth sport often undermine the potential for beneficial developmental outcomes, both from an individual and systemic standpoint.

To conclude on a more encouraging note, at the time of this writing newly elected President Barack Obama had taken the initial measures to redress the aforementioned lack of federal policy through creating a cabinet-level office to oversee youth sport development. According to the Associated Press (16 June 2009), 'the new office will recommend federal policies and programs to the President to enhance opportunities and access for youth participation in sport, with particular focus on youth in urban areas. It will also foster and encourage youth sport, educational and cultural events … '. While the preceding chapter has addressed the consequences of a federalist-based, capitalist-driven sports development system reliant on competition between sectors to produce both elite and recreational sport participation, the recent willingness of the Obama Administration to engage in a discourse about improving the coordination of development sectors offers hope for a more unified, leveraged youth sport development system. Nevertheless, these challenges to the status quo are likely to be met with intense ideological resistance and major structural impediments. The ramifications of decades-long systemic disorganization are beginning to become apparent in terms of decrements in both elite international performance (Wu *et al* 2009) and domestic mass participation (Johnston *et al* 2007). Moving forward, the challenge is to forge a means (be it through federal legislation or not) of integrating the national, regional, and local resources into a more synergistic, sustainable system of youth sport development based on complementary rather than competing sectors.

References

Amateur Sports Act of 1978, Public Law 95-606, 92 Stat. 3045 (1978).

Associated Press. (18 June 2009) *Obama to Create New Office of Youth Sport*. Online. Available http: www. google.com/hostednews/ap/article/ALeqM5i4tlzaLe2DIe8i9YYekbnwphdrBQD98S3T901 (accessed 20 June 2009).

Baker, J. (2003) 'Early specialization in youth sport: a requirement for adult expertise?', *High Ability Studies*, 14(1): 85–94.

Bissinger, H.G. (1991) *Friday Night Lights: A Town, a Team, and a Dream*, New York: Harper Perennial.

Broom, E.F. (1991) 'Lifestyles of aspiring high performance athletes', *Journal of Comparative Physical Education and Sport*, 13(2): 24–54.

Brower, J.J. (1979) 'The professionalization of organized youth sport: social psychological impacts and outcomes', *The ANNALS of the American Academy of Political and Social Science*, 445(1): 39–46.

Centers for Disease Control and Prevention. (2009) 'Prevalence of overweight among children and adolescents: United States, 2003–6', *CDC National Center for Health Statistics, Health E-Stat*. Online. Available http: www.cdc.gov/nchs/products/pubs/pubd/hestats/overweight/overwght_child_03.htm (accessed 14 June 2009).

Chalip, L. (1995) 'Policy analysis in sport management', *Journal of Sport Management*, 9: 1–13.

Chalip, L. and Green, B.C. (1998) 'Establishing and maintaining a modified youth sport program: lessons from Hotelling's location game', *Sociology of Sport Journal*, 15(4): 326–42.

Chalip, L., Johnson, A. and Stachura, L. (Eds) (1996). *National Sports Policies: An International Handbook*, Westport, CT: Greenwood Press.

Chalip, L. and Scott, E.P. (2005) 'Centrifugal social forces in a youth sport league', *Sport Management Review*, 8(1): 43–67.

Devereux, E. (1976) 'Backyard versus Little League baseball: the impoverishment of children's Games', in D. Landers (ed.), *Social Problems in Athletics*, 179–92. Urbana: University of Illinois Press.

Eitzen, D.S. and Sage, G.H. (2003) *Sociology of North American Sport*, 7th edn, Boston: McGraw-Hill.

Fejgin, N. (2001) 'Participation in high school competitive sports: A subversion of school mission or contribution to academic goals?', in A. Yiannakis and M.J. Melnick (eds), *Contemporary Issues in Sociology of Sport*, 95–108. Champagne: Human Kinetics.

Fraser-Thomas, J.L., Côté, J. and Deakin, J. (2005) 'Youth sport programs: an avenue to foster positive youth development', *Physical Education and Sport Pedagogy*, 10(1): 19–40.

Green, B.C. (1992) *The coordination of mass participation and elite sport: does trickle up work?*, Report to the United States Volleyball Association, Colorado Springs: USVBA.

——(1997) 'Action research in youth soccer: assessing the acceptability of an alternative program', *Journal of Sport Management*, 11(1): 29–44.

——(2005) 'Building sport programs to optimize athlete recruitment, retention, and transition: toward a normative theory of sport development', *Journal of Sport Management*, 19(3): 233–53.

Green, B.C. and Chalip, L. (1997) 'Enduring involvement in youth soccer: The socialization of parent and child', *Journal of Leisure Research*, 29: 61–77.

Green, M. (2005) 'Integrating macro- and meso-level approaches: a comparative analysis of elite sport development in Australia, Canada and the United Kingdom', *European Sport Management Quarterly*, 5(2): 143–66.

——(2007) 'Policy transfer, lesson drawing and perspectives on elite sport development systems', *International Journal of Sport Management and Marketing*, 2(4): 426–41.

Green, M. and Oakley, B. (2001) 'Elite sport development systems and playing to win: uniformity and diversity in international approaches', *Leisure Studies*, 20: 247–67.

Guttmann, A. (1988) *A Whole New Ballgame: An Interpretation of American Sports*, Chapel Hill: UNC Press.

Hohler, B. (23 July 2006) 'Sneaker war: ethical questions raised as amateur basketball recruiters engage in a high stakes battle for blue-chip recruits', *Boston Globe*. Online. Available http: www.boston.com/sports/basketball/articles/2006/07/23/36neaker_war/?page=full (accessed 16 June 2009).

Hyman, M. (2009) *Until it Hurts: America's Obsession with Youth Sports and How it Harms our Kids*, Boston: Beacon Press.

Johnston, L., Delva, J. and O'Malley, P. (2007) 'Sports participation and physical education in American secondary schools: current levels and racial/ethnic and socioeconomic disparities', *American Journal of Preventive Medicine*, 33(4): S195–208.

Ogden, D.C. (2002) 'Overgrown sandlots: the diminishment of pickup ball in the Midwest', *NINE: A Journal of Baseball History and Culture*, 10(2): 120–30.

Palm, J. (1991) *Sport for All: Approaches from Utopia to Reality*, Schorndorf: Verlag Karl Hofmann.

Ryan, J. (2000) *Little Girls in Pretty Boxes: The Making and Breaking of Elite Gymnasts and Figure Skaters*, Boston: Grand Central Publishing.

Seefeldt, V. and Ewing, M. (1997) 'Youth sports in America: an overview', *PCPFS Research Digest*, 2(11). Online. Available http: www.fitness.gov/youthsports.pdf (accessed 18 June 2009).

Sparvero, E., Chalip, L. and Green, B.C. (2008) 'Laissez faire sport development: building elite athletes in the United States', in B. Houlihan and M. Green (eds), *Comparative Elite Sport Development*, Oxford: Butterworth-Heinemann.

Stokvis, R. (1989) 'The international and national expansion of sports', in E.A. Wagner (ed), *Sport in Asia and Africa: A Comparative Handbook*, 13–24. New York: Greenwood.

Taylor, W.C., Floyd, M.F., Whitt-Glover, M.C. and Brooks, J. (2007) 'Environmental justice: a framework for collaboration between the public health and parks and recreation fields to study disparities in physical activity', *Journal of Physical Activity and Health*, 4: S50–63.

U.S. Department of Health and Human Services. (2008) *Health, United States, 2008*, Washington, DC: U.S. Government Printing Office.

Van der Smissem, B. (2000) *Recreation and Parks: The Profession*, Champaign: Human Kinetics.

Whitaker, L. (24 July 2006) 'Sneaker wars: shining a light on the mess that summer hoops can be', *SLAM*. Online. Available http: www.slamonline.com/online/blogs/the-links/2006/07/sneaker-wars (accessed 19 June 2009).

Wu, J., Liang, L. and Yang, F. (2009) 'Achievement and benchmarking of countries at the Summer Olympics using cross efficiency evaluation method', *European Journal of Operational Research*, 197(2): 722–30.

14

Sports development and young people in Taiwan

Tien-Chin Tan and Chih-Fu Cheng

Before the turn of the century, there was a relative neglect of this policy area as there was no separate or specific policy document that related to young people and sport beyond the specification of the physical education (PE) curriculum within the school system. After winning the 2000 presidential elections, the new Democratic Progressive Party (DPP) government, for the first time, included the issue of youth sport development in a national policy document, *Challenge 2008: The Key Project for National Development (2002–2007)*, issued by the Executive Yuan (the executive branch of government). In one of the subthemes in the document, *Cultivating Active Young People*, the government attempted to promote health, physical fitness and national competiveness through youth sports (Executive Yuan 2001). Following the publication of the Executive Yuan policy the Ministry of Education issued *The White Paper for Cultivating Active Young People* in 2004, in which it was stated that 'the purpose of school PE is to promote the physical fitness and sport skills through planned physical activity' (MoE 2004: 1). At the present time, there are three key concerns of the Taiwanese government in relation to sports development and young people: elite sport, physical fitness and physical activity/leisure sport. The first concern is strongly linked to the discourse on national pride and sport talent development while the other two are related to health and competiveness in the international arena.

The development of youth sport policy

In line with the *Challenge 2008* policy of the Executive Yuan, the Department of Physical Education (DPE) under the Ministry of Education initiated *The Development Project for School Physical Education (2002–2007)*. The six main policy goals highlighted in the project were i) establishing a Sport College System (*Tiyuban*); ii) selecting and producing talented aboriginal students; iii) improving the development of student baseball; iv) raising the average score of physical fitness tests of students by 2% each year; v) raising the number of sports participation rates of students by 3% each year; and vi) 'One Pupil, One Sport; One School, One Team' (DPE 2002a: 10–11). The six goals can be mapped onto the three central concerns of the DPE, with the first three relating mainly to elite sport development, the fourth related to physical fitness development and the last two related most directly to physical activity/leisure sports development. In order to fulfil the policy goals, the administrative structure of the DPE was designed around its three key policy concerns. Figure 14.1 indicates that the functions of the DPE are divided between three divisions for promoting the projects related to: i) elite sport, ii) health, and iii) physical fitness, physical activities and leisure sport.

Regarding elite sport development, the three most important projects are as follows: i) the establishment of the Sport College System (*Tiyuban*), ii) the *Athletic Development Plan for Talented Aboriginal Students (2003–2007)*, and iii) the improvement of student baseball.

In order to identify and develop young potential athletes, the Sport Colleges network (*Tiyuban*) was initiated from 1998 after the establishment of the Sports Affairs Council (SAC) in 1997 by the Executive Yuan. This system did not develop systematically until the SAC hosted the national conference for elite sport development in 2002. One of the key recommendations of this conference was to systematically develop the Sport Colleges network from primary school level to high schools focused on the key sports suggested by the SAC and identified as medal targets at the 2008 Beijing Olympic Games and the 2009 World Games which were hosted in Kaohsiung, Taiwan. To fulfil this objective the Ministry of Education encouraged local education bureaux (LEBs) to set up sport colleges by offering substantial financial support (Su 2006: 14–17). The four-year budget for sport colleges to produce potential young athletes to prepare for the 2008 Olympics and 2009 World Games was around 407 million NT dollars granted by the MoE and SAC from 2006 to 2009 (Su 2006: 23). Table 14.1 indicates that the number of sport colleges at the high/vocational school level has increased almost threefold since 2001. Although it is not clear how many new sport colleges were established at the primary and secondary school levels before 2008, the figure is still increasing, according to a senior official in the DPE (Interviewee A, 18 June 2009).

Although the number of sport colleges has increased, according to a senior official in the DPE (Interviewee A, 18 June 2009), 'quality is more important than the quantity'. He added that 'the emergent mission of the DPE in relation to sport college system is that these limited

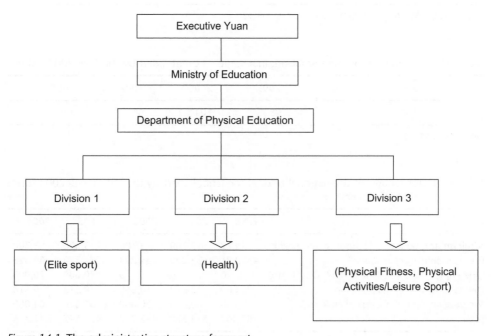

Figure 14.1 The administrative structure for sport

resources have to be scientifically distributed to the schools and athletes, which will make sure that top athletes are produced.' He also emphasized that 'the Ministry of Education is revising the regulations for sport colleges in order to evaluate individual colleges and force out the inefficient.'

In addition to the network of sport colleges, the Ministry of Education has also targeted Taiwanese aboriginal students who were considered to be naturally good at sport. According to the *Athletic Development Plan for Talented Aboriginal Students (2003–2007), issued by the DPE, there are seven sports targeted at talented aboriginal students – baseball, female softball, track and field, gymnastics, judo, taekwondo and weight-lifting (DPE 2003a: 4–5). Table 14.2 indicates the number of talented Taiwanese aboriginal students grant-aided by the DPE since 2003.

As Table 14.3 indicates, around 60 million NT dollars of the annual budget of the DPE was invested in the development for aboriginal athletes each year between 2001 and 2004. The project is overseen by the MoE, which invested around 57 million NT dollars in 2008 with the aim of producing aboriginal medal winners (MoE 2008a). More recently, in 2009 the project, *Athletic Development Plan for Talented Aboriginal Students*, was launched to provide scholarships to support elite aboriginal athletes. Two categories of student athlete have been identified and supported with grants (see Table 14.4) based on their performance during the national athletic intercollegiate games, national high school games and national championships.

Table 14.1 Number of sport colleges, 2001–2008

	Primary school	Secondary school	High/vocational school
2001			46
2004			70
2008	144	236	118

Source: Hong, J.W. (2005: 242–244) and Yu, Z.-Y. (2008: 2)

Table 14.2 The number of talented aboriginal students grant-aided by the DPE 2003–2008

Year	2003	2004	2005	2006	2007	2008
Total	148	138	98	104	60	160

Source: DPE (2009a)

Table 14.3 Distribution of the national budget for school sport by the DPE 1998–2004 (unit: 1,000 NT dollars)

Year	1998	2001	2002	2003	2004
Administrative budget for school PE and health	3,872	3,700	3,300	3,300	3,300
The development of school PE	437,591	433,200	434,294	274,389	294,528
'One Pupil, One Sport; One School, One Team'	0	0	0	70,000	70,000
The development of adapted sport	26,800	17,670	10,368	9,518	9,518
The development of aboriginal athletes	1,200	60,000	50,000	66,320	64,089
Total	469,463	514,570	497,962	423,527	441,435

Source: Hong, J.W. (2005: 322)

Table 14.4 Scholarships for elite aboriginal athletes awarded in 2009 (unit: NT dollars)

	Secondary school	High school	University
Elite student athlete	6,000	8,000	8,000
Potential student athlete	4,000	5,000	4,000

Source: DPE (2009b)

Due to baseball's political symbolism in relation to the national identity of the Taiwanese government and citizens, the government invested substantial money in developing elite baseball (Tan *et al.* 2009: 103–4). In order to enlarge the talent pool for producing more elite baseball players the *Project for Improving Student Baseball* was launched by the DPE in 2003. The strategic goals for this project are incorporated into four linked elements – 'playing' baseball, 'learning' baseball, 'training' for baseball and 'loving' baseball, which cover primary school, secondary school, high school and university levels (DPE 2003b). To support the project four leagues were established, each of which was linked to one level in the educational system. According to a senior official in the DPE, 'the DPE has invested around 50 million NT dollars each year in developing elite baseball since 2003' (Interviewee A, 18 June 2009). Another senior official who is in charge of promoting elite baseball in the DPE emphasized that 'Baseball promotion is one of the key policies for us for the coming years which is why we spend substantial sums in supporting it' (Interviewee B, 18 June 2009).

The recent interest of the government in promoting students' physical fitness is a response to growing concern with the consequences of an increasingly sedentary lifestyle for their long-term health. In order to gather data on the physical fitness levels of Taiwanese students the Ministry of Education introduced a fitness assessment programme in the 1990s. The results of the assessment showed that not only was the level of physical fitness of Taiwanese students worse than that in other developed countries and other Asian countries, but also that 15–20 per cent of pupils in primary schools were identified as overweight (DPE 2002a: 5–6). In order to tackle this problem the Ministry of Education initiated a series of projects, two of which were titled *Physical Fitness 333 Plan (1999–2003)* and, *Healthy Body Shape Plan for Elementary/High School Students (2004–2008)*. The main purposes of these two projects were to encourage students to adopt lifelong exercise habits, an active lifestyle and a balanced diet, in order to improve students' fitness and decrease the percentage of those who were overweight or underweight (MoE 2009a).

Regarding physical activity/leisure sports development, the three main projects were *One Pupil, One Sport; One School, One Team* Plan, *Raising the Swimming Ability of Students,* and *Improving School Sport Fields.* The first project was highlighted in *Challenge 2008: The Key Project for National Development* issued by Executive Yuan in 2002. *One Pupil, One Sport* refers to the aim that each student should acquire at least one sports skill, while *One School, One Team* requires each school to organize at least one sports squad and to take part in regional sports matches. The long-term aims of this project were to increase: i) the sports participation rate of students, ii) the number of students joining school sports clubs, and iii) the number of schools hosting inter-class games and inter-school games (Executive Yuan 2001: 34–35). Tables 14.3 and 14.5 indicate that the DPE's annual budget to support this project has been maintained at around 70–100 million NT dollars since 2003.

Similar to the first project, *Raising the Swimming Ability for Students* (2001–4) (DPE 2001) and *Improvement Plan for School Sport Fields* (2002–5) (DPE 2002b) both attempted to raise the sports participation rate of students by providing free swimming classes within and beyond the curriculum and also by constructing more swimming pools and outdoor and indoor athletic facilities. According to a senior official in the DPE, 'the Department has invested around 200 million NT

Table 14.5 Distribution of the national budget for school sport by the DPE, 2008–2009 (unit: 1,000 NT dollars)

Budget allocation	2008	2009
Administration	3,288	3,269
The development of school PE	593,314	730,677
School health promotion project	106,361	259,961
'One Pupil, One Sport; One School, One Team' plan	105,840	78,340
The development of adapted sport	28,454	28,454
Healthy body shape plan for elementary/high school students	20,327	20,327
Total	857,584	1,121,028

Source: MoE (2008a, 2009b)

Table 14.6 Distribution of the national budget for school sport by the DPE, 2008–2009 (unit: 1,000 NT dollars)

Project	2008	2009
Inter-school games and competitions	228,050	235,486
The promotion of school PE	97,010	98,457
International exchanges related to school PE	17,734	17,734
Upgrading sport universities	20,000	50,000
Construction (athletic fields, swimming pools)	220,000	280,000
Strengthening sport colleges	0	45,000
Other	2,520	4,000
Total	593,314	730,677

Source: MoE (2008a, 2009b)

dollars each year in constructing more swimming pools and outdoor/indoor athletic fields since 2002' (Interviewee D, 13 June 2009). Table 14.6 indicates that the annual budget of DPE invested around 280 million NT dollars in construction in 2009.

Policy delivery

According to a senior official in the DPE, 'the main mission for the DPE is to provide the lead in decision-making and policy-making with the Local Education Bureaux (LEBs) delivering the policies' (Interviewee C, 27 May 2009). As there are only 25 members of staff in the DPE the Department relies not only on the cooperation of units of sub-national government, but also on a number of non-governmental organizations to help in policy delivery. In addition to LEBs, three key organizations are commissioned and funded by the DPE to support youth sport policy implementation (see Figure 14.2). One of these key organizations is the Chinese Taipei School Sport Federation which organizes three senior/junior High School leagues, one each for basketball, volleyball and softball. The 2009 annual DPE budget for promoting this kind of league is around 41 million NT dollars. The second organization is the Chinese Taipei Student Baseball Federation whose main mission is to help the DPE implement the project to improve student baseball, which involves managing four national baseball leagues at primary school, secondary school, high school and university levels. The 2009 annual DPE budget for supporting student baseball is around 45 million NT dollars. The third set of organizations are the research centres and professional associations, including the School Physical Education Research and

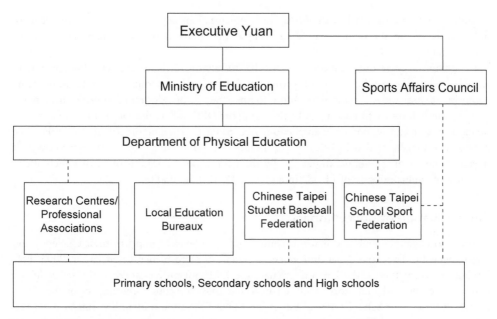

Figure 14.2 The administrative structure for promoting youth sport in Taiwan

Development Centre in National Taiwan Normal University, the National Society of Physical Education of the Republic of China (Taiwan) and the Taiwan Society for Sport Management.

Table 14.7 indicates that these organizations, commissioned by the DPE, play a significant role in helping the DPE promote and implement a wide variety of youth sport policies. Indeed,

Table 14.7 Organizations commissioned by the DPE to contribute to the delivery of youth sport policy

Institutions		Projects
Chinese Taipei School Sport Federation		Organizing senior/junior high school leagues for basketball, volleyball and softball
Chinese Taipei Student Baseball Federation		The improvement of student baseball
Research Centres &	School Physical Education Research & Development Centre	The promotion of school PE
Professional Associations	National Society of Physical Education of the Republic of China (Taiwan)	Physical Fitness 333 Plan (1999–2003), Healthy Body Shape Plan for elementary/high school students (2004–2008) & Happy Life Plan (2007–2011)
	Taiwan Society for Sport Management	Improving the swimming ability of students
	Taiwan Association for Adapted Physical Activity and Health	Athletic Development Plan for talented aboriginal students
	Taiwan Society for Body Culture	Volunteer in school sport
	National Taiwan Normal University	Social inclusion through youth sport
	National Taiwan Sport University (Taichung Campus)	Talented student athletes
	National Changhua University of Education	Happy Life Sport Station Plan

according to a senior official in the DPE, these organizations are not just the passive agents of policy delivery but sometimes play a key role as the 'think tank' for Departmental policy-making (Interviewee C, 27 May 2009).

In addition to these organizations the DPE has to rely on LEBs for project fulfilment within schools. According to the Local Government Act, central government has to respect the authority of local government in relation to the matters of education, culture, and sports. Consequently, in order to encourage LEBs to support DPE policy, the Department relies on its financial power and its power of inspection. According to a senior official in the DPE, 'The only way to make sure that LEBs carry out the policies of the DPE is to use financial power. It means the result of the annual inspection by the Ministry of Education of LEBs which affects the DPE individual subsidy of LEBs' (Interviewee D, 13 June 2009).

The evaluation of policy impact

In order to encourage public officials at central and local level to improve their efficiency and effectiveness the Executive Yuan introduced a system of performance-based pay in 2003. Following the instruction of the Executive Yuan, the DPE not only established the set weighted performance appraisal indicators identified in Table 14.8 to evaluate the impact of the 'Development Project for School Physical Education (2002–7)', but also identified similar indicators for the evaluation of LEBs.

In order to ensure that DPE policy is implemented by local government, the performance appraisal indicators were set by the DPE to enable it to inspect and evaluate LEBs. The outcome of annual inspection by the DPE is a factor in determining annual subsidy that each LEB is awarded. In addition, a pay plan, which included individual and group incentive payments, was introduced by the DPE to provide further encouragement to local civil servants to support central government policy objectives. Table 14.9 indicates that elite sport, physical fitness and sports participation are the three main objectives set for local government in terms of youth sport policy.

According to a senior official in the DPE (Interviewee D, 13 June 2009), the annual PE statistics collected by the School Physical Education Research and Development Centre in National Taiwan Normal University and National Society of Physical Education of the Republic of China (Taiwan) are used by the DPE as an important reference when conducting annual inspections of local government. However, Table 14.10 indicates that the trends in four measures of physical fitness among students in primary, secondary and high schools have generally been downward over the period between 2003 and 2007.

Although data are only available for two years, Table 14.11 provides some reinforcement of the downward trend in physical fitness indicated in Table 14.10. According to the data in

Table 14.8 The weighting between performance appraisal indicators for the 'Development Project for School Physical Education (2002–2007)'

Indicators	Percentage
One pupil, one sport	20
One school, one team	20
Raising the average physical fitness test score of students by 2% each year	15
Raising the sports participation rate of students by 3% each year	15
Improving the development of student baseball	15
Selecting and producing talented aboriginal students	15

Source: DPE (2003c)

Table 14.9 The weighting of performance appraisal indicators used by the DPE to evaluate Local Education Bureaux

Indicators	Percentage
Local sport budget	10
Increasing the capability of primary school PE teachers	10
The results of the Physical Fitness Test	10
Raising the sports participation rate of students	10
Swimming ability of students	5
Reducing the death rate from swimming accidents	5
The participation rate for students joining school sport clubs	10
Increasing the number of sport colleges	5
Hiring full-time coaches	5
Hosting sport competitions at county level	10
Hosting inter-class games and inter-school games	10
Specialist activities related to sports development (hosting games, elite sport training, selection and competition)	10

Source: DPE (2009c)

Table 14.10 Percentage reaching the required level in physical fitness tests for students from primary, secondary and high schools (2003–2007)

Items	Year	Primary school	Secondary school	High school
Sit-and-reach	2003	75.0%	75.0%	75.0%
	2005	77.3%	79.7%	77.3%
	2006	75.6%	78.4%	73.2%
	2007	70.7%	72.9%	66.2%
One-minute sit-ups	2003	75.0%	75.0%	75.0%
	2005	73.5%	76.4%	76.0%
	2006	71.4%	71.9%	73.3%
	2007	66.2%	66.5%	67.3%
Standing long jump	2003	75.0%	75.0%	75.0%
	2005	72.8%	72.8%	76.4%
	2006	73.0%	70.8%	62.5%
	2007	65.7%	72.0%	61.1%
800m/1600m runs	2003	75.0%	75.0%	75.0%
	2005	71.8%	75.6%	75.8%
	2006	74.0%	76.2%	75.7%
	2007	74.4%	73.9%	71.6%

Source: NSPEROC (2009)

Table 14.11 the rate of regular exercise among students slightly decreased between 2005 and 2006. After 2007 the DPE not only changed the definition of regular exercise from '30 minutes on three days per week' to '30 minutes on seven days per week', but also distinguished between exercise taken during school days, weekends and summer or winter holidays.

One consequence of changing the way in which data were collected was that the levels of physical activity reported (see Table 14.12) were generally significantly higher than reported in Table 14.11. More importantly, Table 14.12 also indicates that, while the rate of regular exercise

Table 14.11 Proportion of students at primary, secondary and high schools undertaking regular exercise (30 minutes, 3 days per week) (2005–2006)

Year	Primary school	Secondary school	High school
2005	57.8%	40.7%	25.6%
2006	52.9%	37.5%	25.4%

Source: MoE 2007a: 13

Table 14.12 Proportion of students at primary, secondary and high schools undertaking regular exercise (accumulated 30 minutes per day) (2007–2008)

Time	Year	Primary school	Secondary school	High school
School days	2007	74.6%	63.3%	51.4%
	2008	67.9%	51.7%	40.1%
Weekends	2007	73.2%	59.9%	47.2%
	2008	73.8%	61.3%	53.3%
Summer holidays	2007	74.0%	64.0%	53.4%
	2008	84.6%	72.2%	61.7%
Winter holidays	2007	74.0%	64.0%	53.4%
	2008	74.1%	59.8%	52.3%

Source: MoE 2007b, 2008b

Table 14.13 The average number of sports clubs per school (2005–2008)

Year	Primary school	Secondary school	High school
2005	3.27	3.27	8.48
2006	4.39	5.16	8.76
2007	3.58	4.27	8.00
2008	3.93	4.41	7.17

Source: MoE 2005, 2006, 2007c, 2008c

among students during school time was decreasing, there were more positive trends in the non-school periods.

Regarding the success of the policy of 'One Pupil, One Sport; One School, One Team', the results shown in Tables 14.13–14.15 indicate a lack of significant progress, with the possible exception of sports club membership. According to a senior official in the DPE (Interviewee D, 13 June 2009), 'the two main barriers to the promotion of the policy of "One Pupil, One Sport; One school, One Team" were primarily the limited number of specialized sport teachers, but also the limited sport budget'.

The future of sports policy for young people

As mentioned in an earlier section, six main policy goals were identified by the DPE in the 'Development Project for School Physical Education (2002–7)' all of which were pursued consistently with only slight modifications. In 2007, the DPE integrated the last three policy goals (those concerned with improving fitness scores, participation rates and school team

Table 14.14 The average number of sports teams per school (2005–2008)

Year	Primary school	Secondary school	High school
2005	4.25	5.11	5.66
2006	6.32	6.09	6.57
2007	6.79	6.40	7.26
2008	5.16	5.06	5.62

Source: MoE 2005, 2006, 2007c, 2008c

Table 14.15 The proportion of students participating in school sports clubs (2005–2008)

Year	Primary school	Secondary school	High school
2005	37.1%	22.2%	30.0%
2006	29.7%	17.6%	30.9%
2007	32.0%	21.2%	33.9%
2008	41.7%	27.5%	29.4%

Source: MoE 2005, 2006, 2007c, 2008c

development) into the 'Happy Life Plan (2007–11)' which had four policy goals namely to: i) increase physical activity time; ii) raise the pass rate in the physical fitness test; iii) increase the participation rate in school sports clubs by between 4 per cent and 6 per cent each year; and iv) raise the rate of hosting inter-class games and inter-school games by 20 per cent each year.

In relation to the goal of increasing physical activity time the specific goal set by the DPE is that 'students from all level of schools should do at least 30 minutes per day and a total of 210 minutes per week' (MoE 2007a: 17). However, it should be noted that the primary indicator for this goal is on the accumulation of 210 minutes each week rather than the daily level. The targets adopted for monitoring progress towards the 210 minutes goal is an annual increase of between 10 and 15 per cent from 2008 to 2011 in the proportion of students reaching the 210-minute threshold. For those at primary and secondary schools the target is an increase from 80 per cent achieving the 210 threshold in 2008 to 95 per cent by 2011. Table 14.16 would appear to indicate that the DPE has already made good progress towards its policy goals. However, when the daily target is considered (Table 14.12), it is clear that encouraging the development of a daily routine of physical activity is far more difficult to achieve than the 210-minute weekly threshold.

Table 14.16 The number of students taking regular exercise (a total of 210 minutes per week) (2007–2008)

Time	Year	Primary school	Secondary school	High school
School days	2007	79.3%	69.1%	58.1%
	2008	86.5%	74.1%	68.5%
Summer holidays	2007	46.1%	40.2%	37.1%
	2008	86.3%	75.3%	65.7%
Winter holidays	2007	46.1%	40.2%	37.1%
	2008	76.4%	62.7%	55.4%

Source: MoE 2007b, 2008b

According to a senior consultant of MoE, it would be very difficult to achieve the first policy goal unless the MoE targeted those students who do not like doing physical activity, who are overweight, who have a disability, and those who come from poor communities (Interviewee E, 4 June 2009). In order to increase physical activity time for students from these target groups the MoE initiated, in 2007, the *Happy Life Sport Station Project*. Each primary or secondary school involved in this project is eligible to receive around 0.6 million NT dollars from the Ministry to set up simple indoor sports space and facilities intended to encourage members of target groups to do more physical activity (MoE 2007d). Since 2007 around 209 schools have taken advantage of the initiative and around 93.6 million NT dollars has been invested. As for the results of this initiative, it is too early to make a definitive judgement, although the official website of the MoE claims the initiative has had a positive influence on the participation levels of target groups.

Regarding raising the pass rate for the physical fitness test, in 2008 the MoE suggested using the results of the test as a source of academic credits for students to apply to high schools and universities. The main purpose was to use the test score as a tool to motivate students to take more exercise as well as, hopefully, developing their lifelong exercise habit (MoE 2008d). In addition, the result of the fitness test was also considered to be useful for the development of elite sport. According to a senior official who is in charge of elite sport development, 'the result of the physical fitness test can become one of the indicators for PE teachers or school team coaches to select potential young athletes' (Interviewee B, 18 June 2009).

With regard to encouraging an increase in the participation rate in school sports clubs by between 4 and 6 per cent each year and raising the rate for hosting the inter-class games and inter-school games by 20 per cent each year, the MoE introduced the concept of leagues in which teams composed of students from the same class compete against other class teams from the same school. The winning school team in each age group then represents its school at regional level, then county level and finally at national level finals. The matches are divided into three sections, which are body-shaping exercises for years 3 and 4, fun baseball for years 5 and 6, and relay races for years 7, 8 and 9. In addition matches involving team sports such as volleyball, basketball, baseball, softball and soccer take place within leagues organized from primary school to university level. Like the physical fitness test these matches, from the perspective of the DPE, provide the foundation for the development of elite sport as they improve skills and provide a selection opportunity for elite coaches (Interviewee B, 18 June 2009).

Regarding elite sport development, original policies, including establishing the Sport College System, selecting and producing talented aboriginal students and improving the development of student baseball, continue to be supported by the Ministry of Education. In addition to these established policies, four emergent policies can be identified: i) the introduction of full-time coaches into the education system; ii) the targeting of sports colleges to produce elite athletes; iii) the provision of more opportunities for student-athletes to enter universities; and iv) the attempt to create a scientific training environment for elite student-athletes.

The Ministry of Education started introducing full-time coaches, who have coaching licences but no teaching licences, into the education system after the Legislative Yuan passed a new law in 2008 to allow such appointments. According to the law the main mission for the full-time coaches is to produce potential young athletes (MoE 2008e: 5). According to one LEB director, although the MoE would like to see more full-time coaches recruited into the education system, the LEBs are concerned at the lack of education qualifications held by coaches and by the cost of making those appointments (Interviewee F, 13 June 2009). In order to encourage more LEBs to hire full-time coaches the MoE has offered to cover 50 per cent of the salary of coaches for the first three years. According to a DPE senior official in charge of this project, 'the budget for [the salary contribution] is around 15 million NT dollars this year and 30 million NT dollars in 2010'. He noted that 'there is a quota of 250 full-time coaches for the short term but there will be no limit in the long run' (Interviewee B, 18 June 2009). So far, the Taipei municipal government has agreed to recruit 132 full-time coaches into the education system within three years.

The second emerging policy is to place on sports colleges a greater responsibility for producing elite athletes. According to the former director of the SAC, Chuan-Show Chen (2006), the foundation of the sport selection system is the network of sport colleges from primary to high school level from which talented athletes are selected to be trained in sport universities and university teams. The very best student-athletes should be trained in the National Training Centre (see Figure 14.3).

The third emergent policy is the provision of more opportunities for student-athletes to enter universities. According to a senior official in the DPE, the MoE is asking universities to increase the quota of talented student-athletes that they will accept (Interviewee A, 18 June 2009). An indication of the success of this policy is that one of the strong motivations for student-athletes to enter the sport college system is that their entry to university is considered to be easier than for other applicants. It is often the case that student-athletes are accepted by good universities because of their contribution to the university's sport teams. However, an increasing number of student-athletes feel under pressure to abandon, or at least scale down, their commitment to sport after entering university because of the academic workload and concerns about securing a post-sport career. Although the MoE has allocated 10 million NT dollars for scholarship for 150 elite student-athletes in 2009, according to a senior official in the DPE (Interviewee A, 18 June 2009), the effect could be limited if these student-athletes do not see a sports career as attractive.

The final emerging policy is to attempt to create a scientific training environment for elite student-athletes. According to a senior official in the DPE, most coaches in Taiwan did not realize the extent to which sports science and technology could help them raise the performance of their athletes (Interviewee A, 18 June 2009). In order to help the coaches train elite student-athletes in scientific ways, the MoE is attempting to create regional centres of sports science by

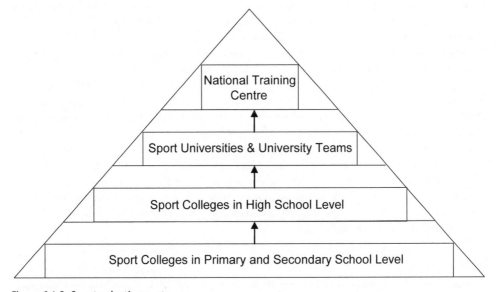

Figure 14.3 Sport selection system

inviting scholars and scientists from universities to become involved. According to a senior official in the DPE (Interviewee A, 18 June 2009), 'This is the initial step for us to set up regional centres of sport science. In the long run, we will follow the lead provided by Japan and Australia to establish a national sport science centre'.

Conclusion

There are three key issues in Taiwanese youth sport: i) the dominant role of elite sport; ii) the apparently unstoppable decline in physical fitness among school students; and iii) the conceptual confusion between physical activity, leisure sport and regular exercise.

Regarding the dominant priority given to elite sport, the goals highlighted in the policy document, 'The Development Project for School Physical Education (2002–7)', the performance appraisal indicators set by the DPE to evaluate LEBs and the distribution by the DPE of the national budget for school sport indicate the priority given to the production of elite student-athletes in order to boost national pride by success on the world stage. As noted by the government 'the results of international sport competition is strongly linked to national confidence and pride' (SAC 2004). A senior official in the DPE acknowledged that the DPE had to accept considerable responsibility for developing elite sport along with the SAC because most elite athletes are produced through the education system (Interviewee A, 18 June 2009).

As for the apparently unstoppable decline in physical fitness among school students, one senior official in the DPE observed that 'the evidence indicates that physical fitness among school students is decreasing globally in modern societies, including Taiwan and China'. He also noted that 'all the government can do [is] attempt to maintain the physical fitness of Taiwanese students at certain level or at least not let it worsen too fast' (Interviewee A, 18 June 2009). Although the Ministry of Education initiated a series of projects to promote physical fitness[1] the evidence in Table 14.10 appears to support the argument of this senior official. However, placing responsibility for the decline in physical fitness on the increasingly sedentary lifestyle of young people might be allowing the government to avoid responsibility rather too easily as it might be argued that part of the explanation rests with the pursuit of international sporting success, which has unbalanced the distribution of government resources leading to the relative neglect of fitness of the general population due to pursuit of medals for the few.

With regard to the confusion between the concepts of physical activity (身體活動), leisure sport (休閒運動) and exercise (運動/健身運動), these three concepts appear to be used interchangeably by the government in the policy documents and in the measurement of *sports* participation. Most government sports policy documents use the terminology of exercise (運動/健身運動) and sports participation (運動參與), while in the most recent statement, 'Happy Life Plan (2007–11)', the concept of accumulated minutes of 'physical activity' (身體活動) is adopted and is used to define 'regular exercise' (規律運動). Furthermore, in the policy, 'One Pupil, One Sport; One School, One Team', it is quite difficult to accept that student participation in sports clubs can be regarded as exercise, physical activity and leisure sport at the same time. Despite this conceptual ambiguity, it is clear that the primary motive of the government is not increased participation as an end in itself but as instrument in improving health, reducing costs to the health service and raising the productivity and national competiveness of Taiwanese athletes in the international arena (MOE 2004).

Note

1 Projects include Physical Fitness 333 Plan (1999–2003), Healthy Body Shape Plan for Elementary/ High School Students (2004–8) and Happy Life Plan (2007–11).

References

Chen, C.-S. (2006). Sport policy in Taiwan. *National Sports Quarterly*, 35 (1), pp. 1–5.

DPE. (2001). *Raising the Swimming Ability for Students (2001–4)*. Taipei: DPE.

——(2002a). *The Development Project for School Physical Education (2002–7)*. Taipei: DPE.

——(2002b). *Improvement Plan for School Sport Fields (2002–5)*. Taipei: DPE.

——(2003a). The introduction and vision of 'Athletic Development Plan for Talented Aboriginal Students'. *Physical Education of School*, 13 (4), pp. 4–11.

——(2003b). *The Project for Improving Student Baseball*. Taipei: DPE.

——(2003c). *The Performance Appraisal Indicator for Practising The Development Project for School Physical Education (2002–7)*. Taipei: DPE.

——(2009a). 'The analysis for athletes granted by the 2008 project of "Athletic Development Plan for Talented Aboriginal Students"'. Retrieved September 8, 2009, from http://epaper.edu.tw/topical.aspx?period_num=363&topical_sn=334&page=0.

——(2009b). The 2009 project of *Athletic Development Plan for Talented Aboriginal Students*. Retrieved September 8, 2009, from http://demo.linkchain.tw/eass/pages/plan.aspx.

——(2009c). *The Performance Appraisal Indicators Set by DPE to Evaluate Local Education Bureaux*. Taipei: DPE.

Executive Yuan. (2001). *Challenge 2008: The Key Project for National Development (2002–7)*. Taipei: Executive Yuan.

Hong, J.W. (2005). *The Management Strategies and Practices for School Physical Education*. Taipei: Shtabook Press.

MoE. (2004). *The White Paper for Cultivating Active Young People*. Taipei: Ministry of Education.

——(2005). *The Annual Statistics of Physical Education (2005)*. Taipei: Ministry of Education.

——(2006). *The Annual Statistics of Physical Education (2006)*. Taipei: Ministry of Education.

——(2007a). *Happy Life Plan (2007–11)*. Taipei: Ministry of Education.

——(2007b). *The Annual Report of Sport Participation (2007)*. Taipei: Ministry of Education.

——(2007c). *The Annual Statistics of Physical Education (2005–8)*. Taipei: Ministry of Education.

——(2007d). *The 'Happy Life Sport Station Project' granted by the Ministry of Education for Primary and Secondary Schools*. Taipei: MoE.

——(2008a). *The Annual Budget of MoE in 2008*. Taipei: MoE.

——(2008b). *The Annual Report of Sport Participation (2008)*. Taipei: Ministry of Education.

——(2008c). *The Annual Statistics of Physical Education (2005–8)*. Taipei: Ministry of Education.

——(2008d). *The Promotion Project to Include the Result of Physical Test as One of Credits to Enter High Schools and Universities*. Taipei: MoE.

——(2008e). *The Regulation for Schools to Recruit Full-Time Coaches*. Retrieved October 15, 2009, from www.edu.tw/files/site_content/EDU01/EDU9725001/2008/9715–2.pdf.

——(2009a). *Physical Fitness Promotion Policy in Taiwan: Retrospect and Prospect*. Taipei: MoE.

——(2009b). *The Annual Budget of MoE in 2009*. Taipei: MoE.

NSPEROC. (2009). *The survey and analysis for physical fitness test among students from primary schools to senior high schools in Taiwan*, offered by the member of staff in National Society of Physical Education of the Republic of China (NSPEROC).

SAC. (2004). *Intermediate Policy Project of the SAC (2005–8)*. Retrieved August 8, 2008, from www.ncpfs.gov.tw/edoc/931029.pdf.

Su, J.Q. (2006). *The key development project for sport colleges in high school level*. Physical Education of School. 16 (1), pp. 13–24.

Tan, T.-C., Cheng, C.-F., Lee, P.-C. and Ko, L.-M. (2009). 'Sport policy in Taiwan, 1949–2008: a brief history of government involvement in sport'. *International Journal of Sport Policy*, **1** (1), pp. 99–111.

Yu, Z.Y. (2008). *The Survey and Report for the Development of Sport Colleges (Tiyuban) (2008)*. Taipei: Physical Education Research & Development Centre.

15

Sports development and young people

The role of international organizations

Roland Naul and Jan Holze

Sports development and young people is presently a topic with many facets. Historically there was a strong link between the evolution of sport in Europe and the targets and goals that European societies were trying to achieve in the education and development of young people. In many cases it was young people who, in their leisure time or in their time at school, gave forms of play and sports their specific character. Scholars of these historical roots find this special relationship between the evolution of sport and the culture of the young in the view of German philanthropists of the late eighteenth century, such as Johann Christoph Gutsmuths, and in the reformed public schools of Thomas Arnold and his followers in the United Kingdom of the nineteenth century. Outside Europe, it should be noted that the beginnings of the sports movement, in America and Asia for example, have to be regarded as closely connected to the evolution of the respective educational systems for young people and the ensuing development of youth sport culture. This connection is seen most prominently when you remember the goals of the young Olympic Movement. In 1894 Pierre de Coubertin was able to reanimate the ancient Olympic Games by inviting the youth of the world – every four years – to engage in fair sporting competition in major cities all over the world. Thus, one of the oldest and most important sports organisations was initiated, the International Olympic Committee (IOC). For over a hundred years, the IOC has stimulated the evolution of sport and youth sport through its various programmes. The current introduction of the Youth Olympic Games by the IOC with the support of the International Federations (IFs) in 2010 underlines this special role (IOC, 2007a).

At the same time groundbreaking changes between the evolution of sport and youth culture are detectable, which creates a gradual separation of the traditional relationship. The evolution of organized sport and its federations is nowadays less a result of new impulses and the input of youth culture but the reaction to other impulses and interests such as technical innovation and economic enterprises. In contrast these impulses and interests in our modern world increasingly clash with the needs and interests of the younger generation, for example where playing is not allowed in streets, squares and neighbourhoods anymore because it has simply become too dangerous. This process does not make it impossible that a new sporting scene can evolve and that kids and youngsters can recapture the lost ground for their activities, as the example of 'parcours' in the high-rise ghetto-like neighbourhoods of big cities shows. It also demonstrates that new youth culture, and especially movement, play and sport, starts outside organized sports and grows rapidly without the involvement of major sports organizations.

In Europe, this pattern of innovation in sport has been obvious over the last 15 years. Informal sports settings, sports activities and fun events incorporated with popular music attract and activate more kids and youths than the regulated competitive and recreational sports within sports organizations (de Knop *et al.* 1996; Naul *et al.* 1998; Telama *et al.* 2002). However, as examples will show later, international sports organizations like the Fédération Internationale de Football Association (FIFA)/Union of European Football Associations (UEFA) and the IOC do countenance new types of sports activities and events, which address social inclusion, and moral demands outside the traditional systems of organized competitive junior sport. Currently, it is possible to identify three prevalent sports settings in which kids and young people experience their physical activity (PA) and sport: curricular and extra-curricular physical and sports education at schools (PESS); physical activities and sport at sport/social clubs outside the education system (PASC); and informal PA settings (IPAS) and sports activities outside schools and sports/ social clubs.

International organizations with activities in the educational and sports sectors play an important role in the first two settings. But there are also international sporting goods companies, social trusts and varied sports organizations, which are especially involved in the third setting with modern lifestyle events and in the frame of social work with 'street work sport culture' (e.g. UEFA and streetfootballworld). National and international sports organizations are today well aware of these transitions and changes in young people's physical activity developments, because recruitment of young people for organized sports – competitive and non-competitive – is more difficult today. Particularly in Western countries, the involvement of young people in organized sports activities occurs increasingly early in childhood. However, young people's commitment to organized sports and participation in organized physical activities is also declining in their later teenage years. The slogan for membership recruitment of young people for sports organizations: 'the earlier – the better' has changed into 'the more attractive and diverse – the longer' to achieve more sustainable membership of young people in sports organizations.

For most international organizations, with activities in the education and sports sector, PESS and PASC are their settings of interest. But there are foundations, like the Dutch Johan Cruyff Foundation, or organizations like 'streetfootballworld', that are only active in the third setting with street work activities and projects of 'social development through sports'.

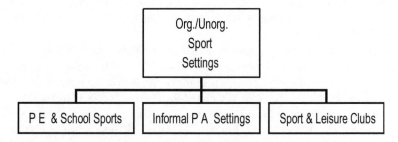

Figure 15.1 The three settings of young people's physical activities

Stakeholders of youth sport development

Central stakeholders in the sports sector

Considered from a genetic and systematic point of view, parents and educators and later teachers and coaches are the central stakeholders for children and young people and their physical and sport-related development. This set of influences is strong before peers increasingly take over this role. In this respect the residential neighbourhood with its places and streets and the schoolyards and sports grounds function as crucial venues for individual sports development. This is before the micro-level, of local sports clubs as part of the organized sport system has the opportunity to mould the sports interests of children and adolescents. Regional and national sports organizations form a movement at quasi-meso-level, which itself is represented world-wide on a macro-level by international federations (IFs) responsible for one sport, such as FIFA for football, the International Association of Athletic Federations (IAAF) for athletics, Federation Internationale de Natation (FINA) for swimming or Fédération Internationale de Gymnastique (FIG) for gymnastics. These IFs influence the international elite sport of young people. They define their own age groups and the rules for participation of young people in competitions. They also organize international tournaments or competitions in their discipline for junior athletes. The programme and regulations of each discipline within the newly created Youth Olympic Games, for example, were defined by these IFs. They are said to be the most influential institutions in relation to the Olympic programme within the IOC. The Olympic summer and winter federations and the recognized federations, in turn, have formed associations: the Association of Summer Olympic International Federations (ASOIF), the Association of International Olympic Winter Sports Federations (AIOWF), the Association of IOC Recognised International Sports Federations (ARISF) and the SportAccord, which also includes other sports federations.

A second group of strong stakeholders for youth sport development are varied commissions and branches of the national umbrella organizations. All national sport federations are associated in these umbrella organizations, along within their youth sport departments. The German Sport Youth (dsj) as the youth organization of the German Olympic Sport Confederation (DOSB) for example represents all sections dealing with youth sport issues in the German Special Federations and the regional Land Sport Federations.

Many countries, especially in Europe, have one main umbrella organization. However, increasingly countries have merged their National Sport Confederations with the National Olympic Committees (NOC). This is the case in the Netherlands (NOC*NSF), in France (CNOSF) or in Germany (DOSB). These national umbrella organizations have again multiple and diverse membership in international sports organizations. One example, the DOSB, is a member of the European Olympic Committee (EOC) like several other national umbrella organizations and at the same time is a member of sport-for-all-oriented associations like the European Non-Governmental Sport Organisation (ENGSO) or The Association For International Sport for All (TAFISA).

In other countries like the UK, Sweden or the Czech Republic a national Olympic committee exists in parallel with the national sport confederation. These federations are members of the international federation of their discipline, for example the British Olympic Association (BOA) is a member of the EOC, but the Central Council for Physical Recreation (CCPR), being the national alliance of governing and representative bodies of sport and recreation, is a member of ENGSO. A central stakeholder of the European-wide youth sport sector is ENGSO Youth, with its 41 national member organizations. ENGSO Youth is the youth organization of

ENGSO and represents the interests of young people under the age of 35 within ENGSO. The Youth Committee, as the governing body in which each member has to be under 35 years of age, is responsible for the development of ENGSO policy in the field of children and youth. This includes finding and administering the financial resources for this objective. It also organizes European youth sports conferences and seminars and develops relationships with other European youth and children's organizations.

Central stakeholders in the education sector

As stakeholders in the educational sector, mention should also be made of parents, teachers, coaches, friends and peers in children's and adolescents' settings. In many cases the local schools are the institutions where young pupils face physical activity and sport for the first time. On a regional and national level it is the responsibility of the ministries for education or family and youth or the ministry for sport and health to set the benchmarks for the development of children and adolescents in schools with national curricula and/or basic regulations for regional and local curricula. On all geographical levels (national, continental or global) special networks for physical education (PE) or associations of physical educators are promoting such programmes for youth sport at schools through diverse activities.

There are three organizations, in this field, that are active in Europe: (1) the European Physical Education Association (EUPEA), a network of national PE teacher associations; (2) the European Network of Sport Science, Education and Employment (ENSSEE), which is primarily an alliance of the higher learning institutes that train physical educators and other professionals; and (3) the European Health and Fitness Association (EHFA), as an association for educators and institutes that deal with health sport outside schools (Petry *et al.* 2008). Furthermore, several global PE societies exist and have an active European branch. Association Internationale des Ecoles Supérieures d'Education Physique (AIESEP); Fédération Internationale d'Education Physique (FIEP), International Society for Comparative Physical Education and Sport (ISCPES); International Association of Physical Education and Sport for Girls and Women (IAPESGW); and International Federation of Adapted Physical Activity (IFAPA) are some of these global players in the education sector for PE in schools and youth sport. They all promote the aims of physical activity and youth sport with their organization's specific focus. Together these international associations, except the IFAPA, founded the International Committee of Sport Pedagogy (ICSP) in 1984. In 1992 the IFAPA joined the ICSP.

In the last 15 years the ICSP has implemented many activities and research projects aimed at supporting a sustainable development of PE and youth sport worldwide.

Another stakeholder to be mentioned within the international organizations in the educational sector is UNESCO. As early as 1978, UNESCO in its International Charter on Physical Education and Sport committed to the regular practice of PE and sport as a right of a child. After the designation of Adolf Ogi as Special Adviser to the UN Secretary-General (at that time, Kofi Annan) on Sport for Development and Peace, UNESCO's mother organization, the UN, supported the sustainable youth sport development in the framework of the Millennium Goals for Development and Peace (2003) and the UN International Year of Sport and Physical Education 2005 (IYSPE). Of note is the emphasis given to social values of sport like fair play, respect and tolerance, which are of interest to the UN as these qualities are elements of their Millennium Development Goals and are also considered to be essential attributes of youth sport and PE projects developed for the UN year of sustainable development.

The list of international organizations who care about the promotion of physical activities and sport for young people would be incomplete if we did not mention those organizations that are neither sports organizations nor organizations that can be classified in the educational sector. They are concerned with health issues, but it is only since the turn of the century that they have taken an increased interest in fostering physical health activities and the promotion of an active lifestyle for children and adolescents. These developments are due to the new pervasive public diseases of children and adolescents, namely overweight and obesity (HBSC-Study of WHO 2004). The World Health Organization (WHO) and especially WHO Europe adhere to a health promotion policy and a strategy of health education with physical activity, play and sport to fight against the rapid and vast increase in obesity among the young. The WHO European Health Ministers Conference set a milestone by approving the *European Charter on counteracting obesity* in Istanbul in 2006 (WHO Europe 2006a). The Charter was followed by another European framework to promote physical activities for health and sports for young people (WHO Europe 2006b; 2007).

Global players in sports development for young people

There are a number of organizations that have engaged for several years in the promotion of sustainable development of sport for young people and that can be considered as global players with distinctive measures and activities in the field. The primary function of these organizations is as policy makers and they can be divided into three groups: education, sport and health, according to their programmes and activities.

Case studies in education: UNESCO and ICSSPE

UNESCO as a promoter of PE

From its foundation after World War II and up to now, UNESCO has been an active stakeholder in the promotion of physical activities and sports for young people (Bailey 1996; Borms 2008). UNESCO in some respects can be seen as the most important supporter of PE and youth sport development. It was on the initiative of UNESCO that WHO was established in 1948, which became an early stakeholder in the promotion of physical activity for health benefits. UNESCO was also an essential driving force for the foundation of the International Council of Sport and Physical Education and Sport (ICSPE) in 1958, which was later, in 1984, named the International Council of Sport Science, Physical Education and Sport (ICSSPE), and has developed as the leading body for the promotion of PE and youth sport worldwide.

To this day, there exists some relations between these two major stakeholders in the educational sector of sports development for young people. Influenced by ICSPE activities in the 1970s (Bailey 1996: 159–63), the first UNESCO meeting of Ministers responsible for the development and implementation of PE and sport in their countries was organized at the UNESCO headquarters in Paris in 1976 (MINEPS I). Only two years later UNESCO published its Charter of Physical Education. The Charter identified a comprehensive list for the development of PE at school. Paragraph two was especially important because it evaluated PE as a compulsory part of general education. However, little progress was reported about the UNESCO recommendations and declarations up to MINEPS III (1999), following the First World Summit on Physical Education, organized by the ICSSPE (cf. Telama 2002).

ICSSPE as an ambassador for PE and youth sport development

UNESCO was the driving force for the ICSPE's promotion of PE up to the 1980s and, when closer collaboration between UNESCO and the ICSSPE was agreed after MINEPS II in 1988, the ICSSPE became the driving force for UNESCO activities regarding PE especially after the First World Summit of PE in late 1999 (Doll-Tepper and Scoretz 2001). Since the mid 1990s there has been a strong global engagement by the ICSSPE to advocate PE in collaboration with UNESCO, WHO and IOC and to initiate ICSSPE-related research projects on PE and health-enhanced physical activity for young people.

Three PE and youth sport-based research projects, financially supported by IOC grants, were conducted by the ICSP on behalf of the ICSSPE. The first research project, Physical Fitness, Sportive Lifestyle and Olympic Ideals of Youth in Europe (cf. Naul *et al.* 1997; Telama *et al.* 2002), focused on six European countries (Belgium, Estonia, Czech Republic, Finland, Germany, Hungary) to investigate aspects of the physical activity of about 7,000 young people (including frequency, intensity, time and type of sports). The study of boys and girls aged 12–15 years collected data related to their basic motor competences, motives, attitudes and their assessment of Olympic ideals such as fair play, solidarity, mutual respect, etc. The major findings of the study were that: more than half of the young people, girls in particular, needed more daily physical activity; physical inactivity started too early in adolescence, but was not a problem exclusive to girls; media consumption dominated physical activity; and physical education needed to be improved for health benefits and moral development.

A second well-received study was conducted on behalf of the ICSP by Hardman and Marshall (2000, 2001), the *World-wide Survey of the State and Status of School Physical Education*, which was supported by PE experts around the world who provided information in a self-report questionnaire. Data analysis proved that regular teaching of PE at school does not exist in many countries in Africa, Asia and Central America. Although for 92 per cent of the countries PE is required as a school curriculum subject, in 29 per cent of countries implementation of statutory policies was inadequate. The officially reported time allocation for teaching PE on the school curricula is reduced in reality by a variety of circumstances in almost every country (for example due to the shortage of qualified teachers or the lack of facilities and equipment). The authors of the survey concluded, 'In spite of official documentation on principles, policies, and aims, actual implementation into practice exposes the realities of situations, which are often far removed from national political ideologies. The findings from the present audit serve to underline such discrepancies' (Hardman and Marshall 2001: 32). Both authors updated the survey (Hardman 2004, 2005; Marshall 2005) but reported only slight progress, 'It is clear that in too many schools in too many countries there is a record of failure in physical education' (Hardman 2004: 11). Only recently, Hardman and Marshall (2009) published fresh data from their second worldwide survey. In general, few real improvements were reported. These were local activities that support networking of schools with other stakeholders to improve daily physical activities, mainly in Western Europe, 'The findings presented in this report tend to draw attention to negative rather than positive features of school physical education and sport' (Hardman and Marshall 2009: 109) and 'Generally, the "reality check" reveals several areas of continuing concern' (Hardman and Marshall 2009: 127) compared to findings of about 10 years ago.

In conjunction with the first worldwide survey, the ICSSPE organized the First World Summit on PE in Berlin in 1999 (Doll-Tepper and Scoretz 2001). A range of statements documented the different benefits of PE and physical activity for young people, supported both by research findings and best practice experiences associated with physical development and individual well-being and also with social inclusion and self-esteem. At the Berlin World Summit the delegates and representatives of governmental and non-governmental institutions adopted the *Berlin Agenda for Action Plan* addressed to governmental authorities worldwide to reinforce the importance of PE and physical activities for young people at school. The most essential paragraphs for required action were: to 'implement policies for Physical Education as a human right for all children'; to 'recognize that quality Physical Education depends on well-qualified educators and scheduled time with the curriculum … '; and to 'recognize that failure to provide Physical Education costs more in health care than the investment needed for Physical Education' (Doll-Tepper and Scoretz 2001: 115). However, future improvements, although anticipated at the UNESCO MINEPS III meeting just after the Berlin Summit at Punta del Este, Uruguay, in December 2000, remained bigger on paper than realized in practice as Hardman and Marshall identified in their 2009 survey.

In principle, it was therefore not really surprising that, at the Second Summit of PE, organized by the ICSSPE in conjunction with the Swiss Federal Office of Sport in December 2005, little progress was recorded in relation to the Berlin Agenda. Nevertheless, new dimensions for PE development were addressed: quality standards for PE and new effective modular strategies to secure and promote PE in the future. However, one highlight of the Second World Summit related to a third research study of the ICSP, which was set up in 2003. The ICSP commissioned Richard Bailey, supported by a group of advisors, to review evidenced-based research findings on the outcome of teaching PE. The study suggested outcomes in five domains of development: physical, lifestyle, affective, social, and cognitive. The results of this review of international research studies entitled 'Sport in Education' (SpinEd) (Bailey 2004, 2005) can be summarized as follows: 'In each of the domains discussed … there is evidence that sport can have a positive and profound effect. … The scientific evidence does not support the claim that these effects will occur automatically' (Bailey 2005: 26). It depends on to what extent parents, teachers and coaches are engaged and are supportive to the potential of PE and school sports.

On behalf of the ICSSPE a third World Summit was scheduled for May 2010 in Iowa, USA. Compared to the two former summits, two essential items were added: instead of the former critical analysis and recording of the never-ending gap between promise and reality of PE in schools, new efforts, concepts and strategies of conduct, for example community-based multi-actor networks of different stakeholders in PE and PA, were targeted in order to combine curricular PE with other organized and unorganized PA in the community at large so as to extend young people's active lifestyle.

Case studies in sport: FIFA, UEFA and the IOC

Fair Play concepts and campaigns of FIFA and UEFA

In many ways organized football is taking up the idea of fair play. FIFA, as the worldwide affiliation of 204 national football associations, is responsible for a very broad spectrum of Fair Play projects and measures whose activities concentrate on three concepts: (1) promoting fair behaviour by players and spectators on the pitch and inside the stadium; (2) promoting the notion of fair play in numerous respects, off the pitch and outside the stadium; and (3) fair play as a tool for demanding human rights.

FIFA is conducting a whole series of campaigns to promote fair behaviour at football matches. These activities date from 1977 and include the FIFA Fair Play Prize, the FIFA Fair Play Award and the FIFA Fair Play Days. The Fair Play Prize is awarded annually during FIFA contests to the team that receives the most points according to the criteria of the Technical Study Group, for its behaviour on the field and its supporters' behaviour on the terraces.

The FIFA Fair Play Award was established ten years later, in 1987, allegedly triggered by what was seen as the fair behaviour of the English national team coach at the 1986 FIFA world championship in Mexico, when 'the hand of God' helped Diego Maradona to a goal. Since then, the distinction has been awarded each year to an individual, a national association, a player or a community 'who has greatly contributed to the promotion of fair play in football' (FIFA 2006a). FIFA Fair Play Days were introduced a further ten years later, in 1997, and are held every year by national and regional football associations and their leagues all over the world, with events and tournaments for children and youngsters.

Since 2004 this Fair Play Day has been celebrated on 21 September every year to link this event to 'another special celebration: the United Nations International Day of Peace' (FIFA 2006b). Here we can already see one recent example of the sporting concept of fair play being linked with the concept of fair play as a 'tool of human rights'.

The first Fair Play Logo was introduced in 1993. Ten years later, in 2003, the logo was changed and given the additional slogan 'My Game is Fair Play'. One of the reasons given for this change was the 'pressing social causes of modern times' (FIFA 2003). We can take this explanation to include not only the social causes associated with modern media's depiction of professional football, but also the context of the socio-political environment and the partnership with political bodies like the UN. FIFA's view is that the new logo and its slogan will help to 'add impact to the values of sporting spirit on and off the pitch, and to highlight football's links with a society in which justice, fairness, and solidarity are integral features' (FIFA 2003). Football sport thus becomes an element of socio-political action, and the idea of fairness becomes a supplementary element of human rights.

At FIFA level we can thus observe a number of fair play concepts that are being implemented and pursued with specific campaigns. This breath of action is also present in the football associations at European level supported by UEFA. As FIFA's continental European association, UEFA and its 53 national associations also support the various fair play campaigns, whereby UEFA concentrates on two projects that are intended to sustainably promote the idea of fair play as a tool for human rights, peace and development. These two campaigns are the Open Fun Football School project and the FARE project: Football Against Racism in Europe (FARE 2009).

The Open Fun Football School project was initiated in 1998 by the Dane Anders Levinson and has since received ethical and financial support from the EU Commission, provincial governments in Denmark, Norway, Sweden and Finland, and UEFA itself (CCPA 2004, accessed Oct 27 2009). The project began in the Balkans, in Bosnia-Herzegovina, with 12 football schools and around 2,250 boys and girls. By 2005 there were 'open schools' in all the new Balkan states, a total of 81 schools catering for around 17,000 children and young people with the support of social workers and football coaches. As a charity programme, it invites children and young people to join in its activities 'regardless of talent, skills, ethnic or social background' (Naul 2007: 42). In 2005 UEFA awarded the project team its prize for the best European Grassroots Project. Similar schools have since been started in other regions (Trans-Caucasus and Jordan, Lebanon and Syria), so that in 2005 the organization's report was able to name a total of 137 schools that cooperated with their countries' national football associations to help a total of 28,000 children and young people. The project's three principal objectives were stated as 'the triple balance' between 'green: development of a grassroots football platform … blue: financially self-sustainable democratic organisation [and] red: openness towards all ethnic, social and political groups [and] equality of sexes' (Naul 2007: 42). Peacemaking and anti-racism through football activities in these war-torn regions are clearly at the forefront of the adopted measures.

The FARE (Football Against Racism in Europe) project maintains its own network of offices in a number of Central European states. The objective of the project is to bring together informally migrants and other ethnic groups in a country by playing football together in Street Kicks, which take place on mobile courts in the inner cities. Similar events were held in

Germany during the 2006 FIFA world championship at every match location. The FARE network receives financial support from the EU Commission under its anti-discrimination programme (Fare 2006).

All these various campaigns are bound by the ten rules of the FIFA Fair Play Code. In its function and its mission this code can be compared with the well-known Fundamental Principles of the IOC Charter, which also stressed fair play as an Olympic Ideal for education.

The IOC as the ambassador of Olympic education

When Pierre de Coubertin resigned as the President of the IOC at the Prague Olympic Congress in 1925 it was bitter for him not to have achieved his key goal of reviving the ancient 'gymnasion' as a modern type of school and a 'permanent factory' for his sports education (Coubertin 2000: 217) and for the promotion of the Olympic ideals. Although the decades up to World War II in Europe did see the development of the kind of sports education envisaged by de Coubertin, the idea of a permanent Olympic Academy did emerge in Greece and Germany.

One of the first steps taken by the IOC, which has to date been a very effective promoter of Olympic education, was the founding and opening of the International Olympic Academy (IOA) in Olympia in 1961. Since then, the Academy has organized worldwide a variety of further education and training seminars for various target groups (such as sports administrators, teachers, coaches and students), both annually and at other regular intervals, on behalf of the IOC. The activities of the IOA during the last 20 years have also aroused considerable interest in the topic of Olympic education (Georgiadis 1995).

A second step in the IOC's promotion of Olympic education was taken with its official promotion of Olympic Youth Camps to coincide with the Olympic Games. This idea was initiated as long ago as the 1912 Stockholm Games, when King Gustav of Sweden permitted over 1,500 boy scouts to pitch their tents near to the Olympic stadium. But it was not until the 1964 Olympic Games in Tokyo that such Youth Camps became a regular occurrence, with the exception of the boycotted games held in Los Angeles in 1984.

A third element in the promotion of Olympic education, which has been particularly long-lasting, was signalled by the resolution enacted by the IOC in 1983 that each national Olympic committee, acting effectively as a decentralized extension of the IOA, should found a National Olympic Academy in order to promote the Olympic idea and encourage and disseminate Olympic educational ideals by means of its own activities in its own country. To date there are approximately 140 such Academies all over the world. One of the principal tasks of these National Olympic Academies is to employ a variety of measures to encourage Olympic education for young people in these countries' schools and sports clubs and to organize appropriate seminars and training courses for teachers and youth coaches.

A significant fourth step in the promotion of Olympic education was taken by the IOC at the 1994 Paris Olympic Centennial Congress, when it expressly demanded the long-term promotion of Olympic ideals as part of the future development of the Olympic Games. From 1994 the manuals published by the IOC to assist cities applying to host the Olympic Games in compiling their bid books have particularly stressed the role of education in any planned cultural programmes. Since the 2002 Winter Olympic Games, each applicant city is not only required to offer an educational programme during the actual Games, but also beforehand, during the seven years between the IOC's deciding vote and the opening ceremony of the Olympic Games.

The decision taken by the IOC on 5 July 2007 at its 119th Session in Guatemala City to initiate a separate Olympic competition for outstanding young sportsmen and women in the

14–18 age groups can be described as a fifth step. The first of these Youth Olympic Games (YOG) will be held in 2010 as a Summer Olympic Games at Singapore and in 2012 as a Winter Olympic Games at Innsbruck, Austria (IOC 2007a).

According to its purposes, the YOG represents an educational and cultural sponsoring programme for the Olympic education of young competitive sportsmen and women. As the initial step in the promotion of Olympic education, it specifically addresses young people who engage in competitive sports, while the second step comes with a bundle of measures for the promotion of Olympic education that aims to address all young people and to further healthy and active lifestyles and ethico-moral behaviours that conform to the Olympic ideals (cf. IOC 2007b).

The EU/CoE, WHO and ENGSO as promoters of PE and sport

The EU/CoE and WHO as promoters of health-enhanced PE and PA

The Council of Europe (CoE) with its Committee for the Development of Sport (Comité pour le développement du sport – CDDS) became a very early supporter of physical fitness and youth sport development in Europe. One early highlight was the development of the EUROFIT test manual as a tool for European-wide measurement of physical fitness for young people, which influenced a variety of related research studies across Europe (CDDS 1988; Pohl 1995).

A second project, jointly developed by the CDDS/EU, was the promotion among EU member states of the *World-wide Survey on Physical Education* (Hardman 2002) and its updated version on behalf of the European Parliament (DG International Policies) in 2007 (cf. Hardman 2007). Both surveys informed the deliberations of the CoE (2003, 2007) which emphasized the necessity of political action in EU member states to redefine the purpose of PE in the school curriculum and to reaffirm the Berlin Agenda of Action. This European Parliament resolution on the 'Role of Sport in Education' in 2007 seems to have been a turning point for the promotion of PE and youth sport development. There has been a clear shift in the debate and recommendations relating to PE and sport for young people, which must be seen in the context of the outcomes of the *European Year of Education through Sport* (2004), the related research studies of the Sport Unit of the Education and Culture DG (Brettschneider and Naul 2004; Janssens *et al.* 2004; Klein 2008) and the impact of the EU White Paper on Sport (2007). The White Paper addressed the Pierre de Coubertin Plan which strongly emphasizes the health benefits and social values of sports.

The 2007 Resolution of the European Parliament states in the first paragraph that 'physical education is the only school subject which seeks to prepare children for a healthy lifestyle and focuses on their overall physical and mental development, as well as imparting important social values such as fairness, self-discipline, solidarity, team spirit, tolerance and fair play' (Paragraph A). Informed by the Pierre de Coubertin Plan and subsequent to the publication of the White Paper, the *EU Physical Activity Guidelines* were released in 2008 which recommended that policy making should be a multi-actor endeavour between school physical education, PA and youth sports, and public health care in local community networks of education, health and sport.

With the White Paper and the *EU Physical Activity Guidelines* the EU Commission took the initiative to address sport-related issues for young people in a comprehensive manner. Although this is not a binding document, the Commission, supported by the White Paper on Sport, provides for the first time a comprehensive vision of its future engagement in the field of sport. In the corresponding Pierre de Coubertin Plan, the Commission sets out a number of sport-related measures involving young people with regard to volunteering, active citizenship, social inclusion and prevention of violence in sport.

European institutions have recognized the specificity of the role sport plays in European society, based on volunteer-driven structures, in terms of health, education, social integration and culture, and that is why sport was mentioned in the Nice Declaration and the Lisbon Treaty. In Article 165 of the Lisbon Treaty sport is introduced as a new area of EU competence. It states: 'The Union shall contribute to the promotion of sporting issues, while taking into account the specific nature of sport, its structure based on voluntary activity and its social and educational function'. Following the treaty's ratification the EU now has a 'soft' competence for sport and the legal basis for a budget for sport. Already in 2009 a first EU Sport Programme named *Preparatory Actions in the Field of Sport* was agreed to support activities that bring an added value to sport for young people at EU level.

However, it is not only the EU that has given more attention to the important role of PE, PA and sport for young people at the beginning of the new millennium. With the rising epidemic of obesity across the world and particularly in Europe (IOTF 2002; WHO 2004), the leading body of public health care, WHO and its European branch (WHO/Europe), identified the importance of PA for young people to counteract overweight and obesity. Following further collaboration and partnership between the EU/European Commission (EC) and WHO the promotion of active lifestyle for young people increased after the EC established its *EU Platform on Diet, Physical Activity and Health* in 2005.

ENGSO: youth sport and social work

In 1998, following the decline of the European Sports Youth Conference, the ENGSO (European Non-Governmental Sport Organisation) General Assembly took the initiative and approved the *ENGSO Guidelines for Children and Youth Sport* that paved the way to establish a working group on Youth in European Sport. Parallel to that initiative eight national sport organizations formed the network *Sport Youth goes Europe*. With the support of the EU and the CoE this network organized conferences and exchanges of best practice. The aim was not to improve national elite sport performance, but to support each country in promoting and developing the social values of sport. One example of social work through sports is the ARCTOS project (Anti-Racism Tools in Sport) which is a non-verbal tool to learn via exemplary situations how to overcome bullying and discrimination in sports clubs (cf. ENGSO Youth 2007). This process culminated in the formation of an ENGSO youth organization, which was formally embraced by ENGSO at the first ENGSO Youth General Assembly in Stockholm in 2003.

Previously in 2002 ENGSO had changed its statutes to involve ENGSO Youth as the official body to deal with children and youth issues at European level. The ENGSO Youth Committee and Youth Assembly are unique in that its members may not continue in active membership after the age of 35 years. The ENGSO Youth Assembly elects its members to the ENGSO Youth Committee every two years.

ENGSO Youth acts as the advocate for children and young people to fight for their right to be physically active. Therefore it has its own projects, budget, statutes and office. Through its work ENGSO Youth was accepted as a member of the European Youth Forum and also became part of the co-management system of the youth sector of the CoE, the Advisory Council on Youth.

Conclusions

A variety of international organizations are engaged in sports development for young people. Important stakeholders are represented in the educational sector as well as in the health and sports sectors. There are some convergent developments between these three main sectors: international sports organizations like FIFA and the IOC not only support organized high-level competitive junior sports (FIFA with world junior football championships; the IOC with new Youth Olympic Games). Both these organizations have also become strong supporters of recreational sports for health benefits, social inclusion and child care projects through sport. The notion of fair play as an Olympic ideal has become a common item of youth sport activities in all three main settings of physical activity for young people. On the other side important stakeholders of the educational sector, like UNESCO and ICSSPE, no longer only promote recreational sports and physical education for a balanced education in harmony of body, will and mind, but are equally involved in the promotion of organized competitive youth sport activities for social purposes in cooperation with international sports organizations. UNESCO and the ICSSPE like some other partners of the two umbrella organizations in the field of education have become strong advocates to justify and to recommend regular school-based PE and extracurricular PA for health, well-being and different psycho-social developments. Closer ties now exist than was the case in previous times for PE, PA and youth sport between traditional stakeholders of the health sector (WHO, WHO/Europe) and the EU/CoE and of course UN/UNESCO/ICSSPE.

Their common efforts to counteract non-communicative diseases of children and youth, like obesity and – as the example of ENGSO shows – to further restore social and gender balances of such young people through PE, PA and sports worldwide are positive and welcome. 'Active Living' with its comprehensive physical, social and moral domains seems to be the unique tie, that may cause closer networking in the future between these three main sectors of international organizations and between the different stakeholders of sports development for young people.

References

Bailey, St. (1996). *Science in the service of physical education and sport*. Chichester: Wiley.
Bailey, R. (2004). *SpinEd. The role of physical education and sport in education. Project Report*. Athens, Greece, December 6–8, 2004 (MINEPS IV).
——(2005). *SpinEd. The role of physical education and sport in education. Final report*. Canterbury: Christ Church College.
Borms, J. (2008). A journey through time – the changing face of ICSSPE. In: Jan Borms (ed.) *Directory of sport science (5th edition)* (pp. 19–73). Berlin: ICSSPE.
Brettschneider, W.D. & Naul, R. (2004). Study on young people's lifestyles and sedentariness and the role of sport in the context of education and as a means of restoring the balance – final report. Accessed on 3 February 2005 from http://europa.eu.int/comm./sport/documents/lotpaderborn.pdf.
CCPA (2004). Open Fun Football Schools. Accessed on 27 October 2009 from www.ccpa.dk/1–41-home.html.
CDDS (1988) *Handbook for the EUROFIT Test of physical fitness*, Rome: Coni.
Coubertin, P. de (2000). *Pierre de Coubertin, 1863–1937. Olympism. Selected Writings*. Lausanne: IOC.
Doll-Tepper, G. and Scoretz, D. (2001) (eds.) *Proceedings. World summit on physical education*. Schorndorf: Hofmann.
Edwards, P. & Tsouros, A. (2006). *Promoting physical activity and active living in urban environments*. Copenhagen: WHO Europe.
ENGSO Youth (2007). *ARCTOS stand up against discrimination in sports!* Frankfurt: ENGSO Youth.
—— (1998). *ENGSO Guidelines for Children and Youth Sport*, Frankfurt: ENGSO.
EU (2007). *White paper on sport*. Brussels: DG EAC.
——(2008). *EU physical activity guidelines*. Brussels: DG EAC.
EUROFIT (1988). *European test of physical fitness*. Rome: CDDS.
European Parliament (2007). Resolution on the role of sport in education. In: K. Hardman & J. Marshall (eds) *Second world-wide survey of school physical education* (pp. 159–66). Berlin: ICSSPE.

FARE: Football against Racism. Accessed on 27 October 2009 from www.farenet.org/default.asp?intPageID=2.

Feingold, R., Crum, B., O'Sullivan, M. & Naul, R. (2002). Sport pedagogy. In: ICSSPE (ed.) *Directory of sport science*. Berlin: ICSSPE.

FIFA (2003). FIFA Fair Play campaign – new slogan, same commitment. Accessed on 20 June 2007 from http://access.fifa.com/de/article/0,0000,70034,00.html.

——(2006a). Fair Play Awards. Accessed on 20 June 2007 from www.fifa.com/aboutfifa/worldwideprograms/footballforhope/fairplay/awards.html.

——(2006b). Fair Play Days. Accessed on 20 June 2007 from www.fifa.com/aboutfifa/worldwideprograms/footballforhope/fairplay/days.html.

Georgiadis, K. (1995). International Olympic Academy: the history of its establishment, aims and activities. In IOA (ed.) *2nd joint international session for directors of national Olympic academies, members and staff of national Olympic committees and international sport federations* (pp. 15–21). Athens: IOA.

Hardman, K. (2002). *Report on school physical education in Europe*. Strasbourg: CDDS.

Hardman, K. (2004). *An up-date on the status of physical education in schools wordwide: Technical report for the World Health Organisation*. www.icsspe.org/document/PEwordlwide.pdf.

Hardman, K. (2007). *Current situation and prospects for physical education in the European Union*. Brussels: DG International Policies.

Hardman, K. & Marshall, J. (2000). *World-wide survey of the state and status of school physical education*. Manchester: University.

Hardman, K. & Marshall, J. (2001). World-wide survey on the state and status of physical education in schools. In: G. Doll-Tepper & D. Scoretz (eds) *Proceedings. World summit on physical education* (pp. 15–37). Schorndorf: Hofmann.

Hardman, K. & Marshall, J. (2009). *Second world-wide survey of school physical education. Final Report*. Berlin: ICSSPE.

Hums, M.A., Wolff, E.A. & Mahoney, M.O. (2008). Sport and human rights. In J. Borms (ed.) *Directory of sport science. 5th edition* (pp. 469–77). Berlin: ICSSPE.

International Olympic Committee (2007a). *Youth Olympic Games*. Lausanne: IOC. http://video.olympic.org/http/yog_uk.pdf.

International Olympic Committee (2007b). *Teaching values. An Olympic education toolkit*. Lausanne: IOC.

Janssens, J., Stegeman, H., van Hilvoorde, L. *et al.* (2004). *Education through sport: an overview of good practice in Europe*. Nieuwegein: Arko Sports Media.

Klein, G. (2008). Education through sport in the European Union: from diversity to definition of models. In G. Klein & K. Hardman (eds) *Physical education and sport education in the European Union* (pp. 15–41). Paris: Editions Revue EP.S.

Knop, P. de, Engström, L.-M., Skirstad, B. & Weiss, M.R. (eds) (1996). *World-wide trends in youth sport*. Champaign, Il: Human Kinetics.

Marshall, J. (2005). A post-Berlin Summit update on school physical education. A European Union perspective. In *ICSSPE Bulletin No. 44*.

Naul, R. (2007). Fair Play in football: international concepts of projects and campaigns. In: M. Lämmer and A. Grassi (eds) *Report of the 12th European Fair Play Congress. Fair play in practice: concepts, projects and campaigns* (pp. 37–49). Cologne/Udine: EPFM.

Naul, R., Hardman, K., Pieron, M. & Skirstad, B. (eds) (1998). *Physical activity and active lifestyle of children and youth*. Schorndorf: Hofmann (Sport Science Studies vol. 10).

Naul, R., Pieron, M., Telama, R., Almond, L. & Rychtecky, A. (1997). *Sporting lifestyle, motor performance, and Olympic ideals of youth in Europe*. Essen: ICSP.

Petry, K., Froberg, K. & Madella, A. (eds) (2006). *Thematic network project AEHESIS. Report of the third year*. Cologne: German Sport University.

Petry, K., Froberg, K., Madella, A. and Tokarski, W. (eds) (2008). *Higher education in sport in Europe*. Maidenhead: Meyer Sport Ltd.

Pohl, A. (1995). Problems of comparing European fitness studies of school children. In: B. Svoboda and A. Rychtecky (eds) *Physical activity for life: east and west, south and north* (pp. 238–45). Aachen: Meyer & Meyer.

Schott, N. & Merkel, K. (2009). Chancen und Wege der Entwicklungszusammenarbeit. In D. Kuhlmann & E. Balz (eds) *Sportentwicklung. Grundlagen und Facetten* (pp. 119–40). Aachen: Meyer & Meyer.

Telama, R. (2002). ICSSPE and Initiatives for Physical Education. *ICSSPE Bulletin* No.34 (pp. 10–12).

Telama, R., Naul, R., Heipponen, H., Rychtecky, A. & Vuolle, P. (2002). *Physical fitness, sporting lifestyle and Olympic ideals of youth in Europe*. Schorndorf: Hofmann (Sport Science Studies vol.11).

UNESCO (1978). *Charter for physical education and sport.* Paris: UNESCO.

United Nations (2003). *Sport for development and peace: towards achieving the millennium development goals.* Geneva: UN, p. 2.

United Nations (2005). *Concept: education, health, development, peace. International year of sport and physical education.* Geneva: UN.

WHO (2004). *Young people's health in context. Health behaviour in school-aged children (HBSC).* Copenhagen: WHO.

WHO Europe (2006a). *European Charter on counteracting obesity.* Copenhagen: WHO.

WHO Europe (2006b). *Physical activity and health in Europe. Evidence for action.* Copenhagen: WHO.

WHO Europe (2007). *The challenge of obesity in the WHO European Region and the strategies for response. Summary.* Copenhagen: WHO Europe.

Wojciechowski, Th. (2009). Sportentwicklung im internationalen Vergleich. In: D. Kuhlmann & E. Balz (Hrsg.) *Sportentwicklung. Grundlagen und Facetten* (pp. 225–38). Aachen: Meyer & Meyer.

Part 4

Sports development and adult mass participation

Introduction: The neglect of adult participation

Barrie Houlihan

As has been observed by a number of writers the concept of 'policy' is often elusive. A 'classical' definition of public policy is offered by Dye (1975: 1) who defines public policy as 'whatever governments choose to do or not to do'. In similar fashion Howlett and Ramesh (2003: 3) who suggest that it is 'at its most simple, a choice made by government to undertake some course of action'. Hogwood and Gunn (1984; see also Hogwood 1987) identified a range of different uses of the term policy including the suggestion that it might refer to aspirations, a set of specific proposals, a decision by government, a programme of activity or the impact of action. Developing Hogwood and Gunn's discussion it is possible to identify three aspects of policy that are particularly useful in understanding sports policy in relation to adult participation, namely policy as aspiration, policy as commitment of resources and policy as a set of actions (programmes and initiatives).

Using elite sport development as an exemplar, it is the case that in many countries it would be relatively easy to track the policy process across these three aspects. Many countries have made public statements of their aspiration to achieve a certain position in the summer Olympics medal table or to win a certain percentage share of the total medals available. Most of the countries have supported their aspirations with a commitment of public resources, often in the form of capital projects (for example, elite training facilities) and revenue funding to pay for coaches or to enable elite athletes to train full time. A significant number have also introduced specific programmes/initiatives to utilise public investment (such as talent identification initiatives or funding programmes). Much the same could be claimed for many of the countries expressing aspirations in relation to youth/school sport. However, an examination of policy for mass/community participation produces a much more mixed picture. Aspirations are often vague and unrealistic rather than precise and feasible; the commitment of resources is, in many countries, modest and unhypothecated; and programmes and initiatives are frequently short term, badly planned and unevaluated.

There are a number of possible explanations for the contrast between these three emerging sub-sectors of sports development. The first is the technical problems of specifying the nature of the problem to be solved or the goal to be sought. While the aims of elite development policy can be specified reasonably clearly (in terms of number of medals, success in particular sport, beating particular rivals, etc.) the aims of community participation are more problematic and fluid. Aims can be specified in terms of collective or personal social objectives (community integration or personal sense of well-being, for example), talent identification and development objectives (based on a percolation model according to which a broad base of participation is needed from which the elite will gradually rise up through the pyramid) or health objectives (regular moderately intensive physical activity for cardiovascular benefits, for example). A second problem is concerned with the delivery infrastructure for community sport. Not only are the infrastructural requirements substantial, but it is not always clear where primary responsibility for service delivery should rest. Unlike youth sport where, in many countries, the education system has already accepted some responsibility and has an existing facility base, there is less clarity of responsibility in relation to community sport, with municipalities and the not-for-profit (voluntary sports clubs) both having a potential primary role. A third problem is the cost of implementing policy aspirations in the area of community sport which, given the scale of the target population, is bound to have some deterrent effect on governments. A fourth possible problem is the political weakness of those advocating on behalf of community sport. In contrast to the lobbying capacity of elite sport (which often includes the National Olympic Committee, Olympic federations, elite sport sponsors and the media) the advocacy groups for community sport are relatively weak and often competing and are thus more easily ignored. A related political problem is the perception of the extent of responsibility that government should accept for community sports. Especially in the more neo-liberal polities it may be argued that responsibility for community sports development rests not with the state, but more properly with the institutions of civil society and the individual citizen. A final challenge lies in the difficulty of measuring success. Acknowledging the methodological problems of establishing a causal relationship between policy programmes and impact it is arguable that there is a clearer relationship between inputs and outcomes in the areas of elite sport development and youth sport development than in the area of community sport. Part of the problem lies in the complexity of the socio-economic factors that mediate between policy programmes and their target audience and part lies in the time lag between programme initiation and behavioural change.

The chapters in this Part of the Handbook provide illustrations of many of these problems. Keech's discussion of England draws attention to the different treatment of elite sport development and mass sport development and the extent to which policy for mass participation has been stuck at the rhetorical level despite the apparent political momentum given to mass participation by the Labour government of 1997. Keech charts a decade or more of hesitation, opacity and confusion within government over its approach to mass participation. Such has been the depth of confusion and indecision about approaches to the promotion of mass participation that current policy seems to have been reduced to relying on the much mythologised 2012 Olympic legacy. A similar tension between the desire for international sporting success and sport for all is evident in Collins' examination of sports development policy in New Zealand. Rather than having separate organisations for elite and mass sport as in the UK, New Zealand has one national organisation, SPARC, which is tasked with balancing the competing pressures. While SPARC can point to a number of national programmes designed to encourage mass adult participation, it has not been immune from the pressures experienced by other countries to divert resources to the pursuit of Olympic and Commonwealth medals on the one hand and tackling the growth in youth physical inactivity on the other. Equally significantly, Collins' chapter highlights the challenge of maintaining the emphasis on sport in the face of pressures to address health by focusing on physical activity, which stretches resources and programmes beyond the boundary of sport.

Thibault's analysis of Canada's policy towards adult sports participation emphasises the degree to which health concerns, rather than any appreciation of the intrinsic value of sports participation, are driving governmental interest in sports participation policy. More significantly, the prevailing policy assumption is that increased adult participation in sport can best be achieved by developing a commitment to sport among the young. Thibault's conclusion echoes many of the findings of earlier chapters insofar as the aspiration to promote adult sports participation rarely translates into the commitment of resources and the design of programmes specifically targeting adult participants. Thibault reports that survey data indicate that 'the majority of adults are involved in essentially inactive roles – as volunteer leaders and administrators and as spectators and attendees of sport events'.

In Japan policy development for adult sports participation is mediated by two central government departments responsible for education and health, respectively. As Yamamoto makes clear, Japanese sports development policy has traditionally been long on rhetoric and short on action and, despite fine-sounding statements about the aim being to enable all citizens to enjoy sport at 'any stage of life, anytime, anywhere', there has been a notable lack of government investment in adult sport. Governmental commitment towards the promotion of adult sports participation has, to some extent, been undermined by the growing concern at the steady decline in children's physical fitness and steady increase in weight. While there has been some progress in promoting adult participation the neo-liberal philosophy of successive Japanese governments has made enthusiastic engagement with the challenges of delivering sport for all difficult to stimulate.

The final chapter in this Part explores the role of international organisations in the promotion of sport-for-all policies. Henry identifies a broad range of governmental and non-governmental international organisations that have an actual or potential interest in adult participation in sport. Of particular note is the role of the Council of Europe which was instrumental in influencing the European governmental agenda with the adoption of the Sport For All Charter in 1976. Despite having very limited resources the Council of Europe has considerable moral authority and has been consistent in reminding its member governments of their obligations under the Charter through periodic reviews of domestic policy. More recently the European Union has become more active in the field of sports policy, although its capacity to influence domestic policy is limited by the principle of subsidiarity. Other organisations reviewed include the IOC, at first sight, an incongruous advocate of sport for all. Overall, the impression gained from the review is that, apart from the Council of Europe, the potential of the other international organisations to influence domestic policy is limited by principles (such as subsidiarity), lack of resources or the prioritisation of more specific target groups such as the young or women.

References

Dye, T. (1975) *Understanding public policy (2nd edn)*, Englewood Cliffs, NJ: Prentice-Hall.
Hogwood, B. (1987) *From crisis to complacency*, Oxford: Oxford University Press.
Hogwood, B. and Gunn, L. (1984) *Policy analysis for the real world*, Oxford: Oxford University Press.
Howlett, M. and Ramesh, M. (2003) *Studying public policy: Policy cycles and policy subsystems*, Oxford: Oxford University Press.

16

Sport and adult mass participation in England

Marc Keech

Sports policy and development in the United Kingdom (UK) has been defined by the irreconcilably dichotomous strands of elite and mass participation sport. A fog of uncertainty has enveloped sports development with regard to mass participation and there are continuing doubts about which organisations are best placed to meet targets that have often been set without full regard to the broader challenge of instigating behavioural changes required from the population. The structure and organisation of sport in the UK is highly complex, with devolved responsibilities in each of the four nations, England, Northern Ireland, Scotland and Wales, so this chapter examines the development of policies aimed at increasing the participation of adults in sport using England as an example. The chapter addresses sports and physical activity development and analyses the extent to which these two elements of policy have been intertwined in the lead-up to the London 2012 Olympics.

Mass participation/adult sports development

From the early 1970s until the mid-1990s an ethos of 'Sport for All', rhetorically at least, underpinned policies aimed at increasing regular participation in sport amongst the adult population in the UK. In 1972, the Advisory Sports Council, which had been established in 1965, was restructured and granted executive powers through a Royal Charter and became known as the Great Britain Sports Council. At this time, although a stated aim of the Sports Council was 'to raise standards of performance in sport and physical recreation' (Coghlan and Webb 1990: 67), the focus was primarily on encouraging participation and improving the provision of new sports facilities for the wider community. Government funding for sport and recreation in the late 1970s and into the early 1980s was increasingly targeted at addressing broader social policy concerns. Policy was largely directed towards mass participation initiatives, or what was 'Sport for All', and the provision of facilities for sport and recreation (Coghlan and Webb 1990; Houlihan 1991; Henry 1993, 2001).

The first Sports Council strategy, *Sport in the Community: the next ten years* (Sports Council 1982), written for the whole of the UK, illustrated the call for more and better local facilities but also identified low participant population groups (housewives, non-car owners, semi- and unskilled workers, low-income groups, older adults, the unemployed and people with disabilities). A target for increasing participation was set with a figure of 1.2 million people doing more sport. With insufficient resources to cover everything mentioned in *Sport in the Community*, two target age groups were identified – 13–24- and 45–49-year-olds. The definition of participation in sport was to have participated at least once in the previous four weeks but between 1983 and 1996 the only age group in which participation increased was the 60–69 years age group. It stagnated or fell in all other age groups (Rowe *et al.* 2004: 8–11) suggesting that, overall, rather than exhibiting a substantive policy aimed at bringing about behavioural change, government/Sports Council policy, where it had been substantive, had been ill-defined, resulting in ineffectual organisations responding to ineffectual policy goals.

Labour's victory at the 1997 general election coincided with the emergence of significant tensions within sports policy. By now, sports policy for the four home nations was devolved and sport's objectives had similar tensions with broader welfare goals. Investment in community facilities was seen as being at odds with the demands to meet the specialist needs of the elite athlete. *A Sporting Future for All* (DCMS 2000) was the first policy paper in England to knit policies since 1960 into one document. *A Sporting Future for All* associated sport with community building and the opportunity that sport presented for moral leadership. The need to ensure that opportunity for progression for talented athletes was identified, as were the health benefits of sports participation. While the Labour government made it clear that it would redirect resources towards increasing participation and community sport, it did not manage to establish a coalition supportive of a more integrated conceptualisation of sports policy objectives (Houlihan and White 2002: 101). *Game Plan: a strategy for delivering the Government's sport and physical activity objectives* (Strategy Unit/DCMS 2002) articulated a clear statement that government perceived sport and physical activity as a potential social instrument to reduce the inequality of opportunities for people to participate in the social structures in British society. Labour's ambitions for sport were clear:

> The message is simple: get more people doing more sport and increase our success rate in top level competition. We recommend that the priorities should be:
>
> - To encourage a mass participation culture (with as much emphasis on physical activity as competitive sport).
> - To enhance international success. Our target is for British and English teams and individuals to sustain rankings within the top 5 countries, particularly in more popular sports.
> - To adopt a different approach to hosting mega sporting events. They should be seen as an occasional celebration of success rather than as a means to achieving other government objectives.
>
> *(Strategy Unit/DCMS 2002: 15)*

There were many in the sports development profession who were unwilling or unable to note the faults in *Game Plan*. The sports policy community generally accepted *Game Plan* uncritically, and it is worth pointing out that some key faults of the document, especially with reference to community sport, were made vociferously, but by academics:

> Like the PAT [Policy Action Team] 10 report in 1999, it [the *Game Plan*] ignores the fact that the main driver underlying these inequalities is the poverty suffered by a quarter of adults and a third of children, and the majority of single parents and disabled people which means they do not have the disposable income to spend on sport and (Physical Activity) for themselves. This cuts them out of any issues regarding motivation, or quality of provision. While the dramatic government interventions in school and youth PE may deliver

increases in youth participation from 2008 onwards, more adults need to participate. For the poor, this means more direct subsidy in the short term, which the [then] Minister [for sport], Richard Caborn, accepted on *You and Yours* (Radio 4, 3 January, 2003), but which is not mentioned in the report.

(Collins 2003: 32–33)

Game Plan had a dramatic impact on the structure of sport in the UK and, in particular, in England. The most high-profile example was the modernisation of Sport England, which resulted in the organisation's transformation from a sports development agency, concerned with mass participation, to a strategic lead agency, responsible for co-ordinating government policy through other organisations. From April 2006, Sport England was made responsible only for community sport, with elite sport being the sole concern of UK Sport. The *Game Plan* not only began a major shake-up of sporting structures across the UK but also explicitly emphasised the symbiotic, and overtly instrumental, relationship between sport (and increased physical activity, in general), education and health policy. There was no recognition that there was not enough public and private investment to sustain current facility and programme provision, let alone attain the overambitious participation targets of 70 per cent of the population participating in five separate sessions of 30 minutes of physical activity each week.

Such concerns have been largely driven by *Game Plan* which, while setting the goal of increasing participation levels in sport and physical activity (a recurring, but difficult to achieve, policy theme over the past 20 to 30 years), makes it clear that if sporting organisations are to lever funding from government in the future then the broader social 'problems' of increasing obesity levels, crime and social cohesion must be addressed. This emerging agenda has raised a number of jurisdictional concerns: concerns that appear to hinge in part on the detail of the role of regional sporting bodies in meeting the broader social objectives identified above, as well as their role in working with NGBs in promoting talented sporting performers.

(Green 2004: 375)

Change for the better?

Sports policy in the UK has undergone another dramatic shift, coinciding with unprecedented media coverage of sports policy issues since the UK was awarded the London 2012 Olympics in 2005. In a hard-hitting article Culf (2007) noted that, when the budget for London 2012 rose to over £9.3 billion (from the originally envisaged £2.735 million):

[T]here in the small print was the cost to the National Lottery distributors, an additional £675m diverted away from their coffers … Sport England's lottery income will be slashed by a further £55.9m in 2009, bringing its contribution to the massive project getting under way in Stratford [the Olympic site in East London] to £395m … for every £1 that Sport England invests at the moment, about £3 is levered in from local authorities and private investors. 'What that really means is that £1.6bn is not going to community sport.'

(Culf 2007; also cited in Collins 2008: 81)

The final sentence in the quote above was from Derek Mapp, then Chair of Sport England and whose short tenure was marked by disagreement with government ministers. Mapp noted that participation in sport would often be complemented by participation in more informal activities and health-related exercise.

'We need to stop looking at sport for sport's sake,' Mapp [said]. 'Those who participate regularly in sport are healthier, there is less crime in the streets, there is less obesity, it creates better business leaders. The benefits of participation are rather more than finding another champion for the 400m. It is not just about getting a six-pack.'

(Culf 2007)

Newly appointed Secretary of State (for the DCMS) James Purnell [who soon after moved to another government department in the 2008 cabinet reshuffle and who dramatically resigned from the government in spring 2009], whose background was in broadcasting not sport, seemed to take exception to Mapp's criticisms, asking Sport England to focus on more traditional sports for a developing legacy to the Olympics and besought the Department of Health to take responsibility for such activities as jogging and walking. ... When Mapp warned Purnell to be careful about this turn, he was asked to resign. He [i.e. Mapp] accurately commented 'I accept that the DoH should be getting people fitter but their contribution in recent years has been very little' (*www.politics.co.uk*) and 'I am bound to say that I think it's unfair. I was mandated to produce an agenda which I was delivering on but now that has changed and I have been dumped on' (*D. Bond, Daily Telegraph, 30 November, 2007*). ... The governing bodies in English sport command only some 6 million members, not all playing. Without exception they argue they need more volunteers to cope with the growing roles government expects of them ... *The Secretary of State's action will almost certainly slow down the uncertain process of increasing mass participation* (emphasis added).

(Collins 2008: 82)

Concomitantly, National Governing Bodies of sport (NGBs) were arguing strongly and loudly for increased funding and a redefined role for sporting organisations. Chief Executive of the Amateur Swimming Association, David Sparkes, and Ed Warner, Chair of UK Athletics, gave evidence to the DCMS Select Committee in which they criticised Sport England's remit as one that was too broad. The Government agreed, announcing what many considered to be a serious 'u-turn' in policy (Revill 2007).

We will never build a world class community sports infrastructure unless we are clear that sport is a good thing and competition is a good thing. There is an old management axiom that the man who has five priorities has none. That is why I am categorically sure that the purpose of Sport England is to deliver sport in England. Call me simple-minded but surely there's a clue in the name. There should be a clear focus on sport development and sports participation. ... That means creating excellent national governing bodies, clubs, coaches and volunteers ... My offer to them is clear. We want to create whole sports plans, with a single funding pot. We will free them up from the bureaucracy and bidding that they complain about today. But, in return, they will need to commit to clear goals to improve participation, coaching and the club structure. And in particular, they will need to show how they will reach groups who do less sport today, whether women, poorer groups or some ethnic minorities.

(Purnell 2007)

As a result of the aggressive lobbying by NGBs and Purnell's belief in their arguments, policy swung again with the emphasis shifting away from sport's role in broader social outcomes to a more narrow focus to what has been commonly termed 'sport for sport's sake'. That is, the development of sport for sport's needs, without a policy focus on broader social objectives, an announcement that received cross-party political support. The review that Purnell announced progressed in a more closed fashion than previous reviews with only those likely to be involved in future policy consulted. Apart from local government receiving little support, the main casualty of the review were County Sports Partnerships (CSPs), sub-regional agencies which, having been incubated in 1999 to develop specific sports, had their role redesigned in 2005 to tackle broader social issues, with increased funding. But in the review conducted in early 2008, CSPs were informed that their funding would be cut and that their roles would be narrowed.

Current policy

The DCMS published its most recent sports strategy in the summer of 2008. Eschewing some principles set out in *Game Plan* and subsequent documents, yet ironically entitled *Playing to Win* the DCMS proclaimed (yet another)

> New era of both sport and physical activity development ... Physical activity by its nature is a cross-Government responsibility and a range of Departments are leading on creating more opportunities to get physically active. Our reforms of sport are set against this backdrop of the Government's drive to raise levels of physical activity.
>
> *(DCMS 2008: 1)*

Furthermore, in addition to the contextual setting of increasing sports participation in order to address broader health and physical activity concerns, the document explained that:

> There has been confusion in the past in the community sport sector, with a lack of clarity over focusing on delivering sport or physical activity; a high level of bureaucracy with competing local, regional and national strategies; and numerous funding streams making it hard for NGBs and sports clubs to get funding. It was essential to review and refocus community sport and Sport England to give greater clarity of purpose; reduce inefficiency and bureaucracy; and make it easier for NGBs and sports to access funding to improve sport and ensure that under-represented groups get equal treatment.
>
> *(DCMS 2008: 14)*

What is openly acknowledged here was that the key changes were a focus on sport by sports organisations and delivery principally through NGBs but drawing in other partners including local authorities. This new approach was predicated on a nationally driven strategy and a more focused role for Sport England. The value of CSPs to the new agenda, and the need for continued core funding for CSPs, has been recognised, but, with funding reduced to £10 million per annum divided equally between the 49 CSPs, it was agreed that the funding should be allocated equally across all CSPs. The intention of this decision was first, to ensure the maintenance of a national network with an agreed set of core services and second, because any banding of CSP funding would require the development of robust criteria which would be a complex process with a high risk of bureaucracy and unfairness as, for example, complexity of service delivery in a shire CSP would have to be balanced against the complexity of inner-city deprivation. However, it is clearly evident and now reasonably well acknowledged that, essentially, there has been a substantial shift from a 'bottom up' mass participation strategy to a nationally defined strategy for each sport (see Table 16.1).

Whilst community (adult/mass participation) sport continues to be ill-defined, the two other strands of sport policy, elite sport and physical education and school sport, have become well-defined and successful elements of government policy. The transformation of elite sport in

Table 16.1 The UK sporting landscape

	1997	2007	2017
PE and school sport	No centrally co-ordinated school sports system Poor school-club links In 2002 an estimated 25% of 5–16-year-olds were doing 2 hours of PE and sport per week Negligible targeted investment	86% of 5–16-year-olds doing 2 hours of PE and sport each week 3,000 community sport coaches 450 school sport partnerships 90 competition managers Over 3,200 secondary school co-ordinators and over 18,000 primary link teachers Over £1.5 billion invested in last five years	A world-leading community sports system, continuing to increase participation year on year All 5–16-year-olds offered 5 hours of sport each week All 16–19-year-olds offered 3 hours of sport a week Competition and coaching at the heart of the school sports system
Community	£32 million annual funding to Sport England Crumbling sports facilities	Over £125 million annual exchequer funding to Sport England 4,000 facilities built or renovated Over £1 billion of investment in facilities since 2001	A world leading community sports system, continuing to increase participation Significantly reduced drop-off at 16 years.
Elite	36th in Olympics medal table, 4th in Paralympic medal table Funding of £70.7 million	10th in 2004 Olympics, 2nd in Paralympics Funding of £216.4 million	Ultimate goal of 4th for London 2012 Olympics medal table and 2nd in Paralympics and sustaining that into 2016 Over £400 million for London 2012 Olympic cycle A legacy of world-leading elite sport infrastructures including high-quality coaching

Source: DCMS 2008: 4

England and the UK had its genesis in the aftermath of the 1996 Olympics, where the British team finished 36th in the medals table, with only a single gold medal. By 2008, the British Olympic team had surpassed all expectations, finishing 4th in the medals table, winning 47 medals (19 gold, 13 silver and 15 bronze). In 2004, the government instigated measurement of participation in physical education and school sport, locating a baseline of participation as 25 per cent of young people receiving two hours a week of physical education and school sport in 2003. With a national Public Service Agreement (PSA) target of 75 per cent of 5–16-year-olds participating in two hours of high-quality physical education and school sport by 2008, and a stretch target of 85 per cent in the same time period, an investment of over £1.5 billion ensured that, by 2008, according to the annual school sport national survey, 90 per cent of pupils in partnership schools (not independent schools) participated in at least two hours of high-quality physical education and out-of-hours school sport in a typical week, exceeding the 2008 PSA target by 5% (DCSF 2008: 2).

The picture of community sport is less encouraging, but remains set against the backdrop of improving levels of health. By 2002 *Game Plan* estimated participation in sport to be approximately 30 per cent participation four times in the most recent four weeks (i.e. an average of once a week). Calls for more systematic understanding of participation were eventually accepted when Sport England commissioned the Active People Survey of sports participation in England. First conducted in 2005–6, at a cost of approximately £3 million, the survey became the most comprehensive picture of participation in sport in any country. In total 363,724 people were interviewed (a minimum of 1,000 in each local authority area) by telephone across England between the period mid-October 2005 to mid-October 2006. Regular participation in sport and recreation was defined as taking part on at least three days a week in moderate intensity sport and active recreation (at least 12 days in the last four weeks) for at least 30 minutes continuously in any one session. Moderate intensity is defined by having walked at a brisk or fast pace and for sports having raised the breathing rate. The key findings of the first survey were:

- 21% of the adult population aged 16 and over (8.5 million people) take part regularly in sport and active recreation.
- 28.4% of adults (11.5 million) have built some exercise into their lives (those described as building some exercise into their lives did at least 30 minutes of moderate intensity sport and active recreation on between one and eleven (inclusive) days in the previous 28 days).
- 50.6% of adults (20.6 million) have not taken part in any moderate intensity sport and active recreation of 30 minutes duration in the last 4 weeks.
- Regular participation in sport and active recreation varies across different socio-demographic groups:

  - Males 23.7%; Females 18.3%;
  - People with a limiting longstanding illness or disability 8.8%; those without 23.3%;
  - Black and other ethnic minority groups 18.6%; adults of white origin – 21.2%; 17.5% of Black Caribbeans regularly participate and 17% of Asians
  - Lowest socio-economic groups 16.3%; highest socio-economic group 25.1%;
  - Participation included recreational walking and cycling. 239 different sports and recreational activities were counted in the survey. Walking was the most popular recreational activity, followed by swimming and going to the gym. Cycling, football, running and jogging, golf, badminton, tennis and aerobics made up the top 10.

(Sport England 2006: 2)

The Active People Survey 2 (2007/8) provides the baseline for Sport England's measurement of the one million target, as part of the Government's drive to get two million people more active by 2012. Over 8.8 million adults (8,835,000) undertook sport and active recreation on three days a week for 30 minutes at moderate intensity. Regular participation has increased from 21.0% (2005/06) to 21.3% (2007/08) representing 283,800 more adults participating in sport and active recreation. Table 16.2 shows there has been a statistically significant increase, which Sport England took to mean 95% certainty that there had been real change (increase or decrease) in participation across all age groups except for the 16–19 and 30–34 age groups in the period between the Active People surveys.

The most recently revised government target is to ensure that two million more people are physically active by 2012. Of these, one million people will be doing more sport (Sport England 2008). The Active People 3 Survey, published on 17 December 2009, was the first survey since the establishment of the one million target, based on the baseline figures from Active People 2 survey. Consistent with Sport England's 2008–11 strategy, this survey included a narrower range of sports (rather than sports and activities) than its predecessors. In 2008–9, 6.93 million

Table 16.2 Participation by age groups

Sports participation APS 1(2005/06) APS 2 (2007/08) by age groups	Number APS 1 (2005/06)	Percentage of population	Number APS 2 (2007/08)	Percentage of population	Participation change (number)	Participation change (%)	Significant difference?
Age 16–19	868,800	32.8	914,200	33.9	45,400	1.07	No
Age 20–24	870,700	26.7	983,900	28.5	113,200	1.78	Yes
Age 25–29	737,600	23.3	838,200	25.0	100,600	1.68	Yes
Age 30–34	723,100	20.5	681,100	20.6	-42,000	0.10	No
Age 35–44	1,370,300	17.6	1,416,400	18.2	46,100	0.55	Yes
Age 45–64	1,303,000	10.6	1,482,900	11.7	179,900	1.09	Yes
Age 65+	444,800	5.5	531,400	6.5	86,600	0.99	Yes

Source: Sport England, 2008a

people (16.6% of the adult population) participated in sport three times a week for 30 minutes at moderate intensity. The actual target is to ensure that 7.815 million people are participating in sport at least three times a week by 2012–13.

The additional one million participation target will be the responsibility of a range of other government departments. Many of these programmes are outlined in the Department of Health's health and physical activity plan, *Be Active, Be Healthy* (DoH 2009). Sport England will receive £392 million from the Government and an estimated £324 million from Lottery funding over the period 2008–11 to deliver community sport. Sport England is required, currently, to continue to work with the network of CSPs to facilitate relationships with, between and on behalf of CSPs, NGBs and local agencies. The caveat, however, was a statement to CSPs in September 2008 that noted that, as the NGBs develop their 2009–13 plans and as Sport England analyses their potential ability to deliver Sport England outcomes, the role of CSPs will inevitably develop and evolve. The new purpose of Sport England, outlined in its strategy, *Grow, Sustain, Excel*, is to build the foundations of sporting success through a world-leading community sports system. Chief Executive Jennie Price outlined how the Sport England strategy would develop. The strategy commits Sport England to deliver on a series of demanding targets by 2012/13:

- One million people doing more sport;
- A 25% reduction in the number of 16-to-18-year-olds who drop out of five key sports;
- Improved talent development systems in at least 25 sports;
- A measurable increase in people's satisfaction with their experience of sport – the first time the organisation has set such a qualitative measure;
- A major contribution to the delivery of the five hour sports offer for children and young people.

(Price 2009; also in Sport England 2008a: 11)

The five-hour offer is the term given to the aspiration that states that, in building upon the work in physical education and school sports policy, all young people aged 5–16 in state-funded education will be able to access five hours of physical education and school sport each week with at least two hours taking place within curriculum time. NGBs are able to facilitate greater involvement through the national school sports competition structure which has emerged in the last three years. But perhaps the single most problematic barrier to the success of current policy will be the fragility of the voluntary sector on which NGBs rely to increase mass participation. Over two million adults (2,044,200) contribute at least one hour a week to volunteering in sport. This is 4.9 per cent of the adult population in England, and sport is the most popular arena for volunteering in England and the UK. Yet, increasing participation in organised sport will necessitate increased and improved club structures, with many more people required to facilitate participation as coaches, administrators and a range of other roles. It is debatable whether those trying to facilitate club-based participation will also be able/willing to participate. The following statement by Sport England indicates the scale of the expectations that the organisation has of NGBs and voluntary sports clubs.

The consultation which underpinned the development of the Sport England strategy (see Figure 16.1) for 2008–11 identified three key challenges facing community sport:

- Increasing participation in sport. Currently 20.9%[1] of the population participate in sport and physical activity three times a week. 50.6% of the population do not participate in at least one session of sport each week.

- Tackling drop-off. Thousands of people drop out of playing sport each year. There is a particular problem at the age of 16, where 25,000 drop out of sport each year.
- Developing talent. England has a successful track record of elite success in a number of sports. We must ensure that we tap into the vast range of sporting potential across the country to maintain the pipeline of talent up to elite levels.

(Sport England 2008b: 7)

One additional issue, openly acknowledged, is that over half of the projected increases in participation are based on the targets of eight key sports. In one sense focusing the target on a narrow range of well-managed, resourced and popular sports means that participation increases are more likely to be achieved. Alternatively, such a narrow focus could lead to failure and a situation that, while targets have been met, a culture of greater participation is not achieved. The role of, and relationship between, NGBs and CSPs also merits consideration. NGBs have recently completed writing the whole sport plans first mentioned in Purnell's 2007 speech. In principal, NGBs have been empowered with greater control over the investment of public funds in their sport. The consequence of increased autonomy is to ensure that national targets are met. Those NGBs already operating to nationally agreed standards will be left to operate accordingly. Weaker NGBs, either in terms of governance or targets, will be given additional help and support by Sport England. CSPs, with strong direction from Sport England, set out an 'offer', detailing what they could provide to facilitate work towards identified targets. It has been determined that CSPs will:

- Deliver cross-sport services to meet NGB priorities and specific services for Sport England.
- Develop and maintain the strategic alliances and local networks that NGBs and Sport England need to drive delivery and secure resources.
- Manage and operate the CSP, ensure sound governance, audit and compliance.

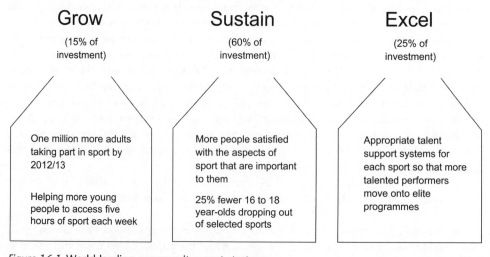

Figure 16.1 World-leading community sport strategy

The role of CSPs will not be one of direct delivery, placing again increased emphasis on local organisations, especially clubs, to increase participation. There are major concerns in local communities as to whether clubs have the capacity and infrastructure to continue to increase participation. Whilst CSPs were instructed to ensure that club and coach development was at the forefront of their revised roles, local authorities are disgruntled by the new approach, especially at a time when public services are under threat from substantial cuts in the near future in the UK. Perhaps as a response to local authorities not achieving the substantial rises in participation required by government policy since 2002, Sport England has greatly reduced its contact with local authorities, instead asking CSPs to fill the policy vacuum created by Sport England's much revamped role. There are now considerable tensions between local authorities and CSPs, exacerbated by the much reduced funding available to the former. Hylton and Totten (2007) offer an insight into the difficulties of increasing community/mass/adult participation:

> Any understanding of why specific activity takes place (or doesn't) at a local level necessitates an understanding of what influences have been brought to bear from the wider policy context. Understanding how community sports development works and why it does what it does at the delivery point to clients is part of a more complex picture of how policy makers and funders influence the scope of activity. This in turn is mediated by factors at a community-engaged level.
>
> *(Hylton and Totten 2007: 83)*

Brutally evident from the lack of identification in the 2008 policy statement, Sport England has forsaken local authority contact and been instructed to co-ordinate the work of CSPs with NGBs. A major question asked of Sport England was whether local government was receptive to CSPs co-ordinating Local Area Agreement delivery plans relating to sport, noting that this would not take cognisance of the context of community engagement in local areas. Local authorities have been lukewarm to this development, citing the lack of organisational capacity of many CSPs to deliver in local areas. CSP performance measures and targets will evolve but will relate to Sport England's strategic outcomes of 'grow, sustain and excel'. The main challenge for Sport England and sports organisations more generally is to align local and national objectives through the delivery of NGB sports outcomes, for example, in volunteering. There is considerable scepticism that CSPs will be able to do this, especially as most of the more organised and larger NGBs seem prepared to 'go it alone' if initial indications are anything to go by.

Sport, health, physical activity and participation

Recent sports reforms are set against the backdrop of the Government's drive to increase levels of physical activity. Intriguingly, early in 2009 the Department of Health announced funding of £60,000 per year to each CSP in order to ensure that some of the physical activity targets would be met, thereby redeveloping their role beyond sport. As many similarities exist between health programmes and sports development programmes, for example in the types of desired outcomes and the service-based nature of provision (Lindsey 2008), the relative sustainability of health programmes recently has led some in Government to believe that sport may benefit from active encouragement to work more closely with health. Tacking health inequalities remains at the forefront of government policy; the financial and associated burdens on the National Health Service are debilitating. For example, obesity alone is estimated to cost the Treasury about £8.2 billion annually, placing immense strain on the National Health Service. According to the Health Survey for England (2005) about 43 per cent of men and 32 per cent of women are overweight and an additional 22 per cent of men and 24 per cent of women are obese (The Information Centre 2006). However, as Coalter (2005) notes:

> Much of the research evidence relates to the health benefits of physical activity, rather than sport per se. Among the least active and least healthy groups, the promotion of an 'active lifestyle' may be a more useful strategy than the promotion of sport and 'fitness'. Nevertheless, the umbrella term 'sport' encompasses a wide range of activities that can be undertaken in a variety of formal and informal contexts and can be adjusted to take account of a wide variety of confidence and skill levels. Furthermore, the social nature of most sporting activities can serve to provide encouragement and support, ensuring the level of frequency and adherence required to obtain physical and psychological health benefits.
>
> *(Coalter 2005: 13)*

The Free Swimming (i.e. no cost to participants) project was a government initiative that aims to increase participation in swimming and to promote physical activity and a healthy lifestyle. The scheme began in April 2009.

> Offering free swimming for those over 60 and under 16 is a key component of our physical activity plans and is a signal of the raised level of our ambitions.
>
> *(DCMS 2008: 18)*

The DCMS is charged with working with other Government departments to ensure Sport England's work on sport is aligned with the work of the Department of Health, Communities and Local Government, Department for Children, Schools and Families, and the Department for Work and Pensions to extend participation in swimming, 'not least because sport plays an important role in helping reduce obesity by getting people more active' (DCMS 2008: 18). Whilst this aspiration is laudable, many local authorities are concerned how they will fund this development and, for others, access in terms of parking is just one example of ensuring people can get to the pools. A lack of integrated transport plans is seen by health professionals as the single largest barrier to instigating a culture of physical activity locally.

Free Swimming is one example of how sport and health development professionals are giving considerable thought locally about how to use community sport to achieve the government targets, while addressing local concerns. Workplaces are a priority setting and larger employers are being asked to consider ways in which physical activity can be built into the working day. One example of this, the 'cycle to work' scheme, involves employers offering interest-free loans to employees so that they can purchase bicycles. Other, more controversial, policies, aimed at alternative areas of policy but which may improve physical activity, currently being quietly mooted, involve taxing people who drive to work. Social marketing is seen as important to changing behaviour, but national campaigns such as the 2005 'Everyday Sport' campaign have had minimal impact. Whereas Sport England is trying to get more people doing more sport, the most effective physical activity interventions have been those that targeted the least active. GP referral schemes have been one example but have usually meant referrals to gyms rather than to sports clubs. Alternative forms of referrals, such as to dance classes for the over 60s, may widen the impact and appeal of 'exercise on prescription'. Some sports are able to offer health-based promotions. Most recently, following the extraordinary success of the British cycling team at both the 2008 Olympics and a series of world championships, and boosted by substantial sponsorship from BSkyB, the British Cycling Federation announced a series of SkyRides, one-day mass participation events in major cities in the UK, on closed roads, for the summer of 2009.

Conclusion

Up until the mid-1990s policy for sport in the UK was vague, insubstantial and ill-defined. Since 1995, when *Sport: Raising the Game*, the first policy paper for sport in the UK, was published, there have been substantial and increasingly rapid attempts to define and redefine sports policy in the UK. Ten years of reorientation and an increasing understanding of what was required of sports development locally, especially in terms of increasing mass/adult participation and addressing broader social concerns, under the 'New' Labour government was dramatically changed by James Purnell's speech in 2007. Since then, a streamlining of sports organisations and agencies has started to demonstrate a much more focused approach from these agencies toward a participation target, but those previously responsible for community/adult participation, in particular local authorities, have become increasingly marginalised within the policy process.

As regards the claims that hosting the Olympic Games in London 2012 will help boost participation, there are many who are sceptical about such legacy claims. No Olympics in recent history has managed to increase mass participation in the host country, and in 2008 Brigid Simmons, chair of the Central Council of Physical Recreation, voiced concerns that there would be no legacy in terms of participation. Criticism of the Government focuses on the way in which existing sports policies have been aggregated into one overarching programme to demonstrate the legacy potential for increased participation. Whilst the Olympics are being seen as the catalyst for increasing participation in sport, there is substantial doubt about whether they will also be a catalyst for increased levels of physical activity. It is also debateable as to whether the structural and organisational uncertainty that has hindered development of increased participation has been solved. Responsibility for increasing participation has been redivided. CSPs have an uncertain future, and NGBs are in the spotlight; they asked for greater responsibility and now they must ensure that participation targets are met in order to secure future investment in community sport.

Note

1 This figure uses the Active People 1 survey data, because the strategy was published prior to the Active People 2 survey.

References

Coalter, F. (2005) *The Social Benefits of Sport: An overview to inform the Community Planning Process*, Edinburgh, SportScotland.

Coghlan, J. with Webb, I. (1990). *Sport and British Politics since 1990*, London, Falmer Press.

Collins, M. F. (2003) 'Sticking to the Plan', *Recreation*, May, pp. 32–4.

——(2008) 'Public Policies on Sports Development', in Girginov, V. (ed.) *Managing Sports Development*, Oxford, Elsevier.

Culf, A. (2007) 'Grassroots participation is the loser as Sport England props up the Games', *The Guardian*, March 22 [retrieved from www.guardian.co.uk/sport/2007/mar/22/Olympics2012.politics, March 23, 2007].

Department for Children, Schools and Families (2008) 'School Sport Survey 2007–8', London, DCSF.

Department of Culture, Media and Sport (DCMS) (2000) *A Sporting Future for All*, London, DCMS.

—— (2008) *Playing to Win: a new era for sport*, London, DCMS.

Department of Health (2009) *Be Active, Be Healthy*, London, DoH.

Green, M. (2004) 'Changing Policy Priorities for Sport in England; the Emergence of Elite Sport Development as a Key Policy Concern', *Leisure Studies,* Vol. 23, No. 4, 365–85.

Henry, I.P. (1993) 'The Politics of Leisure Policy', Basingstoke, Macmillan.

——(2001) 'The Politics of Leisure Policy (2nd edition)', Basingstoke, Palgrave.

Houlihan, B. (1991) *The Government and Politics of Sport*, London, Routledge.

Houlihan, B. and White, A. (2002) *The Politics of Sport Development: Development of Sport or Development through Sport?* London, Routledge.

Hylton, K. and Totten, M. (2007) 'Community Sports Development', in: Hylton, K and Bramham, P. (eds) *Sports Development: policy, process and practice* (2nd Ed.), London, Routledge.

Information Centre, The (2006) 'Statistics on obesity, physical activity and diet', London, The Information Centre.

Lindsey, I. (2008) 'Conceptualising sustainability in sports development', *Leisure Studies*, 27: 3, 279–94.

Price, J. (2009) 'Where we're at', *paper presented to the 2009 Annual Sport England Conference, 'Building Partnerships That Deliver'*, London, March 11, 2009.

Purnell, J. (2007) 'World Class Community Sport', *a speech to the annual Youth Sport Trust School Sport Partnership conference*, Telford, November 28.

Revill, J. (2007) 'U-turn on "sport-for-all" pledge', *The Observer*, 25 November [retrieved from www.guardian.co.uk/uk/2007/nov/25/olympics2012.london, November 27, 2007].

Rowe, N., Adams, R. and Beasley, N. (2004) 'Driving up Participation in Sport: the social context, the trends, the prospects and the challenges', in Rowe, N. (ed.) *Driving up Participation: the Challenge for Sport*, London, Sport England.

Sports Council (1982) *Sport in the Community: the Next Ten Years*, London, Sports Council.

Sport England (2006) 'The Active People Survey: headline findings', London, Sport England.

——(2008a) *Grow, Sustain, Excel: Sport England's Strategy for 2008–2011*, London, Sport England.

——(2008b) 'Active People Survey 2007–8: national KPIs fact sheet', London, Sport England.

Strategy Unit/DCMS (2002) *Game Plan: A Strategy for Delivering the Government's Sport and Physical Activity Objectives*, London, Strategy Unit/DCMS.

17
Sports development and adult participation in New Zealand

Shane Collins

Sport has long played an important cultural and historical role within New Zealand society both as an active pastime and as an activity of national pride with regard to international per-formances. For much of the twentieth century the mandate for sports development remained solely with amateur sporting and community organisations and met with little government interest. Early government intervention was intermittent and limited; however, recent changes to the trajectory of sports development have impacted significantly not only on the direction of sports policy but also on the rationale for, and outcomes sought by, such interventions. Over the last 15 years or so there has been rapid change to the structure and development of sport in New Zealand. Perhaps most notable, has been the way in which the social significance of sport has burgeoned with links to health, education, social and commercial outcomes. Despite the strong cultural significance of sport and increased government interest, there has been limited academic literature regarding the study of sport, particularly prior to the mid-1980s (Collins 2000). While the volume of research on New Zealand sports development has been limited, it is nevertheless growing. More recent academic research has addressed sports development and sports policy issues from a range of historical, social and policy perspectives (Chalip 1996; Collins 2008; Piggin *et al.* 2009; Sam 2003, 2005; Sam and Jackson 2004).

This chapter aims to provide an overview of sports development in New Zealand with particular emphasis on highlighting the increasing intervention by the state and the resulting impact with regard to sports development. In addition, the chapter will discuss the growing links between sports development and other related policy areas, particularly health, economic development, community welfare, youth and promotion of national identity. Developments in New Zealand have been drawn from empirical research that has been conducted over the last fours years. Research has included a review of both academic and organisational documents on sports development activity along with a series of interviews. Interviews were conducted with both governmental and non-governmental senior staff who had been involved in sports development at a senior level over the last eight or so years or still were involved.

Early New Zealand society was heavily influenced by the United Kingdom, with British sporting traditions and activities spreading with the colonisation of New Zealand in the 1800s. By the turn of the twentieth century there were about 14 national sporting associations already formed in New Zealand. National governing bodies[1] (NGBs) began to form towards the end of the nineteenth century with many being established between 1860 and 1900. Government intervention in the early part of the twentieth century was largely restricted to the provision of playing fields, as sport was considered to be the responsibility of the individual and volunteer groups, not the government. Intervention by the state, perhaps unsurprisingly, focused upon concern regarding the health and fitness of young New Zealanders and the implications for the defence of the nation (Perkins et al. 1993).

Post-World War II public sector involvement shifted towards a benign form of social policing that was aimed at reinstating traditional social values, in other words sport was used as a tool to solve urban social problems of the era (Hindson et al. 1994). Participation in sport grew as men returned from the war and attempted to reintegrate into their communities. However, the growth in sporting activity and participation levels was not accompanied by increased resources and few sporting organisations were well resourced (Stothart 2000).

A shift in ethos began to occur during the 1970s whereby sport for sport's sake and ensuring access for all became more important than developing the national fibre of the country's youth (Hindson et al. 1994). At the same time, sporting leaders began calling for increased resources with the goal of achieving greater success on the international stage. Divergent views began to emerge between the two key political parties (National and Labour) based upon what level of state involvement was acceptable. Significantly it was 'community development' that was espoused as the rationale for government involvement (Garrett 1980).

A review of sport was instigated by the new Labour government in 1985 as there was considerable public concern regarding the structure of sport and the growing divide between the supporters of sport and recreation activities (Collins and Stuart 1994). Supporters of sport believed that the recreationists were receiving too much attention, to the detriment of sport, while recreationists were wary that elite sport may receive too much attention (Collins and Stuart 1994). The report, *Sport on the Move*, resulted in the 1987 Recreation and Sport Act and the establishment of the Hillary Commission for Recreation and Sport (Sport Development Inquiry Committee 1985). Funding increased and a range of new initiatives were introduced by the Hillary Commission, which targeted minority groups including women, youth, Māori and older adults (Collins and Downey 2000). *Sport on the Move* advocated a two-pronged approach by government of focusing on both elite and recreational sport, an approach that was to be reiterated in the 2001 Sport Development Inquiry.

Despite supporting increased participation and access to sporting facilities, the inquiry indicated a move away from the welfare-type ethos of Sport for All towards a more neo-liberal approach, according to which the individual should take responsibility for their own actions. Participation in sport was considered to be the responsibility of the individual, as sport should continue to be a 'self help activity, and that no forms of community funding should be established which might reduce or disrupt the independent spirit and motivation of sportsmen and women and their club structure' (Sport Development Inquiry Committee 1985: 66). Government's responsibility to maintain the value of community benefits for sport was clearly articulated throughout the report of the Inquiry Committee with the recommendation that funding from both the Crown and discretionary grants should be directed towards practical support policies at all levels of sport for the benefits of all New Zealanders (Sport Development Inquiry Committee 1985: 67). However, detail of what the practical support policies might consist of was not clarified.

The 1980s saw a focus upon providing opportunities for all with the then newly formed Hillary Commission for Sport, Fitness and Leisure taking the lead in setting the direction of the sport and recreation sector in New Zealand. Somewhat surprisingly, sports policy during this period appeared to be based more upon welfarist type principles, in stark contrast with the then radical neo-liberal approach being adopted across the public sector. A range of programmes including KiwiSport and SportFit were introduced, which encouraged skill development and the promotion of fair play while discouraging a win-at-all costs attitude (Russell *et al.* 1996).

Radical public sector reforms during the 1990s abruptly introduced a new faith in management sciences (James 1997) which impacted significantly upon sporting organisations and the structure of sport. Increased effectiveness of sporting organisations, economic justifications for government support and a user-pays philosophy towards sporting activities were espoused, despite the Hillary Commission continuing to maintain functions that were predominantly based upon a welfarist philosophy (see Russell *et al.* 1996). Towards the end of the 1990s, amidst a general concern for a fragmented sports sector, a Ministerial Taskforce was established. *The Taskforce on Sport, Fitness, and Leisure* (referred to as the Graham Report after its chairman John Graham) was developed during a period of high public interest in sport prompted by the disappointment of a low Olympic medals tally at the 2000 Olympic Games (Sam 2003).

Issues of accessibility were at the forefront of the Graham Report as participation in physical activity was seen as an 'inalienable right', with the implication that recreation and sport opportunities should be available to any sector of the population without undue constraints of cost or access. These principles of equity and access were placed alongside the clear intention to try and develop the concept of lifelong participation in physical activity as 'Lifelong participation in recreation and sport is an integral part of the experience of being a New Zealander' (Ministerial Taskforce 2001: 64). This concept was further expanded as a key principle when it was identified that participation in physical activity 'should be a seamless progression of participatory experiences through all ages and all levels of involvement' (Ministerial Taskforce 2001: 65). Interestingly, the Graham Report identified that it was local, not central, government that needed to be prepared to provide facilities and be aware of, and responsive to, the needs of social sport, while local clubs and Regional Sports Trusts must provide assistance in this area (Ministerial Taskforce 2001: 74).

Worthy of note is the fact that the Taskforce Report, which claimed to represent the voice of sport, called for increased government intervention in sport. It appeared that the Taskforce was prepared to pass control of sport to government when it concluded that, despite the assertion that 'sport should run sport', the variable quality of sports and recreation leadership and administration did not justify the allocation of unmonitored funds (Ministerial Taskforce 2001: 60). This invitation for government to become more involved in sport signalled a significant shift in thinking from 30 years previously. Not surprisingly, themes of efficiency, competitiveness and leadership were central in the development of the taskforce recommendations (Sam 2003). In building a case for government involvement in sport the Taskforce identified health, public good, social cohesion, an enhanced sense of identity and image, crime prevention and economic benefits as reasons for increased government investment in the sport sector while signalling a shift away from an ethos of sport for sport's sake.

As a result of the Graham Report a new crown entity,[2] Sport and Recreation New Zealand (SPARC) was created which, for the first time, placed responsibility for sports policy (which included elite sport, grass-roots sport and physical recreation) under the umbrella of one organisation. The formation of SPARC signalled the beginning of rapid change in the sports sector as, for the first time, there was one organisation mandated to lead New Zealand sport. Upon its establishment SPARC identified three objectives around which its policies, services and investments would be focused:

Being the most active nation.

Having the most effective sport and physical recreation systems.

Having athletes and teams winning consistently in events that matter to New Zealanders.

(SPARC 2002a: 5)

The importance of physical activity and its ability to help address declining health standards was reflected in the rationale for the new crown entity, SPARC. As explained by the then Minister of Sport, Recreation and Fitness, Trevor Mallard, a key driver behind government investment in sport and the formation of SPARC was the need to address 'health issues' (Interview: Minister Sport, Recreation and Fitness, October 2006).

SPARC identified that investment in sports development would also contribute to an array of other key government objectives including achieving wider economic growth targets, supporting a range of other sectors (including technology, services and tourism), and reducing the incidence of cardiovascular disease, some cancers, diabetes, osteoporosis, obesity and depression (SPARC 2002a). The shift away from a narrow focus of sports development on achieving only elite or mass sport goals was reinforced by a senior SPARC official who explained that sport should contribute to 'social development, economic [goals], national identity, environmental [issues] and education' (Interview: October 2006).

To achieve its outcomes SPARC signalled that it would no longer be involved in the delivery of programmes but would accept 'responsibility to provide leadership' (SPARC 2002a: 2). Significantly, SPARC allocates funding to NGBs, Regional Sports Trusts[3] (RSTs), local government and other strategic partners with regard to delivering particular outcomes relating to elite and recreational sport. As such, SPARC is reliant upon other organisations to achieve its outcomes and has moved away from being a provider of programmes to being a strategic partner providing funding, information and other support services to its partners (SPARC 2002a: 9).

In the 2002 corporate document *Our Vision, Our Direction*, the future direction and focus of SPARC for its inaugural four-year period was set out. Low levels of sports participation and the fact that many New Zealanders lacked opportunities to participate in sport were identified as key problems. To address these problems several objectives were identified: a) working with RSTs to become the sports development leaders in their regions; b) investing funds only where they will have a positive result for sports development rather than on the basis of entitlement; c) helping co-ordinate the delivery of services across the sector through key funding contracts; d) working with groups to try and increase the number of volunteers and to make them more effective; e) helping make changes to government policy that will enable the sector to grow; f) improving the linkage between regional sporting infrastructures and schools; and g) targeting key organisations to develop and up-skill people (SPARC 2002a: 13).

SPARC developed two national programmes, *Active Living* and *Active Children*, with the aim of increasing participation in physical activity (see Table 17.1). Policies aimed primarily at increasing the physical activity levels of the post-school group were placed under the *Active Living* programme while policies directed at increasing activity levels of youth (0–24 age group) were placed under the *Active Children* programme. An emphasis on physical activity, rather than on increasing sports or physical recreation participation levels is evident within the programmes, largely driven by the need to address government-related outcomes. As explained by a senior RST official, a key organisation in delivering *Active Living* and *Active Children* programmes, the shift towards physical activity is clear:

> I would say in the last 4 or 5 years we have started to get into this sort of market [physical activity] because of obesity, the health market and the supposed percentage of people that are overweight or obese in this country.
>
> *(Interview: October 2006)*

Several of the programmes that SPARC currently delivers have been extended or continued from the Hillary Commission, and include *Push Play*, *He Oranga Poutama* and *Green Prescription*. What is evident from the strategies developed under the *Active Living* programme is the heavy emphasis on increasing the physical activity levels of the inactive group, which is defined as people who fail to achieve 30 minutes of physical activity a day. Both *Green Prescription* and *Push Play* focus upon increasing awareness of the benefits from physical exercise and target those at most need of increasing their level of physical activity.

Table 17.1 Key SPARC Active Living/Active Children strategies

Programme	Strategy	Description	Focus	Key deliverers
ACTIVE LIVING	Push Play	Increase awareness of and motivation to undertake physical activity	In-active group	Promotional campaign
	Green Prescription	Enables general practitioners and practice nurses to prescribe physical activity to a patient	In-active group	RSTs
	No Exceptions	Strategy aimed at guiding agencies in provision of recreation and sports opportunities for disabled people	Disabled persons	n/a
	Push Play Parents	Provides advice and resources for parents to assist them in getting their children more active	Children aged 0–12 years	Parents
	He Oranga Poutama	Aimed at increasing physical activity levels of Māori	Māori in the 0–5 years age group	Iwi authorities, RSTs, Kaiwhakaheres
ACTIVE CHILDREN	Active Schools	Aim is to increase levels of physical activity through developing physically active culture within primary schools	Primary school-aged children	Schools and RSTs
	Active Schools – SportFit	Aim is to improve delivery of physical activity, sports and health programmes and increase opportunity to participate in sports and physical activity	Secondary school children 13–18 years of age	Schools and RSTs
	Mission On	A cross-government initiative including ministry of Education, Health and Youth Affairs. Includes both national and targeted programmes and aims to embed healthy behaviours for post-school living	Youth	A wide range including general practitioners, RSTs, schools and local government
	Active Movement	Teaches fundamental movement skills	Under 5 years of age	RSTs

The focus on inactive people was also evident in recent research commissioned by SPARC, which aimed to explore the obstacles to physical activity. The target group for this research was the 45 per cent of the New Zealand population who are not physically active but who do have some intention in the next six months of becoming active. While *Push Play* has been credited as being very successful in raising awareness of the key physical activity messages, its influence in increasing participation has been questioned (van Aalst *et al.* 2003: 16–17). This may in part explain the recent change in the focus of *Push Play* from an initiative focused solely on increasing awareness of the benefits of physical activity to motivating people to take action in physical activity (Deloitte 2006).

The increasing importance of health as a motivator for government is also evident in the recently implemented *Mission On* programme. While this initiative addresses the post-school group as well as youth (0–24 age group), a key focus of this programme is upon increasing physical activity and education regarding healthy nutrition, signalling a further expansion in regard to the type of programmes and initiatives developed by SPARC. What is evident is an apparent lack of focus on mass sport and recreational sport:

> We haven't really done anything on how do you develop grassroots sport and that is increasingly on our agenda.
>
> *(Interview: A senior SPARC official, October 2006)*

The 'stretching' of objectives, has drawn government resources towards opposite ends of the activity continuum with an emphasis on elite sport and physical activity (particularly amongst youth) taking priority. As a result, the development of strategies aimed at increasing and maintaining general adult participation in sport and physical recreation have for the most part been overlooked by SPARC. The absence of government policy aimed at the development of grass-roots sport is also driven by a lack of clarity and information on how to address this area:

> Elite and youth [is the current focus] and if we can be criticised and we can, we have tended to get drawn to the two ends of the spectrum so we are driven much more this way to elite. Yes, the whole Push Play has been a big focus. What we are busy talking about internally is how do we develop sport at grassroots level?
>
> *(Interview: A senior SPARC official, October 2006)*

Recognition of the emphasis that has been placed on physical activity, to the detriment of physical recreation, and a renewed prioritisation of sport and physical recreation was highlighted in SPARC's latest planning document where over the next three years a focus will be upon:

> supporting sport and physical recreation in New Zealand. Rather than a general approach to physical activity, we will be putting greater emphasis on delivering physical activity opportunities through sport and recreation. This will mean more of a focus on outdoor recreation than has been apparent in the past.
>
> *(SPARC 2008a: 2)*

The apparent lack of urgency in creating a policy aimed at increasing adult participation in sport appears to be also fuelled by the expectation that taking part in sport or physical activity is the responsibility of the individual. Given the neo-liberal approach that New Zealand has embraced it is not surprising to observe that responsibility for taking part in sport and physical activity rests with the individual, not the state. As explained by a senior RST official, the expectation is that once people leave school they will pay for their own sporting and recreational activities:

> I think traditionally it [participation in sport] has been left to people. If we take 18 year old plus, they are either in tertiary or working and therefore it's over to them to join the clubs or the RSTs or their clubs or activities. It is more in their hands to do it.
>
> *(Interview: October 2006)*

Not only did the establishment of SPARC signal an increase in sports development activity and growing recognition of the importance of sport to the government but, more importantly, this was supported by a significant increase in crown funding. From a relatively modest contribution of NZ$2.7 million in 2001/02, government funding increased to over NZ$58.5 million in 2008, while total overall funding (including sources other than the crown) increased from NZ$35.6 million to NZ$105.3 million in the corresponding period (SPARC 2002b, 2008b). Not surprisingly, the increased funding from government had a flow-on effect to a number of other organisations in the sports sector. Resourcing of all three key areas has risen steadily since 2002 with funding for 'being the most active nation' more than doubling between 2003/2004 and 2007/2008 (see Table 17.2).

The significance of NGBs and RSTs in the development of sport and recreational activity has become increasingly important in delivering government outcomes with 53 per cent of SPARC's investment in the sport sector allocated to NGBs and 25 per cent allocated to RSTs in 2007/2008 (SPARC 2008b). For some RSTs this has resulted in up to 40 per cent of their funding emanating from SPARC. While this new stream of revenue has been welcomed by some RSTs it has also created tensions with regard to how RSTs are perceived by the community as explained by a senior RST official:

> The other thing we have to be mindful of is we do have to get money from the community. The community can get a little funny at times if they think you are getting too much from government, then [they think] 'Do you need our money?'
>
> *(Interview: October 2006)*

Table 17.2 SPARC actual total funding (NZD million)

Financial year	Total funding (for SPARC)	Crown funding (vote funding – sport and recreation)[1]	Winning in events that matter to New Zealanders	Being the most active nation	Having the most effective sports and recreation systems
2001/2002	35.6	2.7	n/a	n/a	n/a
2002/2003	42.2	9.8	n/a	n/a	n/a
2003/2004	53.8	24.9	22.0	19.8	12.0
2004/2005	72.2	36.8	25.3	32.4	14.47
2005/2006	84.3	44.2	31.1	35.9	17.26
2006/2007	98.4	59.4	35.4	34.8	19.6
2007/2008	105.3	58.5	38.4	37.2	20.2

Note: 1 Does not include funding from other government agencies
Source: adapted from Sport and Recreation New Zealand (2002b); Sport and Recreation New Zealand (2003); Sport and Recreation New Zealand (2004); Sport and Recreation New Zealand (2005); Sport and Recreation New Zealand (2006a); Sport and Recreation New Zealand (2007); Sport and Recreation New Zealand (2008b)

While local government was identified as an important provider of sporting opportunities and facilities, funding from SPARC in 2007/2008 was only two per cent of SPARC's investment in key stakeholders. Despite this comparatively low level of crown funding, local government plays a key role in the development of sport in New Zealand, primarily through the provision of sport facilities and, together with RSTs, the development of recreational sport in the community. Increasingly local government is moving away from merely being a provider of facilities and adopting a strictly user-pays approach to the provision of facilities and services – an approach that was adopted by local government during the economic shift of the 1980s.

While elite sport development objectives can be more easily identified and measured (such as numbers of medals won or success in international competitions), the effectiveness of policy initiatives towards increasing participation in sport and/or physical activity remains somewhat unclear due to the lack of longitudinal data. Furthermore, there is difficulty in linking changes in behaviour to particular sports development programmes (Piggin *et al.* 2009). The lack of a survey tool to establish levels of participation has frequently been highlighted as an area of concern, resulting in a *New Zealand Sport and Physical Activity* survey being commissioned for 2007/2008. Given the relatively recent introduction of the surveys it is too soon to identify trends in levels of participation.

Until recently, information on participation levels in New Zealand has been based upon the *Sport and Physical Recreation Survey* that was conducted in 1997/1998, 1998/1999 and 2000/2001. The most recent national activity survey was undertaken in 2007/2008, of which only initial data have been released. Results indicate that participation levels have remained relatively stable between the 2000/2001 and 2007/2008 surveys with the percentage of adults who participated in at least one sport or recreation activity over the previous 12 months decreasing slightly from 97.9 per cent to 95.8 per cent (SPARC 2008c). The 2007/2008 Survey aims to provide a baseline from which future changes can be measured. In 2007/2008 the physical activity levels achieved by New Zealanders (over the age of 16) reached 48.2 per cent (where they participated in at least 30 minutes of moderate intensity physical activity on five or more days of the week) (SPARC 2008c). The top three activities participated in over the previous 12 months for men and women were identical. Walking and gardening were the two most popular activities, while the third (and most popular sporting activity) was swimming.

Research recently conducted by the Secondary Schools Sports Council indicated that the numbers of secondary school children participating in school sport had declined from 56 per cent in 2000 to 51 per cent in 2008. Furthermore, the decline in participation for girls (from 55 per cent in 2000 to 48 per cent in 2008) is higher than that for boys (from 59 per cent in 2000 to 54 per cent in 2008) over the same time period (Secondary School Sports Council 2009). It is difficult to establish the extent to which the relatively recent increase in sports development programmes has impacted upon participation levels. However, it would appear that, while adult participation rates have remained relatively stable between 1998 and 2008, the declining levels of sports participation amongst secondary school children remain a concern.

Alongside the drive to increase participation has been rapid development and investment in elite sport. Investment in elite sport development by government has been closely aligned to its capacity to contribute to a key government goal of building national identity (Collins 2008). As Mallard (Minster for Sport, Recreation and Fitness) explained, 'elite sport and participation in international competition gives us a sense of who we are as New Zealanders, not only this, it lets the rest of the world see who we are' (Interview: October 2006). However, success in elite sport is also considered to assist in achieving other policy-related outcomes including, a) creating a healthy image for marketing New Zealand goods abroad, b) helping attract high-profile sports events to New Zealand, and c) encouraging New Zealanders to be more active (SPARC 2009).

What remains unclear, however, is how the contribution to sport with regard to these outcomes will be measured.

An increasingly business-focused approach has been adopted with regard to sports development since the inception of SPARC, with NGBs and other sporting bodies expected to be able to demonstrate a return on investment (Collins 2008). Along with the rapid increase in investment has been the requirement for NGBs to adopt more effective management systems and processes. The recently developed High Performance Strategy sets out the direction of elite sport development from 2006 to 2012. This new and coordinated approach to elite sport development has resulted in a focus on a relatively narrow band of sports with investment by SPARC now targeted at sports that have the ability to deliver multiple Olympic and Commonwealth medals (SPARC 2006b). The development of elite sport has resulted in national policies being developed that aim to increase the level of coaching, extend the emphasis on the use of sports science, build an effective talent identification system and develop a competition programme that maximises the possibility of elite NZ athletes competing in both international and national competitions. The changes to elite sport development have also resulted in the prioritisation of (Olympic) sports for funding, a huge shift from the funding regimes of previous years. This increasingly hands-on approach of government to elite sport development raises issues regarding the (lack of) autonomy or sporting organisations (Collins 2008).

The influence of SPARC upon NGBs and RSTs in regard to increasing physical activity levels of youth is also evident. NGBs in particular are considered to be the lead agencies for increasing the numbers of participants in their respective sports. In May 2005, SPARC allocated extra funding for the establishment of regional sports development officers within NGBs with the aim of increasing sports participation rates within local communities and encouraging young people to keep playing after they left school (Mallard 2005). Despite this programme, the comparatively small level of funding allocated to sports for increasing participation would indicate that the development of elite sport remains more of a concern than grass-roots or recreational sport. While funding to NGBs has increased, the emphasis is placed upon the development of elite sport in NGBs:

> the bulk [of resources] definitely comes from SPARC they are our major funder [and] contribute between 50 and 60 per cent of our income. We are heavily reliant on them and the bulk of that income is directed to high performance because that is what they are [interested in] investing [in].
>
> *(Interview: A senior NGB official, 24 October 2006)*

It is difficult to accurately identify the level of resourcing directly allocated to NGBs for increasing participation levels due to the structure of the funding streams. While sports development funding allocated to NGBs is considerably less than funding allocated to developing high performance, it is also focused on a number of different areas, only one of which is developing grass-roots sport:

> We get $250,000 a year annually [for sports development]. That's purely as I see it for coaching and development and administration. Now that's separate. We get $1million or nearly $1million for high performance, that's the 2 sums of money that you get. And then there are lots of coaching scholarships but that's all part of the elite programme.
>
> *(Interview: A senior NGB official, October 2006)*

As highlighted earlier, SPARC identified the need to build the capability of sporting organisations to assist in developing an effective and efficient sports delivery network that will assist in keeping New Zealanders involved in sport and physical recreation (2008a). Improved governance and management practices were seen as a sound base upon which the goals of achieving increased participation levels and success in elite sport could be based. In doing this SPARC insisted that NGBs improve their ability to respond to the changing needs of the sector and those involved in sport. This required attracting professional people to organisations that had previously been managed by volunteers while also ensuring the governance and structure of NGBs enhanced rather than inhibited the successful operation of the NGB:

> If you get somebody into the sport whose job it is to run it, with the right mandate and governance structure they will start to solve those problems [and run it better] rather than us sitting in Wellington trying to do that.
>
> *(Interview: A senior SPARC official, October 2006)*

Increased funding of sporting organisations by SPARC was combined with an increased demand for greater accountability and the need for partner agencies to demonstrate a return on investment, which was to be assessed against the ability to assist in achieving SPARC's mission (SPARC 2002a). Most noticeably, in 2006, the allocation of sports development funding to *Athletics New Zealand* was withdrawn due to its inability to impact upon participation levels in the sport. What is perhaps highlighted is the lack of robust baseline data as well as difficulty in understanding the best way in which participation information will be measured. Funding agreements were to be signalled well in advance by SPARC to enhance sporting organisations' and partner agencies' ability to plan more effectively and over a longer period. From the outset SPARC stated that it would assist national organisations 'which demonstrate they can assist us in achieving our mission … the return from these investments will be the subject of negotiation and will be documented in new contracts with SPARC ' (SPARC 2002a: 10).

Striving for increased efficiency amongst sporting organisations by SPARC meant that organisations that did not have, or did not demonstrate, an improved governance structure were less likely to receive support or resourcing from SPARC. The drive by SPARC for more effective management structures and practices amongst NGBs appears to have precedence over policies aimed at advancing their sport. This is not surprising given the incentives from SPARC:

> Well yeah, I suppose our focus at the moment is the implementation and the structures, governance area. But hot on its heels we want to be producing policies that strengthen our clubs and strengthen the membership level.
>
> *(Interview: A senior NGB official, October 2006)*

The landscape of sport in New Zealand over the last 15 years or so has undergone rapid and significant change. For much of the twentieth century the development of sport remained an area where an ethos of voluntarism and autonomy of sporting organisations was considered paramount. Since the late 1990s there has been an increasing acceptance and legitimisation of government intervention in sport with little resistance from sporting organisations. The establishment of a single crown entity in 2002 signalled the increasing salience of sport to government. Mandated to lead the development of sport in New Zealand, SPARC has introduced a number of programmes to lead and shape the development of sport. Since its establishment there has been an acknowledged emphasis on physical activity and youth and elite sport development programmes, with adult participation in sport being largely overlooked as an area of concern. Three major themes have emerged with regard to sports development over the last 15 years or so.

First has been the emphasis that has been placed on increasing physical activity while grass-roots sport and physical recreation have been somewhat overlooked. The range of programmes that have been developed by SPARC, and implemented through a range of non-governmental organisations, have primarily focused upon increasing levels of physical activity amongst youth (along with other high-risk groups). The emphasis on promoting physical activity appears to have been driven by the need to achieve health-related outcomes, a key factor in government's decision to invest in sport. It would appear that the tension and uncertainty that were evident during the 1980s with regard to the level of support for sport and physical recreation have largely remained. However, recent commitments by SPARC to focus on physical recreation and sport rather than the wider sphere of physical activity may indicate a renewed emphasis on the development of sport and physical recreation for all.

The second theme relates to the incredibly business-focused environment in which the development of sport must operate. Sporting organisations must now demonstrate effective governance structures and a return on investment, with failure to achieve agreed objectives sometimes resulting in funding levels being reduced. This not only relates to elite sport development (see Collins 2008) but also to funding allocated to increasing participation levels. However, there remains an acceptance that non-governmental organisations are struggling with changing patterns of behaviour in relation to participation in sport and physical recreation and that there is a lacuna with regard to accurate longitudinal data that is causally linked with sports development programmes (SPARC 2008a; Piggin et al. 2009). Difficulty in measuring the effectiveness of programmes aimed at increasing sports and recreational activity remains a challenge with a national survey aimed at assessing these levels only recently being instigated.

The final theme to emerge relates to the range of social objectives to which the development of sport is increasingly linked. While policy documents and interviews with key governmental and non-governmental senior staff identify sports development with a number of social policy objectives, the two dominant areas have been the promotion of health and national identity. Sport is a relative newcomer to having significant government interest directed at it; it is thus perhaps not surprising that there continues to be some uncertainty regarding the boundaries and direction of sports development at a national level.

Notes

1 National governing body refers to the national organisation for particular sports.
2 Semi-autonomous state agency that forms part of New Zealand's state sector and performs governmental functions.
3 Regional sports trusts are community-based organisations which seek to increase regional levels of physical activity and strengthen regional sport and physical recreation infrastructures.

References

Chalip, L. (1996) 'Critical policy analysis: The illustrative case of New Zealand sport policy development', *Journal of Sport Management*, 10, 310–24.
Collins, C. (2000) 'Australia and New Zealand'. In J. Coakley and E. Dunning (eds) *Handbook of Sports Studies,* London: Sage, 525–9.
Collins, C. and Downey, J. (2000) 'Politics, government and sport'. In C. Collins (ed.) *Sport in New Zealand Society,* Palmerston North: Dunmore Press.
Collins, C. and Stuart, M. (1994) 'Politics and sport in New Zealand'. In L. Trenberth and C. Collins (eds), *Sport Management in New Zealand: An Introduction,* Palmerston North: Dunmore Press, 43–58.

Collins, S. (2008) 'New Zealand'. In B. Houlihan and M. Green (eds) *Comparative Elite Sport Development; Systems, Structures and Public Policy*, Oxford: Elsevier.

Deloitte. (2006) *Sport and Recreation New Zealand. A Review of the Performance of SPARC during the 2002–2006 Period*, New Zealand: Deloitte.

Garrett, T. (1980). 'Government – its role in recreation'. In Shallcrass, J., Larken, B. and Stothart, B. (eds) *Recreation Reconsidered into the Eighties* (pp 41–5), New Zealand: Auckland Regional Authority and New Zealand Council for Recreation and Sport.

Hindson, A., Cushman, G. and Gidlow, B. (1994). 'Historical and social perspectives on sport in New Zealand'. In L. Trenberth and C. Collins (eds) *Sport Management in New Zealand: An Introduction*, Palmerston North: Dunmore Press.

James, C. (1997) 'The policy revolution 1984–93'. In R. Miller (ed.) *New Zealand Politics in Transition*, Auckland: Oxford University Press, 13–24.

Mallard, T. (2005) *Volunteers and Regions get Sport Boost*. Retrieved 13 February 2006, from www.sparc.org.nz/News/Volunteers-and-regions-get-sport-boost

Ministerial Taskforce. (2001) 'Getting set for an active nation: review of the Sport, Fitness and Leisure Ministerial Taskforce', Wellington, New Zealand.

Perkins, H., Devlin, P., Simmons, D. and Batty, R. (1993) 'Recreation and Tourism'. In A. Memon and H. C. Perkins (eds) *Environmental Planning in New Zealand*, Palmerston North: Dumore Press.

Piggin, J., Jackson, S. and Lewis, M. (2009) 'Knowledge, power and politics. Contesting "evidence based" national sport policy', *International Review for the Sociology of Sport, 44*(1), 87–101.

Russell, D., Allen, J. and Wilson, N. (1996). 'New Zealand'. In P. De Knop, L. Engstrom, B. Skirstad and M. Weiss (eds) *Worldwide Trends in Youth Sport*, Champaign, IL: Human Kinetics.

Sam, M. (2003) 'What's the big idea? Reading the rhetoric of a national sport policy process', *Sociology of Sport Journal, 20*(3), 189–213.

——(2005) 'The makers of sport policy: A (task)force to be reckoned with', *Sociology of Sport Journal, 22*(1), 78.

Sam, M. and Jackson, S.J. (2004) 'Sport policy development in New Zealand: Paradoxes of an integrative paradigm', *International Review for the Sociology of Sport, 39*(2), 205.

Secondary School Sports Council. (2009) *Secondary Schools Sports Representation Census 2008*, Wellington: Author.

Sport Development Inquiry Committee. (1985) *Sport on the Move: Report to the Minister of Recreation and Sport*, Wellington: Government Print.

Stothart, B. (2000) 'The development of sport administration in New Zealand: From kitchen table to computer'. In C. Collins (ed.), *Sport in New Zealand Society,* Palmerston North: Dunmore Press, 85–98.

SPARC (2002a) *Our Vision, Our Direction*, Wellington: Sport and Recreation New Zealand.

——(2002b) *Annual Report for the Year Ended June 2002*, New Zealand: Author.

——(2003) *Annual Report for the Year Ended June 2003*, New Zealand: Author.

——(2004) *Annual Report for the Year Ended June 2004*, New Zealand: Author.

——(2005) *Annual Report for the Year Ended June 2005*, New Zealand: Author.

——(2006a) *Annual Report for the Year Ended June 2006*, New Zealand: Author.

——(2006b) *Melbourne 2006. A Review of New Zealand's Performance at the 2006 Melbourne Commonwealth Games*, New Zealand: Author.

——(2007) *Annual Report for the Year Ended June 2007*, New Zealand: Author.

——(2008a) *Statement of Intent 2008–11*, New Zealand: Author.

——(2008b) *Annual Report for the Year Ended June 2008*, New Zealand: Author.

——(2008c) *Sport, Recreation and Physical Activity Participation among New Zealand Adults*, Wellington: Sport and Recreation New Zealand.

——(2009) 'High Performance Strategy'. Retrieved 24 June 2009, from www.sparc.org.nz/high-performance/high-performance-strategy

van Aalst, I., Kazakov, D. and McLean, G. (2003) *SPARC Facts. Results of the New Zealand Sport and Physical Activity Surveys (1997–2001)*, New Zealand: Sport and Recreation New Zealand.

18

Sports development and adult sport participation in Canada

Lucie Thibault

Sports participation leads to important health, social, and economic benefits for Canadians. The link between sports participation and health benefits has been consistently drawn in the literature. For example, sport and physical activity's overall contribution to healthy living, decreased incidences of diabetes, obesity, and heart disease have been underscored in the literature (Bloom *et al.* 2005; Donnelly and Kidd 2003; Katzmarzyk *et al.* 2000; Plotnikoff *et al.* 2004). Sport has also been considered an important tool for social and cultural development. For example, sport's role in national identity, national pride, and national unity has clearly been established in the Canadian context (Bloom *et al.* 2006; Macintosh 1996; Mills 1998; Sport Matters Group 2006). Sport has also been linked to social cohesion and sound character development (Bloom *et al.* 2008; Siegenthaler and Leticia Gonzalez 1997; Weiss 2008).

Regarding sport's contribution to the economy, studies have demonstrated the level of spending by Canadians in sport and sport-related endeavours totalling almost $16 billion[1] annually. This spending represented approximately 2.2 per cent of consumer spending and 1.2 per cent of the Gross Domestic Product in 2004. Furthermore, sports accounted for 2 per cent of the jobs in Canada in 2004. According to a Conference Board of Canada report authored by Bloom *et al.* (2005), consumer spending in sport and sport-related goods and services has increased since 1990. Given the health, social, cultural, and economic importance of sport in the lives of Canadians, one can easily understand why all levels of government (federal, provincial/ territorial, and local) remain involved in various aspects (e.g. leadership, funding, programming, and facilities) of sports participation and sports development.

The following chapter focuses on adults' involvement and participation in sport in Canada. Participation in sport for adult Canadians has been addressed in relation to three distinct roles: active participants, sport volunteers/leaders/administrators, and attendees/spectators (Bloom *et al.* 2005; Ifedi 2008). Therefore, in this chapter, adult involvement in sports participation is addressed in relation to these three roles.

Research about sports participation has focused predominantly on youth involvement (Côté *et al.* 2008; Fraser-Thomas and Côté 2009; Ulrich-French and Smith 2009). This research has targeted increased understanding of youth's participation patterns, motives, and interests in sport. The role of adults in assuming leadership and organisational positions for youth sport has also been addressed (Bloom *et al.* 2005; Clark 2008; Donnelly and Kidd 2003; Ifedi 2008);

however, studies on sports participation rates among adults have been essentially overlooked in the literature (Casper *et al.* 2007; Davey *et al.* 2009). As explained by Casper *et al.* (2007: 253), 'although sport commitment has received widespread theoretical and empirical attention over the past 15 years, its application to adult sport participants has gone largely ignored'. This chapter covers Canadian adult participation in sport and the various roles undertaken in sport by these individuals. In the next section, the focus is on adult active participation in sport.

Adults as active participants

Interest in, and focus on, sports participation among Canadians have increased in recent years due largely to concerns regarding the impact that inactivity is having on their health. In recent media accounts, Canadians' levels of sports participation have been cause for concerns (cf. Brach 2008; CTV 2008; Ferguson 2009; Proudfoot 2008). These media articles were reacting to a survey report from Statistics Canada. In this report, Ifedi (2008) discussed declining rates in sports participation[2] among Canadians aged 15 years and older. Based on two previous Statistics Canada surveys undertaken in 1992 and 1998, Ifedi compared the participation rates of Canadians with data from 2005. He reported that sports participation went from 45.1 per cent in 1992 to 34.2 per cent in 1998, and to 28.0 per cent in 2005. For females, the greatest decrease in sports participation occurred in the 25–34 age category. For males, the greatest decline occurred during the teenage years (i.e. 15–18 years of age). The decline in sports participation has been attributed largely to the ageing population. As reported in the survey, the population 65 years old and over represented 13.1 per cent of the total population – an increase from 8.1 per cent in 1971 and 11.6 per cent in 1991. As Canadians become older, they tend to decrease their involvement in sport. Other factors attributed to decreased sports participation among adults included: time pressures, family responsibilities, careers, lack of interest, and participation in non-active leisure such as watching television and Internet use (Ifedi 2008).

In addition, factors such as gender, education and income were found to affect sports participation. With respect to gender, men's levels of sports participation are higher than women's. Attainment of higher education is correlated to greater involvement in active participation and individuals with higher income levels are also more likely to participate in sport than individuals with low income (Bloom *et al.* 2005; Ifedi 2008). With the relationship between education and income and the costs associated with sports participation, it is not surprising that adults living in poverty may not have the discretionary funds to pay membership fees and for the equipment and clothing necessary for their sports participation and/or their children's sports participation (cf. Frisby *et al.* 2007; Taylor and Doherty 2005). In fact, organisations such as KidSport Canada created in 1993 (KidSport Canada 2008) and Canadian Tire Jumpstart created in 2005 (Canadian Tire 2009) are addressing the expensive nature of sports participation by offering grants to low-income parents to cover the costs of registration, membership, sports equipment, and travel costs for their children's involvement in organised sports. For adults living on low income, some local and regional initiatives have been developed to facilitate their sports participation. These initiatives include subsidies to cover the costs of registration and fees of sport and recreation programmes, subsidies for child care while parents are participating in sport and recreation programmes in low-income neighbourhoods, and leisure programmes developed in conjunction with local partners (e.g. social services agencies, housing associations, and local public health units) (Donnelly and Coakley 2002; Frisby and Fenton 1998; Frisby and Hoeber 2002).

The trend of diminishing levels of sports participation for adults was also discussed in another study. In their examination of how sports participation impacts the economy, health, social cohesion, and skill development, Bloom *et al.* (2005) explained that Canadians are typically unaware of the power of sport. The authors further argued that this lack of awareness may be the reason 'why we are experiencing a national decline in active sport participation' (Bloom *et al.* 2005: 1).

Ifedi (2008) pointed out that declining sports participation does not necessarily mean that Canadians are not physically active. Canadians may undertake regular exercise and physical activities not subsumed under the definition of sport used in the study. For example, in the survey, regular exercise classes, jogging and yoga were not considered as sports participation (Ifedi 2008). In other words, Canadian adults may have chosen fitness (through formal or informal settings) over membership in sports clubs and participation in organised sport in general. However, Bloom *et al.* (2005: 1) argued that 'Canadians were not finding adequate alternatives to sport to keep them fit'. As a result, 'in recent years, more people have become obese or overweight, with negative implications for health' (Bloom *et al.* 2005: 1).

Government initiatives have targeted the elimination of barriers to enhance sports participation for all Canadians (Canadian Heritage 2002a, 2002b, 2007; Sport Canada 2004). One such initiative is the *Canadian Sport Policy*. As noted in the *Canadian Sport Policy*, 'barriers to participation in sport [should] be identified and eliminated, making sport accessible to all' (Canadian Heritage 2002a: 8). Published in 2002, the *Canadian Sport Policy* is focused on the achievement of four goals: enhancing participation, enhancing excellence, enhancing capacity, and enhancing interaction. Sports excellence and sports participation are foundational goals of Canada's sports system while capacity and interaction are support goals for these two foundational goals. Enhanced participation refers to increasing the number of Canadians 'from all segments of society [to be] involved in quality sport activities at all levels and in all forms of participation' (Canadian Heritage 2002a: 16). Enhanced excellence refers to expanding 'the pool of talented athletes' so that they can achieve 'world class results at the highest levels of international competition through fair and ethical means' (Canadian Heritage 2002a: 17). Enhanced capacity refers to 'the essential components of the [sport] system required to achieve the sport participation and excellence goals of this policy – such as coach/instructor education, facilities, sport medicine, sport science, research and the use of technology – [to] meet the needs of athletes/participants' (Canadian Heritage 2002a: 18). Enhanced interaction involves 'increase[d] collaboration, communication, and cooperation amongst the partners in the sport community, government and the private sector, which in turn will lead to a more effective Canadian sport system' (Canadian Heritage 2002a: 19).

Following an unprecedented pan-Canadian consultative process in the late 1990s and early 2000s, the *Canadian Sport Policy* was developed and leaders of all provincial and territorial governments agreed to implement this policy within their jurisdiction. Although the *Canadian Sport Policy* focuses on enhancing sports participation among all Canadians, adults are not specifically among the target groups identified for sports participation initiatives. As outlined in the Canadian Sport Policy, 'certain groups such as girls and women, people with a disability, Aboriginal peoples, and visible minorities continue to be under-represented in the Canadian sport system as athletes/participants and as leaders' (Canadian Heritage 2002a: 8). As a result, a number of initiatives focusing on enhancing sports participation for members of these groups are financially supported by federal and provincial/territorial governments. This does not mean that individuals who do not 'belong' to these target groups are not encouraged to enhance their level of sports participation; however, preference for financial support is given to programmes and initiatives that focus on girls and women, people with a disability, Aboriginal peoples, and visible minorities.

Sport Canada's[3] involvement in sport includes the funding of the sports system in the form of an initiative entitled *Sport Support Program* and another funding programme in collaboration with provincial/territorial governments called *Bilateral Agreements*. The *Sport Support Program* involves financially supporting national sport organisations[4] and national multi-sport/multi-service organisations[5] to enhance high-performance sports programmes as well as sports participation programmes (Sport Canada 2009). The *Sport Support Program* also includes a *Sport Participation Project Stream* component where national sports organisations can apply for funds for projects that focus on enhancing sports participation. This project stream component does give funding preference 'to projects that target one or several of the following groups: children and youth, including those from under-represented groups, such as girls and young women, Aboriginal peoples, persons with a disability, visible minorities, youth at risk, and the economically disadvantaged' (Sport Canada 2004: 4). Sport Canada's concerns with children and youth's participation in sport appears to be based on the premise that lack of attention on this group of Canadians could eventually produce 'in the next 10 to 15 years from now a generation of inactive adults, with many afflicted by ailments caused by inactivity' (Sport Canada 2004: 8). These priorities have been further reiterated in federal and provincial/territorial policy documents guiding the implementation of the *Canadian Sport Policy* (cf. Canadian Heritage 2002b, 2007).

The *Bilateral Agreements* are negotiated contracts between the Government of Canada and each province and territory to fund programmes and initiatives that ensure the successful implementation of the *Canadian Sport Policy* throughout the country (see for example, MacLean 2008a, 2008b; Canadian Heritage 2002b, 2007, 2009). These agreements are particularly focused on the policy goal of enhancing sports participation for Canadians. As part of the programme, any funds invested by the Government of Canada, through Sport Canada, must be matched (with new funds) by the provinces and territories, thus leveraging more resources for sports participation. Each province and territory negotiates its own agreement with the federal government. As such, provinces and territories can customise their needs and wants with respect to sports participation in their jurisdiction. It is important to note that priorities for actions have been set through meetings with federal and provincial/territorial political leaders and bureaucrats responsible for sport (see Canadian Heritage 2002b, 2007). In its initial year, 2003–4, the federal government invested $1.78 million to provincial and territorial governments through the *Bilateral Agreements* – resulting in a $3.56 million investment in sports participation. In subsequent years, the federal government's share of these agreements was: $3.6 million in 2004–5; $4.56 million in 2005–6; $4.85 million in 2006–7; and $5.03 million in 2007–8.[6] It is important to note that most of this funding is earmarked to enhance sports participation among the target groups identified (e.g. girls and women, people with a disability, Aboriginal peoples, and visible minorities). As such, adults outside of these groups are not a priority for this funding. Examples of initiatives funded through the *Bilateral Agreements* include: community-based sport discovery and initiation programmes; school-based sports education and development programmes; programmes aimed at increasing sports participation for seniors and adults with disabilities; and programmes to promote quality, safety, and accessibility of sports in the community.

In addition to the *Canadian Sport Policy* and Sport Canada's sports participation funding through the *Sport Support Program* and the *Bilateral Agreements*, another programme targets lifelong sports participation. As a national initiative to address Canadian involvement in sports participation beyond the *Canadian Sport Policy*, the *Long-term Athlete Development* model (also referred to as *Canadian Sport for Life* and *No Accidental Champion*) was developed by the Canadian Sport Centres[7] and integrated in national sport organisations' strategies (Canadian Sport Centres 2005a, 2005b). Even though the *Long-term Athlete Development* model was originally developed for high-performance purposes (Balyi 2001), it includes a component for individuals who may not have the necessary skills and talent to pursue high-performance sport or for individuals who choose not to pursue a 'career' in high-performance sport. In the *Long-term Athlete Development* model, seven stages are identified (i.e. Active Start, FUNdamentals, Learning to Train, Training to Train, Training to Compete, Training to Win and Active for Life). The last two stages of the model, 'training to win' and 'active for life', target adults. 'Training to win' targets high-performance athletes who are in the final stage of athletic preparation for major competitions, while 'active for life' is the stage for any individual who transitions from competitive sport to sports participation. As such, it is the last stage that targets adult participation in lifelong sport endeavours. It is the intent of the *Long-term Athlete Development* model to ensure 'that a significantly high proportion of Canadians from all segments of society are involved in quality sport activities at all levels and in all forms of participation' (Canadian Sport Centres 2005a: 47). As explained in the *Long-term Athlete Development* model report, 'a positive experience in sport is the key to retaining athletes after they leave the competition stream' (Canadian Sport Centres 2005a: 44). As with the *Canadian Sport Policy*, the *Long-term Athlete Development* model does not focus solely or specifically on adult sports participation but adults' active involvement in sport is covered in these initiatives. It is also important to note that the implementation of the *Long-term Athlete Development* model involves the collaboration of all sport and sport-related organisations in the system (e.g. federal, provincial, and local governments; national, provincial, and local sport organisations; schools, clubs, and community sport and recreation organisations).

In addition to active participation in sport, adults also play a role in the organisation of children's sport and they are also spectators of sport events. In the following section, adults' volunteer involvement in the leadership and organisation of children's sport is discussed.

Adults as sport volunteers/leaders/administrators

Adults' involvement in the organisation of children's sport is an important element for the operation of local sports programmes. As Clark noted,

> Parents are often involved in their children's sports, whether it is on the sidelines shouting encouragement or being more formally involved as a coach, referee, organizer or fundraiser for a team, league or sports club. They also support their children's sports activities.
>
> *(2008: 55)*

To Clark's list of roles held by parents, one could also add their involvement in funding their children's sports' endeavours, the transportation of their children to and from practice and competitions, and their emotional support.

Although active sports participation for Canadian adults has decreased in recent years, adults' levels of involvement as volunteers in Canadian sport increased between 1998 and 2005. In fact, the number of adults involved as amateur coaches increased slightly (1.6 per cent) between 1998 and 2005. Approximately 1.8 million Canadians were involved as amateur coaches in 2005. Volunteering was up by 18 per cent in 2005 (from 1998) when over 2 million adults volunteered in administrative or support positions in amateur sport (Ifedi 2008). This trend of increased involvement however, does not apply to the roles of referees, officials and umpires. Much to the chagrin of leaders of sport organisations, the statistics for referees, officials and umpires decreased by 15 per cent between 1998 and 2005. Sports leaders counted on approximately 800,000 volunteer referees, officials and umpires in 2005 instead of 937,000 individuals in 1998 (Ifedi 2008). Issues with sports officiating have been the object of previous studies (Dorsch and Paskevich 2007; Trudel *et al.* 1996). Dorsch and Paskevich (2007) demonstrated that ice hockey officials underwent a number of stressful situations in their roles. Threats of physical abuse, confrontation with coaches, and verbal abuse by coaches, athletes and spectators were examples of sources of stress for officials and contributed to their feelings of burnout. These issues are not necessarily confined to the sport of ice hockey. Similar issues have been reported by soccer referees, and leaders of national, provincial and local soccer organisations are trying to address the problem (Anderson 2008; Hunter 2001; Lewis 2009). National sport organisations along with Sports Officials Canada are working to address officiating issues and develop strategies to retain current sports officials and recruit more adults to these positions.

Adult involvement in children's organised sport activities is important particularly when safety and supervision are issues. In cases where children need to learn specific skills to undertake a sport (e.g. skating, swimming and skiing), adults play an important role in providing the structure and infrastructure for children to learn these skills in a safe environment. Adults' involvement in children's sports is extremely important. Without their involvement, organized sports for children would not exist as we know then. The nature and type of this involvement, however, are instrumental to the quality of children's experiences in sport. As noted by Donnelly and Kidd:

> In organized youth sports, perhaps the major determinants of the quality of the experience are the relationships with adults – parents, coaches, officials, and administrators. These relationships – and particularly the quality of coaching and mentoring – can realize or dash the expectations for youth sport. The values and practices employed by adults can be powerfully enabling and enriching, or can drive someone out of sport for a lifetime.
>
> *(2003: 10)*

In their report, Donnelly and Kidd (2003) discussed the results of a Canadian poll on sport undertaken by the Canadian Centre for Ethics and Sport and Decima Research, where poor coaching/supervision, too much focus on winning and parental influence/pressure were identified as factors contributing to children's withdrawal from participating in organised sport. In the following section, we discuss adults' involvement as spectators of sport events.

Adults as attendees/spectators

Adults' indirect and inactive involvement in sport has nearly doubled between 1992 and 2005. Ifedi reported data on indirect involvement in sport, more specifically as spectators of sports events. In 1992, five million Canadians reported involvement as spectators/attendees of amateur sports events. In 2005, 9.2 million adults claimed they watched amateur sports. With respect to professional sport spectatorship, other studies have demonstrated that, over a period of two years (2004 and 2005), nearly three million Canadians watch sports events while on trips (business and/or pleasure) of one or more nights (Lang Research 2007). The most popular sports for these Canadians to watch were ice hockey, baseball and basketball.

In another study (national household survey held in 2004) led by the Conference Board of Canada, Bloom *et al.* (2005) reported that more than 11 million Canadian adults attended amateur and professional sports events as spectators. This represented 45.4 per cent of adult Canadians and by far the largest proportion of involvement relative to the other two roles (active sports participants and volunteer leaders and administrators). In their study, Bloom *et al.* (2005) reported 4.6 million Canadian adults involved as sports volunteers while 7.7 million adult Canadians were involved as active participants. As such, most Canadian adults' involvement in sport appears to be in the role of spectator or attendee of sports events and competitions – an alarming trend given efforts devoted to increasing active participation in sport. In fact, 17 per cent (4.2 million adults) of the adult population reported that their attendance at sport events as spectators was their sole involvement in sport. Other adults reported being involved in sports spectating along with volunteering and/or actively participating in sport (Bloom *et al.* 2005). Sports' entertainment value along with its social and cultural importance are certainly underscored in these statistics, however, attendees of sports events do not achieve any physical health benefits from their hours of spectating.

Concluding remarks

As evident from Canadian federal government policy makers and programmers, adults are not the target of specific actions to enhance levels of sports participation. Even though the *Canadian Sport Policy* aims to enhance sports participation for all Canadians, priorities were set to focus on groups that have been considered traditionally under-served. These groups are girls and women, people with a disability, Aboriginal peoples, and visible minorities. From various studies and surveys undertaken regarding adult participation in sport, it is disconcerting to find that the majority of adults are involved in sport in essentially inactive roles – as volunteer leaders and administrators and as spectators and attendees of sports events. Even though, there is a sound rationale for investing funds and efforts for under-served groups to be encouraged to actively participate in sport, the fact remains that all Canadians need to increase their levels of active involvement in sport.

Adults play a crucial role in the sports system. In their various leadership roles (as parents, volunteers, administrators, coaches, officials), they ensure the seamless operation of children's sports clubs, teams, leagues and tournaments. In fact, without adults' and parents' involvement, children's organized sport would likely not exist. Although adults play an instrumental role in the development of amateur sport in general and in sport clubs, teams and leagues for children's sports endeavours, these adults (and the adults attending sports events as spectators) do not reap the health benefits of active participation in sport. With an increasing ageing population and increasing health care costs, adults need to be actively engaged in sport and sport-related activities.

Notes

1 All sums are in Canadian dollars.
2 It is important to note the narrow definition of sport used for Statistics Canada's survey. 'Sport is an activity that involves two or more participants engaging for the purpose of competition. Sport involves formal rules and procedures, requires tactics and strategies, specialized neuromuscular skills and a high degree of difficulty and effort' (Ifedi 2008: 15). This definition was slightly different from the one used in 1998 and 1992.
3 Sport Canada is the federal government department responsible for sport in Canada. It is located within the Department of Canadian Heritage. Its focus includes Canadian involvement in high performance sport and sports participation. For more information on Sport Canada's activities, please see http://pch.gc.ca/pgm/sc/index-eng.cfm
4 National single sport organisations include organisations such as Biathlon Canada, Hockey Canada, Canadian Gymnastics Federation, Equine Canada, Canadian Soccer Association, and Volleyball Canada.
5 Examples of multi-sport organisations include the Canadian Paralympic Committee, the Canadian Olympic Committee, Commonwealth Games Canada, the Canadian Interuniversity Sport, Special Olympics Canada, and the Canada Games Council. Examples of multi-service organisations include the Canadian Centre for Ethics in Sport, the Coaching Association of Canada, Sports Officials Canada, Athletes CAN, Sport Dispute Resolution Centre of Canada, and the Aboriginal Sport Circle.
6 Data on the financial contributions of Sport Canada to the Bilateral Agreements were obtained from Sport Canada's 2003–4 Contribution Recipients (http://pch.gc.ca/progs/sc/contributions/2003-2004-2/2003–4_e.cfm accessed 11 December 2007); 2004–5 Contribution Recipients (http://pch.gc.ca/progs/sc/contributions/2004-2005-2/2004–5_e.cfm accessed 11 December 2007); Sport Canada Contributions Report 2005–6 (http://pch.gc.ca/progs/sc/contributions/2005-2006-2/index_e.cfm

accessed 11 December 2007); Sport Canada Contributions Report 2006–7 (http://pch.gc.ca/pgm/sc/cntrbtn/2006–7/index-eng.cfm accessed 27 September 2009); and Sport Canada Contributions Report 2007–8 (http://pch.gc.ca/pgm/sc/cntrbtn/2007–8/index-eng.cfm accessed 1 August 2009).

7 Canadian Sport Centres are the network of organisations responsible for providing high-performance sport services to Canadian elite athletes (CSC Pacific, CSC Calgary, CSC Manitoba, CSC Ontario, Centre national multisport Montréal and CSC Atlantic) (see Sport Canada 2008).

References

Anderson, K. (2008) Sideline insults drive refs out of minor soccer; Calgary league can't keep up with losses. *Edmonton Journal*, p. B5.

Balyi, I. (2001) Sport system building and long-term athlete development in Canada. *Coaches Review*, 8(1), 25–8.

Bloom, G. A., Loughead, T. M. and Newin, J. (2008) Team building for youth sport. *The Journal of Physical Education, Recreation and Dance*, 79(9), 44–7.

Bloom, M., Gagnon, N. and Hughes, D. (2006) *Achieving excellence: Valuing Canada's participation in high performance sport*. Ottawa, CA: Conference Board of Canada.

Bloom, M., Grant, M. and Watt, D. (2005) *Strengthening Canada: The socio-economic benefits of sport participation in Canada*. Ottawa, CA: Conference Board of Canada.

Brach, B. (2008) Half of Canadian kids don't play sports; Participation plunging nationwide, mostly among boys. *Edmonton Journal*, p. A5.

Canadian Heritage (2002a) *The Canadian sport policy*. Ottawa, CA: Government of Canada. Online. Available HTTP: http://pch.gc.ca/pgm/sc/pol/pcs-csp/2003/polsport-eng.pdf (accessed 23 May 2009).

——(2002b) *The Canadian sport policy. Federal-provincial/territorial priorities for collaborative action 2002–2005*. Ottawa, CA: Government of Canada. Online. Available HTTP: www.pch.gc.ca/pgm/sc/pol/actn/action-eng.pdf (accessed 23 May 2009).

——(2007) *The Canadian sport policy. Federal-provincial/territorial priorities for collaborative action 2007–2012*. Ottawa, CA: Government of Canada. Online. Available HTTP: www.pch.gc.ca/pgm/sc/pol/actn07–12/booklet-eng.pdf (accessed 23 May 2009).

——(2009) *Intergovernmental sport policy development. Federal-provincial/territorial sport committee (FPTSC)*. Ottawa, CA: Government of Canada. Online. Available HTTP: http://patrimoinecanadien.gc.ca/pgm/sc/pubs/FPTSC-eng.cfm (accessed 27 September 2009).

Canadian Sport Centres (2005a) *Long-term athlete development. Resource paper v. 2. Canadian sport for life*. Vancouver, CA: Author. Online. Available HTTP: www.pacificsport.com/Images/PDFs/LTAD_ENG_66p_June5.pdf (accessed 30 August 2009).

——(2005b) *No accidental champions. Long-term athlete development. for athletes with a disability*. Vancouver, CA: Author. Online. Available HTTP: www.pacificsport.com/Images/PDFs/NAC_ENG_June5.pdf (accessed 30 August 2009).

Canadian Tire (2009) *Canadian Tire Jumpstart. About us*. Online. Available HTTP: www.canadiantire.ca/jumpstart/about.html (accessed 26 June 2009).

Casper, J. M., Gray, D. P. and Babkes Stellino, M. (2007) A sport commitment model perspective on adult tennis players' participation frequency and purchase intention. *Sport Management Review*, 10(3), 253–78.

Clark, W. (2008) *Article. Kids' sports*. Ottawa, CA: Statistics Canada [Catalogue no. 11–008-X]. Online. Available HTTP: www.statcan.gc.ca/pub/11–008-x/2008001/article/10573-eng.pdf (accessed 26 August 2009).

Côté, J., Horton, S., MacDonald, D. and Wilkes, S. (2008) The benefits of sampling sports during childhood. *Physical and Health Education Journal*, 74(4), 6–11.

CTV (2008) *Canadians' sports participation plummets: StatsCan*. Toronto, CA: CTV.ca News. Online. Available HTTP: www.ctv.ca/servlet/ArticleNews/story/CTVNews/20080207/sports_080207/20080207?hub=CTVNewsAt11 (accessed 26 June 2009).

Davey, J., Fitzpatrick, M., Garland, R. and Kilgour, M. (2009) Adult participation motives: Empirical evidence from a workplace exercise programme. *European Sport Management Quarterly*, 9(2), 141–62.

Donnelly, P. and Coakley, J. J. (2002). *The role of recreation in promoting social inclusion*. Working paper series. Perspectives on social inclusion. Toronto, CA: The Laidlaw Foundation.

Donnelly, P. and Kidd, B. (2003) Realizing the expectations: Youth, character, and community in Canadian sport. In Canadian Centre for Ethics in Sport (Ed.), *The sport we want: Essays on current issues in community sport in Canada* (pp. 25–44). Ottawa, CA: Canadian Centre for Ethics in Sport. Online. Available HTTP: www.cces.ca/pdfs/CCES-PAPER-TheSportWeWant-E.pdf (accessed 23 May 2009).

Dorsch, K. D. and Paskevich, D. M. (2007) Stressful experiences among six certification levels of ice hockey officials. *Psychology of Sport and Exercise*, 8(4), 585–93.

Ferguson, E. (2009) Busy Canadians get fit with formal exercise; organized sports losing favour, survey discovers. *Calgary Herald*, p. B10.

Fraser-Thomas, J. and Côté, J. (2009) Understanding adolescents' positive and negative developmental experiences in sport. *The Sport Psychologist*, 23(1), 3–23.

Frisby, W. and Fenton, J. (1998) *Leisure access: Enhancing opportunities for those living in poverty*. Vancouver, CA: British Columbia Health Research Foundation. Online. Available HTTP: http://lin.ca/resource-details/4091 (accessed 26 September 2009).

Frisby, W. and Hoeber, L. (2002) Factors affecting the uptake of community recreation as health promotion for women on low incomes. *Canadian Journal of Public Health*, 93(2), 129–33.

Frisby, W., Reid, C. and Ponic, P. (2007) Levelling the playing field: Promoting the health of poor women through a community development approach to recreation. In P. White and K. Young (Eds), *Sport and gender in Canada* (pp. 121–36). Don Mills, CA: Oxford University Press.

Hunter, S. (2001) Lack of refs a real blow: More, and better, officials needed. *The Province*, p. A54.

Ifedi, F. (2008) *Research paper. Culture, Tourism and the Centre for Education Statistics. Sport participation in Canada, 2005*. Ottawa, CA: Statistics Canada [Catalogue no. 81–595-MIE – No. 060]. Online. Available HTTP: www.statcan.gc.ca/pub/81-595-m/81-595-m2008060-eng.pdf (accessed 26 August 2009).

Katzmarzyk, P. T., Gledhill, N. and Shephard, R. J. (2000) The economic burden of physical inactivity in Canada. *Canadian Medical Association Journal*, 163(11), 1435–40.

KidSport Canada (2008) *About us: History*. Online. Available HTTP: www.kidsportcanada.ca/index.php?page=history (accessed 26 June 2009).

Lang Research (2007) *Canadian travel market. Attending professional sporting events while on trips of one or more nights*. Online. Available HTTP: http://dsp-psd.pwgsc.gc.ca/collection_2009/ic/Iu86-30-53-2007E.pdf (accessed 26 September 2009).

Lewis, N. (2009) Marshals to keep soccer parents in line. *Calgary Herald*, p. A1.

Macintosh, D. (1996) Sport and government in Canada. In L. Chalip, A. Johnson, & L. Stachura (Eds), *National sports policies. An international handbook* (pp. 39–66). Westport, CT: Greenwood Press.

MacLean, B. (2008a) *The Government of Canada signs a bilateral agreement to increase sport participation in Newfoundland and Labrador*. St. John's, CA: Government of Canada. Online. Available HTTP: www.patrimoinecanadien.gc.ca/pc-ch/infoCntr/cdm-mc/index-eng.cfm?action=doc&DocIDCd=CHG073251 (accessed 27 September 2009).

——(2008b) *The Government of Canada signs a bilateral agreement for Aboriginal sport in Nova Scotia*. Halifax, CA: Government of Canada. Online. Available HTTP: www.canadianheritage.gc.ca/pc-ch/infoCntr/cdm-mc/index-eng.cfm?action=doc&DocIDCd=CHG073320 (accessed 27 September 2009).

Mills, D. (Chair) (1998) *Sport in Canada: Everybody's business. Leadership, partnership and accountability. Standing Committee on Canadian Heritage. Sub-Committee on the Study of Sport in Canada*. Ottawa, CA: Government of Canada.

Plotnikoff, R. C., Bercovitz, K. and Loucaides, C.A. (2004) Physical activity, smoking, and obesity among Canadian school youth. *Canadian Journal of Public Health*, 95(6), 413–18.

Proudfoot, S. (2008) Sports participation levels slump; Canadian decline in organized sport involvement cuts across age, gender levels. *The Vancouver Sun*, p. A6.

Siegenthaler, K. L. and Leticia Gonzalez, G. (1997) Youth sports as serious leisure. A critique. *Journal of Sport and Social Issues*, 21(3), 298–314.

Sport Canada (2004) *Investing in sport participation 2004–2008. A discussion paper*. Ottawa, CA: Canadian Heritage. Online. Available HTTP: http://dsp-psd.pwgsc.gc.ca/Collection/CH24-16-2004E.pdf (accessed 30 August 2009).

——(2008) *Canadian Sport Centres*. Online. HTTP: www.pch.gc.ca/pgm/sc/csc-eng.cfm (accessed 30 August 2009).

——(2009) *Sport Support Program*. Online. Available HTTP: www.pch.gc.ca/pgm/sc/pgm/spprt-eng.cfm (accessed 30 August 2009).

Sport Matters Group (2006) *Sport, recreation and social development: Discussion paper*. Ottawa, CA: J.W. McConnell Family Foundation. Online. Available HTTP: www.sportmatters.ca/Groups/SMG%20Resources/Social%20Development%20and%20Sport/2006-Sport,%20Rec%20&%20Social%20dev-McConnell.pdf (accessed 23 May 2009).

Taylor, T. and Doherty, A. (2005) Adolescent sport, recreation and physical education: Experiences of recent arrivals to Canada. *Sport, Education and Society*, *10*(2), 211–38.

Trudel, P., Côté, J. and Sylvestre, F. (1996) Systematic observation of ice hockey referees during games. *Journal of Sport Behavior*, *19*(1), 50–65.

Ulrich-French, S. and Smith, A. L. (2009) Social and motivational predictors of continued youth sport participation. *Psychology of Sport and Exercise*, *10*(1), 87–95.

Weiss, M. (2008) Field of dreams: Sport as a context for youth development. *Research Quarterly for Exercise and Sport*, *79*(4), 434–49.

19

Sports development and adult mass participation in Japan

Mayumi Ya-Ya Yamamoto

The definition and the objectives of mass sport development

Mass sport development in Japan can broadly be understood in relation to two policy objectives set by two different ministries with an interest in the policy area, namely, the Ministry of Education, Culture, Sports, Science and Technology (hereafter MEXT) and the Ministry of Health, Labour and Welfare (hereafter MHLW). While MEXT is principally in charge of overall policy for sport and school sport/physical education (PE), the area of concern for MHLW policy is around health, welfare and the well-being of citizens, which embrace the areas of mass participation in physical activities and exercises.

The current sports policy goal in Japan is to 'realise a lifelong sport participation society where all citizens can enjoy sport based on their physical strength, age, skills and interests and objectives at *any stage of life, anytime* and *anywhere*', and this will lead to the realisation of 'a bright, fulfilling, and vital society in the twenty-first century' (emphasis added, MEXT 2006). In September 2000, MEXT published (and revised in 2006) the master plan for sport, the *Basic Plan for the Promotion of Sports (2001–2010)* (hereafter the *Basic Plan*), which outlined a triad policy in sport (increasing lifelong participation in sport, increasing high-performance success in international sports events and widening opportunity for PE and school sport). Policy for mass sport development corresponds to the policy objective to 'establish a lifelong sport participation society'. The quantitative policy objective is to have more than 50 per cent of adults engaged in sports activities at least once a week. To achieve this target, the *Basic Plan* has defined two 'indispensable' areas of policy: i) the development of a minimum of one Comprehensive Community Sports Club (CCSC) per municipality by 2010; and ii) the development of at least one Sports Centre covering a Wide Area (*sic*) in each prefecture. The emphasis on the development of clubs and sports centres is based on the assumption that the development and maintenance of sports clubs and ensuring the widest accessibility will 'enable all lovers of sports, from children to the elderly, to participate in sports according to their interests and goals in their local areas' (MEXT 2006).

As stated, the above-mentioned objective is one of the three-pillar policy objectives set out in the *Basic Plan*. The other two are: i) the improvement of children's physical strength and fitness through the promotion of sport; and ii) the enhancement of international competitiveness.

When the *Basic Plan* was first published in 2000, the decline in children's fitness was not recognised as an urgent policy concern and was initially identified as a 'related policy area' to the lifelong sports participation and competitive sport (MEXT 2000). However, the revised *Basic Plan* of 2006 highlighted the significance, and urgency, of developing the 'human skills (personal capacity development)' of children through improving their physical abilities and fitness. Ever since the hosting of the 1964 Tokyo Olympic Games, the Japanese government has annually conducted the 'Survey into Physical Strength and Exercise Ability (*Tairyoku Undō-nouryoku Chōsa*)' tracking trends in children's physical strength, fitness and abilities as well as their physical development. Through this survey, it has identified that a steady decline in children's fitness and a gradual increase in physical size have taken place since 1985.[1] With this accumulated evidence, a nationwide programme designed to 'raise awareness of the decline in children's physical fitness and to develop an attractive sporting environment' was established as the 'indispensable policy objectives' of mass sport participation (MEXT 2006). By dropping the long-established association with elite sport policy, the roles of education and community sport were emphasised and the idea of the CCSC was introduced to create a pathway between school sports clubs and community.

In light of rapid societal and demographical change in Japan as well as the influence of globalisation, the CCSC system has stimulated huge expectations not only that the clubs will encourage children to experience a wide range of sports and non-sports activities, but also that they will develop and promote the cohesion of community by enabling volunteering by citizens. In 2001 MEXT published a *Manual for the Development of Comprehensive Community Sports Club* to allow upcoming clubs to understand the best practice, particularly in relation to the autonomous management of the clubs (MEXT 2001). It defines 'comprehensive' as being broadly synonymous with 'variety', namely, variety in sports disciplines, age range, interests, skills, and abilities. It further specifies that a wide range of sports and cultural activities should be organised and managed by the citizens of the community who should be recruited from a broad social and demographic background. The CCSC is expected to have a designated facility equipped with a club house and supervised by high-quality coaches (or instructors) to meet the individual needs (MEXT 2001).

It is generally acknowledged that the ideas and values of the CCSC come from the German (community) sports club system (Kurosu 2007; Yamaguchi 2006). Modelled on the German system, the CCSC is expected to feature an autonomous management system that requires not only that a substantial proportion of income should be generated through membership subscriptions, but also that the clubs should provide high-quality management and coaching. The objective of the CCSC initiative is to find interconnections between mass participation in sport and community building based on the assumption that the former will facilitate the latter (Matsuo 2001).

The policy concern of the MHLW is related to the prevention of lifestyle-related diseases, the reduction of the incidence of illness, the promotion of healthy lifestyles, and the improvement of mental well-being. As opposed to the emphasis on mass participation in sport, the MHLW promotes nationwide mass participation in 'physical activity (*shintai-katsudō*)' and 'exercises (*undō*)'. The 'Nation Health Promotion Strategy for the 21st Century (known as *Kenkou Nippon 21*, or *Healthy Nippon 21*)' was published by the MHLW in 2000 as a 'health policy' and its ten-year policy goal is to 'realise a healthy and bright ageing society' (MHLW 2000). The ministry had predicted that, by 2006, Japan would have become an ageing society, where more than 20 per cent of the population would be over 65 years of age. The *Healthy Nippon 21* strategy was aimed at preventing the elderly population from becoming predominantly bedridden and improving the quality of life for all. It also aspired to establish a 'world leading model' for an ageing society (MHLW 2000). As the MHLW is also responsible for the national health care system, one of the objectives through *Health Nippon 21* was to decrease the cost of national health care. To promote health-related exercise nationwide the government enacted the Health Promotion Law in 2002 which obliged citizens to 'be aware of, and understand the significance of, a healthy lifestyle and engaged in promoting health by being conscious of one's health' (Clause 2). With the implementation of the Health Promotion Law, *Healthy Nippon 21* was revised accordingly in 2008 and, together with its *Exercise Guide*, provided a series of performance targets and definitions (Consultative Group for Exercise Requirements and Exercise Guideline 2006). Physical activity was defined as the consumption of more energy than resting; 'exercise' was defined as 'physical activities planned and intended to maintain and improve physical fitness'; while 'lifestyle activity' was defined as 'non-exercise physical activity including activity through one's occupation'. The policy then specified nine areas of health care that can prevent lifestyle-related diseases and lead to an 'extended healthy life span'[2] (MHLW 2000). In relation to the promotion of a 'bright' and 'vivid' society populated by healthy citizens engaged in sport and exercise, the policy areas of MEXT and MHLW resembled each other to a considerable degree. However, the blurred nature of the definitions of what constitutes sport, physical activity and exercise and the distinction between sports promotion and health promotion has created ministerial conflicts. It can also be argued that the overlap between the policies of MEXT and MHLW has attracted criticism that the policy area is 'cluttered' and policy is ineffective.

The history of mass sport development

The slow post-war development of Japanese sport (or rather 'physical education') policy is partly explained by the strong wartime association between the government and physical training and fitness and the subsequent determination to avoid a renewal of the link between militarism and physical education (see for example, Esashi 1973, Kusafuka 1979, 1986). Summarising the development of sports policy in Japan, Saeki argued that there has been 'a long decline' in sports policy since the 1960s (2006: 36–48). He classified post-war sports policy into four phases: i) social physical education in the 1960s; ii) community sport in the 1970s; iii) sport for all in the 1980s; and iv) lifelong sports participation from the 1990s (Saeki 2006).

The initial policy development in the post-war era was the enactment of the Social Education Law in 1949 which identified 'social physical education' as the framework for the promotion of mass sport development (Ministry of Education 1949). As early as 1946, the national athletic/sports competition (*Kokumin Taiiku-taikai*, known as *Kokutai*) was held to bring 'brightness and hope to the devastated life of the citizen' (JASA 1986: 99), and its primary objective quickly became to promote and develop mass participation in sport and to establish associations to organise competitive sport (see Kusafuka 1979; Takahashi and Tokimoto 1996; and Tokimoto 2004).

Despite this early post-war policy development the history of the promotion of mass sport should undoubtedly treat the 1964 Tokyo Olympic Games as the catalyst for modern Japanese sports development policy. The period in the lead-up to the Games in 1964 (the first major international sports event hosted in Japan) and the post-Games period marked the most significant stimulus for the development of national policy in sport. On the award of hosting the Games, the then minister of education, aware of the socio-political situation in Japan, identified the importance of improving the nation's health and nutritional standard and promoting sport and recreation. The minister requested his advisory body, the Advisory Council of Health and Physical Education (ACHPE),[3] to develop a policy. In response, the ACHPE published the policy document, the 'Enhancement of Health and Physical Fitness for Citizens, in particular

Youth, in the Face of Tokyo Olympic Games', in 1960 (ACHPE 1960). This policy document interestingly established policy directions which can still be identified in current policy. Specifically, the policy prioritised the development of physical education in schools and social physical education, which incorporated the development of health education in schools, school safety and the promotion of healthy school lunches. Right after the Games, the Cabinet Office continued advocating further enhancement of nationwide health and physical fitness. In March 1965 the 'National Conference on Physical Fitness Promotion' was convened for the purpose of maintaining and promoting the nation's health and physical fitness, which was to be achieved not only by fostering cross-ministerial cooperation, but also, and importantly, by developing cooperation between departments and agencies across all 47 prefectures and municipal levels.[4]

It is without doubt that the government was particularly concerned to ensure the success of the Japanese squad at the Tokyo Olympic Games and consequently, in 1961, the government enacted the Sports Promotion Law as a cross-party item of legislation. While it specifically restricted the government's intervention in sport and promoted the autonomy and political neutrality of sport (Clause 1.2), the enthusiasm of government at the time was reflected in its objective 'to contribute to the development of the health of the nation and to the development of a bright and high quality lifestyle for citizens' (Clause 1). By defining sport as 'athletic activities and physical activities (including camping and other forms of outdoor activities) that are initiated to develop a healthy mind and body' (Clause 2), the responsibilities of the central and municipal levels of governments were specified as being 'to implement various policy measurement to provide wide opportunities for citizens at any place and for any level of ability' (Clause 3). To achieve this policy goal, the Sports Promotion Law stated that the minister in charge (Ministry of Education/MEXT) should implement a national sports promotion plan. However, it took 39 years to fulfil this commitment, which occurred with the publication, in 2000, of the *Basic Plan for the Promotion of Sports (2001–2010)*. Despite this long delay in developing the policy instruments necessary for the implementation of the mass participation strategy it can be argued that the fundamental values in relation to mass sport development found within the Sports Promotion Law are still guiding current policy.

In order to understand the importance of values in current mass participation policy it is necessary to appreciate the connection between the idea of 'lifelong sport participation' and the notion of 'community sport'. The concept of community sport can be traced back to 1960 when the then minister of education published the policy document, *Social Physical Education: Values and Development* (*Shyakai Taiiku – Kangaekata/ Susumekata*; MOE, 1960; see also Ministry of Education 1948). Faced with rapid post-war economic development and the consequent social changes, such as urbanisation, the government had already anticipated the risk of the collapse of traditional forms of community and societal bonding and the trend towards a more individualistic society. One response was to use the policy of 'social physical education' as a means to (re-)connect individuals within urban society (Matsumura 1988). The policy report published by the ACHPE in 1972 became the impetus for developing community sport. The *Fundamental Policies for the Promotion of Physical Education and Sport* (hereafter *1972 Report*) stressed the idea of lifelong mass sport participation by highlighting the significance of 'creating a healthy society based on human dignity, which is the most important issue for Japan in the future' (ACHPE 1972: 2). While Morikawa (1980: 132–3) argued that the *1972 Report* reflected the 'concern of the government to respond to public anxieties about health and physical fitness and to meet public demand in sport in the 1970s', Kusafuka viewed the report as more directly and narrowly concerned with the promotion of mass sport participation (1986: 25). It should be noted that the policy objective of the *1972 Report* was, and still remains, based on the belief that access was the key to increased levels of participation and thus higher levels of accessibility to sports facilities would lead automatically to higher levels of sports participation. The significance of the *1972 Report* was that it set a national target which was that 'around 20 per cent of the population [over 18 years old] should be able to take up sport once a week by using local sport facilities'. The report underlined the responsibilities of both central and local municipal government to provide sufficient financial support for the development of accessible public sports facilities and 'physical education facilities', including swimming pools, *dōjō* halls, skiing sites and cycling and hiking routes, as well as for the acquisition of land and the training of sports/physical education instructors (ACHPE 1972: 39). Importantly, the idea of community sport, or 'voluntary and autonomous sport group activities', was advocated within this report (ACHPE 1972: 46–55).

It was around the early 1970s when a wider range of government ministries and agencies began to show a stronger interest in welfare and health promotion and identified the significance of community sport, recreation and leisure as potential policy instruments. For example, the then Economic Planning Agency (currently absorbed into the Cabinet Office) published the *New Economic Social Development Plan* which included a promotional plan for sport and recreational facilities (Economic Planning Agency 1970), while the Ministry of Commerce created the Department for the Leisure Development Industry in 1972. Consequently, it can be noted that the relative exclusivity enjoyed by the Ministry of Education in relation to sport was increasingly diluted through the involvement of a range of different ministries and agencies that had developed either an interest in sport or an interest in the related areas of leisure and recreation. Despite the increasing administrative and policy complexity that developed during this period one should not lose sight of the significance of the *1972 Report* in providing the foundation for the promotion of mass participation in sport and physical activities. Seki characterised the report as 'the first systematic "sport policy" in the post war era' (1997: 20).

Another stage in the development in policy for mass sport participation came in 1989 when the ACHPE published a report with a long-term vision into the next century. The report, entitled the *Strategies for the Promotion of Sports for the 21st Century* (hereafter *1989 Report*), used the term 'lifelong sport' for the first time in a policy document. The promotion of lifelong sports participation was stressed in response to the 'transformation of the social environment through urbanisation, the increase in leisure time and the aging society' (ACHPE 1989: 2; see also MESSC 1992). The report acknowledged the 'importance of positive, lifelong engagement in the promotion of health and the improvement of physical fitness/strength' in order to 'live a bright vibrant life' (ACHPE 1989: 7–8). The report stressed the importance of the development of various facilities in order to enable '*anybody* to casually participate in a "lifelong sport" *anywhere* and *at any time*' (emphasis added, ACHPE 1989: 8). In 1990 the Ministry of Education organised the first Sport for All Convention and the national Recreational Festival, both of which have become annual events co-hosted by the Japan Amateur Sports Association (JASA), the National Recreation Association of Japan, the national Federation of Commissioners of Physical Education and the host local municipality.

The significance of the *1989 Report* should also be highlighted because of its recognition of the diverse forms of engagement with sport, particularly the growing importance of 'viewing' sport, as opposed to 'doing' or 'playing' sport. More importantly, the subsequent ACHPE report of 1997 further identified the concept of 'supporting' sport through the voluntary participation of citizens in community sport (ACHPE 1997). The triad of forms of involvement in sport (doing, viewing and supporting sport) are continuously used in a wide range of contexts, especially in relation to mass sport development and the Comprehensive Community Sports Club (MEXT 2006; see also Takahashi and Tokimoto 1999, Kurosu, 2007, Comprehensive Community Sports Club Expert Panel 2009).

Seki criticised the *1989 Report,* characterising it as an 'complete denial' of the policy direction set in the *1972 Report* because of the down-playing of government responsibility which, he argued, 'led the way, and opened the door, for commercialism' (1990: 6). Identifying the 1980s as a period of 'sport policy vacuum', Uchiumi similarly recognised the neo-liberal direction in policy and the increasing reliance on 'private capital resources' for investment in sport (2002: 6). However, it is necessary to recognise the policy continuity between the *1989 Report* and the current policy objectives on the one hand and the discourse set out in the *Basic Plan for the Promotion of Sports* (see Section 1) on the other. It can also be argued that the period of the 1980s laid a firm foundation for policy development in the 1990s, which faced issues such as an ageing society, urbanisation, the desire for an improved quality of life, commercialisation and globalisation. Wider societal change has also influenced the direction of comprehensive education policy. With the Lifelong Education Law enacted in 1990, the roles of sport and physical activity are recognised as providing a wide range of learning opportunities throughout one's life (Central Advisory Council of Education 1991).

Furthermore, the period in the late 1980s and early 1990s can be characterised as one when there was a noticeable growth in interest in sport, leisure, recreation and health/health promotion by the government across a range of ministries and quasi-government agencies, even if their interest was in the utilisation of sport to achieve their respective (non-sports) policy objectives. Although sports policy had largely been confined within the remit of the Ministry of Education (MEXT), it was now prominent within the policy areas of national economy, industry and tourism and reflected the government's growing concern in utilising (or exploiting as some may argue) private finance to stimulate the economy and expanding the domestic demand. The investment in sport and leisure facilities in the late 1980s was, for example, formulated by the Ministry of Internal Affairs and Communication (MIC), the Ministry of Land, Infrastructure, Transport and Tourism (MLIT), and the Ministry of Economy, Trade and Industry (METI) in accordance with the passage of the Comprehensive Resort Region Provisional Law in 1987. As already stated, the Ministry of Health and Welfare (current MHLW) introduced in 1988 the *Active Health Plan* (previously *Health Japan Programme* published in 1978) to develop health promotion through physical activity, for example through the National Health and Welfare Festival (known as 'Nenrinpic') designed to encourage participation by those aged over 65 years. As shown in Table 19.1, multiple ministries annually budget for the area of sport and 'Physical Fitness Promotion', highlighting the cluttered sports promotion policy area.

The policy leadership, organisation and funding of mass sport participation

In Japan, recognised policy areas are overseen by a responsible ministry with policy implementation and service delivery normally undertaken by non-departmental public agencies. As noted before, the lead government administrative unit for the promotion of sports development is MEXT. The responsibility for mass sport development rests with the Division of Sport for All of the Sports and Youth Bureau within MEXT.[5] The Central Council for Education is the advisory body directly appointed by and responsible to the minister of MEXT. In addition, one of the ministry's five subdivisions, the Sports and Youth Division, is specifically dedicated to the areas of overall sports promotion, school health education, promotion of youth education and improvement of physical fitness.

The Division also assesses and monitors applications for government subsidies to quasi government bodies and sports organisations and, if requested by the minister, develops a sports promotion plan. The overall policy area of the 'realisation of a lifelong sport society' has experienced a gradual decrease in its budget in recent years, which is not surprising given the dominance of neo-liberal economic values. The Sport for All Division had expenditure of

Table 19.1 Ministries holding annual budget for the area of sport, as 'Physical Fitness Promotion'

Ministries/agency	Main policy areas	Examples of project areas
Cabinet Office	Development and promotion of specific projects	Development and promotion of policy for the increase and stability of citizens' life
MIC Ministry of Internal Affairs and Communications	Facility management	Managing recreation, sport and welfare facilities; health support services
MEXT Ministry of Education, Culture, Sports, Science and Technology	Facility management	Management of public school facilities; maintenance of PE/sports facilities; management of independent administrative agency under MEXT's authority and supervision
	Development of instructors Organisational development	Development of PE/sports instructors/coaches Subsidising sports bodies; subsidising operations of Independent administrative agencies (e.g. NAASH, JISS, NTC)
	Promotion of specific projects	Promotion of regional sport; promotion of Wide-area Sports Centre; promotion of 'Physical Fitness Activity' programme; management of public school PE-related facilities; promotion of 'Improvement of Children's Physical Fitness Campaign'
MHLW Ministry of Health, Labour and Welfare	Facility management	Management of health-related and child-care facilities
	Development of instructors	Development of skills and abilities of youth labour leaders
	Organisational development	Subsidise 'general sound diet programme' and Union of Elderly People; promotion of *Healthy Nippon 21* project
	Promotion of specific projects	Promotion of 'Total Health Promotion' plan; promotion of health-related exercise
MAFF Ministry of Agriculture, Forestry and Fisheries	Facility management Promotion of specific projects	Management of recreational facilities in forest Promotion of sound diet; facilitation and management of providing milk in school meal
METI Ministry of Economy, Trade and Industry	Promotion of specific projects	Promoting sports/leisure industry and market
MLIT Ministry of Land, Infrastructure, Transport and Tourism	Facility management	Management of tourism industry, parks in urban and greenery places, marina, coast-line, cycle path and large-scale public parks; management of walking and toilet facilities in public places
MOE Ministry of Environment	Facility management Development of instructors Promotion of specific projects	Subsidising natural park Subsidising advisors/instructors for natural park; subsidising volunteer project Subsidising learning environment in natural places and 'Children Park-ranger Project'
Social Insurance Agency	Promotion of specific projects	Promotion of health management project in workplace

¥1,182,772,000 in 2007 which fell to ¥752,886,000 in 2009. The requested budget for 2010 is broadly similar at ¥765,013,000.

The National Agency for the Advancement of Sports and Health (NAASH), under the authority of MEXT, has responsibility for the promotion of sport and health among children and youth. NAASH distributes funding through the Sports Promotion Fund (introduced in 1990 and mainly for elite sport development projects) and the Sports Promotion Lottery (national lottery, or known as *toto*) which is largely distributed to support aspects of mass sport development, including those associated with the maintenance of clubs and activities that form part of the Comprehensive Community Sports Club initiative.[6] The primary non-governmental body, the Japan Amateur Sports Association (JASA) established in 1911, has a long-standing involvement in the promotion of 'sport for all'.[7] Along with two other national non-governmental bodies for sport (the Japanese Olympic Committee and the *Budo-kan*),[8] JASA is eligible to receive government funding for agreed projects, although it can only cover between one-third and two-thirds of the total cost of a project. All 47 Prefectural Sports Associations are affiliated to JASA, which makes it possible to develop nation-wide programmes such as the Japan Junior Sports Club. JASA also organises and manages the Sport Instructors system which provides nine types of recognised qualifications designed to raise the quality of sport experience.[9] JASA's certified instructors system gained additional political salience when, in 2008, the Sport for All Division allocated ¥6.2 million a year funding to a three-year project to develop a training programme for improving and increasing the number and quality of sports instructors in the community.[10]

Under the project to 'realise a lifelong sport society' introduced by the Sports for All Division of MEXT, JASA was assigned, in 1995, the task to develop a model sports club would have the capacity to provide for multiple sports and non-sports physical activities. From 2002 funding through the *toto* was used to support the development of a community sports club as part of the project derived from the *Basic Plan*. From 2004 to 2010, MEXT designated JASA as the primary agency for the promotion of the national project concerned with the 'Development of Comprehensive Community Sports Club'. Unfortunately, consistent levels of funding for the CCSC project have not been achieved, as can be seen from Table 19.2. Peaking in 2005–6, funding declined sharply in 2007–8 and was still half its peak level in 2009–10.

As noted in the previous section and as highlighted in Table 19.1, apart from MEXT, eight other ministries and agencies participated in the National Conference on Physical Fitness Promotion and they annually allocate a budget to sport-related activities (the 'Physical Fitness Promotion Budget') which covers four broad categorises of programme: facility management; development of coaches/instructors; organisational development; and the promotion of specific projects. Because of the number of ministries and quasi-governmental agencies involved, it is often not easy to specify the exact figure for the total expenditure on the promotion of mass participation in sport. For example, in the 2009 financial year, the MLIT allocated the substantial subsidy of ¥83.9 billion to service objectives that included ensuring the wide availability and

Table 19.2 Annual budget for the development and support of Comprehensive Community Sports Club (¥-,000)

2003–4	2004–5	2005–6	2006–7	2007–8	2008–9	2009–10
1,041,000	1,011,000	1,864,000	1,025,000	803,140	834,140	934,000

Source: MEXT (respective years) *MEXT Jigyô Hyôkasho* (MEXT Project Evaluation)

accessibility by the public to sports/recreational facilities and natural parks. It was also reported that ¥105.1 billion was allocated by the same ministry for the maintenance of urban parks and green spaces (Minesaki 2009: 55). As for the Ministry of Health, Labour and Welfare, its 2009 budget allocated ¥11billion to the Physical Fitness Promotion Budget (although this represented a sharp reduction from the ¥48.1 billion allocated in 2002 when the *Health Nippon 21* programme was launched). Under the authority of the MHLW, both the Japan Health Promotion and Fitness Foundation and the Association of Physical Fitness Promotion & Guidance (APFPG) promote similar programmes and provide the certification. The former agency manages and finances the certification system for both Health Promotion Instructors and Health Promotion Practitioners which is intended to provide professional and structured health promotion programmes for individuals,[11] while the APFPG promotes the improvement of 'health physical fitness', especially for the elderly population, and healthy nutrition, and provides the Fitness Instructor for Older Adults certification.

Assessing the success of mass sport development policy and its future development/trajectory

A range of government surveys are available as a basis for the evaluation of the degree of success of the policy for mass sport development. These surveys are: i) National Survey on Physical Fitness and Sport, conducted by the Chief Cabinet Office every three years (since 1976, except for 2004 and 2007); ii) Survey into Physical Strength and Exercise Ability, conducted by MEXT every year (since 1964[12]); and iii) National Survey into Physical Fitness-Physical Ability and Exercise Practice, conducted by MEXT from 2008 (targeted at Year 5 and Year 8 pupils). It is important to note that these surveys are used as reference points by the government in terms of evaluating the effectiveness of overall policy and legitimising the budget requests by each division/bureau and consequently directly affect total government investment. MEXT publishes the annual 'Policy Achievement Evaluation' which involves an examination of the current position and policy progress over the previous 12 months. The annual evaluation assesses the 'effectiveness and efficiency' of current policy instruments and specifies the strategy for the following year (MEXT 2009d).

For example, the overall policy objective in mass sport development, namely to achieve the target of more than 50 per cent of adults participating in sports activities more than once a week, is evaluated in the first of the surveys listed above. Its overall policy progress was rated as 'B' in the MEXT 'Policy Achievement Evaluation' for the financial year 2008. The Sports and Youth Bureau claimed that 44 per cent of adults were participating in sport and exercise activities more than once per week, which is regarded as 'substantial progress to realising a lifelong sport society', and that it compared to survey data from 1994, when only 29.9 per cent of adults participated more than once per week (34.7 per cent in 1997, 37.2 per cent in 2000, and 38.5 per cent in 2004[13]) (MEXT, 2009d: Objective 11). In contrast, national progress in the development of the Comprehensive Community Sports Club network was reported as having been subject to a 'slight delay'. By 2008–9 only 57.8 per cent of municipalities had developed CCSCs making it unlikely that the target of at least one CCSC per municipality by 2010 would be achieved. For the budget request, the Sport for All Division provided its own survey data as shown in Table 19.3 and argued that the policy target would be difficult to meet without additional financial support and additional programmes of action (MEXT 2008a). It should be noted that the measure of 'effectiveness' of policy is quantitative, that is, to achieve 100 per cent coverage of municipalities, and that there is no requirement for the Sport for All Division to evaluate the quality of provision in the clubs.

Table 19.3 Percentage and number of Comprehensive Community Sports Clubs

Establishment of Comprehensive Community Sports Club	2002–3	2003–4	2004–5	2005–6	2006–7	2007–8	2008–9
Percentage of municipalities with CCSCs already established or in progress	13.1%	17.4%	22.5%	33.0%	42.6%	48.9%	57.8%
Already established			394	486	532	631	736
In progress			380	425	406	386	399
Number of municipalities already developed	426	558	702	783	786	894	1,046
Already established			635	1,412	1,758	2,004	2,233
In progress			482	743	658	551	535
Number of Comprehensive Community Sports Clubs	541	833	1,117	2,155	2,416	2,555	2,768

Note: the total number of municipalities is 1,810
Source: Adapted from MEXT (2009b)

As regards the future direction of policy, the change of government in September 2009, from the Liberal Democratic Party (LDP) to the Democratic Party of Japan (the first time the LDP has failed to obtain a majority of seats in the House of Parliament since the end of World War II) is likely to prove highly significant. In particular, the bureaucrat-led policy-making process has been questioned by the Democratic Party of Japan (DPJ) because it is seen as constituting a removal of power from the executive or the cabinet (DPJ 2009a, 2009b). Not only was the process of policy-making subject to criticism, so too was the way public expenditure was allocated, prompting demands for stronger public accountability. The increasing pressure from the central government for public accountability in terms of proving the justification for, and success of, policy will become much stronger.

In this regard poor progress towards the target of 100 per cent Comprehensive Community Sports Club coverage is likely to be viewed as a policy failure. Nevertheless, the DPJ has expressed the intention to enact a new Sports Law,[14] focused on the triad of sport policy – 'doing', 'viewing' and 'supporting' sport – but one that puts more emphasis on achieving a wider degree of accessibility of citizens to sport (DPJ 2009a: 24). The sports policy in Japan has entered a potentially transformational phase, reflected in the policy initiative called 'Towards the Realisation of Leading Sport Nation Status'. The LDP's proposal to the parliament (the Diet) with the renewed Sports Law in July 2009 was abandoned after almost a one-year consultation period in face of the general election. However, the DPJ maintains the similar policy stance where the complete renewal of the 'outdated' Sports Promotion Law of 1961 remains the fundamental policy concern. It is intended to initiate a debate over the creation of a sports ministry or an agency for sport and the depth and the extent of government responsibility in sport. The specific argument can be found in whether it is appropriate to define 'sports rights' or 'human rights for sport', defining physical education and school sport in relation to 'sports policy' and the inclusion of sport for the disabled. It is also being discussed as to whether to identify sport as the concern of central government, in order to achieve wider areas of policy objectives. In addition, with the continuing concern for public health care and promoting health, exercise and well-being, it may be that the area of mass sport development will gain a stronger association with the health policy area, thus strengthening the claim for additional public investment.

Notes

1 The 'Survey into Physical Strength and Exercise Ability' was introduced after the 1964 Tokyo Olympic Games. As nationally conducted with multiple items for testing, the Survey is intended to evaluate the physical fitness and the development of physique (height, weight and seating height) of pupils and students at elementary school (age 6–9, since 1983; age 10–11, since 1965), junior high school and high school as well as 'young adults' (covering 12–29 years old, conducted since 1964). In 1977, the Survey was extended to include all age groups of 30–59 years old, and in 1988, it was expanded to 79 years old. In 2000, the evaluation items and age categories were reviewed and the renewed survey was introduced (categorised as: Primary School, 6–11 years old; Junior High to University, 12–19 years old; Adult, 20–64 years old; and Elderly, 65–79 years old). The 2009 Survey shows a slight increase in 'basic physical ability', the first time since the early 1990s (MEXT 2009a). Since 2008, in addition to this annual survey, MEXT has introduced another targeted survey called 'National Survey into Physical Fitness-Physical Ability and Physical Exercise Practice' (MEXT 2009c). As a three-year project with the budget of ¥2.270 million, this was introduced to analyse the correlation between lifestyle (eating habits and general lifestyle) and physical fitness (same fitness tests are conducted as Survey into Physical Strength and Exercise Ability), and aimed to increase the children's fitness level to the standard in the 1980s. Due to the shortcomings of the existing 'Survey into Physical Strength and Exercise Ability', this new survey was introduced to the selected Year 5 (10–11 years old) and junior high school Year 2 or Year 8 (13–14 years old). The 'National Survey into Physical Fitness-Physical Ability and Physical Exercise Practice' is equivalent to 'National Survey into Study Academic Achievement and Study Ability' which is targeted to Year 6 and junior high school Year 3. See MEXT (2008b).

2 These nine areas are: 1) nutrition and lifestyle; 2) physical activity and exercise; 3) rest and mental health; 4) smoking; 5) alcohol; 6) dental health; 7) diabetics; 8) cardiovascular disease; and 9) cancer. Those nine areas of health are categorised into 70 elements with the specific target respectively.

3 The Advisory Council of Health and Physical Education (ACHPE), or *Hoken Taiiku Shingikai* (known as 'Hotaishin'), was an advisory body for the then Minister for Education. This Advisory Council was restructured into the Central Advisory Council for Education, or *Chūo Kyoiku Shingikai*, in 2001, as part of the Administrative Reform of State Sector enforced by the Koizumi Government (April 2001–September 2006) whose policy was in favour of 'privatisation' of public administrations. The responsibilities of the Sports and Youth Division of the Central Advisory Council of Education are specifically focused on the promotion of sport.

4 The 'National Conference on Physical Fitness Promotion' was initially promoted by the Prime Minister's Office and is currently composed of nine ministries and agencies along with 47 prefectural departments and 233 private organisations (as of April 2009). On the establishment of this National Conference in March 1965, the then Director-General of the Prime Minister's Office highlighted in his speech the triple significance for the nation: development of intelligence, high morale, and physical fitness. Its Secretariat Office is currently placed at the Youth & Sport Bureau of MEXT. See the Japan Health Promotion & Fitness Foundation, URL: www.health-net.or.jp/undou/about/index.html [last accessed 15 March 2010].

5 The organisational name of MEXT in English is taken from the MEXT's Pamphlet (2007). Available from: www.mext.go.jp/list_001/list_016/_icsFiles/afieldfile/2009/03/19/mext_2007_e.pdf [last accessed 15 March 2010].

6 See Nakamura (2002) for the discussions of the process of passage of the Law on Practices of Sports Promotion Lottery, which came into force in November 1998. Also see Yamamoto (2008) for the discussion of how *toto* is distributed in relation to the overall budget for Physical Fitness Promotion.

7 Note that the predecessor of JASA, *Dainippon Taiiku-Kyokai* (Great Japan Amateur Athletic Association, JAAA) was formed specifically for the first participation in the 1912 Olympic Games in Stockholm, and it acted as the National Olympic Committee. In the post-war time, the Japan Amateur Sports

Association was reformed. In the face of controversy over the political pressure on the withdrawal of the Japanese team from the 1980 Moscow Games, the Japanese Olympic Committee (JOC) became independent of JASA in August 1989. Consequently, the responsibilities for elite sport development and mass sport development/Sport for All were divided between the JOC and JASA. See Yamamoto (2009).

8 These are: the JOC and *Budo-kan*. All of these bodies are judicially classified as the 'special public interest agency for public welfare'.

9 The 'publicly recognised' certificate system was changed in 2005 when the government decided not to 'certify' any qualifications or skilled examinations. In 2005, JASA re-launched its 'Sport Instructor System', which is now JASA's 'publically recognised' certificate. See more: www.japan-sports.or.jp/coach/pdf/1.pdf [last accessed 15 March 2010].

10 See detailed project description: MEXT, www.mext.go.jp/a_menu/hyouka/kekka/07110104/007/002.pdf [last accessed 15 March 2010].

11 As for the case of the JASA certified system, the Health Promotion Instructor System was recognised as the national certificate. However, since 2006, it has become a 'publicly recognised qualification' which is recognised by the Japan Health Promotion & Fitness Foundation. In relation to the mass sport development, other relevant certification programmes are 'Japan Recreation Association Instructor System' and 'Disability Sport Instructor System'. Although the effectiveness can be questioned, the Sports Leader Bank system is also in place at the prefectural level. See Sasakawa Sports Foundation (2006), pp. 82–87.

12 As stated, the children's physical fitness and the level of physical strength and abilities are evaluated every year. However, for the first time in 2000, the evaluative items were reviewed and modified.

13 Nevertheless, we should treat these survey data carefully. The *National Survey on Physical Fitness and Sport*, reports that of 3,000, 1,377 were 'active participants'. However, 29.1 per cent of them participate in sport activity three times a week (more than 151 days a year), whereas 30.5 per cent participate 1–2 days a week (51–150 days a year) (Chief Cabinet Secretary Press Office 2006).

14 On 4 March 2010, the Minister for Sport (or Minister in charge of Sport, MEXT/Vice-Minister of MEXT) established a forum and requested some athletes, sports officials and academic experts to provide their opinion. This is to develop Japan as a 'Leading Sport Nation'. See MEXT press release: www.mext.go.jp/b_menu/houdou/22/03/1291345.htm [published 4 March 2010; last accessed 15 March 2010].

References

Advisory Council of Health and Physical Education (ACHPE) (1960) *Enhancement of Health and Physical Fitness for Citizens, in particular Youth, in the Face of Tokyo Olympic Games (Response)*, Tokyo: ACHPE.

ACHPE (1972) *Fundamental Policies for the Promotion of Physical Education and Sport* (1972 Report), Tokyo: ACHPE.

——(1989) *Strategies for the Promotion of Sports for the 21st Century* (*1989 Report*), Tokyo: ACHPE.

——(1997) *Promotion of Education and Sport for a Lifelong Physical and Mental Health*, Tokyo: ACHPE.

Central Advisory Council of Education (1991) *Reformation of Education System in Line with Demand of New Era*, Tokyo: CACE.

Chief Cabinet Secretary Press Office (2006) *National Survey on Physical Fitness and Sport*, Tokyo: Chief Cabinet Secretary Press Office.

Comprehensive Community Sports Club Expert Panel (2009) *The Future Direction of the Development of Comprehensive Community Sports Club*, Tokyo: MEXT.

Consultative Group for Exercise Requirements and Exercise Guideline (2006) *Exercise Guideline for Health Promotion 2006 – for the Prevention of Life-style Related Diseases (Exercise Guideline 2006)*, Tokyo: MHLW.

Democratic Party of Japan (DPJ) (2009a) *The Democratic Party of Japan Policy INDEX 2009*, Tokyo: DPJ.

DPJ (2009b) *Manifesto: DPJ's Policy*, Tokyo: DPJ.

Economic Planning Agency (1970) *New Economic Social Development Plan*, Tokyo: Economic Planning Agency.

Esashi, K. (1973) 'Departure of New Physical Education' in *Study of Post-War Physical Education in School*, M. Maekawa (ed.), Tokyo: Fumaidou, pp. 22–77.

Government of Japan (2002(Health Promotion Law (enacted in August 2002, May 2003 in effect), Tokyo [last updated in June 2009].

Japan Amateur Sports Association (JASA) (1986) *75 Year History of Japan Sports Amateur Association*, Tokyo: JASA.

Kurosu, M. (2006) 'Concept and Reality of the Comprehensive Community Sports Club', in *Modern Sport Perspective*, Kiku, K. (eds), Tokyo: Taishukan, pp. 118–37.

——(2007) *Era of the Comprehensive Community Sports Club: in collaboration with the School Sports Club (Volume I)*, Tokyo: Sobun Kikaku.

Kusafuka, N. (1979) 'The History of Post-war Physical Education Policy: Part 2, process of "democratization" in the post-war Physical Education', *Ritsukmeikan University Human Sciences Research Institute*, vol. 29, pp. 1–77.

——(1986) 'Structure of Japanese Modern Sport', in *Freedom and Modernity of Sport*, T. Fuji, N., K. Kusafuka J. & Kanei, J. (eds), Vol. II, Tokyo: Aoki Shoten, pp. 18–55.

Matsumura, K. (1988) 'Debate on the Lifelong Sport Participation, Sport Community', in *Sport Sociology Lecture*, Morikawa, S. & Saeki, T., pp. 91–6.

Matsuo, T. (2001) 'Publicness in Sport and Comprehensive Community Sports Club', in *White Paper 2000 on Sports Club: towards the realisation of a lifelong sport participation society*, Japan Sports Club Association (ed.), Tokyo: Kouatsu Shyuppan, pp. 115–17.

Minesaki, S. (2009) 'Kokudo Kotsu Shou [Ministry of Land, Infrastructure, Transport and Tourism]', in *Gekkan Taiikushisetsu*, No. 493, April 2009, p. 55.

Ministry of Education (1946) *Social Education Law*, Tokyo: MoE [enacted June 1949].

——(1960) *Social Physical Education: Values and Development [Shyakai Taiiku – Kangaekata/ Susumekata]*, Tokyo: MOE.

Ministry of Education, Science, Sports, and Culture (MESSC) (1992) *White Paper, Japanese Government Policies in Education, Science and Culture*, Tokyo: MESSC.

MEXT (2000) *Basic Plan for the Promotion of Sports (2001–2010)*, Tokyo: MEXT.

——(2001) *Manual for the Development of Comprehensive Community Sports Club*, Tokyo: MEXT.

——(2006) *Basic Plan for the Promotion of Sports (2001–2010)*, Revised edition of 2000, Tokyo: MEXT.

——(2008a) '95. The Development and Support of the Comprehensive Community Sports Club (Extended)', *MEXT Project Evaluation: New and Extended Projects in the Heisei Year 21*, Tokyo: MEXT.

——(2008b) '90. Support Project for Children's Physical Strength based on the National Survey into Physical Fitness-Physical Ability and Exercise Practice (New)', *MEXT Project Evaluation: New and Extended Projects in the Heisei Year 21*, Tokyo: MEXT.

——(2009a) *Survey into Physical Strength and Exercise Ability [Tairyoku Undō-nouryoku Chōsa]*, Tokyo: MEXT.

——(2009b) *Survey into the Current Situation of the Comprehensive Community Sports Club*, Tokyo: MEXT.

——(2009c) *National Survey into Physical Fitness-Physical Ability and Exercise Practice, Heisei Year 20 [Zenkoku Tairyoku-Undo-nouryoku, Undo-Shukan-tou Chosa-Kekka nitsuite]*. www.mext.go.jp/b_menu/houdou/21/01/1217980.htm [last accessed 15 March 2010].

——(2009d) *MEXT Policy Achievement Evaluation: Achievement in the Heisei Year 20*, Tokyo: MEXT.

Ministry of Health and Welfare (MHW) (1978) *Health Japan Programme*, Tokyo: MHW.

MHW (1988) *Active Health Plan*, Tokyo: MHW.

Ministry of Health, Labour and Welfare (MHLW) (2000) *Nation Health Promotion Strategy for the 21st Century [Kenkou Nippon 21, or Healthy Nippon 21]*, Tokyo: MHLW.

Morikawa, S.(1980) *Sports Sociology*, Tokyo: Aoki Shoten.

Nakamura, Y. (2002) *Policy Network in Sport Administration*, Ph.D. thesis, Tokyo: Waseda University.

Saeki, T. (2006) 'History and Current Status of Sport Policy', in *Contemporary Sports Critique*, Nakamura, T. (ed.), pp. 36–48.

Sasakawa Sports Foundation (2006) *Sport for Every One: For Active Sporting Life – Discovery of New Values in Sport*, Tokyo: SSF.

Seki, H. (1990) 'Sport policy towards the 21st Century: "Summary of ACHPE Report" and "72 Report"', *Hitotsubashi University Departmental Bulletin Paper*, 1990, pp. 4–6.

—— (1997) *The Post-war Sports Policy in Japan: its structure and development*, Tokyo: Taishukan.

Takahashi, N. and Tokimoto, T. (1996) 'Development of Physical Education and Sport through Kokutai: An Analysis of speech given by Ministries of Education', *Sangyo Kenkyu Journal (Takasaki Keizai University)*, vol. 32, no. 1, pp. 52–85.

Takahashi, S. and Tokimoto, T. (1999) 'Diversification of Sport Participation and Axis for Sport Participation in the 21st Century', *Chiiki Seisaku Kenkyu [Takasaki Keizai Daigaku, Chiiki Seisaku Gakkai]*, Vol. 2, pp. 35–55.

Tokimoto, T. (2004) *The Administrative Structure for Sport and Sport Policy in the Postwar Japan,* Ph.D. thesis, Tokyo: Nippon Taiiku Daigaku.

Uchiumi, K. 2002, 'The confrontation between "the Right to Play Sport" or the Public Sphere of Sports and Neo-liberalism or Individual Consumption (2): National and Municipal Sports Policies in the 1980s', *Hitotsubashi Journal of Social Studies*, vol. 39, no. 3, pp. 3–97.

Yamaguchi, Y. (2006) *The Comprehensive Community Sports Club that Transformed the Community*, Tokyo: Taishukan.

Yamamoto, M.Y. (2008) 'Japan', in *Comparative Elite Sport Development: Systems, Structures and Public Policy*, B. Houlihan & M. Green (eds), Oxford: Butterworth-Heinemann, pp. 53–82.

——(2009) *The Influence of Non-domestic Factors on Elite Sport Development and Anti-doping Policy: the cases of Japan and the UK/England*, Ph.D. thesis, Loughborough: Loughborough University.

20

Sports development and adult mass participation

The roles of international organisations

Ian Henry

One of the key concepts in relation to an understanding of the role of international organisations in sports policy is that of subsidiary. It is a principle that is overtly adopted to legitimate policy intervention at the European level by the European Union (EU), but it is also applicable to the relationship between local, regional, national, and international/transnational bodies in both the public and third sectors. The principle of *vertical* subsidiarity requires that any policy that can be effectively pursued at a lower level (local, regional or national) should be dealt with at that lower level. Thus the delivery of policy at international level should be limited to those policy domains where effective intervention is only possible through international or transnational agreement and/or enforcement. Thus for example agreements on limits to fuel emissions and pollution are only effective if these have a trans-border dimension, since the impact of domestic pollution is not limited by national boundaries. Sport, however, might be said, particularly in its recreational form, to be a matter for local decision-making, and the provision of opportunities to participate are often the concern of local agencies, in particular local government. Competitive sport, particularly at the elite level, with national competitions and teams representing the nation, would appear to be more likely to be a matter of national policy (though not always a public sector or governmental concern). Relatively few aspects of policy, apart from issues such as regulation of the transnational flow and employment of players, would seem likely to be a concern of transnational policy bodies, whether governmental (e.g. the EU) or sporting (e.g. FIFA).

In addition to vertical subsidiarity, the principle of *horizontal* subsidiarity implies that the organs of the state (ministries, municipalities or quasi-autonomous governmental bodies) will only intervene in sporting affairs where there is evidence of market failure and the failure to achieve public or mixed welfare outcomes. Such would be the case if we consider the protection of young athletes from the pressures of commercial actors, sponsors or coaches (see Figure 20.1).

Thus we might anticipate that intervention in sport, if it is likely to be a matter for governmental bodies, would be at national, or sub-national level in terms of promoting sport for all, and that, at supra-national or international level, government involvement would be fairly limited. Indeed, as far as mass participation is concerned, even major international sporting bodies are less likely to be involved in matters pertaining to sport for all. There are, however, exceptions

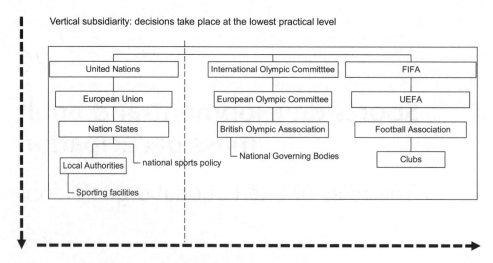

Vertical subsidiarity: decisions take place at the lowest practical level

Horizontal subsidiarity: provision takes place in public sector only if other sectors cannot make provision efficiently

Figure 20.1 Subsidiarity in sport

to this rule and this chapter will address the ways in which intervention at the international level has targeted increasing or sustaining mass participation, albeit in a limited range of contexts.

In this chapter we focus on a small number primarily of governmental and third sector bodies that operate at the continental and the world level, and that have a significant role in promoting mass participation. These are, at the European level, the EU and the Council of Europe; and at the world level, the International Olympic Committee (IOC), the United Nations, and International Federations. This is not to deny that there is considerable activity in other international/transnational groups in relation to sport. However, there is rather less engagement on the part of these bodies with the promotion of adult mass participation in sport. In dealing with our chosen organisations we wish to map out a critical description, identifying what is undertaken by these bodies in relation to promoting mass participation, in what ways such provision is made, for which purposes, and what evidence there is that such interventions are effective.

Sports policy and adult mass participation in Europe: the Council of Europe and the EU

The roles of the EU and the Council of Europe are often confused in the popular imagination. This is probably not surprising when, for example, they share the same flag and anthem and the original impetus behind establishing both bodies in the post-World War II period was in part a shared concern to build institutions that would minimise the possibility of any future conflict. However, their institutions and modus operandi are very separate. The EU came into being in 1957 with the Treaty of Rome with initially six member states and was referred to as the Common Market, since the limited scope of the Treaty (if not the ambition of some of the original promoters of the idea) related to the abolition of tariff barriers between member countries. Subsequently, in the 1970s, with a growing recognition that commercial ties could not be isolated from other forms of common action (such as the formulation of a regional development policy to reduce regional economic and social inequalities and thus increase levels of internal trade), the nomenclature changed from a Common Market to that of European Community. Finally, as the expansion of the EU continued, common action became increasingly difficult to establish on the basis of consensus and the situation was deemed to require the development of a political architecture to ensure that common action could be demanded of members and in many instances legally enforced. This deepening of the relationships between member states is reflected in the Treaties on the EU as amended by the Treaties of Maastricht, Amsterdam, Nice and Lisbon and was prefigured in the adoption of the term 'European Union' rather than 'European Community' in the rhetoric following the introduction of the Maastricht Treaty.

The use of the terms 'international', 'transnational' and 'supra-national' require some clarification in relation to their use in the context of this chapter. 'International' agreements for example refer to agreements between national governments or bodies that are binding by virtue of the agreement of each of the national entities involved. Thus the Council of Europe as an international organisation employs conventions to which individual members are only bound if they 'sign up' to such conventions. 'Transnational' agreements are those that apply similar requirements across a range of national boundaries. 'Supra-national' agreements are those that are binding on those nation states whether or not they have been endorsed by the government of those states. The EU to a degree, in certain policy domains, acts as a supra-national entity in that EU policy is in effect decided upon by the Council of Ministers (in specific policy areas by qualified majority) and may be subsequently imposed on members by the European Court of Justice or the European Commission. Thus the EU is described as a supranational organisation since aspects of national sovereignty have been ceded to the EU. Just as decision-making at the European level has grown in other policy domains with this long journey from Common Market to EU, so also the EU's engagement in sports policy has grown over time, although, as we shall illustrate below, it is only with the enactment of the Lisbon Treaty that the EU has had a legally recognised competence to act in the sports domain per se. Prior to this the EU's engagement in sport had to be justified by reference to other policy domains in which an EU competence had been recognised in earlier treaties, such as in the case of professional sport as trade, or the use of sport to promote social inclusion, or foster regional development.

The Council of Europe

The Council of Europe (CoE) has a slightly longer history than the EU, having been established in 1949. It has 48 members drawn from a far wider geographical range stretching from Greenland in the west to Russia and most of the republics of the former Soviet Union in the east. As we have noted, it is an inter-governmental body in that its various conventions apply only to those states that sign up to each such convention.

Given that it is an intergovernmental body and therefore cannot require its members to conform, the role of the CoE has been characterised as one of providing 'moral leadership' in various policy fields. This is perhaps most clearly illustrated by the CoE's European Court of Human Rights (not to be confused with the European Court of Justice, which is an EU institution concerned with ruling on and enforcing EU regulations). The Court was established under the European Convention on Human Rights and provided a legal resort in respect of fundamental civil and political rights defined in the Convention. The rights and freedoms secured by the Convention include the right to life, the right to a fair hearing, the right to respect for private and family life, freedom of expression, freedom of thought, conscience and religion and the protection of property. The Convention prohibits, in particular, torture and inhuman or degrading treatment or punishment, forced labour, arbitrary and unlawful detention, and discrimination in the enjoyment of the rights and freedoms secured by the Convention.

At the inception of the CoE in 1949, the 10 founding members sought to identify common actions in a range of fields: economic, social, cultural, scientific, legal and administrative. These were given expression in the European Cultural Convention. Sport was added to the range of cultural activities covered by the Cultural Convention in 1976 and the European Sport for All Charter was adopted in the same year, when a Steering Committee for the Development of Sport (CDDS) was established. Since then the moral leadership of the CoE in the field of sport has taken a number of forms such as Conventions against Doping in Sport, Spectator Violence, and the European Sports Charter adopted in 1991, to supersede the European Sport for All Charter. In addition to these Conventions the policy focus of the CDDS had been on enhancing physical education provision for the young and the use of sport in post-conflict contexts (see for example, the Ballons Rouges Projects in Bosnia Herzegovina, 1995–2000 and in the Caucusus, 2000–2004, Council of Europe 2007).

More recently the CDDS had seemed to run out of steam and, with a lack of funding, its ability to operate effectively was called into question. As a consequence in 2007 the CoE adopted a resolution to establish the Enlarged Partial Agreement on Sport (EPAS). The Partial Agreement is an agreement by 30 CoE member countries to engage in the field of sport in collaboration with the countries not belonging to EPAS and representatives of national and international organisations and federations of the sports world. It has the aim

> to promote sport and emphasise its positive values through policy and standard setting, monitoring, capacity building, and the exchange of good practice. It uses existing Council of Europe sports standards such as the European Sports Charter, the Code of Sports Ethics, the European Convention on Spectator Violence and the Anti-Doping Convention as a foundation for its own strategies.
>
> *(Council of Europe 2009)*

While sports policy is addressed across a number of fields, our concern here is with adult participation and this is most clearly reflected in the adoption and promotion of the European Sports Charter and in particular Articles 4 and 6 (see Box 20.1). However, while the Charter acts as an advocacy document, the evaluation of whether signatory countries have lived up to the commitments undertaken in signing up to these conventions has been variable. Three countries, Switzerland, the UK and Estonia have been subject to visits by an evaluation panel following detailed self-assessment of the extent to which they have met the recommendations or requirements of the Charter. The reports of the panels in these cases represent little more than broad expressions of desirable action as the extract in Box 20.2 illustrates. Thus, while the CoE has had a significant role to play in terms of mapping out the policy terrain, its lack of financial resources and lack of institutional power to require actions by members means that its role has perhaps become more marginal. The reduced number of states involved in EPAS is also an indication of the low level of priority accorded to sport by the approximately one-third of all member states that did not sign up to membership of EPAS. While EPAS might exercise influence by carefully targeting its resources to significant policy problems (e.g. the use of sport as a vehicle for promoting inter-culturalism which was a declared policy goal in 2009), it seems unlikely in its current form to have a significant broader impact on adult participation.

Box 20.1 Extracts from European Sports Charter relating to adult sports participation

Article 4

Facilities and activities

1. No discrimination on the grounds of sex, race, colour, language, religion, political or other opinion, national or social origin, association with a national minority, property, birth or other status, shall be permitted in the access to sports facilities or to sports activities.
2. Measures shall be taken to ensure that all citizens have opportunities to take part in sport and, where necessary, additional measures shall be taken aimed at enabling young gifted people as well as disadvantaged or disabled individuals or groups to be able to exercise such opportunities effectively.
3. Since the scale of participation in sport is dependent in part on the extent, the variety and the accessibility of facilities, their overall planning shall be accepted as a matter for public authorities. The range of facilities to be provided shall take account of public, private, commercial and other facilities, which are available. Those responsible shall take account of national, regional and local requirements, and incorporate measures designed to ensure good management and their safe and full use.
4. Appropriate steps should be taken by the owners of sports facilities to enable disadvantaged persons including those with physical or mental disabilities to have access to such facilities.

....

Article 6

Developing participation

1. The practice of sport, whether it is for the purpose of leisure and recreation, of health promotion, or of improving performance, shall be promoted for all parts of the population through the provision of appropriate facilities and programmes of all kinds and of qualified instructors, leaders or 'animateurs'.
2. Encouraging the provision of opportunities to participate in sport at work places shall be regarded as an integral part of a balanced sports policy.

Source: Council of Europe 1992

The EU

As we have already noted, the criterion of subsidiarity is one that is overtly employed to justify the involvement of the EU in a given policy area, and this principle underpins the thinking behind the various founding treaties, and subsequent treaties on EU which defined and subsequently modified the legal areas of competence of the EU. The most recent legislation, the Treaty of Lisbon, which came into force on 1 December 2009 incorporated Article 165, which introduced a 'soft competence', that is a potential for intervention shared with member states, described in the following terms:

Box 20.2 Extracts from the Evaluation Commission's priority recommendations concerning the Estonian submission on meeting the requirements of the European Sports Charter

It is important to pay more attention and investing in work and money on developing existing sports in order to meet needs for 'Sports for All' in Estonia. ....

- Estonia already has a good practice on giving 'ear-marked stimulation money' for building small sports grounds at local level. Therefore, it is important to continue this initiative and to secure strong support for similar purposes.

  ... Recruiting and training of voluntary and professional leaders in sports should continue to be a high priority. In this respect, it is important to find ways to financially support the training and education of sports leaders at all levels.

- The governmental sector should strongly support sports organisations and their ambitions, mainly in order to involve more individuals in the 'Sport for All' activities and to proclaim that sport is a means of increasing physical activity of individuals and of health promotion for the population.
- It is important to concentrate more effort into the pre-school and higher education of Estonian youth.
- The Evaluation Team suggests that the work on data and information collection from various sectors of sport in Estonia continues and is followed by elaboration and analysis of the collected information.

  ......

- The government should add its own resources to that of the NGO 'ear-marked stimulation money' for the construction of small local sports grounds.

Source: Council of Europe Evaluation Team 2003

The Union shall contribute to the promotion of European sporting issues, while taking account of the specific nature of sport, its structures based on voluntary activity and its social and educational function.

... Union action shall be aimed at: ...

—developing the European dimension in sport, by promoting fairness and openness in sporting competitions and cooperation between bodies responsible for sports, and by protecting the physical and moral integrity of sportsmen and sportswomen, especially the youngest sportsmen and sportswomen.

This legislation is the culmination of efforts stretching back at least to the Maastricht Treaty (signed by member states in 1992). The Maastricht Treaty defined a new competence for the EU in respect of culture, and its revision at Amsterdam in 1997 incorporated a declaration on sport, effectively laying down a marker for future definition of the EU's legitimate interest in sport. A role for the EU was partially articulated in an appendix on sport to the Nice Treaty in 2001, but when a New Constitution for Europe (which contained an article for sport for the first time) was put to the member states in 2004/5, having been accepted by the Council of Ministers, it was rejected by some member states in national referendums.

The *White Paper on Sport*, published by the Commission in 2007 (European Commission 2007b) represented an even fuller statement of intent. This document and its accompanying Coubertin Action Plan (European Commission 2007a) set out a range of 53 policy actions under three headings and 18 subheadings (see Box 20.3). Since these two documents were published in 2007, each of these actions had initially to be promoted without reference to a competence, since clearly the Lisbon Treaty had not been approved by the member states at this point. This was possible because much of the White Paper and the Coubertin Action Plan addresses the use of sport in support of other policy goals. Thus mention is made of the role of sport in health and physical activity policy, social cohesion and inclusion, anti-racism, the promotion of volunteering, education of young sportspersons, and the place of sport in the *acquis communautaire* (the body of European legislation) bearing, for example on competition policy, free movement and so on. Much of this has little directly to do with adult mass participation, except in so far as adult participation can foster benefits in terms of health, social cohesion and other such policy goals.

Box 20.3 The principal headings under which actions were recommended in the Coubertin Action Plan

1. *The societal role of sport*
   - Enhancing public health through physical activity
   - Joining forces in the fight against doping
   - Enhancing the role of sport in education and training
   - Promoting volunteering and active citizenship through sport
   - Using the potential of sport for social inclusion, integration and equal opportunities
   - Strengthening the prevention of and fight against racism and violence
   - Sharing our values with other parts of the world
   - Supporting sustainable development

2. *The economic dimension of sport*
   - Moving towards evidence-based sport policies
   - Putting public support for sport on a more secure footing

3. *The organisation of sport*
   - The specificity of sport
   - Free movement and nationality
   - Transfers
   - Players' agents
   - Protection of minors
   - Corruption, money laundering and other forms of financial crime
   - Licensing systems for clubs
   - Media

The principal difference in the situation pre and post the Lisbon Treaty is that the competence, despite its somewhat vague formulation, provides support to the funding or co-funding of community sport by the EU. In addition, it reinforces the role sport plays in support of other important policy areas.

The level of adult participation in sport across Europe does vary considerably as studies such as the COMPASS Report (Gratton 1999), and the more recent Eurobarometer study on sports participation (European Commission 2004) have indicated. Both studies report high levels of participation in Scandinavia and low levels in Southern Europe. The Eurobarometer incorporates a wider range of countries and those from the former communist bloc rank alongside Southern Europe in reflecting low participation levels. Figure 20.2 illustrates this pattern fairly starkly. It remains to be seen whether the development of a European competence in sports policy will be able to reduce such inequalities.

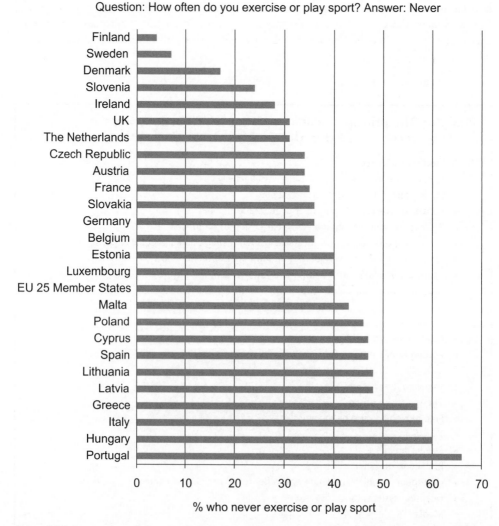

Question: How often do you exercise or play sport? Answer: Never

% who never exercise or play sport

Figure 20.2 Proportion of the population of EU member states who never play sport or exercise

Sports policy and adult mass participation: global organisations

International federations and umbrella organisations

Moving from the European level to the global, there are relatively few bodies that address the direct promotion of adult participation in sport as such. Perhaps the most significant exception is the case of TAFISA (the Trim and Fitness Sport for All Association). This body was founded in 1991 in Bordeaux but has its headquarters in Frankfurt. Although it was originally very much dominated by European members, it has expanded its membership and now claims a membership of more than 150 organisations in 110 countries. TAFISA operates as a lobbying and coordinating body, organising a world congress every two years, and topic-specific regional meetings in between. The organisation also promotes the staging of events, notably the World Walking Day, and International Day, and is seeking with the World Health Organisation to establish an 'Active Cities Award Programme'. Finally, it is also seeking with academic partners to develop and offer a Certified Leadership Course in Sport for All. Independent estimates of the impact of TAFISA's activities in relation to the stimulation of adult participation in sport and recreation are not available, and thus it is difficult to assess the impact of this transnational body and particularly to distinguish its impact from that of local agencies.

The focus of International Federations tends to be on competitive sport at the international level and consequently they have little to do with promotion of mass participation, which is seen as a local concern. Nevertheless, the IAAF (the World athletics body) for example supports courses to develop grass-roots coaching, while FIFA (Football) has a social responsibility strand within its programme including the 'Goal' programme, which funds local infrastructure that can have an impact on mass participation. FINA (swimming) also funds or supports work at beginners levels in terms of coach development, but this is focused on competition activity.

UNESCO

UNESCO (the United Nations Educational, Scientific and Cultural Organisation) is the lead agency for physical education and sport in the United Nations (UN). It operates programmes with five principal themes, namely: Sport for Peace and Development; Quality Physical Education; Traditional Sports and Games; Women and Sport; and Anti-Doping. Of these the two most clearly linked to goals of promoting adult mass participation are those relating to women and sport and the protection of traditional sports and games.

Sport for Peace and Development projects incorporate work by other UN agencies such as UNICEF and tend to be directed towards young people rather than adult populations. Programmes typically promote inter-culturalism through physical education and the practice of sport, employ sport as a means to prevent violence, delinquency and drug consumption, and seek to effect progress towards the achievement of the Millennium Development Goals. The UN designated 2005 as the International Year of Physical Education and Sport (United Nations 2005) engendering within the programme of activities organised for that year a focus on these broad aims.

UNESCO describes itself as 'mandated to improve the quality of physical education, because of its Education for All initiative, as well as its physical education and sport programme and the International Olympic Committee's goal of Sport for All' (UNESCO 2010). Its major activities in this area relate to improving training structures for the teaching of physical education, seeking to ensure universal access to physical education in the primary school sector and the development of university level provision for teachers of physical education. Activity in relation to anti-doping culminated most recently in the development of the International Convention against Doping in Sport which came into being in February 2007. This seeks to harmonise anti-doping procedures so that the force of international law against doping can be applied by all countries.

UNESCO's policy of protection of traditional sports and games (TSG) is as much about protecting cultural heritage as it is a matter of promoting participation. Nevertheless it is a means of valuing cultural practices that involve adult participation in sports, games and physical activity. Following the third International Conference of Ministers and Senior Officials responsible for sport and physical education (MINEPS III), held in Uruguay in December 1999, convened by UNESCO, a number of actions have been taken in relation to TSGs. First, as a result of proposals made at the Conference, UNESCO has been developing both a world heritage list of traditional games and sports and an incentive framework for the promotion and the preservation of these sports, which is intended to lead to the establishment of an 'International Platform' for traditional games and sports (UNESCO 2006). In addition, at the time of writing UNESCO had established a pilot project establishing training camps in traditional wrestling sports for the youth of 22 African countries.

In line with the UN's Convention on the Elimination of All Forms of Discrimination against Women (adopted in 1979) UNESCO has sought to promote equity in the development of national and local sporting projects and programmes. Although this is an aspect of providing moral leadership, few practical projects are associated with this goal beyond the establishment of an Observatory on Women and Sport following the 2004 Conference of Ministers (MINEPS IV) which took place in Athens. Impacts are thus difficult to gauge.

The IOC and promotion of adult participation

The areas of work of the IOC that relate most clearly to promotion of adult participation fall under the remit of the Sport for All Commission. While for many the work of the IOC is synonymous with the staging of the Olympic Games, it should be stressed that success at the Games in terms of winning medals is enjoyed predominantly by a small number of nations. Thus, for many, particularly the smaller National Olympic Committees (NOCs), an emphasis is placed on participation, particularly in the activities associated with the Olympic Day Run which was staged by 160 of the 205 NOCs in 2007 (growing from 5 NOCs at its inception in 1986) (Numan 2008).

The Sport for All Commission was established in 1983. It stages a World Sport for All Conference every two years, with the aim of fostering debate and promoting good practice in relation to sport for all initiatives. It focuses not simply on sport for sport's sake, but also, especially more recently with growing concerns about sedentary lifestyles and obesity, on the health and fitness agenda. However, the concern with health is not exclusive, as the Olympic Day Run illustrates. This event takes on one or more of a number of formats (Numan, 2008), most notably:

- A fun/game format (organisation of games on the Olympic theme)
- A sport/competition format (organisation of one or more sport competitions)
- A gathering format (the bringing together of diverse social groups e.g. men, women and athletes with a disability)
- A symbolic format (that highlights an important theme such as the environment peace)

The Olympic Day Run as an event has an explicit or implicit association with the sport for health message, and its sponsorship by McDonalds has been controversial, given the health sector's critique of the fast food sector. Other values overtly espoused in the Olympic Sport for All area include gender equity, social development through sport, peace through sport, and responsibility for the environment.

The IOC has expressed a preference for referring to the event as Olympic Day, since it has increasingly involved more than a run per se, and, in addition to this event, the Sport for All Commission supports 15 to 20 sport promotion projects per year, largely on a one-off basis.

Other Commissions that have a direct bearing on adult participation include the Women in Sport and the Olympic Solidarity Commissions. The Women in Sport Working Group established in 1995 gained the status of a Commission in 2004. Its core work is in sports promotion among women as well as promotion of the roles that women play in the organisation and management of sport. The actions supported by the Commission involve largely promotional activities rather than direct provision, with initiatives such as the Women and Sport Awards highlighting the contributions of exceptional women and continental seminars seeking to develop capacity among women for management and leadership roles.

Olympic Solidarity acts as a resource provider providing the funding required to support the actions of the other Commissions. Olympic Solidarity manages the broadcasting revenue allotted to the NOCs and it redistributes this through programmes defined on the one hand by the IOC itself (the World Programme) and on the other by the Continental Associations of NOCs (the Continental Programme). Its budget for the quadrennial 2009–12 was as follows:

World Programme	US$134 million
Continental Programme	US$122 million
Olympic Games Subsidies	US$42 million
Administration	US$13 million

(Olympic Solidarity 2008)

Of this sum, US$2.2 million is dedicated to supporting the activities of the Sport for All Commission and US$1.6 million to the activities of the Women in Sport Commission referred to above.

The IOC commissioned two studies of the NOCs' activity in the field of sport for all, in Europe in 2006 (Green and Collins 2007), and in Asia and Oceania in 2008 (Green and Collins 2009). This provides a snapshot of the situation in both contexts, though the response rate was considerably higher in Europe 38 of 49 NOCs responding (78%) compared to 28 of 61 NOCs in Asia and Oceania (46%). Both these studies reviewed the response to the Declarations of the World Sport for All Congresses from 1994 to 2004, which are summarised by the authors in the following manner.

> The main issues raised in the six declarations since 1994 can be summarised as: i) the need to establish / promote public Sport for All policies; ii) the role of Sport for All in promoting public health; iii) the state / 'crisis' of school sport and physical education; and iv) the economic, social and cultural contribution of Sport for All to society.
>
> *(Green and Collins 2009: i)*

While the actual follow-up on the Declaration is described in both cases as being limited and unsystematic, a considerable majority of NOCs in both cases are described as positively engaged in sport for all activities and focusing primarily on sport for health and sport in physical

Ian Henry

education. The promotion of Olympic values through sport was also a significant concern. However, the notion of promoting sport for its own sake, as a human right (a notion explicitly supported by the IOC) is marked by its absence in the descriptions of activities and the rationales for those activities provided by the NOCs themselves.

Conclusions

While sports policy has grown in significance in recent years, it is in respect of elite sport, physical education, health and exercise, social integration through sport and other extrinsic goals rather than in relation to 'sport for sport's sake'. As Green expressed it in the title of an article reviewing trends in sports policy in the UK, policy has moved 'from Sport for All to not about sport at all' (Green 2006). The emphasis on the promotion of access to sport as a right, a rationale based on the intrinsic value of sport in the quality of life of the individual and the community, has declined together with the decline in welfare ideology that underpinned the welfare state.

Adult sports participation is on the agenda of international bodies as a vehicle for the achievement of other goals, but in itself sport for all or mass sport is likely to remain a predominantly local policy concern. Even though exercise is viewed, at least in part, as a counter to the obesity epidemic, since obesity is a non-infectious disease and thus does not travel across borders in the same way as for example, HIV Aids, even bodies such as the World Health Organization may find it difficult to legitimate transnational regulation, since local action may be deemed just as effective. Thus, while various forms of commercial sport seem likely to continue to require international regulation, adult mass participation would seem destined to remain a predominantly intra-national concern.

References

Council of Europe. (1992). *European Sports Charter*. Strasbourg: Council of Europe.
——(2007). 'The Ballons Rouges: sport for internally displaced children'. Retrieved 24 September 2009, from www.coe.int/t/dg4/sport/sportineurope/ballonsrouges_en.asp
——(2009). 'Enlarged Partial Agreement on Sport (EPAS)'. Retrieved 20 January 2010, from www.coe.int/t/dg4/epas/Source/Ressources/F05factsheet_en.pdf
Council of Europe Evaluation Team. (2003). *Evaluation Team Comments on Report by Ministry of Culture and the Estonian Olympic Committee to the Council of Europe on Evaluation of Estonia's Implementation of the European Sports Charter*. Srasbourg: Council of Europe.
European Commission. (2004). *The Citizens of the European Union and Sport*. Brussels: Euroepan Commission.
——(2007a). *Commission Staff Document: Action Plan 'Pierre de Coubertin' – Accompanying document to the White Paper on Sport* (No. COM(2007) 391 final). Brussels: European Commission.
——(2007b). *White Paper on Sport* (No. COM(2007) 391 final). Brussels: European Commission.
Gratton, C. (1999). *COMPASS 1999: A project seeking the coordinated monitoring of participation in sports in Europe*. London: UK Sport and Italian Olympic Committee.
Green, M. (2006). 'From "Sport for All" to Not About "Sport" at All?: Interrogating Sport Policy Interventions in the United Kingdom'. *European Sport Management Quarterly, 6*(3), 217–38.
Green, M. and Collins, S. (2007). *Current Status and Future Visions of Sport for All in Europe: Reflections of the Declarations of the World Sport for All Congresses 1994–2004*: Report by the Centre for Olympic Studies & Research, Loughborough University to the International Olympic Committee (Sports Department).
——(2009). *Current Status and Future Visions of Sport for All in Asia / Oceania: Reflections of the Declarations of the World Sport for All Congresses 1994–2004*: Report by the Centre for Olympic Studies & Research, Loughborough University to the International Olympic Committee (Sports Department).
Numan, J. (2008). *How the Olympic Day Run, a Local/National Event can Become a Communication Tool for the Use and Benefit of its Stakeholders*. Lausanne: MEMOS and University of Poitiers.
Olympic Solidarity. (2008). *Where the Action is: 2009–2012 Quadrennial Plan*. Lausanne: IOC.

UNESCO. (2006). *Collective Consultation in View of Proposing an International Platform to Promote and Develop the Traditional Sport and Games: Reference Document.* Paris: UNESCO.

——(2010). 'Quality Physical Education'. Retrieved 24 January 2010, from www.unesco.org/new/en/social-and-human-sciences/themes/sport/physical-education-and-sport/quality-physical-education/

United Nations. (2005). 'The International Year of Physical Education and Sport 2005: the concept'. In United Nations (Ed.). New York: United Nations.

Part 5

Sport and international development[1]

Introduction: The unproven remedy

Tess Kay

This Part of the Handbook addresses an area of sports development that has seen phenomenal growth in recent years – the use of sport in international development. International development is a long-established policy area, in which the richer nations of the global community provide support to low-income countries to help address acute social and economic problems. In its early phases in the mid-twentieth century, international development work tended to focus on economic and infrastructure issues, such as improving sanitation, transport systems and agricultural practices, but more recently has evolved to put a stronger emphasis on the development of human resources and productive social relationships. Sport is a relatively new addition to this work, but its use has rapidly become widespread. In this Part of the Handbook, several writers examine how and why sport is being used in this way.

The growth of sports-based initiatives within international development work reflects the perceived compatibility of sport with the wider international development agenda. Since 2000 this has been framed by the Millennium Development Goals (MDGs), launched by the United Nations and agreed to by all its 192 member states and by the leading development institutions of the world. The MDGs commit the international community to addressing global poverty, hunger, low education and gender inequity; health issues including the HIV/AIDS pandemic; and also to promoting global partnerships and environmental sustainability. Potentially, sport is believed to have many contributions to make to the Goals, especially in policy areas where young people are a primary target. The expectations about what may be achieved through sport are similar to those attributed to it in the global North – sport is believed to have the capacity to engage young people, provide positive experiences, and through this contribute both to personal development (e.g. increasing self-esteem) and collective benefit (e.g. building community cohesion). Sport is therefore being used in policies to increase education levels, promote healthy lifestyles, support health promotion including HIV-AIDS campaigns, and confront gender inequities by empowering girls.

Plotting the scale and spread of this work is a complex task. Kidd (2008) identified 166 organisations engaged in sport for development and peace projects, while Lyras *et al.* (2009), using different terms of reference, found that the number of known sport for development providers and projects had risen from around 200 in 2005 to over 1500 in 2009. However, the form which sport and development initiatives take varies widely, from transnational programmes to small-scale grass-roots activity, and inevitably it is the projects led by international organisations with their sophisticated PR machines that have become most visible. The best-known instances of sport and development work therefore include, for example, the United Nation's declaration of 2005 as the international year of education and sport; the work of the international organisation Right to Play, based in Toronto and operating in multiple countries; and programmes such as International Inspirations, the UK's 2012 Olympic legacy programme supported by a partnership of UK Sport, UNICEF and the British Council. A number of in-country programmes have also gained significant exposure in policy and academic circles, through their own promotional activities and their participation in research; these include, for example, Magic Bus in India, Go Sisters and the work of EduSport in Zambia, and the Mathare Youth Sports Association project in Kenya. But in addition to these, local workers identify a whole swathe of community-initiated sport and development work that goes undetected, including that undertaken by community, education and health organisations that do not specialise in sport but find it effective in their work. The omission of such activity in published audits underplays both the scale of activity being undertaken, and the pro-active role of indigenous organisations in its initiation. Sport and development work should not be seen, therefore, as primarily the product of externally funded development investment, but as a complex jigsaw resulting from the interaction of internal and external interests.

Positioning sport within this policy area raises some difficult issues. International development is politically complex and sensitive. Aid provided by richer countries can be regarded as a form of interference, control and cultural imperialism, perpetuating the political and economic dominance of donor states and the dependency of recipients. The terminologies 'Majority World' and 'Two-Thirds World' are used by some writers (including Kay (Chapter 22) and Hayhurst *et al.* (Chapter 25), respectively, here) to subvert assumptions about this dependency relationship: they remind us that the economically less developed countries make up the majority of the world's population, and possess rich cultural traditions that are far more widely upheld than those of westernised states. At a more fundamental level they open up the debate about the nature of 'development' itself, challenging assumptions that progression to the capitalist model of the Minority World is self-evidently desirable. Roger Levermore (Chapter 21) captures the distasteful face of this with his example of tobacco companies in Africa cultivating their new market by distributing free cigarettes at a sports event; as a counter-argument this needs little elaboration.

As in the Minority World, sport in the context of international development therefore offers ambiguities and complexities. There are difficulties in operating many projects, which typically rely heavily on partnership working and continuity of funding at the strategic level, and on volunteer effort – especially on the willingness of young people to act as peer leaders – at the point of delivery. Both pose challenges for sustainability of even the most successful initiatives. Additionally, while sport is valued for its potential positive contributions, it can also be regarded more negatively – at the micro-level, for qualities such as its institutionalised competitiveness, aggression and sexism, and at the structural level for its significance as an 'export' of the global North. The reliance of many programmes on meeting the requirements of externally provided funding streams raises further questions about the autonomy of indigenous organisations to develop their sports-based work as they see fit. Together these concerns can fuel debates about whether sport is an appropriate priority for investment in countries facing fundamental issues of poverty, ill-health and hunger.

The most significant challenge facing sport and development work, however, lies deeper. Despite the rhetoric and momentum surrounding it, researchers and policy makers do not know whether sport actually 'works'. As in the Minority World, the central challenge for academics is therefore how to assess the impact of sport. To address this, a number of critical networks have emerged, committed to collaborating to improve research quality and inform policy and practice. But like many sport and development initiatives themselves, such networks risk privileging the voices of the Minority World, and relying on culturally specific research models that reflect the values of the global North. To reach a more appropriate understanding of sport and development involves an altogether more ambitious project: engaging with the debates surrounding decolonising methodology and knowledge that feature prominently in development studies, to develop an understanding of the social impact of sport that originates from the countries in which such work is located.

The chapters that follow reflect the emergence of a critical academic literature examining these complex issues. In Chapter 21 Roger Levermore sets the scene, providing an overview of the growth of sport and development as a policy field, identifying the range of actors and interests involved, and examining how sport reflects a number of the contentious issues encountered in international development work as a whole. Following this, the remaining four chapters illustrate, through a series of detailed case study analyses, individual sport and development initiatives. In Chapter 22 Tess Kay continues these debates, using a case study of the GOAL project in New Delhi, India to examine how sport is being used to contribute to the wider development aim of female empowerment. Kay contrasts the positive response of the participants to the programme with the structural constraints that surround them, raising questions about the extent to which the benefits achieved through such programmes can realistically be translated into wider social gain. Davies Banda's case study of Sport in Action, a sport-for-development non-governmental organization (NGO) in Zambia, follows in Chapter 23. Banda outlines the general aims of the case study project, describes how it is delivered and funded, and turns a critical eye to how the project's targets relate to wider policy goals at community, regional and national level. In doing so he highlights the potential mismatch between national HIV targets and those of sport-for-development in general.

Zambia is also the location for Lyndsay Hayhurst, Margaret MacNeill and Wendy Frisby's examination of the Go Sisters programme, a sports leadership initiative to empower young women that initially operated in Lusaka and by 2013 will have been rolled out to four of the country's seven provinces. Hayhurst and her colleagues especially engage with the issue of sport as a colonising project, arguing that while sport does have potential to play a role in promoting health and other benefits and lessening gendered power imbalances, it also risks acting as a new form of colonialism. The chapter especially examines the potential consequences of this for women at risk of economic marginalisation through the operation of dominant patriarchal market forces, and emphasises the need for local input and cultural adaptation in sport and development work. The Part concludes with Aaron Beacom and Lorna Read's analysis of Right to Play, one of the best known of the transnational organisations now working in the sport and development area. As Beacom and Read show, Right to Play is illustrative of the emergence of sport and development organisations that operate at both the global and localised levels, creating pressure on them to develop sustainable infrastructures. The chapter examines how Right To Play addresses both the creation of a sustainable organisational infrastructure, and ultimately sustainable programmes and results.

Note

1 This is an area in which multiple terminologies are applied, and the chapters in this Part adopt authors' preferences. In this introduction, (i) the use of sport in international development contexts is referred

to as 'sport and development'; alternatives usages are sport 'in' or 'for' development; (ii) the countries in which sport and development work is taking place are referred to as the global South (and the traditional aid-giving richer nations as the global North); the reader is also introduced to the alternative terminologies of the 'Majority' and 'Two-Thirds' world.

References

Kidd, B. (2008) 'A new social movement: Sport for development and peace'. *Sport and Society*. Vol. 11, No. 4, pp. 370–80.

Lyras, A., Wolff, E., Hancock, M. and Selvaraju, U. (2009) *Sport for Development Global Initiative*. Paper presented at the North American Sociology of Sport Conference, Ottawa, Canada, November 2009.

21

Sport in international development

Facilitating improved standard of living?

Roger Levermore

As the following chapters highlight, the use of sport in an attempt to facilitate perceived improvements in international social and economic development is not new. Sport has been used historically (dating back centuries but especially during colonial times and in the post-1960 'independence' era) in (often unsuccessful) attempts to impose order and unity on populations. It has also been used sporadically by non-governmental organizations (NGOs) to promote development. For example, the United Nations Educational, Scientific and Cultural Organization (UNESCO) developed their International Charter on Physical Education and Sport in 1978 and the Mathare Youth Sports Association (MYSA) has been running in the Mathare suburb of Nairobi since 1987. Both have been reasonably well documented by the academic disciplines of sociology, history and of course sports studies (see for example Wagg 1995; Guttmann 1994; MacKenzie 1984; Maguire 1999; Willis 2000). The focus of this chapter is on the significant increase in the last decade in the use of sport to improve the social and economic environments faced by those living in precarious conditions. 'Precarious' here means communities living with one or more of the following:

- Sustained poverty, which includes starvation, poor diets and limited access to (clean) water
- High prevalence of disease (low life expectancy)
- War-torn society and/or unstable/authoritarian political systems
- Low levels of economic development (notably trade and investment) and infrastructure (especially communications networks and limited health care or education systems)
- Significant levels of discrimination and exclusion based on gender, sexual equality, social stratification systems, etc.

Although such conditions might be found in some areas of the world that the World Bank classify as high-income countries, they are more likely to be found in low-income regions.[1] Geographically, this means large areas of sub-Saharan Africa and parts of South America, Asia, the Pacific and eastern/central Europe.

How does sport fit into social and economic development? As Levermore and Beacom (2008) discuss, there is debate that highlights a difference between 'development *of* sport' (enhancing participation and performance in sport), and 'development *through* sport'. Development through sport relates to the role of sport as a vehicle to achieve a range of social and economic development aims or aspirations via specific development initiatives or sports events. However, there can be intended and unintended overlaps of the development of sport and development through sport. For example, FIFA (International Federation of Association Football) introduced two contrasting development initiatives in the last decade. The 'Football for Hope' programme has clear social development objectives for improving education, social integration and promoting empowerment among young people through participation in football and this would therefore mainly be a 'development through sport' initiative (FIFA undated a). In contrast, FIFA's GOAL programme operates primarily to strengthen the football infrastructure in all of its member states and that makes it 'development of sport' (FIFA undated b). Yet, social development is also facilitated through this because it promotes health benefits through sports participation and also an improvement in infrastructure that transfers to the immediate community/vicinity. Although not used in this section of the book, it is useful to note for reference that others who publish in this area – such as Coalter (2007) – categorize these terms as 'sport plus' and 'plus sport'. Sport plus focuses on the development of sport and plus sport concentrates mainly on social and occasionally economic development through sport.

The chapter proceeds by charting the significant increase in development through sport (also termed here 'sport for development'), noting the many different ways in which sport is seen to benefit social and economic development. That is followed by a section that details the array of governmental and non-governmental stakeholders that are (and importantly are not) involved in this. An assessment of some of the key issues associated with sport for development (contrasting motives of those involved, lack of evidence to support grand claims made and the potential of sport to exacerbate unequal power relations exposed in many previous and ongoing development initiatives) is followed by the concluding section which considers how suitable the image of modern, professional sport is for its usage in development.

Mapping the growth of sport as a tool for development and its perceived benefits

Although sport has historically been used with broad development purposes in mind it is really in the last decade that a substantial increase in the use of sport to assist specific development programmes has been seen. This takes two forms, the first of which relates to specific 'bespoke' development initiatives that use sport to assist aspects of mainly social (and occasionally economic) development. In research conducted in 2008, based on the website sportanddev.org, which catalogues an array of sport-in-development programmes, it was shown that over 200 projects were in existence (Levermore and Beacom 2008: 9). At the time of writing (June 2009), this figure is almost certainly above 300. Furthermore, following the 2010 World Cup – heralded the World Cup for social and economic development – there are likely to be approximately 300 initiatives running just on the continent of Africa.

A review of these schemes shows their recent intensification; 93 per cent were formed from 2000 onwards. Most of the schemes – totalling 52 per cent of all programmes – are located in sub-Saharan Africa. Young people are the main focus of these initiatives, with 51 per cent of schemes that specified a target audience (not all complete this), having youth or children as their focus. These schemes are starting to attract considerable interest – and accompanying exposure – from the political elite and the world's media. For example, in 2009 the former UK Prime Minister, Tony Blair, helped establish a policy awareness campaign, 'Beyond Sport' that partners with Virgin Atlantic and Barclays Bank in order to reward/support initiatives that have worked particularly well in promoting their development objectives (John 2009).

In addition to these specific initiatives, there are a growing number of large-scale sports events held in low- or low-to-middle-income countries. This includes the rugby, cricket and football World Cups in South Africa from 1995 to 2010; the Commonwealth Games in New Delhi in 2010; the 2008 Olympic Games in China; the 2007 cricket World Cup in the Caribbean; the 2012 European football championship partly held in Ukraine; and the football World Cup in Brazil in 2014. Hosting these events is said to benefit economic development by attracting tourists as well as stimulating public and private investment (especially into infrastructure) and spilling over to develop employment skills that can be used when the event is over.

It should be noted here that, although the chapter considers the broad application of sport in the development process, its focus is mainly concerned with the discrete benefits that are associated with bespoke sport for development initiatives rather than vague claims made by sports events to generate social and economic development.

But why is sport being considered as a relatively new vehicle in the delivery of social and economic development? On the one hand, there is a view that some perceive sport as a 'pure', non-political vehicle; it has the ability to send out messages in a value-neutral manner and therefore reach communities where communication by development institutions and politicians are met with scepticism. On the other hand, there is the belief that mainstream development strategies have failed and alternative vehicles are required. For example, despite over six decades of these policies, the level of absolute poverty is increasing. The 2008 World Bank Development indicators estimated that around half the world's population live on less than US$2.50 a day. Furthermore, 1.1 billion lack access to water and 2.6 billion lack basic sanitation. This poverty results in 25,000 children under the age of five dying each day (Shah 2009).

Sport has been categorized in at least ten ways in terms of its contribution to development, thus making it a promising new vehicle for development. Examples for each of these categories are given below; the partnership arrangements for them are listed in Table 21.1. Six of these relate to specific benefits linked to discrete sport for development programmes. These are listed by the International Platform on Sport and Development (undated) as being:

- Disability: sport is perceived to be at the forefront in 'normalising' disabled people in society through widespread participation in sport for development projects; it is regarded as being much more advanced than many general development policies in low-income countries. The Landmine Survivors Network, listed in Table 21.1, is a good example of an initiative in this area.
- Gender: using sport to address gender awareness issues to change behaviour and shape policy; particular focus is on female empowerment. See for example, Moving the Goalposts and Goal, listed in Table 21.1. Both of these have received widespread publicity and acclaim. The later chapters by Hayhurst *et al.* on the Go Sisters programme in Zambia and Kay on the GOAL programme in New Delhi look more closely at these types of initiatives.
- Education and child youth development: this is a major focus of sport for development, whereby programmes are organized to provide young people with opportunities to engage further with education/awareness campaigns by facilitating the congregation of young people at sports programmes/events. GOAL and Magic Bus are two examples in Table 21.1 of this aspect of development.
- Health: a major focus for many sport-in-development schemes; initiatives highlight awareness campaigns and there are physical and mental health benefits to participating in sport; particular attention is given to tackling HIV/AIDS. Alive and Kicking (from Table 21.1) educates about the dangers of malaria and HIV/AIDS in its work.

- Peace-building: helps communities to construct relationships that have been destabilized through conflict; this can be through specific initiatives to integrate child soldiers back into society or more broadly through national identity formation – see further details below. For instance, it is the view of the Peres Center for Peace (2003/4) that sport, 'has the invaluable ability to overcome barriers of language, politics, culture, and religion, and as such, is a wonderful tool for peacebuilding'. Football 4 Peace International is an example of this form of sport for development in Table 21.1 (see also Sugden and Wallis 2007).
- Disaster response: sport feeds into humanitarian disaster relief efforts, particularly in providing a suitable environment for stability; this builds social cohesion. Examples from the table include the Landmine Survivors Network and United for UNICEF.

The remaining four benefits are slightly broader. They are:

- The use of sport to promote policy awareness: this differs from the way sport for development programmes use sport (described above) to meet recipients face to face in order to promote health or educational awareness in that 'policy awareness' in this understanding is associated with global campaigns to highlight environmental degradation, child labour abuse, etc. The example of Saga Sports CSR initiative in the table fits into this category (see also Hussain-Khaliq 2004).

  A sub-category of this might arguably include an evolving argument of the right to play sport anywhere in the world, especially for the young, which should be considered a fundamental human right in itself and therefore part of rights/expectations associated with social and economic development (including education, right to food/water, etc.). For example, in 2002, Kofi Annan claimed that sport acts as a formative experience that builds self-esteem, leadership skills and breaks down barriers between communities.[2] The Magic Bus initiative in Table 21.1 highlights the rights of children to play sport.
- National identity formation/unity: some argue that sport (mainly football) is one of the few successful vehicles at driving some form of integrative unity; something that is most noticeable when a national team performs well in an international tournament, arguably projecting a positive image on a world stage. South Africa is one of the countries where the post-apartheid government has visibly attempted to use sport, and sporting occasions, to bolster reconciliation (see for example Höglund and Sundberg 2008).

  A sub-category of this is the use of sport to promote the image of other states, especially those wielding considerable influence, such as the US. The Sports Diplomacy Initiative, highlighted in Table 21.1, is an example of this.
- Economic development: this is occasionally an objective for discrete initiatives (for example, SCORE and Alive & Kicking (listed in Table 21.1) have been established with economic development as a strong characteristic), but is mainly associated with the transference of skills and economic growth initiated through sports events. This is largely via attracting sports tourists who spend money on local services. However, developing micro infrastructures and markets (including remittances from athletes who compete in high-income countries) and building skills for employment through sport are further 'spillover' effects of hosting sports events. Although these figures are disputed by many, the South African government expects the 2010 football World Cup to create 129,000 jobs, contribute R21 billion to its Gross Domestic Product, with 350,000 tourists spending R9.8 million (South African Government undated).

  Furthermore, hosting a series of successful (smaller) events is seen to create a 'virtuous cycle' whereby jobs are created and local industries can benefit. The International Platform on Sport and Development (undated) highlights the success of long standing sports events, such as the Inca Marathon to the Peruvian economy; small craft and manufacturing industries have been established to cater for those that run the marathon or visit to view it, whilst also participating in other tourist activities.

- Partnership formation qualities: as the following section illustrates, sport is regarded – at a time when creating partnerships between traditional and non-traditional actors is seen to be especially important – as being particularly good at strengthening the interaction of business, NGOs and civil society to promote international development. This is because sport is believed to 'connect' with many grass-roots communities as well as providing natural and non-political environments where partners can meet and deliver development. An example of how such partnerships flourish in initiatives is the Kicking Aids Out Network (included in Table 21.1), where coordinated frameworks have been established through the development of a matrix in order to help organizations linked to its plan, goals and resources.

Taken together, all of these 'benefits' point to why some suggest that sport is an apt vehicle to facilitate social and economic development. The United Nations is largely responsible for the escalation in this activity by naming 2005 as their Year for Development and Peace through Sport and Physical Education. Subsequently, the UNDP has declared that sport has a contribution to make to each of the Millennium Development Goals (MDGs). This is particularly the case for:

- MDG2 (achieve universal primary education) through making education more attractive and improving attendance.
- MDG3 (promote gender equality and empower women) by providing a mechanism for girls and women to experience individual development and build collective activity.
- MDG6 (combat HIV/AIDS, malaria and other diseases) through contributing to community-based health education campaigns and by using sports stars as 'ambassadors' who can reach out to often alienated parts of communities (such as young people).
- MDG8 (develop a global partnership for development) as 'sport offers endless opportunities for innovative partnerships for development and can be used as a tool to build and foster partnerships between developed and developing nations to work towards achieving the millennium development goals' (UNDP undated).

Funding, supporting and running sport-in-development: partnerships and new development actors

One reason for the intensification of sport's role in development is the increased number of actors, especially multinational corporations, who have interests in low-income countries and view improvements in development as potentially advantageous to business. These actors are concerned that traditional measures to generate development have not been successful, and are often persuaded that new vehicles – such as sport – are needed. They are joined by sports stars, clubs and federations who often buy in to the idea of the social worth of sport whilst also realising that sport for development can further promote participation of a particular sport.

This is not to say that more traditional development institutions have not been involved in using sport for development purposes. For instance, governments from high-income regions of the world (such as the UK, US, the Netherlands, Canada and Australia) have attempted to harness sport to assist in objectives linked to their international development goals. The belief in the use of sport for development purposes often straddles many departments.

Table 21.1 Selected examples of development partnerships of sport for development

Name of initiative	Description of initiative	'Traditional' development partners involved (e.g. state, World Bank, United Nations, and development NGOs)	'New' development actors (e.g. private sector, including sports federations)	'New' development actors (e.g. 'sport' NGOs)
Alive and Kicking Head Office: London: Initiatives run in Kenya and Zambia	Employs previously unemployed in Africa 'at a fair wage' to hand stitch sports balls. These balls are donated to children in poor communities throughout sub-Saharan Africa. The balls have educational awareness messages printed on them that relate to the dangers of HIV/AIDS, malaria, and TB	None visibly associated	Funding partners: The FA; Elton John Aids Foundation; UK Sport; UEFA has supported in the past	Not known
Beyond Sport Head offices: London and New York	Provides financial grants and mentoring to NGOs to support best practice in sport for development projects. It was established in 2009, with Tony Blair giving it substantial backing. Beyond Sport provides annual awards to projects. The 'Open Fun Football Schools' and 'Goals for a Better Life' received the Sport for Peace and Children's Rights awards in 2009	None visibly associated but UNICEF and the Swiss Academy for Development did attend a recent awards ceremony held by Beyond Sport	Supported by a comprehensive list of multinationals (such as Barclays Bank and Virgin Atlantic) and sports federations (such as the International Olympic Committee, Major League Baseball and US National Basketball Association)	Sport NGOs are beneficiaries of awards
Cricket Against Hunger Run by the World Food Programme and England and Wales Cricket Board Initiatives run globally and especially in the Indian sub continent	The England cricket team raises awareness about the extent of global hunger and remedies to it and the work that can be done to eradicate it. They do this when they tour as the World Food Programme arranges meetings between cricketers and children who receive food aid	United Nations World Food Programme	England and Wales Cricket Board	Not known

Table 21.1 (continued)

Name of initiative	Description of initiative	'Traditional' development partners involved (e.g. state, World Bank, United Nations, and development NGOs)	'New' development actors (e.g. private sector, including sports federations)	'New' development actors (e.g. 'sport' NGOs)
FC Barcelona Solidarity, citizenship and education initiatives promoted across continents, especially Latin America and Africa	Objectives include addressing poverty and ill-health, educational requirements and gender equality of the most disadvantaged children, particularly in low-income countries. In this sense, FC Barcelona Foundation links its work heavily to MDGs 2 and 3 (for further discussion of this, please refer to the debate after the table). A further area of support relates to the 'social normalization' of the most vulnerable especially the disabled and immigrants	UNICEF & UNESCO	Peres Center for Peace	Not known
Football 4 Peace International Located: West Bank and Ireland	Established by British nationals in 2001 to generate interaction of Muslim, Christian and Jewish children in the West Bank and Jewish settlements through football; the scheme, which believes football can established trust, respect, inclusion and responsibility, has subsequently been extended to the borders of the Republic of Ireland and Northern Ireland.	None visibly associated	University of Brighton (UK), German Sport University (Cologne), British Council (Israel), Israel Sports Administration, The FA Financial support is received as part of the 'Football for Hope' programme by FIFA	Not known
Football For Peace Colombia	Stated aims to develop gender awareness and social cohesion, especially by assimilating children back into their communities in Medellin, Colombia through the creation of a soccer league; started in 1996 by the founder of Streetfootballworld	UNICEF	BP funds the scheme	Not known

(Continued on next page)

Table 21.1 (continued)

Name of initiative	Description of initiative	'Traditional' development partners involved (e.g. state, World Bank, United Nations, and development NGOs)	'New' development actors (e.g. private sector, including sports federations)	'New' development actors (e.g. 'sport' NGOs)
Football For Hope Both FIFA and Streetfootballworld are based in Western Europe	Empower children by promoting healthy living initiatives and peace building (e.g. through refugee reintegration in post-conflict societies). These projects have to be aimed at children and young people, and must use football. Financial support is also provided to 39 NGOs that run discrete development through football projects. This ranges from Mali to Tahiti and includes some of the programmes listed in this table	Makes many references to the Millennium Development Goals but no formal link shown with global NGOs	FIFA & funded by official partners	First five centres delegated to run the Football for Hope centres (announced in 2007) were: MYSA, Play Soccer (Ghana), the Association des Jeunes Sportifs de Kigali Espérance (Rwanda), Grassroot Soccer (South Africa) and the Association Malienne pour la Promotion de la Jeune Fille et de la Femme (AMPJF, Mali)
GOAL NAZ (Netball programme) Operates in some major Indian cities	Netball in Delhi and Mumbai is being used to promote self-confidence, communication skills, health and hygiene, economic empowerment and financial literacy to girls aged between 13 and 20 (in poor sections of these cities, i.e. families earning less than US$2 per day). A loan scheme also operates; this is used by participants to further education, work opportunities, etc.	NAZ Foundation has been running since 1994, so might arguably be considered a 'traditional' NGO although sport is a relatively recent addition to the Foundation's work	Standard Chartered Bank is the main institution supporting this programme Partnering is the International Federation of Netball Associations	Supported by international and national NGOs (such as the NAZ Foundation India Trust). NAZ India is the NGO that runs the programme

Table 21.1 (continued)

Name of initiative	Description of initiative	'Traditional' development partners involved (e.g. state, World Bank, United Nations, and development NGOs)	'New' development actors (e.g. private sector, including sports federations)	'New' development actors (e.g. 'sport' NGOs)
Katine football tournament Kenya	The football tournament is part of a wider development project in the Katine community, Kenya, sponsored by the UK newspaper *The Guardian*. In publicizing the tournament, the paper highlights the integrative aspect of such tournaments for children who have lived (and fought) in areas of conflict. Health awareness and education initiatives are also part of this initiative, which is only open to men and boys	Organized partly by COSSEDA (a German-based organization that seeks to build bridges between Europe and Africa for economic development), the Soroti Rural Development Agency	Organized by The Guardian, the Teso League Project, and the Federation of Uganda Football Association (FUFA)	Not known
Kicking Aids Out Network	International network of sport for development NGOs, organizations and national sports agencies that links sports, physical activity and traditional movement games with HIV and AIDS prevention and education; begun as an African initiative aimed at children and youth and developed into an evolving international network of 'southern' and 'northern' partner and member organizations and associates Trained youth leaders who can engage their peers in sports, provide accurate health-related information and create safe spaces for discussion on sensitive issues	None visibly associated	UK Sport, Commonwealth Games Canada and Norwegian Olympic and Paralympic Committee and Confederation of Sports (NIF)	Various

(Continued on next page)

Table 21.1 (continued)

Name of initiative	Description of initiative	'Traditional' development partners involved (e.g. state, World Bank, United Nations, and development NGOs)	'New' development actors (e.g. private sector, including sports federations)	'New' development actors (e.g. 'sport' NGOs)
Landmine Survivors Network HQ Washington, USA	Peer support programme where survivors help each other recover from war injuries and trauma. 'Survivor role models' offer 'encouragement and motivation crucial to helping new survivors find hope, get jobs, and get on with their lives' Leadership skills are particularly emphasized when sports events are organized	International Committee of the Red Cross; Addis Ababa Prosthetic Orthotic Center; Christian Relief and Development Association	Paralympic Committee of Ethiopia	Not known
Laureus (Sport for Good Foundation) Headquarters are in London and projects supported around the world	Funds many partnerships, such as the one for the Peres Center 'Laureus uses the power of sport to help tackle pressing social challenges through a worldwide programme of sports-related community development initiatives' A range of ambassadors (sports celebrities) are used to highlight the benefits of specific projects	None visibly associated	Partners are Daimler, Vodafone, Mercedes-Benz and Richemont	Supports sports NGOs (such as Sport for All in South Africa) in many countries around the world
Magic Bus India	Helps children in slum areas of Indian cities to develop 'life skills' to enable integration into mainstream society through education. Enshrined in this programme is gender equality, the children's right to play sports, and community cohesion through participation in sport	None visibly associated	Standard Chartered, Unilever, and Deloitte sponsor. Run by volunteers from corporations that also fund the scheme	Aided by partnerships with NGOs and local schools

Table 21.1 (continued)

Name of initiative	Description of initiative	'Traditional' development partners involved (e.g. state, World Bank, United Nations, and development NGOs)	'New' development actors (e.g. private sector, including sports federations)	'New' development actors (e.g. 'sport' NGOs)
Mathare Youth Sports Association (MYSA) Nairobi, Kenya	Operating since 1987 in the Mathare township in Nairobi. Organizes sports teams and matches, with a strict code on behaviour and duties that all participants have to adhere to. Stated benefits include HIV/AIDS awareness, leadership training (many of the programmes are run by young people in the community), and other community service work (such as environmental cleanups)	Partners that support it include nine domestic and international development agencies, nine companies in the private sector, 12 governmental departments (local and national as well as support from Norwegian government ministries)	Nine sports institutions Partial funding received through the 'Football for Hope' FIFA programme	Including other sport NGOs such as Play the Game and Streetfootball world
Moving The Goalposts Kenya	An estimated 3,000 girls participate in this girls' youth sport and development initiative. Leadership, economic empowerment and reproductive health rights comprise the core development benefits/objectives	Partners with national government departments (such as Ministries of Health and Education) and traditional NGOs (such as Plan International)	Funders include Mama Cash, British High Commission, Alistair Berkley Trust, Safaricom Foundation, Ford Foundation, and UK Sport	Links with MYSA

(Continued on next page)

Table 21.1 (continued)

Name of initiative	Description of initiative	'Traditional' development partners involved (e.g. state, World Bank, United Nations, and development NGOs)	'New' development actors (e.g. private sector, including sports federations)	'New' development actors (e.g. 'sport' NGOs)
Peres Center for Peace	Sport is one of eight peacekeeping activities associated with this centre. It is used to implement 'a wide array of projects and programmes, utilizing sport to encourage solidarity, mutual understanding, respect and interaction between Palestinian and Israeli children and youth' For example, the Peres Center's 'Twinned Peace Football Schools' initiative encourages interaction between young Palestinians and Israelis through playing sport; peace educational awareness lessons and social activities accompany this	None visibly associated	FC Barcelona	Not known; website indicates that these are run independently by the sports division of the Peres Center
Positive Futures UK initially and now also based in South Africa	Launched in 2000 and now running in 108 local partnership projects in the UK to address anti-social and criminal behaviour of young people. This idea has been transferred to a Positive Futures programme in the Western Cape, South Africa	UK Government Home Office (Lifeline, South Africa)	Individuals and coaches	Not known

Table 21.1 (continued)

Name of initiative	Description of initiative	'Traditional' development partners involved (e.g. state, World Bank, United Nations, and development NGOs)	'New' development actors (e.g. private sector, including sports federations)	'New' development actors (e.g. 'sport' NGOs)
Right To Play HQ in Toronto, Canada	Styled as the largest sport for development INGO An 'international humanitarian organization that uses sport and play programs to improve health, develop life skills, and foster peace for children and communities in some of the most disadvantaged areas of the world. This includes girls, the disabled, child combatants and refugees.' Specifically, it supports the building of 'community infrastructures' through training local community leaders to deliver its programmes Location: regions affected by war, poverty and/or disease in Africa, Asia, the Middle East, and South America	UN agencies (e.g. UNHCR, UNICEF, UNESCO, WHO, ILO), the CORE Initiative, CARE	Celebrated athletes act as role models The International Olympic and Paralympic Movements	Local NGOs

(Continued on next page)

Table 21.1 (continued)

Name of initiative	Description of initiative	'Traditional' development partners involved (e.g. state, World Bank, United Nations, and development NGOs)	'New' development actors (e.g. private sector, including sports federations)	'New' development actors (e.g. 'sport' NGOs)
Sports Coaches Outreach (SCORE) South Africa (particularly the SportBusiness programme)	Trained over 650 international volunteers since 1991 to work in rural communities around southern Africa. A core focus is the development of a local sporting infrastructure, which makes part of this scheme the development of sport. However, a strong component is the desire to create a more sound business environment through a mentor programme in collaboration with local business and transferring general management skills (such as developing business plans). This is linked to SCORE in the Netherlands	Government support (EU, the Netherlands government)	Athletes, Adidas, Nike, IOC, Commonwealth Games Canada, UK Sport	Not known
Sports Diplomacy Initiative United States	Some specific initiatives that link into broader US foreign policy (to improve its image). For example, the use of basketball to facilitate the interaction of different factions within Lebanese society	US Department of State	Varies, country by country. In Ghana it is the Ghana Society for the Physically Disabled	Not known
Sport for Development and Peace International Working Group	This group is comprised of national governments, United Nations, and civil society (over a four-year period that ended in 2008) to make recommendations (particularly to national governments) for the integration of sport into international development initiatives	UN		Administered by Right to Play

Table 21.1 (continued)

Name of initiative	Description of initiative	'Traditional' development partners involved (e.g. state, World Bank, United Nations, and development NGOs)	'New' development actors (e.g. private sector, including sports federations)	'New' development actors (e.g. 'sport' NGOs)
Streetfootballworld Germany	Internet network that creates partnerships between government, business, sports organizations and NGOs to build sports projects. Many initiatives have as their core objective the provision of education, dissemination of information on disease prevention and delivery of employment skills. Over 70 organizations have been linked in this network	Inter-American Development Bank; various German government ministries	Youth Football Foundation; UEFA; FIFA; Sony; Cisco; Ashoka	Not known
'United for UNICEF'	This scheme started in 1999, whereby Manchester United Football Club supports vulnerable children (such as those affected by emergencies like the Indian Ocean Tsunami) through collecting donations at football matches, highlighting UNICEF policy campaigns and using Manchester United staff and players as ambassadors. For example, during the 2007 pre-season tour of South Africa, prominent players visited UNICEF-supported projects in Cape Town and Johannesburg	UNICEF	Manchester United	Local NGOs

(Continued on next page)

Table 21.1 (continued)

Name of initiative	Description of initiative	*'Traditional' development partners involved (e.g. state, World Bank, United Nations, and development NGOs)*	*'New' development actors (e.g. private sector, including sports federations)*	*'New' development actors (e.g. 'sport' NGOs)*
Vodafone	Vodafone Foundation has sport and music at its core; with £100 million spent on corporate social responsibility (CSR) initiatives since 2002. Specific development initiatives supported include support for the Homeless World Cup and Red Dust Role Models ('uses celebrities in the fields of sport, music and entertainment to promote positive lifestyle messages to young people'). Benefits include education, health awareness and welfare	UNICEF	Celebrity athletes support the Red Dust Role Models scheme. Partners with multinationals such as Nike and Qantas	Red Dust Role Model run by local NGOs

Sources: Sport-in-development reports and 'news postings' on relevant websites

In the UK for example, the government's Department for International Development, Department for Culture, Media, and Sport, and Foreign and Commonwealth Office all focus on the use of sport for development purposes.

Governments in the lower-income category are also using sport for development. Countries such as Azerbaijan include sport in their national poverty-reduction strategies and national development plans to stimulate education and highlight health awareness campaigns. Furthermore, a range of traditional development institutions, such as international non-governmental organizations (INGOs) and (domestic) NGOs are also involved in supporting sport-in-development. The UN, UNICEF, UNESCO, World Health Organization (WHO) and ILO recognize that sport can improve the physical and mental health of children and have developed partnerships with NGOs, private interest groups and community-based organizations to encourage participation in sports.

As a result, these relatively new and traditional actors help provide technical assistance, funding and ideas to those that operate specific sport for development programmes or sports events. These are usually non-governmental actors or community-based organizations; few have a long history in development assistance.

Table 21.1 highlights these partnerships, noting how many sport for development initiatives (whether they be programmes or sports events) are a collection of NGOs, government departments, agencies, sports organizations and businesses working together.

In analysing these initiatives, it might be argued that these partnerships come close to the 'novel forms of governance' outlined by Elsig and Amalric (2008) because of the extent to which private interest is diversifying its power into these new areas, whilst also providing more evidence that the state is abrogating its responsibilities in development.

Furthermore, in detailing these discrete initiatives and broader benefits associated with sport-in-development through sports events, it is unsurprising that they are perceived within development studies to be closely aligned to the 'functional' perspectives of neo-modernization and neo-liberalism. These viewpoints – ones that dominate development policy and planning – generally argue that low-income countries need to follow the policies that have worked well in allowing more developed regions of the world to increase their standard of living in the last century. Increases in aid, better governance, addressing corruption, stimulating business, trade and investment and bolstering infrastructure are often associated with one – or both – of these viewpoints. The sport for development movement clearly displays some of these attributes because of its linkage with strengthening infrastructure, endowing individuals with employment skills and allowing for more investment in society, and by being steeped in rhetoric that promises 'transformation' (implying progress from underdeveloped to developed societies) (Levermore 2008c: 29–30).

However, there is an irony that these dominant development perspectives show a level of disinterest and sometimes disdain for the role of sport-in-development. This is partly evidenced by the World Bank's 2007 World Development Report on youth development, in which only two sport for development projects (one being MYSA) are listed. The 'disengagement' of sport and international development by some traditional development agencies is possibly due to:

- A preoccupation with economic growth over social development.
- A continuing view that sport is exclusive, male-dominated and corrupt.
- Resistance to exaggerated claims that sport can be universally applied to an immense range of development problems is evidence of substantive 'over-reach'. For instance, Franz Beckenbauer (former German football captain and an authoritative figure in the world of

football) was quoted in May 2005 by *Süddeutsche Zeitung* as saying: 'Where football is played there is no fighting. If everyone played football, there would be no war – but not everyone plays football.' Less risible are the many 'feel-good' proclamations from those initiatives that support sport for development. For example, the Laureus Foundation (undated) claims that sport 'is a magical concept that affects all that it touches. It brings people together and unites them – for sport is a universal language that unites and inspires'.

- Concern over lack of planning in sport-in-development (both specific programmes and in sports events) and lack of consultation with development experts.
- Rejection of sport as a diversion from more important 'life and death' development issues (such as food security).

There are two issues that are of particular concern in relation to these perspectives. The first relates to contrasting motives that those in sport for development, especially those funding schemes, are understood to have. The second, which often links to contrasting motives, is the lack of accountability or measurement of tangible benefits associated with sport-in-development. Both are detailed in depth in the following section. Yet, more critical viewpoints on development (such as dependency and post-colonialism) share some of these concerns whilst also being wary of the inherent neo-liberalism and unequal power relations that inevitably result from the sport/development relationship, especially with so much funding, technical assistance and ideas emanating from high-income countries. These concerns are also discussed below.

Issues that arise from sport-in-development initiatives

First, there is some concern from across a broad range of development perspectives that the motives of those who engage in sport for development are not always as altruistic as the publicity surrounding their stated aims suggests. As previously noted by the author (Levermore 2008a, 2008b), sport for development partners can enter into agreements with contrasting motives. An oft-quoted example is the re-election to the presidency of FIFA of Sepp Blatter. This has been partially attributed to some of the electorate effectively being offered GOAL money to ensure that they voted for Blatter (Glanville, cited in Turya 2006: 15).

Indeed, many development through sport initiatives lack engagement and consultation with local communities or between partners. In some instances this leads to accusations of initiatives that are examples of 'greenwash strategy' (particularly those hiding well-documented examples of unethical labour practices or that are related to environmental destruction).[3] Undoubtedly, some companies use sport for development as a vehicle by which to further their brand; this is particularly troubling in schemes where companies indirectly market to children (Oxfam 2006). Many of the corporations involved in development through sport are food, soft drinks or tobacco companies, some of which have been criticized for supporting initiatives whilst simultaneously promoting unhealthy products to potential customers, especially the young. For example, allegations of sports events being used as opportunities for cigarettes to be distributed to young people have been recently directed at British American Tobacco in Nigeria, which gave away free cigarettes at sports events (Business Respect 2007).

A related aspect is the way that the influx in funding is revising the work and ethos/orientation of some NGOs in the sport for development movement. Research has pointed to:

a) The way that the 'search for funding' is prioritized over the original objectives of development assistance, and;

b) The encouragement given to organizations that are involved in general sports initiatives to exaggerate their development activities with a view to 'receive' additional funding when 'development through sport' objectives hardly exist.

(Levermore 2008a)

This adds to allegations by funders and mainstream development agencies that some NGOs that use sport for development are untrustworthy, unaccountable and fail to undertake objective and transparent evaluation of the schemes (Levermore 2008b). A result is the second issue of concern here, namely the desire to highlight some form of measurement that provides solid 'proof' that sport does justify its billing as being able to further facilitate development. Whilst some discrete initiatives, such as MYSA and Magic Bus, have been independently evaluated, many other schemes have in-house monitoring procedures, which are more prone to subjective and biased findings.

In the absence of such evaluation many questions are raised, particularly by traditional development actors and funders (Coalter 2007: 87; Kidd 2008). Such concerns extend to claims made about the development promise of major sports events. For example, in the 2007 cricket World Cup, the Caribbean countries that hosted the event incurred widespread debt, which led to the closure of some domestic industries because tourism levels failed to live up to expectations (Levermore 2008c). Furthermore, in South Africa, considerable doubt was expressed over the potential economic benefits of the forthcoming football World Cup, especially as the costs had increased tenfold (from R2.3 billion to R23 billion) since the World Cup was awarded to South Africa in 2003 (Noseweek 2008).

The lack of accountability has undeniably resulted in significant tensions between partners in sport for development projects. Funders complain at the lack of evaluation, which is indicative of an inadequate (business) approach and poor communication by some of the NGOs that implement discrete sport for development initiatives. Yet, this demand for more evaluation is clouded somewhat by the understanding that the environments that development and indeed sport operate within might not be conducive to standard evaluation techniques that international donors are familiar with. This is partially because donors often focus on output produced by initiatives born from corporate responsibility initiatives (termed corporate social responsibility – CSR). This is instead of wider measurement of the process by which CSR programmes are focused or oriented. For example, gendered issues tend to be ignored at the design stage of CSR initiatives (Newell and Frynas 2007). Furthermore, accusations are made that the desired evaluation is too focused on a 'tick box mentality' and that the need for accountability overrides important development objectives. Indeed, demands for evaluation often become highly charged political issues, especially if donors or government departments or development agencies are looking for reasons to suspend aid. Further, implicit in the 'lack of evaluation' argument is a patronising stance that suggests that domestic (Southern) NGOs are incapable of being managed or administered competently or honestly.

These concerns tend to be voiced by institutions based in Northern/Western countries. Yet, there can also be a wariness of the sport for development trend by what might be termed 'Southern' or alternative development perspectives. Similar to criticisms of a raft of mainstream development initiatives, this is partly because sport for development tends to be associated with institutions or development partners based in high-income countries. This view holds that development has imposed a long-standing belief that development is essentially good and that progress – along Western lines of what constitutes development – is possible. These processes are often promoted by Northern donor organizations (governmental or non-governmental) that enter into a relationship with a recipient from the global South (government or non-governmental).

Evidence of this 'top-down' process is clear in sport for development. Table 21.1 demonstrates a pattern whereby schemes that use sport for social worth in high-income countries are run and sometimes transferred to low-income countries. For example, many projects are heavily funded by organizations based in the North. This includes the Football for Hope, Streetfootballworld, Right To Play and Landmine Survivors' Network, whose headquarters are in Zurich, Cologne, Toronto and Washington, respectively. Linked to this is the way that discrete sport for development initiatives use 'Western' sports (football, cricket, basketball, volleyball, etc.) as the centrepiece of their programme. Previous research has highlighted how few indigenous sports are used to facilitate development, as 70 per cent of programmes on the sportanddev.org website that listed sports highlighted the use of football, volleyball, basketball or athletics (Levermore 2008c: 42). One such scheme – Positive Futures – started in the UK in 2000 and is being implemented now in South Africa. This is an example of schemes that have originated in the North and have been transferred to low-income countries.

'Southern' perspectives are particularly disturbed by this pattern because of the belief that sport for development can show a continuation of the exploitation that low-income countries have experienced since colonial times. Sport is viewed as a threat to its intended beneficiaries. Specifically, the 'Trojan horse effect' occurs when sport for development is used principally to further the interests of funders and partners from high-income countries rather than for local communities; this follows a long trend of similar complaints over traditional development initiatives. For example, some multi-national corporations (MNCs) have been accused of using their sport for development funding as a way to improve their publicity or – as the case of the tobacco industry noted above suggests – to strengthen the reach of their brand. Nike has been charged with the former, although the company has received strong support in the sport for development community for its work. This analysis has resulted in some sport for development schemes standing accused of being driven more by donor needs than recipient needs. Again, this parallels weaknesses highlighted in the general development literature, which suggests that the 'partnership' idea has been contrived and imposed on low-income countries; the power inherent in these relationships will rest heavily with international donors, without whom the scheme is unlikely to function (Lister 2000).

Second, sports governing structures and sport for development initiatives can exacerbate unequal political and economic relations that have long existed between the advanced, industrialized world and lower-income countries. This mirrors concerns that sport for development is driven by objectives that are heavily influenced by high-income country priorities, which in turn leads to potential alternative (low-income country) approaches being ignored. Sports federations such as FIFA have also been criticized for being an 'instrument of neo-colonial domination'.[4] Added to this is the perceived one-way flow of sporting men and women migrating from Africa and Latin America to play in sports leagues in North America, Japan, and Western Europe. The few who become successful generate considerable income for their agent, club, league, etc., without much trickling back to their countries of origin. Those who are not successful can be trapped in poverty in the countries to which they migrated (Levermore 2008a).

This 'top-down' dominance has resulted in tension boiling over in some sport for development initiatives. The call for extensive and bureaucratic evaluation from funders results in disruption of day-to-day and long-term development objectives that are required for development to succeed, rather than shorter-term outcomes associated with funders from the business world. Indeed, some NGOs express wariness that the demands of donor-led evaluation causes disruption as well as a fear that some donors have intentions of taking over projects.

Yet, is there evidence of a shift in sport that resists this 'top-down' power relationship? There has been an increase in the awarding and hosting of prestigious sports events to low-income countries. This includes football events such as the 2010 and 2014 World Cups in South Africa and Brazil; the Olympics in Beijing (2008); athletics meetings (Commonwealth Games in India in 2010); major international cricket tournaments (the World Cup in the Caribbean in 2007); and Formula One motor racing. This might represent a shift in power in global sport towards lower-income countries, albeit ones that have displayed a high level of recent economic growth and could be dominant high-income countries in decades to come. A particularly apt example is the Twenty20 cricket Premier league that was established in India in 2008. It was seen as a considerable success; players from the UK, Australia and New Zealand have been lining up to play for these franchises. Furthermore, when the tournament had to relocate for 2009, the UK was amongst countries clamouring to host it. In addition, some sport for development schemes (such as Football 4 Peace International and Kicking Aids Out Network in Table 21.1) have been established in lower-income regions of the world and then their ideas transferred to higher-income regions. Both arguably demonstrate a potential realignment of power relations in the international sporting (and sport for development) world.

Conclusion

This chapter has set out to illustrate the recent growth in the use of sport in attempts to facilitate international development. In some areas – such as sub-Saharan Africa – and for some communities (particularly young people) there has been an explosion of discrete sport for *social* development programmes. This expansion continued apace with the 2010 football World Cup in South Africa. Indeed, such sports events are believed also to hold considerable potential to assist *economic* development. The array of institutions/actors involved in this movement largely has development (improvements in standard of living, alleviating poverty, etc.) objectives at its heart. However, others focus on improving their business opportunities, with development being an unwitting or indirect side effect. This is unsurprising, given that a considerable number of those involved in the sport for development partnerships are commercial entities. In this context, it is reasonable for organizations such as FIFA to expect that football will be the only sport it supports in its sport for development initiatives. Yet, this same logic is part of the reason for traditional and critical development viewpoints to be wary of the use of sport as some 'new' engine that will promote a wide variety of development initiatives. Instead of seeing (mainly professional) sport as a harmless non-political vehicle, many 'outsiders' see sport entirely differently as a tarnished product associated with greed, corruption, foul play, violence and exclusion. In this context, how long might it be before contemporary analyses arrive at Frey's (1988: 66) conclusion that 'in reality, the impact of sport is over played, short-term, and of minor relevance to development'?

However, in defence of sport for development, is the argument that sport has polysemic images associated with it. Therefore, whilst greed and corruption might be associated with professional, elite sport, at the grass-roots level, its traits are viewed as being more laudable and slightly more inclusive. Furthermore, there are few more effective vehicles for reaching young people who have been victim of mainstream development policies that have ignored them or their culturally and age-specific requirements. Indeed, rather ironically, sport is sometimes attractive to young communities because it has a tarnished image, particularly to those involved in anti-social activities.

Moreover, the argument that those in the 'global South' have more important issues to be concerned with other than sport essentially dehumanizes them. They have as much right as anyone to play sport. Indeed, athleticism is often crucial to survival in some sub-Saharan African communities, as forms of sport have long been a part of African society and sport continues to be a compulsory aspect of many African education initiatives (Levermore and Beacom 2008). Therefore, there is a degree of Eurocentrism in disagreeing with the use of sport in the ways highlighted above.

What might help is more independent evaluation – and discussion – of sport for development. This could illustrate successful practices and show how sport compares against other engines of development. Some of these issues are indeed debated in the following case study chapters.

Notes

1 'Low-income countries' is a term used by the World Bank. It categorizes a country to be 'low income' if the Gross National Income per capita is US$975 or lower (2008 figures). In other literature these might be termed underdeveloped, Third World or global South countries. The term 'low-income country' is privileged above other terms here because it is yet to be extensively criticized for carrying the ideological baggage that terms like 'Third World' have. It is also important to note that there is a considerable quantity of programmes that operate in deprived areas of high-income countries.
2 For the full speech see, www.un.org/News/Press/docs/2002/sgsm8119.doc.htm. For further research on the linkage of sport and human rights please see Giulianotti 2004.
3 'Greenwash strategy' is a term given to the difference between rhetoric and practice in ethical/development behaviour by those that support corporate social responsibility (CSR) initiatives. This builds on fears that the primary interests of federations, clubs, and businesses that support CSR and development focus on their own priorities thus hijacking more altruistic developmental creeds.
4 Paul Darby (2002: 168) views football's governing body, FIFA, in such a way, noting that 'FIFA is not uncommonly regarded as an instrument of neo-colonial domination by African and other non-European football associations' and that 'ties between Africa and FIFA are often characterized by ambivalence and wariness on the part of Africans'.

References

Business Respect, 2007, 'CSR News', Issue 111, July.
Coalter, F., 2007, *A Wider Social Role for Sport: Who's Keeping the Score?* London: Routledge.
Darby, P., 2002, *Africa, Football and FIFA: Politics, Colonialism and Resistance*, London: Frank Cass.
Elsig, M., and Amalric, F., 2008, 'Business and Public-Private Partnerships for Sustainability: Beyond Corporate Social Responsibility?', *Global Society*, 22 (3), 387–404.
FIFA, undated a, *Football for Hope: Football's Commitment to Social Development*, Zurich: FIFA, p. 24.
——, undated b, 'About FIFA: GOAL Programme Mission and Goals', accessed from www.fifa.com/aboutfifa/developing/goalprogramme/, 5 May 2009.
Frey, J.H., 1988, 'The Internal and External Role of Sport in National Development', *Journal of National Development*, 1, 65–82.
Giulianotti, R., 2004, 'Human Rights, Globalization and Sentimental Education: The Case of Sport', *Sport in Society*, 7 (3), 355–69.
Guttmann, A., 1994, *Games and Empires*, New York: Columbia University Press.
Höglund, K., and Sundberg, R., 2008, 'Reconciliation through Sports? The case of South Africa', *Third World Quarterly*, 29 (4), 805–18.
Hussain-Khaliq, S., 2004, 'Eliminating Child Labour from the Sialkot Soccer Ball Industry', *Journal of Corporate Citizenship*, 13 (Spring), 101–7.
International Platform on Sport and Development, 2009, 'What is Sport and Development?', accessed from www.sportanddev.org/about_this_platform/ (19 May), accessed 9 July 2009.
——, undated, 'Developing Local Markets through Sport', from www.sportanddev.org/learnmore/sport_and_economic_devel, accessed 9 July 2009.
John, E., 2009, 'The Blair Sport Project', *Observer Sports Monthly*, June, pp. 34–5.
Kidd, B., 2008, 'A new social movement: Sport for development and peace', *Sport in Society*, 11 (4), 370–80.
Laureus Foundation, undated, 'Using the power of sport as a tool for social change', from www.laureus.com/foundation/about, accessed 19 June 2009.

Levermore, R., 2008a, 'Sport-in-International Development: Time to Treat it Seriously?', *Brown Journal of World Affairs*, 14 (2), 121–30.

——, 2008b, 'Playing for Development: Outlining the extent of the use of sport for development', *Progress in Development*, 8 (2), 81–90.

——, 2008c, 'Sport-in-International Development: Theoretical Frameworks', *Sport and International Development* (eds Roger Levermore and Aaron Beacom), Basingstoke, UK and New York: Palgrave, pp. 26–54.

Levermore, R., and Beacom, A., 2008, 'Sport and Development: Mapping the Field', *Sport and International Development* (eds Roger Levermore and Aaron Beacom), Basingstoke, UK and New York: Palgrave, pp. 1–25.

Lister, S., 2000, 'Power in partnership? An analysis of an NGOs relationship with its partners', *Journal of International Development*, 12 (2), 227–39.

MacKenzie, J., 1984, *Propaganda and Empire: The Manipulation of British Public Opinion 1880–1960*, Manchester: Manchester University Press.

Maguire, J., 1999, *Global Sport: Identities, Societies, Civilizations*, Cambridge: Cambridge University Press.

Newell, P., and Frynas, J., 2007, 'Beyond CSR? Business, poverty and social justice: an introduction', *Third World Quarterly*, 28 (4), 669–81.

Noseweek, 2008, 'White Elephant Country', *Noseweek*, 108, from www.noseweek.co.za/article.php?current_article=1822, accessed 1 July 2009.

Oxfam, 2006, *Offside – Labour Rights and Sportswear Production in Asia*, Oxford: Oxfam.

Peres Center for Peace, 2003/4, 'Newsletter', pg. 4, from http://209.85.229.132/search?q=cache: SZf5jxlO9eEJ:www.peres-center.org/ItemImages//2700/NewsletterWinter2003English.pdf+peres +center+%26+value+of+soccer&cd=2&hl=en&ct=clnk&gl=uk, accessed 7 June 2009.

Shah, A., 2009, 'Poverty Facts and Stats', *Global Issues*, from www.globalissues.org/article/26/poverty-facts-and-stats, accessed 15 June 2009.

South African Government, undated, 'South Africa: Fast Facts', from www.southafrica.info/about/facts. htm#2010, accessed 9 June 2009.

Sugden, J. and Wallis, J. (eds), 2007, *Football for Peace: The Challenges of Using Sport for Co-Existence in Israel*, Oxford: Meyer & Meyer Sport.

Turya, M., 2006, 'FIFA – Failing International Football Advancement', *Bulb*, 10, 15.

Tomlinson, A., 2007, 'Lord, Don't Stop the Carnival: Trinidad and Tobago at the 2006 FIFA World Cup', *Journal of Sport and Social Issues*, 31 (3), 259–82.

UNDP, undated, 'A year in sport: Sport and the Millennium Development Goals', from www.un.org/sport2005/a_year/mill_goals.html, accessed 1 July 2009.

Wagg, S., 1995, *Giving the Game Away*, Leicester, UK: Leicester University Press.

Willis, O., 2000, 'Sport and Development: The significance of Mathare Youth Sports Association', *Canadian Journal of Development Studies*, XXI (3), 825–49.

22

Development through sport?

Sport in support of female empowerment in Delhi, India

Tess Kay

Where there is poverty, or exclusion, or some other form of disadvantage, girls are far more likely to be adversely affected than boys. In terms of national development, a country cannot flourish if half of the population is left out of the development process.

(Oxfam 2006: 1)

I thought before the programme came in, before I played netball, I thought that girls can't do much in life, there are very limited things that girls can do, and I was happy and satisfied with that. But the moment this came into my life my entire idea about this has changed, and now I believe the only thing that matters is if you really think that you can do it, and you have the confidence and the will to do it, nothing can stop you.

(Participant, GOAL Project 2008)

This chapter explores issues surrounding the use of sport in support of female empowerment in international development contexts. The chapter is based on work with the GOAL project, a programme for young women operated by the NAZ Foundation (India) Trust. NAZ is a New Delhi-based non-governmental organization (NGO) that has worked in the field of HIV/AIDS and Sexual Health since 1994; sport is a relatively recent addition to the Trust's range of activities. The GOAL programme uses netball as a medium through which young women aged 13–19 can be reached, allowing NAZ to deliver a programme of sport, education and life skills in Delhi's poorer communities. The overarching aim of the project is to empower women to take control of their own lives and, beyond that, to become leaders and social activists in their communities.

Through its focus on women's empowerment the GOAL project sits within a well-established strand of modern international development work in which gender equity has emerged as a core focus for achieving social and economic advancement in the world's poorer countries. This chapter therefore locates its analysis of the programme within this wider policy context. It draws on research undertaken with GOAL in 2008, using this to examine the potential benefits of a sports-based programme with a specific commitment to empowering young women.

Examining the 'benefits' of sport in this way means entering murky waters. When Western researchers attempt to evaluate the social impact of sport in their own cultural settings they face an array of methodological and epistemological challenges (e.g. Coalter 2007; Collins *et al.* 1999; Long *et al.* 2002); when they address impact evaluation in international development contexts, they confront altogether more fundamental issues (Coalter 2009; Levermore and Beacom 2009). As the chapters in this section emphasize, the 'patronizing and colonizing' assumptions (Hayhurst *et al.* this volume) that underpin much of the international development project as a whole inevitably overshadow the role of sport, and sports research, within it.

Within the debates surrounding the colonizing process, the position of researchers is in fact particularly contentious. Linda Tuhiwai Smith (1999) describes the term 'research' as 'probably one of the dirtiest words in the indigenous world's vocabulary', and as 'inextricably linked to European imperialism and colonialism' (Smith 1999: 1). She challenges not just the ontological and epistemological underpinning of Western research and its positivist empiricist roots, but its wider cultural origins:

> From an indigenous perspective Western research is more than just research that is located in a positivist tradition. It is research which brings to bear, on any study of indigenous peoples, a cultural orientation, a set of values, a different conceptualisation of such things as time, space and subjectivity, different and competing theories of knowledge, highly specialised forms of language, and structures of power.
>
> *(Smith 1999: 1)*

Western accounts of 'the impact of sport' in international development thus face questions of legitimacy. Kay (2009) has suggested that evaluation research can be especially problematic, as these studies so frequently require researchers to privilege the positivist forms of knowledge preferred by external, minority world policy makers and donor agencies. The use of these methods is particularly likely to limit local expressions of knowledge and militate against reflexivity, partnership and local capacity building in research. But donor-funded sport for development projects require such data for transparency and accountability, and to counter widely acknowledged issues of poor governance. It would be naïve to expect such requirements to be removed. There are, however, tactical steps that can be taken to enhance the process of knowledge production within these confines, including:

- contextualising sport for development research more fully within broader social science analyses of local social, political, economic and – especially – cultural contexts, especially those produced by indigenous scholars. A key element of this is to avoid homogenising accounts of diverse local populations;
- increasing the extent to which analyses of sport for development are based on direct engagement with local stakeholders, deliverers and participants, underpinned by empirical research conducted in the field; and
- giving greater prominence to reflexive methodologies that can provide a mechanism for the expression of local understandings and knowledge. This is admittedly a limited gesture towards democratising unequal power relationships in a situation circumscribed by the legacy of colonialism; failing to use such methods, however, is a significant gesture to perpetuating them.

The research referred to in this chapter is an illustration of this approach. Drawing on qualitative data obtained in work with local providers and participants, it examines the reported impact of sport for development programmes for young women at the individual and community level.

This focus complements Hayhurst *et al.*'s more strategic application of postcolonial feminist analysis to sport for development in this section, and echoes in particular calls from sport for development researchers to centre Majority World voices in sport for development research (Crabbe 2009; Levermore and Beacom 2009; Nicholls 2009). The reporting of these voices here provides local accounts of how gender inequity is experienced by young women; whether and how the GOAL project contributes to their empowerment; and the wider impact that this has on their own and others' lives.

The remainder of the chapter is presented in four sections. The first establishes the wider policy context for the GOAL project, through a brief discussion of the use of sport in international development and a more detailed examination of the significance of gender within development policy. The second section looks more closely at strategies used within gender equity work in international development, especially approaches to empowering women. The third section reports the case study, outlining the status of women in India and presenting findings of the research that illuminate the sport-empowerment link. The findings indicate that GOAL can have a very positive immediate impact on its participants. The fourth section considers how we should view this in the context of the highly problematic structural challenges to achieving gender equity in Majority World nations.

The policy context: sport and gender equity in the context of international development

'Sport for development' refers to the use of sport in international development work, through which the international community addresses social and economic problems in many of the world's poorer nations. These countries were previously collectively known as 'developing countries' or 'the Third World' but today are more commonly referred to as the 'global South'. This chapter adopts the usage 'Majority World', a term broadly similar to 'Two-Thirds World' (Hayhurst *et al.*, this volume) in intent and designed to remind us that the poorer nations not only constitute by far the majority of the world's population, but possess rich cultural traditions that are more widely upheld than those of Westernised states.

Complex power relations underlie international development initiatives, as the authors in this section have shown. Far from being seen as charitable benevolence, 'aid' is regarded by many as a continuing form of cultural imperialism through which the countries of the Minority World protect their political interests and perpetuate the structural disadvantage of those who lack power within the capitalist system. Nonetheless, since its emergence in the mid-twentieth century international development has become a well-established policy area, working across diverse agendas. During this time it has undergone significant shifts in its focus and approach reflecting the changing nature of the global economy; changing understandings of effective forms of international aid; and changing attitudes to inter-cultural relations.

For the last decade the eight 'Millennium Development Goals' (MDGs), launched in 2000 by the United Nations, have provided a widely recognised framework for international development. The eight strands of work are closely intertwined with each other and address:

- Poverty and world hunger
- Universal education
- Gender equality
- Child health
- Maternal health
- Combating HIV/AIDS

- Environmental sustainability
- Global partnership.

These goals require action at multiple levels of social, political and economic systems and in a variety of contexts from local to transnational. This is therefore a complex policy landscape and it is helpful to see projects such as GOAL as located within this wider policy approach and exposed to some of its challenges. GOAL aims to contribute across multiple areas of young women's lives and to the wider well-being of their families and communities, and this very much reflects the multifaceted approach of development and the prominence of gender work within this. Increasingly, the empowerment of females has come to the fore as a core strategy underpinning wider social and economic advancement in Majority World countries, and sports-based gender programmes need to be viewed in this context. The next section therefore examines the principles behind the current positioning of gender equity within international development.

The gender agenda in international development

The prominence of 'gender' in international development policy is a relatively recent development. When the concept of 'development' was itself first gaining currency in the years following the Second World War, 'issues of gender development were not even considered relevant' (Hunt 2004: 243). Although women and girls were included in development initiatives as the recipients of programmes specifically targeted at females – focusing on issues such as health, family, and child welfare – they were marginalized from core programmes designed to foster structural economic, and therefore social, development. In fact, the failure by development agencies to recognize the economic roles already played by women in many 'Third World' countries led to policies that in many cases increased female exclusion, reduced women and girls' access to resources, and worsened both their economic and social position (Hunt 2004).

During the 1970s revisionist accounts (most notably Boserup 1970) emerged that reconceptualized the significance of women to economic development and exposed the neglect and misunderstanding of women's roles. Over the next two decades pressure grew for the integration of women across the breadth of development. In due course, however, this approach too proved problematic, as it became evident that, when women participated in core programmes that had been constructed on the Westernised model of male bread-winning, they did so on a less favourable basis than men (Kabeer 2003). It became apparent that development based on existing economic, political and cultural structures could not deliver individual equality for women, collective benefit for their families and communities, or structural solutions to gender inequity. A rethink was required that addressed the underlying relationship between gender inequity and development more holistically.

In what might be seen as a third phase in international development approaches to women and girls, the policy focus has progressively shifted from 'women' to 'gender'. This has brought an emphasis on relational perspectives and a recognition that development for women needs to address not just practical requirements but also strategic needs. Importantly, achieving gender equity has been seen – and presented – not just as an issue of social justice for girls and women, but as fundamental to development as a whole. While the saying, 'Poverty has a woman's face', recognizes the disproportionate impact of deprivation on women, the slogan, 'Educate a woman and you educate a community' recognises women's significance as agents of change across the breadth of the development agenda. Thus, organizations such as the World Bank advocate that empowerment of women should be a key aspect of all social development programmes (Herz and Sperling 2004: 21), and this has been supported by a growing body of research that shows that education and empowerment of girls and women lowers poverty, increases family health, reduces birth rates and contributes to a more educated and valuable human resource base (e.g. Tembon and Fort 2008). Such evidence has further strengthened the view that women's equality and empowerment is central to the holistic and sustainable processes of social and economic development that are required to enable Majority World countries to benefit from their full array of human capital (Handy and Kassa 2004).

Gender equity through female empowerment

'Empowerment' is a commonly used approach within gender equity movements and a central concept in international development. Described as both a process and an outcome, empowerment is generally recognised as a strategy for both individual and structural change, therefore operating at multiple levels. In 1998, the Committee on Gender and Population of the International Union for the Scientific Study of Population (IUSSP) attempted to define a concept whose widespread use had fostered ambiguity rather than clarity (Muraleedharan 2005) and stated that:

> Empowerment is about the transformation of power relations; ... it includes both control over resources, and changes in self-perception and confidence in one's self; ... it can be viewed as both an outcome and a process; and ... women's empowerment involves the transformation of power relations at four different levels – the household/family, the community, the market and the state.
>
> *(IUSSP 1997)*

Writers in the international development field corroborate this view, emphasizing in particular the linkages between individual empowerment (e.g. increased self-esteem, confidence and awareness) and structural change. Sen and Battliwala (2000:18) talk in terms of empowerment as 'an inner transformation of one's consciousness that enables one to overcome external barriers to accessing resources or changing traditional ideology'; similarly, Pradhan (2003) describes empowerment as enabling women to overcome 'systemic sources of subordination'. Pradhan thus sees empowerment as 'the process by which the powerless gain greater control over the circumstances of their lives' (2003: 185), and argues that this requires control over ideology (beliefs, values and attitudes) as much as control over resources (physical, human, intellectual and financial). Achieving gender equality is therefore 'as much a question of social values, political commitment and public action as it is of the availability of resources' (Kabeer 2003: 17) and, crucially, is dependent on collective as well as individual impact. A central aim of empowerment in international development contexts is therefore *collective development* that brings women together to jointly address their shared challenges.

The experiences through which women become empowered include awareness building; capacity building and skills development; participation in decision making; and action to bring about greater equality (e.g. Karl 1995). Historically women's empowerment has been based on grass-root initiatives that are designed to meet the specific needs and interest of local women themselves. This is based on the assumption that the capacity to confront gender inequality can only be developed through bottom-up action and participation at community level (e.g. Moser 1998). A further characteristic of empowerment is therefore that it is achieved through a participatory process and cannot be bestowed from the top down (Rowlands 1995; Moser 1998). Friedman (1992; in Muraleedharan 2005: 57) connects political empowerment with social empowerment, in that political empowerment requires a process of social empowerment through which effective participation in politics becomes possible. This involves undoing negative social constructions, so that the people affected can perceive themselves as having the capacity and right to act and have influence (Rowlands 1995: 102).

In international development work, the central strategy to empower women is education of females. This includes formal education (academic learning and skill development) to increase earning capacity, and life skills teaching (on issues such as hygiene, sexual health and reproduction) to enhance quality of life. Education has particular importance in development contexts because of its wider contribution beyond the impact on women themselves (Herz and Sperling 2004). At the aggregate level, the benefits of increased female education include increased labour force participation and expansion of the economy; multiple positive health outcomes for women and their families; lower fertility rates; and intergenerational transmission of knowledge. These impacts are triggered by female education because educated women tend to have fewer children, which reduces dependency ratios and raises per capita spending and eventually lifts households out of poverty, and because increased maternal education also transmits intergenerational benefits by boosting the survival rate, education level, and nutritional status of children (Tembon 2008: 5). Significant as the additional benefits may be, Hanushek (2008: 24) nonetheless argues that the education of girls can be justified on a single premise alone – 'the benefits that educational investment in human capital brings to the economy'. Positioning female education as essential for economic growth and poverty reduction provides a particularly robust policy rationale for investment in this area.

As empowerment involves change beyond the individual, it needs to be supported by accompanying organizational change among a range of actors including policy makers, donor agencies, the state, the private sector and NGOs. 'Gender mainstreaming' within these organizations entails a shift in both cultures and practices. Desia (2005) provides an example of how, in development initiatives in Mumbai, instead of focusing on service delivery or the delivery of technical information only, NGOs with a commitment to social transformation began to focus on raising awareness among poor people about equality, social justice, gender sensitivity, secularism, communal harmony, and human rights. 'The hope is to enable people to achieve a sense of entitlement to equal treatment in matters of human concern, to develop the capacity to reflect on their situation and to question this, and to take action' (Desia 2005: 93).

The widespread use and promotion of female empowerment as a development strategy should not obscure the challenges surrounding this approach. Obstacles arise at the societal, organizational and individual level. Yet 'empowerment' remains a prominent concept within gender equity policies, is gaining rather than losing currency in international development, has often featured in sport's gender equity policies in the Minority World, and is now being widely adopted within sport and international development strategies. The GOAL project is an example of the latter usage, and the following case study therefore examines how the project may contribute to the empowerment of the young women who participate.

Empowerment through sport in India: The GOAL project

This part of the chapter draws on research that was undertaken with the GOAL project in Delhi in May 2008 (Kay *et al.* 2008). At this time GOAL was working in two impoverished communities in the city, Aali Gaon and Deepalaya, using netball as a medium for engaging young women. The focus of the project was on sustained, intense work with relatively small, close-knit groups of participants; approximately 45 young women aged 13–19 were involved across the two sites, most of whom had been taking part for several months and many for more than a year.

The purpose of the research was to develop an understanding of the project through methods that allowed the voices of those involved to come to the fore. The study sought local articulations of both the 'problems' being addressed and the 'solutions' being delivered. This required centring the voices of those directly and indirectly engaged in GOAL. Accounts were obtained through a series of interviews and discussions with young women participants, NAZ project staff, and local education and community personnel who had worked with young people in the two communities for many years. In total information was obtained from 38 individuals, including 19 young women participating at Aali Gaon and 12 at Deepalaya, four NAZ staff, and three other professionals.

The account that follows focuses on the theme of empowerment. First, the challenges, as perceived by the young women and those who worked with them, are identified; second, the extent to which the project delivered individual empowerment is explored; and third, the link between individual empowerment and collective development is scrutinized.

The GOAL project

The GOAL project was established to empower young women to challenge the discriminatory treatment of females in India's strongly patriarchal society. Sport was chosen as a novel way to attract girls to a programme that could provide them with new opportunities and also bring about wider educational, personal and social development benefits. None of the girls participating at the two sites had played netball before: sport was commonly seen as a male preserve and difficult for Indian girls to access. Netball was considered an appropriate introductory sports activity for girls and young women for a number of reasons: it was an accessible and simple game for girls to master; as a 'female' sport it did not challenge male dominance of sport too explicitly; and as a non-contact sport it did not contradict ideas about acceptable behaviour for Indian women.

In 2008 GOAL was offering twice-weekly netball sessions at each of the two sites in which it operated, incorporating educational modules at some sessions to provide a holistic approach to personal development. The topics covered included personal issues such as communication skills, health, sex and sexuality, and HIV/AIDS; social issues including the environment; and economic issues such as micro-finance and computing. The modules were intended to complement the health and well-being, teamwork and leadership promoted through the netball sessions.

The two sites and communities differed. Although both were within the city and close to main traffic routes, at Aali Gaon the immediate environment was almost rural. GOAL sessions took place in a small open area reached by crossing a railway line and surrounded by sparse dwellings and trees. The playing area was a bare dust surface; cows were tethered by some houses and other small animals roamed around the site. The community was socially conservative, and the young women had limited education and little independence; their lives were very much defined by domestic responsibilities in the home. At Deepalaya, the arrangements and participants were different; GOAL activities were delivered in a local school and attended by current (and some former) pupils. The girls at Deepalaya were on average younger than those at Aali Gaon, and more educated; they received more support from their parents for a life outside the home, had more personal time and were not subsumed in domestic work to the extent of the Aali Gaon girls. These relative freedoms should not be exaggerated, however; Deepalaya girls' lives were nonetheless circumscribed by their gender, the low income of their families, and by deeply entrenched societal expectations. There were many commonalities in the two groups' experience of gender inequity.

Being a young woman in Delhi: The experience of gender inequity

Low-income women in India experience the deprivations of poor women elsewhere in impoverished populations. In comparison to men, they are more vulnerable to poverty and poor health, have low levels of education and access to the labour market, and limited social and economic resources. The potential impacts of gender inequity are present throughout the life-cycle: conception and birth bring risks of female foeticide and female infanticide (Oxfam 2006); in childhood many girls become 'nowhere children' (not present in school, or in work, but 'hidden' in domesticity) (Kambhampati and Rajan 2004); in adulthood, women's life expectancy is short, maternal mortality high, female literacy levels low and domestic violence widespread. Many of India's women are therefore invisible, inaudible citizens (Sinha 2003), united by a shared experience of gender inequity, yet divided also by caste, tribe, class and religion (Chanana 2004). For those who are members of the lower status groups among these, India's intensely hierarchical society compounds the gendered impacts of poverty and disadvantage.

Since the 1980s the Government of India has shown increasing concern for women's issues through a range of legislation promoting female participation in education and politics (Kabeer 2003). NGOs have also become active in addressing gender inequity, moving from their traditional focus on health and educational needs to address the underlying causes of deprivation through the economic and social empowerment of women (McNamara 2003). Despite this, the key indicators of women's status remain poor and their problems widespread.

For the young women participating in GOAL, the impacts of gender inequity were evident throughout everyday life. In communities where arranged marriage was prevalent and most young women's futures were structured for them, girls were subordinate in their families. Economically, the lives of the young women in Aali Gaon were particularly difficult. Their fathers were employed in marginalised jobs and the work that the girls did in the home was essential to families because of their low economic position. The expectation that they would stay mainly within their own households, fulfilling domestic responsibilities, limited their wider social engagement.

The girls in both communities were disadvantaged in education. Those from Aali Gaon had either not gone to school or been forced to drop out at an early age, whereas those from Deepalaya had had significantly more schooling, but this too had important limitations. Both groups reported poor-quality teaching and described being intimidated, dismissed or ignored by teachers, particularly over 'sensitive' issues. Their schooling had therefore left them with limited formal education, and little knowledge about the issues that were fundamental to their life chances. They lacked the skills to assert themselves to obtain the information they needed on subjects such as health, fertility and sexuality:

> It's very difficult for us to go and confront a teacher about something, they'll give us a reason like 'right now there are a lot of boys around and I can't answer such a sensitive question', and that is where the matter dies.
>
> *(Deepalaya participant)*

The girls' lack of confidence in this area reflected a deeper inexperience in expressing their views. Their limited social interaction provided few of the communication skills they needed to speak out against the constraints they encountered:

> We never had the opportunity to go out, and when you don't go out, you hardly speak.
>
> *(Aali Gaon participant)*

> I used to tremor or shiver when it came to talking to somebody, I would just hide myself behind a wall or just run away.
>
> *(Deepalaya participant)*

At both Aali Gaon and Deepalaya, the intersection of gender and poverty underpinned the girls' current lives and future aspirations. Their situation presented a substantial challenge for female empowerment.

Experiences of individual empowerment

The girls' experiences on the GOAL project fostered individual empowerment through a range of interrelated benefits. There were significant gains from learning and playing netball: girls' self-esteem and confidence rose as they mastered a new sport and experienced themselves as capable and competent. Netball also required them to work as a team and communicate effectively, and through this their skills developed:

> Because of the team activity that goes on, I have started, I have learnt how to interact, which I would never have done before.
>
> *(Aali Gaon participant)*

Benefits like this equipped them to feel confident about speaking out in other contexts, with both peers and adults:

> Before I was a part of this, I always used to be very shy, even, talking to the people with whom I live every day, like my father, my mother, my brother. I was so uncomfortable even talking to them, I used to shy away. But now it's not like that. I am like a confident girl … Now when we meet, we get to speak.
>
> *(Aali Gaon participant)*

The School Principal at Deepalaya observed how as the girls grew in confidence, they also began to develop decision-making skills:

> You can see the confidence in these girls, I mean the leadership quality and their communication skills and now, they will listen and understand and try and make analytical understanding and then take the right decision which is very important for the children.
>
> *(School Principal, Deepalaya)*

These skills could be applied within their own families:

> The girls, their background is they come from first generation learners and girls are not given that much of importance and their views are not given adequate weighting. So now at least they know how to assert their rights, they know how to speak within their family and be heard which I think is a step in the right direction. They can be very active decision makers in the long run in the families.
>
> *(School Principal, Deepalaya)*

The educational content of GOAL was central to this growth in girls' confidence. The information they obtained through the programme provided self-knowledge and equipped them to manage their own lives:

> I know my own body now, I know which part is functioning how and where, which I had no idea. Even though the body is mine, I was absolutely unaware of my own body.
>
> *(Aali Gaon participant)*

> My biggest learning was something about a killer disease like AIDS. I had no idea about it, and now I know what it is, and I can stand against it, because I have the knowledge, and probably this knowledge would also help me to help the people around me.
>
> *(Aali Gaon participant)*

By delivering educational modules within the context of an enjoyable sports programme, GOAL created an informal environment in which the girls felt safe and comfortable, became accustomed to expressing their views, and developed their social interaction skills with each other and GOAL staff. This improved their teamwork, increased their sense of responsibility and assisted their ability to build relationships with peers and older adults. Many felt they had experienced fundamental change:

> I have changed overall, like the way I talk, the way I present myself ... now I can face people, when I co-ordinate in a team in the field and the sessions, I have become much more confident, I can face the world ... today, in class 9, one of our teachers came and said, 'have you seen the class 7 girls, they are so good at football, and if you have a match with them, I'm sure you guys would lose it'. And I felt sure, it was such a different feeling inside me, and I actually ended up telling my teacher 'just give us a chance and you will see who wins and who loses'. It's not the matter of winning, or losing, it's the matter of having the confidence of going and playing there and I know at this point I can do it.
>
> *(Deepalaya participant)*

The overall impact of the programme was transformative for some girls:

> Now when I have come out to this programme I feel so confident, there is so much self belief in me.
>
> *(Aali Gaon participant)*

From individual empowerment to collective development?

As we have seen earlier, empowerment is not only an individual project: its role is to foster structural change. There was extensive evidence within the research that participating in GOAL had impacts beyond the girls' own individual gains. There were two elements to this: the impact that the girls' experiences had on others around them, and the role the project played in encouraging the girls towards collaborative action.

Indian society, like many cultures within the Majority World, is underpinned by a collectivist ideology. This is especially manifest in family life. The girls made many references to how they shared the knowledge that they gained from the programme with their families and others:

When it comes to the family, whatever we learn there, we go and share it with our families, our mothers and brothers and sisters, so even if they are unaware of other things, they get the knowledge.

(Deepalaya participant)

Our mothers encourage us to go and play and once we get back home, they also look forward to us coming back home because we go home with a lot of information, which we share with them.

(Aali Gaon participant)

Sharing knowledge has the potential to contribute to cultural change by re-educating others, including older and younger generations. Many of the girls reported that their families' expectations of them had shifted as they observed how their daughters were affected by their experiences of the project.

Our mother says 'I could never study, I never got the opportunity, but I don't want that to happen with you, I want you to go on in life and make it big'.

(Aali Gaon participant)

The School Principal saw this as part of a broader trend she had observed in the community, of parents increasingly realizing the importance of education to their daughters:

[This is happening because] before, education was not something that appealed to these people, they wanted their children to work cos that was a helping hand, helping with younger brother and sisters or getting children married off. But now people are gradually understanding the value of education, over a period you see the difference that education brings about, so gradually it is coming into the understanding of the parents, so I see major change.

(School Principal, Deepalaya)

The girls themselves reported how some of the immediate constraints around them were loosening:

People, families, when the sport came up, and the programme was here, they said 'clean, cook, and that's your life'. And there was this line that was drawn that we could never cross. But now that line is going backwards. And we are just, you know, coming out, we have crossed it.

(Aali Gaon participant)

The GOAL staff echoed these views. They were under no illusions that the programme would dramatically change the girls' futures. They believed, however, that it could contribute to gradual cultural change as knowledge was passed to future generations:

We always have to think, you know, where are we taking them? I don't see them becoming professional netball players, because I know they can't reach that. I don't see them being in the corporate world, doing a corporate job, because somewhere down the line in one or two years they will get married. But, the changes we are looking for, as we said, if they get married, and they still have a commitment to be with NAZ, and sharing the information, passing the information, bringing about the change, or when they have daughters, or sons, you know? See, their mothers never taught them, but they being mothers, who have the knowledge, share it. That is what we are about, the chain is broken.

(GOAL Project Manager)

The very experienced Community Worker who worked with GOAL in Aali Gaon felt that the project was making a further contribution to bringing about change by teaching the girls how to work together to achieve it:

One thing which is very important, these girls, during their sessions of the sports, they have developed team spirit, which is a very big thing for them. They will play a game, but team spirit is very very important for their lives. As a team they can fight for their locality, as a team they can fight for any personal issues, now they know, that single person cannot do it, anything, you have to unite, to fight ... Regarding the women issue, girl empowerment, these girls have learnt that we need a team spirit, we need a group relationship, we must be united, we must have a group who has relations with another group, so if they start fighting for any issue, regarding their life, regarding their goal, as women, they can fight.

(Community Coordinator, Aali Gaon)

The girls recognized how the teamwork they had learnt through netball could be applied to other aspects of their lives:

Being in a team and playing is so important because when you are in a team, you're united, and when you're united, you win.

(Aali Gaon participant)

According to those involved in it, the GOAL project offered multiple benefits. Their accounts were a strong testimony to the capacity of sport to provide the basis for a holistic programme to empower and educate girls. Through GOAL, girls developed self-knowledge and confidence that allowed them to expand the parameters of their day-to-day lives. They became more articulate, decisive and effective in communicating and asserting their views. The changes in them spread beyond their own experience, eliciting support in their families and beginning small shifts in their position within their households. The knowledge obtained through the project was shared with siblings, friends and their own mothers, and the girls were also committed to educating future generations. For those in school, the increased confidence and ability to communicate also led to more productive relationships with teachers and shifted the perceptions that some staff held of what young women could achieve. Finally, through participating in the programme, girls from both sites had changed their expectations for the future: their aspirations rose and they gained a confidence that they could make choices about their lives and pursue their preferred goals.

Empowerment through sport? Challenges to strategies to empower women

Those involved in the GOAL project give striking testimonies of its success as a vehicle for personal empowerment. Empowerment is, however, a process of structural as well as individual change, requiring transformation of power relations at multiple levels. How should we relate the experiences of GOAL's participants to the broader project of gender equity?

Empowerment is difficult to achieve and can bring risks. Writing on the use of women's empowerment within HIV/AIDS policies, McCallum captures the magnitude of the challenge when she explains how 'simply providing a woman with negotiating skills is not enough, when what she is trying to shift is a culture that does not respect her right to exert control over her life' (2006: 3). Partial empowerment – for example at the individual level only – may in fact do more harm than good, since power relations operate at multiple levels; change at one level does not guarantee changes at others, and may even lead to backlash or backsliding at other levels (IUSSP 1998). Schuler and Hashemi (1998) provided an illustration of this in their study of a local development initiative in rural Bangladesh, which highlighted how women could be placed at risk when they challenged gender relations. One man in the study explained that 'our wives would not be beaten so much if they were obedient and followed our orders, but women do not listen to us and so they get beaten often' (Schuler and Hashemi 1998; in Muraleedharan 2005).

Further obstacles are evident at the organizational level. Desia's (2005) analysis of NGOs in Mumbai found that, while organizations were quick to absorb new discourses of empowerment and gender equality, there was limited understanding of the underlying approach this entailed. For these NGOs, the replacement of 'women' with 'gender' meant integrating women into development activities along with men, and some used this to resist any specific focus on gender inequalities. Their analysis of gendered power relations did not address organizational dimensions, and formal changes in policy focus therefore had little effect on the lives of local women living in urban poverty. Desia concluded that even the most comprehensive approaches to institutionalizing gender were not adequately emphasizing the importance of organizational change, particularly in organizational norms and culture.

At national and supranational level, Kabeer's (2003) analysis of poverty reduction policy emphasizes the limited extent to which gender mainstreaming has occurred. A key reason for this is the lack of gender expertise across organizations and policy systems, with such expertise tending to be concentrated in sectors traditionally associated with gender and women's issues, and in programmes that directly address women's concerns or gender equality efforts. Although 'the need to institutionalise gender equity in the organisations responsible for making policy has long been recognised' (Kabeer 2003: no page number), progress has been uneven, in richer as well as poorer countries. To date international development policies and programmes show only limited and compartmentalized concerns with gender equity.

Sport for development movements cannot separate efforts to empower women from the need for this to occur alongside structural chance. By empowering individuals, projects such as GOAL provide the foundations upon which this fuller empowerment may be built. There may be resistance within families and local communities, and within organizational and policy structures from local to international level. As McCallum warns, 'simple statements about the need to empower women and build their skills can ignore the complexity of gender relations, the reality of power imbalances and the long hard work involved in shifting entrenched cultural norms' (McCallum 2006: 8). To capitalise on their capacity to achieve individual change, the sport for development movement must also engage with the institutional processes through which gender inequity is constructed beyond the individual.

Acknowledgements

The research reported here was funded by UK Sport and facilitated by the NAZ Foundation. The fieldwork was conducted with Dr Shane Collins, Durham University, and Dr Joanna Welford, De Montfort University, when both were members of the Institute of Youth

Sport, Loughborough University. We are deeply indebted to all research participants for their generous involvement. Some of the data referred to have previously been discussed in Kay (2009).

References

Boserup, E. (1970) *Women's Role in Economic Development*. New York: St. Martin's Press.

Chanana, K. (2004) 'Gender and disciplinary choices: women in higher education in India', Paper prepared for the UNESCO Colloquium on Research and Higher Education Policy 'Knowledge, Access and Governance: Strategies for Change', 1–3 December 2004, Paris.

Coalter, F. (2007) *A Wider Social Role for Sport*. London: Routledge.

——(2009) 'Sport-in-development: accountability or development?' in R. Levermore and A. Beacom (eds) *Sport and International* Development. Basingstoke: Palgrave Macmillan, 55–75.

Collins M., I. Henry, B. Houlihan and J. Buller (1999) *Sport and Social Exclusion*. Loughborough: Loughborough University.

Crabbe, T. (2009) 'Getting to know you: using sport to engage and build relationships with marginalised young people', in R. Levermore and A. Beacom (eds) *Sport and International Development*. Basingstoke: Palgrave Macmillan, 176–97.

Desia, V. (2005) 'NGOs, gender mainstreaming, and urban poor communities in Mumbai', *Gender and Development*, 13, 90–98.

Handy, Femida and Kassa, Menaz (2004) 'Women's empowerment in rural India', Paper presented as the ISTR conference, Toronto, Canada, July 2004.

Hanushek, E. (2008) 'Schooling, gender equity, and economic outcomes', in M. Tembon and L. Fort (eds) *Girls' Education in the 21st Century; Gender Equality, Empowerment, and Economic Growth*. Washington: The World Bank, 23–40.

Hayhurst, L., M. MacNeill and W. Frisby (2009) 'A postcolonial feminist approach to sport, gender and development', in M. Green and B. Houlihan (eds) *Handbook of Sport Development*. London: Routledge.

Herz, Barbara and Sperling, G. (2004) *What Works in Girls' Education: Evidence and Policies from the Developing World*. 2004. Council on Foreign Relations.

Hunt, J. (2004) 'Gender and development' in Kingsbury, D., J. Remenyi, J. McKay, and J. Hunt (eds) *Key Issues in Development*. Basingstoke: Palgrave Macmillan, 243–65.

International Union for the Scientific Study of Population (IUSSP) (1998) 'Seminar on female empowerment and demographic processes: moving beyond Cairo'; www.iussp.org/Activities/scp-gen/gen-rep97.php (accessed 7 July 2009).

Kabeer, N. (2003) 'Gender mainstreaming in poverty eradication and the millennium development goals. A handbook for policy-makers and other stakeholders. Commonwealth Secretariat/IDRC/CIDA'; www.idrc.ca/en/ev-28774-201-1-DO_TOPIC.html (accessed 17 September 2009).

Kambhampati, U. and Rajan, R. (2004) *The "Nowhere" Children: Patriarchy and the Role of Girls in India's Rural Economy*. Reading: Henley Business School.

Karl, M. (1995) *Women an Empowerment: Participation and Decision Making*. London: Zed Books.

Kay, T. A. (2009) 'Developing through Sport: Evidencing Sport Impacts on Young People', *Sport and Society*, 12.9, 1177–91.

Kay, T. A., J. Welford and R. Jeanes with J. Morris and S. Collins (2008) *The Potential of Sport to Enhance Young People's Lives: Sport in the Context of International Development*, Unpublished report to UK Sport and the Department for International Development.

Levermore, R. and Beacom, A. (2009) 'Opportunities, limitations, questions', in R. Levermore and A. Beacom (eds) *Sport and International Development*. Basingstoke: Palgrave Macmillan, 246–68.

Long, J., M. Welch, P. Bramham, K. Hylton, J. Butterfield and E. Lloyd (2002) *Count Me In: The Dimensions of Social Inclusion through Culture and Sport*. Leeds: Leeds Metropolitan University.

McCallum, L. (2006) 'Responding to HIV at individual, community and society level'; www.aidsprojects.com/uploads/File/Responoding%20to%20HIV%20-%20APMG.pdf (accessed 14 July 2009).

McNamara, K. (2003) 'Information and Communication Technologies, Poverty and Development: Learning from Experience', *A Background Paper for the Information and Development Annual Symposium*. Geneva, Switzerland.

Moser, C.O.N. (1998) 'Gender planning in the Third World: meeting practical and strategic needs', *World Development*, 17: 1–19.

Muraleedharan, K. (2005) *Empowering Women Inter-state Comparison of Indian Experiments*. New Delhi: Indian Council of Social Science Research.

Nicholls, S. (2009) 'On the backs of peer educators; using theory to interrogate the role of young people in the field of sport-in-development', in R. Levermore and A. Beacom (eds). *Sport and International Development*. Basingstoke: Palgrave Macmillan, 156–75.

Oxfam (2006) *9. Girls' education in South Asia*, Education and Gender Equality Series, Programme Insights, London: Oxfam.

Pradhan, B. (2003) 'Measuring Empowerment: A Methodological Approach', *Development*, 46, 181–94.

Rowlands, J. (1995) 'Empowerment examined', *Development in Practice*, 5 (2). Oxford: Oxfam.

Schuler, S.R. and Hashemi, S.M. (1998) 'Defining and Studying Empowerment of Women: A Research Note from Bangladesh', JSI Working Paper No.3, Arligton, V.A., in Muraleedharan, K. (2005) *Empowering Women Inter-state Comparison of Indian Experiments*. New Delhi: Indian Council of Social Science Research.

Sen, G. and Battliwala, S. (2000) 'Empowering Women for Reproductive Rights' in Harriet B. Pressure and G. Sen (eds) *Women's Empowerment and Demographic Processes*. New York: Oxford University Press.

Sinha, K. (2003) 'Citizenship degraded; Indian women in a modern state and a pre-modern society', *Gender and Development*, 11.3, 19–25.

Smith, L. T. (1999) *Decolonizing Methodologies: Research and Indigenous Peoples*. New York: Zed Books.

Tembon, M. (2008) 'Overview', in M. Tembon and L. Fort (eds) *Girls' Education in the 21st Century; Gender Equality, Empowerment, and Economic Growth*. Washington: The World Bank, 3–22.

Tembon, M. and Fort, L. (eds) (2008) *Girls' Education in the 21st Century; Gender Equality, Empowerment, and Economic Growth*. Washington: The World Bank, 3–22.

UNESCO (2006) 'Getting girls out of work and into school: policy brief'. Bangkok: UNESCO.

23

Sport in action

Young people, sex education and HIV/AIDS in Zambia

Davies Banda

This chapter presents a case study of a sport-for-development non-governmental organization (NGO) in Zambia. Sport is being recognized for the contribution it can make to Millennium Development Goals (MDGs), particularly as a potential tool for HIV/AIDS preventative programmes. Sports-orientated HIV/AIDS preventative programmes have become a valuable tool for reaching out to populations that are at risk, particularly those aged 15–24 years. The HIV/AIDS pandemic has so far proved to be the greatest pandemic the world has ever faced. Millions of lives both old and young have been lost across the globe but mostly in sub-Saharan Africa. Sports-based HIV/AIDS education programmes have become prominent among young people's activities in the region's deprived communities. The United Nations Inter-Agency Task Force for Sport for Development and Peace stated that such sports programmes are a powerful tool for mobilising societies to communicate key messages such as HIV/AIDS preventative messages (United Nations Inter-Agency Task Force 2003).

Women and girls remain the most vulnerable to the pandemic. In discussing the scourge of HIV/AIDS and sport, the focus will be on young people, gender and sex education programmes. Sex education environments will be used in this chapter to help elaborate the established prominent role of youth-led sex education programmes using sport. Due to the high rate of prevalence among women and girls, the number of projects focused on empowerment of girls and women are a clear indication that HIV/AIDS is a disease of inequalities (UNAIDS 2008).

The chapter starts by presenting a brief history of Zambia and the economic hardships faced by its citizens, and examining how poverty levels have exacerbated the spread of HIV/AIDS. It is in the midst of economic hardships that sport-for-development as a sector emerged and gained its significance based on initiatives to address HIV/AIDS and other MDGs such as gender equality. This chapter, therefore, goes on to explore generally the aims of the case study project; how it is delivered and funded; and how the project's targets relate to wider policy goals at community, regional and national level. In doing so it also highlights the mismatch between national HIV targets and those of sport-for-development in general.

Historical overview

Zambia is a landlocked country that occupies an area of approximately 752,614 square kilometres of the central African plateau from the Zambezi River in the south west to the tip of Lake Tanganyika in the north east (Daniel 1979). Zambia's eight neighbours are the Democratic Republic of Congo in the north, Tanzania to its north east, Malawi to the east, Mozambique to its south east, Botswana and Zimbabwe in the south, Angola on the west and Namibia to the south west and Angola to the west. It was a British colony formerly known as Northern Rhodesia. Lusaka, the capital city, which is host to a majority of the indigenous and foreign sport-for-development NGOs, is centrally positioned.

At the time of gaining its political independence in 1964, Zambia had a stable economy that was supported by its copper production and export earnings. The nation was prosperous but has since moved from being one of the continent's richest nations to being among the poorest nations in the world. At the time of writing this case study, Zambia was placed 165th out of the 177 countries on the UN Human Development Index (HDI) which is used to measure the well-being of a nation's citizens based on standard of living, education and life expectancy (UNDP 2007). According to the UN HDI, the life expectancy in Zambia is 40.5 years with 17 per cent of the adult population infected with HIV/AIDS. The same report commented that 64 per cent of the nation's population lived in poverty in 2006, down from 71 per cent in 1991.

The country's Central Statistics Office (CSO) stated that a majority of the country's poverty-stricken population live in rural areas in households headed by women (CSO 2007). Impoverishment tends to cause more hardship to women than men, making women more vulnerable to infectious diseases such as HIV/AIDS. Schoepf (2004, cited in Kalipeni *et al.* 2004) pointed out that the spread of infectious diseases such as HIV/AIDS is generally propelled by history, political economy and culture. Schoepf stated that the HIV virus silently spread as the African continent went through deepening economic crisis in the late 1970s. At the time when the first case of HIV was diagnosed in Zambia in 1984, the nation was already undergoing critical economic hardships. Poverty levels are believed to have exacerbated the pandemic, although Dr Peter Piot, former Executive Director of UNAIDS, comments that the HIV/AIDS pandemic is not a disease of poverty itself, but a disease of inequalities deeply rooted in society's injustices (UNAIDS 2008).

This case study attempts to highlight some of the initiatives by an indigenous sport-for-development NGO based in Lusaka. Since a majority of NGOs have strategically positioned their offices within the city in proximity to foreign donor offices, there are concerns about duplication between foreign-based sport-for-development NGOs in urban areas (see Banda *et al.* 2008) and about the neglect of rural populations. The case study NGO used here is an exception as it has programmes in the most remote areas of the nation as well as the city. The project therefore attempts to make positive contributions in both rural and urban areas, alleviating societal injustices such as economic and gender inequalities faced by many young people, especially women and girls.

Gender is an important focus for this and many other similar sport-for-development projects because, as Larkin (2000) comments, gender inequalities make females more vulnerable to HIV infection than males. Such inequalities include lower levels of school enrolment, educational achievement and earning capacity among females. There is also a broader relationship between low levels of human development achievement and the prevalence of HIV (Hsu 2005): as nations suffer economically and societal inequalities widen, increases in rates of transmission have been witnessed. These social conditions that facilitate the spread of the HIV pandemic need to be addressed in a much broader way than through the health sector, and sport today is considered a valuable tool for developmental strategies at community level. The sports pro-grammes in this case study show how gender inequalities and low levels of human development are being addressed through the use of sports and life-skills training.

Emergence of NGOs in Zambia

In recent years Zambia has experienced an unprecedented increase in the number of NGOs operating within the nation. The rapid mushrooming of NGOs evident in Zambian communities has been part of a wider trend in development work in Africa, which has seen the level of donor funds available to community-based organizations increase. This also reflects the perception that African governments are both failing and corrupt (Laird 2007; Zaidi 1999), leading international donors to favour working directly with grass-roots organizations. Many regard NGOs as reliable partners in international development (Hulme and Edwards 1997) and a potential solution to poor governance common among low-income countries (Hsu 2005).

Other studies have suggested that the rampant growth of the NGO sector and their prominence in development activities is based on perceptions that such organizations are better placed to effectively enable aid to reach the poorest members of society (see Bebbington and Riddell 1997; Zaidi 1999). The combination of perceived government inefficiencies to deliver public goods, coupled with the neo-liberal principle of minimalist government, has resulted in NGOs being favoured by the international donor community and gaining recognition in development programmes.

The shift of emphasis to NGOs has been accompanied by a tightening of conditions surrounding aid to governments. Lending conditions have been applied to address government inefficiencies and poor governance. In Zambia during the Structural Adjustment Programme (SAP) in 1983, the World Bank/IMF demanded reductions in the size of the cabinet and civil service work-force to reduce inefficiency and promote effective government (Aryeetey-Attoy 1997). These constraints in due course affected most public services, with sport and leisure provision low on government priorities. Physical Education (PE) in schools also suffered considerably. For example, there was lack of equipment and fewer trained teachers to deliver PE lessons. Hence, many schools reallocated PE time to other examinable subjects. These failures by government due to shortage of resources to make sport and leisure opportunities available to young populations in deprived neighbourhoods laid the ground for sport-for-development organizations such as Sport in Action (SIA) to emerge to fill the gaps.

Sport-for-development NGOs emerge

Sport in Action (SIA), a not-for-profit and non-governmental organization was the first regis-tered sport-for-development NGO in Zambia. The founder and current Executive Director is Clement Chileshe, a former High School teacher and schools national basketball coach. SIA uses sport and recreation as a tool through which the quality of lives of people can possibly be improved by providing opportunities that enhance social and economic empowerment to local people. The organization's mission statement is:

> to use sport and recreation as a tool through which the quality of people's lives can be improved by providing a programme that will bring about motivation, self-development and self-reliance through social and economic empowerment.

(www.sportinaction.org)

Working in collaboration with schools and other community groups, SIA delivers a combined package of sport and life skills. Some of its main programmes include: Youth Empowerment Through Sports, which promotes school sport and HIV/AIDS Action clubs; Young Farmers Club through sport, which encourages rural sports and gardening clubs; child empowerment through sport in the course of training camps for young people under 13 years of age; cultural exchange and traditional games that are based on exchange visits (with foreign partners, mostly Norway and Sweden); and promotion of indigenous games for development and physical education.

When SIA started operating in 1998 as a sports organization it was funded by financial contributions from its founding members and in 1999 it was officially registered as a not-for-profit organization. The Norwegian Agency for Development Cooperation (NORAD) was the first foreign donor to recognize the organization's work and fund its activities. At the time of registration of SIA as an NGO, another indigenous organization known as Education Through Sport Foundation (EduSport) founded by Oscar Mwaanga was similarly funded by NORAD. EduSport like SIA also focuses on the use of sport as a means to an end. Sport is viewed not as an end in itself but as a vehicle to address some of the problems faced by society, resulting in sporting outcomes. Such outcomes were and have remained the main attraction for obtaining external funding for most of the NGOs within the sector, though some of the NGOs have now established sports academies focusing on sports development outcomes.

The Norwegian Olympic Committee and Confederation of Sports (known as NIF) played a considerable role in the establishment of sport-for-development NGOs in Zambia. When SIA was becoming established, NIF was already working with the National Sports Council of Zambia (NCSZ) on a community sports project known as the Sport-For-All (SFA) project. Because the SFA was a Norwegian-funded project, the recognition of indigenous sport-for-development NGOs by both NIF and NORAD in 1999 was not well received within government sporting bodies. Animosity developed between government sports bodies and sport-for-development NGOs as the latter were perceived to be diverting donor funds that would otherwise go to government SFA projects. Government officials declined to recognize SIA as a legal entity since the National Sports Act of Parliament recognizes only three sports boards, namely: the National Sports Council; the Professional Boxing and Wrestling Control Board; and the National Olympic committee. Any organization not officially affiliated to any of the three was not allowed to operate by the Ministry of Sport.

The founders of SIA registered the organization as an NGO and not as an affiliate of any of the government's three recognized sporting bodies. Other emerging indigenous organizations began to register their organizations in the same way, leading to the establishment of the sport-for-development NGO sector. A senior official from a large sport-for-development NGO stated that international donors viewed sport-for-development NGOs as being more effective than government agencies, hence more support was made available to the NGOs (Personal interview: 29 August 2008).

There is some evidence that the shift for international donors to working directly with NGOs has been prompted by the failure of government to fulfil its commitment to joint-funding agreements. In the sport-for-development field, Kruse's (2006) review of the Kicking AIDS Out sports programme in Zambia reported that government agencies such as the National Sports Council had failed to deliver programmes due to insufficient government funding, or because of failure by government to provide their counterpart funding when donor funds were made available for projects. The failure prompted the Norwegians to work directly with the newly established sport-for-development NGOs, though they were still committed to the SFA project as well as developing other relations with NGOs.

Recent developments have shown evidence of a government steer for the sector. This is evident in policy documents such as the Fifth National Development Plan (FNDP) 2006–11 (GRZ 2006) and the Zambian Revised National Sport Policy (MSYCD 2009). Both these government policy documents acknowledge the contribution that sport can make in mitigating the impact of the HIV/AIDS pandemic and in achieving outcomes for other MDGs such as gender equity. The government nonetheless has no substantial budget for sport-for-development activities, suggesting that many of its expressed intentions in policy documents may be mere rhetoric.

Sources of funding

Table 23.1 provides data on funding of sports programmes which show how NGOs have become preferred as effective deliverers of community development activities by global North partners. Between 2003 and 2006 the total funding allocation from NORAD for SIA and EduSport was twice the level of funding that the National Sports Council of Zambia received through government programmes. Although it receives no grant from the government, SIA has however been able to jointly deliver externally funded events or programmes with government agencies. Most of the joint-delivered projects have been funded by bilateral or multilateral international donors such as the United Nations Children's Fund (UNICEF).

The trend whereby the sport-for-development sector receives more funding from donors than government programmes continues. This tends to be problematic in terms of sustainability as alternative systems outside mainstream delivery continue to receive more resources than the established mainstream structures. Recent developments, such as the International Inspiration programme under the auspices of the London Organising Committee of the Olympic Games, are however utilizing existing structures such as schools and the PE curriculum to deliver physical activities to young people. Such an approach is more likely to enhance sustainability of programmes than approaches within sport-for-development which only work in parallel with existing structures. For the first time since the emergence of the sport-for-development sector, the central government, through the Ministry of Sport, Youth and Child Development, has allocated US$20,600 (2009 budget) as their counterpart funding for sport and development through the International Inspiration programme.

At present the key funding partners for most of the sport-for-development NGOs in Zambia are three co-operating partners, UK Sport, NIF and Commonwealth Games Canada (CGC). The three have agreed to work co-operatively to achieve sustainable results in sport-for-development through joint investments of time, money and human resources. Some indigenous NGOs express frustrations however in working with these funders, claiming favouritism is shown to NGOs with foreign bases, as more stringent measures are imposed on local NGOs than on

Table 23.1 Foreign donor funding*

	National Sports Council	SIA & EduSport
2003	350,000	650,000
2004	350,000	650,000
2005	350,000	600,000
2006	100,000	555,000
Total	1,150,000	2,450,000

Adapted from Kruse (2006)
* This is NORAD funding to Zambian Sport-for-Development NGOs

organizations with foreign bases. This pattern again reflects notions about corruption in Africa which extends to mistrust for local NGOs and leaders in particular. The current funding situation has not, therefore, resolved the competition for resources evident among NGOs, and competition for resources has hampered attempts to establish effective partnerships within the sector (see Banda *et al.* 2008).

Youth peer leaders as key actors in development

This section looks at the role of young people as key actors in the mode of delivery of SIA programmes and considers the participation of young people in planning, designing and implementation of activities. An illustration is given of the cost-effective utilization of volunteers in sport-for-development as a means of delivering HIV/AIDS preventative messages and other MDG outcomes such as gender equity. This will be based on analyzing participation levels of young people in matters that affect their lives within SIA activities compared to other potential means of active participation with the community.

In sport-for-development, NGO programmes are sustainable local initiatives delivered by volunteers. Though the delivery of programmes or sports activities is locally sustainable through volunteers, NGOs are still very much dependent on donor funding to operate effectively, without which a majority of them would not have been established. Young people have been instrumental in delivering both sporting and non-sporting outcomes in a wide variety of sites throughout the communities.

The use of Youth Peer Leaders has been absolutely central to this work. Sport in Action and EduSport were the first two NGOs in Zambia to introduce the concept of Youth Peer Leaders (YPLs) or 'peer coaches' as they are popularly referred to in sport-for-development. The concept of peer coaches seeks to promote a participatory environment that empowers young people especially in decision making. The use of peer coaches in sport-for-development is based on the broader peer education approach which is a commonly used method in HIV preventative education worldwide. Youth Peer Leaders are volunteers that are trained by NGOs like SIA and have become the main deliverers of programmes within SIA and all other sport-for-development NGOs. The YPLs are involved in planning for sessions, which involves setting of objectives and planning activities to attain objectives. Research studies have shown that YPLs are lacking in some skills and knowledge and need more training to understand the alignment of their objectives and planning of appropriate activities to attain such set objectives (Banda 2003; Kay *et al.* 2006).

With regard to the benefits accrued by YPLs, there are fewer extrinsic benefits than intrinsic ones. Some of the extrinsic benefits come in the form of sports attire from foreign donors and opportunities to travel both locally and abroad. Intrinsic benefits relate to leadership, social and sports-specific skills gained through training and experience as peer leaders (Kay *et al.* 2006). A minority of the YPLs have had opportunities to take paid employment within the NGO, but for the majority, their roles are without any form of financial remuneration, which has posed a great challenge to indigenous sport-for-development NGOs as they tend to lose well-trained staff to NGOs with foreign bases operating within the same sector. Attractive packages from NGOs with foreign bases have lured several young people to abandon indigenous NGOs which heavily depend on these volunteers.

The training that YPLs receive is based on a curriculum designed under the international Kicking AIDS Out (KAO) Network, which has been created to ensure uniformity and quality in training of peer coaches. SIA together with other NGOs was a key actor in drawing up the curriculum for training YPLs in KAO peer-coaching courses. YPLs from SIA were active in delivering training to build the capacity of other KAO network partners. Through the KAO rights-based approach, young people engaged in such programmes are trained as coaches or sports leaders who later lead other peers in both sports and life skills training. The element of collective negotiation, decision making, planning and implementation is vital to the peer leadership process. More broadly, the empowerment of young people is an important strategy in HIV AIDS preventative education.

There are challenges, however, related to young people being active in decision-making forums. However, such skills as taught in KAO courses are usually inculcated away from adult-led contexts which mostly resist empowering young people to make decisions on issues related to risk behaviours. Risk behaviours here relate to behavioural decisions taken by young people that may put them in danger of contracting the HIV virus, or other sexually transmitted diseases, or make them vulnerable to substance abuse. Conflicts between African customs and empowerment approaches adopted by NGOs depict the complexity of the context in which sport-for-development NGOs operate (see Coalter, in Nicholson and Hoye 2008). African customs regard young people as incompetent to actively participate in decision-making processes within a community. These cultural values relating to respect for elders by young people are deeply embedded and influenced by both traditional practices and religious beliefs. SIA has taken an approach that offers young people opportunities to develop skills that can build their competencies to actively participate in decision making at different strategic levels within their communities. SIA officials cited the recent involvement of parents and teachers in SIA forums as an attempt to resolve conflicts between programme objectives, society norms and society's expectations of young people.

Level playing field for both male and female participants

It is the power of sport as a social mobilization tool that has contributed to such NGOs' ability to reach out to large numbers of young people. Although such programmes target both male and female young people, programmes that have attracted funding from global North partners have been those that promote gender equity. This reflects the predominance of female young people between the ages of 15 and 24, who are the highest at-risk group for HIV infection (UNAIDS and WHO 1999). Latest estimates by UNAIDS and WHO still show that women make up 60 per cent of people living with HIV in sub-Saharan Africa (www.who.int/gender/hiv_aids); the Central Statistics Office in Zambia reported that girls aged 20–24 are four times more likely to get infected than boys (CSO 2003).

In UNICEF terms, gender equality means making sure that girls and women have a 'level playing field' with their opposite sex so that all children have equal opportunities to achieve their aspirations (www.unicef.org/gender/).

Like most other nations within the region, Zambia faces challenges of gender inequalities in both rural and urban areas and, in order to show a commitment to addressing gender disparities, has signed all the major international treaties on human rights. The treaties influence how a nation promotes both men's and women's human rights. However, much still needs to be done regarding the rights of women within cultural and economic contexts that foster pronounced gender inequalities. The uneven playing field within cultural and economic settings has contributed to the dominance of females by males and the feminization of poverty due to women being denied equal opportunities in the labour market.

Gender equality is therefore a key component of SIA programmes. SIA has placed gender issues on its agenda in addressing the spread of HIV and empowerment of young women and girls. The organization uses sport, mainly soccer, to address gender issues. Its executive director, Chileshe, stated that the use of soccer as opposed to female-dominated sports is based on challenging traditional stereotypes. The soccer playing field or pitch is regarded as a male pre-serve. Girls within the programme have equal opportunity to practise alongside their male counterparts as sports peer coaches/leaders imparting both sports and life skills to peers of both genders. Apart from the use of soccer to address social issues, traditional movement games, role playing, puppetry and innovative games such as Kicking AIDS Out or Dunking AIDS Out activities (Banda and Mwaanga 2008; Kakuwa 2005; Mwaanga 2002) are used. However, Chileshe states that:

> working with girls within communities especially in proximity to their houses is challenging due to expectations of society on young women and girls. Girls are required to continuously do chores at home whilst young men or boys have time to engage in sporting activities. When girls are noticed as engaging in sporting activities, elder family members will find some extra chores for them to do.
>
> *(Personal interview, 29 August 2008)*

In trying to liberate girls from their labour-intensive domestic lifestyles, boys are encouraged to help in chores to reduce the severe time constraints faced by girls so as to allow girls to take part in activities organized by the NGO (see Saavedra 2005). For example, Chileshe states that the project demands that 'boys have to be allies in the empowerment and self-actualisation process of girls' (Personal interview, 29 August 2008). However, although recognizing the positive role that boys can play in the process of empowering girls and young women, Chileshe points out that male hegemonic tendency among male peer coaches should be strongly addressed when train-ing youth leaders. In domestic or other public settings, imbalances in power relations between women and men continue to be reinforced and such imbalances are impediments in the empowerment and development process of women and girls. Male participants and leaders are very much aware of such settings and away from the organization, may in fact be part of such impediments. Hence, Chileshe emphasizes the need to form alliances between male and female participants in fighting gender inequalities beyond the project's activities.

Youth Peer Leaders, sport and HIV/AIDS education

Bearing in mind the gender disparities mentioned above, SIA has adopted a rights-based approach (UNAIDS 2004) which attempts to achieve the following:

- To promote the rights and participation of young people in HIV/AIDS prevention and care strategies
- To ensure that the rights of marginalized groups within HIV/AIDS-affected communities such as the rights of women and girls to HIV/AIDS prevention and care are protected

However, it is difficult to achieve active participation of young people in decision making about sexual behaviour within forums that are adult-led. For example, young people, particularly girls and young women, are passive listeners when addressed by male elders within a home. Thus, whilst youth-led forums are believed to be favourable for promoting participation of young people in decision making, youth voices tend to be absent in other adult-led settings. This is captured in Table 23.2, which depicts sexual health education scenarios that young people in Zambia and other sub-Saharan Africa nations encounter when growing up. When young people are faced with a plethora of questions about puberty, sex, HIV/AIDS and their own sexuality, the answers to such questions are obtained from several sources such as the scenarios

Table 23.2 Sexual health scenarios

	Home	School	Church or mosque	Sport NGOs, e.g. SIA
Relationship	Parent–child	Teacher–student	Clergy–believers	Peer–peer
Pedagogy[1]	Young people are passive recipients	Teacher-led, mostly didactical	Young people are passive recipients	Peer–peer dialogue. Active in learning process
Youth voice	Mostly absent 'Listen to my word, I know what this world is all about'	Often limited due to examination-driven activities	Limited by religious teachings	Peer–peer dialogue
Youth empowerment	Adults wary of youth empowerment 'Too young to be entrusted with such ...'	Curriculum-driven targets limit impact	Empowerment constrained by doctrines	Involvement in planning, decision making and implementation

Note: [1]Pedagogy here implies good practice in teaching and learning
Source: Banda (2006)

depicted in Table 23.2. Apart from some youth-led organizations such as SIA, Table 23.2 shows that discussions pertaining to sex and sexuality are mostly conducted by adults as instructors (see Buthelezi *et al.* 2007).

Table 23.2 highlights the significance of relationships between young people and adults, the presence of young people's voices, and lastly, pedagogy and channels of empowerment of young people, as factors affecting young people's acquisition of HIV AIDS knowledge and education. In discussing these themes, SIA as a community organization is compared to other contexts that tend to have the presence of an adult as instructor in sex education. The following sections will highlight the advantages SIA has over other community institutions in addressing issues pertaining to youth empowerment, HIV/AIDS and gender equity.

SIA has established partnership work with schools delivering both sports and life skills training. Such partnerships are vital in that they address the barriers to participation that arise from adult power in schools where such power has been institutionalized (Bhana 2009). YPLs utilize games, drills or role play to discuss issues about sex, HIV transmission, gender, sexuality and life-skills. As some have concluded that education is the best vaccine available for prevention against infection (Vandemoortele and Delamonica 2000), partnering with schools and other community-based organizations using sport or KAO drills presents HIV education materials within a broader social context necessary to understand HIV. The informal atmosphere of a sports field setting has potential for active participation of young people in discussing HIV and sex in contrast to classroom-based HIV sessions led by teachers. Problems arise in such settings in that due to the age of the target group (in schools); the main national strategy is abstinence. This poses questions as to whether it is realistic to ignore that young people are sexually active. The appropriateness of such a strategy becomes questionable if lessons are limited to the promotion of abstinence and ignoring other preventative strategies (Kay *et al.* 2006).

Relationship, empowerment and voices of young people

Compared to other settings depicted in Table 23.2, the YPLs approach used by SIA for sexual health education is deemed to promote the involvement of young people in negotiating solutions to health matters, social inequalities, and sexuality issues that affect the target group themselves. In almost all the Zambian tribes, it is culturally inappropriate or taboo for young people to discuss topics of a sexual nature with adults (see also Amuyunzu-Nyamongo et al. 2005). The presence of an adult creates an imbalanced discussion where the process tends to be one-way due to the adult–child relationship. Such adult-led settings are believed to hinder the active participation of young people in discussions due to the authoritative position adopted by the instructors, in this case, the parents, teachers or members of clergy.

The absence of youth voices in such relationships inhibits the effective delivery of HIV/AIDS education and life skills education. For example, Buthelezi et al. (2007: 456) assert that:

> Appropriate and effective life skills curricula in schools and communities are key to HIV prevention among young people. However, unless we are able to develop a climate in which young people are able to discuss sex and sexuality issues openly, it is unlikely that we will be able to develop strategies to tackle the epidemic successfully.

Other projects with peer-led sessions have claimed the effectiveness of such an approach. However, this does not mean to rule out the effectiveness of an instructive model of teaching based on a lived experience by adults which has proved beneficial in some African settings. Research such as Buthelezi et al.'s (2007) suggests, however, that this needs to be complemented by strategies that actively involve and empower young people.

Parents, teachers and community leaders such as members of the clergy often conduct HIV/AIDS education in a hierarchical style, a pedagogical relationship that is seen as denying young people opportunities to fully engage in matters affecting them. Young people are mostly passive recipients in sexual health education forums be it in religious gatherings such as a church, in a home and many times in schools (see Table 23.2). Bhana (2009) stresses that adults take full control as teachers whereas young people are usually accorded a passive learner role. However, although teachers by way of pedagogical expertise are well positioned to design and implement effective HIV/AIDS education programmes, their input into KAO programmes has not developed into collaborative delivery. Their expertise in pedagogy is vital for YPLs to grasp the act of teaching and learning through combined planning and delivery of KAO activities.

In comparison to school settings, SIA has the flexibility to adapt its approach to HIV education whereas schools have a strict observance of the curriculum which mostly is driven by attempts to meet examination targets. Matthews et al. (2006) in their HIV/AIDS education study in South African schools comment that schools usually have an authoritarian approach to curriculum implementation. In contrast, due to its flexible approach, SIA can ensure maximum engagement of youths on HIV prevention initiatives using games, drills or role play as participatory methodologies (see Buthelezi et al. 2007).

In addition, some studies elsewhere have shown that HIV/AIDS education in some schools can be taught didactically as a mere set of facts (Pattman and Chege 2003) ignoring the other social elements such as gender inequality or income inequalities. Campbell (2003) however points out that such 'fact giving' sessions, which adopt an authoritarian approach to teacher–student relationships, promote gender inequalities and inhibit effective student-led HIV education sessions. Indeed, it is the use of the peer-led rights-based approach to HIV education by sport-for-development NGOs that has helped to attract more resources to the sector. Coalter (2007) comments that HIV-related programmes using sport as a social tool have given major impetus and greater coherence to the sport-for-development sector.

Because HIV is a disease of inequalities, it is vitally important that social and economic inequalities are adequately tackled in discussions. This calls into question the depth of KAO training programmes for YPLs. Questions therefore arise whether some YPLs who may themselves have dropped out of school have the ability to fully comprehend the social and economic aspects of the scourge of HIV or whether it is also a mere fact-giving process for them too. Pedagogical issues, questions pertaining to YPLs' understanding of the rationale for the use of the approaches adopted and whether these young leaders are able to explore HIV issues beyond the material they themselves are exposed to in training are all areas that need to be considered in assessing the effectiveness of YPLs.

Contribution to non-sports outcomes and sports outcomes

Besides the use of sport to address broader social issues such as HIV/AIDS preventative education or gender inequalities, SIA also makes significant contribution to traditional sports development – sport as an end in itself and worthwhile activity in its own right. Initially, SIA pursued mostly non-sporting outcomes, but recently has had more significant results in sporting outcomes. These have been achieved in the form of working with physical education teachers in schools and working with national governing bodies of sport, notably the Zambia Basketball Association. For example, SIA holds an annual National High School Basketball tournament. SIA has contributed immensely to the revamping of PE in schools. The organization holds training camps for both teachers and young people which have produced leaders in sport at different levels of both community and national sport administration. The impact in provision of opportunities and upholding the right to play for young people is evident in diverse sites where the programmes of SIA are delivered to young people in deprived communities.

Other authors have suggested that such organizations like SIA play a vital role in compensating for the lack of sports provision by government to engage the young. For example, Coalter argues that such organizations:

> seek to develop forms of social capital by providing young men and women rare opportunities to participate in decision-making, confront exploitative gender relations, encourage ambition and recognize the value of education, develop relationships based on trust and reciprocity and provide opportunities for the development of human capital.

(2007: 88)

Whilst number of participants, variety of sports activities offered, number of sports-coaching camps held and tournaments funded and hosted can be measured, SIA's non-sporting outcomes relating to HIV/AIDS are difficult to measure. Although it is the non-sporting outcomes such as those contributing to combating HIV/AIDS or tackling gender inequalities that attract foreign funding, these outcomes have been difficult to measure for SIA to enable the organization to obtain Global Fund to Fight AIDS, Tuberculosis and Malaria. These funds are disbursed by government and the dilemma lies in the failure to capture the sort of information that HIV-related funders seek to see before funding projects (Banda *et al.* 2008). The type of qualitative measures that are collected mostly by sport-for-development NGOs are a mismatch with the measures of desired outcomes that most donors and the national HIV/AIDS Council require.

For example, national targets demand that organizations receiving funding for HIV/AIDS must contribute towards measurable quantitative targets. These measurable quantitative targets refer to the number of young people coming forth for voluntary counselling and testing (VCT) or the number of condoms distributed in specific areas. Such targets elude the external monitoring and evaluation done by sport-for-development NGOs. In addition to such difficulties, schools where SIA delivers its HIV programmes are not open to condom distribution, making it difficult to achieve condom distribution targets. Apart from such failures to contribute towards measurable quantitative results, HIV prevention activities by SIA reinforce strongly the knowledge about the scourge and instil decision-making and leadership skills through the traditional games, KAO activities, puppetry and sports (see Kruse 2006).

Conclusion

This chapter showed that sport not only has the potential for mobilizing the mass of the population for communicating HIV/AIDS messages, but also that the sports setting and use of peer leaders can be an effective way for youth-led organizations to contribute to the fight against HIV/AIDS. It is clear that the HIV pandemic has provided impetus for the growth of the sport-for-development sector and also that the sector itself has contributed immensely to the provision of sporting opportunities for young people, and also to tackling the spread of HIV. In spite of the growth and recognition of the sector in Zambia, the provision of sport, though valuable itself, is still inadequate to compensate for government inadequacies, especially as SIA and other NGOs have limited resources to meet the demands of young people.

HIV is a disease of inequalities and some of these inequalities relate to gender inequalities. SIA's adoption of the rights-based approach to tackling HIV is the right approach in a cultural context where the rights of girls and women are marginalized. The challenge to the organization lies in sensitizing young males who are brought up in cultural settings that make them feel superior to women. Cultural norms about gender or sexuality marginalizing girls or women need to be tackled in a participatory process involving all participants and the wider community. The involvement of parents and guardians in project committees is one such good step in the right direction.

SIA programmes are a viable tool for breaking barriers in participation for young people in sexual health matters. Through themed games or role-play activities (depicting realities of poverty, gender, sex and disease) which are led by peer leaders, wider social issues linked to HIV can be discussed without the intimidating or dominating presence of an adult. On the contrary, sports activities are mostly considered as 'play or leisure' activities, after the necessary chores of the day have been completed and such activities are usually only a preserve of males and not females, causing girls and women to be denied their right to play. However, to assume that such sports settings are safe zones for girls is not absolutely correct. Sexual abuse by male coaches or officials can be a risk factor for girls or women. Sports settings can be spaces for illicit sexual relationships among participants themselves, which may lead to unsafe sex. Nevertheless, in the main, such settings appear to have helped promote and extend the social world of female participants.

References

Amuyunzu-Nyamongo, M., Biddlecom, A.E., Ouedraogo, C., and Woog, V. (2005). 'Qualitative Evidence on Adolescents' Views on Sexual and Reproductive Health in Sub-Saharan Africa. Occasional Report Number 16. New York: The Alan Guttmacher Institute.

Aryeetey-Attoy, S. (Ed) (1997) 'Geography of Sub-Saharan Africa'. Upper Saddle River, NJ: Prentice Hall.

Banda, D. (2003) 'Evaluating the Role of Sport Orientated Non-government Organisations in the Fight against HIV/AIDS', MSc thesis submitted to the Institute of Sport and Leisure Policy at Loughborough University.

——'When do the youth voices disappear: Monitoring and Evaluation of Community based Projects'. Paper presented at 'Researching Youth Sport' conference. Institute for Youth Sport, Loughborough University, 20 September 2006 (Invited Presentation).

Banda, D., Jeanes, R., Kay, T., and Lindsey, I. (2008) 'Partnerships involving sports-for-development NGOs and the fight against HIV / AIDS'. York St John University, York, November 2008. ISBN 978-1-906604-15-8.

Banda, D. and Mwaanga, O. (2008) Dunking AIDS Out: *Learning About AIDS Through Basketball Movement Games*. York St John University, York. ISBN 978-1-906604-06-6.

Bebbington, A. and Riddell, R. (1997) 'Heavy Hands, Hidden Hands, Holding Hands? Donors, Intermediary NGOs and Civil Society Organisations'. In D. Hulme and M. Edwards (eds.) *NGOs, States and Donors: Too Close for Comfort?* Basingstoke: MacMillan.

Bhana, Deevia (2009) 'They've got all the knowledge: HIV education, gender and sexuality in South African primary schools', *British Journal of Sociology of Education*, 30:2, 165–177.

Buthelezi, T., Mitchell, C., Moletsane, R., De Lange, N., Taylor, M., and Stuart, J. (2007) 'Youth voices about sex and AIDS: implications for life skills education through the "Learning Together" project in KwaZulu-Natal, South Africa', *International Journal of Inclusive Education*, 11:4, 445–59.

Campbell, C. (2003). *Letting them Die: How HIV/AIDS prevention programmes often fail*. Cape Town: Double Storey.

Central Statistical Office (CSO) 'Central Board of Health and ORC Macro'. Zambia demographic and health survey 2001–2. Central Statistical Office. 2003.

——(2007) *Zambia Demographic and Health Survey 2007*. Lusaka: Central Statistical Office.

Coalter, F. (2007) *A Wider Social Role for Sport: Who's Keeping the Score?* London: Routledge.

——(2008) 'Sport-in-development: Development for and through sport?' In M. Nicholson, and R. Hoye (eds) *Sport and Social Capital*. Butterworth-Heinemann.

Daniel, P. (1979) *Africanization, Nationalisation and Inequality: Mining Labour and the Copperbelt in Zambian Development*. Cambridge: Cambridge University Press.

Government of the Republic of Zambia (2006) 'Fifth National Development Plan 2006 – 2010'. Ministry of Finance and National Planning, Lusaka.

Hsu L-N. (2005) 'HIV epidemics in developing countries; looking beyond Health dimensions to the role of development', *International Development Planning Review*, 27, i–xii.

Hulme, D. and Edwards, M. (1997) 'NGOs, States and Donors: An Overview'. In D. Hulme and M. Edwards (eds) *NGOs, States and Donors: Too Close for Comfort?* Basingstoke: MacMillan.

Kakuwa, M. (2005) *Zambian Traditional Games & Activities*. A Kicking AIDS Out Resource Book.

Kalipeni, E., Craddock, S., Oppong, J. and Ghosh, J. (eds) (2004) *HIV/AIDS in Africa: Beyond Epidemiology*. Oxford: Blackwell Publishers.

Kay, T., Jeanes, R., Lindsey, I., Fimusamni, J., Collins, S. and Bancroft, J. (2006) 'Young people, sports development and the HIV-AIDS challenge; Research in Lusaka, Zambia'. Institute of Youth Sport. Loughborough University. April 2007.

Kruse, S. E. (2006) 'Is Sport an Effective Tool in the Fight Against HIV / AIDS?' Oslo: Norad.

Laird, S. E. (2007) 'Rolling Back the African State: Implications for Social Development in Ghana', *Social Policy & Administration*, 41:5, 465–86.

Larkin, J. (2000) 'Women poverty and HIV infection', *Canadian Woman Studies*, 20:9, 137–141.

Matthews, C., Boon, H., Flisher, A.J. and Schaalma, H.P. (2006) 'Factors associated with teachers' implementation of HIV/AIDS education in secondary schools in Cape Town, South Africa'. *AIDS Care*, 18:4, 388–97.

Ministry of Sport (2009) 'Youth and Child Development', National Sports Policy. Department of Sport, Lusaka, Zambia.

Mwaanga, O. (2002) *Manual for HIV/AIDS Education through Movement Games and Sport Activities*. NORAD: Oslo.

Nicholson, M. and Hoye, R. (2008) *Sport and Social Capital*. Butterworth-Heinemann: London.

Pattman, R. and Chege, F. (2003) *Finding our Voices Gendered and Sexual Identities in HIV/AIDS Education*. UNICEF: Nairobi.

Saavedra, M. (2005) 'Women, Sport and Development, Sport and Development International Platform'. Available http://assets.sportanddev.org/downloads/56–women–sport_and_development.pdf

Schoepf, B.G. (2004) 'AIDS, History and Struggles over Meaning'. In Kalipeni, E., Craddock, S., Oppong, J.R., and Ghosh, J. (eds) *AIDS in Africa: Beyond Epidemiology*, pp 15–28. Oxford and Watertown, MA: Blackwell Publishers.

Sport In Action 'Vision and Mission statement'. Online. Available www.sportinaction.org.zm/aboutus.html (accessed 20 July 2009).

UNAIDS and World Health Organisation (WHO) (1999) 'AIDS epidemic update'. Geneva, Switzerland: UNAIDS and WHO.

UNAIDS (Joint United Nations Programme on HIV/AIDS) (2004) *Report on the Global HIV/AIDS Epidemic.* Geneva: UNAIDS and WHO.

UNAIDS (2008) 'Speech by Peter Piot, UNAIDS Executive Director'. 23rd Meeting of UNAIDS Programme Coordinating Board, Geneva, 16 December 2008.

UNICEF 'Gender equality'. Online. Available www.unicef.org/gender/. (accessed 3 June 2009).

United Nations Development Program (2007) *Human Development Report 2007/2008.* Online. Available http://hdr.undp.org/en/media/HDR_20072008_EN_Complete.pdf (accessed 27 August 2010).

United Nations Inter-Agency Task Force (2003) 'Sport for Development and Peace: Towards Achieving the Millennium Development Goals'. United Nations.

Vandemoortele, J. and Delamonica, E. (2000). 'The "Education Vaccine" against HIV'. Online. Available www.tc.columbia.edu/cice/Archives/3.1/31vandemoortele_delamonica.pdf (accessed 19 January 2009).

World Health Organisation. 'Gender Inequalities and HIV'. Online. Available. www.who.int/gender/hiv_aids/en/index.html (accessed 24 July 2009).

Zaidi, S. A. (1999). 'NGO Failure and the Need to Bring Back the State', *Journal of International Development*, 11: 259–71.

24

Right To Play

Sustaining development through sport

Aaron Beacom and Lorna Read

The idea that the development process can be facilitated through sport and play-based interventions is integral to the evolution of modern sporting forms (Guilianotti 2004).[1] It is reflected in the long-held supposition that sport has agency in the promulgation of social norms and values and has been the basis of attempts to promote sport as a conduit for the social, cultural and physical development, particularly of young people (Elias and Dunning 1986; Holt 1989; Macaloon 2006). This supposition has been adopted by policy makers and social commentators throughout the Global North – in particular the United Kingdom (DCMS 2001), Australia (Social Inclusion Unit, Government of South Australia 2005) and Canada (Clark 2008). In the broader international context, a significant global movement has emerged and is becoming embedded within international development frameworks (Sport for Development & Peace International Working Group 2008a). 'Development through sport' has featured in a range of public policy contexts (Australian Sport Commission 2007) and has been embodied in protocols of organizations as various as the United Nations (UN)[2] and the International Olympic Committee (IOC).[3]

Debate over what constitutes sport and how it relates to the development process is wide ranging and has been dealt with elsewhere in this book. Generally speaking, conceptualizations of sport concern themselves with the physical and competitive components of the activity and recognition of the link with wider social and cultural configurations (Bale and Sang 1996). Sport, narrowly defined, typically adopts classification systems that focus on level, intensity and complexity of the competitive activity (Pink 2008). In the context of development through sport a more inclusive interpretation is frequently adopted, taking into account many forms of physical activity that can contribute to the development process (Read and Bingham 2009: xiv). In the context of the UN Task Force on Sport for Development and Peace, sport for the purposes of development includes all forms of physical activity that contribute to physical fitness, mental well-being and social interaction, such as play, recreation, organized or competitive sport and indigenous sports and games (UN 2003). With that in mind, this chapter interprets sport broadly defined as including a wide range of competitive and non-competitive physical activities, including play.[4]

Central to this global movement has been the emergence of a wide range of organizations that seek to engage with various forms of sport and physical culture in the international development context at global and localized levels. Levermore, in the first chapter of this Part has traced the evolution of such organizations within the wider international development arena. He has outlined the shifting nature and priorities of these organizations and their evolving relations with a variety of state and non-state partners who share an interest in international development through sport. It is certainly the case that the reach of such organizations has increased dramatically during the past decade and demand continues to increase. Read and Bingham (2009: xiii) noted that 'sport-based programmes now exist in practically every country from Azerbaijan to Zambia'. This increase in reach, scope and demand for such organizations has created pressure on them to develop a sustainable infrastructure capable of delivering development through sport in the longer term. This chapter will focus on the work of one such organization, the international non-governmental organization (INGO) Right To Play, and how it addresses both the creation of a sustainable organizational infrastructure, and ultimately sustainable programmes and results.

The chapter will consider the origins and growth of Right To Play and the evolution of the organization in keeping with shifts in the wider development arena. It will discuss the extent to which the strategic priorities of the organization have been informed by perceptions regarding what constitutes 'sustainable' development, in particular the organizational development of local infrastructures and capacity, and the emphasis on diversified partnerships.

As in the construction of any case study, the authors recognize the limitations of generalizing from the particular experiences of one organization. The case study by definition provides us with the opportunity for an evaluation of the context, interaction and processes taking place within 'the case' over a limited time period (Bell 2002). In that sense, the study has a direct value in understanding the characteristics of the case in question. In addition, although we cannot generalize from the findings, we can hypothesize that the issues that determine the frame of reference for the case study are generalizable – having enduring value (Silverman 2000). It is in this sense, the authors argue, that the changing international context within which Right To Play operates is generalizable (while the context of each country of operation is specific), and that this study provides insight into the challenges facing a range of actors who seek to secure meaningful and sustainable development through sport.

Background: sustainability and development

The term 'sustainability' is used in a variety of contexts and has acquired a diversity of meanings (Elliott 1999).[5] In particular, linkage of the terms 'sustainability' and 'development' is problematic in the sense that it is not always clear what aspect of an activity is being presented as sustainable and to what end (Gechev 2008). For example, in the context of 'sustainable sport' development programmes, the term can be interpreted as referring to the viability of the programmes from a specifically sports development perspective. Alternatively programmes may be considered in terms of their contribution to wider social, economic and environmental sustainability objectives established by a range of stakeholders in the development process. This may include the United Nations, the donor community, and international financial institutions. Ultimately, these contrasting perspectives on sustainability are not mutually exclusive, and there is value in efforts that emphasize both.

The perception of sustainable development as development in which 'total welfare' does not decrease over time, is dependent on the conservation of economic, environmental and social capital.[6] The UK Government Criteria for Sustainable Development Report (2005) notes that 'just as economic development is sustainable provided economic capital is non-decreasing, sustainable development requires total capital – that is economic capital, human and social capital and environmental capital – to be non-decreasing'.[7] Such sentiments are reflected in discourse related to sport and sustainable development. One example is the shifting perspective of the Olympic movement regarding the sustainability debate. In 1996, the IOC added a paragraph on environmental protection to the Olympic Charter. In 1999, however, it went on to develop its own set of sustainable development protocols in response to Agenda 21 (IOC 1999). This embraced the wider sustainable development agenda which also addressed issues of economic and socio-cultural development. Since then, ensuring that the Olympic Games meet its standards of sustainable development has become one of the 'pillars' of the IOC and is central to the process of bidding for the Games (IOC 2008).

Sustainable development – contrasting Interpretations

While the impetus for the global debate on sustainable development initially came from the biological sciences (Redclift and Sage 1995: 8) it soon became obvious that concern with the human impact on ecosystems linked across a number of areas of human activity.[8] Redclift and Sage (1995) note that economists found in the idea of 'sustainable economic development', apparently juxtaposed terms which, taken together, enabled them to address some of the limitations that had become evident in their discipline. The development community's concern with health, education and social welfare issues soon also became enmeshed with wider debates concerning how sustainable development could be fostered. In a similar way, while this chapter is concerned with the initiation and maintenance of sustainable programmes that can contribute effectively to the development process, such concerns are juxtaposed with the challenge of how to ensure that the wider process of development, in which these programmes are embedded, is itself sustainable.

In terms of this wider process of development, the international community began to mobilize around concepts of community, popular participation, local action and coordination of multi-sectoral activities. If the greatest challenges associated with global poverty were to be overcome, and in a sustainable way, this would require significant collaboration. The Millennium Declaration (UN 2000) established consensus among the international community with respect to the top priorities and corresponding targets in terms of the overall development of the Global South. Embodied in the Millennium Development Goals (MDGs), these priorities and targets are defined by core development objectives and universally accepted human values and rights. For Right To Play, the MDGs represent one of the key international frameworks that underlie all work on long-term programme strategy and design. Right To Play's programmes align to the key priority areas for the governments in countries of operation, and therefore, indirectly to the MDGs. Specifically, development through sport and Right To Play's programmes seek to contribute to MDG2 [Achieve universal primary education]; MDG3 [Promoting gender equality and empowering women]; and MDG6 [Combating HIV/AIDS, malaria and other diseases] (Centre for Community Based Research 2009; O'Reilly 2007; Population Council 2006; Right To Play 2006, 2007; UN 2003).

The *Paris Declaration on Aid Effectiveness* (OECD March 2005) established a series of reforms to help countries meet the MDG targets through a model of partnership and practices that improves the transparency and accountability on the use of development resources. The Paris Declaration has five core elements that set the agenda: (1) ownership – developing countries set their own strategies for poverty reduction and for the improvement in their institutional capacity to tackle corruption; (2) alignment – donor countries align behind these objectives and use local systems; (3) harmonization – donor countries coordinate and simplify procedures and share information to avoid duplication; (4) results – developing countries and donors shift their focus to development results and the measurement of those results; and (5) mutual accountability – donors and partners are accountable for development results. By the end of 2006, as an organization, Right To Play had established strategic direction in alignment with these core elements partly based on recommendations and dialogue with donor countries from which the organization received funding (Norwegian Agency for Development Cooperation [Norad] 2006), and also largely based on analysis of the lessons learned by the organization with its history of implementation up until that date.

In 2008 the Paris Declaration was revisited at the *Third High Level Forum on Aid Effectiveness* (2008) as the expected outcomes had not been met. The Accra Agenda for Action (UNDP 2008) highlighted three major challenges to the achievement of the reforms aspired to in the Paris Declaration. These were: (1) *Country Ownership.* Developing countries' governments need to take stronger leadership in their own development policies. Donors should support such governments by respecting countries' priorities, investing in their human resources and institutions, making greater use of their systems to deliver aid, and increasing the predictability of aid flows. (2) *Building more effective and inclusive partnerships.* In recent years, more development actors – middle-income countries, global funds, the private sector, civil society organizations – have been increasing their contributions and bringing valuable experience to the table. This also creates management and coordination challenges. All development actors are required to work in more inclusive partnerships so that their combined efforts have greater impact on reducing poverty. (3) *Achieving development results and openly accounting for them must be at the heart of all we do.* More than ever, citizens and taxpayers of all countries expect to see tangible results of development efforts. There is a need to demonstrate that the actions of partners translate into positive impacts on people's lives.

Right To Play and the evolution of the international development through sport agenda

The MDGs and the Paris Declaration are examples of key frameworks that have guided the expansion of the development through sport movement over the last decade, providing impetus for the initiatives of organizations such as Right to Play. In addition, the international development principles of partnership, local ownership and participation have also dominated the development through sport agenda. At the same time, the challenge of strengthening the relationship with the mainstream development community in order to ensure long-term sustainability has been recognized across the development through sport community and has been commented upon in the growing body of literature relating to this area (for example Levermore and Beacom 2009).

As development through sport interventions have become established, more numerous and more in demand, the longer-term consequences of these programmes have begun to exercise the minds of practitioners and academics working in the field. It is against this backdrop that the work of Right To Play is assessed as it seeks to nurture self-sustaining programmes that secure long-term social, cultural, educational and physical benefit for communities and also to maintain their relevance over time. Of particular strategic significance, this requires strong partnerships involving collaboration in every aspect of the development process from initiation through to delivery. In other words, the sustainable development through sport debates reflect those taking place within the mainstream development community.

Right To Play – the development of an ideal

As suggested in the introduction, the belief that sport can be a vehicle through which a range of social and economic objectives are achieved has become a default position of the public policy community. While acknowledging recent concern regarding some of the claims relating to the capacity of sport to deliver social and other benefits (Coalter 2007) the conviction regarding the value of sport (supported by a number of recorded successful interventions and ongoing programme evaluations) among many actors, including Right To Play, has underpinned their commitment to development through sport. Right To Play activities evolved from what was originally an Olympic-based movement that sought to engage Olympic athletes in support of people in war-torn countries and areas of distress. This movement was embodied in Olympic Aid, established in 1992 by the Lillehammer Winter Olympic Games Organizing Committee. The principal focus of Olympic Aid was to raise funds and awareness for the interventions by the implementing partner organizations, the Red Cross, Save the Children, Norwegian Refugee Council, Norwegian People's Aid and the Norwegian Church Fund.

Olympic athletes were chosen to be ambassadors of Olympic Aid prior to and during the 1994 Olympic Winter Games in Lillehammer, Norway. The lead Athlete Ambassador was Johann Olav Koss, then four-time Gold Medalist, and now President and CEO of Right To Play. In 2000 Olympic Aid made the transition from a fundraising vehicle to an implementing NGO. In March 2001, the first sport and play programmes began in partnership with the United Nations High Commissioner for Refugees in refugee communities in Angola and Côte d'Ivoire. Olympic Aid also made inroads on other influential fronts, placing sport as a social and human development tool firmly on the agendas of international athletes, the United Nations and humanitarian leaders. During the 2002 Olympic Winter Games in Salt Lake City, Olympic Aid hosted a Roundtable Forum entitled 'Healthier, Safer and Stronger: Using Sport for Development to Build a Brighter Future for Children Worldwide', which positioned sport for development on the agenda of the UN and other leading international organizations. UN Secretary-General Kofi Annan gave the keynote address, while global leaders in health, sport and development participated in a moderated discussion of the role of sport in relation to four development issues: vaccination, tobacco-free sport, HIV/AIDS prevention and the rehabilitation of refugees. Participants included Dr Gro Brundtland (Director General, World Health Organization), Ms Carol Bellamy (Executive Director, UNICEF), Mr Ruud Lubbers (High Commissioner, UNHCR), Archbishop Desmond Tutu, Mr Adolf Ogi (Special Adviser to the United Nations Secretary-General on Sport for Development and Peace) and Dr Jacques Rogge (President, IOC).

In early 2003, in order to meet the growing demands for programme implementation and fundraising, Olympic Aid became Right To Play. Building on the founding legacy of Lillehammer, this transition allowed Right To Play to include both Olympic athletes and other elite sports figures as Athlete Ambassadors; increase relationships with non-Olympic sports; partner with a wider variety of private sector funders; and deepen an implementation strategy. At the moment of transition to an implementing organization, what had become apparent (for Koss) was the need to ensure, first, well-structured programmes that focused on the key development issues facing children and youth in the Global South, and second, that long-term access to sport and play-based activities and programmes would be available.

Currently, Right To Play has programmes in 23 countries in Africa, Asia, the Middle East and South America. The vision of the organization is 'to create a healthier and safer world through the power of sport and play' (Monitor Company Group 2007). The mission is to improve the lives of children in some of the most disadvantaged areas of the world by using the power of sport and play for development, health and peace (Monitor Group Company 2007).

Right To Play – operationalizing an ideal

In his introduction to the June 2008 Right To Play, *Results: Progress Report,* Koss, the President and CEO, argued that the organization 'both remains true to its original founding principles of inclusion and sustainability, while continually adapting to meet the challenges of tomorrow'. Since 2003 the organization has designed and adopted a number of key strategies in alignment with the international development trends that directly relate to sustainability. With respect to sustainable organizational infrastructure (so supply can keep up with demand) two strategies are illustrative of the organization's adaptation, namely: (1) decentralization; and (2) the concentration of resources on a limited number of programmes (and countries), meaning investing in depth as opposed to breadth. In terms of sustainable programmes and results, the organization emphasizes: (1) partnerships (with community-based organizations, local NGOs, international organizations, government ministries); (2) participation of local staff and beneficiaries in all aspects from inception, design of the programme, through implementation and monitoring and evaluation; and (3) inclusion of all children and youth regardless of their age, culture, gender, language, religious beliefs, HIV status, disability, socio-economic status, etc., as one of the 'guiding principles' of Right To Play that has a direct link with sustainability. While the choice of criteria for commenting on the sustainability of Right To Play development interventions is clearly contentious, it seems appropriate to adopt those issues highlighted by the organization itself.

Right To Play: strategic priorities

Having considered how Right To Play emerged as an actor in the development through sport movement and its attempts to embrace the principle of sustainability, this section addresses the key preoccupations that have influenced the strategic direction of the organization as set out in the previous section.

Sustainable organizational infrastructure

Decentralization

In 2005–6 Right To Play began implementation of a decentralization strategy, with a core objective to have professional staff and effective structures in place that could leverage the multiple stakeholders involved in the programme across the local, national and regional levels. In addition, this structure was designed to facilitate sustainability through enhancement of field/ local capacity to plan, implement, manage, monitor and evaluate the programme in order to increase overall reach, outcomes and replication of best practices and lessons learned. The inherent advantages of a decentralized structure include:

- Leadership within each region with long-term vision for growth and sustainability of programmes.
- Capacity to build multi-year strategic plans that align with national development priorities and the local context.
- Professional experience in-field that can effectively manage the partner capacity-building strategy at community, national and regional levels.
- Capacity to manage locally based monitoring and evaluation systems to ensure high levels of knowledge sharing and quality control based on credible data.

- More effective and professional relationships with local embassies, funders, partners and beneficiaries.
- Field-based management of finance, logistics, human resources and administration.

Within its organization Right To Play has developed an information-sharing and quality assurance system to align with its decentralized structure that provides clear lines of responsibility and accountability with respect to data collection, analysis of the data, and information feedback loops. Each level within the structure – which includes community (project) to country, country to region, country/region to partner organization, and region to headquarters – supports and informs the next level. Right To Play also takes advantage of the decentralized staff and resources to create Right To Play Coach Networks at both the country and regional levels. Annual meetings of these networks provide a valuable opportunity for the exchange of lessons learned that can feed back into the planning and future implementation of the programme. A small number of coaches are selected to attend these annual meetings and as such this represents an excellent incentive to motivate coaches to take on leadership roles. For example, in Sierra Leone Right To Play has initiated Community Group Networks and Leaders Associations in Freetown and Makeni. These groups bring together various community partners who are implementing 'Live Safe Play Safe' to discuss strategies for effective programming (Right To Play Evaluation Sierra Leone (2007); Right To Play Evaluation Rwanda (2006) and Right To Play Evaluation Benin, Ghana and Mali (2009)).

The extent of the decentralization is dramatic. In 2009, the shift from an international volunteer model that was central from inception through 2005/2006, to that of a local staff model, is evident in the change from no local field staff (in the original model) to approximately 400 field staff currently. Of these, 3.5 per cent are expats and the remainder are local and national staff. The added value of this decentralization strategy, and the critical importance of emphasis on local expertise (not only international staff are seen as experts) has been supported in programme evaluations (Centre for Community Based Research 2009; Norad 2006; O'Reilly Management and Evaluation Consulting 2007) as evidenced by the following statement: 'by far the greatest strength was hiring local staff. Right To Play is contributing to a change in attitude towards local capacity evidenced by the expertise of its local field staff at workshops, community, events, and partner meetings' (Lisa O'Reilly: Management & Evaluation Consulting 2007, page 35).

Concentration of resources, depth versus breadth

In order to increase the quality of programmes and the likelihood of sustainability, the organization has realized a strategy to focus on depth versus breadth and to concentrate the investment of resources within the current countries and areas of operations. At the institutional level, stages of development have been determined for the countries of operation, specifically: (1) country presence established (country offices and projects); (2) growth of community model programmes; (3) growth through school-based model; and (4) maturation as a country NGO.

A core focus for the organization's growth strategy (Monitor Group Company 2007) is how to ensure the resources necessary to move the current countries through these stages. Ultimately, stage four will represent the institutional investment associated with depth and sustainability of the local organization.

At the programme level, the core delivery methodology has been designed to build local capacity and ultimately, sustainability. As demonstrated in Figure 24.1, through a continuous training cycle there is the possibility for exponential growth in numbers of coaches and

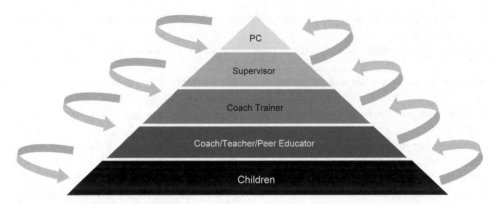

Figure 24.1 Project delivery model

children reached, and the ongoing assurance of programmatic quality control as monitoring systems and checks and balances are embedded across all levels.

In terms of the 400 local staff, almost 300 are at the 'front line' of project/programme implementation, namely the levels of Coaches and Trainers through to Project Coordinators (PCs). To illustrate the depth strategy, in long-standing countries of operation where the delivery methodology has really begun to take hold, from 2007 to date there has been a doubling in numbers of children reached. Examples include Uganda, Mozambique and Thailand (Right To Play Quarterly Monitoring Reports 2007, 2008, 2009). In addition, this exponential growth in reach in the number of children together with the qualitative evidence generated from the programmes, has formed the basis for development of relationships with Ministries of Education in Uganda, Mozambique and Thailand. These relationships will further the scope and potential for sustainability of development through sports programmes in general, and of Right To Play specifically.

Sustainable programmes and results

Partnerships

The principle of partnership within development has continued to gain momentum as recently reinforced by the Accra Agenda for Action (UNDP 2008). The idea of multi-stakeholder partnership – partnership between governments, business and civil society actors – has gained currency and been institutionalized through for example, the United Nations Partnerships for Sustainable Development (United Nations Commission on Sustainable Development 2005b). The term 'partnership' covers a wide spectrum of collaborative arrangements, from permanent national and international institutions, through policy networks bringing together state and non-state actors with a shared policy interest, to time-limited cooperation projects where there is a wide range of resourcing requirements.

Partnership within the sporting environment reflects cross-sectoral interest both in the context of elite performance and in sport as a medium for pursuing a range of social, economic and health objectives. The growth of interest by government departments, government agencies, sports federations, development NGOs and business organizations in the potential of international development through sport, has drawn many new actors into the frame (SDP IWG 2008b) and provided a clear rationale for engagement. The International Business Leaders Forum

(IBLF) has for example, presented the case for business engagement with resourcing of development through sports projects, which bring a range of reciprocal benefits in the areas of corporate communications, procurement and marketing (May and Phelan 2005). Functional and effective partnerships at all levels of the international development context therefore are an imperative for sustainable development through sport. In practice however, bringing together and fostering trust between organizations with contrasting strategic objectives and operational priorities presents a significant challenge.

Right To Play, as an INGO, has an extensive and diversified range of partnerships. In order to ensure sustainability, the organization emphasizes the institutional capacity-building of both Right To Play itself and its partner organizations, within an enabling environment created through advocacy and policy work. Right To Play defines partnership as a collaborative effort where organizations work together to implement a programme, have shared goals, and are involved in the planning, project design and evaluation. Understanding the approach, structure, philosophy and capacities of partner organizations and how the Right To Play programme fits into that context is essential for sustainability (Right To Play Programme Evaluations: Population Council 2006; Norad 2006; Right To Play 2006/2007; Harry Cummings and Associates Inc 2007; O'Reilly 2007; Centre for Community Based Research 2009).

Examples of the activities that Right To Play conducts related to partner organization capacity-building fall into the following categories according to type of partner (i.e. NGO, INGO or Government) and level of partnership (local, national, regional): (1) life skills training of Coaches; (2) work with government ministries to incorporate sport and play for development at a policy level; (3) project management and monitoring and evaluation training for staff of partner organizations; and (4) creation of a civil society structure based on participation in sport and play at the community level. Partnerships also contribute to institutional capacity development of Right To Play through the sharing of expertise in the local community context and strategies to address child development issues.

At the programme level Right To Play depends on partner organizations as a valuable avenue to extend reach and replication of the programme and to develop community ownership, as well as contributing to sustainability through ensuring on-going relevance to the community. At present, there are over 250 local partners across all locations within the 23 countries of operation. A number of evaluations conducted by Right To Play have reinforced the perspective of the value of these partnerships. In Sierra Leone, Rwanda and Ghana there is evidence that Right To Play is strongly engaged in partnerships for promoting HIV and AIDS education with both civil society and government, such as organizations that service children and families, religious organizations, human rights organizations, HIV/AIDS prevention programmes, and the National AIDS Secretariat of Sierra Leone (Centre for Community Based Research 2009). In the Palestinian Territories, there are a small number of partner organizations (UNWRA, National Committee for Summer Camps, Red Crescent – Nablus) displaying signs of 'graduating' from a position of receiving information and support (from Right To Play) to one in which they could contribute, or even lead programme development (O'Reilly: Management & Evaluation Consulting 2007).

Participation

The relationship of sport to empowerment – the social process by which individuals and communities develop the capacity to take control of their own lives – is complex and at times contentious. It is most readily found in feminist literature relating to sport, for example Theberge (1987, 2000) and Hargreaves (1994). More recently writing on sport and development has addressed the subject of the capacity of sport to contribute to the empowerment of women and young girls (Saavedra 2003, 2005). The principle of empowerment has been internalized into the sport for development movement and Youth Empowerment Through Sport (YETS) features as a key element in the 'toolkit for sport development' (Toolkit Sport for Development 2008). In this context, practitioners are encouraged to challenge the assumption that adults are most suited for leadership roles and that development objectives through sport (for example, communication of health-related messages) are more likely to be achieved if resources are directed toward the training of peer leaders. In this sense, groups become empowered to understand and take control of their own behaviour rather than being instructed by others.

There is emerging evidence concerning the efficacy of programmes centred in the development of indigenous human capital and so enhancing a body of local knowledge and expertise necessary to sustain programme delivery in the long term. One example, Moving the Goalposts (MTG), focuses on efforts of such empowerment activity. Saavedra (2009) notes that '[local] girls Committees organize teams, leagues, tournaments and commemorative events. They also undertake training of referees and coaches. Peer education is a central component to their method in tackling poverty and for empowering young girls. MTG provides training in public speaking it also stresses community involvement' (Saavedra 2009: 147). The argument here is that empowering individuals and groups to take control of one aspect of their lives will assist in the development of the skills and confidence necessary to transfer that process to other areas of their lives. In this sense the process becomes central to the socio-cultural aspect of sustainable development.

For Right To Play the design of all programmes is a participatory process that involves needs assessments together with a results-based approach, which emphasizes the context specificity of each programme location. As Figure 24.2 illustrates, the process of programme design for Right To Play is one that also encompasses the variety of stakeholders with which the INGO interacts at all levels.

This method ensures that priorities and needs of local partners and beneficiaries are captured and has been the objective of Right To Play's development through sport programme within each context, for example in Mali in 2006, Benin in 2006 and Azerbaijan in 2007. In all these countries it has been a powerful participatory learning tool and provided a means to actively engage children and youth in their own development as the primary agents of change for future generations. Critical to ensuring longevity and sustainability, is the participation of all 'influencers' in the lives of children and youth, such as coaches, teachers, CBOs and parents. This point has been reinforced in successive evaluations, 'there is the need to involve "traditional institutions" such as parents, traditional leaders, religious leaders' (Norwegian Agency for Development Cooperation 2006; Population Council 2006; Centre for Community Based Research 2009).

It is also through this participatory method that results related to programme objectives can be realized. For example, evaluations of Right To Play's programmes have demonstrated that:

- The emphasis on participation of the whole community and inclusion leads to effective means to decrease stigma and discrimination, for example related to HIV-positive individuals, gender stereotypes, and ethnic violence.
- Through engagement of teachers and community schools it is possible to contribute to an increase in attendance in school (both formal and non-formal settings).
- The focus on youth in a role of community leadership can serve as an entry point with communities to overcome root causes of non-participation.
- Sport and play-based programmes can assist with the strengthening of refugee–host country relations.

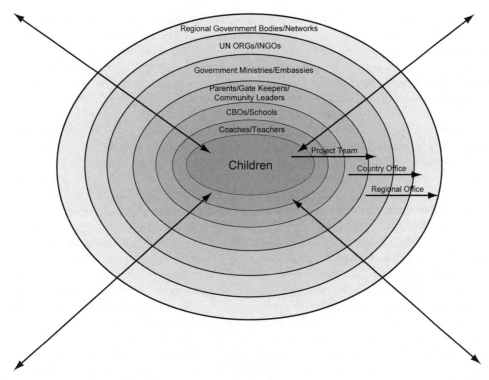

Figure 24.2 Right To Play process of programme design

Inclusion

The characteristics of development through sport programmes and their central objective of alleviating the systemic inequities that result in such poor quality of life for many in developing societies, has led to the inclusion agenda becoming enmeshed within the wider sustainable development agenda. This is the case in relation to a number of groups in society – including women and young girls (Saavedra 2003, 2005), young people generally (Crabbe 2000, 2005) and people with disability. In relation to disability for example, Beacom (2009: 98) argues that the increasing prominence of disability rights and inclusion within the domestic political agenda of Western Liberal democracies, has contributed to the promotion of disability within the international development agenda. This alongside the response of the UN and other international organizations to the rights of the disabled as part of the wider human rights portfolio (UN April 2009), has created a moral imperative for responding to the needs of people with disabilities as part of development through sport. This is accentuated through research that has demonstrated that disability is both; 'a cause and a consequence of poverty – 98 per cent of children with disabilities living in developing countries do not receive an education' (SDP IWG 2008a: 169).

The SDP IWG report makes the ambitious claim that sport for persons with disability is a 'powerful low-cost means to foster greater inclusion and wellbeing' (SDP IWG 2008a: 171). At the same time, the inherently exclusive nature of sport and its potentially divisive impact in the context of persons with disability is generally recognized. Sport can promote exclusion if effective adaptation and the coaching and administrative structures to counter discriminative attitudes and practices are not central to the initiatives (SDP IWG 2008a: 172). Similar arguments are advanced in relation to other marginalized groups. The sustainability of development through sport programmes is then dependent upon, where necessary, challenging social mores and the existing sports culture, and developing activities that promote inclusivity.

Right To Play works to promote the involvement of children and youth who may be marginalized for reasons of gender, disability, ethnicity, social background or religion. A core objective of the organization's programmes is to contribute to the attitudes that underlie a child's exclusion from participation in sport and play activities that often mirror the child's exclusion from participation in other parts of society. Engagement with children and youth also includes efforts to ensure their participation in decision-making with respect to programme development. Sport and play is viewed as a child-friendly tool to overcome the issues in the designated areas of intervention, such as basic education and HIV/AIDS preventative education, and to build trust and positive healthy relationships between children and adults, and among children, which lead to safer environments for children (Right To Play, Life Skills Evaluation 2009).

Also, in response to the inclusion agenda, the organization is committed to significant change in the lives of girls and women and recognizes the gender division between males and females of all ages in the target countries. While sport and play activities often illustrate where this division is prominent, sport and play also provide a powerful means for girls and women to gain critical life skills, such as teamwork, leadership and self-confidence, that help to overcome this division. To illustrate the value of this approach, the principles of inclusion and cooperation are reinforced during all Right To Play activities. The purpose is to normalize respectful behaviour towards children's peers regardless of their differences, and, therefore, gender stereotypes may be broken down within this environment. To date, the organization has achieved an average of 50 per cent participation of girls and women in the programmes, both as participants and as Coaches (Right To Play Quarterly Monitoring Report 2007, 2008, 2009).

Conclusion

If the idea of development is to have substance, it must move beyond nineteenth-century arguments of trusteeship where precedence is given to the objectives of the 'developed' initiator (Cowen and Shenton 1996: 25–7) and recognize the multiplicity of interests and interpretations surrounding the process that we term 'development'. This means much more than dialogue between 'donors' and 'recipients'. It requires a deep understanding of the range of interests and aspirations for development and an acceptance of the implications of 'empowerment' whereby power to make key decisions passes out of the hands of development practitioners and control over the process is relinquished. It recognizes that true partnership requires acknowledgement of the equal value of often contrasting perspectives and trust in the capacity of partners to act in the collective interest. It is against this backdrop that the capacity of Right To Play to develop sustainable programmes has been considered.

This case study identified the principles around which Right To Play has consolidated itself as a key actor within an international movement seeking to achieve meaningful and sustainable development through sport. Sustainability for Right To Play requires emphasis on both the organizational infrastructure, and the programmes and results. Ultimately both must be embedded into the local context through building relationships and partnerships with all 'influencers' and stakeholders. The commitment of the organization to decentralize the decision-making framework relating to programme construction, its acknowledgement of the imperative to empower local communities and invest in the development of local social capital, and its attempts to develop multi-layer partnerships from community-level advocacy groups, through national governments to international organizations, have been considered against a background of increased international interest in the idea of development through sport.

As with other actors engaged in development through sport, Right To Play faces a number of strategic and operational challenges related to sustainability. In particular:

- The need to ensure the level of investment required to move the countries through to institutional and programmatic maturation that will ultimately have the greatest reach to children and youth as participants in development through sport programmes.
- The challenge of continuing to improve the effectiveness and efficiency of decentralization through capacity development of local staff and organizational development.
- The requirement to ensure that resourcing and infrastructure is appropriate to the rising demand. In particular with added emphasis on partnership at the local level and ownership of local staff and organizations, this creates an increase in the requests for programmes from the local stakeholders and beneficiaries themselves.
- As an INGO, finding ways to engage new actors in the process of international development. This can typically include athletes and sports organizations/federations. Simultaneously there is a requirement to garner support from international development agencies to ensure collaboration and cooperation in programme design and implementation.

It remains to be seen what impact the global economic crisis, which was brought to the attention of commentators in the latter part of 2008, has on the development process generally and on development through sport specifically. It is likely to put additional pressure on donor organizations that support the various programmes and to change the priorities of governments in relation to development policy. A critical gauge will be how development organizations (INGOs/NGOs), such as Right To Play, are able to maintain a momentum built on investment to date, encourage local leadership of and demand for sustainable programmes, and remain responsive to the local context.

Finally, while this is a case study and the particular circumstances facing actors will differ to some extent, dependent on the various contexts within which they are operating, it is of value on two levels. On the one hand it is helpful in providing an appreciation of the operation of Right To Play as a key actor in the development through sport movement. Out of such case studies good practice can be identified, which may be transferable to other contexts. It also provides insights into the changing international context within which all actors are operating and the sorts of challenges they are likely to face.

Notes

1 The term 'development' is open to a wide range of interpretations including the UK government's Department for International Development's (DFID) focus on poverty reduction through the promotion of economic growth (Vadera 2007). In the context of this chapter, development broadly defined is interpreted as the enhancement of the human condition through improved social, economic and political conditions. At the same time, it is important to recognize the contentious nature of the term, for example, instances where it is used to legitimize state intervention and the confusion caused when 'the emblem of development is attached to the source of subjective action which is deemed to make development possible' (Cowen and Shenton 1996: 4).

2 In the case of the UN, the declaration of 2005 as the International Year of Sport and Physical Education, created the momentum for the construction and support of a range of international sports-based development initiatives (www.un.org/sport2005/).

3 In the case of the IOC, Olympic Solidarity has the brief to 'plan, organise and control the execution of the support programmes for the NOCs – particularly those that need it most – as stipulated in the

Olympic Charter'. In this role it has engaged directly in a range of development-based initiatives (http://multimedia.olympic.org/pdf/en_report_1072.pdf).

4 It is noteworthy that play, in itself, has been linked to the developmental process at an individual and community level (Huizinga 1955).

5 For example, in relation to business activity, O'Neill *et al.* (February 2009) comment that 'Sustainable entrepreneurship is at the nexus of sustainable development. Advocates see sustainability innovation … being the primary engine by which the holistic economic-environmental-social system is transformed toward sustainability'.

6 Putnam (1993: 167) defines social capital as 'features of social organization such as trust, norms and networks to improve efficiency of society by facilitating coordinated actions'.

7 DETR 'Quality of Life Counts, Criteria for Sustainable Development: Framework and Models Online'. This presents the argument of considering capital as 'both the stock and the quality of the resources – for example the skills, health and knowledge of the population' (http://www.sustainable-development.gov.uk/sustainable/quality99/chap2.pdf).

8 This was reflected in debate surrounding the Rio 'Earth Summit' (UN Conference on Environment and Development 1992), the subsequent Kyoto Protocol of 1997 and later revisions of 'Agenda 21' in subsequent Earth Summits.

References

Australian Sport Commission (2007) *Indigenous Sport and Development*, online. Available www.ausport.gov.au/participating/all/indigenous (accessed 13 December 2007).

Bale, J. and Sang, J. (1996) *Kenyan Running: Movement Culture, Geography and Global Change*, London: Frank Cass.

Beacom, A. (2009) 'Disability Sport and the Politics of Development'. In Levermore, R. Beacom, A. (eds) *Sport and International Development,* Basingstoke: Palgrave, 98–123.

Bell, J. (2002) *Doing Your Research Project* (3rd edn), Buckingham: Open University Press.

Bendell, G. (2005) 'Business – NGO Relations and Sustainable Development', *Greener Management International*, Issue 24 April 2005. Online. Available www.greenleaf-publishing.com/gmi/bendart.htm (accessed 17 February 2008).

Centre for Community Based Research (2009) *An Evaluation of Live Safe Play Safe within the Right to Play Sport and Play Programme in Sierra Leone, Rwanda and Ghana*, Kitchener, Canada: Right To Play.

Clark, W. (2008) *Canadian Social Trends, Kids Sports: Component of Statistics Canada Catalogue no. 11–008-x.* Online. Available www.statcan.gc.ca/pub/11–008-x/2008001/article/10573-eng.pdf (accessed 14 June 2009).

Coalter, F. (2007) *A Wider Social Role for Sport: Who's Keeping the Score?* London: Routledge.

Cowen, M. and Shenton, R. (1996) *Doctrines of Development*, London: Routledge.

Crabbe, T. (2000) 'A Sporting Chance? Using sport to tackle drug use and crime', *Drugs: Education Prevention and Policy*, 7 (4): 381–91.

Crabbe, T. (2005) 'Getting to Know You: Engagement and Relationship Building', *First Interim National Positive Futures Case Study Research Report*. Online. Available www.substance.coop/publications_knowing_the_score (accessed 27 March 2009).

DCMS (February 2001) *Building on PAT 10: Progress Report on Social Inclusion*, London: DCMS. Online. Available www.culture.gov.uk/PDF/social_inclusion.pdf (accessed 14 June 2009).

DCMS (undated) *DCMS Sustainable Development Strategy: Sectors, Sport.* Online. Available www.culture.gov.uk/images/publications/sdsSport.pdf (accessed 20 March 2009).

DEFRA (undated) *Criteria for Sustainable Development – the Framework and Models.* Online. Available www.sustainable-development.gov.uk/sustainable/quality99/chap2.pdf.

DETR (2005) *Quality of Life Counts, Criteria for Sustainable Development: Framework and Models Online.* Available http://www.sustainable-development.gov.uk/sustainable/quality99/chap2.pdf

Elias, N. and Dunning, E. (1986) *Quest for Excitement: Sport and Leisure in the Civilizing Process*, Oxford: Basil Blackwell.

Elliott, J. (1999) *Introduction to Sustainable Development (2nd edn)*, London: Routledge.

Gechev, R. (2008) 'The Institutional Framework for Sustainable Development in Eastern Europe', *Journal of Communist Studies and Transition Politics*, 24 (1): 54–67.

Guilianotti, R. (ed.) (2004) *Sport and Modern Social Theorists*, Basingstoke and N.Y: Palgrave Macmillan.

Hargreaves J. (1994) *Sporting Females: Critical issues in the history and sociology of women's sports*, London: Routledge.

Harry Cummings & Associates Inc (2007) *Evaluation of the SportWorks Programme in Azerbaijan for Right To Play*, Guelph, Canada.

Holt, R. (1989) *Sport and the British*, Oxford: Clarendon Press.

Huizinga, J. (1955) *Homo Ludens: a study of the play element in culture*, Boston: Beacon Press.

IOC (1999) *The Olympic Movement's Agenda 21*, Lausanne: IOC.

IOC (2008) *Factsheet: Environment and Sustainable Development*, Lausanne: IOC Information Centre. Online. Available www.infocentre@olympic.org (accessed 24 December 2008).

Levermore, R. and Beacom, A. (eds) (2009) *Sport and International Development*, Basingstoke: Palgrave.

Macaloon, J. (2006) 'Muscular Christianity after 150 Years', *The International Journal of the History of Sport*, 23 (5): 687–700.

May, G. and Phelan, J. (2005) *Shared Goals: Sport and Business in Partnerships for Development*, London: International Business Leaders Forum / UK Sport. Online. Available www.nextstep2007.org/assets/File//SharedGoalsW.pdf (accessed 15 March 2009).

Monitor Group Company (2007) *Right To Play Growth Strategy 2008 – 2012*, Toronto, Canada.

Norwegian Agency for Development Cooperation (2006) *Review of Right To Play, Organizational Performance Review*.

OECD (2005) *Paris Declaration on Aid Effectiveness*. Online. Available www.oecd.org/dataoecd/11/41/34428351.pdf (accessed 18 May 2009).

Olympic Solidarity Commission (2006) *Olympic Solidarity: Creation and Development*, (2006). Online. Available http://multimedia.olympic.org/pdf/en_report_1072.pdf (accessed 27 September 2008).

O'Neill, G., Hershauer, J. and Golden, J. (2009) 'The Cultural Context of Sustainability Entrepreneurship', *Green Management International*, 55.

O'Reilly, Lisa: Management & Evaluation Consulting (2007) *Evaluation of Right To Play's Programme in the Occupied Palestinian Territory*, Vancouver, Canada.

Pink, B. (2008) *Defining Sport and Exercise: A Conceptual Model*, Adelaide: Australian Bureau of Statistics. Online. Available www.ausstats.abs.gov.au/ausstats/subscriber.nsf/0/BC37A3CD4A82D50DCA2573F6000FF3B7/$File/41490_2008.pdf (accessed 15 March 2009).

Population Council (2006) *Evaluation of the Right to Play Programme*, Mali.

Putnam, R. (1993) *Making Democracy Work: Civic traditions in modern Italy*, Princetown: Princetown University Press.

Read, L. and Bingham, J. (2009) Preface. In: Levermore R. Beacom A. (eds) *Sport and International Development*, Basingstoke: Palgrave.

Redclift, M. and Sage, C. (eds) (1995) *Strategies for Sustainable Development: Local agendas for the South*, Chichester: Wiley.

Right To Play (2006) *Mid-term Evaluation Rwanda Sport Health Project*, Toronto: Right To Play.

Right To Play (2007) *Sierra Leone Mid-Line Evaluation Report*, Toronto: Right To Play.

Right To Play (2008) *Results: Progress Report, June 2008*, Toronto: Right To Play International. Online. Available www.righttoplay.com/site/DocServer/RTP_Results_Magazine_2008.pdf?docID=9661.

Right To Play (2009) *Life Skills Evaluation, Benin, Ghana and Mali*, Toronto: Right To Play.

Right To Play (2007, 2008, 2009) Quarterly Monitoring Reports.

Saavedra, M. (2003) 'Football Feminine – Development of the African Game: Senegal, Nigeria and South Africa', *Soccer and Society*, 4 (2): 222–53.

Saavedra, M. (2005) 'Women, Sport and Development', *Sport and Development International Platform*. Online. Available http://assets.sportanddev.org/downloads/56–women–sport_and_development.pdf (accessed March 2009).

Saavedra, M. (2009) 'Dilemmas and Opportunities in Gender and Sport-in-Development'. In Levermore, R. and Beacom, A. (eds) *Sport and International Development*, Basingstoke: Palgrave, 124–55.

Silverman, D. (2000) *Doing Qualitative Research*, London: Sage.

Social Inclusion Unit (2005) *Social Inclusion Board: Overview of the Social Inclusion Agenda*, Adelaide: Social Inclusion Unit, Government of South Australia. Online. Available www.socialinclusion.sa.gov.au/files/Social%20Inclusion%20Overview.pdf (accessed 14 June 2009).

Sport for Development & Peace International Working Group (2008a) *Harnessing the Power of Sport for Development and Peace: Recommendations for Governments*, Toronto: Right to Play.

Sport for Development & Peace International Working Group (2008b) *Sport for Development and Peace: The UN System in Action*. Online. Available www.un.org/wcm/content/site/sport/sdp_ing_thematicwgs (accessed 27 August 2010).

Sport in Action (undated) *Youth Empowerment Through Sport (YETS)*. Online. Available www.toolk-itsportdevelopment.org/html/topic_82D8DC91-ED55–4A8F-9A38-B (accessed 31 December 2008).

Theberge, N. (1987) 'Sport and Women's Empowerment', *Women's Studies International Forum*, 10 (4): 387–93.

Theberge, N. (2000) *Higher Goals: Women's Hockey and the Politics of Gender*, Albany NY: State University of New York Press.

Toolkit Sport for Development (2008) *Youth Empowerment Through Sport: Background*. Online. Available www.toolkitsportdevelopment.org/./topic_82D8DC91-ED55-4A8F-9A38-BBE4CB1113-DA_F855C526-917C-4B7E-9BBF-7C626B74 (accessed 27 August 2010).

UN (1992) *Report of the UN Conference on Environment and Development*. Online. Available www.un.org/documents/ga/conf151/aconf15126–1annex1.htm (accessed 19 May 2009).

UN (2000) *United Nations Millennium Declaration*. Online. Available www.un.org/millennium/ (accessed 20 May 2009).

UN (2003) *Sport for Development and Peace: Towards Achieving the Millennium Development Goals*, Report from the UN Inter-Agency Task Force on Sport for Development and Peace. Online. Available www.un.org/themes/sport/reportE.pdf (accessed 27 August 2010).

UN (2005a) *International Year of Sport and Physical Education*. Online. Available www.un.org/sport2005/ (accessed 19 May 2009).

UN (2005b) *13th Session of the UN Commission on Sustainable Development*. Online. Available www.un.org/esa/dsd/csd/csd_csd13.shtml (accessed 27 August 2010).

UN (14–16 April 2009) 'Disability and the Millennium Development Goals – Expert Group Meeting on Mainstreaming Disability in MDGs Policies, Processes and Mechanisms: Development For All', *Enable*, Geneva. Online. Available www.un.org/disabilities/default.asp?id=1470 (accessed 14 June 2009).

UNDP (2008) *Third High Level Forum for Aid Effectiveness: Accra Agenda For Action*. Online. Available www.undp.org/mdtf/docs/Accra-Agenda-for-Action.pdf (accessed 18 May 2009).

Vadera, S. (2007) 'Investing in Africa' – Speech by International Development Minister Shriti Vadera at the City of London Corporation and DFID Rwanda and Tanzania's investment symposium, 06 November 2007. Online. Available www.dfid.gov.uk/news/files/speeches/shriti-speech-city-of-london.asp (accessed 6 March 2009).

25

A postcolonial feminist approach to gender, development and EduSport

Lyndsay Hayhurst, Margaret MacNeill and Wendy Frisby

Out of my way bureaucracy and political apathy. Move aside tradition, step down myth … I am a woman and I will Sport to my hearts content. Watch me.

(Lombe Annie Mwambwa 2008)

It has been estimated that approximately 70 per cent of those living in poverty around the world are women and girls (Mohanty 2003). At the same time, international development scholars contend that 'women are increasingly seen, by men as well as women, as active agents of change; the dynamic promoters of social transformation who can alter the lives of *both* women and men' (Sen 2000: 189). In an attempt to build on the 'promise' of women as agents of development and to lessen the dire consequences of poverty, there has been increasing interest in sport for development interventions that specifically target women and girls in the Two-Thirds World[1] by the private sector, governments, and non-governmental organizations (NGOs) (e.g. Kidd 2008; Mwaanga 2005; Nike Foundation 2008).

While boys and men in the Two-Thirds World are also disadvantaged in terms of sports participation, it is well known that the participation levels of girls and women are lower in countries around the world due to various historical, cultural, economic and geopolitical influences that reflect power relations based on class, race, gender, sexuality and nation (Swiss Academy for Development and Cooperation 2008). As a result, girls and women have less access to the potential benefits of participation which are, when fully realised, considered to help overcome the problems historically associated with sport such as exclusion (e.g. due to gender, class and/or racial discrimination, injury, hyper-masculinity, homophobia, violence and abuse) (Kidd 2008; Saavedra 2005, 2009). We argue that sport does have a potential role to play in promoting health and other benefits while lessening power imbalances, as implied in the opening quote by Lombe Annie Mwambwa from Africa, but only if the numerous problems associated with it are not imported from the One-Third World in a colonizing manner. As Darnell (2007: 565) argues, the dominant sport for development discourse describes sport as 'integrative, apolitical and transcendent'. This draws attention away from the potential for sport to be what Cannella and Manuelito (2008: 48) call a new form of colonialism, or another type of Eurocentric and North American error, where dominant patriarchal market forces are used to justify the further economic marginalization of women in the Two–Thirds World (e.g. due to their child-bearing roles and lack of access to education) and legitimize imports from the One–Third World without allowing for local input and cultural adaptation.

Despite increased attention to sport, gender and development, sports feminists have largely ignored the literature on international development, whereas studies on sport for development typically fail to address gender, although there are some notable exceptions (e.g. Brady 2005; Hargreaves 1997; Kay, 2009; Larkin 2007; Saavedra 2005, 2009). The application of new or existing theories is needed to account for the negative effects of global capitalism along with the historical legacies of colonization that contribute to poverty and other social problems, including problems tied to sport. In this way, theory becomes inextricably linked to action and can become a tool for promoting transformation and social justice in ways that generate new insights (Frisby *et al.* 2009). Yet caution must be exercised when challenging entrenched social orders because, as Saavedra (2005: 1) warns: 'female involvement in sport is often a transgression that needs to be explained, encouraged, prevented, or managed, but somehow is not "natural".' As a result, there can be serious risks for girls and women who challenge patriarchy through their involvement in sport and these risks must be carefully taken into account.

The theory that we will begin to explore in this chapter is postcolonial feminism which represents an anti-colonial approach to social science research (Cannella and Manuelito 2008). Postcolonialism refers to ways of critiquing both the material and discursive legacies of colonialism (McEwan 2001). Feminism shares an emphasis on unmasking dominant knowledge claims and how social systems perpetuate injustices, but draws particular attention to how gender intersects with other forms of oppression. While there are many different types of feminist theory, postcolonial feminism critiques Western forms that disregard the different cultural and historical experiences and structural locations of those living outside the One–Third World (McEwan 2001; Mohanty 2003; Spivak 1988).

A helpful departure point for considering postcolonial theory more broadly is to address the significance of the hyphen that is sometimes used between 'post' and 'colonial' to denote different historical periods. Some scholars argue that the hyphen represents a period after colonialism, as post means 'past', therefore suggesting that colonialism and its impacts have 'definitively terminated' (Hall 1996: 243). However, although formal decolonization has taken place in many Two–Thirds World countries, these regions are still reeling from the impacts. In addition, many scholars argue that the Two–Thirds world has more recently been re-colonized through processes of global capitalism, commonly referred to as neocolonialism (Li 2007; Saul 2008). As we are not referring to specific time periods in this chapter, we will use the more common version of the terms postcolonial and neocolonial without the hyphen. Postcolonial feminism is concerned with both the recent impacts of global capitalism, the historical effects of different forms of patriarchy and colonization, and how all of this affects lived experiences (McEwan 2009; Mohanty 2003).

The goal of this chapter is to illustrate the value of postcolonial feminism by discussing two of its key themes and applying them to EduSport and its *Go Sisters* initiative, a sport for development programme in Africa. By taking this approach, we hope to combat one of the critiques of postcolonial feminism that it 'cannot be easily translated on the ground' (McEwan 2001: 102). To briefly contextualize our analysis, we first elaborate on the sport, gender and development movement. We then identify two key themes of postcolonial feminism and apply them to the EduSport case. In the concluding section, we briefly identify other themes that could be further explored and provide a critique of postcolonial feminism given that our aim is to explore and open up further discussion, rather than present a postcolonial feminist approach as a panacea. In this way, we hope to offer a starting point for envisioning new approaches not only to research and knowledge production, but also to international development policy making and practice.

Contextualizing the sport, gender and development movement

In order to understand the interrelationships between sport, gender and development, it is crucial to briefly contextualize the ways gender has been considered in international development. Originating in the 1970s, the gender and development movement was conceptualized as 'Women in Development' (WID), and initiated various international conferences to promote the recognition of women's paid and unpaid work. The momentum behind this movement continued to build in 1976, when the United Nations declared the commencement of the decade for women, resulting in the integration of gender issues into various social policy arenas including sport. While the decade proved useful for addressing many of the issues identified through the application of feminist theory, many fundamental issues were ignored (Chen 1995). Central problems with the WID framework were that it failed to sufficiently challenge hierarchies of class, race and patriarchy (e.g. where women are seen as being inferior to men in various realms of life) (Jennissen and Lundy 2001; Larkin 2007).

In the 1980s a new approach known as 'Gender and Development' (GAD) emerged and its main tenets were to integrate considerations of gender into all international development initiatives (Jackson 1998). The shift in terminology from *women* to *gender* was meant to imply that women alone are not responsible for their situations or for social change, and that additional circumstances must be considered when determining oppression. This approach also emphasized the 'empowerment' of women as a prerequisite for development, but a central problem was the implication that 'people with power can and will give it to people without it' (Smillie 1996: 81). In this way, GAD failed to account either for women's oppression as a product of colonial and neocolonial power relations or for their active agency in resisting them (Larkin 2007; Mohanty 2003). Similar discourses of empowerment are enmeshed in the current development policy agenda.

Another critique of the current development ideology, particularly from a feminist perspective, challenges the implicit Western assumption of 'saving others' in the Two-Thirds World. This poses implications for us as authors of this chapter, as we are white, middle class, Western academics writing about gender in an international development and sports context. Our aim is not to set out an agenda that attempts to 'empower' or 'save' or 'speak for' others. Yet, we do select particular voices from the few available to us in the EduSport case to illustrate the importance of 'having a voice', which certainly points to some of the messy contradictions in applying the theory. Still, we seek to begin a discussion of a theoretical framework that overcomes some of the patronizing and colonizing assumptions underpinning traditional approaches to sports research and development. As Abu-Lughod (2002: 789) aptly points out, 'projects of saving other women depend on and reinforce a sense of superiority by Westerners, a form of arrogance that deserves to be challenged'. Postcolonial feminism provides a lens for questioning how underlying relations of neocolonial power, notions of salvation and solidarity are embedded in research and Two-Thirds/One-Third World relations.

From the mid 1970s onwards, several pertinent gender equity campaigns were formed and position statements issued in Western-based countries to promote the participation of girls and women in sport (Larkin 2007). For example, the Brighton Declaration in 1994 marked an important step in creating women's sports organizations, such as the International Working Group on Women and Sport, subsequently leading to increased lobbying efforts and sports participation (International Working Group on Women and Sport 1994). According to Saavedra (2005), advancements made within the women in sport movement influenced the official gender and development movement, as evidenced by the fact that women in sport were mentioned in the Beijing Platform for Action (United Nations 1995). However, these campaigns were problematic as they mostly ignored women's experiences in sport in the Two-Thirds World (Hargreaves 1999, 2004).

Various researchers have demonstrated that sport is a useful tool for contributing to gender and development in various ways, particularly as a means of enhancing girls' and women's health and well-being, facilitating their self-esteem and self-empowerment, fostering social inclusion and social integration, challenging and transforming gender norms, educating women and girls about HIV/AIDS prevention, and providing them with opportunities for leadership and achievement (Larkin 2007; Nicholls and Giles 2007; Saavedra, 2005; Willis 2000). Yet, Saavedra (2005) cautions sport and gender development organizers and policy makers to be concerned about safety (e.g. particularly with sexual violence in sport), competing obligations (e.g. gendered divisions of labour creates heavy demands on women' and girls' time for leisure) and confronting gender and sexuality norms (e.g. by not over-emphasizing femininity and masculinity to offset fears of homosexuality). These points of contention underscore the importance of using a postcolonial feminist lens to explore how international development practitioners may (or may not) be actively confronting norms and processes that disadvantage girls and women in sport.

Postcolonial and sporting feminisms

There is a dearth of sports feminist literature from outside the One-Third World, and sport, gender and development is a relatively new area of investigation for feminists, development theorists and sport researchers alike (Larkin 2007; Pelak 2005). Drawing on the work of post-colonial feminist scholars, we have identified two key themes which, while not intending to be exhaustive, do represent a starting point for considering the theory's application. The two themes are i) destabilizing neocolonial discourses, and ii) centring Two-Thirds World voices in sport, gender and development initiatives. Below, we give examples related to these two themes to magnify how neocolonialism and postcolonialism operate.

Destabilizing neocolonial discourses that position the One-Third World as advanced and the Two-Thirds World as backward and primitive is a core issue for postcolonial feminism (Mohanty 1988; Ong 1988). According to Sardar (1999), it is in the ability to define, represent and theorize about 'others' that the real colonial power lies. For example, when One-Third World feminists privilege their own perspectives as normative, while essentializing indigenous, Two-Thirds World, and girls and women in the diaspora as victims by 'blaming their cultures', they reproduce colonial discourses and relations of power (Bannerji 2000; McEwan 2009). As Hargreaves (2004: 197) warns 'in sport feminism, specifically, there is a tendency to view sport development for [Two]-Third[s] World women as essentially beneficial and a way of addressing their under-development and bringing them into the modern world', reflecting criticisms of the gender and international development movement more generally. She (1997: 197) argues that 'theorizing is embodied in the life stories of South African sportswomen, and how their experiences are in tension with the dominant structures of race, gender, and class relations'. In her study, several female participants discussed the racial discrimination experienced when participating in sport.

> In our coloured schools, the only sport for girls was netball, because it was the cheapest sport. Most of our schools didn't have hockey, which isn't all that expensive. But in Black schools there was just nothing.
>
> *(Participant quote Hargreaves 1997: 194)*

Pelak (2005: 67) adds that South African women footballers are not a homogeneous and unified group. Instead, they experience and take up gender inequalities in multiple ways, as 'local contexts and histories create different geospatial configurations in the sport football'. She demonstrates the importance of considering categories of difference and encourages researchers to view culture as hybrid, fluid and inherently dynamic to avoid universalizing girls and women's sporting experiences.

This leads to a second central postcolonial feminist challenge that we will focus on, which is best captured in the provocative question asked by Spivak (1988), 'Can the subaltern speak'? Mohanty (2003: 21) argues that it is by hearing subaltern voices that notions that 'gender or sexual difference or even patriarchy can be applied universally and cross-culturally' can be disrupted to radically reconstruct both history and contemporary processes of knowledge production. The need to centre Two-Thirds World voices in sport, gender and development interventions is very much connected to 'questions about on whose authority does one claim to speak on behalf of others' (McEwan 2001: 95). Centring voices from the Two-Thirds World requires the development of new decolonizing methodologies that avoid misrepresenting, essentializing and denying girls and women meaningful input and control over development projects intended for them (e.g. Denzin and Lincoln 2008; Parameswaran 2008; Smith 1999; Swadener and Kagendo 2008). Such decolonizing approaches pay attention to the neocolonial forces that create silences and to the collaborative alliances that can be built to surface and act upon Two-Thirds World voices. It also encourages those in the Two-Thirds World to conduct their own research and sport programming (Parameswaran 2008; Swadener and Kagendo 2008). In the next section, we apply these two postcolonial feminism themes to a discussion of EduSport and *Go Sisters* to illustrate their implications for both sports research and practice.

An exemplar: EduSport and *Go Sisters*

> You will have me heard cattle, walk for miles to fetch water. But you say I can not race or climb the Kilimanjaro.
>
> *(Original spelling, Lombe Annie Mwambwa 2008)*

Indigenous sport and development initiatives such as EduSport and *Go Sisters* in Zambia imagine new educational, economic, sporting and cultural possibilities for girls and women. The historical and material contexts within which these programmes have been organized as a response to colonialism require attention. Situated in sub-Sahara Africa, the Republic of Zambia was occupied by the British in the late nineteenth century and known as Northern Rhodesia until 1964. Drawing on the cultural geography writings of Nash (2002), Power (2003: 121) cogently argues that the material legacies of colonialism are not singular and should be addressed along with postcolonial concerns for culture, difference, development and the 'spatial imagination of progress'. In other words, a postcolonial approach can examine social, political and material inequities *and* the 'mythic' features of progress through development predicted for countries like Zambia (Power 2003: 121). In 2006, the average per capita income was US$770 (World Bank 2006) and had changed little since the 1960s. The prosperous future predicted for Zambia when this Republic replaced the protectorate of British governance did not come to fruition. Indeed, as Power (2003) illustrates, retrogression occurred in many sectors of the national economy, particularly the main copper export sector from the 1970s to 2000s. Growth in the gross domestic product is now rising due to foreign investment in mining and improved copper prices, however Zambia suffers one of the highest per capita foreign debt levels and by 2008 was ranked 112th out of 134 countries in the Global Competitiveness Index 2008–9 (World Economic Forum 2008). Moreover, with an average life expectancy of 42 years, a fertility rate of 5.5 children, an adolescent fertility rate of 125 births per 1,000 girls aged 15–19 years, and a 15.2 per cent HIV rate, Zambians continue to face many challenges (World Bank 2006).

EduSport was founded in 1999 as an NGO in Lusaka, the capital of Zambia, in response to pressing issues of children's rights, poverty and the HIV/AIDS pandemic. EduSport was developed by Africans for Africans with an official mission 'to empower underserved communities through their active participation in Sport' (EduSport 2009). Currently spread over six provinces, the organization hoped to broaden its reach to all ten provinces in the nation by 2010.

> Using the 'Sport in the Development Process' (SDP) approach, we seek to foster community education, development and empowerment. The EduSport concept is based on this belief: that sport with a positive orientation, when integrated into the broader framework of human and social development goals and priorities, is a powerful vehicle for change.
>
> *(EduSport 2009)*

A guiding principal of this programme is '*ubuntu*', which is an indigenous Bantu word meaning '*to do with people*'. For the founders of the programme, ubuntu means sport should be harnessed to serve the local interests and needs of Zambian youth (Mwaanga 2005). As Annie Namukanga, the *Go Sisters* National Program Coordinator, said in email correspondence with us,

> The EduSport Foundation is uniquely Zambian because it was initiated by Zambians for Zambians who, at the time, were affected by and understood the real pool of issues Zambian youth faced and are facing; hence are passionate to use sport in the development process as a vehicle to foster empowerment of socio, economically and at-risk young people through their active participation in sport. … it is important to understand that problems affecting people are better understood by indigenous Zambians. Therefore, it can be the best mode to explain and come up with actual solutions to their own lived problems.
>
> *(Email communication 7 July 2009)*

While the colonizing influences of a British and predominantly Christian hegemony in Lusaka can be detected in EduSport's mandate and motto of '*Greatness through Service*', the conscious attempt to shift gender relations has been a primary mandate of this programme. As one founder claims,

> Before EduSport, boys were brought up to think of girls as sex objects. Now that girls participate in games like football, are peer coaches, and go to school, boys can see they are able to do much in our society.
>
> *(Mwaanga 2005)*

Girls are involved in leadership roles in all EduSport programmes, which gives young women 'the confidence to discuss with boys in communities matters related to sex and negotiate for safer sexual relations' (Namukanga 2009). Leadership opportunities extend to decision-making roles in all EduSport programmes, including *Boys for Girls by Girls* in which girls suggest gender issues to be addressed in peer leadership activities conducted by boys and girls. Overall, the programme has attempted to secure the human rights of girls to education, health and play, while specifically transforming sex education and gender relations across many spheres of social life.

Among the many EduSport initiatives, *Go Sisters* was one of the first to be developed that aims to help girls and young women to pursue equality.

It strives to empower girls by building physical resources, giving social recognition and challenging some traditional gender myths.

(Go Sisters EduSport Website 2005)

Introduced in 2002, Go Sisters is a peer-mentoring programme that promotes sports participation and also encourages girls and young women to stay in school, acquire leadership skills as coaches and referees, organize a variety of team sports at school, and organize tournaments for girls in other communities. These activities have developed in response to the particular challenges facing girls in Zambia including, according to Namukanga,

> sexual harassment, HIV/AIDS, lack of education, lack of social networks, lack of female sports leaders and role models. The program looks at finding innovative ways of engaging girls in positive oriented sport that enhances their empowerment by building physical resources, giving them social recognition and space where they meet to discuss issues affecting their wellbeing and providing them with practical knowledge and skills needed for them to make something out of their lives on the same footing with boys.

(Email communication 7 July 2009)

At the end of 2008, 16 young women between 12 and 18 years of age travelled during holidays to compete in sports and to debate issues affecting their lives with girls in a different community. After the tournament participants were expected to run tournaments for five areas of the capital city Lusaka and eight other communities in the southern province of Zambia. It has become the largest girls' sports movement in a nation where 80% live below the poverty line. When poverty and patriarchy intersect, 'girls are even more affected by AIDS, poverty, illiteracy and unemployment' (Namukanga cited in Clarke and Sewell 2005). Yet, over 200 young women have been trained as peer leaders, 30 school partnerships have been established, and 100 girls have received scholarships to attend school. This NGO now involves approximately 5,000 girls in physical activity movement-based 'empowerment' programmes across Zambia. A policy of gender mainstreaming has been successfully actualized on many levels during a relatively short time span, yet the empowerment discourse that underlies it needs to be scrutinized closely and a postcolonial feminist approach that deconstructs neocolonial discourses is helpful in this regard.

Struggles over empowerment are being waged that reflect wider One-Third World concerns for gender equity. For example, EduSport created Kicking Aids Out (KAO) in 2001 as an international network dedicated to promoting the development of NGOs to promote dialogue about HIV/AIDS and life skills training. Five years later, the National Organisation of Women in Sport Physical Activity and Recreation (NOWSPAR) emerged to serve as a resource and advocate for gender equity in KAO (Mwambwa, cited in Torége 2009). Just as some athletes are playmakers on the field, NOWSPAR has an innovative PlayMaker programme to help women manoeuvre within policy and legal systems. NOWSPAR helps sporting programmes such as Go Sisters move beyond neocolonial notions of individual empowerment to structural change and social justice concerns. 'Women win, women think, women change' is the advocacy motto of NOWSPAR and to empower women, ten strategies for gender equity are advocated including to:

> support women's and girls' sports; join a women's rights organization; challenge the myths; encourage other women and girls; push for gender equity policies; speak out against homophobia; publicize discrimination in your organizations, institutions and schools; develop a media strategy; consider legal alternatives.

(NOWSPAR 2009)

These strategies provide examples of how patriarchy is being challenged through sport. *Go Sisters* and the wider array of EduSport programmes such as *Kicking Aids Out* have achieved some basic levels of sustainability over the past decade, but it has become increasingly difficult to decipher the founding Zambian voices from the voices of the One-Third World in corporate social responsibility initiatives that are tied to the UN Millennium Development Goals.[2] For example, in EduSport's project document for its recent membership in the Nike's Game Changers/ Global Giving programme, sport is considered to be an outstanding vehicle for development for the following reasons.

- Sport is the most popular activity with the young people who are the target group of EduSport.
- Sport can be used to attract, reach out and lobby support from important target stakeholders such as parents, politicians and the business community.
- Sport is a powerful vehicle for overcoming cultural barriers such as issues related to AIDS and sex.
- Physical activity contributes to the betterment of both physical and mental health and also teaches children motor skills, balance and coordination.
- Sports promote self-confidence and build self-esteem, and also teach basic life skills and values which are directly transferable to children's performance in the classroom and across all other spheres of life. Skills such as teamwork, cooperation, communication, self-discipline etc.
- Sport is an international language that cuts across division of race, class, the disabled/abled and gender.
- Sport provides a healthy form of youth recreation and creative self-expression, as an active alternative to boredom, crime, gangsterism and drugs.

(EduSport 2005: 3)

Similar to the apolitical claim of sport as an international language (in item 6 above), a former Secretary General of the United Nations has claimed sport to be a 'universal language' (cited in Ogi 2006: 1). Gender is erased in essentialist notions of sporting activities as a universal language, and this is ironically at odds with the UN's own goal of promoting gender equity and empowering women. The earlier goals of developing sport and life skills in concert with each other have aligned with the rhetoric of the UN Millennium Development Goals in transnational fundraising quests, as illustrated below.

> This *Go Sisters* programme (sic) is trying to contribute to the achievement of the Millennium Development Goals in Zambia – promoting gender equity and empowerment. The programme (sic) is increasing the number of girls taking up leadership roles at the community and district levels. The project has this year trained 45 girls as peer leaders/educators who in turn cascade their life skills and knowledge on health and girls' rights issues to a further number of girls.
>
> *(Mweshi 2008)*

By framing the programme objectives of *Go Sisters* within the UN Millennium Development Goals, the unique local context specific to this programme becomes lost in the harmonizing rhetoric of global development. Of central concern are gender-based development interventions under the auspices of Nike, initiatives that centre on the 'girl effect', a growing but understudied initiative that assumes girls are catalysts capable of bringing 'unparalleled social and economic change to their families, communities and countries' (Nike Foundation 2008). Nike's gender and health-focused development programmes promote microfinance initiatives for girls and women, where small loans supposedly result in their empowerment and the subsequent eco-nomic development of entire nations. Similarly, 'Women Win', one of the first international women's funds to support sport and physical activity programmes around the world as a 'strat-egy for social change and women's empowerment', argues that women's sports programmes need to be aimed at 'women's economic empowerment' (Women Win 2009: 11). This involves building social enterprises and entrepreneurs and promoting organizational sustainability, key features of global capitalism and neocolonialism.

On closer examination, the tension between efforts to develop grass-roots programmes for girls that foster health and other benefits through sport with increased international exposure for corporations like Nike and links to elite sport are apparent when One-Third World develop-ment goals take hold (Hayhurst and Frisby 2010). In recent years, EduSport has received financial support from the Lillehammer Olympic-related Norwegian Agency for Development Co-operation (NORAD) and Nike's Global Giving programme. In the inaugural year of the foundation, Zambian girls were introduced to low-budget recreational football using chimbomba (balls made from tied plastic bags), while an elite team called the 'Kabwata Dream Team' was selected to travel to Norway in 1999 to compete in an unofficial 'World Cup' for women. On Nike's Global Giving Website (2008), the project mission of Go Sisters is cited by Annie Namukanga as challenging patriarchy because, 'playing a male dominated sport and playing it well develops a positive attitude in me about my ability to compete and excel in life'. Yet, material and distributive issues, such as access to equipment and facilities, are ongoing concerns. For example, the marketing manager Patrick Mweshi (2008), who is responsible for providing responses to Nike Global Giving online inquiries about EduSport, claims 'The demand for this girls programme has greatly increased with inadequate sports and training equipment standing as the main challenge'. Thus, the reproduction of neocolonial discourses urging girls to take power over their own health is being emphasized at the expense of redressing the broader determinants of health, reclaiming indigenous games or producing new sport traditions, and enhancing the political-economic status and safety of girls and women in Zambia.

Spivak's (1988) question about hearing subaltern voices highlights the tensions between those participating in Go Sisters and the current trend of market-focused sport, gender and develop-ment programmes that are based on a capitalist ideology of commodification (Cannella and Manuelito 2008: 54). For example, programme prescriptions can be devised that take on qua-lities of products to be manufactured (Li 2007: 269) by romanticizing efforts to empower and give voice to the poor (Parpart 2002: 54). In this way, the rationale of development pro-grammes becomes entangled in neocolonial discourses because more often than not, the entities driving such interventions are increasingly using the market to solve poverty-related develop-ment issues, rather than addressing how globalized and colonial markets exacerbate poverty in the first place (Li 2007).

Concluding comments

Considerable strides have been made with sports programmes like Go Sisters in Zambia, and comparing and contrasting this case with others around the world will illustrate the nuances of different forms of postcolonial, neocolonial and patriarchal power and their influences on the lives of girls and women, men and boys. This will help overcome criticisms from some activists who see the theory as being elitist and too far removed from the devastating and very real material deprivation shaping many lives.

We would be remiss if we did not identify other criticisms of postcolonial feminism. For example, some scholars have expressed concern about the over-emphasis on cultural identities and how they are represented which downplays how structures of transnational capitalism mediate between 'the colonizer and the colonized' (Dirlik 2002: 432). Similarly, an emphasis on 'post' does not mean an end to poverty, hardship and social inequality. And, we certainly question the ability of sport alone to be an antidote to the serious human problems encountered.

Nonetheless, it is by paying attention to such criticisms that postcolonial feminism has much to offer as a theoretical lens for considering the implications and consequences of neocolonialism and postcolonialism in sport, gender and development contexts, as well as potential solutions. Our key argument has been that globalization, colonial oppression and gender are inextricably linked, and that analyses of sport for development initiatives should carefully consider their impact as they intersect with other axes of oppression in local and global relationships. Two main themes that we briefly explored here include destabilizing neocolonial discourses and centring Two-Thirds World voices of girls and women in sport, gender and development initiatives. While these two themes alone do not do justice to the complexities of postcolonial feminism, they do represent a starting point for thinking critically about such projects as a precursor to envisioning new and more appropriate pathways.

To further understand the complexities of sport and gender in development, additional postcolonial feminism themes require application. These include, but are not limited to, destabilizing the historical, political, material and discursive legacies of colonialism; tracking the contemporary influences of globalization; deeper analyses of the intersections between gender, race, class, nation and other interlocking oppressions; and findings new ways to foster the voice and agency of girls and women through decolonizing methodologies (Cannella and Manuelito 2008; McEwan 2001, 2009; Smith 1999). All of this will require participatory approaches to research and development that originate from the very people who have historically been excluded from sport (Frisby et al. 2005). As Probhu (cited in McEwan 2009: 273) argues, 'the use of testimonials, novels, art, images, films and photograph is potentially useful to development researchers in the context of postcolonial critiques and the urgency of moving away from purely economic analyses'.

In keeping with the theme 'having voice', we thought it would be fitting to give women from Africa both the first and last words in this chapter. The quotation below emphasizes the need for those from the One-Third World to assist but 'not become the owners of the problem and the solution'.

> EduSport. … has made its stance to live by and carry the 'Ubuntu' (human centred) philosophy that reflects its work. To address development problems, it is important to be close to the reality of where the problem is. This is because you can only address them through understanding the culture. Outsiders must only help and not become owners of the problem and solution. Real solution [sic] take time and EduSport being situated with the people has time.
>
> *(Email communication Namukanga 7 July 2009)*

Notes

1 Throughout this chapter, we use the terms 'One-Third World' to refer to the Global North and 'Two-Thirds World' to refer to the Global South as discussed by Gustavo Esteva and Madhu Prakash (1998) and C.T. Mohanty (2003). These terms aim to remove the ideological and geographical binaries in other terms (e.g. Third World/First World, North/South).

2 The United Nations Millennium Development Goals aim to fight poverty, and support a framework for designing and implementing development programmes in nations throughout the Two-Thirds World. In 2000, 189 world leaders committed to realizing the goals by 2015. The eight Millennium Development Goals include to:

1. Eradicate extreme poverty and hunger.
2. Achieve universal primary education.
3. Promote gender equality and empower women.
4. Reduce child mortality.
5. Improve maternal health.
6. Combat HIV/AIDS, malaria and other diseases.
7. Ensure environmental sustainability.
8. Develop a global partnership for development.

References

Abu-Lughod, L. (2002) 'Do Muslim women really need saving? Anthropological reflections on cultural relativism and its others', *American Anthropologist,* 104: 783–90.
Bannerji, H. (2000) *The Dark Side of Nation: Essays on Multiculturalism, Nationalism and Gender,* Toronto: Canadian Scholars' Press.
Brady, M. (2005) 'Creating safe spaces and building social assets for young women in the developing world: a new role for sports', *Women's Studies Quarterly,* 33: 35–48.
Cannella, G.S. and Manuelito, K.D. (2008) 'Feminisms from unthought locations: indigenous worldviews, marginalized feminisms, and revisioning anticolonial social science', in N. Denzin, Y. Lincoln and L.T. Smith (eds) *Handbook of Critical and Indigenous Methodologies,* London: Sage.
Chen, M.A. (1995) 'Engendering world conferences: the international women's movement and the United Nations', *Third World Quarterly,* 16: 477–94.
Clarke, W. and Sewell, M. (2005) *The Sage Sets the Stage,* Cambridge: CPI. Online. Available HTTP: www.cpl.biz/isrm/infonotesite/recreation/documents/REOct05pp10–19Keynotes.pdf (accessed 9 June 2009).
Darnell, S.C. (2007) 'Playing with race: Right to Play and the production of whiteness in "development through sport"', *Sport in Society,* 10: 560–79.
Denzin, N.K. and Lincoln, Y.S. (2008) 'Introduction: critical methodologies and indigenous inquiry', in N. Denzin, Y. Lincoln and L.T. Smith (eds) *Handbook of Critical and Indigenous Methodologies,* London: Sage.
Dirlik, A. (2002) 'Rethinking colonialism: globalization, postcolonialism and the nation state', *Interventions,* 4(3): 428–48.
EduSport. (2005) *The Education Through Sport (EduSport) Foundation.* Online. Available HTTP: www.globalgiving.com/pfil/1647/projdoc.doc (accessed 23 April 2009).
EduSport. (2009) *EduSport website.* Online. Available HTTP: www.edusport.org.zm/index.php?option=com_content& task=view&id=15&Itemid=29 (accessed 9 April 2009).
Esteva, G. and Prakesh, M.S. (1998) *Grassroots Post-modernism: Remaking the Soil of Cultures,* London, UK: Zed Books.
Frisby, W., Maguire, P. and Reid, C. (2009) 'The "f" word has everything to do with it: how feminist theories inform action research', *Action Research,* 7: 13–19.
Frisby, W., Reid, C., Millar, S. and Hoeber, L. (2005) 'Putting "participatory" into participatory forms of action research', *Journal of Sport Management,* 19(4): 367–86.
Go Sisters (2004) *Edusport.* Online. Available HTTP: www.edusport.org.zm/index.php?option=com_content&task=view&id=1&Itemid=38 (accessed 12 April 2009).
Hall, S. (1996) 'When was "the post-colonial"? Thinking at the limit', in I. Chambers and L. Curti (eds) *The Post Colonial Question: Common Skies, Divided Horizons,* New York: Routledge.
Hargreaves, J. (1997) 'Women's sport, development, and cultural diversity: the South African experience', *Women's Studies International Forum,* 20: 191–209.
——(1999) 'The Women's International sports movement: local-global strategies and empowerment', *Women's Studies International Forum,* 22: 461–71.
——(2004) 'Querying sport feminism: personal or political'? in R. Giulianotti (ed.) *Sport and Modern Social Theorists,* Basingstoke: Palgrave Macmillan.
Hayhurst, L.M.C. and Frisby, W. (2010) 'Inevitable tensions: Swiss and Canadian sport for development NGO perspectives on partnerships with high performance sport', *European Sport Management Quarterly,* 10: 75–96.

International Working Group on Women and Sport (1994) *Brighton Declaration on Women and Sport*. Online. Available HTTP: www.sportdevelopment.org.uk/brightondeclaration1994.pdf (accessed 10 August 2009).

Jackson, C. (1998) 'Women and poverty or gender and well-being'? *Journal of International Affairs*, 52: 67–77.

Jennissen, T. and Lundy, C. (2001) 'Women in Cuba and the move to a private market economy', *Women's Studies International Forum*, 24: 181–98.

Kay, T. (2009) 'Developing through sport: evidencing sport impacts on young people', *Sport in Society*, 12: 1177–91.

Kidd, B. (2008). 'A new social movement: sport for development and peace', *Sport in Society*, 11: 370–80.

Larkin, J. (2007) *Gender, Sport and Development*. Online. Available HTTP: http://iwg.sportanddev.org/data/htmleditor/file/SDP%20IWG/literature%20review%20SDP.pdf (accessed 4 December 2007).

Li, T.M. (2007) *The Will to Improve: Governmentality, Development and the Practice of Politics*, London: Duke University Press.

McEwan, C. (2001) 'Postcolonialism, feminism and development: intersections and dilemmas', *Progress in Development Studies*, 1: 93–111.

——(2009) *Postcolonialism and Development*, London: Routledge.

Mohanty, C.T. (1988) 'Under western eyes: feminist scholarship and colonial discourses', *Feminist Review*, 30: 61–88.

——(2003) *Feminism Without Borders*, London: Duke University Press.

Mwaanga, O. (2005) *Edusport and Human Rights*, lecture presented at the University of Toronto, Canada.

Mwambwa, L.A. (2008) As I Like It. Online. Available HTTP: www.kickingaidsout.net/personalstories/Documents/As I like it Annie Lombe Mwambwa.docx (accessed 22 June 2009).

Mweshi, P. (2008) *Edusport: Girls End 2008 with Smiles*. Online. Available HTTP: www.globalgiving.co.uk/pr/1700/proj1647a.html (accessed 9 April 2009).

Namukanga, A. (2009) 'Go Sisters'. E-mail (7 July 2009).

Nash, C. (2002) 'Cultural geography: postcolonial cultural geographies', *Progress in Human Geography*, 26 (2): 219–30.

Nicholls, S. and Giles, A.R. (2007) 'Sport as a tool for HIV/AIDS education: A potential catalyst for change', *Pimatisiwin: A Journal of Aboriginal and Indigenous Community Health*, 5: 51–85.

Nike Foundation, (2008) *What We Do*. Online. Available HTTP: www.nikefoundation.org/what_we_do.html (accessed 11 August 2009).

NOWSPAR. (2009) *Advocacy Everybody Matters*. Online. Available HTTP: www.nowspar.com/readmore2 (accessed 23 June 2009).

Ogi, A. (2006) *Achieving the Objectives of the United Nations through Sport* (pamphlet), Geneva: United Nations Publishing Service.

Ong, A. (1988) 'Colonialism and modernity: feminist representations of women in non-western societies', *Inscriptions*, 3: 79–104.

Parameswaran. R. (2008) 'Reading the visual, tracking the global: postcolonial feminist methodology and the chameleon codes of resistance', in N. Denzin, Y. Lincoln and L.T. Smith (eds) *Handbook of Critical and Indigenous Methodologies*, London: Sage.

Parpart, J. (2002) 'Lessons from the field: rethinking empowerment, gender and development from a post – (post?) development perspective', in K. Saunders (ed.) *Feminist Post-Development Thought: Rethinking Modernity, Post-colonialism and Representation*, London, UK: Zed Books.

Pelak, C.F. (2005) 'Negotiating gender/race/class constraints in the new South Africa: a case of women's soccer', *International Review for the Sociology of Sport*, 40: 53–70.

Power, M. (2003) *Rethinking Development Geographies: World Without Boundaries*, London: Routledge.

Saavedra, M. (2005) *Women, Sport and Development*. Online. Available HTTP: http://africa.berkeley.edu/Courses/SportDevelopment/SADplatform-GSAD-148-2005.pdf (accessed 10 August 2009).

——(2009) 'Dilemmas and opportunities in gender and sport-in-development', in R. Levermore and A. Beacom (eds) *Sport and International Development*, New York: Palgrave Macmillan.

Sardar, Z. (1999) 'Development and the locations of eurocentrism', in Munck, R. and O'Hearn, D. (eds) *Critical Development Theory*, London: Zed, 44–62.

Saul, J. (2008) *Decolonization and Empire: Contesting the Rhetoric and Practice of Resubordination in Southern Africa and Beyond*, London: Routledge.

Sen, A. (2000) *Development as Freedom*, New York, NY: Anchor Books.

Smillie, I. (1996) 'Painting Canadian roses red', in M. Edwards and D. Hulme (eds) *Beyond the Magic Bullet: NGO Performance and Accountability in the Post-Cold War World*, West Hartford, CT: Kumarian Press.

Smith, L.T. (1999) *Decolonizing Methodologies: Research and Indigenous Peoples*, New York: Zed Books.
Spivak, G. (1988) 'Can the subaltern speak?', in C. Nelson and L Grossberg (eds) *Marxism and the Inter-pretation of Culture,* Urbana, IL: University of Illinois Press.
Swadener, B.B. and Kagendo, M. (2008) 'Decolonizing performances: deconstructing the global post-colonial', in N. Denzin, Y. Lincoln and L.T. Smith (eds) *Handbook of Critical and Indigenous Methodolo-gies,* London: Sage.
Swiss Academy for Development and Cooperation (SDC, 2008). 'International Platform on Sport and Development'. Online. Available HTTP: www.sportanddev.org/en/in-the-spotlight/launch-of-the-new-international-platform-on-sport-and-development/index.htm (accessed 1 June 2009).
Torége, L. (2009) 'Lombe's Story'. Online. Available HTTP: www.kickingaidsout.net/personalstories/Sider/Lombesstory.aspx (accessed 22 June 2009).
United Nations Division for the Advancement of Women (1995) *Beijing Declaration and Platform for Action*. Online. Available HTTP: www.un.org/womenwatch/daw/beijing/platform (accessed 8 May 2009).
Willis, O. (2000) 'Sport and development: The significance of Mathare Youth Sports Association', *Cana-dian Journal of Development Studies*, XXI: 825–49.
Women Win (2009) *Empowering Girls and Women through Sport and Physical Activity*, Amsterdam: Women Win.
World Bank. (2006) 'Zambia Data Profile 2000–2006'. Online. Available HTTP: http://ddp-ext.worldbank.org/ext/ddpreports/ViewSharedReport?&CF=&REPORT_ID=9147&REQUEST_TYPE=VIEWADVANCED (accessed 26 August 2009).
World Economic Forum. (2008) 'The Global Competitiveness Index: 2008–2009'. (Geneva). Online. Available HTTP: www.weforum.org/documents/PR/GCR_2008–9_rankings.pdf (accessed 16 August 2009).

Part 6
Sports development and elite athletes
Introduction: The irresistible priority

Barrie Houlihan

Over the last 20 years or so elite sport success has, in many countries, become the most distinctive aspect of national sports policy. Government funding and direction of elite sports development policy is an increasingly common feature across a broad range of political systems. The rapidly expanding body of literature analysing elite sports development systems confirms the extent of investment of public resources in dedicated facilities and programmes designed to maximise medals at international sports events (Abbott *et al.* 2002; Digel 2002; Green and Oakley 2001; Green and Houlihan 2005; Houlihan and Green 2008). It is easy to identify the motives of government for the substantial investment in supporting the career ambitions of a tiny minority of their population. For many governments high-level international sport provides both an important diplomatic resource and also a high-profile arena for the practice of diplomacy. The use of sport by the former German Democratic Republic as an essential element in its strategy to achieve recognition as a sovereign state is perhaps the clearest example, while China has used its influence within the International Olympic Committee (IOC) and the major international federations to isolate Taiwan from international sport as part of its continuing challenge to the latter's claims to sovereignty. In the 1970s and 1980s boycotts of various Olympic Games took place or were threatened, prompted by the decision of some countries to maintain sporting contact with the apartheid regime in South Africa and by the ideological rivalry between the Soviet Union and the United States of America.

The decline in the frequency of sports boycotts is mainly due to the collapse of apartheid and communism, but is also partly due to the increased importance of being present at events such as the Olympic Games or the football World Cup. The net benefit of attending major sports events now outweighs the gains obtained through a boycott. Since the late 1980s major sports events have ceased to be arenas for the crude display of political power and have become opportunities for a more subtle deployment of political resources and for the pursuit of a more varied range of political ambitions. This is especially true for the aspiring and actual hosts of major events who can use the bidding process and the hosting of the event to project a range of messages about their country (or region or city) to a global audience: the opportunity cost of not being involved in elite sport events is simply too great. However, if countries are to be in a strong position to exploit the 'soft power' opportunities that their involvement in global sports events provides they need to ensure that they have the necessary domestic resources. While those resources might simply be a willingness to spend vast sums of money developing stadiums and arenas to host events that showcase the country, as is the case with Dubai, for most countries the most important resource is a squad of talented athletes.

For those countries using their hosting or participation in major sports events as an opportunity to demonstrate the vitality of their economy, the modernity of their cities or their pace of social development a set of athletes who embody those values and characteristics is a powerful asset. In more practical terms a successful squad of athletes or a successful team gives important leverage for the consolidation of influence. In other words, countries whose athletes dominate in a particular sport will generally find it easier to be elected to positions of influence within international federations which, in turn, gives opportunities to affect decisions on rule changes, player eligibility and future location of championships.

For these and other reasons governments appear to feel obliged to invest heavily in developing a successful squad of elite athletes. Some countries have taken the short cut of fast-tracking eligibility (and often nationality) of foreign athletes. On many occasions the England cricket team has included players born outside the country in South Africa, Zimbabwe, Ireland and Wales. Many of the small, but rich, states in the Middle East have organised the 'transfer' of athletes from other countries, often giving them local names to obscure their country of origin. However, while such opportunistic practices are not uncommon, most countries seek to develop structures and processes for the development of 'home grown' talent. The chapters in this Part of the Handbook provide ample evidence of the substantial investment by government in elite sports development and the extent to which it dominates broader sports policy activity. McDonald, in his analysis of the UK system of elite sports development, draws attention to the persistence and the naivety of the assumptions that underpin the pyramid model of elite athlete development. McDonald highlights not only the lack of rigorous investigation of the benefits derived from elite sporting success, but also the deep reluctance to challenge the largely self-serving mythologising that has been a feature of sports policy for the last 20 years. Assertions that elite sporting success generates a national 'feelgood factor', or that elite sporting success stimulates community participation both receive scant analysis from within government or indeed from the academic community.

In a country that has such a strong reputation for basing policy on broadly social democratic values and for limited government intervention in sport, Ibsen, Hansen and Storm's study of Denmark illustrates just how difficult it is to resist the lure of medal success. Ibsen and his colleagues trace how, over a 20-year period, the commitment to locate elite sport development programmes firmly within a set of social democratic values that took account of 'the physical, personal and social development of elite athletes' was replaced by a more neo-liberal policy which stressed support for the ambitions of the individual. As the authors note, elite sport had 'not only become socially acceptable, it enjoyed privileged status'. However, the policy of Team Denmark still attempts to maintain a balance between winning medals and the longer-term interests of elite athletes which is absent in many other countries.

Fan Hong provides a marked contrast with Denmark in her analysis of elite sport development in China. China's centralised state-dominated and well-resourced sports system has proved to be exceptionally successful in developing Olympic medal winners. The complex pyramid structure that straddles the education and local government systems based on rigorous selection as young athletes are sifted out at each stage of progress to the elite national and Olympic squads has enabled China to dominate in many of the summer Olympic events. However, as Hong makes clear the success comes at a human cost, and he argues that 'The selection system is brutal ... Only 5 per cent [of the 400,000 boys and girls in the country's sports schools in 2004] would be able to reach the top with the remaining 95 per cent ... leaving their sports schools with no formal primary and secondary education qualifications – only broken dreams. The final contribution to this Part of the Handbook examines the operation of another very different, but equally successful, elite sport development system – that of Australia. Bob Stewart identifies elite sport success as an important element in Australian national identity and illustrates the importance of crisis (in this case failure to win a gold medal in the 1976 Olympic Games) in shaping policy. By the mid 1980s the Australian government had funded the establishment of the highly successful Australian Institute of Sport which subsequently became a model for many other countries seeking to emulate the rapid improvement in Olympic success enjoyed by Australian athletes. The most prominent aspects of the Australian system are the investment in physical infrastructure and coaching on the one hand and a highly targeted funding strategy, which identified the sports where medal success was more easily achieved, on the other. However, as with the example of the UK, the achievements at the elite level have to be balanced against the relative neglect of community sport.

References

Abbott, A., Collins, D., Martindale, R. and Sowerby, K. (2002) *Talent identification and development: An academic review.* Edinburgh: Sport Scotland.

Digel, H. (2002) *Organisation of high performance athletics in selected countries* (Final report for the International Athletic Foundation). Tübingen, Germany: University of Tübingen.

Green, M. & Oakley, B. (2001) Elite sport development systems and playing to win: uniformity and diversity in international approaches. *Leisure Studies*, 20.4, 247–67.

Green, M. & Houlihan, B. (2005) *Elite sport development: policy learning and political priorities.* London: Routledge.

Houlihan, B. & Green, M. (eds) (2008) *Comparative elite sport development: systems, structures and public policy.* Oxford: Butterworth-Heinemann.

26

High-performance sport policy in the UK

An outline and critique[1]

Ian McDonald

At the Olympic Games in Atlanta in 1996, Great Britain won just one gold and came a lowly thirty-sixth in the medal table. Fast forward three Olympic Games to Beijing in 2008. Here, 'Team GB' (as it had now become) won 41 medals including 19 gold and came fourth in the medal table! What explains this dramatic (re-)emergence of Great Britain as an Olympic nation? Even accounting for the fact that Atlanta was an unusually poor Olympics for Great Britain, the improvement in Athens and Beijing is dramatic. It certainly did not happen by accident or by luck. On the contrary, it was the result of the development and systematic application of a comprehensive high-performance sport policy underpinned by a massive investment of financial resources that was unprecedented in the history of sports policy in the UK. This prompts the question as to why such importance is now being given in the UK to high-performance sport, and what are the implications that ought to concern students and scholars of sports politics and policy.

This chapter will outline the historical and political context for the development of high-performance sport policy in the UK. It will become immediately apparent from this discussion that the policy for developing high-performance sport actually means developing Olympic and Paralympic sports rather than sports in general, and it means prioritising Summer Olympic sports rather than Winter Olympic sports. As a sporting event, the Winter Olympics pales in comparison with the profile and impact of the Summer Olympics. In the UK, the Winter Olympics hardly figures on the sporting cultural landscape. It is not difficult to understand the reason for this. Great Britain is not a significant player in the Winter Olympics, and therefore the Games offers limited scope for social and political capital and for international prestige. Also, given the specialist nature of many of the Winter Olympic events, there are fewer opportunities for using these sports for social policy purposes. The vast bulk of the considerable resources being lavished on high-performance sport are directed towards events in the Summer Olympics.

The historical and political context

Most professionals in the sports policy community could probably tell you where they were on 6 July 2005, when, in a hotel in downtown Singapore, Jacques Rogge, the President of the

International Olympic Committee (IOC), announced that London had been awarded the right to host the 2012 Olympic Games. Prime Minister Tony Blair called the win 'a momentous day' for Britain (BBC 2005). But it is difficult now to separate the images of the celebrations that erupted in a packed Trafalgar Square on the night of 6 July from the events the following morning, 7 July 2005, when four separate explosions took place in central London in what turned out to be a series of linked bombings. The resulting carnage led to over 700 people being injured, many seriously, and 56 deaths, including the four British-Asian 'suicide bombers'. National pride and terrorist carnage: these encapsulate both the hope and fear surrounding the 2012 Olympic Games.

For sure, public expectations have been raised after Great Britain's unexpectedly high medal tally in the Beijing Games in 2008, when 'Team GB' surpassed expectations by coming fourth in the medal table. The development of an effective high-performance system has become as much a political imperative as a sporting goal. As Mick Green observed, the embrace of policies for sport and physical activity by the government 'is unprecedented' (2008: 12). Indeed 'sport policy now matters in ways that it never mattered in the past, and it matters at the highest political level' (Ibid: 4). The 2012 Summer Olympics in London is the inevitable point of departure for any understanding and analysis of contemporary sports policy in the UK, with correlatively a focus on UK Sport whose role is to develop elite athletes to represent Great Britain and Northern Ireland (hereafter just Great Britain) at the Olympic and Paralympic Games. The decision to award the Olympic Games to London marked both a beginning and a culmination. It marked the beginning of a build-up to the most important major sporting event ever to be held in the UK. But it was also a culmination: first of the bid campaign of course, but it was also the culmination of a systematic if uneven rise in importance placed on developing high-performance sport in general and on improving the performance of athletes in the Olympic Games in particular.

For most of the post-war period in the UK, the dominant conceptual approach to sport policy was based on the inherent unity between 'sport for all' and 'sport for the elite'. Represented diagrammatically by the notion of the pyramid in which the base constituted mass participation and the apex the elite level, the common sense thinking was that, by increasing the mass base of participation, the quantity and quality of the talent pool from which to develop excellence would increase (see Figure 26.1). This was a notion that can be traced back to the founder of the Modern Olympic Movement, Baron Pierre de Coubertin:

> In order for a hundred people to take part in physical culture, it is necessary for fifty to take part in sport; in order for fifty to take part in sport, twenty must specialise, five must be capable of astonishing feats of prowess.
>
> *(De Coubertin 1966: 131–32)*

Thus the inherent unity rather than the disjuncture between 'sport for all' and high-performance sport was emphasised. However, in practice this model has proved to be naïve. Though it looked neat and coherent in theory, it did not match the reality of two different cultures of sport: high-performance and recreational sport. It was based on the erroneous notion that talented athletes would inevitably emerge from a mass base of participation in sport and recreation. Critics argued that the pyramidal model conflated two distinct cultures of sport: what Eichberg (1989) called 'achievement-sport' (which is constituted on the basis of production of results, maximisation and hierarchisation, e.g. in Olympic and Paralympic sports) and 'fitness sport' (associated with physiological and social-psychological health and well-being, and the ideals of 'sport for all'). This disjuncture was recognised by the veteran British coach, Tom McNab in an article published in *The Guardian* in 2004:

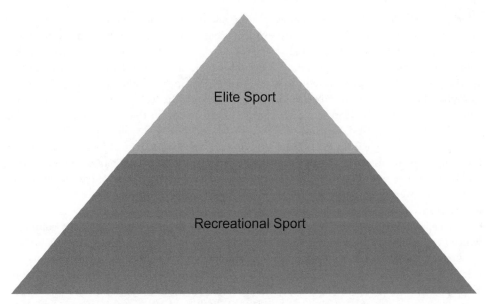

Figure 26.1 The traditional sports development pyramid

> Central to most of the problems of British sport has been the myriad sports bodies and the inability of politicians to understand the workings of the sports ecosystem. Thus, for example, we continue to link participation levels with performance, and confuse competitive sport with health-related exercise.

While sport remained low on the policy agenda, and receiving only derisory political and financial support from government, the lazy and muddled thinking behind the concept of the pyramid didn't matter. For many years, government funding and support for sport had been at best intermittent, normally triggered by a social crisis such as the inner-city riots of the early 1980s (Carrington and McDonald 2007), but often characterised by 'neglect and indeed outright disdain' (Green 2009: 12). In the public imagination, state support for high-performance sport was 'not British' – it was more associated with the fascist regimes of inter-war Europe or the communist regimes of the post-war period than with the 'democratic' regimes of western Europe. In the USSR and East Germany for example, intense scientific interventions to improve sport were perceived as dehumanising and excessively ruthless (Riordan 1977; Hoberman 1992; Beamish and Ritchie 2006).

Meanwhile, in the UK during much of the twentieth century, disdain towards sport by government merely entrenched the amateur culture of the 'blazeratti' (Mackay 1998) that shaped the governance of sport from the late nineteenth century. Even in the post-war period and right up until the early 1980s, organising sporting activity was considered to be the realm of the voluntary sector. When the Sports Council was established in 1972 it was at 'arms-length' from the government. That is, although the Sports Council received funding from the government, it had autonomy in formulating policy, having need only to have 'regard' to the wishes of the government of the day.

The organisation, governance and activity of non-professional and non-commercial sport were seen as the province of the voluntary sector, which prided itself on being resolutely autonomous from political interference. Coaching and talent development were not given priority: the dominant view was that, as sporting talent was natural, the role of coaching was simply to improve and enhance already existing talent rather than identify and 'make' talent. Any complaints from elite athletes and coaches about the lack of support from the sports policy community largely fell on deaf government ears. However, the manifest failure of this laissez-faire approach to high-performance sport was reflected in Britain's declining status in world sport, exacerbated by the success of other nations using more scientific techniques. By the early 1960s, and certainly by the 1990s, there was a change of orientation in the UK and an opening up towards the necessity and benefits of a well-developed policy for elite sport. The decisive turning point came when the post-Thatcher Conservative Government of John Major decided, for complex political reasons, to focus on the development of elite competitive sport. Aligning high-performance sport more closely with public policy necessitated closer government control and scrutiny over sports policy and the need to professionalise/modernise the structure/culture of governance in the sports policy community.

The beginning of the government-initiated shift away from a pluralistic sports culture, in which both achievement sport and fitness sport were accommodated (albeit at very low levels of resourcing), to a prioritising of competitive sport within a culture of 'achievement-sport' (Eichberg 1989) can be identified quite precisely. The creation of the Department of National Heritage (DNH) in 1992 by John Major's Conservative Government registered sports policy as a serious national government responsibility. This was followed by a government policy document, *Sport for 21st Century,* where the then Conservative minister for sport, Iain Sproat, declared that 'the Sports Council will withdraw from the promotion of mass participation, informal recreation, leisure pursuits, and from health promotion … and shift its focus to services in support of excellence' (DNH 1994: 4). This rhetorical declaration of intent was promptly given policy substance. In the landmark policy document, *Sport: Raising the Game* (DNH 1995), John Major declared that his government would 'bring about a sea-change in the prospects of British sport – from the very first steps in primary school right through to the breaking of the tape in an Olympic final' (DNH 1995: 1). Consequently, the thrust of sports policy since the mid 1990s has been to reinvigorate competitive school sport (the mass base), extend the club structure for youth sport (the point at which talent identification begins) and develop a more sophisticated and systematic high-performance system to develop talent and create world-class athletes capable of winning medals at the premier international sports competitions. To be sure, the pyramid concept still lingers on in sports policy, but it is a concept that is applied within the discourse of high-performance sport only (see Figure 26.2).

The focus outlined in *Sport: Raising the Game* was on improving Britain's traditional national sports, reinvigorating competitive school sport and supporting elite athletes in their quest for international success. To this end, the first major restructuring of the Sports Council was declared in 1996 and instituted in 1997. The GB Sports Council was restructured into the English Sports Council (since February 1999 branded as 'Sport England') to sit alongside the already existing sports councils in the other home nations. Sport England's brief was to develop structured sporting opportunities for young people, develop excellence and to distribute monies from the National Lottery Sports Fund that came on stream in 1994. The UK Sports Council (also branded since February 1999 as 'UK Sport') meanwhile was created to work in partnership with a number of organisations (such as the national sports councils, the British Olympic Association (BOA) and the British Paralympic Association (BPA) and especially national governing bodies (NGBs)) to bring success to Britain's athletes in the international arena.

The financial windfall from the bulging coffers of the National Lottery raised expectations in the sports policy community that, at last, real progress could be realised. Ambitious projects were

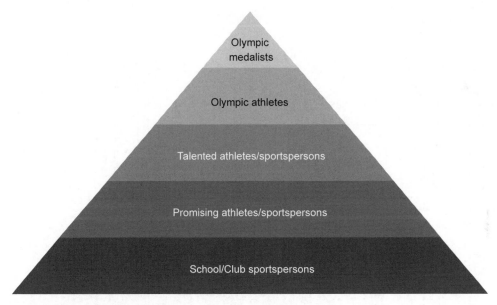

Figure 26.2 The new (high-performance) sports pyramid

designed and given the green light: over £100 million set aside for the construction of a 'British Academy of Sport' (though abandoned by the Labour Government in 1999 in favour of a regional network of academies); and £168 million set aside for a new National Stadium to replace Wembley Stadium in London (it eventually cost £975 million and wasn't completed until 2007). The introduction of lottery funding for elite sport for the first time in 1997 was an important factor in delivering improvements in the Great Britain teams' performance at the Olympic and Paralympic Games in Sydney in 2000 and Athens in 2004.

The Conservative Party was swept from office in the general election of 1997, but the sporting excellence baton was passed smoothly to the new Labour administration. The Labour Government created the Department for Culture, Media and Sport (DCMS), thus giving cabinet status for the first time to sport. Two key policy documents came out of Tony Blair's new Labour Government, *A Sporting Future for All* (DCMS 2000) and *Game Plan* (DCMS 2002). While both of these documents emphasised the government's commitment to developing high-performance sport, they also reflected New Labour's social democratic belief in the importance of equality in sport and of using sport as a means of combating what it termed 'social exclusion' (Collins with Kay 2003).

Figure 26.3[2] is a diagrammatical depiction of the sports policy community in England in 2001. It is a spatial outline of the politics and structure of sports policy. The top horizontal axis represents a continuum of political priorities, ranging from national imperatives (policies designed to enhance feelings of national pride) to social imperatives (policies designed to augment a social welfare agenda). In broad terms, these can be seen as an international-national continuum, with national imperative policies oriented towards actions on the international arena and social imperative policies oriented towards actions in the domestic arena. The bottom horizontal axis represents the substantive sports policy focus along a continuum from high-performance sport to community-based sport. The space between the upper and lower axis sets out a spatial depiction of the sports policy community. The vertical axis represents national level agencies at the upper end, to local or grass-roots agencies at the lower end. The significance and influence of

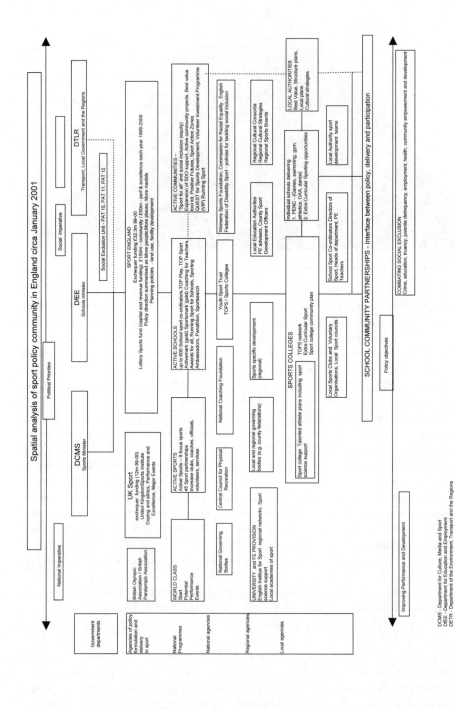

Spatial analysis of sport policy community in England circa January 2001

Government departments

National Imperative	Political Priorities	Social Imperative
DCMS Sports Minister	DfEE Schools minister	DTLR Transport, Local Government and the Regions

Social Exclusion Unit - PAT 10, PAT 11, PAT 12

Agencies of policy formulation and delivery in sport

UK Sport
exchequer funding (12m 99-00)
United Kingdom Sports Institute
Doping and ethics, Performance and Excellence. Major Events

British Olympic Association / British Paralympic Association

SPORT ENGLAND
Exchequer funding £32.3m 99-00
Lottery Sports fund (capital and revenue funding) £150m – community / £50m – perf & excellence each year 1999-2009
Policy direction summarised as More people,More places, More medals
Planning policies – land use, facility development

National Programmes

WORLD CLASS
Start
Potential
Performance
Events

ACTIVE SPORTS
Active Sports – 9 focus sports
45 Sport partnerships
Increase clubs, coaches, officials, volunteers, services

ACTIVE SCHOOLS
up to 600 School sport co-ordinators,TOP Play, TOP Sport
Activemark (gold) Sportsmark (gold), Coaching for Teachers,
Awards for all, Running Sport for Schools, Sporting
Ambassadors, Panathlon, Sportsearch

ACTIVE COMMUNITIES –
"Sport for all' and social inclusion (equity)
Expansion of SDO support, Active community projects, Best value
tool kit, Positive Futures, Sport Action Zones
QUEST for Sports Development, Volunteer Investment Programme
(VIP) Running Sport

National agencies

National Governing Bodies

Central Council for Physical Recreation

National Coaching Foundation

Youth Sport Trust
TOPS / Sports Colleges

Womens Sports Foundation, Commission for Racial Equality, English
Federation of Disability Sport - policies for tackling social inclusion

Regional agencies

UNIVERSITY and FE PROVISION
English Institue for Sport regional networks, Sport
science support
Local academies of sport

Local and regional governing
bodies (e.g. county federations)

Sports specific development
(regional)

Local Education Authorities
PE advisers, County Sport
Development Officers

Regional Cultural Consortia
Regional Cultural Strategies
Regional Sports Boards

LOCAL AUTHORITIES
Best Value, Structure plans,
Local plans
Cultural strategies

Local agencies

SPORTS COLLEGES

Sport college Talented athlete plans including sport

TOPS network
Extra-Curricular
Sport college community plan

Sport college Talented athlete plans including sport
science support

Local Sports Clubs and Voluntary
Organisations, Local Sport councils

Individual schools delivering
1. PENC - (Games, swimming, gym,
athletics, OAA, dance)
2. Extra-Curricular Sporting opportunities

School Sport Co-ordinators Directors of
Sport, Heads of department, PE
Teachers

Local Authority sport
development teams

SCHOOL COMMUNITY PARTNERSHIPS - Interface between policy, delivery and participation

Policy objectives

Improving Performance and Development

COMBATING SOCIAL EXCLUSION
Crime, education, truancy, juvenile delinquency, employment, health, community empowerment and development

DCMS - Department for Culture, Media and Sport
DfEE - Department for Education and Employment
DETR - Department of the Environment, Transport and the Regions

Figure 26.3 Spatial analysis of the sport policy community in England: circa January 2001

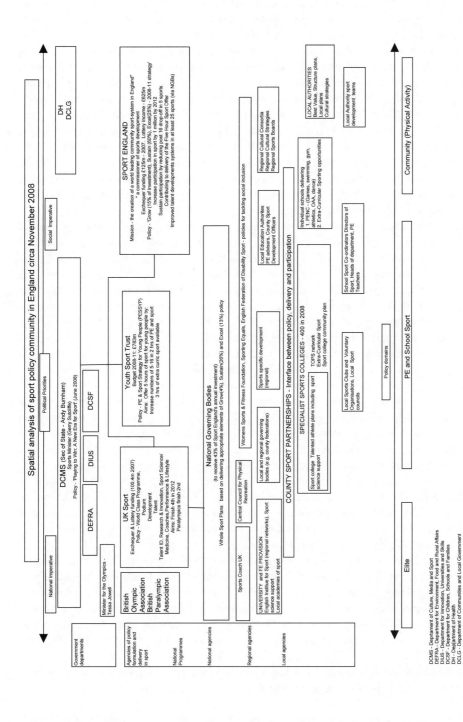

Figure 26.4 Spatial analysis of the sport policy community in England: circa November 2008

the organisations and programmes are indicated by the amount of space they occupy. The key relationships in the sports policy community are indicated by the dark connecting line which represents the spinal column of the sports policy community and identifies the key players and, by extension, the key lines and relations of power.

As the 2001 chart reveals, the sports policy community was dominated at governmental level by the DCMS and the Department of Education and Employment (DfEE). The Department for Transport, Local Government and the Regions (DTLR) was less prominent, perhaps reflecting the declining role of local government in the delivery of sport. At the centre of sports policy in 2001 was Sport England, which received the bulk of Exchequer funding and oversaw the flagship *Active Programmes* delivered by Schools (and especially the Specialist Sport Colleges) with the Youth Sport Trust playing a pivotal role. The year 2001 was a period of transition in the development of UK sports policy. Coming midway between the landmark *Sport: Raising the Game* (1995) and the awarding of the Olympic Games to London (2005), the increasing importance being given to high-performance sport had yet to be consolidated and reflected in organisational structures. However, this was to change.

In 2005 New Labour announced a further restructuring of sport's organisational apparatus at national level. Sport England, was in effect 'stripped' of its responsibilities for elite sport and overall 'control' was passed to UK Sport. Furthermore, the Youth Sport Trust was given responsibility for overseeing developments in school sport and PE. Sport England's remit was reduced to a focus on what was termed 'community sport' tied to the 'legacy' ambitions of the Olympics Games in 2012. Crucially, the reorganisation involved a more significant responsibility for the national governing bodies, who in return for increased public funding for development programmes were required to submit 'whole sport plans' by which they were to set agreed targets and to be subject to greater financial accountability.

In handing greater responsibility for high-performance sport policy to UK Sport and select national governing bodies, perennial concerns about a lack of clear organisation and structure for elite sport were clarified. UK Sport was declared the primary agency responsible for developing elite sports policy and implementing policy in partnership with national governing bodies. The main casualty in this readjustment of organisational position and power in the sports policy community was Sport England. With the Youth Sport Trust taking the lead in developing school sport and PE, and local authorities still bearing the main responsibility for community-based projects, the role of Sport England in high-performance sport is somewhat marginal. Of course, in customary fashion, politicians have dressed up this marginalisation as a form of strategic realignment. For example, Andy Burnham, the Secretary of State for the DCMS, stated that Sport England has 'a new focus' to 'knit together community sport, (state) school sport and elite-level sport in a way that has never quite been managed up to now' (DCMS 2008). However, as the snapshot of sports policy in 2008 illustrates (see Figure 26.4), not only is the centre of gravity for elite sport now firmly with the UK Sport and national governing bodies, supported by the Youth Sport Trust, but the space of the sports policy community is now dominated by the needs of the high-performance sport system. This colonisation of the sports policy space by high-performance sport can be seen as a recent and direct consequence of the decision by the IOC to award the 2012 Olympic Games to London.

Andy Burnham (2008) illustrated the hegemonic dominance of high-performance sport in contemporary sports policy, when he asserted that:

> Sport is about winning and losing. When you play sport, you play to win. Sport's full power is to thrill and captivate ... We are challenging the NGBs in particular to

deliver, but in a new sense of partnership and common endeavour. We've got a once-in-a-lifetime opportunity to make that happen. As Olympic host nation, we have a moment in time. A chance to set a new level of ambition and give sport the prominence that all of us think it should have … To do this we must have a clearer separation between the development of sport, on the one hand, and the promotion of physical activity on the other.

The significance of this statement lies in the way it cites the 2012 Olympic Games to normalise and prioritise the culture of 'achievement-sport' in policy. The prioritisation of achievement sport, declared by the Conservative Government in 1995 in *Sport: Raising the Game* but vigorously challenged at the time, was confirmed under the Labour Government some 13 years later. The Labour Government successfully established the hegemonic positioning of high-performance sport and the consequent marginalisation of other arguably more egalitarian and empowering forms of sport.

UK sport: policies and programmes

For the host nation, qualification is guaranteed for the majority of Olympic and Paralympic events. UK Sport has stated its wider intention to support athletes across the full range of sports so that competitive teams have an opportunity to represent Great Britain and Northern Ireland in every sport at the London 2012 Games (subject to the selection policies of the BOA and the BPA). To facilitate this, in January 2006, the government released yet more funding to UK Sport to ensure that the BOA and the BPA would send to the 2012 Games the largest Great Britain team in recent history – more than 500 Olympic and some 200 Paralympic athletes. This compares to around 300 Olympic and 200 Paralympic athletes who competed in Beijing, and 270 Olympic and 170 Paralympic athletes who competed in Athens in 2004 (NAO 2008).

The preparation for most of these athletes will be conducted with the support of UK Sport's World Class Performance (WCP) programme. Initiated in 1997, the WCP programme has evolved over three previous Olympiads: Sydney (2000), Athens (2004) and Beijing (2008). The beneficial impact of the WCP can be discerned from the rising position of 'Team GB' in the Olympic Medal table (see Table 26.1).

The WCP programme operates at three distinct levels (see Figure 26.5). The bulk of its financial and operational support is allocated to a strand called 'Podium' which is designed to concentrate resources on those athletes who are deemed by their NGB to have a realistic chance of winning a medal at the forthcoming Olympic Games. In addition to receiving the support of the NGB through the performance plan, athletes can seek financial support to allow them to focus on fulfilling the demands of training. The Athlete Personal Award supports

Table 26.1 Great Britain's position and medal tally in the Olympics

Olympics	Position	Gold	Silver	Bronze	Total
1996 Atlanta	36	1	8	6	15
2000 Sydney	10	11	10	7	28
2004 Athens	10	9	9	12	30
2008 Beijing	4	19	13	15	47

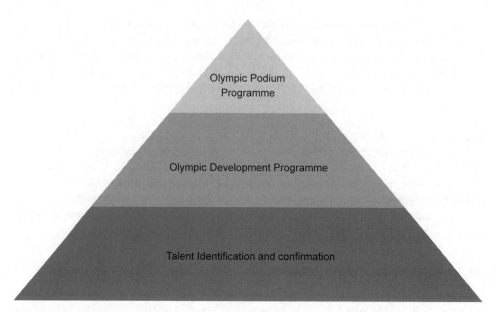

Figure 26.5 UK Sport's World Class Programme pyramid

'Podium' athletes up to a maximum of £26,142 per year. Training and preparation has become thoroughly professionalised, rationalised and in the UK Sport's own jargon on its website, 'ruthless' in what it calls a 'no compromise' investment strategy (www.uksport.gov.uk/pages/no_compromise/):

> Winning medals is incredibly tough and we have to be ruthless about our podium potential in every event, studying every aspect – medals available, athletes, coaches, current performance, future potential, talent selection, cost and above all the opposition – and invest accordingly.

The second level of the World Class Programme is called 'Development' and is aimed at athletes who are deemed to be realistic medal prospects for the next cycle of Olympic Games (Rio de Janeiro will play host to the Games in 2016). The 'Development' programme is for those athletes identified as having clear potential, but who are judged to be some four to six years away from achieving a medal winning position at an Olympic Games. UK Sport is funding over 600 athletes at 'Development' level, many of whom it hopes will enter the Podium programme before 2012 (NAO 2008). The third level of the WCP is the 'Talent Identification and Confirmation Programme'. This programme aims to nurture a wide pool of athletes who may be six years or more away from the 'podium'. UK Sport funds a similar performance pathway for Paralympic athletes, although there are differences in the criteria for entry to each level of the programme. The number of athletes that UK Sport funds at 'Podium' level depends on the Paralympic sport's gold medal potential, and the number of athletes funded at 'Development' level depends on the sport's silver and bronze medal potential.

The WCP programme is delivered by the NGBs, which also select the athletes to be supported. It is a programme that brings NGBs into the heart of delivering high-performance sport development policy. As part of its governance arrangements, UK Sport requires NGBs to acknowledge the primacy of the Olympic and Paralympic medal targets, to have a named

'Accountable Officer' responsible for its use of public money, to have clear financial policies and staff responsibilities, and to consider relevant financial reports at each Board meeting. In return for receiving larger amounts of financial support to cover the costs of taking on this enhanced role, NGBs are required to submit detailed performance plans ('whole sport plans') to UK Sport. In tune with this heightened managerial approach, a monitoring system called 'Mission 2012' is used whereby each governing body is required to consider its athletes' performance and development, as well as the performance system that sits behind them and the leadership and climate that exists within the sport.

All 'Podium' and 'Development' athletes are given an individually tailored performance programme that sets out a pathway for them to achieve the target of winning medals and provides the necessary back-up support such as access to the top coaches in the field, the input of the latest sports science and medical support, warm weather training and acclimatisation and an international competition schedule. Meanwhile, significant levels of investment have gone into providing state-of-the-art physical infrastructure, based primarily on the Institutes of Sport. While each of the other home nations also has their respective Institute of Sport, the English Institute of Sport is a nationwide network of nine regional multi-sport hub sites supplemented by a network of satellite centres.

NGBs are major beneficiaries of the increased funding for high-performance sport. High-profile sports like Athletics saw its funding increase from £11.4 million for the Athens Games to £26.5 million for the Beijing Games. Other Olympic sports in which Great Britain has tended to excel have also been generously funded. The main beneficiaries are Rowing (£10.6 million in 2004 to £26 million in 2008), Swimming (£6.4 million in 2004 to £20.7 million in 2008), Cycling (£8.6 million in 2004 to £22.2 million in 2008) and Sailing (£7.6 million in 2004 to £22.3 million in 2008) (www.uksport.gov.uk/pages/summer_olympic_sports–home/). However, in tune with the performance-related principle of funding allocation, those sports that do not perform as expected are penalised, while those that deliver medals are rewarded. Thus awards for the 2009–13 round reflect the relative success and failure of these sports in Beijing. Athletics, which was deemed to have underperformed and not met its target in Beijing, has been awarded a reduced amount (£25.1 million), whereas Cycling, Swimming, Rowing and Sailing met or exceeded their targets, so have been given an increased budget. Table 26.2 shows how much each sport has received from the UK Sport's World Class Performance Programme since funding began in May 1997.

Since the Olympic Games was awarded to London, funding for high-performance sport has continued to rocket. From April 2006 to March 2013 over £700 million will be allocated to elite sport sourced mainly from the Exchequer and the National Lottery, but with a relatively small contribution from the private sector. Within this amount, the direct funding that UK Sport provides to the NGBs and elite athletes through its WCP programme will double to £588 million (81 per cent of the £700 million), of which £468 million will go to NGBs to provide coaching and other services to their athletes and £120 million (17 per cent) to elite athletes as personal awards (NAO 2008). All this is to ensure that Team GB at least reaches the targets set for London 2012 and, according to reports in The Guardian newspaper (Kelso, 2008), to go one better than Beijing and come third in the medal table.

Critiquing the politics of high-performance sport policy in the UK

The history of sports policy over the past decade or so has been the emergence of the high-performance sport as the main focus of development. After decades of neglect followed by years of inefficient organisation and muddled systems, it seems that there now exists a clear structure and policy for the development of high-performance sport.

Table 26.2 UK sport funding for NGBs for Olympiads

Sport	Sydney Olympiad[1]	Athens Olympiad[2]	Beijing Olympiad	London Olympiad
Archery	n/a	£800,000	£2,834,000	£4,496,700
Athletics	£10,600,000	£11,400,000	£26,513,000	£25,110,900
Badminton	n/a[3]	n/a[3]	£8,759,000	£8,631,700
Basketball	n/a	n/a	£3,694,000	£8,751,800
Boxing	n/a[3]	n/a[3]	£5,005,000	£8,022,300
Canoeing	£4,500,000	£4,700,000	£13,622,000	£16,289,000
Cycling	£5,400,000	£8,600,000	£22,151,000	£26,922,700
Diving	£900,000	£1,400,000	£5,873,000	£5,873,000
Equestrian	£3,000,000	£4,400,000	£11,727,000	£13,651,900
Fencing	n/a	n/a	£3,074,000	£1,259,746
Gymnastics	£5,900,000	£4,100,000	£9,036,000	£10,332,100
Handball	n/a	n/a	£2,986,000	£1,448,327
Hockey	n/a[3]	n/a[3]	£9,882,000	£14,128,700
Judo	£3,900,000	£4,100,000	£6,947,000	£7,636,200
Modern pentathlon	£1,100,000	£2,000,000	£5,920,000	£6,411,400
Rowing	£9,600,000	£10,600,000	£26,042,000	£27,470,000
Sailing	£5,100,000	£7,600,000	£22,292,000	£23,389,800
Shooting	n/a	£1,400,000	£5,056,000	£1,225,350
Swimming	£6,900,000	£6,400,000	£20,659,000	£25,606,000
Synchronised swimming	n/a	n/a	£1,648,000	£3,457,600
Table tennis	n/a[3]	n/a[3]	£2,533,000	£1,207,848
Taekwondo	£600,000	£600,000	£2,667,000	£4,488,300
Triathlon	£1,400,000	£2,600,000	£5,113,000	£5,392,600
Volleyball	n/a	n/a	£4,112,000	£1,359,203
Volleyball – beach	n/a	n/a	n/a	£394,607
Water polo	n/a	n/a	£3,147,000	£1,450,895
Weightlifting	n/a	£300,000	£1,686,000	£680,023
Wrestling	n/a	n/a	£2,125,000	£717,650
Total	£58,900,000	£70,000,000	£235,103,000	£256,588,649

Notes
1 Figures for the Sydney and Athens Olympiads relate just to Podium-level funding. During that time, the home nation sports councils were responsible for supporting Development and Talent level activities.
2 On 1 April 2006 UK Sport became responsible for all performance funding from Talent to Podium, and these figures reflect that total package. These figures also include the cost of sports science and medicine provision not previously incorporated as part of a sport's funding award.
3 Prior to 1 April 2006, governing bodies of sports administered on a home nation basis within the UK were funded by their respective home nation sports councils.
Source: www.uksport.gov.uk/pages/summer_olympic_sports_-_home/

New Labour's support for London's successful bid to host the 2012 summer Olympic Games further demonstrated the importance, if not priority, now placed upon sport generally and elite sport in particular in the early twenty-first century. London's successful bid to host the 2012 Games strengthens the political legitimacy for government to build on developments at the elite level over the past decade.

(Green 2009: 137)

The key elements in the development of a successful high-performance sport policy has been increased funding, especially from the National Lottery, the building of state-of-the-art facilities, a professionalisation of coach education and the adoption of sports science and medicine knowledge. These elements have gone alongside the reform of Sport England and UK Sport and the NGBs. However, the key source of this radical realignment of sports priorities lay within the centre of government itself. For the British Government, as much as the high-performance sport policy community, a successful performance at the Summer Olympics is of paramount sporting and political significance. Such political and sporting momentum has now built up around 2012 that there is little space for critical dissent from the Olympic-inspired sporting policy priorities.

However, given the vast amount of public resources being funnelled into high-performance sport, it is a duty of politicians in a parliamentary democracy to exercise an appropriate level of scrutiny. Indeed, some of the most pointed criticisms and questions have come from within the political system itself. For example, the investment of considerable sums of lottery monies for supporting elite development have been investigated (House of Commons Committee of Public Accounts 2006; National Audit Office 2005). Funding the 2012 Olympic Games means that there will be around £1.7 billion less money available for the other good causes supported by the National Lottery. As well as the £1.1 billion that is to be transferred directly from the other good causes, the newly designated Olympic lottery games are also having a diversionary effect, with an estimated £575 million coming from players who switch from other lottery games. Both the House of Commons Committee of Public Accounts and the National Audit Office have raised questions about the distribution of monies to a narrow elite, especially when other policy goals, such as raising levels of participation in local communities, is compromised as a result. The Chairman of the Public Accounts Committee put the following questions to UK Sport's Director of Performance: 'What is in winning medals for the general public apart from prestige? Why are we not spending more of this money on local swimming pools, for instance?' (cited in House of Commons Committee of Public Accounts 2006: Ev 2).

The fact that there has not been a serious answer to this question is telling. All that the supporters of 2012 and advocates of high-performance sport can reply is that they *believe* it will leave a legacy of 'world-class facilities' and will stimulate mass participation in sport. But there is scant evidence from previous Olympic Games that this belief is sound. As such, the justification for the vast amount of public resources being channelled into high-performance sports policy and the staging of the Olympic Games is a striking example of the 'mythopoeic [myth-making] status of sport' (Coalter 2010: 297). Herein lies the analytical point of departure for scholars and students of sports politics and policy. The forthcoming 2012 Olympic Games in London has ushered in an unprecedented period of government support for high-performance sport. Whether this level of support continues beyond 2012 will largely depend on the political capital that can be gained from the performance of UK athletes at the Olympic Games and the level of international prestige that can be garnered from hosting the Games. This is a highly precarious basis for public policy. However, what any analysis of contemporary high-performance sport policy reveals is that the study of sports policy can no longer (if it ever could) be effectively studied and critiqued through the optic of sports alone. The task facing critical scholars of sports policy is to marginalise the myth-makers in the sports policy community and stimulate a more meaningful discussion about the political and ethical basis of contemporary high-performance sport policy in what De Bosscher *et al.* (2007) aptly if provocatively termed the 'global sporting arms race'.

Notes

1 This chapter stands in an emerging tradition of critical studies of elite sport policy in the UK that has been pioneered by the late Mick Green. His approach was characterised by a commitment to the

empowering possibilities of sport, an understanding of the need to situate the substantive content of policy within a wider political and sporting discourse, and of the need to problematise rather than take for granted the pronouncements of politicians (be they government ministers or sports administrators) about the positive impact of sport on society (Green and Houlihan 2005; Green 2006, 2009). For the most insightful and detailed account of the current politics of UK sports policy, readers are directed to Mick's last published articles, 'Podium or participation? Analysing policy priorities under changing modes of sport governance in the United Kingdom' (2009).

2 I would like to acknowledge the assistance of Dr Marc Keech, my colleague at the University of Brighton, in constructing this chart.

References

BBC (2005) 'London beats Paris to 2012 Games'. http://news.bbc.co.uk/sport2/hi/front_page/4655555. stm (accessed 11 September 2010).

Beamish, R. and Ritchie, I. (2006) *Fastest, Highest, Strongest: A critique of high performance sport*. London: Routledge.

Burnham, A. (2008). *Andy Burnham speech at Lord's – Playing to win – a new era for sport*. www.culture.gov. uk/reference_library/minister_speeches/5184.aspx (accessed 11 September 2010).

Carrington, B. and McDonald, I. (2007) 'The Politics of "Race" and Sport Policy in the United Kingdom' in Houlihan, B. (ed.) *Sport and Society: a student introduction*. London: Sage.

Coalter, F. (2010) 'The politics of sport for development: Limited focus programmes and broad guage problems?'. *International Review for the Sociology of Sport*, 45.3, pp. 295–314.

Collins, M. with Kay, T. (2003) *Sport and social exclusion*, London: Routledge.

De Bosscher, V., Bingham, J., Shibli, S., Van Bottenburg, M. and De Knop, P. (2007) *The Global Sporting Arms Race: An international comparative study of sports policy factors leading to international sporting success*. Oxford: Meyer & Meyer Sport (UK) Ltd.

De Coubertin, P. (1966) *The Olympic Idea: Discourse and essays*. Germany: Carl-Diem-Institut.

Department for Culture, Media and Sport (DCMS) (2000) *A Sporting Future for All*. London: DCMS.

——(2008) *Playing to Win: A new era for sport*. London: DCMS.

Department for Culture, Media and Sport (DCMS)/Strategy Unit (2002) *Game Plan: A strategy for delivering government's sport and physical activity objectives*. London: DCMS/SU.

Department of National Heritage (1994) *Sport for 21st Century*. London: HMSO.

——(1995) *Sport: Raising the game*. London: Department of National Heritage.

Eichberg, H. (1989) 'Body culture as paradigm: the Danish sociology of sport'. *International Review for the Sociology of Sport*, 24, 1, pp. 43–60.

Green, M. (2006) 'From "Sport for All" to not about sport at all? Interrogating sport policy interventions in the United Kingdom', *European Sport Management Quarterly*, 6.3, 217-238.

Green, M. (2008) 'Governing under advanced liberalism: sport policy and the social investment state'. *Public Science*, 40, pp. 55–71.

Green, M. (2009) 'Podium or participation? Analysing policy priorities under changing modes of sport governance in the United Kingdom'. *International Journal of Sport Policy*, 1, pp. 121–44.

Green, M. and Houlihan, B. (2005) *Elite Sport Development: Policy learning and political priorities*. Abingdon: Routledge.

Hoberman, J. (1992) *Mortal Engines, the Science of Performance and the Dehumanisation of Sport*. New York: Free Press.

House of Commons Committee of Public Accounts (2006) *UK Sport: supporting elite athletes (54th Report of Session 2005–06, HC 898)*. London: HMSO.

Kelso, P. (2008) 'Olympics: Britain targets third in 2012 medal table'. *The Guardian*, Monday 25 August. www.guardian.co.uk/sport/2008/aug/25/olympics2008.britisholympicteam1 (accessed 11 September 2010).

Mackay, D. (1998) 'Murky waters dredged up in Bland affair'. *Observer (Sport)*, p. 8.

McNab, T. (2004) 'It's not the taking part that counts: greater participation does not lead to sporting excellence'. *The Guardian*, Wednesday 25 August. www.guardian.co.uk/politics/2004/aug/25/localgovernment. schoolsports (accessed 8 September 2010).

National Audit Office (NAO) (2005) *UK Sport: Supporting elite athletes*. London: NAO.

——(2008) *Preparing for Sporting Success at the London 2012 Olympic and Paralympic Games and Beyond.* London: NAO.

Riordan, J. (1977) *Sport in Soviet Society: Development of sport and physical education in Russia and the USSR.* Cambridge: University of Cambridge.

UK Sport (2008) *Summer Olympic Sports.* www.uksport.gov.uk/pages/summer_olympic_sports – home/ (accessed 11 September 2010).

27

Elite sport development in Denmark

Bjarne Ibsen, Jørn Hansen and Rasmus K. Storm

Denmark is a small country, with a population of only 5.4 million occupying 43,000 sq km. It is part of the Nordic Region and a member of the European Union. In comparative analyses, the Danish welfare model is referred to as 'the Scandinavian model' or 'the institutionalised welfare model', and is epitomised by a large public sector and universal, egalitarian and generous welfare provision.

The same ideals of equality and welfare have also permeated the history of sport in Denmark, where a vigorous movement promoting mass participation emerged early on. Strong national organisations coalesced around sport for all concepts, forming a close-knit network of federations promoting non-competitive sport (mainly gymnastics). Special educational establishments (folk high schools) were also established to provide youngsters with informal training as trainer and organiser, and legislation was passed guaranteeing these organisations, associations and educational establishments significant public sector funding. A sport for all ideology, and practices tailored to its needs, took hold. Elite sport was less accepted than its grass-roots equivalent – certain elements of the sporting and political worlds actively opposed elite sport, particularly the supporting of it with public sector funding. Until Team Denmark (TD) (the national institution for elite sport) was set up in the mid 1980s, progress towards providing support for the elite was, therefore, somewhat haphazard.

This chapter describes the Danish model for elite sport, analyses the factors that contributed to the establishment of TD, and concludes with an examination of the challenges currently facing elite sport in Denmark.

The Danish model of elite sport

TD has been the central co-ordinating body for the development of Danish elite sport since 1985. TD is a state institution, regulated by the Elite Sports Act, which was passed in 1984 and amended most recently in 2004. The Act stipulates that TD's objective is to develop Danish elite sport in a socially and societally responsible manner. This is to be achieved by initiating, co-ordinating and improving the efficiency of measures designed to promote elite sport, and is to be done in collaboration with the National Olympic Committee and Sports Confederation of Denmark (DIF) and associated federations. TD is run by a board of eight members, half of whom are appointed by DIF, the other half, including the chairperson, by the Minister of Culture. The Minister approves TD's statutes, budgets, annual reports and accounts.

The Act also states that TD is responsible for 'developing elite sport in a manner consistent with culture policy' and for 'the physical, personal and social development of elite athletes'. This involves providing adequate training facilities, financial assistance and support in the educational, work and social arenas. TD also provides advice to local authorities, related in particular to the provision of facilities for elite sport, and generates revenue by selling television broadcasting rights and marketing services on behalf of several federations to sponsors and the media. In other words, TD operates in a support and development capacity. The federations retain responsibility for training and for organising competitions and managing participation in competitions.

In 2008, TD's turnover was just under €20 million. The state provided 65 per cent, DIF (whose main source of income is the state (lottery money)) 15 per cent, and the remaining 20 per cent was sourced mainly from sponsors and TV. The bulk of TD's expenses – 62 per cent in 2008 – are attributed directly to the federations' activities for their top athletes, while the remainder is spent on a range of activities organised and funded by TD itself. The latter include partnerships with local authorities, the costs of special testing and training centres for elite sport, research funding, expertise in anti-doping and sports medicine, funding for events and management and communications costs. The spending by TD, however, only represents a small proportion of the total cost of elite sport in Denmark. A 1999 study revealed that elite sport accounted for approximately 60 per cent of the federations' total expenditure. One-fifth of these costs were covered by TD funding (KPMG Consulting 2002). Based on these figures, which are in turn based on uncorroborated data provided by the federations, it is estimated that the total cost of elite sport to the federations is approximately twice as high as TD's total expenditure and that the total annual cost of elite sport at national level is approximately €60 million. However, the cost of elite sport in local voluntary sports clubs and the costs associated with commercial sport would need to be added to this figure, but reliable data are not available for either of the costs.

How TD supports the development of elite sport

TD distinguishes between three levels of elite sport. International elite consists of athletes judged capable of winning medals at European championships, world championships and the Olympic Games. National elite consists of athletes who represent their country or club in senior international competitions, as well as talented youngsters with the potential to reach the international elite as seniors. Club elite consists of athletes who compete at the highest competitive level in Denmark. TD aims its support at the international elite and talented youngsters at national level (Team Denmark 2009).

As mentioned above, almost two-thirds of TD's funds are earmarked for providing financial support to the elite work done by the individual federations. To be eligible for funding, a federation (e.g. football, athletics or rowing) must draw up an analysis of the discipline's potential in terms of development and results. This analysis, which is conducted in collaboration with TD, includes – among other things – a study of the international results achieved by Danish athletes or teams and of the quality and quantity of the training and the level of professionalism of the trainers. It also includes the federation's objectives and strategies for recruiting talent, and takes into account the elite athletes' education/training, nutritional and financial conditions, etc. Finally, the analysis identifies organisational, financial and facility issues deemed to impact upon the development of elite sport. Based on this analysis, TD evaluates whether the federation qualifies for elite support.

Four different types of support are provided. The lowest form is 'advice' on improving the development of elite sport, and involves no direct funding. Federations not yet eligible for actual elite support may receive 'development project' support, the purpose of which is to ensure that the federation will achieve results that match the criteria for elite support within four years. Federations with a small number of elite athletes are eligible for 'individual elite' support. In order to obtain support as an 'elite federation', a federation must have multiple athletes at international level and a tradition of continuously developing elite performers of the highest international standards, that is, winning medals in international championships. Those that qualify as 'elite federations' enter into a fixed-term partnership agreement with TD that sets out the sporting goals for the duration of the agreement.

One key component of TD's activities is its elite centres, where international-level athletes (and others expected to reach that level soon) train together and receive highly qualified expert instruction. The elite centres also offer other forms of help, for example, physiotherapy, massage, sports medicine, physical training and advice about nutrition, education and career strategies. Half of the approximately 30 centres set up are concentrated in one of the three so-called 'Elite Villages' where athletes from various disciplines train together and share the same facilities and experts.

Converging with culture policy, diverging from sports policy

Certain features of the Danish model for elite sport are also characteristic of the Danish welfare and cultural policy model. First, Denmark has a long-standing tradition of state funding for the production and promotion of the arts and cultural activities. In the first half of the twentieth century, the state assumed responsibility for promoting culture in Denmark, for example, the 1922 Radio Act paved the way for the state-owned 'Danish Broadcasting Corporation' and the 1936 Library Act resulted in municipal libraries. Only after World War II did the state also start to assume responsibility for creativity and production. It would be a further two decades before sufficient legitimacy had been amassed to win a majority vote in the Danish parliament in favour of similar legislation for sport.

Second, state involvement is partially legitimised by social and societal concerns. Certain elements of the cultural legislation mentioned above were motivated by the desire to make culture accessible to all social groups and to provide decent economic and social conditions for authors, artists, etc. This was also the thinking behind the 1984 Elite Sports Act. It remains a central objective of state support to ensure that elite athletes enjoy adequate financial support and complete a formal education that will stand them in good stead after their sporting career. It is worthy of note that this support is independent of the elite athlete's economic and social background – an approach symptomatic of the Danish universalist welfare tradition.

However, significant aspects of the elite model diverge from general sports policy in Denmark. First and foremost, responsibility for the development of elite sport lies with a state institution whose authority is endowed by act of parliament. Traditional sports policy, on the other hand, has focused on voluntary organisations and clubs. There are three national umbrella organisations for sport in Denmark (the National Olympic Committee and Sports Confederation of Denmark; the Danish Gymnastic and Sports Association; and the Danish Company Sports Federation) and around 16,000 local sports clubs. Despite the state and local authorities providing a relatively large degree of financial support to exercise and sport, clubs and sporting organisations enjoy a relatively high degree of autonomy, and the role of the public sector is limited to securing the framework for sporting activities, that is, making facilities available and partially funding the activities. In this respect, Danish sports policy clearly differs from the other Scandinavian countries – especially Norway – where a greater degree of state control is the norm. The founding of Team Denmark therefore represented the start of increasing state intervention in sport. A number of state or semi-state institutions for sports development have been established over the last two decades: the Danish Foundation for Culture and Sports Facilities, founded in 1994, which contributes to innovation in sport and culture facilities; the Sports Policy Idea Programme, set up in 1998 but disbanded four years later, was aimed at developing new activities and promoting sport for particular groups; Anti-Doping Denmark, which combats the use in sport of drugs prohibited by the World Anti-Doping Agency; and the Danish Institute for Sports Studies, which was founded in 2004 to analyse different aspects of sport and to stimulate debate on key policy issues.

A second characteristic of sports policy in Denmark is the widespread decentralisation that is also prevalent in other parts of the welfare model. The majority of public services are provided by local authorities, which employ about three-quarters of the public-sector workforce and enjoy extensive autonomy. Around 80 per cent of total public-sector funding for sport is channelled to sports clubs via their local authorities. As far as central government is concerned, sport comes under the formal jurisdiction of the Ministry of Culture, where as few as two to four civil servants oversee policy and advise the minister. The Ministry has only around €7 million at its disposal to fund new sporting initiatives, research, etc. Before TD was set up, the elite sport structure was highly decentralised – individual federations were free to determine the manner in which they promoted elite sport, and the vast majority of training took place in local clubs. One of the main reasons for setting up TD was the perceived need for more effective co-ordination and stronger central control in work done on elite sport. One outcome of this is that elite athletes have been brought together in the centres mentioned above, which provide more intensive and frequent training than the clubs. Another is that the federations in general are now entirely dependent on TD funding for elite activities (apart from soccer and handball).

A history of elite sport in Denmark

The Elite Sports Act 1984 and the establishment of TD in 1985

The establishment of TD in 1985 represented a crucial milestone in the history of Danish sport. It was set up under 'Act No. 643 on the promotion of elite sport', which parliament passed by a clear majority on 13 December 1984. In an unprecedented move, the 1984 Elite Sports Act represented a break with the prevailing political principle of non-interference in the internal activities of sports organisations. Previously, organisations simply received a sum that provided a sound financial framework for the promotion of work considered by politicians to be of general social benefit (Løvstrup and Hansen 2002).

The Act also broke with the politicians' perception hitherto that sport's socially beneficial aspect was first and foremost linked to the promotion of public health and the democratic nature of the voluntary organisations' work in this field. During a 1976 parliamentary debate, not a single Danish politician considered elite sport worthy of state funding. By 1984, the consensus had shifted radically (Løvstrup and Hansen 2002: 105).

Passing the 1984 Act must therefore be interpreted as an expression of dissatisfaction on the part of the politicians with the work done by the main sports association, DIF,[1] to promote elite sport. DIF primarily emphasised the character-building side of sport rather than achievements in international competition. DIF, which is the main organisation for Danish sports, and individual federations, for example, the Danish Football Association (DBU) and the Danish Athletic Federation (DAF), had long clung to the old amateur ideals. As such, DIF preferred, first and foremost, to emphasise sport's character-forming role rather than concentrate unambiguously on performance in international competition. One of many examples of this attitude was the Danish national football team's decision not to enter the 1930 World Cup because FIFA allowed professionals to play. Indeed, DBU was one of the last football associations in the world to accept professionalism in its domestic tournaments, not allowing professional football in Denmark until 1978. Prior to that date, the Danish national team, which generally fared poorly in international competitions, took pride in the fact that, if nothing else, it consisted of 'the world's best amateurs' (Hansen 2006). A number of historical and institutional issues had to be addressed before the final capitulation, as witnessed by the debate that preceded the passing of the Act.

The debate began in earnest in the late 1970s when three issues drew attention to the main problems faced by elite sport in Denmark. First, the coach of the national handball team, Leif Christian Mikkelsen, drew the attention of the Ministry of Culture, at that time overseeing sport policy, to the poor financial and social conditions suffered by his players compared to players in other countries. Second, as mentioned above, the DBU decided to allow professionalism in the domestic league in an effort to boost the fortunes of the national side. Third, the outlook for the 1980 Moscow Olympics was bleak. Denmark had won only one medal in Munich in 1972 and only three in Montreal in 1976 – the country's worst two Olympic performances since World War II (Løvstrup and Hansen 2002).

These issues were crucial in getting the Social Democratic Minister of Culture, Niels Matthiasen, actively involved in the debate. Even though, on principle, he would have preferred the sports organisations to devise their own model for promoting elite sport, it was in the end the Ministry of Culture that took the initiative to set up a committee of enquiry and to draft the bill. This was partly due to the historical institutional barriers that characterised elite sport under DIF, and partly due to the diligence of civil servants in the Ministry of Culture (Løvstrup and Hansen 2002: 106). One consequence was that, at an organisational level, TD was not solely run by representatives of sports organisations. For the first time in Danish history, parliament appointed members of the management of a sports institution, effectively setting TD on the road to public-sector status (Løvstrup and Hansen 2002).

During the parliamentary debate on the report and the subsequent bill, all the parties supported the concept of funding elite sport in Denmark in principle. The general argument in favour of support was that it should be socially and societally sustainable to pursue a career as an elite athlete and a majority voted in favour of funding elite athletes aged 15 and over.

As mentioned above, this bill led to the establishment of TD in 1985. At its inception, TD was neither an association nor a state institution, but a 'self-governing institution',[2] a hybrid complete with a number of inherent contradictions that contained the seeds of potential conflicts of interest between the state, sports organisations, DIF and the national federations. Despite the fact that two-thirds of TD's funding initially came from the state, and also that the Ministry of Culture had appointed two TD board members, the Act did not actually result in a more active state policy for elite sport until it was amended in 2004 (Løvstrup and Hansen 2002: 118).

Greater state influence – the 2004 Elite Sport Act

In general, TD's work on elite sport was perceived as a success story by the political establishment, even though the majority of politicians paid scant heed to its activities. In 1999, 15 years after the legislation was passed, the government of the day thought the time had come for a closer look at whether the 1984 Act 'to a sufficient extent lived up to the challenges of the future' (Ministry of Culture 2001: 5). A working group was assembled, consisting of representatives of sports institutions and the public sector, to look at the Act in greater detail. It failed to reach agreement but, after the 2001 general election, the new right-wing government recommenced committee work in 2002.

Working closely with DIF, the new Minister of Culture, Brian Mikkelsen, of the Conservative Party, paid attention to sport in general and elite sport in particular. In 2004, parliament passed 'Act No. 288 on Elite Sports' which secured considerable influence for both DIF and the Ministry on the composition of TD's board. The new Act retained the idea that TD should develop elite sport in a socially and societally appropriate manner. However, there was widespread agreement that the age limit of 15 years for state funding should be lifted, as it represented a barrier to success in international competition.

TD was still a self-governing institution, but, through the Ministry of Culture, the public sector had secured closer control of it. TD was now subject to the Public Administration Act, and the Ministry had to approve its statutes, budgets, annual reports and accounts (see Act No. 288, the Ministry of Culture).

Danish elite sport policy – from rejection to regulation

Studies of the evolution of the 1984 Act and 2004 amendment reveal that the majority of Danish MPs changed their attitudes in favour of elite sport over a period of nearly 30 years. It may well be the case that politicians gradually developed a greater interest in sport, but at least equally significant was a historic shift in attitudes in Denmark during this period, and not just in the world of sport.

The prevailing attitudes in the 1970s were largely dominated by the anti-authoritarian ideals of the so-called 'youth rebellion' of the late 1960s. Any retrospective study must also take into account the fact that the 1970s saw the culmination of the Danish welfare model and the concept of equality for all. All youngsters were to enjoy equal opportunities to play their part in society, and any negative impact of social background was to be negated. Everybody was to have the right to state benefits, and sport was for all. Denmark therefore acceded to the Council of Europe's 'Sport for All' charter in 1972, and this principle became the overriding aim of sports policy (Korsgaard and Børsting 2002).

The combination of the youth rebellion's anti-authoritarian thinking and the welfare state's focus on equality led to a rejection of the concepts of competition and the elite. As a consequence, the majority of politicians considered it quite natural to support the principle of 'sport for all' and reject the concept of elite sport. Indeed, among the opinion makers of the day, widespread scepticism reigned about sport's competitive element and about 'sporting discipline' (Trangbæk et al. 1995: 106). The majority of politicians involved in a 1976 debate were therefore merely reflecting the Zeitgeist when they asserted that their main interest was in mass sport and stated that they did not wish to 'procure funding for an elite'.

The Danish welfare project changed gradually in the 1980s. As was the case throughout Western Europe, neo-liberal thinking gained ground as society became more diverse. As the middle class became the dominant political force, ideas of social equality took a back seat, replaced by concepts such as careers, incentives and rewards. By the early 1980s, the yuppies had usurped the media space dominated by the hippies in the early 1970s.

As a rule, historical changes of mentality take a long time and are rarely as clear-cut as a first glance would suggest. Aspects of previous attitudes live on in a modified form – parliament did not entirely succumb to the joys of elite sport. The link to the welfare ethos of the 1970s was the specific formulation that state-funded involvement in elite sport was to be 'socially and societally responsible'. As a result, TD is organised in a way that ensures that anyone, regardless of their income, who possesses the talent and will to put in an extraordinary amount of training can reach the top. Instead of the previous rejection of elite sport, the new TD set up provided, in principle, the opportunity to ensure a socially and societally responsible regulation of elite sport (Løvstrup and Hansen 2002: 129).

The impact of the change in attitude outlined above was underpinned by the fact that the Social Democratic-led government of the early 1990s also pursued a differentiated wage policy that was designed to make it easier for the middle class to forge careers in both the private and public sectors. The right-wing government that came to power in 2001 went even further, providing an additional boost to elite sport. As soon as he took office, the Minister of Culture emphasised his support for voluntary sport in general and elite sport in particular. In 2001, sport was written into the programme for government for the first time. In reference to elite sport, the programme stated:

> The potential for Danish elite sport to succeed at international level needs to be enhanced. Team Denmark will work more closely with the voluntary organisations to promote an ethically, socially and societally responsible development of elite sport that provides athletes with the best possible conditions.
>
> *(Programme for government 2001)*

The Programme for government and the 2004 Elite Sports Act completed the process started by the 1984 Act. Elite sport had not only become socially acceptable, it enjoyed a privileged status. It was a development that harmonised with the new government's belief that individuals deserve greater freedom; that systems should yield to the individual. Or, as the prime minister put it when he took office in 2001: 'We will renew Danish society so that it is natural to reward those who set themselves ambitious goals and achieve them' (Information 5 December 2001: 4). They are ideals that have been applied to both elite sport and life in general in the new century.

How successful has elite sport development been?

The general view of the development of TD throughout the years is that TD has been a success. Among other things, it has provided a boost to elite work in collaboration with the specialist federations in a wide range of Danish sports. TD's support activities were evaluated in 2008. The study concluded that the institution effectively exercises its legal duties and makes a serious contribution to work on the development of elite sport (Storm 2008).

TD was awarded top marks for activities related to its core principle – that the development of elite sport must be socially and societally responsible. General acceptance that it is important to study or work alongside a career as an elite athlete and the emergence of flexible educational provision for elite athletes have helped Danish athletes attain a higher level of education than the general population in the same age groups (c.f. Nielsen *et al.* 2000, 2002; Andersen and Storm 2009). Only in sports where Denmark has the largest number of professionals, that is, football (soccer) and handball, is the educational pattern of the athletes slightly different (Nielsen *et al.* 2002; Storm and Almlund 2006).

The study also concludes that if Denmark is to keep pace with international developments in elite sport, then new tools for identifying and developing talent will be needed, as well as better conditions for training and competition.

Pressure on Denmark's ability to compete

These conclusions are stressed as Denmark's ability to compete in sport has come under pressure due to the general trend in international elite sport in recent years, that is, more and more countries investing more and more money into winning medals, for example at the prestigious Olympic Games (c.f. De Bosscher 2007; UK Sport 2006; Green 2004).

Table 27.1 shows the medals won by Danes at summer Olympic Games since 1948. Excluding the 1948 Games, the average medal haul per Olympics has been 5.5. There has been remarkably little variation in the number of medals. In seven of the 15 games, Denmark won six medals. The high points were 1968 and 2004, when Denmark won eight medals. The low points came in the 1970s, when Denmark won just one and three medals, respectively, at the 1972 and 1976 games. The 1980 and 1984 games look better on paper, although Denmark's results would in all probability have been just as poor were it not for the international boycotts that saw several countries refuse to participate. In 1984, four of the six Danish medals were won in rowing and canoeing. Based on the world championships in the 1980s, it seems unlikely that, under normal circumstances, Denmark would have won medals in these events. The Danish medal haul has improved from the 1992 games onwards.

This being said, however, the trend in the number of Olympic medals won cannot be viewed in isolation from the total number of medals awarded at each Olympic Games (market share), which has increased considerably. In 1948, the total number of medals was 408, while in 2008 it was more than twice as many (957). One of the central columns in Table 27.1 indicates Denmark's percentage share of the total number of medals. In 1948, almost one in 20 medals was won by a Danish athlete. Apart from 1956, the proportion remained higher than 1 per cent until it peaked at 1.52 per cent in 1968. Since then, the proportion has been less than 1 per cent and has remained fairly constant since 1980, although 2004 represented a high point, with a share of 0.86 per cent. This is exactly the same as the Danish share in 1956, when Denmark

Table 27.1 Danish medals at summer Olympics 1948–2008

	Gold	Silver	Bronze	Total	Danish share of medals, %	Danish medal points	Share of total medal points, %
1948	5	7	8	20	4.90	37	4.53
1952	2	1	3	6	1.31	11	1.22
1956	1	2	1	4	0.86	8	0.87
1960	2	3	1	6	1.30	13	1.42
1964	2	1	3	6	1.19	11	1.11
1968	1	4	3	8	1.52	14	1.34
1972	1	0	0	1	0.16	3	0.25
1976	1	0	2	3	0.49	5	0.41
1980	2	1	2	5	0.79	10	0.80
1984	0	3	3	6	0.88	9	0.67
1988	2	1	1	4	0.53	9	0.61
1992	1	1	4	6	0.75	9	0.57
1996	4	1	1	6	0.72	15	0.91
2000	2	3	1	6	0.65	13	0.71
2004	2	0	6	8	0.86	12	0.66
2008	2	2	3	7	0.73	13	0.70

entered a very small team. Four medals in 1956 is therefore exactly the same proportion of the total as eight medals in 2004.

The above trends are based exclusively on medals, and for a small nation like Denmark, this is not always the best indicator of results and competitiveness as the number of medals may simply reflect chance, good and bad luck, injuries and marginal differences. Top-eight rankings provide a clearer picture, as they reflect a wider range of results[3] (Storm 2008). Analysis shows that the number of top-eight Olympic results increased from 1988 to 1996 but has since fallen. Denmark has lost ground compared with other countries. This calculation puts Denmark at no. 22 in 1988. Four and eight years later, Denmark's ranking fell to twenty-fourth, despite the marked increase in the number of points in this period. This was partly due to the significant increase in the number of disciplines between 1988 and 1992, and partly due to the fact that the number of nations competing has increased following the collapse of the Soviet Union. Taking this into account, Denmark's overall ranking in international professional sport has declined since the early 1990s. In 2008, Denmark was ranked twenty-eighth. By comparison, Sweden was ranked twenty-fifth and Norway twenty-sixth. The Netherlands, with which Denmark typically compares itself, fared better on every occasion, even though its ability to compete has come under pressure when calculated in terms of top-eight results.

The results indicate that the Danish position in international elite sport has been affected by what several international researchers have dubbed 'the global sporting arms race' (De Bosscher 2007; Houlihan and Green 2008; UK Sport 2006). Its relatively stable budget, with no significant increases, means that TD is likely to find the next few years increasingly challenging in terms of competition results. Combined with a new falling trend in state funding – due to a decreasing income from the state monopoly lottery – pressure is now mounting on the Danish standings (see below).

Changes and probable future developments

Although TD's primary objective is to develop elite sport in a socially and societally responsible manner, medals at major championships are increasingly seen as the measure of success for elite sport policy in Denmark. As described above, there is a great deal of evidence to suggest that Denmark's ability to compete will diminish. Compared with many other countries TD seems to be falling behind in the international sporting arms race in terms of resources. The major challenge for Danish elite sport is therefore to resolve the conflict between Olympic ambitions and political and economic realities. There appear to be three options if Denmark is to maintain or improve its relative international level: provide greater resources; prioritise the allocation of resources more severely; and fine tune the elite development process.

Greater resources

The first option is to pump in greater resources. State funding for TD is derived from the profits generated by 'Danske Spil', the state monopoly that operates the football pools, the lottery and other similar forms of gambling in Denmark. TD receives a fixed share of the annual profits. In the 1980s and 1990s, those profits rose, but in recent years Danske Spil has suffered a decline in turnover as a result of competition from Internet gambling. In 2009, the decline in revenue due to reduced state funding was enhanced by an even larger decline in sponsorship revenue.

To date, the political will has not existed to increase the basic subsidy allocated to TD, and it is unlikely that the individual disciplines will be able to significantly increase their spending on elite activities. At the same time as the federations are having to face up to this fall in Danske Spil's revenues, expectations have also increased that organised sport will help make children and adults more physically active and that this will help prevent health problems.

The government has, however, increased state funding for the development of elite sport by other means. First, it launched an 'Action plan to attract major sporting events to Denmark', for which €35 million has been earmarked for the period 2008–11. About €4 million of this total will be spent on improving talent recruitment. €2.7 million p.a. has been provided for new facilities for events and elite sport. Second, the most recent 2004 amendment to the Elite Sports Act facilitated partnerships between TD and local authorities on elite sport. The results of this new provision include local authorities setting up elite sport institutions to stimulate an elite environment in the local area; assisting athletes to find flexible education/training and jobs; providing financial support for talented athletes to train and compete; and establishing a number of sports schools, which differ from ordinary schools in that pupils have more sports lessons than is the norm in schools. Although these local event or elite sport secretariats typically receive the bulk of their funding directly from the local authority in the form of subsidies, they also generate varying degrees of income from private sponsors – which means that local authorities have a tendency to sponsor local elite sport on purely commercial terms. So far, only 18 of 98 municipalities have been approved as elite sport authorities, and total funding from local authority budgets has been limited. It is also debatable whether these new funds for elite sport represent an efficient use of public resources. TD was originally based on the principle that elite sport should be centralised in order to maximise Denmark's relatively limited resources and small pool of talent.

If resources for elite sport are to be increased it therefore seems likely that more of its funding will have to come from commercial sponsors and media. As a result, TD has focused its attention on the federations 'aggressively developing the commercial potential of their disciplines to improve their financial contribution to elite work' (Team Denmark 2009: 7).

Prioritisation of resources

To date, whether a particular sporting discipline received funding has been determined by both its competitive potential and the federation's ability to live up to TD's organisational and technical requirements. No clear distinction is therefore made between whether the discipline is popular in Denmark or is of interest to a relatively small number of people.

Greater financial pressure could, however, 'force' TD to prioritise disciplines to a greater extent than the organisation is already doing, as a number of other countries do, and focus funding on sports that have major 'medal potential' and/or which are popular in Denmark. The Elite Sports Act allows TD to take a sport's national standing into account in its assessment of whether or not to fund the federation. However, if fewer sports are to be selected for funding by TD, this may have the undesirable consequence that the social and societal objectives will be de-prioritised in disciplines not deemed worthy of funding.

Fine-tuning elite work

The third way to meet the growing demands placed on elite performance in international competition would be to make better and more efficient use of funds – for example, by improving the recruitment of talent, retaining and developing them into elite athletes, and optimising training programmes and participation in competitions.

Several factors have conspired to make talent recruitment and development less than optimal in Denmark from an elite-sports perspective. First, TD was not allowed to provide support to athletes under the age of 15 until 2004. This did not prevent the federations running training and programmes for young elite athletes. Indeed, a scientific study of young elite athletes failed to detect any negative physical or social side effects of elite sport for children (Jensen 1998). The elite sports organisations were therefore of the opinion that abolition of the age limit would provide greater protection for young elite athletes, as TD's objective is to promote elite sport in a socially and societally responsible manner. Second, the federations have tended to concentrate on the best athletes, which triggered funding from TD, at the expense of developing talent, which was not funded to the same extent.

In the wake of the 2004 amendment to the Act, TD now pays greater attention to recruiting talent, and partnerships with local authorities are expected to contribute to this. The evaluation mentioned above suggested that experiments be conducted with selected elite-sport local authorities and a systematic evaluation conducted of the talent potential of volunteers in various disciplines, that is, identifying talent before the athletes themselves choose a particular sport (inspired by the Australian system). However, there is also considerable resistance to what has been dubbed 'Eastern European conditions' due to perceived similarities with the recruitment methods used, for example, in the former East Germany. A more deliberate policy of selecting children for various sports on the basis of early testing in primary schools is therefore most definitely not on the agenda in Denmark. At present, there is no support for setting up special elite sport schools where young children would receive individualised professional training while attending school – despite the fact that the state-run Royal Danish Ballet has had a school of that type for many years.

Once talent has been recruited, it is equally important to retain and develop it. With a limited pool of talent because of the nation's size, Denmark cannot 'afford' to lose the relatively few people who possess the prerequisites to become international elite athletes. The Danish elite-sport model has always – perhaps because of the welfare-state mentality in Denmark – focused on creating a positive environment for young elite athletes, for example, by providing elite-sport classes in senior secondary schools so they have better opportunities to train and take part in competitions but continue to enjoy a 'normal' youth environment. In recent years, greater attention has been paid to the social environment in the elite-sport centres and clubs – some of which are better than others at retaining and developing talented elite athletes. In an attempt to shed light on this, a major research project has started at the University of Southern Denmark to identify and examine the factors that produce successful elite-sport environments. The project will look at the impact of social environments on talented elite athletes' socialisation processes, learning and development of expertise in elite sport, elite-sport coaches' socialisation and the development of expertise in talent identification and development. The sports programmes offered by universities are also changing. In the past, academic programmes were almost exclusively designed to train teachers for senior secondary schools. In recent years, the universities have started running programmes that qualify graduates to work in elite sport.

The evaluation of TD's support concept also suggests that a need exists for even more flexible education/training and job opportunities for elite athletes in the light of the increasing demands placed on them by their training and competition schedules, as well as a need for support for the transition from a career in sport to the labour market (Storm 2008: 19). The federations and other stakeholders have also expressed a wish for enhanced support for sports psychology.

Notes

1 When the Olympic Committee merged with DIF in 1993, the new body was named the National Olympic Committee and Sports Confederation of Denmark, but DIF is still the acronym normally used.
2 The concept of the 'self-governing (selvejende) institution' is uniquely Danish and is not known in other countries. The term is mainly applied to private, non-profit institutions that, unlike associations, do not have individual members and receive public funding to achieve their objectives. A number of so-called free, private kindergartens and schools are 'self-governing institutions'. However, the term is also applied to certain state institutions that enjoy relatively widespread autonomy, for example, the universities.
3 First place generates eight points, second place seven points and so on, up to eighth place, which generates one point. Quarter-finals in disciplines where there is no competition for fifth–eighth place are allocated points as fifth places. The CIS is also included under the Soviet Union (OL 1992). Czechoslovakia is included under the Czech Republic up to and including 1988. (Source: Stamm, H. and M. Lambrecht 2000: 42 and 101, for the years 1964–96. Supplemented with own calculations for the 2000 and 2004 Olympics and world championships, etc. 2006 and 2007)

References

Andersen, M. and Storm, R. (2009) 'Evaluering af Team Danmarks ordning med forlængede ungdom-suddannelser', Copenhagen: Danmarks Evalueringsinstitut og Idrættens Analyseinstitut.
De Bosscher, V. (2007) 'Sports Policy Factors Leading to International Sporting Success', Brussels: VUBPRESS.
Green, M. (2004) 'Power, Policy, and Political Priorities: Elite Sport Development in Canada and the United Kingdom'. In: *Sociology of Sport Journal*. 21: 376–96.
Hansen, J. (2006) 'Fodbold. En kort verdenshistorie', Odense: Syddansk Universitetsforlag.
Houlihan B. and Green, M. (2008) 'Comparative Elite Sport Development. Systems, Structures and Public Policy', Oxford: Butterworth-Heinemann.
Information, 5 December 2001.
Jensen, B. and Andersen, B.H. (1998) 'Børn og eliteidræt – i tal', Copenhagen: Institut for Idræt.
Korsgaard, A. and Børsting, A. (2002) 'Mod statslig involvering – En analyse af dansk idrætspolitik i perioden 1974 – 2000', Odense: Institut for Idræt og Biomekanik, Syddansk Universitet.
KPMG Consulting (2002) 'Eliteidræt – et økonomisk øjebliksbillede på specialforbundenes udgifter til eliteidræt', Brøndby: Danmarks Idræts-Forbund.
Kulturministeriet (2001) Eliteidræt i Danmark. Rapport (Elite sport in Denmark. Report), Kulturministeriet, Lov om eliteidræt – Lov nr. 288 af 26. April 2004, Kulturministeriet.
Løvstrup, I. and Hansen, J. (2002) 'Da eliteidrætten blev stueren – Eliteidræt og idrætspolitik i Danmark', Odense: Syddansk Universitetsforlag.
Nielsen, K., Nielsen, A.G., Christensen, S.M. and Storm R.K. (2002) 'Kontraktspillere i fodbold og håndbold. Undersøgelse af sociale, uddannelsesmæssige og sportslige vilkår for danske kontraktspillere 2002', Copenhagen: Team Danmark.
Nielsen, K., Nielsen, A.G. and Storm, R.K. (2000) 'Den danske subelites vilkår år 2000. Undersøgelse af danske subeliteidrætsudøveres sociale og idrætslige vilkår', Copenhagen: Team Danmark.
Regeringsgrundlaget 2001. www.stm.dk/publikationer/regeringsgrundlag/reggrund01.htm
Stamm, H. and Lambrecht, M. (2000) 'Der Schweizer Spitzensport im internationalen Vergleich. Eine Empirische Analyse der Olympische Spiele 1964–98', Schriftenreihe der Gesellschaft zur Förderung der Sportwissenscahaften an der ETH Zürich, Band 21, Zürich: Studentendruckerei Uni.
Storm, R.K. (2008) 'Team Danmarks Støttekoncept. Evaluering af støttekonceptet 2005–2008', Copenhagen: Danish Institute for Sports Studies.
Storm, R. and Almlund, U. (2006) 'Håndboldøkonomi.dk – fra forsamlingshus til forretning'. Bind 1 & Bind 2. Copenhagen: Danish Institute for Sports Studies.
Storm, R.K. and Brandt, H.H. (red.) (2008) 'Idræt og sport i den danske oplevelsesøkonomi. Mellem forening og forretning', Frederiksberg: Forlaget Samfundslitteratur.
Team Denmark (2009) 'Team Danmarks støttekoncept 2009–2012', Brøndby: Team Denmark.

Trangbæk, E., Hansen, J., Ibsen, B., Jørgensen, P. and Nielsen, N.K. (1995) 'Dansk idrætsliv Bind 2. Velfærd og fritid 1940–96', Copenhagen: Gyldendal.

UK Sport (2006) 'Sports Policy Factors Leading to International Sporting Success. An International Comparative Study', London: UK Sport.

28

Sports development and elite athletes in China

Fan Hong[1]

After the modern Olympic movement was introduced to China at the beginning of the twentieth century (Guoqi 2008), a seminar organized in October 1908 by the Tianjin YMCA raised the famous 'Three Questions about the Olympics'. When would China send its first athlete to participate in the Olympic Games? When would Chinese athletes win their first gold medal at the Olympic Games? When would the Olympic Games be held in China? (Hong *et al.* 2008) China spent 100 years in finding the answer to these questions.

China sent its first athlete, Liu Changchun, to participate in the Los Angeles Olympics in 1932 but he failed to win a medal for his beloved motherland. China won its first Olympic gold medals at the Los Angeles Olympics in 1984. China hosted the Olympic Games in Beijing in 2008. It 'grabbed a total of 100 medals at the Beijing Games – a happy coincidence as the country has dreamed for 100 years to be the Olympic host – and overtook the United States to top the gold medal table with 51 golds' (Na *et al.* 2008). China's quest for global power and Olympic glory had been achieved and it successfully transformed from the 'sick man of East Asia'[2] to a world sports superpower in just 100 years!

The triumph of Chinese sport is deeply rooted in China's elite sport system. It is called 'Ju Guo Ti Zhi' in Chinese and translates as 'whole-country support for the elite sports system'. This system channelled all resources for sport in the country into elite sport and effectively produced hundreds of thousands of young elite athletes in a short time in pursuit of ideological superiority and national status. Its main characteristics are centralized management and administration and guaranteed financial and human resources from the whole country to ensure maximum support (Qin 2004).

This chapter will examine China's elite sports system from a historical perspective and analyze the following aspects of the elite sports infrastructure: government policy; financial resources; athlete's selection and training; retired athlete's education and re-employment; coaching; and sports facilities.

China's elite sports system: a historical overview

China's sports system underwent dramatic transformation between 1949 when the People's Republic was established to the present. Between the 1950s and 1970s the administrative and

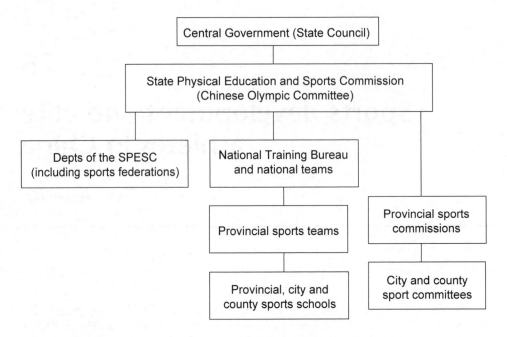

Figure 28.1 The administrative structure of Chinese sport (1952 to mid 1990s)

management structure were centralized. The national governmental body, the State Physical Education and Sports Commission (SPESC), was responsible for the formulation and implementation of sports policy; administration of national sports programmes and organizations; training elite athletes; and organizing national and international competitions. The model of the Chinese sports administrative system reflected the wider social system in China. Both the Party and state administrations were organized in a vast hierarchy with power flowing down from the top (see Figure 28.1).

Since the 1980s, the sports system has been transformed from a centralized system to a multi-level and multi-channel system. The turning point was when it changed its name from the State Physical Education and Sports Commission (国家体育运动委员会) to the China General Administration of Sport (CGAS – 国家体育总局) in 1998. The CGAS was reduced in size. Its function was formulation and supervision of the implementation of sports policy. The original sports departments were transformed into 20 sports management centres to manage its training and commercial interests (see Figure 28.2). Individual sports federations were located in these management centres. The change in title and structure was both symbolic and pragmatic. The aim was for Chinese sport to stand more on its own feet and rely less on government support.

However, with regard to the 20 sports management centres, it is evident that, except for football, basketball and table tennis, they are far from self-supporting. The centres remain partially dependent on money from central government and local government. With the approach of the Beijing Olympic Games, central government could do nothing but increase its financial support in order to maximize the chances of success in the Games. Therefore, the reform of the sports management system before 2008 was in reality old wine in a new bottle. However, after the Beijing Olympics in 2008 the central government and the CGAS both emphasized that the sports reform must continue and that sports commercialization and fitness programmes for the nation must be promoted further. However, the unique 'Ju Guo Ti Zhi' must remain since it

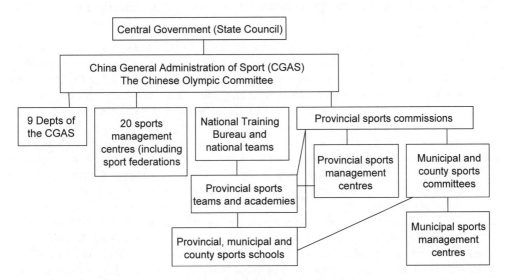

Figure 28.2 The administrative structure of Chinese sport (1998–2009)

proved at the Beijing Olympics to be a most effective way to project the image of China and to establish national identity in the world. The traditional centralized system remains and still plays an important role in the Chinese elite sports system (Hong *et al.* 2005).

The development of elite sport in China

The beginning of the elite sports system in China (pre-1956)

Due to foreign invasions and political and social unrest during the first half of the twentieth century, competitive sport[3] in China remained underdeveloped before 1949. The Republic of China managed to participate in three Olympics between 1932 and 1948, but did not win a single medal.

The People's Republic of China (PRC) was established in Beijing in 1949. Sport and physical education initially was an important element in the PRC's domestic policy of building a strong nation state. China's experience at the Helsinki Olympic Games in 1952 stimulated the government's determination to utilize sport as a valuable tool to help to restore the new China in international politics. Consequently, competitive sport was promoted by the government as a vehicle for expressing Chinese national representation and identity on the international stage.

A competitive sports system was formally set up after the SPESC issued 'The Competitive Sports System of the PRC' in 1956. Forty-three sports were officially recognized as competitive sports; rules and regulations were defined; professional teams were set up at provisional and national levels which would compete with each other at regional and national championships; the National Games would take place every four years to promote sport. Competitive sport was regarded as an effective way to unite the nation though sports events. At the same time the SPESC issued 'The Regulations for the Youth Spare-Time Sports Schools' in 1956. The Soviet Union's spare-time sports school model was adapted to train and foster talented athletes from a very young age. By September 1958 there were about 16,000 spare-time sports schools (业余体校) with approximately 777,000 students throughout the country (Wu 1999).

The development of the elite sports system during the Great Leap Forward (1958–1960)

The late 1950s saw the initiation of the Great Leap Forward (GLF). The movement resulted from the desire of the leaders of the Chinese Communist Party (CCP) to 'drag China out of the mire of poverty and backwardness during their own lifetime' (Rodzinski 1999). The slogan of the GLF was 'Go all out, aim high and achieve greater, faster, better and more economic results.' Objectives of the Campaign were set as 'surpass Great Britain in 10 years and the US in 15 years' in terms of steel production and heavy industry (Dajun 1995). However, this approach led to 'the cherishing of totally unrealistic expectations and the formulation of grandiose, but badly planned and clumsily implemented schemes, the execution of which heaped insupportable burdens on the Chinese people' (ibid.: 107). The campaign ended in November 1959, and was followed by the Great Famine which resulted in millions of deaths (Chengrui 1998).

Although the GLF primarily focused on agriculture and heavy industry, it touched every aspect of Chinese society. The Great Leap Forward of Sport began in February 1956 when the State Physical Culture and Sport Commission (SPCSC) issued the 'Ten-Year Guideline for Sports Development'. It aimed to promote mass sport and elite sport simultaneously and to reach the world level within a decade. The major target was to 'have four million people achieve the standard of the Labour and Defense System (LDS 准备劳动与卫国体育制度) which was adopted from Soviet Union in 1954. It aimed to cultivate eight million athletes and five thousand elite athletes in ten years between 1956 and 1966' (SPCSC 1958). By mid 1958, inspired by the booming campaign in agriculture and heavy industry, the SPCSC believed that, 'the goal of surpassing the capitalist West in general has stimulated the development of sport … therefore, the old Ten-Years Guideline would no longer suit the current situation and will damage people's enthusiasm' (Yannong 2007: 161). Therefore, the SPESC revised the Guideline in September 1958 and the new Guideline required 150–200 million people to achieve the standard of the LDS, and to cultivate 50–70 million athletes and 10–15 thousand elite athletes (ibid).

Guided by the 'Ten-Year Guideline for Sports Development', the SPESC initiated the 'Sports Great Leap Forward Campaign' in 1957. Its ambition was to catch up with the world's most competitive sports countries in ten years. It planned that, by 1967, China's basketball, volleyball, football, table tennis, athletics, gymnastics, weight-lifting, swimming, shooting and skating performers were to be among the very best in the world. China would produce 15,000 professional full-time elite athletes.

At the same time, mass sport was promoted throughout the country. Two hundred million men and women were expected to pass the fitness grade of LDS. One million seven hundred and twenty thousand sports teams would be formed among factory workers and 3,000,000 among peasants by 1967. It was expected that Chinese sport would develop under the 'two legs walking system': elite and mass sports developing simultaneously (Shaozu 1999: 102–6). However, the failure of the GLF and the Great Famine in 1960 resulted in a change of direction.

The consolidation of the elite sports system (1961–1966)

In 1960, the Party changed its slogan to 'Readjustment, consolidation, filling out and raising standards' and, in 1961, the SPESC changed its policy for producing elite sports stars (PRCGAS 1982: 60 & 72). The government was determined to use the best of its limited resources to provide special and intensive training for potential athletes in particular sports so that they could compete on the international sporting stage. Consequently, physical education institutes, whose major responsibility was to train physical education teachers and instructors for mass sports, were reduced in number from 29 in 1959 to 20 in 1960. In contrast, professional sports teams increased from 3 in 1951 to more than 50 in 1961. In 1963 the SPESC also issued the 'Regulations for Outstanding Athletes and Teams' to improve the system. Under the instruction of the SPESC a search for talented young athletes took place in every province (ibid: 102). Meanwhile ten key sports were selected from the previous 43. They were: basketball, volleyball, soccer, table tennis, track and field, gymnastics, weightlifting, swimming, skating and shooting (ibid: 103). The Party concentrated all the resources on a few elite athletes in order to produce high performances on the international sports stage. It was a turning point of Chinese sports ideology and system which had changed from 'two legs' to 'one leg' – the elite one.

The decline and recovery of elite sport during the Cultural Revolution (1966–1976)

The Cultural Revolution was initiated by Mao Zedong in early 1966 as he believed that he was losing control and that his enemies had changed the colour of the Party from Red (Communism) to Black (Capitalism and Revisionism). The aim of the Cultural Revolution was to regain and consolidate his power (Rodzinski 1999: 416) and to prevent China changing its colour (Hong 1999).

The turbulence of the Cultural Revolution reached the field of sport too. The confrontation ultimately focused on the relationship between elite sport and mass sport. The former was regarded as the representative of bourgeois and capitalist ideology and the latter as communist and proletarian. He Long, the Sports Minister, was accused of neglecting mass sport and of supporting Liu Shaoqi and Deng Xiaoping's revisionist and capitalist sports policy (Jarvie et al. 1999: 85). He was condemned and jailed. He died in prison in 1975 (Hong 1999).

The Revolutionary Communist Central Committee, the State Council and the Central Military Commission jointly issued a Military Order on 12 May 1968 to disband the SPCSC and the provincial and local sports commissions. PLA officers and soldiers were sent to replace the cadres. Most of the sports administrators were attacked by the Red Guards and revolutionary rebels. More than 1,000 cadres from the SPCSC were sent to a May Seventh Cadre School in Shanxi province to be 're-educated' by doing physical labour (ibid). Administrators and coaches of provincial and local sports commissions were sent to the countryside to be 're-educated' as well. The whole training system in China was dismantled. Sports schools were closed down. Provincial and local sports teams were dismissed. National squads stopped participating in international competitions. Sports facilities were destroyed by the Red Guards and revolutionary rebels. Sports stadia became venues for denunciation meetings. Top athletes, outstanding coaches and sports scientists and scholars were condemned as counter-revolutionaries, capitalist-roaders and rightists and suffered mentally and physically (ibid). Some of the athletes died in the violent revolutionary storm. For example, three famous world-class table tennis players committed suicide in 1969 as they could not endure the torture anymore.

Elite sport was attacked violently between 1966 and 1970 due to Mao's decision to wipe out his political enemies and to consolidate Maoist ideology. In 1971 the situation began to change due to political and diplomatic reasons when China felt the threat from the Soviet Union and sought the United States as a new ally. Sport, with its non-political image, was used as a medium to approach western enemies (ibid). Ping-Pong Diplomacy played its part to establish the relationship with the United States. At the same time, under the slogan 'Friendship First, Competition Second', sport was used to strengthen the relations between China and its old allies including socialist countries, African countries and South American countries – the so-called Third World (Hong 2001). In 1972, the Chinese Table Tennis Teams visited Asia, Africa, South America, Europe and America. Seventy-two countries and regions communicated with China through the visit of the Chinese sports delegations (Yannong 2007: 383).

The rise of the elite sports system since the early 1980s

Mao's death in 1976 brought the end of the Cultural Revolution. The Third Plenary Session of the 11th Central Committee which was held in September 1978 marked a new era for China. The Maoist's 'class struggle-oriented' political policy was replaced by economic reformation and the 'open-door' policy. It was hoped that, through economic reformation and communication with advanced countries in the West, China would catch up with the rest of the world and again be a modernized and strong country (ibid).

Sports policy also underwent transformation in the new era. The SPCSC held a national sports conference in 1980 and officially established its strategy for the future development of sport. It focused on elite sport. Wang Meng, then Sports Minister, stated, on the one hand, that China was still a poor country and was restricted in the amount of money it could invest in sport. On the other hand, elite sport was an effective way to boost China's new image on the international stage. Therefore, the solution was to bring elite sport into the existing planned economy and administrative system, which could assist in the distribution of the limited resources of the whole nation to medal-winning sports (Wang 1982). It was hoped that international success of Chinese athletes would, in return, bring pride and hope to the nation, which were badly needed in the new era of transformation (Rong 1987).

Based on this strategy, the conference drafted the blueprint for Chinese sport in the 1980s and 1990s. Elite sport was set as the priority both in the short term and long term. The short-term plan required the national team to be placed among the top ten at the 1980 Olympics, and to be placed among the top six at the 1984 Olympics. The long-term plan required China to become a sports superpower, level with the USA, by the end of the twentieth century (Hao 2008).

China joined the USA and some Western European countries to boycott the 1980 Olympics in Moscow due to the Soviet invasion of Afghanistan. China then participated in the 1984 Olympics in Los Angeles after an absence of 32 years from the Olympics. There, Chinese athletes won 15 gold medals which placed China fourth in the Olympic medals tally. China's success at the Olympic Games inspired Chinese from all walks of life and stimulated a stronger call for the promotion of elite sport from both the central government and ordinary Chinese people. 'Develop elite sport and make China a superpower in the world' became a popular slogan in China (Hong *et al.* 2005).

Immediately after the Los Angeles Games the central government issued 'A Notification about the Further Promotion of Sport' in October 1984. It stated:

> Sport has a close relationship with people's health, the power of the nation and the honour of the country. It plays an important role in promoting people's political awareness, achieving modernization targets, establishing foreign relations, and strengthening the national defense. Therefore, the Party and the society have recognized the importance of sport in our society and will develop sport in China further. ... The remarkable achievement in sport, especially the success at the 1984 Olympics, has restored our self-confidence and national pride. It has stimulated a patriotic feeling among all the Chinese both at home and abroad and enhanced China's international influence ... Our policy is to develop both

the mass sport and the elite sport, and to strive for greater success in the international sport arena'.

(CCP Central Committee 1984)

After the conference, the Society of Strategic Research for the Development of Physical Education and Sport (?体育发展战略研究会) produced the 'Olympic Strategy' (奥运战略) for the SPESC in 1985. The new strategy was to build up China's international image by transforming China into a leading sports power (Hong *et al.* 2005). To achieve this goal China would continue its strategy of using the resources of the state to develop elite sport. One year later, the SPESC issued the 'Decisions about the Reform of Sports System (Draft)' which reinforced the importance of the 'Olympic Strategy' and confirmed the importance of elite sport in serving the modernization of the country in the twentieth century. The major objective of the sports policy was to raise the standard of elite sport (State Physical Culture and Sport Commission 1986). The clauses of the policy clearly indicated its elite sport-oriented nature. Six out of the nine objectives directly related to elite sport:

- Improving the level of sport leadership and strengthening the SPCSC's overall role of leadership, coordination and supervision
- Establishing a scientific training system
- Improving the sports competition system
- Enhancing and promoting Chinese traditional indigenous sports
- Developing sports scientific research gradually
- Reforming the sport and physical education system
- Enhancing political thought on sport
- Establishing a sports prize-winning system
- Developing a flexible and open policy to international sport (Jarvie *et al.* 2008: 100)

Under the 'Olympic Strategy' and sports reformation policy China's elite sport developed rapidly in the 1980s and 1990s. The famous 'Ju Guo Ti Zhi' (whole country support for the elite sports system, 举国体制) was reinforced. In the 1980s when China was slowly recovering from the Cultural Revolution the nation's limited economic and educational resources and human capital were channelled to this system. All the efforts were being made to serve the goal of winning Olympic medals. As the Minister of Sport, Wu Shaozu, stated in 1994, 'The highest aim of Chinese sport is to achieve success at the Olympic Games. We must concentrate our resources on it. To raise the flag at the Olympics is our major responsibility' (Shaozu 1999).

The 'Ju Guo Ti Zhi' brought China remarkable success on the international sports stage. From the 1984 Los Angeles Olympic Games to 2008 Beijing Olympics Chinese athletes climbed the ladder of the gold medals with a world record speed (see Figure 28.3) from 15 gold medals and fourth place on the gold medal table in 1984 to 51 gold medals and first place in 2008. China's dream came true at the Beijing Olympic Games when it beat the USA and became a world sports superpower in just 24 years!

Dimensions of elite sport infrastructure

Resources

There are three major sources of income that support China's sports system: government sport budget; commercial and sponsorship income; and lottery funding (see Figure 28.4). Table 28.1 clearly shows that Chinese sport remains largely dependent on government funding.

Fan Hong

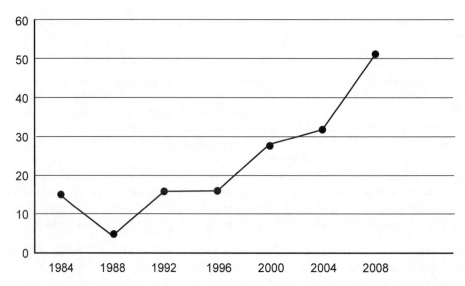

Figure 28.3 The number of gold medals won by China in the Summer Olympics (1984–2008)

Together with the rise of the Chinese economy, both government funding and commercial and sponsorship income have increased dramatically since the mid 1990s.

With regard to lottery funding, when the sports lottery (体育彩票) system was introduced in 1998, the Ministry of Finance and the People's Bank of China announced that 60 per cent of the income would be used to promote mass sport and 40 per cent would be allocated to elite sport. According to the General Administration of Sport's report on the distribution of lottery funding in 2004, 1,190 million RMB went to elite sport and 1,750 million RMB was channelled to mass sport (Dong *et al.* 2005: 13).

As mentioned earlier, in the 1980s the 'Olympic Strategy' stressed that all available sport resources in China should be concentrated on elite sport. Consequently, the government invested most of its public funding for sport in elite sport and the proportion of the government's sports budget spent on elite sport compared with mass sport became extremely skewed. Between 1990 and 1999, only 1.88 per cent of the national and provincial sports budget was invested in mass sport programmes (ibid). Gao Min, a former director of the Mass Sport Department in the SPESC claimed in 2004, 'Our department had two million RMB for developing mass sport each year … There was less than one million RMB sports budget to invest in mass sport for each provincial government'. One former senior staff member from the Policy and Regulation Department in the SPESC confirmed this situation. He stated in 2006, 'So far, we have not had the money to subsidize the development of mass sport' (ibid).

Athletes

Selection and training

China has one of the most effective systems in the world for systematically selecting and producing sports stars from a very young age. As discussed, this system was officially created in 1963

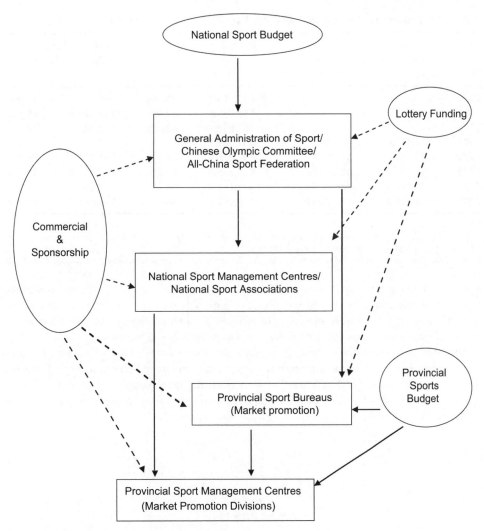

Figure 28.4 The income of China's sports system
Source: Tan, T.C. 2008

when the SPESC issued the 'Regulations for Outstanding Athletes and Teams'. Under the instructions of the SPESC, the selection of talented young athletes took place in every province (PRCGAS 1982: 102). Over the years it has developed into a well-organized and tightly structured three-level pyramid: primary, intermediate and high level. The sports schools at county, city and provincial levels formed the base of the pyramid. After several years' training about 12% of talented athletes from sports schools were selected to go on to provincial teams and become full-time athletes. From there, outstanding athletes progress to the top: the national squads and Olympic teams (see Figure 28.5). The system remains in place today.

In terms of selection procedures, it is between the ages of six and nine years when boys and girls with some talent in particular sports are first identified. They then join local sports schools across the country where they train for three hours per day, four to five times per week. After a period of hard training the promising ones are promoted to 'semi-professional' training: four to

Fan Hong

Table 28.1 Chinese sports budget 1994–2001 (Unit: 10 thousand RMB)

Year	General administration of sport	Local governments	In total		Commercial and sponsorship income	
1994	–	–	133,515.4	58.0%	96,526.6	42.0%
1995	–	–	153,958.5	54.5%	128,416.5	45.5%
1996	–	–	207,652.9	52.5%	187,744.7	47.5%
1997	47,317.0	354,043.0	401,359.6	–	–	–
1998	26,251.0	379,975.0	406,226.0	71.5%	161,913.0	28.5%
1999	31,846.0	383,739.0	415,585.0	65.8%	216,123.0	34.2%
2000	76,791.0	428,405.0	505,196.0	58.2%	363,256.0	41.8%
2001	103,126.0	572,266.0	675,392.0	56.7%	515,695.0	43.3%

Notes
1 The sports budget in this table does not include the capital costs of the construction of basic sports facilities
2 In the 1990s, 1 US$ was equivalent to about 5 RMB yuan
Source: China General Administration of Sport, Statistic Year Book of Sport (Internal Information) 1994–2002 (Tan 2008)

five hours training per day, five to six days per week. Before the 1990s, the sports schools, which were part of the local sports commission, provided coaching and training facilities and met all costs of training and competition. In addition, the young athletes were provided with a free meal once a day. After the 1990s, the cost was partially borne by parents.

After this 'semi-professional' training, young athletes with potential are selected for the provincial sports academies or training centres. They live on campus and train four to six hours per day, five or six days per week. Their aim is to reach the second stage and become full-time professionals in provincial teams or professional clubs and eventually to reach the third stage to become members of the national squads and Olympic teams (see Figure 28.6).

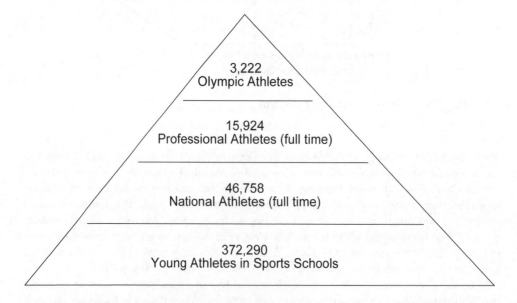

Figure 28.5 Pyramid of China's selective system for elite sport and the number of athletes at each level in 2004 (Hong et al. 2005)

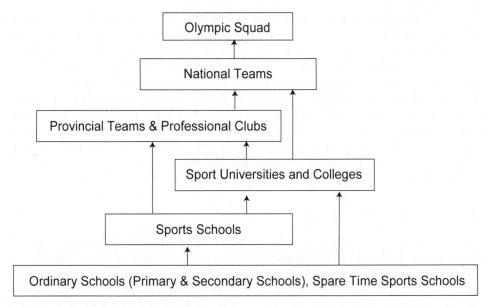

Figure 28.6 China's sport selection system

The selection system is brutal and is the core of the 'Ju Guo Ti Zhi' (the whole country support for the elite sports system). In 2004 there were nearly 400,000 young boys and girls training at more than 3,000 sports schools throughout China (Dai 2005). Only 5 per cent would be able to reach the top, with the remaining 95 per cent of these young athletes leaving their sports schools with no formal primary and secondary education qualifications – only broken dreams.

In recent years, sport universities and colleges became a new source for provincial teams, professional clubs and national squads (see Figure 28.6). For example, since 2006, all the athletes of the Sichuan Provincial Water Polo Team were selected from the Chengdu Sport University Water Polo Team. In addition to the provincial team, the Chengdu Sport University Water Polo Team also provided athletes to the National Water Polo Squad. Between 2004 and 2008, more than ten athletes became national squad members.

Athletes in provincial teams, professional clubs and national teams are full-time professionals. They receive wages from provincial and national governmental bodies and sponsors. Their average income is 2,000–4,000 RMB monthly. World champions and Olympic medalists receive additional income from rewards provided by national and provincial governments, sponsorships and advertising. For example, Liu Xiang, the Olympic gold medallist, following his victory at the 2004 Athens Games, received a reward of more than one million RMB from the Shanghai government since he is a native Shanghainese, with further financial rewards being received from the SPESC, and from sponsorship and advertising. However, these full-time athletes receive their pensions only from their provincial sports bodies. One major consequence of the priority given to Olympic success is that local governments, especially the local sports commissions, have suffered, and will continue to suffer, from the 'Olympic drainage', a unique system within the elite sports system which is discussed below.

Provincial and local sports teams and commissions have responsibility for nurturing and training elite athletes for the national teams and rewarding them when they win medals. There-fore, when the Olympic Games or international competitions finish athletes return to their home teams, and their provincial sports commissions have to reward the winners with huge amounts of money. For those who are not lucky enough to win medals the local sports authority has a responsibility to look after them and to pay them wages and pensions. Therefore, local sport authorities are constantly short of money for sport, for they have already spent most of their budget on training and have nothing left to pay the rewards, wages, pensions and other costs. For example, in Liaoning Province, where athletes have won more medals than any other province, the local sports commission is facing a huge financial burden due to the large amount of money it has to pay to the current Olympic and World Champions and to pay in wages and pensions to those ex-Olympic gold medalists and ex-World Champions. 'Able to produce gold medalists but unable to reward and feed them' is the harsh reality facing local sports governing bodies (Hong *et al.* 2005).

The training of Olympic athletes

Elite athletes are selected to join national teams according to their performance at the National Games, National Championships, regional Games and other domestic sports competitions. The national teams consist of experienced team managers, head coaches, and coaches who are appointed by the SPCSC and sports management centres, and elite athletes who are selected from the provincial sports teams cross China. According to Chinese sports tradition, when it prepares for international competitions there are two teams for each event: the national team and the resource team. For example, at the Beijing Olympics in order to ensure success, 'The Strategic Plan for Winning Olympic Medals in 2008' required an expansion in the number of teams. Therefore, some key events had three teams: the national team, the youth team and the resource team. All elite athletes in China whose age allowed them to perform at the 2008 Games were selected and allocated to different teams according to their current ability and future potential. Each national team was to be given specific targets for the number of medals expected; no team effort was being spared to ensure success. Managers, coaches and athletes were working under enormous pressure. One head coach of a national team revealed that he felt that it was like having a sword hanging over his head every day. National teams and youth teams trained in their national training centres. The resource teams trained in provincial sports commission training centres and at those universities which had superior training facilities. In 2002, China had 1,316 full-time Olympic athletes in national teams. In 2004, an additional 706 athletes joined national teams and 1,200 joined youth teams. In total, by the end of 2004 there were 3,222 full-time elite athletes training for the 2008 Olympic Games, plus others training in resource teams (Yang 2002).

Support for retired elite athletes

After retirement, athletes have to adjust to a new life. In general, professional athletes in China have four options. The first is to become an official, the second is to become a coach or physical education teacher, the third is to establish a sports agency or company and the fourth is to study at university. After the establishment of the 'Ju Guo Ti Zhi' in the early 1980s, the Chinese government issued a series of policies and decrees to support retired elite athletes.

In general, at the beginning of the period of sports reform during the 1980s and 1990s provincial and local governments had the responsibility of assigning jobs to retired athletes. The policy was that athletes who ranked among the first six places at national level sports events would be offered jobs by the provincial sports commissions. The majority of them became coaches and sports development officers of provincial governments. Athletes who ranked below the first six places nationally would be the responsibility of municipal and county governments. They were allocated to local government departments, schools and state-owned enterprises.

As the market economy reform deepened in the late 1990s, the government's policy began to encourage retired athletes to search for jobs by themselves. If athletes chose to find jobs by themselves, provincial and local governments would provide them with an amount of settlement allowance (Hong and Zhouxiang 2008).

In 2002 CGAS, the State Commission Office for Public Sector Reform, the Ministries of Education, Finance, Human Resources and Labour and Social Security jointly issued the decree 'Suggestions on Re-employment for Retired Athletes'. It required governments at all levels to support retired athletes and offer them jobs and education opportunities.

Some economically advanced regions, such as Guangdong, Fujian, Jiangsu, Shanghai and Beijing, acted quickly. Athletes could be offered a comfortable settlement allowance and good job opportunities. For example, according to Guangdong province's 'Measures for Retired Athletes' in 2004, athletes who performed well at the Olympics, international championships, world cups, the Asian Games, and those who won a medal at national level could be employed as cadres in government departments. Athletes who won medals at international and national sports events would be offered big bonuses and jobs in Guangzhou or any other cities in Guangdong province.

In Fujian province, the 'Measures for Retired Athletes' established by the provincial government in 2005 stated that professional athletes could receive settlement allowance if they chose self-employment or to find jobs by themselves. On August 2005, the Sport Commission of Fujian province paid 10,510,000 RMB to 140 retired athletes. Chen Hong, a badminton player who won a gold medal at the national games received 200,000 RMB (Jie 2009).

A sea change for the retired athletes nationally happened in 2006 when the 'Notifications on the Strengthening of the Insurance System for Elite Athletes' was issued. It was a joint venture between the CGAS, the Ministry of Finance and the Ministry of Human Resources. It detailed regulations on social insurance, endowment insurance, medical insurance, unemployment insurance, injury insurance and housing allowance for retired athletes (General Administration of Sport 2007). One year later, another decree entitled 'Tentative Administrative Measures for the Employment of Elite Athletes' was jointly issued by CGAS, the Ministry of Human Resources, the Ministry of Education, the State Commission Office for Public Sector Reform, the Ministry of Finance, the Ministry of Labor and Social Security and the Ministry of Public Security. It clearly defined regulations for the recruitment, training and retirement of elite athletes. It required that every provincial government and sports commission must establish its measures for retired elite athletes with the aim being to protect their rights (ibid).

However, due to China's unbalanced economic development caused by geographical differences, these policies have failed to take effect in some economically disadvantaged provinces. For example, the conditions in Liaoning province are still far from being satisfactory. The provincial and local governments have difficulties in offering the majority of the retired elite athletes suitable jobs or a sufficient amount of settlement allowance (Nafang Daily 2007).

Higher educational opportunities for elite athletes

Research conducted in 2002 by Deng Yaping, a former table tennis world champion and Olympic gold medalist, provided an insightful case study on retired athletes in China. She argued that the elite system had a negative impact on those children who began from a very young age to play table tennis and who aimed to become professional players in the future. They spent their first 15 years doing nothing but playing table tennis and they dreamed of becoming world champions. However, there were nearly 1,000 full-time table tennis players in China but only 20 of them could be selected for the national team. The majority had to retire at the age of 25. Deng argued that, because of their lack of a formal schooling, suitable jobs were difficult to find outside the table tennis world. Disillusionment and depression were at least two of the negative outcomes for the many who did not make it to the very highest level (Deng 2002).

However, the government has produced policies intended to give elite athletes the opportunity to enjoy formal higher education; to help them to acquire specialist knowledge and skills; and to prepare them for the job market. The first policy document was issued by the SPESC in 1987 entitled the 'The Notification about Higher Education for Elite Athletes'. It stated that winners in the first three places at the Olympics, world cups and world championships could enter universities without taking the National Universities Entrance Examination. This policy was further strengthened in 2002 when the CGAS, the State Commission Office for Public Sector Reform, the Ministry of Education, the Ministry of Finance, the Ministry of Human Resource and the Ministry of Labour and Social Security jointly issued the 'Recommendations on the Re-employment for Retired Athletes'. It widened the entrance requirement for elite athletes and encouraged them to go to universities. Athletes who finished in the first eight places at international sports events, in the first six places at Asian sports events, or captured the first three places at the national sports competitions, could enter universities without taking the National Universities Entrance Examination (General Administration of Sport of China 2007).

Young athletes also received support from government policy. According to the 'Notification on University Recruitment with Sport Talented Students' and the 'Standard for University Recruitment with Sport Talented Students' issued by the Ministry of Education in 2005, secondary school graduates, who achieved the titles of the 'First Rank Athletes' and the 'Second Rank Athletes' and also captured one of the first three places at provincial sports competitions, could enter universities without taking the National Universities Entrance Examination. By the end of 2006, 235 universities recruited young athletes under these policies (Ministry of Education 2006). The government and universities also provided scholarships for elite athletes who chose to study at universities and colleges. According to the 'Interim Procedures for Scholarships for Elite Athletes' issued by the CGAS in 2003, elite athletes and retired elite athletes could apply for government scholarships. The amount awarded ranges from 3,000 to 15,000 RMB which would cover their tuition fees and/or living costs.

Training facilities

Since the foundation of China's elite sport system, all the sports schools have been well equipped. They have their own training facilities, including gymnasia, football pitch, basketball court, table tennis court and swimming pool. Historically, they are the result of the investment by the local sports commissions. Consequently, the public can share these facilities, however, the training of the young athletes takes priority.

At the provincial level, each province provides its sports teams with a training camp, which is normally situated in the capital city of the province and which is close to the sports research centre. For example, the Sichuan Rhythmic Gymnastics Squad and Water Polo Squad established their training base in Chengdu Sport University. In addition, each provincial team develops its own individual training base outside the capital city of the province. Taking Guangdong Synchronized Swimming Squad as an example, its training base is located in Shantou, a county 150 miles from the Guangzhou, the capital of the province.

At national level, there are several national training centres in Beijing for different sports such as gymnastics, diving, swimming, synchronized swimming, modern pentathlon, fencing, weight-lifting and athletics. In addition, each national team has its own training camp outside Beijing. These training camps have first class training facilities which are jointly sponsored by the local government and the General Administration of Sport, for example:

- Haigen camp in Yunnan province: swimming and women's football.
- Hongta camp in Yunnan province: women's long distance running. It is believed that these athletes benefit from the high attitude environment in Yunnan province.
- Haikou camp in Hainan province: sailing.
- Sanya camp in Hainan province: beach volleyball.
- Zhongshan camp in Guangzhou: table tennis.
- Shenzhen camp in Guangdong province: judo and cycling.
- Guangzhou camp: shooting, handball, throwing disciplines, boxing and baseball.
- Fuzhou camp in Fujian province: athletics (high jump).
- Xinzhuan camp in Shanghai: athletics (hurdles).

Universities also provide venues and training facilities for national teams, for example, a National Team Training Centre was established at Beijing Sport University in 2006. The total investment of this training centre is 206 million RMB. The national rhythmic gymnastics team, trampoline team, track and field team and modern pentathlon team trained in this centre for the 2008 Beijing Olympics. After the 2008 Olympics, this national training centre continued to serve various national teams. In general, the national teams spend more than eight months in their training camps outside Beijing. It is believed that these isolated bases with first class training facilities would minimize distractions and improve athletic performance.

In summary, through the Olympic medal-oriented policy, the centralized sports administrative and management system and the selection and training system facilities, the entire Chinese elite sport system is focused on producing a handful of exceptional athletes to win gold medals at the Olympic Games and world championships.

Coaching and sports science research

Coaches in China, from the county level to national level, are employed on a full-time basis by sports commissions throughout China. To become a coach at a local sports school one has to obtain a higher diploma or a bachelor's degree in physical education and sports studies and pass coaching certificate tests. By June 2005, there were 29,317 full-time coaches with bachelor's degrees working in sports schools and elite sports teams at provincial and national levels (Qoing 2007) (see Figure 28.7).

In terms of training methods, the People's Army's training method: 'hard, disciplined, intensive training and practice according to real battle' was adopted in 1963. In 1964, however, a new training method was introduced. It included 'three non-afraids': non-afraid of hardship, difficulty and injury, and 'five toughnesses': toughness of spirit, body, skill, training and competition (Hong 2003). It has become a legendary Chinese sports method and continues to influence China's training system in the twenty-first century. For example, Wang Junxia, holder of world records from 1,500 to 10,000 metres and recipient of the prestigious Jesse Owens Trophy in 1994, ran 170 km in four days in her training sessions. She is not alone. Almost all the girls in her team trained, and still train, under the same methods and routine. Nevertheless, since the late 1980s the emphasis has been on more scientific training methods including

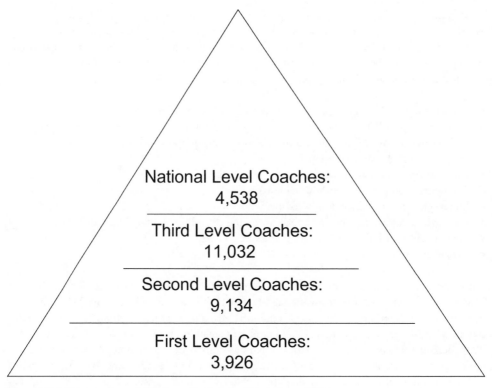

Figure 28.7 The number of full-time coaches in China, June 2005

coaching techniques, sports science, sports psychology, sports medicine, and better facilities and equipment.

There are thirty-six sports research centres at provincial level, seven of which are in the major cities of Beijing, Shanghai, Guangzhou, Tianjin, Xi'an, Chengdu and Chongqing. The National Institute of Sports Science is in Beijing under the direct leadership of CGAS. All the sports researchers who work in these research centres are employed as full-time staff and are required to link their research directly to training athletes to win medals.

Experts and researchers in universities also contribute directly and indirectly to training gold medalists in the areas of coaching techniques, sports psychology, sports medicine, sports physiology and biomechanics and sports sociology. During the past decade, in order to prepare the Beijing Olympics, several Olympic research centres were established in universities. In these university research centres all the initial funds and the majority of the on-going revenue funding are provided by the university and from commissioned research projects. The current university research centres are as follows :

- Olympic Research Centre at Beijing Sport University (established 1994)
- The National Team Management Centre in Beijing Sport University (2005)
- The Humanistic Olympic Studies Centre in Renmin University of China (2000)
- The Olympic Culture Research Centre in Beijing Union University (2000)
- China Paralympics Research Centre at Xi'an Sport University (2006)

- The Beijing Olympic Education Research Centre at Beijing Normal University (2006)
- Beijing Institute of the Olympiad at Beijing Institute of Physical Education (2005).

Competition opportunities

In order to select and train elite sport stars from a young age, local and provincial competitions are held on a regular basis. In general, individual sports have their national championships once every year to give athletes experience and to select talented young athletes for the provincial and national teams. Regional and provincial sports meetings take place every two years and the National Games every four years.

Most of the competitive sports events in the National Games are Olympic events. The SPCSC officially stated in 1993 that the National Games must be directly linked to the Olympic Games and function as a training ground for the Olympic Games. Consequently, the National games take place two years prior to the Olympic Games. All the competition events are Olympic events except Wushu (Chinese Martial Arts). The slogan is 'Let the national competitions serve the Olympics' (变全运为奥运) and 'Training the athletes in Chinese competitions and preparing them to fight for China at international games' (国内练兵，一致对外). Furthermore, Chinese athletes regularly participate in international sports competitions. All the costs of participation in the Olympic Games, world championships and the Asian Games are met by the CGAS and relevant sports management centres. The International Relations Department in CGAS, the sports management centres and sports associations are responsible for facilitating and organizing all international competitions.

Conclusion

China's determination to achieve first place in the Olympic medals table has resulted in the promotion of its elite sports system since the early 1980s. The 2008 Olympics in Beijing proved it is an effective way to make China a world sports superpower. It is likely that elite sport will continue to develop in the traditional form of 'Ju Guo Ti Zhi', a product of the planned economy, and will receive major support from the government. This unique system, which has played such an important role in China's political life, will continue to fulfil China's ambitions to be one of the global economic and political superpowers in the twenty-first century.

Notes

1 I wish to thank Lu Zhouxiang for his brilliant assistance with the format and notes.
2 A derogatory term used for China by Western powers and Japan from the late nineteenth century to the end of the Second Sino-Japanese War in 1945.
3 The terms for 'Competitive sport' and 'Elite sport' in Chinese are the same words – Jing Ji Ti Yu 竞技体育。This chapter will use the term of competitive sport in the period of pre-1980s and elite sport in the post-1980s era since the concepts of Jing Ji Ti Yu have developed since the 1980s.

References

CCP Central Committee, 1984, *A Notification about the Further Promotion of Sport*, October 5.
Chengrui, L., 1998, *Population Change Caused by The Great Leap Movement*, Demographic Study, No.1, p. 97–111.
Dai Q., 2005, 'Zhongguo tijy yexu yige xinshidai' [Chinese Sport Needs a New Era], *Xinwen Zhoukan* (*Chinese News Weekly*, 7 September).

Dajun G. (ed.), 1995, *The History of the People's Republic of China* (1949–93), Beijing Normal University Press, Beijing.

Deng, Yaping, 2002, 'From Boundfeet to Olympic Gold in China: The Case of Women's Chinese Table Tennis', unpublished MA thesis, Nottingham University.

Dong Xinguang, Liu Xiaoping and Bai Yonghui, 2005, 'The Problems Aroused by the Neglect of Construction due to Mass Sports and its Solution', *Sport Culture Guide*, 4, p. 13–15.

Gaotang, R. (ed), 1987, *The History of Contemporary Chinese Sport*, China Social Science Press (Zhongguo Shehui Kexue Chubanshe), Beijing.

General Administration of Sport of China, *Support for Athletes in the New Era*, Online. Available www.gov.cn/gzdt/2007–10/18content_778919.htm (accessed 2 June 2009).

Guoqi, X., 2008, *Olympic Dreams China and Sports 1895–2008*, Harvard University Press, Cambridge.

Hao Qin (ed.), 2008, *The History of Sport in China 1980–1992*, Renmin Tiyu Press, Beijing.

Hong F., 1999, 'Not all bad! Communism, Society and Sport in the Great Proletarian Cultural Revolution: A revisionist Perspective', *The International Journal for the History of Sport*. 16(3), p. 47–71.

——, 2001, 'Two Roads to China: The Inadequate and Adequate', *The International Journal for the History of Sport*, 18(2), p. 148–67.

——, 2003, *Women's Sport in the People's Republic of China: Body, Politics and the Unfinished Revolution*, in Lise Hartmann-Tews and Gertrud Pfister, *Sport and Women: Social Issues in International Prespective*, Routledge, London, p. 227–8.

Hong, F., McKay D. and Christensen K. (eds), 2008, *China Gold: China's Quest for Global Power and Olympic Glory*, Berkshire Publishing Group, Great Barrington.

Hong, F., Wu, P. and Xiong, H., 2005, 'Beijing Ambitions: An Analysis of the Chinese Sports System and Its Olympic Strategy for the 2008 Olympic Games', *The International Journal of the History of Sport*, 22(4), p. 510–29.

Hong, F. and Zhouxiang, L., 2008, *On the Rights to Sport*, Sichuan Science & Technology Press, Chengdu.

Jarvie, G., Hwang, D.-J. and Brennan, M., 2008, *Sport Revolution and the Olympics*, Berg Publishers, Oxford.

Jie, S., *The Hard Life of Retried Athletes*, Online. Available www.ce.cn/sports/typl/200508/25/t20050825_778919.htm (accessed 2 June 2009).

Meng, W., 1982, *The Report to the 1980 National Sports Conference, Sports Policy Documents (1949–1981)*, People's Sport Press, Beijing, p. 150.

Na, M., Xing, H. and Mingwei, H., n.d., 'Chinese people cheerful and proud for success of Beijing Olympic Games', Online. Available http://news.xinhuanet.com/English/2008-08-05/content_9701874.htm.

Qin, H., 2004, 'Lun zhongguo tiyu' Juguo tizhi' de gainian, detain yu gongneng [Definition and Characters and Functions for the Chinese Elite Sport System], *Tiyu* [Physical Education], p. 9.

——, 2008, *The History of Sport in China 1980–92*, Renmin Tiyu Press, p. 11.

Qoing, Z., 2007, *Coaches in China, General Administration of Sport in China*, 2007-02-07.

Rodzinski, W., 1999, *The Walled Kingdom*, Fontana Press, p. 406.

Rong Gaotang (ed.), 1987, *The History of Contemporary Chinese Sport*, China Social Science Press, Beijing.

Shaozu, W. (ed.), 1999, *The History of Sport of the PRC*, China Books Press, Beijing.

SPCSC, 1958, *Reports on the Ten-Year Guidelines for Sports Development*, 1958-09-08.

State Physical Culture and Sport Commission, 1986, *Decisions about the Reform of Sports System (Draft)*, 15 April.

Tan, T.C., 2008, *Chinese Sports Policy and Globalisation: The Case of the Olympic Movement Elite Football and Elite Basketball*, Loughborough University.

The Ministry of Education established the Standard for University Recruit Students with Sport Talent in 2006, Online. Available http://www.eol.cn/article/20060209/3172211.shtml (accessed 4 June 2009).

The Policy Research Centre of the Sports Ministry (PRCGAS), 1982, *Policy Documents for Sport (1949–1981)*, People's Sport Press, Beijing.

Wang Meng, 1982, 'The Report to the 1980 National Sports Conference', Sports *Policy Documents (1949–1981)*, People's Sport Press, Beijing.

Wei Bifan, 2007, 'They Prosecuted the "Devil Coach"', *Nanfang Daily*, 2007-01-02.

Wu Shaozu (ed.), 1999, *The History of Sport of the PRC*, China Books Press, Beijing.

Yang S.A., n.d., 'Woguo jingji tiyu de shili xianzhuang, xingshi, renwu ji duice fengxi [the Analysis of our Elite Sport]', *Zhongguo tijy keji [China Sport Science and Technology]*, (1), p:3–9. (Deng is Deputy Minister of the China General Administration of Sport and Head of the Department of Competitive Sport in the General Administration of Sport).

Yang Suan, 2002, 'Woguo jingji tiyu de shili xianzhuang, xingshi, renwu ji duice fengxi' [The Analysis of our Elite Sport], *Zhongguo tiyu keji* [China Sport Science and Technology], (1), p. 19–21.

Yannong, F., (ed.), 2007, *The History of Sport in China*, Vol. 5, 1949–79, People's Sport Press, Beijing, p. 161.

29

Sports development and elite athletes

The Australian experience

Bob Stewart

Australia is an island continent that contains a population of 21 million within a landmass of around 7.7 million square kilometres, which makes it one of the least densely populated nations on earth. Most of its inhabitants live on the coastal fringes, and while it has been mythologised as a land of laconic bushmen (White 1981), in reality over 70 per cent of all Australians live in cities, making it one of the most urbanised countries in the world (Salt 2003). Australia is also an ancient nation, having been inhabited by aboriginals for at least 40,000 years, but it has only 220 years of permanent European settlement. It is an English-speaking country, having been established as a British penal colony in 1788, and given political independence in 1901 when it became a federated nation of six states and one territory. Since then it has evolved into a highly industrialised and cosmopolitan society governed by a democratically elected national parliament, six state parliaments, and two territory parliaments.

Australia's identity and how it sees its place in world affairs has always been problematic, and is particularly apparent when it tries to define itself in relation to its surroundings (White 1981). It occupies a strategic place in the Asia–Pacific region but has a weak cultural connection to many of its Asian and Pacific neighbours. It is caught between its Anglo-Irish origins and a desire to integrate into the wider Asian community. At the same time, it has augmented its British colonial roots with millions of migrants from Continental Europe, and more recently from Asia and South America. However, the broadening of Australia's migration base did not come easily, and for much of its early history Australia opposed migration from non-western European countries. During the 40 years immediately after its Federation in 1901, Australia had a white–Australia policy, which meant that Asian migrants were often denied entry (Rickard 1988).

Australia's economic development has also taken many twists and turns. It was traditionally an exporter of primarily rural products and raw materials, and until the 1950s it was often said that Australia rode on the sheep's back (Hancock 1961). However, in recent times Australia has relied extensively on its mining and service sectors to fuel its growth (Catley 2005). Primary industry has ended up supporting less than 10 per cent of the workforce and the most recent United Nations human development index ranks Australia as the third most developed country in the world. This high level of national wealth was achieved through a combination of

'explosive productivity growth', low inflation, a rapid expansion in the finance, business and communication industries, and growth in global trade (Edwards 2000: 10). Despite the chronic disadvantage suffered by aboriginal communities, Australia has also used a system of industrial conciliation and arbitration and progressive taxes to ensure an even spread of wealth and income, and 'tangible equality' between workers and households (Hancock 1961: 154). However, the income gap between rich and poor has been progressively widening in recent years, and the egalitarian myth that has been projected to the world is under threat (O'Conner et al. 2001). Australia's enigmatic history has created a diverse society, but it has also produced many social fractures and cultural tensions.

While Australia is divided in all sorts of ways, with the main tensions being economic, religious, racial, and gender-based (O'Conner et al. 2001), there are many occasions when Australians are strongly united, and for the most part this occurs when the nation is represented in major sporting events. Indeed, the one thing that defines Australia's global image is sport. Sport has, more than any other cultural practice, the capacity to unite Australians, whatever their background (Magdalinski 2000). As a result, international sporting successes have been the primary means of securing a strong sense of 'we-ness', nationhood and national identity (Australian Sports Commission 1999a; Coakley et al. 2009: 415; Hancock 1961; White 1981). Whereas for the first 60 years of the twentieth century, Australia's commercial sector rode on the 'sheep's back', it is also fair to say that for the last 60 years Australia's cultural identity has ridden on the back of its players and athletes (Blainey 2000; Booth and Tatz 2000).

This is not to say, however, that Australia's national government was always heavily involved in sport. Indeed, for the first 80 years after Federation there was virtually no national government funding for elite sport development. Olympic and Commonwealth Games teams were given travel cost assistance, and the Australian national surf livesaving programme was heavily subsidised (Booth 2001), but beyond that it was expected that sport would not only run its own affairs, but also fund them (Stewart et al. 2004). While the institutional framework for the delivery of sport altered in 1972 with the election of the Whitlam Labor Government, and a mandate for it to change the political landscape (Crowley, 1986), it was not concerned with changing the elite sport development landscape. Although one of its first initiatives was to ban all racially selected sports teams from touring Australia, it was not interested in funding stadium construction, providing financial support to talented young players and athletes, training coaches, or using sports science to improve sporting performance. Its focus was on recreational sport and the delivery of community services (Stewart et al. 2004).

The catalyst for a radical change in elite sport policy

However, this all changed in the mid 1970s when Australia was traumatised by a significant national incident. The trauma did not result from the defeat of the Whitlam Government in 1975, but rather from the collective shock that followed from the failure of its athletes to win a gold medal at the 1976 Montreal Olympic Games. Given Australia's previous successes – it won eight gold medals at Munich in 1972 – and the role of sport in sustaining a strong national identity, it was viewed as a catastrophe. Enquiries were conducted into the national sporting system, and delegations were sent overseas to examine successful sports systems, and report back to the government (Houlihan 1997). The newly elected Fraser Government – and a highly conservative one when contrasted with the reformist Whitlam Government – was not initially interested in supporting sport, since it believed sport was better off as an autonomous, apolitical enterprise. However, the government also understood that sport was crucial to the nation's identity and self-image, and that Australian players and athletes could no longer successfully compete in international competitions without a radical shift in the way government viewed sport. It also wondered how it might reclaim Australia's position as a major player on the sports stage (Cashman 1995). The Fraser Government was consequently confronted by a serious policy problem. It was clear that the international sports world had changed and that the traditional arms-length approach to sport would take it into a developmental black hole. Having examined the recommendations of a number of related reports and enquiries, it was decided to take a completely new policy position on elite sport development (Houlihan 1997). There was unanimous agreement, not just in government, but also amongst sport's policy communities – which included coaches, national sporting bodies, sports scientists, coaches, athletes, and even the media – that a national body had to be established that would take responsibility for the full-time training and long-term development of the nation's most talented players and athletes. This was a major policy shift, and completely transformed the way in which government viewed the role of sport in society, and how the sports sector would be supported to ensure ongoing international success (Stewart *et al.* 2004).

The evolution of elite sport policy

The Commonwealth Government's elite sport development policies exploded into the public arena in 1981 when the Australian Institute of Sport (AIS) was established at Bruce, a suburb of Canberra, the national capital. Its primary goal was to assist elite athletes to improve their international sporting performances, and its initial operations were supported by extensive capital spending that included an infrastructure comprising an athletic stadium, an indoor sports centre, outdoor tennis courts, and a netball centre. The generous capital budget was complemented by an equally supportive operating budget which provided full-time employment of 26 coaches and the offering of live-in six-month scholarships for 150 athletes in eight different sports (Daly 1991). Over the next two years international-standard facilities were established for gymnastics and aquatics, and, by the beginning of 1985, training and playing facilities had been constructed for weight-lifting, basketball, netball and soccer (Australian Sports Commission 2003b). These initiatives reflected a totally new role for government in the training and development of talented young players and athletes (Houlihan 1997). It was finally conceded that the mythology about Australia being an inherently sporting nation where international-standard players and athletes would inevitably rise to the top of the talent pool without any government interference was nothing more than a fantasy (Adair and Vamplew 1997; Booth and Tatz 2000). Instead, a talent pathway had to be built that added value to player and athlete sporting performance across each phase of their lifecycle.

At the same time, the AIS centre was a risky policy initiative since Australian sport had no history of government control and external strategic guidance. Moreover, the national governing bodies for specific sports were not only uncertain about how to best connect to the AIS model, but were also – for the most part – not well resourced. There was a consequent collective sigh of relief when AIS athletes won seven of the 12 swimming medals for Australia at the 1984 Olympics at Los Angeles. In addition, the AIS-trained gymnastic team was close to winning medals for the first time in Olympic Games history, and three AIS athletes won medals on the running track. The national euphoria was instant; it immediately infected the Commonwealth Government, and John Brown, the Minister for Sport, announced a 60 per cent increase in AIS funding for the 1985/86 financial year (Stewart *et al.* 2004).

This funding increase not only enabled the AIS to consolidate its Canberra facility, but also allowed for the development of a strong network of regional elite training centres. Following the 60 per cent funding increase in the 1985/86 budget, residential satellite centres were being established in Perth for field hockey, Brisbane for squash and diving, and Adelaide for cricket and cycling (Australian Sports Commission 1998: 2). This coincided with the establishment of the Australian Sports Commission (ASC) in 1984, whose role was to co-ordinate and deliver the national government's increasingly ambitious sports objectives. In 1989 the government merged the AIS with the ASC in order to first, eliminate duplication, and second, ensure greater accountability and transparency in the wake of over-zealous spending by AIS senior management. The CEO at the time, Dr John Cheffers, conceded that he had induced a serious budget deficit, but in his defence claimed that athletes could not produce their best performances in a constrained climate where economic rationalism overwhelmed innovation (Stewart *et al.* 2004). In the meantime, the ASC confirmed that the AIS would continue to be the focal point for elite athlete development, and during the 1990s the Institute consolidated its activities and successfully delivered many international sporting successes (Australian Sports Commission 1999a).

By the beginning of the twenty-first century there was no doubt in the minds of Australia's sports policy communities that the AIS model was superior to anything that had preceded it. Moreover, it was also clear to them that if it were not for the ASC's support of national sporting bodies, the availability of the AIS world class training facilities, and the scholarship assistance to young athletes, Australia's international sporting credentials would have been at rock bottom. The international reputation of Australia's sports development capacity was forever etched into the minds of the global sporting community in 2000 when Sydney hosted the Olympic Games. Not only were 315 of the 620 team members AIS scholarship holders, but 31 of the 58 medals were won by former or current AIS athletes (Australian Sports Commission 2001). The 58-medal tally was the greatest ever for an Australian team, and came on the back of a population of only 20 million people at the time. Furthermore, notwithstanding the home-site advantage, it demonstrated the massive strength of Australia's elite sport development system. Moreover, most of the members of the world champion teams in non-Olympic sports that included netball, rugby and cricket were former AIS scholarship holders. All of these successes solidified the national pride of Australians and allowed the nation, in conjunction with our medical research, and our minerals and mining sector to secure an international presence and global status. However, our international sporting successes beg the question as to how it was achieved, and what structures and systems made it all happen.

Explaining Australia's international sporting successes

There are many factors that can be used to explain Australia's international sporting success, but first and foremost it is fundamentally the result of government initiatives that began in the early 1980s and which were explained in the previous part of this chapter. They set the policy parameters that not only gave a clear articulation of what needed to be done to secure international sporting success, but also provided the capital and operational funding to make it all happen (Adair and Vamplew 1997; Green 2007; Green and Houlihan 2005; Houlihan 1997; Stewart *et al.* 2004). The current elite sport development arrangements are multi-faceted and, when viewed collectively, constitute an impressive and, in some respects, a formidable system of integrated initiatives for the development of elite level players and athletes.

The policy statements

Many government-sponsored reports and policy statements were generated during the 1980s and 1990s which set the scene for further sporting successes. During the 1989–90 period the House of Representatives Standing Committee on Finance and Public Administration published *Going for Gold* and *Can Sport be Bought?*, which argued the case for: first, an increase in income support for elite athletes to ensure additional intensive training and overseas competition; second, an increase in spending on international-standard sports facilities; and, finally, greater assistance to national sporting bodies for improving the quality of their management structures and systems. A further impetus to elite sport came from the establishment of the Olympic Athlete Program (AOP) in 1994, which guaranteed athletes vying for selection to the Sydney 2000 Olympics access to additional financial support. These developments were subsequently enshrined in the government's 2001 policy statement titled *Backing Australia's Sporting Ability: A More Active Australia*, which became a sporting manifesto for the neo-liberal Howard Government, which had been elected in 1996. While BASA – as it came to be known – aimed to strike an even balance between community sport and elite sport development, the high-performance area ended up receiving the majority of the funding allocation. This has continued to the present. A review of the national government's sports policy is currently under way, a policy framework document entitled *Australian Sport: Emerging Challenges, New Directions*, has been published, and the driver of the review, the Independent Review Panel, is expected to table its report no later than 2010. However, there is little evidence to suggest that it will challenge the existing policy arrangements, which gives priority to elite sport development (Australian Sports Commission 2008b). There is in fact consensus that 1) sport is a vital part of our national culture, 2) it is pivotal to our sense of nationhood, and 3) government should do whatever it takes to sustain our international sporting reputation (Australian Government 2008).

The national government budgeting arrangements

Throughout the 1980s and 1990s the national government budget allocation to sport consistently increased and in the lead-up to the 2000 Olympic Games, had increased from around $90 million per year to more than $150 million per year. However, these figures were inflated by special one-off capital and operating grants to the Australian Olympic Committee (AOC) and the Sydney Organising Committee for the Olympic Games (SOCOG). The BASA policy document, which covered the period 2001/2–2004/5 budgeted for an average annual allocation of just under $125 million a year, which included grants to national sporting organisations and operating funds for the ASC and AIS. The Howard Government made further budget increases in 2006 when it allocated $192 million to sport, which was a record amount. The government's commitment to sports development continued with the election of the Kevin Rudd-led Labor Government in 2007, and although it professed to be government 'for the people', it continued to give priority to elite sport. Indeed, in its desire to see sport continue its role as a flagship for signifying Australia's national identity, it allocated just under $220 million to sport in the 2008/9 budget. This constitutes a serious commitment to maintaining Australia's global sporting status.

The structural arrangements

The AIS is, structurally speaking, part of the Australian Sports Commission. At the same time, it is relatively autonomous in an operational sense, and is organised around a number of functional divisions, the main ones being 1) Sport Programmes, 2) Athlete and Coach Services, and 3) National Programmes.

The foundation division of the AIS is Sport Programmes, and it is this area that drives its training, coaching and competition programmes. While all its elite development programmes were originally delivered at the Canberra centre, many structural modifications were made to the model in the 1980s and 1990s, and now its elite development programmes are provided at both the Canberra site and so-called satellite sites in major cities around the nation. Most of the programmes are residential – that is they require athletes to live on a central site for the duration of the training programme – but some are based around various State Institutes and involve more of a daily commuting experience for its participants. In all, 35 different sports activities are supported by AIS programmes (Australian Sports Commission 2008a: 73).

The residential programmes at the Canberra AIS site include archery, artistic gymnastics, athletics, men's and women's basketball, boxing, netball, rowing, men's soccer, swimming, men's and women's volleyball and men's water polo. The satellite residential programmes are not only held around Australia, but also overseas. Adelaide runs the track cycling, Brisbane offers cricket, diving and squash, Melbourne delivers the golf and tennis programmes, Perth offers men's and women's field hockey, while the road cycling programme is based in Italy.

All other elite sports development programmes are run on a dispersed basis, where the co-ordinating authority may be centralised, but athletes may be located in a number of states, and programmes customised to meet local needs. Most of the athletes in these dispersed programmes are in part supported by their State Sport Institutes, which are administered locally (Australian Sports Commission 2008b). The Australian football programme is administered from Melbourne, the alpine skiing, rugby union, rugby league, women's slalom canoeing, and sailing programmes are administered from Sydney, the softball programme is administered from Brisbane, the sprint canoeing programme is administered from the Gold Coast, while the women's soccer programme is administered from Canberra. The sports programme location arrangements are summarised in Table 29.1 below.

Table 29.1 Australian Institute of Sport Program Locations

Location	Residential: central & satellite	Non-residential: dispersed
Adelaide	Cycling	
Brisbane	Cricket	Softball
	Diving	
	Squash	
Canberra	Archery	Football (soccer)
	Athletics	
	Basketball	
	Boxing	
	Football (soccer)	
	Gymnastics	
	Netball	
	Rowing	
	Triathlon	
	Swimming	
	Volleyball	
	Water polo	
Gold Coast	Flat-water canoe/kayak	Sprint canoe
Melbourne	Golf	Australian football
	Tennis	Winter sports
Perth	Hockey	
Sydney	Slalom canoe	Alpine ski
		Rugby league
		Rugby union
		Sailing

Source: Australian Sports Commission (2008a) *Annual Report 2007–2008*, pp. 187–188

The athlete scholarship arrangements

The key to the success of these programmes is that there is the opportunity for players and athletes to secure scholarships that are awarded to those who are nominated by their national sporting associations. Athletes must submit an application form which is assessed by the appropriate national sporting body, which recommends to the AIS programme directors that an offer be made. The scholarships enable athletes to use all the facilities at the training location, and obtain specialist coaching. Funds are also used to give athletes national and international competition. In the case of residential facilities, accommodation is provided at no cost to the athletes.

In 2002 the AIS supported 25 sports and offered scholarships to 627 athletes, but these figures had increased to 37 sports and 700 students, respectively, in 2008 (Australian Sports Commission 2008a). At any one time there are more than 200 athletes on scholarship. The AIS employs around 70 coaches and a core of sport scientists who offer world standard/best practice training and coaching services. The 2003 ASC grant allocation to AIS scholarships was $15.3 million, but in 2008 had increased to $20.7 million (Australian Sports Commission 2003a, 2008a).

The sport science support arrangements

The Sport Science and Sport Medicine Division has established an international reputation for innovation and technology enhancement. It developed the ice jacket that was used at the Atlanta Olympic Games, and soon after designed the ultra-light carbon fibre track cycle. It also produced a high-altitude training simulator and, more recently, developed swim analysis systems to support the national swimming team. In 2008 the Biomechanics Department established an 'on-field data collection and real-time feedback system' at the Perth Hockey Stadium, and used it to analyse player movements and performance (Australian Sports Commission 2008a: 76). The Sport Science and Sport Medicine Division has also been in the vanguard of drug testing. Working in conjunction with the Australian Drug Testing Laboratory, it developed a test for artificial erythropoietin (EPO) which is a drug commonly used by endurance athletes to illegally improve their performance.

The talent search arrangements

The AIS also has a strong talent search programme. The AIS recognises that Australia's relatively small population of 21 million severely limits the pool from which talented athletes can be drawn and developed, which is estimated to be around 200,000, in contrast to the USA figure of two million (Australian Government 2008b: 3). It therefore makes sense to provide a time-efficient way of locating and identifying young people with the physical attributes and aptitude to become elite athletes. To this end, the AIS in conjunction with national sporting bodies and state sport academies has established a national talent search programme which it has titled the National Talent Identification and Development programme (NTID). The NTID programme has been divided into three stages or phases. In phase one state talent search co-ordinators target secondary schools and, with the assistance of physical education teachers, conduct a battery of screening tests which identify students with outstanding athletic potential. The aim is to locate those young people who are very strong, very fast, very agile, very well co-ordinated, are bio-mechanically superior and have a lot of endurance. In phase two the abilities and aptitudes of students are matched with specific sports to ensure the best possible performance outcome. In phase three students are invited to participate in a talented athlete programme, run by either the national sporting body or the state sports academy.

The talent search programme originated in 1988 when the AIS rowing programme coaches undertook a national search for young athletes who had the attributes to become elite rowers. The programme was so successful that it was extended to include athletics, cycling, canoeing, swimming, rowing, triathlon, water polo and weight-lifting as a fast-track means of training young athletes for the 2000 Olympics. Since then the talent search programme has been consolidated into an integrated initiative that combines AIS leadership with state academy screening of the athletic potential of school students. While the talent search programme has been accused of being overly mechanistic in the way it examines the potential of young athletes, it has delivered a number of successful outcomes. It has recently been extended into regions of high population growth, and has been complemented by an on-line talent identification tool supported by 20 talent assessment centres scattered across regional Australia (Australian Sports Commission 2008a: 83).

The talent search programme brings to the foreground the whole nature/nurture debate, and whether hard work and good coaching can compensate for an average athletic inheritance. According to AIS officials, the key to high achievement is a 'superior genetic foundation' (Drane 2003: 72). In other words, the best coaching will take athletes so far, and the evidence suggests that a young athlete who is not in the top 50 per cent of athletic ability will never reach international standard. On the other hand, recent AIS experience showed that athletically gifted and multi-skilled sports men and women with only limited structured sports experience behind them can reach international standards with intensive and high-quality training. For example, in 1993 Cycling Australia and the AIS developed a pilot talent identification project that focused on South Australian secondary schools. The project discovered a number of talented young cyclists, three of whom went on to become world junior champions. In particular, Alayna Burns gained seventh place in the 3,000 metres individual pursuit at the Sydney Olympic Games. More recently Natalie Bale and Luke Morrison won medals at the world junior championships in rowing and kayaking, respectively. Neither Natalie nor Luke had a long history in these sports.

The ASC-targeted funding arrangements

One of the great strengths of Australia's elite sport development programme is the close relationship that has been built up between the ASC, the AIS and sport's national governing bodies, which are more commonly known as national sport organisations (NSOs). The ASC has a pivotal role in funding the scholarship and high-performance programmes of NSOs, while the AIS provides coaching and sports science expertise. The ASC elite development grant scheme, which is divided into 1) AIS scholarships and 2) allocations to NSO high-performance activities, is especially crucial for the ongoing conduct of elite athlete development programmes by NSOs, and there has been a gradual but significant increase in funding over recent years. Not all sports are funded equally and, in general, those sports that secure the most scholarship and high-performance funds are those sports that have a strong participation base, do not have access to large TV rights fees or gate receipts, but at the same time can deliver success on the international sporting stage. The best funded sports for 2007/8 were swimming ($5.7 million), rowing ($5.4 million), cycling ($5.3 million), athletics ($5.2 million), hockey ($5.0 million), basketball ($4.3 million) and sailing ($3.6 million). The allocations are significantly lower for diving ($1.4 million), golf ($860,000), judo ($468,000), badminton ($185,000) ice racing ($85,000) and fencing ($36,000) (Australian Sports Commission 2008a: 183–84). Table 29.2 provides a

Table 29.2 Sample of national sport organisation funding for elite sport development 2002/3–2007/8

National sporting body	Funding 2002–2003 ($m.)	Funding 2007–2008 ($m.)
Swimming	3.3	5.7
Athletics	2.4	5.2
Rowing	3.1	5.4
Field hockey	2.8	5.0
Cycling	2.4	5.3
Basketball	2.2	4.3
Sailing	2.3	3.6
Soccer	2.1	2.8
Canoeing	2.0	2.9
Volleyball	0.8	2.7
Golf	0.5	0.9
Judo	0.4	0.5
Diving	0.4	1.4
Badminton	0.2	0.2
Ice racing	0.2	0.1
Fencing	0.03	0.04

Source: Australian Sports Commission (2003a) *Annual Report 2002–2003*; Australian Sports Commission (2008a) *Annual Report 2007–2008*

comparison between selected sports, and the changes that have occurred between 2002/3 and 2007/8.

The NSO high-performance programmes are the driving force behind the development of international-standard sporting achievement. They combine scholarships, coaching assistance, sports science advice, access to international-standard facilities, and exposure to elite level competition to optimise the athletes' potential. While each NSO works within the funding guidelines provided by the ASC, they all have their own distinctive approach to high-performance development.

Explaining the targeted funding

When assessing the scholarship and high-performance programmes funded through the Commonwealth Government's sports development policy, the first thing to note is that there has been a continual growth in funding to NSOs over the last 30 years. Whereas in 1980 NSOs were allocated just over $3 million for elite sport development, by 1990 the annual grant – including AIS scholarships – to NSOs had increased to nearly $32 million. The 2002–3 annual grant to NSOs was calculated to be $65 million, with another $4 million going to a variety of sports organisations that serviced athletes with disabilities. For 2007–8 it was a record $74 million. By any measure, and taking into account inflation, this constitutes a massive increase in national government funding of national sporting bodies.

The other striking feature of the government's sports funding policy is that the money is not distributed evenly across the sports sector. Ever since the establishment of the AIS in 1981, a minority of sports have been targeted for funding. When the AIS began its operations, basketball, gymnastics, netball, soccer, swimming, tennis, track and field and weight-lifting were selected for special attention. It was not immediately clear as to why these sports were chosen in preference to some other cluster of national sporting bodies. Swimming and netball were selected because they were sports in which Australia already performed well internationally, but the same could not be said of gymnastics and weight-lifting. Neither was it clear why soccer was preferred over rugby union, rugby league and Australian football. The only sensible explanation was that in this early period of the government's policy arrangements, decisions were based less on evidence and more on political clout and influence. This meant the senior officials of those NSOs with strong policy-maker connections were better able to sustain their arguments for their sports being included in the top eight (Stewart et al. 2004). In the end, all of the 153 available AIS scholarships in 1981 were allocated to these eight sports.

Throughout the 1980s there was a constantly changing set of funding priorities. In 1983 for instance, field hockey was the highest funded sport with an annual grant of $235,000, followed by basketball ($165,000) and athletics ($150,000). The next best funded sports were cricket, Australian football, gymnastics, swimming, tennis, yachting and baseball, with grants of between $100,000 and $140,000 (Australian Sports Commission 1996: 59–62). In 1989 the ASC reviewed its sports priorities and decided to target the seven sports in which it could achieve the best results on the international sporting stage. Basketball, swimming, and track and field were retained, but netball, gymnastics, soccer, tennis, and weight-lifting were omitted and replaced by canoeing, cycling, hockey and rowing.

In 1990 swimming had replaced hockey as the highest funded sport. It received $2.2 million from the Commonwealth Government, while the combined allocation for men's and women's hockey was $2.1 million. Athletics had maintained its favoured status with a grant of $1.9 million, as too did basketball, which attracted $1.7 million of Commonwealth Government funds. The only other sports to receive more than $1 million were cycling ($1.3 million), gymnastics ($1.1 million), netball ($1 million) and canoeing ($1 million). Non-Olympic sports, even where they had a strong participation base were not favourably treated at this time. Cricket, which had many more players than any of the sports listed above, received $610,000, rugby league obtained $193,000, while Australian football, the nation's most popular spectator sport was allocated $200,000. In contrast, volleyball and water polo, which both had relatively low participation levels, received $670,000 and $750,000 respectively (Australian Sports Commission 1991). These anomalies were defended on the grounds that first, professional team sports like cricket, rugby league and Australian football were already financially secure, and second, funds should be targeted to sports that could produce international success. Despite these arguments, there was a groundswell of opinion that funding should be more inclusive (Stewart et al. 2004).

THE CURRENT POSITION

Over the last ten years, there has been a broadening of the NSO funding base for elite sport development, and in 2008 there were 700 scholarships spread across 27 sports. However, when the current funding arrangements for NSOs are closely examined it is clear that the distribution of funds is still directed mainly to a few high-profile sports (Australian Sports Commission 2008a). The first point to be made is that not all sports are eligible for funding. Sporting bodies have to satisfy a number of conditions before they can be eligible to receive grants from the Commonwealth Government. First, they must be recognised as a sport. The ASC defines a sport as any activity involving competition, the use of physical exertion, and the use of skill to achieve a result (Australian Sports Commission 2001). In addition, they must be seen to be the national governing body for a sport, and responsible for the national development of the sport. In addition, they have to satisfy a number of administrative and structural requirements. First, they need to be legally incorporated. Second, they must have an operable strategic plan that covers at least three years. Third, they must have produced an audited financial report for the previous three years, Fourth, they must have links with affiliated associations in at least four states. Fifth, they must have a doping policy that is consistent with ASC guidelines. Finally, they must belong to an international sports federation that is linked to the General Association of International Sport Federations (GAISF) or the International Olympic Committee (IOC), or the sport must have been played in Australia for more that 75 years and have a significant number of participants (Australian Sports Commission 2008a). On the basis of these criteria, some 125 organisations are designated or recognised as NSOs.

However, only 90 of these recognised national sporting bodies are eligible to receive grants from the ASC. To receive a grant for use in high-performance activities and elite athlete development, the NSO must demonstrate that it is internationally competitive, has a broad base of public and media interest, and that the world championships have an international profile. To increase the probability of funding, NSOs need to show that they have in excess of 2000 registered and active participants, have a history of international competition, belong to an international federation that has at least 25 active member countries, have achieved a top 16 result in a world championship, or have been played for more than 75 years in Australia with a sizeable participation base (Australian Sports Commission 2001).

In 2008 the ASC funded 56 NSOs, which means that the remaining 34 eligible sporting bodies were not funded. These 56 funded NSOs were allocated funds from a total elite development pool of $74 million, but when the distributions are analysed it is clear that most of the recipients received only a modest share of the total pool of elite development funds. The bulk of the grants go to ten sports, as Table 29.2 illustrates. In 2008 the top ten NSOs attracted $43 million, or 62% of all grant monies for elite sport development, with the remaining 80 NSOs sharing the balance. As indicated previously, this skewed distribution can be explained by the government's insistence that funding be used to achieve the best possible performance outcomes. While the BASA policy was in part framed by the desire to increase participation, the primary goal was to achieve as much international success as possible. To this end, sports that had a high likelihood of producing world champions, Olympic Games medallists, and Commonwealth Games medallists were given the greatest support. This means there is a strong bias to 1) sports that are represented in the Olympics, and 2) Olympic sports that have a history of delivering top five and top ten finishes.

The bias toward a select number of Olympic sports is put into stark relief when participation rates are compared to funding levels. For example, swimming and hockey receive a combined total of $10.7 million from the Commonwealth Government for elite sport development. By any measure these funds have delivered significant international success. Both the men's and women's teams have consistently been in the world top five, while Australia's swimmers are only marginally less successful than the dominant USA team. However, both have only a moderate participation base of 135,000 and 335,000, respectively. Netball, in contrast, which is not represented at the Olympic Games, has a participation base of around 540,000, but an ASC elite development grant of $2.5 million. The differences between funding and participation are even more marked when sailing and water polo are examined. Both of these Olympic sports are well funded by the Commonwealth Government, receiving $3.6 million and $2.3 million, respectively, in 2008. However, only 88,000 people sail competitively, while the participation level for water polo is no more than 30,000. Rowing is similarly favoured by a sizeable funding arrangement despite low levels of participation. Its $5.4 million elite development allocation makes it the third best-funded NSO, but it governs a sport with only 47,000 participants. Golf, on the other hand, has 650,000 players who participate in an organised setting, but can only attract $850,000 of Commonwealth Government funds in 2008.

The key to understanding the Commonwealth Government funding arrangement for sport is to view it as an exercise in both rational and values-based decision making. At one level there is a clearly defined logic to the funding process whereby sports are targeted for their capacity to produce international successes and medals. At another level the funding process is infected by biases and preferences in which certain sports are seen to be more needy, deserving or appropriate. The funding process is also influenced by the capacity of some NSOs to gain the ear of Ministers and their advisors more than others. This mix of 1) rational, evidence-based decision making and 2) decision making that reflects the political clout of certain segments of the sports policy community, suggests that future funding arrangements will shift in response to a number of factors. First, there will be changing views abut the capacity of different sports to deliver an international profile. Second, there will be changes in the ability of NSOs to convince the Minister that their sport has untapped potential. Finally there will be changing notions of which sports deserve additional support on ethical or equity grounds.

Case studies in elite sport development

Australian sport has been a major beneficiary of the Commonwealth Government's major policy shift in the early 1980s. Nearly 30 years on, Australia has been able to maintain its high international ranking despite a major surge in competition from Europe and Asia. Not only has Australia been able to maintain its reputation for excellence in its traditional fields of strength like swimming and rowing, but has also been able to secure a vast improvement in sports like gymnastics and kayaking. The following cases are provided as illustrations of how Australia's government-led sports development system works in practice, and what results can flow from it.

Case 1: Athletics Australia's high-performance programme

Athletics Australia is one of Australia's most prominent sporting bodies, and track and field in general has an iconic presence in the annals of Australian sporting history (Booth and Tatz 2000). While athletics has a relatively low participation base, it has produced many internationally recognised athletes including Cathy Freeman, a former Olympic 400 metres track champion, Jana Pittman, a former world 4,000 metres hurdles champion, and Steve Hooker, the current Olympic pole vault champion. It is relatively well funded, since it receives an annual grant of nearly $6 million from the ASC. Although it also receives a sizeable sponsorship from Telstra, Australia's largest telecommunication company, its government grant accounts for 78 per cent of its annual revenue (Athletics Australia 2008: 8).

Athletics Australia prides itself on the nationwide spread of its high-performance programme. This has been achieved through a three-tier structure. First, the head coach is located in Sydney under the umbrella of the Australian Olympic Committee. This allows him to work closely with the Australian Olympic Committee, which is an important funding source leading up to the Olympic Games. Second, the high-performance manager is located at the AIS in Canberra, and works closely with the AIS coaching staff. Finally, Athletics Australia provides financial support for the delivery of high-performance coaching and training programmes at each of the State sports academies. While this approach leads to a duplication of coaching programmes, it ensures a high degree of access and opportunity for elite athletes around the nation (Athletics Australia 2008). Most of the high-performance funds support the employment of coaches, but funds are also used to support participation at international competitions, training camps, sports science, medical and physiotherapy services, and direct financial support for selected athletes.

The success of the high-performance programme is measured primarily by the number of athletes who achieve an international ranking. Athletics Australia had been frequently criticised for its inability to produce a solid base of top-ten rankings. When compared to cycling, swimming, and rowing, Australian athletes appear to under achieve. Athletic Australia officials defend its performance by noting that 1) unlike cycling, swimming and rowing, nearly every country in the world has a track and field programme, and 2) the track and field resources have to be spread thinly through multiple running and field event (Athletics Australia 2008: 12). As a result, an athletics top-ten ranking should be weighted more heavily than a similar ranking in any other Olympic sport. However, this argument should not hide the fact that, on the whole, Australian track and field athletes struggle to attain and sustain international excellence.

Case 2: Archery Australia's high-performance programme

Unlike athletics, archery is a minor sport in Australia, and has produced nothing approaching a national sporting hero. It goes virtually unreported until its appearance in the Olympics every four years. At the same time, Australian archers have occasionally achieved international success. There have been four individual world target champions, while in the team events Australia obtained fourth place at the Atlanta Olympic Games and first place in the 1998 world indoor championships.

Australian archers claimed media attention for the first time at the 2000 Sydney Olympic Games when Simon Fairweather won a gold medal. Fairweather's ground-breaking performance set off a chain of events that culminated in archery being invited to participate in the AIS elite athlete programme. In effect, Archery Australia convinced the ASC that, given appropriate support, archery could further enhance Australia's international sporting reputation. The ASC consequently established an archery training centre at the AIS in Canberra, and allocated funds for both AIS scholarships and a high-performance programme. In 2003 $499,000 was allocated to the AIS scholarship programme, while $310,000 was allocated to the high-performance programme. The combined funding increased to just over $1 million in 2008 (Australian Sports Commission 2008a). This additional funding had a number of important impacts on Australian archery. First, it allowed it to not only recruit the services of its head coach, Ki-Sik Lee, a Korean, who was one of the world's leading archery coaches, but also secure another high-quality replacement, Kyo Moo Oh, a former Olympic gold medallist, in 2006. Second, by creating a strong archery infrastructure it provided a national focus for elite development. Third, the scholarships enabled a number of young archers to gain exposure to international competition, sustain high-quality coaching, and ongoing sports science support. Finally, the high-performance funds allowed Archery Australia to appoint a high-performance manager who could co-ordinate the elite development programmes, establish a nationwide talent identification process around regional competitions and tournaments, conduct regular coaching camps, and manage a schedule of international competitions.

Since the 2000 Olympics a number of junior Australian archers have won medals at international competitions, and there is a strong feeling amongst Archery Australia officials that, because of its inclusion in the AIS programme, Australia could achieve a top-five ranking by 2010. The archery case demonstrates that in an internationally competitive sports world, sustained success will only come with government support. In this case, the critical support came in the form of funding to support facility development, the establishment of a centre for training of elite competitors on a full-time basis, a systematic talent identification and development programme, and the appointment of world class coaches.

Concluding comments

It is clear that ever since the AIS opened its doors to Australia's elite athletes in 1981, and the ASC took on responsibility for implementing the Commonwealth Government's radically new sports policy in 1985, there has been a strong bias to high-performance sport, and a low priority given to community sport. While this preference for elite sport development has been criticised for failing to address the disadvantages faced by women, non-English-speaking migrants and aboriginals (Australian Government 2008), it has produced many international successes over many years (Australian Sports Commission 2008b). The AIS, through its capacity to produce so many high-quality players and athletes, has become an international benchmark for elite athlete development. By any measure it constitutes a successful policy initiative, and despite the occasional argument that it takes away scarce resources from important public health and community recreation programmes, sports policy communities have embraced its underlying assumptions and strategic direction. Moreover, the Australian public would not seem to like it any other way.

References

Adair, D. and Vamplew, W. (1997) *Sport in Australian History*, Melbourne: Oxford University Press.
Athletics Australia (2008) *Submission to the Independent Sports Panel*, Melbourne: Athletics Australia.
Australian Government (2008) *Australian Sport: Emerging Challenges, New Directions*, Canberra: Australian Government.
Australian Sports Commission (1991) *Annual Report: 1990–91*, Canberra: Australian Sports Commission.
——(1996) *Annual Report: 1995/96*, Canberra: Australian Sports Commission.
——(1998) *Excellence: The Australian Institute of Sport*, Canberra: Australian Sports Commission.
——(1999a) *Annual Report: 1998–99*, Canberra: Australian Sports Commission.
——(1999b) *The Australian Sports Commission: Beyond 2000*, Canberra: Australian Sports Commission.
——(2001) *Annual Report: 2000–2001*, Canberra: Australian Sports Commission.
——(2003a) *Annual Report 2002–2003*, Canberra: Australian Sports Commission.
——(2003b) *The AIS at a Glance*, Retrieved 15 December 2008 from www.ais.org.au/overview.
——(2008a) *Annual Report: 2007–2008*, Canberra: Australian Sports Commission.
——(2008b) *Submission to the Commonwealth Government's Independent Review of Sport in Australia*, Canberra: Australian Sports Commission.
Blainey, G. (2000) *A Shorter History of Australia*, Sydney: Vintage Books.
Bloomfield, J. (1973) *The Role and Scope of the Development of Recreation in Australia – for the Department of Tourism and Recreation of the Australian Government*, Canberra: AGPS.
Booth, D. (2001) *Australian Beach Cultures: the History of Sun, Sand and Surf*, London: Frank Cass.
Booth, D. and Tatz, C. (2000) *One-eyed: a View of Australian Sport*, Sydney: Allen & Unwin.
Cashman, R. (1995) *Paradise of Sport*, Melbourne: Oxford University Press.
Catley, B. (2005) *The Triumph of Liberalism in Australia*, Sydney: Macleay Press.
Coakley, J., Hallinan, C., Jackson, S. and Mewett, P. (2009) *Sport in Society: Issues and Controversies in Australia and New Zealand*, Sydney: McGraw Hill.
Crowley, F. (1986) *Tough Times: Australia in the 1970s*, Melbourne: Longman.
Daly, J. A. (1991) *Quest for Excellence: The Australian Institute of Sport*, Canberra: Australian Government Publishing Service.
Drane, R. (2003) Full Medal Racket, *Inside Sport*, December, pp. 68–9.
Edwards, J. (2000) *Australia's Economic Revolution*, Sydney: University of New South Wales Press.
Green, M. (2007) Olympic glory or grass roots development? Sport policy priorities in Australia, Canada and the United Kingdom, 1960–2006, *International Journal of the History of Sport*, 24 (7) pp. 143–6.
Green, M. and Houlihan, B. (2005) *Elite Sport Development: Policy Learning and Political Priorities*, London: Routledge.
Hancock, W. (1961) *Australia*, Melbourne: Jacaranda Press.
Houlihan, B. (1997) *Sport Policy and Politics: a Comparative Analysis*, London: Routledge.
Houlihan, B. and White, A. (2002) *The Politics of Sport Development: Development of Sport or Development through Sport?* London: Routledge.

House of Representatives Committee on Finance and Public Administration (1989) *Going for Gold: First Report on an Inquiry into Sports Funding and Administration (The Martin Report)*, Canberra.

——(1990) *Can Sport be Bought: Second Report on an Inquiry into Sports Funding and Administration (The Martin Report)*, Canberra.

Magdalinski, T. (2000) The reinvention of Australia for the Sydney 2000 Olympic Games, in J. Magan and J. Nauright (eds) *Sport in Australasian Society: Past and Present*, pp. 305–22, London: Frank Cass.

Oakley, R. (1999) *Shaping Up: A Review of Commonwealth Involvement in Sport and Recreation in Australia – A Report to the Federal Government*, Canberra: Commonwealth of Australia.

O'Conner, K., Stimson, R. and Daly, M. (2001) *Australia's Changing Economic Geography: A Society Dividing*, Melbourne: Oxford University Press.

Rickard, J. (1988) *Australia: A Cultural History*, London: Longman.

Salt, B. (2003) *The Big Shift: Welcome to the Third Australian Culture*, South Yarra: Hardie Grant Books.

Stewart, R., Nicholson, M., Smith, A. and Westerbeek, H. (2004) *Australian Sport: Better by Design? The Evolution of Australian Sport Policy*, London: Routledge.

White, R. (1981) *Inventing Australia: Images and Identity*, St Leonards: Allen and Unwin.

Part 7

Issues in the practice of sports development

Introduction: Managing complexity and fluidity

Barrie Houlihan

The management challenges within the sports development field are multiple and complex. The variety of target or client groups, the fluidity and frequent lack of specificity of long-term objectives and the variety of delivery mechanisms and agencies make it impossible to identify a particular 'business model' as an archetype. Effective management is particularly daunting in relation to the development of community sport where the extent of variation in the organisational environment is especially great. The chapters in this Part address some of the most pressing issues that face those with management responsibility for service delivery.

Sports development in many countries is synonymous with volunteering, with sports volunteering vying with volunteering in religious organisations or educational institutions as being the most common form of voluntary activity. As Schulz, Nichols and Auld make clear, without the huge contribution from volunteers the infrastructure of sports development would be radically different. Yet as the authors note, there has been relatively little research exploring the particular challenges of managing this invaluable resource. Management approaches in sports clubs tend to be borrowed from classical management theory and a rational systems perspective which, as is made abundantly clear, provide a questionable basis for managing voluntary sports clubs. In arguing for the inappropriateness of the rational systems approach to the management of voluntary sports clubs, the authors examine the distinctive features of volunteering in sports and leisure contexts; they distinguish between long-term regular club volunteering and event volunteering; they examine how expectations vary and the adaptations to management that need to be adopted. In conclusion, the authors remind us that the very concepts of 'managing' and 'being managed' are often antithetical to the concept of, and motivation for, volunteering.

As Brackenridge and Telfer make clear, the abuse of children in a sports context can take a wide variety of forms, many of which, such as sexual violence and rape, would be abuse whether they took place within a sports context or not. However, there are some forms, such as overtraining and playing while injured, which are specific to sport, but which are not specific to young people and are perhaps indicative of a wider malaise within high-level sport. Research into the variety of forms that abuse can take and the extent of abuse within sport has a remarkably short history and the history of the policy response to the abuses uncovered is shorter still. While the authors note the action taken by a wide range of governmental and sports bodies, their most significant conclusions relate to the considerable variation in the acknowledgement of the issue of child abuse in sport and the many aspects of child abuse in sport that remain to be thoroughly researched.

Gray and O'Leary examine a range of legal issues commonly encountered in sports development work and begin by reminding the reader of the particular and, one might add, the peculiar relationship between sport and the law. In general the courts have been reluctant to become involved in sports-related disputes, preferring to leave the settling of disputes to sports organisations or their nominated tribunals such as the Court of Arbitration for Sport. Yet, as the authors note, sports development 'sits on the cusp of general and sports-specific law'. Thus while many aspects of employment law, for example, apply just as clearly to sports development as they do to any other form of employment, much of the practice of sports development – the actual playing of sport – occupies more ambiguous legal territory. The authors provide a valuable initial guide to the foundation of the law as it is likely to affect sports development, as well as illustrations of some of the applications of the law within the sports development field. The primary message of the chapter is to highlight the complexity of the legal framework within which sports development officers and others work and the importance of an awareness of the key legal duties of those involved in sports development.

As Bloyce and Green note, the values that sports development officers bring with them to their role is a neglected aspect of sports development. Given the centrality of the inter-personal relationship between the sport, leader/development officer and the participant to the quality of the experience of sport, this chapter addresses a particularly important issue for policy makers and programme managers. In many respects the range of values expressed by sports development officers reflect the broader tensions within sports development, such as that between an instrumental view of sports participation and an emphasis on the intrinsic value of involvement in sport. However, the degree of heterogeneity should not be exaggerated, as the authors emphasise the 'shared fund of common-sense understandings' and the generally highly pragmatic approach of sports development officers to their role. John Lyle's discussion of 'sport development, sports coaching and domain specificity' provides a valuable complement to the chapter by Bloyce and Green, as it focuses on the experience of the participant and the importance of understanding how the individual progresses through the various stages of participation. As Lyle argues, the design and delivery of effective sports development require an appreciation of the stages of participation and an understanding of the different populations that participate in sport. The chapter concludes with the outline of a coach development model that complements the four main areas of participation – children, general participation, performance development and high-performance coaching.

Biddle and Foster's chapter also emphasises the need for a better understanding of the behaviour and motivations of the participant. Their concern is with the factors that contribute to health-related behavioural change through physical activity and sport and, as such, they address a central priority of much public policy making in relation to sports development. At the heart of the chapter is an examination of the factors that are associated with different levels of physical activity and an evaluation of some of the interventions that have been designed on the basis of behavioural research. The authors conclude that while a number of interventions aimed at the inactive have produced positive effects on behaviour for periods of between six and twelve months, many struggle to show strong longer-term effects.

Iain Lindsey's contribution marks a shift of focus from attempts to understand the values and/ or behaviour of those involved in sports development to a concern with the organisation of the delivery of sports development. As the author notes, partnership working has become ubiquitous within the sports development sector. Growing out of a broadly neo-liberal agenda, the emphasis on partnerships has been criticised as disguising the withdrawal of government from its responsibilities for service provision, but has also been lauded as an important shift in priorities from concerns of the providers (i.e. debates about who should provide) to the concerns of the service user (i.e. whether the service meets the requirements of the user). While Lindsey concludes that partnership working offers potential benefits in terms of greater efficiency and effectiveness, he emphasises the extent to which these benefits require considerable management skills and investment of resources. Of particular importance are financial resources, which Ian Jones discusses in his chapter on funding and sustaining sports development. As is the case in many countries, financial support for sports development from the national treasury is only one of a range of sources of finance – others include lotteries of various kinds, which though controlled by the government are not formally considered public expenditure, and private contributions from sponsorship or match-funding schemes for example. The significance of the introduction of the national lottery in the UK has been substantial, not because it added to the overall amount of finance available, as it is arguable whether the income from the national lottery compensated for the long-term decline in the flow of public finance to sports development through local authorities. What makes the national lottery income so significant is that it is generally money that is unencumbered by long-term commitments and can be used to pump-prime new projects and to leverage additional funds from the voluntary, commercial and public sectors, thus giving government an enhanced capacity to determine the strategic direction of sports development. However, a constant theme in any discussion of finance for sports development is the extent to which the funding is sustainable. As the author notes, the challenge of programme sustainability has received relatively little attention, but remains the most pressing management challenge.

Paul Downward, in the final chapter in this Part, uses economic theory to provide a sharper insight into the nature of market segmentation in the area of sports development and the implications for public sector provision. In particular the author explores the circumstances under which different patterns of provision by sports clubs, government and the commercial sector will emerge, arguing, for example, that clubs emerge in circumstances of market or government failure, and then relates the patterns suggested by the application of economic theory to the actual pattern found in the UK. His conclusion is that market segmentation is the product of the interaction between individual preferences, property rights associated with sport and public policy initiatives. Further, with reference to the role of public policy, he concludes that sports development policy interventions will 'only be successful if [they are] applied to willing parties who are somehow constrained from undertaking the sports that they wish to'.

30

Issues in the management of voluntary sport organizations and volunteers

John Schulz, Geoff Nichols and Christopher Auld

In Australia, Canada, parts of Europe, and the United Kingdom, the provision of sport has a long tradition of reliance on volunteers. Volunteers perform a variety of duties ranging from coaching, maintaining grounds, and providing transportation through to senior management and development roles such as chairpersons, club secretaries, and treasurers. Volunteers come from a variety of backgrounds: some are (ex-)players who wish to pass on the experiences that they received; some are parents supporting their children's involvement; and others are individuals helping their local community (Cuskelly *et al.* 2006a).

Voluntary sport organizations (VSOs) vary considerably in size and complexity. The largest area of sports volunteering activity is within sports clubs run by their members, and the majority of these operate within a governing body structure. In England there are over 100,000 sports clubs run by volunteers, involving over eight million volunteers (Taylor *et al.* 2003). In Australia, over 1.7 million people volunteer in sport and over a third of these contribute 140 hours or more of their time each year (ABS 2009). Research in European countries suggests that between 2.6 per cent (France) and 6 per cent of the population regularly volunteer in sport (see Coalter 2007). Volunteers are important in all facets of the sports governing body structure which may have local, regional, and national levels; even at national governing body level, volunteers play critical roles as administrators and policy makers. The relative importance of paid staff varies considerably between national governing bodies (NGBs): the few wealthy ones, such as the Rugby Football Union in England, employ considerable numbers of paid staff, both centrally and across the country, but small NGBs rely almost entirely on volunteers. In relation to this chapter, the most important feature of volunteering within sports clubs is that the clubs are relatively small and are run by volunteers themselves. Paid staff are most likely at the NGB level and, while their influence over clubs is restricted by the considerable autonomy of the clubs, they have indirect 'control' by directing and implementing policy.

Another important area of sports volunteering is events. These vary far more in size than do sports clubs. The 2012 London Olympics will require 70,000 volunteers; the nearest comparable event in the UK, the 2002 Commonwealth Games in Manchester, required 10,500 volunteers (Ralston *et al.* 2004). However, there are innumerable small local events, run by clubs, local government, or a wide variety of other organizations. Unlike sports clubs, events are more likely to be managed by paid staff. Secondly, they are more likely to involve volunteers whose commitment is restricted by time and event; what has been termed 'episodic volunteers' (Auld 2004).

From an academic perspective, the struggle to manage volunteers and VSOs appears to stem largely from incomplete understandings of what it means to volunteer and the process of managing sports organizations. This chapter explores three 'management' issues currently facing sport: first, the differences between managing VSOs and other types of organizations; second, the differences between managing volunteers and employees; and, finally, the differences in managing episodic volunteers.

What is different about VSOs?

One observation about the management of VSOs is that the volunteers tasked with this role usually have little training or experience to guide their practice. Many rely on popular press management ideas or their own place of business or employment's practices; and assume that the principles of managing for-profit organizations apply to VSOs. Consequently, there is a tendency for VSOs to adopt management processes and approaches developed in for-profit contexts without giving adequate thought to the differences in organizational mission, character and culture. What further clouds the situation is that the public and private sector organizations, who interact with VSOs have a tendency to view practices, evaluate programmes, and offer advice from the perspective of their own organizational practices and experiences, which are far removed from the values and expectations of the members of voluntary-based organizations (see Jeavons 1993; Paton and Cornforth 1991). This confusion creates problems for VSOs, and there is evidence of VSOs being pressured to adopt processes that are not always sustainable or suitable for their operations (Mills and Schulz 2009; Nichols and James 2008; Taylor *et al.* 2003). For instance, Nichols and James suggest that small-sized clubs that currently have informal cultures are not eligible to receive government support unless they adopt more formal operating arrangements. However, many of these clubs do not have sufficient volunteers to do so.

The dominant approach to management in VSOs is to draw on classical management theory and to adopt a rational systems perspective. This approach assumes that the organization is a formal, purposely designed mechanism for the delivery of sport (Slack and Parent 2006). Decisions about the organization's structure and operating procedures are reached from the rational assessment of the organization's needs, goals, and external influences (Morgan 2006; Scott 2003). The two main processes within rational management are setting specific goals and formalization. Specific goals provide criteria for selecting among alternative activities and guide decisions about the organization's structure and design. For instance, they specify which tasks are performed, what kinds of personnel are employed, and how resources are allocated. An organization is formalized when the rules governing behaviour are precisely and explicitly formulated, and when the roles and role relations are prescribed independently of the personal attributes and relations of individuals occupying positions in the structure. Most volunteer training programmes follow this style of management and focus on: setting aims and objectives; defining and formalizing roles and responsibilities, through task or job descriptions and organizational charts; and focusing on strategic and operational plans (see for example McCurley and Lynch 2006). Researchers of VSOs also use these concepts for their analyses. Kikulis and her colleagues (see Kikulis *et al.* 1992) studied change in Canadian sports organizations and how that influenced formalization, goal-setting and decision-making within organizations. Similar research has been undertaken in other countries with a volunteer-based sporting infrastructure (see for instance Greece – Papadimitriou 2002; Norway – Jakobsen *et al.* 2005; Malaysia – Yusof *et al.* 2009; and the UK – Taylor 2004). While this research provides a good insight into the relationship between systems in organizations, there is little evidence to suggest that this style of management is appropriate for VSOs.

The use of a rational systems perspective for the management of VSOs is questionable for a variety of reasons. First, it is difficult for a VSO to identify its aims and objectives. Sporting organizations, at all levels, are expressions of the ideologies and aspirations of the beliefs found within the membership, and are not the value-free instruments of task accomplishment assumed by traditional management approaches (Slack and Thiabult 1988; Whitson and MacIntosh 1988). At a club level, VSOs comprise a variety of internal constituencies (players, relatives, coaches, officials, paid staff and board members) who function together to achieve a variety of, often disparate, goals. At an NGB level, membership comprises of representatives of regional sporting bodies, elected board members and paid staff. In addition to the internal constituencies, VSOs work with external organizations, such as government and third sector organizations, which also represent additional constituencies. Each of these organizations brings different perceptions to the partnership and potentially conflicting expectations of the way other organizations should function and the criteria used for judging effectiveness. Papadimitriou and Taylor (2000) argue that there are clear differences between players, volunteers, technical staff and board members' perceptions of organizational effectiveness of regional and national level sporting organizations. Similarly, Schulz (2005) identified the different management preferences of regional governing bodies' volunteers and paid staff. However, it is not so clear-cut; Auld (1994, 1997) found that the values of paid staff and volunteer committee members are quite compatible, whereas the real difference lies between management committees and ordinary members of clubs. Furthermore, the perspectives of volunteers vary between different size and level organizations, organizations in different geographic locations, and organizations with different access to resources (Amis *et al.* 1995).

Second, followers of rational management approaches argue that the most effective nonprofit organizations are those that ensure a clear separation between governance and delivery (Brooks 2002; Inglis *et al.* 1999). Boards should focus on setting policy goals and leave latitude to staff to deliver the services. However, in sport, especially at the higher governing body level, the policy/implementation split between volunteers and staff is a far too simplistic understanding and does not exist in most organizations. The model does not take into account member representation on the board, nor does it consider board members' involvement in the delivery of the programmes, which is what happens in sport (Auld and Godbey 1998; Hoye and Cuskelly 2003). There is also evidence to suggest that staff have substantial input into policy development, which further clouds the governance and delivery roles (Shilbury 2001). One concern is that the policy/implementation split favours paid staffing arrangements over volunteers in regional and national governing bodies (see Auld 1997; Schulz and Auld 2006). Due to a variety of circumstances, staff often need to make decisions amongst themselves, which eliminates the need for a formal decision-making chain of command. This leaves final approval only symbolically with the volunteer committee. What this creates is a system where policy decision-making is dominated by staff in an NGB, or head offices whose perceptions of the organization may differ markedly from the volunteers in clubs who are left to implement the new policies. In this sense, rational management allows organizations to adopt structures and practices that favour staff opinion and not volunteer capacity. In Canada, the shift in the structure of NGBs, from volunteers supported by professionals, to a structure controlled by professionals and assisted by volunteers was considered by some to be a far more efficient delivery system (Kikulis *et al.* 1992). However, the bureaucracy that goes hand in hand with this type of process jeopardizes the democratic nature of VSOs (Cuskelly *et al.* 2006a) and ultimately reduces a sporting organization's legitimacy in the eyes of players, members, volunteers and parents.

Third, rational management structures are designed to function independently of the current role incumbents and work best with 'average' people. Role descriptions are tightly formulated and individuals are recruited to fill these roles. This process ensures that any turnover of staff does not affect the organization's ongoing performance. Whilst this process appears sensible, unlike other organizations the roles in VSOs need to be more flexible and are usually determined by availability of volunteers and not by experience or organizational need. For instance, many club-level VSOs have a history of a loyal core of volunteers who 'muck in, stay with the organization longer, and take on more duties as other volunteers leave' (Cuskelly *et al.* 2006a: 25). Important roles such as the secretary or treasurer are often filled by people who accept the nomination for the role for the sake of the organization rather than to enhance their own skills or experience (Schulz 2005). Similarly, those who represent the club at regional levels, often do so to support their club. Furthermore, while the relative freedom of volunteers may mean that they are potentially more unreliable than employees (a major concern of some managers – Nichols 2009), some volunteers are exceptionally loyal to their organization. A substantial number of volunteers – 'stalwarts' – have been in a senior administrative position in clubs and on regional committees for many years and make far above the average contribution in terms of hours (Cuskelly and Harrington 1997; Nichols 2005). Rational approaches do not recognize the commitment and loyalty of volunteers and in a way treat volunteers as a simple means for organizations to reach their goals, which can ultimately affect involvement and retention.

Finally, rational management relies on market forces to determine the size of the organization and to sustain the organization. Typically, the cost of production is passed on to clients who then evaluate the price. However, this is problematic in organizations that are funded or subsidized by grants and where the price of the service is determined by what clients can afford. At club levels, the members and volunteers of the club absorb much of the cost of delivery. For example, parents provide transport for children to away games and coaches pay for their own training and accreditation. To complicate matters, the people who are responsible for the delivery of programmes are often beneficiaries of the programme (Pearce 1993). Players are often simultaneously on boards or acting as coaches for teams. As mentioned previously, the sustainability of a VSO is usually determined by availability and generosity of volunteers, rather than the organization's income generation.

Unfortunately, this discussion leaves VSOs with a dilemma. The blanket application of traditional management processes to a VSO is fraught with difficulties and, at present, there are few alternative models or ideas. Despite recent attempts to break down the 'one size fits all' approach to management (Cuskelly *et al.* 2006b) or to criticize it (Nichols and James 2008), rational management approaches appear to dominate the thinking about management of VSOs.

What is different about volunteers?

Similar to the management of VSOs, management theory is often applied and adapted to the volunteer without sufficient regard to the differences between volunteering and employment. Volunteering has to be understood as a leisure activity, which implies it is generally more freely engaged in than paid work. Consequently, 'volunteers are not as dependant on their organizations as are employees, and their independence ... leads to less volunteer subordination to the system of organizational behavior' (Pearce 1993: 128). Therefore, managerial authority is not based on a manager's control over a volunteer's need to earn a wage or to maintain a position in the work-place hierarchy. A refined understanding of volunteering as leisure gives further insight into managing volunteers.

Three types of volunteering as leisure

Volunteering can be thought of as three overlapping types: unpaid work or service, activism, and serious leisure (Billis 1993; Rochester 2006). This can be related both to how volunteers think of themselves, and to how managers think of volunteers.

Unpaid work is the non-profit paradigm commonly adopted by management studies. It reflects an economic model of voluntary work filling a gap left by the private and public sector (Weisbrod 1978). It incorporates an element of altruism, the individuals for whom net costs are most apparently exceeding benefits being the ones most strongly associated with volunteering (Cnaan et al. 1996; Meijs et al. 2003: 20). This way of thinking about volunteering is the closest to paid work and is usually the assumption that underpins the adaptation of human resource management (HRM) theory to volunteers. It tends to lead managers to think of volunteers' rewards, apart from payment, as the same as those of employees (McCurley and Lynch 1998). Although this is an untested research question, it is likely that, if volunteers regard their volunteering as primarily unpaid work, they will expect to be managed in a similar way to paid employees.

Volunteering as activism is where individuals associate freely around a set of shared values. Some have argued that volunteering and activism are different, as one is associated with practical action to improve society (for example, providing sports opportunities for disadvantaged children) and the other is concerned more with political action to change the structure of society (such as campaigning for more resources from government for sports for children, or to reduce social inequalities). In practice, it is difficult to distinguish volunteering from activism, as there is considerable overlap (Musick and Wilson 2008: 23). In both cases volunteers are bound together to promote a common cause, set of beliefs or values. The greater freedom of volunteers to choose volunteering organizations, in contrast to choice of paid employment, means that volunteers' own values are important in directing this choice. Alignment of the volunteers' values to the objectives of the organization will extend to values about how the organization meets those objectives and how volunteers are managed. For example, a volunteer working in an organization to promote the positive development of young people will expect to be treated with the same respect and consideration as the young people they are working with themselves: the means must be consistent with the ends.

A third way of conceptualizing volunteering is as serious leisure, defined by Stebbins (2004: 5) as:

> The systematic pursuit of an amateur, a hobbyist or a volunteer activity sufficiently substantial and interesting in nature for the participants to find a (non-work) career therein acquiring and expressing a combination of its special skills, knowledge and experience.

For Stebbins, volunteer activity is only one type of serious leisure, distinguished from other types by 'its altruism, which invariably propels it', and the 'unselfish regard for another or a set of others' (Stebbins 1996: 219). Within volunteering, a narrower field of activity is defined as 'career volunteering'. This involves sustained voluntary activity, in contrast to a single act or single donation of money. A career in serious leisure will have 'turning points and stages of achievement and involvement' (Stebbins 1997: 119) and is usually connected to an organization. This concept has gained much popularity in leisure studies (e.g. Jones and Symon 2001; Mackellar 2009), and has been applied to groups of volunteers (Cuskelly *et al.* 2003; Nichols and King 1999). This concept is particularity valuable in understanding the very strong ties of many volunteers with the organizations they are connected to: such as the 'stalwart' sports club members mentioned earlier. These volunteers' sense of identity is so bound up with the organization they are volunteering in that they are extremely loyal. These volunteers will also have built up considerable expertise and experience. They will value this being used, but may resent it being disregarded. They may be very resistant to change and may appear to present a problem to succession planning.

As Figure 30.1 suggests, the three circles overlap, and therefore a volunteer could be placed in any one of the seven segments. Current management approaches tend to view all volunteers as unpaid work but, as this discussion has suggested, this may be far from the case. The following section provides an example of the need to adapt an HRM concept when applied to volunteers.

The psychological contract

The psychological contract is a popular HRM concept (Dick 2006; Lester *et al.* 2007; Robinson and Wolfe Morrison 2000; Rousseau and Tijoriwala 1998; Sels *et al.* 2004) that has been

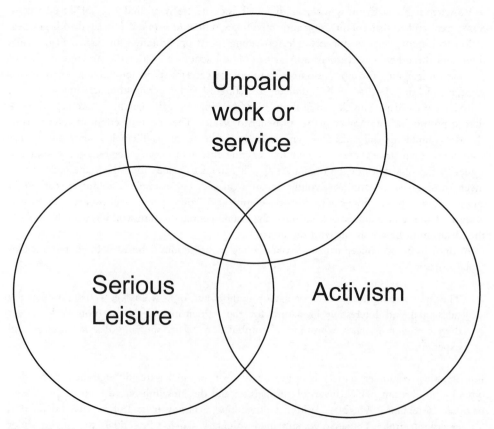

Figure 30.1 Three perspectives on volunteering as leisure (Billis 1993)

applied recently to the management of volunteers (Caldwell *et al.* 2008; Farmer and Fedor 1999, 2001). A psychological contract is 'an individual's belief in mutual obligations between that person and another party such as an employer' (either a firm or another person) (Rousseau and Tijoriwala 1998: 679) and is therefore very subjective. Contracts have been categorized and measured with reference to their content (what employees expect from the employment relationship), their features (covered by adjectives such as 'explicit – unwritten'), or by employees' evaluation (such as the degree of fulfilment or violation). However, its application to volunteers has not sufficiently acknowledged the differences between volunteers and paid staff. Specifically, it seldom considers the difficulties of translating categories of expectations (the content of the contract) from paid work to volunteering; it tends to treat the psychological contract as a tool used by management for control, rather than as an explanation of a relationship; and rarely looks outside the volunteer/management relationship for sources of mutual expectations.

Research by Liao-Troth (2001, 2005) compared the psychological contracts of employees and volunteers with reference to their content (what employees expect from the employment relationship). He concluded (in contrast to Pearce 1983) that the psychological contracts were similar except for the economic benefits – a view consistent with the 'unpaid work' paradigm. Liao-Troth adapted a version of Rousseau's instrument (1998) which measured employees' expectations of the content of their work by their agreement to a set of statements, with responses being measured on a scale. However, while this research found that the expectations of employees and volunteers were similar (the two groups were selected because they were doing similar jobs in the same organization), some of the scale items were difficult to apply in other volunteer situations. For example, when Taylor *et al.* (2006) tried to use the statements used by Liao-Troth (2001) to code interviews with volunteers and administrators of community rugby clubs, they had difficultly relating interview content to some of the statements. In this context statements like 'dress in a professional manner', 'meet minimum acceptable standards for performance', and 'protect confidential information' had little resonance to the experience of volunteers. In addition, 'professional' and 'acceptable' were ambiguous terms, so the meaning to volunteers may vary, and will be different to the meaning attributed by employees. Therefore, in applying the psychological contract to volunteers, one consideration is the usefulness of applying quantitative measures derived from studies of employees. Liao-Troth's research had an objective of comparing employees and volunteers and therefore the measures used had to be the same. However, if the objective was just to understand volunteers, the design of quantitative research instruments could be based on volunteer motivation theory. This was Starnes's (2007) approach in a study of 85 volunteers in 'not-for-profit' organizations in Alabama. Another starting point could be the theory underpinning Figure 30.1. Alternatively, a more interpretative approach could be used such as Smith's (2004) study of volunteers in the Junior League of Chicago, or Ralston *et al.*'s (2004) study of volunteers in the 2002 Commonwealth Games.

A second limitation of adapting the psychological contract directly from HRM applications is that HRM theory is underpinned by assumptions that its function is to help managers achieve their objectives (Pinnington and Lafferty 2003) and that managers have the power and authority to set these objectives. This was explicitly acknowledged in an early application of the concept to volunteer management, it being introduced as a tool that can 'direct employee behavior without necessarily requiring managerial surveillance' (Farmer and Fedor 1999: 351). An implication of this view of management is that in studying employees, it is very rare to juxtapose the expectations of employees and managers (an exception being Dick 2006). One reason for this is that it is difficult to identify exactly whom the employee has a relationship with – they may have a set of different managers (Freese and Schalk 2008). However, more fundamentally, if the object of understanding expectations is managerial control, then managers do not need to know their own expectations – they just need to know the expectations of the employees. As noted above, the assumption that the manager's role is to control may not be as applicable to volunteers because, especially at the level of grass-roots organizations, where volunteers are themselves managers, there is a strong egalitarian ethos. This ethos represents more than just an equality of the way people are treated in an organization. It extends to a greater equality of rights in determining the purpose and objectives of the organization and thus challenges the assumption that these are set entirely by management.

A second reason for juxtaposing expectations of volunteers and managers is precisely because managers will need to adapt their expectations from those of managing paid employees. Managers may have to reappraise their own assumptions about management. The ability of managers to do this will determine their relationship to the volunteers. Thus, Nichols and Ojala (2009) compared perspectives of managers and volunteers at events, and Hagan (2008) compared them in museums.

A third limitation of the psychological contract within the HRM paradigm is that, following the lead of Rousseau and Tijoriwala (1998), it limits its examination of expectations to those derived specifically from the manager–employee relationship. This is common to most applications of the concept since 1998. Once the source of expectations is broadened beyond the manager–employee relationship to 'socio-cultural and institutional influences … from which the psychological contract is derived' (Dick 2006: 46) it makes it harder to identify exactly what these are. However, earlier in this chapter it has been argued that this is relevant to managing volunteers precisely because of the expectations of greater freedom in volunteering as leisure, in contrast to in paid work; and that those expectations will vary according to how volunteering is experienced: as unpaid work, activism or serious leisure.

What is different about event volunteers?

As the previous discussions suggest, the effectiveness of a VSO is often reliant on long-term volunteers; however the viability of many sports events, either large or small, generally depends on the short-term or episodic volunteer. Not only is the involvement of these volunteers critical to underwriting the financial and logistical success of events but event volunteers are amongst the more conspicuous components of an event and are likely to have frequent interactions with participants and/or spectators (Auld *et al.* 2009). Therefore, stakeholder perceptions of event quality and success may be partially dependent on the nature of their experiences with event volunteers.

Despite this apparent importance, and while event volunteers feature prominently in the pre-event legacy rhetoric, this interest fades somewhat rapidly once the event is over (Auld *et al.* 2009). This trend is also reflected in the relatively low level of event volunteer research. Furthermore, much of this research does not fully acknowledge nor address the potential differences between managing continuous versus episodic volunteers. Therefore, event organizers may not be aware of the specific characteristics and requirements of event volunteers and consequently may not always manage their volunteers in a manner appropriate to the context in which they operate.

There is increasing recognition that event volunteers and regular sports volunteers may possess different sets of attributes. For example, Dolnicar and Randle (2007) suggested that volunteers can be segmented according to their motivations and the specific sport context, and Treuren and Monga (2002) argued that event volunteers exhibited significantly different demographic characteristics to those indicated by the volunteering literature. However, Dolnicar and Randle

(2007: 137) also argued that 'data-based studies of variety amongst volunteers seem to be limited'. The main differences addressed by research to date can be broadly categorized into three main areas: motivation, satisfaction, and behaviour (Cuskelly *et al.* 2006a).

Event volunteer motivations

Farrell *et al.* (1998) suggested that sports event volunteer motivations are different to other categories of sports volunteers. Farrell and his colleagues found that event volunteers were more likely to rank external traditions and commitments as less important than were non-event volunteers and therefore it seemed that the specific features of sports events attracted volunteers for reasons that were different to factors that attracted regular or continuous volunteers.

While Slaughter (2002) and Coyne and Coyne (2001) also argued that the motivations of event volunteers were different, they further suggested that such motivations may change over time and were related to the length of time that the volunteer has been involved with the event. Taking their results together, it appears that event volunteer motivations may become more altruistic as time goes on (i.e. perhaps over a period of years), rather than the initial concentration on more personal factors such as social interaction. These findings as well as those of Farrell *et al.* are also reflected in research conducted by Ralston *et al.* (2004) and Reeser *et al.* (2005). Both of these studies not only highlighted motivational factors such as altruism, but also other motivational influences related to the specific characteristics of events such as opportunities to be involved with something 'unique' and interact with elite athletes. Importantly, Reeser *et al.* (2005) concluded that reciprocity was a key motivation for event volunteers, who in addition to those factors outlined above, wanted to be involved in something which benefited not only themselves but also other stakeholders (e.g. event organizers and participants). The perception of volunteering as a reciprocal and fair exchange was recently reinforced by MacNeela (2008: 132) who found that volunteers frequently emphasized the experience 'as a pragmatic choice oriented toward fair exchange' and that such exchanges tended to be characterized as equitable rather than as an obligation.

Cuskelly *et al.* (2006a) summarized the key findings from these studies, suggesting that sports event volunteers tend to be motivated for reasons that differ from regular volunteers; that their motivations may change over time if involved on a regular basis with the same event; and therefore, they should not be perceived or managed as a homogeneous group.

Event volunteer satisfaction

Similar to the motivation research, in the event volunteer context, there has not been a great deal of emphasis on satisfaction research. However, the findings that are available also tend to indicate that event volunteers may exhibit different characteristics to their non-episodic counterparts. The nature of, as well as involvement in, the event appear to be important antecedent factors that influence event volunteer satisfaction (Elstad 1997; Farrell *et al.*1998; Kemp 2002). Other factors include the opportunity to develop networks, experience feelings of job competence, recognition, and the nature and amount of communication between volunteers (Elstad 1997; Farrell *et al.* 1998). Moreover, a number of authors have emphasized the importance of effective management to volunteer satisfaction (Auld and Cuskelly 2001; Kemp 2002; Reeser *et al.* 2005).

The difficulty for event managers, however, is that a number of factors important to event volunteer satisfaction may not be under their direct control (Auld 2004; Auld and Cuskelly 2001; Cuskelly *et al.* 2004; Rundle-Thiele and Auld 2009). Consistent with Herzberg's Two

Factor Theory, Kemp (2002) argued that internal factors only serve to avoid dissatisfaction and consequently, external factors are critical to enhancing satisfaction. Therefore, event managers should concentrate their efforts to increase event volunteer satisfaction on those event elements over which they have some degree of control, especially the nature of the work itself and management practices such as: communication; matching roles and expectations; mentoring; and workloads and rosters. These issues are likely to be especially critical in the event context due to the elevated levels of work pressure associated with inflexible deadlines and the overall highly stressful nature of event management.

Event volunteer behaviour

A number of studies have concentrated on volunteer behaviour in the sports event context especially concentrating on key phases in the event lifecycle, (pre, during and after the event) and how these impact on sustained volunteerism and retention. This research recognizes that volunteer behaviour is a function of the interactions between the dispositional attributes of the individual volunteer and the in situ context of the organization/event and its management protocols (see Penner 2002). Importantly, this research also reinforces the importance of effective management practices in sustaining volunteer involvement and enhancing retention. For example, Harrington *et al.* (2000) found that motorsport event volunteers resented the lack of appreciation and the manner in which they were treated by organizers.

The outcomes from this research clearly suggest that if event managers are to enhance commitment and influence retention behaviour then they must recognize the critical role played by the different event stages and shape their efforts accordingly (Hanlon and Cuskelly 2002; Hanlon and Jago 2004). For example in the pre-event stage, Hanlon and Jago (2004) recommended that such factors as the status and timing of the event, recognition and rewards were critical. Moreover, even at this early stage of the event lifecycle they argued it was important to encourage a sense of autonomy and ownership within the volunteers. Role development, support processes and recognition were crucial in the latter stages.

More recently Auld *et al.* (2009) found that event volunteers want to be able to make a meaningful contribution to the events in which they are involved and this is especially problematic if the event manager over recruits volunteers (in anticipation of high drop-out rates), therefore possibly diminishing the impact that each volunteer perceives they can have. Auld and his colleagues argued that event volunteers should be managed so that they: feel they can commit and contribute to the event (even if it means long hours); are supported by effective training; experience a degree of control over their work environment; and don't feel inconvenienced or taken for granted.

Effective event volunteer management does not just focus on the event implementation phase but begins with the pre-recruitment and orientation phases and extends right through to the post-event (and between events) periods. Thus event managers need to adopt an 'event volunteer lifecycle' approach to ensuring that their volunteers are managed in a manner conducive to influencing satisfaction, commitment and retention. Furthermore, although the external factors 'unique' to the nature of the event itself are important, as argued by Cuskelly *et al.* (2004) and Rundle-Thiele and Auld (2009), managers should not ignore the intrinsic appeal of event volunteering and hence the importance of good management practices. Consequently, managers should focus on enhancing the feelings by event volunteers that they: have the freedom to use their skills; can develop their skills further if required through effective orientation and training opportunities; are able to make a meaningful contribution; can interact with other volunteers, participants and spectators; and are highly valued for their contributions.

Conclusion

As the discussion in this chapter has suggested, managing volunteers and VSOs is very different from managing businesses and employees. Rational management approaches are questionable in a VSO context, the relationship between clubs and volunteers is very different from the manager–employee relationship in other organizations, and even the volunteer management practices for clubs and events differ considerably. Volunteering in sport takes place in clubs, schools, colleges and universities; and takes place in festivals and events. It takes place in organizations that use sport in their programme, and organizations providing opportunities for particular disadvantaged groups. Therefore, a discussion of the management of sports volunteers has to be continually qualified by the type of organization and the motivation and behaviour of its volunteers. A final complicating issue and comment comes from the perspective of many volunteers. 'Management' is not a priority concern and 'many of them find … managerial activities loathsome' (Pearce 1993: 156). The challenge for those people given the responsibility to manage sport clubs and events is to transform current practices and make them meaningful and appropriate for volunteers.

References

ABS. (2009). *Volunteers in Sport*. Report No: 4440.0.55.001, Australia Bureau of Statistics, Australia.

Amis, J., Slack, T., and Berrett, T. (1995). The structural antecedents of conflict in voluntary sport organizations. *Leisure Studies, 14*, 1–16.

Auld, C. (1994). Changes in professional and volunteer relationships. Implications for managers in the leisure industry. *Australian Journal of Leisure and Recreation, 4*, 14–21.

——(1997). Professionalisation of Australian sport administration: the effects on organizational decision-making. *European Journal of Sport Management, 4*, 17–39.

——(2004). Behavioural characteristics of student volunteers. *Australian Journal on Volunteering, 9*:2, 8–18.

Auld, C. and Cuskelly, G. (2001). Behavioural characteristics of volunteers: implications for community sport and recreation organizations. *Australian Parks and Leisure, 4*:2, 29–37.

Auld, C., Cuskelly, G., and Harrington, M. (2009). Managing volunteers to enhance the legacy potential of major events. In Baum, T., Deery, M., Hanlon, C., Lockstone, L. and Smith, K. (Eds), *People and work in events and conventions: A research perspective*. Oxfordshire: CABI (pp 181–92).

Auld, C. and Godbey, G. (1998). Influence in Canadian National Sport Organizations: perceptions of professionals and volunteers. *Journal of Sport Management, 12*, 20–38.

Billis, D. (1993). Organizing public and voluntary agencies. In C. Rochester. (2006). *Making Sense of Volunteering: A Literature Review*. London: Volunteering England.

Brooks, A. (2002). Can nonprofit management help answer public management's 'Big Questions'? *Public Administration Review, 62*, 259–66.

Caldwell, S., Farmer, S., and Fedore, D. (2008). The influence of age on volunteer contributions in a non-profit organization. *Journal of Organizational Behaviour, 29*, 311–33.

Cnaan, R., Handy, F., and Wadsworth, M. (1996). Defining who is a volunteer. *Nonprofit and Voluntary Sector Quarterly, 25*, 364–83.

Coalter, F. (2007). *A Wider Role for Sport*. London: Routledge.

Coyne, B. and Coyne, E. (2001). Getting, keeping and caring for unpaid volunteers for professional golf tournament events. *Human Resource Development International, 4*:2, 199–214.

Cuskelly, G., Auld, C., Harrington, M., and Coleman, D. (2004). Predicting the behavioural dependability of sport event volunteers. *Event Management, 9*, 73–89.

Cuskelly, G. and Harrington, M. (1997). Volunteers and leisure: evidence of marginal and career volunteerism in sport. *World Leisure, 39*, 11–18.

Cuskelly, G., Harrington, M., and Stebbins, R. (2003). Changing levels of organizational commitment amongst sport volunteers: A serious leisure approach. *Loisir/Leisure, 27*, 191–212.

Cuskelly, G., Hoye, R., and Auld, C. (2006a). *Working with Volunteers in Sport: Theory and Practice*. London: Routledge.

Cuskelly, G., Taylor, T., Hoye, R., and Darcy, S. (2006b). *The Advantage Line: Identifying Better Practice for Volunteer Management in Community Rugby Clubs*. A report for the Australian Rugby Union.

Dick, P. (2006). The psychological contract and the transition from full to part-time police work. *Journal of Organizational Behaviour, 27,* 37–58.

Dolnicar, S. and Randle, M. (2007). What motivates which volunteers? Psychographic heterogeneity among volunteers in Australia. *Voluntas, 18,* 135–55.

Elstad, B. (1997). Volunteer perception of learning and satisfaction in a mega-event: the case of the XVII Olympic Winter Games in Lillehammer. *Festival Management and Event Tourism, 4,* 75–83.

Farmer, S. and Fedor, D. (1999). Volunteer participation and withdrawal: a psychological contract perspective on the role of expectations and organizational support. *Nonprofit Management and Leadership, 9,* 349–67.

——(2001). Changing the focus on volunteering: an investigation of volunteers' multiple contributions to a charitable organization. *Journal of Management, 27,* 191–211.

Farrell, J., Johnston, M., and Twynam, G. (1998). Volunteer motivation, satisfaction, and management at an elite sporting competition. *Journal of Sport Management, 12,* 288–300.

Freese, C. and Schalk, R. (2008). How to measure the psychological contract? A critical criteria-based review of measures. *South African Journal of Psychology, 38,* 269–86.

Hagan, J. (2008). *The Volunteer and the Professional – Presence, Development, Policy, and Management.* Dissertation completed as part requirement for the degree of MSc Heritage Tourism Development at University of Sunderland.

Hanlon, C. and Cuskelly, G. (2002). Pulsating major sport event organizations: a framework for inducting managerial personnel. *Event Management, 7,* 231–43.

Hanlon, C. and Jago, L. (2004). The challenge of retaining personnel in major sport event organizations. *Event Management, 9,* 39–49.

Harrington, M., Cuskelly, G., and Auld, C (2000). Career volunteering in commodity-intensive serious leisure: motorsport events and their dependence on volunteers/amateurs. *Loisir et Société/Society and Leisure, 23*:2, 421–52.

Hoye, R. and Cuskelly, G. (2003). Board-Executive relationships within voluntary sport organizations. *Sport Management Review, 6,* 53–74.

Inglis, S., Alexander, T., and Weaver, L. (1999). Roles and responsibilities of community nonprofit boards. *Nonprofit Management and Leadership, 10,* 153–67.

Jakobsen, S., Gammelsæter, H., Fløysand, A., and Nese, G. (2005). *The Formalization of Club Organization in Norwegian Professional Football.* Bergen Open Research Archive. Norwegian School of Economics and Business Administration.

Jeavons, T. (1993). The role of values: management in religious organizations. In D. Young, R. Hollister, and V. Hodgkinson (Eds), *Governing, Leading, and Managing Nonprofit Organizations.* Jossey Bass Wiley.

Jones, I. and Symon, G. (2001). Lifelong learning as serious leisure: policy, practice and potential. *Leisure Studies, 20,* 269–84.

Kemp, S. (2002). The hidden workforce: volunteers' learning in the Olympics. *Journal of European Industrial Training, 26,* 109–16.

Kikulis, L., Slack, T., and Hinings, B. (1992). Institutionally Specific Design Archetypes. A Framework for Understanding Changes in NSOs. *International Review for the Sociology of Sport, 27,* 343–67.

Lester, S., Kickul, J., and Bergman, T. (2007). Managing employee perceptions of the psychological contract over time: the role of employer social accounts and contract fulfillment. *Journal of Organizational Behaviour, 28,* 191–208.

Liao-Troth, M. (2001). Attitude differences between paid workers and volunteers. *Nonprofit Management and Leadership, 11,* 423–42.

——(2005). Are they here for the long haul? The effects of functional motives and personality factors on the psychological contracts of volunteers. *Nonprofit and Voluntary Sector Quarterly, 34,* 510–30.

Mackellar, J. (2009). An examination of serious participants at the Australian Wintersun Festival. *Leisure Studies, 28,* 85–104.

MacNeela, P. (2008). The give and take of volunteering: motives, benefits, and personal connections among Irish volunteers. *Voluntas, 19,* 125–39.

McCurley, S. and Lynch, R. (1998). *Essential Volunteer Management* (3rd edition). London: Directory of Social Change.

——(2006). *Volunteer Management: Mobilizing all the Resources of the Community* (2nd edition). Kemptville, ON: Johnstone Training and Consultation, Inc.

Meijs, L., Handy, F., Cnaan, R., Brudney, J., Ascoli, U, Ranade, S., Hustinx, L., Weber, S., and Weiss, I. (2003). All in the eyes of the beholder? Perceptions of volunteering across eight countries. In P. Dekker and L. Halman (Eds), *The Values of Volunteering: Cross Cultural Perspectives*. New York: Kluwer Academic / Plenum Publishers (pp. 19–34).

Mills, H. and Schulz, J. (2009). Exploring the relationship between task conflict, relationship conflict, organizational commitment, and job satisfaction in Voluntary Sport Organizations in the UK. *Sport Management International Journal, 5*, 5–18.

Morgan, G. (2006). *Images of Organization (3rd edition)*. Newbury Park: Sage.

Musick, M. and Wilson, J. (2008). *Volunteers: A Social Profile*. Bloomington, IN: Indiana University Press.

Nichols, G. (2005). Stalwarts in sport. *World Leisure, 2*, 31–7.

——(2009). Case study: Newham Volunteers – London; England. In K. Holmes and K. Smith (Eds), *Managing Volunteers in Tourism Attractions, Destinations and Events*. London: Elsevier Butterworth-Heinemann.

Nichols, G. and James, M. (2008). One size does not fit all: implications of sports club diversity for their effectiveness as a policy tool and for government support. *Managing Leisure, 13*, 104–14.

Nichols, G. and King, L. (1999). Redefining the recruitment niche for the Guide Association in the United Kingdom. *Leisure Sciences, 21*, 307–20.

Nichols, G. and Ojala, E. (2009). Understanding the management of sports event volunteers through psychological contract theory. *Voluntas International Journal of Voluntary and Nonprofit Organizations, 20*, 369–87.

Papadimitriou, D. (2002). Amateur structures and their effect on performance: the case of Greek voluntary sports clubs. *Managing Leisure, 7*, 205–19.

Papadimitriou, D. and Taylor, P. (2000). Organizational effectiveness of Hellenic National Sports Organizations: a multiple constituency approach. *Sport Management Review, 3*, 23–46.

Paton, R. and Cornforth, C. (1991). What's different about managing in voluntary and nonprofit organizations. In J. Batsleer, C. Cornforth and R. Paton (Eds), *Issues in Voluntary and Non-profit Management*. Workingham, England: Addison-Wesley.

Pearce, J. (1983). Job attitudes and motivation differences between volunteers and employees from comparable organizations. *Journal of Applied Psychology, 68*, 646–52.

——(1993). *Volunteers: The Organizational Behaviour of Unpaid Workers*. London: Routledge.

Penner, L. (2002). The causes of sustained volunteerism: an interactionist perspective. *Journal of Social Issues, 58*, 447–67.

Pinnington, A. and Lafferty, G. (2003). *Human Resource Management in Australia*. Victoria, Australia: Oxford University Press.

Ralston, R., Downward, P., and Lumsdon, L. (2004). The expectations of volunteers prior to the XVII Commonwealth Games, 2002: a qualitative study. *Event Management, 9*, 13–26.

Reeser, J., Berg, R., Rhea, D., and Willick, S. (2005). Motivation and satisfaction among polyclinic volunteers at the 2002 Winter Olympic and Paralympic Games. *British Journal of Sports Medicine, 39*:4, e20.

Robinson, S. and Wolfe Morrison, E. (2000). The development of psychological contract breach and violation: a longitudinal study. *Journal of Organizational Behaviour, 21*, 525–46.

Rochester, C. (2006). *Making Sense of Volunteering: A Literature Review*. London: Volunteering England.

Rousseau, D. (1998). *The Psychological Contract Inventory*. Pittsburgh: Heinz School of Public Policy, Carnegie Mellon University.

Rousseau, D. and Tijoriwala, S. (1998). Assessing psychological contracts: Issues, alternatives and measures. *Journal of Organizational Behaviour, 19*, 679–95.

Rundle-Thiele, S. and Auld, C. J. (2009). Should I stay or should I go? Retention of junior sport coaches. *Annals of Leisure Research, 12*:1, 1–21.

Schulz, J. (2005). Paid staff in voluntary sporting organizations. Do they help or hinder? In Nichols, G. and Collins, M. (Eds), *Volunteers in Sports Clubs*. Eastbourne: Leisure Studies Association.

Schulz, J. and Auld, C. (2006). Perceptions of role ambiguity by chairpersons and executive directors in Queensland sporting organizations. *Sport Management Review, 9*, 183–202.

Scott, W. (2003). *Organizations: Rational, Natural and Open Systems (5th edition)*. Upper Saddle River, NJ: Prentice Hall.

Sels, L., Janssens, M., and Van Den Brande, I. (2004). Assessing the nature of psychological contracts: a validation of six dimensions. *Journal of Organizational Behaviour, 25*, 461–88.

Shilbury, D. (2001). Examining board member roles, functions, and influence: A study of Victorian sporting organizations. *International Journal of Sport Management, 2*, 253–81.

Slack, T. and Parent, M. (2006). *Understanding Sport Organizations (2nd edn)*. Champaign, Il: Human Kinetics Publishers.

Slack, T. and Thiabult, L. (1988). Values and beliefs: their role in the structuring of national sport organizations. *Arena Review, 12,* 140–55.

Slaughter, L. (2002). Motivations of long term volunteers at events. In: Jago, L., Deery, M., Harris, R., Hede, A., and Allen, J. (Eds), *Proceedings of Event and Place Marketing Conference*, Australian Centre for Event Management, Sydney, Australia (pp. 232–52).

Smith, J. (2004). What they really want: assessing psychological contracts of volunteers. *The Journal of Volunteer Administration, 22,* 18–21.

Starnes, B. (2007). An analysis of psychological contracts in volunteerism and the effect of contract breach on volunteer contributions to the organization. *The International Journal of Volunteer Administration, XXIV,* 31–41.

Stebbins, R. (1996). Volunteering: a serious leisure perspective. *Non-profit and Voluntary Sector Quarterly, 25,* 211–24.

——(1997). Serious leisure and well-being. In J. Haworth (Ed.), *Work, Leisure and Well-being.* London: Routledge (pp. 117–30).

——(2004) Volunteering as Leisure/Leisure as Volunteering: An International Assessment. Wallingford, Oxon, UK: CAB International.

Taylor, P. (2004). Driving up participation: sport and volunteering. In Sport England (2004). *Driving up Participation: The Challenge for Sport.* London: Sport England.

Taylor, P., Nichols, G., Holmes, K., James, M., Gratton, C., Garrett, R., Kokolakakis, T., Mulder C., and King, L. (2003). *Sports Volunteering in England.* London: Sport England.

Taylor, T., Darcy, S., Hoye, R., and Cuskelly, G. (2006). Using psychological contract theory to explore issues in effective volunteer management. *European Sport Management Quarterly, 6,* 123–47.

Treuren, G. and Monga, M. (2002). Are special event volunteers different from non-SEO volunteers? Demographic characteristics of volunteers in four South Australian special event organizations. In: Jago, L., Deery, M., Harris, R., Hede, A.-M., and Allen, J. (Eds), *Proceedings of Event and Place Marketing Conference*, Australian Centre for Event Management, Sydney, Australia (pp. 275–304).

Weisbrod, B. (1978). *The Voluntary Non-profit Sector.* Lexington, Massachusetts: Lexington Books.

Whitson, D. and MacIntosh, D. (1988). The professionalization of Canadian amateur sport questions of power and purpose. *Arena Review, 12,* 81–96.

Yusof, A., Omar-Fauzee, M., Abdullah, M., and Shah, P. (2009). Managing Conflict in Malaysian Sports Organizations. *International Bulletin of Business Administration, 4,* 46–50.

31

Child protection and sports development

Celia H. Brackenridge and Hamish Telfer

Children and young people comprise a significant proportion of sports participants, mainly through engagement in school-based physical education and in out-of-school clubs and community programmes (Kirk 2005; Sport England 2010). They are the lifeblood of sport – its future 'playforce' – medallists and recreational athletes, administrators and coaches. Without a healthy and positive foundation in sport this source of talent is compromised. The purpose of this chapter is to explore some of the ways in which children are harmed in sport and the policy goals being pursued to prevent such harms.

The chapter opens by examining definitions of child abuse and protection in the international context and by identifying how these terms form part of a more general discourse that has political connotations. Next, a summary of available knowledge on this subject is provided. The arguments for and against including formal child protection policy and practice in sports development are then considered, followed by an account of child protection policy and practice in sport. The status confusion that often attends notions of 'junior' in sport is discussed, with particular attention paid to how this confusion is compounded at the elite level and the implications this has for child protection. Very few attempts have been made to evaluate child protection in sport but a summary of the available studies is given before some final reflections on a future agenda for protecting child athletes.

What is meant by child abuse and protection?

Violence and abuse to children within their own families was recognised as a problem only in the 1960s and 1970s after medical doctors detected physical signs such as bruising and internal injuries that were inconsistent with accidental falls. The suspicion was that children were being 'battered' in their own homes by their own parents or relatives. This revelation cased public shock since it gave a *public* label to a previously *private* matter. In so doing, it challenged the authority and autonomy of the family, more specifically the father.

Child abuse takes many forms: in the context of sport, the National Society for the Prevention of Cruelty to Children (NSPCC) describes four main types of abuse: sexual, physical and emotional abuse, and neglect (Slinn 2008). Bullying is often added to this list as it is now recognised as a widespread problem, especially in youth settings such as local communities, schools and sport (Brackenridge *et al.* 2006). Whereas many people think of sexual abuse as the most shocking and damaging form of abuse, it is actually neglect and life-threatening physical abuse and violence that often cause more serious, long-lasting damage to individuals.

The United Nations International Children's Emergency Fund (UNICEF) uses the term 'violence' to cover physical, sexual and psychological/mental forms of maltreatment, including abuse and assault. This descriptor has a much wider compass than the term 'child abuse': arguably, it also carries greater discursive and political power. Two important definitions of violence come from Article 19 of the *UN Convention on the Rights of the Child* (United Nations 1990):

> All forms of physical or mental violence, injury and abuse, neglect or negligent treatment, maltreatment or exploitation, including sexual abuse.

and from the *World Report on Violence and Health* (World Health Organization/Krug *et al.* 2002):

> The intentional use of physical force or power, threatened or actual, against a child, by an individual or group, that either results in or has a high likelihood of resulting in actual or potential harm to the child's health, survival, development or dignity.

In the context of sport, violence to child athletes, by either their peer athletes or from authority figures, may be expressed through:

- Discrimination and harassment on the basis of sex, race or sexual orientation
- Sexual violence
- Groomed or forced sex/rape
- Use of pornography
- Sexual degradation
- Sexualised initiations, bullying and hazing
- Physical maltreatment
- Overtraining
- Playing while injured
- Peer aggression
- Parental maltreatment
- Doping/drug abuse
- Alcohol abuse
- Emotional and psychological abuse
- Neglect
- Child labour and trafficking.

(adapted from UNICEF (in press))

'Child protection' is the term given to describe the legal, organisational and cultural system that is designed to prevent children and young people under 18 years old from being abused. When first applied in the education and training work of the National Coaching Foundation (now Sports Coach UK) and various national governing bodies of sport (NGBs) in the UK this term gave rise to some concerns that child protection might be prioritised above the protection of coaches and other adults involved in youth sport: the Australian Sports Commission (ASC) neatly sidestepped this debate by adopting the phrase 'member protection' for their policies (ASC 2004). As with race issues in sport, the terminology adopted by policy makers to describe child protection work is thus a reflection of political tensions and vested interests: these, themselves, reflect wider social debates about threats to the security of adulthood in a late modern society and consequent policy focus on childhood (Parton 2006).

A term closely related to child protection is 'welfare', used as an umbrella description for the overall system of harm prevention, child protection, safety, social and educational services to which all children should be entitled under their human rights. It is a benign-sounding label but one that suffers rather from connotations of need and helplessness associated with the politics of the 'welfare state' (Henry 2001). For many in sport 'welfare' is the antipathy of the rugged individualism associated with striving for athletic success: but it is also a useful general term describing both the nature of services for children and also the ways in which they are delivered. Providing for the welfare of athletes requires integrated delivery of biopsychosocial services and requires that they be regarded as whole people rather than simply performance machines (Leahy 2008).

In the UK, the government has moved away from a narrow conception of child protection towards what is now termed 'safeguarding', a more holistic and proactive approach to children's services, under the policy banner *Every Child Matters* (ECM) (DfES 2004). ECM has five outcomes:

- to be healthy
- to stay safe
- to enjoy and achieve
- to make a positive contribution
- to achieve economic well-being.

These outcomes are of both *intrinsic* benefit to the child (e.g. personal safety and enjoyment) and of *extrinsic* benefit for the state (e.g. make a positive contribution and achieve economic well-being). All elements of civil society that engage with children in the UK – whether from the public, private or voluntary sector, *including* sport – are compelled to pursue these outcomes. Safeguarding of children is thus no longer simply the preserve of social workers, teachers and the family but is *everyone's* responsibility.

All children, whether elite athletes or not, are rights bearers whose best interests are enshrined in the *UN Convention on the Rights of the Child* (David 2005). This is much more than simply a piece of paper, espousing rights-related rhetoric. It is an agenda for change that applies to all aspects of civil society, sport included. It has been signed by all countries (bar the United States of America and Somalia) and its implementation is monitored through a global network of state and non-governmental organisation mechanisms coordinated by the UN Committee on the Rights of the Child. Child protection/safeguarding/violence prevention matters because, without it, there is the possibility that the child's rights will be overlooked or even violated.

What is known about child abuse within sport?

Over the past 10–15 years the sports and exercise science communities have begun to acknowledge the need for research and prevention work on abuse in sport (David 2005; Fasting *et al.* 2003, 2004; Lackey 1990; Volkwein *et al.* 1997). Even so, since research on the topic is so new, relatively little is known about it compared with other social problems such as racism or social inclusion.

Logically, investigations into the nature and prevalence of abuses to athletes have preceded studies of policy impacts. Most of the scientific research on child abuse in sport has therefore concentrated on behaviour rather than policy (Fasting and Brackenridge 2005; Cense 1997; Leahy *et al.* 2002). The research that has been published varies in both quality and scope, yet it is important for empirical data to underpin the development and implementation of abuse prevention policies and for work on abuse inside and outside sport to be brought together in mutually reinforcing ways.

Research into child abuse in sport began by examining various forms of sexual exploitation, especially sexual abuse cases that led to legal action (Brackenridge 2001). However, of the published studies on this subject, very few deal exclusively with abuses to athletes under 18 years of age: some include retrospective accounts by adults of their experiences as child athletes (e.g. Brackenridge 1997; Cense 1997), some include accounts by athletes aged both under and over 18 (e.g. Fasting *et al.* 2003; Leahy *et al.* 2002) and others focus only on adults (e.g. Auweele *et al.* 2008; Volkwein *et al.* 1997).

In recognition of limitations in its own knowledge and policy work, in 2007 UNICEF commissioned a global review of violence against children in sport (Brackenridge *et al.* 2010). That review revealed a number of gaps in knowledge, policy and practice related to violence prevention. For example, the research literature is dominated by studies of sexual abuse with only a few studies of emotional abuse now emerging (such as Gervis 2009; Gervis and Dunn 2004; Stirling and Kerr 2007, 2008) and very little work focussing specifically on physical violence to children. Journalistic and policy items about camel jockeys seem to be the exception here, having led to some changes in regulations for this middle eastern sport (Amodeo 2005; Asghar *et al.* 2005; Shea 2006; The Economist 2002; The Ecologist 2005; UNICEF 2006). There are also reported concerns about children involved in Thai boxing (UNICEF undated.) and bull fighting (Lacey 2007).

Under-researched areas of sports abuse, uncovered by the UNICEF research, include:

- male victims and female perpetrators
- emotional and physical abuse and neglect
- peer abuse/bullying/hazing and homophobic bullying
- female–female abuse
- abuse at the recreational level of sport
- policy links beyond sport, for example, with social work, child welfare groups and probation
- the child's voice, which is absent in most research and policy
- age-specific data
- male–male abuse.

Internationally, progress in relation to research, policy and practice in child athlete welfare has been very variable. The leading countries are listed in Table 31.1 but, even so, very little monitoring and evaluation has been conducted. Policy development in these countries is not thought to have followed these empirical investigations. Finally, large geographic gaps are thought to exist in relation to both research and policy in: Central and South America, Africa, the Middle and Far East, and the Pacific Rim.

Despite the paucity of research, some general trends have emerged from published studies:

- the majority of young athletes do not appear to experience abusive behaviour in their sport
- the higher the level in sport, the greater is the risk of both sexual exploitation and emotional abuse
- child protection and elite performance coaching are sometimes seen to be antithetical
- males, especially coaches, are responsible for most cases of sexual exploitation but both male and female coaches engage in emotionally abusive behaviour
- abusive parent behaviour in sport is very problematic
- there is some evidence that athletes are better able to resist harassment within sport than outside it (Fasting *et al.* 2008)
- sport authority figures appear to present a greater sexual harassment threat to athletes than schoolteachers do to their pupils

Table 31.1 Estimated international progress in research, policy and practice for child protection in sport[1]

Country	Research	Policy	Practice
Australia	Quant and qual	Good	Good
Canada	Quant and qual	Good	Good
UK	Qual (quant pending)	Good	Good
Netherlands	Qual (quant pending)	Good	Good
Denmark	Quant and qual	Limited	Not known
Norway	Quant and qual	Limited	Not known
USA	Some quant	Limited	Not known
Czech Republic	Quant and qual	None	Not known
Belgium	Some quant	None	Not known
Germany	Some quant	None	Not known
Greece	Some quant	None	Not known

Note: 1 Some research has been conducted in Japan and Mexico but this has not been disseminated in the global scientific or policy communities

Several myths about abuse and protection in sport persist:

- that team sports are safer than individual sports
- that touching an athlete in sport is always an unsafe practice
- that athletes in sport with less clothing cover experience more abuse
- that there are some abuse-free sports
- that athletes are in more danger from strangers than those inside sport
- that coaches are the only abusers in sport
- that sport will take care of its own athletes.

Why is child protection policy important for sports development?

Sport is a significant contributor to the economy and has been widely adopted as a mechanism for international development (Gratton *et al.* 2005; Madden and Crowe 1997; Santo 2005). Arguably, however, children's sport has been ignored by international policy analysts, perhaps because it has been thought of as non-serious in relation to weighty issues such as child poverty, malnutrition or HIV/AIDS.

Children's sport has been largely modelled on adult forms, with the transition from novice to elite status following a fairly linear pathway (Lavallee and Wylleman 2000). Most youngsters who show talent and achieve success early on proceed with their chosen sport, unless enticed to switch within performance families, for example from gymnastics to diving, or from cycling or swimming to triathlon.

Generally, success breeds success: it is easier for a promising young athlete to stay in the system than to drop out. But it is also clear that some elite young athletes succeed *despite* rather than *because of* the sporting system. In other words, even if they are unhappy, there is no realistic possibility of such athletes retiring, dropping out, or switching to a different sport or to a less intense performance level. There are complex reasons for this and both social and psychological forces are involved. Social forces include: family pressures, community expectations, national or civic pride. Psychological forces include: sheer habit, fear of failure, desire for social approval or recognition, loss of identity, and fear of the unknown or of retribution. Some elite child athletes suffer unhappiness because they are being abused, either outside or inside their sports environment. For such athletes, the perceived compulsion to stay in sport and yet to remain silent about their trauma can compound the feelings of inadequacy and alienation that have been generated by the abuse.

Sport is regarded by UNICEF as an especially powerful medium for realising the Millennium Development Goals, agreed at the United Nations Millennium Summit in September 2000 (United Nations 2000). These are eight goals that the 192 member states of the United Nations aspire to achieve by the year 2015. Sport is thus conceived as a valuable vehicle for achieving organisational or *extrinsic* goals. But it is also vital that the *intrinsic* merits of sport – pleasure, satisfaction, well-being, fun – are also recognised, for without them the flame of motivation and enthusiasm for sport is likely to be extinguished. Another compelling reason why those working with elite child athletes should pay attention to the *UN Convention on the Rights of the Child* lies in the moral potential of sport. Sport is loaded with expectations about fair play and ethical purity so it is especially hypocritical if sport is simultaneously a site of child abuse and rights violations.

The vast majority of sports participants are young people, many of whom are legally defined as children, that is, under 18 years of age, although a wide variety of ages of consent exists in different countries, ranging from 12 to 21, with further variations between males and females, heterosexuals and homosexuals (AVERT 2009). Most sports structures differentiate between 'junior' and 'senior' competition categories, and some have many intervening layers of age-group sport. Very few neatly divide junior from senior along the same lines as legal definitions. Many among the population of elite athletes are below 18 years old and are thus 'children'. In 'early specialisation' (Coté *et al.* 2007) or early peaking sports these young elite athletes have to manage the responsibilities associated with intense training and competition, including media exposure, travel away from home (often overseas), separation from family support systems and routines, and reliance on adult advisors such as coaches, team managers and medical staff: all of these factors can increase their vulnerability to abuse. So, it is not uncommon for the young elite athlete to be treated like an adult. Conversely, in late peaking sports, elite athletes are often treated as if they were children (infantilised) with controls imposed over their diet, weight, training, sleep, and their social, financial and even sex lives. The age-status confusions associated with elite competition present some of the most difficult policy challenges to sports administrators.

Embedding child protection in sports policy and practice

Several major scandals within sport in the UK during the 1990s – mainly about sexual abuse by male coaches of female and male athletes – led to the establishment, in 2001, of a dedicated Child Protection in Sport Unit, co-funded by the NSPCC and Sport England (Boocock 2002; www.thecpsu.org.uk). The Unit's six-year *Strategy for Safeguarding Children and Young People in Sport* (CPSU 2006b: 3), adopted throughout the sport system, endeavours to set out the safeguarding priorities for sport from recreational to elite level in the run-up to the London 2012 Olympic and Paralympic Games. Before the Strategy only half of national NGBs had adopted a child protection policy. *National Standards for Safeguarding and Protecting Children in Sport* were introduced in 2003 and endorsed by the government (CPSU 2003). By 2006, 45 state-funded NGBs and 29 county sports partnerships had achieved recognition at the first or preliminary level (of three) of these standards (CPSU 2006b: 4). The Standards cover:

- Policy
- Procedures and systems

- Prevention
- Codes of practice and behaviour
- Equity
- Communication
- Education and training
- Access to advice and support
- Implementation and monitoring
- Influencing.

The effect of these standards has been to raise sharply the awareness of sports organisations, coaches and teachers of the many different aspects of welfare that need to be provided if sport is to be safe for young athletes. Associated training, delivered to hundreds of thousands of coaches through the UK, has also had a marked and beneficial impact on coaching practice (Brackenridge 2006; Brackenridge *et al.* 2002, 2003; Woodhouse 2001). The standards provide a clear roadmap for bringing the worlds of sport and child welfare together and demonstrating in practice the values and principles to which signatories to the UN Convention on the Rights of the Child have agreed. However, *some* elite coaches and *some* sports managers have been reluctant to accept these kinds of measures, arguing that they interfere with performance goals or that they apply only to the recreational level of sport (Collins 2006). Indeed, some social commentators argue that child protection in general is a bandwagon that has reduced rather than enhanced children's rights (Furedi 2002; Douglas and Michaels 2004).

The practical consequences of the safeguarding standards in the UK are that NGBs now have policies and procedures in place, have appointed designated welfare or child protection officers at national (and many at club) level and have a host of arrangements for enhancing the safety and well-being of young athletes. In parallel with this, event managers (for camps, tournaments and competitions) also have access to detailed guidance on planning and delivering safe sporting competitions such as the UK School Games, sports development and leadership camps and multi-sports events like the International Children's Games (Kinder *et al.* 2008; Tiivas and Morton 2003). Minimum requirements for all youth sport event venues include:

- A written Welfare Plan
- Codes of Practice for all young people and staff members or volunteers engaged in the event/sessions
- Outlets and resources for counselling and support
- Transport and supervision procedures for children to get to and from the event/sessions
- Health and safety policy and procedures
- Substance misuse policy and procedures
- Photography and media policy and procedures
- Record-keeping procedures (incident forms, referrals, reports, etc.)
- Medical forms for parents/carers and guardians to complete for all children involved in the programme/sessions
- Background/police (safeguarding) checks on all those working or volunteering and who will be in unsupervised contact with children.

If the UK has so many policy provisions for safeguarding young elite athletes, does this reflect a particularly bad record of child abuse and harm in sport? No. It simply reflects that, along with colleagues in Australia (www.ausport.com; ASC 1998a–d), Canada (www.CAAWS.com), The Netherlands (Cense 1997) and a few other countries, the UK has recognised a problem in sport and started to address it by conducting research, promoting advocacy and pursuing policy change. Perhaps the greatest challenge remaining is to embed the principle of athlete participation, not in the physical sense understood in sport but in the *political* sense as used by the UN Committee on the Rights of the Child – that is, giving a voice to the child athlete, then listening and responding to that voice.

Evaluating child protection in sport

Child protection impacts in sport have been measured in football (Brackenridge *et al.* 2003), rugby league (Hartill and Prescott 2007), swimming (Myers and Barrett 2002) and local authority leisure services (Brackenridge 2002), and some work has also been done to evaluate child protection training (Woodhouse 2001).

Prevalence of violence and violence-related behaviour is notoriously difficult to measure, for many reasons. As mentioned above, with little legal, policy or academic agreement about what constitutes violence to children, definitions and age boundaries vary from study to study and country to country. Violence is a sensitive subject, which many victims and most perpetrators are reluctant to discuss or report. Athletes, in particular, are often hesitant to report such problems because of their marginal status or silenced by virtue of this status. For those who do speak out, there may be negative consequences such as being dropped from the team, being isolated by peers or being revictimised by the perpetrator (Cense 1997; Leahy *et al.* 2004).

Research methods issues also help to explain the lack of reliable data in this field. It is difficult to compare studies across cultures because of variations in definition, sampling, ethics and consent, under-reporting and non-response. Ethical research practice stipulates that children cannot consent but merely assent to be research participants and, even then, there is a question over the their freedom to refuse or to speak freely since children's sport is largely adult-controlled (Coakley and Donnelly 1999; Orlick 2006).

Establishing validity and reliability in child abuse research is very difficult (Dahlberg *et al.* 2005). Some researchers use proxy measures to assess prevalence, such as number of child abuse-related hospital visits or number of child abuse-based court convictions, but such measures are rather crude and often underestimate the true scale of violence. Longitudinal studies are the most accurate for obtaining trend data but are also expensive and therefore rare: no such studies are known to have been conducted on child abuse in sport although one incidence study (measuring the number and type of reported cases each year) is available for swimming in England (Myers and Barrett 2002) and another in the same sport is underway.

Sports research on violence suffers from the same limitations as do mainstream violence studies. For example, many of the published studies on the subject do not distinguish between grades of violent behaviour (harassment, physical injury or sexual abuse, for example); some do not differentiate athletes under 18 years old from adult athletes in their research samples; some use legal definitions and others adopt everyday norms as threshold measures (Fasting *et al.* 2000; Leahy *et al.* 2002); and, some do not differentiate on the basis of gender, rendering invisible the gendered nature of violence.

Sports psychologists and sports sociologists approach the study of child violence from different perspectives and thus adopt different methods and tolerances of what counts as violence. For example, some psychology research measures violence as a one-off *event* or perhaps a series of events (number of fouls in a game, number of red or yellow cards issued by a referee) but this can also mask prevalence: sociologists would argue perhaps that violence arises from a (social) *process* whereby unequal power relations are exercised by those with authority over those without it. This might assist with explanation of violence but may overlook the fine details of violent behaviour that are required to underpin successful violence prevention interventions. There are certainly, as yet, no standardised scales by which to measure violence to children in sport.

Street play and adult-free recreation may be the only locations where children have real autonomy over their sport (but even then, they are often under the surveillance of adults). In contrast, children in organised, competitive sport usually lack authority: they are excluded from decision-making and may even have their voices silenced by coaches, assertive parents or carers, or even by senior athletes (Kirby and Wintrup 2002). Participation in sport is therefore defined as a *physical* but not a *political* right and, as a consequence, children are rarely allowed to shape their own competitive sporting experiences and may be subjected to violence if they fail to comply with the wishes of sports authority figures. This exclusion from the right to participation as defined by the United Nations Convention on the Rights of the Child renders children vulnerable to a range of violences, from bullying to sexual abuse, to commercial trafficking (David 2005). As yet, we have virtually no idea of the prevalence, scale or depth of violence to children in sport, or of the consequences of violence for their well-being.

David Banda, from Zambia, has worked and coached in Zambia and Botswana, and has researched HIV/AIDS and sports development projects. He argues:

> There is need for research in issues of abuse in this [sport for development] sector due to the vulnerability of the participants that attend sports sessions organised by sport for development NGOs. This vulnerability is mainly to do with power relations – abuse is always about the misuse of power by those who have more power within the organisation. People that have the 'saviour' decision on ways out of ones' poverty circles.
>
> *(Banda, personal communication 2007)*

Questions about the politics of research apply to most social science projects but they become sharply relevant in the field of sport for development. Almost by definition, the moral direction of sport for development is one of 'doing good'. Widespread use is made of sport as a social and economic panacea – not unlike nineteenth-century rational recreation and Muscular Christianity – and sport for development programmes are packed full of assumptions about their benefits (Coalter 2007). The expectations of sponsors and gatekeepers thus bear heavily on the research manager. No government agency wants to hear that its international development funds have had no positive effect or, worse, may have damaged local conditions. No international peace organisation wants to learn that sport cannot deliver social inclusion, reduce community crime or integrate rival youth groups.

Looking to the future

In summary, factors affecting progress in the development of knowledge about violence and abuse prevention in sport are known, anecdotally, to include:

- level of awareness and political support – some countries are in denial about the possibility of abuse occurring in sport; some regard it as inevitable (a kind of 'casting couch' system for aspiring athletes) and others refuse to sanction research or policy development on the grounds that it would bring sport into disrepute; in other countries the subject remains a taboo one that engenders danger for anyone who dares to raise it in public;

- geography and coordination – language differences mean that information has not been widely shared between countries; the various international sports authorities have only recently begun to acknowledge the issue and it has not therefore appeared on many national sports research or policy agendas;
- definitions and legislative requirements between and within countries – ages of consent vary very widely, making it difficult to arrive at a common set of concepts of athlete welfare and protection;
- resources – many countries have very limited resources for sports development and prefer to channel these into performance enhancement (e.g. coaching or talent identification) rather than research on violence prevention;
- links to international federations – not all sports delivery agencies are affiliated to international sports federations. Even those that are do not necessarily have to conform to agreed standards of child welfare or protection;
- ability to share (confidential) information between and within countries and organisations regarding offenders – there is no agreed protocol in sport for the sharing of information between nations about alleged or convicted offenders, meaning that some former coaches with convictions for sexual abuse of athletes, for example, have been able to move inside and between countries and to continue coaching;
- human rights orientation – notwithstanding the almost-universal acceptance of the UNCRC, different countries adopt very different operational interpretations of children's rights in sport, leading to a wide spectrum of cultural practices and norms. In short, what is regarded as child abuse in sport in one country might be regarded as normal elite coaching in another (David 2005).

Child abuse and exploitation is a familiar theme in the international development and social policy literature (UNICEF 2006; Heinemann and Verner 2006), but it has yet to be recognised in many of the major international child welfare organisations or in mainstream academic sources dealing with sport. Only within the past few years have international agencies accepted the need for international standards for the welfare and protection of child athletes. This has begun to change with, for example, the publication of an IOC Consensus Statement on Sexual Harassment and Abuse in Sport in (IOC 2007) and the commissioning of the UNICEF global review of violence to children in sport (Brackenridge *et al.* 2010). Further, under the auspices of its Medical Commission, the IOC is also developing a model of athlete protection for athletes at the Youth Olympic Games (Margo Mountjoy, IOC Medical Commission, personal communication, December 2008). Through a combination of international and NGO pressure, and partnerships between agencies working for children and for sport, the safety and welfare of child athletes is at last beginning to find its place in sports development policy and practice.

References

Amodeo, C. (2005) 'Hope for child camel jockeys', *Geographical*, 77(3): 6.
Asghar, S. M., with Farhat, S. & Niaz, S. (2005) *Camel Jockeys of Rahimyar Khan: Findings of a participatory research on life and situation of child camel jockeys*, Peshawar, Save the Children Sweden, Pakistan Programme.
Australian Sports Commission (2004) *Supporting sport: Member protection*. www.ausport.gov.au/supporting/ethics/member_protection. Retrieved 30 Dec 2008.
——(1998a) *Harassment Free Sport: Guidelines for Sport Administrators*, ACT: ASC.
——(1998b) *Harassment Free Sport: Guidelines for Sport Organisations*, ACT: ASC.
——(1998c) *Harassment Free Sport: Guidelines for Athletes*, ACT: ASC.
——(1998d) *Harassment Free Sport: Guidelines for Coaches*, ACT: ASC.

Auweele, Y.V., Opdenacker, J., Vertommen, T., Boen, F., Van Niekerk, L., De Martelaer, K. and De Cuyper, B. (2008) 'Unwanted sexual experiences in sport: Perceptions and reported prevalence among Flemish female student-athletes', *International Journal of Sport and Exercise Psychology*, 16(4): 354–65.
AVERT (2009) *Worldwide Ages of Consent*. www.avert.org/aofconsent.htm. Retrieved 1 Jan 2009.
Banda, D. (2007) *Child Protection Issues*. Personal communication, Oct 2007.
Boocock, S. (2002) 'The child protection in sport unit', *Journal of Sexual Aggression*, 8(2): 99–106.
Brackenridge, C.H. (1997) '"He owned me basically": Women's experience of sexual abuse in sport', *International Review for the Sociology of Sport*, 32(2): 115–30.
——(2001) *Spoilsports: Understanding and Preventing Sexual Exploitation in Sport*. London: Routledge.
——(2006) 'Measuring the implementation of an ethics initiative: Child protection in Scottish sport', *Commonwealth Games International Conference*, Melbourne, Australia, 10–13th Mar.
——(2002) '"So what?" Attitudes of the voluntary sector towards child protection in sports clubs', *Managing Leisure – An International Journal*, 7(2): 103–24.
Brackenridge, C.H., Bringer, J.D., Cockburn, C., Nutt, G., Pawlaczek, Z., Pitchford, A. and Russell, K. (2002) *Child Protection in Football Research Project 2002*. Unpublished report to The Football Association.
Brackenridge, C.H., Cockburn, C., Collinson, J.A., Ibbetson, A., Nutt, G., Pawlaczek, Z., Pitchford, A. and Russell, K. (2003) *Child Protection in Football Research Project 2003*. Unpublished report to The Football Association.
Brackenridge, C.H., Rivers, I., Gough, B. and Llewellyn, K. (2006) 'Driving down participation: Homophobic bullying as a deterrent to doing sport', in: C. C. Aitchison (ed.) *Sport and Gender Identities: Masculinities, Femininities and Sexualities*. London: Routledge, pp. 122-139.
Brackenridge, C.H. Fasting, K., Kirby, S. and Leahy, T. (2010) *Protecting Children from Violence in Sport: A review with a focus on industrialized countries*. Florence: United Nations Innocenti Research Centre Review, www.unicef-irc.org/publications/pdf/violence_in_sport.pdf.
Brackenridge, C.H. *Exercising Rights: Preventing Violence against Children in Sport*. Florence: UNICEF Innnocenti Research Centre.
Canadian Association for the Advancement of Women and Sport (CAAW+S), www.caaws.ca (n.d.)
Cense, M. (1997) *Red Card or Carte Blanche. Risk Factors for Sexual Harassment and Sexual Abuse in Sport. Summary, Conclusions and Recommendations*. Arnhem: Netherlands Olympic Committee*Netherlands Sports Federation/TransAct.
Child Protection in Sport Unit (2006) *Strategy for Safeguarding Children and Young People in Sport*. London: NSPCC.
——(2003) *National Standards for Safeguarding and Protecting Children in Sport*. London: NSPCC.
——(n.d.) www.thecpsu.org.uk
Coakley, J.J. and Donnelly, P. (1999) *Inside Sports: Using Sociology to Understand Athletes and Sport Experiences*. London: Routledge.
Coalter, F. (2007) *A Wider Role for Sport: Who's Keeping the Score?* London: Routledge.
Collins, T. (2006) 'The experience of elite coaches and child welfare', presentation to a one day conference on *Safeguarding the Elite Child Athlete*, hosted by Brunel University and the NSPCC, London, 4th May.
Coté, J., Strachan, L. and Fraser-Thomas, J. (2007) 'Participation, personal development and performance', in N.L. Holt (ed.) *Positive Youth Development Through Sport*. International Studies in Youth Sport. London: Routledge. pp. 34–46.
Dahlberg, L.L., Toal, S.B., Swahn, M. and Behrens, C.B. (2005) *Measuring Violence-related Attitudes, Behaviors, and Influences among Youths: A compendium of assessment tools*. 2nd ed., Atlanta, GA: Centers for Disease Control and Prevention, National Center for Injury Prevention and Control.
David, P. (2005) *Human Rights in Youth Sport: A critical review of children's rights in competitive sports*. London: Routledge.
Department for Education and Skills (DfES). (2004) *Every Child Matters*. London: HMSO.
—— (2004) *Every Child Matters: Change for Children*. Department for Education and Skills: London. DfES/1081/2004.
Douglas, S. and Michaels, M. (2004) *The Mommy Myth: The idealization of motherhood and how it has undermined all women*. New York: Free Press.
Fasting, K. and Brackenridge, C.H. (2005) 'The grooming process in sport: Case studies of sexual harassment and abuse', *Auto/Biography*, 13(1): 33–52.
Fasting, K., Brackenridge, C.H. and Sundgot-Borgen, J. (2000) *Females, Elite Sports and Sexual Harassment. The Norwegian Women Project*. Oslo: Norwegian Olympic Committee.

——(2003) 'Experiences of sexual harassment and abuse amongst Norwegian elite female athletes and non-athletes', *Research Quarterly for Exercise and Sport*, 74(1): 84–97.

Fasting, K., Brackenridge, C.H., Miller, K.E. and Sabo, D. (2008) 'Participation in college sports and protection from sexual victimization', *International Journal of Sport and Exercise Psychology*, 6(4): 427–41.

Furedi, G. (2002) *Paranoid Parenting: Why ignoring the experts may be best for your child*. Chicago: Chicago Review Press.

Gervis, M. (2009) *An Investigation into the Emotional Responses of Child Athletes to their Coaches' Behaviour from a Child Maltreatment Perspective*. Unpublished doctoral thesis, Brunel University.

Gervis, M. and Dunn, N. (2004) 'The emotional abuse of elite child athletes by their coaches', *Child Abuse Review*, 13(3): 215–23.

Gratton, C., Shibli, S. and Coleman, R.J. (2005) 'The economics of sport tourism at major events', in Higham, J. (ed.) *Sport Tourism Destinations: Issues, opportunities and analysis*, Ch. 17, pp. 233–47. Oxford, Elsevier Butterworth-Heinemann.

Hartill, M. and Prescott, P. (2007) 'Serious business or "any other business"? Safeguarding and child protection policy in British rugby league', *Child Abuse Review*, 16(4):237-251.

Heinemann, A. and Verner, D. (2006) *Crime and Violence in Development: A literature review of Latin America and the Caribbean*. World Bank Policy Research Working Paper No. 4041. http://ssrn.com/abstract=938907.

Henry, I.P. (2001) *The Politics of Leisure Policy*. 2nd ed. Basingstoke: Palgrave.

——(2005) *Consensus Statement on Training the Elite Child Athlete*. Available at http://multimedia.olympic.org/pdf/en_report_1016.pdf. Retrieved 1 Nov 2007.

Kinder, E., Brackenridge, C. and Tiivas, A. (2008) *Model Safeguarding Standards – Where do coaches fit in?* Unpublished document prepared for a UNICEF.UK Sport Workshop, 27 Feb.

Kirby, S. (1986) *High Performance Female Athlete Retirement*. Unpublished doctoral thesis, University of Alberta, Edmonton, Canada.

Kirby, S. and Wintrup, G. (2002) 'Running the gauntlet: An examination of initiation/hazing and sexual abuse in sport', *Journal of Sexual Aggression*, 8(2): 49–68.

Kirk, D. (2005) 'Physical education, youth sport and lifelong participation: The importance of early learning experiences', *Physical Education Review*, 11(3): 239–55.

Krug, E.G. *et al.* (Eds) (2002) *World Report on Violence and Health*. Geneva: World Health Organisation.

Lacey, M. (2007) 'Child matadors draw olés in Mexico's bullrings', 19th Nov, *New York Times*. www.nytimes.com/2007/11/19/world/americas/19bullfight.html?_r=1. Retrieved 2 Jan 2009.

Lackey, D. (1990) 'Sexual harassment in sports', *Physical Educator*, 47(2): 22–6.

Lavallee, D. and Wylleman, P. (2000) *Career Transitions in Sport: International perspectives*. Morgantown, WV: Fitness information Technology.

Leahy, T. (2008) 'Biopsychosocial support systems and the role of the sports scientist', speech to the annual conference of the British Association of Sport and Exercise Sciences, Brunel University, 4th Sep.

Leahy, T., Pretty, G. and Tenenbaum, G. (2004) 'Perpetrator methodology as a predictor of traumatic symptomatology in adult survivors of childhood sexual abuse', *Journal of Interpersonal Violence*, 19: 521–40.

——(2002) 'Prevalence of sexual abuse in organized competitive sport in Australia', *Journal of Sexual Aggression*, 8(2): 16–36.

Madden, J.R. and Crowe, M. (1997) *Economic Impact of the Sydney Olympic Games*. Report of a collaborative study by NSW Treasury and the Centre for Regional Economic Analysis, New South Wales Treasury Research & Information Paper, TRP 97-10, Sydney.

Mountjoy, M. (2008) personal communication, December 2008.

Myers, J. and Barrett, B. (2002) *In at the Deep End: A New Insight for All Sports*. London: NSPCC.

Orlick, T. (2006) *Cooperative Sports and Games: Joyful Activities for Everyone*. Champaign, IL: Human Kinetics.

Parton, N. (2006) *Safeguarding Childhood: Early Intervention and Surveillance in a Late Modern Society*. Basingstoke: Palgrave Macmillan.

Pinheiro, P.S. (2006) *World Report on Violence Against Children*. Details at www.violencestudy.org. Retrieved 14 Nov 2007.

Hartill, M. and Prescott, P. (2007) 'Serious business or "any other business"? Safeguarding and child protection policy in British rugby league', *Child Abuse Review*, 16(4): 237–51.

Santo, C. (2005) 'The economic impact of sports stadiums: Recasting the analysis in context', *Journal of Urban Affairs*, 27(2): 177–92.

Shea, N. (2006) 'Robot camel jockeys', *National Geographic*, 208(5): 2.

Slinn, N. (2008) *Safeguarding Children in Sport: A Guide for Sportspeople*. Leeds: NSPCC/Coachwise.

Sport England (2010) *The PE & Sport Strategy for Young People*. www.sportengland.org/support–advice/ children_and_young_people/PESSYP.aspx. Retrieved 26 Mar 2010.

Stafford, I. and Balyi, I. (2005) *Coaching for Long-term Athlete Development*. Leeds: Coachwise.

Stirling, A. and Kerr, G. (2008) 'Defining and categorizing emotional abuse in sport', *European Journal of Sport Science*, 8 (4): 173–81(9).

——(2007) 'Elite female swimmers' experiences of emotional abuse across time', *Journal of Emotional Abuse*, 7(4): 138.

The Ecologist. (December 2004/January 2005) 'Outsourcing 2: Robots to Qatar', *Ecologist*, 34(10): 8.

The Economist (2002) 'The camel jockeys of Arabia', *Economist*, 31 August, 364(88): 32.

Tiivas, A. and Morton, J. (2003) *Safe Sport Events*. London: Child Protection in Sport Unit/NSPCC.

UNICEF (undated) *Children and Thai Boxing*. Unpublished internal document.

United Nations. (2000) *Millennium Development Goals*. www.un.org/millenniumgoals/ 2000. Retrieved 2 August 2007.

——(1990) *Convention on the Rights of the Child*. Geneva York: United Nations.

Volkwein, K., Schnell, F., Sherwood, D. and Livezey, A. (1997) 'Sexual harassment in sport: Perceptions and experiences of American female student-athletes', *International Review for the Sociology of Sport*, 23(3): 283–95.

Woodhouse, T. (2001) *Impact Study of the NCF Good Practice and Child Protection Coach Education Workshop*. Unpublished report, University of Gloucestershire/Sports Coach UK.

32

Legal issues in sports development

James T. Gray and John O'Leary

Law and sport enjoy a fascinating relationship. Although it may be true to say that 'the law of the land never stops at the touchline' (Grayson and Bond 1993) it is also true that the application of legal rules to sport has resulted in some juridical redefinition. For example, a fight on the street raises issues of criminal and civil liability, whilst the same activity undertaken under the auspices of, say, the World Boxing Council, might be considered boxing and enjoy a limited immunity from the law that bears no close philosophical scrutiny.

Legally speaking, sports development sits on the cusp of general and sports-specific law. For instance, issues relating to employment and discrimination are firmly in the domain of ordinary legal principles. On the other hand, those legal principles applied to sporting activity enjoy an increasingly noteworthy position for the sports development officer.

As sports development spans an increasingly wide range of social activities, it is subject to a broader range of legal principles – too many to be covered in a chapter of this nature. As a result, the object of this chapter is a limited one: to give the reader a general understanding of the law as it applies to certain elements of sports development and offer some practical guidance on its application. The first part examines the foundation of the law. The second part examines the application of the law to sport and recreation. Although the chapter focuses on the law of the United Kingdom, special reference is made to examples from the United States where legal issues relating to facilities and risk assessment are more developed and could be a harbinger of which sports development officers should be cognizant.

The foundation of the law

The law relating to sports and recreation participants

One of the most significant issues facing sports development is the effective management of participant health and safety during sports activities (although this is not to deny the importance of this concern to sports workers as well). Sport and recreation-based injury or illness, may occur at any time before, during and after competitions or practices and it is vital that those people working in the sports development field are aware of their legal duties and responsibilities. To the non-lawyer, legal liability issues seem frightening and may prompt the organisers of sport and recreation to question whether any physical or competitive activity is a risk worth taking. Fortunately, there are many legal decisions that confirm the value of sport and recreation within society and these decisions also provide useful guidance as to how legal liability can either be avoided or reasonably managed.

In general, accidental injury and illness are usually dealt with through the law of negligence, whilst the deliberate infliction of injury is addressed by the law relating to civil trespass to the person or the criminal law. For sports development officers, civil law can be understood in the context of the risk of financial loss when sponsoring or organising sports and recreation activities. Criminal law, on the other hand, can be viewed as the government's method to punish wrongdoing, through fines and imprisonment. Both the civil and criminal law has been interpreted to protect the health and safety of people engaged in sports and recreation opportunities.

The law of negligence can provide a useful checklist for those involved in sports development. A successful negligence action may be brought against a defendant sport and recreation provider if all of the following elements are proven:

- A duty of care is owed by provider to user.
- The provider has breached that duty owed to the user.
- The breach of that duty by the provider caused the damage sustained by the user.
- There was damage suffered by the user.

If any one of these elements is not proven, the defendant sports and recreation provider will not be held legally liable for the alleged negligent conduct. As a general rule, the law works on the basis that individuals owe a duty of care to other individuals to 'avoid acts or omissions which you can reasonably foresee would be likely to injure your neighbour'. This statement by Lord Atkin in the landmark case of Donoghue v Stevenson (1932) has become the foundation on which the tort of negligence is based. Today, assessing specifically whether someone is your 'sport and recreation neighbour' has become a complex legal issue. For instance, the leading authority in identifying 'legal neighbourliness' is Caparo Industries plc v Dickman (1990) which requires the courts to ask three questions:

1. Was the damage reasonably foreseeable?
2. Was there a relationship of proximity between the defendant and the claimant?
3. Is it just, fair and reasonable to impose a duty in this situation?

A classic example of the interaction between sport and legal duties arose in the case of Alcock v Chief Constable of South Yorkshire (1991). This case concerned the 'nervous shock' suffered by friends and families of those killed as a result of the Hillsborough disaster. The House of Lords restricted the duty in nervous shock cases to those who had close familial and geographic proximity to the victims in order to limit legal actions against the South Yorkshire Police. This case illustrated that the law neither imposes liability in all situations where a sports and recreational injury occurs nor for all types of injury. Liability is limited to those people whom the sports development officer should reasonably have had in mind when contemplating the reasonable risks of sports and recreation activity.

There is no question, however, that sporting activities conducted under the auspices of sports development officers would usually satisfy the above test. Sports development officers and, those under their direction, will owe a duty to those undertaking sports and recreation activities. The courts are sympathetic to the pressures and demands on government agencies in providing sports and recreation opportunities for the benefit of its citizens. As a result of this public policy position, courts would usually refute the idea that government agencies would owe a duty for policy decisions related to the offering of sports activities. Courts, however, might be willing to accept that a duty exists at the operational stage (X v Bedfordshire County Council 1995). This distinction is best explained thus. Sports development officers' decisions relating to the offering (or not) of sport or recreation services (policy decisions) are likely to be non-justiciable whilst responsibility for the way an activity is arranged or executed (the operational stage) may well be subject to judicial scrutiny.

The establishment of a duty relationship then leads to the next question. Was there a breach of that duty? The standard imposed by the law would be of the 'reasonable sports development officer' (Woodroffe-Hedley v Cuthbertson 1997). It is important to appreciate that, by reasonableness, the law evaluates how the reasonable sports development officer might act in a given circumstance and not what the 'perfect' sports development officer would do. For instance, in Bolton v Stone (1951) a woman struck by a cricket ball hit out of the ground was unable to recover from her injuries. While a cricket ball had been hit out of the ground on a few previous occasions, this occurrence was judged by the court to be infrequent. This reasoning led the House of Lords to conclude that the ignoring of such a risk was a course of action that the reasonable cricket club might have taken and, therefore, was considered reasonable under these circumstances. The duty is owed to users individually and so may vary according to the needs of a particular person. For example, greater care is owed to disabled sports participants (Morrell v Owen and Others 1993) or those who are young or new to a sport (Smoldon v Whitworth v Nolan 1997).

However, the inexperience, or lack of expertise, of a sports development officer actually controlling the activity would not be a satisfactory defence. While the law may anticipate a lower standard of care during the 'heat of sport and recreation activity' (Wooldridge v Sumner 1963) the law would not protect the organisers of an event who would be expected to carry out all reasonable steps to ensure the health and safety of participants. Of course, the practical ways of achieving this may vary between sports development officers. For example, the safe distance for spectators to stand during an activity can vary from sport to sport. While spectators could be safe while standing closely to competitors during a golf competition, the same would not be true during a rugby match. If the issue is one of the appropriateness of a particular technique, arrangement or method then expert witnesses (who could be former competitors, coaches, or administrators) can be called to establish the suitability of the methods used when a sport and recreation-based injury or illness is sustained (Bolam v Friern Hospital Management Committee 1957). Examples of where legal liability may be imposed on sports and recreation providers could include:

- a failure to provide adequate first aid and emergency treatment (Watson v British Boxing Board of Control 2001);
- inappropriate sports equipment (especially safety equipment such as pads, gloves, helmets, etc);
- inappropriate facilities, for example, pitches fit for play;
- inadequate supervision;
- competitive sport based on unequal strength, size and ability of the competitors;
- inappropriate training and medical examinations.

The standard test for causation is the 'but for' test (Devon County Council v Clarke 2005) which operates as a way to connect the breach of duty to the resulting damage. For example:

- But for 10-year-olds playing football with 16 year olds this injury would not have occurred.
- But for playing rugby on a frozen pitch this injury would not have been sustained.

By applying the principle of 'res ipsa loquitur' (the thing speaks for itself – see Ward v Tesco Stores 1976) the court may require the organisers of sport to prove how they acted reasonably rather than relying on the claimant to show how they had not. For example, assume a child is injured by another child swinging a hockey stick. On a subsequent occasion another child is seen swinging a hockey stick and the supervisor takes no action. The court may impose liability on the organisers for the earlier incident (even though there was no evidence on that occasion that the supervisor was negligent) on the basis that the subsequent occurrence evidences negligent practices. Causation is also a useful legal means for establishing limits of legal liability. An injury of a type that is an unforeseeable consequence of the organisation or operation of an event will not usually be subject to liability (The Wagon Mound No.1 1961). Assuming the claimant is able to prove all of the three elements of negligence, damages in the form of financial compensation will be payable for the injuries or harm sustained.

The deliberate (intentional) infliction of harm is dealt with by criminal law or the civil tort of trespass to the person (depending on whether the action brought is criminal or civil). The criminal law is, however, a reluctant actor when it comes to on-field offences because it is often difficult to distinguish what is within (and, therefore, outside) the playing culture of a particular sport. Sports workers are unlikely to become embroiled in criminal actions by one participant against another unless they are deemed to be conspiring with the offender (an unlikely scenario). Bullying by a sports worker is unlikely to involve the criminal law unless the bullying is of a physical nature. Bullying is likely to be an ongoing issue for sports development officers and there is a need to be able to distinguish between those forms of support and encouragement that are legitimate and those that cross the line into intimidation.

The criminal law however has less difficulty in its applicability when the alleged behaviour is of a sexual nature. Sports development staff should be highly attuned to possible claims of sexual impropriety. The policy of the Amateur Swimming Association, for example, is that swimming instructors should not make physical contact with children during swimming lessons. Care needs to be taken to ensure that appropriate policies are adopted in relation to issues such as the photographing and videoing of swimmers.

Although the coach/organiser/convenor of the event may be held directly liable under these principles, liability may also be imposed on sports providers under the principle of vicarious liability. Those ultimately responsible for the activity will be held liable for those volunteers and employees (deemed to be 'servants' for the purposes of legal liability) who are acting in the course of the organisers' business on the grounds that they are more likely to have the capacity to compensate. This places the sports development officer in a difficult position. If the person actually carries out the activity in breach of the instructions imposed on them by the organiser it is likely that the organiser will still be held vicariously liable (they are still, after all, carrying out the duty even if they are doing so in an unauthorised manner – see Rose v Plenty 1976). The organiser would need to show that the person in breach was acting outside of their 'employment' in order to escape legal liability. This places a particular burden on the sports development officer to ensure that volunteers and employees act in accordance with their instruction. For example, a coach detailed to teach touch rugby may, against strict instruction, teach rugby tackling to a group of children. It is likely that the organisers would be held liable for any injuries sustained. The coach was not acting outside his employment, merely doing his job in an unauthorised manner. In practice, this means that sports workers cannot 'wash their hands' of responsibilities for participant injury (be it physical, emotional or sexual – see Lister v Hesley Hall 2002) even if the primary responsibility for the injury lies with a third party.

The law relating to sport and recreation-based employment

The full range of employment law issues relating to sports development is worthy of a handbook in its own right. The purpose of this section, therefore, is to provide a general overview of some of the more important issues. For an additional, more detailed analysis, reference should be made to a sports text (Gardiner *et al.* Sports Law) or employment law text (Smith and Thomas 2009). This section begins with an overview of employee rights and qualification. It then considers specific issues relating to sports development.

Many important duties and obligations flow from the establishment of an employer–employee relationship. For example, employees have a right to a maximum working week and holidays and holiday pay (Working Time Regulations 1998), maternity (Employment Rights Act 1996) and paternity entitlements (Employment Act 2002), a safe place of work (common law and the Health and Safety at Work Act 1974), and a redundancy payment (Employment Rights Act 1996). They also have the right not to be wrongfully (common law) or unfairly dismissed (Employment Rights Act 1996) as well as to be treated fairly regardless of race, sex, disability, age, sexual orientation, and religion (Equality Act 2010). The more general issues of discrimination in the execution of a sports development officer's work will be considered later. Issues surrounding this contractual nexus will be important, not only for the relationship between the sports development officer and her employer, but may also be important in the regulation of the relationship between the sports development officer and others 'employed' to deliver sporting activities on their behalf.

Identifying when an employment relationship exists is a crucial question and one that has confounded the courts for over one hundred years. This is not an issue that should unduly concern the sports development officer who will usually have an established, conventional employment relationship with his or her employer. The difficulty is that, in the opinion of the courts, it is the 'relationship' that is crucial and not the 'documentation' (employment contracts do not have to be in writing) or the 'labels' the parties give each other. Hence, it is not beyond the realms of possibility that a 'volunteer' helper may be considered an employee by the courts. So, one of the key aspects of legal knowledge in this area is the ability to conduct relationships with others safe in the understanding of whether an employer–employee relationship is being established. It may seem rather bizarre to the non-lawyer that the law does not have a simple definition of who is, exactly, an employee. Such is the wide range of relationships and diverse activities undertaken within those relationships that the best the law can offer are important factors in indentifying when this relationship does exist. Top of this list is the authority or control (over what and how the person carries out their duties – see Yewens v Noakes 1880) and mutuality of obligations (the mutual ties that bind typical employment relations – see O'Kelly v Trusthouse Forte 1984), but other factors such as exclusivity, tools of the trade, profit and loss also play a part in some leading judgements (Market Investigations v Minister of Social Security 1969). For example, a worker considered as casual labour might be considered an employee by the courts if work is offered on a regular basis, a uniform is provided, holiday entitlement is given or if there develops a mutual reliance between the parties (Carmichael v National Power plc 1999). Or an hourly paid worker coaching football practice to a number of groups on an ongoing basis may be considered differently to 'employed' sports development staff but may possess equal employment status in the eyes of the law.

An employee acquires some legal rights on employment (such as anti-discrimination rights) but unfair dismissal rights, for example, are not acquired until the employee completes one year of continuous employment (Employment Rights Act 1996). Again, an employment law text will detail employment rights and qualification periods (see the references as cited above).

The law regulating part-time employment is also important when considering the appointment of non-regular employees. For instance, the Part-Time Workers (Prevention of Less Favourable Treatment) Regulations 2000 state that part-time employees can expect the same terms, conditions and benefits as full-time employees. This would include staff development opportunities in the form of training courses, etc.

It is in the nature of sports and recreation development that some of the work will take place outside normal working hours and those involved in sports development need to be flexible in response to a diverse range of expectations. Even though it may not be specifically stated in any written terms, the courts are likely to imply terms relating to travel in association with work (mobility clauses – see Courtaulds Northern Spinning Ltd v Sibson 2004) as well as the need to work 'unsociable' hours (e.g. evenings and weekends – see Johnson v Nottinghamshire Combined Police Authority 1974). Courts will also imply a need for flexibility in terms of the changing nature of the employment (Cresswell v Board of Inland Revenue 1984). This would mean that those employed in sports and recreation development would be expected to upgrade their expertise and vary their activities according to market demand. It is unlikely that sports development personnel who were required to change the nature or scope of the programmes they deliver would later be able to claim unfair dismissal or redundancy (on the grounds that the contract is now not what the parties may have originally agreed. See Chapman v Goonvean & Rostowrack China Clay Co Ltd 1973). Needless to say disharmony is best avoided when clearly stated, written terms of employment are given to each employee on commencement of their employment with the sports development agency (that each employee should receive a statement of particulars of employment is a statutory requirement under the Employment Rights Act 1996).

In addition, 'Respect' is an important concept in the law of employment. Respect is owed by the employer to the employee and vice versa. 'Disrespect' on the part of either party could be subject to legal action (Woods v W.M. Car Services Ltd 1982). Disrespect by employees either towards the employer or the client could amount to a dismissible offence, and by the employer to the employee to constructive dismissal (also, interestingly, by the failure on the part of the employer to react appropriately to disrespect shown by a client to the employee – see Western Excavating v Sharp 1978). A common example of lack of respect is the use of foul or abusive language directed at an employer or client (Isle of Wight Tourist Board v Coombes 1976). This is important since coaches, athletes, and sports and recreation administrators may use abusive language as a motivational tool.

Discrimination in the provision of sport

For the purposes of this section discrimination refers to bias between sports development staff and their clients. Please refer to the law relating to employment for an overview of the impact of discriminatory work practices by sports development employers (see recommended texts above).

United Kingdom discrimination law works on the basis of 'equality of opportunity' rather than 'positive discrimination' which is just another form of discrimination. This is not a consistent principle worldwide. For example, South Africa and Malaysia both operate systems of 'positive discrimination' in team selection. An example of this might be the use of racial quotas in team selection. With respect to sex discrimination issues, the United States federal government passed Title IX of the Education Amendments of 1972 (Section 20 U.S.C. §§1681–88). This law provides, in pertinent part that, 'no person in the United States shall, on the basis of sex, be excluded from participation in, be denied the benefits of, or be subjected to discrimination under any educational program or activity receiving Federal financial assistance.' Since sport and recreation is considered part of the American educational experience from grade school to university, these opportunities are subject to the provisions of Title IX. However, this American federal law does not apply to sports and recreation development organisations so long as the membership of these associations has traditionally been limited to persons of one sex and principally to persons of less than 19 years of age. Organisations specifically exempted from Title IX include the Young Men's Christian Association, Young Women's Christian Association, Girl Scouts, Boy Scouts, and the Camp Fire Girls §1681 (a)(6)(B).

Difficulties arise when national anti-discrimination laws conflict with the purposes and philosophy of sport. For example, should a sports development officer refuse permission for a pregnant woman to play netball? How should a football coach deal with heading practice when the group includes, say, a Muslim girl or Sikh boy? Should boys and girls be segregated to play touch rugby? In which dressing room should a transsexual change? The legal answer to these issues must be to allow the widest participation possible and to make the necessary accommodation to promote this ideal. One area where the law is clear is covered by s.195 of the Equality Act 2010, 'A person does not contravene this Act, so far as relating to sex, only by doing anything in relation to the pratication of another as a competitor in a gender-affected' (s.195(1)).

The application of the law to sport and recreation

Like museums, libraries, and airports, sports and recreation facilities are a public reflection of the community that is often responsible for planning, designing, financing, and operating these edifices. Sometimes, a visitor's first impression of a sports and recreation facility, and its host municipality, is a lasting one. Further, for many people their first encounter with a sport-based competition or event is the facility. For example, spectators will make snap judgements regarding the facility's accessibility, its comfort, and its sight lines of the competition. Further, people will quickly determine if facility food and beverages suit their tastes and their budget. Much of the foregoing will shape how visitors react to a town or city, and how its inhabitants understand themselves and its environs.

Additionally, a facility's worthiness can be evaluated during times of crisis. For instance, the word 'Hillsborough' will always be associated with tragedy and disaster. Similarly, 'Munich' will forever be tainted with terrorism and 'Atlanta' connected to bombings. Facility and event negligence, which consists of the legal elements of duty, breach, cause and harm, is applied when the health and safety of competitors, spectators and sport-based personnel are at stake.

Ongoing sports facility and event challenges pertain to issues of inclusion and sustainability. As it pertains to inclusion, since the passage of the Americans with Disabilities Act in 1990 (ADA), United States-based facilities and events are required to provide 'reasonable accommodations' for the disabled. During the last 20 years, numerous lawsuits and, plenty of legal commentary, established the parameters of reasonable accommodations. For instance, to prove a Title III ADA claim a plaintiff must establish the following: 1) the individual is disabled; 2) the sport business is a 'private entity' operating a 'place of public accommodation'; 3) the person is denied the opportunity to 'participate in or benefit from services or accommodations on the basis of disability'; and 4) that reasonable accommodation could be made which does not fundamentally alter operations of the sport business, its event, or its competition (American with Disabilities Act, ADA Title III Technical Assistance Manual, Covering Public Accommodations and Commercial Facilities). In the United Kingdom similar principles operate with a need to show a (legal) disability on the part of the claimant and the need to make reasonable adjustments on the part of the defendant.

A new development within the sports and recreation facility industry has been 'sustainability'. Given the recognised fragility of the earth to absorb waste along with its limited capacity to provide energy resources at its current level, many within the sports and recreation facility industry have recognised that venues should be 'sustainable'. It is anticipated that, as energy costs remain high for consumers and the amount of waste associated with facilities and events continues to be significant, identifying 'environmentally friendly' and 'economically efficient' strategies is imperative for venue operators. Further, it is anticipated that sustainability initiatives will become increasingly subject to legislative regulation, judicial scrutiny, media commentary, and public awareness (Yessin 2006).

Sports venue leadership for the twenty-first century

Leadership is vital to managing sports or recreation facility legal liability. Effective leadership can motivate facility and event staff members to maximise their abilities in order to perform their assigned tasks correctly. Given the demanding legal challenges, along with lucrative business opportunities for venue and event operators, leadership is crucial in assisting any organisation in running its venue efficiently and effectively. In addressing issues relative to health, safety, disability, and sustainability, facility owners, and their executive team, should possess the ability to lead within a changing sport, legal and business environment (Vecchio 1997).

Leadership, as is the case with sports and recreation facility law, is constantly evolving. Similarly the study of leadership, and that of the law, continues to be interpreted by many, and has been redefined by scholars and practitioners on an ongoing basis for centuries. While tomes of leadership commentary are available, for purposes of this chapter, leadership will be defined as one's ability to effectively cope with change. For instance, there are 10 leadership characteristics connected with change that are applicable to sports and recreation facility and event legal issues. Leaders are expected to:

- manage the dream;
- embrace errors;
- encourage reflective backtalk;
- encourage dissent;
- possess the Nobel Factor (optimism, faith, and hope);
- understand the Pygmalion effect in management (if you expect great things, your colleagues will give them to you – stretch, don't strain, and be realistic about expectations);
- have the Gretzky Factor (a certain 'touch');
- see the long view;
- understand stakeholder symmetry;
- create strategic alliances and partnerships.

(Bennis 1994)

471

James T. Gray and John O'Leary

Applied sports and recreation facility leadership – the communication and legal dilemma

As the abovementioned leadership traits are applied within a sports and recreation facility and event legal setting, possessing competent communication skills, in order to apply these 10 leadership characteristics, is paramount. While it may appear obvious, one should recognise that communication can usually be verbal or written. However, commonplace verbal and written communication skills may have unintended consequences in an increasingly digital world. For example, there is an expectation by many within society, and perhaps it is an unreasonable one, that communication should be provided 'on demand'. With the advent of mobile telephones, texting, videophones, 'Blackberry', 'Twitter', and 'Instant Messaging', there may not be sufficient time to either reflect on one's words or enjoy the ability to retract one's communication given the permanency and memory capacity of electronic mail and recording devices. Instant leadership communication is a 'double-edged sword' where it could avert or minimise legal liability for a sports or recreation facility and event (i.e. providing reasonable medical treatment to a spectator injured during a sports event), while this same leadership communication technology can create a legal record to prove facility legal liability (i.e. failure to observe reasonable standard operating procedure for the treatment of spectator medical injuries).

The legal aspects of sports and recreation event management and organisation

When planning and organising a sports event, there should be a reasonable opportunity to identify and assess the goals associated with it. During this initial assessment period an adequate amount of time should be allocated for sports and recreation facility and event organisers to engage in a strengths, weaknesses, opportunities and threats ('SWOT') analysis. Initially created by American professor, Albert S. Humphrey, a SWOT evaluation helps to identify the 'internal' strengths or accomplishments and the 'internal' weaknesses or challenges of a sports event organisation. For instance, this analysis can identify the experience and expertise of those planning a sports event or managing a facility. It can also elicit an examination of the 'institutional history' pertaining to a specific sports event and its planning, and enhance the development of a collective continuity or memory connected with event and facility planning.

When applying a SWOT analysis to the external opportunities and 'external' threats segments it should account for all relevant social, cultural, economic and political forces found outside an organization. For instance, an external threat could be an economic one such as insufficient funding for an event when discretionary income is limited due to economic uncertainty. From a legal perspective, this lack of funding may hinder the event's ability to provide a safe environment for a competition or to provide reasonable medical treatment for injuries sustained during a sports event. Similarly, examples of external opportunities could include community goodwill and favourable media exposure derived from the staging of a successful sports event. These opportunities could result in contracts to renew financial sponsorship support, or providing 'in-kind' assistance such as computer software facility advice, or event product donations such as food and beverages (Coate 2007).

One of the legal challenges connected with event organisation is that it requires sufficient sports event and facility skills and relevant planning attributes. This experience requires one to understand sports event and facility legal history in order to reasonably predict future legal challenges. This demand, in sum, can be simultaneously invigorating, frustrating, empowering, and unsettling for those involved in the legal aspects of sports event and facility planning.

Strategic planning and organisation does have its pitfalls both from a business and legal perspective. Amongst the biggest impediments to successful planning and organisation are the following:

- Top management assuming that it can delegate its planning function, and, thus, not become directly involved.
- Top management becoming so involved in current problems that it spends insufficient time on planning. As a consequence, planning becomes discredited at lower levels.
- Failing to clearly define and develop enterprise goals as a basis for formulating long range goals.
- Failing to adequately involve major line managers in the planning process.
- Failing to actually use plans as a standard for assessing managerial performance.
- Failing to create a congenial and supportive climate for planning.
- Assuming that comprehensive planning is something separate from other aspects of the management process.
- Creating a planning programme that lacks flexibility and simplicity and fails to encourage creativity.
- Top management failing to review and evaluate long-range plans that have been developed by department and division leaders.
- Top management making intuitive decisions that conflict with formal plans.

(Sawyer 2005)

The legal aspects of sports facility and event risk assessment

Risk assessment includes the ability to identify risks, classify risks, and plan to either prevent or react to risks. The primary goal of risk assessment is to eliminate, transfer or reduce the prospective monetary losses while effectively managing a sports facility or event. The 'DIM' process is one way that risk assessment can be applied in the sports setting. This process involves three elements: 1) developing the risk management plan, 2) implementing the plan, and 3) managing the risk management plan (Nilson 2003).

The DIM method of risk assessment is a flexible framework useful for any facility or event ranging from youth football grounds to municipal basketball stadia and from community fitness centres to public golf courses. With respect to developing a sports and recreation-based risk management plan, identifying risk or issues is paramount. For instance, if one is unable to recognise a problem, then the risk of incurring legal liability becomes greater. In other words, within the sports and recreation facility and event setting, ignorance is certainly not bliss. In fact, negligence law demands that sports and recreation providers carry out their duty to provide a safe environment for all within their purview. Risk identification can be accomplished by performing surveys of spectators, completing inspections of facilities, or conducting interviews with employees connected with sports facilities or events.

In classifying threats, one could adopt a risk assessment matrix where dangers can be categorised by frequency such as 'often', 'average', and 'seldom', as well as recognising the severity of harm such as 'high loss', 'moderate loss' and 'low loss'. For instance, a 'low loss' with 'often frequency' could be a beverage spill at a concession stand. A 'high loss' with 'seldom frequency' occurrence could include the death of a spectator or a competitor. Once the classifications of risks and its assessment are completed then one should decide to avoid, transfer or retain the risk identified (Griffiths 2005).

Within sports facility and event risk assessment the transfer of risk usually involves the use of two types of insurance – 'Personal Injury Liability Insurance' and 'Property Insurance'. Personal injury liability insurance can provide protection when a person is injured such as a spectator, a participant or an employee. However, one should recognise that there are financial limitations found in insurance policies based on each occurrence and in aggregate. For instance, a policy may pay a maximum of US$250,000 for each occurrence with a maximum of US$1 million during the policy term. In addition, insurance policies should be understood as a contract with agreement negotiated as to term, premiums and exclusions. Exclusions serve as protection for insurance companies when explicit events or occurrences are specifically eliminated from coverage. These exclusions can be based on geography (i.e. domestic coverage only, no international application available) or events (i.e. no coverage for scuba diving, but coverage extended to beach volleyball injuries) (Zevnik 2004).

As it pertains to the implementation of the risk assessment plan, communication is crucial. In other words, a plan that remains on a shelf collecting dust and is otherwise ignored, is wasted effort and enhances legal liability exposure. To achieve effective communication, employees should be made aware of the plan and empowered to implement it, or suggest changes to it as needed. For instance, holding periodic half-day continuing education seminars during employment time is best practice in reducing or eliminating legal liability.

In managing the plan, a 'command and control' system should be established where an individual or a committee possesses authority to lead and motivate those who are expected to implement and monitor the plan. Further, people should be convinced to embrace the plan and be encouraged to recommend amendments, as required, when sport-based legal issues either evolve or change.

Conclusion

Many sports development officers love sport and recreation. It is their passion. It is the reason why they entered the industry and do their jobs. Further, they are entrusted by their communities with the mission of providing safe sports and recreation opportunities in an inclusive, welcoming environment where all can develop, grow and enjoy. Similarly, the law, as applied to sport and recreation, has been interpreted by the courts, legislators, and legal commentators, as a system to simultaneously protect the health and safety of participants, employees and providers as much as reasonably possible.

In order for sports development officers to realise all their professional potential while fulfilling the legal duties owed to their communities and constituents, ongoing continuing sports and recreation legal education should be recognised and implemented. In this regard, sports and recreation providers should incorporate sports and recreation law seminars into their daily operating procedures. This risk prevention mindset is wonderfully highlighted by the American author and inventor, Benjamin Franklin, who once famously said: 'An ounce of prevention is worth a pound of cure'. His eighteenth-century counsel is as sound now, as it was then.

Leadership is crucial in maintaining a legally sound sport and recreation-based risk management strategy. For instance, a manual that is neither read nor used is a waste of time and money. Instead, effective leadership would encourage sports and recreation development officers to cultivate their ability to identify problems or issues before they occur while using the manual for the basis of their analysis.

Similarly, leadership should foster excellent communication between and amongst sports and recreation providers, employees and participants. This type of communication should become 'routine' to the extent possible. For example, scheduled meetings between management and employees as well as using participant surveys can be a means to maintain communication between various stakeholders. In sum, the adage of 'two heads are better than one' describes that, when a spirit of cooperation is present, legal problem solving is augmented.

References

Cases

Alcock v Chief Constable of South Yorkshire [1991] 1 WLR 814

Bolam v Friern Hospital Management Committee [1957] 2 All ER 118

Bolton v Stone [1951] 1 All ER 1078

Caparo Industries plc v Dickman [1990] 2 WLR 358

Carmichael v National Power plc [1999] WLR 2042

Chapman v Goonvean & Rostowrack China Clay Co Ltd [1973] 1 WLR 678

Courtaulds Northern Spinning Ltd v Sibson [2004] ICR 451

Cresswell v Board of Inland Revenue [1984] ICR 508

Devon County Council v Clarke [2005] EWCA Civ 266

Donoghue v Stevenson [1932] AC 562

Isle of Wight Tourist Board v Coombes [1976] IRLR 413

Johnson v Nottinghamshire Combined Police Authority [1974] 1 WLR 358

Lister v Hesley Hall [2002] AC 215

Market Investigations v Minister of Social Security [1969] 2 QB 173

Morrell v Own and Others [1993] The Times 14th December

O'Kelly v Trusthouse Forte [1984] QB 90

Rose v Plenty [1976] 1 WLR 141

Smoldon v Whitworth v Nolan [1997] PIQR 13

The Wagon Mound No.1 [1961] AC 388

Ward v Tesco Stores [1976] 1 WLR 810

Watson v British Boxing Board of Control [2001] QB 1134

Western Excavating v Sharp [1978] QB 761

Woodroffe-Hedley v Cuthbertson [1997] QBD Unreported

Woods v W.M. Car Services Ltd [1982] ICR 693

Wooldridge v Sumner [1963] 2 QB 43

X v Bedfordshire County Council [1995] 2 AC 633

Yewens v Noakes 1880 LR 6 QBD, 530, CA

Statutes and regulations

Americans with Disabilities Act, ADA Title III Technical Assistance Manual, Covering Public Accommodations and Commercial Facilities, Retrieved 26 June 2009 www.ada.gov/taman3.html.

Employment Act 2002

Employment Rights Act 1996

Equality Act 2010

Health and Safety at Work Act 1974

Part-Time Workers (Prevention of Less Favourable Treatment) Regulations 2000

Title IX of the Education Amendments of 1972 §§1681–88

Working Time Regulations 1998

Articles and books

Bennis, W. (1994) *On Becoming a Leader*, Cambridge, MA: Perseus Books.

Coate, P. (ed.) (2007) *Focus on Strategic Management*, Emerald Group Publishing Limited, Retrieved from ebrary 26 June 2009.

Gardiner, S. *et al.* (2006) *Sports Law*, London: Cavendish.

Grayson, E. & Bond, C. (1993) Making Foul Play a Crime, *Solicitors Journal* 693, 16 July.

Griffiths, P. (2005) *Risk Based Auditing*, Ashgate Publishing Limited. Retrieved from ebrary 26 June 2009.

Humphrey, A. (2009) *SWOT Analysis*. Retrieved 26 June 2009 www.businessballs.com/swotanalysis freetemplate.htm

Nilson, C. (2003) *How To Manage Training: A Guide to Design and Delivery of High Performance* (3rd edn), American Management Association (AMACOM) Retrieved from ebrary 26 June 2009.

Sawyer, T. H. (2005) Editor in Chief, *Facility Design and Management for Health, Fitness, Physical Activity, Recreation, and Sports Facility Development*, (11th edn), L.L.C, Champaign, Illinois: Sagamore Publishing.

Smith, I. & Thomas, G. (2007) *Smith & Wood's Employment Law*, Oxford: OUP.

Vecchio, R. P. (Ed.) (1997) *Leadership: Understanding the Dynamics of Power and Influence in Organizations*, Notre Dame, Indiana: University of Notre Dame Press.

Yessin, G. (2006) *Sustainable Development Law (SDL)* Research Guide. Retrieved 26 June 2009 www.nyulawglobal.org/globalex/Sustainable_Development_Law.htm

Zevnik, R. (2004) *The Complete Book of Insurance: Understand the Coverage You Really Need*, Naperville, Illinois: Sphinx Publishing.

33

Sports development officers on sports development

Daniel Bloyce and Ken Green

This chapter examines a relatively neglected aspect of sport; namely, the views and experiences of sports development officers (SDOs). In the process it explores the reality of 'doing' sports development from the perspective of SDOs themselves in order to enhance our understanding of sports development in practice. The chapter draws on a preliminary study of 16 SDOs (nine males; seven females) employed in 10 different local authorities within the West Midlands and north-west of England (see Bloyce *et al.* 2008). The local authorities for whom the SDOs worked were purposively selected to represent a variety of cities, new towns and rural locations, as well as the various patterns of political control, typical of the two regions. Pertinent among the themes that emerged from the interviews were the SDOs' views of the nature and purposes of sports development, their experiences of sports development in practice and their perceptions of the ways in which their working environments had impacted upon their 'philosophies' (in sociological terms: their ideologies) and practices.

SDOs' views of the purpose(s) of sports development

In terms of their views of the role of an SDO in principle (rather than in practice), there was near universal agreement among the SDOs that sports development should revolve around what Houlihan and White (2002) have termed 'the development of sport'. For some SDOs sports development was believed to be primarily about increasing participation in sport and providing sporting opportunities for all groups, especially young people and the socially excluded. For example, one SDO stated that: 'It is a matter of promoting sport to everyone. I mean the big thing here … is targeting hard-to-reach children. I think as part of sports development you have to do that' (SDO A). In response to a question asking for her views on the nature and purposes of sports development, another SDO explained:

> I think it is to facilitate and aim for people to develop, such as provide opportunities whether it be participation, volunteer coaches, clubs or schools to be able to give them the resources that they require for them to be able to develop sport.
>
> *(SDO B)*

Other SDOs spoke more directly about the ways in which sports development should be associated more closely with performance rather than participation in the sense of talent identification and the development of sporting excellence. Interestingly, SDOs who believed that sports development could and should emphasise sports performance viewed this as occurring alongside, but not to the exclusion of, 'sport for all'. SDO C, for example, commented that sports development should, 'in an ideal world', be about 'providing opportunities for grassroots ... but, I also think that we should maintain [a] level of elite and excellence'. Another SDO claimed that 'sports development is about increasing the number of people participating in sport ... but for me it should be about achieving success internationally too' (SDO D). SDOs who viewed sports development as having the twin goals of participation and performance often considered the former to be a necessary condition of the latter; in other words, they viewed grass-roots development in the form of 'sport for all' to be an integral aspect of talent identification and development. Indeed, as SDO E put it:

> In an ideal world ... the role of the [sports development] officer should be ... going back to the sports development continuum – we as officers should be increasing the number of people participating, to the point where we need more resources, just basically getting more people involved in sport as possible and also achieve success internationally at the highest level ... and then these role models impact again on the base level of sport and become a positive cycle whereby we are achieving so much, so that people are getting involved. That would be my ideal world.

In particular, the SDOs believed that the goal of talent identification and development would be achieved most effectively by developing links and pathways between schools and sports clubs: 'It is a case of getting good links from school development ... and creating a pathway for kids to feed through into their local club, and from their local club, if they are still a talent, into regional or county level and then even further' (SDO F). Indeed, whether they viewed performance or participation, or both, as the main aim of sports development, SDOs pointed to schools and clubs as a primary vehicle for realising their goals.

Alongside their stated beliefs that the role of sports development was to facilitate participation and performance, a leitmotif of the SDOs' 'philosophies' was a taken-for-granted acceptance of the intrinsic and extrinsic worth of sport. They tended, in other words, either explicitly or implicitly, to assume that sports development work should not only promote sport because of its supposed intrinsic worth but also because of its suitability as a means of achieving external social and political goals, such as health promotion and national glory. While it was apparent that many of the SDOs believed implicitly in the merits of an extrinsic role for sports development, it was also evident that they were acutely aware of the constraints of the practice of sports development.

SDOs' views of the 'reality' of sports development

The view that sports development represents some kind of panacea for a range of perceived social problems – a perception commonplace in much government sport policy – was apparent in the comments of SDOs in the study. One SDO, for example, outlined the general benefits, as she saw it, of sports development: 'Sport helps people learn social values they can take on for the rest of their lives' (SDO G). Many SDOs described in more specific terms the ways in which they thought sport could be an effective tool for achieving a range of social outcomes, such as the improvement of health and community regeneration. The following quote was quite typical of the views of most of the SDOs in the study:

Whenever we get the chance to outline and promote the value of sport generally, we should take it, because accountants and politicians and people who run organisations, authorities and countries should be told that it's not just about bottom line pounds, shillings and pence, it's really about the value that sport and the provision of sport facilities can bring to a community.

(SDO H)

Some SDOs pointed to examples of the ways in which the reality of sports development could be influenced by the shifting policy priorities beyond their own local authority, particularly at the national level, such as Sport England:

Sports development can be driven by Sport England. If their priorities change then so do the priorities in sports development. It used to be sport for sports sake but now it's more like sport for other reasons. Mainly at the moment it's health and childhood obesity … targeting young people at risk from social exclusion … that is what we're about.

(SDO I)

The contemporary policy focus on health issues was widely cited by SDOs as a justification for re-orientating their sports development activity away from the development of sport per se, towards using sport and physical activities as vehicles of social policy designed to achieve health outcomes. One SDO said, 'at the moment we're concentrating more on the health side, obviously, because of Sport England's priorities and obesity concern' (SDO J).

All told, there was general agreement among the SDOs that they and their colleagues were increasingly being required to focus on broader targets that were perceived as falling outside the proper remit of sports development. In this respect tension was apparent between official expectations (e.g. from Sport England, the government, the local councillors within the local authority), the reality of SDOs' situations as they perceived them and aspects of their 'philosophies'. Indeed, there were dissenting voices in relation to the extrinsic goals introduced to sports development by various government strategies. One SDO commented, for example, that 'Personally, I think the role of sports development should be encouraging people to take part in sport for sports sake and enjoying playing sport, I think there's enough other professionals that can deal with obesity, depression that kind of thing' (SDO G).

Occasional dissenting voices notwithstanding, it was evident that not only did many SDOs accept and share the view that sports development (and, for that matter, sport itself) could and should be viewed instrumentally, many also accepted the legitimacy of sports development being guided by politicians rather than by 'professionals'. For example, as SDO H put it:

It's important that people know not only does sport improve your health, it can reduce crime, it provides life-long learning achievements, such as how to win and lose and play by the rules, it can regenerate communities, it can regenerate cities, sport can provide a feel good factor that nothing else can … It's made me realise the value of sport needs to be pushed and pushed.

This, in itself, suggests that sports development officers are a long way from seeing themselves, let alone acting, as a profession despite the fact that they lay claim to particular expertise and appear to be positioning themselves not only as purveyors of specialised knowledge but also at the node where the needs of various government departments and agencies and sports organisations meet.

Explaining SDOs' 'philosophies'

The final section of the chapter seeks to explain SDOs' 'philosophies' in terms of the networks or figurations of which they are and have been a part. For ease of explanation, we will divide the analysis up into three dimensions: the personal, local and national.

SDOs in their figurations: The personal dimension

For all the SDOs in the study, valuing sport had been and/or remained central to their lives and identities. Their 'love of sport' had influenced their choice of employment and, unsurprisingly, was influencing their views of their roles as SDOs and the aims of sports development. Positive experiences in sport had led to them placing a premium on sports performance – and the identification and nurturing of talent – as well as 'mere' participation for its own sake. The way the SDOs thought about sports development had been shaped by their deep-seated predispositions (or habitus) towards sport. One SDO, for example, explained how her own personal sporting experiences had an ongoing influence on her values, thoughts and practices in sports development:

> I'm biased because I enjoy sport and I don't understand people who don't enjoy sport. ... but the job of the sports development team ... should be to encourage people to take part in sport because they want to go out and to kick a football, or go out to enjoy tennis, not because they think 'Oh, well, this is going to help me lose weight'.
>
> *(SDO G)*

A male SDO commented that it was because he was 'good' at sport that he first was motivated to pursue a career in the sports industry. He stated that: 'I started because I was good at it and it made me feel good, and I recognised that I had a talent in terms of playing sport, and then that carried over into coaching, and now sports development ... I've seen first hand the powers it [sport] has had on me' (SDO E). Being good at sport was a main motivation for another of our SDOs who had actually been an international sportsman: 'I was originally interested in sport development because it was supporting the elite end ... which I guess is close to my heart [because I was involved] at the elite end' (SDO C). It was the competition of sport – and the perceived 'competitive nature' of SDOs generally – that one of our subjects commented on had been a significant motivation for her involvement in sports development: 'Like most SDOs, I am into sport, and am hardworking because of my competitive nature, I'm always striving to do my best and [willing] to put in the hours, unsociable hours, to make sure others are getting the same opportunities [to take part in sport]' (SDO I).

It seems that there is a taken-for-granted acceptance among SDOs of the intrinsic and extrinsic worth/value of sport and that the role of an SDO is to facilitate participation and performance. Put another way, sports development work should, to varying degrees, be about the promotion of sport, the development of sporting opportunities, and developing gifted and talented young people in order to help achieve goals associated with international success. Thus, SDOs' 'philosophies' (again, in sociological terms, their ideologies) and, for that matter, their reasons for entering sports development – what has been referred to as the anticipatory phase of occupational socialization (Lawson 1988) – is best understood in terms of SDOs' habitus: in other words, their 'second nature' (Elias 1978). Their biographies, and particularly their early and profound attachments to sport, appeared to have developed a typical orientation towards sports development for enjoyment, and particularly competitive sport, among many SDOs. The responses of these SDOs lent weight to a conceptualisation of childhood and youth as 'the main "transmission belt" for the development of habitus' (Van Krieken 1998: 156): habituses that have come to characterise social groups such as SDOs. Thus, the sporting experiences of SDOs as youngsters act, in effect, to socialise them into particular views regarding the nature and purposes of sports development: into particular 'philosophies' or, more exactly, ideologies.

As in the case of PE teachers (see Green 2003), the biographies of prospective SDOs, and particularly their own childhood experiences of sport, appear to have an ongoing influence on their values, thoughts and practices. In terms of explaining *why* SDOs think the way they do about their subject, it is important to remind ourselves that their emotional ties to, and identification with, sport forms what Elias would describe as 'a deep-anchorage in the personality structure' (or habitus) of young sports men and women (Elias; cited in Mennell and Goudsblom 1998: 251). It becomes a significant dimension of their individual and collective identities and one which 'cannot easily be shaken off' (Elias; cited in Mennell and Goudsblom 1998: 251), not least because what people value tends to be shaped by what they have experience of, as well as competence in. In line with the findings of a number of authors writing on the theme of the socialisation of PE teachers, for example (see Dewar and Lawson 1984; O'Bryant *et al.* 2000), for many SDOs in the study, valuing sport was a pervasive and enduring influence being, as it was, central to many of their lives and identities.

Although habitus is formed in early life, it remains susceptible to development as networks of relationships become ever more complex and compelling, especially in and around the world of work. In this regard, SDOs are related to an increasingly large number and wider range of people at one and the same time, in other words, to those connected in one way or another to the subject matter of sports development (such as coaches, representatives of various sporting lobbies, government and the media). It is somewhat unsurprising, therefore, to find that SDOs' 'philosophies' – as well as their practices – represent something of a 'working' compromise. SDOs respond to the immediate pressures of their working situation as involved participants in the 'hurly-burly' of sports development and view the attendant constraints as more urgent if not more important. In this sense, SDOs' views on their subject sometimes appeared more reactive than proactive. Indeed, along with Evans' (1992: 243) view that where, among physical educationalists, 'tension' exists 'between the operational ideology and the fundamental ideology' we would conclude that this tends, on the part of SDOs, to lead to 'some modification in the latter'.

All in all, in the process of expressing their views on the nature and purposes of sports development, it became apparent that SDO's 'philosophies' had not only been shaped by their habituses but also by their experiences of 'doing' sports development.

SDOs in their figurations: The local dimension

The socially constructed nature of SDOs' 'philosophies' is, of course, a process and, as such, does not cease on completion of university education – which all of the SDOs interviewed had experienced. Making sense of their views requires appreciation of the ways in which prospective SDOs' sporting backgrounds interact at one level with their occupational socialisation but also with the broader professional and socio-political contexts, as well as the prevailing ideologies found therein. Thus, what SDOs think, as well as what they do, may at least partially be explained in terms of dealing with the constraints of the day-to-day practice of sports development via the culture of the workplace and the values, beliefs, attitudes and norms to be found therein.

Most of the SDOs in the study saw themselves as more or less 'at the mercy' of the expectations of the local councillors who were, in effect, their employers, but who were viewed as not really understanding or even placing much importance on sports development and what the SDOs were doing. Where councillors did exert pressure this typically took the form of antici- pating 'development through sport' (Houlihan and White 2002): in other words, the promo- tion of sport for some wider good. A significant source of pressure on SDOs in their eyes is a consequence of national level pressure on local authorities (that is on councillors from govern- ment) via local legislation (such as 'Best Value', which required local authorities to measure the impact of the services that they provide, including sports development), but also through national policies and strategies towards sport and health (Bloyce and Smith 2010). En bloc the SDOs were critical of what they regarded as the increasing burden of paperwork associated with government dictat. SDO K, for example, stated:

> Don't talk to me about Best Value! Yes we've been through a Best Value review recently. We actually went through it with the leisure centres which was unfortunate really because I don't think it concentrated enough on Sports Development. We have got associated action plans to do with Best Value and self improvement but our biggest initiative around Best Value I see is QUEST which is a service standard. It's the equivalent of a kite mark/ club mark for SD. We're actually assessed externally on several management issues, so we've got research, policy and planning, strategy, management style, marketing and communication, health and safety, lots of different issues.

Another SDO commented that 'sometimes it's a bit frustrating because doing these exercises takes us away from what you should be doing, all the fact finding, paper work and procedure. We should be doing real sports development work' (SDO I).

A further strategy perceived by the SDOs as having added a significant burden to their roles was the expectation that SDOs in local authorities would work with a range of partners – such as those that constitute County Sport Partnerships, sports clubs, youth organisations and other community-based bodies – in order to achieve their own sports development policy outcomes. There was a near universal acceptance among the SDOs in our sample that, whilst being con- strained to work with a range of other groups to deliver sports development services helped generate much needed funding, partnership working also meant that resources and services were often duplicated or, in some cases, left unfulfilled. One female SDO described her experiences of this as follows:

> On the partnership side … so many things are being replicated and people are doing the same thing because [they] have got their own agendas and their own tick-boxes … If you actually pooled resources and pulled things together you could actually do a couple of very effective programmes … rather than doing 50 small ones which don't help … Everyone in sports development needs to have the same kind of agenda, but it's not going to happen.
>
> *(SDO L)*

In this respect, SDOs recognised that they were being required to deliver such programmes by working with more and more organisations, most of which operated beyond sport. One SDO described how the shifting policy agenda (particularly in relation to social inclusion) of the local council for which he worked impacted on his role in the following way:

> When the council did their own survey, they found that people don't feel safe on the streets so community safety is high on the council agenda, which led to the creation of the

youth-only zone and creating opportunities for young people in disadvantaged areas [to take part in sport].

(SDO M)

However, at the same time as being potentially rather burdensome, many of the developing partnerships were seen as having a positive impact in the form, among other things, of much needed resources (that sometimes resulted from aligning sports development service outcomes more closely to the priorities of other, more financially secure, public service providers such as Primary Care Trusts [PCTs]. As one SDO put it, 'There is no statutory requirement to do it [sport development] … [but] budgets always impinge on sport because it's a bit of a Cinderella service' (SDO H). Thus, one SDO commented:

> Working within partnerships impacts upon my role in a positive way … There are negatives, if the communication breaks down, but if everything is up and running then I don't see any problems … you can share facilities, knowledge, you can make joint bids together and get the funding because funding is key within local government and sports development.
>
> *(SDO A)*

A similar point was made by SDO N who commented that 'working with other organizations is positive; there are opportunities for more money and more funding so if we have a limited budget here we can tap into what they have got. We can share the pressures of the work, and we can work together on different things.'

All the SDOs recognised that sports development was becoming an increasingly complex network of interested parties and partnership organisations and that this emerging and developing network was having enabling as well as constraining effects on them. Indeed, the increasing expectation that they would become involved in more and more partnerships contributed to a strong feeling among them that their jobs were becoming driven by the pressure towards partnership. As far as the SDOs were concerned, this pressure had resulted in the relative neglect of what might be termed intrinsic, sports-related outcomes (such as the delivery of sport and physical activity programmes) in favour of targeting the extrinsic, non-sport-related goals of government such as health promotion and social inclusion. This was perceived as having changed the nature as well as the purposes of sports development and the SDO role. One SDO summed up the general feeling thus: 'I don't find myself being very practical in this job; it is very office-based now and I get very little time to go out and about and do any practical activity' (SDO O).

Evidently, the personal and local dimensions to figurations are intimately related to developments at the national level, even though these are less transparent to SDOs and their influence on SDOs' 'philosophies' less overt. As SDO O again commented, 'our strategies are more localised, although they do link with regional and national strategies, and we have similar objectives to [the national] government [objectives]'.

SDOs in their figurations: The national dimension

An adequate appreciation of ideological developments within sports development over time – including contemporary views on the nature and purposes of sports development – requires an account of broader socio-political developments that have shaped sports development, as well as the habituses of SDOs. According to Houlihan and White (2002: 160), such is the prevailing vulnerability of sports development within local government in England it 'remains a pre-cariously balanced service tolerated rather than deeply embedded within the range of obliga-tions of local government'. One consequence of this, they argue, is that SDOs working within local authorities 'are finding it increasingly difficult to sustain a perception of their work as being defined primarily by sports outcomes and there appear to be a marked number who are taking a pragmatic decision to redefine their service outcomes in terms of cross-cutting issues and integrate their activities more tightly with those of larger directorates' (Houlihan and White 2002: 222). Indeed, the broader changes in, and growing complexity of, the figurations of which SDOs are a part has meant that over the last decade, in particular, local authority SDOs' justifications for their roles have become overtly extrinsic. As one SDO from our study put it:

> It [sports development work] reflects what's going on nationally and national thinking. You do try to do that, particularly if you are trying to access national pots of money through Sport England ... We've had to change considerably over the past few years ... in that we try to reflect national initiatives ... like the obesity debate ... So we've met the expectation that alliances will be formed within local authorities which ... bring people together in one group. Health people, sports people, education people, PCTs [Primary Care Trusts] ... anyone who could be involved in the health and sport agenda ... to apply for funding to drive sport forward.
>
> *(SDO H)*

Another SDO recognised that the national government was directly impacting on the kinds of programmes and strategies that he was being asked to provide by his employers:

> It does change, obviously the government bring out agendas for health and crime and things like that, so that obviously affects the role, new programmes are always coming on board for the socially disadvantaged, people with disabilities, things like that ... and then you have to go out there and let the clubs ... and the participants know that this is what the latest fad is ... The latest ones are the crime and health agenda.
>
> *(SDO P)*

SDOs are increasingly and enthusiastically championing the perceived role of sport and sports development in contributing positively to the achievement of broader social objectives, parti-cularly those related to the achievement of improving health and greater social inclusion (Coalter 2007). The following statement from one of the SDOs in the study illustrates this point:

> I think the role of the SDO used to be very sports-specific, whereas now its become ... incorporated with healthy eating and general walking ... We're all coming on board together to try and work together ... to try and help the process of healthy living which is now being drummed into us ... Government try to push for a more healthy living ... sports development can do that by us linking in with people like the Primary Care Trust, the NHS [National Health Service], other clubs, Weight Watchers, and the British Heart Foundation.
>
> *(SDO G)*

All in all, SDOs are constrained to move beyond simply extolling the intrinsic benefits of sports participation and provide a more persuasive justification for using public funds to develop sport.

Nonetheless, while bemoaning some of the unforeseen consequences of this development they appear, on the whole, to be willing partners, who already subscribe to the current rhetoric of government.

Conclusion

This chapter has briefly explained SDOs' 'philosophical' (or, rather, ideological) orientations. Starting from the premise that such 'philosophies' cannot be adequately explained by studying the SDOs in isolation, it has been argued that their everyday 'philosophies' (in sociological terms, their professional ideologies) need to be understood in terms of their deeply rooted attachments to sport and the dynamic occupational context that circumscribes their working lives.

While SDOs cannot be described as a homogenous group, neither are they particularly heterogeneous. Indeed, many appear to share similar habituses at the personal level and are constrained by similar circumstances at the local and national dimensions of their networks. Consequently, there is an impression of a group habitus in the sense of a shared fund of common sense understandings and justificatory ideas or ideologies at the local level – what might be termed, 'articles of faith' – that SDOs share with each other in the course of their normal, everyday working lives. The particular networks of relationships that SDOs inhabit make some interpretations of sports development more likely than others. As such, SDOs' 'philosophies' tend to be *practical* 'philosophies', that is to say, 'philosophies' bearing the hallmarks of their prior sporting practice and their increasingly demanding sports development contexts.

From a (figurational) sociological perspective, it is argued that normative views on the nature and purposes of sports development must be understood as the (often unintended) outcomes of (longer-term) social developments. In the process of being constrained to move beyond simply extolling the intrinsic benefits of sports participation towards providing a more persuasive justification for their existence (not least to their local authority paymasters) – in the form of the externalities that sports development is said to accrue – many SDOs appear to have gone native; that is to say, they appear to have been readily persuaded of the extrinsic value of sport. In this regard, local authorities and government appear to have been pushing at an open door.

References

Bloyce, D. & Smith, A. (2010). *Sport policy and development: An introduction*. London: Routledge.

Bloyce, D., Smith, A., Mead, R. & Morris, J. (2008) 'Playing the game (plan)': a figurational analysis of organizational change in sports development in England. *European Sport Management Quarterly*, 8 (4), 359–78.

Coalter, F. (2007). *A wider social role for sport. Who's keeping the score?* London: Routledge.

Dewar, A. & Lawson, H. (1984). The subjective warrant and recruitment into physical education. *QUEST*, 30: 15–25.

Elias, N. (1978). *What is sociology?* London: Hutchinson.

Evans, J. (1992). A short paper about people, power and educational reform: authority and representation in ethnographic research subjectivity, ideology and educational reform: the case of physical education. In: A. Sparkes (Ed.) *Research in Physical Education and Sport: Exploring Alternative Visions*. London: Falmer Press.

Green, K. (2003). *Physical Education Teachers on Physical Education. A Sociological Study of Philosophies and Ideologies*. Chester: Chester Academic Press.

Houlihan, B. & White, A. (2002). *The Politics of Sports Development: Development of sport or development through sport?* London: Routledge.

Lawson, H. (1988). Occupational socialization, cultural studies and the physical education curriculum. *Journal of Teaching in Physical Education*, 7: 265–88.

Mennell, S. & Goudsblom, J. (1998). *Norbert Elias: On civilization power and knowledge*. Chicago: The University of Chicago Press.

O'Bryant, C., O'Sullivan & Raudensky, J. (2000). Socialization of prospective physical education teachers: the story of new blood. *Sport, Education and Society*, 5(2): 177–93.

Van Krieken, R. (1998). *Norbert Elias*. London: Routledge.

34

Sports development, sports coaching, and domain specificity

John Lyle

Sports development may be rationalised as a contribution to broad policy outcomes focused on, for example, health and well-being, social cohesion, regeneration and national prestige. However, the outputs from sports development (for example, participation rates, standards of performance and diffusion through the population) are derived from the accumulation and aggregation of myriad episodes and programmes of sport-related activity. In this chapter I deal with the folly of treating this participation profile, and those who lead/coach within it, as homogeneous or susceptible to common policies and practices.

Insufficient attention has been paid to models of sports participation, that is, an understanding of how (and why) individuals progress through the various stages of participation. It is difficult to imagine how any strategic sports development can be conducted without such an understanding of these broad patterns. However, at the operational level, attention to these participant populations is required because they bring within them different participant needs, and the different forms of sports leadership that are appropriate to them. There is a universal acceptance that it is inappropriate to treat all participants in the same way; their abilities, cultural backgrounds, motives, social and educational history, and so on should be acknowledged. However, it is equally inappropriate to assume that sports leaders and coaches are a homogeneous group and capable (or motivated) to operate equally effectively with all participant populations. The purpose of the chapter is to provide evidence that there are clear distinctions between coached populations.

It would be inappropriate to spend time on discussing the use of the term sports development, but it is necessary to define the scope of the assumptions within the chapter. I have previously described sports development as 'purposeful intervention to bring about more extensive, better quality, more widely accessible sports participation and/or improved standards of performance' (Lyle 2008: 217). I also noted that intervention could be categorised at a number of levels – strategic facilitation, organisational and administrative, and delivery. The term has commonly been used to refer to 'community sport' or to an 'introduction to sport for young people'. In this instance it is intended that the term should apply to all sports activity, and not to a subset of occupational activity. There is a presumption (perhaps more in intention than reality) that there is a more or less integrated infrastructure of participation from the toddler's first gymnastics lesson to Olympic preparation and on to forms of adult recreation. Within this I assume all of the individual and collective benefits that might accrue from such participation. More importantly, this purposeful facilitation, promotion, development and provision of sport are dependent, for the most part, on some form of active leadership.

Sports development refers to various layers of activity (Lyle 2008) that can be differentiated by their dependence on the coach/leader, and by distinctive practices and behaviours. Sports coaching is domain specific (Lyle 2002; Lyle and Cushion 2010; Trudel and Gilbert 2006) and these domains (categorised using terms such as participation, recreation, high performance, community, development, club, school, elite and talent development) are characterised by distinctive participant motives, intensities of commitment, standards of performance, leadership roles, social expectations and values, organisational arrangements, and delivery patterns. The clear inference to be drawn from this is that sports development is domain specific. Therefore, the chapter will demonstrate that the juxtaposition of environment, motive and form of sport intervention in the coached and coaching populations creates a domain specificity that, at a national level, requires a coherent and coordinated approach. In particular, the understanding of participant populations on which this 'system-wide' approach should be based should focus on progression and transition between stages and populations.

The chapter is structured in the following way. First, I examine the Participant Development Model (North 2009) and other conceptions of stages of participation, both to illustrate the range of participant populations and for their strengths and weaknesses as development tools. Second, evidence is presented to illustrate the relative scale of these populations and to interpret the data for the relative emphases placed on these populations. Third, the concept of 'guided' and 'coached' populations is examined, along with some evidence of the diversity of coaching deployment. Finally, the evidence presented is interpreted in the context of the Coach Development Model (North 2009) and the implications for sports development.

Participant populations

The first part of the chapter focuses on the division of the sporting population into its constituent parts. It will be argued that this is a necessary stage in adequately addressing the needs of individuals within these subdivisions and fulfilling a sports development agenda. The basis for discussing participant populations is the Participant Development Model (PDM). North (2009) gives a detailed description of the genesis of the 'model', highlighting its characteristic of being 'participant-needs led' in contrast to the traditional and ubiquitous 'pyramid' model (Houlihan and White 2002). The PDM is a key feature of the UK Coaching Framework, the UK-wide strategic framework for the development of a 'world-leading coaching system in the UK' (sports coach UK 2008a). Perhaps more interesting is that governing bodies of sport are 'required' to have a sports-specific version of the PDM. The guidance notes for the construction of a sport's Whole Sport Plan for 2009–13, on which funding is based, makes it clear that a Long Term Participant-Development Model is an expectation (sports coach UK 2008b). The generic model provided in the notes identifies a number of participant populations: active start, fundamentals, learning to play and participate, talent development, high performance, developing performance, sustaining performance, developing participation, sustaining participation, and learning and relearning.

North's (2009: 12–16) description of the PDM clarifies the distinctive participant populations, and identifies a number of aspects of the 'model' that impact on sports development. The most obvious is that sporting provision should be individualised where feasible to meet the participant's needs. When taken in aggregate the provision associated with each participant population is intended to provide a range of opportunities that will make it easier to establish inclusive participation. Thus ability and motive can be accommodated, in addition to more participant-friendly provision, designed to attract 'equity target groups such as participants with a disability, women and girls, and black and ethnic minority groups' (p. 14). The model also attempts to provide an age/stage dimension that acknowledges that, for example, both children and adults may have recreation, development and performance 'stages' in their progress through sports participation.

Two further features of the PDM are particularly relevant for sports development. The first of these is the embedding of long-term development principles in the 'model'. This is a recognition that there are common patterns of development in how individuals develop their capabilities, and in how their 'sports careers' develop. These principles are to be found in Balyi's model of Long Term Athlete Development (Balyi and Hamilton 2003; Stafford 2005) and recognition of the need for varying but intensive levels of commitment (Ericsson *et al.* 1993). The second feature is that of 'segmentation', that is, the identification of sporting populations in which there is a commonality of life stages, motives and prior sporting experiences. The implication is that sporting interventions and opportunities can be shaped to these populations in ways that are more likely to be effective. The population segments identified are as described above, other than talent development having been subdivided into early talent development and late talent development. Although these generic populations are identified, North makes it clear that the 'model' should be made sport specific, and examples of sport-specific models are provided (2009: 88–103). It cannot be assumed, of course, that there are no perceived weaknesses in the model, and I turn now to a critical interpretation of the PDM.

The PDM is a good attempt to delineate a prescriptive framework for sports development. It describes how the sports population could be 'structured', rather than how it is presently configured; in other words a 'model for' rather than a 'model of'. This is congruent with much of

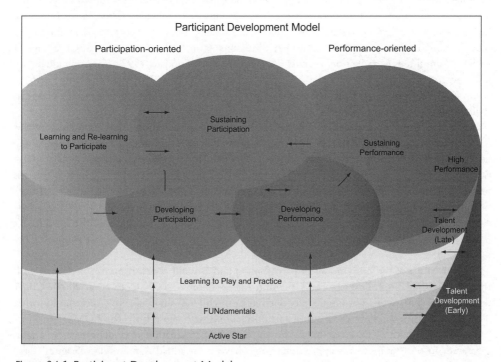

Figure 34.1 Participant Development Model

public policy (and thereby aspiration) in that it is most often based on 'ideas' rather than empirically tested practice (Coote *et al.* 2004). It is also important to note, however, what the PDM represents and does not represent. It is not a model – it is a framework. The progressions or transitions from stage to stage are not identified, diluted further by claims such as 'moving seamlessly' from segment to segment, and being distant from current practice. There is limited attention to 'how' individuals move through the various stages and domains. Therefore, the PDM is aspirational, prescriptive and idealised. This is not a bad thing. It provides a template or guide to the development of sport and assistance to sports organisations and agencies. There are two obvious issues, each derived from the adoption of this approach by governing bodies of sport. First, governing bodies tend to have more influence in some provision sectors (clubs) than in others (adult recreation). The PDM embraces all provision. Therefore, schools, some community groups, professional sport and commercial sector instruction tend not to be so directly impacted by the governing body-led development. Second, although there is an intuitive validity about the classification of segments, when sports translate the PDM into their language, it appears often to be put in the context of organised competition and the various stages/levels of that competition. For example, Scottish Rugby uses the classifications beginners/learners, club competition (youths/age groups), club competition (adults), club recreational players, representative players (youths) and representative players (adults). These classifications are based on competition structures, which are themselves reflective of standard of performance.

The segments themselves are open to some challenge. In particular the neatness and order of children's participation may be neither accurate nor desirable. There is no direct evidence that children/young people make decisions, on emerging from the learn to play/practice stage, to become part of participation development or performance development. The 'model' to this extent makes sense from a developmental/process perspective but (even allowing for a degree of looseness of boundaries) does not accord with personal experience. For the most part, the 'avenues of transmission' (provision) at these age groups will embrace a large range of young people and of very varying standards. This 'development' phase is a key stage in modelling participation and is important for a number of reasons: (a) modelling identifies this as a stage at which 'committed participation' occurs (McDonald and Tungatt 1992); (b) individuals are unlikely to move to 'recreational' participation until they have experienced some form of committed involvement; (c) this is a talent search stage; and (d) models suggest this as a stage at which 'participation' and 'performance' will begin to diverge.

There is an issue about the 'distance' between practice and aspiration. The importance of this is that policy rhetoric may be adopted by agencies but may not bring about change if the intended practice is some way distant from the current practice. The identification of populations may not accord with the existing structures and organisations within which a sport is practised. I am certainly not 'reifying' existing arrangements, merely pointing to the challenges of organisational realignment that might be required if a system-wide approach is being advocated. The PDM and its related assumptions provide an appropriate reminder of the need to ask 'How does my activity fit into the bigger picture?' 'What are the entry and exit routes for my participants?'

The PDM is not the only model of participation and a useful comparison can be drawn with that of Côté and his colleagues (see Côté and Fraser-Thomas 2007; Côté *et al.* 2003). Côté's development framework was empirically derived from children's retrospective sporting histories. The resulting categories are shown in Table 34.1, along with those from the PDM.

In Table 34.1 the PDM has been shown with its participation and performance strands separated. In both frameworks approximate ages have been added. Côté and colleagues' categories were derived from a conference presentation (Côté 2008) and the PDM from an internal

Table 34.1 The comparison of participant populations

Côté and colleagues	Participant Development Model	
	Active Start Phase 0–6 years	
Sampling Years 6–12	Fundamentals Phase 5/6–8/9 years	
Children	Beginner Child	
	Learning to Play and Practice Phase 8–12 years	
	Beginner Child	
		Talent Development Early 8+
		Child Performer
Specialising Years 13–15		Talent Development
Young adolescents		Late 12/13+
		Child Performer
Recreational Years 13+	Developing Participation	
Adults/adolescents	12+	
	Young Person Participant	
Investment Years 16+		Developing Performance
Late adolescents/adults		Young Person Performer
Investment Years 16+		Sustaining Performance
Late adolescents/adults		Adult Performer
Recreational Years 13+	Sustaining Participation	
Adults/adolescents	18+	
	Adult Participant	
Investment Years 16+		Elite Performance
Late adolescents/adults		Young person/Adult Performer
Recreational Years 16+	Learning/Relearning	
Adults/adolescents	Adult Participant	

sports coach UK paper (sports coach UK 2008c). Much of the debate surrounding Côté's work has been centred on the balance of 'sampling and specialisation'. When presented as in the table above, a degree of linearity becomes evident. It is worth recalling that the central purpose of the chapter was to demonstrate that there are very distinction participant populations. Table 34.1 suggests that there may well be some measure of agreement about these populations, but, of course, the issues of demarcation and boundary criteria are always present.

Ultimately the practical questions are about the forms of sports development practice – interventions, facilitation, programmes – that can be put in place to support each of these segments and, of course, the important transition and progression phases. The chapter will examine the relationship of these different segments to sports coaching, but before doing so, examines the evidence for the relative size of each participant population.

Participant population distributions

The 'driver' for this part of the chapter was twofold. First, the traditional pyramid model gave a misleading impression of the relative sizes of the participant populations, and, second, it was accompanied by rhetoric that implied that movement between segments was relatively easy and determined by the participants' needs and ambitions (Lyle 2004). It seemed from a lifetime of engagement in sport that this was rather simplistic, if not naïve, and that a realistic picture of the scale of participant populations would provide valuable insights about the scale of the likely transitions. The data, of course, are useful for sports development planning.

John Lyle

Table 34.2 The comparative scale of competition activity

Activity	Participation rate	Participation rate	Competition activity	
	At least once in past 12 months (%)	At least once in last 4 weeks (%)	Organised, competitive activity in last 4 weeks (%)	
			Percentage of number in that sport	Percentage overall
Swimming	49	23	2	1
Cycling	30	19	1	<1
Keep fit	24	15	0	0
Soccer	20	11	31	6
Snooker/pool	17	8	3	1
Jogging	13	7	5	1
Tennis	10	0	0	0

Source: Data fram future (2000)

A comparison between those participants who might be termed 'recreational' and those who take part in sports competition reinforces the relatively small proportion of the population who 'compete'. In a small-scale survey of adults (n = 940) carried out in the UK (Futre 2000) the overall 'participation rates' of a sample of the population are demonstrated to be very significantly influenced by the impact of non-competitive activity. The data from the seven most popular activities (not including walking) (shown in Table 34.2) illustrate the limited scale of competition sport.

The data are used merely to illustrate that the proportion of the sample that participates 'regularly' in sport (accepting that 'once in the previous four weeks' is a poor measure) is dominated by what might be termed 'lifestyle' activities. The proportion taking part in competition is very low. The survey was carried out on adults; given the much larger participation rates in the under-16s, the proportion of competition activity would be higher.

Another issue is the illusory progression implied in development models. It is perhaps understandable that 'progression' should not be presented as unlikely. On the other hand, to underestimate the barriers is not helpful. Eady's (1993) earlier picture of individuals 'progressing smoothly ... and moving easily between levels' (1993: 14) simply does not describe the reality of the meritocracy in sport. In addition, there are myriad social barriers to equal progression and achievement in sport. Rowe (2003) describes a social inequality in the proportion of elite sportspersons who emerge from the already inequitable mass participation. In a survey of national squad members in 14 sports, individuals from socio-economic grouping AB were twice as likely to be represented as their prevalence in the population would suggest.

Using the broad categories from the traditional pyramid model (foundation, participation, performance and excellence) it is possible to illustrate that the scope for progression is much less than is often assumed (or implied in representations of the pyramid model). Table 34.3 uses a variety of data to provide a more realistic assessment of the relative proportions of these stages of development.

These categories of participation have been overtaken by the PDM and other more recent terminology. However, the data make it clear that the proportion of those who become sportspersons (and we might interpret that in its broadest sense) is a small proportion of the adult population. Those who form the committed performers are also a very small proportion. In

Table 34.3 The relative scale of participation domains

	Pyramid[1]	Compass[2]	Soccer[4]	Swimming[4]
Excellence[5]	13	1	0.6	0.1
Performance[3]	42	9	6	1
Participation[3]	66	14	20	49
Foundation[6]	100	100	100	100

Notes
1 Pyramid data calculated on the proportional area of each section of the conventional triangle
2 Estimate using the UK participation data from the Compass Survey (UK Sport/Sport England/CONI 1999).
3 Performance = competitive, organised and intensive + regular competition and organised; Participation = intensive + regular recreational
4 Data taken from Futre (2000)
5 Excellence is (perhaps considerably over-) estimated at 10% of performance levels
6 Foundation is assumed to apply to all

Table 34.3 the proportion of 'excellent' performance is likely to be overestimated. To reinforce the central message of the chapter, these are distinct populations, who require distinctive forms of development.

A more up-to-date set of data is provided by North (2009). These data are derived from a wide range of survey evidence, and point out both the distinctive participant populations and the relative scale of these segments. Throughout the document North uses the measure of 'sports participation as once in the last week' (2009: 31). However, the data also allow him to distinguish usefully between guided and unguided sport. 'Guided' sport is those forms of participation that have been organised, led or coached by another individual, and help to distinguish more general forms of physical activity from organised sport. Indeed, this might spawn a new mantra in sports development between 'provide or guide'. 'Provide' implies the recreational facilities and open spaces within which self-directed activity can take place, and might be contrasted with 'guided' activity in which a form of leadership is present. A further distinction might be between 'guided' in the voluntary or commercial sectors, and the programmes/ initiatives provided by 'sports developers'.

The data reinforce the skewed nature of sports participation and the intensity and leadership implied. (Using data largely from the sports coach UK 2008 national surveys) the overall proportion of the population who took part in sport (in the last week) was 38 per cent. The rate for children (16 years and under) was 82 per cent and that for adults was 31 per cent. More interestingly, the overall proportion of the population taking part in 'guided sport' was 13 per cent, with a very clear distinction between children (50 per cent) and adults (7 per cent). However, of those adults who had participated in the last week, the proportion 'receiving' guided sport was 22 per cent. These data begin to 'describe a picture' of the scale of the population that might be influenced by various forms of sports leadership. To illustrate further the differences, the proportions of the population who take part in two or more hours of guided sport per week can be described: for 9–11-year-olds it is 36 per cent, for 17–21-year-olds it is 12 per cent, and just 4 per cent of 30–39-year-olds take part in two or more guided hours per week.

Some idea of the relative scale of the guided provision can be obtained from the total number of hours in each segment. Table 34.4 was compiled from the data in North (2009: 39). The data are also presented by age groups. These show that the total number of guided hours for years 5 to 16 accounts for 61 per cent of the total, and years 5 to 21 for 74 per cent of the total. In Table 34.4, adult performance can be thought of as the 'club sector'. The 'recreation'

Table 34.4 Guided hours per domain

	Guided sporting hours	
Children (extracurricular)	619,260	23%
Children (foundation)	693,493	26%
Adult participation	141,357	5%
Adult performance	759,538	29%
Talent development	442,456	17%
Total	2,656,104	100%

Source: Data from North (2009)

Table 34.5 Participant populations within two sports

Age groups				Participation stages			
Triathlon	%	Rugby League	%	Triathlon	%	Rugby League	%
<17 years	13	<16 years	66	Beginner	19	Beginner	12
18–24 years	10	17-20 years	13	Club	38	Club	71
>24 years	77	>20 years	21	Representative	26	Representative	17
Total	100	Total	100	Recreational	17	Recreational	1

Source: Data derived from project commissioned by sports coach UK

element of adult participation accounts for a small proportion of the total. Overall, the children's segments of participation (including talent development) form a very sizable proportion of the whole. Data were not available for the 'high-performance' sector. Given the intensity of preparation and performance in that sector, the number of guided hours would be very high, but it might be argued that this sector constitutes a very specialised aspect of sports development.

As might be expected, there will be sport-specific differences in the distribution of participant populations. This can be illustrated from data generated by the author from a coaching workforce development project. Table 34.5 shows the distribution of members across the segments in two sports, one a team sport with a traditional pattern of younger age-group players (rugby league), and the other an individual sport participated in mostly by adults (triathlon). The variation in populations does not negate the analysis by 'stage of development', but reinforces the message about the specificity of participation domains and appropriate development needs.

It seems clear that sports development in its many forms will have to deal with participant populations that have no homogeneity across the participation segments. Coached populations differ in many ways: age, motive, ability, stage of development and so on. In order to reinforce this point, and to examine a key feature of development activity, the chapter turns now to the nature of coaching across the participant populations.

Coaching domains

It is not unreasonable to begin with the assumption that sports development activity relies on sports leaders/coaches, and that a major concern of developers would be to ensure that the role, characteristics and competences of the coach match those of the participant population in its particular context. Thus far, evidence has been presented to suggest that the term 'participation' is too imprecise, and that developers need to appreciate the range of participation contexts that are created by the individual's sports development pathway. In this section a similar message is conveyed in relation to coaching. Once again an aspirational model is available, the Coach Development Model (CDM), that suggests a similar differentiation of coaching roles to match those of the PDM.

Much has been written about the role of the coach, and the distinctions between the coach's role and other sports leaders (Lyle 2002). These debates focus on the 'boundary markers' that distinguish a coaching role from that of teaching, leading, facilitating or instructing. There is insufficient space here to explore these nuances, but a baseline assumption can be made that sports development will normally rely on qualified leaders, and these leaders normally have sport-specific coaching awards, validated by a governing body of sport. The next most obvious question is, 'are these coaches/leaders appropriately qualified, and are they equipped to service the needs of the varying participant populations?' The coaching qualifications can be thought of as a minimum level of competence, but individuals will also have a distinctive set of motives for coaching, previous experiences, prior education, and so on. It will also be shown that the varying levels of award (usually from 1 through to 5) are designed to equip the coach to operate in a specific context.

The CDM is an aspirational framework of coaching roles and attendant qualifications that is intended to complement the PDM (North 2009) (see Figure 34.2). For practical purposes the number of domains (populations being coached) has been grouped into four – children's

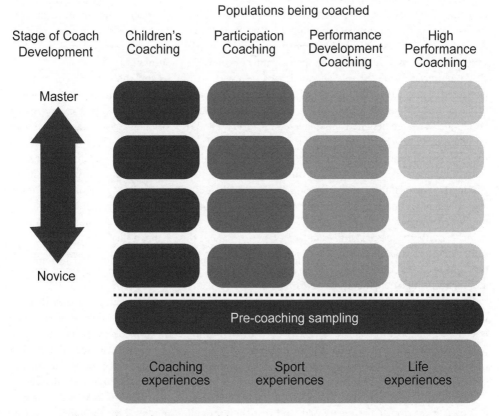

Figure 34.2 The Coach Development Model

coaching, participation coaching, performance development coaching and high performance coaching. It is intended that coaches are able to specialise; not only that their education and training is relevant to the participant group, but that they are able to become 'expert' within that domain.

It is important to stress that the CDM is aspirational, and that, at the time of writing, there are no governing body of sport coaching award schemes that have fully embraced this framework. Governing bodies have devised sport-specific versions to match their PDMs (see North 2009: 88–103). Existing award structures in gymnastics and swimming acknowledge a 'teacher' route, to distinguish it from 'coaching', and some sports have 'instructor' awards. However, the current position is that the award system is not matched to the populations identified in the PDM.

The coaching literature does acknowledge the notion that there are 'coaching domains' (Lyle 2002; Lyle and Cushion 2010; Trudel and Gilbert 2006). Lyle (2002: 52–57) expands upon three domains – participation, development, and performance – that have some resonance with the PDM. The significant issue is that these domains have a particular configuration of participant aspirations, stages of development, levels of commitment, and delivery organisation that impact on the coach's behaviour and practice. This becomes evident in the coach's leadership style, methods of communication, demands on technical knowledge, planning, goal setting and emphasis on competition. The coaching role and 'style' appropriate to a basketball programme that is part of a social inclusion community programme will differ from that of a primary school taster programme, and differ again from a talent search programme for aspiring young players. It is here that some of the sports development issues arise in relation to participant populations and coaching. For example, does the level of award held by a leader/coach equip them to operate in that context; is the leader providing a 'programme' that suits the needs of that population; does the coach's 'style' suit the population and its aspirations; is the 'programme' provided sufficient to act as a catalyst for the participant's development journey?

To appreciate some of this dilemma, it is necessary to understand the level of competence conferred by sports coaching awards. Although the emerging CDM intends that coaches' development be considered on a continuum from novice to expert, the existing reality is that coaching awards are designed and delivered by 'level'. The UK Coaching Certificate-endorsement framework for coaching awards (sports coach UK, no date) recognises four levels of award and four functional roles. In their original conception, these were assistant coach (qualified to assist a more experience coach, but not to operate independently), coach (capable of operating independently, and planning and delivering short programmes), senior coach (designing, delivering and managing annual coaching programmes), and master coach (dealing with longer-term, specialised programmes). Although the levels of award held by coaches are not intended to coincide with the participant's standard of performance, this is the reality in most sports. To some extent this is understandable, since the levels of commitment that require 'advanced' coaching are created by the reward environment in which they operate, and the greater rewards are linked to higher standards of performance.

I have been engaged in a number of coaching workforce development projects with governing bodies of sport that have involved an audit of coaches' practice. The following evidence is generated from those projects and is used to demonstrate the link between coaching and participant domains. The CDM has not progressed to the stage at which the 'model' distribution of coaches across levels and domains has been proposed. A distribution is proposed from the evidence contained in North's report (2009), and this is compared to evidence from the audit.

The data in Table 34.6 are being used to illustrate the point that the link between coaching and participant domains is recognised, and that they provide some 'food for thought' for sports development. The pattern of data differs from the survey-generated 'guidelines', partly because

Table 34.6 Distribution of coaching awards by domain[4]

| Level of award | Proportions by level[1] | | | | | | |
	Children	Participation	Performance	Elite	Total	Guide[2]	Proposed[3]
Level 4	3%	4%	5%	15%	*4%*	12%	5%
Level 3	11%	12%	17%	31%	*13%*	19%	15%
Level 2	29%	32%	43%	29%	*32%*	36%	45%
Level 1	37%	32%	23%	15%	*33%*	33%	35%
Unqualified	20%	21%	11%	10%	*18%*		

| | Proportions by domain[1] | | | |
	Children	Participation	Performance	Elite
Level 4	47%	21%	21%	11%
Level 3	47%	23%	23%	7%
Level 2	51%	23%	23%	3%
Level 1	64%	23%	12%	1%
Unqualified	61%	27%	10%	2%
Total	*56%*	*24%*	*17%*	*3%*
Guide[2]	53%	29%	18%	n/a

Notes
1 Audit data from a sample of 1,674 coaches across 12 sports in Scotland, 2007–2008
2 'Guide' data taken from North (2009)
3 Proposed distribution generated from work with Scottish Governing Bodies of sport
4 The data are indicative; categorisations of domains are not always completely consistent

of the inclusion of unqualified coaches. These individuals could have been omitted from the calculations but they were part of the audit and constitute a significant grouping. It is interesting that they are distributed across domains, but their deployment is centred on the children's domain. The distribution by level shows the expected decrease in proportion as the level of award increases, and also that the proportion of Level 3 and Level 4 coaches is higher with 'elite' athletes. Sports developers should note that the proportion of coaches with lower than Level 2 awards (that is, unqualified or Level 1), and therefore not qualified to operate unsupervised, is almost 60 per cent in the children's domain. The data also show that 80 per cent of all coaches were deployed in the children's or participation domains.

Table 34.7 Distribution of coach deployment by club and local authority

Participant domains	Clubs[1]	Local authorities[2]
Elite	3%	2%
Performance	8%	5%
Performance development	17%	7%
Learning to play/train	30%	30%
Fundamentals	21%	25%
Participation/ recreation	21%	31%

Notes
1 Club data from a sample of 2,737 club coach deployments, across 12 sports in Scotland, 2007–2008
2 Local authority data from a sample of 1,161 coach deployments across seven sports in Scotland, 2007–2008

Table 34.8 Distribution of deliverers in the primary school domain

Deliverer category[1]	Proportion
Teachers	32%
Parents	18%
Pupils	5%
Community coaches	26%
Sports development officers	7%
Others	11%

Note
1 Sample of 5,341 deliverers across 12 sports in Scottish primary schools, 2005/2006

Similar data were collected on the deployment of coaches in clubs and local authorities. These data confirm the relative 'weightings' of the participant domains. Table 34.7 was generated from the workforce development projects mentioned above.

The learning to play/train and fundamentals domains are predominantly for children, and confirm the majority deployment to that domain. Not surprisingly, the local authority deployments place less emphasis on 'performance'-related activity, although the proportion of participation/recreation is relatively high.

Although the focus in this section is on the coaching/participant domains, it is important to acknowledge that not all 'deliverers' of sports activity are qualified coaches. The proportion of unqualified coaches identified in a previous table refers to active coaches deployed within clubs. More general surveys (see Townend and North 2007) suggest that between 38 per cent and 50 per cent of coaches are qualified, although this would appear to embrace a fairly generous interpretation of the role and the commitment. North (2009) identifies coaches, leaders, fitness instructors and teachers as deliverers of sport. The final table uses data obtained from **sport**scotland to illustrate the range of providers in one domain. Active Schools is a school-based sports development initiative in Scotland; monitoring data are collected on sport-related activity from all schools. Table 34.8 identifies the proportion of different deliverers for non-curricular primary school activity (usually aged between 5 and 11).

Although it seems unlikely that all deliverers (particularly teachers, pupils and parents) would have a Level 1 or above coaching award, many will have been trained to deliver appropriate activities to younger children, and may have 'leader' awards. Once again the simple message for sports developers is that domains can be identified, and that even with a predictable participant population, there is a quite diverse profile of deliverers.

Conclusion

The purpose of the chapter was to reinforce two messages. First, sports development is a layered framework of facilitated sport-related activity. This applies to all stages and levels of performance and participation, and for the most part, is 'guided' by a coach, leader, instructor, teacher or other deliverer. The distinction between guided activity and the facilitation of largely self-directed activity is a useful one. Second, the effectiveness and impact of sports development cannot be assured without an understanding and appreciation of the participant's development journey in and through sport. This journey creates a number of participant populations that have been captured in the Participant Development Model. Not surprisingly, a Coach Development Model has been proposed to complement this. Its purpose is to ensure that the participant's needs are met by coaches having appropriate qualifications and training.

It was acknowledged that these models are aspirational, and the messages are prescriptive. Nevertheless, it is difficult to argue with the principles on which they are based. Evidence was presented to demonstrate that participant populations differ in scale and participant needs, although the pre-eminence of the children's domain was clear. Progression and transition from population to population (or stage to stage) is not 'seamless' and not determined solely by the participants' aspirations. A significant amount of work is yet to be done on these transitions, on making the models sport-specific, and on bridging the gap between current and aspirational provision. It seems almost unremarkable that domain specificity should be acknowledged, and that coaches/leaders should be specialists. However, it would be difficult to gainsay the assertion that minimally qualified coaches/leaders continue to operate in the children's domain, and that much of sports development activity takes place without consideration of the individual participant's development journey.

The evidence paints a clear picture of the scale of the children's learning domain, the developing performance domain, and the developing and sustaining participation domains. This is 'where the action is' if measured solely by the scale of provision and the deployment of coaches. It can also be argued that the children's domain is important as a basis for further sustained activity and personal development. This activity takes place across all sectors – school partnerships, clubs, local authorities, sport-specific development schemes, and so on. Nevertheless, the evidence presented on the current deployment of coaches and the training of coaches suggests that we have some way to go before there is an equitable distribution of opportunities for specialisation across the domains.

Acknowledgement

Figures 34.1 and 34.2 are reproduced from *The Coaching Workforce 2009–2016* with kind permission of The National Coaching Foundation (brand name sports coach UK). All rights reserved. Sports coach UK subscription and membership services provide a range of benefits to coaches, including insurance and information services. For further details please ring 0113-290-7612 or visit www.sportscoachuk.org

References

Balyi, I. and Hamilton, A. (2003) 'Long term athlete development update: trainability in childhood and adolescence', *Faster, Higher, Stronger*, 20: 6–8.

Coote, A., Allen, J. and Woodhead, D. (2004) *Finding out what works: building knowledge about complex-community based initiatives*, London: King's Fund.

Côté, J. (2008) 'Coaching expertise defined by meeting athletes' needs', paper presented at the 2008 International Coaching Conference, Twickenham, London, 18–20 November 2008.

Côté, J., Baker, J. and Abernethy, B. (2003) 'From play to practice: a developmental framework for the acquisition of expertise in team sports', in J. Starkes and K.A. Ericsson (eds) *Expert performance in sports: advances in research on sport expertise*, Champaign, Il: Human Kinetics (89–110).

Côté, J. and Fraser-Thomas, J. (2007) 'Youth involvement in sport', in P.R.E. Crocker (ed.) *Introduction to sport psychology: a Canadian perspective*, Toronto: Pearson (266–94).

Eady, J. (1993) *Practical sports development*, Harlow: Longman.

Ericsson, K.A., Krampe, R.T. and Tesch-Romer, C. (1993) 'The role of deliberate practice in the acquisition of expert performance', *Psychological Review*, 100(3): 363–406.

Futre, D. (2000) 'Modelling sports participation: an exploratory investigation into participation in sport in Newcastle Upon Tyne', unpublished thesis, Northumbria University.

Houlihan, B. and White, A. (2002) *The politics of sports development*, London: Routledge.

Lyle, J. (2002) *Sports coaching concepts: a framework for coaches' behaviour*, London: Routledge.

——(2004) Ships that pass in the night: an examination of the assumed symbiosis between sport-for-all and elite sport. *Innovation in Cooperation: Proceedings of the 12th EASM European Sport Management Congress*, Ghent, Publicatiefond voor Lichamelijke Opvoeding vzw (26–37).

——(2008) 'Sports development and sports coaching', in K. Hylton and P. Bramham (eds) *Sport development: policy, process and practice, 2nd edition*, London: Routledge (214–35).

Lyle, J. and Cushion, C. (2010) 'Narrowing the field: some key questions about sports coaching', in J. Lyle and C. Cushion (eds) *Sports coaching: professionalisation and practice*, Edinburgh: Elsevier (243–52).

McDonald, M. and Tungatt, D. (1992) *Community development in sport*, London: Community Development Foundation.

North, J. (2009) *The coaching workforce 2009–2016*, Leeds: National Coaching Foundation.

Rowe, N. (2003) 'The social landscape of sport in England – a review of the research evidence and public policy implications', www.uida.es/economia (accessed 5 July 2004).

sports coach UK (2008a) *The UK coaching framework executive summary*, Leeds: Coachwise.

——(2008b) 'Completion of the coaching element of your Whole-Sport Plan', www.sportscoachuk.org/Resources/SCUK/Documents/ (accessed 17 June 2009).

——(2008c) 'Participant Development Model – core purpose, philosophy and values', Internal unpublished paper.

——(no date) 'UK coaching certificate', www.sportscoachUK.org/investing+in+coaching/UK+Coaching+Certificate/ (accessed 13 April 2009).

Stafford, I. (2005) *Coaching for Long Term Athlete Development*, Leeds: Coachwise.

Townend, R. and North, J. (2007) *Sports Coaching in the UK II*, Leeds: sports coach UK.

Trudel, P. and Gilbert, W. (2006) 'Coaching and coach education', in D. Kirk, M. O'Sullivan and D. McDonald (eds) *Handbook of research in physical education*, London: Sage (516–39).

UK Sport/Sport England/CONI (1999) *Compass 1999: sports participation in Europe*, London: UK Sport.

35

Health behaviour change through physical activity and sport

Stuart J.H. Biddle and Charlie Foster

There is a t-shirt on sale depicting humans evolving from apes to active hunter-gatherers, and then to sedentary people at a screen. The accompanying caption says 'something somewhere went terribly wrong'! This captures nicely the irony of contemporary lifestyles and health. In western market economies, we live longer than previous generations and have superior health care systems and medicines than ever before. Yet, at the same time, we have changed the way we live to create different health problems – those of non-communicable disease. These include cardiovascular disease, obesity, diabetes, and cancers and are considered lifestyle diseases. As such, in theory at least, we should be able to reverse such trends and improve physical and mental health, and quality of life, by changing such destructive behaviours.

As a result of the scenario just described, a great deal of thought and investment has gone into the burgeoning field of 'physical activity for health'. Whereas in the past, physical activity was not considered such an important health behaviour, or was viewed simply as 'sport' for youth or higher performance competitors, it is now a very high priority in public health. Two key reasons for this are that, first, physical activity can have a significant impact on a wide range of health conditions, including those stated above. Second, population surveillance of physical activity levels suggests that large numbers of people are insufficiently active to gain such health benefits. This means that the 'population attributable risk' of physical inactivity is very high and therefore successful physical activity behaviour change could have a significant impact on public health.

Behavioural epidemiology framework

The behavioural epidemiology framework was first advocated in physical activity by Sallis and Owen (1999). Behavioural epidemiology is concerned with the distribution and aetiology of behaviours that may be associated with disease outcomes and how these relate to the occurrence of disease in the population. Such behaviours could be smoking, lack of physical activity, sedentary behaviour, diet, etc. In relation to physical activity, this framework has five main phases, with phases 1–4 discussed here (see Figure 35.1):

- *to establish the link between physical activity and health*. This is now well documented for many diverse health conditions and well-being in adults (Hardman and Stensel 2009) and young people (Stensel *et al.* 2008).

- *to develop methods for the accurate assessment of physical activity*. This is a challenge. Often, large-scale surveillance of population trends rely on self-report, a method that has significant problems with validity and reliability. Recent 'objective' methods, such as accelerometers, heart rate monitors or pedometers, are useful but do not necessarily give all of the information required, such as type of activity or the setting in which the activity takes place. Nevertheless, it is recommended that objective assessment is undertaken, supplemented by other tools, including self-report or geographic information systems (GIS) and global positioning systems (GPS), if possible.
- *to identify factors that are associated with different levels of physical activity*. It is important to identify factors that might be associated with the adoption and maintenance of particular types of behaviour. This area is referred to as the study of 'correlates' (association) or 'determinants' (assuming some measure of causality) of physical activity (Biddle and Mutrie 2008).
- *to evaluate interventions designed to promote physical activity*. Once a variable is identified as a correlate of physical activity (e.g. family support), then interventions can manipulate this variable to test if it is, in fact, a determinant (Baranowski *et al.* 1998).
- *to translate findings from research into practice*. If interventions work, it is appropriate to translate such findings into ecologically valid settings.

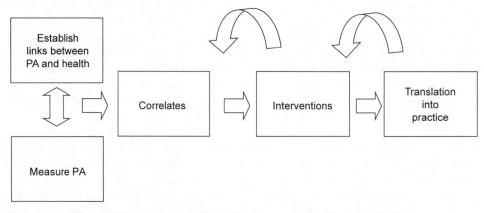

Figure 35.1 The behavioural epidemiology framework applied to physical activity

Phase I: Synopsis of health benefits

Space does not allow more than cursory coverage of the health benefits of regular physical activity. The Chief Medical Officer's report in England (Department of Health 2004) summarised such evidence and concluded that physical activity has preventive health effects on cardiovascular disease, overweight and obesity, Type 2 diabetes, musculo-skeletal health, psychological health, and some cancers. It is clear that physical activity is a significant behaviour in the context of public health (Hardman and Stensel 2009).

Phase II: Defining and measuring physical activity and sport

Physical activity is an umbrella term referring to all physical movement of an individual that results in energy expenditure significantly above resting levels (Caspersen *et al.* 1985). Typically, therefore, in this regard we think about walking, cycling and stair climbing, as well as sport-related activities and 'exercise'. *Exercise* is one element of physical activity and refers to planned, structured and repetitive bouts of activity that are highly correlated with gains in different components of physical fitness. Typically, this might include jogging, lifting weights and stretching exercises. *Sport*, on the other hand, is one form of physical activity (and usually exercise) that is structured around rules and competition, and has elements of skill, strategy or chance (Rejeski and Brawley 1988). However, while many sports are quite physically active, and therefore have overlap with exercise, not all are. Some sports (e.g. darts, snooker and pool) are less physically active but nonetheless constitute sports.

Defining terms is important if we are interested in enhancing health through physical activity, sport or exercise. We need to know if the behaviour selected can enhance health, and then we need to understand how to change the behaviour, and this requires more subtle definitions of the behaviour. Assuming 'exercise' is the same as 'sport', for example, would be a mistake.

Phase III: Correlates of physical activity

One of the primary aims of research into physical activity for health is to find ways of increasing physical activity in those with less than optimal levels. Before successful interventions can be initiated it is important to establish what factors might be associated with participation (referred to as 'correlates'). A great deal of research effort has been invested in this area for more than 20 years and a number of reviews now exist for young people (Sallis *et al.* 2000; van der Horst *et al.* 2007) and adults (Trost *et al.* 2002). Correlates are typically grouped into demographic, biological, psychological, socio-cultural, and environmental factors. For young people, Sallis *et al.* (2000) addressed correlates of physical activity, with van der Horst *et al.* (2007) also reviewing correlates of 'insufficient physical activity' (i.e. low levels of activity) as well as sedentary behaviours.

Demographic. Age and gender have been consistent correlates of physical activity in youth, with males and children often reporting more activity than females and adolescents. Particularly in girls, participation falls steadily in the teenage years, although the updated review by van der Horst *et al.* (2007) showed no evidence of age effects for physical activity in children and data were inconclusive for adolescents, albeit with fewer studies over a shorter time frame than reported by Sallis *et al.* (2000). Data on ethnicity is more sparse, but trends suggest greater activity for 'white' ethnic groups, but clearly this distinction is likely to mask many other possible differences and similarities.

For adults, clear inverse associations were reported by Trost *et al.* (2002) in a review of studies on age, and also showed males to be more active than females. Education and related socio-economic status markers showed that lower levels of these indicators were associated with less physical activity.

Biological. The most frequently studied biological correlate for young people is weight status (e.g. body fat or BMI). This has not been shown to be related to physical activity when reviewed by Sallis *et al.* and van der Horst *et al.* While an association between physical activity and overweight/obesity has been demonstrated (Steinbeck 2001), and indeed would be expected, associations in childhood can be difficult to detect due to measurement issues such as maturity and measurement error, particularly for self-reported physical activity. For adults, however, an inverse association is evident between overweight/obesity and physical activity (Trost *et al.* 2002).

Psychological. For children, there is little consistency in the results reported by Sallis *et al.* (2000) and van der Horst *et al.* (2007). Part of this may be explained by a simple lack of studies reported on some correlates. Across the two reviews, physical activity is positively associated with intentions and 'preference' for physical activity. Recent studies have also shown self-efficacy (confidence) to be associated with greater levels of physical activity in children.

For adolescents, reviews show that higher levels of perceived competence and self-efficacy are associated with greater physical activity. Biddle *et al.* (2005) reported that the strength of the association between physical activity and perceived competence for adolescent girls was small, but small to moderate for self-efficacy. 'Goal orientation/motivation' and 'achievement orientation' were identified by van der Horst *et al.* and Sallis *et al.* as being positively associated with physical activity in adolescents. This construct is likely to be some form of 'task orientation' – a style or 'orientation' of motivation where the individual defines competence and success in self-referenced terms. The individual is motivated to learn from mistakes, to exert effort and improve (Biddle *et al.* 2003).

The psychological literature is clear that the motivation to take part in behaviours of free choice, such as physical activity in leisure-time, is predicted by strong intentions (Ajzen 2001), and this was supported in the review by Sallis *et al.* (2000). Intention is a key mediating variable in the Theory of Planned Behaviour (see later). Intentions to act are the immediate antecedent of behaviour, and research supports an association between intentions and physical activity. Planning how best to implement intentions may strengthen this relationship further (Gollwitzer and Sheeran 2006) and help close the gap between intentions and behaviours.

Issues of body image and appearance seem to be important for adolescent girls in the context of physical activity decision making. Specifically, the correlates of perceived body attractiveness, importance of appearance, and physical self-worth were positive and small to moderate in their strength of association with physical activity in adolescent girls (Biddle *et al.* 2005).

Trost *et al.*'s (2002) review of adult correlates of physical activity located 38 new studies published since those used in the summary produced by Sallis and Owen (1999) (i.e. 1998–2000). Of those addressing psychological correlates of physical activity, there was evidence for a consistent positive association with physical activity, across both reviews, for the variables of enjoyment, expected benefits, intention, perceived health, self-motivation, self-efficacy, stage of behaviour change and self-schemata for exercise, and negative associations for barriers and mood disturbance.

The strongest evidence is for self-efficacy and is likely to be more important for behaviours that require effort, such as structured fitness programmes. The correlate of enjoyment is associated with intrinsic motivational states (Deci and Ryan 2002). However, enjoyment might be seen as both an antecedent of behaviour, thus acting as a motivator ('I exercise to seek enjoyment'), or an outcome ('I enjoyed that session of exercise'), thus acting as reinforcement.

Behavioural. Previous physical activity and healthy diet have been associated with physical activity in youth. The variable of 'previous physical activity' suggests that some measure of 'tracking' takes place, that is, the more active children remain so as they age. Evidence for tracking, however, is not as strong as we sometimes might think. Statistical associations for activity patterns between different ages are, at best, 'moderate' and sometimes 'small'. Of course, this will depend on the periods of the life course being studied and the length of time between assessments. Associations are weaker between adolescence and adulthood than childhood to adolescence (Malina 1996), and associations decline as the length of assessment period increases (Telama *et al.* 2005). Moreover, in Trost *et al.*'s (2002) review of correlates of physical activity in adults, physical activity history in childhood/youth was not associated with adult activity, whereas an association was found for activity history in adulthood. Other behavioural factors associated with physical activity for adults include smoking (a negative association) and healthy diet (a positive association).

Sedentary behaviour during the after-school and weekend periods are associated with less physical activity in youth (Atkin *et al.* 2008). For adolescents, sports participation is related to overall physical activity levels, including girls (Biddle *et al.* 2005; Vilhjalmsson and Kristjansdottir 2003).

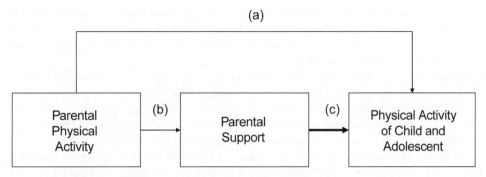

Figure 35.2 Relationships between parental physical activity, parental support and youth physical activity

Socio-cultural. Sallis *et al.* (2000) did not find any socio–cultural variables associated with physical activity in children whereas parental support was associated in the review by van der Horst (2007). Peer and parental support were found to be correlates of physical activity for adolescents. One variable often thought to be associated with activity in young people is that of parental physical activity. However, the evidence for this is weak. A review by Gustafson and Rhodes (2006) showed that parental activity was most likely mediated in its influence on activity by parental support, as suggested in Figure 35.2. Social support is associated with physical activity in adults (Trost *et al.* 2002).

Environmental. The study of environmental factors associated with physical activity is a more recent trend (Davison and Lawson 2006). Reviews show that access to facilities (children) and 'opportunities to exercise' (adolescents) are associated with higher levels of physical activity. In addition, time outdoors is associated with more activity in children, and this is likely to be related to spending less time on sedentary entertainment (Ferreira *et al.* 2006; Sallis *et al.* 2000). For adults, environmental factors that are related to physical activity include access to facilities and a positive environment, such as enjoyable scenery and neighbourhood safety.

Theories underpinning physical activity behaviour change

Theory provides a unifying framework from which to understand physical activity behaviours and, ultimately, behaviour change. It underpins the planning and implementation of physical activity research, particularly for interventions (Bartholomew *et al.* 2001). There have been a number of social psychological theories that have been used to advance understanding of why people might choose to be active or not. These include Social Cognitive Theory (Bandura 1986), Theory of Planned Behaviour (Ajzen 2001; Hagger *et al.* 2002), and the Transtheoretical Model (Marshall and Biddle 2001; Prochaska and Marcus 1994). In addition, the Health Action Process Model (Schwarzer 2008), Common Sense Model of Illness Perceptions (Hagger and Orbell 2003; Leventhal *et al.* 1998), Health Belief Model (Harrison *et al.* 1992), and Behavioural Choice Theory (Epstein and Roemmich 2001) have also been used and have a place in intervention planning. Space only allows a brief look at some of these frameworks.

Social Cognitive Theory

Social Cognitive Theory (SCT) can be attributed to the work of Bandura (1977). SCT suggests that we learn and modify our behaviours through an interaction between personal, behavioural, and environmental influences – 'reciprocal determinism'. In other words, we are not merely a function of the environment, nor are we merely passive in following our psychological characteristics. Moreover, our own and others' behaviour can influence us. Put together, all three factors influence how we think, feel and act.

SCT comprises a self-regulation component in which we regulate our behaviour based on our own goals, behaviours and feelings. For example, people may adopt a certain goal to be physically active that helps motivate action. In addition, we reflect on our actions, particularly in respect of thinking about the consequences of our behaviours ('outcome expectancies') and our own capabilities to enact the behaviours of choice ('efficacy expectancies').

Self-efficacy. The element of SCT concerning self-reflection of our capability has led to Bandura's most significant contribution, that of 'self-efficacy'. This is situation-specific confidence to undertake a certain behaviour, and we have already identified this construct as an important correlate of physical activity. Self-efficacy refers to efficacy beliefs and is the 'can I?' question. This will be most influential for behaviours that challenge us, such as being more physically active. If someone believes they can adopt and maintain the behaviour in question, they are more likely to do so.

Research on self-efficacy in physical activity not only shows this to be an important antecedent of behaviour (i.e. a correlate), but also an outcome of participation by showing that positive experiences in physical activity can enhance feelings of efficacy (McAuley and Blissmer 2000; McAuley and Morris 2007).

There are four main sources of information that we might use to develop our levels of self-efficacy. These are prior behaviour (success and performance attainment), watching others (imitation and modelling), encouragement (verbal and social persuasion), and creating feelings of relaxation and upbeat mood (judgements of physiological states), and these can form strategies for interventions.

Theory of Planned Behaviour

The Theory of Planned Behaviour (TPB) assumes that intention is the immediate antecedent of behaviour and that intention is predicted from attitude, normative beliefs, and perceptions of behavioural control (see Figure 35.3). Ajzen and Fishbein (1980) suggested that the attitude component of the model is a function of the beliefs held about the specific behaviour, as well as the evaluation, or value, of the likely outcomes. Such beliefs can be instrumental (i.e. 'exercise helps me lose weight') and affective ('exercise is enjoyable'). The latter may be more effective for sustainable behaviour change.

The normative beliefs ('subjective norm') component is comprised of the beliefs of significant others and the extent that one wishes to comply with such beliefs. Perceived behavioural control (PBC) is defined by Ajzen (1988: 132) as 'the perceived ease or difficulty of performing the behaviour' and is assumed 'to reflect past experience as well as anticipated impediments and obstacles'. Figure 35.3 shows that perceived control links with both intentions and behaviour. This suggests that the variable has a motivational effect on intentions, such that individuals wishing to be physically active, but with little or no chance of doing so, possibly because of barriers, are unlikely to be active regardless of their attitudes or the normative factors operating.

The construct of PBC is underpinned by a set of control beliefs and the perceived power of these beliefs. Control beliefs refer to the perceived presence of factors that may help or impede the behaviour, and perceived power refers to the perceived impact that helping or inhibiting factors may have on the behaviour (Ajzen 1991). PBC is thought to accurately predict

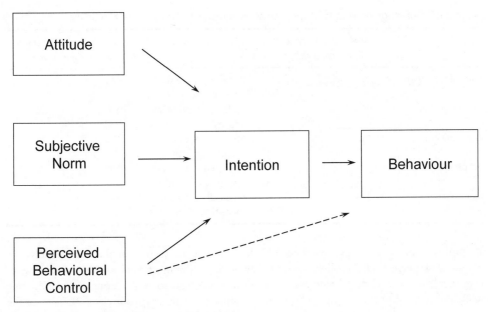

Figure 35.3 The Theory of Planned Behaviour

behaviour under circumstances only when perceived control closely approximates actual control (hence the use of broken line in Figure 35.3).

Two meta-analyses have been conducted using the TPB, or elements of the model. Hausenblas *et al.* (1997) showed that intention had a large effect on exercise behaviour, and attitude had a large effect on intention. Similar findings were reported by Hagger and colleagues (2002) in showing correlations of 0.35 between attitude and behaviour, 0.60 between attitude and intention, and 0.51 between intention and behaviour.

There is a less than perfect correlation between intentions and behaviour. To help bridge the gap between intentions and behaviour, 'implementation intentions' have been proposed (Gollwitzer 1999). These are goals and plans that involve specifying when, how, and where performance of behaviour will take place.

Transtheoretical Model

Research concerning the Transtheoretical Model (TTM) in physical activity is now quite extensive (Marshall and Biddle 2001; Riemsma *et al.* 2002). The model proposes that behaviour change involves moving through 'stages of change'. The term 'transtheoretical model' is used to describe the wider framework that encompasses both the 'when' (stages) and the 'how' of behaviour change, including the processes (strategies) of change and moderators of change such as decisional balance (pros and cons of change) and self-efficacy.

Studies on physical activity assess the stages of precontemplation, contemplation, preparation, action and maintenance. These are described in Table 35.1. The stages of change are concerned with the temporal patterning of behaviour change. By also identifying processes of change we are able to better understand why and how this temporal shift might take place. Processes of change, therefore, are important for interventions by helping move people between stages. Processes of change are defined by Marcus *et al.* (1992) as various strategies and techniques that people use to help them progress through the different stages of change over time. Typically,

Table 35.1 Defining the stages of the Transtheoretical Model in physical activity

Stage	Meeting criterion level of physical activity?	Current behaviour	Intention to meet criterion level of physical activity?
Precontemplation	No	Little or no physical activity	No
Contemplation	No	Little or no physical activity	Yes
Preparation	No	Small changes in physical activity	Yes
Action	Yes	Physically active for less than 6 months	Yes
Maintenance	Yes	Physically active for more than 6 months	Yes

10 processes of change have been identified, with five of these described as cognitive or 'thinking' strategies and the other five as behavioural or 'doing' strategies. Cognitive processes (e.g. increasing knowledge, being aware of health risks) tend to peak during the action stage while behavioural processes (e.g. enlisting social support, reminding yourself) peak later, in the maintenance stage. The meta-analysis by Marshall and Biddle (2001) showed that movement from precontemplation to contemplation and from preparation to action are characterised by sharper increases in behavioural process use compared to other stage transitions and that nine of the 10 processes followed similar patterns of change across the stages. This argues against the presence of a stage-by-process interaction whereby some processes are thought to be more important or likely at certain stages.

One strategy that can assist people to make successful behaviour change is to weigh up the advantages of change ('pros') against the disadvantages or costs ('cons'). This 'decisional balance' exercise is one that has been at the core of the TTM. Research suggests that in the early stages of behaviour change the cons outweigh the pros of change. Those in preparation see more equality between the pros and cons, whereas those who are in maintenance will perceive more pros than cons. Changing perceptions of pros and cons, therefore, may assist in behaviour change.

Marshall and Biddle (2001) also showed that self-efficacy increased with each stage progression, as proposed by the model. The pattern of increase was not linear, however, with effects being moderate between precontemplation and contemplation, small to moderate from contemplation to preparation, moderate from preparation to action, and moderate to large from action to maintenance.

The TTM is not without its critics. Riemsma *et al.* (2002) conducted a systematic review to assess the effectiveness of stage-based approaches in behaviour change interventions. This included seven intervention trials concerning physical activity, and only one showed a positive effect for behaviour change, with two showing mixed effects. Similarly, Adams and White (2005) have questioned the long-term effectiveness of such interventions. However, several commentators suggest that short-term effectiveness has been demonstrated, and that further work is required before dismissing the model or replacing it with something else (Brug *et al.* 2005).

Other theoretical frameworks

There are numerous other theories and frameworks that have been applied to the study of physical activity behaviour and, as stated, space precludes covering them all (see Bartholomew *et al.*

2001, for comprehensive coverage). One that has been used in the study of sedentary behaviour in children and offers a useful heuristic is 'behavioural choice theory' (BCT) (Epstein and Roemmich 2001). Based on 'behavioural economics' (Zimmerman 2009), BCT proposes that choosing a specific behaviour (e.g. playing a sport or being physically active in other ways) will be a function of the accessibility and reinforcement value of the behaviour. In using this approach to explain and modify young people's propensity for sedentary technological pursuits, Epstein and colleagues have shown that making alternative active behaviours more accessible, and sedentary pursuits less reinforcing, reductions in sedentary behaviour and increases in physical activity are possible (Epstein and Roemmich 2001; Epstein et al. 1995). The challenge is to find ways of making sport and physical activity more appealing (reinforcement value) and easy to do (accessible) relative to competing behaviours, such as sedentary behaviours. This is a significant challenge given the current ubiquitous nature of attractive sedentary entertainment.

Phase IV: Intervention effectiveness

The struggle to develop successful approaches to change and maintain physical activity first developed in the 1980s as part of large cardiovascular risk reduction community programmes. In the 1990s, interventions focused on adapting and applying theories of behaviour change in face-to-face contexts, leading to a switch, around the year 2000, to look at broader policy interventions across communities or within settings like schools or workplaces. More recently, new interventions have emerged reflecting not only an increasing awareness of the possible impact of policy interventions and changing the built environment but also new opportunities offered by mediated interventions, such as the internet, e-health and mobile phone technology (Napolitano and Marcus 2002). This section provides an overview of the evidence base for four types of interventions: (i) policy, (ii) environmental change, (iii) community-based interventions, and (iv) individualised interventions (Foster and Cavill 2009).

What types of physical activity interventions exist at policy or population level? Much of the evidence base for the effectiveness of physical activity interventions is for small-scale interpersonal or group interventions. It has been said that this demonstrates the 'inverse evidence law' in which there is the least evidence about the approaches that we think might have the greatest potential (Ogilvie et al. 2005).

Policy interventions

The published literature on the effectiveness of policy interventions to promote physical activity is sparse. The review by Cavill et al. (2006) found three types of policy approaches: (i) national policy on health and physical activity; (ii) environmental change interventions; and (iii) community-based interventions.

Pucher and Djikstra's (2003) review of national transport policies reported an association between having national transport related policies that include an environmental modification component and improved levels of walking and cycling compared to countries without such policies. A national or regional planning policy can contribute to increased physical activity, such as by insisting on locating mixed land use building (housing, retail and industry). Moreover, mass transit systems have increased population levels of walking and cycling, particularly in more urbanised areas (Schwanen et al. 2004).

Perhaps the best examples of city-wide approaches to use policies to encourage physical activity can be seen in Europe. The gradual impact of policies to support a range of active travel initiatives, delivered at a city-wide level, has led to reported increases in population levels of cycling and walking (e.g. Copenhagen, Odense, Amsterdam and London) (National Institute for Health and Clinical Excellence 2009; Ogilvie *et al.* 2004, 2007). Finally, the Agita Sao Paulo programme, in Brazil, combined policy, environmental and community-based physical activity initiatives to produce an intervention that delivered actions at each section of a socio-ecological model for different population groups. The evaluation of this programme over six years, using random stratified population samples (pre/post design), has reported increases in walking, moderate levels of physical activity, and knowledge of physical activity and the programme itself (Matsudo *et al.* 2004).

Environmental interventions

The National Institute for Health and Clinical Excellence (NICE), in England and Wales, has recently published public health programme guidance on physical activity and the environment based on a series of systematic reviews (National Institute for Health and Clinical Excellence 2009). Transport interventions show positive benefits for the promotion of active travel by changes in the built environment via a range of options. These have included:

- re-allocation of road space to support physically active modes of transport (as an example, this could be achieved by widening pavements and introducing cycle lanes);
- restricting motor vehicle access (for example, by closing or narrowing roads to reduce capacity);
- introducing road-user charging schemes;
- introducing traffic-calming schemes to restrict vehicle speeds (using signage and changes to highway design);
- creating safe routes to schools (for example, by using traffic-calming measures near schools and by creating or improving walking and cycle routes to schools).

Other systematic reviews have also found some evidence to support the impact of large-scale environmental changes on physical activity (Foster and Hillsdon 2004; Ogilvie *et al.* 2007). Studies have included the provision and improvement of sports and exercise facilities, changes to policies to encourage adults to have greater access and time to use new facilities, and the construction of new local opportunities to walk and cycle using cycling and walking paths. Five of six studies have reported a small effect of their interventions in increasing physical activity levels either as a direct change in self-reported physical activity, cardiovascular fitness or trail usage (Gordon *et al.* 2004; Linenger *et al.* 1991; Merom *et al.* 2003; Peel and Booth 2001; Vuori *et al.* 1994). Two studies have demonstrated that a combination of changes to working practices, policies and the physical environment encouraged adults to maintain their vigorous physical activity and fitness (Linenger *et al.* 1991; Peel and Booth 2001). Despite the appeal of changing the environment or providing new opportunities for physical activity (e.g. cycle paths), the evidence base for these approaches in terms of promoting physical activity is still small. Some evidence does exist of an effect upon physical activity behaviour in the short term but this evidence base is weakened by the poor quality of study methodology.

Community-based interventions

Community-based physical activity interventions can span many different types, delivered across different settings (Cavill and Foster 2004). Community is often defined as a geographical area, such as a city or town, defined by geopolitical boundaries (Sharpe 2003). However, it could also include dimensions related to age, culture, ethnicity, gender and race. One advantage of community interventions is that they tend to use a 'seeking stance' (King 1998), where the health promoter actively seeks out the target community. This contrasts with a 'waiting stance', such as that adopted by health care professionals who respond to the needs and demands of people using their service.

Community interventions can be categorised into three groups: a) comprehensive integrated community approaches; b) community-wide campaigns using mass media; and c) community-based approaches using person-focused techniques. These interventions use three types of outcome variable: proximal variable (e.g. changes in knowledge, self-efficacy and awareness), intention to be more active, and changes in self-reported physical activity.

Community-integrated approaches include actions across a range of settings. Three large cardiovascular health programmes – the Minnesota Heart Health Project (Luepker et al. 1994), the Stamford Five Cities Project (Young et al. 1996), and the Pawtucket Heart Health Project (Eaton et al. 1999) – include physical activity as a focus of their actions alongside healthy eating and smoking reduction. Change in physical activity across these programmes could be described as modest at best with small and unsustained changes. Other process measures from these programmes showed high levels of participation in community events and that mass media campaigns increased awareness and knowledge, while the longer-term setting-specific programmes contributed more to increased physical activity (Blake et al. 1987; King 1998).

Community-wide campaigns using mass media have produced significant changes in proximal variables. Reviews have shown that mass media approaches alone are effective at raising awareness of physical activity messages, but have little long-term impact on behaviour (Kahn et al. 2002; Marcus and Forsyth 1999). Evaluation of such approaches is limited as it tends to focus too much on behaviour change, without measuring any changes in the proximal variables, such as knowledge or attitudes, which are more amenable to change through communication campaigns (Cavill and Bauman 2004). The 'Active for Life' campaign in England, run by the then Health Education Authority, reported similar findings with significant changes in knowledge about the new physical activity recommendations, but no changes seen in physical activity.

One recent example of a successful mass media campaign – Project VERB – has reported changes in knowledge, attitude and physical activity. In 2001, the US Congress gave US$ 125 million to the Centres for Disease Control and Prevention (CDC) to launch a campaign that would help children develop habits to foster good health over a lifetime and to use methods that are employed by the best marketers for children. The funding was the largest ever given to the CDC for a single initiative. VERB was the largest youth campaign conducted in the world, focusing on 'tweens' (9–13 year olds), and was very comprehensively evaluated using formative, process and outcome evaluations. These evaluations reported that the more children who reported seeing VERB messages, the more physical activity they reported and the more positive their attitudes were about the benefits of being physically active. Selected communities received 'high doses' of advertising and special campaign activities. These were compared with a comparison group that received only the national dose of advertising. After two years, 'tweens' in the high-dose communities reported higher awareness and understanding of VERB, greater self-efficacy, more sessions of free-time physical activity per week, and were more active on the day before being surveyed than those in the comparison group. Parents' awareness of VERB was also associated with positive attitudes, beliefs and behaviour. The links to communities were thought to be particularly important; the campaign used a social marketing approach to deliver its message through the mass media, school and community promotions, and partnerships (Asbury et al. 2008; Wong et al. 2008).

Community-based approaches using person-focused techniques

This category includes programmes that use methods and strategies, such as one-to-one counselling, classroom instruction, and cognitive-behavioural strategies, but use them in community facilities and settings such as church halls or community centres (Sharpe 2003). These approaches have reported significant changes in physical activity, sustained up to one year (Foster *et al.* 2005; Ogilvie *et al.* 2004, 2007). Characteristics of successful interventions include those tailored to people's needs, targeted at the most sedentary or at those most motivated to change, and delivered either at the level of the individual (brief advice, supported use of pedometers, telecommunications) or household (individualised marketing), or through groups. Interventions that provide people with professional guidance about starting an exercise programme, and then provide ongoing support, may be more effective in encouraging the uptake of physical activity.

New approaches

New media technologies have been embraced by physical activity promoters. These include mobile communications (mobile phones, PDAs), computers and the internet. A growing body of evidence from small efficacy studies has shown small sustained changes in physical activity. These 'mediated interventions' are based on the same theories of health behaviours, such as Social Cognitive Theory, as non-mediated approaches and have often adapted the same strategies to be delivered in new ways. For example, Robbins *et al.* (2006) targeted low-active 11–13-year-old American girls in schools and used a computer-mediated approach, as well as counselling, to increase physical activity. The girls received tailored feedback and nurse counselling over 12 weeks based on their computerised assessment of their current activity status, while a control group received activity guidelines only. Support materials were also provided to parents of girls in the intervention group and follow-up phone calls were made to the intervention girls. However, no significant differences were observed between the groups at follow-up for physical activity.

Sedentary behaviour interventions

As the epidemiology for the association between sedentary behaviour (usually defined as sitting time) and health outcomes develops there is no doubt that more interventions focusing on reducing sedentary behaviour time will emerge. Some small studies have tried to increase both physical activity and reduce sedentary behaviour, but nearly all studies are with young people rather than adults. For example, Epstein *et al.* (2008) recruited 4 to 7-year-olds whose BMI was at or above the 75th BMI percentile for age and gender and who participated in high levels of sedentary screen time. A randomised controlled trial (RCT) design was used. After baseline television and computer use was monitored for 3 weeks, families were stratified and randomised into either a control or intervention group. Screen time was monitored and budgeted by a TV/computer allowance device, however, those in the control group had free access to televisions and computers. Families in the intervention group received monthly leaflets providing alternatives to sedentary behaviour and tips for parents to reduce such behaviour. Parents were also instructed to praise children for reducing TV viewing and computer use and for participating in non-sedentary alternatives. Both groups showed a reduction in screen time, with the intervention group showing larger reductions in comparison to the control group and remaining similar through to 24 months. Statistically significant between-group differences were observed at 6 and 24 months.

Interventions: Conclusions

There is now a strong and increasingly mature evidence base to demonstrate that a number of face-to-face, environmental and policy interventions can increase and maintain changes in physical activity for between 6 months to a year. We note that these studies have focused on trying to stimulate physical activity behaviour in the inactive and wonder if there is a need in the future to consider developing interventions to keep the active still active (i.e. strategies for maintenance). Such approaches would have to re-visit health behaviour models from smoking and substance misuse and apply constructs and strategies for relapse prevention. The impact of life events and key changes in someone's personal and social circumstances have considerable impact on physical activity behaviour. Such events might include changes in employment status, residence, physical status, relationships and family structure (Allender *et al.* 2008). These events offer future physical activity interventions a focus for action.

The field of physical activity health research is increasingly focused on interventions. Many of these struggle to show strong effects, at least in the medium to long term. This may be due to a lack of intervention fidelity. This refers to the extent that the intervention was delivered as intended. Community-based interventions are difficult to implement and more needs to be documented about exactly what was delivered in the intervention. For example, Pate *et al.* (2003) provide an interesting and candid account of the difficulties encountered in trying to engage young people in an intervention. The use of detailed process evaluation, through checklists and interviews, should prove useful in better documenting how an intervention was delivered, what worked, and what did not work.

References

Adams, J., & White, M. (2005). Why don't stage-based activity promotion interventions work? *Health Education Research, 20*(2), 237–43.

Ajzen, I. (1988). *Attitudes, personality and behaviour.* Milton Keynes: Open University Press.

——(1991). The Theory of Planned Behavior. *Organizational Behavior and Human Decision Processes, 50*, 179–211.

——(2001). Nature and operation of attitudes. *Annual Review of Psychology, 52*, 27–58.

Ajzen, I., & Fishbein, M. (1980). *Understanding attitudes and predicting social behaviour.* Englewood Cliffs, NJ: Prentice-Hall.

Allender, S., Hutchinson, L., & Foster, C. (2008). Life-change events and participation in physical activity: a systematic review. *Health Promotion International, 23*, 160–117.

Asbury, L., Wong, F., Price, S., & Nolin, M. (2008). The VERB campaign: applying a branding strategy in public health. *American Journal of Preventive Medicine, 34*(6, Suppl.), S183–S187.

Atkin, A. J., Gorely, T., Biddle, S. J. H., Marshall, S. J., & Cameron, N. (2008). Critical hours: Physical activity and sedentary behavior of adolescents after school. *Pediatric Exercise Science, 20*, 446–56.

Bandura, A. (1977). *Social learning theory.* Englewood Cliffs, NJ: Prentice Hall.

——(1986). *Social foundations of thought and action: a social cognitive theory.* Englewood Cliffs, NJ: Prentice Hall.

Baranowski, T., Anderson, C., & Carmack, C. (1998). Mediating variable framework in physical activity interventions: How are we doing? How might we do better? *American Journal of Preventive Medicine, 15*(4), 266–97.

Bartholomew, L. K., Parcel, G. S., Kok, G., & Gottlieb, N. H. (2001). *Intervention mapping: designing theory- and evidence-based health promotion programs.* Mountain View, CA: Mayfield.

Biddle, S. J. H., & Mutrie, N. (2008). *Psychology of physical activity: determinants, well-being and interventions (2nd Edition).* London: Routledge.

Biddle, S. J. H., Wang, C. K. J., Kavussanu, M., & Spray, C. M. (2003). Correlates of achievement goal orientations in physical activity: a systematic review of research. *European Journal of Sport Science, 3*(5), www.humankinetics.com/ejss.

Biddle, S. J. H., Whitehead, S. H., O'Donovan, T. M., & Nevill, M. E. (2005). Correlates of participation in physical activity for adolescent girls: a systematic review of recent literature. *Journal of Physical Activity and Health, 2*, 423–34.

Blake, S., Jeffery, R., & Finnegan, J. R. (1987). Process evaluation of a community-based physical activity campaign: The Minnesota Heart Health Program. *Health Education Research, 2,* 115–21.

Brug, J., Conner, M., Harre, N., Kremers, S., McKeller, S., & Whitelaw, S. (2005). The transtheoretical model and stages of change: a critique. Observations by five commentators on the paper by Adams, J. and White, M. (2004) Why don't stage-based activity promotion interventions work? *Health Education Research, 20*(2), 244–58.

Caspersen, C. J., Powell, K. E., & Christenson, G. M. (1985). Physical activity, exercise and physical fitness: definitions and distinctions for health-related research. *Public Health Reports, 100,* 126–31.

Cavill, N., & Bauman, A. (2004). Changing the way people think about health-enhancing physical activity: do mass media campaigns have a role? *Journal of Sports Sciences, 22*(8), 771–90.

Cavill, N., & Foster, C. (2004). How to promote health enhancing physical activity: Community interventions. In P. Oja & J. Borms (Eds), *Health Enhancing Physical Activity. Perspectives Vol. 6.* London: Meyer & Meyer.

Cavill, N., Foster, C., Oja, P., & Martin, B. W. (2006). An evidence-based approach to physical activity promotion and policy development in Europe: contrasting case studies. *Promotion & Education, 13,* 104–11.

Davison, K., & Lawson, C. (2006). Do attributes in the physical environment influence children's physical activity? A review of the literature. *International Journal of Behavioral Nutrition and Physical Activity, 3*(1), www.ijbnpa.org/content/3/1/19

Deci, E. L., & Ryan, R. M. (Eds). (2002). *Handbook of self-determination research.* Rochester: The University of Rochester Press.

Department of Health. (2004). *At least five a week: Evidence on the impact of physical activity and its relationship to health. A report from the Chief Medical Officer.* London: Author.

Eaton, C., Lapane, K., Garber, C., Gans, K., Lasater, T., & Carleton, R. (1999). Effects of a community-based intervention on physical activity: the Pawtucket Heart Health Program. *American Journal of Public Health, 89,* 1741–4.

Epstein, L. H., & Roemmich, J. N. (2001). Reducing sedentary behaviour: role in modifying physical activity. *Exercise and Sport Sciences Reviews, 29*(3), 103–8.

Epstein, L. H., Roemmich, J. N., Robinson, J. L., Paluch, R. A., Winiewicz, D. D., Fuerch, J. H., *et al.* (2008). A randomised trial of the effects of reducing television viewing and computer use on body mass index in young children. *Archives of Pediatric and Adolescent Medicine, 162*(3), 239–45.

Epstein, L. H., Saelens, B. E., & O'Brien, J. G. (1995). Effects of reinforcing increases in active behavior versus decreases in sedentary behavior for obese children. *International Journal of Behavioral Medicine, 2,* 41–50.

Ferreira, I., van der Horst, K., Wendel-Vos, W., Kremers, S., van Lenthe, F. J., & Brug, J. (2006). Environmental correlates of physical activity in youth: A review and update. *Obesity Reviews, 8*(2), 129–54.

Foster, C., & Cavill, N. (2009). *Expert testimony – The effectiveness of physical activity promotion interventions. Report submitted to NICE CVD PDG Committee.* London: NICE.

Foster, C., & Hillsdon, M. (2004). Changing the environment to promote health enhancing physical activity. *Journal of Sports Sciences, 22,* 755–69.

Foster, C., Hillsdon, M., & Thorogood, M. (2005). Interventions for physical activity. *Cochrane Database of Systematic Reviews, Issue 1. Art. No.: CD003180. DOI: 10.1002/14651858.CD003180.pub2.*

Gollwitzer, P. M. (1999). Implementation intentions: Strong effects of simple plans. *American Psychologist, July,* 493–503.

Gollwitzer, P. M., & Sheeran, P. (2006). Implementation intentions and goal achievement: A meta-analysis of effects and processes. *Advances in Experimental Social Psychology, 38,* 69–119.

Gordon, P., Zizzi, S., & Pauline, J. (2004). Use of a community trail among new and habitual exercisers: A preliminary assessment. *Preventing Chronic Disease [serial online],* Oct. Available from: www.cdc.gov/pcd/issues/2004/oct/2004_0058.htm.

Gustafson, S. L., & Rhodes, R. E. (2006). 'Parental correlates of physical activity in children and adolescents'. *Sports Medicine, 36,* 79–97.

Hagger, M. S., Chatzisarantis, N. L. D., & Biddle, S. J. H. (2002). 'A meta-analytic review of the Theories of Reasoned Action and Planned Behaviour in physical activity: Predictive validity and the contribution of additional variables'. *Journal of Sport & Exercise Psychology, 24,* 3–32.

Hagger, M. S., & Orbell, S. (2003). 'A meta-analytic review of the common-sense model of illness representations'. *Psychology and Health, 18,* 141–84.

Hardman, A. E., & Stensel, D. J. (2009). *Physical activity and health: The evidence explained (2nd Edition)*. London: Routledge.

Harrison, J. A., Mullen, P. D., & Green, L. W. (1992). 'A meta-analysis of studies of the Health Belief Model with adults'. *Health Education Research: Theory & Practice, 7*, 107–16.

Hausenblas, H. A., Carron, A. V., & Mack, D. E. (1997). Application of the theories of reason action and planned behavior to exercise behavior: A meta-analysis. *Journal of Sport and Exercise Psychology, 19*, 36–51.

Kahn, E. B., Ramsey, L. T., Brownson, R. C., Heath, G. W., Howze, E. H., Powell, K. E., *et al.* (2002). 'The effectiveness of interventions to increase physical activity: A systematic review'. *American Journal of Preventive Medicine, 22*(4S), 73–107.

King, A. C. (1998). 'How to promote physical activity in a community: research experiences from the US highlighting different community approaches'. *Patient Education and Counseling, 33*, S3–S12.

Leventhal, H., Leventhal, E., & Contrada, R. J. (1998). 'Self-regulation, health and behaviour: a perceptual cognitive approach'. *Psychology and Health, 13*, 717–34.

Linenger, J. M., Chesson, C. V., & Nice, D. S. (1991). 'Physical fitness gains following simple environmental change'. *American Journal of Preventive Medicine, 7*, 298–310.

Luepker, R., Murray, D., Jacobs, D., Mittelmark, M., Bracht, N., Carlaw, R., *et al.* (1994). 'Community education for cardiovascular disease prevention: risk factor changes in the Minnesota Heart Health Program'. *American Journal of Public Health, 84*, 1383–93.

Malina, R. M. (1996). 'Tracking of physical activity and physical fitness across the lifespan'. *Research Quarterly for Exercise and Sport, 67*(3, Suppl.), S48–S57.

Marcus, B. H., Banspach, S. W., Lefebvre, R. C., Rossi, J. S., Carleton, R. A., & Abrams, D. B. (1992). 'Using the stages of change model to increase the adoption of physical activity among community participants'. *American Journal of Health Promotion, 6*, 424–9.

Marcus, B., & Forsyth, L. (1999). 'How are we doing with physical activity?' *American Journal of Health Promotion, 14*, 118–24.

Marshall, S. J., & Biddle, S. J. H. (2001). 'The Transtheoretical Model of behavior change: a meta-analysis of applications to physical activity and exercise'. *Annals of Behavioral Medicine, 23*, 229–46.

Matsudo, S., Matsudo, V., Araújo, T., Andrade, D., Andrade, E., Oliveira, L., *et al.* (2004). 'Physical activity promotion: Experiences and evaluation of the Agita São Paulo program using the ecological mobile model'. *Journal of Physical Activity and Health, 1*, 81–97.

McAuley, E., & Blissmer, B. (2000). 'Self-efficacy determinants and consequences of physical activity'. *Exercise and Sport Sciences Reviews, 28*, 85–8.

McAuley, E., & Morris, K. S. (2007). 'Advances in physical activity and mental health: quality of life'. *American Journal of Lifestyle Medicine, 1*(5), 389–96.

Merom, D., Bauman, A., Vita, P., & Close, G. (2003). 'An environmental intervention to promote walking and cycling: the impact of a newly constructed Rail Trail in Western Sydney'. *Preventive Medicine, 36*, 235–42.

Napolitano, M. A., & Marcus, B. H. (2002). 'Targeting and tailoring physical activity information using print and information technologies'. *Exercise and Sports Science Reviews, 30*, 122–8.

National Institute for Health and Clinical Excellence. (2009). *Public Health Guidance 8 – Physical activity and the environment*. London: NICE.

Ogilvie, D., Egan, M., Hamilton, V., & Petticrew, M. (2004). 'Promoting walking and cycling as an alternative to using cars: Systematic review'. *British Medical Journal, 329*, 763–6.

——(2005). 'Systematic reviews of health effects of social interventions: 2. Best available evidence: how low should you go?' *Journal of Epidemiology and Community Health, 59*, 886–92.

Ogilvie, D., Foster, C. E., Rothnie, H., Cavill, N., Hamilton, V., Fitzsimons, C. F., *et al.* (2007). 'Interventions to promote walking: Systematic review'. *British Medical Journal, 334* (www.bmj.com DOI: 10.1136/bmj.39198.722720.BE).

Pate, R. R., Saunders, R. P., Ward, D. S., Felton, G., & Trost, S. G. (2003). 'Evaluation of a community-based intervention to promote physical activity in youth: Lessons from Active Winners'. *American Journal of Health Promotion, 17*(3), 171–82.

Peel, G. R., & Booth, M. L. (2001). 'Impact evaluation of the Royal Australian Air Force health promotion program'. *Aviation, Space and Environmental Medicine, 72*, 44–51.

Prochaska, J. O., & Marcus, B. H. (1994). 'The transtheoretical model: Application to exercise'. In R. K. Dishman (Ed.), *Advances in exercise adherence* (pp. 161–80). Champaign, IL: Human Kinetics.

Pucher, J., & Dijkstra, L. (2003). 'Promoting safe walking and cycling to improve public health: Lessons from The Netherlands and Germany'. *American Journal of Public Health, 93*, 1509–16.

515

Rejeski, W. J., & Brawley, L. R. (1988). 'Defining the boundaries of sport psychology'. *The Sport Psychologist, 2*, 231–42.

Riemsma, R., Pattenden, J., Bridle, C., Sowden, A., Mather, L., Watt, I., *et al.* (2002). 'A systematic review of the effectiveness of interventions based on a stages-of-change approach to promote individual behaviour change'. *Health Technology Assessment, 6*(24). www.ncchta.org/execsumm/summ624.shtml

Robbins, L., Gretebeck, K. A., Kazanis, A., & Pender, N. J. (2006). 'Girls on the Move program to increase physical activity participation'. *Nursing Research, 55*(3), 206–16.

Sallis, J. F., & Owen, N. (1999). *Physical activity and behavioral medicine.* Thousand Oaks, CA: Sage.

Sallis, J. F., Prochaska, J. J., & Taylor, W. C. (2000). 'A review of correlates of physical activity of children and adolescents'. *Medicine and Science in Sports and Exercise, 32*, 963–75.

Schwanen, T., Dijst, M., & Dieleman, F. M. (2004). 'Policies for urban form and their impact on travel: The Netherlands experience'. *Urban Studies, 41*, 579–603.

Schwarzer, R. (2008). 'Modeling health behavior change: How to predict and modify the adoption and maintenance of health behaviors'. *Applied Psychology: An International Review, 57*, 1–29.

Sharpe, P. (2003). 'Community-based physical activity intervention'. *Arthritis Rheumatism, 15*, 455–62.

Steinbeck, K. S. (2001). 'The importance of physical activity in the prevention of overweight and obesity in childhood: a review and an opinion'. *Obesity Reviews, 2*(2), 117–30.

Stensel, D. J., Gorely, T., & Biddle, S. J. H. (2008). 'Youth health outcomes'. In A. L. Smith & S. J. H. Biddle (Eds), *Youth physical activity and sedentary behavior: Challenges and solutions* (pp. 31–57). Champaign, IL: Human Kinetics.

Telama, R., Yang, X., Viikari, J., Valimaki, I., Wanne, O., & Raitakari, O. (2005). 'Physical activity from childhood to adulthood: A 21-year tracking study'. *American Journal of Preventive Medicine, 28*(3), 267–73.

Trost, S. G., Owen, N., Bauman, A. E., Sallis, J. F., & Brown, W. (2002). '"Correlates of adults" participation in physical activity: Review and update'. *Medicine and Science in Sports and Exercise, 34*, 1996–2001.

van der Horst, K., Chin A. Paw, M. J., Twisk, J. W. R., & Van Mechelen, W. (2007). A brief review on correlates of physical activity and sedentariness in youth. *Medicine and Science in Sports and Exercise, 39*(8), 1241–50.

Vilhjalmsson, R., & Kristjansdottir, G. (2003). 'Gender differences in physical activity in older children and adolescents: The central role of organised sport'. *Social Science & Medicine, 56*, 363–74.

Vuori, I. M., Oja, P., & Paronen, O. (1994). 'Physically active commuting to work: Testing its potential for exercise promotion'. *Medicine and Science in Sports and Exercise, 26*, 844–50.

Wong, F., Greenwell, M., Gates, S., & Berkowitz, J. (2008). 'It's what you do! Reflections on the VERB campaign'. *American Journal of Preventive Medicine, 34*(6, Suppl.), S175–S182.

Young, D. R., Haskell, W. L., Taylor, C. B., & Fortmann, S. P. (1996). 'Effect of community health education on physical activity knowledge, attitudes, and behavior: The Stanford Five-City Project'. *American Journal of Epidemiology, 144*, 264–74.

Zimmerman, F. J. (2009). 'Using behavioral economics to promote physical activity'. *Preventive Medicine, 49*(4), 289–91.

36

Partnership working and sports development

Iain Lindsey

Partnership working has become ubiquitous as a *modus operandi* across all sports development sectors. Not just representing a way of working, partnerships have been established as an important structure in the design and delivery of sports development policies and programmes. Although partnerships and partnership working are not necessarily new to sports development practice (Thilbault *et al.* 1999; Babiak 2007; Lindsey 2009), their current importance is demonstrated in a variety of recent sports development policy documents. In England, for example, national policy has called for the 'creation of effective partnerships at every level to deliver for and through sport' (Sport England 2004: 18).

Similarly, a governmental review on sport in Canada stated that

> The future of sport in Canada depends on strong leadership, partnerships and accountability. It is necessary to create stronger partnerships between the public and private sectors and between the various levels of government throughout this country.
>
> *(Mills 1998: 1, cited in Babiak and Thilbault 2008)*

The prominence of partnerships is also apparent in international policies for sports development. In considering the contribution of sport to development and peace, the United Nations (2006: 61) recognised that:

> Local development through sport particularly benefits from an integrated partnership approach to sport for development involving the full spectrum of actors in field-based community development including all levels and various sectors of Government, sports organisations and federations, NGOs and the private sector.

These exemplar policy statements also give an indication of the (potential) variety of different types of partnerships involving sports development organisations. Partnerships now exist between organisations involved in sport at both a grass-roots and elite level (see Houlihan and Lindsey 2008 and Babiak and Thilbault 2008, respectively, for examples). Sports development partnerships may encompass intra-organisational, inter-organisational and cross-sectoral members.

Sports development organisations are also increasingly required to develop partnerships with agencies from other policy areas such as health and education (Bloyce *et al.* 2008).

The wide variety of types of relationship that, in policy and practice, are termed as partnerships raises a definitional question as to what defines a particular relationship as a 'partnership'. Moreover, the definitional issue is complicated by the variety of terms used, sometimes indiscriminately, to describe similar relationships in sports development. For example, Lindsey (2009) chooses to use the term 'collaboration'. Wolfe *et al.* (2002) examine a 'sports network' and, within the North American context, the term 'inter-organisational relationship' appears to predominate in the work of a number of authors (e.g. Alexander *et al.* 2008; Babiak 2007). While there is no attempt made here to offer a categorical definition of partnership, it is worthwhile in this introduction to briefly identify the similarities between those definitions offered in the sports development literature. Commonly partnerships are considered to comprise two or more organisations (or different sections of a single organisation) that are involved, to a lesser or greater extent, on a voluntary basis in a long-term pattern of engagement (Babiak and Thilbault 2008; Lindsey 2009). In addition, some definitions also include a specification that partnerships are directed towards a purpose that is mutually beneficial to their organisational members (Babiak 2007). These, largely agreed, characteristics of partnerships will serve as a guide throughout the remainder of the chapter.

Accompanying the wide variety and large number of partnerships that now exist in sports development, the emergence of a growing body of research examining the implications of partnerships for sports development policy and practice can be identified. The academic study of partnerships remains in its infancy and mainly has been clustered in work undertaken in the United Kingdom and Canada. In addition, partnerships have been the focus of recent research in international sports development efforts in Zambia in particular. Commonly adopting a single- or multiple-case study approach, research has examined partnerships in both the delivery of local and elite sport development services (e.g. Frisby *et al.* 2004 and Babiak and Thilbault 2008, respectively) as well as those partnerships that encompass sports development and other services such as education (e.g. Lindsey 2006) and health (e.g. Lindsey and Banda forthcoming).

The purpose of this chapter is to review the emerging body of literature on partnerships in sports development. Initially, this review will allow a greater understanding to be developed of the contextual factors that have contributed to, and continue to affect, the emergence of partnership working as an important *modus operandi* in sports development. Subsequently, distinct sections will review literature related to sports development that covers the range of desired outcomes of partnership working, the variety of forms that partnerships have taken and the different roles of specific agencies and processes within partnerships. Although there remain significant methodological difficulties in evaluating the effectiveness of sports development partnerships (Houlihan and Lindsey 2008), a common thread throughout the chapter will be the identification of factors that influence the effectiveness of partnerships both generically and in specific instances. The chapter will conclude by identifying key issues related to partnership working for future sports development policy, practice and research.

Contextual influences on partnership working in sports development

For Babiak (2007: 338), the increasing importance of partnerships in sport has been 'precipitated by environmental factors such as globalisation, changing technologies, economic challenges, and evolving social expectations'. Similarly, Frisby *et al.* (2004: 109) suggest that, in local leisure services in Canada, there has been 'strategic shift [towards] pursuing partnerships with a wider range of partners in response to a number of social, political and economic pressures'. However, few authors provide a comprehensive account of historical trends of such environmental factors which fully explains the current 'propartnership bias' (Babiak 2007: 371) in national and international sports development. Although current contextual influences on partnerships will be considered later in this section, it is first worthwhile to briefly consider two historical accounts that situate the current prominence of partnership working in sports development within broader, historical changes in the provision of public services more generally.

Although the historical accounts of the changing political and organisational context of sports development offered by both Houlihan and Lindsey (2008) and Lindsey (2009) are primarily UK-focused, many of the antecedents of partnership working that they identify may be common elsewhere, particularly in those countries that would be considered as neo-liberal in Esping-Andersen's (1990) typology. Drawing on more general analyses of public policies, these authors suggest that the antecedents of the current prominence of partnership working lie in the neo-liberal reforms of the 1980s and 1990s. During this period, policies such as privatisation led to a greater array of organisations being involved in the delivery of public services especially those such as sports development that commonly were the responsibility of local authorities (Johnson 1990). Moreover, sports services were also affected by the concurrent reform of the management of public services (commonly termed the 'new public management') which led to an emphasis on the efficiency of discrete services with relationships between different agencies determined by contractual- and market-based mechanisms (Robinson 1999; Henry 2001).

Subsequently, in the late 1990s and in the early part of the twenty-first century, marked in the United Kingdom by the election of the New Labour government in 1997, there was a reappraisal of the implications of these neo-liberal reforms. Increasingly there was a recognition that previous reforms had led to fragmented systems of delivery in sports development as well in other public services (Houlihan 2000; Oakley and Green 2001) which had failed to resolve persistent social problems, including low participation in sport and physical activity, and cut across different policy areas (Houlihan and Lindsey 2008). This analysis led to an increased focus on partnership working as a way in which these problems could be addressed through a more 'joined up' approach to public service delivery. As Houlihan and Lindsey (2008: 226) suggest, partnerships came to be 'seen as flexible, innovative and adaptive and part of the solution to the problems of "overloaded" and under-performing government'.

As a result, across different counties, individuals and organisations involved in sports development are now subject to significant pressure to adopt partnership-based approaches. As Babiak (2007) suggests, the degree to which such pressure from national governments and agencies is exerted in an explicit way may vary. For example, as identified earlier, the promotion of partnership working is very prominent and explicit in a number of national sports policies. The provision of funding for particular sports development programmes is also now commonly conditional on a partnership-based mode of implementation (Lindsey 2006; Alexander et al. 2008). Related to more implicit pressures, individuals from an elite Canadian Sports Centre were reported to feel driven to form partnerships in order to 'maintain their status, influence and position within the larger [Canadian] sport system' (Babiak 2007: 351).

Despite the strength of national pressures to work in partnership, more detailed examination of national factors suggests a more nuanced picture as to their influence on sports development partnerships. Broadly, Lindsey (2010) questions the extent to which national agencies can promote effective partnership working in local sports development. Moreover, Babiak (2007: 368) suggests that the factors influencing partnership formation in sports development are often 'conflicting or contradictory'. There may also be difficulties in developing effective partnerships when such relationships 'operate within a prescribed framework with clear objectives set by dominant powers' (McDonald 2005: 594). In a more concrete example, Babiak and

Thilbault (2008, 2009) note that changes in Canadian governmental priorities affected the ongoing operation of partnerships involving elite Canadian Sports Centres by changing the balance of power within these relationships. Similarly, in an English context the consulting company, Knight, Kavanagh & Page (2005), suggests that County Sports Partnerships have been affected by Sport England 'changing the goalposts' in terms of their policy advice.

Besides these national factors, authors also identify that more local-orientated issues influence partnership working in sports development. For example, in research on a United Kingdom-wide sports facility development programme, Lindsey (2006) found that the differences between the four home countries resulted in different forms of local partnerships being predominately developed in each country. In addition, the form of these partnerships was also affected by other factors within their particular local context (Lindsey 2006). The Institute of Youth Sport's (2006) evaluation report contains a similar finding regarding the adaptation of the structure of individual School Sport Partnerships dependent on particular local needs and contexts.

As with national factors, research also highlights the influence of locally orientated issues on the ongoing effectiveness of particular sports development partnerships. A first theme prominent in research conducted in a variety of different countries is the difficulty developing effective partnerships between organisations that may also have divergent and competing interests. For example, individuals involved in elite sport development in Canada believed that 'competition violated the "true spirit" of collaboration and led to tension and frustration between partners' (Babiak and Thilbault 2009: 134). Similarly, reflecting on research on sports development partnerships in England, Houlihan and Lindsey (2008: 239) state that 'an important barrier to realising the benefits of partnerships is often the general congestion in the policy area and the need to compete with other agencies and partnerships for similar policy space'. The connection between organisational fragmentation, competition and difficulties in partnership working is reinforced by research undertaken by Lindsey and Banda (forthcoming). These authors found that partnership working was hindered by the variety of different agencies involved in sports development in Zambia and the need for a number of these agencies to compete for similar sources of funding.

A second locally orientated theme in the literature is the effect of change within organisations that are members of sports development partnerships. Lindsey (2009) contrasts the relative positive and negative effects of local organisational stability and change on the ongoing development of youth sports development partnerships in two English case studies. More specifically, local managers of sports development programmes in Canada were frustrated that organisational restructuring led to continual changes in the individual representatives involved in particular partnerships (Frisby *et al.* 2004). Change within organisations may also result in the adoption of different objectives, a factor identified by Babiak and Thilbault (2009) as affecting partnerships in elite sport development in Canada.

Desired outcomes of partnership working in sports development

While there is recognition that there are strong, but somewhat inconsistent, contextual forces that promote the adoption of partnerships and partnership working in sports development, the literature suggests that partnerships are also developed in order to achieve a wide variety of potential benefits or outcomes. However, while desired outcomes are considered to a lesser or greater extent in almost all of the published research on sports development partnerships, as yet a significant gap in the literature is the lack of a comprehensive classification schema to differentiate between these desired outcomes. Where attempts have been made to distinguish between different desired outcomes of partnerships (e.g. Babiak 2007; Lindsey and Banda forthcoming), the case study nature of the research means that the generalisability of classifica-tory schema, whether deductively applied from categorisations developed in other fields of lit-erature or inductively derived from research data, remains open to question. Similarly, it is acknowledged that the range of different desired outcomes of sports development partnerships identified in this section is by no means exhaustive nor offers a definitive way in which these outcomes can be classified. Equally significantly, the initial examination of the range of desired outcomes is a prerequisite for the subsequent discussion, that concludes the section, of the implications resulting from the outcomes desired of partnership working in sports development.

Identified outcomes that are desired of sports development partnerships range from those that could be considered as being particularly limited and practical in scope to those that may have widespread and strategic importance both for the members of a particular partnership as well as for other organisations and individuals. Closer to the former end of the range are those part-nerships that offer an opportunity for member organisations to share information. In Zambia, Lindsey and Banda (forthcoming) recognise the commonality of such a desired outcome among partnerships of non-governmental organisations, including those concerned with sports devel-opment. Similarly, an evaluation study by Knight, Kavanagh & Page (2005) identifies that information sharing between member organisations was one of the early impacts of County Sports Partnerships in England. While the sharing of information could lead to improvements in the practice of individual organisations, it may also be a precursor to other collective desired outcomes of partnership working. For example, a collective benefit such as the avoidance of duplication (recognised by both Lindsey (2009) and Thilbault *et al.* (1999) as a desired outcome of sports development partnerships in specific local contexts) would be initially dependent on sharing of information regarding current practices.

In turn, avoidance of duplication may be considered as one of a broader cluster of desired outcomes connected to increased efficiency in sports development work. Amongst partners in the elite sport system in Canada, desired outcomes related to efficiency included the achieve-ment of economies of scale and increased purchasing power (Babiak 2007). Moreover, a desire for similar efficiencies amongst local providers of sport has been recognised both in three case study metropolitan areas in Canada (Thilbault *et al.* 1999) and in County Sports Partnerships in England (Knight, Kavanagh & Page 2005). Slightly different to the internal nature of efficiency gains, and linked to one of the contextual partnership drivers discussed previously, partnerships have also been recognised as a mechanism through which members can achieve their desire to garner external funding. Reporting on interviews with local authority sports development officers in England, Bloyce *et al.* (2008) emphasise the strong motivation for accessing funding that underpinned a number of partnerships with agencies from health and other sectors.

Beyond efficiencies, partnership working in sports development may also be desirous for enabling greater effectiveness through the synergies between different agencies involved. For example, Lindsey (2009) found that partnerships were widely valued in one of two local case studies as a mechanism through which the resources and skills of different organisations could be combined in order to enhance the delivery of sport and physical activity opportunities for young people. In a similar vein, using the term 'reciprocity', Alexander *et al.* (2008) found that two partners in a local sports development programme wished to 'integrate' the different capacities of each of their respective organisations in order to enable more effective delivery of the programme itself. Combining the skills of different organisations through partnerships may be particularly important where sports development programmes are designed to deliver more socially orientated objectives (Frisby *et al.* 2004). Interviewees from sporting organisations in Zambia highlighted the need to combine their own skill in delivering sports activities with the specific expertise of health-based organisations in order to effectively utilise sport as a tool to educate young people about issues connected to HIV/AIDS (Lindsey and Banda forthcoming).

A final cluster of desired outcomes of partnership could be considered as representing those that could have greatest strategic significance. Lindsey (2009) describes how, in one English local authority area, partnerships were utilised as a mechanism to integrate and coordinate sports development policy and planning. Similar outcomes are desired of the development of partnerships at a variety of levels throughout the entire 'delivery system' of sport in England (Sport England 2005). Partnership working may not only be valued for the potential to 'join up' policy but also, as Thilbault et al. (1999) note, as a way in which citizens may have a greater input into decision making. The recognition by these authors that improved citizen input into partnership decisions is not always achieved could be considered as indicative of the more widespread challenges that partnerships have in achieving desired outcomes.

In fact, authors suggest that one of the challenges of partnership working is reconciling the different outcomes desired by those individuals and organisations involved. While Lindsey (2009) identifies the positive impact that shared understanding of desired outcomes had on one well-regarded partnership between local youth sports development agencies, more commonly authors cite examples where difficulties in partnership working were connected to differences in desired outcomes. For example, Houlihan and Lindsey (2008) consider the differences between the objectives of schools and clubs in School Sport Partnerships in England as problematic. Similarly, Babiak and Thilbault (2008: 300) recognise that the 'incongruity of objectives led to tensions among [the] partners' of an elite-orientated Canadian Sports Centre. While it may be inevitable that partners desire different outcomes to some extent (Babiak 2007), the example of a partnership between a local government agency and national sport organisation presented by Alexander et al. (2008) suggests that this may not automatically lead to partnership failure. Instead, what appears to be important is a mutual understanding of desired outcomes and a need for 'space to negotiate a shared sense of purpose and common objectives' (Houlihan and Lindsey 2008: 239). This shared space, in turn, leads to questions regarding the structure of partnerships, which is considered in the next section.

Partnership structures in sports development

The importance of understanding issues related to partnership structure is emphasised by the suggestion within the sports development literature that particular forms of partnership are more or less likely to achieve certain desired outcomes (Babiak 2007; Lindsey 2006, 2009). However, the complexity of issues related to partnership structure is highlighted by a number of authors. An early evaluation of County Sports Partnerships by Knight, Kavanagh & Page (2005) highlights some confusion amongst individuals involved as to the desired and actual structure of these partnership bodies. In a similar vein, Lindsey (2006) identifies significant differences in local partnership structures adopted within a single, national sports development programme in the United Kingdom. The large diversity in the forms of partnerships involving sports development organisations in Zambia is also an issue emphasised by Lindsey and Banda (forthcoming). Therefore, this section will review the literature concerning partnership structure in sports development focusing on three specific, but interrelated themes: partnership membership; the degree of formality associated with partnerships; and the distribution of power and resources within partnerships.

The number of members of a specific sports development partnership can vary enormously. Babiak and Thilbault (2008) model the partnerships involving an elite Canadian Sports Centre as a number of separate, yet overlapping, bilateral relationships between specific organisations.

Contrastingly, local partnerships examined by Lindsey (2006) in a sports facility development programme in Northern Ireland encompassed over 15 members. The predominant issue identified by a number of authors is the complexities and challenges inherent in partnerships that include a large number of members or when an organisation is involved in a large number of partnerships. This issue is raised in different sports development contexts: local sport and leisure services in England (Lindsey 2009) and in Canada (Frisby et al. 2004), elite sport development in Canada (Babiak and Thilbault 2008, 2009) and in the utilisation of sport as a tool to address HIV/AIDS in Zambia (Lindsey and Banda forthcoming). Specifically in this last context, Lindsey and Banda contrast the strength of partnerships comprising of two member organisations with the difficulties encountered in partnerships comprising a greater number of members.

Another issue identified in the literature is the type of members involved in sports development partnerships. In Canada in particular, partnerships that involve both public and private sector organisations have been identified as problematic both in the development of local leisure services (Frisby et al. 2004) and elite sport development (Babiak and Thilbault 2009). More generally, there appears to be difficulties in developing effective partnerships when there are differences in the ethos of particular members (Thilbault et al. 1999; Lindsey 2009). Furthermore, Lindsey and Banda (forthcoming) suggest that there may be 'cross-cultural difficulties in approaches to partnership interaction' where such partnerships span different countries.

Besides differences in their membership, partnerships vary as to the degree that their structure and operation is formalised in documents, memoranda of understanding, service level agreements or, in some cases, contracts. Furthermore, the literature on sports development partnerships includes contributions that are divergent in their assessment of the relative importance of formalised or informal partnership structures. In some cases, authors are critical of the lack of formal partnership agreements (e.g. Frisby et al. 2004) or identify the success of partnerships in which formal agreements specify 'clear lines of authority and responsibility' (Alexander et al. 2008). Alternatively, interviewees in studies by Babiak (2007), Babiak and Thilbault (2008) and Lindsey (2009) believed that formalisation of partnerships may restrict, and actually conflict with, the development of cooperative relationships between partners. The complexity of this issue is further elucidated by Babiak and Thilbault (2008), who recognise that informal partnerships may become overly reliant on relationships between individuals whose affiliation or position with their organisation may change, resulting in negative consequences for the partnership itself.

By its very nature, partnership working in sports development involves, to differing extents, sharing and pooling of the resources held by individual members. Financial, human and facility-based resources are among, but not the only, resources that members could contribute to a particular sports development partnership (Thilbault et al. 1999). The structure of the resource contributions of individual partnership members, and the power that specific resource contributions could bring, is an issue that is considered by a number of authors. The most common perspective in the literature on sports development partnerships is that resource and power imbalances may impede effective partnership working. For example, in the partnerships that included an elite-orientated Canadian Sports Centre, Babiak and Thilbault (2008: 294) found the 'contribution of some founding partners to be less than the others which caused resentment among some partners'. Moreover, these authors suggest that differences in resource contributions and imbalances in power contribute negatively to the effectiveness of partnerships. A similar finding is presented in the English sports development context by Knight, Kavanagh & Page (2005), who suggest that the greater power held by the host organisation of County Sports Partnership 'compromised' decision making in some of the cases that they examined. However, it is perhaps inevitable that there will be imbalances in resource contributions and power within partnerships. A more realistic conclusion that could be drawn from Alexander *et al.*'s (2008) study of a locally orientated sports development partnership in Canada is that issues of resource and power balance need to be overcome through mutual recognition and management by all partners.

Agencies and processes of partnership working in sports development

Alongside the structure of partnerships and the relationships between members, the capacities of individual partnership members and the processes of interaction, as hinted above, are also important in contributing to, or impeding, the effectiveness of partnerships. As in previous sections, synthesis of research on specific sports development partnerships enables the identification of facets of agencies and processes that influence partnership effectiveness. The section will commence by examining issues related to roles and capacities of specific agencies within partnerships, which will be followed by a similar review of important partnership processes.

A common facet of the sports development literature is the identification that specific skills and capacities are required for effective partnership working. For example, Frisby *et al.* (2004: 110) rhetorically ask whether 'local governments have the managerial capabilities and capacities to fulfill these new [partnership] roles'. Similar issues are raised both in other research (e.g. Thilbault *et al.* 1999; Lindsey 2009) and in evaluations of specific partnership-based initiatives such as County Sport Partnerships and School Sport Partnerships in England. These evaluation reports call for specific training for sports development staff in order to develop necessary skills in partnership working (Knight, Kavanagh & Page 2005; Institute of Youth Sport 2006). What is less apparent from the literature is exactly what skills are required for effective partnership working. Of the research that considers this issue, Thilbault *et al.* (1999) note the need for negotiation skills, while Lindsey (2009) identifies that, as Huxham and Vangen (2000) more generally identify, both facilitative and manipulative skills may be required by individuals and organisations working in partnership. In fact, in one of Lindsey's (2009) local case studies there was a suggestion that some of these skills were already well developed among sports development staff due to the ongoing and long-term need of a non-statutory service to be aligned and integrated with other, more prominent local government services.

The need for sports development agencies to have specific skills may be particularly pertinent for those individuals and organisations that perform a leadership role within specific partnerships. Drawing from research on a variety of sports development partnerships in England, Houlihan and Lindsey (2008: 238) suggest that 'of particular importance [in the success of partnerships] is the presence of an organisational actor that can fulfill a leadership role'. However, these authors also strike a cautionary note as they identify that the leadership organisation in one particular sports development initiative had 'excessive influence on County Sport Partnership policy'. As a result, a delicate balance may have to be achieved by specific organisational actors between providing leadership within a partnership and the perceptions of power that may accompany such a role. What may also be problematic is the need for organisational actors responsible for leading partnerships to have sufficient human resources to fulfil such a role. Frisby *et al.* (2004: 123) found that the 'leisure services departments [of local authorities] that we studied lacked the capacity to effectively manage the numerous and complex partnerships they were engaged in'. Similarly, in the Canadian elite sport context, Babiak and Thilbault (2009: 125) reported that 'challenges existed because of the lack of human resources to accomplish all of the duties necessary to sustain the partnerships' that a Canadian Sports Centre was managing.

Besides the individually orientated skills and capacities identified, the importance of specific processes within sports development partnerships is also highlighted in the literature. For example, in their research on an elite-orientated Canadian Sports Centre, Babiak and Thilbault (2008: 299) found that 'informal processes, specifically mutual trust, played a key role in overcoming the challenges and the tensions that inevitably arise when dealing with partners'. Similarly, in different sports development contexts, Frisby et al. (2004); Alexander et al. (2008); Wolfe et al. (2002) and Lindsey (2009) all recognise the need for trust between those involved in specific partnerships. As Babiak and Thilbault (2008) themselves recognise, trust may be a multi-layered concept, an idea reinforced by Lindsey (2006) who identifies one partnership in which there was a high level of trust between individuals despite significant tensions between the organisations which these individuals represented. In fact, it may be particularly relevant that both Babiak and Thilbault (2008) and Lindsey (2009) identify instances in which trust between individuals was built through prior, personal associations in sporting contexts as well as being developed in a more professional sports development environment. However, partnerships which are overly reliant on trust between individuals could be negatively affected by staff turnover in sports development organisations (Frisby et al. 2004).

For Lindsey (2009), the issue of individual trust developed in an external sporting environment highlights the benefits of high levels of interaction and communication between members. Alexander et al. (2008) also identify the connection between trust and communication within sports development partnerships. Reflecting the issue of formality in the previous section, it may be that communication within partnerships may also occur both informally and through more formal channels (Institute of Youth Sport 2006). Although the quality of communication within sports development partnerships is not a common focus of the literature, Knight, Kavanagh & Page (2005: 14) do recognise that communication in English County Sports Partnerships was often 'not as good as partners would like'.

Another aspect of sports development partnerships that appears to contribute to their development and continued effectiveness is the derivation and distribution of benefits through partnership working. Similar to other processes, the sports development literature suggests that the derivation of individual and collective benefits could either contribute to improvements or hinder continued partnership working. Knight, Kavanagh & Page's (2005) report on County Sports Partnerships stresses the need for all members to be able to identify how they may benefit from involvement in the partnership. More specifically in the case of local partnerships in both England (Lindsey 2009) and Canada (Alexander et al. 2008), research identified that the achievement of outcomes that were mutually beneficial to partner organisations helped to foster and enhance partnership working between these same organisations. Conversely, in research on an elite-orientated Canadian Sport Centre, Babiak and Thilbault (2008) identified problems where one organisation was perceived as deriving benefits that were disproportionate to their contribution to the partnership. The potential for the derivation of partnership benefits to be problematic is perhaps heightened by the difficulty assessing the exact contribution that partnership working has made to specific outcomes (Frisby et al. 2004; Houlihan and Lindsey 2008).

The identification that the derivation of benefits could contribute to, or hinder, the continued development of partnership working is indicative of a broader issue within the literature, namely that sports development partnerships are themselves subject to continual processes of change. While the influence of changing contexts on partnerships was noted previously, Babiak and Thilbault (2008) considered the nature of relationships within partnerships to be 'evolving' over time. Moreover, for Wolfe et al. (2002), the main driver of change within networks encompassing national governing bodies of sport in Ireland was changes in the relationships between specific organisations in these networks.

Irrespective of the driving factors, processes of partnership change are themselves complex. In research on a partnership between a provincial sports organisation and a local government sport and recreation department, Alexander *et al.* (2008) found that a staged model of partnership evolution, inclusive of partnership formation, management and outcome, did not sufficiently capture the interrelated nature of partnership evolution. Moreover, Babiak and Thilbault (2008: 290) identify both the complex nature and facets of partnership change in the context of an elite-orientated Canadian Sport Centre: 'partner organisations appeared to engage in an iterative process of negotiating purpose, coalition building and adjusting to changes in membership throughout the partnership'. Similarly, an evaluation by the Loughborough Partnership (2008) found ongoing, and connected, changes in the role and structure of partnerships involved in the development of school sports facilities. Collectively, these findings suggest that partnership change processes are interlinked and can affect the desired outcomes of partnerships, the structure of partnerships and the continued interaction between members.

Conclusions

The purpose of this chapter has been to review the existing research literature on partnership working in sports development. While the context, desired outcomes, structures and processes of sports development partnerships have been examined sequentially throughout the chapter, the issues raised are commonly interconnected and, as a result, emphasise the complexity inherent in partnership working. In contrast, these complexities are often overlooked in the exhortations to increase and enhance partnerships that are common in recent sports policy documents. This concluding section will first examine some of the interrelated issues that point to the complexity of partnership working in sports development. Implications of the issues raised within the chapter for policy makers, sports development practitioners and researchers will then be considered in turn.

Space, and the emergent nature of the research literature, precludes identification of all the interconnections between issues connected to partnership working in sports development. However, identifying examples of these interconnections may be beneficial in demonstrating the implications of complex interplay between different influences within and on sports development partnerships. An initial link between the wider context and the structure of sports development partnerships has been drawn earlier in the chapter and in specific research (Lindsey 2006). In turn, it has been suggested that the degree of formality in partnership structures may affect (or reflect) the trust engendered between members (Babiak and Thilbault 2008). Relating to the range of desired outcomes of partnership working identified in this chapter, it could also be suggested that only those partnerships with higher levels of integration and trust between members are likely to realise the more strategically orientated purposes such as joint planning and provision (see, for example, Lindsey and Banda forthcoming). While recognising the limitations of this single line of argument, what it suggests is that the effectiveness of sports development partnerships may depend on a complex interaction between a variety of different factors that may be within and beyond the control of sports development policy makers and practitioners.

Despite this complexity, it is also important to draw some clear conclusions that may enable policy makers and practitioners to improve the effectiveness of sports development partnerships. For policy makers, the complexity of the organisational context of sports development partnerships is a key issue. The recognition of the challenges in developing effective partnerships between a large number of organisations suggests that policy makers should focus on enhancing partnerships between existing organisations rather than adding new partnerships and organizations to an already fragmented context. This conclusion is strengthened by the evidence that suggests that top-down direction alone may not realise the types of partnership desired (Lindsey

2010) and, in fact, may lead to undesired and unintended outcomes (Bloyce *et al.* 2008). For sports development practitioners, training in partnership working skills that has been recommended could be enhanced to develop a greater awareness of the variety of purposes of partnerships and issues regarding the design of partnership structures. Including all these elements in training would help to ensure that the structure and processes of partnerships are developed in order to meet clearly defined purposes. Moreover, an improved recognition of the evolving nature of sports development partnerships may enable practitioners to continually enhance the effectiveness of these relationships whilst taking a positive approach to overcoming the inherent challenges in doing so.

Given that this chapter has focused on existing research, there are even stronger implications to be drawn for researchers with an interest in sports development partnerships. These implications relate to both the methods employed and the focus of enquiry. In terms of methodology, the majority of research on partnership working in sports development has been undertaken through (one or multiple) case studies with the principle source of data being interviews with partnership members. Although a number of common issues have been identified in this chapter, the commonality of a case study approach ensures that the generalisability of research findings remains open to question (Babiak and Thilbault 2008). For this reason, there are significant opportunities for research that engages a wider variety of sports development agencies, possibly through quantitative methods, to assess the extent to which the issues identified in this chapter are common to a greater range of partnerships. Another research method that, given its potential applicability, appears under-used in examining partnership working in sports development is ethnography. For example, when used in previous studies, observation methods (e.g. Alexander *et al.* 2008) have typically been a secondary research method to interviews, and the impact of observation data on findings has been unclear.

Beyond the potential to utilise alternative research methods, further research on partnership working in sports development would benefit from introducing further diversity in research approaches. Only in a limited number of studies (e.g. Alexander *et al.* 2008) has longitudinal data been collected. Given the evidence of the evolving nature of individual sports development partnerships, this is a particular weakness of the existing literature and presents a significant opportunity for future researchers (Babiak and Thilbault 2008). Ongoing involvement with specific sports development partnerships may also allow researchers to adopt action research approaches as, for example, Huxham and Vangen (2005) have done in other policies fields. Action research approaches may also help sports development practitioners gain the increased understanding of partnership working that was called for earlier in these conclusions. A final suggested research approach that may also enhance understanding of partnership working in sports development is cross-country comparative analysis. As Lindsey and Banda (forthcoming) suggest, there may be cross-cultural differences in the understanding and practice of partnership working. Specifically, comparative analysis may allow a greater understanding of both contextual influences and partnership working processes to be developed.

These suggestions may help to broaden and deepen the literature on partnership working in sports development. Methodological innovation should be undertaken alongside a more comprehensive examination of specific issues concerning sports development partnerships. Three issues appear to be particularly pertinent. First, related to a theme within this book, existing research has not adequately considered differences between partnerships involved in the development of sport and those concerned with development through sport. Existing research has tended to implicitly focus on partnerships with one or other of these two objectives. As a result, while the different memberships of 'development of' and 'development through' sports partnerships can be identified, a more sophisticated analysis of differences in the issues and implications of these two approaches for partnership working is impossible. Second, previous research has almost exclusively focused on the identification of partnership working issues for those individuals and agencies involved in specific partnerships. Research is required that examines the implications of sports development partnerships for individuals and agencies not included (or excluded) from these structures, for organisations such as sports clubs that may be at the periphery of sports development partnerships, and for the intended beneficiaries of sports development policies and practices. Such research may support the examination of a third issue requiring further study, namely analysis of the effectiveness of sports development partnerships. While this chapter has considered *issues affecting* the effectiveness of sports development partnerships, as yet, there have been few systematic attempts to evaluate the contribution that partnerships make to sports development outcomes (Babiak and Thilbault 2008). Although such an evaluation is methodologically difficult (Houlihan and Lindsey 2008), the ubiquity of partnership working in sports development means that attempts to do so are necessary.

To conclude, it is perhaps ironic that the challenges that sports development partnerships present may require partnership-based solutions. While sports development policy makers and practitioners may be able to take steps to improve partnerships with which they are involved, the academic community has a significant responsibility to undertake research that can enhance this improvement process. Conversely, research on sports development partnerships is impossible without further support from individuals and agencies that are involved in, and influence, them. Academics, policy makers and practitioners with a stake in sports development partnerships have a significant challenge ahead of them!

References

Alexander, T., Thilbault, L. & Frisby, W. (2008) 'Avoiding separation: sport partner perspectives on a long-term inter-organisational relationship'. *International Journal of Sport Management and Marketing*. Vol. 3, No. 3, pp. 263–80.

Babiak, K. (2007) 'Determinants of interorganizational relationships: the case of a Canadian nonprofit sport organization'. *Journal of Sport Management*. Vol. 21, No. 3, pp. 338–76.

Babiak, K. & Thilbault, L. (2008) 'Managing inter-organisational relationships: the art of plate spinning'. *International Journal of Sport Management and Marketing*. Vol. 3, No. 3, pp. 281–302.

——(2009) 'Challenges in multiple cross-sector partnerships'. *Nonprofit and Voluntary Sector Quarterly*. Vol. 38, No. 1, pp. 117–43.

Bloyce, D., Smith, A., Mead, R. & Morris, J. (2008) '"Playing the Game (Plan)": a figurational analysis of organizational change in sport development in England'. *European Sport Management Quarterly*. Vol. 8, No. 4, pp. 359–78.

Esping-Andersen, G. (1990) *The Three Worlds of Welfare Capitalism*. Cambridge: Polity Press.

Frisby, W., Thilbault, L. & Kikulis, L. (2004) 'The organizational dynamics of under-managed partnerships in leisure service departments'. *Leisure Studies*. Vol. 23, No. 2, pp. 109–26.

Henry, I. (2001) *The Politics of Leisure Policy 2nd ed*. Houndmills: Palgrave.

Houlihan, B. & Lindsey, I. (2008) 'Networks and partnerships in sport development'. In V. Girginov, ed. *Management of Sport Development*. Oxford: Butterworth-Heinemann.

Houlihan, B. (2000) 'Sporting excellence, schools and sport development: the politics of crowded policy spaces'. *European Physical Education Review*. Vol. 6, No. 2, pp. 171–93.

Huxham, C. & Vangen, S. (2000) 'Leadership in the shaping and implementation of collaborative agendas: how things happen in a (not quite) joined up world'. *Academy of Management Journal*. Vol. 43, No. 6, pp. 1159–75.

——(2005) *Managing to Collaborate: the Theory and Practice of Collaborative Advantage*. Abingdon: Routledge.

Institute of Youth Sport (2006) *School Sport Partnerships: Annual Monitoring and Evaluation Report for 2006*. Loughborough: Institute of Youth Sport, Loughborough University.

Johnson, N. (1990) *Reconstructing the Welfare State: A Decade of Change 1980–1990*. London: Harvester Wheatsheaf.

Knight, Kavanagh & Page (2005) *Active Sports/CSP Impact Study Year 3: Final Report*. Bury: Knight, Kavanagh & Page.

Lindsey, I. (2006) 'Local partnerships in the United Kingdom for the New Opportunities for PE and Sport initiative: a policy network analysis'. *European Sports Management Quarterly*. Vol. 6, No. 2, pp. 167–84.

——(2009) 'Collaboration in local sport services in England: issues emerging from case studies of two local authority areas'. *International Journal of Sport Policy*. Vol. 1, No. 1, pp. 71–88.

——(2010) 'Governance of lottery sport programmes: national direction of local partnerships in the new opportunities for PE and sport programme'. *Managing Leisure*. Vol. 15, No. 3, pp. 198–213.

Lindsey, I. & Banda, D. (forthcoming) 'Sport and the fight against HIV / AIDS in Zambia: A "partnership" approach?'. *International Review for the Sociology of Sport*.

Loughborough Partnership (2008) 'Evaluation of the New Opportunities for PE and Sport Programme: Year Five Report'. Loughborough: Institute of Youth Sport, Loughborough University.

McDonald, I. (2005) 'Theorising partnerships: governance, communicative action and sport policy'. *Journal of Social Policy*, Vol. 34, No. 4, pp. 579–600.

Mills, D. (1998) *Sport in Canada: Everybody's Business*. Ottawa: Standing Committee on Canadian Heritage.

Oakley, B. & Green, M. (2001) 'Still playing the game at arm's length? The selective re-investment in British Sport, 1995–2000'. *Managing Leisure*, Vol. 6, No. 2, pp. 74–94.

Robinson, L. (1999) 'Following the quality strategy: the reasons for the use of quality management in UK public leisure facilities'. *Managing Leisure*, Vol. 4, No. 4, pp. 201–17.

Sport England (2004) *The Framework for Sport in England: Making England an Active and Successful Nation: A Vision for 2020*. London: Sport England.

——(2005) *Policy Statement: The Delivery System for Sport in England*. London: Sport England.

Thilbault, L., Frisby, W. & Kikulis, L.M. (1999) 'Interorganizational linkages in the delivery of local leisure services in Canada: responding to economic, political and social pressures'. *Managing Leisure*, Vol. 4, No. 3, pp. 125–41.

United Nations (2006) *Sport for a Better World: Report on the International Year of Sport and Physical Education 2005*. Geneva: United Nations Office of Sport for Development and Peace.

Wolfe, R., Meenaghan, T. & O'Sullivan, P. (2002) 'The sports network: insights into the shifting balance of power'. *Journal of Business Research*, Vol. 55, No. 7, pp. 611–22.

37

Funding and sustaining sports development

Ian Jones

The funding landscape for sports development is a complex and ever-changing one, yet crucial to the delivery of any objectives related to either increased grass-roots participation or improved performance in sport on the world stage. Jackson and Nesti suggest, first, that 'many SDOs and deliverers of sport development programmes more prosaically have identified a lack of funding as the major obstacle to achieving equality of opportunity' (2001: 151), and second, that 'if there is to be a realistic chance of Sport England's strategy achieving its objectives, the mission of More People, More Places, More Medals is implicitly underpinned by another catchline of More Money' (2001: 156–57). The purpose of this chapter is not to provide a detailed overview of all of the sources of funding for sports development, as changes to policy and practice often mean that such information becomes outdated very quickly. Instead, the chapter provides first, a brief overview of the changing environment within which funding has been distributed. Second, some of the sources of funding for both grass-roots and elite sport development are described. Finally, issues related to funding and the sustainability of sports development are discussed. Much of the focus is on funding provided by the public sector, and some important areas, for example the contribution in financial terms of volunteers who contribute to sport (see, for example, Nichols *et al.* 2004) are not dealt with as part of the chapter.

The funding context

The funding of sports development takes place within a complex environment, one that can only really be summarised within this chapter. Public sector funding, especially, is subject to a number of factors that influence the volume and distribution of money to support sport. As Hylton and Bramham (2008: 44) argue

> The public sector is political, and must continually search for political ideas to legitimate state regulation, taxation and policy provision. Whereas the commercial and voluntary sectors are in their different ways self-referencing, self-contained and self-sustaining, the public sector is more open to changing discourses, shifting rationales in order to justify the distinctive function of the state and its precise relationship with the other two leisure providers.

Public policy for sport has, as Coalter (2007) suggests, been largely characterised by the two intentions of providing sport and physical activity to the population as a social right of citizenship, and as a consequence of the wider assumed benefits associated with a physically active population, such as improved physical and mental health, reduced burden on the National Health Service, increased social capital, and the promotion of ethnic and cultural harmony (see, for example, Collins 2003 or Lawson 2005). As we will see, the balance between the two intentions has shifted over time, in line with the dominant political ideologies within which they have been implemented, although with some degree of continuity, due partly to the number of quangos that have been developed to administer sports policy within the United Kingdom (for example relative stability is provided through bodies such as Sport England, Sportscotland, or UK Sport). Collins (2008) summarises four broad phases of sports development policy. These are:

- Developing the facility base and facility management (1960s–1982)
- A strategy of targeting and the evolution of sports development (1982–1991)
- Shifting priorities to performance and excellence (1992–1997)
- Social inclusion and more medals (1997 to date).

Policies for the promotion of sport generally began to emerge within Western society in the years immediately preceding the Second World War; however it was not until the 1960s that central government began to take a systematic interest in funding sport, and the 1970s that the idea that access to sport and physical activity was a human right was developed, largely influenced by the establishment of the Sports Council in 1972 and the 1975 European Sport for All Charter (Kidd and Donnelly 2000). As a consequence, policies focused upon capital funding to create new sports facilities, and on providing sport and physical activity opportunities. The stimulus for this investment was a perceived public need, rather than an expressed public demand. Investment tended to be focused upon target groups, specifically those perceived as disadvantaged in some way with the aim, for example, in relation to those considered to be at risk of youth offending of diverting such individuals from potential crime and delinquency into active participation. Such perceived benefits to individuals were promoted by the Labour Governments of the 1970s which encouraged a more welfarist ideology, whereby sports participation was considered to be of potential benefit not only to the individual, but also to the wider community. One high-profile initiative to emerge during this period was Sport for All. Coalter (2007), however, notes that such policies were open to accusations of inefficiency and ineffectiveness, as well as acting as a form of regressive taxation. He goes on to suggest that subsidies to support sports provision at a local level during this period 'were perceived to generate artificially high levels of demand among groups who could afford to take responsibility for their own consumption' (Coalter 2007: 12), and despite being, according to Collins (2003: 36) focused on 'Sport for the Disadvantaged' rather than Sport for All, they had, according to Coalter (2007: 12), 'demonstrably failed to attract the disadvantaged groups for whom they were intended', simply acting as subsidies for those who could already afford to participate in sport and physical activity, and whose sporting needs could have more appropriately been met by the commercial or voluntary sectors. Such schemes also failed to demonstrate any convincing evidence in terms of increased sports participation, partly due to the lack of systematic monitoring and evaluation.

The second phase of sports development, 1982 to 1991, that of targeting and evolution of sports development, addressed the problem of poor monitoring and data collection to some extent, but with a clear emphasis upon financial performance, and the justification of key decisions through producing long-term detailed, and financially underpinned strategies. A key policy document in this period was *Sport in the Community* (Sports Council 1982). Here, the first mention of specific targets for increased participation emerged, as well as a focus on developing performers at higher levels. A five-year review of the strategy (Sports Council 1987) suggested, however, that first, insufficient resources had been made available to repair, replace or update facilities developed within the first phase of the sports development process. Second, inequalities within society had shown a marked increase, with greater need for help for disadvantaged groups from the public sector. With a perception that much valuable money was being leaked out through inefficient management of public sector operations, a move towards greater efficiency was the obvious next stage. This vehicle for achieving greater financial efficiency was Compulsory Competitive Tendering (CCT), which was introduced within a political context that aimed to drive down costs through increased economic efficiency. Such increased efficiency (and the ability to demonstrate that efficiency) allowed a clearer focus on providing appropriate, and affordable services. Unfortunately, the target-driven focus of CCT was largely negated by the difficulty again in being able to develop quantifiable, conceptually underpinned measures, other than those based around financial measures. The scheme 'almost certainly held down or reduced usage by poor and under represented groups like people with a disability, ethnic minorities, and one parent families for whom such public services were intended' (Collins 2003: 20).

The appointment of John Major as Prime Minister in 1990 did give the United Kingdom a Prime Minister with a clear interest in sport, and this was pivotal in many of the policy decisions made in the next phase of sports development, that of shifting priorities to performance and excellence, where elite sport became an important element of the funding landscape (Green 2004). One key policy decision from Major's Conservative Government can be seen to have had far-reaching implications for the funding landscape – the introduction in 1994 of The National Lottery, a scheme which has 'changed the complexion of financial support for the sporting endeavours of the country' (Jackson and Nesti 2001: 160). Although initially of great benefit to local sport, the lottery quickly developed a focus upon elite sport, reflecting the ideas of the White Paper *Sport: Raising the Game* (Department of National Heritage 1995), which highlighted four key themes: those of improving both the quality and quantity of sport in schools; extending the sporting culture, through greater partnership working; developing the provision of sport in higher and further education; and the development of excellence.

The fourth phase, that of 'social inclusion and more medals' emerged in 1997. From the late 1990s onwards, the Labour Government focused on a policy of social inclusion, whereby the use of sport and physical activity as a tool for welfare for the individual became to be seen as less important than the ideas of equality, inclusiveness, and the stress upon building up the social networks and capacity for sustainable participation. The Best Value process, introduced in 2002, resulted in a change of emphasis from that of CCT, which on elements of quality and customer satisfaction, as well as financial indicators. The principles of Best Value were based upon local accountability and transparency and continuous improvement in service delivery to all groups of residents and businesses. Best Value was also outcome based, rather than outcome driven, thus providing an attempt to achieve a balance between the need to provide services to all as a right of citizenship, and an over stretched public budget.

The prioritisation of overcoming social exclusion, rather than poverty, was highlighted in the subsequent Policy Action Team (PAT) reports. These reports, of which there were 18 in total, were commissioned by the Social Exclusion Unit (SEU) in an attempt to provide some 'joined-up thinking' to deal with issues of exclusion from activities such as sport and physical activity (Social Exclusion Unit 2002). The PAT 10 report emphasised the role that sport and leisure could have in dealing with the key issues raised by the Labour Government, especially in terms of its emphasis upon personal and civic responsibility (Coalter 2007). A number of policy documents made explicit links between participation and such wider benefits to the community. The notion of social capital becomes important here, and sport's potential role in enhancing social capital, reflecting the changes in policy from the provision of sport *to* disadvantaged groups and communities, to the provision of sport *for* disadvantaged groups and communities.

Subsequent initiatives such as *A Sporting Future for All* (DCMS 2000) and *Game Plan* (DCMS 2002) have been important in shaping current governmental policy, and have, to some extent been able to integrate the ideas of both providing access to sport and physical activity for the benefit of the individual and for the community. The four key objectives identified in Game Plan were:

- Increasing mass participation
- Improving success in popular sports
- Improving the approach to hosting major events
- Simplifying the fragmented funding arrangements and reforming the organisational framework (Collins 2008).

Subsequent recommendations emerged from the Carter Report (2005), which focused much more on the means by which policies should be delivered, rather than the policies themselves. Lord Carter stressed the need for greater and more robust evidence upon which to base policy, the need for sustained, rather than short-term marketing strategies to promote participation, a renewed infrastructure, with a single 'supply chain' from Central Government to local delivery of sport, and greater commercial assistance for delivery. In 2008, the Strategic Paper *Playing to Win – a New Era* set out the current government's ambition to become a world leading sporting nation, intending to capitalise upon the hosting of the 2012 Olympic and Paralympic Games in London. This objective demonstrates a clear focus upon performance sport, and concomitant improvements in support mechanisms to achieve such aims, for example by the development of the UK Coaching Framework, as well as inclusionary policies to combat social exclusion from sport and physical activity. Some of the sources by which these visions are funded are outlined below.

Sources of funding

A number of sources of funding are available to fund sports development within the United Kingdom. These include local authorities, the Sports Councils, the National Lottery, the private sector, and charitable sources. Traynor and Lillya (2009) outline the key funding sources:

- Local and central government (other than that distributed through Sports Councils and the National Lottery)
- The National Lottery
- Sports Councils
- National governing bodies
- Sponsorship
- Charities
- European sources
- Sources within the local community.

It is not the purpose of the chapter to identify every source of funding, and the processes by which funding is allocated. Instead, some of the key issues in terms of the key providers, their objectives for funding, and some of the issues regarding the sustainability of such funding will be outlined.

Local authorities are a key source of funding, spending approximately £1 billion each year on sport, representing almost half of all funding available (Traynor and Lillya 2009). Funding is delivered for both capital and revenue purposes; however, funding is extremely competitive, especially when sport is competing against areas such as housing, education and social services, for example. There is no uniform approach to sports development across different local authorities, and each may have different priorities, and in some local authorities, sport may be part of a wider 'Leisure Services' department, with additional competition from sectors such as museums and tourism, for example. The White Paper *Strong and Prosperous Communities* (DCLG 2006) set out a number of changes to the role of local government, intending to strengthen the influence of local communities, through rebalancing the relationship between central government, local government and local people towards a more 'reciprocal', rather than top-down, framework for the allocation of funding. The key changes from the White Paper are:

- Reduced control of central government
- Increased freedom of local government
- Greater flexibility of local government to respond to challenges
- Greater power to local communities
- Increased focus on local, rather than national targets
- Greater co-ordination and 'joined-up thinking' in terms of delivery services.

Local authorities are the key player in leading and developing local strategic partnerships (LSPs), comprising of stakeholders from the public, private and voluntary sectors, which are intended to enable the more effective identification and delivery of a sustainable community strategy, forming the basis of a Local Area Agreement (LAA). Funding for LAAs was initially divided between four 'blocks' dealing with Children and Young People, Healthier Communities and Older People, Safer and Stronger Communities and Economic Development. The *Strong and Prosperous Communities* White Paper was beneficial for sport, however, in that it both removed perceived inflexibility in funding areas that did not necessarily fit into one of these themes, but also in that it specifically suggested that sport should be part of a wider fourth theme, that of *Economic Development and the Environment*. To date, 80 local authorities have identified adult participation in sport and active recreation as a targeted priority for their LAA (Communities and Local Government 2009). Partnership working has become key in the delivery of such strategies, and thus, there is a strong need for sporting bodies and related stakeholders at a local level to ensure sufficient representation within an LSP to ensure strategies are delivered.

The National Lottery remains a key funder of sport in the UK, despite a shift in emphasis towards elite and Olympic sport (see below). Sport is one of four causes supported by the lottery (the others being: (a) charities, health, education and the environment, (b) arts, and (c) heritage). In total, the lottery has contributed over £23 billion to these causes. Over recent years the average amount available for distribution to the various good causes has been £1.3 billion of which 16.66 per cent is currently allocated to sport, giving sport approximately £230 million of the £1.38 billion income in 2008–9. Funding raised through the lottery is distributed through a variety of bodies, including the Sports Councils, UK Sport and the Olympic Lottery Distributor. The Olympic Lottery Distributor will receive £1,085 million in 13 instalments from the National Lottery Distribution Fund plus £750 million from a dedicated Olympic lottery game. The largest distributor is the BIG Lottery Fund, created in 2006 through

Table 37.1 Total funding allocated through selected funding distributors, 1995 to March 2010

Lottery distributor	Number of projects funded	Total funding allocated
UK Sport	12,203	£452m
Sport England	19,626	£3,060m
Sport Scotland	8,586	£225m
Sports Council for Wales	7,383	£144m
Sports Council of Northern Ireland	3,360	£150m

the merging of the community and the new opportunities funds, and which is responsible for distributing 50 per cent of money allocated to the various good causes. Cumulative funding totals since the introduction of the National Lottery are shown in Table 37.1. A key element of lottery funding is the emphasis upon partnership working, and the need for applicants to demonstrate active and viable partnerships, not only for the scope of the project, but also beyond. Despite the focus on elite sport, the National Lottery remains a key funding source for many initiatives.

The five Sports Councils in the United Kingdom have a key role in the distribution of money through both government and lottery funding. UK Sport focuses on high-performance sport, whereas the other four Sports Councils (Sport England, sportscotland, the Sports Council for Wales and the Sports Council for Northern Ireland) have a much broader remit. The current Sport England strategy, for example, runs until March 2011, and addresses three key challenges facing community sport:

- Increasing participation in sport
- Tackling drop-off
- Developing talent.

The strategy focuses on five key targets:

- One million people doing more sport
- A 25% reduction in the number of 16- to 18-year-olds who drop out of five key sports
- Improved talent development systems in at least 25 sports
- A measurable increase in people's satisfaction with their experience of sport – the first time the organisation has set such a qualitative measure
- A major contribution to the delivery of the five-hour sports offer for children and young people.

(Sport England 2008)

Again, as with the role of LSPs within Local Authority funding, partnership working has become a key value underpinning delivery. To achieve this, a number of new principles have been developed, for example by providing: longer-term commitment to partners such as County Sports Partnerships, rather than funding on a yearly cycle; greater support for innovation; greater flexibility in the way that funding is distributed to ensure it meets the needs of applicants;

minimal bureaucracy while ensuring accountability. The strategy is designed to ensure a more appropriate allocation of funds, which are grouped into a number of key funding streams:

- Funding of National Governing Body Whole Sport Plans
- Five-Hour Sport Offer Funding
- Funding to National Partners (e.g. sports coach UK or Skills Active)
- Core funding to County Sports Partnerships
- A series of 'managed' rounds of lottery funding for projects specifically aligned with Sport England's strategic objectives
- A targeted programme of investment in facilities
- A small grants scheme
- A dedicated innovation fund.

Funding is distributed in two ways: first, through solicited applications, in conjunction with organisations such as national governing bodies, county sports partnerships and local authorities to finance aspects of their work concerned with community sport objectives. The amount available is approximately £158 million a year. Second, a maximum of £45 million per year is available for open funding. This funding stream is available for any sports organisation including sports clubs, voluntary sports clubs, community organisations, local authorities and schools, colleges and universities. The key criteria upon which funding decisions are made are those linked with the overall strategy of Sport England in terms of 'grow, sustain and excel', thus priority is given to applications that demonstrate outcomes in terms of increasing participation, sustaining such participation through ensuring a high-quality experience and reducing drop-out from physical activity, and developing talent within sport.

Funding streams for grass-roots participation are always competing against funding for elite sport programmes. Elite Sport Development has been a 'key policy concern' since the mid-1990s (Green 2004) and is currently the responsibility of UK Sport, which receives funding from the Department of Culture, Media and Sport (DCMS) to address three strategic priorities, those of World Class Success, Worldwide Impact, and World Class Standards. To achieve these, eight 'Primary Activities' were agreed between DCMS and UK Sport, these being:

World Class Success:

- Support athletes to succeed in world class events
- Develop skilled people to support UK world class athletes
- Drive the development of a world class high performance system for the UK.

Worldwide Impact:

- Establish the UK as an authoritative and leading player in world class sport
- Develop an international development assistance programme in and through sport
- Develop a sports-focused strategy for staging major international events across the UK.

World Class Standards:

- Lead a world class anti-doping programme for the UK (this responsibility transferred to a new agency, UK Anti-Doping, in December 2009)
- Work with athletes and others to promote the highest standards of conduct in sport.

(DCMS 2005)

In the 2006 Budget statement the Government announced a £600 million package for the remaining three years of the Beijing cycle and for the London cycle, comprising £200 million of Exchequer funding matched by £100 million of private sector investment, and supported by £300 million of lottery investment (DCMS 2009). This was followed in December 2008 by the announcement of an actual total of £550 million of public funds to UK Sport to support its elite programme. This consisted of additional Exchequer funding of £29 million to UK Sport over the four years to 2012 plus a projected uplift in lottery income – at the expense of grass-roots sport – of £21 million, enabling UK Sport to set a target to attain a place in the top four in the Olympic Games, and second place in the Paralympic Games in 2012 and to win more medals in more sports than in Beijing. In total, 28 Olympic sports are due to receive a total of over £256 million, and 19 Paralympic sports will receive over £47 million in funding (UK Sport 2009). The principles of UK Sport funding are that of a 'no compromise' strategy, whereby funding is provided to those sports that are capable of winning medals, and funding is not awarded to, or may be removed from, those national governing bodies failing to meet such criteria. Criteria are assessed through factors such as results at the previous Olympic Games, the sport's overall track record in significant competition, its projected medal capability at major events, and the effectiveness of its 'athlete pipeline', that is, the process of talent identification and successful athlete development. Hence, sports that have shown success such as cycling and swimming have received increased funding compared to sports such as athletics and gymnastics. Sports such as shooting, volleyball and table tennis have all had significant reductions in their financial allocations in the funding round for the London Olympics. Despite the focus on 'more medals', the DCMS, in early 2009, announced that it had reached the 'limit of public investment in sport', and that further funding would have to come from private fundraising initiatives, such as that from the creation of a fundraising partnership for elite sport, aimed at bringing together UK Sport, the British Olympic Association, the British Paralympic Association and the London Organising Committee of the London Olympic and Paralympic Games (LOCOG) to raise private sector funds for elite sport, thus demonstrating a shift in emphasis from a focus on lottery funding (adopted for the Sydney and Athens Olympic funding rounds), to Exchequer and lottery money (for the Beijing Olympics), to a mix of lottery, Exchequer and private sector funding (for the London, and presumably, subsequent Games).

The focus on Olympic sport has, however, a potentially harmful impact upon grass-roots sport, perhaps suggesting that the dual strategy of social inclusion and more medals is problematic. A London Assembly report (2008) noted the difficulty of achieving both fourth place in the 2012 Olympics and meeting the target of increased and sustained grass-roots participation. As Traynor and Lillya (2009: x) suggest:

> The issue that the government is 'robbing Peter to pay Paul' is highlighted … by the following figures; Sport England is contributing £50.5 million to the Olympics Aquatic Centre and Velopark – money that could pay for 19 sports halls with courts, 20 five-lane swimming pools, 721 multi use games areas or 841 grass pitches.

The argument that diverting funding to elite sporting events such as the London Olympics will benefit grass-roots sport and result in increased participation is, at best, weak. The Game Plan (Strategy Unit 2002) document was clear on this, noting that hosting events such as the Olympic Games was simply not effective in creating a sustained increase in sports participation. However, this focus on the demonstration effect of major sports events has also impacted upon National Lottery funding for grass-roots projects, with funding being redistributed to the Olympics, and UK Sport reducing that available through the other funding streams of the lottery.

Funding of sports development and its sustainability

Whichever funding stream is accessed, the concern with sustainability has become ubiquitous in sports development, yet has received little attention within the academic literature (Lindsay 2008) despite sustainability having, to some extent, taken precedence over other criteria that guide the choice of funding recipients, especially those concerned to provide community sports participation. Girginov and Hills (2008: 2094) note that sustainability, in terms of sports development, is a complex issue as there is no static target. Instead, this

> renders sustainable sports development into a construction process aimed at creating value but with an unknown end point. It also places local actors centre stage, as any meaningful vision of change in individuals, communities and organisations produced by sports has to be derived from local symbols, knowledge and behaviours.

Girginov and Hill's analysis stresses the importance of developing the appropriate skills and abilities of a range of stakeholders based at a local, rather than national, level for policies aimed at developing participation, rather than elite success. The different groups of stakeholders can be identified through Lindsay's (2008) framework which, although based upon health-related literature, is useful in terms of identifying four forms of sustainability and clarifying the concept. The four forms are:

- Individual sustainability – this refers to the extent to which any impact upon individuals as a result of any funding or initiative leads to a sustained change in behaviour, such as through continued regular participation at a grass-roots level, or through a sustained involvement upwards through the various performance levels, from grass roots to elite.
- Community sustainability – this refers to the wider impacts of the use of any such funding, for example does it enhance the community's skills, abilities and resources? Does it change community attitudes towards participation, and does funding lead to improved relations between sports providers and the wider community? It can also refer to the extent to which the community is able to engage with itself, rather than central or local government, to achieve sustainable funding (Adams 2008), and whether there is civic confidence in the programmes being funded (Collins 2003).
- Organisational sustainability – is the extent to which the organisations receiving the funding have the ability and motivation to deliver the funded schemes, through having appropriate skills and resources not only for the period of the funding, but for a sustained period beyond. Thus, as well as having the capacity to deliver the programme itself, sustainability requires capacity to be developed in aspects such as planning, budgeting, fundraising, advertising and promotion. A key element of sustainable funding is that of being able to develop income generation schemes to enable longer-term strategic planning, rather than crisis fundraising. Organisational sustainability seems more likely when there is a 'bottom up' approach, with local people being able to take active leadership roles (Collins 2003).
- Institutional sustainability – this refers to the wider policy context, and the extent to which the funding landscape allows programmes and initiatives to be maintained, for example the extent to which the global recession may impact upon sports development, especially given the need for sponsorship to sustain funded programmes, which seems to be a critical success factor for sustained activity (Collins 2003).

As well as defining these four forms, Lindsay (2008) also identifies three processual issues that can be related to the sustaining of a particular funded strategy. These are:

- Project design and implementation factors – this can refer to a variety of factors related to the actual programme, scheme or initiative being funded, for example whether the programme is effective and appropriately designed to meet its needs, and whether there are any proposals for sustaining the programme when funding has ceased, for example through charging participants, making the scheme attractive to potential sponsors and charities, ensuring that all required capital expenditure is spent before funding ends, and so on. Some funding streams, for example the National Lottery Big Lottery Fund (BIG), make this an obligatory aspect of any application for funding.
- Factors in the organisation setting – referring to the strength and capability of the organisation itself to deliver programmes, and the extent to which the programme is integrated within the organisation. If there is one particular individual leading the project, for example, what would be the impact upon the sustainability of the project if they were to leave?
- Environmental factors – the extent to which the political, social, economic, legal, environmental and technological factors influence delivery of the programme. Thus a change in local government may well impact the potential sustainability of a programme, as may a downturn in the local economy.

Environmental factors are, essentially, beyond the control of organisations seeking funding, yet are a key issue in terms of the institutional and organisational sustainability of projects. Collins (2003) outlines a number of issues that relate to environmental factors. The first of these is the 'policy lifespan', influenced by the continual pressure to adapt, modify, or even completely redesign programmes and initiatives to maintain a sense of appeal and currency, especially with a change of government, or personnel within government. Projects are set up that provide funding at an initial stage, but changing priorities and initiatives may fail to give such projects enough time to bed in, or may promote a feeling amongst organisations that there is little point in setting up a sustainable infrastructure if there are likely to be subsequent changes. A lack of institutional sustainability may also influence organisational sustainability through a pressure to provide rapid results, and the limitations provided by offering funding cycles of two, three or four years. Collins (2003) suggests that, from his own experiences, this leads to issues whereby the first year of any project may involve a period of time setting up networks and relationships, whilst demonstrating an initial 'honeymoon' effect, which may lead to positive results in the second year. Subsequent years are more difficult, with reducing capability, leading to a downsizing of the project as funding from government begins to diminish, and the ambitions of the organisation reduce in accordance with likely future funding. In reality, according to Collins, schemes require at least seven to 10 years to establish.

Although issues of sustainability can be addressed in developing proposals to gain funding, Girginov and Hills' (2008) suggestion that sustainable sports development is a moving target makes it difficult to address, especially as key performance indicators (KPIs), especially for schemes funded by the various Sports Councils, tend to address performance, rather than the sustainability of such projects. As Robinson (2004) highlights, performance management exists to demonstrate that public money has been spent appropriately and efficiently, to manage stakeholder expectations, and to motivate individuals to assist with meeting the overall goals set. Thus, generic KPIs, such as numbers and throughput of participants, coaching hours delivered, numbers of volunteers involved and so on, are less appropriate to address issues of sustainability. KPIs need to be appropriately targeted towards issues of sustainability as far as possible, a difficult task given that KPIs focus upon what has happened, rather than addressing what may happen. The KPIs outlined in the current Sport England Strategy fail, it could be argued, to address the issue of sustainability in any meaningful form, focusing overly upon measurable outcomes.

Conclusion

The concept of sports development has undergone a significant degree of evolution in the last 50 years, towards a much more holistic – and ambitious – approach focusing on both inclusion and success. This new agenda is supported through increasing reliance upon public funding, especially that sourced from central and local government, and the National Lottery. Whilst a perfect funding model for sport would seem to be, in reality, unattainable, the current funding arrangements do raise a number of key issues. At a local level, the lack of consistency between local authorities, combined with the relative lack of emphasis given to sport compared with other local authority functions, is clearly problematic, leading to significant variations in provision, and a subsequent lack of a cohesive strategy at a local level. At a national level, the reliance of national governing bodies upon government funding, as well as reliance upon the Department for Children, Schools and Families for the provision of resources for school sport, leads to potential problems of sustainability, given the complex, and ever changing political and economic environment within which funding decisions are made. This situation is reinforced with a focus upon key performance indicators, with a subsequent emphasis upon short-term measurable outcomes, rather than a focus on sustainability, a focus which, it could be argued, needs to underpin the next phase of sports development within the UK.

References

Adams, A. (2008). Building organisational and management capacity for the delivery of sports development, in Girginov, V. (Ed.) *Management of Sports Development*, London: Butterworth-Heinemann, pp. 203–24.

Carter, P. (2005). *Review of National Sport Effort and Resources*, London: DCMS.

Coalter, F. (2007). *A Wider Social Role for Sport: Who's Keeping the Score*, London: Routledge.

Collins, M. (2003). *Sport and Social Exclusion*, London: Routledge.

——(2008). Public policies on sports development: can mass and elite sport hold together? in Girginov, V. (Ed.) *Management of Sports Development*, London: Butterworth-Heinemann, pp. 59–88.

Communities and Local Government (2009). *Local Priorities*, available at www.localpriorities.communities. gov.uk/LAAResults.aspx (accessed 07/06/09).

DCMS (2008). *Playing to win: A new era for sport*. London: DCMS.

Department of Communities and Local Government (DCLG) (2006). 'Strong and Prosperous Communities: The Local Government White Paper', DCLG/TSO.

Department of Culture, Media and Sport (DCMS) (2000). *A Sporting Future for All*, London: HMSO.

——(2002). *Game Plan: a strategy for delivering Government's sport and physical activity objectives*, London: DCMS/Strategy Unit.

——(2009). 'Written Ministerial Statement on the new fundraising partnership for elite sport', London: HMSO.

Department of National Heritage (DNH) (1995). *Sport: Raising the Game*, London: HMSO.

Girginov, V. and Hills, L. (2008). 'A sustainable sports legacy: creating a link between the London Olympics and sports participation', *International Journal of the History of Sport*, 25 (14), 2091–116.

Green, M. (2004). 'Changing policy priorities for sport in England: the emergence of elite sport development as a key policy concern', *Leisure Studies*, 23 (4), 365–85.

Hylton, K. and Bramham, P. (2008). 'Models of sport development', in Girginov, V. (Ed.) *Management of Sports Development*, London: Butterworth-Heinemann, pp. 41–58.

Jackson, D. and Nesti, M. (2001). 'Resources for sport', in Hylton, K., Bramham, P., Jackson, D., and Nesti, M. (Eds) *Sport Development: Policy, Process and Practice,* London: Routledge, pp. 149–70.

Kidd, B. and Donnelly, P. (2000). 'Human rights in sport', *International Review for the Sociology of Sport,* 35 (20), 131–48.

Lawson, H. (2005). 'Empowering people, facilitating community development, and contributing to sustainable development: the social work of sport, exercise, and physical education programs', *Sport, Education, Society*, 10 (1), 135–60.

Lindsay, I. (2008). 'Conceptualising sustainability in sports development', *Leisure Studies*, 27 (3), 279–94.

Nichols, G., Taylor, P., James, M., Garrett, R., Holmes, K., King, L., Gratton, C. and Kokolakakis, T. (2004). 'Voluntary activity in UK sport', *Voluntary Action*, 6 (2), 31–54.

Robinson, L. (2004). *Managing Public Sport and Leisure Services*, London: Routledge.

Social Exclusion Unit (SEU) (2002). *The Social Exclusion Unit's Policy Action Team Approach to Policy Development: The Views of Participants*, London: Cabinet Office.

Sport England South West (2005). 'Regional Plan Bulletin No. 3 Community Investment Fund'.

Sport England (2008). *Sport England Strategy 2008–2011*, available at www.sportengland.org/text/.../sport_england_strategy.htm (accessed 12/06/09).

——(2009). *Sustainable facilities*, available at www.sportengland.org/funding/sustainable_facilities.aspx (accessed 04/06/09).

Sports Council (1982). *Sport in the Community: the Next Ten Years*, London: Sports Council.

——(1987) *Sport in the Community: into the 90's*, London: Sports Council.

Strategy Unit (2002). *Game Plan: A Strategy for Delivering Government's Sport and Physical Activity Objectives*, London: Strategy Unit/Department of Culture, Media and Sport.

Traynor, T. and Lillya, D. (2009). *Sports Funding Guide*, Liverpool: Directory of Social Change.

UK Sport (2009). 'London 2012 – Sport by Sport Funding Breakdown', available at www.uksport.gov.uk/pages/summer_olympic_sports–london_2012/ (accessed 6/06/09).

38

Market segmentation and the role of the public sector in sports development[1]

Paul Downward

This chapter examines the origins and current emphases of sports supply in the UK, drawing primarily upon economic theory. In this regard the chapter focuses upon sports development as deriving from the interplay between rational individual agents and the form by which the supply of resources to meet their needs emerges. The implication of this discussion will be that markets and their role in sports development can only be understood in connection with the development of other forms of organisation, which includes the public sector provision of services and facilities and voluntary formal organisations such as club-sport systems, as well as entirely informal activity.

To facilitate this discussion the next section briefly discusses the definition of sports development. Some basic economic concepts are then introduced as bases of an economic explanation of how and why sports have developed as they have. The subsequent section then explores how regulatory and policy changes have taken place in the UK, as vehicles for promoting organisational change, and indicating how, from an economic perspective, policy tensions can be said to exist that will affect future sports development.

Sports development

Sports development is a difficult concept to define (Hylton and Bramham 2008). In part this is because 'sport' lacks clear definition. It is reasonable to assume that for many people sport comprises an intrinsically competitive activity, but the 1992 European Sports Charter, revised in 2001, argues that,

> Sport embraces much more than traditional team games and competition. Sport means all forms of physical activity which, through casual or organised participation, aim at expressing or improving physical fitness and mental well-being, forming social relationships or obtaining results in competition at all levels.

Consequently, as Gratton and Taylor (2000: 7) note, definitions of sport involve 'the criterion of general acceptance that an activity is sporting, e.g. by the media and sports agencies'.

Moreover, Downward *et al* (2009) show there is international variance in what activities constitute sport, even in official documentation and review.

There are also different domains in which sport takes place. Downward *et al* (2009) identify three major components of the sports 'economy' covering professional team sports, sports events and mass participation sports. In the former case, competition takes place in league structures and other forms of knockout tournament. In the latter two cases, both individuals as well as teams *can* compete in environments in which either multiple sports are involved, or individual sports, and competition can be between professional as well as amateur participants. Generally now elite sport is professional. Amateur sports leagues are also prevalent for team sports. Events in this sense are simply less regular tournaments of a limited duration, relative to leagues. The amateur component of both team and individual sports naturally forms part of the mass participation sector of sports, but as part of a formal setting through sports club structures. Self-organised, informal sports then comprises the majority of sports participation.

The 'development' of sport, then, can be understood in the context of this supply structure and by reference to some form of policy initiative aimed at changing the nature of sports activity. Hylton and Bramham (2008: 4) suggest that this 'must be ... devising better and more effective ways of promoting interest, participation or performance in sport'. For example the traditional sports continuum, presented in Figure 38.1, is widely cited in public policy documentation connected with sports development.[2] In this figure, levels of sports participation in terms of frequency, intensity and ultimately competition are measured on the vertical dimension, whilst numbers of participants are measured on the horizontal dimension.

The continuum maintains that if more people can be attracted to sport as beginners, or children learning the foundation skills for sport, regular sports participation will occur, with subsequent desires to enhance skills and performance through regular training which may then, ultimately, result in excellent performance in competition generally, but also at an elite level. In economic language this means that the sports development continuum postulates a supply chain through which casual mass participation may become more formalised, competitive and feed into elite activity.

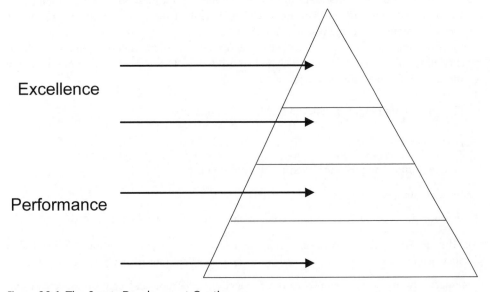

Figure 38.1 The Sports Development Continuum

Hylton and Bramham (2008: 4) also note that many definitions of sports development tend to obscure 'the arguably more important issues of who has the responsibility for this activity, and … where, how, why, and ultimately what should be done'. However, answers to such questions noted by the authors are typically based around differences in opinion associated with the objective of an active sports policy either to address broader social, economic, health and cultural aims or, in contrast, to promote sport for sport's sake. As reviewed later in the chapter, elements of both these objectives have figured in sports policy in the UK. At this point, however, it should be noted that an economic approach to sports development also asks a more fundamental question. 'Should there be an active comprehensive public policy agenda for sports development?'[3] To address such a question naturally raises the need to outline some key economic principles.

Key economic principles

It is widely accepted that economics is

> … the science which studies human behaviour as a relationship between ends and scarce means which have alternative uses

> *(Robbins 1940: 16)*

Consequently economic analysis seeks generalised understanding of behaviour concerned with how society allocates resources to alternative actions. To address this, economics first postulates that *individuals* make rational choices between alternative courses of action, and hence this is why resources get committed to satisfy these choices. It is assumed that the goal of choice is for individuals to *maximise utility*, that is to seek to maximise welfare, as judged *by themselves* (see also Becker 1976). In this way aggregate outcomes in society are represented as the sum of individual decisions. Further, following Friedman (1953) the methodology of economics is to test the predictions of a theory, deduced from its assumptions, regardless of the realism of the latter. This means that it is the outcomes of decisions, as alternative states of the world, that are the focus of attention for economists, more than the specific historical, social and cultural means by which the outcomes emerge. The approach is inherently static and comparative, emphasising *equilibria* as outcomes from individual actions.[4]

Normative impetus from economics consequently rests on comparison of equilibria, with the benchmark for maximum economic welfare being *efficiency*. There are a number of dimensions to efficiency. Efficiency applies in production where:

The maximum output is achieved for the minimum input

or equivalently:

The maximum output is achieved for the minimum cost

and in consumption where:

Prices reflect the true opportunity costs of alternative uses of resources

in the aggregate where: any reallocations of resources, for example through individual or policy action, cannot improve the welfare of one agent without reducing it for the other.

Respectively, these are examples of the production, allocation and Paretian aspects of efficiency. An extremely important set of results in economics (referred to as the Fundamental

Theorems of Welfare Economics) is that a perfectly competitive market system is sufficient to produce economic efficiency. These theorems underpin the normative basis of most economic policy that market forces, capturing voluntary individual free choice, are the best form of institutional mechanism to allocate resources in society and, further, that this is the reason why market forms of organisation tend to emerge in transactions. The conclusion is that markets work in the individual's best interests and that observed behaviour in society can be viewed as optimal for the individual, unless there are problems in the ability of markets to function.

For markets to work effectively, property rights, defined as

> the rules (whether formal and legal or informal custom) which specify which individuals are allowed to do what with resources and the outputs of those resources. Property rights define which of the technologically feasible economic decisions individuals are permitted to make
>
> *(Gravelle and Rees 2004: 9)*

need to be well specified. If so, then they define *private goods* which can be bought and sold on markets, but this need not be restricted to legal forms of activity.

If property rights are not clearly defined, then markets fail to produce an efficient allocation of resources.[5] Externalities can occur and this means that the private benefits and costs received by, or paid to, an individual in a transaction/exchange of resources, do not correspond to those that, if aggregated, indicate that society is better off or not (Mishan 1981). Positive externalities arise when the social benefits of consumption exceed those of the private individual, or the social costs of production are less than the private costs of production. Negative externalities occur in the opposite sense.

The impact of externalities on the allocation of resources, with a corresponding explanation of how resources come to be supplied to consumers, can be understood with reference to whether resources are *rival or non-rival* (Samuelson 1954, 1955) and whether they are *exclusive or non-exclusive* (Musgrave 1969; Musgrave and Musgrave 1973). If resources are non-rival and non-exclusive they are described as public goods. Non-rivalry means that one individual's consumption does not reduce the availability of the good for others to consume because of scarcity. Non-exclusivity means that it is impossible to exclude individuals from the consumption of resources. Public goods by definition, therefore, cannot be supplied by markets but can provide a rationale for government intervention to supply the resource to consumers. However, this does require an ethical judgement that government intervention should correct market failure. Public goods do not of necessity imply public sector activity. The case for that intervention needs to be made.

These two conditions show that a variety of economic goods exist as illustrated in Table 38.1.

Table 38.1 Types of economic good

Characteristic	Rival	Non-rival
Excludable	Private goods (supplied by markets)	Club goods (supplied to members of a club)
Non-excludable	Common property resource (over-consumed unless exclusion is enforced)	Public goods (can provide a rationale for public sector provision)

Common property resources might reflect national parks, or natural resources such as the sea.[6] It is difficult to exclude people from walking in the park, or fishing in the sea – though possible – but walking in the park or fishing in the sea are rivalrous in as much as the benefits of isolation, or the fishing stock available to others are affected by agents. Economic theory predicts that these resources will be overexploited unless some form of regulation is enforced.

Of most significance for this chapter is when consumption is excludable but non-rival. This defines a *club good* which is

> a voluntary group deriving mutual benefit from sharing one or more of the following: production costs, the members characteristics, or a good characterised by excludable benefits ... thus, the utility jointly derived from membership and the consumption of other goods must exceed the utility associated with non-membership status.
>
> *(Cornes and Sandler 1986: 159)*

This suggests that clubs emerge so that like-minded individuals voluntarily combine to supply and to consume resources amongst a shared group, but others can be excluded, for example, by price such as a membership fee. Congestion can also limit club membership, as having too many members will undermine the production and consumption of the resource. For example, it may reduce the 'exclusivity' of the club, or make it difficult to access the facilities provided by the club.

Based on these ideas economics predicts that, dependent on the different allocation of property rights associated with different elements of sport, it is to be expected that the private sector market, voluntary clubs or government can best meet sports participants' needs. This, of course, begs the theoretical question of how much sport will be supplied by each institutional mechanism. To develop these predictions requires thinking about the scale of the desire to consume resources as sport, coupled with the institutional mechanism that will most efficiently supply the resources.

Insight can be derived from Weisbrod (1978, 1988, 1998) who argues that voluntary club-based activity comes into existence to correct *government failure* as well as *market failure*.

It is argued that, in the case of there being small-scale and heterogeneous demands for the use of resources, the government or the market will be unable to supply consumers. Demand is too localised for markets to develop, whilst government agencies will be unable to meet the varied demands underpinned by the heterogeneous preferences of individuals, by following bureaucratic rules.[7] It is under such circumstances that informal participation arises which, following Becker (1965, 1974, 1976), results from the participant acting as a consumer-producer of sport combining their skills, time, goods and equipment to engage in an activity.

It follows, then, that clubs, government or private-sector activity will develop and be possible as the nature of these demands changes. For example, as participation becomes more formalised, and competition becomes desirable, then some specialisation in roles will need to take place. According to economic theory *it is such developments that lead to clubs arising*. There becomes a requirement for coaches, for players and for those that manage the running of the club and competition to have distinct roles and, of course, competitions require governance across clubs – hence the formation of National Governing Bodies. As well as sports clubs emerging and developing, economic theory suggests two other possibilities as the scale of demands increase.

In the first case, if participation grows and becomes more homogeneous, then this enhances the possibility that the government and/or the private sector could supply the sport. However, to the extent that individuals prefer control over their consumption, economics predicts that the private sector will meet such demands *unless* governments intervene instead. Consequently, if governments retreat from provision, or fail to meet individual preferences, then markets will emerge with well-specified property rights.

In the second case, economic theory predicts that, should tastes for spectatorship of sports develop and grow, then a further evolution of clubs will occur. In particular, commercial prospects become apparent and roles change such that participants become employees (players) and club support systems become employers (club owners and management, etc.) which contract to supply spectators with sports contests whilst seeking profits and/or success in sports competition (Andreff and Staudohar 2000, 2002; Downward *et al* 2009).[8]

The impetus for such governance changes can be understood more clearly with reference to transaction cost theory, developed in a number of seminal contributions by Williamson (1970, 1975, 1985) and others. This theory indicates that alternative governance structures will evolve to produce efficient bases for transactions in economics, by reducing transaction costs. For example, with standardised products/services and repeat purchases, then market exchanges can be efficient. Likewise, if coordination of activities is important, then networks can improve on markets and formal authoritarian hierarchies can improve on networks. Figure 38.2 illustrates the main ideas.

The bilateral transactions part of Figure 38.2 might represent the set of 12 communication channels required by four individuals engaging in informal sport. If competition and rules need to be agreed upon and monitored, then Figure 38.2 shows that a network such as a sports club system is more efficient in coordinating the participants within and across sports. Note that only six lines of communication are involved. The final part of Figure 38.2 is a formal contractual hierarchy, as might be indicative of professional clubs. This is more efficient still as agent 'A' is not the hub of a wheel of communication, as with the network, but has strategic oversight in the organisation and authority to instruct the others in their actions. There are only three lines of communication.

Of course elements of combined organisation will be relevant in practice across systems of relationships. For example commercial organisations will be hierarchical, comprising internally related agents of the relevant skills, etc., but will act in markets with other firms and customers as part of a bilateral transaction model. The point is that the economic theory predicts that particular organisational forms emerge as a direct consequence of the specific needs of those engaged in transactions.

Having outlined the relevant economic theory and suggested predictions of behaviour, it is now possible to show how this can be used to explain 'market segmentation' in sports development in the UK. Subsequently, the economic concepts just outlined can then be employed to explore some challenges that are faced in current sports development policy.

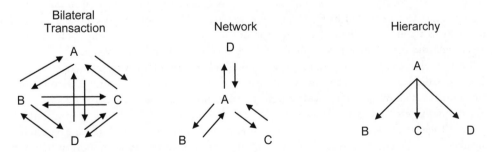

Figure 38.2 Organisational efficiency

UK sports policy and delivery

Space precludes a detailed review of the UK's historical delivery structure, but the voluntary sports club system is the oldest form of organisational delivery, having roots at least in the nineteenth century with governing bodies for cricket, football and rugby developing. As Houlihan (1977), Green (2004) and Green and Houlihan (2005) note in the early twentieth century, there was a lack of sports policy other than connected with raising general physical fitness, with a commensurate lack of private sector provision.

As Gratton and Taylor (1991) note, the first major sports policy development in the UK was the Wolfenden Committee report of 1960 'Sport and the Community', in which a recommendation for the establishment of a Sports Development Council was made, as well as a public recognition of the lack of sports facilities. The Advisory Sports Council was established in 1965 and its role was to advise the government on cooperation between statutory bodies and the pre-existing largely voluntary sports sector.

In 1966 the Council embraced the Council of Europe's 'Sport for All' policy as one of its aims, as well as working towards the development of elite athletes. This advisory role changed with the formation of the executive Sports Council in 1971 by Royal Charter. These developments in the UK were informed again by the broader policy direction in Europe and, as Henry (2001) argues, by the 'welfare-reformist' principles of the then current UK government. Such concerns were consolidated with the publication of the European Sport for All Charter in 1975 which, in Article 1, argued that 'Every individual shall have the right to participate in sport'. Explicit within the Charter were suggestions for achieving Sport for All, which included a high level of government support from public funds, a planned approach to facility development, administrative machinery to develop and coordinate policy, and finally, a willingness to use legislation. There was a policy presumption that externalities prevented the private sector or informal sector meeting the needs of sports participants.

To facilitate this policy the Sports Council developed national 'Provision for Sport' plans and allocated grant funding, as well as coordinated large-scale local authority investment to facilitate participation. As Gratton and Taylor (1991) note, a large-scale investment programme, particularly in swimming pools, was undertaken. Targets for the increase in sporting infrastructure were put forward and achieved. However, following the publication of three white papers; 'Sport and Recreation' (1975), 'Policy for inner cities' (1977) and 'Recreation and Deprivation in Urban Areas' (1997), a focus upon the need to target non-participants emerged in policy discussion which led to the publication of 'Sport in the Community: The Next Ten Years' (1982) and 'Sport in the Community: Into the 1990s' (1988). In these documents the policy impetus changed from one of providing facilities to having a focus upon increasing the *use* of facilities. This was, in part a result of ideological change in economic policy towards market-based provision. In the 1980s a broad policy sweep encouraged the privatisation of public services and the deregulation of markets that were dominated by monopoly government agencies, and a focus upon the individual making appropriate choices for their welfare. This process began with the conservative governments of Margaret Thatcher and John Major.

Two developments occurred during this period, and are consistent with the economic predictions of the last section. The first was the rapid growth of commercial, private sector sports provision. These now cater for a wide range of health and fitness interests, including swimming and racquet sports, and in the latter case often work as centres of excellence with governing bodies. Table 38.2 describes some of the current provision in the UK. Rising consumer incomes and preferences for sport, coupled with the standardised provision of sport in the form of fitness and health made these rapid developments possible.

Table 38.2 Private Sector Health and Fitness Clubs 2007

Company/owner	Brand(s)	Clubs	Members	Average members/club
Fitness First Holdings Ltd	Fitness First/ Fitness First for Women/Kaizen	183	452,000	2,470
Whitbread plc	David Lloyd	59	325,000	5,508
Virgin Active Ltd	Virgin Active	72	288,301	4,004
LA Fitness plc	LA Fitness/ Promise	87	261,000	3,000
Esporta Group Ltd	Esporta	53	220,000	4,151
Bannatyne Fitness Ltd	Bannatyne Health Club/Just Fitness	61	180,000	2,951
Cannons Health & Fitness Ltd	Cannons	52	177,000	3,404
JJB Sports plc	JJB Health Clubs	39	175,000	4,487

Source: Mintel (2007)

Secondly, a general policy emphasis upon cutting public expenditure had a direct impact on public sector sports supply under an extension to the Local Government Act (1988). In 1989, compulsory competitive tendering (CCT) was advocated for local authority services. Provision of sports and leisure services could only be retained by the public authorities if they had competed for the right to provide such services with other private sector companies according to a sealed bid auction. The only exceptions were facilities provided solely for educational and community group establishments. In practice, CCT applied often to the running and maintenance of facilities still owned by the local authorities (Gratton and Taylor 1991; Henry 2001). CCT was, however, replaced when the Local Government Act (1999) placed a duty on local authorities to provide Best Value (BV) services instead. The impetus for this policy came from the first New Labour government and reflected the White Paper 'Modernising Government' (1999). The aim was to remove the excessive emphasis on costs that had occurred with CCT (Coalter 1995; Nichols and Taylor 1995). The underpinning objective of BV in local authorities is

> to secure continuous improvement in the way in which its functions are exercised, having regard to a combination of economy, efficiency and effectiveness.
>
> *(Sport England 1999b: 3)*

This implies that resources are used most efficiently (efficiency), that costs are minimised (economy) and that objectives are achieved (effectiveness); impetuses clearly distilled from the normative dimensions of economics, discussed earlier, though there is no presumption that commercial objectives *per se* should dominate.[9]

The concurrent development of sports participation with these policy changes can be seen from Table 38.3. This reveals the well-documented stagnation in sports participation, but identifies this as particularly the case for local authority facilities and possibly sports clubs, if these are included in the 'elsewhere' category. With home and local park activities being stable categories of participation, and probably sites of informal activity, this would suggest that over time it is the traditional public sector and sports club systems that are shrinking in relative terms. It should be noted that this development is not coincident with cuts in public sector provision (Mintel 2005).

Table 38.3 Location of sports provision

Location	1998, %	2000, %	2003, %	2005, %
Local authority sports centre	50	48	46	38
Private club or gym	32	33	34	32
Local park	23	22	22	24
Home	24	23	21	22
School/college/university	17	16	14	13
Local authority sports ground	12	9	11	8
Place of employment	8	7	6	4
Elsewhere	31	25	25	26
Sample size	*1,126*	*1,187*	*1,062*	*971*

Source: Mintel (2005)

Over the same period the informal sector has also been characterised by innovative change. For example, five-a-side football, as well as being played in an entirely self-organised manner, has also been increasingly supplied by companies such as the Powerleague Group PLC, which was established in December 1999. The group has 43 centres throughout the UK with more than 450 floodlit pitches and an average of 130,000 players each week. This has prompted the Football Association to work with such providers, as the source of much of the investment and growth in participation in football. Similar innovative growth has occurred in activities like bicycle motocross (BMX) and snowboarding, which began as 'sub-cultural' activity, but have also grown into formalised Olympic forms.

The economic concepts discussed above predict these outcomes concordant with the relaxation of government intervention, because the commercial and informal sites for participation better meet individual preferences. Significantly whilst all the data suggest that sports participation is *not* growing, it is clear that the location of its practice is switching and it is shifting away from traditional sources of participation.

Current public-sector supply structures and policy emphases also changed over the period. The emphasis of sports policy shifted with large relative increases in funding towards elite sports. Gratton and Taylor (1991) note that by 1985 direct government spending on elite sports had reached approximately £164m, compared to £2,411m allocated to mass participation. However, the largest proportion of the grants allocated by the Sports Council were targeted at the governing bodies of sports for the coaching, training and administration of sports as well as the staging of events. Consequently a greater prescription of the use of funds occurred with their allocation. Requirements for funding coincided with the need for development plans and targets being established. A series of National Centres of Excellence were established, and UK Sport was established by Royal Charter in 1996, to take the lead in promoting sports policy and distributing public investment, from the newly founded National Lottery, with national sports councils now presiding over the interests of the home nations of the UK: Sport England, sportscotland, The Sports Council for Wales and The Sports Council for Northern Ireland. The Youth Sport Trust was also established in 1994 to enhance the sporting and physical education opportunities for children primarily within school, but it also encourages participation in sport and supports talent development outside school in connection with governing bodies, corporate partners and other agencies.

Current sports policy and provision in the UK underwent a significant overhaul following the publication of 'Game Plan, a strategy for delivering Government's sport and physical activity objectives' in 2002 (DCMS/Strategy Unit 2002). This document identified two main objectives for government policy (202: 12), which have recently been reaffirmed in 'Playing to win: A new era for sport' (DCMS 2008):

1. A major increase in participation in sport and physical activity, primarily because of the significant health benefits and to reduce the growing costs of inactivity.
2. A sustainable improvement in success in international competition, particularly in the sports which matter most to the public, primarily because of the 'feelgood factor' associated with winning.

It is argued that there is positive feedback between investment in elite sport and participation in sport (DCMS/Strategy Unit 2002: 84). Further, the public policy emphasis has consolidated around not providing facilities, but encouraging the options available to individuals (DCMS/Strategy Unit 2002: 78).

A key feature of the policy reviews was the reorganisation of the delivery system as the previous arrangements were criticised for their complexity and the blurred functions between the agencies, particularly concerning UK Sport and Sport England (Carter 2005; DCMS/Strategy Unit 2002). As a result, UK Sport now has sole responsibility for elite sport, the Youth Sport Trust for school and young people's sport (under the age of 16 years) and it was the intention that mass sports participation generally would be targeted through the regional sports councils working, in England, with County Sports Partnerships (CSPs). These partnerships were developed to coordinate National Governing Body and local authority inputs to sport in a set of local Community Sports Networks (CSNs) in which local provision of sport by the education, private, public and voluntary sports club sectors were drawn together. In the other countries of the UK the separate sports councils retained responsibility for sport (DCMS 2008).

Further refinement has, however, taken place. In particular, since 2008, Sport England now takes full responsibility for 'community' sport (Sport England 2008). Moreover, the focus for the development of community sport has shifted from broader social and welfare emphases towards the needs of sport. Sport England's current key policy objectives are: developing talent that can progress to elite level (Excel), encouraging participation across the community (Grow), and enhancing the satisfaction of participants of their experiences generally whilst reducing the post-16-year-old drop-out rates in sport (Sustain).

Importantly the new strategy recognises that 'A modern network of sports clubs will be the centrepiece of people's sporting experience' (Sport England 2008: 3). Consequently it is now National Governing Bodies (NGBs) working under 'commission' by Sport England that will work to ensure that policy objectives are met. The implication is that the sports club system will pick up and develop youth sport from the Youth Sport Trust, whilst CSPs work with NGBs and other wider constituencies of partners in promoting and coordinating sport at the regional and sub-regional levels (Sport England 2008: 13). It follows that they may also act as agents coordinating the wider policy impacts of sport, but this is not at all clear. This raises the question, will such initiatives work?

The economic concepts discussed earlier suggest problems with this strategy. The first point to note is that the convoluted changes to the supply structure and their apparent complexity are linked developments from an economic point of view as network-based organisational structures struggle to define and to meet clear objectives. In this regard the contrast between the clear lines of accountability associated with UK Sports' funding of elite performance, in which budgets have been cut for sports regarded as unsuccessful in delivering Olympic medals, and the changing delivery structure of mass participation sport is noticeable.

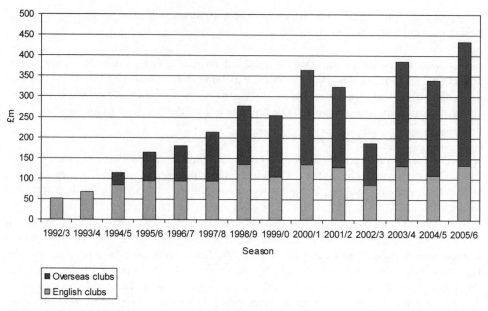

Figure 38.3 Transfer spending in the Premier League

Focussing directly upon current sports development policy initiatives also reveals internal tension. For example, if one takes the Excel dimension of the strategy, then the existing sports club system needs to develop and to move elite performers through the sports continuum. Will this be likely? It is clear that in some highly commercial sports, like football, clubs already have their own commercial incentives to obtain talent. As illustrated in Figure 38.3, at the top flight levels the market system implies buying talent rather than taking on the more complex task of developing it. Rugby Union is clearly undergoing similar dynamics since becoming professional. Moreover, access to the top-flight clubs is now increasingly facilitated by Academies. These have the potential to put limitations on the opportunities of young players to engage in other activities as part of a healthy lifestyle either directly because of restrictions, or because of the time commitments required to 'Excel', and despite the pronouncements of Long Term Athlete Development, in which adolescents and young adults should essentially be 'training to train' and 'training to compete'. The often implicit demands that this puts on athletes has opportunity costs for other activity.[10]

It is also the case that the sports delivery system is struggling to match the demands of encouraging participation through their clubs, and yet to engage in professional practice. For example, a National League Rugby Union side, Nottingham RUFC, has been attempting to qualify for the Premiership, but has subsequently been on the verge of financial collapse by failing to match its revenues with its playing costs (http://news.bbc.co.uk/sport1/hi/rugby_union/english/7708626.stm). Whilst this financial dynamic is not at all uncommon in professional sports, what is significant here is that rugby clubs, unlike football clubs, often still promote and run amateur mini, junior and colts sides that are also put in jeopardy. Economic theory suggests, of course, that such an organisational mix is not an efficient way of dealing with commercial pressures, which is why, historically, professional clubs evolved from amateur clubs.

Leaving aside commercially active team sports, it is important to recognise that sports clubs also find the mass participation versus elite development agendas difficult to coordinate. In recent research LIRC (2003) noted, as typical, the comment of one swimming volunteer who remarked that,

> At the end of the day we are a competitive swimming club. We are not a community or social group. We are not here to look after [the disadvantaged], although we will help where we can we are not in a position to arrange transport [from disadvantaged areas], we are not in a position to reduce their fees. We will train people that want to train but we cannot be used as a social service organisation.

This suggests that the current sports club system has potentially similar difficulties matching its needs to broader policy needs.

If one now focuses upon the Grow dimension of the strategy, leaving aside the implicit argument of the last section that the formal mass participation elements of sport may be declining overall, there are problems in targeting the sports club system to develop participation, that is to enter the sports continuum. Table 38.4 reports the participation rates for a number of sports from the 2005 Active People survey for the 12-month period prior to the survey.

In the second column the participation rate in the sample is recorded. The third column shows the proportion of overall participation that is club-based. It is quite clear that the lowest participation rates are connected with the sports that have the highest level of club-based activity. This suggests that the opportunities for growth are going to be extremely limited for the competitive sports club sector. In this regard it should be noted as above, that sectors such as health and fitness and keep-fit are now readily met by the private sector market.

This, of course, also puts some pressure on the Sustain elements of the strategy. If the sports club system is relatively small then it may have, at best, a minor role in reducing post-16-year-old drop-out – which is one of the policy targets. More importantly, however, whilst data on sports participation satisfaction are not yet available, there is ample evidence that the key input to sports clubs, that is the volunteers, are not entirely satisfied. LIRC (2003) and Downward *et al* (2009) note the increasing demands of volunteering, which requires increasingly specialised skills as a response to governing bodies and sports agencies requiring more accreditation and formalisation of their activities. In the UK, comparing Gratton *et al* (1997) and LIRC (2003), volunteering hours increased by approximately 45 per cent (183m to 266m) between 1995 and 2002, whilst the number of volunteers increased by approximately 35 per cent (1.49m to 2.01m). However, it should be recognised that this comparison includes volunteering in education and events. Focusing purely on sports clubs and National Governing Bodies, volunteer hours increased by approximately 40 per cent (from 170m to 237m) and the number of

Table 38.4 Sports participation and club participation

Sport	Participation, %	Club, %
Indoor swimming	29.1	9.4
(Non-utility) cycling	14.8	2.2
Indoor football	3.9	14.9
Health fitness/gym	18.6	40.0
Keep fit/aerobics	10.9	21.8
Outdoor football	8.2	18.4
Rugby Union	0.8	45.7
n = 28117		

volunteers by 33 per cent (from 1.19m to 1.6m) (LIRC 2003: 22). The implication is that volunteering is essential to the supply of sports and 'remains the bedrock of opportunity in many sports' (LIRC 2003: 33) but that more hours per volunteer are being required to support sport. This puts supply constraints upon sports development.

Conclusions

The above discussion has used economic analysis to conceptualise sports development, to examine aspects of the historical development of sports participation as well as to identify challenges that will be faced for current sports development strategy. The essence of the discussion has been that, from an economic perspective, sports participation and supply opportunities, that is, 'market segmentation', develop out of an interplay between individual preferences, the property rights associated with sport, and policy initiatives promoting public sector involvement. A consequence of this discussion is that sports development policy is only relevant for, and will only be successful if it is applied to, willing parties who are, somehow, additionally constrained from undertaking the sports that they wish to. Failure to account for this may induce policy failure. Currently a case can be made that the informal and private sectors meet the needs of their relatively robust sectors of participants, but that this cannot be said for public sector provision, in which much is asked by policy makers. Further current sports development policy is targeted at clubs in which only a minority of participants are involved and in which accountability is putting pressure on the system.

Notes

1 This chapter draws partially upon ideas first discussed and presented in Downward *et al* (2009).
2 See for example Brentwood Borough Council Sports Development Strategy 2007–11, Guernsey Sports Commission, Sports Development Unit, Sport England (1999a,b).
3 It is acknowledged that a 'policy' of no active intervention in itself can be seen as an 'active' policy, but issues of such semantics are not addressed here. Suffice it is to say that the distinction rests in either seeing it as the policy maker's position to advocate and to encourage sports participation, and provide opportunities for this to take place, versus a policy of leaving individuals to make decisions for themselves.
4 Of course there is no belief in economics that the world is static, but that equilibria capture relatively stable sets of outcomes. What constitutes 'relative stability' is then a matter of specific empirical enquiry.
5 It should be noted that market failure is defined as a lack of efficiency.
6 Of course a national park is the outcome of a policy decision, common grazing land too. This illustrates that the boundaries of the categories are fuzzy.
7 In this way voluntary clubs through active membership necessarily adjust their behaviour in the specific interests of their membership. Public sector agencies, in contrast, may have to meet multiple stakeholders' needs and necessarily compromise across them. For example, 'Perhaps the greatest difficulty for government-operated clubs is trying to ascertain what the members really want in terms of provision, maintenance and fees. These decisions must be made prior to citizen utilisation, a utilisation that reveals preferences. In a member-owned club, members have an incentive and an ability to reveal their preferences for provision during meetings. Governments may be more interested in pleasing constituents with large political influence than in setting up an efficient club' (Cornes and Sandler 1986: 192).
8 There is debate concerning the overriding motive for professional sports clubs in economic theory, with the US literature tending to emphasise profit maximisation and the European literature win per cent maximisation – as an indication of team owner utility maximisation (Downward *et al* 2009 discuss these issues further).

9 As Downward *et al* (2009) show, Best Value contains potentially contradictory statements from an economic perspective as 'economy' and 'efficiency' are necessarily compromised if, say, equity targets are important.

10 For example consider the following quotation from the Leicester Tigers Academy 'You are not competing to just get in to any rugby club academy, you are competing against hundreds of others for a place at one of the world's most successful and historic rugby clubs. The expectations and standards required of you on and off the pitch as a Tiger are second to none and higher than any other club. Therefore commit yourself to the programme, work hard, push your self and train to the standard expected of you.' It is entirely legitimate of a commercial organisation to expect this of its funded trainees. The issue here is, does this objective match that of broader social objectives?

References

Andreff, W. and Staudohar, P. D. (2000). 'The evolving European model of professional sports finance', *Journal of Sports Economics*, 1(3), pp. 257–276.

—— (2002) 'European and US sports business models', in Barros C., Ibrahimo M. and Szymanski S. (Eds.) *Transatlantic sport: The comparative economics of North American and European sports*, Cheltenham: Edward Elgar.

Becker, G. (1965) 'A Theory of the Allocation of Time', *Economic Journal*, 75, 299: 493–517.

——(1974) 'A Theory of Social Interactions', *Journal of Political Economy*, 82, 1063–91.

——(1976) *The Economic Approach to Human Behaviour*, The University of Chicago Press.

Brentwood Borough Council Sports Development Strategy 2007–11 (2009) www.brentwood.gov.uk/pdf/pdf_1246.pdf (accessed 8/6/09).

Cabinet Office (1999) *Modernising Government*, White Paper, London: The Stationery Office.

Carter, P. (2005) *Review of National Sport Effort and Resources*, DCMS, London.

Coalter, F. (1995) 'Compulsory competitive tendering for sport and leisure management: a lost opportunity?', *Managing Leisure*, 1, 3–15.

Cornes, R. and Sandler, T. (1986) *The Theory of Externalities, Public Goods*.

Council of Europe (1975) *European Sport for All Charter*, Strasbourg: Council of Europe.

DCMS/Strategy Unit (2002) *Game Plan: A strategy for delivering government's sport and physical activity objectives*, London: DCMS/Strategy Unit.

—— (2008) *Playing to win*, London: DCMS/Strategy Unit.

Department of the Environment (1975) *Sport and Recreation*, London: HMSO.

—— (1975) *Recreation and Deprivation in Urban Areas*, London: HMSO.

—— (1977) *Policy for the Inner Cities*, London: HMSO.

Downward, P.M., Dawson, A. and Dejonghe, T. (2009) *Sports Economics: Theory Evidence and Policy*, London: Butterworth Heinemann.

European Sports Charter (2001) Available at (accessed 15/11/10) https://wcd.coe.int/ViewDoc.jsp?Ref=Rec(92)13&Sector=secCM&Language=lanEnglish&Ver=rev&BackColorInternet=9999CC&BackColorIntranet=FFBB55&BackColorLogged=FFAC75

Friedman, M. (1953) *The Methodology of Positive Economics in Essays in Positive Economics*, Chicago: University of Chicago Press.

Gratton, C. Nichols, G. Shibli, S. and Taylor, P. (1997) *Valuing Volunteers in UK Sport, Sports Council*, England.

Gratton, C. and Taylor, P. (1991) *Government and the Economics of Sport*, Longman: Harlow.

—— (2000) *Economics of Sport and Recreation*, London: E. and F.N. Spon.

Gravelle, H. and Rees, R. (2004) *Microeconomics*, London: Prentice Hall.

Green, M. (2004) 'Changing Policy Priorities for Sport in England: The Emergence of Elite Sport Development as a key Policy Concern', *Leisure Studies*, 23, 4: 365–385.

—— (2005) Elite Sport Development: Policy Learning and Political Priorities, London: Routledge.

Guernsey Sports Commission (n.d.) *Sports Development Unit*, www.guernseysports.com/guernsey_sports_our_activities.asp?PageID=94 (accessed 8/6/09).

Henry, I. (2001) *The Politics of Leisure Policy*, London: Palgrave.

Houlihan, B. (1997) *Sport, Policy and Politics: A Comparative Analysis*, London: Routledge.

Hylton, K. and Bramham, P. (2008) *Sports Development: Policy, Process and Practice (2nd ed.)*, London: Routledge.

LIRC (Leisure Industries Research Centre 2003) *Sports volunteering in England 2002: A report for Sport England*, Sheffield: Sheffield Hallam University.

Local Government Act 1988, London: HMSO.

Local Government Act 1999, London: HMSO.

Mintel (2005) *Fitness Classes* http://academic.mintel.com.

——(2007) *Health and Fitness Clubs* http://academic.mintel.com.

Mishan, E.J. (1981) *Introduction to Normative Economics*, Oxford: Oxford University Press.

Musgrave, R.A. (1969) *Provision of Social Goods*, in Margolis, J. and Guitton, H. (eds) *Public Economics: An Analysis of Public Production and Consumption and their Relations to the Private Sectors*, London: Macmillan.

Musgrave, R.A. and Musgrave, P.B. (1973) *Public Finance in Theory and Practice*, New York: McGraw-Hill Book Company.

Nichols, G. and Taylor, P. (1995) *The Impact on Local Authority Leisure Provision of Compulsory Competitive Tendering, Financial Cuts and Changing Attitudes'*, *Local Government Studies* Vol 21, No. 4, pp. 607–22.

Robbins, L. (1940) *An Essay on the Nature and Significance of Economic Science*, London: Macmillan and Co.

Samuelson, P.A. (1954) *The Pure Theory of Public Expenditure*, *Review of Economics and Statistics*, 36, 4: 387–89.

——(1955) *Diagrammatic Exposition of a theory of Public Expenditure*, *Review of Economics and Statistics*, 37, 4: 350–56.

Sports Council (1982) *Sport in the Community: The next Ten Years*, London: Sports Council.

Sport England (1999a) *Best Value Through Sport*, London.

——(1999b) *Best Value Through Sport: Case Studies*, London.

—— (2008) *Sport England Strategy 2008-2011*, London.

Weisbrod, B.A. (1978) *The Voluntary Nonprofit Sector: An Economic Analysis*, Lexington: Lexington Books.

——(1988) *The Non-Profit Economy*, Lexington: Heath.

——(1998) *To Profit or not to Profit: The Commercial Transformation of the Non Profit Sector*, Cambridge: Cambridge University Press.

Williamson, O. (1970) *Corporate Control and Economic Behavior: An Inquiry into the Effects of Organization Form on Enterprise Behavior*, Prentice Hall, Englewood Cliffs, N.J..

——(1975) *Markets and Hierarchies: Analysis and Antitrust Implications*, New York: Free Press.

——(1985) *The Economic Institutions of Capitalism: Firms, Markets, Relational Contracting*, London: Collier Macmillan.

Wolfenden Report (1960) *Sport and the Community*, chairman Sir John Wolfenden, London: Eyre and Spottiswood.

Part 8

Assessing the impact of sports development

Introduction: The problems of policy evaluation

Barrie Houlihan

Questions such as 'Is our programme meeting its objectives?', 'Are we receiving value for money from this project?', 'Is our programme reaching the target group?', and 'Is the balance between expenditure on facilities and sports leaders appropriate?' are as familiar as they are daunting, but are being asked with increasing urgency as the competition for scarce public and private resources intensifies. In common with many areas of public policy that aim to change behaviour, the managers of sports development programmes face a stiff challenge in identifying valid measures of progress, especially sustained progress. Studies of the impact of sports development initiatives abound with examples of the selection of inappropriate indicators, inconsistent measurement and dubious generalisation. The failure to take on the challenge of effective policy evaluation allows the critics of the policy to argue that the absence of evidence equates to the absence of impact.

The importance of tackling the issue of evaluation notwithstanding, it has to be acknowledged that the prospect of developing a technique that would enable the identification of a clear causal relationship between particular policy inputs (specific schemes or programmes) and measurable change in physical activity and sports participation patterns is very remote given the complexity and dynamism of the socio–economic environment within which the initiatives and programmes function. The recognised 'gold standard' for evidence-based policy, the laboratory-based randomised control trial, has far less utility in assessing the relationship between sports development programmes and complex behavioural outcomes.

At one level, programme evaluation is a straightforward process and involves discovering whether or not a programme or intervention has achieved its goals – whether or not the policy works (Shadish *et al.* 1991). However, behind that statement lie a series of complications that makes fulfilling that apparently simple requirement a substantial challenge. The complications can be grouped under the following headings: clarity of, and extent of agreement on, policy/programme goals; the explicit or implicit theory of behaviour change incorporated into the policy/programme; the purpose of the evaluation; and the evaluation methodology, validity of data and thresholds of evidence.

In many policy areas policy/programme goals suffer from ambiguity, multiplicity and impermanence (Chun and Rainey 2005; Daft 2004; Hogwood and Gunn 1984), all of which are particularly evident in relation to sports development. As is clear from the earlier chapters in this volume, the objectives set for sports development have, at different times, been drawn from policy areas as varied as health, community safety/social control, international relations and economic regeneration. Evaluating policy effectiveness in the face of multiple, overlapping and often vaguely specified objectives poses severe challenges for evaluation.

Closely linked to problems associated with defining programme goals is the identification of the theory of change on which policy is based. All policy is based on a set of explicit or implicit assumptions about how the policy is intended to bring about the desired change in behaviour (Clarke 1999; Fitz-Gibbon and Morris 1996). For the sports development policy-maker or manager the specification of the underlying theory of behaviour change is often reasonably straightforward. For example, an increasing number of countries now offer cash incentives to successful elite athletes. With regard to participation in community sport, reference is normally made to a range of health behaviour change models such as the health belief model (Rosenstock et al. 1994) and the stages of change model (Prochaska et al. 1992).

A further complication in relation to evaluation is that policy/programme evaluation often has a dual purpose – to prove (summative) and also to improve (formative). The main audience for summative evaluation is funders and policy makers; the focus for (usually quantitative) data collection is on impact/outcome measurement; the frequency of data collection is limited; and the evaluator is independent. By contrast, formative evaluation is targeted primarily at programme managers with whom there should be regular interaction; the focus of data collection is on processes and procedures; both quantitative and qualitative data are collected, with the latter seen as important; reporting is frequent and is a focus for discussion (Herman et al. 1987).

The selection of the evaluation methodology cannot be separated from issues relating to validity and standards of proof. It is often the case that funders set thresholds of proof that are not only unrealistic given the complexity of a policy area (programmes to reduce recidivism or illiteracy or to encourage the adoption of a healthy lifestyle), but are also higher than those used by criminal and civil courts. The difficulties of designing a realistic evaluation protocol (realistic in terms of implementation costs – money, time and expertise; cultural sensitivity and clarity of interpretation) are compounded by the tendency to over-concentrate on the pursuit of objective outcome measures and endow them with an uncritical privileged status – treating succession and regular conjunction as causal relationships (Campbell and Boruch 1975; Cook et al. 2010; Mark and Cook 1984) and failing to acknowledge the limitations of experimental methods in expressing the nature of causality and change going on within social programmes (Pawson and Tilley 1994).

Looking beyond the confines of sports development programmes, it is likely that there are lessons to be learnt from the extensive evaluation work being conducted in similarly complex policy areas: policing (Bennett 1991), recidivism (Vass 1990), recreational drug use (Ennett et al. 1994; Weiss et al. 2005) and quality of life (Jenkinson and McGee 1997). In all these areas evaluators have been tackling problems of establishing causal relationships between policy (often with a strong educational element) and perceived change, identifying and calibrating change/ impact and translating evaluation results into useful management information. Of particular potential interest is the increasingly popular use of evaluation based on 'logic models' (McLaughlin and Jordan 1999; Stinchcomb 2001; Weiss 1997; Yampolskaya et al. 2004).

The three chapters in this final Part of the Handbook address the core concerns of sports development policy evaluation and provide ample evidence of the progress that has been made over the last 10 years or so. Coalter, in reviewing the problems of the evaluation of both sports development and development through sport programmes, notes that in addition to the problems that beset evaluation in more politically salient policy areas, sport suffers from its 'essentially marginal status in both domestic and international aid policy'. What the author highlights with particular clarity is the degree to which evaluation, just like policy-making, takes place in a highly political environment, often far removed from the rational model of policy evaluation projected by the rhetoric of evidence-based policy. In reviewing a range of approaches to sports development policy evaluation and a number of practical attempts to evaluate the impact of sport on social problems such as crime and health, Coalter makes a strong case for a theory-based approach to evaluation which among its many attractions encourages a closer dialogue between policy-makers and external evaluators.

De Bosscher and van Bottenburg explore the relationship of sport for all to elite sport and the logic that implicitly underpins the continuing support for a pyramid model of sports development, where a broad base of participation is considered a necessary condition for the production of a large cohort of elite athletes. The authors use data from the SPLISS study of six countries, which measured over one hundred factors considered critical to elite sport success and which were then grouped into nine clusters or pillars, one of which was sports participation. The authors found 'hardly any relationship' between the scores for sports participation and performance at the Olympic Games of 2004 and 2008. However, in their conclusion the authors note the paucity of useful data on which to evaluate the impact of participation levels on elite success. While there is substantial data collection on these two aspects of sports development as separate elements of sports development, data that would allow analysis of their inter-relation are scarce. With this caveat in mind, De Bosscher and van Bottenburg concluded that, on the basis of the SPLISS research, 'a broad base of sports participation is not always a necessary condition for success', but qualify this conclusion by noting that it may still be 'an influence on success'.

The final chapter assesses the impact of sports development on sports participation. Van Bottenburg and De Bosscher begin by exploring the variation in the mix of sports providers (voluntary, commercial, educational and public) across the world, trends in participation and policy development. This exploration is followed by an analysis of the interconnection between them and especially between participation trends and policy. The authors emphasise the importance of not assuming a causal relationship between policy and participation and conclude that there appears to be little relationship between policy and trends in participation. They identify an s-curve in participation 'in a variety of countries in spite of differences in their existing sporting cultures and structures, their general political contexts and specific sport policy actions'. Arguing that the explanation for the similarity in trends must consequently lie in broader social developments, they highlight the problem of trying to establish causality between policy and observed outcomes.

References

Bennett, T. (1991) The effectiveness of a police-initiated fear-reducing strategy, *British Journal of Criminology*, 31.1, 1–14.

Campbell D.T. and Boruch, R.F. (1975) Making the case for randomised assignment to treatment. In Lumsdaine, A. and Bennett, C.A. (eds) *Evaluation of experience: Some critical issues in evaluating social programs*, New York: Academic Press.

Chun, Y.H. and Rainey, H.G. (2005) Goal ambiguity in US Federal agencies, *Journal of Public Administration and Research*, 15.1, 1–30.

Clarke, A. (1999) *Evaluation research*, London: Sage.

Cook, T.D., Scriven, M., Coryn, C. and Evergreen, S. (2010) Contemporary thinking about causation: A dialogue with Tom Cook and Michael Scriven, *American Journal of Evaluation*, 31.1, 105–17.

Daft, R.L. (2004) *Organization theory and design*, St Paul, MI: West.

Ennett, S.T., Tobler, N.S., Ringwalt, N.S. and Flewelling, F.L. Resistance education: A meta-analysis of project DARE outcome evaluations, *American Journal of Public Health*, 84.9, 1394–401.

Fitz-Gibbon, C.T. and Morris, L.L. (1996) Theory-based evaluation, *Evaluation Practice*, 17.2, 177–84.

Herman, J., Morris, L. and Fitz-Gibbon, C. (1987) *Evaluator's handbook*, Newbury Park, CA: Sage.

Hogwood, B.W. and Gunn, L.A (1984) *Policy analysis for the real world*, Oxford: Oxford University Press.

Jenkinson, C. and McGee, H. (1997) Patient assessed outcomes: Measuring health status and quality of life. In Jenkinson, C. (ed.) *Assessment and evaluation of health and medical care: A methods text*, Buckingham: Open University Press.

Mark, M.M. and Cook, T.D. (1984) Design of randomised experiments and quasi-experiments. In L. Rutman (ed.) *Evaluation research methods: A basic guide*, Beverly Hills, CA: Sage.

McLaughlin, J.A. and Jordan, G.B. (1999) Logic models: A tool for telling your program's performance story, *Evaluation and Program Planning*, 22, 65–72.

Pawson, R. and Tilley, N. (1994) What works in evaluation research? *British Journal of Criminology*, 34, 291–306.

Prochaska, J., DiClemente, C. and Norcross, J. (1992) In search of how people change – applications to addictive behaviors, *American Psychologist*, 47.9, 1102–14.

Rosenstock, I., Strecher, V. and Becker, M. (1994) The health belief model and HIV risk behaviour change. In DiClemente, R. and Peterson, J. (eds) *Preventing AIDS: Theories and methods of behavioural interventions*, New York: Plenum Press.

Shadish, W., Cook, T. and Leviton, L. (1991) *Foundations of program evaluation: Theories of practice*, Newbury Park, CA: Sage.

Stinchcomb, J.B. (2001) Using logic modelling to focus evaluation efforts: Translating operational theories into practical measures, *Journal of Offender Rehabilitation*, 33, 47–66.

Vass, A.A. (1990) *Alternatives to prison: Punishment, custody and the community*, London: Sage.

Weiss, C. (1997) 'How can theory-based evaluation make greater headway?' *Evaluation Review*, 21, 501–24.

Weiss, C., Murphy-Graham, E. and Birkland, S. (2005) An alternate route to policy influence: Evidence from a study of the Drug Abuse Resistence Education program, *American Journal of Evaluation*, 26, 12–31.

Yampolskaya, S., Nesman, T.M., Hernandez, M. and Koch, D. (2004) Using concept mapping to develop a logic model and articulate a program theory: A case example. *American Journal of Evaluation*, 25.2, 191–207.

39

Sports development's contribution to social policy objectives

The difficult relationship between politics and evidence

Fred Coalter

In the 1990s sport became an increasingly important aspect of both national and international social policy. For example, in the United Kingdom sport became an important aspect of 'New' Labour's social inclusion agenda. The expected contribution of sport is summarised by *Policy Action Team 10*'s (DCMS 1999: 23) statement that 'sport can contribute to neighbourhood renewal by improving communities' performance on four key indicators – health, crime, employment and education'. Similar, if less well-developed, policies can be seen in Australia (Australian Sports Commission 2006) and Canada (Bloom *et al.* 2005).

In the area of international development policy the UN declared 2005 as the International Year of Sport and Physical Education arguing that,

> The world of sport presents a natural partnership for the United Nations system. By its very nature sport is about participation. It is about inclusion and citizenship. Sport brings individuals and communities together, highlighting commonalties and bridging cultural or ethnic divides. Sport provides a forum to learn skills such as discipline, confidence and leadership and it teaches core principles such as tolerance, cooperation and respect. Sport teaches the value of effort and how to manage victory, as well as defeat.
>
> *(United Nations 2005a: v)*

This increased emphasis on sport can be explained by 'paradigm shifts' in the analysis of the nature of, and presumed solutions to, social issues. However, the assertions of such wide-ranging contributions of sport to the solution of a range of social problems were also accompanied by an increased concern about accountability and evidence. This chapter deals with the nature of the paradigm changes, the associated assumptions about sport's contribution, the nature of the accompanying emphasis on accountability and evidence and the potential of a new approach to monitoring and evaluation that bridges the current gap between policy makers and researchers.

Paradigm shifts and an economy of remedies

Social inclusion

In the UK the 'New' Labour government's politics and policies were based on a so-called Third Way between the perceived failures of 'old' Labour's top-down policies of state control, state provision and anti-individualism and the Thatcherite neo-liberal, free-market policies underpinned by an extreme individualism. In this regard the Third Way represented an attempt to modernize and reform all aspects of government, to strengthen civil society, to address issues of 'social exclusion' and to encourage 'active citizenship' (Giddens 1998). Or, as stated by Tony Blair, 'to create a modern civic society for today's world, to renew the bonds of community that bind us together' (quoted in Keaney and Gavelin n.d: 2).

This perspective resulted in an increased policy emphasis on social processes, relationships and the organizational capacities of communities (Blunkett 2003; Forrest and Kearns 1999). It represented a broad shift from urban regeneration policies based on the investment of economic capital and the development of physical infrastructure to community development, civic infrastructure and human and social capital. Given this increased policy interest in issues of civil society, volunteerism and community self-help, it is unsurprising that there would be an increased interest in the voluntary sector and organisations within civil society.

In this regard, *Policy Action Team 10* (DCMS 1999: 25) stated that:

> Participation in the arts and sport has a beneficial social impact. Arts and sport are inclusive and can contribute to neighbourhood renewal. They can build confidence and encourage strong community groups. However, these benefits are frequently overlooked both by some providers of arts and sports facilities and programmes and by those involved in area regeneration programmes.

Such policies were also part of a wider strategy to reform aspects of welfare, with a move away from passive definitions of welfare rights to notions of obligations and active citizenship. This is illustrated by David Blunkett's (2003) assertion that 'New' Labour was seeking ways 'to empower people in their communities to provide the answers to our contemporary social problems'.

Such perspectives served to revive and reinforce sport's traditional claims about its ability to provide an 'economy of remedies' (Donnison and Chapman 1965) to a variety of social problems. Consequently, sports policy shifted from the traditional social welfare approach of developing sport *in* communities to a broader and vaguer attempt to develop communities *through* sport (Coalter 2007).

Sport-for-development

Such shifts in problem definition and policy development have been paralleled in the area of international aid and development (Renard 2006), which have also led to a rapid growth of the so-called 'sport-for-development' movement (Coalter 2010; Kidd 2008; Levermore 2008). Woolcock and Narayan (2000) argue that in the late 1990s there was a broad shift in the 'aid paradigm', based on recognition that the concentration of development policy on the economic dimension was too narrow. Others were concerned with corrupt governments, a widespread lack of transparency and failures of governance, with aid serving to underpin economic inefficiency, mismanagement and governments who were not accountable to electorates (Calderisi 2006; Moyo 2009).

The new approach, like the Third Way, placed an emphasis on the strengthening of aspects of civil society, social capital and culture (Hognestad 2005). In a parallel with 'New' Labour, Portes and Landolt (2000: 530) suggest that the new emphasis represented an attempt to repair the damage done by previous policies in which,

> the removal of state protection giving way to unrestrained market forces has produced growing income disparities and an atomised social fabric marked by the erosion of normative controls. ... the trend is visible enough for policy-makers to seek ways to sensitise or create anew community bonds and social institutions.

In addition to these broad shifts in the aid paradigm, the publication in 2000 of the United Nations' eight Millennium Development Goals (MDGs) also had major implications for sport-for-development. The new rhetorical commitment to sport was based on its supposed ability to offer an economy of solutions, as 'the United Nations is turning to the world of sport for help in the work for peace and the effort to achieve the Millennium Development Goals' (United Nations 2005b: v).

The MDGs represented an attempt to achieve a comprehensive and coordinated strategic approach to tackling the issues of development and were based on more precise definitions of priority areas for investment. Significantly, many of these were focused on personal and 'social inclusion' issues – strengthening education, improving community safety and social cohesion, helping girls and women and youth at risk and addressing issues of public health (Kidd 2008). The latter included HIV/AIDS, which was to provide the sport-and-development movement with a major opportunity, becoming a central component of many programmes and resulting in the establishment of the Kicking-Aids-Out! network of sport-for-development organisations (www.kickingaidsout.net). The defining of such 'people-centred' objectives clearly resonated with many of sport's traditional claims about its contribution to personal and social development.

Portes and Landolt (2000: 546) conclude that non-governmental organizations are an attractive proposition for aid agencies because they can increase the yield of aid and investment via volunteer labour and an openness and accountability not characteristic of government and its agencies. Within this context, widespread and ambitious claims made by the sport-for-development-and-peace lobby (Kidd 2008) appear to offer an economy of remedies (see Sport for Development International Working Group (2008) for an example). Investment in sport is relatively cheap and its high dependence on both foreign and indigenous volunteers provides a substantial value-added for relatively small sums of aid.

Coming in from the margins: inflated promises and lack of intellectual clarity

The wide-ranging claims for sport's (or more precisely, sports') contribution to social and economic development bring to mind Pawson's (2004: no page number) argument that the majority of social policy interventions can be characterised as 'ill-defined interventions with hard-to-follow outcomes'. Some of the reasons for the formulation of such ambitious, wide-ranging and vague claims are to be found in the processes of lobbying and alliance-building central to policy processes. It is worth looking briefly at these issues, because these processes of policy formulation have substantial implications for the nature of evidence which is deemed to be relevant, both in terms of programme design and outcome assessment.

Weiss (1993: 96) emphasises the essentially political nature of much policy formulation, resource bidding and programme development, arguing that:

> Because of the political processes of persuasion and negotiation that are required to get a program enacted, inflated promises are made in the guise of program goals. Furthermore, the goals often lack the clarity and intellectual coherence that evaluation criteria should have. ... Holders of diverse values and different interests have to be won over, and in the process a host of realistic and unrealistic goal commitments are made.

In the area of sports policy these problems are probably exacerbated by sport's essentially marginal status in both domestic policy and international aid policy (Levermore 2008). For example, Kidd (2008) comments that, despite the rhetorical and symbolic legitimation provided by a human rights discourse (Sport for Development International Working Group 2008) and UN support, sport-for-development-and-peace initiatives are heavily dependent on others for funding. The available funding is often from non-sporting sources, such as aid agencies that have very specific development agendas – with the necessity for sport to persuade them that it could contribute to their core agendas.

It is understandable that aid-dependent, often marginally viable and volunteer-based organizations make inflated promises in order to obtain funding – an apparent economy of remedies is always a very attractive proposition to a funder. It must also be acknowledged that over-ambitious and theoretically weak grant submissions are often encouraged, or at the very least condoned, by many funding agencies. In this regard Howells (2007), the Executive Director of South African-based Sport Coaches Outreach, argues that aid is given within the predefined (often political) parameters or objectives of the developer. Further, the necessity to compete for limited resources frequently leads to projects being developed to fit the funding criteria, with the potential to compromise beneficiaries' needs, promote organizational mission drift and an acceptance of donor targets with insufficient implementation capacity (Howells 2007). For example, although many sport-for-development organizations viewed the people-centred MDGs as a major opportunity to apply for funding, Renard (2006) suggests that donors' insistence on addressing MDGs may lead to the development of programmes that do not reflect local issues and needs (and often work against simple sports development). This mission drift is paralleled in the area of sport and social inclusion in the UK, because of the new policy imperatives to address cross-cutting agendas (crime, health, social inclusion, education, social regeneration) and contribute to 'joined-up government' (Audit Commission 2009).

The lobbying and alliance-building central to much policy formulation and bids for funding seems to be aided in sport by its mythopoeic nature (Coalter 2007). Mythopoeic concepts are those whose demarcation criteria are not specific, but are based on popular and idealistic ideas that are produced largely outside sociological analysis and research and that 'isolate a particular relationship between variables to the exclusion of others and without a sound basis for doing so' (Glasner 1977: 2–3). Such myths contain certain elements of truth, but elements that become reified and distorted and 'represent' rather than reflect reality, standing for supposed, but largely unexamined, impacts and processes. The strength of such myths lies in their 'ability to evoke vague and generalised images' (Glasner 1977: 1). It is this status of sport that underpins the sports evangelism (Giulianotti 2004) that characterises many domestic and international sports' self-interest and their commonsense 'repertoires' and 'tacit knowledge' (Rossi et al. 2004). For example, Kidd (2008: 374) argues that many of the spokespeople for this 'movement' have been successful elite athletes and have 'imbibed the developmental rhetoric of sport throughout their lives and saw themselves as living testimonials'. In such circumstances ad hominem 'evidence' is widespread, with little perceived need to consider issues of the causes of the problems to which sport is presumed to offer solutions, the extent to which sport might contribute to solutions, or the nature and processes of sport which might lead to desired outcomes.

All this seems to reflect Weiss's (1993: 96) more general argument that, in relatively marginal policy areas, it is quite common to have 'inflated promises [with] goals lacking the clarity and intellectual coherence that evaluation criteria should have'. In the policy areas of both sport and social inclusion and sport-for-development this has often resulted in situations where, as Kruse (2006: 27) argues, 'intermediate objectives are missing, providing targets for how much and when results were expected' and 'indicators are used in the application for funds, but not for actual monitoring and reporting', with the absence of clear targets 'making it difficult to assess performance'.

Referring to sports research more generally, Coalter (2007) argues that, in addition to lack of clarity in definitions of sport, participation and outcomes, there is a more general lack of systematic and robust programme evaluation, with an over-concentration on outputs; cross-sectional designs, with limited longitudinal data; convenience sampling; general lack of control groups; and a failure to control for a wide range of potentially intervening and confounding variables. It is within these contexts that we can consider issues of effectiveness and outcome measurement.

A new emphasis on effectiveness

In parallel with the increased emphasis on sport's potential contribution to a variety of social and developmental issues, governments and funding agencies have also placed increased emphasis, however rhetorical, on the monitoring and evaluation of the effectiveness of their investments. For example, the Business Plan for the UN International Year of Sport and Physical Education (UN 2005a: 11) refers to the need for 'monitoring and evaluation of sport and development programs and ... the selection of impact indicators that would show the benefits of sport and development programs in the field'. A UNICEF publication on monitoring and evaluation of such programmes (UNICEF 2006: 4) states that 'there is a need to assemble proof, to go beyond what is mostly anecdotal evidence to monitor and evaluate the impact of sport in development programme.'

Similar emphases can be seen in the UK, where 'New' Labour introduced an emphasis on 'evidence-based policy making' as a central component of its approach to modernizing government and policy-making processes. This philosophy is stated clearly in the 1999 White Paper, Modernising Government (Section 2: 2).

> This Government expects more of policy makers ... better use of evidence and research in policy making and better focus on policies that will deliver long term goals ... policy decisions should be based on sound evidence ... Good quality policy making depends on high quality information, derived from a variety of sources – expert knowledge; existing domestic and international research; existing statistics; stakeholder consultation; evaluation of previous policies.

This was re-affirmed by David Blunkett in a speech in 2000 to the Economic and Social Research Council:

> This Government has given a clear commitment that we will be guided not by dogma but by an open-minded approach to understanding what works and why. This is central to our agenda for modernising government: using information and knowledge much more effectively and creatively at the heart of policymaking and policy delivery.

Evidence-based policy making: cynical or naïve?

However, despite the increased emphasis on 'evidence-based policy' and the need for evidence of effectiveness, it is useful to reflect on the precise meaning of such rhetoric and its place in the more pragmatic world of policy making. For example, Matarasso (1998: 5) argues that, 'the decision-making processes of public administration, like the civil courts, depend on the balance of probabilities rather than the elimination of reasonable doubt'. However, some political scientists have gone beyond this 'weak evidence' perspective to suggest that it is essential to recognise that 'evaluation is a rational exercise that takes place in a political context' (Weiss 1993: 94). The implication is that it is naive to confuse research findings with *evidence* and fail to understand that research, however robust, competes for attention with a range of other more influential factors – *politics* in all senses of the term (Solesbury 2001).

For example, Davies (2004), from the UK Government Chief Social Researcher's Office in the Prime Minister's Strategy Unit, argues that policy making involves a range of factors that work to filter and interpret the validity and value of evidence. Some of these factors are listed below.

Values

Policy making takes place within the context of values, ideologies and political beliefs (often underpinned by mythopoeic views about sport) and the tension between these and empirical evidence 'is the very stuff of contemporary politics in an open democratic society and is unlikely to disappear because of the advent of evidence-based policy' (Davies 2004: 5). For example, Pisani (2008), in the closely allied field of HIV/AIDS prevention, argues that many programmes are based on false assumptions and the systematic ignoring of morally or politically uncomfortable evidence. For example, despite clear evidence that the use of condoms and needle exchanges substantially reduces infection rates, such policies are opposed by those who reject birth control and argue that needle exchanges simply encourage drug use.

Experience, expertise and judgement

The experienced-based 'tacit knowledge' of decision makers (and sports evangelists) informs the judgement of the validity and, more importantly, relevance of evidence (Rossi *et al.* 2004).

Habit and tradition

This refers to the difficulties involved in changing traditional and habitual ways of doing things on the basis of sometimes limited evidence (Rossi *et al.* 2004). In a comment that could easily apply to many sport-for-development projects, Pisani (2008: 288) argues that this results in the monitoring of implementation being more important than the evaluation of outcomes:

> You almost never have to show you've prevented any infections. You can be judged a success for just doing what you said you were going to do, like build a clinic, or train some nurses or give leaflets to 400 out of the nation's 160,000 drug injectors.

Lobbyists, pressure groups and consultants

Such groups have a major influence on policy making and frequently use evidence in less systematic and more selective ways than proposed by proponents of evidence-based policy and practice. As in many policy areas, sport is characterised by several 'policy entrepreneurs' and high-profile lobbyists. For example, Kidd (2008) outlines the increasingly vociferous and well-connected sport-for-development lobby, led by Johan Koss of Right to Play, which sought to convince the United Nations and other agencies about the contribution that sport could make to their aid agendas.

Resources

Concerns with finite resources and cost-effectiveness mean that policy making is not a simple matter of 'what works', but what works, at what cost and with what outcomes. Consequently, lobbying is more likely to be effective if it promises a relatively cheap economy of remedies to long-standing and seeming intractable problems – something which sports lobbyists regularly promise.

Further, Weiss (1993) points out that the programmes which researchers seek to evaluate are not neutral experiments, but are the products of political decisions and, in sport as in many other areas, are often the product of complex negotiations and partnerships (which are often as important as the programmes that they deliver). In addition, Weiss (1993: 96) reminds us of realpolitik by arguing that 'a considerable amount of ineffectiveness may be tolerated if a program fits well with prevailing values, if it satisfies voters, or if it pays off political debts.'

Perhaps this explains John Maynard Keynes' view that 'there is nothing a government hates more than to be well-informed; for it makes the process of arriving at decisions much more complicated and difficult' (quoted in Solesbury 2001: 7). Such political considerations and compromises can lead to 'inflated promises [with] goals lacking the clarity and intellectual coherence that evaluation criteria should have' (Weiss 1993: 96). In such circumstances weak evaluation evidence of vague programme outcomes has to compete for attention with other factors that carry much more weight in the political process – which will include the political and professional investment in previous policy decisions, the political and economic costs of changing policy (the dreaded U turn), the lack of an affordable alternative and the frequent desire to 'do something' – to confuse movement with progress.

Within this context it is interesting to reflect on some attitudes to the nature and role of research and evaluation. For example, at the first Next Step conference in 2003 Johann Koss stated correctly that 'we do not evaluate enough and so we invite people to do research into things like sport and development, sport and peace'. However, he continued by stating that 'we need to prove what we say that we do'. Like many policy advocates or evangelists, Koss views the outcomes of research as being pre-given – performing the function of *proving success* and thereby supporting further influence and investment.

Admitting the difficulties

Despite Koss's rather optimistic views about 'proving success', it has to be acknowledged that providing robust evidence for the wider individual and collective impacts of sport presents some significant methodological problems (many of which are common to most social science research on social interventions). The measurement of cause and effect, of the relationship between inputs, participation and desired outcomes presents a number of difficulties.

- Participation in sport is just one of many things that people do. Therefore its impact will depend on the relative salience of the experience compared to other factors (e.g. criminal sub-cultures; wider social and cultural norms). Further, even where there are some measured changes, it is often difficult to disentangle the effects of participation in sport from parallel social influences and developmental processes – for example, in relation to anti-social behaviour, young people tend to reduce their involvement in such behaviour as they mature and in relation to the prevalence of HIV/AIDS, wider sources of information and influence may explain increased understanding of how infection can be prevented.

- Effects will be determined by the frequency and intensity of participation and the degree of participants' adherence over time. Although these factors are especially important for fitness and health benefits, they also have clear implications for the development of technical and social skills and attitudes and values. For example, Taylor *et al* (1999) illustrate that the length of involvement in recidivism programmes is related to their impact on attitudes and behaviour (although the nature of the experience is more important).

- Even if sports participation does assist in the development of certain types of *individual* competence, confidence and attitudes (intermediate impacts), this cannot simply be taken to imply that these will be transferred to wider social or community benefits (intermediate and social outcomes). This problem relates to what can be referred to as 'displacement of scope' – the claims for sport seem to include, and frequently confuse, issues of individual development (e.g. increases in self-confidence; self-esteem); individual behavioural change (reduced criminality; changed sexual behaviour); collective community impacts (social cohesion; social capital) and the more ambitious 'peace' and 'development'.

- Most fundamentally, the nature and extent of any impact on individual participants will depend on the nature of the experience. Sports are not a homogenous, standardised product or experience and will vary widely between programmes and participants. Clearly, participation in sport (however defined) is a necessary condition to obtain any of the hypothesised benefits. However, as these outcomes are only a possibility (Svoboda 1994) there is a need to consider *sufficient conditions* (the conditions under which the potential outcomes are achieved). It cannot be assumed that any, or all, participants will automatically obtain the presumed benefits in all circumstances, and we have little understanding about which sports and sports *processes* produce what *outcomes,* for which *participants* and in what *circumstances*. As Patrikson (1995: 128) argues,

> Sport, like most activities, is not a priori good or bad, but has the potential of producing both positive and negative outcomes. Questions like 'what conditions are necessary for sport to have beneficial outcomes?' must be asked more often.

In a similar vein, Coakley (1998: 2) argues that we need to regard 'sports as *sites* for socialisation experiences, not *causes* of socialisation outcomes'.

Families of mechanisms

Despite the policy rhetoric, sport (however defined) does not have causal powers, and outcomes are essentially contingent (i.e. not guaranteed and variable between programmes and participants). Even the most robust outcome-based evaluations are unable to *explain* either success or failure – the 'how and why?' questions. In this regard Pawson (2001a) argues for a configurational approach to causality, in which outcomes can only be understood as being *produced* by the interaction of a particular and often complex combination of circumstances. This perspective, which emphasises the need to understand mechanisms and processes, is closely allied to theory-based evaluation, which Weiss (1997: 520) argues is most appropriate 'when prior evaluations show inconsistent results' – clearly the case for sport-for-development (Coalter 2007).

Theory-based evaluation is less of a method and more of a framework for analysis. The key idea of theory-based evaluation is that we can express policy makers' and programme providers' beliefs and assumptions in terms of a 'programme theory' (or theory of change (Granger 1998)) – a sequence of causes and presumed effects (Weiss 1997). Not only does this approach seek to describe actual mechanisms, but it 'aims to surface the theoretical underpinnings of the program in advance and use the theories to help structure the evaluation' (Weiss 1997: 510). Theory-based evaluation allows an in-depth understanding of the working of

> the program or activity – the 'program theory' or 'program logic'. In particular it need not assume simple linear cause-and-effect relationships ... By mapping out the determining or causal factors judged important for success, and how they might interact, it can then be decided which steps should be monitored as the progress develops, to see how well they are in fact borne out. This allows the critical success factors to be identified.
>
> *(The World Bank 2004: 10)*

This approach shifts the focus from families of programmes (sports projects) to *families of mechanisms*, with the key issue being the assumed programme *mechanisms* that underpin policy makers' and providers' investment decisions and presumably inform the design and delivery of the programme. While outcome measurement is not precluded, the emphasis is on *process evaluation* – is the basic plan theoretically sound and plausible, what are the key variables to be studied and key stages at which to collect information, is the programme being delivered as theoretically intended?

It is worth illustrating this approach via two examples – one from the sport and social inclusion agenda and one from the sport-for-development agenda.

Sport and crime

If we take one of the most common elements of the social inclusion agenda – crime prevention – there are a series of questions that we can ask about programme theories or theories of change. First, the policy makers' understanding of the *causes* of crime will heavily influence the nature of the programme provision. A possible range of perceived causes and presumed 'solutions' might be (Coalter 2007; Nichols 2007; Schafer 1969):

- Boredom [opportunity-led crime]: diversionary schemes.
- Differential association via peer/criminal sub-cultures: introduction to new peers/role models via sports programmes.
- Adolescent development needs for catharsis/excitement/competition: certain types of adventure programmes.
- Lack of self-discipline: sports training/performance/deferred gratification.
- Educational failure and blocked aspirations/achievement/low self-esteem: sports provide opportunity for a sense of achievement, increased self-efficacy and improved locus of control.

The first thing to notice is that the presumed causes of crime, even in this rather simple typology, are varied and will probably interact. Second, it is essential to question the extent to which such analyses of the causes of crime are correct and in what circumstances. If the initial diagnosis of the causes of the problems to be addressed is incorrect, then it is highly likely that the programmes will be ineffective in addressing the issues. More generally, the programme theory for many of the proposed sports programmes seems to be that they will produce a series of *intermediate impacts*, such as improved cognitive and social skills, reductions in impulsiveness and risk-taking behaviour, improved self-confidence/efficacy and self-esteem, increased locus of control and self-discipline and all of these, in various combinations, are presumed to reduce the propensity to commit crime.

However, irrespective of the assumptions about the determinants of crime, the nature of the programme processes are a major consideration – do they produce such intermediate impacts and if so, how? Here there is an emerging view that the nature of the activity (i.e. 'sport') is less important than the nature of the social environment and social relationships involved in the activity (Fox 2000; Morris *et al.* 2003; Nichols 2007; Shields and Bredemeier 1995; Taylor *et al.* 1999; West and Crompton 2001). As Coakley (1998: 2) argues, 'sports are *sites* for socialisation experiences, not the *causes* of socialisation outcomes'. The emerging evidence suggests that programmes are most likely to work via voluntary participation in relatively small groups, in environments that emphasise task orientation rather than competition (Biddle 2006), and where quality leadership provides a number of 'protective factors' (Witt and Crompton 1997; West and Crompton 2001) (e.g. adult support and affirmation).

These complex circumstances and contingent outcomes are reflected in Taylor *et al*'s (1999: 50) summing up of their evaluation of programmes using sport to reduce recidivism:

> All programmes agree that physical activities do not by themselves reduce offending. All agree that there are personal and social development objectives that form part of a matrix of outcomes. These developments may, sooner or later, improve offending behaviour, but their impact is unpredictable in scale and timing. To expect anything more tangible is unrealistic.

HIV/AIDS: kicking AIDS out?

The second example comes from sport-for-development, where the majority of programmes make some claim to contribute to the reduction of HIV/AIDS (in part driven by funders' objectives and the legitimating role of the HIV/AIDS reduction as one of the MDGs). There is little general discussion as to how sports participation can contribute to changed sexual behaviour, other than as a vehicle for the dissemination of relevant knowledge. The approach to this can broadly be divided into a traditional didactic approach, in which sport is used as 'fly paper' to attract young people to AIDS education programmes that they otherwise would not attend. The second, more sophisticated, approach is via the use of symbolic games integrated into sports programmes (www.kickingaidsout.net). However, the basic underlying theory seems to be the rather simple, but unwarranted, assumption (Grunseit and Aggleton 1998), that increased knowledge and understanding – often provided via age-and sex-appropriate peer leaders – will lead to changed sexual behaviour. There is limited research as to the effectiveness of either approach, but that which does exist is not encouraging (Botcheva and Huffman 2004; Kruse 2006).

However, it is possible to develop a slightly more sophisticated *programme theory* (Weiss 1997), which seems to be implicit in some programmes and which would provide the basis for a process-led approach to monitoring and evaluation. I must emphasise that this 'programme theory' (Figure 39.1) is somewhat basic and based almost wholly on my fieldwork observations and discussions, but it serves to illustrate the generic point about needing to construct the assumptions and theories of behaviour change that inform programmes. There is no claim that this is definitive or effective, or that the programmes are targeted at relevant high-risk groups. For example, Pisani (2008) argues that many such programmes are not targeted at relevant high risks groups (e.g. sex workers; intravenous drug users), often for ideological, political or moral reasons.

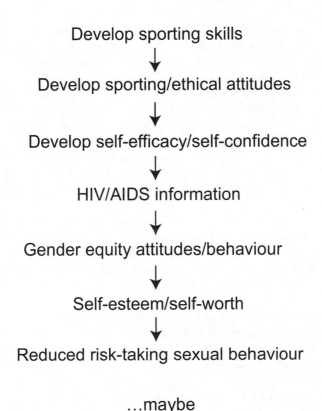

Develop sporting skills

↓

Develop sporting/ethical attitudes

↓

Develop self-efficacy/self-confidence

↓

HIV/AIDS information

↓

Gender equity attitudes/behaviour

↓

Self-esteem/self-worth

↓

Reduced risk-taking sexual behaviour

…maybe

Figure 39.1 A speculative logic model of sports-based HIV/AIDS education and sexual behaviour change

The logic outlined in Figure 39.1 (each stage of which can be monitored and evaluated), is that the process of developing practical sporting skills (via effort and practice) leads to the increase in a sense of self-efficacy and self-confidence (the ability to set and work towards certain goals; the ability to overcome certain obstacles).

In addition, by operating within an ethical framework, it is assumed that participants will develop a certain degree of moral reasoning via an emphasis on sporting and ethical attitudes (e.g. respecting opponents; the need for fair play and obeying rules; collective responsibility). Within this context of the developing individual, information about health and HIV/AIDS is provided and the approach adopted, either via traditional didactic methods or via a more symbolic and integrated approach, may be significant. There also may be an assumption that those involved in sport and concerned about fitness may be more receptive to health messages and are developing an awareness that they can take some control over their fitness and health. This information is communicated within the context of an emphasis on gender equity and respect. This entails both increasing young women's self-confidence (often via peer leadership roles) and changing young men's attitudes to young women, frequently by playing the same game (soccer). The issue of gender relations, power and respect are regarded by many as central to addressing the issues of HIV/AIDS, especially when communicated via the role model approach of peer leadership (Kruse 2006).

These various *intermediate impacts* may also lead to an increase in self-esteem and feelings of self-worth, although this is a much misused and misunderstood concept (see Coalter 2007; Emler 2001; Fox 1992) that needs care in both measurement and interpretation.

Consequently, this hypothetical programme theory/theory of change suggests that it is a *combination* of increased self-efficacy, the understanding of relevant information, changed gender attitudes and improved self-worth which *may* lead to a reduction in risky sexual behaviour, an outcome that is exceptionally difficult to measure. Nevertheless, if the programme theory is regarded as plausible and the programme is delivered consistently as theoretically intended (not an easy task in the circumstances in which many such organisations operate), then it provides a plausible basis for assuming that it has *maximised the possibility* of achieving the desired outcomes of safer sexual behaviour (even if this cannot be measured directly).

In both cases – crime reduction and changed sexual behaviour – the programme theory, with its broadly sequential steps of presumed cause and effect, provides the basis for a systematic process-led monitoring and evaluation of the relative effectiveness of the programme. Consequently, the notion of a theory of change relates to such (usually unexamined) questions as:

- To what extent are programmes designed and delivered on the basis of a believable theory of the complex causes and nature of the problems that they seek to address (Rossi *et al* 2004) – anti-social behaviour, crime, educational under-achievement, low self-esteem, risky sexual behaviour, lack of community cohesion? Here it is useful to note Pawson's (2006: 9) comment that programme design is frequently 'a research free zone'.
- Why do we assume that participation in particular sports programmes or types of sport can have certain impacts on certain types of participants and communities?
- What are the properties and processes of participation in a specific sports programme that might lead to such outcomes?
- Can we define clearly the theory of the relationship between participation in the specific sports programmes and a range of *intermediate impacts* (e.g. increased self-efficacy; increased physical self-worth; increased self-esteem; increased self-confidence)?

Here it is worth noting an increasingly widespread development that both illustrates the limitations of a 'sport only' approach and further complicates issues of monitoring and evaluation – *sport plus*. This term refers to programmes in which sport's contribution is complemented and supported by a range of parallel education and training programmes. Nearly all sport-for-development programmes are sports plus and in the UK, as programmes aimed at crime prevention have matured, projects have gone 'beyond sport and physical activities, rather than viewing them as an end in themselves. Increasingly, there is an understanding of the potential to introduce a wider programme of interventions' (Home Office 2005: 5). The wider programme of interventions included training and mentoring, linked educational programmes, healthy lifestyle programmes, drug-prevention programmes and leadership training (Leisure Futures 2002). Consequently, while sport plays a central role in such programmes, there is an increasing acceptance that it must be complemented by *development* and that sport cannot achieve the desired outcomes on its own (Deane 1998).

A much more difficult question relates to a theoretical understanding of how, and to what extent, such achieved individual changes will result in changed behaviours (reduced criminal behaviour; improved educational performance; reduction or cessation of drug use; changed sexual behaviour; reduced community conflict).

Conversations and knowledge creep

Both Pawson and Weiss argue for configurational and theory-based approaches to evaluation for sound methodological reasons. For example, Weiss (1997: 154) suggests that theory-based evaluation, by shifting focus from categories of activities to the categories of mechanisms by which change is achieved, 'can track the unfolding of events, step-by-step, and thus make causal attributions on the basis of demonstrated links. If this were so, evaluation would not need randomized control groups to justify its claims about causality'. The approach provides *explanations* for particular outcomes and a basis for informed generalisation, or as Pawson (2001b: 4) suggests, 'a tailored, "transferable theory" – (this programme theory works in these respects, for these subjects, in these kinds of situations)'.

However, and returning to the earlier sections of this chapter about the relationship between policy making and 'evidence', they both have associated 'political' agendas. A major attraction of theory-based approaches to evaluation is that they seem to provide an opportunity to close the distance between academic research and policy makers. Weiss (1980) argues that a theory-based approach entails a 'conversation' between researchers, policy makers and practitioners, Pawson (2006: 169) refers to 'sense-making' and Pawson and Tilley (2000: 201) refer to mutual 'teaching and learning interactions'.

An approach based on programme theories requires sports policy makers, providers and managers to articulate much more clearly and precisely the nature of their programme theories, tacit knowledge and professional repertoires. It would require them to consider how participation in their specific sports *programmes* (i.e. not 'sport') is presumed to lead to certain intermediate impacts (changes in values, attitudes, competencies) which then lead to broader intermediate outcomes (changes in behaviour). The attraction is clear for Bailey *et al* (2009: 31), who suggest that,

> One of the key tasks for researchers is to work with programme developers and sponsors to analyse the outcomes for which they are hoping. More importantly, the analysis reveals assumptions (and micro-assumptions) that have been made about the ways in which programme activities will lead to intended outcomes. A theory of change approach to evaluation argues that this clarification process is valuable for all parties, particularly in making explicit powerful assumptions that may or may not be widely shared, understood or agreed.

Weiss (1997) provides a broad outline of the potential advantages of theory-based evaluation for a range of closely inter-related interest groups:

Programme designers are encouraged to think harder and deeper about their assumptions, the kind of programmes that they design and the mechanisms by which those programmes work.

Practitioners. It may be that members of the same organisation or programme have different theories about how the programme works. If they can work through their differences and agree on a common set of assumptions about what they are doing and why, they can increase the force of the intervention. As process monitoring is inherently participatory it can develop a greater ownership and understanding of the philosophical and theoretical basis of the programme by those delivering it.

Programme managers. A major advantage is that the evaluation provides feedback about which chain of reasoning breaks down and where it breaks down.

Managers and funders of similar programmes elsewhere. If they understand the what, how and why of programme success (and failure), they can undertake new ventures better prepared to reproduce those elements of the programme that are associated with the successful transition to the next link in the chain of assumptions and to rethink and rework those elements that do not lead to the next interim marker.

Policy makers. Theory-based evaluation provides explanations – stories of means and ends – that communicate readily to policy makers.

Programme evaluator. The theory-based evaluation approach helps evaluators to focus the study on key questions. It provides information on short-term and intermediate outcomes, which are linked, according to the best available knowledge, to the long-term outcomes of interest.

The value of such an approach lies not only in strengthening the relationship between researchers and practitioners, but also in the fact that it is inherently developmental and can contribute to improved coherence and effectiveness in policy formulation and programme delivery. It has the potential to contribute to capacity-building, develop a greater sense of ownership, understanding and integration and develop an organisational ability to reflect on and analyse attitudes, beliefs and behaviour (Coalter 2006; Shah *et al.* 2004).

There is also a broader 'politics of methodology' strategy underpinning this proposed approach. Several writers (Solesbury 2001; Weiss 1997; Weiss and Bucuvalas 1980a, 1980b) suggest that, because of the political, bureaucratic and interest-ridden nature of organisational decision making, there are few examples of direct and immediate influence of research on decisions – 'killer facts' that change policy direction. Research results tend to reach policy makers and practitioners in diverse ways and the diffusion of research into practice is a rather hit and miss affair. It is suggested that, in the absence of killer facts, there is a long, gradual, cumulative process, vividly summarised in the title of Weiss's (1980) article – 'knowledge creep and decision accretion'. Weiss and Bucuvalas (1980b: 156, quoted in Pawson and Tilley 2000: 13) found that there was a:

> Diffuse and undirected infiltration of research ideas into [decision-makers'] understanding of the world ... they absorbed the concepts and generalisations from many studies over extended periods of time and they integrated research ideas ... into their interpretation of events ... [there was a] gradual sensitisation to the perspectives of social science.

Limited focus programmes and broad gauge problems

However, even if all of the above was achieved we are still left with a rather fundamental issue – are the 'solutions' that sport is offering relevant to some of the problems that it seeks to address? As we have noted, this is also a major component of a theory-based approach – the need to understand the *causes* of the behaviour that sports programmes wish to change (e.g. crime; educational under-achievement; weak social capital; risky sexual behaviour). Improving our understanding of the mechanisms involved to improve the effectiveness of sports programmes' ability to achieve desired *intermediate impacts* may be of little use if the initial diagnosis of the causes of problems (and therefore the solutions) is incorrect.

There has been a tendency for a lack of in-depth consideration of the relationship between causes and programme content and process, or the extent to which there is evidence that what they are offering can contribute to a solution (Crabbe 2000; West and Crompton 2001; Williams and Strean 2006). The frequent failure to address such issues is reflected in Weiss's (1993: 103) concerns that many social interventions fail because they are 'fragmented, one-service-at-a-time programs, dissociated from people's total patterns of living'. Pawson (2006: 5) laments the frequent failure to recognise that many social intervention programmes are 'complex systems thrust amidst complex systems'.

In part this is because of the frequently individualistic assumptions that underpin many sports programmes, with a strong emphasis placed on aspects of individual character-building, self-efficacy, self-control, self-esteem, self-discipline and self-confidence. Consequently, it is suggested that there is a need to recognise that actions and choices take place within the material, economic and cultural realities within which the 'empowered' live (Morris *et al.* 2003; Mwaanga 2003). Or, as Weiss (1993: 105) puts it,

> We mount limited-focus programs to cope with broad-gauge problems. We devote limited resources to long-standing and stubborn problems. Above all we concentrate attention on changing the attitudes and behaviour of target groups without concomitant attention to the institutional structures and social arrangements that tend to keep them 'target groups'.

For example, it is worth noting Mwaanga's (2003) argument that raising the expectations and educational aspirations of young women without changing their economic circumstances may have limited impact on their more instrumental sexual behaviour. Or, the literature that emphasises the deep-rooted cultural nature of sexual behaviour and associated risks of HIV/AIDS (McNeill 2009; Pisani 2008). Such analyses illustrate the complexity of the issues which is often ignored in policy rhetoric and which too often reduces complex social issues to individual behaviours. In fact, an over-concentration on traditional intermediate individual outcomes is, in many cases, misguided, with a clear need to develop a more informed, grounded and contextual understanding (Burnett 2001). One might argue that there are moral and political dangers of de-contextualised, rather romanticised, communitarian generalisations about the 'power' of sport-in-development.

Conclusion

Rather than seeking simply to assert sport's almost magical properties, or commission 'research' that proves 'success' (however defined), what is required is a developmental approach based on the de-reification of 'sport' and a concentration on understanding the social processes and mechanisms that *might* lead to desired outcomes for *some* participants or some organisations in *certain circumstances* (Pawson 2006). From this perspective, monitoring and evaluation need to pursue *understanding* via participatory, process-centred and formative evaluation (Coalter 2006, 2007; Shah *et al.* 2004). In addition to improving the design and implementation of sport-for-development programmes and defining more realistic and contextually relevant outcomes, such an approach could have a more strategic political function. Hopefully it would provide the basis for a constructive dialogue, or 'conversation' (Pawson 2006; Weiss 1993), between a variety of policy makers, funders and sport-for-development organisations and the development of real partnerships. However, we are still left to ponder Pisani's (2008: 300) warning that 'doing honest analysis that would lead to programme improvement is a glorious way to be hated by just about everyone'.

References

Audit Commission (2009) *Tired of Hanging Around: Using sport and leisure activities to prevent anti-social behaviour among young people*, London, Audit Commission.

Australian Sports Commission (2006) *The Case for Sport in Australia*, Canberra: Australian Sports Commission.

Bailey, R.P., Armour, K., Kirk, D., Jess, M., Pickup, I., Sandford, R. and BERA Physical Education and Sport Pedagogy Special Interest Group (2009) 'The educational benefits claimed for physical education and school sport: an academic review'. *Research Papers in Education*, 24(1), pp. 1–27.

Biddle, S.J.H. (2006) 'Defining and measuring indicators of psycho-social well-being in youth sport and physical activity', in Vanden Auweele, Y., Malcolm, C. and Meulders, B. (eds) *Sport and Development*, Leuven: Lannoocampus.

Bloom, M., Grant, M. and Watt, D. (2005) *Strengthening Canada: The socio-economic benefits of sport participation in Canada*, Ottawa: Conference Board of Canada.

Blunkett, D. (2000) *Influence or Irrelevance: Can social science improve government*. Speech to the Economic and Social Research Council, 2 February.

Rt Hon David Blunkett MP, Home Secretary, 'Edith Kahn Memorial Lecture', June 2003.

Botcheva, L. and Huffman, M.D. (2004) *Grassroot Soccer Foundation HIV/AIDS Education Program: An intervention in Zimbabwe*, White River Junction, VT: Grassroot Soccer Foundation.

Burnett, C. (2001) 'Social impact assessment and sport development: Social spin-offs of the Australia–South Africa Junior Sport Programme', *International Review for the Sociology of Sport*, 36(1): 41–57.

Calderisi, R. (2006) *The Trouble with Africa: Why foreign aid isn't working*, New York: Palgrave Macmillan.

Coakley, J. (1998) *Sport in Society: Issues and controversies*, 6th edn, Boston, MA: McGraw Hill.

——(2004) *Sport in Society: Issues and controversies*, 8th edn, Boston, MA: McGraw Hill.

Coalter, F. (2006) *Sport-in-development: A monitoring and evaluation manual*, London: UK Sport.

——(2007) *Sport a Wider Social Role: Who's Keeping the Score?* London: Routledge.

——(2010) 'The politics of sport-for-development: limited focus programmes and broad gauge problems?' *International Review for the Sociology of Sport*, Special issue: 'Interrogating boundaries of "race", ethnicity and identity', 45(3): 295–314.

Crabbe, T. (2000) 'A sporting chance? Using sport to tackle drug use and crime', *Drug Education, Prevention and Policy*, 7(4): 381–91.

Davies, P. (2004) *Is Evidence-based Government Possible?* Jerry Lee Lecture. 4th Annual Campbell Collaboration Colloqium, Washington.

Deane, J. (1998) 'Community Sports Initiatives: An Evaluation of UK Policy Attempts to Involve the Young Unemployed. The 1980's Action Sport Scheme', in *Sport in the City: Conference Proceedings*, Loughborough and Sheffield: Loughborough University, Sheffield Hallam University and University of Sheffield, vol. 1, Sheffield, 2–4 July 1998, pp.140–59.

Department of Culture, Media and Sport (1999) *Policy Action Team 10: Report to the Social Exclusion Unit – Arts and Sport*, London: HMSO.

Department for International Development (2005) *Guidance on Evaluation and Review for DFID Staff Evaluation Department*, London: Department for International Development.

Donnison, D.V. and Chapman, V. (1965) *Social Policy and Administration*, London: Allen & Unwin.

Emler, N. (2001) *Self-esteem: The costs and causes of low self-worth*, York: Joseph Rowntree Foundation.

Forrest, R. and Kearns, A. (1999) *Joined-up Places? Social cohesion and neighbourhood regeneration*, York: YPS for the Joseph Rowntree Foundation.

Fox, K.J. (2000) 'The effects of exercise on self-perceptions and self-esteem', in S.J.H. Biddle, K.K. Fox and S.H. Boutcher (eds) *Physical Activity and Psychological Well-being*, London: Routledge, pp. 88–117.

Fox, K.R. (1992) 'Physical education and the development of self-esteem in children', in N. Armstrong (ed.) *New Directions in Physical Education*, vol. 2, *Towards a National Curriculum*, Leeds: Human Kinetics.

Giddens, A. (1998) *The Third Way*, Cambridge: Polity Press.

Giulianotti, R. (2004) 'Human rights, globalization and sentimental education: the case of sport', *Sport in Society* 7(3): 355–69.

Glasner, P.E. (1977) *The Sociology of Secularisation*, London: Routledge & Kegan Paul.

Granger, R.C. (1998) 'Establishing causality in evaluations of comprehensive community initiatives', in K. Fulbright-Anderson, A.C. Kubisch and J.P. Connell (eds) *New Approaches to Community Initiatives*, vol. 2, *Theory, Measurement and Analysis*, Washington, DC: Aspen Institute: www.aspenroundtable.org/vol2/granger.htm

Grunseit, A.C. and Aggleton, P. (1998) Lessons learned: an update on the published literature concerning the impact of HIV and sexuality education for young people, *Health Education*, 98(2): 45.

Hognestad, H. (2005) *Norwegian Strategies on Culture – and Sports Development with Southern Countries*, a presentation to the Sports Research Forum, Australian Sports Commission, Canberra, 13–15 April.

Home Office (2005) *Positive Futures Impact Report: Staying in Touch*, London: Home Office.

Howells, S. (2007) 'Organisational sustainability for sport and development', A paper presented at the *2nd Commonwealth Sport for Development Conference*, Glasgow, 12 June 2008.

Keaney, E. and K. Gavelin. (n.d.) *Sport, Physical Activity and Civil Renewal: Literature Review*, London: Institute of Public Policy Research.

Kidd, B. (2008) 'A new social movement: Sport for development and peace', *Sport in Society*, Vol 11, No 4: 370–80.

Kruse, S.E. (2006) *Review of Kicking AIDS Out: Is Sport an Effective Tool in the Fight Against HIV/AIDS?*, draft report to NORAD, unpublished.

Leisure Futures (2002) *Positive Futures: A Review of Impact and Good Practice*, London: Sport England.

Levermore, R. (2008) 'Sport: a new engine of development', *Progress in Development Studies*, 8, 2: 183–90.

Matarasso, F. (1998) *Beyond Book Issues: The social potential of library projects*, Stroud: Comedia.

McNeill, F.G. (2009) '"Condoms cause AIDS": Poison, prevention and denial in Venda, South Africa', *African Affairs*, 108(432): 353–70.

Morris, L., Sallybanks, J., Willis, K. and Makkai, T. (2003) *Sport, Physical Activity and Anti-Social Behaviour*, Research and Public Policy Series, 49, Canberra: Australian Institute of Criminology.

Moyo, D (2009) *Dead Aid: Why aid is not working and how there is a better way for Africa*, London: Penguin.

Mwaanga, O. (2003) *HIV/AIDS At-risk Adolescent Girls' Empowerment through Participation in Top Level Football and Edusport in Zambia*, MSc thesis submitted to the Institute of Social Science at the Norwegian University of Sport and PE, Oslo.

Nichols, G. (2007) *Sport and Crime Reduction*, London: Routledge.

Patriksson, M. (1995) 'Scientific Review Part 2', in *The Significance of Sport for Society – Health, Socialisation, Economy: A Scientific Review*, prepared for the 8th Conference of European Ministers responsible for Sport, Lisbon, 17–18 May 1995, Strasbourg: Council of Europe Press.

Pawson, R. (2001a) *Evidence Based Policy*, vol. 1, *In Search of a Method*, ESRC UK Centre for Evidence Based Policy and Practice, Working Paper, 3, London: Queen Mary University of London.

——(2001b) *Evidence Based Policy*, vol. 2, *The Promise of 'Realist Synthesis'*, ESRC UK Centre for Evidence Based Policy and Practice, Working Paper, 4, London: Queen Mary University of London.

——(2004) 'Evaluating ill-defined interventions with hard-to-follow outcomes', paper presented to ESRC seminar understanding and evaluating the impact of sport and culture on society, Leeds Metropolitan University, January.

——(2006) *Evidence-based Policy: A Realist Perspective*, London: Sage.

Pawson, R. and Tilley, N. (2000) *Realistic Evaluation*, London: Sage.

Pisani, E. (2008) *The Wisdom of Whores: Bureaucrats, brothels and the business of AIDS*, London: Granta Books.

Portes, A. and Landolt, P. (2000) 'Social Capital: Promise and Pitfalls of its Role in Development', *Journal of Latin American Studies*, 32: 529–47.

Renard, R. (2006) *The Cracks in the New Aid Paradigm*, Discussion Paper, Antwerpen, Belgium, Institute of Development Policy and Management.

Rossi, P.H., Lipsey, M.W. and Freeman, H.E. (2004) *Evaluation: A systematic approach*, 7th edn, Thousand Oaks, CA: Sage.

Schafer, W. (1969) 'Some social sources and consequences of inter-scholastic athletics: The case of participation and delinquency', *International Review of Sport Sociology*, 4, 63–81.

Shah, M.K., Kambou, S., Goparaju, L., Adams, M.K. and Matarazzo, J.M. (eds) (2004) *Participatory Monitoring and Evaluation of Community- and Faith-based Programs: A step-by-step guide for people who want to make HIV and AIDS services and activities more effective in their community*, Core Initiative.

Shields, D.L.L. and Bredemeier, B.J.L. (1995) *Character Development and Physical Activity*, Champaign, IL: Human Kinetics.

Solesbury, W. (2001) *Evidence Based Policy: Whence it came and where it's going*, ESRC UK Centre for Evidence Based Policy and Practice, Working Paper, 1, London: University of London.

Sport for Development International Working Group (2008) *Harnessing the Power of Sport for Development and Peace*, Toronto: Right to Play.

Svoboda, B. (1994) *Sport and Physical Activity as a Socialisation Environment, Scientific Review Part 1*, Strasbourg: Council of Europe, Committee for the Development of Sport (CDDS).

Taylor, P., Crow, I., Irvine, D. and Nichols, G. (1999) *Demanding Physical Activity Programmes for Young Offenders Under Probation Supervision*, London: Home Office.

UNICEF (2006) *Monitoring and Evaluation for Sport-Based Programming for Development: Sport recreation and play*, Workshop Report, New York, NY: UNICEF.

United Nations (2000) *United Nations Millennium Declaration: Resolution adopted by the General Assembly*. New York, UnitedNnations http://www.un.org/millennium/declaration/ares552e.pdf

—— (2005a) *Business Plan International Year of Sport and Physical Education*, New York, NY: United Nations.

——(2005b) *Sport for Development and Peace: Towards achieving the millennium development goals*, New York, NY: United Nations.

US Department of Health and Human Services (1999) *Framework for Program Evaluation in Public Health*, Atlanta, GA: US Department of Health and Human Services, Centers for Disease Control and Prevention (CDC).

Weiss, C.H. (1980) 'Knowledge Creep and Decision Accretion', *Knowledge: Creation, Diffusion, Utilisation*, 1(3): 381–404.

——(1993) 'Where Politics and Evaluation Research Meet', *Evaluation Practice*, 14(1): 93–106.

——(1997) 'How Can Theory-based Evaluation Make Greater Headway?', *Evaluation Review*, 21(4): 501–24.

Weiss, C.H. and Bucuvalas, M. (1980a) 'Truth tests and utility tests: decision-makers' frames of reference for social science research', *American Sociological Review*, 45: 302–13.

——(1980b) *Social Science Research and Decision Making*, New York: Columbia University Press.

West, S.T. and Crompton, J.L. (2001) 'A Review of the Impact of Adventure Programs on At-risk Youth', *Journal of Park and Recreation Administration*, 19(2): 113–40.

White Paper: *Modernising Government*. Presented to Parliament by the Prime Minister and the Minister for the Cabinet Office by Command of Her Majesty, March 1999. London. The Stationery Office.

Williams, D.J. and Strean, W.B. (2006) 'Physical activity as a helpful adjunct to substance abuse treatment', *Journal of Social Work Practice in the Addictions*, 4(3): 83–100.

Witt, P.A. and Crompton, J.L. (1997) 'The Protective Factors Framework: A Key to Programming for Benefits and Evaluating Results', *Journal of Parks and Recreation Administration*, 15(3): 1–18.

Woolcock, M. and Narayan, D. (2000) 'Social Capital: Implications for Development Theory, Research, and Policy', *The World Bank Research Observer*, 15(2): 225–49.

World Bank (2004) *Monitoring and Evaluation: Some tools, methods and approaches*, Washington, DC: World Bank.

40

Elite for all, all for elite?

An assessment of the impact of sports development on elite sport success

Veerle De Bosscher and Maarten van Bottenburg

A global sporting arms race ... and the search for the high-performance bible

Without her individual talent, Tia Hellebaut would never have developed her impressive high jumping career, nor would Pieter van Den Hoogenband his swimming career or innumerable elite athletes their career in a range of other sports. But neither would they have done so without the network of sports clubs where they developed as athletes; without the training and competition opportunities; without the guidance from coaches, physiotherapists, doctors, dieticians and sports scientists; without the support services from national governing bodies, governments, Olympic Committees and/or private partners, who made the athletic career more attractive for athletes. Talent, whether it is in sport, arts, economy or science, is an individual quality that can only be fully expressed in a specific social environment and with the support of others (Van Bottenburg 2009). Over the years, this has raised questions among researchers and policy makers about the extent to which success at international competitions can be affected by policy. Nations are searching for the ways to increase success by investing strategically in elite sport development (De Bosscher *et al.* 2008). As the supply of success at dominant international competitions (such as the Olympic Games) remains essentially fixed in the future (e.g. the IOC has indicated that it would like the number of events to be capped at around 300), and the demand for success is increasing (more nations taking part and more nations winning medals), the 'market' adjusts by raising the 'price of success' (Shibli 2003). As the competition gets stronger, nations will have to invest even more just to maintain their success. This has led to what Oakley and Green (2001b) called a global sporting arms race. During the last decennium, this global sporting arms race has intensified considerably. Research has shown that many nations have invested substantially in high-performance sport, even doubling budgets over a four-year cycle, without obtaining a return on their investment in terms of international performances (De Bosscher *et al.* 2008a; Van Bottenburg 2009). This makes policy makers even more aware of the need for a thorough search for effectiveness and efficiency in their management processes and policies. The Olympic Games have evolved from a competition among individuals to a competition among nations.

Elite sports have become a business, where nations are searching for a competitive advantage and where the rules are determined by what rival nations do.

As a result, many nations have sought to increase their success by copying best practice from other competitors, leading to an increasing trend towards institutionalisation of elite sport and increased government involvement in many sports (Bergsgard *et al.* 2007; Houlihan and Green 2008). Policy makers of various nations are searching for a common 'Bible' on high-performance sport. Consequently the elite sport systems of leading nations have become increasingly homogenous. Several authors state that, more than ever before, they are based around a single model of elite sport development with only slight variations (Bergsgard *et al.* 2007; Clumpner 1994; Green and Houlihan 2005; Oakley and Green 2001a). On the other hand, there is an increasing belief among researchers that there is no one globally successful elite sport system: many systems can be successful depending on the sport and the nation (De Bosscher *et al.* 2009); there are many ways to skin a cat. Houlihan and Green (2008: 17) explain this variation by, among other reasons, path dependency: initial policy decisions can determine future policy choices. Historical developments constrain future policy decisions. Furthermore policy transfer and lesson-drawing in elite sport policies are often shaped by the socio-economic and cultural foundations of a country.

A particular example that illustrates this point is the autonomous development of sport-for-all and elite sport and the continual strain between both in many nations. In most countries sports policy is directed towards two aims: to (a) increase sports participation for the wider population and (b) increase success for a few athletes at the elite level. The extent to which both are prioritised differs considerably amongst nations and this explains part of the divergence found in the keys to elite sporting success. Whereas some nations may treat the development of elite athletes essentially as an extension of sport-for-all, others may prioritise international success by developing elite sport more autonomously. As an example De Bosscher *et al.* (2008a, 2008b) found in their comparative study of six nations that the pathway to the podium was clearly a more explicit and possibly overriding concern in the UK, the Netherlands, Italy and Canada than it was in Norway and Belgium (Wallonia and Flanders), two nations with a sport-for-all oriented policy. In the case of Norway, according to Augestad and Bergsgard (2008), this is illustrated by the strong resistance towards the establishment of a talent identification system at young age (younger than 13 years old), a position which has been incorporated into the sports confederation 'regulations for Children's sport', which indicate that play and socialisation in sport are more important than competition. This reveals the presence of strong democratic tendencies in the Norwegian sports system, which clearly influences their policy choices. Nations that emphasise sport-for-all may look for relatively cheaper ways to the podium and strategies for success that fit within their overall culture. This raises the question of whether such ways exist. Still, from a top down perspective, considering its population of 4.5 million inhabitants, Norway is relatively successful in international competitions. The country won 10 medals in Beijing, which is an increase of 4 in comparison with Athens (although fewer were gold). This is striking in a context of increasing competition, where many nations have lost market share. Furthermore, Norway performs extremely well at winter sports (19 medals in Turin). Considering the relatively small budget spent on high-performance sports in Norway (De Bosscher *et al.* 2008a), this raises interesting questions for policy makers about why this occurs. It is not clear whether Norway has gained an advantage at the elite level because of its sport-for-all oriented policy and its more restrictive approach towards the involvement of young children in the talent development process, or because Norway is also well developed in all other areas of elite sport development and has a relatively efficient elite sport system (De Bosscher *et al.* 2009). With this knowledge, it may be that Norway, and probably a few other

Scandinavian countries where sport-for-all is highly developed (Van Bottenburg *et al.* 2005), could be interesting benchmarking nations, even for elite sport, because they show that, with a small population and limited funding for elite sports, success is still possible in spite of the increasing competition. It may be that these nations have found more effective ways to invest in elite sport over a longer term, which should not surprise us considering the intensification of the link between sport-for-all and elite sport, as a key success determinant. This article aims to open a dialogue about the divergent developments of sport-for-all and elite sport and more particularly on the role that a broad sports participation may play in increasing success at the elite level. We will use existing research to endeavour to assess the impact of sport-for-all at the bottom of the pyramid on international sporting success. To illustrate this, we will go into more depth on the results of a large-scale study, SPLISS, which aimed to increase insight into the sports policy factors leading to international sporting success and to identify the possible relationship between policy and success. We realise that we cannot draw firm conclusions about possible causal relationships between grass-roots and elite sport by zooming in on the specific results of this broader study with regard to the particular question of sports participation. This chapter seeks rather to initiate a debate on this dual development and on the state of the art in elite sport development research in relation to sport-for-all.

Status questions about the pyramid theory

An ongoing discussion has emerged in many nations on the role that sport-for-all plays in elite sport development. The relationship between the two is often used by policy makers as a justification for their often high levels of investment in the careers of only a few sportspeople. However, little conclusive research has been conducted that shows this relationship. As Houlihan *et al* (2009: 5) stressed:

> Sport is replete with deeply entrenched 'storylines', not only that elite success has a powerful demonstration effect on the mass of the public, but also that sport participation has a positive impact on the behaviour of the young, that international sport improves relations between nations and that sport can strengthen community integration. Storylines are not necessarily false, but their persistence and impact is not related to the quality or quantity available.

Traditionally, scholarship related to athletic pathways has been dominated by the so-called pyramid metaphor. According to this theory, thousands of people practising sport at the base lead to a few Olympic champions and, at the same time, the existence of champion role models encourages thousands of people to take up some form of sport (IOC 2000). In this paper we will focus on the causal pathway heading up the pyramid and ask to what extent high-performance sport benefits from a broad sports participation base.

During the twentieth century the internal differentiation and the scale of participation in sport increased and a global competition system developed, gradually leading to selection mechanisms to find the best athletes. A link was created between the youngest athletes at the lowest level and in the smallest towns and the winning of gold medals (Van Bottenburg 2003). In the second half of the twentieth century, this conception of the sports pyramid came to be regarded as incomplete. The original concept was revised and reinterpreted and sport-for-all became an alternative to elite sport (Heinilä 1971). Ongoing differentiation in the sporting world has led to the creation of new, additional structures. Apart from sports clubs, informal sports participation, fitness, and outdoor sports all became much more prevalent. The pyramid theory was criticised, because many people practise a sport without any desire to move up to a higher level. Nor can elite sport at present be regarded as a simple extension of sport-for-all. Elite sport has developed into a relatively autonomous world, one that functions in accordance with different principles from those of sport-for-all. Whereas elite sport policy focuses on a group of athletes that is limited in number by definition, with policy implemented in accordance with relatively strict regulations that increasingly take the interest of the media, business community and consumers into account, sport-for-all policy concentrates on developing a wide range of organisations and facilities for mass use and is primarily concerned with the well-being of the practitioners themselves. Accordingly sport-for-all and elite sport are developing in different directions, so that the mutual connection between the two is placed under increasing strain. They continue to grow apart and athletes are obliged at increasingly younger ages to choose between the sport-for-all approach and the elite sport approach (Eichberg, cited in Bale and Philo 1998). Instead of the single pyramid model, there are three independent and autonomous models of sports involvement/participation (Figure 40.1):

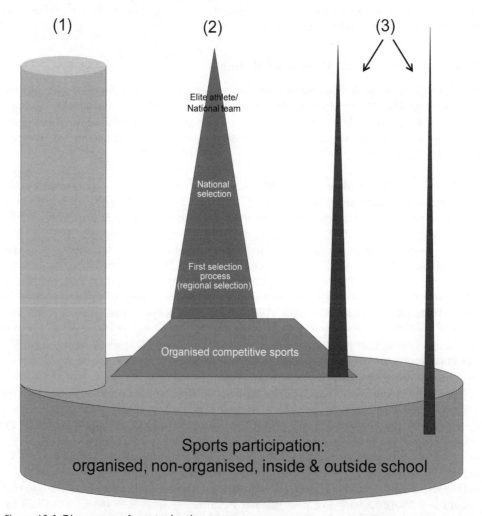

Figure 40.1 Divergence of sports development

- The non-organised or informal sports participation pillar.
- The traditional pyramid, presenting a continuous progression from the lower level of organised sports participation to the highest competition levels.
- An autonomous elite sport pyramid, focusing solely on elite career development, selecting athletes either from a sport's participant base or from outside a sport's participant base.

According to Van Bottenburg (2003) we should not jump to the conclusion that this divergence is a negative development. It has helped to enrich the world of sport. All the levels and forms in which sport is practised remain inextricably linked and all are part of a single, global sporting system. Although developing independently, these processes are not static but dynamic and continually subject to change. However, there is a dearth of literature on the interaction between these developments. Green (2005) and Sotiriadou *et al.* (2008) tried to scrutinise the pyramid model of sports development more closely. They state that the logic of the pyramid analogy is sound in terms of the link between top and bottom but that the pyramid model does not capture the increasingly sophisticated nature of the sports system. The pyramid does not illustrate the internal interrelationships and processes within sports systems that assist in the design of appropriate playing pathways to promote player movement vertically and/or laterally. They therefore tried to gain a deeper understanding of the different stages of an athletic pathway: (1) the entrance (or attraction, recruitment), to find out what factors influence athletes' decisions to participate in a sport in which they may become successful later; (2) the retention, to find out what factors keep them involved and enhance their commitment to the sport; and (3) the advancement (or nurturing), or how athletes move up the pyramid and experience different transitions. This kind of knowledge may have important implications for policy makers and national sports organisations in the way they plan and manage athletic programmes at different levels. Sotiriadou and Shilbury (2009, in press) endeavour to show how national sport organisation (NSOs) and other interest groups (such as the National Olympic Committees (NOC's), regional institutes, sponsors, spectators, supporters) take part in that process.

The connection between sport-for-all and elite sport

Participation and competitive standards are linked by the endeavour to create a deep pool of athletes from which a corps of elite competitors can develop (Green 2005; Van Bottenburg 2003). However, there is a lack of scholarly evidence for such relationships. Some examples show that this pyramid analogy can be discussed, because it is possible to imagine ways of building high-level competition systems without relying on a broad participation base. Green (2005) uses the example of some winter sports in the United States, such as bobsledding, that rely primarily on recruitment of athletes initially developed for other sports, for example from football and track and field. As another example, Australia used to be successful in diving and cycling, two sports with a low participation base (Elphinston 2004). However, these are sports that worldwide don't have a broad participation base. There are scarcely any figures on the correlation between the scale of sports participation and the scale of sporting success. The reason is the lack of internationally comparable data. De Bosscher and De Knop (2003) found that success in tennis was highly correlated among 43 European nations both with the number of registered tennis players ($r = 0.724$; $p = 0.000$) and the number of tennis courts ($r = 0.858$; $p = 0.000$). Furthermore, these factors were more important than population and wealth of a country. Van Bottenburg (2003) found a significant correlation between the percentage of the population participating in organised sports and the number of medals won per million

Veerle De Bosscher *et al.*

inhabitants in 20 European nations (0.535; p = 0.007). Furthermore, when looking at the entire range of sport-for-all, which means also taking non-organised sport into account, he found that the correlation primarily depends on the intensity, competitiveness and the degree of organisation in sporting practice. This correlation was higher (r = 0.789; 0.035) and was not significant for the percentage of the population practising sport more broadly. He concluded that this supply function of sport-for-all does not take place automatically. Specific organisations and facilities are required, which have to ensure that there is a good atmosphere, proper sports accommodation, training opportunities, skilled coaches and sufficient volunteers. Stewart, Nicholson, Smith and Westerbeek (2004) analysed this on a sport-by-sport level and looked at the correlation between the number of registered sports club members (organised sports participation) and international success over a longer period in Australia. They did not find any correlation in six sports over a 14-year period. For example, while Australia is one of the best swimming nations in the world, the participation rate is only 2% of all sports.

A similar analysis in Flanders, the northern (Dutch-speaking) region of Belgium, could only partly confirm these findings. Braeckmans *et al.* (2005) analysed six sports over a period of 11 years and only found a significant correlation in two sports: tennis (r = 0.969; p < 0.01) and cycling (r = 0.687; p = 0.014). Some sports even correlated negatively. Interestingly, when we extend this analysis to a correlation between the number of registered members and success in year X to success three years later (year X+3), correlations tend to be more positive. There is a logic for this, as approximately 10 years are required in order to become a top athlete in a particular sport (Bloom 1985; Ericsson 2003). Table 40.1 shows these correlations and appendix 1 provides a graph of these figures by sport. With the exception of tennis and swimming, the correlations have increased considerably with success in these sports three years later. This finding could indicate that the correlation with success is a long-term process. Of course, there are a range of other variables influencing success.

Clearly, these kinds of studies are fragmentary and mean little in terms of the interdependency of elite sports and sports for all. Questions are raised concerning the strength of the relationship between the two, on causality and on how this relationship occurs. A lack of comparable data hinders further in-depth analysis of the nature of this relationship. There are after all a range of other variables that influence both success and sports participation figures. The correlations do however indicate that this relationship is ambiguous and may vary by sport. Further research, for example on an international level, is needed to get a deeper understanding of the pyramid analogy. Notwithstanding the range of counter-examples, it should be admitted that almost all top athletes have their roots somewhere in sport-for-all (whether or not from

Table 40.1 Correlation between the number of registered members and success (top eight places at EC, WC, OG) from 1992 to 2006 in seven sports in Flanders

	Correlation in year X	Correlation in year X+1
Athletics	−0,352	0,289
Baseball	0,107	0,337
Gymnastics	−[1]	−0,095
Judo	−0,164	0,483
Tennis	0,969	0,632
Triathlon	−0,551	0,581
Swimming	−0,379	−0,920

Note
1 No correlation was possible because the success score was zero

different sports or even informal sports participation) and they play according to virtually identical rules at top levels as at the lowest levels of competitive sport. Many top athletes start practising a sport at a very young age and in a different sport to the one in which they later excel (Van Bottenburg 2003). Current elite sport developments oblige young talents to choose ever earlier, which raises the question of the effects of early specialisation.

The next section will go into more depth on the impact of sport-for-all on elite sport at an overall sports level by focusing on the results of an international comparative study, which included a range of criteria to evaluate sports participation in six nations.

Does sports development have an impact on elite sport success? Results from the SPLISS study

We will try to answer the question of whether high-performing nations also have higher sports participation by focusing on some of the results that were obtained from the SPLISS study. SPLISS reflects the common purpose of a group of researchers who initiated an international comparative study of elite sports policies in six nations: Belgium, Canada, Italy, the Netherlands, Norway and United Kingdom. 'SPLISS' stands for 'Sports Policy factors Leading to International Sporting Success' (see De Bosscher et al. 2008a). For the purpose of this chapter we will specifically look at how sport-for-all was developed in these nations and whether this is possibly related to their international success.

Instruments

As a starting point, this study used a nine-pillar model for international comparison derived from previous research as a basic analytical framework (De Bosscher et al. 2006). This draft model was developed because of an identified gap in existing research and the lack of an empirically grounded, coherent theory on the factors that determine international sporting success. From a comprehensive body of literature at the meso (policy) and micro (athlete) level, additionally extended with two surveys with experts and of athletes, it was eventually concluded that all key success drivers, which can be influenced by policy, can be distilled down into nine key areas or 'pillars' (Figure 40.2), situated at two levels, according to a multidimensional approach to measure the effectiveness of national sports organisations (Chelladurai 2001):

- Inputs are reflected in pillar 1, as the financial support for sport and elite sport: countries that invest more in (elite) sport can create more opportunities for athletes to train under ideal circumstances.
- Throughputs are the processes ('what' is invested and 'how' it is realised) in elite sports policies, which may lead to increasing success in international sporting competitions. They refer to the efficiency of sports policies, that is the optimum way that inputs can be managed to produce the required outputs. All the other pillars (2–9) are indicators of the throughput stage.

The athlete has a central place in these nine pillars. Research has shown that on average 8–10 years and 10.000 training hours of deliberate practice are necessary to become an elite athlete (Ericsson 2003). Therefore this model focuses on the traditional pyramid and the support services that are needed to enable athletes to move up the pyramid. It presents the policy factors that are important during the different stages as identified by Wylleman et al. (1998), that is, the initiation or participation phase, the development phase, the perfection phase and the

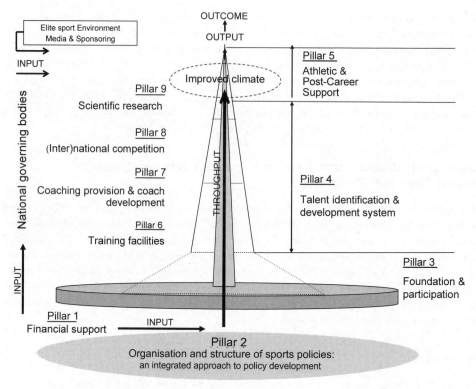

Figure 40.2 SPLISS model: a conceptual model of nine pillars of sports policy factors leading to international sporting success
Source: De Bosscher et al. 2006

discontinuation phase. These stages are similar to those that have been used by Green (2005) and Sotiaradou *et al.* (2008).

When these nine pillars are compared to other recent international comparative studies on elite sport systems conducted by Bergsgard *et al.* (2007), Digel *et al.* (2006), Green and Houlihan (2005) and Houlihan and Green (2008), they show a high degree of overlap between what different authors consider to be an elite sport system. However, only the SPLISS study considered sports participation as a key success determinant. The departing point was that, although sports participation may not be a necessary condition for success, it influences success to a large extent because of the continuous supply of young talent and the higher level of training and competition. The next section will therefore look at how the sample nations compared regarding their level of sports participation, and will attempt to indicate a possible relationship with success. By doing this for every pillar, the SPLISS study aimed to increase the theoretical knowledge of the relationship between elite sport policies (input and throughputs) and a nation's success (outputs) and accordingly increase insight into the factors that shape elite sport policies and the pathways to success in different nations.

SPLISS methods

Without going into depth on the methods of the SPLISS study (see De Bosscher *et al.* 2008a, 2009, 2010) the key point was that it tried to: (1) operationalise the nine pillars into measurable concepts by identifying detailed critical success factors (CSFs) for each pillar and by focusing solely on the meso-level, or the factors that can be fashioned by policy; and (2) by trying to go beyond the descriptive level of comparison by developing a scoring system. This allowed initial analysis that could indicate possible relationships with success. Data were collected through an overall sports policy research instrument and through surveys with 1,090 athletes, 273 coaches and 71 performance directors in the sample nations in order to measure the competitive position of nations in elite sport quantitatively. A total of 103 CSFs were aggregated into a final percentage score for each pillar. Although the quantification of qualitative information, such as policies, could be criticised on a number of grounds, the researchers emphasised that the scoring system is in this respect rather a supportive and tangible way of understanding elite sport policies more broadly in relation to sporting success than an isolated competitiveness measurement or ranking system by itself (De Bosscher *et al.* 2009). In this respect the SPLISS study complemented the existing literature on elite sport policy development which tried to gain a deeper understanding of the factors, including social, economic, political and cultural differences, that shape policy.

To simplify the presentation of results and to identify any specific characteristics and trends in the overall results for the nine pillars, each nation was allocated a colour-coded score or 'traffic light' (black and white in this paper), varying from a policy area 'very well developed' to 'little or no development' (Figure 40.3).

SPLISS results for pillar 3: sports participation

This study analysed sports participation at two different levels: opportunities for children to engage in sport during school time (physical education) and in sport outside school (sports participation). Apart from the organised sports participation, several sources in the literature indicate that the recognition of physical education and sport in schools, the access to sport-for-all and the number of individuals participating in sport were drivers for success, with the former communist countries often taken as an example (e.g. Broom 1986; Chelladurai *et al.* 1987; Riordan 1991; Sedlacek *et al.* 1994). Taking all the indicators of sports participation into account, 14 critical success factors for pillar 3 have been evaluated on a five-point scale according to predefined standards. The factors were weighted to reflect an expert group's view of their relative importance (De Bosscher *et al.* 2007; De Bosscher *et al.* 2008a, 2009).

The results are shown in Figure 40.3 and Table 40.2.

Figure 40.3 shows that there is relatively small variation in pillar three, except from two nations with a fairly low level of development: Italy and Wallonia. Time devoted to physical education is roughly similar in most nations. Italy's score is explained by its lack of coordination

	UK	ITA	NED	CAN	NOR	FLA	WAL
Evaluation	○	◉	◎	NA	◎	○	◉
Assessment by athletes and coaches			no assessment on this pillar				

○ policy area very well developed
○ good level of development
◎ moderate level of development
◍ fairly low level of development
● low level of development
NA data not available

Figure 40.3 Comparative analysis in six sample nations of pillar 3: participation in sport

Veerle De Bosscher *et al.*

Table 40.2 Critical success factors pillar 3[1]

W	Physical education and school sport	UK	ITA	NED	NOR	FLA	WAL
	Physical education and school sport						
	Nursery education						
1	National statutory amount of minimum time PE	1	1	1	5	5	1
1	Weekly average amount of time PE (minutes per week)	1	1	3	3	3	1
	Primary education						
1	National statutory amount of minimum time PE	3	1	3	5	5	5
1	Weekly average amount of time PE (minutes per week)	3	1	3	3	3	3
1	Regular extracurricular competitions	5	3	3	1	5	5
	Secondary education						
1	National statutory amount of minimum time PE	5	5	5	5	5	5
1	Weekly average amount of time PE (minutes per week)	2	3	3	3	3	3
1	Regular extracurricular competitions	5	3	3	1	5	5
	Sports participation						
3	Participation in sport at least once a week	3	3	3	na	3	3
3	Percentage of population participating in a sports or outdoor club	4	2	5	4	4	4
6	Total number of sports club members	4	3	2	2	1	1
3	Sports club members per head of population	4	2	3	5	3	3
1	Total number of registered sports clubs	5	4	2	2	2	2
3	Existence of quality stimulation projects in sports clubs	3	1	5	na	5	1
	Total points	96.00	64.00	86.00	67.00	87.00	69.00
	MAX	135.00	135.00	135.00	105.00	135.00	135.00
	Number of times na	0.00	0.00	0.00	2.00	0.00	0.00
	Total score for pillar 3 (%)	71.11	47.41	63.70	63.81	64.44	51.11

Notes:
na, data not available; W, weight; italic text, results deriving from the overall sports policy questionnaire
levels of development: 1, low level of development; 5, very well developed
1 Data collection dated from 2004
Source: De Bosscher *et al.* (2007)

in Physical Education (PE) (schools decide independently whether they will offer PE) and a relatively small base of organised sports participants. The score for Wallonia is at the threshold of a moderate level of development and can in part be explained by its relatively low number of club members and the lack of quality projects for sports clubs. The UK has a good level of development on this pillar mainly because of its larger number of sports club members. The number of sports club members may be seen as the most important criterion in relation to elite sporting success in pillar three because in most nations talented athletes are usually selected from an organised and competitive sports system at grass-roots level. In relative terms, Norway is the leading nation for the percentage of the population who are sports club members (48%)

followed by the United Kingdom (36%). However, in absolute terms, Canada, Italy and the United Kingdom have an advantage, as they have a greater number of sports participants and registered sports club members than the other sample nations. This confirms the earlier pyramid discussion that these nations can fish for talent in a larger pool of sports participants and sports clubs than Flanders, the Netherlands, Norway and Wallonia. It should also be noted that, in the UK and Canada, institutions of secondary and higher education also have the responsibility to act as the first rung on the talent development ladder, unlike in the other nations. Up to 400 Specialist Sports Colleges (SSCs) thus form an important part of a planned, coordinated and integrated organisational and administrative model of elite sport development in the United Kingdom (Green and Houlihan 2005). Canadian Interuniversity Services (CIS) represents over 12,000 athletes and 550 full- and part-time coaches who are training and working in Canadian universities. Furthermore the Canadian Colleges Athletic Association (CCAA) is the sole coordinating body for college sport comprising 9,000 intercollegiate athletes, 700 coaches and 150 sports administrators in total (Sport Canada 2006). These findings may therefore skew the comparative analysis to some extent.

As most athletes have their roots in sports clubs, this pillar refers not only to the number of sports participants but also to the quality delivered at club level. Although quality in sports clubs is definitely a criterion that needs to be explored in greater depth on a sport-by-sport basis, some nations have set up national projects to stimulate quality management in sports clubs. An example of this can be found in Flanders, where subsidy criteria for national governing bodies are partly based on initiatives for increasing quality in sports clubs. Some sports, such as gymnastics, korfball, football and hockey have developed a specific total quality management system with the aim of delivering quality labels for their clubs, accompanied by appropriate consultancy. Another example is IKSport (Integral Quality in Sports clubs), which was designed to introduce 'Total Quality Management' in sports clubs in Flanders and the Netherlands.

Measuring success

By extending this analysis, the core question is whether these results relate to the success of these nations in high-performance sport. Measuring success is a tremendously difficult exercise, because ranking the sample countries may vary markedly by the index type that is used: for winter or summer sports, Olympic or non-Olympic sports and absolute or relative measurements (according to population and wealth) (De Bosscher et al. 2007). For convenience we will use the ranking according to performances in Olympic summer Games (see Table 40.3), as all nations participate in summer sports and these were also the focus of the policy analysis for pillar 3.

With the exception of Italy and Great Britain, which have switched places in Beijing compared to Athens, all four other nations kept the same rank. We find hardly any relationship between the scores for pillar 3 (sports participation), in Figure 40.2 and Table 40.1, and the success ranking in Table 40.2. Italy is the best performing nation in Athens and has only a low level of development on pillar 3. On the other hand Wallonia also appears to score fairly low on both measurements. Among the other nations there is relatively little variation.

Preliminary conclusions on the SPLISS study

These figures should be regarded as suggestive rather than conclusive. First, it was not possible to quantify levels of sports participation very exactly. The figures do give a rough indication of the level of sports participation, but don't include detailed measures of some essential features

Table 40.3 Relative ranking of the sample nations according to different performance measures in Olympic sports, using market share

Nation	Market share (%)[1]	
	OG Athens	OG Beijing
Italy	3.4 % (1st)	2.9 % (2nd)
Great Britain	3.1 % (2nd)	5.3 % (1st)
Netherlands	2.1 % (3rd)	1.9 % (3rd)
Canada	1.3 % (4th)	1.8 % (4th)
Norway	0.9 % (5th)	1.1 % (5th)
Belgium	0.3 % (6th)	0.3 % (6th)
(Flanders)[2]	(0.17 %)	(0.2 %)
(Wallonia)	(0.13 %)	(0.1 %)

Notes

1 Market share: a standardised measure of total achievement in an event whereby total medals won are converted into 'points' (gold=3, silver=2, bronze=1) and the points won by a given nation are subsequently expressed as a percentage of the total points awarded (SIRC 2002)

2 In Belgium, figures are divided according to the number of athletes involved in winning medals from Flanders and Wallonia

such as the quality of local sports clubs, the organisation and structure of national governing bodies and how strongly these are developed. Because some determinants are intangible (Van Hoecke 2000; Zeithaml *et al.* 1993) and complex to measure, more insight into the underlying processes, and further research at a sport-by-sport level, are needed. Second, the SPLISS study measured a range of critical success factors, assuming that there was a logical explanation for a possible relationship with success. The analysis shows that perhaps not all criteria are connected with success. Looking at the scores in Table 40.2, while both Flanders and Norway have the best scores on physical education (PE) and school sport, they do not differ in terms of weekly average amount of time devoted to PE from the other nations. It could be argued that the way sport is embedded in the school system, as for example in the United States, or the provision of daily opportunities to practise sport during school time, are factors that encourage the broader development of the talent pyramid. Moreover, it should be noted that both Italy and the UK have the highest number of sports club members, which is, according to Van Bottenburg (2003), a more important indicator for success. He found a significant correlation between the percentage of organised sports participants and the number of medals won per million inhabitants (r = 0.535).

While the SPLISS study attempted to increase insight in terms of identifying a relationship between nine pillars (pillar three in particular) and success, we could not be conclusive on this point. This can be explained by many factors, such as the limited number of sample nations compared, the range of confounding elements influencing success, the complexity of international comparisons and struggle to find comparable data, the difficulty in defining and measuring elements of sports policies, just to mention a few (De Bosscher *et al.* 2009, 2010). The study did not lead to further evidence that may confirm the pyramid theory and furthermore, it may raise questions over whether pillar three should be excluded from the SPLISS model, supporting the view that policies should stimulate the further autonomous development of high-performance sport in order to find more effective ways of developing elite sport policy.

The unclear correlation between the degree of success and extensive participation in sport-for-all raises new, supplementary questions. Does the chance of elite sport success increase to the extent that a few sports strongly dominate in a country and decrease to the extent that participation is more widely distributed over a greater number of sports? Or does a wider variety of sports actually help to increase the chances of young people finding the sport they most enjoy and which they are best at? We will therefore extend our analysis to some other findings, with regard to the number of sports that are prioritised by nations and accordingly, the number of athletes.

Prioritisation of (Olympic) sports

Several authors pointed out that it may be more efficient in elite sport to target the resources on a relatively small number of sports through identifying those that have a real chance of success at world level (Clumpner 1994; Oakley and Green 2001a; Wells 1991). This strategy was followed by the former communist nations and later by several other nations. In this respect, we looked at the number of national governing bodies (NGBs) funded for sport and elite sport in the six sample nations.

Table 40.4 shows that some nations, such as the Netherlands, support a broad spectrum of sports for elite performances, 63 NGBs in total, including non-Olympic sports such as billiards, bridge and chess. On the contrary, in Flanders only 26 NGBs receive funds for elite sport, in Norway 30, in Wallonia 36 and in the UK 40.

Furthermore we also looked at elite sport expenditure as a proportion of total sport expenditure. This criterion may indicate whether governments emphasise elite sport development rather than grass-roots development or both. Canada (67.3%) and UK (52.6%) are the biggest NGB-funders on elite sport development, followed by the Netherlands (47.2%). Interestingly, compared with the other nations, the Netherlands also appears to have the most athletes per million inhabitants ranked in the world top eight and top three, as is presented in Table 40.5.

With 28.3 athletes per million inhabitants ranked in the world top eight, the Netherlands has 15 times more athletes than Wallonia, 10 times more than Flanders, seven times more than the UK, and four times more than Canada. This score is partly related to the diverse range of sports (over 60) on which Dutch elite sports policy is focused. Until 2003, federations and athletes in many sports were eligible for subsidies and stipends if they had reached the top eight in the world regardless of whether their sport was football, swimming, athletics, draughts or aeromodelling. In 2003, NOC*NSF tightened up this policy, by reducing the number of 'first

Table 40.4 Number of National Governing Bodies (NGBs) that are recognised and funded in six nations (2003)

	CAN	FLA	ITA	NED	NOR	UK	WAL
Number of recognised & funded NGBs for sport	55	68	77*	72	55	120[1]	64
Number of NGBs funded for elite sport	47	26	41	63	30	40	36
Elite sport funding (% of total funding for NGB's)	67.3%	25.0%	17.9%	47.2%	21.1%	52.6%	42.3%

Note
1 UK: This number will include, for some sports, separate governing bodies for England, Scotland, Wales and Northern Ireland
* This number includes 43 federations + 18 associated disciplines + 16 enti di promozione sportive

Table 40.5 Number of world top eight and top three athletes in the sample nations

	Number of athletes in the world top 8 (2003)	Athletes/million inhabitants
Canada	227 (Olympic Summer and Winter sports)	7.10
Flanders	17 (Olympic Summer sports)	2.83
The Netherlands	461 (343 Olympic (of which 111 in team sports) and 118 non-Olympic disciplines; 40 are in Winter sports)	28.3 (21.4 if only Olympic disciplines; 14.6 if team sports are left out)
United Kingdom	240 (mainly Olympic Summer sports) 462 athletes are in WCPP and World Class Podium programme, of which 20 in Winter sports	3.98
Wallonia	8 (Olympic Summer sports)	1.84

	Number of athletes in the world top 3 (2003)	Athletes/million inhabitants
Canada	82 (Olympic Summer and Winter sports)	2.54
Italy	119 (Olympic Summer and Winter sports)	1.97
United Kingdom	97 (mainly Olympic Summer sports)	1.61
The Netherlands	47 (Olympic Summer and Winter sports)	2,88
Flanders	4 (Olympic Summer sports)	0,67
Wallonia	2 (Olympic Summer sports)	0.45

Source: De Bosscher *et al.* 2007; De Bosscher *et al.* 2008a

category sport disciplines' that are eligible for subsidies and stipends. In 2009, 57 sports are still subsidised.

Nevertheless, even within Olympic disciplines, the number of athletes in the Netherlands is still much higher than in the other nations (three times more than Canada and five times more than the UK). In terms of world top three rankings the number of athletes in the UK and Italy are broadly comparable, while again the Netherlands has the highest number of Olympic medal-winning athletes per million inhabitants. This could be a significant finding for Dutch policy, which supports athletes from a relatively broad level of abilities in world terms. One possible explanation for this finding is that supporting many athletes of a lower standard than some of the other sample nations results in the production of more top eight (and top three) athletes.

Conclusions on the prioritisation of (Olympic) sports

Despite the general tendencies in many nations to target resources on a relatively small number of sports, these figures in the Netherlands are striking and may have policy implications. Generally speaking it is fair to say that young people have a wide variety of preferences when it comes to sport. In the Netherlands, young people as a whole participate in more than a hundred different kinds of sport (Van Bottenburg 2003). Van Bottenburg (2003) states that a positive response to such diversity is desirable, not only in terms of encouraging sport, but also in terms of promoting elite sport. The above figures suggest that perhaps the Dutch success can be explained by its support of so many sports, because this variety offers Dutch youngsters more opportunities to practise a sport that they like, to develop their individual qualities and perhaps to move up the pyramid. Meanwhile, it offers opportunities to national governing bodies to develop their sport at a higher international level. The conclusion reached by Van Bottenburg (2003) is that all-round sports engagement at a young age and delayed specialisation of talent helps to promote the development of top athletes. Many top athletes start practising a sport at a very young age, often before they are seven years old. Usually their sporting career starts with a different sport from the one in which they later excel. In the first years of their sporting career, the future elite athletes often participate in several sports consecutively or simultaneously, before specialising in the sport in which they will later climb to the top. Van Bottenburg (2003) also indicates that smaller countries in particular should certainly take the positive effects of delayed specialisation into account. These countries must nurture every talent, whereas countries with a large pool from which to recruit can allow 99 talents out of a hundred to drop out.

Discussion and conclusion

While a correlation between the scale of sports participation and the scale of sporting success would seem to speak for itself, there are scarcely any data available in this regard. The main reason is the lack of internationally comparable data (Van Bottenburg 2003). Sports policy and scholarly sports research often treat sport-for-all and elite sport as separate phenomena. They focus on either sport-for-all or elite sport and pay little attention to their relationship and mutual influence. Although sport-for-all and elite sport are still closely interwoven, they are developing in different directions. On the one hand, several new sporting practices have emerged and new frameworks have been created for these sporting practices in addition to the traditional organisational structures. On the other hand, elite sport is more than ever before growing into a relatively autonomous entity, which indeed stems from sport-for-all, but increasingly has its specific dynamics and follows its own logic, due to processes of specialisation, commercialisation and professionalisation (Digel 2001). The critical question for policy makers is how to deal with this ambiguous and changing pyramid process. Should this divergent development be reinforced or should elite sport and sport-for-all in fact be more closely integrated? As elite sport systems are being copied all over the world, policy makers enter into debates over the organisational structure in their countries regarding the separation of both worlds. Norway and the UK have proven to have relatively efficient elite sport structures, with respectively Olympiatoppen and UK Sport being responsible solely for elite sport (and not sport-for-all). These structures were both created after a 'focussing event' (Chalip et al. 1996), which acted as a catalyst for significant and sustained investment in elite sport (De Bosscher et al. 2008). Similar questions are posed with regard to the structures of national governing bodies (federations) in many nations. The requirements in high-performance sport and increased professionalisation and commercialisation are often too high for the many volunteers who often serve on the boards of the governing bodies. This leads to increasing strains and the restructuring of the relationship between elite sport and sport-for-all. One typical example is the way that nations search to maximise their pool of potential talent, seeking innovative ways of effective talent scouting and talent transfer that deliver a higher return on investment. One way to do so is the system-related scientific selection process which was typical of former communist countries (Fisher and Borms 1990; Riordan 1989) and which aims to identify potential elite athletes from outside a sport's participation base. A similar system still currently exists in Australia. Here approximately 10,000 young people around the age of 14 are introduced to the most physiologically appropriate sport of their choice and a selection of these young people is offered intensive training under professional guidance (Oakley and Green 2001a). So far, the system has been particularly successful in discovering international talent in athletics, cycling, weight-lifting and women's rowing (Robinson 1997). None of these successes can be explained by a high sports participation base. However, these sports can be considered as sports that worldwide have a smaller participation base. It could be different for sports like football, basketball, hockey or tennis. In this respect, a prudent deduction could be that the more globalised the sports are, the more difficult to perform at a high level without a broad sports participation base and vice versa.

Accordingly the United Kingdom for example, has set up four projects as a hunt for new talent in the run-up to London 2012 (Bingham 2008; UK Sport 2009):

- Sporting Giants: a selection of tall people (a minimum of 190 cm for men and 180 cm for women), between 16 and 25 and with some sort of athletic background, who may have the potential to become part of the performance programme in the Olympic sports of handball, rowing and volleyball. Fifty-eight athletes were selected from a pool of 4,800 applications.
- Girls4Gold is a search for highly competitive sportswomen between the ages of 17 and 25 years old with the potential to become Olympic champions in cycling and other targeted Olympic sports (bob skeleton, canoeing, modern pentathlon, rowing and sailing).
- Talent Transfer: UK Sport has analysed the records of over 1,200 retired or nearly retired athletes previously involved in UK Sports World Class Programmes, to investigate their suitability to switch sports, and extend their athletic career.
- Pitch2Podium: young football and rugby players who have been unsuccessful in securing a professional contract are selected and provided with a second-chance opportunity to succeed in a new Olympic sport.

By starting these projects, the UK wants to boost intake for both high-performing and 'new' sports. These projects are strong examples of the autonomous development of high-performance sport without dependence on a broad sports participation base. However, in most of these projects (maybe with the exception of the systematic talent selection process), selected athletes will nonetheless have roots in sport-for-all, albeit from other sports or in a wide variety of sports. Green and Houlihan (2005) refer to Tihanyi (2001: 29) who said that 'it is much too late to develop Olympians at the level of the training centres. This process must be incubated, nurtured and brought to fruition at the club level'. After all, most of these athletes will not follow the traditional pyramid, but are still selected because they appear to have some talent as former sports practitioners; talents which they have most often developed in sports clubs.

In conclusion we can state that a broad base of sports participation is not always a necessary condition for success, but it may influence success to a large extent because of the continuous supply of young talent and the higher level of training and competition (De Bosscher 2007). The latter claim is also based on the fact that sports are social products where 'training with better athletes makes athletes better'. Van Bottenburg (2003) found that the correlation primarily depends on the intensity, competitiveness and the degree of organisation in sporting practice. Furthermore, it is quite likely that sport-for-all also serves a supply function with respect to coaching and training and it creates employment opportunities for many coaches (Van Bottenburg 2003). Similarly with regard to sports infrastructure, the number of sports facilities may influence success because of the possibility of influencing the number of talented athletes who move up to the top.

The pyramid still exists at competition level, and many sports clubs, especially in European countries, are focused on competition and selection from the juniors and measure the club's success by the achievements of the first teams. Therefore the traditional club structures are still the backbone of the player pathway. While the pyramid is often under strain from the perspective of sport-for-all, because sports clubs can't cater for the wide variety of demand for sport at the grass-roots level, this does not detract from the fact that developing a broader sporting pyramid on a sport-by-sport level may enlarge the pool of talents specialising in a sport and possibly the number of athletes who finally make it to the top. Looking at these arguments, policy makers might need to rethink their policies and indeed question whether elite sport and sport-for-all should be more closely integrated and whether developing quality of sport at the grass-roots level may be an effective way to develop sustained long-term success strategies at the elite level. While almost all nations invest in increasing sports participation rates, only a few nations developed projects to improve the quality in sports clubs in order to improve the level of athletic talent development in sports clubs (De Bosscher et al. 2007). For a long time national sports organisations (federations) have organised coaches' courses, competitions and other services towards clubs, but the level of quality stimulation projects and services for improvement of the talent development processes are often limited. A study in Flanders with 140 top-level athletes revealed that 60% of all athletes were older than 16 when they first received special attention as a rising talent from their governing body. Furthermore, 41% of the coaches and 47% of the athletes indicated that this was too late (De Bosscher, V., De Knop, P. and Truyens, J. 2008b), while governing bodies reported that the level of the initial talent selection from sports clubs is inferior. Similar results were found in the Netherlands (Van Bottenburg 2009). These figures are striking and should attract the attention of Flemish and Dutch policy makers. They show that sports clubs may have a higher impact on athletic career development than one might initially think. Importantly, Van Bottenburg (2003) states that therefore sport-for-all does not supply elite sport automatically. Specific organisations and facilities are required and national sports organisations play an indispensable role in this regard. As was indicated by Green (2005: 249) 'there is a need to rethink the design and integration of our sport programmes to optimize athlete recruitment, promote athlete commitment and sustain athlete transitions and advancement'. It is therefore important to think of strategies to improve the level of youth sports academies and general quality in sports clubs in order to develop more potential top athletes. The SPLISS study suggested that small countries especially could see the development of grass-roots sport (pillar three) as a long-term investment to achieve a competitive advantage in high-performance sport (De Bosscher 2007). Norway is a good example in this respect. While this approach is very different from current elite sport policy in many top nations, which look for focused investment and for narrower talent pyramids, it should be noted that there is only limited evidence for the effectiveness of 'all inclusive' talent selection and monitoring systems, and little evidence that all talents will be discovered through the system (Bloom 1985; Mac-Curdy 2006). Furthermore there are drawbacks to early specialisation such as overtraining (Dalton 1992), physical and psychological limitations (Wiersma 2000) and drop-outs (Weiss and Petlichkoff 1989). There are only a handful of sports (such as gymnastics, tennis and swimming) where early specialisation is necessary to make it to the top. Most sports benefit from a more diverse development of their athletes, in other words, from athletes practising several sports at young age. In this regard it can be argued that nations could profit from multidimensional sports development at a young age rather than early specialisation and performances.

While many nations are searching for a common bible for elite sport, this paper argues that policy makers should promote quality at the grass-roots level as a key to developing competitive advantage in their elite sport system. The contribution of sport-for-all to elite sporting success is under-researched and is underestimated by policy makers. Future success can be pursued through quality programmes in sports clubs, good competition structures and strong national sports federations, from which both sport-for-all and elite sport would benefit. Therefore, the question of whether elite sporting success could be increased through developing sport-for-all should be re-addressed in the agendas of policy makers. It is not just about athletic pathways, but also about the development of coaches, umpires, managers and administrators. Especially for small nations whose number of potential athletes is smaller, this may be a way to survive in an increasingly competitive environment where immense amounts of money are being invested in order to win medals. At the end, the question is: who benefits most from this global sporting arms race?

Appendix

Number of registered sports members compared to points on the elite sport index to measure sporting success (top eight places at EC, WC, OG) in seven sports in Flanders.

Note

1 Flanders is the northern, Dutch-speaking part of Belgium, Wallonia the southern, French and German-speaking part. In Belgium the Flemish community (Flanders) and the French/German-speaking community (Wallonia) have separate sports policies at each level, from local to national (including three separate ministers of sport). Apart from the Olympic Committee (BOIC), whose main task is to select athletes for the Olympic Games, there is no national (federal) policy or structure for sport, nor are there expenditures on sport at federal level. Therefore Flanders and Wallonia have participated in this research as if they were two distinct nations. As the study includes to a large extent qualitative data, it is not possible to sum policies of Wallonia and Flanders into one final evaluation. Instead of excluding Belgium as a nation, it was decided with the consortium group to separate the two regions.

References

Augestad, P. & Bergsgard, N.A. (2008). Norway. In B. Houlihan & M. Green (Eds). *Comparative elite sport development* (pp. 195–217). London: Elsevier.

Bale, J. and Philo, C. (Eds) (1998). *Body cultures: essays by Henning Eichberg*. London: Routledge.

Bergsgard, N.A., Houlihan, B., Mangset, P., Nordland, S.I. & Rommetveldt, H. (2007). *Sport policy. A comparative analysis of stability and change*. London: Elsevier.

Bingham, J. (2008). The road to 2012: The development of elite sport in the UK. Paper presented during congress 'topsport in de lage landen' [elite sport in the low countries]. Antwerp, Belgium.

Bloom, B.S. (1985). *Developing talent in young people*. New York: Balantine.

Braeckmans, P., De Bosscher, V. & Van Hoecke, J. (2005). *Onderzoek naar de relatie tussen topsport en breedtesport in Vlaanderen* [Research in Flanders into the relationship between sport for all and elite sport]. Un-published masters thesis, Vrije Universiteit Brussel, Brussels, Belgium.

Broom, E.F. (1986). Funding the development of the Olympic athletes: A comparison of programs in selected Western and socialist countries. *Proceedings of the third International Seminar on Comparative Physical Education and Sport* (pp. 21–4). Champaign: Human Kinetics.

Chalip, L., Johnson, A. & Stachura, L. (Eds) (1996). *National sport policies: An international handbook*. Westport, CT: Greenwood.

Chelladurai, P. (2001). *Managing organisations, for sport & physical activity. A system perspective*. Scotsdale: Holcomb Hathaway publishers.

Chelladurai, P., Szyszlo, M. & Haggerty, T.R. (1987). 'System-based dimensions of effectiveness: The case of national sport organisations'. *Canadian Journal of Sport Sciences, 12*, 111–19.

Clumpner, R.A. (1994). 21st century success in international competition. In R. Wilcox (Ed.). *Sport in the global village* (pp. 298–303). Morgantown, WV: FIT.

Dalton, E.R. (1992). Overuse injuries in adolescent athletes. *Sports Medicine*, 13, 58–70.

De Bosscher, V., Bingham, J., Shibli, S., van Bottenburg, M. & De Knop, P. (2008). 'A global sporting arms race. An international comparative study on sports policy factors Leading to international sporting success'. Aachen, Germany: Meyer & Meyer.

De Bosscher, V. & De Knop, P. (2003). 'The influence of sports policies on international success: An international comparative study' [Abstract]. In NOC*NSF (Ed.), *Proceedings of the 9th World Sport for All Congress. Sport for All and Elite Sport: Rivals or partners?* (p. 31). Ahrnem, the Netherlands: NOC*NSF.

De Bosscher, V., De Knop, P. & Truyens, J. (2008). *Hoe succesvol zijn we in topsport? De ontwikkeling van een Belgische Topsportindex*. Tussentijds rapport, Vrije Universiteit Brussel.

De Bosscher, V., De Knop, P. & Van Bottenburg, M. (2007). Sports Policy Factors Leading to International Sporting Success. Published doctoral thesis. Brussels, BE: VUBPRESS.

——(2009). 'An analysis of homogeneity and heterogeneity of elite sport systems in six nations'. *International Journal of Sports Marketing and Sponsorship*, 10(2), 111–31.

De Bosscher, V., De Knop, P., van Bottenburg, M. & Shibli, S. (2006). 'A conceptual framework for analysing Sports Policy Factors Leading to International Sporting Success'. *European Sport Management Quarterly*, 6(2), 185–215.

De Bosscher, V., De Knop, P., van Bottenburg, M., Shibli, S. & Bingham, J. (2009). 'Explaining international sporting success. An international comparison of elite sport systems and policies in six nations'. *Sport Management Review*, 12, 113–36.

De Bosscher, V., Shibli, S., van Bottenburg, M., De Knop, P. & Truyens, J. (2010). Developing a methodology for comparing the elite sport systems and policies of nations: a mixed research methods approach. *Journal of Sport Management*, 24, 5.

Digel, H. (2001). 'Talentsuche und talentfoerderung im internationalen vergleich [An international comparison of talent detection and talent development]'. *Leistungssport, 31*, 72–8.

Digel, H., Burk, V. & Fahrner, M. (2006). 'High-performnce sport. An international comparison'. *Edition Sports international*, 9. Weilheim/Teck: Bräuer.

Eichberg, H., edited by J. Bale and C. Philo (1998). *Body cultures. Essays on sport, space and identity*. London: Routledge.

Elphinston, B. (2004). *Win to win models in sport. The Australian Experience 1896–2004*. Paper presented at the IOC-technical seminar, Warschau, Poland.

Ericsson, K.A. (2003). 'Development of elite performance and deliberate practice: An update from the perspective of the expert performance approach'. In K. Starkes & K.A. Ericsson (Eds). *Expert performance in sports. Advances in research on sport expertise* (pp. 49–85). Illinois, Champaign, IL: Human Kinetics.

Fisher, R.J. & Borms, J. (1990). 'The search for sporting excellence'. *Sport Science Studies*, 3, 5–89.

Green, M. (2005). 'Integrating macro- and meso-level approaches: A comparative analysis of elite sport development in Australia, Canada and the United Kingdom'. *European Sport Management Quarterly*, 2, 143–66.

Green, M. & Houlihan, B. (2005). *Elite sport development. Policy learning and political priorities*. London and New York: Routledge.

Houlihan, B., Bloyce, D. & Smith, A. (2009). 'Developing the research agenda in sport policy'. *International Journal of Sport Policy*, 1(1), 1–12.

Houlihan, B. & Green, M. (2008). *Comparative elite sport development. Systems, structures and public policy*. London: Elsevier.

IOC (2000). '*Sport for All/Sport pour Tous*', Lausanne: International Olympic Committee.

MacCurdy, D. (2006). *Talent identification around the world and recommendations for the Chinese Tennis Association*. Retrieved April 13, 2009, from www.itftennis.com/shared/medialibrary/pdf/original/IO_18455_original.PDF.

Oakley B. & Green, M. (2001a). 'The production of Olympic champions: International perspectives on elite sport development system'. *European Journal for Sport Management*, 8, 83–105.

——(2001b). 'Still playing the game at arm's length? The selective reinvestment in British sport, 1995–2000'. *Managing Leisure*, 6, 74–94.

Riordan, J. (1989). 'Soviet sport and Perestroika'. *Journal of Comparative Physical Education and Sport*, 6, 7–18.

——(1991). *Sport, politics and communism*. Manchester: Manchester University Press.

Robinson, E. (1997). *Youngsters with stars in their eyes*. The Financial Times.

Sedlacek, J., Matousek, R., Holcek, R. & Moravec, R. (1994). 'The influence of the political changes on the high performance sport organisation in Czechoslovakia'. In R. Wilcox (Ed.). *Sport in the global village* (pp. 341–47). Morgantown, WV: FIT.

Shibli, S. (2003). *Analysing performance at the Olympic Games: Beyond the final medal table*. Paper presented at the 11th Congress of the European Association for Sport Management, Stockholm, Sweden.

Sotiriadou, K. & Shilbury, S. (2009). 'Australian elite athlete development: An organisational perspective'. *Sport Management Review*, 12(3), 137–48.

Sotiriadou, K., Shilbury, S. & Quick, S. (2008). 'The attraction, retention/transition and nurturing process of sport development: Some Australian evidence'. *Journal of Sport Management*, 22, 247–72.

Sport Canada (2006). 'Canadian Interuniversity Services'. Retrieved January 18, 2006, from www.pch.gc.ca/sportcanada/index_e.cfm.

Stewart, B., Nicholson, M., Smith, A. & Westerbeek, H. (2004). *Australian Sport: Better by design? The evolution of Australian sport policy*. London and New York: Routledge.

Tihanyi, J. (2001). 'Discontent on deck', SwimNews, pp. 6–9.

UK Sport (2009). *UK Sport*. Retrieved May 11, from the UK Sport website, www.uksport.gov.uk/.

Van Bottenburg (2003). *Top-en breedtesport: een Siamese tweeling? [Elite sport and sport for all: a Siamese twin]* In K. Breedveld (Ed.). *Rapportage Sport 2003* (pp. 285–312). Den Haag, NL: Sociaal en cultureel planbureau.

Van Bottenburg, M. (2009). *Op jacht naar goud. Het topsportklimaat in Nederland, 1998–2008*. [The hunt for gold. The elite sport climate in the Netherlands, 1998–2008]. Niewegein: Arko Sports Media.

Van Bottenburg, M., Rijnen, B. & Van Sterkenburg, J. (2005). *Sports participation in the European Union. Trends and differences*. Hertogenbosch: W.J.H. Mulier Inistitute and Nieuwegein: Arko Sports Media.

Van Hoecke, J. (2000). *De ontwikkeling van IKGym: een relevante toepassing van de principes van integrale kwaliteitszorg en servicemanagement binnen de (traditioneel) georganiseerde sport* [The development of IKGym: a relevant application of the principles of total quality management and service management within the (traditional) organised sport]. Doctoral dissertation, Vrije Universiteit Brussel. Ghent, Belgium: PVLO.

Weiss, M.R. & Petlichkoff, L.M. (1989). 'Children's motivation for participation in and withdrawal from sport: Identifying the missing links'. *Pediatric Exercise Science*, 1, 195–211.

Wells, H.J.C. (1991). 'Developing sporting excellence in Hong Kong'. *Journal of Comparative Physical Education and Sport*, 1, 28–34.

Wiersma, L.D. (2000). 'Risks and benefits of youth sport specialization: Perspectives and recommendations'. *Pediatric Exercise Science*, 12, 13–22.

Wylleman, P., De Knop, P. & Sillen, D. (1998). *Former Olympic athletes' perceptions of retirement from high-level sport*. Paper presented at the 28th Congress of the International Association of Applied Psychology, San Francisco, United States, August.

Zeithaml, V., Berry, L. & Parasuraman, A. (1993). 'The nature and determinants of customer expectations of service'. *Journal of the Academy of Marketing Science,* 21, 1–12.

41

An assessment of the impact of sports development on sports participation

Maarten van Bottenburg and Veerle De Bosscher

There are many definitions of sports development, reflecting the past and current mix of objectives of the various principal agents involved and the changing political, economic, ideo-logical and cultural background in which they operated. These definitions can all be positioned along two axes: first, the axis between encouraging people to become physically active on the one hand (sport for all) and producing elite athletes through talent development on the other (elite sport); and second, the axis between creating the pathways and structures to enable people to participate and perform in sport on the one hand (development of sport) and using sport as a vehicle to achieve non-sport policy goals on the other (development through sport) (Houlihan and White 2002). In assessing the impact of sports development on sports participation, this chapter focuses on a specific part of the space created by these two axes. While Chapter 40 concentrated on the development *through* sport, this chapter will focus on the development *of* sport; and contrary to the previous chapter, which explored the impact of sports development on elite sport, this chapter will tackle its impact on sports participation.

For several reasons this impact of sports development on sports participation is difficult to assess. In the first place, both the terms 'sports development' and 'sports participation' are by no means constants but historically fluid and socially contextual in their meaning (Houlihan and White 2002; Van Bottenburg *et al.* 2005; Bloyce and Smith 2010). It cannot be expected, therefore, to create a uniform model to determine the impact of sports development on sports participation which is valid throughout the world. In the second place, the analysis is limited in establishing the extent to which this impact varies from country to country, because analyses of sports development – let alone its relationship with sports participation – are still lacking in many (especially non-Western) countries. This chapter will be confined to (mostly English) secondary literature published about sports development and sports participation in a limited number of (mostly Western) countries. In the third place, even in those countries where both sports development and sports participation have been richly documented, the impact of the former on the latter is hard to assess because sports development policies are increasingly inter-woven with other policy areas and often made in a variety of institutional settings at multiple levels of government and within a mix of public, not-for-profit and commercial organizations (Bergsgard *et al.* 2007).

Against these difficulties, the growing body of scholarly literature on sports development increasingly enables us to describe and evaluate from an international comparative perspective the impact of policies designed to increase levels of participation, at least for some countries. From this literature, several striking similarities between sports participation trends and policies in these countries come to the fore, especially when viewed over the longer term. This raises interesting questions about the underlying dynamics. At the same time, national, local and sport specific variations and dissimilarities in sports development policies and sports participation levels and trends are easy to recognize, creating a fascinating and complex puzzle to solve about their relationship. This chapter tries to take a step in that direction. First, the main similarities and differences in sports participation trends and levels will be discussed in a variety of mainly Western countries. After this, the most significant similarities and differences in sports development policies in these countries will be analyzed, followed by a discussion of the impact of sports development policies on sports participation and the influence of broader societal processes in this respect.

Sports participation trends

Over the longer term, Western countries show a remarkable similarity in their sports participation trends. With some simplification, this trend can be characterized by an S-shaped curve: after a long initial period of slow but steady growth in sports participation from the introduction of modern sports until the middle of the twentieth century, nearly all Western countries experienced a massive increase in sports participation between the 1960s and 1980s. This was followed by a period of partial and temporary stagnation and, with respect to some age groups in some countries, even a slight decline in the 1990s, but overall and in the longer term sports participation continued to grow, albeit moderately. This goes for both formal, competitive and informal, recreational forms of sports participation, with plausibly an earlier growth in formal, competitive sport after the mid-twentieth century, but also clearer signs of stagnation or decline of this kind of sports participation in the late twentieth century (Van Bottenburg et al. 2005).

In France, for example, sports participation increased from 28 per cent of the population in 1967 to 74 per cent in 1986, to fall back slightly to 72 per cent in 2000.[1] In Denmark, the share of the population engaged in sports and physical activities increased from 15 per cent in 1964 to 43 per cent in 1987 and 51 per cent in 1998. In Austria, sports participation increased from 36 per cent of the population in 1979 to 69 per cent in 1997, to fall back slightly in the years thereafter. In Spain, the same trend can be witnessed, with a growth in sports participation from 22 per cent of the population in 1975 to 34 per cent in 1985 and 39 per cent in 1995, followed by a period of stagnation. In Italy, the number of informal sports participants multiplied by five in the last two decades of the twentieth century, while the membership of sports federations decreased after 1990. Although the percentages of the population practicing sport cannot be compared between these countries, due to differences in the definitions of 'sports participation', the similarities in their sports participation trends point towards common underlying processes (Van Bottenburg et al. 2005).

In other countries, like Australia, Belgium, Canada, France, Germany, Italy, the Netherlands, New Zealand, and Norway, the same trends can be witnessed in organized sports, with membership figures increasing sharply from the 1950s to the 1980s, followed by a period of slower growth, stagnation or a slight decline in the course of the 1990s (Kamphorst and Roberts 1989; Scheerder et al. 2002; DaCosta and Miragaya 2003; Cushman et al. 2005; Van Bottenburg et al. 2005). Figures 41.1–41.3 show long-term developments in membership of national sports organizations in the Netherlands, Germany and Spain, providing evidence of the S-shaped sports participation trend; here with respect to organized sports participation.[2] Unfortunately, data on informal sports participation cannot be traced back further than the 1970s in most countries and the 1960s in a few others.

The growth in sports participation was accompanied by a differentiation of the sports world. Sport penetrated society to such an extent that German scholars (Bette 1989; Dietrich and Heinemann 1989; Cachay 1990; Digel 1990) came to speak of a *Versportlichung der Gesellschaft*

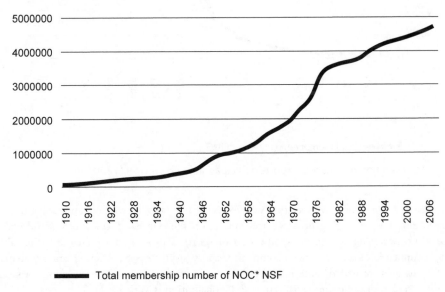

Figure 41.1 Evolution of organised sports participation in the Netherlands, 1910–2006

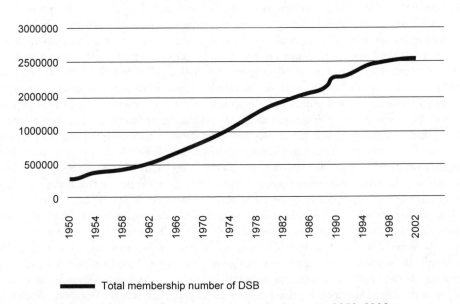

Figure 41.2 Evolution of organised sports participation in Germany, 1950–2002

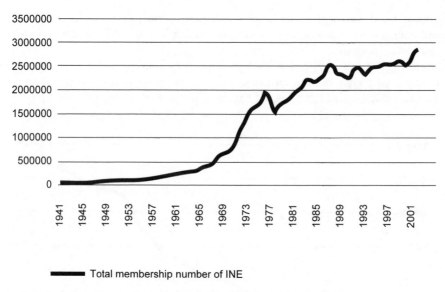

Figure 41.3 Evolution of organised sports participation in Spain, 1941–2001

(sportification/sportization of society), which resulted in a more diffuse and polymorphous sports world. Two diverging processes took place: on the one hand, the sports world experienced a *Versportlichung des Sports* (sportization of sport), a process in which the 'citius, altius, fortius' – principle of the organized, competitive sport (*sportliche Sport*, Dietrich and Heinemann 1989) – has been provided quite radically, influenced by processes of specialization, professionalization, scientization, commercialization and globalization (Crum 2001). This raised the levels of competence and skills to ever greater heights and turned elite sport into a relatively autonomous system, characterized by Joseph Maguire as 'a global achievement sport monoculture' (Maguire 1999: 165), which involves talent identification and development, the provision of sports services to create an excellence culture, the targeting of resources to a relatively small group of sports and athletes, systematic methods of coaching and training, and well-structured competitive programmes (Green and Oakley 2001; De Bosscher *et al.* 2008). In opposition to this trend, a process of 'de-sportization of sport' (*Entsportlichung des Sports*) can be distinguished, in which a growing number of casual, unstructured, uncompetitive forms of sport and physical activity (*nicht-sportliche Sport*, Dietrich and Heinemann 1989) have emerged and become popular. In these sports – as diverse as jogging, surfing, rock-climbing, mountain-biking, snowboarding, rafting, skateboarding, paragliding, aerobics and street dance – most people participate without the need of a formal club structure or competitive environment. They do not desire to move up to a higher level. They are motivated by having fun, experiencing nature, seeking adventure, socializing with friends, achieving body effects (improvement to one's physique) or health improvement; and not or rarely to triumph over others (Dietrich and Heinemann 1989; Crum 2001).

This growth of casual, unorganized sports was part of a wider process of what has been called 'informalization': the spread of more 'permissive' ways of behaving in the 1960s and early 1970s (Wouters 1986). In the field of sports, this process of informalization was pushed and accelerated by an increase in leisure time and income in many Western societies, a shift from physically demanding factory work to sedentary office work, and the realization of a social welfare policy aimed at improving the quality of life and physical fitness among the population. In many countries, the growth in informal sports participation has been evident since the 1970s.

However, there is evidence that this growth lagged behind the organized and competitive sports participation until the 1980s or even the 1990s. In the Netherlands, for example, the percentage of the sporting population participating in training and competition reached its peak in the mid 1980s and declined afterwards. Sports club membership as a percentage of the sporting population continued to grow until the early 1990s, before a slow decline set in (Kamphuis and Van den Dool 2008). In the last two decades, this decline has continued, pushed by a growing number of sports participants moving into middle age and the elderly age group. As a result, a majority of the populations in most Western countries participate in sport today in an informal, unorganized way (DaCosta and Miragaya 2003).

As a consequence of the internal differentiation, the sports world cannot be represented as a pyramid model anymore. Until the mid-twentieth century, the principle of selection and competition used to be so predominant that the entire sports world could be regarded as a single pyramid, broad based and rising to a peak at the top.[3] This pyramid model was based on the declaration of Pierre de Coubertin that every thousand athletes produced a hundred exceptional talents, and these one hundred produced in turn a single world class athlete (Lenk 1974). As Frank Pfetsch (Pfetsch 1975) remarked as long as 35 years ago, this pyramid still exists (in competitive sport), but ongoing differentiation in the sporting world has led to the creation of new kinds of sports activities and structures, some of which have hardly any relationship with the achievement-oriented competition sport. Sport has become a strongly differentiated and diffuse phenomenon, that is practised for many different ends, in diverse ways and in divergent contexts and organizational forms. How people experience sport is related to this. More than ever before, people have the tendency to label their leisure-time physical activities as 'sport'. One of the consequences of this is that sport today encompasses a broad spectrum with the Olympic games at one extreme, as the ultimate manifestation of organized competitive sport, and at the other, all kinds of physical activities that people perceive as sporting behaviour.

As such, sport is not practised anymore only in schools and clubs. These institutions have lost their monopoly position as the prevailing providers of sports opportunities. What Barrie Houlihan and Anita White (Houlihan and White 2002) observe with respect to the UK, holds true for other countries as well, although the exact timing may differ: by the early 1980s the commercial leisure industry rapidly moved into the mass participation sport and recreation market and increasingly overlapped with and competed against public and voluntary providers. Moreover, people increasingly made use of public facilities and services to take part in sport, like jogging in the streets, cycling on paths and tracks, mountain biking on designated trails, basketball on a public court, skating on public half-pipes, or volleyball on the beach.

Although these processes took place all over the world, each country developed a distinctive culture and structure of sports participation. Everywhere the level of sports participation increased substantially in the second half of the twentieth century, but these levels are different between countries and, within countries, between social groups. As far as we know, the highest sports participation levels can be found in the western world, first and foremost in the Scandinavian countries, followed by the western Europe, Australia, New Zealand, and the United States. The sports participation level in eastern and southern European countries is lower, but still higher than in most Latin American, African and Asian countries. These differences are strongly related to socio-economic differences (Kamphorst and Roberts 1989; Van Bottenburg 2001; DaCosta and Miragaya 2003; Van Bottenburg et al. 2005).

This socio-economic relationship can also be discerned within individual countries. In general, the rule applies that men play more sport than women and young people more than old people. The likelihood of sports participation is also greater for those with a higher level of educational achievement, income and professional status. Further to this, there are various other social differences that can be found with respect to levels of sports participation, such as the disparities between people from richer and poorer regions, and between those of native and immigrant origin. However, as the level of affluence increases within countries, these differences tend to diminish. In a number of northern and western European countries, the levels of sports participation have levelled out and the differences between the young and old have become less pronounced (Van Bottenburg *et al.* 2005).

All around the world, sports participation takes place on the basis of at least four types of providers of sport and recreation facilities and services: the voluntary clubs sector, the commercial sector, the educational system and public authorities. However, as a product of its sports tradition and policy system, in each country the sports structure is characterized by a different mix of these modes. In most northern and western European countries – and especially Germany, Belgium, the Netherlands, Denmark, Sweden and Norway – the voluntary sector (local clubs, community leagues) is the largest within the overall sports structure, with the municipalities playing an important role in supporting the clubs (club facilities, club subsidies) and delivering sporting activities (sports programmes, public sports facilities). The commercial sector is less dominant here, but of increasing significance. In contrast to these countries, the educational and commercial systems predominate in the USA and to a lesser extent in Canada. In the USA, schools, colleges and universities, and commercially managed sports centres form the main organizing principles of sports participation, whereas a sports club tradition is lacking and the government hardly takes any role. Here, the educational system creates the arenas for the introduction of young people to sport and for the development of sporting abilities. The UK, Australia and New Zealand seem to have a mix between the north-western European and northern American configurations with the educational and the voluntary club system as the main vehicles for the development of sport (Bergsgard *et al.* 2007). In the more eastern and southern parts of Europe, the voluntary sector is weaker and the supporting role of local authorities is more limited. In eastern Europe, the sports participation structures still show the marks of their long-term dependence on the state-regulated and financed educational system (schools and universities), but they also show new commercial and voluntary structures rising (Girginov and Sandanski 2008).

Sports policy trends

In the western world, modern sports generally emerged within voluntary sports clubs and the educational system, preserving a large degree of autonomy from the government and business sector (Houlihan 1997; DaCosta and Miragaya 2003; Riordan and Krüger 2003; Bloyce and Smith 2010). That does not mean that the sports sector developed without any governmental support at all. Defence and health were prime reasons for several governments to promote sports like swimming, shooting and gymnastics, and – especially in the English-speaking world – competitive ball games in the school system from the late nineteenth century onwards. Moreover, local authorities supported sports clubs by creating and maintaining facilities. But this was primarily a 'help to self help' as Nils Asle Bergsgard and his co-authors observe with respect to Germany (Bergsgard *et al.* 2007). De facto, one cannot speak of a coherent public sports policy until halfway through the twentieth century.

After the Second World War, this governmental approach to sport changed. In many countries, governments showed an increased willingness to accept sport and leisure as legitimate areas of public policy and public spending. This was first legitimated by a growing concern with the socialization of the youth and then connected to the welfare state ideology (Houlihan and White 2002). In the 1960s and 1970s, sport and recreation came to be seen as a right of every citizen; a merit good which needed and justified public funding. This welfare policy perspective on sport expressed itself in the adoption of a new philosophy to promote 'sport for all'. This philosophy elaborated on a new sports development approach in Germany (called 'der zweite Weg') and Scandinavia (called 'Trim'), in which sport was no longer equated with organized, competitive sport only, but also included 'various forms of physical activity, from spontaneous unorganized games to a minimum of physical exercise regularly performed' (Council of Europe 1970, cited in ICSPE/UNESCO 1980). The adoption of this philosophy by the Council of Europe in 1966 and UNESCO in 1975 led among other things to an internationally accepted charter which stated that 'every individual shall have the right to participate in sport' (Sport for All Charter, adopted by the Conference of European ministers responsible for sport in 1975, cited in Scheerder *et al.* 2007).[4] In fact, these charters lumped together sports development programmes that existed in various countries under diverse names, like 'Physical Fitness and Sports' in the United States, 'Recreation Canada' and 'Fitness Canada' in Canada, 'Come alive' in New Zealand, 'Life be in it' in Australia, Trim or Trimm in Norway, Sweden, Denmark, Germany, the Netherlands and Japan, 'Kuntourheilu' in Finland, 'Zabar' in Israel, and 'Deportes para todos' in Spain and Brazil. Other countries, like Brazil, Cameroon, Colombia, Egypt, France, Spain, Tunisia, and the United Kingdom started using the term 'Sport for All' or translations ('Sport pour Tous', 'Deportes Para Todos') of this term (ICSPE/UNESCO 1980; De Knop *et al.* 2006).

As Bergsgard *et al.* (2007: 203) observe, 'the 1960s and 1970s were a "golden age" for sport for all policies', at least in industrialized countries. The European Sport for All Charter included an article that declared that 'since the scale of participation in sport is dependent, among other things, on the extent, the variety and the accessibility of facilities, the overall planning of facilities shall be accepted as a matter for public authorities' (Scheerder *et al.* 2007). And indeed, many countries increased their sports budgets, made possible by a long-lasting period of economic growth, during which the gross national income and tax revenues in industrialized countries multiplied. These rising sports budgets were mainly used for investments in sports facility development, like the construction, maintenance and exploitation of playing fields, swimming pools, and sports centres at the municipal level. This improvement of the sports infrastructure led to a dramatic increase in participation opportunities which met the needs of a growing number of citizens, especially among the youth.

At the end of the 1970s, the government ambitions with respect to sport and recreation in the welfare states were significantly tempered by a worldwide economic crisis. National debt, the unemployment rate and interest payments rose in many countries leading, in the 1980s, to a global wave of liberalization and privatization of public utilities and services, a radical re-shaping of the welfare state and a concomitant lowered profile of public policy directed towards sports facility provision. Instead of concentrating their efforts on the creation of sports facilities, governments focused on specific target groups, like ethnic minorities, the elderly, and disabled people. In that respect, more influence was ascribed to sports development officers. In the 1960s and 1970s, sports development policies tried to increase sports participation primarily by a massive construction of sports facilities, because the infrastructure lagged behind the sports participation needs. In the 1980s, however, the demand and supply of sports facilities were thought to be much more in balance, decreasing the effects of a further enhancement of facility provision. Sports development policies were now expected to be more effective if directed towards specific groups of under-participating sections of the population. The relatively low sports participation level of these target groups was no longer explained by a lack of facilities, but in relation to broader socio-economic problems and cultural disadvantages. Therefore, in many countries, sports development officers were instructed to get these target groups involved in sports programmes and empower them to create their own sports practices, based on a pro-active and interventionist approach (ICSPE/UNESCO 1980; Houlihan and White 2002; Bergsgard *et al.* 2007).

This changing spearhead of sports development policies was the forerunner of a more significant transformation that would alter the fundamentals of sports policy after the 1980s (Bloyce and Smith 2010). The desired outcomes of sports development policy changed in many countries from 'development of sport' to 'development through sport'. It was not focused anymore on an increase of sports participation per se; the emphasis came to be placed on the use of the malleable character of sport as a tool for achieving non-sport goals, like health enhancement, social inclusion, and community building. This broader social value of sport was repeatedly stressed both by national sports organizations which lobbied for more political recognition, and by the sports departments of local and national governmental organizations that were increasingly under pressure to demonstrate that they delivered public value for public money. This resulted in a powerful and successful lobby which marked the beginning of a new period in national sports policies in general and their sports development policies in particular. In this period, which has lasted until the present day, there was again a significant and sustained increase in public investments in sport. This was accompanied by growing governmental interference in sport (Houlihan and White 2002; Coalter 2007), which has become so strong that some authors have come to speak of a 'politicization of sport' (Bergsgard *et al.* 2007).

This new policy agenda zeroed in on the differentiation of the sports world. On the one hand, the policy focus moved from promoting sport and exercise to enhancing physical activity, and from young people to adults and the elderly. The 'sport for all' campaigns of the third quarter of the twentieth century were supplanted by, for example, a 'Europe on the move' campaign. In this campaign, the emphasis was put on physical activities which avoid risk and are regularly done in a moderately intensive fashion and can be incorporated into people's everyday way of life, such as cycling, walking and gardening. From this health perspective, other traditional values of the sports world, fun and sociability, took more of a back seat (Van Bottenburg *et al.* 2005).

On the other hand, the policy focus moved from sport for all to high-performance sport. Although there have been significant differences between countries, especially with respect to the timing of this policy change and the role of the government in the prioritization of elite sport policy (see below), in the longer run most countries followed the same path and adopted a strategic approach towards elite sport development. As the power struggle between nations to win medals in major international competitions intensified over the last two decades, this policy approach required increasing investments in elite sports by governments and sports organisations all over the world (Oakley and Green 2001; De Bosscher *et al.* 2008). These investments often put pressure on sport for all budgets, legitimated by a discourse that claimed positive effects of sporting successes on national pride and international prestige (Green 2006; Van Hilvoorde *et al.* 2010).

These governmental ambitions to use sport as a means to achieve non-sporting objectives have created a steering problem in sports policy. After all, for the 'development of sport' the governments in most Western countries rely to a large extent on voluntary sports organisations. This particularly holds true for countries with a strong sports club system, like Belgium, Denmark, Germany, the Netherlands, Norway and Sweden, but also goes for countries like the UK, Australia and Canada, where governments and the school systems are more directly involved with the organisation of sport. In all these countries, sports policy is made at the level of national sports organisations and national and local governments, while the implementation of this policy substantially depends on the ability and willingness of volunteers in relatively autonomous local sports clubs. These volunteers, however, are basically motivated for reasons of having their own children as participants or participating themselves (Skille 2008). The organisation of their sporting passion is the raison d'être of sports clubs. Ergo, it is quite unlikely that development through sport is anything more than a by-product of the energy they spend in the development of sport (Houlihan and White 2002).

The limited capacity of sports clubs to meet the government ambitions with respect to development through sport, has generated criticism of the local and national voluntary sport organizations. In the Netherlands, this has had three consequences: the foundation of a new, powerful organization for sports policy implementation, which is heavily dependent on state subsidy; an emphasis on professionalization and modernization of national governing bodies of sport and local sporting clubs; and changes in the distribution and destination of government subsidies to the voluntary sport system. These subsidies are distributed less to national sports organizations and more to local authorities; and less based on the membership numbers of national sports organizations and more on their contribution to governmental policy goals. There are indications that the same decline in deference towards voluntarism in the sports sector can be witnessed in other countries. Initially, public resources in sport were directed in many countries through the voluntary sector. However, since the 1990s, this privileged position of sports organizations has eroded. First, federal or central administrations have shifted the distribution of public spending on sport – at least partly – from national governing sports bodies to local authorities. Second, contractual relations with voluntary sports organizations have been introduced, accompanied with an increased emphasis on outcomes and proof of effectiveness in terms of value for money. Third, these voluntary organizations have increasingly been put under pressure to adopt a more 'business-like' approach, like the commercial leisure industry that has moved rapidly into the mass participation market since the early 1980s. One of the implications of these changes has been that sports development is not consigned anymore to voluntary organizations, but is increasingly based on networks and partnerships of voluntary, commercial and governmental organizations, with all the coordination problems involved (Houlihan and White 2002; Bergsgard et al. 2007; Bloyce and Smith 2010).

These analogies in the sports policies of different countries with diverging state systems and sports structures can only be explained if the sports policy processes are put in a broader, historical and comparative context. Sports policies do not develop in a vacuum, but are influenced by both general societal processes and developments in other policy areas. Moreover, national sports policies influence each other, as can be learned from the international 'sport for all' campaigns in the 1970s and the increasingly homogeneous elite sport systems in the last decades, although we do not yet exactly know how this policy adoption in various countries takes place. At the same time, however, these processes have worked out differently in each country so that the sports development policy and its impact on sports participation exhibit unique characteristics as well.

The literature gives the impression that this (difference in) impact is particularly determined by the balance of power between the state, market and society in the sports sector, and – more specifically – the capability of national, provincial and local authorities, commercial agencies, schools and universities, and the voluntary sports organizations to influence the sports policy making process at the national level, and contribute to the provision and development of sport at the local level. Moreover, the consequences of these influencing forces for sports development activities in each country seem to be strongly linked to critical junctures in the history of national sports policies. The choices made during these critical junctures close off alternative options and lead to the establishment of institutions that generate self-reinforcing path-dependent processes (Capoccia and Kelemen 2007).

The inclusion of sports competitions in extra-curricular activities of high schools and universities in the USA, instead of a separate organization of sports competitions in independent sports clubs that became tradition in most European countries, was such a watershed with diverging consequences for the further development of the American and European sporting formation and cultures (Stokvis 2009). Mick Green and Shane Collins offer another telling case study of this mechanism, showing that the intervention by the Australian government in the early 1980s to give priority to elite sport in sports development instead of focusing on the provision of sporting facilities and opportunities for the masses, as remained the case in Finland, created self-reinforcing, positive feedback processes in both countries, leading to a steady and consistent path of elite sport development in Australia and sport for all in Finland (Green and Collins 2008). Interestingly, Bergsgard et al. show that there are good reasons to assume that the same diverging historical processes took place in other liberal welfare states, like Canada and the United Kingdom, on the one hand, and social democratic welfare states, like Norway and Germany, on the other; although the authors are right in underlining that these differences are not categorical but matters of degree (Bergsgard et al. 2007).[5]

The tension between the perception of sports development as providing sports opportunities for everyone or selecting and targeting resources at the most gifted athletes also differed at the level of the national sports governing bodies. Hartmann-Tews demonstrates, for example, that sports clubs in Germany succeeded earlier and better in broadening the country's scope towards a democratization in participation than the sports clubs in Great Britain. In Germany, the Deutsche Sport Bund (DSB) started as early as 1959 with the promotion of recreational leisure sport (*Freizeitsport*) for children, women, unemployed and the elderly, in addition to the traditional achievement-oriented understanding of sport. With this dual strategy, the DSB and its member associations tried to regain recognition and acceptance in society after being strongly linked with German nationalism before and during the Second World War. The sports clubs in Great Britain, on the other hand, did not open up to the same extent and remained achievement-oriented to a larger extent (Hartmann-Tews 1999). As Houlihan and White observe with respect to the United Kingdom, 'among national governing bodies, sports development was only slowly being accepted as a legitimate activity, and then only in terms more akin to marketing and recruitment than to any wider community-related definition' (Houlihan and White 2002: 49). Interestingly, the consequence of this was not so much that the overall sports participation levels came to diverge between the two countries, but that the increasing participation rates in Germany led to a growing voluntary sector, whereas in Great Britain the growing number of people active in sport has been far more attracted by commercial enterprises and the public sector (Hartmann-Tews 1999).

In several countries, the decision to allocate money from public lotteries for sport seems to be another critical juncture that highly influenced the further development of sport. What specifically set the development along a particular path, in this respect, was the question as to who 'owned' and distributed this lottery money. In Belgium, Canada, England, Germany, Italy, the Netherlands, Norway, and undoubtedly several other countries, the lottery money has become an important source of income for sport (Bergsgard et al. 2007; De Bosscher et al. 2008). However, there are important differences between these countries with respect to the introduction, ownership and distribution of this source of income. In Norway, for example, lottery money has financed sport since 1946 and has become the dominant form of state funding of sport over the years. Here, the lottery money is distributed to both elite sport and sport for all through the Norwegian sports federation and Olympic Committee, with the national government taking a firmer grip in the last decade on how this money for sport is to be used (Bergsgard et al. 2007). In Britain, lottery funding did not start until the mid-1990s. These lottery resources altered the pattern of resource dependencies between the main organizations responsible for sports development, strengthening the position of the central government, weakening the influence of local authorities, and giving more prominence to national governing sports bodies and the British Olympic Association. This was reflected in an increased emphasis on elite sport. In Canada and Germany, profits from lotteries are used at the provincial (Canada) and Länder (Germany) level to support sport. As a result, the level of support given to recreational sport and elite sport varies considerably between parts of these countries (Bergsgard et al. 2007).

The impact of sports development on sports participation

In this chapter, we consciously decided to discuss the trends in sports participation and sports policy separately and one after the other, to prevent us from automatically presenting one trend as the cause or effect of the other, or making any implicit suggestion in that direction without critically examining its relationship. In this last section, we will examine the interconnection of both trends.

Our first observation in this respect is that there is a high degree of synchronization in sports participation trends between countries. This applies for both the S-curve in the sports participation figures and the differentiation process within the growing sports world. Both processes took place in the second half of the twentieth century in a variety of countries, in spite of differences in their existing sporting cultures and structures, their general political contexts and specific sports policy actions. This suggests that these sports participation trends – in the longer term – were influenced by underlying mechanisms. Sport developed into a mass phenomenon in most industrialized countries mainly because of broader societal developments, independent of specific sports development policies.

Our second finding is that many governments and sports organizations have invested heavily in sports development, both in terms of money and people, and have been rewarded with substantial increases in participation and sporting successes (Bergsgard et al. 2007; De Bosscher et al. 2008). In the 1960s and 1970s, this sports policy was mainly demand led. As Bergsgard et al. observe, governments invested mainly in sports facilities during this period, leading to 'a dramatic increase in participation opportunities which met latent demand from the grassroots participants as well as the needs of the elite performer' (Bergsgard et al. 2007: 209). The sport for all policy in this period was successful because it was underpinned by wider economic and socio-cultural developments in society: the increase in affluence and leisure time, the reduction in manual work, the expansion of higher education, the levelling out of income differences, individualization and informalization of interpersonal relations, and the emancipation of the working class, women, youth and the elderly (Van Bottenburg et al. 2005). The growth in facility provision certainly played a role in increasing sports participation levels, but when this trend 'began to stutter and then stall' in the course of the 1980s, the sport for all policies were redefined and began to drop down the political agenda (Bergsgard et al. 2007: 203). As Houlihan and White conclude: 'the facility building programme simply released latent demand, and, when that demand had been satisfied, growth in participation slowed, then levelled off' (Houlihan and White 2002: 47).

Third, we think that there is evidence for claiming that sports development policies at the national, regional and local level have influenced overall trends in sports participation. The overall patterns in sports participation are more or less the same, but the sports participation level is much higher in some countries than in others. Moreover, there are clearly smaller differences in sports participation between social groups (related to income, education, gender, age groups and ethnicity) in these countries compared to other ones. And there are differences as well with respect to the organizational settings within which these groups participate in sport, varying from schools and universities, sports clubs, commercial sports centres, and public sports facilities and sports programmes (Van Bottenburg *et al.* 2005). There are good arguments to assume that these differences are related to earlier sports development policies that influenced the sporting culture and structure in each country. Differences in national policies towards sports develop- ment have contributed to differences in attitudes and perceptions with respect to sport, physical activity and leisure, and to differences on the supply side in the sports sector, resulting in different needs, impulses and opportunities to participate in sport among the population (Hartmann- Tews 1999; Bergsgard *et al.* 2007). Whether these effects can be considered as results of national 'Sport for All' campaigns is, however, difficult to assess. Sport for All was an extremely flexible concept (Houlihan and White 2002). McIntosh and Charlton's review found that early state- ments of the policy were constantly being revised and amended, and included a wide array of objectives, with respect to grass-roots sport, community sport and elite sport (McIntosh and Charlton 1985; Green 2006).

Our fourth observation is that the sports development policy agenda encouraged and fol- lowed the differentiation of the sports world from the 1980s, leading to diverging policy objectives with respect to physical activity on the one hand, and elite sport on the other. The welfare theme was supplanted by one of health in most industrialized countries. In line with this, sports development policies have shifted further from supporting club-based sports partici- pation to the promotion of 'health-enhancing physical activities', in whatever context they may occur. Moreover, the attention in this sports policy is focused more on adults and the elderly than ever before. This change in policy focus cannot only be found at the governmental level. In their competition for public resources, sports organizations do their best to incorporate this trend in their rationales as well; this often leads to tensions between 'intrinsic' goals of local sports clubs and 'extrinsic' goals of national governing bodies.

Fifth, the emphasis on health is illustrative of a fundamental change in sports policy during recent decades, shifting from 'development of sport' to 'development through sport'. This change has also put community sports development (striving for regeneration, social inclusion, crime reduction) and elite sport (with national pride and international prestige as intended results) higher on the agenda, although the evidence of these societal effects is circumstantial and inconclusive. With respect to the subject of this chapter, this policy change implies that sports participation per se is no longer – or less and less – the ultimate sports development policy objective. It still might be the pursued output, but more and more as a means to achieve a broader societal outcome. For an increasing number of sports development officers of local authorities, development through sport has become their primary and guiding goal (Houlihan and White 2002). They have undoubtedly been successful in organizing sports activities, encouraging specific target groups to participate, and building social capital in disadvantaged communities (see Coalter's contribution to this volume). Yet, it proves to be hard to raise the sports participation levels among these groups substantially and structurally.

A sixth observation is that physical activities, club-based sports and elite sports increasingly fight for attention and resources. There is hardly any country where elite sport has not been given higher priority since the 1980s. Remarkably, elite sport has especially been prioritized by the governments of neo-liberal societies, like Australia, Canada and the United Kingdom. In social democratic and conservative welfare states like Norway and Germany, the confedera- tions of sport have played central roles in the coordination of sport and sports policies. As the policy of these confederations is defined and controlled by the national sports organiza- tions, whose policies are, in their turn, determined by the local sports clubs, there is less support for the prioritization of a relatively small number of elite athletes in a relatively small number of targeted sports. It is in these countries that we find the strongest sport for all values (Bergsgard *et al.* 2007).

Finally, there is evidence that the impact of sports development on sports participation depends on the governance structure in the sports sector. The historical role that the educational system, voluntary sports organizations, commercial sports providers, and national, regional and local authorities played in the policy making, funding and implementation of sports development differs from country to country, with long-lasting path-dependent consequences of critical junctures in this long-term process.

Notes

1 These figures are based on a population survey and refer to both organized and unorganized sport participation.
2 The data represent the total number of memberships and not members of the national sports associations affiliated to the national sports federation. Therefore, these figures are not identical to the overall number of organized sports participants. Moreover, especially with respect to earlier years, the reliability of the data can be questioned for all three countries. Nevertheless, it is plausible to assume that the main trends in these numbers of memberships of the national sports federations do not fundamentally differ from the trends in the overall number of organized sports participants.
3 In many countries, this model became widely used by sports organizations. In the UK, the model was modified in 1988 into a pyramid composed of four relatively discrete levels: from foundation, participation and performance to excellence (Houlihan and White 2002: 41).
4 The UNESCO charter stated that 'every human being has a fundamental right of access to physical education and sport' (International Charter of Physical Education and Sport, adopted by the General Conference of UNESCO in 1978, cited in ICSPE/UNESCO 1980).
5 In some western countries that were forerunners in governmentally supported elite sport development, like Australia and Canada, there are signs of a political reconsideration of the explicit prioritisation of elite sport (Bergsgard *et al.* 2007). The report on the future of Australian sport, written by an independent sport panel, argues for example that 'a pre-occupation with elite performance and winning medals has led some NSOs to neglect grassroots participation.' It concludes that 'if we are truly interested in a preventative health agenda through sport, then much of it may be better spent on lifetime participants than almost all on a small group of elite athletes who will perform at that level for just a few years' (Australian Government 2009: 21, 8). As the last quote indicates, however, this 'renewed modest enthusiasm for participation programmes' (Bergsgard *et al.* 2007: 207) still expresses an instrumental attitude in the governmental thinking regarding sports policy.

References

Australian Government (2009). The Future of Sport in Australia. Report of the Independent Sport Panel chaired by Mr. David Crawford. Commonwealth of Australia.
Bergsgard, N. A., Houlihan, B., Mangset, P., Nodland, S. I., and Rommetvedt, H. (2007). *Sport policy. A comparative analysis of stability and change.* Amsterdam: Elsevier.
Bette, K. H. (1989). *Körperspuren. Zur Semantik und Paradoxie moderner Körperlichkeit.* Berlin/New York: Walter de Gruyter.
Bloyce, D., and Smith, A. (2010). *Sport policy and development. An introduction.* London/New York: Routledge.
Deutsche Sport Bund / Deutscher Olympischer SportBund (1971–2005). *Bestandserhebung.* Frankfurt: DSB/DOSB.
Cachay, K. (1990). Versportlichung der Gesellschaft und Ersportung des Sports. Systemtheoretische Anmerkungen zu einem gesellschaftlichen Phänomen. In H. Gabler, and U. Göhner, *Für einen besseren Sport. Themen, Entwicklungen und Perspektiven aus Sport und Sportwissenschaft* (pp. 97–113). Schorndorf: Verlag Karl Hofmann.
Capoccia, G., and Kelemen, D. (2007). The study of critical junctures. Theory, narrative, and counterfactuals in historical institutionalism. *World Politics, 59* (3), 341–69.

Coalter, F. (2007). *A wider role for sport: who's keeping the score?* London: Routledge.

Crum, B. (2001). *Over de versporting van de samenleving.* Haarlem: De Vrieseborch.

Cushman, G., Veal, A., and Zuzanek, J. (2005). *Free time and leisure participation. International perspectives.* Cambridge: CABI Publishing.

DaCosta, L., and Miragaya, A. (2003). *Worldwide experiences and trends in sport for all.* Aachen: Meyer and Meyer Sport.

De Bosscher, V., Bingham, J., Shibli, S., Van Bottenburg, M., and De Knop, P. (2008). *The global sporting arms race. An international comparative study on sports policy factors leading to international sporting success.* Oxford: Meyer and Meyer Sport.

De Knop, P., Scheerder, J., and Vanreusel, B. (2006). *Sportsociologie. Het spel en de spelers.* Maarssen: Elsevier Gezondheidszorg.

Dietrich, K., and Heinemann, K. (1989). *Der nicht-sportliche Sport.* Schorndorf: Verlag Karl Hofmann.

Digel, H. (1990). Die Versportlichung unserer Kultur und deren Folgen für den Sport. Ein Beitrag zur Uneigentlichkeit des Sports. In H. Gabler, and U. Göhner, *Für einen besseren Sport. Themen, Entwicklungen und Perspektiven aus Sport und Sportwissenschaft* (pp. 73–96). Schorndorf: Verlag Karl Hofman.

Girginov, V., and Sandanski, I. (2008). Understanding the changing nature of sports organisations in transforming societies. *Sport Management Review,* 21–50.

Green, M. (2006). From 'Sport for All' to not about 'sport' at all? Interrogating sport policy interventions in the United Kingdom. *European Sport Management Quarterly, 6* (3), 217–38.

Green, M., and Collins, S. (2008). Policy, politics and path dependency: sport development in Australia and Finland. *Sport Management Review, 11,* 225–51.

Green, M., and Oakley, B. (2001). Elite sport development systems and playing to win: uniformity and diversity in international appraches. *Leisure Studies, 20,* 247–67.

Hartmann-Tews, I. (1999). The idea of Sport for All and the development of organised sport in Germany and Great Britain. *Journal of European Area Studies, 7* (2), 145–56.

Houlihan, B. (1997). *Sport, policy and politics. A comparative analysis.* London/New York: Routledge.

Houlihan, B., and White, A. (2002). *The politics of sports development. Development of sport or development through sport?* London/New York: Routledge.

ICSPE/UNESCO. (1980). *'Sport for all' programmes throughout the world. A report prepared by professor Peter McIntosh for the Inernational Council of Sport and Physical Education for submission to UNESCO in November 1980.* n.p.

INE (2003). *Licencias federados anos.* Madrid: Instituto Nacional de Estadistica.

Kamphorst, T., and Roberts, K. (1989). *Trends in sports. A multinational perspective.* Culemborg: Giordano Bruno.

Kamphuis, C., and Van den Dool, R. (2008). Sportdeelname. In K. Breedveld, C. Kamphuis, and A. Tiessen-Raaphorst, *Rapportage Sport 2008* (pp. 74–101). Den Haag: Sociaal en Cultureel Planbureau.

Krüger, A. (2003). Germany. In J. Riordan, and A. Krüger, *European cultures in sport. Examining the nations and regions* (pp. 67–88). Bristol: Intellect.

Lenk, H. (1974). *Leistungssport: Ideologie oder Mythos?* Stuttgart: Kohlhammer.

Maguire, J. (1999). *Global sport. Identities, societies, civilizations.* Cambridge: Polity Press.

McIntosh, P., and Charlton, V. (1985). *The impact of Sport for All policy 1966–1984 and a way forward.* London: Sports Council.

NOC*NSF. (1993–2008). *Ledentallen [Membership figures].* Arnhem: NOC*NSF.

Oakley, B., and Green, M. (2001). The production of Olympic champions: international perspectives on elite sport development systems. *European Journal for Sport Management, 8,* 83–105.

Pfetsch, F. (1975). *Leistungssport und Gesellschaftssystem. Sozio-politische Faktoren im Leistungssport. Die Bundesrepublik Deutschland im internationalen Vergleich.* Schorndorf: Verlag Karl Hofman.

Riordan, J., and Krüger, A. (2003). *European cultures in sport. Examining the nations and regions.* Bristol: Intellect.

Scheerder, J., Taks, M., Vanreusel, B., and Renson, R. (2002). *30 jaar breedtesport in Vlaanderen: participatie en beleid. Trends 1969–1999 [30 years of sport participation in Flanders: participation and policy. Trends 1979–1999].* Ghent: PVLO.

Scheerder, J., van Tuyckom, C., and Vermeersch, A. (2007). *Europa in beweging. Sport vanuit Europees perspectief.* Ghent: Academia Press.

Skille, E. (2008). Understanding sport clubs as sport policy implementers: a theoretical framework for the analysis of the implementation of central sport policy through local and voluntary sport organizations. *International Review for the Sociology of Sport, 43* (2), 181–200.

Stokvis, R. (2009). Sport en middelbaar onderwijs in de VS en Nederland. *Sociologie, 5* (4), 484–501.

Van Bottenburg, M. (2001). *Global games*. Urbana/Chicago: University of Illinois Press.

Van Bottenburg, M., Rijnen, B., and Van Sterkenburg, J. (2005). *Sports participation in the European Union*. Nieuwegein: ARKO Sports Media.

Van Hilvoorde, I., Elling, A., and Stokvis, R. (2010). How to influence national pride? The Olympic medal index as a unifying narrative. *International Review for the Sociology of Sport, 45* (1), 87–102.

Wouters, C. (1986). Formalization and informalization: changing tension-balances in civilizing processes. *Theory Culture and Society, 3* (2), 1–18.

Index